# GLOBAL MARKETING MANAGEMENT

## 5TH EDITION

# GLOBAL MARKETING
# MANAGEMENT

## 5TH EDITION

**Masaaki Kotabe**
*Temple University*

**Kristiaan Helsen**
*Hong Kong University of Science and Technology*

WILEY

**JOHN WILEY & SONS, INC.**

# DEDICATION

*To my sons and SDK*
—M.K.

*To my mother and A.V.*
—K.H.

| | |
|---|---|
| Vice President & Executive Publisher | George Hoffman |
| Executive Editor | Lise Johnson |
| Senior Editor | Franny Kelly |
| Production Manager | Dorothy Sinclair |
| Senior Production Editor | Valerie A. Vargas |
| Marketing Manager | Diane Mars |
| Creative Director | Harry Nolan |
| Senior Designer | James O'Shea |
| Production Management Services | Elm Street Publishing Services |
| Senior Illustration Editor | Anna Melhorn |
| Photo Associate | Sheena Goldstein |
| Assistant Editor | Maria Guarascio |
| Editorial Assistant | Emily McGee |
| Associate Media Editor | Elena Santa Maria |
| Cover Photo Credit | © Daniel lvascu/iStockphoto |

This book was set in 10/12pt Times Ten Roman by Thomson Digital and printed and bound by Courier-Kendallville. The cover was printed by Courier-Kendallville.

ISBN-13 978-0-470-38111-3

Printed in the United States of America

10 9 8 7 6 5 4 3 2

# ABOUT THE AUTHORS

**Masaaki "Mike" Kotabe** holds the Washburn Chair Professorship in International Business and Marketing, and is Director of Research at the Institute of Global Management Studies at the Fox School of Business at Temple University. Prior to joining Temple University in 1998, he was Ambassador Edward Clark Centennial Endowed Fellow and Professor of Marketing and International Business at the University of Texas at Austin. Dr. Kotabe also served as Vice President of the Academy of International Business in the 1997–1998 term. He received his Ph.D. in Marketing and International Business at Michigan State University. Dr. Kotabe teaches international marketing, global sourcing strategy (R&D, manufacturing, and marketing interfaces) and Asian business practices at the undergraduate and MBA levels, and teaches theories of international business at the Ph.D. level. He has lectured widely at various business schools around the world, including Austria, Brazil, China, Colombia, Finland, Germany, Indonesia, Japan, Korea, Mexico, Norway, Sweden, and Turkey. For his research, he has worked closely with leading companies such as AT&T, Kohler, NEC, Nissan, Philips, Sony, and Seven & I Holdings (parent of 7-Eleven stores), and served as advisor to the United Nations' and World Trade Organization's Executive Forum on National Export Strategies.

Dr. Kotabe has written many scholarly publications. His numerous research papers have appeared in such journals as *Journal of Marketing, Journal of International Business Studies, Strategic Management Journal*, and *Academy of Management Journal*. His books include *Global Sourcing Strategy: R&D, Manufacturing, Marketing Interfaces* (1992), *Japanese Distribution System* (1993), *Anticompetitive Practices in Japan* (1996), *MERCOSUR and Beyond* (1997), *Marketing Management* (2001), *Market Revolution in Latin America: Beyond Mexico* (2001), *Emerging Issues in International Business Research* (2002), and *Global Supply Chain Management* (2006).

He currently serves as Editor of the Journal of International Management, and also serves and/or has served on the editorial boards of Journal of Marketing, Journal of International Business Studies, Journal of International Marketing, Journal of World Business, Journal of the Academy of Marketing Science, Advances in International Management, Journal of Business Research, and Thunderbird International Business Review, among others. He also serves as Advisor to the Institute of Industrial Policy Studies (IPS) National Competitiveness Report. Dr. Kotabe has been elected a Fellow of the Academy of International Business for his significant contribution to international business research and education.

**Kristiaan Helsen** has been an associate professor of marketing at the Hong Kong University of Science and Technology (HKUST) since 1995. Prior to joining HKUST, he was on the faculty of the University of Chicago for five years. He has lectured at Nijenrode University (Netherlands), the International University of Japan, Purdue University, the Catholic University of Lisbon, and China Europe International Business School (CEIBS) in Shanghai, China. Dr. Helsen received his Ph.D. in Marketing at the Wharton School of the University of Pennsylvania.

His research areas include promotional strategy, competitive strategy, and hazard-rate modeling. His articles have appeared in journals such as *Marketing Science, Journal of Marketing, Journal of Marketing Research*, and *European Journal of Operations Research*, among others. Dr. Helsen is on the editorial board of the *International Journal of Research in Marketing*.

Professors Kotabe and Helsen recently published the *SAGE Handbook of International Marketing* (2009), an authoritative collection of chapters written by expert researchers from around the world that provides an in-depth analysis of international marketing issues that must be understood and addressed in today's global and interdependent markets. The *Handbook* brings together the fundamental questions and themes that have surfaced, and promises to be an essential addition to the study of international marketing.

# PREFACE

## THREE FUNDAMENTAL ISSUES ADDRESSED IN THE FIFTH EDITION

◆ ◆ ◆ ◆ ◆ ◆ ◆

We have continued to receive many letters and e-mail messages as well as comments on Amazon.com from instructors and business executives around the world who used the previous editions of *Global Marketing Management*. Their comments have been unanimously favorable. Thanks to the increased desire in many parts of the world for access to our book in their own languages, our book has been translated into Chinese, Japanese, Portuguese, and Spanish. However, we just cannot be sitting on our laurels. As the world around us has been constantly changing, the contents and context of our book also must change to reflect the *climate of the time*. Today, the worst global financial crisis since the Great Depression of 1929 has changed the global marketing environment completely. A continued global economic growth has proved to be a false assumption. Now there are even political tides against freer trading environments. Although we currently live in a very unfortunate global economic environment, we are fortunate enough to capture various changes in the marketplace and describe them in this fifth edition of our book.

In our mind, the role of a textbook is not only to describe today's realities but also to extrapolate logically from them how the future will unfold. After all, that is how marketing executives have to act and make *correct* decisions based on the facts they have gathered. Today's realities are a product of past realities, and the future will be an uncharted course of events lying ahead of us. We constantly strive to help you better understand state-of-the-art marketing practices on a global basis with relevant historical background, current marketing environments, and logical explanations based on a massive amount of knowledge generated by marketing executives as well as by academic researchers from around the world.

Therefore, the fifth edition of our book builds on three major changes that have taken place in the last decade or so. *First*, the landscape of the global economy has changed drastically, particularly as a result of the global financial crisis and ensuing global recession. The emergence of Brazil, Russia, India, and China, among others, as economic superpowers has occurred during the same period. For example, China's role as the world's factory is well established; India's increased role in information technology development is obvious; and Brazil and Russia are still rich in mineral resources that are becoming scarce around the world.

*Second,* the explosive growth of information technology tools, including the internet and electronic commerce (e-commerce), has had a significant effect on the way we do business internationally. This still continues to be an evolving phenomenon that we need to take a careful look at. On one hand, everyone seems to agree that business transactions will be faster and more global early on. And it is very true. As a result, marketing management techniques, such as customer relationship management and global account management, have become increasingly feasible. However, on the other hand, the more deeply we have examined this issue, the more convinced we have become that certain things will not change, or might even become more local as a result of globalization that the internet and e-commerce bestow on us.

*Third*, it is an underlying human tendency to desire to be different when there are economic and political forces of convergence (often referred to as globalization). When the globalization argument (and movement) became fashionable in the 1980s and 1990s, many of us believed that globalization would make global marketing easier. As we explain later in the text, marketing beyond national borders, indeed, has become easier, but it does not necessarily mean that customers want the same products in countries around the world. For example, many more peoples around the world try to emphasize cultural and ethnic differences and accept those differences than ever before. Just think about many new countries being born around the world as well as regional unifications taking place at the same time. Another example is that while e-commerce promotion on the internet goes global, product delivery may need to be fairly local in order to address local competition and exchange-rate fluctuations as well as the complexities of international physical distribution (export declarations, tariffs, and non-tariff barriers). From a supply-side point of view, globalization has brought us more products from all corners of the world. However, from a demand-side (market-ing-side) point of view, customers have a much broader set of goods and services to *choose from*. In other words, marketers now face all the more divergent customers with divergent preferences—far from a homogeneous group of customers.

Indeed, these changes we have observed in the last decade or so are more than extraordinary. In this fifth edition, we have expanded on these issues in all the chapters wherever relevant. We have added many new examples that have occurred in this period. However, we do not sacrifice logical depth in favor of brand-new examples. This revision required a lot of work, as did previous editions in the past. But it was well worth the effort because we are confident that enlightened readers like you will be very satisfied with the results.

We strongly believe that cases provide students not only with lively discussions of what goes on with many companies but also an in-depth understanding of many marketing-related concepts and tools as used by those companies. In this revision, we added many new cases and retained and updated several cases from earlier editions that our textbook users and their students voted as *favorites*.. We have more than 40 cases in this edition. The cases represent many products and services and many regions and countries as well as many nationalities. Six cases are included in the textbook itself, and the rest are placed on the textbook website for easy download www.wiley.com/college/kotabe.

Many users of the previous editions continue to commend our book as probably the most academically rigorous and conceptually sound, and yet full of lively examples with which students can easily identify in order to drive across important points. We combine the academic rigor and relevance (fun of reading) of materials to meet both undergraduate and MBA educational requirements. We keep this tradition in our fifth edition.

## ◆◆◆◆◆◆◆◆ OUR PEDAGOGICAL ORIENTATION

Marketing in the global arena is indeed a very dynamic discipline. Today, there are many international or global marketing management books vying for their respective niches in the market. It is a mature market. As you will learn in our book, in a mature market, firms tend to focus closely—or maybe, too closely—on immediate product features for sources of differentiation and may inadvertently ignore the fundamental changes that may be re-shaping the industry. Often those fundamental changes come from outside the industry. The same logic applies to the textbook market. Whether existing textbooks are titled international marketing or global marketing, they continue to be bound by the traditional bilateral (inter-national) view of competition. While any new textbook has to embrace the traditional coverage of existing text-books, we intend to emphasize the multilateral (global) nature of marketing throughout our book.

Some textbooks have replaced the word, "international," with "global." Such a change amounts to a repackaging of an existing product we often see in a mature product market, and it does not necessarily make a textbook globally oriented. We need a paradigm shift to accomplish the task of adding truly global dimensions and complex realities to a textbook. You might ask, "What fundamental changes are needed for a paradigm shift?" and then, "Why do we need fundamental changes to begin with?"

Our answer is straightforward. Our ultimate objective is to help you prepare for this new century and become an effective manager overseeing global marketing activities in an increasingly competitive environment. You may or may not choose marketing for your career. If you pursue a marketing career, what you will learn in our book will not only have direct relevance but also help you understand how you, as a marketing manager, can affect other business functions for effective corporate performance on a global basis. If you choose other functional areas of business for your career, then our book will help you understand how you could work effectively with marketing people for the same corporate goal. Our book is organized as shown in the flowchart.

We believe that our pedagogical orientation not only embraces the existing stock of useful marketing knowledge and methods but also sets itself apart from the competition in a number of fundamental ways, as follows:

**Global Orientation**

As we indicated at the outset, the term "global" epitomizes the competitive pressure and market opportunities from around the world and the firm's need to optimize its market performance on a global basis. Whether a company operates domestically or across national boundaries, it can no longer avoid the competitive pressure and market opportunities. For optimal market performance, the firm should also be ready and willing to take advantage of resources on a global basis, and at the same time respond to different needs and wants of consumers. In a way, global marketing is a constant struggle with economies of scale and scope needs of the firm and its responsiveness and sensitivity to different market conditions. While some people call it a "glocal" orientation, we stay with the term, "global," to emphasize marketing flexibility on a global basis.

Let us take a look at a hypothetical U.S. company exporting finished products to Europe and Japan. Traditionally, this export phenomenon has been treated as a bilateral business transaction between a U.S. company and foreign customers. However, in reality, to the executives of the U.S. company, this export transaction may be nothing more than the last phase of the company's activities they manage. Indeed, this company procures certain components from long-term suppliers in Japan and Mexico, other components in a business-to-business (B2B) transaction on the internet with a supplier in Korea and from its domestic sources in the United States, and then assembles a finished product in its Singapore plant for export to Europe and Japan as well as back to the United States. Indeed, a Japanese supplier of critical components is a joint venture, majority-owned by this American company, while a Mexican supplier has a licensing agreement with the U.S. company that provides most of technical know-how. A domestic supplier in the United States is in fact a subsidiary of a German company. In other words, this particular export transaction by the U.S. company involves a joint venture, a licensing agreement, a B2B transaction, subsidiary operation, local assembly, and R&D, all managed directly or indirectly by the U.S. company—and add the realities of market complexities arising from diverse customer preferences in European, Japanese, and North American markets. Now think about how these arrangements could affect the company's decisions over product policy, pricing, promotion, and distribution channels.

Many existing textbooks have focused on each of these value-adding activities as if they could be investigated independently. Obviously, in reality they are not independent of each other and cannot be. We emphasize this multilateral realism by examining these value-adding activities as holistically as possible.

At the same time, we are fully aware of the increased importance of the roles that emerging markets and competitive firms from those markets play in fundamentally

# Global Marketing Management
## 5th Edition

### Globalization

1. Globalization Imperative

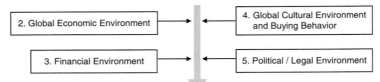

### Global Marketing Environment

2. Global Economic Environment → ← 4. Global Cultural Environment and Buying Behavior

3. Financial Environment → ← 5. Political / Legal Environment

### Development of Competitive Strategy

6. Global Marketing Research

7. Global Segmentation and Positioning ↔ 8. Global Marketing Strategies

9. Global Market Entry Strategies

### Global Marketing Strategy Development

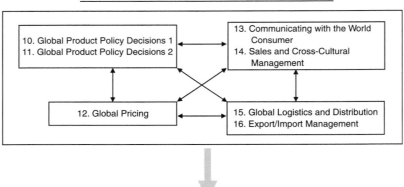

10. Global Product Policy Decisions 1
11. Global Product Policy Decisions 2

13. Communicating with the World Consumer
14. Sales and Cross-Cultural Management

12. Global Pricing

15. Global Logistics and Distribution
16. Export/Import Management

### Managing Global Operations

17. Planning, Organization and Control of Global Marketing Operations

18. Marketing in Emerging Markets

19. Global Marketing and the Internet

reshaping the nature of global competition. In this fifth edition, we have added Chapter 18 to highlight various marketing issues related to the emerging markets.

To complement our global orientation, we offer an interdisciplinary perspective in all relevant chapters. We are of the strong belief that you cannot become a seasoned marketing executive without understanding how other functional areas interface with marketing. The reverse is also true for non-marketing managers. Some of the exemplary areas in which such a broad understanding of the interface issues is needed are product innovation, designing for manufacturability, product/components standardization, and product positioning. In particular, Japanese competition has made us aware of the importance of these issues, and leading-edge business schools have increasingly adopted such an integrated approach to business education. Our book strongly reflects this state-of-the-art orientation.

**Interdisciplinary Perspective**

Market orientation is a fundamental philosophy of marketing. It is an organizational culture that puts customers' interests first in order to develop a long-term profitable enterprise. In essence, market orientation symbolizes the market-driven firm that is willing to constantly update its strategies using signals from the marketplace. Thus, marketing managers take market cues from the expressed needs and wants of customers. Consequently, the dominant orientation is that of a firm reacting to forces in the marketplace in order to differentiate itself from its competitors. This reactive "outside-in" perspective is reflected in the typical marketing manager's reliance on marketing intelligence, forecasting, and market research.

**Proactive Orientation**

   While not denying this traditional market orientation, we also believe that marketing managers should adopt an "inside-out" perspective and capabilities to shape or drive markets. This aspect of the link between strategic planning and marketing implementation has not been sufficiently treated in existing textbooks. For example, recent trends in technology licensing indicate that it is increasingly used as a conscious, proactive component of a firm's global product strategy. We believe that it is important for marketers to influence those actions of the firm that are some distance away from the customer in the value chain, because such actions have considerable influence on the size of the market and customer choice in intermediate and end product markets.

A book cannot be written devoid of its authors' background, expertise, and experience. Our book represents an amalgam of our truly diverse background, expertise, and experiences across North and South America, Asia, and Western and Eastern Europe. Given our upbringing and work experience in Asia, Western Europe, and Latin America, as well as our educational background in the United States, we have been sensitive not only to cultural differences and diversities but also to similarities.

**Cultural Sensitivity**

   Realistically speaking, there are more similarities than differences across many countries. In many cases, most of us tend to focus too much on cultural differences rather than similarities; or else, completely ignore differences or similarities. If you look only at cultural differences, you will be led to believe that country markets are uniquely different, thus requiring marketing strategy adaptations. If, on the other hand, you do not care about, or care to know about, cultural differences, you may be extending a culture-blind, ethnocentric view of the world. Either way, you may not benefit from the economies of scale and scope accruing from exploiting cultural similarities—and differences.

   Over the years, two fundamental counteracting forces have shaped the nature of marketing in the international arena. The same counteracting forces have been revisited by many authors in such terms as "standardization vs. adaptation" (1960s), "globalization vs. localization" (1970s), "global integration vs. local responsiveness" (1980s), "scale vs. sensitivity" (1990s), and more recently—let us add our own—"online scale vs. offline market sensitivity." Terms have changed, but the quintessence of the strategic dilemma that multinational companies (MNCs) face today has not changed and will probably remain unchanged for years to come.

However, the terminology no longer expresses an either/or issue. Forward-looking, proactive firms have the ability and willingness to accomplish both tasks simultaneously. As we explain later in the text, Honda, for example, developed its Accord car to satisfy the universal customer needs for reliability, drivability, and comfort, but marketed it as a family sedan in Japan, as a commuter car in the United States, and as an inexpensive sports car in Germany, thereby addressing cultural differences in the way people of different nationalities perceive and drive what is essentially the same car.

With our emphasis on global and proactive orientations, however, we will share with you how to hone your expertise, be culturally sensitive, and be able to see how to benefit from cultural similarities and differences.

## Research Orientation

We strongly believe that theory is useful to the extent that it helps in practice. And there are many useful theories for international marketing practices. Some of the practical theories are a logical extension of generic marketing theories you may have encountered in a marketing course. Others are, however, very much unique to the international environment.

Many people believe—rather erroneously—that international or global marketing is just a logical extension of domestic marketing, and that if you have taken a generic marketing course, you would not need to learn anything international. The international arena is just like a Pandora's box. Once you move into the international arena, there are many more facts, concepts, and frameworks you need to learn than you ever thought necessary in order to become a seasoned marketing manager working globally. To assist you in acquiring this new knowledge, various theories provide you with the conceptual tools that enable you to abstract, analyze, understand, and predict phenomena, and formulate effective decisions. Theories also provide you with an effective means to convey your logic to your peers and bosses with a strong, convincing power.

We also apply those theories in our own extensive international work advising corporate executives, helping them design effective global strategies, and teaching our students at various business schools around the world. Our role as educators is to convey sometimes-complex theories in everyday language. Our effort is reflected well in our textbook. This leads to our next orientation.

## Practical Orientation

Not only is this book designed to be user-friendly, but it also emphasizes practice. We believe in experiential learning and practical applications. Rote learning of facts, concepts, and theories is not sufficient. A good marketing manager should be able to put these to practice. We use many examples and anecdotes, as well as our own observations and experiences, to vividly portray practical applications. This book also contains real-life, lively cases so you can further apply your newly acquired knowledge in practice, and experience for yourself what it takes to be an effective international marketing manager.

Therefore, this book has been written for both upper-level undergraduate and MBA students who wish to learn practical applications of marketing and related logic, and subsequently work internationally. Although we overview foundation materials in this book, we expect that students have completed a basic marketing course.

To further enhance your learning experience, Professor Syed Anwar of West Texas A&M University kindly shares his excellent international marketing one-stop search website, *Marketing & International Links*[1] with you.

## Internet Implications

As we stated earlier, we extensively address the implications of the internet and e-commerce in global marketing activities. E-commerce is very promising, but various environmental differences—particularly cultural and legal as well as consumer-needs differences—are bound to prevent it from becoming an instantaneous freewheeling tool for global marketing. What we need to learn is how to manage *online scale and*

---

[1] http://wtfaculty.wtamu.edu/~sanwar.bus/otherlinks.htm#Marketing_&_International_Business_Links

*scope economies* and *offline sensitivities to different market requirements*. We try our best to help you become internet-savvy. The internet is addressed in all the chapters where relevant. In particular, Chapter 19 provides an in-depth analysis of global marketing issues in the age of the internet. We admit that there are many more unknowns than knowns about the impact of the internet on global marketing activities. That is why we point out areas in which the internet is likely to affect the way we do business and have you think seriously about the imminent managerial issues that you will be dealing with upon graduation. Chapter 19 serves not as an epilogue to the fifth edition but as a prologue to your exciting career ahead of you.

While this book is designed to be user-friendly, it also emphasizes practice. We believe in Instructor Support Materials. To accomplish our stated goals and orientations, we have made a major effort to provide the instructor and the student with practical theories and their explanations using examples, anecdotes, and cases to maximize the student's learning experience. Some of the specific teaching features are:

- **Global Perspectives**—Included in every chapter, Global Perspectives provide concrete examples from the global marketing environment into the classroom. They are designed to highlight some of the hottest global topics that students should be aware of and may actually act on in their careers. The instructor can use these inserts to exemplify theory or use them as mini-cases for class discussion.

- **Long Cases**—Long Cases are designed to challenge students with real and current business problems and issues. They require in-depth analysis and discussion of various topics covered in the chapters, and help students to experience how the knowledge they have gained can be applied in real-life situations. There are more than 40 cases covering various aspects of marketing situations as well as products, regions, and nationalities of firms. Six of them are included at the end of the text and the rest are placed on the textbook website for easy download.

- **Short Cases**—Short Cases are included at the end of each chapter and designed to address various specific issues explained in the chapters. These cases are useful in demonstrating to students the relevance of newly learned subject matters and are useful for open class discussions.

- **Maps**—The maps provided show the economic geography of the world. Students should be knowledgeable about where various economic resources are available and how they shape the nature of trade and investment and thus the nature of global competition. Global marketing cannot be appreciated without an understanding economic geography.

- **Review Questions**—Students may use the review questions to test themselves on and summarize the facts, concepts, theories, and other chapter materials in their own words. We strongly believe that by doing so, students will gain active working knowledge, rather than passive knowledge acquired by rote learning.

- **Discussion Questions**—These questions facilitate discussions that can help students apply the specific knowledge they learned in each chapter to actual business situations. They are designed to serve as mini-cases. Most of the issues presented in these questions are acute problems multinational marketing managers are facing, and have been adapted from recent issues of leading business newspapers and magazines.

- **The Instructor's Manual**—The Instructor's Manual is designed to provide major assistance to the instructor while allowing flexibility in course scheduling and teaching emphasis. The materials in the manual include the following:
  a. **Teaching Plans**—Alternative teaching plans and syllabi are included to accommodate the instructor's preferred course structure and teaching schedules. Alternative teaching schedules are developed for the course to be taught in a semester format, on a quarter bases, or as an executive seminar.
  b. **Discussion Guidelines**—For each chapter, specific teaching objectives and guidelines are developed to help stimulate classroom discussion.

c. **Test Bank**—A test bank consists of short essay questions and multiple-choice questions. This test bank is also computerized and available to adopters on IBM compatible computer diskettes.

d. **PowerPoint Slides**—These are available on the web to assist the instructor in preparing presentation materials.

e. **Home Page on the Web**—Make sure to visit our website http://www.wiley.com/college/kotabe/ for useful instructional information.

f. **Global Marketing Management System Online, 3.0 (GMMS03)**—developed by Dr. Basil J. Janavaras, professor of International Business at Minnesota State University, is a Web-based global marketing management research and planning program. As a bonus, each student who purchases the fifth edition of *Global Marketing Management* will receive a complimentary registration code that will provide access to the software. This practical, realistic program guides students through the systematic and integrative process of gathering, evaluating, and using certain types of information to help them to determine which markets to enter with a particular product or service and to create a marketing plan for the country with the optimal market environment for penetration. It is both interactive and experiential. More specifically, the program enables students to do the following:

- Perform a situation analysis of a company in a global context.
- Research global markets.
- Identify high potential country markets for selected products or services.
- Conduct in-depth market and competitive analysis.
- Determine the best entry mode strategies.
- Develop international marketing plans and strategies.

A Student Guide, Glossary, and targeted Web-based resources are provided in sample student projects as models to guide first-time users through the GMMSO process. An Instructor's Manual is also available to those who use the GMMSO. It includes the following:

- Frequently asked questions/answers/suggestions.
- Schedules for quarters and semester modules.
- Table that correlates the software content with the content in the text.
- Outlines for the presentation and the final paper.
- PowerPoint presentation of the entire GMMSO for instructional purposes.

Additional benefits for Instructors:

- Monitor both individual & group-progress and review completed projects online.
- Integrate knowledge from this and other courses.
- Bridge the gap between theory and the real world of business.
- Obtain technical support.

If you are interested in using the GMMSO class project, register online at www.gmmso3.com or contact your local Wiley representative for details at: www.wiley.com/college/rep

Finally, we are delighted to share our teaching experience with you through this book. Our teaching experience is an amalgam of our own learning and knowledge gained through continued discussion with our colleagues, our students, and our executive friends. We would also like to learn from you, instructor and students, who use our book. Not only do we wish for you to learn from our book but we also believe that there are many more things that we can also learn from you. We welcome your sincere comments and questions. Our contact addresses are as follows:

Masaaki Kotabe
Ph. (215) 204-7704
e-mail: mkotabe@temple.edu

Kristiaan Helsen
Ph. (852) 2358-7720
e-mail: mkhel@ust.hk

# ACKNOWLEDGMENTS

This book would have never materialized without the guidance, assistance, and encouragement of many of our mentors, colleagues, students, and executives with and from whom we have worked and learned over the years. We are truly indebted to each one of them. We also thank the many reviewers for their constructive comments and suggestions that helped us improve our argument and clarity, and raise the quality of our book.

The first co-author would like to extend thanks to his colleagues around the world. At Temple University, Dean Moshe Porat at the Fox School of Business, for emphasizing international business education and research as the school's primary focus of excellence, and providing plentiful opportunities for this co-author to meet with and discuss with leading practitioners/executives of international business those emerging issues that are shaping and re-shaping the way business is conducted around the world. A good deal of credit also goes to Dan Zhang for having educated me with so many fascinating business examples and cases from around the world throughout the revision process.

Various colleagues outside Temple University have helped the first co-author in the writing process. Tim Wilkinson (Montana State University) offered an interesting insight into the workings of the European Union and its marketing peculiarities. Amal Karunaratna (University of Adelaide, Australia) assisted in providing interesting examples from "Down Under." Taro Yaguchi (Omori & Yaguchi Law Firm, Philadelphia) offered an update on ever-changing laws and treaties that affect firms marketing internationally. Sae-Woon Park (Changwon National University, Korea), who has many years of export management and export financing practices, assisted in documenting the most up-to-date and state-of-the-art export practices in use today.

The second co-author would like to extend his thanks to MBA students at the University of Chicago, Nijenrode University, Hong Kong University of Science and Technology, and MIM students at Thammasat University (Bangkok). He also acknowledges the valuable comments on Chapter 13 from Chris Beaumont and John Mackay, both with McCann-Erickson, Japan. Professor Niraj Dawar (University of Western Ontario, Canada) offered helpful insights on marketing in emerging markets. A word of gratitude for their feedback and encouragement is given to two colleagues who spent their sabbatical at HKUST: Jerry Albaum (University of Oregon) and Al Shocker (University of Minnesota); and special thanks to Romualdo Leones for some of the photo materials used in the new edition.

The textbook becomes ever more useful when accompanied by good resources for instructors and students. Preparing good resources is no small task. Chip Miller of Drake University deserves a special credit not only for preparing the excellent Resource Guide and Test Bank to go with the book but also for providing useful examples and insights throughout the revision process.

A very special word of appreciation goes to the staff of John Wiley & Sons, Inc., particularly, Franny Kelly and Maria Guarascio, and Cynthia Mondgock of iD8 Publishing Services, for their continued enthusiasm and support throughout the course of this project.

Finally and most importantly, we are deeply grateful to you, the professors, students, and professionals, for using this book. We stand by our book, and sincerely hope that our book adds to your knowledge and expertise. We would also like to continuously improve our product in the future.

As we indicated in the Preface, we would like to hear from you, our valued customers. Thank you!

# BRIEF CONTENTS

# CONTENTS

**The following additional cases appear on the textbook's website:**

# GLOBALIZATION IMPERATIVE

HAPTER OVERVIEW

1. WHY GLOBAL MARKETING IS IMPERATIVE
2. GLOBALIZATION OF MARKETS: CONVERGENCE AND DIVERGENCE
3. EVOLUTION OF GLOBAL MARKETING
4. APPENDIX: THEORIES OF INTERNATIONAL TRADE AND THE MULTI-NATIONAL ENTERPRISE

Marketing products and services around the world, transcending national and political boundaries, is a fascinating phenomenon. The phenomenon, however, is not entirely new. Products have been traded across borders throughout recorded civilization, extending back beyond the Silk Road that once connected East with West from Xian to Rome on land, and the recently excavated sea trade route between the Roman Empire and India that existed 2,000 years ago. However, since the end of World War II, the world economy has experienced a spectacular growth rate never witnessed before in human history, primarily led by large U.S. companies in the 1950s and 1960s, then by European and Japanese companies in the 1970s and 1980s, and most recently by new emerging market firms, such as Lenovo, Mittal Steel, and Cemex. In particular, competition coming recently from the so-called BRIC countries (Brazil, Russia, India, China) has given the notion of global competition a touch of extra urgency and significance that you see almost daily in print media such as the *Wall Street Journal, Financial Times, Nikkei Shimbun, and Folha de São Paulo*, as well as in TV media such as BBC, NBC, and CNN. With a few exceptions, such as Korea's Samsung Electronics (consumer electronics) and China's Haier (home appliances), most emerging-market multinational companies are not yet household names in the industrialized world, but from India's Infosys Technologies (IT services) to Brazil's Embraer (light jet aircrafts), and from Taiwan's Acer (computers) to Mexico's Cemex (building materials), a new class of formidable competitors is rising.[1]

---

[1]"A New Threat to America Inc." *Business Week*, July 25, 2005, p. 114; and also read Martin Roll, *Asian Brand Strategy: How Asia Builds Strong Brands*, New York: Palgrave Macmillan, 2006.

In this chapter, we will introduce to you the complex and constantly evolving realities of global marketing. Global marketing refers to a strategy for achieving one or more of four major categories of potential globalization benefits: cost reduction, improved quality of products and programs, enhanced customer preference, and increased competitive advantage on a global basis. The objective is to make you think beyond exporting and importing. As you will learn shortly, despite wide media attention to them, exporting and importing constitute a relatively small portion of international business. We are not saying, however, that exporting and importing are not important. In 2006, the volume of world merchandise trade grew by 8 percent, while world gross domestic product recorded a 3.5 percent increase, which confirms that the trend in world merchandise trade grows by twice the annual growth rate of output since 2000. Total merchandise trade volume reached $16.3 trillion in 2008, compared to $6 trillion in 2000.[2] In recent years, improved market conditions in the United States and Europe, as well as strong growth in the Emerging Markets, such as China and India, steadily improved the world economy after the devastating terrorist attacks in the United States on September 11, 2001. However, the aftermath of the U.S.-led war against Iraq, the high oil prices, and most recently, the unprecedented global recession triggered by the subprime mortgage crisis in the United States in 2008, among other things, continue to curb a full-fledged recovery in the world economy. Indeed, at the time of this writing in early 2009, as the global economy is currently experiencing the worst recession since the Great Depression of 1929–1932, World Bank predicts that the world trade volume will shrink in 2009 for the first time in over 25 years,[3] and the specter of economic nationalism—the country's urge to protect domestic jobs and keep capital at home instead of promoting freer international trade—is hampering further globalization.[4] Although sometimes bumpy, it is expected that the drive for globalization will continue to be promoted through more free trade, more Internet commerce, more networking of businesses, schools and communities, and more advanced technologies.[5]

---

## ◆ ◆ ◆ ◆ ◆ ◆ ◆ ◆  WHY GLOBAL MARKETING IS IMPERATIVE

We frequently hear terms such as *global markets*, *global competition*, *global technology*, and *global competitiveness*. In the past, we heard similar words with *international* or *multinational* instead of *global* attached to them. What has happened since the 1980s? Are these terms just fashionable concepts of the time without some deep meanings? Or has something inherently changed in our society?

***Saturation of Domestic Markets.***   First, and at the most fundamental level, the saturation of domestic markets in the industrialized parts of the world forced many companies to look for marketing opportunities beyond their national boundaries. The economic and population growths in developing countries also gave those companies an additional incentive to venture abroad. Now companies from emerging economies, such as Korea's Samsung and Hyundai and Mexico's Cemex and Grupo Modelo, have made inroads into the developed markets around the

---

[2]*The World Factbook 2009*, https://www.cia.gov/library/publications/the-world-factbook/index.html.

[3]World Bank, *Global Economic Prospect 2009*, www.worldbank.org/gep2009.

[4]"The Return of Economic Nationalism," *Economist*, February 7, 2009, pp. 9–10.

[5]The reader needs to be cautioned that there may be limits to the benefit of globalization for two primary reasons. First, firms in poor countries with very weak economic and financial infrastructures may not be able to (afford to) adjust fast enough to the forces of globalization. Second, poor countries could be made worse off by trade liberalization because trade tends to be opened for high-tech goods and services exported by rich countries – such as computers and financial services – but remains protected in areas where those poor countries could compete, such as agricultural goods, textiles or construction. See, for example, Joseph E. Stiglitz, *Globalization and Its Discontents*, New York: W.W. Norton & Co., 2003. For an excellent treatise on various paradoxes of globalization, refer to Terry Clark, Monica Hodis, and Paul D'Angelo, "The Ancient Road: An Overview of Globalization," in Masaaki Kotabe and Kristiaan Helsen, ed., *The SAGE Handbook of International Marketing*, London: Sage Publications, 2009, pp. 15–35.

world. The same logic applies equally to companies from developed countries, such as Australia and New Zealand, geographically isolated from the other major industrialized parts of the world. Dôme Coffees Australia is building a multi-national coffee shop empire by expanding into Asia and the Middle East. Inevitably, the day will come when Starbucks from the United States and Dôme Coffees from Australia will compete head-on for global dominance.[6]

***Emerging Markets.*** During the twentieth century, the large economies and large trading partners have been located mostly in the Triad Regions of the world (North America, Western Europe, and Japan), collectively producing over 80 percent of world gross domestic product (GDP) with only 20 percent of the World's population.[7] However, in the next 10 to 20 years, the greatest commercial opportunities are expected to be found increasingly in ten Big Emerging Markets (BEMs)—the Chinese Economic Area, India, Commonwealth of Independent States (Russia, Central Asia, and Caucasus states), South Korea, Mexico, Brazil, Argentina, South Africa, Central European countries, Turkey, and the Association of Southeast Asian Nations (Indonesia, Brunei, Malaysia, Singapore, Thailand, the Philippines, and Vietnam). Accordingly, an increasing number of competitors are expected to originate from those ten emerging economies. In the past 20 years, China's real annual GDP growth rate has averaged 9.5 percent a year; while India's has been 5.7 percent, compared to the average 3 percent GDP growth in the United States. Clearly, the milieu of the world economy has changed significantly and over the next two decades the markets that hold the greatest potential for dramatic increases in U.S. exports are not the traditional trading partners in Europe, Canada, and Japan, which now account for the overwhelming bulk of the international trade of the United States. But they will be those BEMs and other developing countries that constitute some 80 percent of the "bottom of the pyramid."[8] As the traditional developed markets have become increasingly competitive, such emerging markets promise to offer better growth opportunities to many firms.

***Global Competition.*** We believe something profound has indeed happened in our view of competition around the world. About thirty years ago, the world's greatest automobile manufacturers were General Motors, Ford, and Chrysler. Today, companies like Toyota, Honda, BMW, Renault, and Hyundai, among others, stand out as competitive nameplates in the global automobile market. Now with a 15-percent market share in the United States, Toyota's market share is larger than Ford's 14 percent. In early 2008, Toyota surpassed General Motors to become the world's largest automaker in terms of worldwide output.[9] Similarly, while personal computers had been almost synonymous with IBM, which had previously dominated the PC business around the world, today, the computer market is crowded with Dell and Hewlett-Packard (HP) from the United States, Sony and Toshiba from Japan, Samsung from Korea, Acer from Taiwan,[10] and so on. Indeed, Lenovo, a personal computer company from China, acquired the IBM PC division in 2005, and now sells the ThinkPad series under the Lenovo brand. The deal not only puts Lenovo into third place in the industry, it also challenges the world top players, Dell and HP/Compaq, respectively.[11] Nike is a

---

[6]"Bean Countess," *Australian Magazine*, December 9–10, 2000, p. 50+.

[7]L. Bryan, *Race for the World: Strategies to Build A Great Global Firm*, Boston, MA: Harvard Business School Press, 1999.

[8]C. K. Prahalad, *The Fortune at the Bottom of the Pyramid: Eradicating Poverty through Profits*, Philadelphia, PA: Wharton School Publishing, 2004.

[9]"Toyota's Global Sales Top GM by 277,000 Units in 1st Half," Nikkeinet Interactive, www.nni.nikkei.co.jp, July 24, 2008.Catches GM in Global Sales," CNNMoney.com, January 23 2008.

[10]"Why Taiwan Matters: The Global Economy Couldn't Function without It, but Can It Really Find Peace with China?" *Business Week*, May 16, 2005, pp. 74–81.

[11]"Can China's Lenovo Brand in the Land of Dell?" *B to B*, October 10, 2005, p. 1 and p. 45.

JTB Photo/Photolibrary Group Limited

Globe-trotting companies are vying for customers' "mind share" in many parts of the world such as in Piccadilly Circus, London, England.

U.S. company with a truly all-American shoe brand, but all its shoes are made in foreign countries and exported to many countries. Pillsbury (known for its Betty Crocker recipes and Häagen-Dazs ice cream brand) and 7-Eleven convenience stores are two American institutions owned and managed, respectively, by Diageo from the United Kingdom and Seven & i Holdings Co. from Japan. On the other hand, the world of media, led by U.S. media giants, has become equally global in reach. MTV, targeting teenage audiences, has 35 channels worldwide, 15 of them in Europe, produces a large part of its channel contents locally. CNN has 22 different versions. In 1996, 70 percent of the English-language version of CNN International was American; today that share has shrunk to about 8 percent.[12] The video game industry is truly global from day one; Nintendo's Wii, Sony's Playstation 3, and Microsoft's Xbox now vie for customers in the Triad regions simultaneously.

***Global Cooperation.***    Global competition also brings about global cooperation. This is most obvious in the information technology industry. IBM and Japan's Fujitsu used to be archrivals. Beginning in 1982, they battled each other for fifteen years in such areas as software copyright. But in October 2001, they developed a comprehensive tie-up involving the joint development of software and the mutual use of computer technology. IBM would share its PC server technology with Fujitsu and the Japanese company would supply routers to IBM.[13] Japan's Sony, Toshiba, and U.S. computer maker IBM are jointly developing advanced semiconductor processing technologies for next-generation chips. As part of the project, IBM transfers its latest technologies to Sony and Toshiba, and the partner companies each send engineers to IBM's research center in New York to work on the joint project.[14] Similarly, in the automotive industry, in 1999 French carmaker Renault SA took a 36.8 percent stake in Japanese carmaker Nissan Motor Corp. The two companies began producing cars on joint platforms in 2005. To help pave the way for that, in March, 2001 the two carmakers decided that they would combine their procurement operations in a joint-venture company that would eventually handle 70 percent of the companies' global purchasing. The joint venture is headquartered in Paris, with offices in Japan and the United States.[15]

[12]"Think Global," *Economist*, April 11,2002.

[13]"Fujitsu, IBM Negotiate Comprehensive Tie-up," *Nikkei Interactive Net*, www.nni.nikkei.co.jp, October 18, 2001.

[14]"IBM, Sony, Toshiba Broaden and Extend Successful Semiconductor Technology Alliance," IBM Press Room, http://www-03.ibm.com/press/us/en/pressrelease/19103.wss, January 12, 2006," *Nikkei Interactive Net*, www.nni .nikkei.co.jp, April 2, 2002.

[15]"Nissan and Renault Look to Boost Joint Procurement Efforts," Japan Times, November 29, 2002.

***Internet Revolution.*** The proliferation of the Internet and e-commerce is wide reaching. The number of Internet users in the world reached 1.4 billion by March 2008, which amounts to almost three times that of 2000. According to Internet World Stat,[16] 41.2 percent of the Internet users come from Asia, followed by 24.6 percent and 15.7 percent from Europe and North America, respectively. Although the Middle East and Africa account for only 6.3 percent of Internet users, these two regions rank top two in their usage growth of over ten times between 2000 and 2008. In the same period, Internet usage in Asia and Latin America/Caribbean grew by 475 percent and 861 percent, respectively. As a result, the total global e-commerce turnover ballooned more than 33 times from $385 billion in 2000 to $12.8 trillion in 2006, taking up 18 percent of the global trade of commodities in 2006. Developed countries led by the United States are still leading players in this field, while developing countries like China are emerging, becoming an important force in the global e-commerce market.[17]

Compared to business-to-consumer (B2C) e-commerce, business-to-business (B2B) e-commerce is larger, growing faster, and has less unequal geographical distribution globally.[18] Increases in the freedom of the movements of goods, services, capital, technology, and people, coupled with rapid technological development, resulted in an explosion of global B2B e-commerce. The share a country is likely to receive of the global B2B e-commerce, on the other hand, depends upon country-level factors such as income and population size, the availability of credit, venture capital, and telecom and logistical infrastructure; tax and other incentives, tariff/nontariff barriers, government emphasis on the development of human capital, regulations to influence firms' investment in R&D, organizational level politics, language, and the activities of international agencies.[19]

Who could have anticipated the expansion of today's e-commerce companies, including Amazon, eBay, and Yahoo in the United States; QXL Ricardo and Kelkoo in Europe; Rakuten and 7dream in Japan, and Baidu in China? The Internet opened the gates for companies to sell direct-to-consumers easily across national boundaries. Many argue that e-commerce is less intimate than face-to-face retail; however, it actually provides more targeted demographic and psychographic information.

Manufacturers that traditionally sell through the retail channel may benefit the most from e-commerce. Most importantly, the data allow for the development of relevant marketing messages aimed at important customers and initiate loyal relationships on a global basis.[20] With the onset of satellite communications, consumers in developing countries are equally familiar with global brands as consumers in developed countries, and as a result, there is tremendous pent-up demand for products marketed by multinational companies (which we also refer to as MNCs).[21]

What's more, the Internet builds a platform for a two-way dialogue between manufacturers and consumers, allowing consumers to design and order their own products from the manufacturers. Customized build-to-order business model is already an established trend. Dell Computer is a pioneer that does business globally by bypassing traditional retail channels. It accepts orders by phone, fax, or on the Internet.[22] General Motors started providing a build-to-order Web service for its

---

[16]http://www.internetworldstats.com, accessed July 20, 2009.

[17]Annual Report on the Development of Global E-Commerce Industry: 2006-2007, http://market.ccidnet.com/pub/report/show_17192.html, accessed July 20, 2009.

[18]B2B and B2C, among others, have become trendy business terms in recent years. However, they are fundamentally the same as more conventional terms, consumer marketing and industrial marketing, respectively, except that B2B and B2C imply the use of the Internet, Intranet, customer relationship management software, and other information technology expertise. In our book, we will not use use these trendy terms unless they are absolutely necessary in making our point.

[19]Nikhilesh Dholakia, "Determinants of the Global Diffusion of B2B E-commerce," *Electronic Markets*, 12 (March 2002), pp. 120–29.

[20]Andrew Degenholtz, "E-Commerce Fueling the Flame for New Product Development," *Marketing News*, March 29, 1999, p. 18.

[21]D. J. Arnold, and J. Quelch, "New Strategies in Emerging Markets," *Sloan Management Review* 40(1), 1998, pp. 7–20.

[22]However, Dell's direct sales on the Internet fails to work in some emerging markets, particularly where customers want to see products before they buy. Such is the case in small cities in China. See "Dell May Have to Reboot in China," *Business Week*, November 7, 2005, p. 46.

Brazilian customers in 2000. Mazda's Web Tune Factory site, being one of the first Japanese auto build-to-order models, allows consumers to choose their own engine specifications, transmission type, body color, wheel design and other interior and exterior equipment.[23] However, as presented in **Global Perspective 1-1**, we would also like to stress as a caveat that the proliferation of e-commerce and satellite communications does not necessarily mean that global marketing activities are going culture- and human contact-free. Learning of foreign languages will probably remain as important as ever.

# GLOBAL PERSPECTIVE 1-1

## THE INTERNET WORLD AND CULTURAL AND HUMAN ASPECTS OF GLOBAL MARKETING

Cultural differences greatly affect business relationships in the world of e-commerce, but this is often underestimated, especially in international team-building efforts. Language issues are not the only source of the problem. Foreign companies need acceptance by the local market and understanding of the local business culture. The Internet's awesome communications power can be turned into a conduit for miscommunication if such cultural factors are ignored. Knowing what level of communication is appropriate for a certain level of trust is particularly important in a Web-based environment, where face-to-face contact may be more limited.

Think, for example, a typical mid-sized manufacturer in, say, Taiwan, China, or Thailand. Would it enter into a strategic business relationship with companies and people they encounter only through computerized interactions? The short answer is yes; they will enter into such relationships. However, we qualify our positive reply by adding that the initial courtship ritual must continue to have personal face-to-face, one-to-one, or what we feel is becoming a new "screen-to-screen" relationship dimension as with a traditional business model. In China, which has a long tradition of distrust and a culture of relationship building known as "guanxi," information, a key source of power in this business culture, is only passed selectively to individuals who are proven trustworthy or known as insiders. This kind of culture has considerable impact on B2B e-commerce adoption and diffusion in China. In this context, such sociocultural tensions cannot be solved with only the Internet's technical power. In fact, traditional personal face-to-face communications are still critical in building trust and relationships.

However, after the initial mating ritual, you can and already do see tremendous transactional business-to-business activity in these countries. There is nothing to say that e-commerce can or should replace the human element in relationship building. In fact, e-commerce is a new form of personalized relationship building that even the highest context cultures engage in. eBay and the other online auction companies are perfect examples of such new electronic relationship and trust building. Even in the Eastern cultures, we see numerous gambling sites springing up where the only aspects of the relationship are anonymous e-commerce-related.

The critical factor will be the Web site evolving into the first step in developing the personal international business relationship. Unless the Web site makes the first connection based on sensitivity to the cross-cultural aspects of interface design, human factors, navigation currency, time and date conventions, localization, internationalization, and so on, the ability to "connect" will be stilted.

In the information technology sector, one can look at Dell and Gateway, which both do very strong business in the Asia/Pacific region. The networking company, Cisco Systems, serves as an example of the morphing of electronic and personal relationships. While they have done a tremendous job of building global relationships and partnerships on an in-country face-to-face level, almost 90 percent of their business (i.e., sales transactions) is conducted over the Web.

Has the Web replaced the need for the personal business courtship? Absolutely not. Has it added a new element to the same relationship after the bonds are formed? Most definitely. Will there be new electronic forms of relationship building that replace the old model of face-to-face in a karaoke bar? . . . Yes, it is happening already. Starting with video/teleconferences in the boardroom and expanding downward to Microsoft NetMeetings using a Webcam on the desktop.

Just think, one decade or so ago very few of us would hardly dream that most Web-enabled adolescents communicate more through instant messaging than they do on the phone or in person. In ten years, technology will give us HDTV screen quality with real time audio and video bandwidth. This surely will not completely replace face-to-face interaction among global sellers and buyers, but it will for certain offer a viable substitute for those who grew up chatting online.

*Sources*: Frank Cutitta, GINLIST@LIST.MSU.EDU, April 17, 1999; Nitish Singh, Vikas Kumar, and Daniel Baack, "Adaptation of Cultural Content: Evidence from B2C E-Commerce Firms," *European Journal of Marketing*, 39 (1/2), 2005, pp. 71–86; Jing Tan, Katherine Tyler, Andrea Manica, "Business-to-Business Adoption of eCommerce in China," *Information & Management*, 44, April 2007, pp. 332–51; and Maris G. Martinsons, "Relationship-Based e-Commerce: Theory and Evidence from China," *Information Systems Journal*, published online, April 15, 2008.

---

[23]Setsuko Kamiya, "Mazda lets buyers fine-tune Rodster," The Japan Times Online, www.hapantimes.co.jp, January 5, 2002.

**EXHIBIT 1-1**
CHANGE IN THE WORLD'S 100 LARGEST COMPANIES
AND THEIR NATIONALITIES

| Country | 1970 | 1980 | 1990 | 2000* | 2009* |
|---------|------|------|------|-------|-------|
| United States** | 64 | 45 | 33 | 36 | 29 |
| Germany** | 8 | 13 | 12 | 10 | 15 |
| Japan | 8 | 8 | 16 | 23 | 10 |
| France | 3 | 12 | 10 | 7 | 10 |
| Britain** | 9 | 7 | 8 | 6 | 6 |
| Italy** | 3 | 4 | 4 | 3 | 5 |
| China | 0 | 0 | 0 | 3 | 5 |
| South Korea | 0 | 0 | 2 | 0 | 4 |
| Spain | 0 | 0 | 2 | 1 | 3 |
| Netherlands** | 4 | 5 | 3 | 6 | 2 |
| Russia | 0 | 0 | 0 | 0 | 2 |
| Switzerland | 2 | 3 | 3 | 4 | 1 |
| Belgium** | 0 | 1 | 1 | 1 | 1 |
| Brazil | 0 | 1 | 1 | 0 | 1 |
| Mexico | 0 | 1 | 1 | 1 | 1 |
| Norway | 0 | 0 | 0 | 0 | 1 |
| Finland | 0 | 0 | 1 | 0 | 1 |
| Luxembourg | 0 | 0 | 0 | 0 | 1 |
| Malaysia | 0 | 0 | 0 | 0 | 1 |
| Venezuela | 0 | 1 | 1 | 1 | 1 |
| Sweden | 0 | 0 | 2 | 0 | 0 |
| Austria | 0 | 0 | 1 | 0 | 0 |
| South Africa | 0 | 0 | 1 | 0 | 0 |
| Canada | 0 | 2 | 0 | 0 | 0 |
| Australia | 1 | 0 | 0 | 0 | 0 |
| Total** | 102 | 103 | 102 | 103 | 100 |

*Source: Fortune*, various issues up to 2009.

**Fortune* Global 500 criteria changed to include services firms (including retailing and trading)

**Includes joint nationality of firms (joint nationality has been counted for both the countries), so the total may exceed 100.

An examination of the top 100 largest companies in the world also vividly illustrates the profound changes in competitive milieu and provides a faithful mirror image of broad economic trends that we have seen over the past thirty some years (see **Exhibit 1.1**). In particular, the last decade was characterized by the long-term recession in Japan and a resurgence of the U.S. economy that had once been battered by foreign competition in the 1980s. Take Japan, which has suffered several recessions since 1995 and many political changes, as an example. The number of Japanese companies on the list fell from 23 in 2000 to 10 in 2009. The number of U.S. and European firms ranking in the largest 100 has stayed relatively stable since 1990. Although the United States boasts the largest number of firms in the top 100 list, a list of countries with large firms is getting more decentralized. One of the biggest changes since 1990 has been the emergence of China.[24] As economic reform progressed and Chinese companies improved their accounting standards, their presence grew steadily. Five Chinese companies are on the 2009 *Fortune Global 100* list. Because of the rising tide of petrodollars, a Chinese company, Sinopec, was lifted into the top 10 for the first time. The current world economy has changed so drastically from what it was merely a decade ago.

The changes observed in the past thirty years simply reflect that companies from other parts of the world have grown in size relative to those of the United States despite the resurgence of the U.S. economy in the 1990s. In other words, today's environment is characterized not only by much more competition from around the world but also by more fluid domestic and international market conditions than in the past. As a result, many U.S. executives are feeling much more competitive urgency in product development, materials procurement, manufacturing, and marketing around the world. It does not necessarily mean that U.S. companies have lost their competitiveness, however. The robust economy in the United States in the late 1990s met a slow down in 2000 due to

---

[24]See "The China Price," *Business Week*, December 6, 2004, pp. 102-120; "How China Runs the World Economy," *Economist*, July 30, 2005, p. 11.

the crash of dot.com's bubble economy, and was worsened by the terrorist attacks on September 11, 2001. But the strong consumer demand has saved its economy. On the other hand, many Asian countries have recovered from the 1997 Asian financial crisis (see chapter 3 for details).

The same competitive pressure equally applies to executives of foreign companies. For example, while its Japanese home market was the incredible shrinking market in the 1990s, Toyota's new strategy has been to de-Japanize its business and make the U.S. market its corporate priority. By 2001, Toyota had already accomplished its goal by selling more vehicles in the United States (1.74 million) than in Japan (1.71 million), with almost two-thirds of the company's operating profit coming from the U.S. market. Now Toyota's top U.S. executives are increasingly local hires. As Mark Twain once wrote, "if you stand still, you will get run over." This analogy holds true in describing such competitive pressure in this era of global competition.

It is not only this competitive force that is shaping global business today. Particularly in the past several years, many political and economic events have affected the nature of global competition. The demise of the Soviet Union, the establishment of the European Union and the North American Free Trade Agreement, deregulation, and privatization of state-owned industries have also changed the market environments around the world. Furthermore, the emerging markets of Eastern Europe and the rapidly re-emerging markets of Southeast Asia also add promise to international businesses.

The fluid nature of global markets and competition makes the study of global marketing not only interesting but also challenging and rewarding. The term *global* epitomizes both the competitive pressure and the expanding of market opportunities all over the world. It does not mean, however, that all companies have to operate globally like IBM, Sony, Philips, or Samsung. Whether a company operates domestically or across national boundaries, it can no longer avoid competitive pressure from other parts of the world. Competitive pressure can also come from competitors at home. When Weyerhaeuser, a forest products company headquartered in Seattle, Washington, began exporting newspaper rolls to Japan, it had to meet the exacting quality standard that Japanese newspaper publishers demanded—and it did. As a result, this Seattle company now boasts the best newspaper rolls and outperforms other domestic companies in the U.S. market as well. Even smaller firms could benefit from exacting foreign market requirements. When Weaver Popcorn Co. of Van Buren, Indiana, started to export popcorn to Japan, Japanese distributors demanded better quality and fewer imperfections. This led to improvements in Weaver's processing equipment and product, which helped its domestic as well as international sales.[25] Furthermore, e-commerce comes in handy for those smaller firms with international marketing ambitions. For example, LaPebbles.com, a small handcrafted jewelry maker based in the northeastern part of the United States, can tap into potentially large global markets. So can small firms based in foreign countries looking to the U.S. market as well. Therefore, even purely domestic companies that have never sold anything abroad cannot be shielded from international competitive pressure. The point is that when we come across the term global, we should be made aware of both this intense, competitive pressure and expanding market opportunities on a global basis.

◆ ◆ ◆ ◆ ◆ ◆ ◆ ◆ ◆    ## GLOBALIZATION OF MARKETS: CONVERGENCE AND DIVERGENCE

When a country's per capita income is less than $10,000, much of the income is spent on food and other necessity items, and very little disposable income remains. However, once per capita income reaches $20,000 or so, the disposable portion of income increases dramatically because the part of the income spent on necessities does not

---

[25] Doug LeDuc, "Overseas Markets Spur Growth for Van Buren, Ind.-Based Popcorn Maker," *The News-Sentinel*, (April 19, 1999).

rise nearly as fast as income increases. As a result, a billion people, constituting some 16 percent of the population, around the world with per capita income of $20,000 and above have considerable purchasing power. With this level of purchasing power, people, irrespective of their nationality, tend to enjoy similar educational levels, academic and cultural backgrounds, and access to information. As these cultural and social dimensions begin to resemble each other in many countries, people's desire for material possessions, ways of spending leisure time, and aspirations for the future become increasingly similar. Even the deeply rooted cultures have begun to converge.[26] In other words, from a marketing point of view, those people have begun to share a similar "choice set" of goods and services originating from many parts of the world. What does it mean?

In one sense, we see young people jogging in Nike shoes (an American product made in China), listening to System of a Down (an Armenian rock band) or Thalia Sodi (a Mexican pop singer) on Apple Computer's iPod (an American product) in Hong Kong, Philadelphia, São Paulo, Sydney, and Tokyo. Similarly, Yuppies (young urban professionals) in Amsterdam, Chicago, Osaka, and Dallas share a common lifestyle: driving a BMW (a German car assembled in Toluca, Mexico) to the office, listening to Sumi Jo's and Sissel Kyrkjebø's new CD albums (purchased on their business trips to Korea and Norway, respectively), using a Dell notebook computer (an American product made by Quanta, a Taiwanese company in Taiwan) at work, calling their colleagues with a Nokia cellular phone (a Finnish product), signing important documents with an exquisite Parker Pen (made by a French-based company owned by a U.S. company), and having a nice seafood buffet at Mövenpick (a Swiss restaurant chain) on a Friday. In the evenings, these people spend their spare time browsing various Web sites using Google search engine (an American Internet company) to do some "virtual" window-shopping on their PCs (powered by a microprocessor made in Malaysia by Intel, an American company). The convergence of consumer needs in many parts of the world translates into tremendous business opportunities for companies willing to risk venturing abroad.

The *convergence* of consumer needs at the macro level may be evident, but it does not necessarily mean that individual consumers will adopt all the products from around the world. Globalization does not suffocate local cultures, but rather liberates them from the ideological conformity of nationalism.[27] As a result, we have become ever more selective. Therefore, you find one of your friends at school in the United States driving a Toyota Tacoma (a compact Japanese truck made by General Motors and Toyota in Fremont, California), enjoying Whoppers at a Burger King fast food restaurant (an ex-British company, now American), and practicing capoeira (a 400-year-old Brazilian martial art); another friend in Austria is driving a Peugeot 107 (a French car made by Toyota in the Czech Republic, also marketed as Citroën 1 and Toyota Aygo), enjoying sushi at a sushi restaurant (a Japanese food), and practicing karate (an ancient Japanese martial art); and a cousin of yours is driving a Ford Escape (an American sports utility vehicle jointly developed with Mazda, a Japanese automaker), munching on pizzas (an American food of Italian origin), and practicing soccer (a sport of English origin, known as football outside the United States and some few other countries). In other words, thanks to market globalization, not only have we become more receptive to new things, but we also have a much wider, more divergent "choice set" of goods and services to choose from to shape our own individual preferences and lifestyles. This is true whether you live in a small town in the United States or in a big city in Europe. In other words, the *divergence* of consumer needs is taking place at the same time. For example, Pollo Campero, a Latin American fried chicken chain from Guatemala, which offers a crunchy bite of chicken with a Latin service in a Latin-American environment, has been catching on quietly in the United

---

[26]For an excellent story about global cultural convergence, read "Global Culture" and "A World Together," *National Geographic*, 196 (August 1999), pp. 2–33.
[27]Mario Vargas Llosa, "The Culture of Liberty," *Foreign Affairs*, issue 122, January/February 2001, pp. 66–71.

States, the land of Kentucky Fried Chicken (KFC), to cater to Americans' increased appetite for a different kind of chicken.[28] From a marketing point of view, it is becoming more difficult—not easier—to pinpoint consumers' preferences in any local market around the world, the more globalized the markets become.

As presented in **Global Perspective 1-2**, the European Union (EU) market offers a vivid example of how market forces of convergence and divergence are at work. One thing is clear. There is no such a thing as a static market in an era of globalization.

---

*G*LOBAL PERSPECTIVE 1-2

**MARKET CONVERGENCE AND DIVERGENCE AT WORK IN THE EUROPEAN UNION**

Will Euroland survive? Rejection of the proposed EU Constitution by France and The Netherlands in 2005 caused anguish for political and EU economic elites. An "ever closer union" had been seen—until the no vote called it into question—(see Chapter 2 for details), as the European answer to globalization, political security, and economic growth. European leaders aren't the only ones who are concerned. Insightful American and Japanese business managers are also worried because, contrary to popular belief, the chief economic beneficiaries of European integration are American and Japanese multinational corporations.

Historically, Europe, due to national, cultural, and ethnic differences, has had heterogeneous and fragmented markets. These markets produced small to mid-sized firms capable of adapting to, and prospering from, highly differentiated environments. Even the largest European companies tended to operate at the national, rather than Pan-European, level, avoiding the many encumbrances of functioning across borders where market conditions were so dissimilar. For instance, for many years Unilever sold a fabric softener in ten countries under seven different brand names, using a variety of marketing strategies and bottle shapes.

Typical European firms pursued niche strategies, emphasizing craftsmanship, specialization, and networks of relationships. Europe, with its myriad laws, languages, and customs, historically constituted a market environment with significant entry and operating barriers. Foreign firms could not use economies of scale or scope inherent in large homogeneous markets; they were unable to compete on the basis of low cost or low price. High labor costs, heavy taxation to support welfare states, and high expectations of European retailers and consumers, all worked together to shape an environment that favored the creation of specialized, premium products rather than mass-consumption products. This put U.S. multinationals in Europe at a competitive disadvantage.

The traditional European advantage was based on the notion that a less homogeneous marketplace requires a more individualized marketing strategy. This approach is at odds with the strategy of many American firms—preserving the ability to reduce costs through economies of scale and scope. Historically, market fragmentation shielded Europe from U.S. competition. Such fragmentation constituted location-specific advantages that

were either costly to overcome, or were simply impenetrable by many smaller U.S. companies. However, the creation of the European Union changed the rules of the game.

One major purpose of the EU is to create extensive homogeneous markets in which large European firms are able to take advantage of economies of scale and therefore are better able to compete with their U.S. counterparts. EU reformers hope to create an economy analogous to the United States, in which low inflation coexists with high growth, thereby leading to low unemployment.

The formation of the EU has resulted in extremely large levels of U.S. and Japanese foreign direct investment (FDI) in Europe. Why? First, it was feared that the EU would become "Fortress Europe" through the implementation of significant protectionist measures against firms from outside the EU. Under these circumstances, FDI constitutes tariff jumping in anticipation of negative actions that may or may not occur in the future. Second, the elimination of internal borders creates a single market, amenable to the large economies of scale and scope preferred by U.S. and Japanese multinationals.

Numbers tell the story. The average FDI inflows into the European Community (as the EU was known until November 1, 1993) amounted to $65.6 billion from 1985–1995. The inflow in 1999 (the year the euro, a new currency adopted by eleven EU member countries, was launched) was $479.4 billion—a 700 percent increase. By 2000 Japanese investment in the EU was roughly six times more than EU investment in Japan. In 1980 the total FDI stock of European Community was $216 billion, by 2005 it was $3,123 billion. Finally, FDI stock as a percentage of GDP was 8.5 percent in 1987 (the year that plans for the Maastricht Treaty were presented). In 2002, the year in which euro notes and coins replaced local currencies, it was 34.6 percent.

Four decades ago the French intellectual, J. J. Servan-Schreiber complained bitterly about the U.S. presence in Europe in a best-selling book entitled, *The American Challenge* (1967). The Europeans now face similar competitive dynamics. Ironically, in their quest for economic competitiveness, they may have made themselves more vulnerable to the ambitions of U.S. and Japanese multinationals.

What can European firms do to cope with the onslaught of U.S. and Japanese multinationals? Large European firms can

---

[28]"From Guatemala with Love," *Chain Leader*, September/October 2005, pp. 28–32.

counter U.S. competitors by exporting or investing directly in the United States and other markets. Red Bull, the Austrian company that created the energy drink category, expanded throughout Europe after the Maastricht Treaty came into force in 1993. In 1997 it was big enough to take on the American market and by 1999 its sales were $75 million. Today, Red Bull is popular around the world. In 2006, more than 3 billion cans were sold in over 130 countries. And in 2007, the company sales amounted to 3.08 billion euro. On March 24, 2008 Red Bull introduced its first foray into the cola market

with a product named "Simply Cola." Mergers and acquisitions resulting from unification, also enhance the ability of EU firms to enter the United States. For example, in June of 2000 the French firm Publicis Group acquired Saatchi & Saatchi, the U.K.-based advertising firm, as a means of strengthening its position in the American market.

Smaller European firms are likely to consider pursuing a universal niche-market strategy. For instance, Iona Technologies, PLC, an Irish software firm, has successfully internationalized by pursuing a global niche-market strategy.

Finally, there remain EU customers who continue to prefer the more expensive, high-quality European products. Keeping this market segment from erosion by U.S. and Japanese competitors is key in retaining the viability of the EU market. The irony is that, if the failure of the EU Constitution is just the first event in a cascade of reversals for the integrationists, the newly refragmented markets may once again play a major role in strengthening the competitive position of smaller European firms.

*Source*: Lance Eliot Brouthers and Timothy J. Wilkinson, "Is the EU Destroying European Competitiveness?", *Business Horizons*, 45 (July–August 2002), 37–42; *EU Foreign Direct Investment Yearbook 2007*, Luxembourg: Office for Official Publications of the European Communities, 2007; "Buyers Bullish on Red Bull, Sales Up," *New Europe*, February 25, 2008, Issue 770, http://www.neurope.eu/articles/83145.php, accessed July 20, 2009; and "United Europe Celebrates Ethnic Diversity," *CNN.com*, November 20, 2008.

---

The United States, which enjoys one of the highest per-capita income levels in the world, has long been the most important single market for both foreign and domestic companies. As a result of its insatiable demand for foreign products, the United States has been running a trade deficit since 1973—for three consecutive decades (more on this in Chapter 2). In the popular press, the trade deficits have often been portrayed as a declining competitiveness of the United States. This assumes—rather erroneously—that U.S. companies engaged only in exports and imports and that international trade takes place between independent buyers and sellers across national boundaries. In order to appreciate the complexities of global competition, the nature of international trade and international business must first be clarified, followed by a discussion of who manages international trade.

First of all, we have to understand the distinction between international trade and international business. Indeed, **international trade** consists of exports and imports, say, between the United States and the rest of the world. If U.S. imports exceed U.S. exports, then the nation would register a trade deficit. If the opposite were the case, then the United States would register a trade surplus. On the other hand, **international business** is a broader concept and includes international trade and foreign production. U.S. companies typically market their products in three ways. First, they can export their products from the United States, which is recorded as a U.S. export. Second, they can invest in their foreign production on their own and manufacture those products abroad for sale there. This transaction does not show up as a U.S. export. And third, they can contract out manufacturing in whole or part to a company in a foreign country, either by way of licensing or joint venture agreement. Of course, not all companies engage in all three forms of international transaction. Nonetheless, foreign manufacture, independently or contractually, is a viable alternative means to exporting products abroad. Although it is not widely known, foreign production constitutes a much larger portion of international business than international trade.

The extensive international penetration of U.S. and other companies has been referred to as *global reach*.[29] Since the mid-1960s, U.S.-owned subsidiaries located around the world have produced and sold three times the value of all U.S. exports. Although more recent statistics are not available, this 3:1 ratio of foreign manufacture to international trade had remained largely unchanged in the 1980 and 1990s, and it becomes much more conspicuous if we look at U.S. business with the European Union,

**International Trade versus International Business**

---

[29] Richard J. Barnet and R. E. Muller, *Global Reach: The Power of the Multinational Corporations* (New York: Simon and Schuster, 1974).

A Global Reach: Executives increasingly use a global map to visualize their strategy.

Charles Thatcher/Tony Stone Images New York, Inc.

where U.S.-owned subsidiaries sold more than six times the total U.S. exports in 1990. Similarly, European-owned subsidiaries operating in the United States sold five times as much as U.S. imports from Europe.[30] This suggests that experienced companies tend to manufacture overseas much more than they export. On the other hand, Japanese companies did not expand their foreign manufacturing activities in earnest until about twenty years ago. According to one estimate, more than 90 percent of all the cases of Japanese FDI have taken place since 1985.[31] Despite their relative inexperience in international expansion, Japanese subsidiaries registered two-and-a-half times as much foreign sales as all Japanese exports worldwide by 1990.[32]

**Who Manages International Trade?**

As just discussed, international trade and foreign production are increasingly managed on a global basis. Furthermore, international trade and foreign production are also intertwined in a complex manner. Think about Honda Motors, a Japanese automobile manufacturer. Honda initially exported its Accords and Civics to the United States in the 1970s. By mid-1980s the Japanese company began manufacturing those cars in the United States in Marysville, Ohio. The company currently exports U.S.-made Accord models to Japan and elsewhere and boasts that it is the largest exporter of U.S.-made automobiles in the United States. Recently, Honda announced that it would start manufacturing its "world car" in Thailand, Brazil, and probably China, due to the low cost, and then export it mainly to Europe and Japan. It is expected that eventually all Honda cars in Japan will be produced and imported from aboard.[33] Similarly, Texas Instruments has a large semiconductor manufacturing plant in Japan, marketing its semiconductor chips not only in Japan but also exporting them from Japan to the United States and elsewhere. In addition to traditional exporting from their home base, these companies manufacture their products in various foreign countries both for local sale and for further exporting to the rest of the world, including their respective home countries. In other words, multinational companies (MNCs) are increasingly managing the international trade flow from within. This phenomenon is called **intra-firm trade**.

Intra-firm trade makes trade statistics more complex to interpret, since part of the international flow of products and components is taking place between affiliated companies

---

[30]Peter J. Buckley and R. D. Pearce, "Overseas Production and Exporting by the World's Largest Enterprises," *International Executive*, 22 (Winter), 1980, pp. 7–8; Dennis J. Encarnation, "Transforming Trade and Investment, American, European, and Japanese Multinationals Across the Triad," a paper presented at the Academy of International Business Annual Meetings, November 22, 1992.

[31]Masaaki Kotabe, "The Promotional Roles of the State Government and Japanese Manufacturing Direct Investment in the United States," *Journal of Business Research*, 27 (June 1993), pp. 131–46.

[32]Encarnation.

[33]"Honda to Re-Import 'World Car' Produced in Thailand," *Nikkei Interactive Net*, www.nni.nikkei.co.jp, December 18, 2001; "Honda Could Bring a Small Car to Europe from Thailand," *Automotive News Europe*, December 13, 2004, p. 3.

within the same corporate system, transcending national boundaries. Although statistical information is scarce, one United Nations official report shows that in 1999, 34 percent of world trade was intra-firm trade between MNCs and their foreign affiliates and among those affiliates, and that additional 33.3 percent of world trade constituted exports by those MNCs and their affiliates. In other words, two-thirds of world trade is managed one way or another by MNCs.[34] These trade ratios have been fairly stable over time.[35]

Although few statistics are available, service industries are going through the same evolution as manufacturing industries on a global basis. Indeed, some similarities exist in intra-firm trade of services. In 2007 alone, world commercial services exports rose by 18 percent to $3.3 trillion. Among the top global service exporters and importers, the United States was still ranked the largest exporter, providing $454 billion of services to the rest of the world. The United States was also the top importer of services, receiving $440 billion worth of services.[36] As stated earlier in the chapter, however, the severe global recession is expected to reduce the global trade for the first time in over 25 years.[37] Today, approximately 16 percent of the total value of U.S. exports and imports of services were conducted across national boundaries on an intra-firm basis.[38] Government deregulation and technological advancement have facilitated the tradability of some services globally and economically.

---

# EVOLUTION OF GLOBAL MARKETING                        ◆ ◆ ◆ ◆ ◆ ◆ ◆

Marketing is essentially the activity, set of institutions, and processes for creating, communicating, delivering, and exchanging offerings that have value for customers, clients, partners, and society at large.[39] Marketing is not only much broader than selling, it also encompasses the entire company's *market orientation* toward customer satisfaction in a competitive environment. In other words, marketing strategy requires close attention to both customers and competitors.[40] Quite often marketers have focused excessively on satisfying customer needs while ignoring competitors. In the process, competitors have outmaneuvered them in the marketplace with better, less-expensive products. It is widely believed that in many cases, U.S. companies have won the battle of discovering and filling customer needs initially, only to be defeated in the competitive war by losing the markets they pioneered to European and Japanese competitors.[41]

**What Is Marketing?**

---

[34]Khalil Hamdani, "The Role of Foreign Direct Investment in Export Strategy," presented at 1999 Executive Forum on National Export Strategies, International Trade Centre, the United Nations, September 26–28, 1999.

[35]United Nations Center on Transnational Corporations, *Transnational Corporations in World Development: Trends and Perspectives*, New York: United Nations, 1988; Organization for Economic Cooperation and Development, *Intra-Firm Trade*, Paris, OECD, 1993; William J. Zeile, "U.S. Affiliates of Foreign Companies," *Survey of Current Business*, August 2005, pp. 198–214.

[36]*World Trade Report 2008*, Geneva, World Trade Organization, www.wto.org, 2008.

[37]World Bank, *Global Economic Prospect 2009*, www.worldbank.org/gep2009.

[38]Janet Y. Murray and Masaaki Kotabe, "Sourcing Strategies of U.S. Service Companies: A Modified Transaction-Cost Analysis," *Strategic Management Journal*, 20, September 1999, 791-809; Masaaki Kotabe and Janet Y. Murray, "Global Procurement of Service Activities by Service Firms," *International Marketing Review*, 21 (6), 2004, 615–633; for detailed statistics, see Michael A. Mann, Laura L. Brokenbaugh, Sylvia E. Bargas, "U.S. International Services," *Survey of Current Business*, 80, October 2000, pp. 119–61.

[39]This is the definition of marketing adopted by the American Marketing Association in October 2007, and is strongly influenced by Drucker's conception of two entrepreneurial functions—marketing and innovation—that constitute business. Recent thinking about marketing also suggests the task of the marketer is not only to satisfy the current needs and wants of customers, but also to innovate on products and services, anticipating and even creating their future needs and wants. See Peter F. Drucker, *The Practice of Management* (New York: Harper & Brothers, 1954), pp. 37–39; and also Frederick E. Webster, Jr., "The Changing Role of Marketing in the Corporation," *Journal of Marketing*, 56 (October 1992), pp. 1–16.

[40]Aysegül Özsomer and Bernard Simonin, "Antecedents and Consequences of Market Orientation in a Subsidiary Context," *Enhancing Knowledge Development in Marketing*, 1999 American Marketing Association Educators' Proceedings, Summer 1999, p. 68.

[41]Robert M. Peterson, Clay Dibrell, and Timothy L. Pett, "Whose Market Orientation is Longest: A Study of Japan, Europe, and the United States," *Enhancing Knowledge Development in Marketing*, 1999 American Marketing Association Educators' Proceedings, Summer 1999, p. 69.

It is increasingly difficult for companies to avoid the impact of competition from around the world and the convergence of the world's markets. As a result, an increasing number of companies are drawn into marketing activities outside their home country. However, as previously indicated, different companies approach marketing around the world very differently. For example, Michael Dell established Dell Computer because he saw a burgeoning market potential for IBM-compatible personal computers in the United States. After his immediate success at home, he realized a future growth potential would exist in foreign markets. Then his company began exporting Dell PCs to Europe and Japan. In a way this was a predictable pattern of foreign expansion. On the other hand, not all companies go through this predictable pattern. Think about a notebook-sized Macintosh computer called the PowerBook 100 that Apple Computer introduced in 1991. In 1989, Apple enlisted Sony, the Japanese consumer electronics giant, to design and manufacture this notebook computer for both the U.S. and Japanese markets.[42] Sony has world-class expertise in miniaturization and has been a supplier of disk drives, monitors, and power supplies to Apple for various Macintosh models. In an industry such as personal computers, where technology changes quickly and the existing product becomes obsolete in a short period of time, a window of business opportunity is naturally limited. Therefore, Apple's motivation was to introduce the notebook computer on the markets around the world as soon as it could before competition picked up.

Companies generally develop different marketing strategies depending on the degree of experience and the nature of operations in international markets. Companies tend to evolve over time, accumulating international business experience and learning the advantages and disadvantages associated with complexities of manufacturing and marketing around the world.[43] As a result, many researchers have adopted an evolutionary perspective of internationalization of the company just like the evolution of the species over time. In the following pages we will formally define and explain five stages that characterize the evolution of global marketing. Of course, not all companies go through the complete evolution from a purely domestic marketing stage to a purely global marketing stage. An actual evolution depends also on the economic, cultural, political, and legal environments of various country markets in which the company operates, as well as on the nature of the company's offerings. A key point here is that many companies are constantly under competitive pressure to move forward both *reactively* (responding to the changes in the market and competitive environments) and *proactively* (anticipating the change). Remember, "if you stand still, you will get run over."

Therefore, knowing the dynamics of the evolutionary development of international marketing involvement is important for two reasons. First, it helps in the understanding of how companies learn and acquire international experience and how they use it for gaining competitive advantage over time. This may help an executive better prepare for the likely change needed in the company's marketing strategy. Second, with this knowledge, a company may be able to compete more effectively by predicting its competitors' likely marketing strategy in advance.

As shown in **Exhibit 1.2**, there are five identifiable stages in the evolution of marketing across national boundaries.[44] These evolutionary stages are explained below.

**Domestic Marketing**

The first stage is **domestic marketing**. Before entry into international markets, many companies focus solely on their domestic market. Their marketing strategy is developed based on information about domestic customer needs and wants, industry trends,

---

[42]"Apple's Japanese Ally," *Fortune* (November 4, 1991), pp. 151–52.

[43]Anna Shaojie Cui, David A. Griffith, S. Tamer Cavusgil, "The Influence of Competitive Intensity and Market Dynamism on Knowledge Management Capabilities of Multinational Corporation Subsidiaries," *Journal of International Marketing*, 13 (3), 2005, pp. 32–53).

[44]This section draws from Balaj S. Chakravarthy and Howard V. Perlmutter, "Strategic Planning for A Global Business," *Columbia Journal of World Business* (Summer 1985), pp. 3–10; Susan P. Douglas and C. Samuel Craig, "Evolution of Global Marketing Strategy: Scale, Scope and Synergy," *Columbia Journal of World Business* 24 (Fall 1989), pp. 47–59.

**EXHIBIT 1-2**
EVOLUTION OF GLOBAL MARKETING

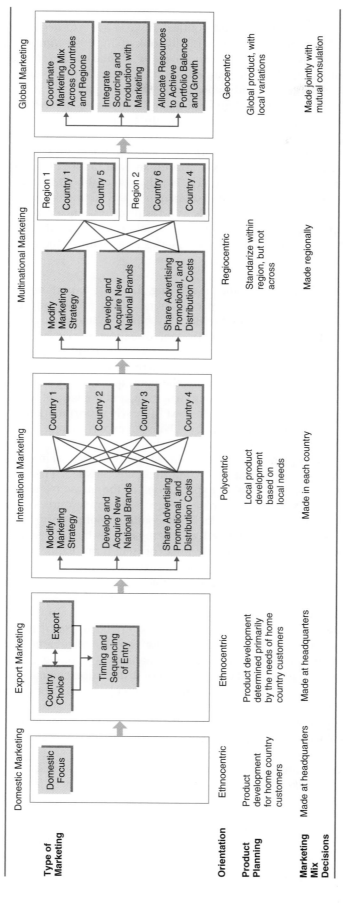

*Sources:* Constructed from Susan P. Douglas and C. Samuel Craig, "Evolution of Global Marketing Strategy: Scale, Scope and Synergy," Columbia Journal of World Business, 24 (Fall 1985). p. 50; and Balai S. Chakravarthy and Howard V. Perlmutter, "Strategic Planning for a Global Business," Columbia Journal of World Business, 20 (Summer 1985), p. 6.

economic, technological, and political environments at home. When those companies consider competition, they essentially look at domestic competition. Today, it is highly conceivable that competition in a company's home market is made up of both domestic competitors and foreign competitors marketing their products in the home market. Domestic marketers tend to be *ethnocentric* and pay little attention to changes taking place in the global marketplace, such as changing lifestyles and market segments, emerging competition, and better products that have yet to arrive in their domestic market. *Ethnocentrism* is defined here as a predisposition of a firm to be predominantly concerned with its viability worldwide and legitimacy only in its home country[45]—that is, where all strategic actions of a company are tailored to domestic responses under similar situations. As a result, they may be vulnerable to the sudden changes forced on them by foreign competition. For example, U.S. automakers suffered from this ethnocentrism in the 1960s and 1970s as a result of their neglect of imminent competition from Japanese automakers with more fuel-efficient cars that would eventually seize a market opportunity in the United States as a result of the two major oil crises in the 1970s.

**Export Marketing**

The second stage is **export marketing**. Usually, export marketing begins with unsolicited orders from foreign customers. When a company receives an order from abroad, initially it may fill it reluctantly, but it gradually learns the benefit of marketing overseas. In general, in the early stage of export marketing involvement, the internationalization process is a consequence of incremental adjustments to the changing conditions of the company and its environment, rather than a result of its deliberate strategy. Such a pattern is due to the consequence of greater uncertainty in international business, higher costs of information, and the lack of technical knowledge about international marketing activities. At this early export marketing stage, exporters tend to engage in *indirect exporting* by relying on export management companies or trading companies to handle their export business.

Some companies progress to a more involved stage of internationalization by *direct exporting*, once three internal conditions are satisfied. First, the management of the company obtains favorable expectations of the attractiveness of exporting based on experience. Second, the company has access to key resources necessary for undertaking additional export-related tasks. Such availability of physical, financial, and managerial resources is closely associated with firm size. Particularly small companies may have few trained managers and little time for long-term planning, as they are preoccupied with day-to-day operational problems; consequently, they find it difficult to become involved in exporting. Third, management is willing to commit adequate resources to export activities.[46] The company's long-term commitment to export marketing depends on how successful management is in overcoming various barriers encountered in international marketing activities. An experienced export marketer has to deal with difficulties in maintaining and expanding export involvement. These difficulties include import/export restrictions, cost and availability of shipping, exchange rate fluctuations, collection of money, and development of distribution channels, among others. Overall, favorable experience appears to be a key component in getting companies involved in managing exports directly without relying on specialized outside export handlers. To a large degree an appropriate measure of favorableness for many companies consists of profits. An increase in profits due to a certain activity is likely to increase the company's interest in such activity.[47]

External pressures also prod companies into export marketing activities. Saturated domestic markets may make it difficult for a company to maintain sales volume in an

[45]Chakravarthy and Perlmutter, pp. 3–10.
[46]S. Tamer Cavusgil, "On the Internationalization Process of Firms," *European Research*, 8 (November 1980), pp. 273–79.
[47]Masaaki Kotabe and Michael R. Czinkota, "State Government Promotion of Manufacturing Exports: A Gap Analysis," *Journal of International Business Studies*, 23 (Fourth Quarter 1992), pp. 637–58.

increasingly competitive domestic market; it will become much more serious when foreign competitors begin marketing products in the domestic market. Export marketers begin paying attention to technological and other changes in the global marketplace that domestic marketers tend to ignore. However, export marketers still tend to take an ethnocentric approach to foreign markets as being an extension of their domestic market and export products developed primarily for home country customers with limited adaptation to foreign customers' needs.

Once export marketing becomes an integral part of the company's marketing activity, it will begin to seek new directions for growth and expansion. We call this stage **international marketing**. A unique feature of international marketing is its *polycentric* orientation with emphasis on product and promotional adaptation in foreign markets, whenever necessary.[48] Polycentric orientation refers to a predisposition of a firm to the existence of significant local cultural differences across markets, necessitating the operation in each country being viewed independently (i.e., all strategic decisions are thus tailored to suit the cultures of the concerned country). As the company's market share in a number of countries reaches a certain point, it becomes important for the company to defend its position through local competition. Because of local competitors' proximity to, and familiarity with, local customers, they tend to have an inherent "insider" advantage over foreign competition. To strengthen its competitive position, the international marketer could adapt its strategy, if necessary, to meet the needs and wants of local customers in two alternative ways. First, the company may allocate a certain portion of its manufacturing capacity to its export business. Second, because of transportation costs, tariffs, and other regulations, and availability of human and capital resources in the foreign markets, the company may even begin manufacturing locally. BMW has been exporting its cars to the United States for many years. In 1992, the German company invested in a manufacturing plant in South Carolina in order to be more adaptive to changing customer needs in this important market, and to take advantage of rather inexpensive resources as a result of the dollar depreciation against the euro. Accordingly, BMW South Carolina has become part of BMW Group's global manufacturing network and is the exclusive manufacturing plant for all Z4 roadster and X5 Sports Activity Vehicles.[49]

If international marketing is taken to the extreme, a company may establish an independent foreign subsidiary in each and every foreign market and have each of the subsidiaries operate independently of each other without any measurable headquarters control. This special case of international marketing is known as **multidomestic marketing**. Product development, manufacturing, and marketing are all executed by each subsidiary for its own local market. As a result, different product lines, product positioning, and pricing may be observed across those subsidiaries. Few economies of scale benefits can be obtained. However, multidomestic marketing is useful when customer needs are so different across different national markets that no common product or promotional strategy can be developed. Even Coca-Cola, which used to practice globally standardized marketing strategy, changed its strategy when it found that its structure had become too cumbersome and that it was insensitive to local markets. In 2000, the company decided to return to a more multidomestic marketing approach and to give more freedom to local subsidiaries. Local marketing teams are now permitted to develop advertising to local consumers and even launch new local brands.[50]

At this stage, the company markets its products in many countries around the world. We call this stage **multinational marketing**. Management of the company comes to realize the benefit of economies of scale in product development, manufacturing, and marketing by consolidating some of its activities on a regional basis. This *regiocentric* approach suggests

**International Marketing**

**Multinational Marketing**

---

[48]Warren J. Keegan, "Multinational Product Planning: Strategic Alternatives," *Journal of Marketing*, 33 (January 1969), pp. 58–62.

[49]http://www.bmwusa.com/about/, accessed January 27, 2006.

[50]Isabelle Schuiling and Jean-Noël Kapferer, "Real Differences between Local and International Brands: Strategic Implications for International Marketers," *Journal of International Marketing*, 12 (4), 2004, pp. 97–112.

that product planning may be standardized within a region (e.g., a group of contiguous and similar countries), such as Western Europe, but not across regions. Products may be manufactured regionally as well. Similarly, advertising, promotion, and distribution costs may also be shared by subsidiaries in the region. In order for the company to develop its regional image in the marketplace, it may develop and acquire new regional brands to beef up its regional operations. Caterpillar now has a regional headquarters in Europe that has united and integrated its geographically diverse organizations, and a unique joint venture with Mitsubishi Heavy Industries to meet the exacting Japanese quality standards for the Japanese market and beyond.

## Global Marketing

The international (country-by-country) or multinational (region-by-region) orientation, while enabling the consolidation of operations within countries or regions, will tend to result in market fragmentation worldwide, nonetheless. Operational fragmentation leads to higher costs. When many Japanese companies entered the world markets as low-cost manufacturers of reliable products in the 1970s, well-established U.S. and European multinational companies were made acutely aware of their vulnerability as high-cost manufacturers. Levitt,[51] an arduous globalization proponent, argues:

> Gone are accustomed differences in national or regional preference. Gone are the days when a company could sell last year's models—or lesser versions of advanced products—in the less developed world. . . . The multinational and the global corporation are not the same thing. The multinational corporation operates in a number of countries, and adjusts its products and practices in each—at high relative costs. The global corporation operates with resolute constancy—at low relative cost—as if the entire world (or major regions of it) were a single entity; it sells the same things in the same way everywhere.

**Global marketing** refers to marketing activities by companies that emphasize the following:

1. *Standardization efforts*—standardizing marketing programs across different countries particularly with respect to product offering, promotional mix, price, and channel structure. Such efforts increase opportunities for the transfer of products, brands, and other ideas across subsidiaries and help address the emergence of global customers

2. *Coordination across markets*—reducing cost inefficiencies and duplication of efforts among their national and regional subsidiaries

3. *Global Integration*—participating in many major world markets to gain competitive leverage and effective integration of the firm's competitive campaigns across these markets by being able to subsidize operations in some markets with resources generated in others and responding to competitive attacks in one market by counterattacking in others.[52]

Although Levitt's view is somewhat extreme, many researchers agree that global marketing does not necessarily mean standardization of products, promotion, pricing, and distribution worldwide, but rather it is a company's proactive willingness to adopt a global perspective instead of country-by-country or region-by-region perspective in developing a marketing strategy. Clearly, not all companies adopt global marketing. Yet an increasing number of companies are proactively trying to find commonalities in their marketing strategy among national subsidiaries (see **Global Perspective 1-3**). For example, Black & Decker, a U.S. manufacturer of hand tools, adopted a global perspective by standardizing and streamlining components such as motors and rotors while maintaining a wide range of product lines, and created a universal image for its products. In this case, it was not standardization of products per se but rather the company's effort at standardizing key components and product design for manufacturability in the manufacturing industry and core, supplementary services in the service

---

[51]Theodore Levitt, "The Globalization of Markets," *Harvard Business Review*, 61 (May–June) 1983, pp. 92–102.

[52]Shaoming Zou and S. Tamer Cavusgil, "The GMS: A Broad Conceptualization of Global Marketing Strategy and Its Effect on Firm Performance," *Journal of Marketing*, 66, October 2002, pp. 40–56.

## 𝒢LOBAL PERSPECTIVE 1-3

### GLOBALIZING THE BUSINESS TERMS BEFORE GLOBALIZING THE FIRM

International was the first word that William Hudson, president and CEO of AMP Inc., Harrisburg, Pennsylvania, told his corporate colleagues to cut from their business vocabularies. Why? The term creates a "Chinese wall" that divides a globalizing company into "domestic" and "international" sides, he explained to A. T. Kearney Inc. officers meeting in Chicago. "It's almost as if you don't jump over that wall" to work or team together, he said.

Another banished word: "subsidiary." It conveys "a parent/child relationship," said Mr. Hudson. Headquarters tends to lord its power over foreign and domestic operations and "make them feel like inferior souls." Revising the business lexicon is not easy, Mr. Hudson readily admitted. "Every now and then [one of the words] shows up on a . . . slide when

*Sources:* Jon Erlendsson, "Globalization and Innovation," http://www.hi.is/~joner/eaps/cq_globi.htm, accessed December 15, 2005; and Herman E. Daly, "Globalization versus Internationalization: Some Implications," http://www.globalpolicy.org/globaliz/econ/herman2.htm, accessed August 10, 2008.

somebody makes a presentation. And I've got to put up my hand and say: 'Erase that word.'"

Next, what is the difference between internationalization and globalization? According to Herman E. Daly, "Internationalization refers to the increasing importance of international trade, international relations, treaties, alliances, etc. Inter-national, of course, means between or among nations. The basic unit remains the nation, even as relations among nations become increasingly necessary and important. Globalization refers to global economic integration of many formerly national economies into one global economy, mainly by free trade and free capital mobility, but also by easy or uncontrolled migration. It is the effective erasure of national boundaries for economic purposes . . ." Briefly speaking, the key difference between internationalization and globalization lies in that internationalization takes place between individual nations, between individual companies operating in different countries, and between individual citizens of different countries; globalization, however, increasingly ignores national boundaries.

---

industry, to achieve global leadership in cost and value across common market segments around the world.

Global marketing does not necessarily mean that products can be developed anywhere on a global basis. The economic geography, climate, and culture, among other things, affect the way in which companies develop certain products and consumers want them. First, the availability of resources is a major determinant of industry location. The U.S. automobile industry was born at the dawn of the twentieth century as a result of Henry Ford having decided to locate his steel-making foundry in Detroit midway between sources of iron ore in the Mesabi range in Minnesota and sources of bituminous coal in Pennsylvania. Similarly, in the last quarter of the twentieth century, Silicon Valley, in and around Palo Alto, California and Silicon Hill, in Austin, Texas, emerged as high-tech Meccas as a result of abundant skilled human resources (thanks to leading universities in the areas), aided by warm, carefree environments—a coveted atmosphere conducive to creative thinking. For the same reason, Bangalore in India has emerged as an important location for software development. Brazil boasts that more than half of the automobiles on the road run on a hundred percent pure alcohol, thanks to an abundant supply of ethanol produced from subsidized sugar cane. Even bananas are produced in abundance in Iceland, thanks to nature-provided geothermal energy tapped in greenhouses.[53] Since Germans consume the largest amount of bananas, about 33 lbs (or 15 kg) on a per capita basis, in the European Union, Iceland could become an exporter of bananas to Germany![54]

Obviously, the availability of both natural and human resources is important in primarily determining industry location as those resources, if unavailable, could become a bottleneck. It is to be stressed that consumer needs are equally important

**The Impact of Economic Geography and Climate on Global Marketing**

---

[53]"Iceland Information," http://www.vjv.com/information/country/europe_west/iceland_info.html, accessed December 15, 2005.

[54]Paul Sutton, "The Banana Regime of the European Union, the Caribbean, and Latin America," *Journal of Interamerican Studies and World Affairs*, 39, Summer 1997, pp. 5–36.

as a determinant of industry location.[55] As the Icelandic banana example shows, the fact that Germans consume a large amount of bananas gives Icelandic growers a logistical advantage. Ask yourself why cellular phones have been most widely adopted in Finland, and why fax machines and ink-jet printers have been most widely developed in Japan. In Finland and other Scandinavian countries, it snows heavily in winter but it is very damp snow owing to the warm Gulf Stream moderating what could otherwise be a frigid climate. The damp snow frequently cuts off power lines. Thus, Scandinavians always wished for wireless means of communication, such as CB radios and cellular phones. Companies such as Nokia in Finland and Ericsson in Sweden have become world-class suppliers of cellular technology.[56] Similarly, Japanese consumers always wanted machines that could easily produce and reproduce the complex characters in their language. Thus, Japanese companies such as Canon, Epson (a subsidiary of Seiko Watch), and Fujitsu have emerged as major producers of fax and ink-jet printers in the world. For outdoor activity-loving Australians, surfing is a national sport. No wonder that Quicksilver, an Australian company that knows quite well how to design sportswear that is functional as well as aesthetic, has conquered the European market from skateboarders beneath the Eiffel Tower to snowboarders in the Swiss Alps and surfers in Spain.[57] Similarly, Billabong, another Australian surfing goods retailer with a keen eye for what outdoor sports lovers want to wear, is expanding into the U.S. market with a broad range of leisure-related products following the acquisition of Element, a U.S. skateboarding clothing company, and Von Zipper, a U.S. sunglasses and snow goggles brand.[58] Indeed, as the old proverb says, "necessity is the mother of invention."

The point is that what companies can offer competitively may be determined either by the availability of natural and human resources or by the unique consumer needs in different countries or regions or by both. Global marketers are willing to exploit their local advantages for global business opportunities. Then ask yourself another question about an emerging societal need around the world: environmental protection. Where are formidable competitors likely to originate in the near future? We think it is Germany. Germans have long been concerned about their environmental quality as represented by the cleanliness of the Rhine River. When phosphorus—a major whitening agent in laundry detergent, polluted the Rhine —, the German government was the first in the world to ban its use. Now German companies are keen on developing products that are fully recyclable. In a not too distant future recyclable products will become increasingly important. Naturally, marketing executives need to have an acute understanding of not only the availability of various resources but also emerging consumer and societal needs on a global basis.

So far we focused on complex realities of international trade and investment that have characterized our global economy in the past twenty years. Some vital statistics have been provided. The more statistics we see, the more befuddled we become by the sheer complexities of our global economy. It even seems as though there were not a modicum of orderliness in our global economy, it being just like a jungle. Naturally, we wish the world had been much simpler. In reality, it is becoming ever more complex. Luckily enough, however, economists and business researchers have tried over the years to explain the ever-increasing complexities of the global economy in simpler terms. A simplified yet logical view of the world is called a **theory**. Indeed, there are many different ways—theories—of looking at international trade and investment taking place in the world. For those of you interested in understanding some orderliness in the complex world of international trade and investment, we encourage you to read the appendix to this chapter. Some theoretical understanding will not only help you appreciate the competitive world in which we live, but also help you make better strategy decisions for a company you may join shortly or a company you may own.

---

[55]Michael E. Porter, *The Competitive Advantage of Nations*, New York: Free Press, 1990.

[56]Lilach Nachum, "Does Nationality of Ownership Make Any Difference and If so Under What Circumstances," *Journal of International Management*, 9, 2003.

[57]"Global Surfin' Safari: Quiksilver Rides Wave In Europe and Far East," *Women's Wear Daily*, June 30, 2005, pp. 1–8.

[58]"Skateboarding Springs into Billabong," *The Australian*, July 4, 2001, p. 21.

## SUMMARY ✦ ✦ ✦ ✦ ✦ ✦ ✦ ✦ ✦ ✦ ✦ ✦ ✦ ✦ ✦ ✦ ✦ ✦ ✦ ✦ ✦ ✦ ✦ ✦ ✦

World trade has grown from $200 billion to more than $17 trillion in the last 30 years, although the current global recession is expected to reduce world trade for the first time in over 25 years. Although world trade volume is significant in and of itself, international business is much bigger than trade statistics show. Companies from Western Europe, the United States, and Japan collectively produce probably more than three times as much in their foreign markets than they export. And about a third of their exports and imports are transacted on an intra-firm basis between their parent companies and their affiliated companies abroad or between the affiliated companies themselves.

What this all means is that it is almost impossible for domestic company executives to consider their domestic markets and domestic competition alone. If they fail to look beyond their national boundaries, they may unknowingly lose marketing opportunities to competitors that do. Worse yet, foreign competitors will encroach on their hard-earned market position at home so fast that it may be too late for them to respond. International markets are so intertwined that separating international from domestic business may be a futile mental exercise.

Historically, international expansion has always been a strategy consideration after domestic marketing, and has therefore been reactionary to such things as a decline in domestic sales and increased domestic competition. Global marketing is a proactive response to the intertwined nature of business opportunities and competition that know no political boundaries. However, global marketing does not necessarily mean that companies should market the same product in the same way around the world as world markets are converging. To the extent feasible, they probably should. Nonetheless, global marketing is a company's willingness to adopt a global perspective instead of country-by-country or region-by-region perspective in developing a marketing strategy for growth and profit.

What companies can offer competitively may be determined either by the availability of natural and human resources or by the unique consumer needs in different countries or regions or by both. Global marketers should be willing to exploit their local advantages for global marketing opportunities. The proliferation of e-commerce on the Internet accelerates such global marketing opportunities.

## KEY TERMS ✦ ✦ ✦ ✦ ✦ ✦ ✦ ✦ ✦ ✦ ✦ ✦ ✦ ✦ ✦ ✦ ✦ ✦ ✦ ✦ ✦ ✦ ✦ ✦ ✦ ✦ ✦

| | | | |
|---|---|---|---|
| Domestic marketing | Export marketing | International marketing | Multidomestic marketing |
| Electronic commerce (E-commerce) | Global marketing | International trade | Multinational marketing |
| | International business | Intra-firm trade | Triad regions |

## REVIEW QUESTIONS ✦ ✦ ✦ ✦ ✦ ✦ ✦ ✦ ✦ ✦ ✦ ✦ ✦ ✦ ✦ ✦ ✦ ✦ ✦ ✦

1. Why is international business much more complex today than it was twenty years ago?

2. What is the nature of global competition?

3. Does international trade accurately reflect the nature of global competition?

4. Why are consumption patterns similar across industrialized countries despite cultural differences?

5. How is global marketing different from international marketing?

6. Why do you think a company should or should not market the same product in the same way around the world?

7. What is proactive standardization?

8. How is the Internet reshaping the nature of global marketing?

## DISCUSSION QUESTIONS ✦ ✦ ✦ ✦ ✦ ✦ ✦ ✦ ✦ ✦ ✦ ✦ ✦ ✦ ✦ ✦ ✦ ✦ ✦

1. The United States and Japan, the two largest economies in the world, are also the largest importers and exporters of goods and services. However, imports and exports put together comprise only 20 to 30 percent of their GDPs. This percentage has not changed much over the last three decades for both of these countries. Does this imply that the corporations and the media may be overemphasizing globalization? Discuss why you agree or do not agree with the last statement.

2. Merchandise trade today accounts for less than 2 percent of all the foreign exchange transactions around the world. Can

one deduce that merchandise plays an insignificant role in today's economies? Why or why not?

3. A major cereal manufacturer produces and markets standardized breakfast cereals to countries around the world. Minor modifications in attributes, such as sweetness of the product, are made to cater to local needs. However, the core products and brands are standardized. The company entered the Chinese market a few years back and was extremely satisfied with the results. The company's sales continue to grow at a rate of around 50 percent a year in China.

Encouraged by its marketing success in China and other Asian countries, and based on the market reforms taking place, the company started operations in India by manufacturing and marketing its products. Initial response to the product was extremely encouraging and within one year the company was thinking in terms of rapidly expanding its production capacity. However, after a year, sales tapered off and started to fall. Detailed consumer research seemed to suggest that while the upper-middle social class, especially families where both spouses were working, to whom this product was targeted, adopted the cereals as an alternative meal (i.e., breakfast) for a short time, they eventually returned to the traditional Indian breakfast. The CEOs of some other firms in the food industry in India are quoted as saying that non-Indian snack products and the restaurant business are the areas where multinational companies (MNCs) can hope for success. Trying to replace a full meal with a non-Indian product has less of a chance of succeeding. You are a senior executive in the international division of this food MNC with experience of operating in various countries in a product management function. The CEO plans to send you to India on a fact-finding mission to determine answers to these specific questions. What, in your opinion, would be the answers:

    a. Was entering the market with a standardized product a mistake?

    b. Was it a problem of the product or the way it was positioned?

    c. Given the advantages to be gained through leveraging of brand equity and product knowledge on a global basis, and the disadvantages of differing local tastes, what would be your strategy for entering new markets?

4. Globalization involves the organization-wide development of a global perspective. This global perspective requires globally thinking managers. Although the benefits of globalization have received widespread attention, the difficulties in developing managers who think globally has received scant attention. Some senior managers consider this to be a significant stumbling block in the globalization efforts of companies. Do you agree with the concerns of these managers? Would the lack of truly globally thinking managers cause problems for implementing a global strategy? And how does the proliferation of e-commerce affect the way these managers conduct business?

5. The e-commerce business in China has entered a golden period, with transaction volume of online trading reaching 21.86 billion yuan (US$2.64 billion) in 2004. With 94 million Internet users, more than 40 million people conducted transactions on the Internet in 2004, compared with 10.7 million in 2001, and more than 60 percent of people expressed their willingness to try online trading in 2005. Among net citizens, roughly 20 million people have had the experience of playing games online. China's largest e-game operator, Shanda Interactive Entertainment Limited has accumulated a huge amount of wealth in just a couple of years. In May 2004, Shanda was listed on the NASDAQ and generated US$373 million in the online games market; 39.3 percent of this market is from China. Now the company is shifting its business focus from the computer platform to the TV platform—including games, music and literature—through a set-top box to penetrate those 340 million households that already own a television. With 1.3 billion in population, the Chinese market is inviting to both online and offline businesses. In terms of online businesses, what do you foresee as opportunities and threats to multinational corporations, especially in emerging economies?

# SHORT CASES

## CASE 1-1

### GLOBAL MARKETING REQUIRES A VERY LOCAL ATTENTION: A LESSON FROM VODAFONE'S LOSS OF JAPAN UNIT

As the world's leading mobile telecommunications company, Vodafone Group, a British company, has a significant presence in Europe, the Middle East, Africa, Asia Pacific, and the United States through the Company's subsidiary undertakings, joint ventures, associated undertakings and investments. According to the latest data, the Company had a total market capitalization of approximately £99 billion on December 31 2007. However, the company's road to success is not always smooth. Vodafone's five years of struggle in Japan from 2001 until its final sale of the unit in March 2006, proves that global marketing does not necessarily mean that a global company can treat all markets the same way. In essence, think globally, but act locally.

Since entering the Japanese market in 2001 by taking over J-Phone Co., a local cellular provider, the company had seen its reputation slip with its handsets being viewed dull and its service second rate. Vodafone was focused on building a global brand and cutting costs by producing large numbers of handsets to sell throughout the world. In Japan, however, this came at the expense of products and services to suit the nation's finicky and tech-savvy consumers. In July 2004, Vodafone's unit in Japan, Vodafone KK, became the first of the three carriers to report a monthly net loss of customers from the period one year earlier. Four years after its entry into Japan, Vodafone ended up being slower than Japanese rivals to roll out flashy new handsets and competitive price plans. It failed to gain market share, far lagging behind two other of Japan's major cellular carriers, NTT DoCoMo and KDDT. The two winners simply out-hustled Vodafone by coming up with cooler designs and must-have services. AU attracted plenty of buzz with a high-speed music download service, for instance. Vodafone's struggle in Japan shows that it is not always an advantage to act like a big global player.

For a long time, Vodafone KK had been accustomed to getting management directives from its London headquarters. After its steady decline in Japan from 2001 to 2005, Vodafone's Japanese unit realized that more ideas should have originated in Japan, instead of trying hard to make European handsets fly in the Japanese market. In early 2005, Vodafone dispatched Bill Morrow to Tokyo to run its Japan operations with a largely modified marketing strategy. There were signs that Vodafone did make some headway in Japan since then with its transition from 2G to 3G, a greater range of new tailored handsets and services, much better content and a stronger network, as can be reflected by numbers: In January, 2005, Vodafone lost 59,000 subscribers on a net basis, an alarming figure. One year after, by comparison, it pulled in 17,600, after signing up 63,700 subscribers in December 2005. That pushed total subscribers above the 15.1 million mark.

However, reviving in Japan was not easy after a long-time loss largely due to lack of local attention. The worst thing was that time was running out. In spite of its endeavor to recover its Japan market, by early 2006, Vodafone was still far behind its rivals with its market share of 16.7 percent compared to 24.1 percent for KDDI's AU brand and 55.8 percent for DoCoMo.

As a closure, on March 17, 2006, Vodafone sold its 97.7 percent holding in Vodafone Japan to SoftBank, which had planned to get into cellular in 2007, for $15.5 billion after the company had struggled to gain traction in Japan. With this deal Vodafone finally relieved its executives of the headache of trying to fix a unit with sinking profitability and little hope of catching bigger rivals NTT DoCoMo and KDDI unit AU.

*Sources*: Ian Rowley, "Vodafone's Bad Connection In Japan," *BusinessWeek.com*, February 21, 2005; Ian Rowley, "Can Vodafone Get Through?" *BusinessWeek.com*, February 28, 2006; and Kerry Capell, "Vodafone's Tough Calls," *BusinessWeek.com*, February 28, 2006 (4). Ian Rowley and Kenji Hall, "Softbank-Vodafone Deal Rings True," *BusinessWeek.com*, March 17.

**DISCUSSION QUESTIONS**

1. Why would a firm such as Vodafone need to have a global marketing strategy even though its product development, as well as the rest of its marketing strategy, needs to be localized for tech-savvy consumers in Japan?

2. What alternative strategy might Vodafone have used to set a strong market position in Japan from the very beginning?

3. What implications can you draw from Vodafone's loss of its Japan unit with regard to global firms' tapping into the convergence among global consumers?

# $\mathcal{C}$ASE 1-2

## KEEPING WITH THE TIMES—MCDONALD'S, I'M LOVIN' IT!

McDonald's, the world's largest restaurant chain with over 30,000 outlets in more than 115 countries, brings to mind many terms: golden arches, Big Macs, McNuggets, affordable meals, brand value, and American capitalism, to name just a few. How did McDonald's become one of the world's best-known brands? Needless to say, being in the food industry entails different menus for different parts of the world based on varying tastes and preferences. At the time, McDonald's made its foray into foreign markets it was almost impossible to have a mass marketing or global strategy in terms of McDonald's menu items. Therefore, the company adopted a strategy to appeal to those different preferences. According to the company, the secret to its successful brand is a type of multidomestic strategy, which the company used successfully by being able to offer different menus in different countries.

Previously, McDonald's even extended this strategy to marketing for its restaurants in foreign markets. Remember the yellow and red-garbed clown that attracted kids to McDonald's? McDonald's had maintained the same image for years and by the start of the twenty-first century, it was not working anymore. Additionally, the growing health consciousness among consumers the world over caused the restaurant chain to suffer decreasing profitability. Nevertheless, by 2005, the year that marked its fiftieth anniversary, McDonald's was on its way to regaining its stardom.

With time, it is necessary for companies to keep abreast of the changes that are taking place in the environment. Today, many firms are shifting from a multidomestic or multinational strategy to a more global one. It is believed that one reason for this is the growing convergence in consumer behavior, especially for food and apparel. For example, consumers all over the world are moving toward a healthy lifestyle that includes a healthy diet and exercise. For firms, a global strategy allows them to minimize overall costs, and specifically marketing costs, by repeating commercials with few alterations, justifying high advertising expenditure to release a perfect ad. McDonald's is one of several companies that have adopted a global marketing strategy. McDonald's has had to revive its global business over the past five years, one of the ways to do it being to replace its previous shoddy image with a hip new one.

In the year 2003, the company launched its first truly global marketing campaign called "I'm lovin' it." The new promotion effort aimed at changing the company's image in markets all over the world sends the same message to its global consumers with small changes for local tastes and preferences. Thus, even though there is still a significant divergence in McDonald's menus, the new global marketing campaign instilled a distinct global brand value in the minds of consumers. McDonald's invested heavily in the campaign, employing celebrities, such as singer Justin Timberlake and popular music group Destiny's Child who draw a global audience, to appear in its advertisements. In addition, McDonald's introduced more healthy foods in its menus such as salads. The "I'm lovin it" marketing campaign was targeted at consumers in all age groups from kids and young adults to seniors. The conceptualization of the ad was also global. It was the brainchild of a Germany-based firm Heye and Partner; the company settled on this agency after consulting with several marketing agencies in many different countries. The campaign has been one of the most successful of its time. The strategy worked, and in just one year, the company's revenues were up by more than 10 percent. As for the novel marketing drive, the company won *Advertising Age* magazine's Marketer of the Year Award for 2004. As for its recent comeback, McDonald's is truly lovin' it.

### DISCUSSION QUESTIONS

**1.** Why do firms such as McDonald's need to have a global marketing strategy even though its national menus are localized?

**2.** What alternative strategy could McDonald's have used to regain its market?

**3.** For the future, how should McDonald's tap into the convergence among global consumers?

# FURTHER READING

"A Survey of Globalization: Globalization and Its Critics," *Economist*, September 29, 2001: 1–30.

Bhagwati, Jagdish, "The Globalization Guru," *Finance & Development*, 42, September 2005, pp. 4–7.

Clark, Terry, Monica Hodis, and Paul D'Angelo, "The Ancient Road: An Overview of Globalization," in Masaaki Kotabe and Kristiaan Helsen, ed., *The SAGE Handbook of International Marketing*, London: Sage Publications, 2009, pp. 15–35.

de La Torre, José, and Richard W. Moxon, "Introduction to the Symposium E-Commerce and Global Business: The Impact of the Information and Communication Technology Revolution on the Conduct of International Business," *Journal of International Business Studies*, 32(4th Quarter, 2001): 617–639.

Dunning, John H., ed., *Making Globalization Good: The Moral Challenges of Global Capitalism*, New York: Oxford University Press, 2003.

Eden, Lorraine and Stefanie Lenway, "The Janus Face of Globalization," *Journal of International Business Studies*, 32(Third Quarter, 2001): 383–400.

Eroglu, Sevgin, "Does Globalization Have Staying Power?" *Marketing Management*, 11 (March/April 2002): 18–23.

Friedman, Thomas L., *The Lexus and the Olive Tree*, Revised ed., New York: Farrar, Straus & Giroux, 2000.

Gwynne, Peter, "The Myth of Globalization?" *Sloan Management Review*, 44 (Winter 2003): 11.

Jain, Subhash C., *Toward a Global Business Confederation: A Blueprint for Globalization*, Westport, CT: Praeger, 2003.

Kogut, Bruce, "What Makes a Company Global?" *Harvard Business Review*, 77 (January/February 1999): 165–70.

Luo, Xueming, K. Sivakumar, and Sandra S. Liu, "Globalization, Marketing Resources, and Performance: Evidence From China," *Journal of the Academy of Marketing Science*, 33 (Winter 2005): 50–65.

Mahajan, Vijay and Kamini Banga, *The 86 Percent Solution: How to Succeed in the Biggest Market Opportunity of the Next 50 years*, Upper Saddle River, N.J.: Wharton School Publishing, 2006.

"Measuring Globalization," *Foreign Affairs*, 122, January/February 2001: 56–65.

Merchant, Hemant, *Competing in Emerging Markets*, New York: Routledge, 2008.

Prahalad, C. K., *The Fortune at the Bottom of the Pyramid: Eradicating Poverty through Profits*, Philadelphia, PA: Wharton School Publishing, 2004.

Roll, Martin, *Asian Brand Strategy: How Asia Builds Strong Brands*, New York: Palgrave Macmillan, 2006.

Stiglitz, Joseph E., *Globalization and Its Discontents*, New York: W. W. Norton & Co., 2003.

Tétreault, Mary Ann, and Robert A. Denemark, ed., *Gods, Guns, and Globalization: Religious Radicalism and International Political Economy*, London: Lynne Rienner Publishers, 2004.

# APPENDIX: THEORIES OF INTERNATIONAL TRADE AND THE MULTINATIONAL ENTERPRISE

Theories are a simplification of complex realities one way or another. A few important theories will be explained here. Each of the theories provides a number of fundamental principles by which you can not only appreciate why international trade and investment occur but also prepare for the next impending change you will probably see in a not-so-distant future. These theories are arranged chronologically so that you can better understand what aspect of the ever-increasing complexities of international business each theory was designed to explain.

***Comparative Advantage Theory.*** At the aggregate level, countries trade with each other for fundamentally the same reasons that individuals exchange products and services for mutual benefit. By doing so, we all benefit collectively. Comparative advantage theory is an arithmetic demonstration made by the English economist, David Ricardo, almost 190 years ago that a country can gain from engaging in trade even if it has an absolute advantage or disadvantage. In other words, even if the United States is more efficient than China in the production of everything, both countries will benefit from mutual trade by specializing in what each country can produce relatively more efficiently.

Let us demonstrate comparative advantage theory in its simplest form: the world is made up of two countries (the United States and China) and two products (personal computers and desks). We assume that there is only one PC model and only one type of desk. We further assume that labor is the only input to produce both products. Transportation costs are also assumed to be zero. **Exhibit 1.3** presents the production conditions and consumption pattern in the two countries before and after trade. As shown, U.S. labor is assumed to be more productive absolutely in the production of both personal computers (PC) and desks than Chinese labor.

Intuitively, you might argue that since the United States is more productive in both products, U.S. companies will export both PCs and desks to China, and Chinese companies cannot compete with U.S. companies in either product category. Furthermore, you might argue that as China cannot sell anything to the United States, China cannot pay for imports from the United States. Therefore, these two countries cannot engage in trade. This is essentially the **absolute advantage** argument. Is this argument true? The answer is no.

If you closely look at labor productivity of the two industries, you see that the United States can produce PCs more efficiently than desks compared to the situation in China. The United States has a three-to-one advantage in PCs, but only a two-to-one advantage in desks over China. In other words, the United States can produce three PCs instead of a desk (or as few as one-third of a desk per PC), while China can produce two PCs for a desk (or as many as half a desk per PC). Relatively speaking, the United States is comparatively more efficient in making PCs (at a rate of three PCs per desk) than China (at a rate of two PCs per desk). However, China is comparatively more efficient in making desks (at a rate of half a desk per PC) than the United States (at a rate of one-third of a desk per PC). Therefore, we say that the United States has a **comparative advantage** in making PCs, while China has a comparative advantage in making desks.

Comparative advantage theory suggests that the United States should specialize in production of PCs, while China should specialize in production of desks. As shown in Exhibit 1.3, the United States produced and consumed 100 PCs and 20 desks, and China produced and consumed 40 PCs and 30 desks. As a whole, the world (the United States and China combined) produced and consumed 140 PCs and 50 desks. Now as a result of specialization, the United States concentrates all its labor resources on PC production, while China allocates all labor resources to desk production. The United States can produce 60 more PCs by giving up on the 20 desks it used to produce (at a rate of three PCs per desk), resulting in a total production of 160 PCs and no desks. Similarly, China can produce 20 more desks by moving its labor from PC

## EXHIBIT 1-3
### COMPARATIVE ADVANTAGE AT WORK

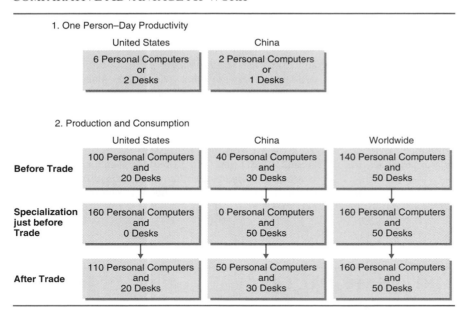

1. One Person–Day Productivity

| United States | China |
|---|---|
| 6 Personal Computers or 2 Desks | 2 Personal Computers or 1 Desks |

2. Production and Consumption

| | United States | China | Worldwide |
|---|---|---|---|
| Before Trade | 100 Personal Computers and 20 Desks | 40 Personal Computers and 30 Desks | 140 Personal Computers and 50 Desks |
| Specialization just before Trade | 160 Personal Computers and 0 Desks | 0 Personal Computers and 50 Desks | 160 Personal Computers and 50 Desks |
| After Trade | 110 Personal Computers and 20 Desks | 50 Personal Computers and 30 Desks | 160 Personal Computers and 50 Desks |

production to desk production (at a rate of half a desk per PC), with a total production of 50 desks and no PCs. Now the world as a whole produces 160 PCs and 50 desks.

Before trade occurs, U.S. consumers are willing to exchange as many as three PCs for each desk, while Chinese consumers are willing to exchange as few as two PCs for each desk, given their labor productivity, respectively. Therefore, the price of a desk acceptable to both U.S. and Chinese consumers should be somewhere between two and three PCs. Let us assume that the mutually acceptable price, or **commodity terms of trade** (a price of one good in terms of another), is 2.5 PCs per desk. Now let the United States and China engage in trade at the commodity terms of trade of 2.5 PCs per desk. To simplify our argument, further assume that the United States and China consume the same number of desks after trade as they did before trade, that is, 20 desks and 30 desks, respectively. In other words, the United States has to import 20 desks from China in exchange for 50 PCs (20 desks times a price of a desk in terms of PCs), which are exported to China from the United States. As a result of trade, the United States consumes 110 PCs and 20 desks, while China consumes 50 PCs and 30 desks. Given the same amount of labor resources, both countries respectively consume 10 more PCs while consuming the same number of desks. Obviously, specialization and trade have benefited both countries.

In reality, we rarely exchange one product for another. We use foreign exchange instead. Let us assume that the price of a desk is $900 in the United States and 6,300 yuan in China. Based on the labor productivity in the two countries, the price of a PC should be $300 (at a rate of a third of a desk per PC) in the United States and 3,150 yuan (at a rate of half a desk per PC) in China. As we indicated earlier, U.S. consumers are willing to exchange as many as three PCs for each desk worth $900 in the United States. Three PCs in China are worth 9,450 yuan. Therefore, U.S. consumers are willing to pay as much as

9,450 yuan to import a $900 desk from China. Similarly, Chinese consumers are willing to import a minimum of two PCs (worth 6,300 yuan in China) for each desk they produce (worth $900 in the United States). Therefore, the mutually acceptable exchange rate should be:

$$6{,}300 \text{ yuan} \leq \$900 \leq 9{,}450 \text{ yuan, or}$$

$$7.0 \text{ yuan} \leq \$1 \leq 10.5 \text{ yuan.}$$

An actual exchange rate will also be affected by consumer demands and money supply situations in the two countries. Nonetheless, it is clear that exchange rates are determined primarily by international trade.

From this simple exercise, we can make a few general statements or **principles of international trade**.

Principle 1: Countries benefit from international trade.

Principle 2: International trade increases worldwide production by specialization.

Principle 3: Exchange rates are determined primarily by traded goods.

By now you might have wondered why U.S. workers are more productive than Chinese workers. So far we have assumed that labor is the only input in economic production. In reality, we do not produce anything with manual labor alone. We use machinery, computers, and other capital equipment (capital for short) to help us produce efficiently. In other words, our implicit assumption was that the United States has more abundant capital relative to labor than China does. Naturally, the more capital we have relative to our labor stock, the less expensive a unit of capital should be relative to a unit of labor. The less expensive a unit of capital relative to a unit of labor, the more capital we tend to use and specialize in industry that requires a large amount of capital. In other words, the capital–labor endowment ratio affects what type of industry a country tends to specialize in. In general, a capital-abundant country (e.g., the United States) tends to specialize in capital-intensive industry and export capital-intensive products (personal computers), and import labor-intensive products (desks). Conversely, a labor-abundant country (China) tends to specialize in labor-intensive industry and export labor-intensive products (desks), and import capital-intensive products (personal computers). This refined argument is known as **factor endowment theory** of comparative advantage.

The factor endowment theory can be generalized a bit further. For example, the United States is not only capital-abundant but also abundant with a highly educated (i.e., skilled) labor force. Therefore, it is easy to predict that the United States has comparative advantage in skill-intensive industries such as computers and biotechnology and exports a lot of computers and genetically engineered ethical drugs around the world, and imports manual labor-intensive products such as textiles and shoes from labor-abundant countries such as China and Brazil. **Global Perspective 1-4** clearly shows that labor productivity alone shows a very erroneous impression of industry competitiveness.

Now you might have begun wondering how comparative advantage arguments will help businesspeople in the real world. Suppose you work as a strategic planner for Nike. Shoe manufacturing is extremely labor-intensive, while shoe designing is becoming increasingly high-tech (i.e., skill-intensive). The United States is a relatively skill-abundant and labor-scarce country. Therefore, the country has a comparative advantage in skill-intensive operations but has a comparative disadvantage in labor-intensive operations. There are two ways to use your knowledge of comparative advantage arguments. First, it is easy to predict where competition comes from. Companies from countries like China and Brazil will have a comparative advantage in shoe manufacturing over Nike in the United States. Second, you can advise Nike to establish shoe-manufacturing plants in labor-abundant countries instead of in the labor-scarce United States. As we said earlier, shoe designing has become increasingly high-tech, involving computer-aided designing and development of light, shock-absorbent material, which requires an extremely high level of expertise. Therefore, based on the comparative advantage argument, you suggest that product designing and development be done in the United States, where required expertise is relatively abundant. Indeed, that is what Nike does as a result of global competitive pressure, and has exploited various countries' comparative advantage to its advantage (no pun intended). Nike has product designing and development and special material development conducted in the United States and has manufacturing operations in labor-abundant countries like China and Brazil.

The comparative advantage theory is useful in explaining inter-industry trade—say computers and desks—between countries that have very different factor endowments. It suggests efficient allocation of limited resources across national boundaries by specialization and trade, but hardly explains business competition, because computer manufacturers and desk manufacturers do not compete directly. Further, it fails to explain the expansion of trade among the industrialized countries with similar factor endowments. Trade among the twenty or so industrialized countries now constitutes almost 60 percent of world trade, and much of it is intra-industry in nature. In other words, similar products are differentiated either physically or only in the customers' minds and traded across countries. Thus, BMW exports its sports cars to Japan, while Honda exports its competing models to Germany. BMW and Honda compete directly within the same automobile industry. This type of intra-industry competition cannot be explained by comparative advantage theory.

### International Product Cycle Theory.

When business practitioners think of competition, they usually refer to intra-industry competition. Why and how does competition tend to evolve over time and across national boundaries in the same industry? How then does a company develop its marketing strategy in the presence of competitors at home and abroad? **International product cycle theory** addresses all these questions.

## 𝒢LOBAL PERSPECTIVE 1-4

It is correct to say, "the best way to improve living standards is to encourage investment in sophisticated industries like computers and aerospace." Is it correct to say, "the best way to improve living standards is to encourage investment in industries that provide high value added per worker"? The real high-value industries in the United States are extremely capital-intensive sectors like cigarettes and oil refining. High-tech sectors that everyone imagines are the keys to the future, like aircraft and electronics, are only average in their value added per worker, but are extremely skill-intensive industries. Look at these statistics:

| Value Added Per Worker | Thousands |
| --- | --- |
| Cigarettes | $823 |
| Petroleum refining | $270 |
| Automobile | $112 |
| Tires and inner tubes | $101 |
| Aerospace | $86 |
| Electronics | $74 |
| All manufacturing | $73 |

*Source:* Adapted from Paul Krugman, "Competitiveness: Does it Matter?" *Fortune* (March 7, 1994), pp. 109–15.

Several speculations have been made.[59] First, a large domestic market, such as the United States, makes it possible for U.S companies to enjoy **economies of scale** in mass production and mass marketing, enabling them to become lower-cost producers than their competition in foreign countries. Therefore, those low-cost producers can market their products in foreign markets and still remain profitable. In addition, an **economies-of-scope** argument augments an economies-of-scale argument. Companies from a small country can still enjoy economies of scale in production and marketing by extending their business scope beyond their national boundary. For example, Nestlé, a Swiss food company, can enjoy economies of scale by considering European, U.S., and Japanese markets together as its primary market. Second, technological innovation can provide an innovative company a competitive advantage, or **technological gap**, over its competitors both at home and abroad. Until competitors learn about and imitate the innovation, the original innovator company enjoys a temporary monopoly power around the world. Therefore, it is technological innovators that tend to market new products abroad. Third, it is generally the per-capita income level that determines consumers' **preference similarity**, or consumption patterns, irrespective of nationality. Preference similarity explains why intra-industry trade has grown tremendously among the industrialized countries with similar income levels.

Combining these forces with the earlier comparative advantage theory, international product cycle theory was developed in the 1960s and 1970s to explain a realistic, dynamic change in international competition over time and place.[60] This comprehensive theory describes the relationship between trade and investment over the product life cycle.

One of the key underlying assumptions in the international product cycle theory is that "necessity is the mother of invention." In the United States, where personal incomes and labor costs were the highest in the world particularly in the 1960s and 1970s, consumers desired products that would save them labor and time, and satisfy materialistic needs. Historically, U.S. companies developed and introduced many products that were labor- and time-saving or responded to high-income consumer needs, including dishwashers, microwave ovens, automatic washers and dryers, personal computers, and so on. Similarly, companies in Western Europe tend to innovate on material- and capital-saving products and processes to meet their local consumers' needs and lifestyle orientation. Small and no-frill automobiles and recyclable products are such examples. Japanese companies stress products that conserve not only material and capital but also space to address their local consumers' acute concern about space limitation. Therefore, Japanese companies excel in developing and marketing small, energy-efficient products of all kinds.[61]

International product cycle theory suggests that new products are developed primarily to address the needs of the local consumers, only to be demanded by foreign consumers who have similar needs with a similar purchasing power. As the nature of new products and their manufacturing processes becomes widely disseminated over time, the products eventually become mass-produced standard products around the world. At that point, the products' cost competitiveness becomes a determinant of success and failure in global competition. Your knowledge of comparative advantage theory helps your company identify where strong low-cost competitors tend to appear and how the company should plan production locations.

As presented in **Exhibit 1.4**, the pattern of evolution of the production and marketing process explained in the international product cycle consists of four stages: introduction, growth, maturity, and decline. Let us explain the international product cycle from a U.S. point of view. It is to be reminded, however, that different kinds of product innovations also occur in countries (mostly developed) other than the United States. If so, a similar evolutionary pattern of development will begin from those other industrialized countries.

In the *introductory stage*, a U.S. company innovates on a new product to meet domestic consumers' needs in the U.S. market. A few other U.S. companies may introduce the same product. At this stage, competition is mostly domestic among U.S. companies. Some of those companies may begin exporting the product to a few European countries and Japan where they can find willing buyers similar to U.S. consumers. Product standards are not likely to be established yet. As a result, competing product models or specifications may exist on the market. Prices tend to be high. In the *growth stage*, product standards emerge and mass production becomes feasible. Lower prices spawn price competition. U.S. companies increase exports to Europe and Japan as those foreign markets expand. However, European and Japanese companies also begin producing the product in their own local markets and even begin exporting it to the United States. In the *maturity stage*, many U.S. and foreign companies vie for market share in the international markets. They try to lower prices and differentiate their products to outbid their competition. U.S. companies that have carved out market share in Europe and Japan by exporting decide to make a direct investment in production in those markets to protect their market position there. U.S. and foreign companies also begin to export to developing countries, because more consumers in those developing countries can afford the product as its price falls. Then, in the *decline stage*, companies in the developing countries also begin producing the product and marketing it in the rest of the world. U.S., European, and Japanese companies may also begin locating their manufacturing plants in those developing countries to take advantage of inexpensive labor. The United States eventually begins to import what was once a U.S. innovation.

The international product cycle argument holds true as long as we can assume that innovator companies are not informed about conditions in foreign markets, whether in other industrialized countries or in the developing world. As we amply indicated in Chapter 1, such an assumption has become very iffy. Nor can it be safely assumed that U.S. companies are exposed to a very different home environment from European and Japanese companies. Indeed, the differences among the

[59]Mordechai E. Kreinin, *International Economics: A Policy Approach*, 5th ed. (New York: Harcourt Brace Jovanovich, 1987), pp. 276–78.

[60]See, for example, Raymond Vernon, "International Investment and International Trade in the Product Cycle," *Quarterly Journal of Economics*, 80 (May 1966), pp. 190–207; "The Location of Economic Activity," *Economic Analysis and the Multinational Enterprise*, John H. Dunning, ed. (London: George Allen and Unwin, 1974), pp. 89–114; and "The Product Cycle Hypothesis in a New International Environment," *Oxford Bulletin of Economics and Statistics*, 41 (November 1979), pp. 255–67.

[61]Vernon, 1979.

**EXHIBIT 1-4**
INTERNATIONAL PRODUCT CYCLE

| | Introduction | Growth | Maturity | Decline |
|---|---|---|---|---|
| Demand Structure | Nature of demand not well understood<br>Consumers willing to pay premium price for a new product | Price competition begins<br>Product standard emerging | Competition based on price and product differentiation | Mostly price competition |
| Production | Short runs, rapidly changing techniques<br>Dependent on skilled labor | Mass production | Long runs with stable techniques<br>Capital intensive | Long runs with stable techniques<br>Lowest cost production needed either by capital intensive production or by massive use of inexpensive labor |
| Innovator Company Marketing Strategy | Sales mostly to home-country (e.g., U.S.) consumers<br>Some exported to other developed countries (e.g., Europe and Japan) | Increased exports to the other developed countries (e.g., Europe and Japan) | Innovator company (e.g., U.S.) begins production in Europe and Japan to protect its foreign market from local competition | Innovator company (U.S.) may begin production in developing countries |
| International Competition | A few competitors at home (e.g., U.S.) | Competitors in developed countries (e.g., Europe and Japan) begin production for their domestic markets<br>They also begin exporting to the United States | European and Japanese companies increase exports to the United States<br>They begin exporting to developing countries | European and Japanese competitors may begin production in developing countries<br>Competitors from developing countries also begin exporting to the world |

*Source:* Expanded on Louis T. Wells, Jr., "International Trade: The Product Life Cycle Approach," in Reed Moyer, ed., *International Business: Issues and Concepts* (New York: John Wiley, 1984), pp. 5–22.

industrialized countries are reduced to trivial dimensions. Seeking to exploit global scale economies, an increasing number of companies are likely to establish various plants in both developed countries and developing countries, and to cross haul between plants for the manufacture of final products. As an explanation of international business behavior, international product cycle theory has limited explanatory power. It does describe the initial international expansion (exporting followed by direct investment) of many companies, but the mature globetrotting companies of today have succeeded in developing a number of other strategies for surviving in global competition.

### Internalization/Transaction Cost Theory.
Now that many companies have established plants in various countries, they have to manage their corporate activities across national boundaries. Those companies are conventionally called multinational companies. It is inherently much more complex and difficult to manage corporate activities and market products across national boundaries, rather than from a domestic base. Then why do those multinational companies invest in foreign manufacturing and marketing operations instead of just exporting from their home base? International product cycle theory explains that companies

reactively invest abroad when local competitors threaten their foreign market positions. Thus, the primary objective of foreign direct investment for the exporting companies is to keep their market positions from being eroded. Are there any proactive reasons for companies to invest overseas?

To address this issue, a new strand of theory has been developed. It is known as **internalization** or **transaction cost theory**. Any company has some proprietary expertise that makes it different from its competitors. Without such expertise no company can sustain its competitive advantage. Such expertise may be reflected in a new product, unique product design, efficient production technique, or even brand image itself. As in the international product cycle argument, a company's expertise may eventually become common knowledge as a result of competitors copying it or reverse-engineering its product. Therefore, it is sometimes to an innovator company's advantage to keep its expertise to itself as long as possible in order to maximize the economic value of the expertise. A company's unique expertise is just like any information. Once information is let out, it becomes a "public good"—and free.

In other words, the multinational company can be considered an organization that uses its internal market to produce and distribute products in an efficient manner in situations where the true value of its expertise cannot be assessed in ordinary external business transactions. Generating expertise or knowledge requires the company to invest in research and development. In most circumstances, it is necessary for the company to overcome this appropriability problem by the creation of a monopolistic internal market (i.e., internalization) when the knowledge advantage can be developed and explored in an optimal manner on a global basis.[62] The motive to internalize knowledge is generally strong when the company needs to invest in business assets (e.g., manufacturing and marketing infrastructure) that have few alternative uses, uses those assets frequently, and faces uncertainty in negotiating, monitoring, and enforcing a contract. Such a situation suggests a high level of transaction costs due to specific assets and contractual uncertainty involved.[63]

### Resource-Based View and Appropriability Theory.

Now that many companies have established subsidiaries and other affiliates in various countries, they have to manage their far-flung corporate operations to their competitive advantage. The **resource-based view** of the firm suggests that companies can be conceived of as controlling bundles of various resources, also called capabilities. These capabilities are developed through previous experience and over time. When resources are *valuable, rare, difficult to imitate* (inimitable), and *non-substitutable*, they can lead to sustainable competitive advantage.[64] Resources and capabilities do not only include physical assets but also skills, technologies, and more intangible endowments, such as productive routines and other organizational competencies as well. An individual subsidiary as a resource node or bundle of resources and capabilities with its own unique resource profile plays a significant role in maintaining the multinational company's competitive advantage. Furthermore, its subsidiary's intraorganizational linkages give rise to competitive advantages due to scope and scale economies and other relational benefits.

However, the company's organizational resources can only be sources of sustained competitive advantage if competitors that do not possess these resources cannot obtain them easily. The company's expertise can be channeled through three routes to garner competitive advantage: appropriability regime, dominant design, and operational/marketing capabilities.[65] **Appropriability regime** refers to aspects of the commercial environment that govern a company's ability to retain its technological advantage. It depends on the efficacy of legal mechanisms of protection, such as patents, copyrights, and trade secrets. However, in today's highly competitive market, legal means of protecting proprietary technology have become ineffective as new product innovations are relatively easily reverse-engineered, improved upon, and invented around by competitors without violating patents and other proprietary

protections bestowed on them. It is widely recognized that the most effective ways of securing maximum returns from a new product innovation are through lead time and moving fast down the experience curve (i.e., quickly resorting to mass production).[66] Obviously, the value of owning technology has lessened drastically in recent years as the inventor company's temporary monopoly over its technology has shortened.

**Dominant design** is a narrow class of product designs that begins to emerge as a "standard" design. A company that has won a dominant design status has an absolute competitive advantage over its competition. In an early stage of product development, many competing product designs exist. After considerable trial and error in the marketplace, a product standard tends to emerge. A good case example is Sony's Betamax format and Panasonic's VHS format for VCRs. The Betamax format was technologically superior with better picture quality than the VHS format, but could not play as long to record movies as the VHS. Although the Sony system was introduced slightly earlier than the Panasonic system, the tape's limited capability to record movies turned out to be fatal to Sony as the VHS tape was increasingly used for rental home movies and home recording of movies. Thus, VHS emerged as the worldwide standard for videocassette recording.

Was it simply the act of the "invisible hand" in the marketplace? The answer is clearly no. Panasonic actively licensed its VHS technology to Sanyo, Sharp, and Toshiba for production and supplied VHS-format videocassette recorders to RCA, Magnavox, and GTE Sylvania for resale under their respective brand names.[67] When Philips introduced a cassette tape recorder, a similar active licensing strategy had been employed for a quick adoption as a dominant standard around the world. Despite various government hurdles to stall the Japanese domination of emerging HDTV technology, Sony is currently trying to make its format a standard by working its way into Hollywood movie studios. It is clear that a wide adoption of a new product around the world, whether autonomous or deliberated, seems to guarantee it a dominant design status.

**Operational and marketing ability** is in almost all cases required for successful commercialization of a product innovation. The issue here is to what extent this ability is specialized to the development and commercialization of a new product. Indeed, many successful companies have highly committed their productive assets to closely related areas without diversifying into unrelated businesses. This commitment is crucial. Take semiconductor production for example. A director at SEMATECH (a U.S. government-industry semiconductor manufacturing technology consortium established in Austin, Texas, to regain U.S. competitive edge in semiconductor manufacturing equipment from Japanese competition) admits that despite and because of a rapid technological turnover, any serious company wishing to compete on a state-of-the-art computer chip with the Japanese will have to invest a minimum of a billion dollars in a semiconductor manufacturing

[62]Alan M. Rugman, ed., *New Theories of the Multinational Enterprise* (London: Croom Helm, 1982).

[63]Oliver E. Williamson, "The Economics of Organization: The Transaction Cost Approach," *American Journal of Sociology*, 87 (1981), pp. 548–77.

[64]Jay B Barney, "Firm Resources and Sustained Competitive Advantage," *Journal of Management*, 17(1, 1991), pp. 99–120.

[65]David J. Teece, "Capturing Value from Technological Innovation: Integration, Strategic Partnering, and Licensing Decisions," in Bruce R. Guile and Harvey Brooks, eds., *Technology and Global Industry: Companies and Nations in the World Economy* (Washington, D.C.: National Academy Press), pp. 65–95.

[66]Richard C. Levin, Alvin K. Klevorick, Richard R. Nelson, and Sidney G. Winter, "Appropriating the Returns from Industrial Research and Development," *Brookings Papers on Economic Activity*, 3 (1987), pp. 783–831.

[67]Richard S. Rosenbloom and Michael A. Cusumano, "Technological Pioneering and Competitive Advantage: The Birth of VCR Industry," *California Management Review*, 29 (Summer 1987), pp. 51–76.

equipment and facility. General Motors invested more than $5 billion for its Saturn project to compete with the Japanese in small car production and marketing. A massive retooling is also necessary for any significant upgrade in both industries. Furthermore, the software side of manufacturing ability may be even more difficult to match, as it involves such specialized operational aspects as JIT (just-in-time) manufacturing management, quality control, and components sourcing relationships. Irrespective of nationality, those multinational companies that are successful in global markets tend to excel not only in product innovative ability but also in manufacturing and marketing competencies.[68] It is clear that innovative companies committed to manufacturing and marketing excellence will likely remain strong competitors in industry.

These three sources of competitive advantage are not independent of each other. Given the relative ease of learning about competitors' proprietary knowledge without violating patents and other legal protections, many companies resort to mass production and mass marketing to drive down the cost along the experience curve. To do so requires enormous invest-

ment in manufacturing capacity. As a result, the efficacy of appropriability regime is highly dependent on investment in manufacturing and marketing ability. Similarly, a wide acceptance of a product is most likely necessary for the product to become a dominant design in the world for a next generation of the product. Thus, mass production and marketing on a global scale is likely to be a necessary, if not sufficient, condition for a company to attain a dominant design status for its product.

It is apparent that patents, copyrights, and trade secrets are not necessarily optimal means of garnering competitive advantage unless they are strongly backed by strengths in innovative manufacturing and marketing on a global basis. Likewise, companies strong in manufacturing without innovative products also suffer from competitive disadvantage. In other words, it takes such an enormous investment to develop new products and to penetrate new markets that few companies can go it alone anymore. Thus, to compete with integrated global competitors, an increasing number of companies have entered into strategic alliances so as to complement their competitive weaknesses with their partners' competitive strengths.

---

[68]Masaaki Kotabe, "Corporate Product Policy and Innovative Behavior of European and Japanese Multinationals: An Empirical Investigation," *Journal of Marketing*, 54 (April 1990), pp. 19–33.

## SUMMARY ◆ ◆ ◆ ◆ ◆ ◆ ◆ ◆ ◆ ◆ ◆ ◆ ◆ ◆ ◆ ◆ ◆ ◆ ◆ ◆ ◆ ◆ ◆ ◆ ◆

Three theories that cast some insight into the workings of international business have been reviewed. These theories are not independent of each other. Rather, they supplement each other. Comparative advantage theory is useful when we think broadly about the nature of industrial development and international trade around the world. International product cycle theory helps explain why and how a company initially extends its market horizons abroad and how foreign competitors shape global competition over time and place. Internalization or

transaction cost theory provides some answers to how to manage multinational operations in a very competitive world.

There are other theories to supplement our understanding of international business, however, they are beyond the scope of this textbook and are probably unnecessary. Now you can appreciate how international business has expanded in scope over time. With understanding of these theories, we hope you can better understand the rest of the book.

## KEY TERMS ◆ ◆ ◆ ◆ ◆ ◆ ◆ ◆ ◆ ◆ ◆ ◆ ◆ ◆ ◆ ◆ ◆ ◆ ◆ ◆ ◆ ◆ ◆ ◆ ◆

| | | | |
|---|---|---|---|
| Absolute advantage | Factor endowment theory | Economies of scale | Preference similarity |
| Comparative advantage | International product cycle theory | Economies of scope | Internalization theory |
| Commodity terms of trade | | Technological gap | Transaction cost theory |

# ECONOMIC ENVIRONMENT

2

## CHAPTER OVERVIEW

1. INTERTWINED WORLD ECONOMY

2. COUNTRY COMPETITIVENESS

3. EMERGING ECONOMIES

4. EVOLUTION OF COOPERATIVE GLOBAL TRADE AGREEMENTS

5. INFORMATION TECHNOLOGY AND THE CHANGING NATURE OF COMPETITION

6. REGIONAL ECONOMIC ARRANGEMENTS

7. MULTINATIONAL CORPORATIONS

At no other time in economic history have countries been more economically interdependent than they are today. Although the second half of the twentieth century saw the highest ever sustained growth rates in **Gross Domestic Product** (GDP) in history, the growth in international flows in goods and services (called international trade) has consistently surpassed the growth rate of the world economy. Simultaneously, the growth in international financial flows—which includes foreign direct investment, portfolio investment, and trading in currencies—has achieved a life of its own. Thanks to trade liberalization heralded by the General Agreement on Tariffs and Trade (GATT) and the World Trade Organization (WTO), the GATT's successor, the barriers to international trade and financial flows keep getting lower. From 1997 to 2007, global GDP grew more than 30 percent, while total global merchandise exports increased by more than 60 percent (see **Exhibit 2-1**).[1]

However, the beginning of the 21st century was beset with a recessionary world economy. For example, growth in the value of the United States' trade decelerated throughout 2001. Western Europe's merchandise exports and imports values increased by about 2 percent during the same period. Overall, the year 2001 witnessed the first decline in the volume of world merchandise trade since 1982 and the first decrease in world merchandise output since 1991. On the other hand, the transition economies

[1]*World Trade Report 2008*, http://www.wto.org/, Geneva, World Trade Organization, 2008.

**EXHIBIT 2-1**

GROWTH (IN PERCENT) IN THE VOLUME OF WORLD MERCHANDISE TRADE AND GDP, 1997–2007

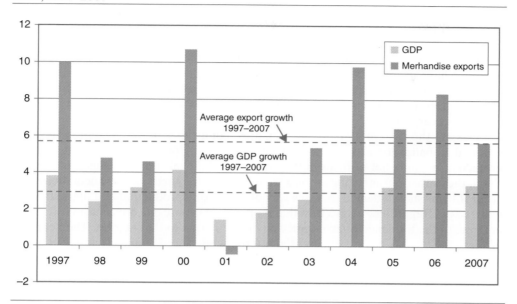

*Source: World Trade Report 2008: Trade in a Globalizing World,* www.wto.org, World Trade Organization, 2008.

recorded an outstanding trade growth performance in an adverse global environment. A further strengthening of trade and investment links between the European Union and Central and Eastern Europe contributed largely to this outcome. Africa and the Middle East also expanded their imports despite a fall in prices of oil and other commodities in 2001. Overall, global GDP growth edged up only by about 1 percent due chiefly to a more resilient services sector.[2] Since then, however, the world economy had continued to recover. In 2007, the world GDP maintained a strong increase of 3 percent, and the volume of world merchandise trade grew by 5.5 percent.[3] As stated in Chapter 1, however, U.S. subprime home loan-led financial turmoil has led to an unprecedented global economic slowdown since late 2008. At the time of this writing in early 2009, World Bank predicts that global GDP growth will slip from 2.5 percent in 2008 to 0.9 percent in 2009. Developing country growth is expected to decline from a resilient 7.9 percent in 2007 to 4.5 percent in 2009. Growth in developed countries will likely be negative in 2009.[4]

Expanding world markets will likely remain a key driving force for the 21st century economy. Although the severe slump in Asia in the late 1990s, the renewed financial crisis in South America and the slump in the U.S. and European economies in 2001, and now the worst global recession since the 1930s point up the vulnerabilities to the global marketplace, the long-term trends of fast-rising trade and rising world incomes still remain uncertain.

Since the second half of the 1990s, there have been some strong anti-globalization movements for various reasons including economics, environmental concern, and American cultural hegemony, among others. Let us focus just on economics here. Some in developed countries argue that globalization would result in increased competition from low-income countries, thus threatening to hold down wages, say, in the United States. However, real wages in the United States increased at a 1.3

---

[2]WTO News: 2002 Press Release, "Disappointing Trade Figures Underscore Importance of Accelerating Trade Talks," October 7, 2002, http://www.wto.org/, accessed November 12, 2002.

[3]*World Trade Report 2008.*

[4]"World Trade to Shrink in 2009: World Bank," newsroomamerica.com, December 9, 2008.

percent annual rate in the 1990s, much faster than the 0.2 percent annual gain of the 1980s.[5]

Globalization has helped improve the economies of emerging and developing countries more than those of developed countries. The gap in real GDP growth rate between emerging countries and developed countries, widened from zero in 1991 to about five points in 2008. Helping poorer countries catch up economically has long been among the benefits touted for globalization. Unfortunately, the current global recession has caused exactly the reverse—the economic downturn has been sharpest in countries that opened up most to world trade, especially East Asian countries. For example, Taiwan's exports are over 60 percent of GDP, and its economy may fall well over 10 percent in 2009.[6]

Despite the current global recession, most countries in the 21st century have not shunned globalization and are likely to continue their globalization trend. It has been protected by the belief of firms in the efficiency of global supply chains. But like any chain, these are only as strong as their weakest link. A dangerous miscalculation could occur if firms should decide that this way of organizing production and marketing has had its day.[7] Regardless, even a firm that is operating in only one domestic market is not immune to the influence of economic activities external to that market. The net result of these factors has been the increased interdependence of countries and economies, increased competitiveness, and the concomitant need for firms to keep a constant watch on the international economic environment.

---

◆ ◆ ◆ ◆ ◆ ◆ ◆ ◆  **INTERTWINED WORLD ECONOMY**

There is no question that the global economy continues to become more intertwined. Whether the world economy was in a growth mode or is in a severe recession mode, the current global recession has made all of us aware that countries are ever more interdependent of each other. The United States is a $14.3 trillion economy in 2008, and its U.S. trade deficit of $813 billion is about 6 percent of the U.S. GDP. In 2008, about 15 percent of what Americans consumed was imported in the United States (measured based on the ratio of the country's imports to its GDP). The United States is relatively more insulated from external shocks than Britain or Thailand. In 2008, the imports/GDP ratios for Britain and Thailand are about 23.2 percent and 58.5 percent, respectively.[8] Nonetheless, the U.S. economy, too, is getting increasingly intertwined with the rest of the world economy.

The importance of international trade and investment cannot be overemphasized for any country. In general, *the larger the country's domestic economy, the less dependent it tends to be on exports and imports relative to its GDP.*[9] Let's compute trade dependence ratios (total trade/GDP) using the available statistics. For the United States (GDP = $14.3 trillion in 2008), international trade in goods (sum of exports and imports) rose from 10 percent of the GDP in 1970 to 25 percent in 2008. For Japan (GDP = $4.8 trillion), with about one-third of the U.S. GDP, forms 31 percent in 2008. For Germany (GDP = $3.8 trillion), trade forms about 72 percent of the GDP. For Netherlands (GDP = $910 billion), trade value exceeds GDP, for as high as 112 percent of GDP (due to re-export); and for Singapore (GDP = $193 billion), trade is more than

---

[5]"Restating the '90s," *Economist*, April 1, 2002, pp. 51–58.

[6]"Turning their Back on the World: The Integration of the World Economy is in Retreat on Almost Every Front," *Economist*, February 19, 2009.

[7]Ibid.

[8]Computed from trade statistics in U.S. Central Intelligence Agency, *The World Factbook 2009*, https://www.cia.gov/library/publications/the-world-factbook/.

[9]In other words, smaller economies are more susceptible than larger economies to various external shocks in the world economy, such as the recession in the Unite States that would import less, sudden oil price surge, and exchange rate fluctuations. Read "Restoring the Balance: The World Economy is Still Growing Rapidly, but is Also out of Kilter," *Economist*, September 24, 2005, p. 13.

**EXHIBIT 2-2**

TOP 10 EXPORTERS AND IMPORTERS IN WORLD MERCHANDISE TRADE, 2008

| Rank | EXPORTERS | Value ($billion) | Export Dependence* (%) | Value per capita ($) | Rank | IMPORTERS | Value ($billion) | Import Dependence** (%) | Value per capita ($) |
|---|---|---|---|---|---|---|---|---|---|
| 1 | Germany | 1,530 | 40.1 | 18,574 | 1 | United States | 2,190 | 15.3 | 7,208 |
| 2 | China | 1,465 | 34.7 | 1,101 | 2 | Germany | 1,202 | 31.5 | 14,592 |
| 3 | United States | 1,377 | 9.6 | 4,532 | 3 | China | 1,156 | 27.4 | 869 |
| 4 | Japan | 777 | 16.0 | 6,104 | 4 | France | 718 | 24.1 | 11,209 |
| 5 | France | 630 | 21.1 | 9,835 | 5 | Japan | 696 | 14.4 | 5,468 |
| 6 | Italy | 566 | 23.6 | 8,453 | 6 | United Kingdom | 646 | 23.2 | 10,167 |
| 7 | Netherlands | 538 | 59.2 | 32,321 | 7 | Italy | 567 | 23.6 | 8,677 |
| 8 | United Kingdom | 469 | 16.8 | 7,184 | 8 | Netherlands | 485 | 53.3 | 29,137 |
| 9 | Canada | 462 | 29.5 | 13,910 | 9 | Canada | 437 | 27.9 | 13,158 |
| 10 | Belgium | 373 | 70.3 | 35,852 | 10 | Belgium | 375 | 70.7 | 36,044 |

*Exports/GDP × 100
**Imports/GDP × 100

*Source:* Computed from trade statistics in Central Intelligence Agency, *World Factbook 2009, https://www.cia.gov/library/publications/the-world-factbook/.*

340 percent of its GDP![10] These trade statistics are relative to the country's GDP. In absolute dollar terms, however, a small relative trade percentage of a large economy still translates into large volumes of trade (See **Exhibit 2-2**). As shown in the last column for exports and imports in Exhibit 2-2, the per-capita amount of exports and imports is another important statistic for marketing purposes as it represents, on average, how much involved or dependent each individual is on international trade.

For instance, individuals (consumers and companies) in the United States and Japan—the world's two largest economies—tend to be able to find domestic sources for their needs since their economies are diversified and extremely large. The U.S. per capita value of exports and imports is $4,532 and $2,190 in 2008. For Japan, its per capita value of exports and imports is $6,104 and $5,468, respectively. On the other hand, individuals in smaller and rich economies tend to rely more heavily on international trade, as illustrated by the Netherlands with the per capita exports and imports of $32,321 and $29,137, respectively. Although China's overall exports and imports amounted to $1.47 trillion and $1.16 trillion, respectively, the per capita exports and imports amounted to only $1,101 and $869, respectively, in 2008. One implication of these figures is that the higher the per-capita trade, the more closely intertwined is that country's economy with the rest of the world. Intertwining of economies by the process of specialization due to international trade leads to job creation in both the exporting country and the importing country.

However, beyond the simple figure of trade as a rising percentage of a nation's GDP lies the more interesting question of what rising trade does to the economy of a nation. A nation that is a successful trader—i.e., it makes goods and services that other nations buy and it buys goods and services from other nations—displays a natural inclination to be competitive in the world market. The threat of a possible foreign competitor is a powerful incentive for firms and nations to invest in technology and markets in order to remain competitive. Also, apart from trade flows, foreign direct investment, portfolio investment, and daily financial flows in the international money

---

[10]Computed from trade statistics in U.S. Central Intelligence Agency, *The World Factbook 2009*, https://www.cia.gov/library/publications/the-world-factbook/.

"The repairs will take awhile. We need a part from
Mexico, a part from Brazil and one from Taiwan."

Chon Day/The Cartoon Bank, Inc.

Even a simple "domestic" job involves inputs
from various countries in an intertwined world.

markets profoundly influence the economies of countries that may be seemingly
completely separate.

**Foreign Direct
Investment**

**Foreign direct investment**—which means investment in manufacturing and service
facilities in a foreign country with an intention to engage actively in managing them—
is another facet of the increasing integration of national economies. As shown in
**Exhibit 2-3**, the overall world inflow of foreign direct investment (FDI) increased

**EXHIBIT 2-3**
FOREIGN DIRECT INVESTMENT INFLOWS (IN US$ BILLION), 1980–2007

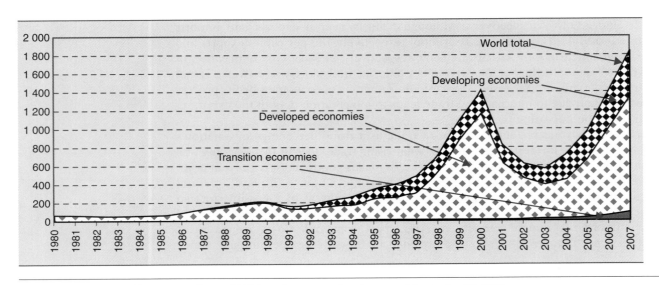

*Source:* UNCTAD, *World Investment Report 2008,* http://www.unctad.org/, accessed September 18, 2008.

*Note:* CIS = Commonwealth of Independent States (Russia, Central Asia, and Caucasus states)

twenty-five fold from 1980 to 2000 when it peaked at $1,411 billion. Then the global recession that ensued after the September 11, 2001 terrorist attacks on the U.S. soil dampened FDI flows significantly for a few years. Since 2004, global FDI inflows have continued growing, reaching the highest level ever recorded of $1,833 billion in 2007. Although the continued rise in FDI flows across regions largely reflects strong economic growth and performance in many parts of the world, global FDI flows also largely resulted from a weakening U.S. dollar in 2007. Although not yet available in the latest official statistics, the ongoing worldwide financial and economic crisis (and the sudden appreciation of the U.S. dollar) has changed the FDI situation drastically. In 2008, FDI flows declined by more than 20 percent, and a further decrease in FDI flows is expected in 2009 (at the time of this writing).[11]

Two things should be noted. In the past, foreign direct investment was considered as an alternative to exports in order to avoid tariff barriers. However, these days, foreign direct investment and international trade have become complementary.[12] For example, Dell Computer uses a factory in Ireland to supply personal computers in Europe instead of exporting from Austin, Texas. Similarly, Honda, a Japanese automaker with a major factory in Marysville, Ohio, is the largest exporter of automobiles from the United States. As firms invest in manufacturing and distribution facilities outside their home countries to expand into new markets around the world, they have added to the stock of foreign direct investment. Second, although not shown in the exhibit, the composition of FDI has shifted from manufacturing to services in all regions. FDI in services increased from being one-quarter of the world inflow FDI stock in 1970s to 49 percent in 1990, and to 62 percent with an estimated value of $6 trillion in 2005. Most notably, although FDI outflows in services are still dominated by developed countries, they are no longer controlled by firms from the United States, but much more evenly distributed among developed countries than before. By 2002, Japan and the European Union had emerged as significant sources of outward FDI in service sectors. Developing countries' outward FDI in services has also grown gradually since the 1990s.[13]

The increase in foreign direct investment is also promoted by efforts by many national governments to woo multinationals and by the leverage that the governments of large potential markets such as China and India have in granting access to multinationals. For example, in 2006, China's FDI inflow still reached $69 billion, even though this was the first time it declined in seven years due mainly to reduced flows to financial services. Meanwhile, China gradually became a source of FDI. China's outflows increased by 32 percent to $16 billion in 2006, and its outward FDI stock reached $73 billion, the sixth largest in the developing world.[14] Sometimes trade friction can also promote foreign direct investment. Investment in the United States by Japanese companies is, to an extent, a function of the trade imbalances between the two nations and by the consequent pressure applied by the U.S. government on Japan to do something to reduce the bilateral trade deficit. Since most of the U.S. trade deficit with Japan is attributed to Japanese cars exported from Japan, Japanese automakers, such as Honda, Toyota, Nissan, and Mitsubishi, have expanded their local production by setting up production facilities in the United States. In 1986, Japanese automakers exported 3.43 million cars from Japan and assembled only 0.62 million cars in the United States. By 1992, the number of exported cars equaled the number of U.S.-built Japanese cars at 1.7 million cars each. Since then, Japanese automakers have manufactured more cars in the United States than exporting from Japan. In 1997, they produced 2.31 million cars in the United

[11]"Assessing the Impact of the Current Financial and Economic Crisis on Global FDI Flows," UNCTAD News, http://www.unctad.org/Templates/Page.asp?intItemID=3665&lang=1, February 4, 2009.

[12]"Trade by Any Other Name," *Economist*, October 3, 1998, pp. 10–14.

[13]UNCTAD, *World Investment Report 2008*.

[14]UNCTAD, *World Investment Report 2007*.

States and imported 1.27 million cars from Japan. During the 1986–1999 period, Japanese automakers also increased their purchases of U.S.-made components almost thirteen fold from $2.5 billion in 1986 to 31.9 billion in 1999.[15] As of April 2008, Toyota conducts its business worldwide with 53 overseas manufacturing companies. It has design centers in California and in France on the Côte d'Azur, and with its engineering centers located in the Detroit area and in Belgium and Thailand.[16] This localization strategy reduced Japanese automakers' vulnerability to political retaliation by the United States under the Super 301 laws of the **Omnibus Trade and Competitiveness Act of 1988**.

## Portfolio Investment

An additional facet to the rising integration of economies has to do with **portfolio investment** (or **indirect investment**) in foreign countries and with money flows in the international financial markets. Portfolio investment refers to investments in foreign countries that are withdrawable at short notice, such as investment in foreign stocks and bonds. In the international financial markets, the borders between nations have, for all practical purposes, disappeared.[17] The trading of enormous quantities of money on a daily basis has assumed a life of its own. When trading in foreign currencies began, it was as an adjunct transaction to an international trade transaction in goods and services—banks and firms bought and sold currencies to complete the export or import transaction or to hedge the exposure to fluctuations in the exchange rates in the currencies of interest in the trade transaction. However, in today's international financial markets, traders trade currencies most of the time without an underlying trade transaction. They trade on the accounts of the banks and financial institutions they work for, mostly on the basis of daily news on inflation rates, interest rates, political events, stock and bond market movements, commodity supplies and demand, and so on. As mentioned earlier, the weekly volume of international trade in currencies exceeds the annual value of the trade in goods and services.

The effect of this proverbial tail wagging the dog is that all nations with even partially convertible currencies are exposed to the fluctuations in the currency markets. A rise in the value of the local currency due to these daily flows vis-à-vis other currencies makes exports more expensive (at least in the short run) and can add to the trade deficit or reduce the trade surplus. A rising currency value will also deter foreign investment in the country and will encourage outflow of investment.[18] It may also encourage a decrease in the interest rates in the country if the central bank of that country wants to maintain the currency exchange rate and a decrease in the interest rate would spur local investment. An interesting example is the Mexican meltdown in early 1995 and the massive devaluation of the peso, which was exacerbated by the withdrawal of money by foreign investors. And more recently, the massive depreciation of many Asian currencies in the 1997–1999 period, known as the Asian financial crisis, is also an instance of the influence of these short-term movements of money.[19] Unfortunately, the influences of these short-term money flows are nowadays far more powerful determinants of exchange rates than an investment by a Japanese or German automaker.

Another example is provided by Brazil, which was a largely protected market until 1995. Liberalization is on the way as a result of the formation in 1994 of the Southern Common Market (Mercado Común del Sur, or MERCOSUR) (to be explained later in

---

[15]"JAMA Members Set New Records in Their Purchase of U.S.-Made Auto Part," Japan Auto Trends, *Today's JAMA*, March 2000, http://jamaserv.jama.or.jp/e_press/index.html, accessed October 30, 2002.

[16]"The Car Company in Front," *Economist*, January 27, 2005, pp. 65–67.

[17]Kenichi Ohmae, *The Borderless World* (New York: Harper Collins Books, 1990).

[18]"Beware of Hot Money," *Business Week*, April 4, 2005, pp. 52–53.

[19]Masaaki Kotabe, "The Four Faces of the Asian Financial Crisis: How to Cope with the Southeast Asia Problem, the Japan Problem, the Korea Problem, and the China Problem," *Journal of International Management*, 4 (1), 1998, 1S–6S.

the chapter). Since the debt crisis of 1982, Brazil had suffered a chronic hyperinflation that ruined its economy and competitiveness. Brazil's new currency, *real*, was launched in 1994 both as the instrument and as the symbol of a huge effort for Brazil to catch up with the developed world. Financial markets first attacked the Brazilian *real* in March 1995, in the wake of Mexico's peso devaluation. Brazil responded by adopting a pegged exchange rate, under which the *real* devalued by 7.5 percent a year against the U.S. dollar. Then, the Asian financial crisis and the crash of many Asian currencies (with as much as 75 percent in the case of Indonesian currency, *rupiah*, in a matter of a few months) in 1998 reverberated again in Brazil and Mexico as well, because portfolio investors started viewing all emerging markets with a jaundiced eye. Worse yet, in 2002, Argentina caused another financial crisis in Latin America, triggered by one of the largest government debt default ever. The Brazilian *real* was under pressure, falling from R1/US$ in July 1994 to R3.63/US$ in October 2002—a whopping 72 percent depreciation since its introduction. The central bank had to sell dollars and buy *real* to shore up the value of the *real*. This led to a credit crunch, causing a slowdown in export growth, only to be temporarily stabilized by the International Monetary Fund's $30 billion rescue loan to Brazil in 2002.[20] There were also adverse effects on the Indian stock markets as well. The point is that, at least in the short run, these daily international flows of money have dealt a blow to the notion of economic independence and nationalism.

## COUNTRY COMPETITIVENESS

◆ ◆ ◆ ◆ ◆ ◆ ◆

**Country competitiveness** refers to the productiveness of a country, which is represented by its firms' domestic and international productive capacity. Human, natural, and capital resources of a country primarily shape the nature of corporate productive capacity in the world, and thus the nature of international business. As explained in the Appendix to Chapter 1, a country's relative endowment in those resources shapes its competitiveness.

Country competitiveness is not a fixed thing. The dominant feature of the global economy is the rapid change in the relative status of various countries' economic output. In 1830, China and India alone accounted for about 60 percent of the manufactured output of the world. Since then, the share of the world manufacturing output produced by the twenty or so countries that are today known as the rich industrial economies moved from about 30 percent in 1830 to almost 80 percent by 1913.[21] In the 1980s, the U.S. economy was characterized as "floundering" or even "declining," and many pundits predicted that Asia, led by Japan, would become the leading regional economy in the 21st century. Then the 1997–1999 Asian financial crisis changed the economic milieu of the world (to be explained in detail in Chapter 3). Since the September 11, 2001 terrorist attacks, the U.S. economy has grown faster than any other developed countries at an annual rate of 3–4 percent. However, even the U.S. economic growth rate pales in comparison to China and India, two leading emerging economic powers in the last decade or so. China and India have grown at an annual rate of 7–10 percent and 4–7 percent, respectively, since the dawn of the 21st century.[22]

**Changing Country Competitiveness**

---

[20]"A Matter of Faith–Will a big bail-out led by the IMF allow Brazil to avoid defaulting?" *Economist*, August 15, 2002; Brazilian economy has since stabilized and started growing again, which is reflected in the *rea*'s appreciation to R2.28/US$ as of late 2005.

[21]Paul Bairoch, "International Industrialization Levels from 1750 to 1980," *Journal of European Economic History*, 11 (1982), pp. 36–54.

[22]United Nations Conference on Trade and Development, *Trade and Development Report 2005*, Geneva: United Nations.

**EXHIBIT 2-4**
GLOBAL COMPETITIVENESS RANKING[23]

| Country | Score In 2008/9 | Rank in 2005 | Rank In 2008/9 | Country | Score In 2008/9 | Rank In 2005 | Rank In 2008/9 | Country | Score In 2008/9 | Rank In 2005 | Rank In 2008/9 |
|---|---|---|---|---|---|---|---|---|---|---|---|
| United States | 5.74 | 2 | 1 | Hong Kong | 5.33 | 28 | 11 | Iceland | 5.04 | 7 | 21 |
| Switzerland | 5.61 | 8 | 2 | United Kingdom | 5.30 | 13 | 12 | Ireland | 4.99 | 26 | 22 |
| Denmark | 5.58 | 4 | 3 | South Korea | 5.28 | 17 | 13 | Israel | 4.97 | 26 | 23 |
| Sweden | 5.53 | 3 | 4 | Austria | 5.23 | 21 | 14 | New Zealand | 4.93 | 16 | 24 |
| Singapore | 5.53 | 6 | 5 | Norway | 5.22 | 9 | 15 | Luxembourg | 4.85 | 25 | 25 |
| Finland | 5.50 | 1 | 6 | France | 5.22 | 30 | 16 | Qatar | 4.83 | * | 26 |
| Germany | 5.46 | 15 | 7 | Taiwan | 5.22 | 5 | 17 | Saudi Arabia | 4.72 | * | 27 |
| Netherlands | 5.41 | 11 | 8 | Australia | 5.20 | 10 | 18 | Chile | 4.72 | 23 | 28 |
| Japan | 5.38 | 12 | 9 | Belgium | 5.14 | 31 | 19 | Spain | 4.72 | 29 | 29 |
| Canada | 5.37 | 14 | 10 | Israel | 5.05 | 26 | 20 | China | 4.70 | * | 30 |

*Source*: World Economic Forum, *Global Competitiveness Report 2005–2006* and *Competitiveness Report 2008–2009*, http://www.weforum.org/.

Obviously, a decade is a long time in the ever-changing world economy, and indeed, no single country has sustained its economic performance continuously.

**Human Resources and Technology**

Although wholesale generalizations should not be made, the role of human resources has become increasingly important as a primary determinant of industry and country competitiveness as the level of technology has advanced. As shown in **Exhibit 2-4**, according to World Economic Forum's *Global Competitiveness Report,* Singapore, one of the four Asian Tigers, consistently ranked among the world's top ten economies. Another one of the four Asian Tigers, Taiwan, also ranked within top 10 (No. 5) in 2005 and within top 20 (No. 17) in 2008/9. These two Asian countries have virtually no natural resources to rely on for building their competitiveness. Clearly, human resources are crucial for the long-term economic vitality of natural resource-poor countries. All the top-10 ranked countries, with the exception of the United States and Canada, are scarce in natural resources.

Similarly, three of the top 10 countries in 2008/9 are Nordic countries, led by Denmark, followed by Sweden and Finland. Although the rankings change to some extent, Norway and Iceland also kept within the top 20 and top 30, respectively. Nordic countries share a number of characteristics that make them extremely competitive, such as very healthy macroeconomic environments and highly transparent and efficient public institutions, with general agreement within society on the spending priorities to be met in the government budget. While the business communities in the Nordic countries point to high tax rates as a potential problem area, there is no evidence that these are adversely affecting the ability of these countries to compete effectively in world markets, or to provide to their respective populations some of the highest standards of living in the world. Indeed, the high levels of government tax revenue have delivered world-class educational establishments, an extensive safety net, and a highly motivated and skilled labor force.[24]

Although the United States kept its top positions of No. 2 and No. 1 in the reports of 2005–2006 and 2008–2009, respectively, the prognosis for the future U.S. competitive-

---

[23]The World Economic Forum has been producing *The Global Competitiveness Report* for over a quarter of a century, and its unique mix of hard and soft data has made it possible to accurately capture the broad range of factors seen to be essential to a better understanding of the determinants of growth.

[24]World Economic Forum, *Global Competitiveness Report 2005-2006* and *Global Competitiveness Report 2008-2009*, http://www.weforum.org/.

**EXHIBIT 2-5**
CHANGE IN COUNTRY INNOVATIVENESS: A KEY TO A COUNTRY'S LONG-TERM COMPETITIVENESS

| Rank Year | 1980 | 1986 | 1993 | 1995 | 1999 | 2005 (expected) |
|---|---|---|---|---|---|---|
| 1 | Switzerland | Switzerland | Switzerland | U.S.A. | Japan | Japan |
| 2 | U.S.A. | U.S.A. | Japan | Switzerland | Switzerland | Finland |
| 3 | Germany | Japan | U.S.A. | Japan | U.S.A. | Switzerland |
| 4 | Japan | Germany | Germany | Sweden | Sweden | Denmark |
| 5 | Sweden | Sweden | Sweden | Germany | Germany | Sweden |
| 6 | Canada | Canada | Denmark | Finland | Finland | U.S.A. |
| 7 | France | Finland | France | Denmark | Denmark | Germany |
| 8 | Netherlands | Netherlands | Canada | France | France | France |
| 9 | Finland | Norway | Finland | Canada | Norway | Norway |
| 10 | U.K. | France | Australia | Norway | Canada | Canada |
| 11 | Norway | Denmark | Netherlands | Netherlands | Australia | Australia |
| 12 | Denmark | U.K. | Norway | Australia | Netherlands | Austria |
| 13 | Austria | Australia | U.K. | Austria | Austria | Netherlands |
| 14 | Australia | Austria | Austria | U.K. | U.K. | U.K. |
| 15 | Italy | Italy | New Zealand | New Zealand | New Zealand | New Zealand |

*Source:* Adapted from Michael E. Porter and Scott Stern, *The New Challenge to America's Prosperity: Findings from the Innovation Index*, Washington, D.C.: Council on Competitiveness, 1999, pp. 34–35.

ness might not be as good as it currently appears. Seemingly contradictory to the current U.S. situation, U.S. Council on Competitiveness[25] reported in 1999 that the U.S. technological competitiveness had peaked in 1985 and that the United States might be living off its historical assets that were not being renewed (See **Exhibit 2-5** showing the change in the innovative capability of leading countries over the years). Although a more recent country innovativeness report is not available, this report clearly pointed to the rise of Finland as a technological powerhouse. Other conclusions include that although the United States and Switzerland had been the most innovative in the last three decades, other OECD nations have been increasingly catching up to the U.S. and Swiss levels. In particular, Denmark and Sweden have registered major gains in innovative capacity since the mid-1980s. Another interesting observation is that despite its economic slowdown in the 1990s, Japan has maintained its innovative capacity over the years without little sign of weakening. The recent strong recovery of the Japanese economy seemed to underscore its technological strengths, among other things.[26] Finally, although not shown in Exhibit 2-5, Singapore, Taiwan, South Korea, India, Israel, and Ireland have upgraded their innovative capacity over the past decade, becoming new centers of innovative activity.[27]

One major lesson here is that we should not be misled by mass media coverage of the current economic situations of various countries. While mass media coverage is factual and near-term focused, it may inadvertently cloud our strategic thinking. In other words, the current performance of the U.S. economy should not erroneously lull us into believing that U.S. companies are invincible in the global economy.[28] Information technology (IT) characterizes one of the most dynamic and turbulent industries today. As presented in **Global Perspective 2-1**, no one can be sure of the U.S. dominance even for the next decade.

---

[25]Michael E. Porter and Scott Stern, *The Challenge to America's Prosperity: Findings from the Innovation Index*, Washington, D.C.: Council on Competitiveness, 1999.

[26]"The Viagra Economy," A Survey of the World Economy Economist, September 24, 2005, 12–14; and "Japan: The Sun Also Rises," *Economist*, October 6, 2005, pp. 3–6.

[27]Michael E. Porter and Scott Stern, *The Challenge to America's Prosperity: Findings from the Innovation Index*, Washington, D.C.: Council on Competitiveness, 1999, p. 7.

[28]Paul Krugman, "America the Boastful," *Foreign Affairs*, 77 (May/June 1998), pp. 32–45.

❖ ❖ ❖ ❖ ❖ ❖ ❖ ❖ ❖ ❖ ❖ ❖ ❖ ❖ ❖ ❖ ❖ ❖ ❖ ❖ ❖ ❖ ❖ ❖ ❖ ❖ ❖ ❖ ❖ ❖

## 𝒢LOBAL PERSPECTIVE 2-1

### INFORMATION TECHNOLOGY COMPETITIVENESS OF THE UNITED STATES, THE EUROPEAN UNION, JAPAN, AND BEYOND

Is it possible that in the foreseeable future, the industrial competitiveness of the United States, especially in information technology (IT), could be beaten by the European Union (EU) and Japan? Due to the pace at which technology advances, it is often the case that the life cycle of a product gets shorter. So, no one can deny that a new software company with higher and more innovative technology could replace Microsoft Windows, even overnight. Another key consideration is that it is impossible for the U.S. to be ahead of the other two members of the Triad in every sector. Take mobile phone industry. In Japan, people now use their mobile phones not only as a telephone but also as a computer terminal. In this industry, the U.S. lags behind the EU and Japan in terms of both popularity and technology. By introducing even more sophisticated mobile phones, the EU and Japan have found themselves turning into information-based societies more quickly than the U.S.

The EU has launched its ambitious plan, called eEurope, since 2002. It aims to develop modern public services and a dynamic environment for e-business through widespread availability of broadband access at competitive prices and a secure information infrastructure. Its primary goal is the development and delivery of services and applications such

as eHealth, eBusiness, eGovernment and eLearning, making broadband crucial to European growth and quality of life in the years ahead. A widespread secure broadband infrastructure is essential for these societal goals.

The Japanese government has also launched a similar plan to realize an information-oriented society. For example, by May 2003, a higher percentage of homes in Japan than in the United States had broadband, and Japan had moved well beyond the basic connections still in use in the United States. Today, nearly all Japanese have access to "high-speed" broadband, with an average connection speed 16 times faster than in the United States—for only about $20 a month. Even faster "ultra-high-speed" broadband, which runs through fiber-optic cable, has become available throughout the country for $30 to $40 a month by the end of 2005. And that is to say nothing of Internet access through mobile phones, an area in which Japan is even further ahead of the United States.

It is now clear that Japan and its neighbors will lead the charge in high-speed broadband over the next several years. South Korea already has the world's greatest percentage of broadband users, and in 2004 the absolute number of broadband users in urban China surpassed that in the United States. These countries' progress will have serious economic implications. By dislodging the United States from the lead it commanded not so long ago, Japan and its neighbors, as well as Europe, have positioned themselves to be the first states to reap the benefits of the broadband era: economic growth, increased productivity, technological innovation, and an improved quality of life.

*Sources:* Thomas Bleha, "Down to the Wire," *Foreign Affairs*, 84, May/June 2005, pp. 111–124; "Widespread and Affordable Broadband Access is Essential to Realize the Potential of the Information Society," *eEurope*, http://europa.eu.int/information_society/eeurope/2005/all_about/broadband/index_en.htm, accessed December 15, 2005.

❖ ❖ ❖ ❖ ❖ ❖ ❖ ❖  **EMERGING ECONOMIES**

Large economies and large trading partners have been located mostly in the **Triad Regions** of the world (North America, Western Europe, and Japan, collectively producing over 80 percent of world GDP with 20 percent of the World's population) in much of the 20th century.[29] However, in the next 10 to 20 years, the greatest commercial opportunities are expected to be found increasingly in ten **Big Emerging Markets** (BEMs)—the Chinese Economic Area (CEA: including China, Hong Kong region, and Taiwan), India, Commonwealth of Independent States (Russia, Central Asia, and Caucasus states), South Korea, Mexico, Brazil, Argentina, South Africa, Central European countries,[30] Turkey, and the Association of Southeast Asian Nations (ASEAN: including Indonesia, Brunei, Malaysia, Singapore, Thailand, the Philippines

---

[29]Lowell Bryan, *Race for the World: Strategies to Build A Great Global Firm*, Boston, MA: Harvard Business School Press, 1999.
[30]Poland, Czech Republic, Slovakia, Slovenia, Hungary, Estonia, Latvia, Lithuania, Romania, and Bulgaria. See an excellent article, "The Rise of Central Europe," *Business Week*, December 12, 2005, pp. 50–56.

and Vietnam). For instance, in the past 20 years, China's real annual GDP growth rate has averaged 9.5 percent a year; while India's has been 5.7 percent, compared to the average 3 percent GDP growth in the United States. Companies like Hewlett-Packard (HP) are benefiting a lot from BEMs. For example, growth in such markets as Brazil, Russia, India, and China is helping HP shrug off the effects of a slowdown in the U.S. and prompted the company to raise its sales forecast for 2008. However, we should also realize that, an increasing number of competitors are expected to originate from those emerging economies.

Accordingly, an increasing number of competitors are also expected to originate from those emerging economies. According to trade statistics compiled in *World Factbook 2009*, published by the U.S. Central Intelligence Agency (See **Exhibit 2-2**),[31] the world's ten largest exporting countries accounted for more than half of the world merchandise trade in 2008: Germany ($1,530 billion), China ($1,465 billion), the United States ($1,377 billion), Japan ($777 billion), France ($630 billion), Italy ($566 billion), Netherlands ($538 billion), United Kingdom ($469 billion), Canada ($462 billion), and Belgium ($373 billion). A look at the trade data in recent years turns out two notable changes attesting to the globalization of the markets. First, since taking over the United States as the largest exporting country for the first time in 2004, Germany has steadily kept its leading position. Second, China then passed the United States and has become the second largest exporting country since 2007. Although not in the top 10 exporting countries group, Korea, Russia, Singapore, and Mexico are immediately behind.

As a result, over the next two decades, the markets that hold the greatest potential for dramatic increases in U.S. exports are not the traditional trading partners in Europe and Japan, which now account for the overwhelming bulk of the international trade of the United States. But they will be those BEMs. Already, there are signs that in the future the biggest trade headache for the United States may not be Japan but China and India.[32] China's trade surplus with the United States ballooned from $86 billion in 2000 to $256.2 billion in 2007; it had already surpassed Japan's trade surplus position with the United States by 2000.[33] India has increasingly become a hotbed as sources of information technology (IT), communications, software development, and call centers particularly for many U.S. multinationals. Russia is extremely rich in natural resources, including oil and natural gas, which are dwindling in the rest of the world, and has gradually warmed up to international commerce, and will potentially become a major trading nation. As these three leading emerging economies, among others, are likely to reshape the nature of international business in the next decade, the profiles of these countries will be highlighted here (See **Exhibit 2-6** for summary country profile).

Marketing in emerging markets requires is contextually different from marketing in developed countries. Companies that have succeeded in developed countries may or may not be able to approach those emerging markets the same way. When they enter huge emerging markets in rapidly developing economies, Western companies typically bring with them U.S., Japanese, or Western European quality standards, dismissing local goods as inferior. They know there is a great hunger in those countries for Western goods in the same way as developed-country consumers and businesses might buy in New York, London, or Tokyo. However, they forget that, in spite of the lust for high-quality Western goods, relatively few developing-country customers can afford them. In terms of price and quality, most developing-country customers weight more on the former and choose not-up-to-Western-standards but good enough and inexpensive

---

[31]https://www.cia.gov/library/publications/the-world-factbook.

[32]The economic role of smaller emerging economies cannot be ignored. Read, for example, "Good Morning, Vietnam: Intel' Deal to Build a Factory is Likely to Spur More Western Investment," Business Week, March 13, 2006, pp. 50–51.

[33]*Statistical Abstract of the United States, 2009*, http://www.census.gov/compendia/statab/2009edition.html.

**EXHIBIT 2-6**
LEADING EMERGING ECONOMIES IN 2008

|  | Brazil | Russia | India | China |
|---|---|---|---|---|
| Population | 196 million | 141 million | 1,148 million | 1,330 million |
| Population Growth Rate | 1.23 percent | -0.47 percent | 1.58 percent | 0.63 percent |
| GDP in current US$ | $1.67 trillion | $1.76 trillion | $1.24 trillion | $4.22 trillion |
| GDP in current US$ based on purchasing power parity | $2.03 trillion | $2.23 trillion | $3.32 trillion | $7.80 trillion |
| GDP per capita based on purchasing power parity | $10,300 | $15,800 | $2,900 | $6,100 |
| GDP real growth rate | 5.2 percent | 6.0 percent | 7.3 percent | 9.8 percent |
| Inflation rate | 5.8 percent | 13.9 percent | 7.8 percent | 6.0 percent |
| Current account balance | −$27.3 billion | $97.6 billion | −$38.3 billion | $368.2 billion |

*Sources:* Compiled from IMF statistics and U.S. Central Intelligence Agency, *The World Factbook 2009*, https://www.cia.gov/library/publications/.

local products. The local companies making these "good enough" products costing up to 75 percent less than Western brands are actually serious challengers of their developed-country rivals, especially given that they will finally produce ever-better products as they gain scale, lower costs, and invest in R&D.

Take Nokia for example. The world's largest supplier of mobile handsets entered the Chinese market early in 1991. As most Western companies usually do, it did market research and identified distributors in the wealthiest cities and sold them product "by the container load." By 1999, the company outperformed any other domestic or foreign companies and became the No. 1 with a 30 percent share of the handset market. However, Nokia did not realize that, while Nokia was focusing on the biggest cities with Western-grade handsets, local challengers were gradually taking up the populous countryside by selling "good enough" handsets. Soon Nokia and local challengers' positions were reversed. Nokia's market share fell from 30 percent in 1999 to the low teens in 2003; and the local challengers' share jumped from just 2.5 percent in 1999 to nearly 30 percent. Undoubtedly, Nokia was paying the price for focusing its China strategy on the high-end market. The large loss woke up Nokia to renovate its strategy: it set up its own distribution and sales network across China and introduced cheaper new handsets with fewer bells and whistles, quickly expanding from 10 cities to hundreds of cities. And this reinvention of strategy worked. By 2005, the company created a new peak of sales by selling 51 million—or 35 percent—of the handsets sold in China.[34]

Like Nokia, many developed-country firms fail to fully understand the competitive environment in those emerging markets. They enter these emerging markets ready to sell existing high-end products to increasingly prosperous city dwellers. It might work for a while, but not forever. A valuable lesson from the Nokia example is to have the right products at the right price. There is no doubt about the attractiveness and potential of the emerging markets. To succeed, however, developed-country companies need a new reference. We will further explore issues related to the emerging markets in Chapter 18.

# EVOLUTION OF COOPERATIVE GLOBAL TRADE AGREEMENTS

◆ ◆ ◆ ◆ ◆ ◆ ◆

In the aftermath of World War II, the then-big powers negotiated the setting up of an **International Trade Organization** (ITO), with the objective of ensuring free trade among nations through negotiated lowering of trade barriers. ITO would have been an international organization operating under the umbrella of the United Nations with statutory powers to enforce agreements. However, when the U.S. government announced, in 1950, that it would not seek congressional approval, ITO was effectively dead. Instead, to keep the momentum of increasing trade through the lowering of trade barriers alive, the signatories to ITO agreed to operate under the informal aegis of the **General Agreements on Tariffs and Trade** (GATT). GATT provided a forum for multilateral discussion among countries to reduce trade barriers. Nations met periodically to review the status of world trade and to negotiate mutually agreeable reductions in trade barriers.

The main operating principle of GATT is the concept of **Normal Trade Relations** (NTR) status (formerly known as **Most Favored Nation** or MFN status). The NTR status meant that any country that was a member state to a GATT agreement and that extended a reduction in tariff to another nation would have to automatically extend the same benefit to all members of GATT. However, there was no enforcement mechanism, and over time many countries negotiated bilateral agreements, especially for agricultural products, steel, textiles and automobiles. GATT was successful in lowering trade barriers to a substantial extent (e.g., developed countries' average tariffs on manufactured goods from around 40 percent down to a mere 4 percent) during its existence from 1948 to 1994. However, some major shortcomings limited its potential and effectiveness. The initial rounds of GATT concentrated only on the lowering of tariff barriers. As trade in services expanded faster than the trade in goods and GATT concentrated on merchandise trade, more and more international trade came to be outside the purview of GATT. Second, GATT tended to concentrate mostly on tariffs, and many nations used non-tariff barriers, such as quota and onerous customs procedure, to get around the spirit of GATT when they could not increase tariffs. Finally, as developed nations moved from manufacturing-based economies to services- and knowledge-based economies, they felt the need to bring intellectual property within

**General Agreements on Tariffs and Trade**

---

[34]Harold Sirkin and Jim Hemerling, "Price Trumps Quality in Emerging Markets," *BusinessWeek.com*, June 4, 2008, http://www.businessweek.com/.

the purview of international agreement, because that was where the competitive advantage lay for firms in the developed nations.

**World Trade Organization**

The World Trade Organization (WTO) was created in the eighth round of GATT talks—called the **Uruguay Round**—that lasted from 1986 to 1994. The WTO took effect on January 1, 1995. The WTO has statutory powers to adjudicate trade disputes among nations to oversee the smooth functioning of the multilateral trade accords agreed upon under the Uruguay Round. *Its main function is to ensure that trade flows as smoothly, predictably and freely as possible.* As of February 28, 2009, the WTO had 153 member countries.[35] This round was successful in bringing many agricultural products and textiles under the purview of GATT. The Uruguay Round created an environment in which a global body of customs and trade law is developing. In particular, the Uruguay Round ensured the ultimate harmonization of the overall customs process and the fundamental determinations that are made for all goods crossing an international border: admissibility, classification, and valuation.[36] It also included provisions for trade in intellectual property for the first time and provided for many services.

Then, the WTO's ninth and latest round–called the **Doha Development Agenda** (**Doha Round**, for short) was launched in Doha, Qatar in November, 2001. Most notably, the inaugural meeting at the Doha Round also paved the way for China and Taiwan to get full membership in the WTO[37] (See **Global Perspective 2-2** on China's

◆ ◆ ◆ ◆ ◆ ◆ ◆ ◆ ◆ ◆ ◆ ◆ ◆ ◆ ◆ ◆ ◆ ◆ ◆ ◆ ◆ ◆ ◆ ◆ ◆ ◆ ◆ ◆ ◆ ◆ ◆ ◆ ◆ ◆ ◆ ◆ ◆

### 𝒢LOBAL PERSPECTIVE 2-2

#### CHINA'S ACCESSION TO THE WTO AND ITS IMPLICATIONS

After fifteen years of arduous negotiation, China joined the World Trade Organization (WTO) in December 2001. The United States reached a bilateral agreement with China on WTO accession that secures broad-ranging, comprehensive, one-way trade concession on China's part, in which China made specific commitments to open its market to U.S. exports of industrial goods, service and agriculture to a degree unprecedented in the modern era. For example, China promised to reduce import tariffs from an average of 24.6 percent to 9.4 percent within three to five years. The United States also offered extension of permanent Normal Trade Relations (NTR) to China, as China entered the WTO. The House vote was called one of the most important trade and foreign policy decisions the United States had made in many years. Because of the accession, the markets of WTO members were also opened to China.

Trade officials from the United States, Europe, and Japan have portrayed China's entry into the WTO as an antidote to their growing trade deficits with China. But the reality is that China's agreement to reduce tariffs, phase out import quotas, open new sectors of its economy to foreign investment, and otherwise follow WTO rules will not reverse this imbalance in trade. China's accession to the WTO has begun to boost its economic reforms in the world's most populous nation. There is no doubt that China and its 1.3 billion people benefit tremendously from its WTO accession. It has allowed China to expand trade, attract foreign investment and give private firms a greater role in the economy, but more importantly, it has increasingly integrated China with the rest of the world economy. According to the United Nations Conference on Trade and Development (UNCTAD), although global inflows of foreign direct investment (FDI) declined from 2001 to 2003,

*(continued)*

---

[35]New members that joined the WTO in the 21st century are Albania, Armenia, Cambodia, Cape Verde, China, Croatia, Former Yugoslav Republic of Macedonia (FYROM), Georgia, Jordan, Lithuania, Moldova, Nepal, Oman, Saudi Arabia, Chinese Taipei, Tonga, Ukraine, and Viet Nam. At the time of writing this chapter, the application of 31 countries were being considered for accession: Afghanistan, Algeria, Andorra, Azerbaijan, Bahamas, Belarus, Bhutan, Bosnia and Herzegovina, Cape Verde, Comoros, Equatorial Guinea, Ethiopia, Vatican, Iran, Iraq, Kazakhstan, Lao People's Democratic Republic, Lebanese Republic, Republic of Liberia, Libya, Montenegro, Russian Federation, Samoa, Sao Tomé and Principe, Serbia, Seychelles, Sudan, Tajikistan, Uzbekistan, Vanuatu, Yemen.

[36]Paulsen K. Vandevert, "The Uruguay Round and the World Trade Organization: A New Era Dawns in the Private Law of International Customs and Trade," *Case Western Reserve Journal of International Law*, 31 (Winter 1999), pp. 107–38.

[37]Anne McGuirk, "The Doha Development Agenda," *Finance & Development*, 39 (September 2002), 4–7.

*(continued)*

China experienced an increased trade inflow of 14 percent ($ 53 billion in 2003) and became the world's largest FDI recipient. China is actively attracting FDI in manufacturing and service sectors from multinational corporations. Multinational corporations have found China's workforce not only cheap and vast but also educated and disciplined. Meanwhile, as an emerging FDI outward investor, firms in China have invested in neighboring countries and in Africa, Latin America, North America, and Europe to access to natural resources, markets, and strategic assets such as technology and brand names. In 2002, China's outward investment flows exceeded $35 billion, reaching more than 160 countries.

*Sources:* "Analysis: Chinese Threat to Japan Manufacturers." *Nikkei Net Interactive*, May 29, 2001; Nicholas R. Lardy, "Sweet and Sour Deal," *Foreign Policy*, March/April 2002, 20–21; Bill Powell, "It's All Made in China Now," *Fortune*, March 4, 2002; "Tilting at Dragons," *Economist*. October 25, 2003, pp. 65–66; "The China Price," *Business Week*, December 6, 2004, pp. 102–24.

Entry into the WTO membership followed Beijing winning the right to host the 2008 Olympic games and Shanghai hosting the Asia Pacific Economic Cooperation (APEC) leaders' summit. Driven by government's open policy to foreign investment since 1980s and accession by WTO as an important trade partner to the world, China is emerging as the virtual factory of the world, driving a profound shift in global investment flows.

How will this affect other economies such as the United States, Japan, and Europe? With China's increased trade surplus with the United States, the deflationary crisis in Tokyo, as well as European manufacturers becoming vulnerable to the "Made in China" shock, should China be blamed for the rich countries' economic problems? On the one hand, China has presented business opportunities for firms to offshore manufacturing and services jobs with low-waged, skilled workforce and also lowered its import tariffs since its entry into the WTO; on the other hand, China has cost some firms to lose global market share and job opportunities by conducting cheap-currency strategy.

accession to the WTO). This new round places the needs and interests of developing countries at the heart of its work (**Exhibit 2-7** gives an idea of the "intended" scope of the Doha Round). Agricultural tariffs are five times higher on average than those for industrial products. High tariffs undermine the ability of developing countries to trade their way out of poverty—it is estimated that two-thirds of the world's poorest people are dependent on agriculture. The United States currently spends up to $19 billion on farm-production subsidies, which heavily distort trade. The EU spends over

**EXHIBIT 2-7**

AGENDA FOR THE DOHA ROUND

- Implementation-related issues and concerns
- Agriculture
- Services
- Market access for non-agricultural products
- Trade-related aspects of intellectual property rights (TRIPS)
- Relationship between trade and investment
- Interaction between trade and competition policy
- Transparency in government procurement
- Trade facilitation
- WTO rules: anti-dumping
- WTO rules: subsidies
- WTO rules: regional trade agreements
- Dispute Settlement Understanding
- Trade and environment
- Electronic commerce
- Small economies
- Trade, debt and finance
- Trade and transfer of technology
- Technical cooperation and capacity building
- Least-developed countries
- Special and differential treatment

*Source:* World Trade Organization, http://www.wto.org/english/thewto_e/minist_e/

CLARO CORTES IV/Reuter/Landov LLC

Although WTO is a global institutional proponent of free trade, it is not without critics. In December 2005, the sixth ministerial conference of the WTO in Hong Kong was greeted by jeers and riots triggered by labor unions, environmentalists, and other onlookers who were opposed to free trade for various reasons.

$75 billion.[38] The reluctance of some of the world's richest countries to substantially reduce high farm tariff and non-tariff barriers stymied the opportunity to secure other reforms that would deliver huge benefits to the world trading regime. Broadly speaking, the United States was under pressure to reduce trade-distorting farm subsidies, while Europe and India tried to keep too many farm products from deeper tariff cuts, and some developing countries were under pressure to reduce industrial tariffs further and faster. The agenda also included new trade talks–an action program to resolve developing countries' complaints about the implementation of Uruguay Round agreements, and an accord on **Trade Related Aspects of Intellectual Property Rights** (TRIPS) ensuring that patent protection does not block developing countries' access to affordable medicines. As these countries eventually failed to come to an agreement on farm product issues, the Doha Round of multilateral trade talks did not make much progress in other areas and eventually collapsed on July 29, 2008.[39]

Incidentally, the WTO is not simply an extension of GATT. The GATT was a multilateral agreement with no institutional foundations. The WTO is a permanent institution with its own secretariat. The GATT was applied on a provisional basis in strict legal terms. WTO commitments are full and permanent and legally binding under international law. Although GATT was restricted to trade in merchandise goods, WTO includes trade in services and trade-related aspects of intellectual property. It is to be noted that GATT lives on within WTO. Some of the major issues and agendas in WTO are highlighted below.

***Dispute Settlement Mechanism.*** The WTO dispute settlement mechanism is faster, more automatic, and therefore much less susceptible to blockages than the old GATT system. Once a country indicates to WTO that it has a complaint about the trade practices of another country, an automatic schedule kicks in. The two countries have three months for mutual "consultations" to iron out their differences. If the disputants cannot come to a mutually satisfactory settlement, then the dispute is referred to the Dispute Settlement Mechanism of WTO, under which a decision has to be rendered within six months of the setting up of the panel to resolve the dispute. The decision of the panel is supposed to be legally binding. However, trade experts have revealed deep ambivalence about the WTO's experiment with binding adjudication, and there is little clear sense of where the system should go from here. Litigation draws

[38]"A Stopped Clock Ticks Again," *Economist,* October 13, 2005, pp. 76–79.
[39]"So Near and Yet So Far: Trade Ministers Have Come Too Close to a Deal to Let the Doha Round Die," *Economist,* August 2, 2008, p. 14; and "After Doha," *Economist,* September 6, 2008, pp. 85–86.

◆ ◆ ◆ ◆ ◆ ◆ ◆ ◆ ◆ ◆ ◆ ◆ ◆ ◆ ◆ ◆ ◆ ◆ ◆ ◆ ◆ ◆ ◆ ◆ ◆ ◆ ◆ ◆ ◆ ◆ ◆

## $\mathcal{G}$LOBAL PERSPECTIVE 2-3

### TRADE BARRIERS AND POLITICS

The United States thinks of itself as a leading exponent of free trade and frequently brings actions against other nations as unfair trading partners. On March 20, 2002, President George W. Bush announced that U.S. would impose tariffs of up to 30 percent on most steel imports, as a means to save the domestic steel industry. But this temporary steel tariff has set a dangerous precedent for the others, opening the floodgates on new tariffs by other World Trade Organization (WTO) members. In response to the U.S. action, the European Union (EU) immediately filed for a complaint to the WTO, and decided to impose six-month protective tariffs of 14.9 percent–26 percent on 15 kinds of steel imports that exceed current quotas. Japan also notified the WTO of its plans to impose 100 percent retaliatory tariffs on U.S. steel imports. China is also preparing to erect new trade barriers in retaliation for the U.S. steep tariffs. In May 2002, Chinese government announced its plan to levy tariff-rate quotas on imports of nine steel products, which would impose tariffs ranging from 7 percent to 26 percent once imports of those products exceed a designated amount. Further, if the WTO panel rules that the U.S. steel tariffs conflict with WTO agreements, China says it will impose

*Sources:* Campion Walsh, "EU's Lamy Warns US Steel Tariffs A Dangerous Example," *Dow Jones Newswires*, May 21, 2002; Owen Brown, "EU, China Discuss Campaign Against US Steel Tariffs," *Dow Jones Newswires*, April 4, 2002; Andrew Batson, "China Prepares Retaliation Against US Steel Tariffs," *Dow Jones Newswires*, May 21, 2002; "WTO Approves EU Bid for Panel On US Steel Tariff Hikes," *Dow Jones Newswire*, June 3, 2002; Dan Bilefsky and Edward Alden, "Test for Bush as EU retaliates on Gluten Tariffs," *Financial Times*, January 21, 2001; "U.S. Puts Tariff on Canadian Lumber amid Allegations of Unfair Subsidies," *Wall Street Journal*, March 22, 2002; and "Steel, Rolled," *Economist*, August 31, 2002, p. 54.

24 percent tariffs on a list of U.S. products including waste paper, bean oil and electric compressors.

The WTO agreed to step into the escalating dispute, agreeing to the EU request for a panel to rule on the legality of the U.S. decision. The panel could take up to a year to rule on the legality of the U.S. tariffs and either side can appeal the ruling, but a decision by the appellate body would then be final. The U.S. argument is the safeguard practice: under WTO rules, countries can impose temporary increases in tariffs to give time for a domestic industry to restructure to improve competitiveness. But according to the EU, Japan, China and South Korea, the U.S. action breaks WTO rules: there was no overall increase in steel imports—a precondition for safeguards action—and that some of the moves target the wrong steel products. Although the U.S. government decided to take back some of its earlier tariffs under pressure from the EU, the U.S. protectionism on its steel industry remains a volatile trade dispute.

The U.S. protectionism on its steel industry is considered a major setback for the world trade system, but it is not something new. In January 2001, the European Commission announced it would retaliate against U.S. restriction on wheat gluten imports in 1998 by imposing a tariff on corn gluten feed exported from the United States, which could cost U.S. exporters up to $29.1 million a year. WTO panel ruled that the US had failed to establish a causal link between wheat gluten imports and losses being suffered by US companies. Thus the EU is allowed to offset the damage with similar restriction on imports from the United States. In March 2002, U.S. government levied tariffs averaging 29 percent on a popular type of Canadian lumbers, but this was said to be an act of retaliation for Canada's "unfair trade practices."

---

on different skills, resources, and even cultural attitudes than does diplomacy, with a possibility placing certain nations at a real disadvantage.[40] As **Global Perspective 2-3** shows, the United States frequently violates the WTO principles and resorts to unilateral trade sanctions against foreign trading partners.

Finally, although WTO is a global institutional proponent of free trade, it is not without critics. In December 1999, WTO launched what would have become the beginning of a ninth round of negotiations inaugurated in Seattle, the United States. However, its Seattle meeting was only to be greeted by jeers and riots triggered by labor unions, environmentalists, and other onlookers who were opposed to free trade for various reasons. As a result, the meeting was postponed until 2001 under so much uncertainty, which resulted in the Doha Round mentioned earlier. Indeed, contrary to

---

[40]Susan Esserman and Robert Howse, "The TWO on Trial," *Foreign Affairs*, 82 (January/February 2003), pp. 130–40.

## 𝒢LOBAL PERSPECTIVE 2-4

### ANTI-GLOBALIZATION MOVEMENT

Oppositions to corporate and economic globalization have been growing for many years, but have received media attention only since the late 1990s. Anti-globalization movement, launched by a French farmer, quickly spread the network to other parts of the world. The growing trend toward anti-globalization activism is directed, first, against multinational corporate power and, second, against global agreements on economic growth made by international trade institutions, such as the World Trade Organization (WTO), the World Bank, and International Monetary Fund (IMF).

The movement is often described as "multi-generational, multi-class, and multi-issue." Participants protest against

capitalism, free trade, international investment (especially from the West to the Third World), cultural and economic globalization, wars, and Western politics. During the last few years, massive anti-globalization protests have accompanied international meetings in cities such as Seattle, Quebec City, Genoa, and Washington, D.C. The anti-globalization movement became front-page stories when its protesters gathered during the WTO meeting in Seattle in late 1999, when the activists almost disrupted the meeting. Later protests focused on the World Bank and IMF. Their main slogan is "Here, another world is possible."

There are two kinds of people in the movement: Reformists and Radicals. Reformists are often engaged in a serious exchange of ideas and proposals on socioeconomic and environmental changes, which ask for a broader international participation in decision-making. Protests organized by radicals often go violent and disruptive. Campaigners cyber-attacked international businesses' websites, burned their properties, and destroyed international meetings. Multinational companies are often accused of social injustice, unfair labor practices—including slave labor wages, living and working conditions—as well as a lack of concern for the environment, mismanagement of natural resources, and ecological damage.

*Sources:* Konstantin Lezhandr, "The Future of Europe's Anti-globalization Activists," *Itogi*, April 24, 2002, p. 26; "Anti-Globalization: A Spreading Phenomenon," *Perspectives* (Canadian Security Intelligence Report #2000/08), http://www.csis-scrs.gc.ca/eng/miscdocs/200008_e.html; Sean Higgins, "Anti-Globalization Protesters Discover New Enemy: Israel," *Investor's Business Daily*, April 23, 2002, p. A16; James Petras, "Porto Alegre 2002: A Tale of Two Forums—Correspondence; Anti-Globalization Social Forum," *Monthly Review* 53, April 1, 2002, p. 56; Julian Nundy, "Fire Destroy McDonald's Site in France; Police Suspect Arson," *Bloomberg News,* May 7, 2002.

the globalization forces at work, anti-globalization sentiment has been building over the years (See **Global Perspective 2-4**).

***Trade Related Aspects of Intellectual Property Rights (TRIPS).*** Trade Related Aspects of Intellectual Property Rights (TRIPS) Agreement, concluded as part of the GATT Uruguay Round, mandates that each member country accord to the nationals of other member countries the same treatment as its nationals with regard to intellectual property protection (see Chapter 5 for details). However, it is not an international attempt to create a universal patent system. In March 2002, the WTO's TRIPS Council has started work on a list of issues at the November 2001 Ministerial Conference in Doha. These include specific aspects of TRIPS and public health, geographical indications, protecting plant and animal inventions, biodiversity, traditional knowledge, the general review of the TRIPS Agreement, and technology transfer. One hot issue is to find a solution to the problems countries may face in making use of compulsory licensing if they have too little or no pharmaceutical manufacturing capacity. During a special session, WTO members have also embarked on two-phase program for completing negotiations on a multilateral registration system for geographical indications for wines and spirits.[41]

***Global E-Commerce.*** Due to an explosive use of the Internet, a global effort to regulate international e-commerce has become increasingly necessary (See Chapter 19

---

[41]Compiled from TRIPS Material on the WTO Website, http://www.wto.org/english/tratop_e/trips_e/trips_e.htm; "Patently Problematic," *Economist,* September 14, 2002, pp.75-76; and Donald Richards, "Trade-Related Intellectual Property Rights," *Review of International Political Economy*, 12, August 2005, pp. 535–51.

for the impact of the Internet on various marketing activities). According to the Internet World Statistics, the number of Internet users reached 1.46 billion by July 2008, a four-time increase from 2000 to 2008.[42] To address this issue, the WTO's Work Program on Electronic Commerce has been working on how to define the trade-related aspects of electronic commerce that would fall under the parameters of WTO mandates. The Work Program submitted a report to the organization's General Council on March 31, 1999 in which it sought to define such services as intellectual barriers to trade in the context of electronic commerce. Probably the best thing the WTO can do to assist the development of electronic commerce in global trade is to meet its stated goal of assisting in the creation of an environment in which electronic commerce can flourish. According to WTO documents, such an environment requires liberalized market policies and predictable trade regimes that encourage the massive investments in technology that is required for electronic commerce to work.[43]

The U.S. is taking the lead in bringing e-commerce-related issues to the table. A U.S. document that was presented to the Work Program's general meeting on March 22, 1999, clearly outlined both the issues raised by the introduction of e-commerce in international trade and the importance of e-commerce to the global economy. The United States also proposed that the WTO examine services that may emerge as more viable in terms of international trade through e-commerce. For example, with widespread use of the Internet, has the notion of retailing across borders—previously inhibited by different time zones and the high cost of international communications—now become commercially viable? Now that networked appliances increasingly are used, will remote monitoring, testing and diagnostics of such devices become increasingly important? Much has yet to be clarified and resolved.

## INFORMATION TECHNOLOGY AND THE CHANGING NATURE OF COMPETITION

As the nature of value-adding activities in developed nations shifts more and more to information creation, manipulation, and analysis, the developed nations have started taking an increased interest in international intellectual property protection measures. Imagine a farmer in the nineteenth century headed into the twentieth century. The intrinsic value of food will not go away in the new century, but as food becomes cheaper and cheaper to produce, the share of the economy devoted to agriculture will shrink (in the United States agriculture contributes less than 3 percent to the GDP) and so will the margins for the farmer. It would be advisable to move into manufacturing, or at least into food processing, to maintain margins.

An analogous situation faces a content maker for **information-related products** such as software, sheet music, movies, newspapers, magazines, and education in the late-twentieth century headed into the twenty-first century. Until now, content has always been manifested physically—first in people who knew how to do things; then in books, sheet music, records, newspapers, loose-leaf binders, and catalogs; and most recently in tapes, discs, and other electronic media. At first, information could not be "copied": it could only be re-implemented or transferred. People could build new machines or devices that were copies of or improvements on the original; people could tell each other things and share wisdom or techniques to act upon. (Reimplementation was cumbersome and re-use did not take away from the original, but the process of building a new implementation—a new machine or a trained apprentice—took considerable time and physical resources.)

Later, with symbols, paper, and printing presses, people could copy knowledge, and it could be distributed in "fixed" media; performances could be transcribed and

---

[42]Internet World Stats, http://www.internetworldstats.com/stats.htm, accessed September 1, 2008.

[43]David Biederman, "E-Commerce and World Trade," *Traffic World*, 258 (April 26, 1999), p. 22.

recreated from musical scores or scripts. Machines could be mass-produced. With such mechanical and electronic media, intellectual value could easily be reproduced, and the need (or demand from creators) to protect intellectual property arose. New laws enabled owners and creators to control the production and distribution of copies of their works. Although reproduction was easy, it was still mostly a manufacturing process, not something an individual could do easily. It took time and money. Physical implementation contributed a substantial portion of the cost.

## Value of Intellectual Property in Information Age

However, with the advent of the Information Age, firms face a new situation; not only is it easy for individuals to make duplicates of many works or to re-use their content in new works, but the physical manifestation of content is almost irrelevant. Over the Internet, any piece of **electronically represented intellectual property** can be almost instantly copied anywhere in the world. Since more and more of value creation in the developed nations is coming from the development and sale of such information-based intellectual property, it is no surprise that developed nations are highly interested in putting strong international intellectual property laws in place. For instance, a recent survey of more than 200 largest firms in United Kingdom disclosed that 83 percent of those firms had experienced different types of cyber crime in 2003. Further, according to an international specialist in computer forensics, roughly 70 percent of UK business professionals have stolen corporate intellectual property through personal e-mails when leaving the employer. Obviously, it is costly for corporations to protect their intellectual property, and to adjust for losses in productivity and perceived damage to corporate brand and share price.[44] The U.S. insistence on the inclusion of provisions relating to intellectual property in WTO's TRIPS agreement is a direct consequence, and is understandable as cyber crime affects all parties with intellectual property. Technology-based protection of electronic information through hardware, software, or a combination thereof in the form of encryption and digital signatures has been suggested as the means of circumventing the problem of unauthorized copying.[45]

Controlling copies (once created by the author or by a third party), however, becomes a complex challenge. A firm can either control something very tightly, limiting distribution to a small, trusted group, or it can rest assured that eventually its product will find its way to a large non-paying audience—if anyone cares to have it in the first place. But creators of content on the Internet still face the eternal problem: the value of their work generally will not receive recognition without wide distribution. Only by attracting broad attention can an artist or creator hope to attract high payment for copies. Thus, on the Internet, the creators give first performances or books (or whatever) away widely in hopes of recouping with subsequent works. But that breadth of distribution lessens the creator's control of who gets copies and what they do with them. In principle, it should be possible to control and charge for such widely disseminated works, but it will become more and more difficult. People want to pay only for what is perceived as scarce—a personal performance or a custom application, or some tangible manifestation that cannot easily be reproduced (by nature or by fiat; that is why the art world has numbered lithographs, for example).

The trick may be to control not the copies of the firm's information product but instead a relationship with the customers—subscriptions or membership. And that is often what the customers want, because they see it as an assurance of a continuing supply of reliable, timely content. Thus, the role of marketing may be expected to assume increasing importance. A firm can, of course, charge a small amount for mass copies. Metering schemes will allow vendors to charge—in fractions of a penny, if desired—according to usage or users rather than copies. However, it will not much change the overall approaching-zero trend of content pricing. At best, it will make it much easier to charge those low prices.

---

[44]DeeDee Doke, "Sniffing Out the Evidence," *Personnel Today*, May 11, 2004, pp. 20–22.

[45]Ravi Kalaktota and Andrew B. Whinston, *Frontiers of Electronic Commerce* (Reading, Mass.: Addison Wesley, 1996). See Chapter 15.

There are other hurdles for content creators with the emergence of electronic commerce (e-commerce). One is the rise of a truly efficient market for information. Content used to be **unfungible**: it was difficult to replace one item with another. But most information is not unique, though its creators like to believe so. There are now specs for content such as stock prices, search criteria, movie ratings, and classifications. In the world of software, for instance, it is becoming easier to define and create products equivalent to a standard. Unknown vendors who can guarantee functionality will squeeze the prices of the market leaders. Of course the leaders (such as Microsoft) can use almost-free content to sell ancillary products or upgrades, because they are the leaders and because they have reinvested in loyal distribution channels. The content is advertising for the dealers who resell, as well as for the vendors who create. This transformation in the form of value creation and ease of dissemination implies a jump in economic integration, as nations become part of an international electronic commerce network. Not only money but also products and services will flow faster.

The other consequence of fungible content, information products, and electronic networks is an additional assault on the power of national governments to regulate international commerce. Ford uses a product design process whereby designers at Dearborn, Michigan, pass on their day's work in an electronic form to an office in Japan, which then passes the baton along to designers in Britain, who pass it back to Dearborn the next day. When the information represented in the design crosses borders, how do the governments of the United States, Japan, and Britain treat this information? How will such exchanges be regulated? Less-open societies like China and Malaysia, recognizing the power of electronic networks, are already attempting to regulate the infrastructure of and access to the electronic network.

## Proliferation of E-Commerce and Regulations

The similar problem applies to electronic commerce. The rapid proliferation of e-commerce led by Internet and e-commerce providers, such as AOL, Yahoo, Amazon. com as well as by traditional marketers that have gone into e-commerce, such as Dell Computer, Victoria's Secret, and Nokia, has spawned a type of international commerce and transactions that countries' regulations have not kept pace with. In terms of e-commerce, how do countries control online purchases and sales? If one looks at Europe, each country has different tax laws and Internet regulations, as well as consumer protection laws. In addition, import and export formalities still apply to goods bought electronically. How to monitor electronic commerce transactions remains a problem for most national governments.[46]

One such example is illustrated by the launch of Viagra by Pfizer in 1998. The company celebrated the most successful drug launch in history with the introduction of Viagra, the first pill that allows effective oral treatment for men who suffer from erectile dysfunction (impotence). Since that time the name Pfizer has become a synonym for Viagra and vice versa, due to a media hype that arose after this launch of the first of so-called "lifestyle drugs" to treat undesired symptoms that suppress quality of life. The Internet attracted the portion of patients from all over the world who are not willing to talk about their problem even to their doctors. The Internet quickly filled up with "virtual" pharmacies that promised to supply Viagra via a mouse click. Internet pharmacies sometimes try to conceal their location, set up in offshore places and sell their items in a gray area of doing business. Customers who are not willing to disclose their erectile dysfunction can easily order Viagra without consultation of their physician, but run the risk to become victims of fraud. Internet pharmacies that are selling genuine Viagra pills have found a way to get around prescription by their customers' physicians in the following way: An online-consultation form can be filled out within a few minutes (at a consultation fee of $65–$75). The pharmacy's physician

---

[46]Kim Viborg Andersen, Roman Beck, Rolf T. Wigand, Niels Bjùrn-Andersen, and Eric Brousseau, "European e-Commerce Policies in the Pioneering Days, the Gold Rush and the Post-Hype Era," *Information Polity*, 9 (3/4), 2004, pp. 217–32.

then will issue the prescription based on the information ("honestly") given by the candidate.[47] This procedure allows the customer to retain a high degree of anonymity, while the pharmacy fulfills the obligation to distribute Viagra only after a physician's consultation.

Pfizer and counterfeiting experts have warned the public not to buy from Internet pharmacies.[48] In reputable pharmacies cases of fraud usually do not occur, but there are tens of other fraud websites that will exploit the patient's unwillingness to talk about impotence. The Federal Trade Commission (FTC) is in charge of cases where entities are trying to mislead potential customers and commit fraud. The FTC sent out some warnings about products that claim to be related to Viagra, and no prescription is necessary. The warnings advise people to check credentials of suppliers. Fraud on the Internet can be found in reports where businesses set up to sell counterfeit pills managed to have about 150.000 customers in about a year. The owner of these "enterprises" advertised pills under names similar to Viagra, like Viagrae. Pfizer sued and the FTC was able to find that this name was only one small part in a larger fraud to distribute large amounts of phony pills.[49]

Regulating international e-commerce obviously requires cross-border cooperation. The rising problems resulted in numerous international treaties. For example, in May 2001, the Council of Europe, working with Canada, Japan, South Africa and the United States, approved the 27th draft of the Convention on cyber crime—the first international treaty on crime in cyberspace. The treaty requires participating countries to create laws regarding various issues including digital copyrights and computer-related fraud. It offers international businesses the best hope for legal recourse if they become the victim of cyber crime in e-commerce. The United Nations Commission on International Trade Law (UNCITRAL), the core legal body within the United Nations system in the field of international trade law, has also formed a Working Group on Electronic Commerce to re-examine these treaties.[50]

## ◆ ◆ ◆ ◆ ◆ ◆ ◆ ◆   REGIONAL ECONOMIC ARRANGEMENTS

An evolving trend in international economic activity is the formation of multinational trading blocs. These blocs take the form of a group of countries (usually contiguous) that decide to have common trading policies for the rest of the world in terms of tariffs and market access but have preferential treatment for one another. Organizational form varies among market regions, but the universal reason for the formation of such groups is to ensure the economic growth and benefit of the participating countries. Regional cooperative agreements have proliferated after the end of World War II. There are already more than 120 regional free trade areas worldwide. Among the more well-known ones existing today are the European Union and the North American Free Trade Agreement. Some of the lesser-known ones include the MERCOSUR (Southern Cone Free Trade Area) and the Andean Group in South America, the Gulf Cooperation Council in the Arabian Gulf region (GCC), the South Asian Agreement for Regional Cooperation in South Asia (SAARC) and the Association of South East Asian Nations (ASEAN). The existence and growing influence of these multinational groupings implies that nations need to become part of such groups to remain globally competitive. To an extent, the regional groupings reflect the countervailing force to the increasing integration of the global economy—it is an effort by governments to control the pace of the integration.

---

[47]See e.g., www.qualitymed.com, www.medservices.com, or www.MDHealthline.com.

[48]"Black Market Filled Phony Viagra Tablets," article at www.cafecrowd.com, accessed August 10, 1999.

[49]See "FTC: Watch for Viagra Knock-Offs," at www.msnbc.com/news/2090, accessed August 10, 1999.

[50]Bill Wall, "An Imperfect Cybercrime Treaty," *CIO*, February 15, 2002; and Jason R. Boyarski, "United Nations Working Group Focuses on E-Commerce," *Intellectual Property & Technology Law Journal*, 13 (October 2001).

Market groups take many forms, depending on the degree of cooperation and inter-relationships, which lead to different levels of integration among the participating countries. There are five levels of formal cooperation among member countries of these regional groupings, ranging from free trade area to the ultimate level of integration—which is political union.

Before the formation of a regional group of nations for freer trade, some governments agree to participate jointly in projects that create economic infrastructure (such as dams, pipelines, roads) and that decrease the levels of barriers from a level of little or no trade to substantial trade. Each country may make a commitment to financing part of the project, such as India and Nepal did for a hydroelectric dam on the Gandak River. Alternatively, they may share expertise on rural development and poverty alleviation programs, may lower trade barriers in selected goods such as in SAARC, which comprises India, Pakistan, Sri Lanka, Bangladesh, Nepal, Maldives, and Bhutan. This type of loose cooperation is considered a precursor to a more formal trade agreement.

A **Free Trade Area** has a higher level of integration than a loosely formed regional cooperation and is a formal agreement among two or more countries to reduce or eliminate customs duties and non-tariff trade barriers among partner countries. However, member countries are free to maintain individual tariff schedules for countries that do not belong to the free trade group. One fundamental problem with this arrangement is that a free trade area can be circumvented by nonmember countries that can export to the nation having the lowest external tariff in a free trade area, and then transport the goods to the destination country in the free trade area without paying the higher tariff applicable if it had gone directly to the destination country. In order to stem foreign companies from benefiting from this tariff-avoiding method of exporting, *local content laws* are usually introduced. Local content laws require that in order for a product to be considered "domestic," thus not subject to import duties, a certain percentage or more of the value of the product should be sourced locally within the free trade area. Thus, local content laws are designed to encourage foreign exporters to set up their manufacturing locations in the free trade area.

### Free Trade Area

The North American Free Trade Agreement (NAFTA) is the free trade agreement among Canada, the United States, and Mexico. It provides for elimination of all tariffs on industrial products traded between Canada, Mexico, and the United States within a period of ten years from the date of implementation of the NAFTA agreement—January 1, 1994. NAFTA was preceded by the free trade agreement between Canada and the United States, which went into effect in 1989. The United States has a free trade area agreement with Israel as well. Canada signed a trade deal with the Andean Group in 1999 as a forerunner to a possible free trade agreement.[51] Mexico also established a formal trans-Atlantic free trade area agreement with the European Union without U.S. involvement in 2000,[52] and with Japan in 2005.[53] On the other hand, the United States also reached a free trade agreement with Chile on December 11, 2002,[54] formed the Central American-Dominican Republic Free Trade Agreement (CAFTA-DR) with Costa Rica, the Dominican Republic, El Salvador, Guatemala, Honduras, and Nicaragua, effective on January 1, 2006,[55] and most recently concluded another free trade agreement with Colombia on February 27, 2006.[56]

---

[51]"Canadian Companies Get Andean Boost," *World Trade*, 12 (September 1999), p. 14.

[52]"Mexico Turns To Europe," *Europe*, July/August 2001, pp. 18–19.

[53]Joseph P. Whitlock, "US Has Stake in Japan-Mexico FTA," *Journal of Commerce*, 6 (23), June 6, 2005, pp. 34–34.

[54]"U.S. and Chile Reach Free Trade Accord," *New York Times*, http://www.nytimes.com, December 11, 2002.

[55]"CAFTA-DR to Build Options over Time," *Marketing News*, February 1, 2006, pp. 13–14.

[56]"United States and Colombia Conclude Free Trade Agreement," U.S. Department of State, http://www.state.gov/p/wha/rls/62197.htm, accessed August 20, 2008.

Another free trade group is the European Free Trade Association (EFTA) comprising Iceland, Liechtenstein, Norway, and Switzerland. Although Austria, Finland, and Sweden used to be EFTA member countries, they have joined the European Union (EU) and Switzerland has been negotiating with EU to become a member.[57] It appears that some, if not all of, the remaining EFTA members may gradually merge into the European Union (which we discuss later). In the meantime, Singapore and EFTA have also agreed to form a free trade area effective on January 1, 2003.[58] MERCOSUR is a free trade area consisting of Brazil, Argentina, Uruguay, and Paraguay with Chile, Bolivia, Peru, and Venezuela as associate members,[59] with the intention to lower internal trade barriers and the ultimate goal of the creation of a customs union.[60]

One probably the most ambitious free trade area plan is also in the works. The Free Trade Area of the Americas (FTAA) was proposed in December, 1994, by thirty-four countries in the region as an effort to unite the economies of the Western Hemisphere into a single free-trade agreement, which was originally planned for completion by January 2005. For various political oppositions and reluctance from some major countries, such as Brazil and Venezuela, the negotiations for the agreement were stalled even at the most recent Summit of the Americas in November 4–5, 2005.[61] If completed, however, the FTAA agreement would encompass an area from the Yukon to Tierra del Fuego with 800 million people and about $13 trillion in production of goods and services, making it the most significant regional trade initiative presently being pursued by the United States. Regional cooperative agreements in the 1990s such as NAFTA and MERCOSUR have made trading within the continent much easier, but the South America markets are still less open than those of East Asia. Despite the fact that many doubted the U.S. government's power to stand up to domestic industries crying for protection, many are seeing FTAA as more than a remote hypothesis and are already preparing for it. Brazil, member of the MERCOSUR and South America's largest economy, is not so sure about the agreement, but cannot afford the loss if the rest of the Americas rush to sign the deal without it.[62]

Japan had not been keen on regional free trade area agreements, as it preferred a broader multilateral free trade regime as espoused by WTO. However, under pressure from an increasing number of successful regional trade agreements, Japan has also decided to join this fray, aiming to offset the economic challenges posed by the EU and the NAFTA zones, by having formed a free trade agreement with Singapore, recently another with Mexico,[63] and having resumed free trade area talks with the ASEAN[64] (see **Global Perspective 2-5** on Japan's further push for free trade areas in Asia). Immediately after the collapse of the Doha Round of multilateral trade negotiations in late July 2008, India also reached a free trade agreement with the ASEAN. The ASEAN also announced another regional free trade deal with Australia and New Zealand.[65] Such regional free trade agreements are clearly on the rise.

---

[57]Sieglinde Gstöhl, "Scandinavia and Switzerland: Small, Successful and Stubborn towards the EU," Journal of European Public Policy, 9 (August 2002), pp. 529–49.

[58]"Singapore-EFTA Agreement Sets New Standards," *Managing Intellectual Property*, (July/August 2002), pp. 11–12.

[59]At the time of this writing, Venezuela is expected to become a permanent member of MERCOSUR in December 2005. See "Venezuela to Fully Join Mercosur," BBC News, http://news.bbc.co.uk/, October 17, 2005.

[60]Maria Cecilia Coutinho de Arruda and Masaaki Kotabe, "MERCOSUR: An Emergent Market in South America," in Masaaki Kotabe, *MERCOSUR and Beyond: The Imminent Emergence of the South American Markets* (Austin, TX: The University of Texas at Austin, 1997).

[61]"Hemisphere Meeting Ends without Trade Consensus," New York Times, November 6, 2005.

[62]"A Really Big Gree-Trade Zone," *Business Week*, December 23, 2002, p. 40; and Alan M. Field, "Grand Illusion?" *Journal of Commerce*, April 7, 2008, pp. 18–22.

[63]Joseph P. Whitlock, "US Has Stake in Japan-Mexico FTA," *Journal of Commerce*, 6 (23), June 6, 2005, pp. 34–34.

[64]"Japan To Propose E Asia Development Concept In Singapore," *NikkeiNet Interactive*, http://www.nni.nikkei.co.jp, August 24, 2008.

[65]"Regional Trade Agreements: A Second-Best Choice," *Economist*, September 6, 2008, p. 16.

## $\mathcal{G}$LOBAL PERSPECTIVE 2-5

### FREE TRADE AREAS IN ASIA

The global trend of forming strategic trade blocs is accelerating, given the success of the EU and the NAFTA. The United States, already has a NAFTA under its belt, is now creating a pan-American trade area. Since the United States and European countries now have entered the final stages of creating huge economic zones, Japan figured that it is time to catch up.

In January 2002, the Japanese government, having criticized and opposed free trade areas (FTAs) for years, had its first-ever free trade agreement with Singapore. Now it is proposing an East Asia Free-trade Area no later than 2012. The grouping, dubbed by Japanese officials as "ASEAN plus five," would represent a third of the world's population and would cover the ten-member Association of Southeast Asian Nations (ASEAN), as well as Japan, mainland China, South Korea, Hong Kong and Taiwan. Indeed, Japan's exports to China outstripped those to the United States for the first time

*Sources:* Yoshikuni Sugiyama, "Economic Forum—Japan Does About-Face on Asia FTAs," *Yomiuri Shimbun*, September 11, 2001; "Japan to Reopen Trade Pact Talks with ASEAN in April," *NikkeiNet Interactive*, http://www.nni.nikkei.co.jp, March 11, 2006; "Japan-China-Bound Exports Outstrips Shipments to U.S. for 1st time after WWII," *NikkeiNet Interactive*, August 21, 2008; and "Japan To Propose E Asia Development Concept In Singapore," *NikkeiNet Interactive*, August 24, 2008.

in the postwar, making the fast-growing Asian economy the country's largest trading partner, in August 2008. With progress in ASEAN-India economic ties also being under way, the establishment of a Pan-Asian economic zone covering a wide area from East Asia to South Asia may be possible. As a result, the creation of a Pan-Asian economic zone that would include "ASEAN plus five" and India is also being advocated.

Japan proposed a new initiative calling for region-wide cooperation in promoting deregulation, improvement of distribution networks and other measures in East Asia at a meeting of economic ministers from Asian countries held in Singapore in 2008. The initiative for creating a "large industrial artery in East Asia" covers Japan, China and South Korea, the Association of Southeast Asian Nations (ASEAN), India and other economies. The initiative also examines the possibility of streamlining rules on customs procedures and tax systems, which vary widely among East Asian countries, and consider ways to use capital in the private sector more effectively. The proposal is aimed at facilitating economic integration in East Asia, which has a population of 3.1 billion, to build the foundations for the region's role as a global growth hub. Japan seeks to use the broad development proposal to set the stage for concluding an economic partnership agreement among 16 nations in the region, including India, Australia and New Zealand.

---

**Customs Union**

The inherent weakness of the free trade area concept may lead to its gradual disappearance in the future—though it may continue to be an attractive stepping-stone to a higher level of integration. When members of a free trade area add common external tariffs to the provisions of the free trade agreement then the free trade area becomes a **customs union**.

Therefore, members of a customs union not only have reduced or eliminated tariffs among themselves, but also they have a common external tariff of countries that are not members of the customs union. This prevents nonmember countries from exporting to member countries that have low external tariffs with the goal of sending the exports to a country that has a higher external tariff through the first country that has a low external tariff. The ASEAN (Brunei, Cambodia, Indonesia, Laos, Malaysia, Myanmar, the Philippines, Singapore, Thailand, and Vietnam) is a good example of a currently functional customs union with the goal of a common market. The Treaty of Rome of 1958, which formed the European Economic Community, created a customs union between West Germany, France, Italy, Belgium, Netherlands, and Luxembourg.

**Common Market**

As cooperation increases among the countries of a customs union, they can form a **common market**. A common market eliminates all tariffs and other barriers to trade among members of the common market, adopts a common set of external tariffs on nonmembers, and removes all restrictions on the flow of capital and labor among member nations. The 1958 Treaty of Rome that created the European Economic Community had the ultimate goal of the creation of a common market—a goal that was substantially achieved by the early 1990s in Western Europe.

The **Maastricht Treaty**, which succeeded the Treaty of Rome, entered into force on November 1, 1993, calling for the creation of a union (and hence the change in name to European Union). At a historic summit on December 13, 2002, EU agreed to add ten new member countries, creating the 25-member **European Union** effective on May 1, 2004, with a total economy larger than that of the United States.[66] In 2007, two countries, Bulgaria and Romania, became new additional members of EU, expanding the total number of EU member to 27.[67] Those new members are mostly Eastern and Central European countries once part of the Soviet empire. Now German banks can freely open branches in Poland, and Portuguese workers can live and work in Luxembourg.

**Monetary Union**     The Maastricht Treaty also laid down rules for, and accomplished, the creation of a **monetary union** with the introduction of the euro–a new European currency in January 1999, which began its circulation since January 2002. As per the Maastricht Treaty, the EU's sixteen member countries[68] have adopted the euro so far. The United Kingdom, Denmark and Sweden have not accepted the third stage and the three EU members still use their own currency today. A monetary union represents the fourth level of integration with a single common currency among politically independent countries. In strict technical terms, a monetary union does not require the existence of a common market or a customs union, a free trade area or a regional cooperation for development. However, it is the logical next step to a common market, because it requires the next higher level of cooperation among member nations.

**Political Union**     The culmination of the process of integration is the creation of a **political union**, which can be another name for a nation when such a union truly achieves the levels of integration described here on a voluntary basis. The ultimate stated goal of the Maastricht Treaty is a political union with the adoption of a constitution for an enlarged European Union. However, the member countries have varying levels of concern about ceding any part of their sovereignty to any envisaged political union. In May 2005, France shocked the whole Europe by voting against the EU constitution with a decisive margin. Meanwhile, in June, Dutch voted more strongly against the constitution. According to the analyst, the rejection from Dutch and French are a terrible blow to the morale of true believers in political union in EU. In order for the constitution to come into force, all twenty-five members of EU must ratify it. Since France has always been politically central to the EU, as one of the six founders and one of the twelve members that have joined the European currency, it is extremely difficult for the EU to handle the current crisis. Previously some political leaders urged voters to approve the constitution to make Europe more efficient, dynamic, and democratic. However, French consider the constitution as a means for the EU members to impose "Anglo-Saxon" free market policies on them. They voted against the constitution to protect their jobs, employment rights, and social benefits from low-cost, low-tax, deregulated countries.[69]

◆ ◆ ◆ ◆ ◆ ◆ ◆ ◆     ## MULTINATIONAL CORPORATIONS

Although no steadfast definition of **multinational corporations** (MNCs) exists, the U.S. government defines the multinational company for statistical purposes as a company that owns or controls 10 percent or more of the voting securities, or the equivalent, of at

---

[66]As of the beginning of 2006, the European Union consists of 25 countries including: Austria, Belgium, Cyprus, Czech Republic, Denmark, Estonia, Finland, France, Germany, Greece, Hungary, Ireland, Italy, Latvia, Lithuania, Luxembourg, Malta, Poland, Portugal, Slovakia, Slovenia, Spain, Sweden, the Netherlands, United Kingdom.
[67]http://europa.eu/index_en.htm, Accessed on March 1, 2009.
[68]The euro member countries, as of March 1, 2009, are Austria, Belgium, Cyprus, Finland, France, Germany, Greece, Ireland, Italy, Luxembourg, Malta, the Netherlands, Portugal, Slovakia, Slovenia, and Spain.
[69]"Dead, But Not Yet Buried," *Economist*, June 4, 2005, pp. 47–48.

**EXHIBIT 2-8**
OUTWARD FOREIGN DIRECT INVESTMENT (FDI) STOCK AND EMPLOYMENT IN
FOREIGN AFFILIATES, 1982–2006

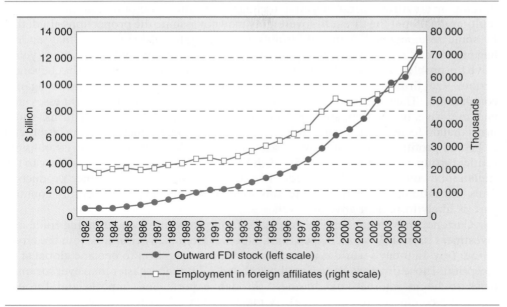

*Source: World Investment Report 2007*, http://www.unctad.org/, accessed August 20, 2008.

least one foreign business enterprise. Many large multinationals have many subsidiaries and affiliates in many parts of the world. In the early 1970s, Howard Perlmutter, a professor at the Wharton School in Philadelphia, predicted that by 1985 around 80 percent of the noncommunist world's productive assets would be controlled by just 200–300 companies. As shown in **Exhibit 2-8**, now some 78,000 multinational companies have 780,000 affiliates in foreign countries. In 2006, foreign affiliates employed about 73 million people around the world, compared to 24 million in 1990. The stock of outward foreign direct investment (FDI) increased from $627 billion in 1982, to $1.8 trillion in 1990, and to $12.5 trillion in 2006. Foreign affiliates' sales account for 52.1 percent of world GDP as of 2006. By far the highest share of FDI in the primary industries has been in mining (grouped along with quarrying) and petroleum. While FDI stock and flow estimates are not available for mining and petroleum separately, data on cross-border mergers and acquisitions (M&As) suggest that both these industries have attracted increasing volumes of investment in recent years. During 2005 and 2006, the value of cross-border M&As in petroleum (representing an annual average of $63 billion) was nearly twice that in mining. Although FDI stock in manufacturing has experienced a consecutive decline over fifteen years since 1990, world inflow FDI stock in services climbed from 49 percent of the region's total inward stock in 1990 to 62 percent in 2005, with an estimated value of $6 trillion. During the same period, world inflow FDI stock in manufacturing fell from 41 percent to 30 percent. Outward FDI in services continues to be dominated by developed countries, although FDI is more evenly distributed among them than before. By 2002, Japan and the European Union had emerged as significant sources of outward FDI in service sectors. Developing countries' outward FDI in services has also grown gradually since the 1990s.[70]

The forces of economies of scale, lowering trade and investment barriers, need to be close to markets, internalization of operations within the boundaries of one firm, and

---

[70]World Investment Report 2008, http://www.unctad.org/, accessed March 1, 2009.

the diffusion of technology will continue to increase multinationals' influence in international trade and investment. The sovereignty of nations will perhaps continue to weaken due to multinationals and the increasing integration of economies. Some developing countries harbor negative feelings about the sense of domination by large multinationals, but the threat to sovereignty may not assume the proportions alluded to by some researchers.[71] Although established multinationals' sheer size may appear hegemonic and have some monopolistic power in smaller economies, they have yet to solve the problem associated with their large size. Current trends indicate that beyond a certain size firms tend to become complacent and slow and they falter against competition. They are no longer able to remain focused on their businesses and lack the drive, motivation, and a can-do attitude that permeates smaller firms. Those firms that do focus on their core businesses shed unrelated businesses, as the latter tend to be less profitable or even incur losses.[72] For example, Novartis, the Swiss pharmaceutical group, recently sold off its Swedish Wasa biscuits and crackers subsidiary to the Italian food company, Barilla, in order to concentrate on its health science products.[73] Thus, the nation-state, while considerably weaker than its nineteenth century counterpart, is likely to remain alive and well.

Currency movements, capital surpluses, faster growth rates, and falling trade and investment barriers have all helped multinationals from many countries join the cross-border fray. In today's world it is not unusual for a startup firm to become global at its inception. Those firms are known as "born global."[74] It is now easier than ever for small firms to be in international business through exports and imports and through electronic commerce (e-commerce). A major survey of companies with fewer than 500 employees by Arthur Andersen & Co. and National Small Business United, a trade group, found that exporters averaged $3.1 million in revenue, compared with $2.1 million for all companies in the survey in 1996, and also reported that exporters' profits increased 4.4 percent while the overall average was 2.6 percent. Exporters are also more technology-savvy: 92 percent have computers (versus 79 percent overall) and 70 percent use the Internet (versus 44 percent overall).[75]

---

[71]Raymond Vernon, *Sovereignty At Bay,* New York: Basic Books, 1971.

[72]John A. Doukas and L. H. P. Lang, "Foreign Direct Investment, Diversification and Firm Performance," *Journal of International Business Studies,* 34 (March 2003), pp. 153–72.

[73]Paul Betts, "Barilla Pays SFr475m for Wasa Biscuits," *Financial Times,* (April 27, 1999), p. 33.

[74]Alex Rialp, Josep Rialp, Gary A. Knight, "The Phenomenon of Early Internationalizing Firms: What do We Know after a Decade (1993-2003) of Scientific Inquiry?" *International Business Review,* 14 (April 2005), pp. 147–66.

[75]"Export Energy," *Business Week,* November 17, 1997.

---

## SUMMARY ◆ ◆ ◆ ◆ ◆ ◆ ◆ ◆ ◆ ◆ ◆ ◆ ◆ ◆ ◆ ◆ ◆ ◆ ◆ ◆ ◆ ◆ ◆ ◆ ◆

The severe global recession since late 2008 has slowed down the world economy. Nevertheless, the world economy is increasingly intertwined, and virtually no country is immune from the economic events in the rest of the world. It is almost as if participation in the international economy is a *sine qua non* of economic growth and prosperity—a country has to participate in the world economy in order to grow and prosper—but participation is not without its risks. Events outside one country can have detrimental effect on the economic health of that country. The Asian financial crisis that started in 1997 with a precipitous depreciation of Thailand's *baht,* Indonesia's *rupiah,* Malaysia's *ringgit,* and Korea's *won,* among others, is an example of a situation where withdrawal of funds by portfolio investors caused a severe economic crisis. In effect, participating in the international economy imposes

its own discipline on a nation, independent of the policies of the government of that nation. This is not to suggest that countries should stay outside the international economic system because of the risks. Those countries that have elected to stay outside the international economic system—autarkies like Burma and North Korea—continue to fall farther behind the rest of the world in terms of living standards and prosperity.

Various forces are responsible for the increased integration. Major emerging economies have begun to reshape the nature of international trade and investment. Growth in international trade continuously outpaces the rise in national outputs. Transportation and communications are becoming faster, cheaper, and more widely accessible. The nature of value-adding activities is changing in the advanced countries from manufacturing to services and information manipulation. Such changes are a result of and are a force behind the rapid advancement in telecommunications and computers. Even developing nations, regardless of their political colors, have realized the importance of telecommunications and electronic commerce and are attempting to improve their infrastructure. The capital markets of the world are already integrated for all practical purposes, and this integration affects exchange rates, interest rates, investments, employment, and growth across the world. Multinational corporations have truly become the global operations in name and spirit that they were envisaged to be. Even smaller companies are leapfrogging the gradual expansion pattern of traditional multinational companies by adopting e-commerce that has no national boundaries. In short, to repeat an old maxim, the world is becoming a global village. When Karl Marx said in 1848 that the world was becoming a smaller place, he could not have imagined how small it truly has become.

## KEY TERMS ◆ ◆ ◆ ◆ ◆ ◆ ◆ ◆ ◆ ◆ ◆ ◆ ◆ ◆ ◆ ◆ ◆ ◆ ◆ ◆ ◆ ◆ ◆ ◆ ◆

Common market

Country competitiveness

Customs union

Big Emerging Markets (BEMs)

Foreign direct investment

Free trade area

General Agreements on Tariffs and Trade (GATT)

Gross domestic product (GDP)

Maastricht Treaty

Monetary union

Multinational corporation (MNC)

Normal Trade Relations (NTR) status [formerly, Most Favored Nation (MFN) status]

Political union

Portfolio (indirect) investment

Trade Related Aspects of Intellectual Property Rights (TRIPS) Agreement

World Trade Organization (WTO)

## REVIEW QUESTIONS ◆ ◆ ◆ ◆ ◆ ◆ ◆ ◆ ◆ ◆ ◆ ◆ ◆ ◆ ◆ ◆ ◆ ◆ ◆

1. What are some of the visible signs that reflect the current increased economic interdependence among countries? What are some reasons for this growth in interdependence and for the rise in global integration?

2. What is GATT, and what is its role in international transactions?

3. How is the WTO different from GATT? What functions is WTO expected to perform?

4. In what ways have the U.S. foreign direct investment and trade patterns changed over the past decade?

5. Cooperative inter-relationships between countries (regional groupings) can be classified into five broad categories. What are these categories, and how do they differ from each other?

6. Do current measures of balance of payments accurately reflect a country's transactions with the rest of the world? What are the concerns?

7. What challenges do the content creators and information providers face due to the advent and popularity of the electronic media? Are there current mechanisms to protect their rights? What are the macroeconomic implications for industrialized countries?

8. What are some of the forces influencing the increase in size of multinational corporations? Are there any forces that are influencing them to downsize?

## DISCUSSION QUESTIONS ◆ ◆ ◆ ◆ ◆ ◆ ◆ ◆ ◆ ◆ ◆ ◆ ◆ ◆ ◆ ◆ ◆ ◆

1. Recently in response to a dispute with both the U.S. and the EU's possible action toward imposing tariffs on cheap textile products from China, China took countermeasure actions to exclude those products from the existing export tariffs to ward off damages to its economy. To resolve the issue, in June 2005, EU signed an agreement with China imposing new quotas on ten categories of textile goods, limiting growth in those categories to between 8 percent and 12.5 percent a year. The agreement was in hope of providing EU's domestic manufacturers time to adjust to a world of unfettered competition. But for most retailers in Europe, which had already placed orders for mountains of new goods from China, it turned out to be a disaster since tens of millions of garments piled up in warehouses and customs checkpoints, when Chinese textile manufacturers exceeded their quotas right after the restriction. As a matter of fact, less than a month after the agreement, men's trousers hit their import quota, followed rapidly by blouses, then bras, T-shirts and flax yarn. It is estimated that France lost about a third of its jobs in the sector between 1993 and 2003. Italy has also seen its firms suffer since the euro transition. Nevertheless, it is not clear as to how the quota restriction on Chinese goods would help domestic producers, especially when there are so many low-cost firms in low-wage countries like Bangladesh and Costa Rica waiting to take up any Chinese slack. According to an EU official, the action against China was designed to help workers in those very countries in that "The EU also considered the effect the Chinese market share was having on other developing countries that have historically been dependent on our market. Who will protect jobs in Tunisia and Morocco?" While large retailers will probably

be able to find new sources for their autumn and winter lines under the quota restriction, it seems that smaller stores may be driven into bankruptcy as the clothes they have bought would be buried in warehouses around Europe. Do you think the EU textile war with China will eventually save their domestic businesses? Should U.S. follow the EU to impose textile quota on Chinese imports to protect domestic businesses? Why or why not?

2. A justification of developing countries against product patents for pharmaceutical products has been that if they were enforced, life-saving drugs would be out of reach for all but the very rich. A similar argument is being used in a populist move in the U.S senate for reducing the patent lives of innovative drugs, in a bid to reduce health care costs. Some senators and the pharmaceutical industry leaders claim that this move would discourage medical innovation and slow down the development of drugs for the cure of such diseases as AIDS and cancer, and thereby increase the costs of taking care of current and future patients. How would you react to the arguments and counterarguments for reducing patent lives, and what would be your stance on this issue? In your opinion, what would be the international repercussions if this bill were to pass? How do you think other developed and developing countries would react?

3. Today, some 150 million EU citizens shop online from websites such as Amazon.com and eBay, spending on average $1248 (800 euros) per capita. However, only one-fifth of them buy goods and services from another EU state. The EU's consumer chief is currently planning new rules to make it easier and safer for the bloc's 490 million consumers to shop online in any corner of the 27-nation EU. As the latest step from Brussels to make itself more friendly and relevant to people's everyday lives, particularly after the rejection of the EU's Lisbon Treaty in Ireland, this move is expected to tear down barriers to cross-border web shopping barriers to boost competition, offer businesses a bigger market and cut prices for consumers. What advantages and difficulties do you think EU has in setting such rules? What can EU members benefit individually or as a whole from such a move? Are there any implications from the move, if successfully set, for the rest of the world? Why or why not?

4. Information technology is having significant effects on the globalization activities of corporations. Texas Instruments is now developing sophisticated chips in India. Motorola has set up programming and equipment design centers in China, India, Singapore, Hong Kong, Taiwan, and Australia. Similarly, a large number of U.S. and European corporations are looking at ways to transfer activities such as preparing tax returns, account statements, insurance claims, and other information processing work to Asia. Although until now it was only blue-collar employees in the industrialized countries who faced the threat of competition from low-wage countries (which could be countered to some extent through direct and indirect trade barriers), this new trend in movement of white-collar tasks may be a cause for concern to industrialized countries, as the sophistication of these tasks increases. This movement of white-collar jobs could be a cause for social concern in the near future. Do you foresee social pressures in developed countries having the potential of reversing the trend of movement of white-collar tasks to developing countries? Given the intangibility of information, are there any effective ways of controlling the movement of information across borders?

5. The effects of the formation of regional trade blocs on international trade could be interpreted in two ways. One way is to view regional blocs as one step forward in the process of ensuring completely free trade between countries on a global basis. On the other hand, the formation of regional blocs could be seen as a step backward toward an era of greater protectionism and greater trade tensions between the regions. Which view would you agree with, and why?

6. Electronic commerce (e-commerce) blurs the distinction between a good and a service. Under WTO, goods tend to be subject to tariffs; services are not, but trade in services is limited by restrictions on "national treatment" or quantitative controls on access to foreign markets. For example, a compact disc sent from one country to another is clearly a good, and will be subject to an import tariff as it crosses the national border. But if the music on the disc is sent electronically from a computer in one country to another on the Internet, will it be a good or a service? Customized data and software, which can be put on CD, are usually treated as services. What kind of confusion would you expect with WTO overseeing increased transaction on the Internet?

# SHORT CASES

## CASE 2-1

### RUSSIA: A HUGE EMERGING CAR MARKET ISOLATED FROM OIL CRISIS

High oil prices are causing pain for carmakers in America as people there are sacrificing their fancy for pick-up trucks and sport-utility vehicles for more frugal small vehicles. In May 2008, General Motors announced a 30 percent fall in car sales, compared with a year earlier; Ford posted a 19 percent drop, and sales of its F-150 pick-up fell behind Toyota's Camry and Corolla for the first time. But far in Russia, the high oil price is powering the expansion of the market rather than painful restructuring. Thanks to abundant natural resources, Russia has been witnessing a rising economy since decade ago. With nearly doubled and steadily rising real disposable income, cars are no longer unaffordable for many Russians.

Currently, car ownership in Russia is still low at about 200 per 1,000 people, compared with the over 500 in most of Western Europe and the around 800 in American (even in other former communist countries in Central Europe, the number is between 300 and 350). But the car market there is expanding: in 2007 Russia's sales of new cars grew 36 percent by volume and 57 percent by value; sales of passenger vehicles exceeded 2.7million. According to analysts, Russia could outstrip Germany as Europe's biggest market by 2008, with sales reaching around 3.3 million; by 2012 Russians will be buying more than 5 million new cars a year, of which nearly 90 percent will be foreign brands.

However, all of the growth has been met by foreigners. Sales of Russian brands have stayed flat for the past few years—hovering between 750,000 and 800,000. Early in 2002, a few years before foreign carmakers' rushing into Russia, the Russian government slapped a 25 percent duty on imported used cars when domestic carmakers were struggling with challenges from imported second-hand cars. Unfortunately, later new imports took their place as the sale of used imports fell. The new rivals took 48 percent of the market by value in 2005. This time, instead of raising import duties again, Russian government passed a measure intended to encourage foreign makers to set up local assembly plants so as to revive the Russian car industries. According to the terms, to qualify for relief from import duty, foreign carmakers have to build a factory with a capacity of more than 25,000 vehicles a year—a minimum investment of at least $100m. Within five years of production starting, the local content in each car had to reach 30 percent.

This triggered a scramble by the world's biggest car firms to build factories in Russia. On the crowded list are American firms Ford and GM's Chevrolet, Japan's Toyota, Suzuki, Nissan, Isuzu, and Mitsubishi, South Korea's Kia, Hyundai and Daewoo, and European makers Renault, Volkswagen, Fiat and BMW. Chinese carmakers like Chery, Great Wall, and SsangYong are also trying to head into Russia.

Doubtlessly, the foreign carmakers' rush into Russia is promoting this country's car industry as the government expected. Currently, assembly of foreign models alone has attracted significant investment over $2 billion in the first stage. And investment plans already announced suggest that new capacity could reach 1.6m units by 2012. However, foreign carmakers' expansion on the Russian market is at the expense of Russian ones.

In 1990 Russian carmakers built 1.2 million passenger vehicles, but in 2007 they sold just 756,000. AvtoVAZ, which makes more than 90 percent of the Russian-brand passenger cars, is still selling its Ladas in provincial Russia because of its low price, the large number of dealers, and few alternatives there. Currently, the main threat to Lada comes from very cheap Chinese cars and the possible change in the used-car business policy. Although so far the likes of Chery and Great Wall from China haven't received permissions from the Russian authorities to set up in Russia, such situation may not last long. And if as expected the 18 percent VAT on used cars sold by dealers is abolished, Lada's price advantage will vanish. Now AvtoVAZ's main hope lies in the 25 percent stake recently acquired by Renault for $1 billion. Based on Renault platforms, the largest Russian carmaker is expecting to bring new Ladas to market by 2010.

Another local producer, Severstal-Auto, has decided to focus on small vans and trucks rather than taking on foreign car brands due to the potentially large demand from the fast-growing retail sectors. Severstal already has a joint venture with Fiat to produce its Albea and Linea saloons. In May 2008, the first Fiat Ducato van was successfully driven off the firm's new production line in Elabuga, a "free economic zone" in Tatarstan. Severstal also makes small and medium-sized Isuzu trucks. Another possible section of this company probably will be high-margin services—actually Severstal is as well thinking about building a dealer network so as to sell services such as adapting vehicles for school and hospitals, providing full-service leasing arrangements and offering credit terms with local banks.

### DISCUSSION QUESTIONS

**1.** Do you think it is a good idea for the Russian government to take the measure of encouraging foreign carmakers to build factories in Russia instead of setting trade barriers as it did in 2002 to help relieve its carmakers from the challenges from the imported used cars? Why or why not?

**2.** What obstacles might foreign carmakers encounter when they expand to Russia's market?

**3.** Russia's domestic carmakers are facing fierce competitions from foreign counterparts as many local firms in other countries might do upon the arrivals of foreign firms. Do you think the strategies of Russia's domestic carmakers will work? Why or why not? Are there any other strategic options? What implications can you draw from the case regarding competitions between domestic firms and foreign firms as a common worldwide issue?

*Sources::* "Crisis? What Oil Crisis?" *Economist*, June 7, 2008, pp. 73–74; "VW Opens Huge Factory Near Moscow," *BusinessWeek.com*, November 29, 2007; and "Russian Car Boom Catches Eye of Japan, Germany," *JapanTimesOnline*, May 28, 2007.

# CASE 2-2

## BOEING VERSUS AIRBUS? OR THE U.S. VERSUS THE EU? LET THE WTO DECIDE!

So, who gets to decide which party wins when two of the world's largest aircraft manufacturers engage in a trade war? Well, apparently, the World Trade Organization (WTO), which received its biggest international trade petition in 2005 since its establishment in 1995: The case to settle the dispute between U.S.-based Boeing and European Airbus. Airbus is jointly owned by European aerospace companies EADS and BAE Systems.

The dispute is not new. It dates back to the 1980s when the two behemoths went head on against each other in the market for civil aircraft. In 1992, the two rivals attempted to reach a settlement. Airbus had been largely reliant on 'launch aid' from European governments such as those of France, Germany and the United Kingdom (UK) while Boeing also received subsidies from American government agencies, mainly the Department of Defense and NASA (National Aeronautics and Space Administration). Airbus' launch aid consisted of loans for product development that were written off if the products failed in the market. However, if the product were a success, the governments would continue to get royalties even after the loans were paid off. Under the bilateral settlement in 1992, the companies and the countries involved agreed that Boeing's aid from external parties would not exceed 4 percent of its revenues and Airbus's loans would be maintained at 33 percent of its development costs for an aircraft.

But the newfound peace in 1992 did not last too long. Both parties remained suspicious that the other was breaking the terms of the bilateral contract. What exacerbated the situation was when Airbus launched five new products since the 1992 agreement, its final blow to Boeing being its most recent A380 model. Boeing meanwhile managed to introduce only one new product in the same time period. Furthermore, Airbus became a profitable company and was on par with Boeing's market position and therefore, according to Boeing, Airbus no longer needed help from the European governments. In May 2004, U.S. Trade Representative Robert E. Zoellick met with European Commissioner for Trade, Pascal Lamy to suggest that both parties agree to rule out the use of new subsidies for aircraft. But, the Europeans refused to make any promises. In fact, Airbus continued to seek launch aid from the government. And so the discussions went on.

In October 2004, the U.S. filed a complaint with the WTO against Airbus and the EU retaliated by immediately filing a countersuit with the WTO against Boeing. Their reasons remained the same—EU government aid versus American subsidies. But, in order to avoid an expensive legal encounter, once again, the two parties decided to engage in bilateral negotiations with the expectation that they would reach a settlement by April 11, 2005. But it was not meant to be. Boeing and its supporters maintained their stance against Airbus, which instead insisted that Boeing's Japanese suppliers had obtained soft loans from their government and therefore Boeing benefited from these indirect subsidies as well. Finally, in June 2005, both parties re-approached the WTO.

The WTO's trade agreement on Subsidies and Countervailing Measures disallows government subsidies or subsidies from public bodies to a particular company or industry. The U.S. side of the appeal to the WTO includes its claim that Airbus breached these WTO's rules when it accepted around $15 billion in loans from the EU governments. On the other hand, the EU claims that Boeing broke the WTO rules when it received around $23 billion in subsidies. It will be interesting to see who wins the case, Boeing or Airbus and since their respective governments are solidly intertwined with the companies, the U.S. or the European Union.

The last time the WTO adjudicated a similar case was back in the 1990s, the case being Brazil's Embraer versus Canada's Bombardier, both medium-sized jets manufacturers. However, in that case, even though the WTO granted a 'guilty' verdict to both parties, there was no special action taken by either party. Their governments continued to grant subsidies to the companies. According to experts, it is likely that the WTO would find both parties guilty in the Boeing-Airbus case as well, which may once again lead the firms to pursue another bilateral agreement.

While the outcome of the WTO's decision might chart out the course of future competition between Boeing and Airbus, the importance of the case sheds light on the role of the WTO in world trade negotiations and policy. Even though a lot of countries still have bilateral trade agreements, more countries are turning to the WTO to arbitrate their disputes. With a growing membership that rests at 148 at present, the WTO's authority on trade matters is being recognized and its world trade rules supersede bilateral and other similar trade pacts. In the meantime, Boeing and Airbus wait for a verdict.

## DISCUSSION QUESTIONS

**1.** On one hand, the WTO's role in international trade is becoming more significant. On the other hand, its verdict on the Brazil's Embraer versus Canada's Bombardier case did not seem to solve the problem. Discuss.

**2.** Why does the Boeing-Airbus case, a dispute between two firms, extend to their governments?

**3.** What issues should the WTO take into consideration before making a decision? How should the WTO make a decision?

*Sources:* "In the Race," *Aviation Week & Space Technology,* October 10, 2005, pp. 22–23, and various other sources.

## FURTHER READING ◆ ◆ ◆ ◆ ◆ ◆ ◆ ◆ ◆ ◆ ◆ ◆ ◆ ◆ ◆ ◆ ◆ ◆ ◆ ◆ ◆ ◆

Bezmen, Trisha L. and David D. Selover, "Patterns of Economic Interdependence in Latin America," *International Trade Journal*, 19 (Fall 2005), pp. 217–67.

Johansson, Johny K. *In Your Face: How American Marketing Excess Fuels Anti-Americanism*, Upper Saddle River, NJ: Financial Times Prentice Hall, 2004.

Johnson, Joseph and Gerard J. Tellis, "Drivers of Success for Market Entry into China and India," *Journal of Marketing*, 72 (May), 2008: 1–13.

Kotler, Philip, Somkid Jatusripitak, and Suvit Maesincee, *The Marketing of Nations: A Strategic Approach to Building National Wealth*, New York: Free Press, 1997.

"Latin America: A Time of Transition," *Finance and Development*, 42(4), December 2005.

Rugman, Alan, *The Regional Multinationals*, Cambridge: Cambridge University Press, 2005.

Montealegre, Ramiro, "Four Visions of E-Commerce in Latin America in the Year 2010," *Thunderbird International Business Review*, 43(6) (2002): 717–35

Moore, Mike, ed., *Doha and Beyond: The future of the Multilateral Trading System*, New York: Cambridge University Press, 2004.

Schulz, Michael, Fredrik Soderbaum, and Joakim Ojendal, ed., *Regionalization in a Globalizing World: A Comparative Perspective on Forms, Actors, and Processes*, New York: Zed Books, 2001.

Shenkar, Oded. *The Chinese century: The Rising Chinese Economy and its Impact on the Global Economy, the Balance of Power, and Your Job*, Upper Saddle River, N.J.: Wharton School Publishing, 2005.

Sohn, Byeong Hae, "Regionalization of Trade and Investment in East Asia and Prospects for Further Regional Integration," *Journal of the Asia Pacific Economy*, 7 (June 2002): 160–81.

"The China Price," *Business Week*, December 6, 2004, pp. 102–24.

"The Tiger in Front: A Survey of India and China," *Economist, March* 5, 2005.

The European Union: A Guide for Americans, Washington, DC: Delegation of the European Commission, 2002.

"Vachani, Sushil, Mavericks and Free Trade: Chile's Pivotal Role in the Formation of the FTAA," *Thunderbird International Business Review*, 46 (May/Jun 2004), pp. 237–53.

# FINANCIAL ENVIRONMENT

3

When international transactions occur, foreign exchange is the monetary mechanism allowing the transfer of funds from one nation to another. The existing international monetary system always affects companies as well as individuals whenever they buy or sell products and services traded across national boundaries. The dollar's strengths, vis-à-vis other major currencies at the dawn of this new century, affected not only foreign but also U.S. companies as well. For example, in the fourth-quarter of 2001, Amazon.com posted its first-ever profit of US$5.1 million, thanks to reduced U.S. dollar payments on its euro-denominated debt.[1] Similarly, due to the stronger yen compared to the U.S. dollar in early 2008, Japanese multinational corporations, such as Toyota, reported a reduction in their profits as these companies' overseas businesses in the United States collect sales in U.S. dollars but report profit in Japanese yen. Every one-yen increase in the Japanese currency relative to the U.S. dollar is expected to trim Toyota's operating profit by around 35-billion yen (which would amount to a whopping $350 million at 105 yen/$).[2] It is obvious that the current international monetary system has a profound impact not only on individuals and companies but also on the U.S. balance of payments at the aggregate level.

This chapter examines international trade in monetary terms. In fact, the international monetary system has changed rather drastically over the years. Given the drastic realignment in recent years of the exchange rates of major currencies, including the U.S.

---

[1] Raizel Robin, "New Age Profit," *Canadian Business*, February 18, 2002.
[2] "The Yen Also Rises," *Economist*, May 19, 2008.

dollar, the European euro, and the Japanese yen, the current international monetary system may well be in for a major change. The adoption of the euro as a common currency in the European Union in 1999 is just one example of the many changes to come. Although international marketers have to operate in a currently existing international monetary system for international transactions and settlements, they should understand how the scope and nature of the system has changed and how it has worked over time. Forward-looking international marketers need to be aware of the dynamics of the international monetary system.

Since the last decade—particularly, the second half of the last decade—of the twentieth century, the global financial market has been anything but stable and has proved to be one of the most turbulent periods in recent history. The seemingly unstoppable rapid economic growth of Asia came to a screeching halt in 1997, and the introduction of the euro in the European Union in 1999 has drastically changed the European economic environment. The beginning of the 21st century has not been smooth, either. As described in Chapter 2, the financial crisis in South America and the slump in the U.S. and European economies since 2001 have also made us aware how vulnerable the global economy can be. Then the worst of such vulnerability has manifested itself again in an unprecedented global recession triggered by the U.S. subprime mortgage loan-led credit crisis that has quickly spread around the world since late 2008. These events profoundly affect international marketing practices. We are convinced that these epoch-making events need your special attention and that your understanding of them will allow you to become seasoned marketing decision makers in crucial areas such as product development, brand management, and pricing, among others, when developing marketing strategy on a global basis. It is another way to tell you that you have to be up-to-the-minute with ever-changing events that could affect your understanding of the class material, let alone your future career. In this chapter, we also provide a special detailed examination of the implications of the Asian and South American financial crises and marketing in the Euro Area.

## HISTORICAL ROLE OF THE U.S. DOLLAR        ◆ ◆ ◆ ◆ ◆ ◆ ◆

Each country also has its own currency through which it expresses the value of its products. An international monetary system is necessary because the vast majority of countries have their own monetary unit or currency that serves as a medium of exchange and store of value. The absence of a universal currency means that we must have a system that allows for the transfer of purchasing power between countries with different national currencies. For international trade settlements, the various currencies of the world must be exchanged from one to another. This is accomplished through foreign exchange markets.

Periodically, a country must review the status of its economic relations with the rest of the world in terms of its exports and imports, its exchange of various kinds of services, and its purchase and sale of different types of capital assets and other international payments, receipts and transfers. In the post-World War II period, a number of institutions came into existence to monitor and assist countries as necessary in keeping their international financial commitments. As a result, a new system of international monetary relations emerged, which promoted increased international trade through the 1950s and 1960s. In the early 1970s, however, a weakening U.S. dollar caused the existing system to show strains and eventually break down.

The U.S. trade deficit has pushed the value of the U.S. dollar downward in the last forty years. Since 1960, the dollar has fallen by approximately two-thirds against the euro (using Germany's currency as a proxy before 1999) and the Japanese yen.[3] Despite this long-term trend, the value of the dollar also fluctuates up and down significantly in

---

[3]"The Passing of the Buck?" *Economist*, December 4, 2004. pp. 71–73.

the short and intermediate term, and it remains stronger than commonly expected. Whether a strong dollar is in the best interest of the United States or not is debatable, but a strong dollar certainly reflects global confidence in U.S. economic leadership. However, the dollar could become an overvalued currency and make the current account deficits unsustainably large. A sharp downward shift of dollar value could have an enormous impact on global economy. During the annual G8 Summit meetings in June 2002, one of the most urgent issues was whether enough had been done to cushion against a collapse of the dollar.[4]

For example, within two years after the euro's introduction in 1999, the dollar appreciated 20 percent against the euro. However, from 2001 to 2008, the dollar kept depreciating against the euro by as much as 60 percent because of the weak U.S. economy, increased fear of rising U.S. inflation rates, uncertainty about the aftermath of a U.S.-led war with Iraq, and rising oil prices.

Because of the weakening of the dollar and other issues, the monetary stability of the world became unsettled beginning with the 1970s and continuing into the early 1980s. As the 1980s advanced, the U.S. economy stabilized and the value of the dollar against other currencies climbed to an all-time high. This caused U.S exports to become costlier, and foreign imports to become cheaper, resulting in an adverse trade balance. In the fall of 1985, leading industrialized countries joined the United States effort to intervene in the foreign exchange markets to decrease the value of the dollar. The dollar had steadily fallen and remained weak since mid-1980s. However, the current severe global recession has demonstrated an unexpected aspect of the dollar: When the global economy is in an unprecedented level of turmoil as it has been since late 2008, the world still considers the U.S. dollar as a last-resort currency to hold on to. As a result, the dollar has since appreciated dramatically against most other foreign currencies but depreciated against Japanese yen. For example, as of February 4, 2009, the U.S. dollar appreciated 15 percent against euro, 39 percent against Australian dollar, and a whopping 46 percent against Korean won, and depreciated almost 20 percent against Japanese yen from a year earlier. Clearly, the currency market has been far from stable.

---

## ♦ ♦ ♦ ♦ ♦ ♦ ♦ ♦ DEVELOPMENT OF TODAY'S INTERNATIONAL MONETARY SYSTEM

**The Bretton Woods Conference**

Post–World War II developments had long-range effects on international financial arrangements, the role of gold, and the problems of adjustment of balance of payments disequilibria. Following World War II, there was a strong desire to adhere to goals that would bring economic prosperity and hopefully a long-term peace to the world. The negotiations to establish the postwar international monetary system took place at the resort of Bretton Woods in New Hampshire in 1944. The negotiators at Bretton Woods recommended the following:[5]

Each nation should be at liberty to use macroeconomic policies for full employment.

1. Free floating exchange rates could not work. Their ineffectiveness had been demonstrated in the interwar years. The extremes of both permanently fixed and floating rates should be avoided.

2. A monetary system was needed that would recognize that exchange rates were both a national and international concern.

In order to avoid both the rigidity of a fixed exchange rate system and the chaos of freely floating exchange rates, the Bretton Woods Agreement provided for an

---

[4]Jesper Koll, "Dangers of a Falling Dollar," *Wall Street Journal*, June 12, 2002.

[5]Carlo Cottarelli and Curzio Giannini, *Credibility without Rules? — Monetary Framework in the Post-Bretton Woods Era*, Washington, D.C.: International Monetary Fund, 1997.

adjustable peg. Under this system, currencies were to establish par values in terms of gold, but there was to be little, if any, convertibility of the currencies for gold. Each government was responsible for monitoring its own currency to see that it did not float beyond 1 percent above or below its established par value. As a nation's currency attained or approached either limit, its central bank intervened in the world financial markets to prevent the rate from passing the limit.

Under this system, a country experiencing a balance-of-payments deficit would normally experience devaluation pressure on its current value. The country's authorities would defend its currency by using its foreign currency reserves, primarily U.S. dollars, to purchase its own currency on the open market to push its value back up to its par value. A country experiencing a balance-of-payments surplus would do the opposite and sell its currency on the open market. An institution called the **International Monetary Fund** (IMF) was established at Bretton Woods to oversee the newly agreed-upon monetary system. If a country experienced a fundamental or long-term disequilibrium in its balance of payments, it could alter its peg by up to 10 percent from its initial par value without approval from the International Monetary Fund. Adjustment beyond 10 percent required IMF approval.

In the 1960s, the United States began to experience sequential balance of payments deficits, resulting in downward pressure on the dollar. Since the U.S. government was obligated to maintain the dollar at its par value, it had to spend much of its gold and foreign currency reserves in order to purchase dollars on the world financial markets. In addition, the U.S. dollar was the reserve currency, convertible to gold under the Bretton Woods Agreement; the U.S. Treasury was obligated to convert dollars to gold upon demand by foreign central banks.

Furthermore, many central banks engaged in massive dollar purchases on the foreign exchange markets to counteract the downward pressure on the dollar and related upward pressure on their own currencies. The continued defense of the dollar left central banks around the world with massive quantities of dollars. These countries, knowing that the dollars they held were in fact convertible to gold with the U.S. Treasury, attempted to hold back, demanding gold in exchange. However, it became clear by 1971 that the dollar was quite overvalued, and devaluation of the dollar versus gold was inevitable. Central banks increasingly presented U.S. dollar balances to the U.S. Treasury for conversion to gold, and gold flowed out of the U.S. vaults at an alarming rate.

This situation led President Richard Nixon to suspend the convertibility of the dollar to gold on August 15, 1971. This effectively ended the exchange rate regime begun at Bretton Woods more than twenty-five years earlier.

## The International Monetary Fund

The International Monetary Fund (IMF) oversees the international monetary system. The IMF was a specialized agency within the United Nations, established to promote international monetary cooperation and to facilitate the expansion of trade, and in turn to contribute to increased employment and improved economic conditions in all member countries.

Its purposes are defined in the following terms:[6]

To promote international monetary cooperation through a permanent institution, providing the machinery for consultations and collaboration on international monetary problems.

1. To facilitate the expansion and balanced growth of international trade, and to contribute thereby to the promotion and maintenance of high levels of employment and real income, and to the development of the productive resources of all members as primary objectives of economic policy.

---

[6]International Monetary Fund, *The Role and Function of the International Monetary Fund* (Washington, D.C.: International Monetary Fund, 1985).

2. To promote exchange stability, to maintain orderly exchange arrangements among members, and to avoid competitive exchange depreciation.

3. To assist in the establishment of a multilateral system of payments in respect to current transactions between members and in the elimination of foreign exchange restrictions that hamper the growth of world trade.

4. To give confidence to members by making the general resources of the fund temporarily available to them under adequate safeguards, thus providing them with the opportunity to correct maladjustments in their balance of payments without resorting to measures destructive of national or international prosperity.

5. In accordance with the above, to shorten the duration and lessen the degree of disequilibrium in the international balance of payments to members.

Today the IMF has 186 members.[7] Its accomplishments include sustaining a rapidly increasing volume of trade and investment and displaying flexibility in adapting to changes in international commerce. To an extent, the IMF served as an international central bank to help countries during periods of temporary balance of payments difficulties, by protecting their rates of exchange. This helped countries avoid the placement of foreign exchange controls and other trade barriers.

As time passed, it became evident that the IMF's resources for providing short-term accommodation to countries in monetary difficulties were not sufficient. To resolve the situation, and to reduce upward pressure on the U.S. dollar by countries holding dollar reserves, the fund created special drawing rights in 1969. **Special drawing rights (SDRs)** are special account entries on the IMF books designed to provide additional liquidity to support growing world trade. The value of SDRs is determined by a weighted average of a basket of four currencies: the U.S. dollar, the Japanese yen, the European Union's euro, and the British pound. Although SDRs are a form of fiat money and not convertible to gold, their gold value is guaranteed, which helps to ensure their acceptability.

Participant nations may use SDRs as a source of currency in a spot transaction, as a loan for clearing a financial obligation, as security for a loan, as a swap against a currency, or in a forward exchange operation. A nation with a balance of payment problem may use its SDRs to obtain usable currency from another nation designated by the fund. By providing a mechanism for international monetary cooperation, working to reduce restrictions to trade and investment flows, and helping members with their short-term balance of payment difficulties, the IMF makes a significant and unique contribution to economic stability and improved living standards throughout the world.

In the wake of the 1997–1998 Asian financial crisis, the IMF worked on policies to overcome or even prevent future crisis. After 1997, the external payments situation was stabilized through IMF-led aid programs, and financial packages were being geared to encourage the adoption of policies that could prevent crises in selected developing countries. Backed by an IMF quota increase of $90 billion, the IMF would make a contingent short-term line of credit available before a crisis breaks out, but only if a country adopts certain policies that would limit its vulnerability. The line of credit is expected to be short-term and to charge interest rates above market rates to discourage misuse.[8] In September, 2002, the IMF also approved $30 billion in emergency loans to Brazil battered by the financial crisis in Argentina. The announcement pushed various developing market currencies higher as investors welcomed both the vote of confidence in Brazil and the broader implications of the loan announcement for emerging market assets. Now as the global financial crisis has spread since late 2008, net capital inflows into emerging markets, which were $929 billion in 2007, are expected to fall to a meager $165 billion in 2009. Again, IMF is channeling a massive amount of capital to those

---

[7]International Monetary Fund Homepage, http://www.imf.org/, accessed July 11, 2009.

[8]Suk H. Kim and Mahfuzul Haque, "The Asian Financial Crisis of 1997: Causes and Policy Response," *Multinational Business Review*, 10 (Spring 2002), pp. 37–44; and Ramon Moreno, "Dealing with Currency Crises," *FRBSF Economic Letter*, Number 99-11, April 2, 1999.

countries to stem any precipitous collapse not only of their economies but also of the global trading regime itself.[9] These loans signal that there is still a commitment by international organizations to countries with major financial problems.[10]

## The International Bank for Reconstruction and Development

Another creation of the Bretton Woods Agreement was the International Bank for Reconstruction and Development, known as the **World Bank**. Although the International Monetary Fund was created to aid countries in financing their balance of payment difficulties and maintaining a relatively stable currency, the World Bank was initially intended for the financing of post-war reconstruction and development and later for infrastructure building projects in the developing world. More recently, the World Bank has begun to participate actively with the IMF to resolve debt problems of the developing world, and it may also play a major role in bringing a market economy to the former members of the Eastern bloc. Each year the World Bank lends between US$15–20 billion to developing country governments to support projects for economic development and poverty reduction. The World Bank is the largest external fund provider for education and HIV/AIDS programs, strongly supports debt relief, and is responding to the voices of the poor people. The organization greatly supports developing country governments to build schools and health centers, provide water and electricity, fight disease, and protect the environment.[11]

Comstock Inc.

Various foreign currencies and gold coins, nuggets, and bars as means to measure and store economic value.

## Fixed versus Floating Exchange Rates

Since the 1970s all major nations have had floating currencies. An IMF meeting in Jamaica in 1976 reached consensus on amendments to the IMF Articles of Agreement that accepted floating rates as the basis for the international monetary system. The amended agreement recognized that real rate stability can only be achieved through stability in underlying economic and financial conditions. Exchange rate stability cannot be imposed by adoption of pegged exchange rates and official intervention in the foreign exchange markets.

There are two kinds of currency floats, and these are referred to as free or managed or as clean or dirty. The **free (clean) float** is the closest approximation to perfect competition, because there is no government intervention and because billions of units

[9]"Supersizing the Fund," *Economist*, February 5, 2009; also see "2008–2009 Global Financial Crisis" at http://wtfaculty.wtamu.edu/~sanwar.bus/otherlinks.htm#GlobalFinCrisis, an excellent website maintained by Professor Syed Anwar of West Texas A&M University.

[10]"Special Summary of Stories on IMF $30B Package for Brazil," *Dow Jones Newswire*, August 8, 2002; "IMF Improves Terms on Emergency Aid," *Finance & Development* (42), March 2005, p. 3.

[11]The World Bank, http://www.worldbank.org/, accessed December 20, 2005.

of currency are being traded by buyers and sellers. Buyers and sellers may change sides on short notice as information, rumors, or moods change, or as their clients' needs differ.

A **managed (dirty) float** allows for a limited amount of government intervention to soften sudden swings in the value of a currency. If a nation's currency enters into a rapid ascent or decline, that nation's central bank may wish to sell or buy that currency on the open market in a countervailing movement to offset the prevailing market tendency. This is for the purpose of maintaining an orderly, less-volatile foreign exchange market.

In March 1973, the major currencies began to float in the foreign exchange markets. The advocates for floating exchange regime argued that it would end balance of payments disequilibria because the value of each currency would float up or down to a point where supply equaled demand. It has not worked that way, at least in part due to the reluctance of governments to permit extreme changes in the value of their currencies. Governments have intervened in the currency markets to moderate or prevent value changes. In reality, however, the supposed benefits of floating exchange rates have not been borne to date. For example:Floating exchange rates were supposed to facilitate balance of payments adjustments. However, not only have imbalances not disappeared, they have become worse, as attested to by the recent Asian and Latin American financial crises.

1. Currency speculation was expected to be curtailed. But speculation has since been greater than ever. Similarly, short-term speculations worsened the Asian and Latin financial crisis.

2. Market forces, left to their own devices, were expected to determine the correct foreign exchange rate balance. But imbalances have become greater than ever, as have fluctuations in rates.

3. Autonomy in economic and monetary policy was hoped to be preserved, allowing each country free choice of its monetary policy and rate of inflation. But this has also not materialized.

As a result, international marketers have had to cope with the ever-fluctuating exchange rates (see **Exhibit 3.1**). Refer back to the enormous change in Toyota's operating profits as a result of a small change in the yen/dollar exchange rate illustrated in the opening paragraph of this chapter. Even a small fluctuation in exchange rates cannot be ignored, since it has an enormous impact on a company's operating profit.

**Currency Blocs**  Although currencies of most countries float in value against one another, those of many developing countries are pegged (or fixed) to one of the major currencies or to a basket of major currencies such as the U.S. dollar, Special Drawing Rights, or some specially chosen currency mix. In general, developing countries that depend on their trading relationships with a major country, such as the United States, for economic growth tend to use the currency of the principal country.

For example, Chinese currency, *renminbi* (yuan), had been pegged to the U.S. dollar for a decade at 8.28 yuan to the dollar. Based on its growing trade surplus with the United States as well as its sustained real GDP growth in the past twenty years of 9.5 percent, China has been accused of pursuing a cheap-yuan policy and has been pressured to revalue its currency. In the past, in order to prevent the yuan from rising against the dollar, the Chinese central bank had to buy huge amounts of U.S. Treasury securities. The Chinese government believed that the fixed exchange rate would provide stability to the Chinese economy as it relied so much on trade with the United States. However, as the dollar continued to fall against other key currencies, the Chinese central bank decided on July 21, 2005 to abandon the yuan's peg to the dollar in favor of a link to a basket of several currencies, including the euro and the yen, and revalued the yuan by 2.1 percent against the dollar. On September 23, 2005, the Chinese central bank further decided to let the yuan float against the major currencies by up to 3 percent a day against the euro, yen and other non-dollar currencies, compared with 1.5 percent previously. Daily movements against the dollar, meanwhile, remained

**EXHIBIT 3-1**

FOREIGN EXCHANGE RATE FLUCTUATIONS OVER THE PAST 30
YEARS (FOREIGN CURRENCY UNITS/U.S. DOLLAR)

| Year | Deutsche Mark | French Franc | Japanese Yen | Swiss Franc | British Pound |
|------|------|------|------|------|------|
| 1980 | 1.96 | 4.55 | 203 | 1.76 | 0.42 |
| – | – | – | – | – | – |
| 1985 | 2.46 | 7.56 | 201 | 2.08 | 0.69 |
| – | – | – | – | – | – |
| 1990 | 1.49 | 5.13 | 134 | 1.30 | 0.52 |
| 1991 | 1.52 | 5.18 | 125 | 1.36 | 0.53 |
| 1992 | 1.61 | 5.51 | 125 | 1.46 | 0.66 |
| 1993 | 1.73 | 5.90 | 112 | 1.48 | 0.68 |
| 1994 | 1.55 | 5.35 | 100 | 1.31 | 0.64 |
| 1995 | 1.43 | 4.90 | 103 | 1.15 | 0.65 |
| 1996 | 1.50 | 5.12 | 94 | 1.24 | 0.64 |
| 1997 | 1.73 | 5.84 | 121 | 1.45 | 0.64 |
| 1998 | 1.82 | 6.10 | 139 | 1.53 | 0.60 |
| 1999 | | 0.94 euro* | 108 | 1.69 | 0.66 |
| 2000 | | 1.08 | 108 | 1.69 | 0.66 |
| 2001 | | 1.12 | 122 | 1.69 | 0.69 |
| 2002 | | 1.06 | 125 | 1.55 | 0.67 |
| 2003 | | 0.88 | 116 | 1.35 | 0.61 |
| 2004 | | 0.80 | 108 | 1.24 | 0.55 |
| 2005 | | 0.80 | 116 | 1.24 | 0.55 |
| 2006 | | 0.79 | 113 | 1.24 | 0.54 |
| 2007 | | 0.68 | 111 | 1.13 | 0.50 |
| 2008 | | 0.72 | 91 | 1.07 | 0.62 |
| 2009** | | 0.72 | 92 | 1.09 | 0.62 |

*Source:* International Monetary Fund, *Balance of Payments Statistics Yearbook* (Washington, D.C.: U.S. Government Printing Office); and "World Value of the Dollar," *Wall Street Journal*, March 17, 2009.

*The euro was introduced in 1999 and completely replaced the currencies of member countries in 2002.
**Exchange rate as of July 10, 2009.

limited to only 0.3 percent.[12] On May 16, 2007, however, China again took steps to let its currency trade more freely against the dollar and to cool its sizzling economy and its soaring trade surplus[13]. The yuan is now allowed to fluctuate against the dollar by 0.5 percent a day, up from 0.3 percent. The renminbi exchange rate rose from 8.28 yuan/$ in July 2005 to 6.84 yuan/$ in February 2009, a jump of 21 percent in three years.

Today, the global economy is increasingly dominated by three major currency blocs. The U.S. dollar, the EU's euro, and the Japanese yen each represent their "sphere of influence" on the currencies of other countries in the respective regions (i.e., North and South America, Europe, and East Asia, respectively).[14] After its launch, the euro immediately became the world's second leading international currency. The U.S. dollar is still likely to remain the dominant international currency for the time being. However, the current financial crisis seems to indicate that companies based in countries with more stable currencies than the U.S. dollar, such as Japan, have seriously started to move away from the U.S. dollar as the international transaction currency.[15]

Due to the large size of the euro-area economy, the stability attached to the euro, and the ongoing integration of national financial markets in Europe into broad, deep and liquid Pan-European financial markets, the euro is gradually becoming an international currency.[16] Although the U.S. dollar has lost some of its role as the

---

[12]"Yuan Step at a Time," *Economist*, January 22, 2005, p. 74; and "Patching the Basket," *Economist*, October 1, 2005, p. 71.

[13]"China Eases Controls to Allow Yuan Float Freely against Dollar," *SeekingAlpha.com*, August 30, 2007.

[14]Michael H. Moffett, Arthur I. Stonehill, and David K. Eiteman, *Fundamentals of Multinational Finance*, 2nd ed., Reading, Mass.: Addison-Wesley, 2006.

[15]"Japan Firms Rethink Using Dollar as Settlement Currency," NikkeiNet Interactive, www.nni.nikkei.co.jp, October 9, 2008.

[16]"The Passing of the Buck?" *Economist*, December 4, 2004. pp. 71–73.

international transaction currency, it remains a currency of choice that many Latin American companies use for operating purposes. The Japanese yen has increasingly become a regional transaction currency in Asia. In other words, U.S. companies will find it easier to do business with companies in Latin America as business planning and transactions are increasingly conducted in dollar denominations. On the other hand, those U.S. companies will increasingly have to accept yen-denominated business transactions in Asia and euro-denominated transactions in Europe, thus being susceptible to exchange rate fluctuations. Considering increased trade volumes with Asian and European countries as well as with Latin American countries, it has become all the more important for U.S. marketing executives to understand the dynamic forces that affect exchange rates and predict the exchange rate fluctuations.

---

## ◆ ◆ ◆ ◆ ◆ ◆ ◆ ◆     FOREIGN EXCHANGE AND FOREIGN EXCHANGE RATES

Foreign exchange, as the term implies, refers to the exchange of one country's money for that of another country. When international transactions occur, foreign exchange is the monetary mechanism allowing the transfer of funds from one nation to another. In this section, we explore what factors influence the exchange rates over time and how the exchange rates are determined.

**Purchasing Power Parity**

One of the most fundamental determinants of the exchange rate is **purchasing power parity (PPP)**, whereby the exchange rate between the currencies of two countries makes the purchasing power of both currencies equal. In other words, the value of a currency is determined by what it can buy.

The following formula represents the relationship between inflation rates and the exchange rate, say, in the United States and Europe's eurozone:

$$R_t = R_0 * \frac{(1 + Infl_{euro})}{(1 + Infl_{US})}$$

where
$\quad$ R = the exchange rate quoted in euro/$,
$\quad$ Infl = inflation rate,
$\quad$ t = time period.

For example, if the inflation rate in the eurozone were 2 percent a year and U.S. inflation were 5 percent a year, the value of the dollar would be expected to decline by the difference of 3 percent, so that the real prices of goods in the two countries would remain fairly similar. If the current exchange rate ($R_0$) is 0.675 euro to the dollar (€0.675/$), then

$$R_t = 0.675 * \frac{(1 + .02)}{(1 + .05)} = €0.656/\$.$$

In other words, the dollar is expected to depreciate from €0.675/$ to €0.656/$ in a year. The U.S. dollar will be able to buy slightly more less euro. Or, stated in reverse, the euro will be able to buy slightly more U.S. dollars.

In fact, the *Economist* publishes a PPP study every year based on McDonald's Big Mac hamburger, sold all over the world. It is known as the Big Mac Index to show whether currencies are at their "correct" exchange rate. Look at the recent Big Mac Index to see how actual exchange rates "deviate" from the Big Mac Index (see **Exhibit 3.2**). The average price for a Big Mac is $3.54 in the United States in 2009. For example, the cheapest burger in the chart is in South Africa, at 47 percent of the U.S price, or $1.68. This implies that the South African rand is 53 percent undervalued

**EXHIBIT 3-2**
THE BIG MAC INDEX

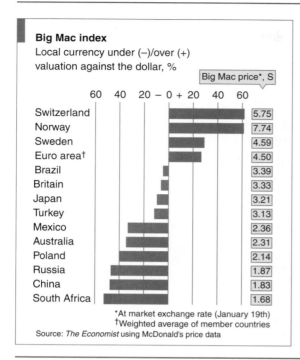

*At market exchange rate (January 19th)
†Weighted average of member countries
Source: *The Economist* using McDonald's price data

*Source:* "Big Mac Index," *Economist,*
July 26, 2009.

relative to the U.S. dollar, based on the Big Mac dollar-PPP. On the same basis, the euro is 27 percent overvalued, the Swedish krona a whopping 98 percent overvalued, and the yen 9 percent undervalued. We can observe that, in general, major European currencies are overvalued relative the U.S. dollar, while Asia-Pacific currencies are undervalued. Theoretically, over the long run, exchange rates tend to go toward the direction of PPP index. If the dollar is overvalued relative to a foreign currency (i.e., the foreign currency is undervalued relative to the dollar), people using that foreign currency will find it more expensive to buy goods from the United States. Conversely, people living in the United States will find it cheaper to import goods from a country with an undervalued currency.

**Forecasting Exchange Rate Fluctuation**

Actual exchange rates can be very different from the expected rates. Those deviations are not necessarily a random variation. As summarized in **Exhibit 3.3**, many inter-related factors influence the value of a floating currency. In particular, the nation's inflation rate relative to its trading partners, its balance of payments situation, and world political events are the three most fundamental factors.

Although accurately predicting the actual exchange rate fluctuations is not possible and it is not related directly to marketing executives' jobs, seasoned marketers can benefit from the knowledge. Exchange rate fluctuations have an enormous direct impact on the bottom line for the company—profitability.

**Coping with Exchange Rate Fluctuations**

When the fast-food operator Kentucky-Fried Chicken (KFC) opens new restaurants in Mexico, for example, it often imports some of the kitchen equipment, including fryers, roasters, stainless steel counters, and other items for its stores from U.S. suppliers.

In order to pay for these imports, the Mexican subsidiary of KFC must purchase U. S. dollars with Mexican pesos through its bank in Mexico City. This is necessary because Mexican pesos are not readily accepted currency in the United States. Most likely, KFC-Mexico will pay for the imported merchandise via a bank cashier's check from its

## EXHIBIT 3-3
### FACTORS INFLUENCING FOREIGN EXCHANGE RATES

MACROECONOMIC FACTORS

1. **Relative Inflation:** A country suffering relatively higher inflation rates than other major trading partners will cause depreciation of its currency.
2. **Balance of Payments:** Improvement (deterioration) in the balance of payments for goods and services is an early sign of a currency appreciation (depreciation).
3. **Foreign Exchange Reserves:** A government may intervene in the foreign exchange markets to either push up or push down the value of its currency. The central bank can support (depreciate) the domestic currency by selling its foreign currency reserves to buy its own currency (selling its domestic currency to buy foreign currency).
4. **Economic Growth:** If the domestic economy is growing fast relative to major trading partners, the country's imports tend to rise faster than exports, resulting in deterioration of the trade balance and thus depreciation of its currency. However, if the domestic economic growth attracts a large amount of investment from abroad, it could offset the negative trade effect, thus potentially resulting in appreciation of the domestic currency.
5. **Government Spending:** An increase in government spending, particularly if financed through deficit spending, causes increased inflationary pressures on the economy. Inflation leads to domestic currency depreciation (as in 1).
6. **Money Supply Growth:** Many countries' central banks attempt to stave off recession by increasing money supply to lower domestic interest rates for increased consumption and investment. Increase in money supply usually leads to higher inflation rates and subsequently currency depreciation.
7. **Interest Rate Policy:** As in 6, the central bank may also control its discount rate (interest rate charged to banks) to raise domestic lending rates so as to control inflation. Higher interest rates discourage economic activity and tend to reduce inflation and also attract investment from abroad. Reduced inflation and increased investment from abroad both lead to currency appreciation.

POLITICAL FACTORS

1. **Exchange Rate Control:** Some governments have an explicit control on the exchange rate. The official rate for domestic currency is artificially overvalued, thereby discouraging foreign companies from exporting to such a country. However, as long as there is a genuine domestic demand for imported products, the black market tends to appear for foreign currency. Black market exchange rates for a domestic currency tend to be much lower than the government-imposed artificial rate. Thus, a wide spread between the official exchange rate and the black market rate indicates potential pressures leading to domestic currency devaluation.
2. **Election Year or Leadership Change:** Expectations about imminent government policy change influence exchange rates. In general, pro-business government policy tends to lead to domestic currency appreciation as foreign companies are willing to accept that currency for business transactions.

RANDOM FACTORS

Unexpected and/or unpredicted events in a country, such as assassination of political figures and sudden stock market crash, can cause its currency to depreciate for fear of uncertainty. Similarly, events such as sudden discovery of huge oil reserves and gold mines tend to push up the currency value.

*Source:* Developed from a discussion in Chapter 3 of David K. Eiteman, Arthur I. Stonehill, and Michael H. Moffett, *Multinational Business Finance,* 9th ed., New York: Addison-Wesley, 2001.

local bank in Mexico City, denominated in U.S. dollars. If the exchange rate on the date of purchase is 10.19 Mexican pesos per U.S. dollar and their debt is $10,000 dollars, then KFC-Mexico must pay 101,900 pesos, plus a commission to the bank, for the dollars it sends to the U.S. supplier. The bank in Mexico acquires the dollars on the open foreign exchange market or through other banks for the purpose of satisfying the foreign exchange needs of its customers.

This is the case when currency is freely convertible with minimal government foreign exchange controls, as has been true in Mexico. However, this is not always the case. Governments have often limited the amount of domestic currency that can leave a country, in order to avoid capital flight and decapitalization. One example of this was South Africa in the 1980s, where it was illegal to buy foreign currency or take domestic currency out of the country without government approval. If a company in South Africa required foreign manufactured goods, it had to solicit authorization for the purchase of foreign exchange through the national treasury in order to make payment.

Even more rigid exchange controls existed in the former Soviet Union and other Eastern bloc countries prior to the fall of communism, where trade in foreign currency was a crime meriting harsh punishment. The problem with such tight exchange controls is that often they promote a black market in unauthorized trade in the controlled currency. In such cases, the official rate of exchange for a currency will tend to be overvalued, or in other words, possessing an officially stated value that does not reflect its true worth. The black market will more likely reflect its true worth on the street.

Another issue affecting foreign exchange concerns fluctuation in the rates of exchange, whereby currencies either appreciate or depreciate with respect to one another. Since the 1970s most of the world's currencies have been on a floating system, often fluctuating with wide variations. For example, in 1976, the Mexican peso traded at an exchange rate of 12.5 per dollar, but in 1993 it had fallen to 3,200 pesos per dollar.

This peso depreciation reflected much greater inflation in Mexico compared to the United States, and the fear of political/financial instability in Mexico prompted Mexican residents to buy dollars for security. In 1993, the Mexican government dropped three zeroes off the currency, creating a new peso (nuevo peso) worth 3.2 pesos per dollar. This rate climbed again with the depreciation that began in December 1994 to the 11 pesos per dollar range by 2004. Since then, the peso has begun to appreciate a little against the U.S. dollar as the dollar has weakened. As of June 2008, the exchange rate rose to10.29 peso/$. On the other hand, in the early 1980s, the Japanese yen traded at approximately 250 yen per dollar, but by 1996 had appreciated to 94 yen per dollar (before losing value slightly to approximately 108 yen per dollar in 2008). This long-term depreciation of the dollar against the yen reflected continuing U. S. trade deficits with Japan, as well as a higher level of inflation in the United States relative to Japan.

Many countries attempt to maintain a lower value for their currency in order to encourage exports. The reason for this is that if the dollar depreciates against the Japanese yen, for example, U.S.-manufactured goods should become cheaper to the Japanese consumers, who find that their supply of yen suddenly purchases a greater quantity of dollars; and Japanese and other foreign goods more expensive to Americans. The depreciation of the U.S. dollar should then help to reduce the United States' deficit with its trading partners by increasing exports and reducing imports, in the absence of other countervailing factors.

Directly related to the issue of floating currency is the concept of transaction gain or loss on the import or export of merchandise. Returning to the example of KFC-Mexico's import of $10,000 in kitchen equipment, if that company ordered the equipment in January 2008 (when the exchange rate was 10 pesos per dollar) for payment in June 2009 (when the exchange rate had fallen to 11.5 pesos per dollar), they would incur a foreign exchange transaction loss. This happens because the company would have to buy dollars for payment in the month of June at a depreciated rate, thus paying more pesos for every dollar purchased. Only if they had the foresight (or good luck) to buy the dollars in January 2008 at the more favorable rate could they avoid this foreign exchange loss. A more detailed illustration follows:

| | |
|---|---|
| Cost of imported equipment in pesos at exchange rate in effect at order date (10 pesos per dollar) | 100,000 pesos |
| Cost of imported equipment in pesos at exchange rate in effect at payment date (11.5 pesos per dollar) | 115,000 pesos |
| Foreign exchange loss in pesos | 15,000 pesos |

Conversely, if the peso were to appreciate prior to the payment date, KFC-Mexico would have a transaction gain in foreign exchange.

**Spot versus Forward Foreign Exchange**

If payment on a transaction is to be made immediately, the purchaser has no choice other than to buy foreign exchange on the **spot (or current) market**, for immediate delivery. However, if payment is to be made at some future date, as was the case in the KFC-Mexico example, the purchaser has the option of buying foreign exchange on the spot market or on the **forward market**, for delivery at some future date. The advantage of the forward market is that the buyer can lock in on an exchange rate and avoid the risk of currency fluctuations; this is called **currency hedging**, or protecting oneself against potential loss.[17]

The sound management of foreign exchange in an environment of volatile floating rates requires an astute corporate treasurer and effective coordination with the purchasing or marketing functions of the business.[18] If they see their national currency or the currency of one of their subsidiaries declining, they may purchase a stronger foreign currency as a reserve for future use. Often, if the corporation's money managers are savvy enough, significant income can be generated through foreign exchange transactions beyond that of normal company operations.[19] However, in recent years, many companies seem to be reducing hedging because exchange rate fluctuations have become so erratic and unpredictable. According to a survey conducted by the University of Pennsylvania's Wharton School and Canadian Imperial Bank of Commerce, only one-third of large U.S. companies engage in some kind of foreign-currency hedging.[20]

For example, Merck, a pharmaceutical giant, hedges some of its foreign cash flows using one- to five-year options to sell the currencies for dollars at fixed rates. Merck argues that it can protect adverse currency moves by exercising its options or enjoy favorable moves by not exercising them. But many well-established companies see no strong need to hedge for protection against currency risk. The reason is that fluctuations in the underlying business can spoil the hedge's effectiveness. For companies with a strong belief in hedging, the sustained rise in the dollar over the past several years proved a serious test. Coca-Cola hopes to limit the negative impact of unfavorable currency swings on earnings to 3 percent annually over the long term. However, Coca-Cola's profits from foreign sales were knocked off by 10 percent due to the stronger dollar in 1998, instead. Eastman Kodak used to use aggressive hedging strategy, but abandoned such practice recently as it realized that hedging was not necessary since the ups and downs of currencies would even out in the long run.[21]

---

[17]Alternatively, there is **operational hedging**, which is to shift production and procurement abroad to match revenues in foreign currency when exchange rate fluctuations are very difficult to predict (i.e., successful currency hedging is increasingly difficult). For example, by producing abroad all of the products a company sells in foreign markets, this company has created an "operational hedge" by shielding itself from fluctuating exchange rates. See, for example, Christos Pantzalis, Betty J. Simkins, Paul A. Laux, "Operational Hedges and the Foreign Exchange Exposure of U.S. Multinational Corporations," *Journal of International Business Studies*, 32 (4), 2001, pp. 793–812.

[18]Raj Aggarwal and Luc A. Soenen, "Managing Persistent Real Changes in Currency Values: The Role of Multinational Operating Strategies," *Columbia Journal of World Business* (Fall 1989), pp. 60–67.

[19]Stephen D. Makar and Stephen P. Huffman, "Foreign Currency Risk Management Practices in U.S. Multinationals," *Journal of Applied Business Research*, 13, Spring 1997, pp. 73–86.

[20]Peter Coy, De'Ann Weimer, and Amy Barrett, "Perils of the Hedge Highwire," *Business Week*, October 26, 1998, p. 74.

[21]Ibid.

However, it does not necessarily mean that currency hedging is less important to any company. Who should consider financial hedging more seriously? For an export-oriented economy, which is heavily dependent on the export of dollar-based products, such as Norway, currency hedging strategies remain vital.[22] While more young companies have started getting involved with international imports or exports, currency hedging has also become more accessible to them, thanks to a growing number of services offered by large banks as well as business-to-business Web sites. Currency hedging allows small business owners to greatly reduce or eliminate the uncertainties attached to any foreign currency transaction.

Forward currency markets exist for the strongest currencies, including the EU's euro, the British pound, Canadian dollar, Japanese yen, Swiss franc, and U.S. dollar. The terms of purchase are usually for delivery of the foreign currency in either thirty, sixty, or ninety days from the date of purchase. These aforementioned currencies are often called hard currencies, because they are the world's strongest and represent the world's leading economies.

Traditionally weaker currencies, such as the Indian rupee or the Colombian peso, are rarely used in forward currency markets, because there is no worldwide demand for such a market; nearly all international transactions are expressed in terms of a hard currency. **Exhibit 3.4** illustrates the daily quotes for foreign exchange on the spot and forward markets. In the second column, the foreign currency is expressed in terms of how many dollars it takes to buy one unit of foreign currency. The third column indicates the inverse, or how many units of a foreign currency it would take to purchase one dollar. For example, on July 11, 2009, one Japanese yen was worth $0.01082; or more conventionally, the value of the yen was expressed as 92.42 yen per dollar. Similarly, on the same day, one euro was worth $1.3949; or conversely, one U.S. dollar could buy 0.7169.

## Exchange Rate Pass-Through

The dramatic swings in the value of the dollar since the early 1980s have made it clear that foreign companies charge different prices in the United States than in other markets.[23] When the dollar appreciated against the Japanese yen and the German mark in the 1980s, Japanese cars were priced fairly low in the United States, justified by the cheaper yen, while German cars became far more expensive in the United States than in Europe. In the 1990s, when the dollar began depreciating against the yen and the mark, Japanese and German auto makers had to increase their dollar prices in the United States. Japanese auto makers did not raise their prices nearly as much as German competitors. Obviously, they "price to market."[24] As a result, Japanese carmakers did not lose as much U.S. market share as did German car makers.

One of the success factors for many Japanese companies in the U.S. markets seems to be in the way they used dollar–yen exchange rates to their advantage, known as the **target exchange rate**. Japanese companies, in particular, are known to employ a very unfavorable target exchange rate (i.e., hypothetically appreciated yen environment) for their costing strategy to make sure they will not be adversely affected should the yen appreciate. Therefore, despite close to a twofold appreciation of the yen vis-à-vis the dollar from 240 yen/$ in to 110 yen/$ in a decade, the dollar prices of Japanese products have not increased nearly as much. The extent to which a foreign company changes dollar prices of its products in the U.S. market as a result of exchange rate fluctuations is called **exchange rate pass-through**. Although accurately estimating the average increase in dollar prices of Japanese products is almost impossible, our estimate suggests

---

[22]Ranga Nathan and Nils E. Joachim Hoegh-Krohn, "Norwegian Institutional Investors: Currency Risk," *Derivatives Quarterly*, 6 (Fall 1999), pp. 59–63.

[23]Terry Clark, Masaaki Kotabe, and Dan Rajaratnam "Exchange Rate Pass-Through and International Pricing Strategy: A Conceptual Framework and Research Propositions," *Journal of International Business Studies*, 30 (Second Quarter 1999), pp. 249–68.

[24]"Pricing Paradox: Consumers Still Find Imported Bargains Despite Weak Dollar," *Wall Street Journal* (October 7, 1992), p. A6.

**EXHIBIT 3-4**

FOREIGN EXCHANGE RATES.

Friday, July 10, 2009
U.S.-dollar foreign-exchange rates in late New York trading

| | IN US$ | PER US$ | | IN US$ | PER US$ |
|---|---|---|---|---|---|
| **Americas** | | | **Europe** | | |
| Argentina peso | 0.2631 | 3.8008 | Czech Rep. koruna | 0.05368 | 18.629 |
| Brazil real | 0.5005 | 1.9980 | Denmark krone | 0.1873 | 5.3390 |
| Canada dollar | 0.8587 | 1.1646 | Euro area euro | 1.3949 | 0.7169 |
| 1-mos forward | 0.8588 | 1.1644 | Hungary forint | 0.00503 | 198.81 |
| 3-mos forward | 0.8590 | 1.1641 | Norway krone | 0.1532 | 6.5274 |
| 6-mos forward | 0.8593 | 1.1637 | Poland zloty | 0.3188 | 3.1368 |
| Chile peso | 0.001819 | 549.75 | Romania leu | 0.3307 | 3.0239 |
| Colombia peso | 0.0004754 | 2103.49 | Russia ruble | 0.03059 | 32.690 |
| Ecuador US dollar | 1 | 1 | Sweden krona | 0.1260 | 7.9365 |
| Mexico peso | 0.0731 | 13.6724 | Switzerland franc | 0.9219 | 1.0847 |
| Peru new sol | 0.3306 | 3.0248 | 1-mos forward | 0.9222 | 1.0844 |
| Uruguay peso | 0.04320 | 23.15 | 3-mos forward | 0.9230 | 1.0834 |
| Venezuela b. fuerte | 0.46570111 | 2.1473 | 6-mos forward | 0.9245 | 1.0817 |
| | | | Turkey lira | 0.6446 | 1.5513 |
| **Asia-Pacific** | | | UK pound | 1.6208 | 0.6170 |
| Australian dollar | 0.7787 | 1.2842 | 1-mos forward | 1.6207 | 0.6170 |
| China yuan | 0.1464 | 6.8327 | 3-mos forward | 1.6205 | 0.6171 |
| Hong Kong dollar | 0.1290 | 7.7504 | 6-mos forward | 1.6203 | 0.6172 |
| India rupee | 0.02050 | 48.7805 | | | |
| Indonesia rupiah | 0.0000986 | 10142 | **Middle East/Africa** | | |
| Japan yen | 0.01082 | 92.42 | Bahrain dinar | 2.6525 | 0.3770 |
| 1-mos forward | 0.010824 | 92.39 | Eqypt pound | 0.1790 | 5.5869 |
| 3-mos forward | 0.010831 | 92.33 | Israel shekel | 0.2507 | 3.9888 |
| 6-mos forward | 0.010845 | 92.21 | Jordan dinar | 1.4119 | 0.7083 |
| Malaysia ringgit | 0.2795 | 3.5778 | Kenya shilling | 0.01302 | 76.800 |
| New Zealand dollar | 0.6276 | 1.5934 | Kuwait dinar | 3.4751 | 0.2878 |
| Pakistan rupee | 0.01224 | 81.699 | Lebanon pound | 0.0006634 | 1507.39 |
| Philippines peso | 0.0207 | 48.216 | Saudi Arabia riyal | 0.2666 | 3.7509 |
| Singapore dollar | 0.6837 | 1.4626 | South Africa rand | 0.1216 | 8.2237 |
| South Korea won | 0.0007759 | 1288.83 | UAE dirham | 0.2723 | 3.6724 |
| Taiwan dollar | 0.03026 | 33.047 | | | |
| Thailand baht | 0.02935 | 34.072 | SDR* | 1.5466 | 0.6466 |
| Vietnam dong | 0.00006 | 17806 | | | |

*Special Drawing Rights (SDR); from the International Monetary Fund; based on exchange rates for U.S., British and Japanese currencies.
*Source: Wall Street Journal*, July 10, 2009.

about 30 percent price increase, or pass-through, over the same period. If this estimate is accurate, Japanese companies must have somehow absorbed more than 70 percent of the price increase. This cost absorption could result from smaller profit margins and cost reductions as well as effective use of the unfavorable target exchange rate for planning purposes. According to Morgan Stanley Japan Ltd.'s estimate in the 1990s,[25] Toyota could break even at an unheard of 52 yen to the dollar. In other words, as long as the Japanese currency does not appreciate all the way to 52 yen to the dollar, Toyota is expected to earn windfall operating profits.

The emergence of the Internet as a global purchasing tool also brings a whole new aspect to the concept of pass-through, particularly at the retail setting. Now that retailers can sell to the world through one web site, it is increasingly difficult for them to set different prices for each country. One can already see this with software purchased and downloaded over the Net. Consumers in England will not pay £120 for a software

---

[25]Valerie Reitman, "Toyota Names a Chief Likely to Shake Up Global Auto Business," *Wall Street Journal* (August 11, 1995), pp. A1, A5.

program that they know sells for $100 in the United States. Online commerce will limit price flexibility in foreign markets.

This pass-through issue will be elaborated on in Chapter 12.

## BALANCE OF PAYMENTS

◆ ◆ ◆ ◆ ◆ ◆ ◆

The balance of payments of a nation summarizes all the transactions that have taken place between its residents and the residents of other countries over a specified time period, usually a month, quarter, or year. The transactions contain three categories: current account, capital account and official reserves. There is also an extra category for statistical discrepancy. **Exhibit 3-5** shows the balance of payments for the United States 1990–2007.

The balance of payments record is made on the basis of rules of credits (transaction that result in an inflow of money) and debits (i.e., transactions that result in an outflow of money), similar to those in business accounting. Exports, like sales, are outflows of goods, and are entered as credits to merchandise trade. Imports, or inflows of goods, are represented by debits to the same account. These exports and imports are most likely offset by an opposite entry to the capital account, reflecting the receipt of cash or the outflow of cash for payment.

When a German tourist visits the United States and spends money on meals and lodging, it is a credit to the U.S. trade in services balance reflecting the U.S. rendering of a service to a foreign resident. On the other hand, this transaction would represent a debit to the trade in services account of Germany, reflecting the receipt of a service from a U.S. resident (or company) by a resident of Germany. If the foreign resident's payment is made in cash, the credit to trade in services is offset by a debit (inflow) to short-term capital. On the other hand, if a foreign resident purchases land in the United States, paying cash, this is represented on the United States balance of payments as a debit to short-term capital (representing the inflow of payment for the land) and a credit to long-term capital (representing the outflow of ownership of real estate).

**EXHIBIT 3-5**
U.S. BALANCE OF PAYMENTS, 1990–2007

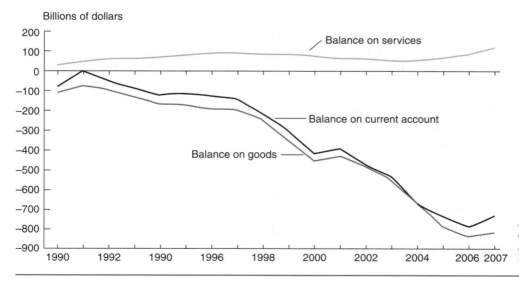

Sources: constructed from *Statistical Abstract of the United States 2009*, Washington, DC: U.S. Census Bureau, 2009.

This is based on the principle of double-entry accounting, so theoretically every debit must be offset by a credit to some other account within the balance of payments statement. In other words, the balance of payments statement must always balance, because total debits must equal total credits. A deficit (debit balance) in one account will then be offset by a surplus (credit balance) in another account. If the statement does not balance, an entry must be made as statistical discrepancy. But in reality, there is no national accountant making accounting entries for every international transaction. In the United States, the Department of Commerce, which prepares the balance of payments statement, must gather information from a variety of sources, including banks and other business entities concerning the inflow and outflow of goods, services, gifts, and capital items.

The **balance of payments on goods** (also know as **trade balance**) shows trade in currently produced goods. Trade balance is the most frequently used indicator of the health of a country's international trade position. The **balance of payments on services** shows trade in currently transacted services. The **balance of payments in current account** (**current account balance**, for short) shows trade in currently produced goods and services, as well as unilateral transfers including private gifts and foreign aid. The goods or merchandise account deals with tangibles such as autos, grain, machinery, or equipment that can be seen and felt, as well as exported and imported. The services account deals with intangibles that are sold or bought internationally. Examples include dividends or interest on foreign investments, royalties on trademarks or patents abroad, food or lodging (travel expenses), and transportation. Unilateral transfers are transactions with no quid pro quo; some of these transfers are made by private individuals and institutions and some by government. These gifts are sometimes for charitable, missionary, or educational purposes, and other times they consist of funds wired home by migrant workers to their families in their country of origin. The largest unilateral transfers are aid, either in money or in the form of goods and services, from developed to developing countries.

Although not shown in Exhibit 3-5, the mirror image of the balance of payments in current account (goods, services, and unilateral transfers), as a result of double entry accounting, is the capital account. The balance of payments in capital account (**capital account**) summarizes financial transactions and is divided into two sections, short- and long-term capital accounts. Long-term capital includes any financial asset maturing in a period exceeding one year, including equities. Subaccounts under long-term capital are direct investment and portfolio investment.

**Direct investments** are those investments in enterprises or properties that are effectively controlled by residents of another country. Whenever 10 percent or more of the voting shares in a U.S. company are held by foreign investors, the company is classified as a U.S. affiliate of a foreign company and therefore a foreign direct investment.[26] Similarly, if U.S. investors hold 10 percent or more of the voting shares of a foreign company, the entity is considered a foreign affiliate of a U.S. company.

**Portfolio investment** includes all long-term investments that do not give the investors effective control over the investment. Such transactions typically involve the purchase of stocks or bonds of foreign investors for investment. These shares are normally bought for investment, not control, purposes.

Short-term capital includes only those items maturing in less than one year, including cash. The official reserves account registers the movement of funds to or from central banks.

A key point to remember here is that the deficit or surplus is calculated based not on the aggregate of all transactions in the balance of payments, but on the net balance for certain selected categories.

There are three particularly important balances to identify on the balance of payments statement of a country, including the balance of the merchandise trade

---

[26]Department of Commerce, *U.S. Direct Investment Abroad* (Washington, D.C.: Bureau of Economic Analysis, 2008).

account, the current account (including merchandise trade, trade in services and unilateral transfers) and the basic balance (the current account and long term capital). Everyone knows about the U.S. deficit in merchandise trade, but what is less commonly known is that the U.S. regularly runs a surplus in trade in services. This surplus offsets a small part of the deficit in the merchandise account (see **Global Perspective 3-1**).

Many observers have commented that since the 1980s, the United States has been able to continue its import binge via the sale of long-term investments, including real estate and ownership in companies. This belief was heightened by the high-profile sale of such U.S. landmarks as the legendary Hollywood studio MGM to Sony of Japan in 2005 and Anheuser-Busch to InBev of Belgium in 2008. These foreign companies invested in U.S. capital assets, paying in cash that was then recycled in payment for merchandise imports by U.S. residents. The criticism was made that the U.S. was selling off capital assets for short-term merchandise imports like a wealthy heir who sells off the family jewels to finance a profligate lifestyle. Meanwhile, others viewed the increase in foreign investment in the United States as proof of the nation's vitality and long-term attractiveness to investors.

## $\mathcal{G}$LOBAL PERSPECTIVE 3-1

### BALANCE OF PAYMENTS AND COMPETITIVENESS OF A NATION

The Information Age characterizes the world we live in today, but some people do not seem to recognize it.

Each time the U.S. trade statistics are reported, we hear the dismal news of a trade deficit of $707 billion in 2004. But when it comes to U.S. balance of payments, many people do not look beyond the "trade" statistics.

When we say trade statistics, we talk about exports and imports of goods. Trade of services is not included. When the United States incurred an $819 billion trade deficit in goods in 2007, its trade deficit was partly—albeit weakly—offset by a $119 billion trade surplus in services. Such services—the hallmark of the Information Age—include telecommunications, education, financial services, and a host of other intangibles.

These and other services did not only have just one good year. Around the world, service companies are expanding rapidly, ringing up sales at a fast pace. Indeed, worldwide, services accounted for about $3 trillion in international trade in 2008.

Why, then, don't we notice this important development? It is primarily because many of us are still measuring our economic performance based on the facts of an earlier era, which meant apples, steel, sneakers and the like—tangible merchandise and nothing else. Many just do not realize a new day has

dawned—one in which advertising exports can mean as much as auto exports.

Take the Department of Commerce, which collects U.S. trade data. The department keeps track of more than 10,000 different kinds of tangible goods. But when it comes to services, the agency collects trade data for only a few service categories. Services excluded from Department of Commerce data, or addressed only partially, include such significant ones as public relations, management consulting, legal services, and many financial and information-related services. While accurate estimates are difficult, it is believed that exports of services would be 70 percent higher than reported in Department of Commerce trade data.

What is wrong with underplaying the importance of services? First, it misleads the public about the nation's true competitiveness. Second, it induces government officials to develop trade policy on mistaken premises. Third, and worst of all, the growth of services could be thwarted because many non-tariff barriers to trade in services—such as discriminatory licensing and certification rules, and bans of the use of internationally known company names—do not get as much policy attention as tariffs on goods and thus could harm U.S. service companies trying to sell various services abroad.

There is also a word of caution. The increased importance of services in the U.S. balance of payments does not necessarily mean that the United States can ignore manufacturing businesses. First, exports of services have been historically too small to offset the staggering deficits in goods. Second, if the United States loses mastery and control of manufacturing, the high-paying and thus important service jobs that are directly linked to manufacturing—such as product designing, engineering, accounting, financing and insurance, and transportation—may also wither away. Manufacturing and those services are tightly linked and may not be separable.

*Sources:* Based on Daniel J. Connors, Jr. and Douglas S. Heller, "The Good Word in Trade is 'Services'," *New York Times*, September 19, 1993, p. B1; Stephen S. Cohen and John Zysman, *Manufacturing Matters: The Myth of the Post-Industrial Economy*, New York: Basic Books, 1987; *World Trade Report 2007*, Geneva: World Trade Organization, 2007; and "U.S. International Trade in Goods and Services: Annual Revision for 2007," *News*, U.S. Census Bureau, Bureau of Economic Analysis, June 10, 2008.

**The Internal and External Adjustments**

According to the theory of international trade and balance of payments, a surplus or deficit in a country's basic balance should be self-correcting to some extent. This self-correction is accomplished through the internal and external market adjustments. The market adjustment mechanisms bring a nation's deficit or surplus within the basic balance back into equilibrium. This is a natural event where the economy of a nation corrects its prior excesses by moving back toward the middle.[27]

The **internal market adjustment** refers to the movement of prices and incomes in a country. The following is a hypothetical example of such an adjustment process in the case of a Current Account surplus country, such as Japan.

1. As Japan continues to export more than it imports resulting in a surplus in the Current Account, its internal money supply grows, the result of receiving payment from foreigners for their purchases of goods, services, and investments originating in Japan. The payments are made to Japanese residents and may be deposited in banks either in Japan or abroad, either in yen or foreign currency. But wherever and however payment is made, it becomes an asset of a Japanese resident.

2. As Japan's money supply increases, domestic residents of Japan spend more, because they have more money available to spend. Japan's money supply is increasing because foreigners are buying Japanese goods in greater quantities than Japanese are buying foreign goods.

3. As local residents in Japan spend more (i.e., have greater demand for products and services), domestic prices rise. In other words, inflation occurs.

4. As domestic prices increase, Japanese residents find that foreign goods are relatively cheaper.

5. Because the Japanese find foreign goods cheaper, they import more goods from abroad. This begins to reduce Japan's current account surplus and bring it back into balance.

The **external market adjustment** concerns exchange rates or a nation's currency and its value with respect to the currencies of other nations. The following is a hypothetical description of the application of the external adjustment to a surplus nation, in this case again, Japan:

Japan exports more than it imports, resulting in a surplus in its current account. So, foreigners must pay Japanese residents for the goods they purchase from Japan. Payment will likely be made in Japanese yen.

1. Because Japanese residents export more than they import, there is more demand for yen by foreigners than demand for dollars by Japanese residents. This excess in relative demand for yen causes it to appreciate in value with respect to other currencies. Remember, it appreciates because foreigners must pay Japanese suppliers for their goods and services.

2. The appreciated yen causes Japanese goods, services, and investments to be more expensive to foreign residents who convert prices quoted in yen to their local currencies.

3. All other things being equal, this should cause foreigners to buy fewer Japanese goods and thus shrink Japan's trade surplus.

However, other factors, such as a country's taste for foreign goods and general habits of consumption, must be taken into account, as well as the quality and reputation of a country's manufactured goods. Many other factors beyond domestic prices and foreign exchange values affect Japan's trade balance with the United States, and these have become a topic of serious discussion between the governments of these two nations.

---

[27]Mordechai E. Kreinin, *International Economics: A Policy Approach*, Mason, OH: Thomson South-Western, 2006, pp. 241–52.

# ECONOMIC AND FINANCIAL TURMOIL AROUND THE WORLD

◆ ◆ ◆ ◆ ◆ ◆ ◆

Since the last few years of the twentieth century we have observed some unprecedented economic and financial crises in some parts of the world that have caused significant slowdowns in the growth of the world economy and international trade and investment. Excessive borrowing by companies, households or governments lie at the root of almost every economic crisis of the past two decades from East Asia to Russia and to South America, and from Japan to the United States. In this section, we highlight the Asian financial crisis of 1997–1998, the South American financial crisis of 2002 that spread out of Argentina to other parts of South America, and most recently the severe global recession triggered by the U.S. subprime mortgage loan crisis, to illustrate the global ripple effect of local and regional economic downturn.

Chronologically speaking, China's devaluation of its currency, Yuan, from 5.7 yuan/$ to 8.7 yuan/$ in 1994, set the stage for an ongoing saga of the Asian financial crisis. The mechanism of how the Asian financial crisis occurred is summarized in **Exhibit 3-6**.

The currency devaluation made China's exports cheaper in Southeast Asia where most currencies were virtually pegged to the U.S. dollar. According to Lawrence Klein, a Nobel Laureate in economics, the Southeast Asian countries' strict tie to the U.S.

**Asian Financial Crisis and its Aftermath**

**EXHIBIT 3-6**
MECHANISM OF THE ASIAN FINANCIAL CRISIS

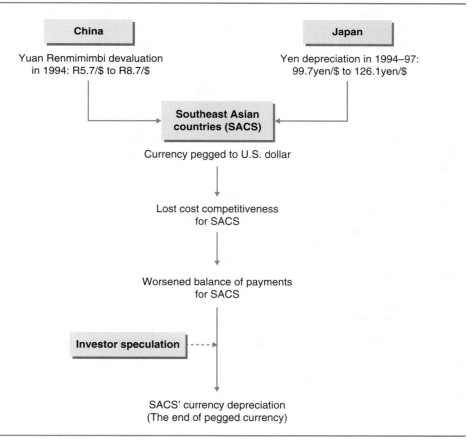

dollar cost them between 10 and 20 percent of export loss spread over three or four years.[28]

Separately, Japan's post-bubble recession also caused its currency to depreciate from 99.7 yen/$ in 1994 to 126.1 yen/$ in 1997, resulting in two pronged problems for Southeast Asian countries. First, recession-stricken Japan reduced imports from its Asian neighbors; second, the depreciated yen helped Japanese companies increase their exports to the rest of Asia. Consequently, Southeast Asian countries' trade deficits with China and Japan increased abruptly in a relatively short period. Southeast Asian countries' trade deficits were paid for by their heavy borrowing from abroad, leaving their financial systems vulnerable and making it impossible to maintain their currency exchange rates vis-à-vis the U.S. dollar. The end result was the sudden currency depreciation by the end of 1997. For example, Thailand lost almost 60 percent of its baht's purchasing power in dollar terms in 1997. Malaysian ringgit lost some 40 percent of its value in the same period. Korean won was similarly hit toward the end of 1997 and depreciated 50 percent against the U.S. dollar in less than two months. The worst case was Indonesia whose rupiah lost a whopping 80 percent of its value in the last quarter of 1997. In a way, it would amount to a U.S. dollar bill becoming worth only 20 cents in three months!

The Asian financial crisis in the latter half of the 1990s had escalated into the biggest threat to global prosperity since the oil crisis of the 1970s. The region's once booming economies were fragile, liquidity problems hurt regional trade, and losses from Asian investments eroded profits for many Japanese companies. Similarly, among Western companies, quite a few U.S. companies that had large investments in Asia reported less than expected earnings. Others feared that the Asian crisis would wash ashore to the seemingly unrelated regions of the world, including the United States and Europe.[29] For example, the unsettling ups and downs of the Dow Jones Industrial Average reflected the precarious nature of U.S. investments in Asia. Economists blamed Asia for nipping the world's economic growth by one percentage point in 1998–1999.[30]

Now the Asian market has recovered from the crisis since the beginning of this century. The acceleration of Asia's economic growth since 2000 can be largely credited to the recovery of the Japanese economy.[31] In 2003, Asia's GDP grew at 3.5 percent, exceeding the average growth rate for the 1990s. Further, Asian developing countries' GDP growth continued to exceed 5 percent. Asia's merchandise trade growth was realized primarily by intra-regional trade, which rose by 20 percent to $950 billion in 2003. Further, China's surging import demand and increased purchase of investment goods, semi-manufactured goods and machinery parts have sustained output and exports in many East Asian economies. Asia's developing economies had sustained robust growth boosted by domestic demand, regional trade, and a steady inflow of investment until 2008.

**The South American Financial Crisis and Its Aftermath**

Starting from the end of 2001, we witnessed the largest debt default in Argentina. Unlike the Asian financial crisis, Argentina's problems took a long time to develop, giving enough signs to investors and analysts.[32] However, the trouble has turned out to be much worse than anyone would have imagined. By April 2002, Argentine currency had lost nearly 40 percent of its value since the government freed it from the dollar in December 2001. Unemployment rate reached about 25 percent and bank accounts

---

[28]"Panel Discussion One: An Overview of the Crisis," *Journal of International Management*, Supplement, 4 (1), 1998, pp. 7S–17S.

[29]"Europeans, Despite Big Stakes Involved, Follow U.S. Lead in Asia Financial Crisis," *Wall Street Journal*, January 16, 1998: A11.

[30]This section builds on Masaaki Kotabe, "The Four Faces of the Asian Financial Crisis: How to Cope with the Southeast Asia Problem, the Japan Problem, the Korea Problem, and the China Problem," *Journal of International Management*, 4 (1), 1998, 1S–6S.

[31]"The Sun Also Rises," *Economist*, October 8, 2005, pp. 3–6.

[32]Martin Crutsinger, "Shock Waves From Argentina Crisis Could Yet Reach U.S. Economy," *AP Newswire* (April 28, 2002).

remained frozen. Several presidents failed to slow down the recession. The economy contracted by 1 percent in 2001, and a whopping 8 percent in 2002.[33] In December 2001, the government stopped payment on much of its $141 billion in foreign debt—the biggest government default in history. Thousands of commercial establishments were closed in a week.

The first reason behind the crisis lies in its own monetary system. For a decade, Argentine government fixed peso at one U.S. dollar, which overvalued the currency and caused a lack of competitiveness when other currencies depreciated. Three months after peso was freed from the dollar, the rate became 3 pesos to the dollar, with a depreciation of 67 percent.[34] The second reason is its unbelievable government debt. Argentina has years of chronic government deficit spending. The debt sent the interest rate up and caused so many businesses to close. As more companies were closed and more people were laid off, the government's tax income have shrunk and increased the debt burden. Finally, as IMF refused to make an advance payment on a previously agreed loan to allow Argentina to make its next debt payment, the economy became paralyzed. The Argentina crisis inevitably hurt its neighbors, such as Brazil, South America's largest economy that conducts nearly one-third of its trade with Argentina. The Mexican peso had weakened 5 percent within two months since the end of March 2002. The Brazilian real had retreated 6.4 percent over the same period, and several other regional currencies had also slid while their counterparts from Asia and Europe were in their 12-month high. After the Argentine crisis, both international bank loans and capital inflows in Latin America declined. International financial flows to Latin America have declined substantially since the crisis in Argentina.[35]

The property boom in the United States since early 1990s and the availability of easy mortgage loans through the Federal Reserve's loose monetary policy helped pump up the property bubble, much like what had happened in Japan a decade earlier. In the process, a huge amount of easy mortgage loans had been offered to the subprime mortgage market, that is, those customers who could otherwise not afford to purchase houses. Easy money and loose regulations allowed banks to securitize the expected cash flows from a pool of underlying assets such as home mortgages and sell those securities on the open market. Not only domestic but also foreign—particularly, European and Japanese—banks and securities companies purchased them. Then an onslaught of defaults in the subprime mortgage market in the United States in recent years has snowballed into a global credit crisis, causing the collapse of the securities market around the world.[36] The current global recession is the worst of its kind since the Great Depression of 1929–1932.

As the credit market has dried up, businesses that rely on consumer credit have suffered dearly. For example, when the credit crisis became evident by the end of 2009, the December sales of cars and light trucks in the United States fell by 36 percent compared with a year ago; in France, car sales were down by 16 percent despite government incentives designed to prop up the market; in Spain, car sales were off by almost 50 percent; and in Japan, by 22 percent.[37] Car sales have since continued to decline. Toyota, now the world's largest and most profitable automaker, reduced domestic production by 40 percent in January 2009 as its exports dropped almost 60 percent from a year earlier.[38] You can see the severity of the current global recession as such a precipitous sales decline is extraordinary by any means.

**The U.S. Subprime Mortgage Loan Crisis and the Subsequent Global Financial Crisis**

---

[33]Terry L. McCoy, "Argentine Meltdown Threatens to Derail Latin Reforms," *The Orlando Sentinel*, (April 22, 2002), p. A15.

[34]Ian Campbell, "As IMF Fiddles, Argentina Burns," *United Press International* (March 28, 2002).

[35]Patricia Alvarez-Plata and Mechthild Schrooten, "Latin America after the Argentine Crisis: Diminishing Financial Market Integration," *Economic Bulletin*, 40, December 2003, pp. 431–36.

[36]"Ruptured Credit," *Economist*, May 15, 2008.

[37]"The Big Chill," *Economist*, January 15, 2009.

[38]"Toyota, Nissan Japan Output Drop As Exports Sink," NikkeiInteractive.net, http://www.nni.nikkei.co.jp/, February 25, 2009.

## Financial Crises in Perspective

There is some commonality across the recent financial problems facing Asian and South American countries and in how they could affect businesses and consumers in the region. The Asian financial crisis has to be placed in a proper perspective that the "economic miracles" of the East and Southeast Asian countries have already shifted the pendulum of international trade from cross-Atlantic to cross-Pacific in the last decade. Companies from the United States and Japan, in particular, have been helping shape the nature of the cross-Pacific bilateral and multilateral trade and investment. Today, as a result, North America's trade with these five Asian countries alone exceeds its trade with the European Community by upwards of 20 percent. The trend is irreversible. Although the recent stock market turmoil and the subsequent depreciation of the foreign exchange rates of many Asian countries may have set back their economic progress temporarily, the fundamental economic forces are likely to remain intact.

Now we are in the midst of a severe global recession. Again and again, the unbridled asset appreciation, whether it is stock prices or property value, and the availability of easy credit appear to lead to an eventual collapse of a financial system. The United States is no exception. As we discussed in Chapter 2, the fundamental source of "easy" money in the United States is the persistent current-account deficits in the United States, matched by surpluses in emerging markets, notably China. In other words, the United States has been living beyond its economic means by borrowing money from foreign creditors. It is a stark reminder to the rest of the world that no country could sustain its livelihood for good on borrowed money.[39]

In order for countries to sustain their strong economic performance, the importance of several necessary conditions needs to be stressed. Those include: strong financial institutions—commercial and investment banks, stock exchanges; transparency in the way the institutions do business; financial reporting systems that are consistent with free markets where capital and good flow competitively; and supply of a managerial pool to shepherd these economies through very difficult transitional periods. While the Asian countries remain strong and attractive with respect to their "economic" fundamentals, the recent events have demonstrated that institutional environment of the countries needs reforms (See **Global Perspective 3-2** for a new lurking problem in emerging economies).

## Responses to the Regional Financial Crises

For illustrative purposes, let us use the Asian financial crisis of 1997–1998 and explain how domestic and foreign companies coped with the sudden recessionary environment brought about by the crisis. Such implications apply to any regional and global financial crisis.

Reeling from the initial shock of the financial crisis, marketing executives have begun to cope with the realities of marketing their products in a completely changed world–from the world that was once believed to keep growing with ever increasing prosperity to a world that has decimated the burgeoning middle class by snapping more than 50 percent of the consumers' spending power. Marketers are facing two dire consequences of the crisis: namely, declining markets and increased competition from existing competitors. Their major task is to figure out how to keep current customers and gain new ones and maintain profitability in the long run.

Although Asia's current recession caused by its financial crisis is a serious one, other countries or regions have also experienced economic slumps over the years. Recession is usually defined as an economic situation in which the country's GDP has shrunk for two consecutive quarters. Based on this definition, the United States has experienced 29 recessions since 1894, approximately once every four to five years. First, we examine how consumers react to an economic slump. Second, we show different ways in which competing companies cope with the recession and the changed consumer needs.

---

[39] "When a Flow becomes a Flood," *Economist*, January 22, 2009.

## $\mathcal{G}$LOBAL PERSPECTIVE 3-2

### RISING INFLATION IN EMERGING ECONOMIES

Inflation has risen far more over the past few years. Taken as a whole, the average world inflation rate had grown to 5.5 percent in 2008, the highest since 1999. With the relatively low inflation rates of 3.9 percent in the United States and 3.3 percent in the euro area, this high world average resulted from the soaring inflation in emerging economies.

As of May 2008, China's official rate of consumer-price inflation had risen from 3 percent a year ago to 8.5 percent, a 12-year high. Russia's inflation rate had increased from 8 percent to over 14 percent. Indonesian inflation was already 9 percent and likely to reach 12 percent soon as the government raised the price of subsidized fuel by 25–30 percent. India's wholesale price inflation rate was also at a four-year high of 7.8 percent. In the Middle East, most Gulf oil producers were also witnessing double-digit inflation rates.

Although inflation in Latin America remained relatively low, Brazil's rate still rose to 5 percent in 2008 from less than 3 percent in early 2007. Chile's had changed from 2.5 percent to 8.3 percent. In Argentina where the officially published inflation rate was recorded as 8.9 percent, economists estimated that its true figure was 23 percent, up from 14.3 percent in

*Sources: Economist*, May 24, 2008, p.17; and "An Old Enemy Rears its Head," *Economist*, May 24, 2008, pp. 91–93.

2007. When it comes to Venezuela, where the national money went through a currency change of taking three zeros to the new Bolivar Fuerte on January 1, 2008, the inflation rate may even have reached as high as 29.3 percent, making this country the most alarming one.

This rising inflation in emerging economies should be mainly ascribed to the surge in the prices of food and oil. For example, in China food prices had risen by 22 percent in 2007, whereas non-food prices had gone up by only 1.8 percent. But a real dangerous reason, although only partly explaining the recent jump in prices, is the loose monetary conditions in emerging economies. The initial shock to food prices may have come from the supply side, but the strength of income and money growth helps to validate higher prices.

Unfortunately, many policymakers in emerging economies view the rise in inflation as a short-term supply shock and consequently see little need to raise interest rates. In order to keep prices from rising further, they are instead using price controls and subsidies. Money supplies are growing almost three times as fast as in the developed world. Many central banks are still not fully independent. As inflationary expectations are not properly contained, the risk of a wage-price spiral could trigger another huge inflation as we had experienced in the 1970s. And this is what the globe is really worried about.

***Consumer Response to the Recession.*** As we all know from our own personal experiences, we tend to become more selective in choosing products and stay away from impulse buying in a recessionary period. In other words, consumers begin to spend their money more wisely and emphasize value for the money. We may consume less of some products but we may even consume more of certain other products. General changes in the consumption pattern in an economic downturn are summarized in **Exhibit 3-7**.

Although a recession alters the mood of a country, it does not necessarily affect consumption of all products in the same way. If you now travel to any major city in Asia, such as Kuala Lumpur in Malaysia, you will hardly notice any change in shopping behavior at first glance. Finding a parking spot at One Utama, a large shopping mall on the outskirts of Kuala Lumpur, is as difficult now as it was a year ago. Young Malaysian couples shop for groceries and kitchenware, while moviegoers flock to a cinema multiplex showing Columbia Pictures' *Spider-Man*. The coffee houses such as Starbucks are successful as ever, teeming with trendy customers, and high-tech aficionados are trying out the latest iPhones. In sharp contrast, if you visit the huge upscale Meladas Casa Mobili store, you will see few middle-class families buying its exquisite Italian furniture there. Indeed, the most susceptible to a recessionary downturn usually are big ticket items, such as cars, home furnishings, large appliances, and travel. Those relatively unaffected are alcohol, tobacco, small appliances, packaged goods, and computer items.[40]

---

[40]James Chadwick, "Communicating through Tough Times in Asia," *Economic Bulletin*, August 1998, pp. 25–29.

**EXHIBIT 3-7**
CHANGES IN THE CONSUMPTION PATTERN DURING A RECESSION

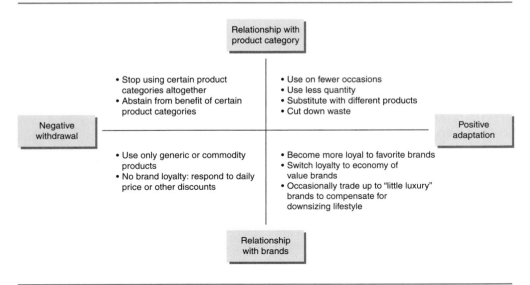

*Source:* Adapted from James Chadwick, "Communicating through Tough Times," *Economic Bulletin*, August 1998, p. 27.

***Corporate Response to the Recession.*** Different companies have reacted differently to the recession, based on their different corporate objectives. In general, there are short-term and long-term orientations in crisis management. Short-term orientation dictates that the corporate goal is to maximize year-to-year profit (or minimize loss), whereas long-term orientation tolerates some short-term loss for the benefit of future gains. Although any definitive value judgment should not be made of the two different orientations, short-term orientation tends to serve stockholders' speculative needs, while long-term orientation tends to cater to customer needs. A short-term oriented solution is to pull out of the market, at least temporarily as long as the markets remain in a recession. Long-term oriented solutions are to modify marketing strategies in various ways to address the consumer needs completely changed during the recession.

- **Pull-out.** Pulling out of the market is an easy way out, at least, financially in the short run. Immediately after Indonesia's rupiah depreciated by almost 80 percent in a couple of months, J.C. Penney and Wal-Mart had no second thought but simply left the Indonesian market. Similarly, Daihatsu, a small Japanese automobile manufacturer, decided to pull out of Thailand. While pull-out strategy may be the least painful option in the short run, it could cause some irreparable consequences in the long run, and particularly so in many Asian countries where long-term, trustworthy, and loyal relationships are a vital part of doing business and short-term financial sacrifices are revered as an honorable act. A better strategy would be to cut the planned production volume and maintain corporate presence on the market as General Motors did in Thailand.[41]

- **Emphasize a product's value.** Weary consumers become wiser consumers. In a prosperous time, middle-class consumers may have resorted to some impulse buying and conspicuous consumption. But during the current recession, they want to maintain their current lifestyle and standard of living. However, they want to feel vindicated that the product or service they purchase is worth the money they pay for. Marketers will have to develop a promotion that emphasizes the value contained in the product. For example, Procter&Gamble's new Pantene shampoo line, which

---

[41] "Asia's Sinking Middle Class," *Far Eastern Economic Review*, April 9, 1998, p. 12.

sells for $2.20 to $7.30, is one of the most expensive shampoos available in Hong Kong. Its advertising campaign promotes Pantene's extra moisturizers and other high-tech ingredients to tell clearly the benefits of Pantene over other less expensive brands.[42]

Another way to add value is to enhance the perceived quality image of a product. For example, in Thailand, an advertising campaign for a relatively cheap Clan MacGregor scotch whiskey made locally under license emphasizes the product value: "Even if you have to buy something cheap, you are getting something of real value." This is stated in reference to three times more expensive imported Johnnie Walker Black Label whiskey. This ad helps enhance Clan MacGregor's quality image in the minds of consumers.[43]

- **Change the product mix.** If a company has a wide array of product lines, it can shift the product mix by pushing relatively inexpensive product lines while de-emphasizing expensive lines. This strategy is suited to ride over a slump by generating sufficient cash flow not only to cover the fixed costs of business operations but also to maintain the corporate presence on the market. Particularly in Asia, the company's dedication to the market as perceived by local customers will win many favorable points in the long run. For example, Burberry's, a British fashion retailer, has replaced its expensive jackets in window displays with relatively inexpensive T-shirts, stressing that everyone still afford some luxury even in hard times.[44]

- **Repackage the goods.** As stated earlier, middle-class consumers want to maintain their lifestyle and quality of life as much as possible. It means that they will keep buying what they have been buying but consume less. Companies like Unilever are repackaging their products to suit consumers' declining purchasing power. Unilever has reduced the size of its Magnum-brand ice-cream packs and made it cheaper, offers giveaways on its Lux soaps (buy six, get one free), and marketing its detergents in smaller and cheaper refillable packs.[45]

- **Maintain stricter inventory.** Japanese companies have long taught us that their just-in-time inventory management practices not only reduce unnecessary inventory but also improve their product assortment by selling only what customers want at the moment. Even if companies are not practicing just-in-time inventory management, it would make a lot of sense to keep inventory low. Essentially, inventory is a tied-up capital of unsold merchandise that can be costly to the company. For example, the Kuala Lumpur store of Swedish furniture retailer, Ikea, has not restocked certain slow-selling items.[46]

- **Look outside the region for expansion opportunities.** Asia's recession is still a regional problem although there is some risk that it will bring down the rest of the world with it to cause a global economic crisis. Nevertheless, market opportunities can be found outside the recession-stricken part of Asia. This strategy is not only a part of geographical diversification to spread out the market risk but also an effective way to take advantage of cheaper Asian currencies which translate to lower prices in other foreign countries. For instance, Esprit, the Hong Kong based retailer, is now marketing very aggressively in Europe. Despite the Asian slump, its revenues increased 52 percent during fiscal 1998 with most of the gain coming from the European market.[47] Hewlett-Packard and Dell Computer, among others, which depend heavily on less-expensive components now made in Asia, have begun to trim the prices of their products.[48]

---

[42]"Multinationals Press On in Asia despite Perils of Unstable Economies," *Asian Wall Street Journal*, September 4–5, 1998, p. 12.

[43]"Asia's Sinking Middle Class," p. 12.

[44]"Asia's Sinking Middle Class," p. 13.

[45]"Asia's Sinking Middle Class," p. 12.

[46]"Asia's Sinking Middle Class," p. 13.

[47]"With Asia in collapse, Esprit pushes aggressively into Europe," *Asian Wall Street Journal*, January 4, 1999, p. 2.

[48]"Asia Crisis May Benefit U.S. Companies," *New York Times on the Web*, January 19, 1998, at www.nytimes.com.

- **Increase advertising in the region.** It sounds somewhat antithetical to the strategy stated above. However, there is also a strong incentive to introduce new products now. It is a buyer's market for advertising space. Television stations are maintaining advertising rates but giving bonus airtime, effectively cutting advertising costs. As a result, Unilever can better afford to reach the large middle-class market segment in Hong Kong that its SunSilk shampoo targets. American Express is launching the Platinum card for the first time in Malaysia, and it is targeted at the highest-income consumers whose wealth has been cushioned by investment overseas.[49]

    Historical evidence also suggests that it is usually a mistake to cut advertising budgets during a recession.[50] For example, Oxy, a South Korean household products manufacturer, like many other hard-hit companies, slashed its advertising budget by a third, while its competitors halted their advertising completely. Before the slump, Oxy had commanded an 81 percent of the closet dehumidifier market with its Thirsty Hippo model. Now instead of losing sales, Oxy boosted its market share to 94 percent at the expense of its rivals.[51]

- **Increase local procurement.** Many foreign companies operating in Asian countries tend to procure certain crucial components and equipment from their parent companies. Now that Asian currencies depreciated precipitously, those foreign companies are faced with those imported components and equipment whose prices have gone up enormously in local currencies. Companies with localized procurement were not affected easily by fluctuating exchange rates. As a result, many companies scurried to speed steps toward making their operations in Asian countries more local. Japanese companies seemed to be one step ahead of U.S. and European competitors in this localization strategy. Since the yen's sharp appreciation in the mid-1980s, Japanese manufacturers have moved to build an international production system less vulnerable to currency fluctuations by investing in local procurement.[52]

---

◆ ◆ ◆ ◆ ◆ ◆ ◆ ◆ ◆   ## MARKETING IN THE EURO AREA

**Historical Background**

Initially, the European Union (formerly, European Economic Community) consisted of 6 countries, including Belgium, Germany, France, Italy, Luxembourg, and the Netherlands. Denmark, Ireland, and the United Kingdom joined in 1973; Greece in 1981; Spain and Portugal in 1986; Austria, Finland, and Sweden in 1995. The European Union consisted of fifteen developed European countries until 2004, when ten more countries joined the European Union—Cyprus, the Czech Republic, Estonia, Hungary, Latvia, Lithuania, Malta, Poland, Slovakia, and Slovenia. In 2007, two more countries, Bulgaria and Romania, became new members of the European Union (EU), expanding the total number of EU member countries to twenty-seven. These twelve Central and Eastern European countries are, in general, less developed than the previous fifteen countries. Hence, due to the great differences in per capita income and historic national animosities, the European Union faces difficulties in devising and enforcing common policies.

On January 1, 1999, eleven countries (Austria, Belgium, Finland, France, Germany, Ireland, Italy, Luxembourg, Portugal, Spain, and the Netherlands) embarked on a venture that created the world's second largest economic zone (officially, the Euro Area and more commonly, the Eurozone)—after the United States. Later five countries (Cyprus, Greece, Malta, Slovakia, and Slovenia)[53] joined the Eurozone with a total

---

[49]"Multinationals Press On in Asia despite Perils of Unstable Economies," p. 12.

[50]James Chadwick, "Communicating through Tough Times in Asia," pp. 26–28.

[51]Karene Witcher, "Marketing Strategies Help Asian Firms Beat a Downturn," *Asian Wall Street Journal*, December 7, 1998, p. 9.

[52]"Manufacturers Reshape Asian Strategies," *Nikkei Weekly*, January 12, 1998, pp. 1, 5.

[53]Eurozone membership years are as follows: Greece in 2001, Slovenia in 2007, Cyprus and Malta in 2008, and Slovakia in 2009.

**EXHIBIT 3-8**
16 EUROZONE COUNTRIES (AS OF JANUARY 1, 2009)

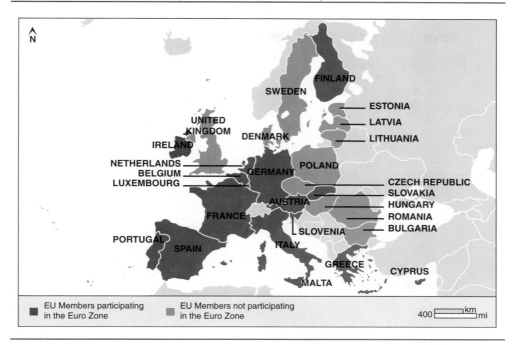

membership of sixteen countries as of January 1, 2009 (See **Exhibit 3-8**). The seeds for the euro had been laid almost exactly three decades ago. In 1969, Pierre Werner, a former prime minister of Luxembourg, was asked to chair a think tank on how European monetary union (EMU) could be achieved by 1980. The Werner report published in October 1970 outlined a three-phase plan that was very similar to the blueprint ultimately adopted in the Maastricht Treaty, signed on February 7, 1992. Just like the Maastricht treaty, the plan envisioned the replacement of local currencies by a single currency. However, EMU was put on hold following the monetary chaos created by the first oil crisis of 1973. The next step on the path to monetary union was the creation of the European monetary system (EMS) in the late 1970s. Except for the United Kingdom, all member states of the European Union joined the Exchange Rate Mechanism (ERM). The ERM determined bilateral currency exchange rates. Currencies of the then nine member states could still fluctuate but movements were limited to a margin of 2.25 percent. The EMS also led to the European currency unit (ecu)—in some sense the predecessor of the euro. Note that this newly bred currency never became a physical currency.

The foundations for monetary union were laid at the Madrid summit in 1989 when the EU member states undertook steps that would lead to free movement of capital. The Maastricht treaty signed shortly after spelled out the guidelines toward EMU. Monetary union was to be capped by the launch of a single currency by 1999. This treaty also set norms in terms of government deficits, government debt and inflation rate that applicants had to meet in order to qualify for EMU-membership. As stated earlier, there are now sixteeen member countries in the Eurozone. Monetary policy for this group of countries is run by the European Central Bank headquartered in Frankfurt, Germany. Three of the developed EU member states, namely the United Kingdom (not surprisingly), Sweden, and Denmark, decided to opt out and sit on the fence. The new EU members may choose to adopt the euro in the future when they meet the EU's fiscal and monetary standards and the member states agreement. The Eurozone economies combined represent about a third of world's gross domestic product and 20 percent of

## EXHIBIT 3-9
### THE EURO-BANK NOTES AND COINS

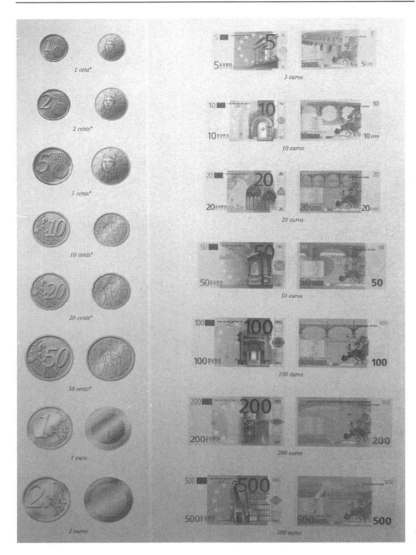

*Source:* Courtesy of Forestier
Yves/Corbis Sygma

overall international trade, with a population of roughly 320 million people. Each of these countries has committed itself to adopt a single currency, the euro, designated by the € symbol. The euro bank notes and coins are shown in **Exhibit 3-9**.

On January 1, 2002, the euro notes and coins (see **Exhibit 3-10** for some spelling rules) began to replace the German mark, the Dutch guilder and scores of other currencies. By July 1, 2002, the local currencies ceased to exist. Those of you who traversed Europe before 2002 may remember the financial strains of exchanging one European currency for another one. Now this hassle became a thing of the past. The creation of the euro has been described as "the most far-reaching development in Europe since the fall of the Berlin Wall."[54] According to the Economic and Monetary Union (EMU), it has already helped create a new culture of economic stability in Europe, to weather the recent slowdown in the world economy, and to avoid the kind of damaging intra-European exchange rate tension. With the euro in place, the citizens of euro area countries are now looking forward to the benefits of increased price

---

[54]"The Long and Arduous Ascent of Euro-Man," *Financial Times*, December 15, 1998, p. 4.

**EXHIBIT 3-10**

THE EURO–OFFICIAL SPELLING RULES

One indication of the confusion surrounding the euro is the spelling of the word "euro." Here are the "official" rules:

- **Question 1:** Upper-case or lower-case?
  **Answer:** lower-case. In English but also in almost all other official EU languages, the spelling should always be lower-case, that is, euro and not Euro. One notable exception is Denmark—one of the four euro-out countries—where it is spelled Euro.

- **Question 2:** Plural: euros or euro?
  **Answer:** euro. This rule sounds puzzling but that is the official plural form in English (and also in Dutch and Italian, for example). Some of the Community languages (e.g., French, Spanish) add an "s."

*Source:* The European Union's Server at http://www.europa.eu.int

transparency, more intense competition in the market place and greater financial integration in Europe.[55] Although some of the benefits of the euro to firms and consumers are clear, many policy questions are still left unanswered.

Now, in order to protect all the member states, EU has made agreements to maintain the economic stability within the Eurozone and avoid any financial crisis. For example, under the Europe's Stability and Growth pact, the EU's executive body would recommend that public warnings be issued to any country that fell foul of European deficit control agreements. Some countries such as France complains that there was too much stress on budget stability and not enough on growth, thus seeking to loosen the constraints imposed on national budgets.[56]

## Ramifications of the Euro for Marketers

Will the euro be the final stage leading to a "United States of Europe"? What opportunities does the euro create for firms operating in the Eurozone? What are the possible threats? Answers to these and many other euro-related questions are murky at best (See **Global Perspective 3-3**).

What is clear is that the switch to the euro has a wide-ranging impact on companies doing business in the Eurozone. There have been gains but also plenty of pain. Massive investments in computer infrastructure and logistical expenses have been needed to put in place the changeover. For example, Allianz, the German insurance group, spent $124 million in euro-related data processing and devoted the equivalent of 342 years' worth of extra manpower into its euro-changeover enterprise. DaimlerChrysler pumped $120 million in its euro-conversion projects.[57] A consensus estimate was that switching to the euro would have cost companies around $65 billion.[58] On top of these upfront investments, there was also the cost of lost revenues from price harmonization within the Eurozone. Apart from these immediate bottom-line effects, EMU also has a strategic impact on companies' operations. For marketers, the key challenges include:

- **Price Transparency.** Before the introduction of the euro, drug prices varied as much as 250 percent within Europe, and German cars in Italy cost up to 30 percent less than in their home market.[59] Conventional wisdom says that prices will slide down to the same level throughout the Eurozone. The reason for that is that the single currency makes markets more transparent for consumers and corporate purchase departments. Now that retailers in different Eurozone member states display their prices in euro, price differentials have become clear to the consumer. Customers can then easily compare prices of goods across countries.[60] Savvy shoppers will bargain-hunt

---

[55]"Three and a Half Years on the Benefits of the Single Currency are Evident," The European Commission, Brussels, June 19, 2002.

[56]"France Challenges EU Deficit Pact," *CNN News*, http://www.cnn.com/, June 18, 2002.

[57]"The Euro. Are You Ready?" *Business Week*, December 14, 1998, p. 35.

[58]"The Euro. Are You Ready?" p. 35.

[59]"When the Walls Come Down," *Economist*, July 5, 1997, p. 69.

[60]John Paul Quinn, "The Euro: See-Through Pricing Arrives," *Electrical Wholesaling*, April 2002, pp. 22–24.

## 𝒢LOBAL PERSPECTIVE 3-3

### THE EURO PROBLEM

In 2005, many countries in European Union were grumbling about the euro, complaining that euro had weakened the financial advantages that firms previously had in stable economies. The euro area's three largest economies, France, Germany, and Italy were struggling with how to stimulate economic growth. Germany, for example, was battling with unfriendly growth rates and double-digit unemployment; Italy entered its second recession in two years in the first quarter of 2005; France voiced their complains with the rejection of the European constitution. According to a government minister in Italy, the euro should be blamed for Italy's poor economic performance and he even advocated reintroducing the lira.

Three years later, new economic figures showed that the first quarter in 2008 was surprisingly strong for the Eurozone. The GDP in the Eurozone rose at an annual rate of 2.8 percent, far stronger than in either the United States or Britain. Solidity in the north made up for fragility in the south. Spain's growth was only 1.2 percent, making this its weakest quarter for over a decade. But Germany's economy grew by 6 percent, as construction firms took advantage of warm weather. France managed a solid 2.4 percent. Yet this could be a high-water mark for the Eurozone economy. A bellwether survey of German firms by Ifo in Munich, showed confidence dropping in April 2008 to its lowest in more than two years. French business confidence, which had briefly improved, wilted as well; and Italian firms have sunk further into gloom. The monthly survey of euro-area purchasing managers showed manufacturing industry in April 2008 growing at its slowest pace since August 2005.

*Sources:* "Three and a Half Years on the Benefits of the Single Currency are Evident," The European Commission, Brussels, June 19, 2002; "Can This Union Be Saved?" *Economist*, Global Agenda, June 3, 2005; "Too Good to Last," *Economist*, May 17, 2008, pp. 63–64.

So what's wrong with the euro, which was once believed to create "the most far-reaching development in Europe since the fall of the Berlin wall"? Can the united currency be unified across the EU? Ideally, currency zones should be solid and homogenous enough to exhibit little regional variation in business cycles. One potential problem for the one-size-fits-all monetary policy would be make some countries in the region lingering in recession, while others experience rapid growth. This is exactly what happened in the EU region with a few countries, such as Ireland growing so fast while its large economies, like Germany and Italy, stagnating.

In Europe, the lack of adjustment mechanism from the European Central Bank to mitigate imbalances across different regions pushes the EU into a situation of survival, instead of creating a new culture of economic stability in Europe. Wide differences in social insurance and retirement programs across the region, as well as the language and cultural barriers, do not seem to easily drive convergence of the labor market. Furthermore, policy makers have recently unsuccessful to force fiscal policies into rough alignment and strong public resistance has made government unwilling, or unable, to implement some structural reforms.

When growth in the euro area is weak and business confidence is declining, what are the disadvantages of the euro to be in a weak position for its member countries? How would less productive economies cope with competition in the euro area when devaluation was no longer an option? Would a single interest rate for different economies cause problems? And finally, unlike the United States, which has central controls on national budget, how could Europe survive with a single currency without effective controls on national budgets?

---

cross-border or search the Internet for the best deal. Significant price gaps will also open up arbitrage opportunities leading to parallel imports from low-priced to high-priced markets. Ultimately, manufacturers are forced to make their prices more uniform. While the logic of this argument sounds strong, there is some skepticism about whether the greater transparency achieved via the euro will really push prices downwards. For one thing, one could argue that anyone capable of browsing the Internet or handling a pocket calculator already enjoys the benefits of full price transparency. Hence, whether a single currency will enlighten shoppers a great deal is debatable. For many goods and services, cross-border transaction costs (e.g., shipping bulky goods), cost differentials (e.g., labor, energy), standard differences (e.g., televisions in France) and different tax regimes will still justify significant price gaps. Shrewd companies can also find ways to "localize" their products by offering different features or product configurations. One important point to remember is that transparency is two-way. For many firms, not only will the cost of their end product become more comparable but also the cost of supplies sourced from within the Eurozone.[61] In fact, in a 1997 survey of 2,100 companies within the European

---

[61]"US Sop Giants' Million-$ Chances to Score," *Financial Times*, December 16, 1998, p. 4.

Union, 65 percent of the respondents viewed "greater price transparency" as one of the key areas of cost saving (ranked second behind "reduction of exchange risks or costs").[62] Pricing implications of the euro will be discussed further in Chapter 12.

- **Intensified Competitive Pressure.** Many analysts predict that competitive pressure will intensify in scores of industries following the launch of the euro. Pressure to lower prices has increased. Most likely, the single currency spurs the pace of cross-border competition. But then again, intensified competition should be seen as the outcome of an ongoing process of which the euro is one single step. The euro plays a role but it is surely not the sole driver that accelerates rivalry within the European Union. To prepare their defenses, several companies have taken measures to lower their costs. This desire to cut costs has also spurred a wave of mergers and acquisitions to build up economies of scale. The Dutch supermarket chain Ahold, for example, is scouting opportunities in Britain, France, Germany, and Italy. By building up muscle, Ahold will be able to negotiate better prices with its suppliers.

- **Streamlined Supply Chains.** Another consequence of the euro is that companies will attempt to further streamline their supply channels. When prices are quoted in euro, singling out the most efficient supplier becomes far easier. Cutting back the number of suppliers is one trend. Numerous firms also plan to build up partnerships with their suppliers. Xerox, for instance, is cutting its supplier base by a factor of 10.[63]

- **New Opportunities for Small and Medium-Sized Companies.** The euro is most likely also a boon for small and medium-sized enterprises (SMEs). So far, many SMEs have limited their operations to their home markets. One motivation for being provincial has often been the huge costs and hassle of dealing with currency fluctuations. According to one study, currency volatility has deterred almost a third of German SMEs from doing business abroad.[64]

- **Adaptation of Internal Organizational Structures.** The euro also provides multinational companies (MNCs) an incentive to rethink their organizational structure. In the past, firms maintained operations in each country to match supply and demand within each country often at the expense of scale economies. Given that currency volatility, one of the factors behind such setups, significantly lessens with the introduction of the euro, many MNCs doing business on the continent are trimming their internal operations.[65] For instance, Michelin, the French tire maker, closed down 90 percent of its 200 European distribution sites. The pharmaceutical concern Novartis streamlined its European production and eliminated overlapping operations.[66] In the long run, firms like Michelin and Novartis will enjoy tremendous benefits of economies of scale. Once again, the euro should be viewed here as a catalyst stimulating a trend that has been ongoing for a number of years rather than a trigger.

- **EU Regulations Crossing National Boundaries.** As the EU matures and the member governments expand its authority, Europeans have found that the EU has increasingly become a force for social regulation that crosses ethnic and national boundaries. Its officials are regulating what people can eat, how they can travel, even how they incinerate their trash. Many cases have been filed for national violations of EU farming, fishing, educational, fiscal, consumer, transportation, taxation, and environmental policies. Countries stand accused of failing to enact laws that conform to EU policies, or of failing to enforce such laws.[67] Companies have been struggling through EU's complex regulatory process. As a result, various industry associations are now trying to clarify exactly where EU-wide rules end and member state laws begin. For

[62] www.euro.fee.be/Newsletter

[63] "Business Performance Will Need Sharper Edge," *Financial Times*, November 5, 1998, p. VIII; and John K. Ryans, "Global Marketing in the New Millennium," *Marketing Management*, 8 (Winter 1999), pp. 44–47.

[64] "When the Walls Come Down," *Economist*, July 5, 1997, p. 70.

[65] "Faster Forward," *Economist*, November 28, 1998, p. 84.

[66] "The euro," *Business Week*, April 27, 1998, p. 38.

[67] Jeffrey Smith, "EU Rules Leave a Bad Taste in Italians' Mouths," *Washington Post*, August 7, 2000, p. A01.

example, a workshop organized by international food and nutrition policy consultancy, European Advisory Services (EAS), in February 2008, aimed to guide companies toward developing multi-country strategies and successfully introducing food supplements and functional ingredients into the European market.[68]

---

[68]"EAS Clarifies EU and National Boundaries for Companies Launching Food Supplements," WNII, whatsnewiningredients.com, February 14, 2008.

[69]Masaaki Kotabe and Ricardo Leal, *Market Revolution in Latin America: Beyond Mexico*, New York: Elsevier Science, 2001.

---

# SUMMARY ❖ ❖ ❖ ❖ ❖ ❖ ❖ ❖ ❖ ❖ ❖ ❖ ❖ ❖ ❖ ❖ ❖ ❖ ❖ ❖ ❖ ❖ ❖ ❖ ❖ ❖

The international financial environment is constantly changing as a result of income growth, balance of payments position, inflation, exchange rate fluctuations, and unpredictable political events in various countries. The International Monetary Fund and World Bank also assist in the economic development of many countries, particularly those of developing countries, and promote stable economic growth in many parts of the world. In most cases, the change in a county's balance of payments position is an immediate precursor to its currency rate fluctuation and subsequent instability in the international financial market.

Thanks to the huge domestic economy and the international transaction currency role of the U.S. dollar, many U.S. companies have been shielded from the changes in the international financial market during much of the postwar era. However, as the U.S. economy depends increasingly on international trade and investment for its livelihood, few companies can ignore the changes.

Having been more dependent on foreign business, many European and Japanese companies have honed their international financial expertise as a matter of survival, particularly since the early 1970s. Accordingly, European countries and Japan have been better able to cope with foreign exchange rate fluctuations than the United States.

International marketers should be aware of the immediate consequences of exchange rate fluctuations on pricing. As increased cost pressure is imminent in an era of global competition, cost competitiveness has become an extremely important strategic issue to many companies. Astute companies have even employed an adverse target exchange rate for cost accounting and pricing purposes. Although accurate prediction is not possible, international marketers should be able to "guesstimate" the direction of exchange rate movements in major currencies. Some tools are available.

The Asian and South American financial crises, and the recent unprecedented global recession triggered by the U.S. subprime mortgage loan crisis as well as the introduction of the euro in the European Union are highlighted. We do not mean to imply that other issues, such as the collapse of the Russian economy, the recession in the United States and the EU, and global warming, are not equally important and do not have many business implications. We are sure that you are convinced of the importance of keeping constantly abreast of events around you to understand and cope with the ever-changing nature of international business.

We expect that companies from various Asian countries will become ever-leaner and more astute competitors in many different ways. South America is also expected to recover.[69] U.S. and other foreign companies doing business in Asia and South America should not pull out of the Asian markets simply because it is very difficult to do business there. Doing so will likely damage corporate reputation and customer trust. U.S. and other foreign companies should have longer-term orientation in dealing with Asian and Latin American consumers and competitors by developing strategies that emphasize value and reducing operational costs thereby reducing susceptibility to occasional financial upheavals.

On the other hand, the European Union (EU) is going through a different kind of economic and political metamorphosis. The EU's new common currency, the euro, has begun to change the way companies do business in Europe. Price comparison across European countries has become easier than ever before. The ease of doing business across countries will permit small and medium-sized companies to go "international" in the region. Competitive pressure is bound to increase. European companies can also enjoy broader economies of scale and scope, making themselves more competitive in and outside the EU. Again, U.S. and other foreign companies should not take for granted the changing face of the EU market and competition originating from it.

# KEY TERMS ❖ ❖ ❖ ❖ ❖ ❖ ❖ ❖ ❖ ❖ ❖ ❖ ❖ ❖ ❖ ❖ ❖ ❖ ❖ ❖ ❖ ❖ ❖ ❖

| | | | |
|---|---|---|---|
| Balance of Payments | Euro Area (Eurozone) | International Monetary Fund (IMF) | Special Drawing Rights (SDRs) |
| Bretton Woods Conference | Exchange rate pass-through | Managed float | Spot market |
| Currency bloc | External market adjustment | Operational Hedging | Target exchange rate |
| Currency hedging | Fixed exchange rate | Portfolio investment | Trade balance |
| Current account balance | Forward market | Purchasing power parity (PPP) | World Bank |
| Direct investment | Free float | | |
| Euro | Internal market adjustment | | |

# REVIEW QUESTIONS ◆ ◆ ◆ ◆ ◆ ◆ ◆ ◆ ◆ ◆ ◆ ◆ ◆ ◆ ◆ ◆ ◆ ◆ ◆ ◆ ◆

How did the U.S. dollar become the international transaction currency in the post–World War II era?

1. Which international currency or currencies are likely to assume increasingly a role as the international transaction currency in international trade? Why?

2. Why is a fixed exchange rate regime that promotes the stability of the currency value inherently unstable?

3. Discuss the primary roles of the International Monetary Fund and World Bank.

4. What is the managed float?

5. How does a currency bloc help a multinational company's global operations?

6. Using the purchasing power parity argument, estimate whether the U.S. dollar is overvalued or undervalued relative to the German deutsche mark, the French franc, and the Japanese yen.

7. Describe in your own words how knowledge of the spot and forward exchange rate market helps international marketers.

8. Why is the exchange rate pass-through usually less than perfect (i.e., less than 100 percent)?

9. Define the four types of balance of payments measures.

10. Describe the sequence of events that took place to cause the Asian financial crisis in the late 1990s.

11. What are the advantages and disadvantages of having euro as a common currency in the European Union?

# DISCUSSION QUESTIONS ◆ ◆ ◆ ◆ ◆ ◆ ◆ ◆ ◆ ◆ ◆ ◆ ◆ ◆ ◆ ◆ ◆ ◆ ◆ ◆ ◆

The Big Mac Index of the *Economist* has been introduced as a guide in the popular press to whether currencies are at their "correct" exchange rate. Although the merits of this index have been mentioned, this index has various defects. Identify and explain the defects associated with this index.

1. Fujitsu, a Japanese computer manufacturer, was recently quoted as taking various steps to prevent wild foreign exchange fluctuations from affecting the company's business. One step being taken is the balancing of export and import contracts. In 2001, the company entered into $3.4 billion of export contracts and $3.2 billion of import contracts. For the year 2002, these figures were expected to be balanced. Explain how this measure would help the firm. What are the advantages and disadvantages of this measure? Are there any alternate courses of action that would give the same end results?

2. In a referendum in September 2000, Denmark citizens voted to reject membership of Europe's single currency euro. The result was pretty close, with 53.1 percent of voters rejected the membership and 46.9 percent favoring adoption. Many feared that rejection would deepen divisions within the European Union and Denmark would be left out of the integration and cooperation; others believe that a single currency would erode Danish sovereignty. Do you believe that rejection of membership will create a "two-speed" Europe?

3. In July 2005, China dropped its decade-long currency peg to the U.S. dollar, an instead re-pegged to a basket of currencies. China reevaluated yuan to make the currency effectively 2.1 percent stronger against the U.S. dollar. On May 16, 2007, China again took steps to let its currency trade more freely against the dollar and to cool its sizzling economy and contain its soaring trade surplus with the United States. The yuan was allowed to fluctuate further against the dollar by 0.5 percent a day, up from 0.3 percent. Under the new currency system, China has not yet surrendered control of the currency. It has moved away from a fixed exchange rate but not all the way to a flexible or free-floating one. American manufacturers and labor unions hope yuan's reevaluation will help U.S. factory sales and jobs by making U.S. goods more affordable abroad. For China, the currency move will make Chinese exports a little more expensive abroad. Many Asian countries have been trying to compete with China's low-cost manufacturing, and after China's yuan reevaluation, Malaysia announced it would drop its peg to the U.S. dollar as well. In the short run, the change in China's currency management system could be almost unnoticeable. In the longer run, however, the impact on trade and on the world financial system could be huge. Based on what you learned from this chapter, what would be the impacts on the world's economy, if China and other Asian countries truly allowed their currencies to float, or, instead, keep holding them within narrow bands against the dollar?

As presented in **Global Perspective 3-3**, many countries in European Union are complaining that the euro has weakened the financial advantages that firms previously had in stable economies. The euro area's three largest economies, France, Germany, and Italy are now struggling with how to stimulate economic growth. Germany, for example, is battling with unfriendly growth rates and double-digit unemployment; Italy entered its second recession in two years in the first quarter of 2005; France expressed their complaints through their rejection of the European constitution. According to a government minister in Italy, the euro should be blamed for Italy's poor economic performance and he even advocated reintroducing the lira. So the question is, can the united currency be unified across the EU? Ideally, currency zones should be solid and homogenous enough to exhibit little regional variation in business cycles. However, the current one-size-fits-all monetary policy would possibly make some countries in the region lingering in recession, while others experience rapid growth. Witnessing the rapid growth of a few countries, such as Ireland while other large economies like Germany and Italy, stagnate, should EU make any changes to its currency system? Or what needs to be done to adjust the EU problem?

## SHORT CASES

 ASE 3-1

### SAMSUNG'S SURVIVAL OF THE ASIAN FINANCIAL CRISIS

The Asian financial crisis severely affected the Korean economy, reflecting on its currency and balance of payments situation. Several Korean companies went bankrupt in its aftermath, the epicenter of which was the year 1997. Others such as Daewoo and Hyundai are still struggling to hang on almost eight years after the crisis. Among those that survived is the successful South Korean *chaebol* (conglomerate) Samsung with revenues of over $50 billion and over 60 related and unrelated divisions under its umbrella. Samsung is known all over the world for its flat screen liquid display panels and superior memory chips as well as for finished products like cell phones and other consumer electronics. The company's electronics division Samsung Electronics is now one of the largest technology companies in Asia competing head on with older Japanese electronics firms such as Sony and Panasonic for global market share.

Samsung rose to global fame in the late 1980s and early 1990s when it introduced its DRAM (dynamic random access memory) chips in the West and developments in chip technology soon led it to present its 1 megabit chip, the first in the world and a technological breakthrough at the time. Samsung went on to later introduce upgrades on its chips in the years that led up to the crisis of 1997 and even though it was successful in chip manufacturing, it was losing out to its competitors in consumer electronics and white goods. When the Asian financial crisis hit, many companies shut down shop but Samsung steeled itself and persevered among falling prices for chips and its other products. In order to boost profitability, the company laid-off around 30 percent of its workforce after the crisis but continued to invest in innovation to bring it out of the red. So, how did Samsung make a turnaround? Well, it turned to the huge North American and Western European markets, known for their penchant for technologically advanced products and greater purchasing power among consumers compared with Asian consumers.

Samsung had to work hard to gain market share in these markets. In the years after the crisis, it set up subsidiaries in Western countries. One of its main targets was the large U.S. market. The company realized that to succeed in the U.S. and

the global arena, key factors would include better design to be able to charge premium prices and therefore generate increased revenues. The company set out and did just that. It focused on research in digital technology, design, and utility and brought in designers from the best design schools in the Western hemisphere. Their designers were sent all over the world to draw inspiration for electronics architecture. Thus, Samsung sought to differentiate itself from its global rivals through superior design. Its efforts paid off. By the year 2005, Samsung had captured the higher end TV market in the U.S. market and its brand was the best selling in such items in the country. It also is the largest maker of DRAMs and LCD monitors. Every year, the company increases its design staff and budget. Its design staff evaluates consumer tastes and advises engineers on products. According to a ranking of the IDEA Biggest Award Winners between 2003 and 2007, Samsung ranked the first with a total number of 15, much higher than Apple and Hewlett-Packard (HP) with 11, respectively.

In a way, the Asian financial crisis proved to be an indirect blessing for the company. Due to the crisis, the Korean government stepped in to revive the industry and that enabled firms like Samsung to take the necessary measures to get back to profitability such as laying off workers, which in Korea is a contentious issue due to the highly unionized workers. Also, it pushed the company to look beyond at larger markets. Somewhere in the midst of all the chaos that surrounded companies during and after the Asian financial crisis, the company made a big decision, to transform itself from a me-too producer of electronics to one of the most innovative companies and leading brands in the world. In 2005, it is known for its "cool" products. Between 1998 and 2006, the company raised its R&D expenditures to around $6 billion, which constitutes 9.5 percent of its sales value. Today, the company that could have easily sunk in the crisis has brand equity worth more than $15 billion and its market capitalization is greater than that of Sony and other Japanese electronics leaders that have been around much longer than Samsung has.

### DISCUSSION QUESTIONS

1. What did Samsung do differently from other firms that also faced the Asian financial crisis?

2. What should Samsung do to continue to bring in profits in the future?

3. What can global firms do to reduce vulnerability to financial crises?

*Sources:* Seung-Ho Kwon; Dong-Khee Ree; Chung-Sok Sub. "Globalization Strategies of South Korean Electronics Companies after the 1997 Asian Financial Crisis," *Asia Pacific Business Review*, 10 (Spring/Summer 2004), pp. 422–40; "The Lessons for Sony at Samsung," *Business Week*, October 10, 2005 pp. 37–38; "Winners Over The Past Five Years," *BusinessWeek.com*, July 30, 2007; and Samsung, http://www.samsung.com/.

ASE 3-2

## MANUFACTURING LOCATION: THE UNITED STATES OR CHINA

In this era of globalization, American factories and supplier networks in many industries have withered, with a large migration to developing countries, especially to China. In electronics, for instance, a lot of component manufacturers have moved to China in the past decade. The furniture industry has undergone a similar transformation. The same also goes for lighting fixtures, household appliances, and more. One reason accounting for the migration is what American managers call the China Price, the once-formidable 40 percent to 50 percent cost advantage enjoyed by Chinese manufacturers—and demanded by customers.

However, today the global industrial landscape appears to be starting a realignment, as the dollar has plunged by 30 percent against major world currencies since 2002 and the cost of fuel has surged. The euro's breathtaking appreciation against the dollar has spurred European manufacturers of cars, steel, aircraft, and more to shift production to the United States. Meanwhile, the soaring cost of fuel is making it pricier to send goods across the Pacific. In the case of China, the dollar dropped from 8.3 yuan/$ in 2002 to 6.8 yuan/$ in June 2008. Wages in China are rising 10 percent to 15 percent a year. And shipping rates are driven up by spiking oil prices—the cost of sending a 40-foot container from Shanghai to San Diego has soared by 150 percent, to $5,500, since 2000. If oil hits $200 a barrel, that could reach $10,000. Will the surging shipping costs drive the United States to bring jobs in manufacture back from China?

If global shipping costs continue to rise, some businesses could eventually move their factories back to the United States, but that process will take years. In the short term, China is still irreplaceable. One reason for China being able to keep its edge in the face of soaring costs is its rising productivity, a factor widely overlooked by the world. For the past decade, U.S. manufacturing productivity growth has averaged 4.8 percent, which is doubtlessly impressive for an industrialized nation, and bodes well for U.S. industry when the economy recovers. But on the other side of the Pacific, productivity at medium and large Chinese manufacturers—the backbone of country's export boom—has averaged nearly 19 percent over the same period. In circuit-board industry, for instance, a decade ago the U.S. accounted for one-third of global circuit-board output. Today that is down to 10 percent, with China manufacturing 80 percent. According to Douglas Bartlett, chairman of Bartlett Manufacturing, a U.S. manufacturer of high-end circuit boards used in defense and medical

*Source:* "Can the U.S. Bring Jobs Back from China?", *BusinessWeek.com*, June 19, 2008.

systems, Chinese boards are still 40 percent to 50 percent cheaper than the ones Bartlett makes in the United States, in part because Chinese producers have superior technology.

Another reason lies in that China's price edge against the United States will remain for a long time in spite of the soaring yuan, if not for a decade as contended by some analysts. While the United States has become a "midprice" alternative to Western Europe thanks to the plunge in the dollar, its cost structure in relation to China has changed only marginally. Take industrial compressors, which are used to power equipment such as office air-conditioning systems, for example. Three years ago it cost 38 percent less to make a 1.5-ton compressor in a factory in China than in a U.S. plant. The big driver was Chinese wages and benefits, which were 65 percent below those in the United States. Today, after accounting for rising labor costs in China, the strengthening yuan, and higher shipping rates, Chinese-made compressors are still about 30 percent less expensive.

Actually, expecting the United States to recapture industries that have already gone to China may not be realistic. In other words, the bulk of goods made in China—clothing, toys, small appliances, and the like—probably will not be coming back, because they require abundant cheap labor. If anything, their manufacture will go to other lower-wage nations in Asia or Latin America. And in industries from machinery to motorcycles, China's productivity gains have nearly offset rising wages and fuel prices.

But in areas where the United States is at the forefront of innovation—renewable energy, nano materials, solid-state lighting—the United States may have as good a chance as anyone of being a strong player. The new cost equation likely will influence U.S. companies' decisions about where to locate production in the future. The challenge will be to persuade reluctant venture capitalists and corporations to invest again in modern U.S. manufacturing facilities.

### DISCUSSION QUESTIONS

1. According to this case, U.S. companies will not bring back jobs from China in industries whose products are currently made in China but can be a strong player in areas where the United States is at the forefront of innovation. Do you agree with the opinion? Why or why not?

2. Besides shipping costs, are there any other possible advantages for U.S. firms to manufacture inside the country or any other possible disadvantages for them to manufacture in China? If yes, what are they? If not, why not?

## FURTHER READING ◆ ◆ ◆ ◆ ◆ ◆ ◆ ◆ ◆ ◆ ◆ ◆ ◆ ◆ ◆ ◆ ◆ ◆ ◆ ◆

Beaverstock, Jonathan V., Michael Hoyler, Kathryn Pain, and Peter J. Taylor, "Demystifying the Euro in European Financial Centre Relations: London and Frankfurt, 2000-2001," *Journal of Contemporary European Studies*, 13, August 2005, pp. 143–57.

Cohen, Benjamin J. "The International Monetary System: Diffusion and Ambiguity,"_International Affairs, 84_ (May), 2008: 455–70.

Dhanani, Alpa, "The Management of Exchange-Rate Risk: A Case from the Manufacturing Industry," *Thunderbird International Business Review*, 46 (May/June 2004): 317–38.

Hildebrand, Doris, "Legal Aspects of Euro-Marketing," *European Journal of Marketing*, 28 (7), 1994: 44–54.

"In Search of Elusive Domestic Demand," *Economist*, October 15, 2005: 44–45.

Knox, Andrea, "Pricing in Euroland," *World Trade*, January 1999: 52–56.

Kotabe, Masaaki and Ricardo Leal, *Market Revolution in Latin America: Beyond Mexico*, New York: Elsevier Science, 2001.

Mudd, Shannon, Robert Grosse, and John Mathis, "Dealing with Financial Crises in Emerging Markets," *Thunderbird International Business Review*, 44 (May–June 2002): 399–430.

# GLOBAL CULTURAL ENVIRONMENT AND BUYING BEHAVIOR

**4**

**HAPTER OVERVIEW**

1. DEFINITION OF CULTURE

2. ELEMENTS OF CULTURE

3. CROSS-CULTURAL COMPARISONS

4. ADAPTING TO CULTURES

5. CULTURE AND THE MARKETING MIX

6. ORGANIZATIONAL CULTURES

7. GLOBAL ACCOUNT MANAGEMENT (GAM)

8. GLOBAL CUSTOMER RELATIONSHIP MANAGEMENT (CRM)

Buyer behavior and consumer needs are largely driven by cultural norms. Cultural backgrounds also influence consumers' information processing and buying motivations.[1] Managers running a company in a foreign country need to interact with people from different cultural environments. Conducting global business means dealing with consumers, strategic partners, distributors and competitors with different cultural mindsets. Cultures often provide the cement for members of the same society. A given country could be an economic basket case compared to the rest of the world, but its cultural heritage often provides pride and self-esteem to its citizens. Foreign cultures also intrigue. A stroll along Hong Kong's Nathan Road, Singapore's Orchard Road, or Shanghai's Nanjing Road reveals the appeal of Western cuisine and dress codes among Asian citizens. At the same time, cultures may also foster resentment, anxiety, or even division. When plans for Euro-Disney were revealed, French intellectuals referred to the planned theme park as a "cultural Chernobyl."[2] Many Japanese sumo-wrestling

---

[1] For a good overview of recent research insights on how cultural backgrounds impact consumer decision-making see Donnel A. Briley and Jennifer L. Aaker, "Bridging the Culture Chasm: Ensuring That Consumers Are Healthy, Wealthy, and Wise," *Journal of Public Policy & Marketing*, 25 (2006), pp. 53–66.

[2] In contrast, the Hong Kong government actively pursued Disney in the hope of setting up a Disney theme park in the territory. Hong Kong Disneyland, Disney's second theme park in Asia, opened in September 2005.

fans resent the rising prominence of foreigners like the Bulgarian Malhlyanov, better known by his sumo name of Kotooshu meaning "Zither of Europe."[3]

To be able to grasp the intricacies of foreign markets, it is important to get a deeper understanding of cultural differences. From a global marketing perspective, the cultural environment matters for two main reasons. First and foremost, cultural forces are a major factor in shaping a company's global marketing mix program. Global marketing managers constantly face the thorny issue of the degree to which cultural differences are a major factor in shaping a company's global marketing mix program. Cultural blunders can easily become a costly affair for MNCs. Some of the possible liabilities of cultural gaffes include embarrassment, lost customers, legal consequences, missed opportunities, huge costs of damage control, and tarnished brand or corporate reputations.[4] Second, cultural analysis often pinpoints market opportunities. Companies that recognize cultural norms that their competitors have so far ignored often gain a competitive edge. For instance, several Japanese diaper makers were able to steal market share away from Procter & Gamble by selling diapers that were much thinner than the ones marketed by P&G, thereby better meeting the desires of Japanese mothers.[5] (Japanese homes have less space than most European or American houses.)

Evolving trends, as mapped out by changes in cultural indicators, also lead to market opportunities that savvy marketers can leverage. Consider for a moment the opportunities created by the "little emperors and empresses" in China, who altogether provide a market of around 300 million children. Children in China impact consumption patterns in three ways: (1) they have spending power, (2) they have "pester power," and (3) they act as change agents. Giving pocket money to children is increasingly common in China. Chinese children—who are most often single children because of China's one-child policy—also have a tremendous amount of "pester power." Finally, children are important change agents for scores of new consumer products because they are often the first ones to be exposed (via friends, television) to the innovation. Capitalizing on these trends, Pepsi-Cola launched a fruit drink ("Fruit Magix") in China that targeted children.[6]

Within a given culture, consumption processes can be described via a sequence of four stages: access, buying behavior, consumption characteristics, and disposal (see **Exhibit 4-1**):

- *Access.* Does the consumer have physical and/or economic access to the product/service?
- *Buying behavior.* How do consumers make the decision to buy in the foreign market?
- *Consumption characteristics.* What factors drive the consumption patterns?
- *Disposal.* How do consumers dispose of the product (in terms of resale, recycling, etc.)?[7]

Each of these stages is heavily influenced by the culture in which the consumer thrives.

This chapter deals with the cultural environment of the global marketplace. First we describe the concept of culture, and then we explore various elements of culture. Cultures differ a great deal, but they also have elements in common. We will discuss several schemes that can be used to compare cultures. Cultural mishaps are quite likely to occur when conducting global business. As a global business manager, you should be aware of your own cultural norms and other people's cultural mindset. To that end, we

---

[3]"Big in Bulgaria, Huge in Japan," *Financial Times*, Dec. 30/31, 2005, p. W3.

[4]Tevfik Dalgic and Ruud Heijblom, "International Marketing Blunders Revisited—Some Lessons for Managers," *Journal of International Marketing* 4, no. 1 (1996): 81–91.

[5]Alecia Swasy, *Soap Opera: The Inside Story of Procter & Gamble* (New York: Random House, 1993).

[6]Amit Bose and Khushi Khanna, "The Little Emperor. A Case Study of a New Brand Launch," *Marketing and Research Today* (November 1996): 216–21.

[7]P. S. Raju, "Consumer Behavior in Global Markets: The A-B-C-D Paradigm and Its Applications to Eastern Europe and the Third World," *Journal of Consumer Marketing*, 12 (5), 1995, pp. 37–56.

**EXHIBIT 4-1**
THE A-B-C-D PARADIGM

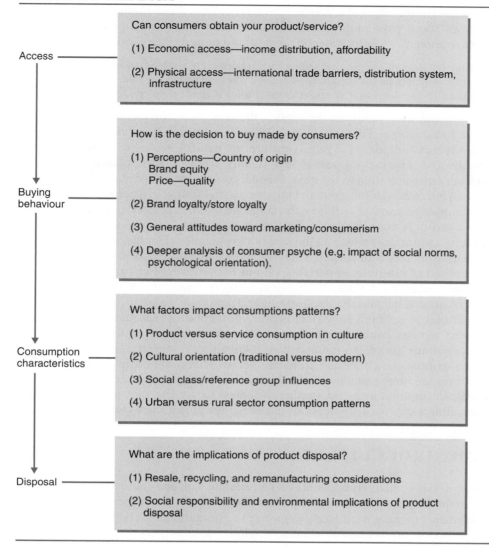

Access — Can consumers obtain your product/service?

(1) Economic access—income distribution, affordability

(2) Physical access—international trade barriers, distribution system, infrastructure

Buying behaviour — How is the decision to buy made by consumers?

(1) Perceptions—Country of origin
Brand equity
Price—quality

(2) Brand loyalty/store loyalty

(3) General attitudes toward marketing/consumerism

(4) Deeper analysis of consumer psyche (e.g. impact of social norms, psychological orientation).

Consumption characteristics — What factors impact consumptions patterns?

(1) Product versus service consumption in culture

(2) Cultural orientation (traditional versus modern)

(3) Social class/reference group influences

(4) Urban versus rural sector consumption patterns

Disposal — What are the implications of product disposal?

(1) Resale, recycling, and remanufacturing considerations

(2) Social responsibility and environmental implications of product disposal

*Source:* P.S. Raju, "Consumer Behavior in Global Markets: The A-B-C-D Paradigm and Its Applications to Eastern Europe and the Third World," *Journal of Consumer Marketing* 12, No. 5 (1995): 39. Reprinted with permission.

will discuss several ways to adapt to foreign cultures. Cultural forces shape the company's marketing mix. The chapter will also discuss the influence of culture on a firm's marketing mix policy. This chapter will primarily consider national cultures. However, organizations are also governed internally by their own organizational culture. We will look at the different types of organizational cultures that exist. We round out the chapter by looking at two very important customer management areas in a global setting, namely, global customer account management and customer relationship management.

## DEFINITION OF CULTURE ◆ ◆ ◆ ◆ ◆ ◆ ◆

Culture comes in many guises. A Google search on "culture" resulted in around 469 million hits. Social scientists have not come to any consensus on a definition of culture. The literature offers a host of definitions. Wikipedia gives the following definition: "all the ways of life including arts, beliefs and institutions of a population that are passed down from generation to generation."[8] The Dutch cultural anthropologist Hofstede defines culture as "the collective programming of the mind which distinguishes the members of one group or category from those of another."[9] Triandis, a well-known social psychologist, refers to culture as "the shared perceptions of the social environment."[10] Terpstra and David offer a more business-oriented definition:

> Culture is a learned, shared, compelling, interrelated set of symbols whose meanings provide a set of orientations for members of society. These orientations, taken together, provide solutions to problems that all societies must solve if they are to remain viable.[11]

Despite the wide variety of definitions, there are common elements that span the different formulations. First of all, people *learn* culture.[12] In other words, it is not biologically transmitted via the genes (nurture, not nature). A society's culture is passed on ("cultivated") by various peer groups (family, school, youth organizations, and so forth) from one generation to the next. Second, culture consists of many different parts that are all *interrelated*. One element (say, one's social status) of a person's culture does have an impact on another part (say, the language that this person uses). So, a person's cultural mindset is not a random collection of behaviors. In a sense, culture is a very complex jigsaw puzzle in which all the pieces hang together. Finally, culture is *shared* by individuals as members of society. These three facets—cultures being learned, shared, and composed of interrelated parts—spell out the essence of culture.

Cultures may be defined by national borders, especially where countries are isolated by natural barriers. Examples are island nations (e.g., Japan, Ireland, Australia) and peninsulas (e.g., South Korea). However, most cultures cross national boundaries. Also, most nations contain different subgroups (*subcultures*) within their borders. These subgroups could be defined along linguistic (Flemish versus Walloons in Belgium) or religious (Buddhist Sinhalese versus Hindu Tamils in Sri Lanka) lines. Few cultures are homogeneous. Typically, most cultures contain subcultures that often have little in common with one another. Needless to say, the wide variety of cultures and subcultures creates a tremendous challenge for global marketers.

## ◆◆◆◆◆◆◆◆ ELEMENTS OF CULTURE

Culture consists of many components that interrelate with one another. Knowledge of a culture requires a deep understanding of its different parts. In this section, we describe those elements that are most likely to matter to international marketers: material life, language, social interactions, aesthetics, religion, education, and values.

**Material Life**  A major component of culture is its material aspect. *Material life* refers primarily to the technologies that are used to produce, distribute, and consume goods and services within society. Differences in the material environment partly explain differences in the level and type of demand for many consumption goods. For instance, energy consumption is not only much higher in developed countries than in developing nations but also relies on more advanced forms such as nuclear energy. To bridge material environment differences, marketers are often forced to adapt their product offerings. Consider, for instance, the soft drink industry. In many countries outside the United States, store shelf space is heavily restricted, and refrigerators have far less capacity (smaller kitchens) compared to the United States. As a result, soft drink

---

[8]http://en.wikipedia.org/wiki/Culture, accessed October 30, 2008.

[9]Geert Hofstede, *Cultures and Organizations: Software of the Mind* (London: McGraw-Hill, 1991), p. 5.

[10]Harry C. Triandis, *The Analysis of Subjective Culture* (Oxford: Wiley-Interscience, 1972).

[11]Vern Terpstra and Kenneth David, *The Cultural Environment of International Business* (Cincinnati, OH: South-Western Publishing Co., 1991), p. 6.

[12]Some biologists have made a compelling case that culture is not a uniquely human domain in the sense that animals (especially primates) can also possess a culture. A good introduction to this perspective is Frans de Waal, *The Ape and the Sushi Master* (London: Penguin Books, 2001).

# GLOBAL PERSPECTIVE 4-1

## INFILTRATING THE RURAL MARKETPLACE

Having conquered urban markets in Asia, consumer goods behemoths, such as Unilever, Procter & Gamble, and Coca-Cola, are setting their sights on the millions of potential consumers in remote, rural communities of the region.

Selling shampoo, soap, or detergents to rural consumers is often very demanding. And yet, the market opportunities offered by these consumers are tremendous. In Indonesia, 135 million people (64 percent of the population) live in areas where many of them can afford inexpensive, fast-moving consumer goods. In India, 75 percent of the population (700 million people) is spread out over 627,000 villages. India's rural market contributes almost 50 percent of Unilever's total sales in India. The share is even higher for major categories such as detergents and beverages. Fifty percent of consumer durables in India are sold in the rural markets.

Many of these villages are virtually untouched by the mass media. As one India-based advertising executive stated: "often the nearest thing to brand villagers have experienced is a home-made mud skin care product from a neighboring village." According to the same source, the two biggest barriers are the near-complete absence of a guaranteed 24-hour power supply and the road conditions. To cope with unreliable power supply, many soft drink makers have tried to develop coolers that can survive up to eight hours of power cuts. Add to these

further hurdles such as high illiteracy rates, low exposure to mass media, and low incomes, and one can imagine that conventional marketing approaches are largely ineffective when reaching out to rural consumers. Instead, multinational corporations need to come up with creative and innovative tools to sell their wares.

To relay marketing messages to villagers, marketers need to resort to unconventional media. To promote its brands in rural India, Hindustan Lever (Unilever's India subsidiary) relies on vans with TV sets and satellite dishes that are set up in village squares. These vans provide local entertainment (e.g., songs from Hindu movies) along with ads for Unilever-branded products. Lever's goal is to establish a physical presence in places where villagers meet frequently such as wells and markets. Lever even uses some form of product placement in local folk performances. Local advertising agencies are asked to write a story around a Lever brand. The story is then developed into a stage performance in any one of the local dialects. Sampling can also be a very effective promotion tool, especially in places where people have never experienced products such as shampoos or toothpaste.

Besides communication, other concerns are availability and affordability. Unilever uses teams of "motorbike cowboys" and boat salesmen to sell its goods in Vietnam. Soft drink makers like Pepsi and Coca-Cola have launched 200 ml bottles priced between 10 and 12 cents in India. A battery-free radio designed by Philips for the rural market enables Indian consumers to save 1200 rupiahs (about $25) per year. Kodak India has developed a camera pack targeting India's rural consumers. Graphics on the pack visually demonstrate usage instructions.

*Sources*: "Marketing in the Field," *Ad Age Global* (October 2001): 8; "Village Leverage," *Far Eastern Economic Review*, August 24, 2000, pp. 50–55; "Unilever's Jewel," *Business Week International*, April 19, 1999, pp. 22–23; "Striving for Success—One Sachet at a Time," *Financial Times*, December 11, 2000, p. 9; and "Rural Consumers Get Closer to Established World Brands," *Ad Age Global* (June 2002): p. 5.

bottlers sell one- or one-and-a-half liter bottles rather than two-liter bottles. In markets like China and India, the road infrastructure is extremely primitive, making distribution of products a total nightmare. In India, Coca-Cola uses large tricycles to distribute cases of Coke along narrow streets.[13]

Technology gaps also affect investment decisions. Poor transportation conditions, unreliable power supply, and distribution infrastructure in many developing countries force companies to improvise and look for alternative ways to market and deliver their products. In rural areas of countries like India, conventional media are incapable of reaching the whole universe of consumers. As is illustrated in **Global Perspective 4-1,** global marketers in such countries need to come up with innovative ways to access rural consumers. Governments in host nations often demand technology transfers as part of the investment package. Companies that are not keen on sharing their technology are forced to abandon or modify their investment plans. When the Indian government asked Coca-Cola to share its recipe, Coke decided to jump ship and left the India marketplace in 1977. The soft drink maker returned to India in 1992.

---

[13]"Coke Pours into Asia," *Business Week*, October 21, 1996, pp. 22–25.

**Language**    In developing a line of talking dolls targeted at children in China, a major hurdle for Fisher-Price engineers was the Mandarin "sh" sound, which involves a soft hiss that was difficult to encode on sound-data chips. In the end, Fisher-Price was able to resolve the issue of recording the phrase "It's learning time" in Mandarin.[14]

The Fisher-Price problem is just one illustration of many language-related challenges that international marketing managers need to wrestle with. Language is often described as the most important element that sets human beings apart from animals. Language is used to communicate and to interpret the environment. Two facets of language have a bearing on marketers: (1) the use of language as a communication tool within cultures and (2) the huge diversity of languages across and often within national boundaries.

Let us first consider the communication aspect. As a communication medium, language has two parts: the *spoken* and the so-called *silent* language. The spoken language consists of the vocal sounds or written symbols that people use to communicate with one another. Silent language refers to the complex of nonverbal communication mechanisms that people use to get a message across. Edward Hall identified five distinctive types of silent languages: space, material possessions, friendship patterns, time, and agreements. Space refers to the conversation distance between people: close or remote. The second type, material possessions, relates to the role of possessions in people's esteem of one another. Friendship patterns cover the notion and treatment of friends. Perceptions of time also vary across cultures. Differences exist about the importance of punctuality, the usefulness of "small talk," and so forth. The final type refers to the interpretation of agreements. People in some cultures focus on the explicit contract itself. In other cultures, negotiating parties put faith in the spirit of the contract and trust among one another.

Not surprisingly, a given gesture often has quite different meanings across cultures. In Japan, scribbling identifying cues on business cards is a major violation of basic business etiquette. On the other hand, foreigners (*gaijin*) are not expected to engage in the bowing rituals used for greeting people of various ranks.[15] Other examples abound of silent language forms that are harmless in one society and risky in others. It is imperative that managers familiarize themselves with the critical aspects of a foreign culture's hidden language. Failure to follow this rule will sooner or later lead to hilarious or embarrassing situations.

The huge diversity of languages poses another headache to multinational companies. Language is often described as the mirror of a culture. The number of "living" languages is estimated to be 6,912, though most of these are spoken by very few people.[16] Differences exist across and within borders. Not surprisingly, populous countries contain many languages. In India, Hindi, spoken by 30 percent of the population, is the national language but there are 14 other official languages.[17] Papua New Guinea, an island nation in the southern Pacific Ocean, has around 715 indigenous languages. Even small countries show a fair amount of language variety. Switzerland, with a population of nearly 7.5 million people, has four national languages: German (spoken by 63.7 percent of the population), French (20.4 percent), Italian (6.5 percent), and Romansch (0.5 percent).[18]

Even within the same language, meanings and expressions vary a great deal among countries that share the language. A good example is English. English words that sound completely harmless in one English-speaking country often have a silly or sinister meaning in another Anglo-Saxon country. Until fifteen years ago, Snickers bars were sold under the brand name Marathon in the United Kingdom. Mars felt that the Snickers name was too close to the English idiom for female lingerie (knickers).[19] Cert,

---

[14]"Fisher-Price Talks Mandarin," *The Wall Street Journal*, June 2, 2008, p. 28.

[15]"When Fine Words Will Butter no Parsnips," *Financial Times*, May 1, 1992.

[16]http://gamma.sil.org/ethnologue, accessed on September 12, 2008.

[17]These are: Bengali, Telugu, Marathi, Tamil, Urdu, Gujarati, Malayalam, Kannada, Oriya, Punjabi, Assamese, Sindhi, and Sanskrit. Hindustani, a mixture of Hindi and Urdu, is not an official language, though widely spoken.

[18]Note though that only the first three are official languages, http://www.cia.gov/cia/publications/factbook/geos/sz. html, accessed December 30, 2005.

[19]Masterfoods recently launched a new energy bar in the United States under the Snickers Marathon brand name.

a London-based consultant, offers a few rules of thumb about talking to non-native English speakers in English:

1. *Vocabulary.* Go for the simplest words (e.g., use the word *rich* instead of *loaded*, *affluent*, or *opulent*). Treat colloquial words with care.

2. *Idioms.* Pick and choose idioms carefully (for instance, most non-U.S. speakers would not grasp the meaning of the expression *nickel-and-diming*).

3. *Grammar.* Express one idea in each sentence. Avoid subclauses.

4. *Cultural references.* Avoid culture-specific references (e.g., "Doesn't he look like David Letterman?").

5. *Understanding the foreigner.* This will be a matter of unpicking someone's accent. If you do not understand, make it seem that it is you, not the foreigner, who is slow.

Language blunders easily arise as a result of careless translations of advertising slogans or product labels. Toshiba once had a commercial jingle in China that went "Toshiba, Toshiba." Unfortunately, in Mandarin Chinese, Toshiba sounds a lot like "let's steal it" (*tou-chu-ba*). The English version of a newspaper ad campaign run by Electricité de France (EDF), the main electricity supply firm in France, said that the company offered "competitive energetic solutions" and was "willing to accompany your development by following you on all of your sites in Europe and beyond."[20] Certain concepts are unique to a particular language. For example, an expression for the Western concept of romance does not exist in languages such as Chinese, Thai, Malay, and Korean.[21] **Exhibit 4-2** shows an example of *Chinglish*.[22] The exhibit is part of a hotel manual that one of us found in a guesthouse in Shanghai.

## EXHIBIT 4-2
### NOTICE TO GUESTS

1. Show the valid ID card as stated when registering with the Front Office.

2. Please don't make over or put up your guest or your relatives or your friends for the night without registering.

3. Please don't damage and take away, the furniture and equipment in the hotel or something borrowed from the Main Tower and change their usages. If happened, We will claim for damage and loss.

4. Please don't take the things which are subject to burning, explosion, rolling into the Main Tower. Please throw the cigrettend march into the ashtray when smoking in the room. Please don't smoking when lying in the bed.

5. Please don't commit illegal behaviours like gambling, smuggling, whoring, selling drugs. Please don't pick fruit and flower and vomit anywhere, Please don't take the animal and usuall smell things into the hotel.

6. Keep quiet in the hotel, please don't fight and get truck and create a disturbance in the hotel. The security department will handle the person who damage Severely, the order, endanger others' rest, even body safety, according to public security clauses.

7. Guest are advised to deposit their valuables in the Front Office safe. In case of burglary or theft, the hotel haven't responsibility for it.

8. Please don't use dangerous electrical equipment except hairdrier, shaver.

9. The service hour of the hotel is 8:00 am to 10:00 pm the visitor should leave the hotel before 11:00 pm.

10. Please pay attention to and observe all regulations of the hotel. The hotel have access to depriving the quantity of staying of the people who transgress the rules above the neglect the dissuading.

*Source:* Hotel manual of a guesthouse in Shanghai.

---

[20]"The Case of the Misleading Coffin," *Financial Times*, June 21, 1999, p. 12.

[21]Jocelyn Probert and Hellmut Schütte, "De Beers: Diamonds Are for Asia," INSEAD-EAC, Case Study 599-011-1 (1999).

[22]See http://www.pocopico.com/china/chinglish.php for some other amusing cases of Chinglish.

Mistranslations may convey the image that the company does not care about its customers abroad. Several techniques can be used to achieve good translations of company literature. With **back translation**, a bilingual speaker—whose native tongue is the target language—translates the company document first in the foreign language. Another bilingual translator—whose native tongue is the base language—then translates this version back into the original language. Differences between the versions are then resolved through discussion until consensus is reached on the proper translation.

Firms doing business in multilingual societies need to decide what languages to use for product labels or advertising copy. Multilingual labels are fairly common now, especially in the pan-European market. Advertising copy poses a bigger hurdle. To deal with language issues in advertising copy, advertisers can rely on local advertising agencies, minimize the spoken part of the commercial, or use subtitles. We will revisit these issues in much more detail in Chapter 13.

In markets such as China, marketers also need to decide whether to keep the original brand or company name or whether to adopt a localized brand identity. Many multinationals in China have localized their brand names by creating equivalent names that sound like their global name with a positive meaning in Chinese. Hewlett-Packard, for instance, adopted *Hui-Pu* as its Chinese brand name. Hui means "kindness" and Pu means "universal." Other companies take a different track and translate their name using characters that do not necessarily have the same sound as the original name. In 2002, Oracle, following a brainstorming session with its Chinese executives, adopted the name *Jia Gu Wen*. The literal translation means the recording of data and information—a nice fit with Oracle's core business. Apparently, the meaning of the phrase stems from a time when tortoise shells were used to record the prophecies from an oracle during the Shang dynasty (16th to 11th century B.C.E.).[23] **Global Perspective 4-2** discusses how language was a key driver behind the overhaul of Oracle's marketing organization.

---

## $\mathcal{G}$LOBAL PERSPECTIVE 4-2

### ORACLE CORPORATION—MARKETING BY LANGUAGE

In 2000, Oracle Corporation, the leading California-based software maker, revamped its marketing organization by setting up regional teams by language instead of country-specific teams. Oracle expected that the move might save up to $100 million each year. A team based in France handles all French-language marketing in countries such as France, Belgium, Switzerland, and Canada. A Spanish-language team runs the marketing in Spain and Latin America. Teams for seven other languages—English, Japanese, Korean, Chinese, Portuguese, Dutch, and German—cover Oracle's other markets. Through this overhaul, Oracle not only hopes to save money but also to gain more consistency and control over its marketing messages. Given that Oracle is a high-technology company, localization is less of an issue. Mark Jarvis, Oracle's senior vice president, worldwide marketing, notes that: "Our product is identical in every market, and the way we sell it is identical, so why would we want local teams changing the message?"

Oracle also decided to get rid of its 60-plus country-specific websites. According to Jarvis: "Sixty-two websites are a great excuse for high costs—you need 62 Webmasters, and you have 62 opportunities to have the wrong logo, wrong tagline or wrong marketing message. All of that becomes really simple when you have one Website managed at headquarters." First-time visitors to www.oracle.com now need to register their country. They receive local information when they log in afterward. Oracle uses the Web as its key marketing tool because it is cheap, direct, and can have a much higher response rate than more traditional forms of direct marketing. One piece of direct mail that went out to 500 CEOs had a 0.1 percent response rate. Personalized e-mail targeting the same audience had a 76 percent response rate.

*Source*: "Marketing by Language: Oracle Trims Teams, Sees Big Savings," *Advertising Age International* (July 2000): 4, 38.

---

[23]"Ancient Symbolism in a New Oracle Logo," *Ad Age Global* (May 2002): 12.

The movie *Iron & Silk* is a neat illustration of the cultural misunderstandings that arise in cross-cultural interactions. The movie is based on the true-life story of Mark Salzman, a Yale graduate who, after his studies, went to China to teach English in a Chinese village. During his first day of class, his students, out of respect for their teacher, insist on calling him "Mister Salzman." Mark prefers to be addressed on a first-name basis. Ultimately, students and teacher settle on "teacher Mark" as a compromise.

A critical aspect of culture is the social interactions among people. Social interplay refers to the manner in which members of society relate to one another. Probably the most crucial expression of social interactions is the concept of kinship. This concept varies dramatically across societies. In most Western countries, the family unit encompasses the **nuclear family**, being the parents and the children. The relevant family unit in many developing countries is the **extended family,** which often comprises a much wider group of only remotely related family members. The way families are structured has important ramifications. Family units fulfill many roles, including economic and psychological support. For instance, Sri Lankan banks promote savings programs that allow participants to build up savings to support their parents when they reach retirement. Such saving programs would be unthinkable in the United States. Views on marriage and the role of husband and wife can also be unique to a particular culture. Attitudes toward love and marriage in China are far more materialistic than in most other countries. Marriage is seen as a partnership toward achieving success. Chinese women select prospective husbands based on financial status and career prospects rather than love, which is considered a luxury. Role expectations are very traditional: the man should be provider and protector; the woman should do the cooking, be a good mother, and be virtuous.[24] In countries where extended families are the norm, major purchase decisions are agreed upon by many individuals. Within such communities, members of an extended family will pool their resources to fund the purchase of big-ticket items (e.g., sewing machines).

In Chinese cultures, *guanxi* is an important form of social interaction in business contexts. *Guanxi*, which roughly means "connections," is crucial in numerous situations: negotiating a distribution deal, getting a business license, setting up joint ventures. Important forums for building up *guanxi* in China are executive education programs, where senior executives from different industries and cities can meet.[25] **Exhibit 4-3** spells out five rules that are helpful in successfully cracking the *guanxi* code.

Countries also vary in terms of the scope of the decision-making authority. A study by Asia Market Intelligence (AMI), a Hong Kong-based research firm, looked at the decision-making influence of husbands and wives on grocery shopping. The study showed that even in Asia's most conservative societies, men are heavily involved in

**Social Interactions**

**EXHIBIT 4-3**
RULES TO START CRACKING THE *GUANXI* CODE IN CHINA

1. Be prepared to carry stacks of business cards, but don't waste time trying to swap one with every person in the room. *Guanxi* is about building trust, not a personal database.

2. Never pass up an invitation to play golf or other sports with the locals. Wine tastings and art auctions are good places to network.

3. When someone promises to "open doors" for you be suspicious. Increased transparency in China means that everybody has to jump through the same hoops.

4. Tap into your own alma mater's alumni associations in China. Even consider enrolling in local executive MBA programs.

5. In traditional *guanxi*, if someone does you a favor, one day you will have to repay (in *The Godfather* fashion). These days, however, people are more willing to give without expecting something in return.

*Source:* "You Say *Guanxi*, I Say Schmoozing," *BusinessWeek*, November 19, 2007, p. 85.

---

[24]Probert and Schütte, "De Beers: Diamonds Are for Asia," p. 11.
[25]"You Say *Guanxi*, I Say Schmoozing," *BusinessWeek*, November 19, 2007, pp. 84–85.

grocery shopping. The reasons for the rising number of men doing the family grocery shopping vary, including more women entering the workforce and changing attitudes toward gender roles.[26]

Another important aspect of social interactions is the individual's reference groups—the set of people to whom an individual looks for guidance in values and attitudes. As such, reference groups will have an enormous impact on people's consumption behavior patterns. The consumer research literature identifies three kinds of reference groups[27]: membership groups—those to which people belong; anticipatory groups—groupings of which one would like to be a part; and dissociative groups—groups with which individuals do not want to be associated. Reference groups are especially influential for consumer products that are socially visible, such as most status goods and luxury items. Knowledge on reference group patterns could provide input in formulating product positioning strategies and devising advertising campaigns. A good example is a campaign that Allied Domecq developed to reposition Kahlúa in Asia. During the Asian recession in the late 1990s, Allied Domecq wanted to revamp Kahlúa, a Mexican coffee liqueur brand, as the brand of choice among young Asians. To reach out to its target audience, Allied Domecq sponsored a dance program on MTV Networks Asia called "Party Zone Mixing with Kahlúa." The prime motivation behind the sponsorship was that "Young adults throughout Asia look to MTV as a trendsetter and representative of their lifestyle."[28] The "chav" phenomenon in Britain is a good illustration of the importance of dissociative reference groups. Chavs belong to a social underclass of young, white, undereducated, and mostly unemployed individuals. Chavs have adopted the classic Burberry fashion-brand as their clan plaid, though most of what they purchase is counterfeit. Not surprisingly, Burberry is not very pleased with the popularity of its label among chavs.[29]

**Aesthetics**   *Aesthetics* refers to the ideas and perceptions that a culture upholds in terms of beauty and good taste. Cultures differ sharply in terms of their aesthetic preferences, though variations are mostly regional, not national. In the Asia-Pacific region, aesthetic expressions are driven by three principles: (1) complexity and decoration (multiple forms, shapes, and colors), (2) harmony, and (3) nature displays (e.g., mountains, flowers, trees).[30]

Aesthetics plays a major role in designing the visuals of the product, including components such as the packaging and the logo. A series of studies of the design of brand logos in Singapore and China suggested that companies should select logo designs that are elaborate (complex, depth, active), harmonious (symmetry, balance), and natural.[31]

Color also has different meanings and aesthetic appeals. This is illustrated in **Exhibit 4-4**, which shows color associations in eight different countries. As you can see, three colors—blue, green, and white—appear to convey universal meanings in all eight countries: "peaceful," "gentle," "calming." However, other colors reveal striking cultural differences in the emotions they create. For example, black is seen as "masculine" in Hong Kong and the United States but "formal" in Brazil.[32] In Chinese

[26]"As More Women Enter Work Force, More Men Enter the Supermarket," *Asian Wall Street Journal* (March 8, 2001), pp. N1, N7.

[27]James F. Engel, Roger D. Blackwell, and Paul W. Miniard, *Consumer Behavior* (Hinsdale, IL: Dryden, 1986), pp. 318–24.

[28]"Kahlua Gets New Sales Face in Asia," *Advertising Age International,* March 8, 1999, pp. 5–6

[29]http://www.telegraph.co.uk/news/main.jhtml?xml=/news/2005/01/01/nchav01.xml&sSheet=/news/2005/01/01/ixhome.html

[30]Bernd H. Schmitt and Yigang Pan, "Managing Corporate and Brand Identities in the Asia-Pacific Region," *California Management Review*, 38 (Summer 1994), pp. 32–48.

[31]Pamela W. Henderson, Joseph A. Cote, Siew Meng Leong, and Bernd Schmitt, "Building Strong Brands in Asia: Selecting the Visual Components of Image to Maximize Brand Strength," *International Journal of Research in Marketing*, 20 (December 2003), pp. 297–313.

[32]Thomas J. Madden, Kelly Hewett, and Martin S. Roth, "Managing Images in Different Cultures: A Cross-National Study of Color Meanings and Preferences," *Journal of International Marketing*, 8 (4), 2000, pp. 90–107.

**EXHIBIT 4-4**
THE MEANING OF COLOR

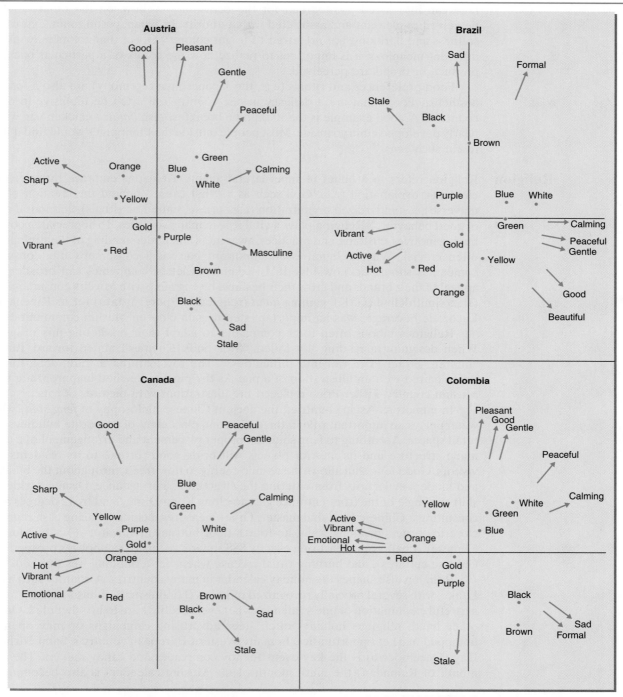

*Source:* Thomas J. Madden, Kelly Hewett, and Martin S. Roth, "Managing Images in Different Cultures: A Cross-National Study of Color Meanings and Preferences," *Journal of International Marketing* 8, No. 4 (2000): 96–97 (Figure 1). Reprinted with permission from the American Marketing Association.

cultures, red is perceived as a lucky color. During the Beijing 2008 Olympics, many MNCs marketing in China draped their brands in red. Even Pepsi changed its iconic blue can into a red painted can for the occasion.[33] Yellow, on the other hand, is perceived as pleasant and associated with authority. In Japan, pastel tones, expressing softness and harmony, are preferred to bright colors.[34] Given that colors may invoke different meanings, it is important to realize how the colors of a particular package, product, or brand are perceived.

Food preferences and rituals (e.g., the Japanese tea ceremony) are also a form of aesthetics. Foods that are a delicacy in one country can often be repulsive in other countries. A good example is the Philippine breakfast dish *balut*: a chicken egg with a nearly developed embryo inside. Most people outside the Philippines would find it hard to eat such eggs.[35]

**Religion**     Religion refers to a belief in supernatural agents. Religions embrace three distinct elements: explanation (e.g., God seen as a "first cause" behind the creation of the universe), a standardized organization (e.g., priests, churches, rituals), and moral rules of good behavior.[36] Religion plays a vital role in many societies. To appreciate people's buying motives, customs, and practices, awareness and understanding of their religion is often crucial. When religion is an important part of a consumer's life, consumer companies should acknowledge it. In Islamic societies, companies can broaden the appeal of their brands and grow their business by engaging with Muslim consumers. For GlaxoSmithKline (GSK), gaining *halal* (religiously "pure") status for its Ribena and Lucozade beverages was an important step to gain clout in Muslim communities.[37]

Religious taboos often force companies to adapt their marketing mix program. When designing a reading toy called "Storybook Rhymes" aimed toward Turkish children, Fisher-Price ran into difficulties.[38] The toy featured a traditional Turkish poem paired with an illustration of a pig. As the pig was deemed inappropriate for a Muslim country, Fisher-Price replaced the illustrations with pictures of cats.

In numerous Asian countries, the ancient Chinese philosophy of *feng shui* (wind-water) plays an important role in the design and placement of corporate buildings and retail spaces. According to feng shui, the proper placement and arrangement of a man-made structure and its interior objects will bring good fortune to its residents and visitors. Good feng shui allows the cosmic energy to flow freely throughout the building and hinders evil spirits from entering the structure.[39] For instance, Disney decided to shift the angle of the front entrance gate to Hong Kong Disneyland by 12 degrees after consulting a Chinese feng shui master. Other measures included placing cash registers close to corners or along walls, no fourth-floor buttons in elevators (4 is bad luck in Chinese), a ballroom measuring exactly 888 square meters (8 symbolizes prosperity in Chinese cultures), and burning ritual incense whenever a building was finished.[40]

Religion also shapes the holiday calendar in many countries. A country such as Sri Lanka, with several officially recognized religions (Hinduism, Buddhism, Islam), forces a careful examination of one's calendar whenever meetings are to be scheduled. On the other hand, religious holidays often steer advertising campaigns or may open up untapped market opportunities. In many Western European countries, Saint Nicholas Day (December 6) is the key event for toy companies and candy makers. The holy month of Ramadan (the ninth month of the Muslim calendar) is also becoming an

---

[33]http://www.youtube.com/watch?v=dzFuIQe88jU, accessed October 30, 2008.

[34]Bernd H. Schmitt, "Language and Visual Imagery: Issues in Corporate Identity in East Asia," *Journal of World Business* (Winter 1995): 28–36.

[35]http://www.youtube.com/watch?v=RXucin9iIaE, accessed October 30, 2008.

[36]Jared Diamond, "The Religious Success Story," *New York Review of Books*, November 7, 2002, pp. 30–31.

[37]"Muslims offer a new Mecca for marketers," *Financial Times*, August 11, 2005, p. 6.

[38]"Fisher-Price Talks Mandarin," *The Wall Street Journal*, June 2, 2008, p. 28.

[39]Bernd Schmitt and Alex Simonson, *Marketing Aesthetics: The Strategic Management of Brands, Identity, and Image* (New York: The Free Press, 1997), pp. 275–76.

[40]"Disney bows to feng shui," *International Herald Tribune*, April 25, 2005, pp. 1, 6.

increasingly commercialized event. In major Mideastern cities such as Cairo and Amman, Ramadan has a Christmas-like atmosphere these days.[41] During the 2008 Ramadan Coca-Cola ran a 60-second TV commercial dubbed "Iftar Street"[42] in sixteen Muslim countries.[43] The spot featured two male leads being caught in a traffic jam. When they spot a Coke delivery truck, the two begin distributing Coke bottles among the rest of the commuters. As the sun sets, the group begins eating and drinking to celebrate the end of the fasting day.[44] In several Muslim countries Coca-Cola also decorated Coke cans with a crescent moon and star, well-recognized symbols in Islam, to celebrate Ramadan.

The role of women in society is sometimes largely driven by the local religion. In Islamic societies, conducting market research that involves women is extremely difficult. For instance, mixing men and women in focus groups is prohibited in Saudi Arabia. Likewise, UPS, the courier firm, only hires men in India to make delivery rounds in deference to local cultural sensibilities.[45]

Religious norms also influence advertising campaigns. In Iran, all ads need to be cleared by Islamic censors. This approval process can take up to three months. Iranian authorities frowned on one print ad created for Chiquita because they considered showing only three bananas on a full-page ad a waste of space.[46] Also in Iran, Gillette's local advertising agency had a hard time placing an ad for the Gillette Blue II razor. Islam dictates that its followers refrain from shaving. Ultimately, Gillette's account executive was able to convince the advertising manager of one local newspaper by using the argument that shaving sometimes becomes necessary, such as in the case of head injuries resulting from a car accident.[47] In Egypt, Coca-Cola's business was hampered by rumors that its logo read "no Mohammed, no Mecca" when read backwards and in Arabic script—a heresy for local Muslims. Coke called on Egypt's Grand Mufti, the country's most senior authority on Sunni Islam, to issue a religious opinion. The Mufti ruled that Coke was *halal*.[48] Rumors also affected Wrigley's sales in Indonesia when an e-mail circulated that claimed the company used pig extract in the manufacturing of its chewing gum products. Hush Puppies, the U.S.-based shoe brand, lost market share in Malaysia when consumers there discovered that its shoes contained pigskin.[49]

## Education

Education is one of the major vehicles for channeling culture from one generation to the next. Two facets of education that matter to international marketers are the level and the quality of education. The level of education varies considerably between countries. Most developed countries have compulsory education up to the late teens. In some countries, however, especially Muslim societies, education is largely the preserve of males. As a consequence, males are often far better-educated than females in such societies. One powerful indicator of the education level is a country's illiteracy rate. In countries with low literacy levels, marketers need to exercise caution in matters such as product labeling, print ads, and survey research. One baby food company attributed its poor sales in Africa to the product label that was used. The label's picture of a baby was mistakenly thought by the local people to mean that the jars contained ground-up babies.[50]

[41]"Parts of Mideast Are Split Between Ramadan as Time for Prayer and Partying," *Asian Wall Street Journal*, December 5, 2002, pp. A1, A8.

[42]*Iftar* refers to the evening meal for breaking the fast during the Ramadan holiday.

[43]http://541aesthetic.wordpress.com/2008/09/16/media-hong-kong-mccann-indonesia-launches-global-coke-tvc-drive-for-ramadan/, accessed October 30, 2008.

[44]http://hk.youtube.com/watch?v=I7bsW4zdYKo, accessed on October 30, 2008, shows the Indonesian version of Coca-Cola's 2008 Ramadan TVC.

[45]"Late to India, UPS Tries to Redraw its Map," *Wall Street Journal*, January 25/27, 2008, p. 4.

[46]"Multinationals Tread Softly While Advertising in Iran," *Advertising Age International*, November 8, 1993, p. I-21.

[47]"Smooth Talk Wins Gillette Ad Space in Iran," *Advertising Age International*, April 27, 1992, p. I-40.

[48]"U.K. Supermarket Sainsbury Travels Mideast's Rocky Road," *Advertising Age International*, July 2000, p. 19.

[49]"Muslim Market Minefield," *Media*, February 8, 2002, pp. 16–17.

[50]David A. Ricks, *Blunders in International Business*, (Cambridge, MA: Blackwell Publishers, 1993).

**EXHIBIT 4-5**
CROSS-COUNTRY PERFORMANCE SCIENCE SKILLS
AMONG HIGH SCHOOL STUDENTS (PISA 2006)

| Country | Mean Score on Science Scale |
|---------|------------------------------|
| Finland | 563 |
| Hong Kong | 542 |
| Canada | 534 |
| Japan | 531 |
| Australia | 527 |
| Korea | 522 |
| Germany | 516 |
| United Kingdom | 515 |
| France | 495 |
| USA | 489 |
| Spain | 488 |
| Russia | 479 |
| Italy | 475 |
| Turkey | 424 |
| Thailand | 421 |
| Mexico | 410 |
| Indonesia | 393 |
| Brazil | 390 |
| Qatar | 349 |
| Kyrgyzstan | 322 |

*Source:* OECD PISA 2006 database

Companies are also concerned about the "quality" of education. Does education meet business needs? Chinese software companies produce less than 1 percent of the world's software, despite the presence of many skilled programmers. One reason for the slow development of China's software industry is cultural. Managers able to supervise large-scale projects are scarce: "Chinese people individually are very, very smart but many, many people together are sometimes stupid."[51] High-tech companies operating in India face similar problems. Indian colleges produce plenty of engineering graduates but 85 percent of them according to one estimate are not ready for work after graduation.[52]

PISA is a triennial survey sponsored by the OECD that gauges skills in literacy, science, and mathematics of 15-year old students in participating countries.[53] More than 400,000 students from 57 countries took part in the 2006 survey. **Exhibit 4-5** shows how students compare in their science skills. As you can see, there are some huge differences, even among countries with a similar level of economic development. Top performers include students from Finland (563), Hong Kong (542), and Canada (534). At the bottom of the scale are Azerbaijan (382), Qatar (349), and Kyrgyzstan (322). U.S. students (489) rank in the middle—higher than their Russian counterparts (479) but below most Far Eastern and European students.[54]

Shortages in certain fields often force companies to bid up against one another for the scarce talent that is available or to employ expatriates. Many companies try to build up a local presence by hiring local people. However, a shortage of qualified people in the local market usually forces them to rely on expatriates until local employees are properly trained.

People's thought processes can also differ across cultures. Richard Nisbett, a social psychologist at the University of Michigan, has done extensive research in this area. The work is summarized in his book *Geography of Thought*. In general, East Asians (i.e., Chinese, Japanese, Koreans) tend to be more holistic, looking at the whole, making

---

[51]"China Takes Pivotal Role in High-Tech Production," *International Herald Tribune*, December 5, 2002, p. 2.

[52]"Wanted: Employees for India's Tech Sector," *Wall Street Journal*, July 17, 2008, p. 28.

[53]PISA stands for the Programme for International Student Assessment.

[54]See the project's website for further information and additional datasets—http://www.pisa.oecd.org.

**EXHIBIT 4-6**
DENTSU LIFESTYLE SURVEY

| | Beijing | Mumbai | Tokyo | Singapore | Bangkok |
|---|---|---|---|---|---|
| Beliefs (% who agree with statement) | | | | | |
| Children should look after aged parents | 67% | 85% | 15% | 77% | 78% |
| Parents should not rely on their children | 21 | 11 | 39 | 9 | 8 |
| Cannot say | 12 | 5 | 46 | 14 | 14 |
| Men work, women stay at home | 20 | 37 | 21 | 26 | 24 |
| Concerns (% agree) | | | | | |
| Personal safety | 73 | 38 | * | * | * |
| Economic development | 70 | 62 | 48 | 67 | 87 |
| Cost of living | 60 | * | 56 | 50 | 62 |
| Education and culture | 46 | 49 | * | 39 | 49 |
| Moral civilization | 38 | * | * | * | * |
| Health and welfare | * | 48 | 68 | 55 | 49 |
| Pollution | * | * | 46 | * | 39 |
| Employment | * | * | 37 | * | * |
| Citizens' rights | * | * | * | 35 | * |
| National security | * | 50 | * | * | * |
| Image as a nation (% agree) | | | | | |
| Hard working | 86 | 59 | 65 | 65 | ** |
| Takes good care of family | 63 | ** | ** | 21 | 31 |
| Funny | ** | 53 | ** | ** | ** |
| Polite | 41 | 47 | 30 | 29 | 38 |
| Bad at negotiating | ** | ** | 45 | ** | ** |
| Loyal to company | ** | ** | 42 | ** | ** |
| Closed society | ** | ** | 36 | ** | ** |
| Clean | ** | ** | ** | 37 | ** |
| Appreciates nature | ** | ** | ** | ** | ** |
| What the state must do (% agree) | | | | | |
| Adopt policies according to public opinion | 65 | 56 | 68 | 50 | 67 |
| Grant full social benefits | 68 | 68 | 65 | 56 | 63 |
| Regulate individual rights for greater good | 47 | 67 | 11 | 42 | 51 |
| Promote competition based on ability | 33 | 26 | 25 | 26 | 38 |
| Adopt Western systems | 21 | 38 | 8 | 24 | 36 |
| Have a strong leader push social reform | 11 | 35 | 5 | 18 | 14 |

*Not among top five concerns.

**Not among top 10 concerns.

*Source:* Dentsu Institute for Human Studies.

little use of categories, clear logic. East Asians also appear to recognize multiple perspectives, contradictions, and search for a middle way. Western people, however, are more analytical in their thought processes, relying on rules, paying attention to categories and objects. Their thinking and behavior is much more rule-based (*Ten steps to . . .*) than that of East Asians.

**Value Systems**

All cultures have value systems that shape people's norms and standards. These norms influence people's attitudes toward objects and behavioral codes. Value systems tend to be deeply rooted. Core values are intrinsic to a person's identity and inner self. One study of the decision-making process made by executives from the People's Republic of China showed that even after almost four decades of communist philosophy, traditional Chinese values (e.g., saving face, long-term exchange relationships, respect for leaders) heavily influence market entry and product decisions.[55] **Exhibit 4-6** is an excerpt of a study commissioned by Dentsu, a Japanese advertising agency, on the beliefs and attitudes of Asian citizens. Note that the data were gathered between November 1996 and January 1997—prior to the start of the Asian crisis. The figures show that talk about

[55]David K. Tse, Kam-hon Lee, Ilan Vertinsky, and Donald A. Wehrung, "Does Culture Matter? A Cross-Cultural Study of Executives' Choice, Decisiveness, and Risk Adjustment in International Marketing," *Journal of Marketing* 52, no. 4 (October 1988): 81–95.

"Asian values" may be a bit premature—there appears to be little common ground among Asian citizens. For instance, 85 percent of Mumbai citizens agree that children should look after aged parents, compared to a mere 15 percent agreement for Tokyo citizens.

For marketers, a crucial value distinction is a culture's attitude toward change. Societies that are resistant to change are usually less willing to adopt new products or production processes. Terpstra and David (1991) suggest several useful guidelines that are helpful to implement innovations in cultures hostile toward changes:[56]

1. Identify roadblocks to change.
2. Determine which cultural hurdles can be met.
3. Test and demonstrate the innovation's effectiveness in the host culture.
4. Seek out those values that can be used to back up the proposed innovation.

From an international marketer's vantage point, a society's value system matters a great deal. Local attitudes toward foreign cultures will drive the product positioning and design decisions. In many countries, goods with American roots are strongly valued. U.S. companies are able to leverage on such sentiments by using Americana as a selling point. McIlhenny sells Tabasco with the same product label and formulation worldwide, emphasizing its American roots.

◆ ◆ ◆ ◆ ◆ ◆ ◆ ◆ ◆ ## CROSS-CULTURAL COMPARISONS

Cultures differ from one another but usually share certain aspects. Getting a sense of the similarities and dissimilarities between your culture and the host country's culture is useful for scores of reasons. Cultural classifications allow the marketing manager to see how much overlap is possible between the marketing programs to be implemented in different markets. Furthermore, most cultural traits tend to be regional instead of national. For example, Walloons in French-speaking Belgium have much more in common, culture-wise, with the French than with the Flemish of northern Belgium. This section gives you an overview of the most common classification schemes.

**High- versus Low-Context Cultures**

One of the characters in the movie *Chan Is Missing* is a lawyer who describes a confrontation between her client who was involved in a traffic accident and a policeman at the scene of the accident. The client is a recent immigrant from mainland China. The policeman asks her client whether or not he stopped at the stop sign, expecting a yes or no for an answer. The Chinese immigrant instead starts talking about his driving record, how long he has been in the United States, and other matters that he feels are relevant. The policeman, losing his patience, angrily repeats his question. The events described in the movie are a typical example of the culture clash that arises when somebody from a high-context culture (China) is faced with a person from a low-context culture (United States).

The notion of cultural complexity refers to the way messages are communicated within a society. The anthropologist Edward Hall makes a distinction between so-called **high-context** and **low-context** cultures.[57] The interpretation of messages in high-context cultures rests heavily on contextual cues. Little is made explicit as part of the message. What is left unsaid is often as important (if not more) as what is said. Examples of contextual cues include the nature of the relationship between the sender and receiver of the message (for instance, in terms of gender, age, balance of power), the time and venue of the communication. Typical examples of high-context societies are Confucian cultures (China, Korea, Japan) and Latin America. Outsiders find high-context cultures often completely mystifying.

---

[56]Terpstra and David, *The Cultural Environment of International Business,* pp. 124–125.
[57]Edward T. Hall, *Beyond Culture* (New York: Doubleday, 1977).

Low-context cultures have clear communication modes. What is meant is what is said. The context, within which messages are communicated, is largely discounted. The United States, Scandinavia, and Germany are all examples of low-context cultures. In many areas of international marketing, the distinction between high- and low-context cultures does matter. For example, in the field of personal selling, many U.S. companies like to rotate salespeople across territories. In high-context societies, where nurturing trust and rapport with the client plays a big role, firms might need to adjust such rotation policies. In the field of international advertising, campaigns that were developed with a high-context culture in mind are likely to be less effective when used in low-context cultures, and vice versa.

Recent research in social psychology also reveals key cultural differences between East (high-context) and West (low-context) in how people perceive reality and reasoning.[58] For instance, one study contrasted the eye movements of Chinese and American students scanning pictures of objects placed within surroundings. American students focused on the central object while Chinese students spent more time on the background, putting the object in context. An analysis of crime reports in newspapers found that English-language papers focus on the personality traits of perpetrators while Chinese papers stress the context (e.g., the perpetrators' background). High- and low-context cultures also differ on their view of logic. Westerners have a deep-seated distaste for contradictions. Easterners, however, appreciate them.[59]

The Dutch scholar Geert Hofstede developed another highly useful cultural classification scheme.[60] His grid is based on a large-scale research project he conducted among employees of more than sixty IBM subsidiaries worldwide. The first dimension is labeled **power distance**. It refers to the degree of inequality among people that is viewed as being acceptable. Societies that are high in power distance tolerate relatively high social inequalities. Everyone has his or her rightful place in society; status symbols play a vital role; the ideal boss is a benevolent dictator or a good patriarch. Members of such societies accept wide differences in income and power distribution. Examples of high power distance countries are Malaysia (PD score = 104), the Philippines (94), Latin American countries such as Mexico (81) and Venezuela (81), Arab countries (80), India (77), and West Africa (77). Low power distance societies tend to be more egalitarian. In Norway, for example, driving fines are linked to income: one drunk Norwegian driver was fined a record 500,000 kroner (around US$79,000) after having hit three parked vehicles and punched a policeman.[61] The rich and powerful in low power distance societies try to look less powerful; status symbols are frowned upon; the ideal boss is a resourceful democrat. Low power distance countries include the United States (40), Germany (35), Great Britain (35), Scandinavia (e.g., Norway and Sweden score: 31, Denmark: 18), and Israel (13).

The second dimension is labeled **uncertainty avoidance**, referring to the extent to which people in a given culture feel threatened by uncertainty and rely on mechanisms to reduce it. Societies with strong uncertainty avoidance possess a need for rigid rules and formality that structure life. What is different is threatening. Examples of countries that score high on uncertainty avoidance are Greece (112), Portugal (104), Japan (92), France (86), and Spain (86). Consumers in such countries value naturalness and freshness. The British cosmetics firm Lush is a prime example of a company that has leveraged this desire. Its stores sell cosmetics *au naturel* with the motto "as natural as beauty gets." All products are sold with an expiration date. Lush has been very successful in Japan—a strong uncertainty avoidance country.[62] In weak uncertainty avoidance cultures, people tend to be more easygoing, innovative, and entrepreneurial.

**Hofstede's Classification Scheme**

[58]"Where east can never meet west," *Financial Times*, October 21, 2005, p. 8.

[59]See also, Richard Nisbett, *The Geography of Thought* (New York: Free Press, 2004.)

[60]Geert Hofstede, *Cultures and Organizations*, McGraw-Hill, 1991.

[61]http://news.bbc.co.uk/2/hi/europe/3870967.stm

[62]www.lush.com

What is different is intriguing. Some weak uncertainty avoidance countries are India (40), Malaysia (36), Great Britain (35), Hong Kong (39), and Singapore (8).

The third dimension is called **individualism**. As the label suggests, this criterion describes the degree to which people prefer to act as individuals rather than as group members ("me" versus "we" societies). In societies that are high on individualism, the focus is on people's own interests and their immediate family's. In such cultures, a child early on realizes that one day it will need to stand on its own feet. There is little need for loyalty to a group. In **collectivist** societies, the interests of the group take center stage. Members in such societies differentiate between in-group members who are part of its group and all other people. They expect protection from the group and remain loyal to their group throughout their lives. Individualist countries are the United States (91), Australia (90), and Great Britain (89). Collectivist countries are South Korea (18), Taiwan (17), Indonesia (14), and Venezuela (12).

The fourth distinction, **masculinity**, considers the importance of "male" values such as assertiveness, status, success, competitive drive within society, and achievement versus "female" values like a people orientation, solidarity, and quality of life. "Masculine" societies are those in which values associated with the role of men prevail. Cultures where people favor values such as solidarity, preserving the environment, and quality of life, are more "feminine." Not surprisingly, Japan (95) is a very masculine society. Other high scorers include Austria (79), Italy (70), and Mexico (69). Thailand (34), Chile (28), the Netherlands (14), and Sweden (5) are low-scoring countries on the masculinity trait.

Follow-up research on Hofstede's work in Asia led to a fifth dimension: **long-termism**.[63] This criterion refers to the distinction between societies with a pragmatic, long-term orientation and those with a short-term focus. People in long-term-oriented societies tend to have values that center around the future (e.g., perseverance, thrift). On the other hand, members of short-term-oriented cultures are concerned about values that reflect the past and the present (e.g., respect for tradition). China (118), Hong Kong (96), Japan (80), and South Korea (75) score high on the long-term dimension. However, the United States (29), Great Britain (25), Canada (23), and the Philippines (19) score very low on this criterion.

**Exhibit 4-7 (A** and **B**) and portrays how different countries score on the various dimensions. One must be cautious when applying these schemes to global buyer behavior. It is important to bear in mind that the five dimensions and the respective country scores that were derived in Hofstede's work were not determined in a consumption context. In fact, questions have been raised about the ability of these values to make meaningful predictions about consumption patterns.[64] Countries with the same scores may have entirely different buying behaviors. Similarly, countries that have completely different scores on a given cultural dimension could have very similar consumption patterns.

Several researchers have looked at the influence of culture on consumption patterns. Luxury articles are often used as a badge of one's success. They are more appealing to members of masculine cultures than to people in feminine cultures. Indeed, one study found that the masculinity of a culture correlates positively with the ownership of expensive (more than $1500) watches (r = 0.56) or multiple (>4) watches (r = 0.53), sales of jewelry (r = 0.44), and the ownership of a suit or dress priced over $750 (r = 0.68).[65] These findings are also confirmed by further anecdotal evidence. According to a study done by Morgan Stanley Dean Witter, Japanese customers (including those traveling overseas) represent 88 percent of the sales of Louis Vuitton, 48 percent of Gucci, and 38 percent of Hermès. One in three Japanese women and one

[63]Geert Hofstede and Michael H. Bond, "The Confucius Connection: From Cultural Roots to Economic Growth," *Organizational Dynamics* 16, no. 4 (Spring 1988): 4–21.

[64]Marieke de Mooij, *Advertising Worldwide* (New York: Prentice-Hall, 1994), p. 159.

[65]Marieke de Mooij and Geert Hofstede, "Convergence and Divergence in Consumer Behavior: Implications for International Retailing," *Journal of Retailing* 78 (2002): 61–69.

**EXHIBIT 4-7A**
UNCERTAINTY AVOIDANCE VERSUS POWER DISTANCE

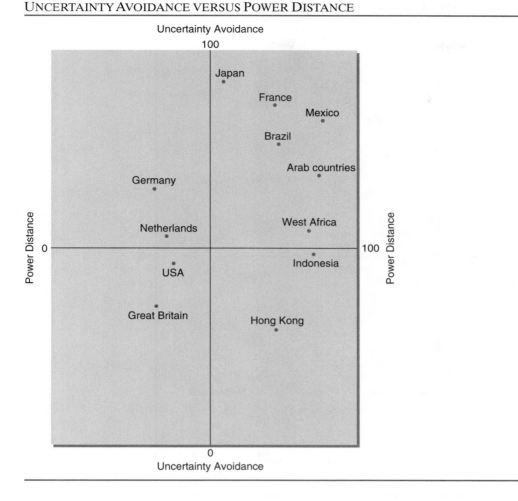

in three men own a Vuitton product. Many Japanese teenage girls want Louis Vuitton because "everyone has it."[66]

GLOBE (Global Leadership and Organizational Behavior Effectiveness) is a large-scale research program involving the efforts of a team of 160 scholars. The study explored cultural values and their impact on organizational leadership in 62 cultures.[67] The GLOBE researchers developed a scale of nine cultural dimensions based on a survey of 17,000 middle managers in three industries: banking, food processing, and telecommunications. The first three—uncertainty avoidance, power distance, and collectivism I (societal collectivism)—are the same as Hofstede's contructs described above. The remaining six culture dimensions are:

**Project GLOBE**

1. *Collectivism II (in-group collectivism).* The degree to which individuals express pride, loyalty, and cohesiveness in their organizations or families.

2. *Gender egalitarianism.* The degree to which an organization or society minimizes gender role differences and gender discrimination.

3. *Assertiveness.* The extent to which individuals are assertive, confrontational, and aggressive in social relationships.

---

[66]"Addicted to Japan," *Newsweek International* (October 14, 2002), p. 44.

[67]Robert J. House, Paul J. Hanges, Mansour Javidan, Peter W. Dorfman, and Vipin Gupta, *Culture, Leadership, and Organizations: The GLOBE Study of 62 Societies,* SAGE Publications, 2004.

**EXHIBIT 4-7B**
MASCULINITY VERSUS INDIVIDUALISM

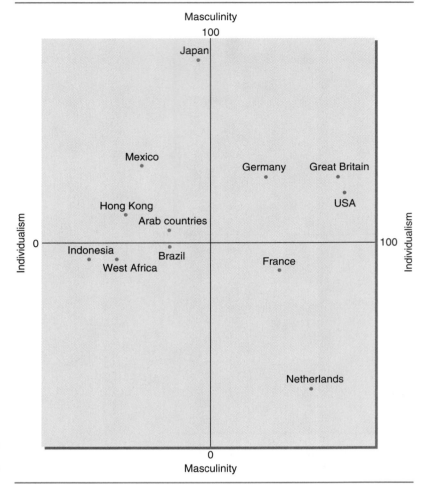

*Source:* Based on: Geert Hofstede, "Management Scientists are Human," *Management Science* 40, No. 1 (January 1994): 4–13.

4. *Future orientation.* The degree to which individuals in societies engage in future-oriented behaviors such as delaying gratification, planning, and investing in the future.

5. *Performance orientation.* The extent to which a society encourages and rewards group members for performance improvement and excellence.

6. *Humane orientation.* The extent to which a culture encourages and rewards people for being fair, altruistic, generous, caring, and kind to others.

**Exhibit 4-8** maps a subset of the countries on four of the dimensions. GLOBE has some overlap with the Hofstede scheme that we discussed earlier. However, there are some notable differences. The study and the measurements are far more recent—in fact, the project is still ongoing. The GLOBE scheme includes nine cultural dimensions instead of just four. The project also assigned scores to each country on the nine cultural dimensions from two angles, namely cultural practices reported in terms of *As Is* and values recorded in terms of *What Should Be.* (Exhibit 4-8 is based on the *As Is* part.)

**World Value Survey (WVS)**

Our final classification scheme is based on the **World Value Survey** (WVS) conducted by a network of social scientists at leading universities worldwide.[68] This survey assessed people's values and beliefs in about eighty countries, covering 85 percent

---
[68]See the project's website for further background information: http://www.worldvaluessurvey.org/organization/index.html

**EXHIBIT 4-8**
PROJECT GLOBE

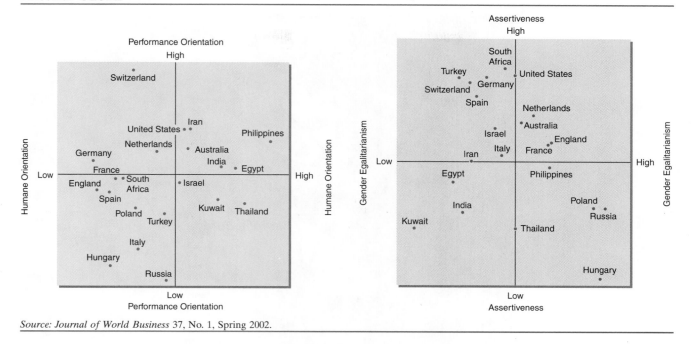

*Source: Journal of World Business* 37, No. 1, Spring 2002.

of the world's population. The first wave of the survey was carried out in the early 1980s; the most recent wave took place in 1999–2001. The WVS scheme differs from the previous ones in two respects: it has been done multiple times (the last data collection was the fourth wave), and the population covered by the sample is much broader than in other similar studies.

The chart in **Exhibit 4-9** shows how cultural attitudes in the surveyed countries stack up against one another. Most of the cross-cultural variations (70 percent) can be captured by two dimensions. The first one is the Traditional/Secular-rational dimension (vertical axis in Exhibit 4-9). This measure captures the relative importance of religious values as opposed to secular norms within society. Societies with a traditionalist orientation stress family values, parent–child ties, and deference to authority. The second category is the Survival/Self-expression dimension (horizontal axis in Exhibit 4-9). At one end of the spectrum are the survival values related to economic and physical security. At the other end are the self-expression values. Usually, as countries grow wealthier and modernize, the emphasis is on moving from Traditional toward Secular orientation and from Survival toward Self-expression values. Not all countries obey this rule though: countries such as the United States, Portugal, Ireland, and Mexico uphold Traditional values and Self-expression values at the same time (the lower-right quadrant in Exhibit 4-9).

## ADAPTING TO CULTURES  ◆ ◆ ◆ ◆ ◆ ◆ ◆

To function in the global marketplace, you need to become sensitive to cultural biases that influence your thinking, behavior, and decision-making. Given the diversity of cultures, cultural mishaps easily arise when global marketers interact with members of a "foreign" culture. Some of these cultural gaffes are relatively harmless and easily forgiven. Unfortunately, many cultural mistakes put the company and its products in an unpleasant situation or even create permanent damage. There are numerous firms whose globalization efforts have been derailed by cultural mishaps.

**EXHIBIT 4-9**
WORLD VALUE SURVEY (WVS)

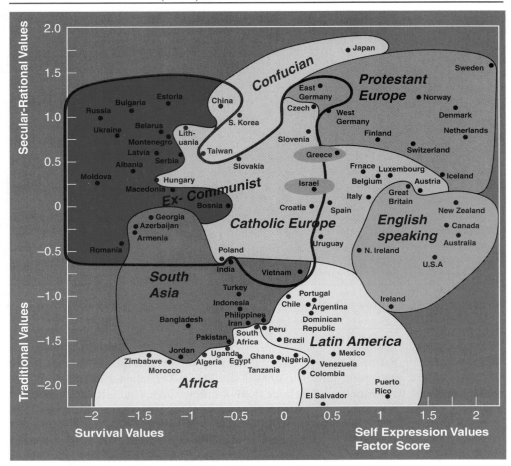

*Source:* Ronald Inglehart and Christian Welzel. *Modernization, Cultural Change and Democracy.* Cambridge University Press, 2005, page 63.

Lack of cultural sensitivity takes many forms. Most of us hold cultural stereotypes that distort cultural assessments. Cultural blinders that occur at the subconscious level are difficult to detect. When cultural misassessments do show up, it is usually after the fact. Therefore, cultural adaptation is absolutely necessary to make marketing decisions in line with the host culture. Such adaptation is hampered by the tendency to use a **self-reference criterion (SRC)**, a term coined by J. A. Lee, a cultural anthropologist. The SRC refers to people's unconscious tendency to resort to their own cultural experience and value systems to interpret a given business situation. Lee outlined a four-step procedure that allows global marketers to identify cross-cultural differences and take the necessary actions to cope with them. The four-step correction mechanism goes as follows:[69]

**Step 1:** Define the business problem or goal in terms of your own cultural traits, customs, or values.

**Step 2:** Define the business problem or goal in terms of the host culture's traits, customs, or values.

**Step 3:** Isolate the SRC influence in the problem and examine it scrupulously to see how it interferes with the business problem.

---

[69]J. A. Lee, "Cultural Analysis in Overseas Operations," *Harvard Business Review* (March–April 1966): 106–14.

**Step 4:** Redefine the business problem, but this time without the SRC influence, and solve for the "optimal" business goal situation.

Even more dangerous than SRC interference is to fall into the trap of **ethnocentrism**, the belief that one's own culture is superior to another culture. Procter & Gamble's experience in Mexico exemplifies cultural adaptation. Ace detergent, which P&G launched in Mexico in the early 1950s, was clobbered by the local brands. Ace, developed for U.S. washing machines, had a low-suds formula. At that time, many Mexicans washed their clothes in the river. High-suds detergents were therefore preferable. Eventually, the formula was changed to have a higher-suds content. P&G also adapted the packaging: smaller sizes, using plastic bags (to keep the detergent dry) instead of cardboard.

Campbell Soup's experience in China is another nice illustration of cultural adaptation.[70] When Campbell entered China in the early 1990s, it sold the same ready-to-eat soups that you find in American stores. Sales were marginal. Now, Campbell is trying to crack China with broths that fit with the Chinese tradition of making soup from scratch. Likewise, Kraft Foods tweaked its celebrated Oreo sandwich cookie in China to boost sales. After finding out that traditional Oreos were too sweet, the company introduced reduced-sugar versions. In 2006, Kraft totally reframed Oreo for the China market launching a layered chocolate wafer sandwich with a square rather than round shape. The company also developed a proprietary handling process to withstand the extreme weather conditions in the country.

The lesson offered by the experience of marketing behemoths such as P&G, Kraft, and Campbell Soup is that there is no magic bullet to avoid cultural mishaps. P&G mistakenly believed that what works in the United States would also work across the Rio Grande. Although Lee's four-step SRC-correction procedure appears flawless, it is often difficult to put into practice. When commenting about the Russian luxury market, Marcello Bottoli, the president and CEO of Samsonite, stated: "The key is having local people in local markets. There are cultural habits that a westerner or an expat just can't overcome."[71] This keen observation clearly applies to most other markets.

Still, companies can rely on several techniques to prepare managers for cross-cultural differences.[72] Immersion through prolonged stays in the foreign market often helps. Intensive foreign-language training is one of the more common tools to foster cultural sensitivity. Language skills, however, are not sufficient to become a successful international manager. Other qualities like humility—a willingness to accept the fact that you will not be as competent as in your own environment—also play an important role.[73] Numerous resources exist to familiarize managers with other aspects of the host country's cultural environment. An online resource is the Lonely Planet publisher's website (www.lonelyplanet.com). Many providers of cultural training programs (e.g., Berlitz International) offer a cultural orientation for executives. Such programs range from environmental briefings to "cultural assimilator" exercises where participants are exposed to various simulated settings that could arise during their assignment.

## CULTURE AND THE MARKETING MIX ◆ ◆ ◆ ◆ ◆ ◆ ◆

Culture is a key pillar of the marketplace. The success of international marketing activities is to a large extent driven by the local culture. These cultural variables may act as barriers or opportunities. In this section we show how culture and the firm's marketing mix interact. **Global Perspective 4-4** shows how Population Services

---

[70]"Kraft Reinvents Iconic Oreo to Win in China," *The Wall Street Journal*, May 1, 2008, p. 28.

[71]"The Pitch in Russia: Luxury with Cultural Sensitivity," *International Herald Tribune*, November 30, 2007, p. 30.

[72]Howard Tu and Sherry E. Sullivan, "Preparing Yourself for an International Assignment," *Business Horizons* (January–February 1994): 67–70.

[73]"Culture Shock for Executives," *Financial Times*, April 5, 1995, p. 12.

---

## GLOBAL PERSPECTIVE 4-3

### PREVENTING HIV/ AIDS IN MYANMAR

Condoms were seldom used in Myanmar (Burma) just a decade ago. Yet, today they are one of the country's fastest growing consumer goods—more than 40 million were purchased in 2005. This compares to only 4.4 million in 1997 (see Table). This rapid increase reflects increased awareness of HIV/AIDS among the local population. HIV/AIDS rates in Myanmar among high-risk groups are among the highest in the region now: up to 2.2 percent of adult Burmese have been infected.

The surge in sales of condoms is largely the result of Population Services International (PSI). PSI is a non-profit organization based in Washington, D.C. For the first 16 years after its founding in 1970, PSI concentrated on the area of family planning through social marketing. In the late 1980s, PSI has also entered the areas of malaria and HIV/AIDS prevention. The group, which had a 2005 budget of $297m, has program offices in almost 70 countries.

PSI launched its social marketing campaign in Myanmar in 1996, despite criticism of pro-democracy groups. PSI supplies about 75 percent of all the condoms used in Myanmar. Heavy subsidies allow them to be sold for one-third of the production cost. Guy Stallworthy, PSI's Myanmar country director, points out that "Price is the number one issue here—you are not going to get a mass market with an expensive product . . . Consumers don't have much money but they are discerning and want to buy quality things . . . if you can somehow make quality affordable, you are bound to be a winner in this country."

Apart from pricing, promotion is a major challenge. When PSI first imported condoms in Myanmar, the brand

*Sources:* "A Golden Opportunity: Preventing HIV/AIDS in Myanmar," http://www.psi.org/resources/pubs/myanmar_profile.pdf, accessed February 22, 2006 and "A Chameleon Enlists in War on Aids," *Financial Times* (February 20, 2006): 6.

name was written in Burmese. However, PSI found out that the Burmese associated Burmese-language packaging with inferior quality. In 1998, PSI changed to *Aphaw* ("trusted companion") in English, with usage instructions in Burmese.

CONDOMS DISTRIBUTED IN MYANMAR SINCE THE LAUNCH OF APHAW (IN MILLIONS)

| Year | Private Sector | Public Sector | PSI Social Marketing | Total Condom Market |
|------|---------|--------|-----------|--------|
| 1997 | 1.4 | 1.2 | 1.8 | 4.4 |
| 1998 | 2.2 | 2.1 | 3.3 | 7.6 |
| 1999 | 2.8 | 2.0 | 6.8 | 11.6 |
| 2000 | 7.0 | 1.5 | 7.9 | 16.4 |

*Source:* www.psi.org, accessed February 22, 2006

PSI built up its own national distribution network, with 28 sales representatives and 50 wholesalers. Aphaw condoms are available in every town and major village. PSI developed its own advertising mascot: a chameleon (a "pothinnyo") wearing a traditional sun hat. These days, PSI's mascot has an 82 percent recognition among urban Burmese. PSI collaborated with cultural troupes to produce traveling theatrical performances to educated communities about the risks of HIV/AIDS. It also produced soap operas and feature films to stem the spread of HIV/AIDS. In 2005, PSI's mascot made its TV debut when PSI sponsored the broadcast of English Premier League soccer matches on local television. At 0.8 per capita per year, condom use is still minimal compared to Thailand or Cambodia. PSI's goal is to raise condom use to one per capita per year by 2008.

---

International adapts marketing tools to local Burmese tastes to make condoms acceptable in Myanmar.

**Product Policy**    The PowerpuffGirls is a karate superheroes show aired on the Cartoon Network with a huge following among American preteens. When in 2001 the show debuted in Japan with a "Japanese look" it failed miserably. To boost its appeal, Cartoon Network decided to revamp the characters. Toei, a well-established Japanese animation house, was brought in to assist with the overhaul. The characters Blossom, Buttercup, and Bubbles were given Japanese names, more realistic outfits (e.g., miniskirts, hip-hugging belts), and the lives of Japanese junior-high-school students. As Japanese kids prefer more narrative plots, the shows were made 15 to 20 minutes long (compared to the 7 to 11 minutes shows in the United States). They also introduced new themes in line with Japanese girls' expectations such as love themes and acceptance of people who are different ("Monsters can be anyone who is different from us. If we change our attitude, they can become our friends"). The show became successful not just among Japanese girls but also attracted animation-obsessed adult men (*otaku*). As a result, Cartoon Network launched special items tied to show such as bookmarks and pop music targeting the show's adult Japanese fans.[74]

In recent years, doughnuts have been catching on in Asia as a luxury treat.[75] International doughnut chains such as Dunkin' Donuts and Krispy Kreme have modified their product offerings in the region to cater toward Asian palates. Dunkin' Donuts Taiwan, for instance, offers localized flavors such as green tea and honeydew melon. Doughnut chains also lowered the sugar content as Asians have a lower preference for sweet foods.

Certain products, in particular, food, beverages, and clothing are obviously more culture-bound than other products. Products or services can also be banned or restricted due to cultural reasons. In March 2004, the government of Saudi Arabia banned the import and sale of mobile phones with cameras after reports of "misconduct" (photographing women) by owners of such phones.[76]

The implied meanings of brand names also exemplify the role of culture in global marketing. Sometimes the brand name can hurt sales as P & G experienced with its Ariel laundry detergent in Middle Eastern countries like Egypt. The detergent was being tied with Ariel Sharon, Israel's former prime minister. Kit Kat, on the other hand, gained a strong following among Japanese students, especially during exam periods. The name of the chocolate bar, made by Nestlé,[77] closely resembles a Japanese expression, "kitto katsu," used by students to wish each other good luck prior to exams. The phrase roughly translates as "I hope you will win." Often Japanese parents will buy Kit Kats as lucky charms for their children during exam days.[78]

Cultural norms sometimes open up new product opportunities. In most Asian countries, white skin is associated with positive values that relate to beauty, class, and an upscale lifestyle. Dark skin is linked with hard labor and toil. In India, the skin whitener market has been growing at an annual rate of around 20 percent. Multinationals such as Unilever, Avon, and Beiersdorf have been able to cash in on this phenomenon by marketing skin whiteners. Indeed, for Avon, its top-selling product in India is VIP Fairness Cream. The cream that retails for 160 rupees promises a fairer skin in one month.[79] In Vietnam, Unilever customized its brands to reflect local customs. The Vietnamese version of SunSilk shampoo includes extracts from a seed known as *bo ket*, which Vietnamese women have long used to keep their hair shiny black. Unilever also decided to sell a local fish sauce under the Knorr brand name. The sauce is bottled on Phu Quoc, an island where the fish sauce originated. Unilever vowed that it would protect the good name and purity of Phu Quoc fish sauce.[80]

## Pricing

Customers' willingness to pay for your product will vary across cultures. Products that are perceived as good value in one culture may have little or no value in other cultures. In Western countries, a high price is often seen as a signal of premium quality for many product categories. Such beliefs sometimes also exist in less developed markets. For instance, multinational pharmaceuticals such as Pfizer benefit from a belief in much of the developing world that branded medicines are worth paying a premium because of the perception that generic drugs are less safe and less effective. In Venezuela, a monthly standard dose of Lipitor, Pfizer's cholesterol-lowering drug, costs between $100 and $125, compared to less than $50 for a generic.[81] However, in emerging markets, charging a high price is often regarded as gouging the customer for many product categories.

[74]"Cartoon Characters Get Local Makeovers in Asia," *The Wall Street Journal*, October 16, 2007, p. 28.

[75]"Doughnuts Catching on in Asia as a High-end Western Treat," *International Herald Tribune*, June 13, 2007, p. 12.

[76]"Saudi ministries picture the future as embargo on mobiles draws in King Fahd," *Financial Times*, November 23, 2004, p. 7.

[77]In the United States, Kit Kat is made (under license) by Hershey's.

[78]http://news.bbc.co.uk/2/hi/asia-pacific/4230471.stm.

[79]"Creams for a Lighter Skin Capture the Asian Market," *International Herald Tribune*, April 24, 1998, p. 2.

[80]"Unilever has a taste for success in Vietnam," *Financial Times*, December 2, 2003, p. 9.

[81]"Drug Firms See Poorer Nations as Cure for Sales Problems," *The Wall Street Journal Asia*, July 8, 2009, pp. 14-15.

One example of how pricing and culture interact is the practice of odd pricing in which prices end with 9 (or 5) ($19.99 instead of $20). Specific price points like End-9 prices are known to increase unit sales substantially. This sales effect is due to the fact that these "magic prices" signal good value to the customers. In Chinese-speaking cultures like Hong Kong, however, the price points used often end with 8 instead of 9.[82] In Chinese cultures, the number 8 is associated with prosperity and good luck. This symbolism stems from the fact that the digit 8's pronunciation in Chinese, *ba*, is similar to *fa*, which means to "get rich".[83]

**Distribution** Cultural variables may also dictate distribution strategies. Plagued with lifestyle changes, Avon, the U.S. cosmetics maker, has been forced to fine-tune its direct selling model. In places like Taiwan and China, Avon experimented with alternative distribution modes for selling its products. Some of the alternatives include the use of kiosks, small counters in department stores, the Internet, and selling products on home-shopping TV channels.

Retailers must often fine-tune their practices when entering foreign markets. Wal-Mart learned this lesson the hard way in Germany, a market that the mega-retailer was never able to crack. Grocery bagging turned out to be a no-no for German shoppers, as they do not like strangers handling their groceries. When clerks followed orders to smile, male customers took that as a come-on.[84] After many years of sustained losses, Wal-Mart sold its 85 German stores to its German rival Metro in July 2006.

Companies often need to tweak their distribution model in emerging markets; even their model is a key success factor in their home market. A good example is Dell's direct sales model, which has long been the computer maker's holly grail. In countries such as Russia, Dell is pushing into traditional retailing by opening company-owned retail stores. Countries such as Russia lack the home delivery services needed to support Dell's direct sales and customers have little experience with e-commerce.[85] In China, where face-to-face contact is important when selling computers, Dell overhauled its direct-sales model when it announced a deal in September 2007 to sell computers through Gome, a major Chinese electronics retailer.[86] McDonald's offers another example.[87] In many developing world cities, McDonald's now offers delivery service. The model works well in traffic-congested cities with cheap labor. In Egypt, where the delivery setup originated in 1995, deliveries account for 27 percent of McDonald's revenue.

**Promotion** Of the four marketing mix elements, promotion is the most visible one. People who do not buy your product for whatever reason may still be exposed to your advertising. Culture will typically have a major influence on a firm's communication strategy. Key events of a country's cultural calendar (e.g., Chinese New Year, Ramadan) often create major marketing opportunities (see **Exhibit 4-10**). The manner in which customers process marketing communications often hinges on their cultural values. One recent study found that North Americans are persuaded more by promotion-focused information (benefits to be gained) whereas Chinese consumers are driven by prevention-focused messages (problems that can be avoided).[88] Advertising styles that are effective in certain cultures can be counterproductive in other cultures. In high-context cultures (e.g., Spain, Italy, Japan), communication styles tend to be more indirect and subtle, making use of less copy and more symbols. In low-context cultures (e.g., Germany,

[82]Lee C. Simmons and Robert M. Schindler, "Cultural Superstitions and the Price Endings Used in Chinese Advertising," *Journal of International Marketing*, 11 (2), 2003, pp. 101–11.

[83]Note that the Beijing Olympics 2008's opening date was August 8, 2008 (8-8-08).

[84]"Wal-Mart: Local Pipsqueak," *BusinessWeek*, April 11, 2005, pp. 25–26.

[85]"Where Dell Sells With Brick and Mortar," *BusinessWeek*, October 8, 2007, p. 78.

[86]"China Chapter of Dell's Retail Adventure Opens," *Financial Times*, September 25, 2007, p. 7.

[87]"Knock Knock, It's Your Big Mac," *BusinessWeek*, July 23, 2007, p. 36.

[88]Donnel A. Briley and Jennifer L. Aaker, "When Does Culture Matter? Effects of Personal Knowledge on the Correction of Culture-Based Judgments," *Journal of Marketing Research*, 18 (2006), pp. 395–408.

## EXHIBIT 4-10
MCDONALD'S CHINESE NEW YEAR PROMOTION (HONG KONG)

Courtesy Kristiaan Helsen

Scandinavia), on the other hand, advertising uses more copy, factual data, and reasoning.[89] Advertising in countries such as the United States and the United Kingdom often uses a lecture-format style in which a celebrity "lectures" the audience about the good points of the product being advertised. Cultures in these countries are low in power distance and high in individualism. One study compared the reactions of Chinese and U.S. subjects to different advertising appeals. Not surprisingly, the study found that Chinese consumers favored a collectivistic appeal, whereas their U.S. counterparts preferred an individualistic appeal.[90]

Country of origin strategies may also need to be customized across countries. In collectivist cultures, local brands are likely to benefit from touting their local roots. However, one study suggests that in individualist countries, country of origin appeals will be beneficial only when the local brand is superior.[91] Therefore, buy-local

[89]Marieke de Mooij, *Global Marketing and Advertising. Understanding Cultural Paradoxes* (Thousand Oaks, CA: SAGE Publications, 1998), pp. 157–58.

[90]Yong Zhang and James P. Neelankavil, "The Influence of Culture on Advertising Effectiveness in China and the USA. A Cross-Cultural Study," *European Journal of Marketing* 31 (1997): 134–49.

[91]Gürhan-Canli, Zeynep, and Durairaj Maheswaran, "Cultural Variations in Country of Origin Effects," *Journal of Marketing Research* 37 (August 2000): 309–317.

## $\mathscr{G}$LOBAL PERSPECTIVE 4-4

### SELLING RAZOR BLADES IN JAPAN

Gillette, now owned by Procter & Gamble, is the dominant razor brand in Western Europe, Russia, China, and the United States. In Japan, however, Gillette is a distant second, behind Schick, which has more than half of the Japanese market and which entered Japan much earlier than its rival. The wet shaving market in Japan is worth about US$310 million with potential to grow much further. After introducing the Fusion brand in 2006, Gillette's market share jumped from 21 to 33 percent, following a long spell of stagnant growth. Japan has been a difficult market to penetrate for a number of reasons: most Japanese males prefer electric razors over razor blades, Japanese men shave less frequently than men in Western countries.

*Sources:* "A Battle for Hearts and Chins in Japan," *International Herald Tribune*, June 26, 2007, p. 12; and "Procter and Gillette Learn From Each Other's Marketing Ways," http://www.nytimes.com/2007/04/12/business/media/12adco.html?_r=1&pagewanted=print&oref=slogin, accessed July 22, 2008.

With Fusion, Gillette customized its product and promotion strategy to local tastes. P&G found that Japanese men were particularly interested in product features. So when Gillette launched Fusion, it used the name "Fusion 5+1," stressing the fact that the razor comes with five blades and a trimmer on the back. It further positioned the Fusion razors against Schick's four-bladed Quattro Titanium razor by labeling its packages with "Superior versus four-blade products." Gillette also joined with a local barber's association to run the shaving bar in Tokyo's financial district. Several barbers now sell Fusion blades in their shops.

When in summer 2007 Gillette debuted the Phantom razor, a black and silver version of the Fusion, Gillette used local athletes and celebrities such as Kosuke Kitajima, a breaststroke gold medalist. It also changed the brand name to Air as the original name did not translate very well in Japan.

campaigns in highly individualist countries such as Australia and the United States may be counterproductive unless the product has superior quality.

Local cultural taboos and norms also influence advertising styles. In the United States, Gidget, a talking Chihuahua, is the advertising mascot for Taco Bell, a Mexican-style fast-food chain owned by Yum! Brands. However, Gidget does not feature in Taco Bell's Singapore ads. Singapore's large Muslim population was the main motivation for dropping Gidget—Muslims view dogs as unclean animals.[92] Global Perspective 4-3 describes how Gillette tailors its products and advertising strategies to local tastes in Japan.

## ◆◆◆◆◆◆◆◆ ORGANIZATIONAL CULTURES

So far, we have looked at the importance of national cultures for international marketing operations. At the same time, most companies are also characterized by their **organizational (corporate) culture**. Deshpandé and Webster[93] defined organizational culture as "the pattern of shared values and beliefs that help individuals understand organizational functioning and thus provide them with the norms for behavior in the organization" (p. 4). Shared beliefs relate to leadership styles, organizational attributes, bonding mechanisms within the organization, and overall strategic emphases.[94] As you can see in **Exhibit 4-11**, organizational culture types can be described along two dimensions. The vertical axis distinguishes between organizations with *organic* (emphasis on flexibility, spontaneity, individuality) and *mechanistic* processes (emphasis on control, stability, order). The horizontal axis describes whether

---

[92]"As Taco Bell Enters Singapore, Gidget Avoids the Ad Limelight," Ad Age International, January 11, 1999, pp. 13–14. 64 "A Campaign Too Far for Carlsberg," *Financial Times*, August 11, 1998, p. 8.

[93]Rohit Deshpandé and Frederick E. Webster, "Organizational Culture and Marketing: Defining the Research Agenda," *Journal of Marketing*, 53, (no. 1) (1989): 3–15.

[94]Rohit Deshpandé, John U. Farley, and Frederick E. Webster, "Corporate Culture, Customer Orientation, and Innovativeness in Japanese Firms: A Quadrad Analysis," *Journal of Marketing* 57, no. 1 (1993): 23–37.

**EXHIBIT 4-11**
A MODEL OF ORGANIZATIONAL CULTURE TYPES

**Organic Processes (flexibility, spontaneity)**

| | |
|---|---|
| TYPE: Clan<br>DOMINANT ATTRIBUTES:<br>  Cohesiveness, participation, teamwork,<br>  sense of family<br>LEADER STYLE: Mentor, facilitator,<br>  parent-figure<br>BONDING: Loyalty, tradition, interpersonal<br>  cohesion<br>STRATEGIC EMPHASES: Toward developing<br>  human resources, commitment, morale | TYPE: Adhocracy<br>DOMINANT ATTRIBUTES:<br>  Entrepreneurship, creativity, adaptability<br><br>LEADER STYLE: Entrepreneur, innovator, risk<br>  taker<br>BONDING: Entrepreneurship, flexibility, risk<br><br>STRATEGIC EMPHASES: Toward innovation,<br>  growth, new resources |
| **INTERNAL MAINTENANCE**<br>**(smoothing activities, integration)**<br>TYPE: Hierarchy<br>DOMINANT ATTRIBUTES: Order, rules and<br>  regulations, uniformity<br>LEADER STYLE: Coordinator,<br>  administrator<br>BONDING: Rules, policies, and procedures<br><br>STRATEGIC EMPHASES: Toward stability,<br>  predictability, smooth operations | **EXTERNAL POSITIONING**<br>**(competition, differentiation)**<br>TYPE: Market<br>DOMINANT ATTRIBUTES: Competitiveness,<br>  goal achievement<br>LEADER STYLE: Decisive, achievement-<br>  oriented<br>BONDING: Goal orientation, production,<br>  competition<br>STRATEGIC EMPHASES: Toward competitive<br>  advantage and market superiority |

**MECHANISTIC PROCESSES (control, order, stability)**

*Note:* Adapted from Cameron and Freeman (1991) and Quinn (1988).

*Source:* Rohit Deshpandé, John U. Farley, and Frederick E. Webster, "Corporate Culture, Customer Orientation, and Innovativeness in Japanese Firms: A Quadrad Analysis," *Journal of Marketing,* 57, 1, 1993, pp. 23–37.

the organizational emphasis is on *internal maintenance* (integration, efficient and smooth operations) or *external positioning* (competitive actions and achievement, differentiation). This scheme leads to four organizational culture types labeled *clan, adhocracy, hierarchical,* and *market.* Exhibit 4-11 lists for each of these organizational forms the dominant attributes, leadership styles, primary means of bonding, and strategic emphases.

*Clan cultures* (top left quadrant) stress cohesiveness, participation, and teamwork. They are often headed by a patriarch. The bonding glue is loyalty and tradition. Commitment to such firms runs high. In contrast, *adhocracy cultures* (top right quadrant) are driven by values like entrepreneurship, creativity, adaptability, flexibility, and tolerance. Effectiveness in such cultures is viewed in terms of finding new markets and new opportunities for growth. The head of such organizations is usually an entrepreneur or an innovator. Such firms are committed to innovation and new product development. The third form is the *hierarchy culture* (bottom left quadrant), which emphasizes order, rules, and regulations. Such organizations tend to be very formalized and structured. Maintaining a smooth-running operation is very important for such firms. Organizational effectiveness within hierarchical cultures is defined by consistency and achievement of clearly stated goals. Finally, *market culture-like* organizations (bottom right quadrant) value competitiveness, tasks and goal achievement, and productivity. These organizations tend to be production-oriented. The major concern is getting the job done.

Most multinational firms have elements of several types of cultures. Despite the fact that managers these days are exposed to similar business concepts and technologies, cultural differences in management style and practice persist.[95] **Exhibit 4-12** lists the seven distinct business cultures based on a recent survey that polled 700 managers worldwide. Multinational firms, regardless of size, must heed such differences. Not

[95]"United in a World of Difference," *Financial Times,* October 15, 2004, p. 8.

**EXHIBIT 4-12**
SEVEN DISTINCTIVE BUSINESS CULTURES

| Business culture | Description | Prime example |
|---|---|---|
| 1. Go-getting | Staff highly enthusiastic about their work. Risk-taking attitude. Decisions made in highly charged debates, not via consensus. | United States |
| 2. Worker bee | Tasks may overlap, responsibilities are shared. Decisions are consensual. Strong sense of pride. | Hong Kong |
| 3. People who care | Employers assist poor performers. Spend time making sure staff members are happy. | Sweden |
| 4. Easy going | Workers do their tasks freely. Emphasis on getting the job done. | Australia |
| 5. Stalwart | Roles, functions clearly defined. Aversion to change for change's sake. | United Kingdom |
| 6. Mechanistic | Managers work "by the book." Culture egalitarian but with strong sense of individual responsibility. | The Netherlands |
| 7. Family entrepreneurs | Roles and functions are structured on "family" principles. Management is patriarchal. | India |

*Source:* Based on "United in a World of Difference," *Financial Times*, October 15, 2004, p. 8.

all MNCs succeed. Kia Motors America exemplifies how a strongly hierarchical company culture can create cultural discord. The American subsidiary of Hyundai, a Korean carmaker, experienced a major management shakeup in recent years. One important reason behind the exodus of talent was that many of the former U.S. executives deeply disliked Hyundai's authoritarian management style with little tolerance for disagreement.[96]

In general, Anglo-Saxon companies are much more market-type cultures than German or French firms. Perhaps not surprisingly, Japanese companies are also much more clan-driven than companies in other countries. The same study also found that organizations with a market culture tend to have a better business performance. On the other hand, firms governed by a clan or hierarchy culture are poor business performers. Cross-cultural gaps resulting from a merger are fairly common. DaimlerChrysler, was formed by the merger of Daimler and Chrysler, went through a stormy honeymoon period, not the least of which were the cross-cultural clashes stemming from the merger. The old Daimler was bureaucratic and very formal, whereas the old Chrysler was spontaneous. The company's German managers moved toward a less formal way of doing business under the influence of their U.S. counterparts.[97] In May 2007, Daimler sold Chrysler to Cerberus Capital Management, a private investment firm, for US$6 billion.

In the balance of this chapter, we focus on two customer-related areas that are becoming increasingly important to global marketers: global account management and global customer relationship management.

## ◆ ◆ ◆ ◆ ◆ ◆ ◆ ◆ ◆  GLOBAL ACCOUNT MANAGEMENT (GAM)

In business-to-business contexts and in manufacturer-distributor relationships, one major consequence of having a global presence is dealing with global customers. The coordination of the management of such customer accounts across national boundaries is referred to as **global account management (GAM)**.

Global customer accounts, due to their sheer size, often have major leverage over their suppliers. In their drive to squeeze costs, these customer accounts will often strive for global contracts with global prices. Global retailers, such as Carrefour, Wal-Mart, and Royal Ahold, try to gain a cost advantage over their local competitors by negotiating the best terms with their suppliers. At the same time, global customers can also offer tremendous opportunities. Indeed, one survey of global account managers indicated that sales to their global customers had grown on average by 10 to 15

---

[96]"My Way or the Highway at Hyundai," *BusinessWeek*, March 17, 2008, pp. 48–51.
[97]"The DaimlerChrysler Emulsion," *The Economist*, July 29, 2000, pp. 65–66.

percent per year.[98] Effective global account management could ultimately lead to a win-win for both parties.

A research project of global customer account practices singled out the following areas that might require a globalized treatment:

- *Single point of contact.* Global customers prefer a single point of contact rather than multiple points. This will improve vendor–supplier relationships.
- *Coordination of resources for serving customers.* They also demand better coordination of their suppliers' resources.
- *Uniform prices and terms of trade.* Global customers will also often push for a uniform price, typically meaning the lowest price—unless the supplier can reasonably justify cross-border price gaps. Other non-price elements in the contract, such as shipping policies, warranties, volume discounts, could also be vulnerable to single-policy demands.
- *Standardized products and services.* They also often expect that their suppliers are able to deliver standardized products or services, unless good reasons can be provided.
- *Consistency in service quality and performance.* Coupled to the previous requirement, global accounts request a high degree of consistency in service support quality and performance.
- *Support in countries where the company has no presence.* Finally, global customers will also prefer a supplier who is able to service agreements with them in all countries where the customer operates, including the ones where the supplier has no presence.

The first key question that a vendor should ask is which customer accounts should be designated as global accounts. Obviously, one crucial factor will be the preferences and the organizational setup of the client. Even if a customer desires a global relationship, global account management is not always the right response. One other key criterion is the balance of power between the customer and the company. A major driver here will be the degree of internal coordination in each of the parties. If the vendor is less globally integrated than the customer, then the vendor might be vulnerable. Hence, a global account relationship would have limited appeal for the vendor. The other criterion is the extent of strategic synergies that can flow from a global relationship. If the relationship merely focuses on sales transactions, then globalization will most likely imply lower prices and increased pressure for volume discounts. Global account relationships are much more rewarding when they are triggered by strategic synergy rationales. Synergies can be achieved in areas where the two partners can collaborate, such as product innovation, brand building, and market development.

Effective GAM strives to capture the scale and scope benefits of an integrated approach while maintaining the local responsiveness to cope with the account's local needs. The success of a global account relationship depends on the right implementation. The following guidelines contribute to effective implementation:

- *Clarify the role of the global account management team.* Usually, a global account manager is designated who will be dedicated to the global account. Often, the manager will be based in the country where the customer is headquartered. Typically, the account manager will report to the local country manager and to company headquarters. Global account managers often end up working very closely with their customers; sometimes they or some of their support staff members even have an office at the customer's premises.

---

[98]David Arnold, Julian Birkinshaw, and Omar Toulan, "Can Selling Be Globalized? The Pitfalls of Global Account [FN 96, cont.'d] Management," *California Management Review* 44, no. 1 (Fall 2001): 8–20.

[99]David B. Montgomery and George S. Yip, "The Challenge of Global Customer Management," *Marketing Management* (Winter 2000): 22–29.

[100]This section draws from Arnold, Birkinshaw and Toulan, "Can Selling Be Globalized," pp. 11–19 and David Arnold, Julian Birkinshaw, and Omar Toulan, "Implementing Global Account Management in Multinational Corporations," Working Paper No. 00-103 (Marketing Science Institute, 2000).

- *Make incentive structure realistic.* Having the right incentive mechanisms in place is crucial. This is also a major headache for companies: if a global account places an order, how should the commission be split between the global account manager and the local unit? Many companies simply pay the commission twice, but that can be an expensive solution.

- *Pick the right global account managers.* Being a successful local or regional salesperson is not always a promise for turning into a good global account manager. Other skills that matter include the ability to coordinate efforts internally, having a long-term perspective, nurturing the account—not milking it. Given that GAM is primarily a matter of internal coordination, good coordination and communication skills are probably most valuable.

- *Create a strong support network.* The strength of the support network is another success factor. Global account managers will need support staff, solid customer information (profitability, worldwide sales), communication materials, and so forth. Having solid internal support systems in place is known to be one of the most critical variables in making GAM programs successful.[101]

- *Make sure that the customer relationship operates at more than one level.* Customer relationships should be established at all levels—above and underneath the global account manager, right down to the local field and support team.

- *Ensure that the GAM program remains flexible and dynamic.* A supplier's GAM program should maintain a fit with the customer's changing needs. The Xerox–BMW relationship is a good example. BMW wanted to make its vehicle ownership manuals personalized and less expensive to make. Most manuals included at least four languages and were quite thick, wasting paper and leading to high printing costs. Xerox cooperated with BMW to offer a new manual with the buyer's name in the buyer's preferred language and other personalized features. The new manual is 80 percent thinner.[102]

## ✦✦✦✦✦✦✦✦ GLOBAL CUSTOMER RELATIONSHIP MANAGEMENT (CRM)

**Customer relationship management (CRM)** or **database marketing** is the strategic process of managing interactions between the company and its customers, with the objective of maximizing the lifetime value of the customers for the company and satisfying the customers by being customer-focused. A successful CRM program will create a formidable competitive edge and can boost profits substantially. Multinational corporations apply CRM programs across national boundaries. In China, Volkswagen decided to implement a CRM project by building a data warehouse that can store information about millions of dealers and prospective customers. The system would allow VW to track prospective customers from the awareness stage to purchase interest, offering insights into reasons for purchase and nonpurchase. VW spent around $3.75 million to develop the customer database.[103]

Several benefits can be derived from globalizing CRM programs. In some industries (e.g., travel, rental car, credit cards), global customers account for a major share of the business. Furthermore, just as in other areas of global marketing, country units can share ideas and expertise on CRM programs. Typically, customer relationships evolve through distinct phases, each with its unique requirements. The first phase is customer acquisition. This phase involves prospect evaluation, acquisition management, and recovery of "old" customers (brand switchers, inactive customers). The second phase focuses on retention. The most critical areas here include customer evaluation (lifetime

---

[101]See Arnold, et al., "Implementing Global Account Management."

[102]Shi, Linda H., et al., "Global Account Management Capability: Insights from Leading Suppliers," *Journal of International Marketing* 13, no. 2 (2005): 93–113.

[103]"Shanghai VW Drives Tailor-Made CRM Plan," *Ad Age Global* (April 2002): 12.

value), consumer complaint management, retention mechanisms (e.g., loyalty programs), up-selling (meaning, the firm tries to sell higher-margin items to its current client) or cross-selling (meaning, the firm tries to sell other products in its portfolio to the existing client) and referral management. The final possible phase is the termination of the relationship. This may happen because of customer-related factors such as the customer simply losing interest in the category or switching to another supplier.

Many reasons can motivate the rollout of a CRM program. The German company Otto Versand is the world's largest mail-order company and one of the largest Internet retailers worldwide. It decided to introduce CRM for the following reasons:[104]

**Motivations**

- Decreasing customer loyalty, which puts pressure on the company to improve programs for customer retention and recovery.
- Deteriorating customer response rate in customer acquisition leading to higher acquisition costs. CRM can help here by offering better-qualified customer addresses and guidelines on effective acquisition strategies.
- More demanding customers.
- Highly differentiated target segments, which require differentiated marketing campaigns and, in the extreme case, one-on-one marketing.
- Emergence of the Internet, which allows richer communication and interactive marketing.

These motivations overlap to some extent with the reasons why KLM, the Dutch airline, embraced CRM:[105]

- Air travel has become a commodity, putting pressure on margins.
- New entrants (e.g., discount carriers in Europe) have changed the rules of competition.
- Product differentiation has become increasingly tough.
- Competitors in Europe and the United States are investing in CRM.
- Customers are unique; they increasingly expect tailored services.
- Customers are better informed about product offerings and the market (knowledge transparency).

The benefits of effective CRM programs are potentially huge. The key ones include the following:

**Gains from CRM**

- *Better understanding of customers' expectations and behavior.* This knowledge allows the MNC to develop differentiated strategies. The ultimate goal of CRM is to be able to offer the right product or service to the right customer at the right price and via the proper distribution channel.
- *Ability to measure the customer's value to the company.* Putting value—in terms of current and projected margin contribution—on the customer also facilitates more effective resource allocation. Such insights help the company decide which target customers to nurture, to grow, to protect (against competitive inroads), or to economize on.
- *Lower customer acquisition and retention costs.* In principle, a successful CRM program should enable the MNC to do a better job in acquiring and keeping

[104]Norbert Sellin, "Automated Direct Marketing Campaigns at Otto," in "Customer Relationship Management: Strategies and Company-wide Implementation," Conference Summary, Report No. 02–112 (Marketing Science Institute, 2002), pp. 11–12.

[105]Lesley McDermott, "Targeting the Right Customers," in "Customer Relationship Management: Strategies and Company-wide Implementation," Conference Summary, Report No. 02-112 (Marketing Science Institute, 2002), pp. 11–12.

customers. Obviously, this benefit might not materialize if the major competitors also adopt CRM programs.

- *Ability to interact and communicate with consumers in countries where access to traditional channels is limited.* Access to conventional tools, such as TV, press, or radio, might be restricted because of an underdeveloped media infrastructure, government regulations, or high charges. Alternatively, the prospect might be a very particular niche, which is hard to reach with more common tools. A good example is Western Union's operations in Asia.[106] Western Union's business model is that people can transfer money overseas without the need for a bank account. This has made the firm very popular among low-paid foreign expatriate workers who often do not have a bank account. Given the niche qualities of this customer group, spending marketing money on mass media would create a lot of wastage. Instead, Western Union developed a customer database that facilitates direct mailing campaigns. Under such circumstances, CRM offers a valuable alternative to reach the target customers.

**Challenges**　Marketing programs can get much mileage out of CRM systems. However, to capture the full benefits of a CRM program in the global marketplace, several challenges have to be met:

- *Customer database.* The success of a CRM program depends to a large degree on the quality of the customer database. Setting up a high-quality customer database can be time-consuming and expensive. Access to customer data in some countries can be a major struggle—creative and inspired thinking is often necessary to come up with innovative ways to gather customer data. Audi's Asia Pacific division used an online campaign in Singapore and South Korea to build up its database of prospective customers. To encourage prospects to offer personal data, Audi offered users the chance to win tickets to an Audi driving clinic.[107]

- *Clutter.* One major risk of CRM is that, given all the hype, everybody and his brother jumps on the bandwagon. Indeed, as we saw earlier, this was one reason KLM adopted CRM. As a result, breaking through the clutter can prove to be a major task. When customers start receiving e-mails from every airline he or she ever flew with, those personalized e-mails most likely get the spam treatment.

- *Cultural and language differences.* Obviously, just as with other endeavors in global marketing, cultural and language differences can prove to be major obstacles, especially when the customer database covers multiple countries. Chinese names, for instance, can be written in multiple ways, creating the risk of duplication.

- *Privacy and other government regulations.* Privacy and personal data protection are highly sensitive issues in many countries. Often, it is difficult—for legal or cultural reasons—to buy a database from third parties. Companies should make themselves familiar with local regulations and laws covering these issues.

- *Local talent.* Qualified staff to run and support CRM projects is often scarce and difficult to find in many countries.

- *Local infrastructure.* CRM is also difficult to run in countries where the direct marketing infrastructure is still underdeveloped.

**Guidelines for Successful CRM Implementation**　Experience and lessons from implementation of CRM programs have led to the following insights:

- Make the program business-driven rather than IT-driven. CRM is more than just a data-mining exercise; it goes way beyond technology and having a database in place.

- Monitor and keep track of data protection and privacy laws in those countries where CRM systems are being used or are in the planning stage.

---

[106]"Finance Firm in Loyalty Push to Fend Off Rivals," *Media*, September 6, 2002, p. 10.

[107]"Audi in Web Drive to Collect Data," *Media*, October 18, 2002, p. 18.

- Remember that the effectiveness of CRM starts with the database. A good database is money in the bank; a bad database is money wasted.

- Make sure that the information and rewards being sent out to customers are relevant, targeted, and personal.

## SUMMARY ◆ ◆ ◆ ◆ ◆ ◆ ◆ ◆ ◆ ◆ ◆ ◆ ◆ ◆ ◆ ◆ ◆ ◆ ◆ ◆ ◆ ◆ ◆ ◆ ◆ ◆ ◆ ◆ ◆ ◆

Global marketing does not operate in a bubble. Culture is an intrinsic part of the global marketing environment. Cultural diversity brings along an immense richness. "Foreign" cultures may offer a breeding ground for new product ideas. Cultural changes may open up new market opportunities. At the same time, cultural diversity also poses enormous challenges to international marketers and managers in general. Usually, cultural blunders are easily forgiven. Occasionally, however, failure to respect the local culture will create resentment and may even lead to permanent damage of the firm's overseas business operations. Companies like Coca-Cola and KFC learned this lesson the hard way in India. When Coca-Cola reentered India in 1992 after a long absence, it acquired Thums Up, a leading local brand. It subsequently tried to promote its global brand by piggybacking Thums Up's distribution network, at the expense of the local brand. Loyal customers of Thums Up were not pleased. In the end, Coke decided to promote Thums Up rather than substitute it with its global brands. KFC, on the other hand, retrenched in the Indian marketplace, cutting down on the number of outlets from four to just one. Its formula of selling fried chicken in a country where tandoori chicken is preferred never caught on.[108]

Preventive medicine is more effective than having to lick your wounds afterward. Dictums, such as "When in Rome . . . ," are nice catch phrases but unfortunately, it is seldom easy to learn what it means to "do as the Romans."

Sensitivity to the host culture is a nice attribute, but for most people it will always remain an ideal rather than an accomplishment. There simply are no tricks-of-the-trade or shortcuts. In fact, an often-fatal mistake is to overestimate one's familiarity with the host culture.

In this chapter we analyzed what is meant by culture. We examined several elements of culture in detail. Cultures have differences but also share certain aspects. We examined several frameworks that you can use to analyze and classify different cultures. Once you are aware of the differences and parallels, the next and most formidable task is to become sensitive to the host culture. We described several procedures to foster cultural adjustment. Cross-cultural training is one route toward cultural adaptation. The ideal, however, is to immerse oneself in the foreign culture through intensive language training, prolonged visits, or other means.

The interface between culture and the various marketing mix instruments was studied. Future chapters (Chapters 11 through 16) that look more closely at the global marketing mix will revisit these interactions. In this chapter, we also examined the notion of corporate or organizational culture. As we saw, to some extent corporate cultures are driven by the culture in which the company originated. Finally, we explored two increasingly important areas on the consumer front, namely, global customer account management (GAM) and global customer relationship management (CRM).

## KEY TERMS ◆ ◆ ◆ ◆ ◆ ◆ ◆ ◆ ◆ ◆ ◆ ◆ ◆ ◆ ◆ ◆ ◆ ◆ ◆ ◆ ◆ ◆ ◆ ◆ ◆ ◆ ◆

Back translation
Collectivist culture
Customer relationship marketing (CRM)
Database marketing
Ethnocentrism

Extended family
Global account management (GAM)
High- (low-) context culture
Individualism (collectivism)

Long-termism (short-termism)
Masculinity (femininity)
Nuclear family
Organizational (corporate) culture

Power distance
Project GLOBE
Self-reference criterion (SRC)
Uncertainty avoidance
World Value Survey (WVS)

## REVIEW QUESTIONS ◆ ◆ ◆ ◆ ◆ ◆ ◆ ◆ ◆ ◆ ◆ ◆ ◆ ◆ ◆ ◆ ◆ ◆ ◆ ◆ ◆ ◆ ◆

**1.** How does language complicate the tasks of global marketers?

**2.** Describe the importance of reference groups in international marketing.

**3.** What can marketers do to launch new products in countries that tend to resist change?

**4.** How do high-context cultures differ from low-context ones?

**5.** What are some possible issues in applying Hofstede's classification scheme in a global marketing context?

---

[108]"Hard to Sell to a Billion Consumers," *Financial Times*, April 25, 2002, p. 14.

# DISCUSSION QUESTIONS ◆ ◆ ◆ ◆ ◆ ◆ ◆ ◆ ◆ ◆ ◆ ◆ ◆ ◆ ◆ ◆ ◆ ◆ ◆ ◆ ◆ ◆

1. Focus group research conducted by advertising agencies like Leo Burnett shows that Asia's youngsters (the proverbial X-generation) mimic American trends, but at the same time, they are pretty conservative. Gangsta rap, for instance, is extremely popular in Malaysia. But many of the values that Asian youths hold are quite traditional: family relations, respect for elders, marriage, and so on. Discuss this seeming contradiction.

2. A recent survey in China of 400 urban children aged 7 to 12 showed that 81.3 percent dreamed of international travel, 61.9 percent wanted space travel, 60.2 percent wanted to be more beautiful, and almost 90 percent wanted to be more intelligent. Given these aspirations, what market opportunities do you see for Western companies that target China's child population?

3. What are some of the possible infrastructural roadblocks (e.g., in terms of transportation, storage) that ice cream manufacturers would face in South East Asia?

4. One of the cultural dimensions singled out by Hofstede is the individualism/collectivism distinction. What would this categorization imply in terms of setting up a sales force for international marketers? For instance, what incentive schemes might work in an individualist culture? Collectivist?

5. Countries showing strong uncertainty avoidance such as France, Germany, and Italy have witnessed a rise in the consumption of mineral water since 1970. In fact, according to one study, the correlation between mineral water consumption and the uncertainty avoidance score for 1996 was almost 0.75. What might explain the linkage between uncertainty avoidance and mineral water consumption? What other products might find opportunities in strong uncertainty avoidance countries?

6. Download the results for the 2005 Global Sex Survey results from the Durex website (http://www.durex.com/us/ gss2005result.pdf). The survey interviewed more than 317,000 people from 41 countries about their sexual attitudes and behavior. According to the survey 44 percent of all adults claim to be satisfied with their sex lives. At the top of the contentment chart are lovers in Belgium (57 percent), Poland (56 percent), Netherlands (54 percent), the United States (52 percent), and Switzerland and the United Kingdom (51 percent). At the bottom of the satisfaction scale are lovers in China (22 percent), Japan (24 percent), Hong Kong (30 percent), Portugal (33 percent), Indonesia (34 percent), Israel and Italy (36 percent), and Taiwan (37 percent). What might explain these differences? Examine some of the other findings in the survey. What do they imply for Durex, one of the world's leading manufacturers of condoms?

7. Certain Muslim countries like Saudi Arabia do not allow advertisers to show a frontal picture of a woman with her hair. This creates a challenge for companies like Unilever or Procter & Gamble that want to advertise hair-care products (e.g., shampoo). How would you tackle this challenge?

8. Visit the Culturgrams website and download the free sample (www.culturgram.com/culturgram/freedownload.htm). Read the sample. What cultural differences exist between your culture and the one described in the sample? What are the similarities, if any?

9. A survey conducted by the Thailand Marketing Research Society (TMRS) among 1200 Thai youngsters (13 to 18 years) in the summer of 2002 showed that loss of "Thai identity" was picked as one of the top five most serious issues. At the same time, Thai teenagers are growing more skeptical about advertising and Western brands. What do these findings suggest for Western marketers?

# SHORT CASES

# ᴄASE 4-1

## SELLING BRATZ DOLLS IN ASIA – "HOOKER CHIC" DOES NOT CATCH ON

Bratz is a range of streetwise dolls marketed by MGA Entertainment (www.mgae.com). The dolls have taken the United States and Europe by storm. Global sales in 2004 hit US$2.5 billion, compared to Barbie's $3 billion. You only need to take a stroll in any toy store in the United States or Europe to witness the impact of Bratz. Instead of Barbie's signature pink, the shelves are black and purple—the colors of Bratz. In Europe and the United States, the Barbie look is now *passé* among teenage girls in spite of an image and lifestyle makeover. Many observers of the industry wonder whether Barbie has any future left.

What made Bratz a runaway success in the United States and Europe is that Bratz dolls resonate far more strongly with today's generation of teenage girls who have grown up with MTV and lifestyle magazines like *Dolly* and *Seventeen*. Some commentators refer to the Bratz dolls' funky image as "hooker chic." Barbie, however, reflects the bygone era of 1950s Americana.

In Asia, however, the story is completely different. Bratz dolls caused some hoopla when they were first launched[109] in the region, but since then reactions have been rather muted.

*Source:* "Asia balks at Bratz's 'hooker chic' image," *Media*, December 16, 2005, p. 16, http://www.mgae.com.

There has been virtually no marketing since then. The success story of Bratz in Europe and the United States has so far not been replicated in Asia. There are a couple of possible causes behind Bratz failure to catch on. A range of distributors across different markets, each with inputs at the local level, has made it difficult to coordinate promotional efforts. Barbie reflects a nostalgic image of America. However, many Asian girls (and their mothers) are not familiar with Bratz. MGA may also have misjudged the Asian market. Play-patterns and role models Asian girls differ from their American and European peers. Barbie and Hello Kitty dolls still hold strong allure among Asian girls (and even women). One important factor in Asia is the mother: in Asia, it is typically the mother who buys toys. The funky image of Bratz dolls with their hip looks, heavy make-up, and short skirts might be far too risqué for mothers in Asia.

### DISCUSSION QUESTIONS

**1.** Examine what cultural factors hindered the take-off of Bratz in Asia despite the dolls' phenomenal success in the United States and in Europe.

**2.** Discuss what MGA Entertainment can do to boost the sales of Bratz dolls in Asia.

# ᴄASE 4-2

## SELLING VIDEO GAMES IN GERMANY

Germany has been one of the most challenging markets in Europe for game companies to penetrate. With 38 million households, Germany represents a huge opportunity for the gaming industry. But so far, the promise has been elusive. For instance, while 24 percent of UK households own a Sony PlayStation 2, merely 6 percent of German households have the console. Gerhard Florin, the head of European operations for Electronic Arts (EA), a leading game publisher, noted that: "If we could get German game-playing up to the level of the UK, Europe would become EA's largest market, even overtaking the United States. Germany is not a technological laggard: Internet usage (around 57.1 percent) is among the highest in Europe.

According to industry analysts, sociocultural factors explain the slow adoption of videogames in Germany. One important element is the low birth rate: the average German woman has 1.4 children compared to 1.6 per woman in Britain. German parents are also more strict, steering their children away from video games

*Source:* "Gunning for players," *Financial Times*, February 1, 2005, p. 9.

toward homework. German children tend to be older when they finally take up the hobby—starting at five-to-six compared to three-to-four for British children. There is also a strong reading culture. Mr. Florin observed that: "Germans feel they are supposed to spend their time on their education or career."

Gaming companies are trying hard to change the image of gaming in Germany. Sony is promoting a more family-friendly image. Companies also tailor their games to comply with German decency standards, among the strictest in the world. For instance, games based on World War II leave out Nazi insignia; spurting blood is changed to green, suggesting an alien has been killed rather than a human. Companies also hope that a new generation of handheld game consoles will boost the market. According to a Sony executive: "Most German parents say they don't want kids sitting in front of the TV screen playing games. But they don't mind giving them a handheld console in the back of the car."

Discuss what other marketing initiatives gaming companies can take to stimulate their sales in Germany

## FURTHER READING ✦ ✦ ✦ ✦ ✦ ✦ ✦ ✦ ✦ ✦ ✦ ✦ ✦ ✦ ✦ ✦ ✦ ✦ ✦ ✦ ✦

Baligh, H. Helmy. "Components of Culture: Nature, Interconnections, and Relevance to the Decisions on the Organization Structure." *Management Science* 40, no. 4 (1994): 14–27.

Briley, Donnel A. and Jennifer L. Aaker. "Bridging the Culture Chasm: Ensuring that Consumers are Healthy, Wealthy, and Wise." *Journal of Public Policy & Marketing* 25 (2006), pp. 53–66.

De Mooij, Marieke and Geert Hofstede. "Convergence and Divergence in Consumer Behavior: Implications for International Retailing." *Journal of Retailing* 78 (2002): 61–69.

Hall, Edward T. *Beyond Culture.* Garden City, NY: Anchor Press, 1976.

Hofstede, Geert. *Cultures and Organizations: Software of the Mind.* London: McGraw-Hill, 1991.

Hofstede, Geert. *Culture's Consequences: International Differences in Work-Related Values.* Beverly Hills, CA: Sage Publications, 1980.

Hofstede, Geert, and Michael Bond. "The Confucius Connection: From Cultural Roots to Economic Growth." *Organizational Dynamics* (1988): 4–21.

House, Robert J., Paul J. Hanges, Mansour Javidan, Peter W. Dorfman, and Vipin Gupta. *Culture, Leadership, and Organizations: The GLOBE Study of 62 Societies.* SAGE Publications, 2004.

Madden, Thomas J., Kelly Hewett, and Martin S. Roth. "Managing Images in Different Cultures: A Cross-National Study of Color Meanings and Preferences." *Journal of International Marketing* 8, no. 1 (2000): 90–107.

Nisbett, Richard. *The Geography of Thought: How Asians and Westerners Think . . . and Why.* Free Press, 2004.

Parker, Philip M. *Cross-Cultural Statistical Encyclopedia of the World.* Volumes 1, 2, 3, and 4. Westport, CT: Greenwood Press, 1997.

Ricks, David A. *Blunders in International Business.* Cambridge, MA: Blackwell Publishers, 1993.

Schwartz, Shalom H., and Lilach Sagiv. "Identifying Culture-Specifics in the Content and Structure of Values." *Journal of Cross-Cultural Psychology* 26, no. 1 (January 1995): 92–116.

Sebenius, James K. "The Hidden Challenge of Cross-Border Negotiations." *Harvard Business Review* (March 2002): 76–85.

Shi, Linda H., Shaoming Zou, J. Chris White, Regina C. McNally, and S. Tamer Cavusgil, "Global Account Management Capability," *Journal of International Marketing* 13, no. 2 (2005): 93–113.

Terpstra, Vern, and Kenneth David. *The Cultural Environment of International Business.* Cincinnati, OH: South-Western Publishing Co., 1991.

Triandis, Harry C. "The Self and Social Behavior in Differing Cultural Contexts." *Psychological Review* 96, no. 1 (1989): 506–20.

# POLITICAL AND LEGAL ENVIRONMENT

## CHAPTER OVERVIEW

1. POLITICAL ENVIRONMENT—INDIVIDUAL GOVERNMENTS

2. POLITICAL ENVIRONMENT—SOCIAL PRESSURES AND POLITICAL RISK

3. TERRORISM AND THE WORLD ECONOMY

4. INTERNATIONAL AGREEMENTS

5. INTERNATIONAL LAW AND LOCAL LEGAL ENVIRONMENT

6. ISSUES TRANSCENDING NATIONAL BOUNDARIES

Business has been considered an integral part of economic forces. Indeed, economics was once called *political economy*, and as such, business could not be conducted devoid of political and legal forces. Although we tend to take political and legal forces for granted most of the time in doing business domestically, they could become central issues in international business and cannot be ignored. It is human nature that we tend to look at other countries' political and legal systems as peculiar because they differ from ours. We might even make some value judgment that our own country's political and legal system is always superior to other countries' and that they should change their system to our way. This ethnocentrism, however, hinders our proper understanding of, and sensitivity to, differences in the system that might have major business implications. By the very nature of their jobs, international marketers cannot afford to be ethnocentric as they interact with a multitude of political and legal systems, including their own at home.

International marketers should be aware that the economic interests of their companies could differ widely from those of the countries in which they do business and sometimes even from those of their own home countries. There are various international agreements, treaties, and laws already in place for them to abide by. Furthermore, there is an increased level of visible distrust of multinational firms around the world, calling for creating codes of conduct for them.[1]

---

[1]S. Prakash Sethi, *Setting Global Standards: Guidelines for Creating Codes of Conduct in Multinational Corporations,* Hoboken, NJ: Wiley, 2003.

In this chapter, we will examine political and legal forces that affect the company's international marketing activities from the following three perspectives: the political and legal climates of the host country, those of the home country, and the international agreements, treaties, and laws affecting international marketing activities transcending national boundaries. Although political and legal climates are inherently related and inseparable because laws are generally a manifestation of a country's political processes, we will look at political climate first, followed by legal climate.

◆ ◆ ◆ ◆ ◆ ◆ ◆ ◆ ◆ ## POLITICAL ENVIRONMENT—INDIVIDUAL GOVERNMENTS

Government affects almost every aspect of business life in a country. First, national politics affect business environments directly, through changes in policies, regulations, and laws. The government in each country determines which industries will receive protection in the country and which will face open competition. The government determines labor regulations and property laws. It determines fiscal and monetary policies, which then affect investment and returns. We will summarize those policies and regulations that directly influence the international business environment in a country.

Second, the political stability and mood in a country affect the actions a government will take—actions that may have an important impact on the viability of doing business in the country. A political movement may change prevailing attitudes toward foreign corporations and result in new regulations. An economic shift may influence the government's willingness to endure the hardships of an austerity program. We will discuss the strategic importance of understanding political risk in an international business context.

**Home Country versus Host Country**

Whenever marketing executives do business across national boundaries, they have to face the regulations and laws of both the home and host countries. A **home country** refers to a country in which the parent company is based and from which it operates. A **host country** is a country in which foreign companies are allowed to do business in accordance with its government policies and within its laws. Therefore, international marketing executives should be concerned about the host government's policies and their possible changes in the future, as well as their home government's political climate.

Because companies usually do not operate in countries that have been hostile to their home country, many executives tend to take for granted the political environment of the host country in which they currently do business. Sweeping political upheavals, such as the Cuban crisis in the 1960s, the Iranian Revolution in the 1980s, the breakup of the Soviet Union in the late 1980s, the Persian Gulf War in the 1990s, the Kosovo crisis in Yugoslavia[2] in 1999, the suicide bombings in Indonesia during the last few years, and more recently, the U.S.-led war against Iraq have already made many business executives fully aware of dire political problems in some regions, and many companies have since stayed away from those areas. Despite the fact that those major political upheavals provide the largest single setting for an economic crisis faced by foreign companies, what most foreign companies are concerned about on a daily basis should be a much larger universe of low-key events that may not involve violence or a change in government regime but that do involve a fairly significant change in policy toward foreign companies.[3] In recent years, the end of apartheid in South Africa also signals foreign companies' cautious yet optimistic attitude toward resuming business relations with this African country.[4] Similarly, Vietnam has begun to attract foreign direct

---

[2]As a series of ethnic tensions since 1980, the former Yugoslavia is now divided into seven independent states: Serbia, Croatia, Bosnia and Herzegovina, Kosovo, Macedonia, Slovenia, and Montenegro.

[3]Stephen J. Kobrin, "Selective Vulnerability and Corporate Management," in Theodore H. Moran, ed., *International Political Risk Assessment: The State of the Art, Landegger Papers in International Business and Public Policy*, Georgetown University, Washington, D.C. 1981, pp. 9–13.

[4]"South Africa: Investment Climate Statement," *Tradeport*, www.tradeport.org/ts/countries/safrica/climate.html, April 10, 1999, accessed on August 20, 1999.

investment to spur its domestic economic growth and shift toward a more market-based economy.[5]

The U.S.–China diplomatic relationship, which was re-established in the mid-1970s under the Nixon administration, illustrates the intertwined nature of home and host government policies. As a result, the Chinese government finally opened its economy to foreign direct investment—mostly through joint ventures—in the 1980s. The first pioneer foreign companies have stood to gain from the host government policies designed to protect the domestic producers they teamed up with in China. Thus, the United States' Chrysler, Germany's Volkswagen, and France's Peugeot, with their respective Chinese partner companies, were such beneficiaries. However, the U.S.–China relationship has since been anything but smooth. The United States, in particular, has been openly critical of China's human rights "violations" since the Tiananmen Square massacre of 1989 and has tried to make its trade policy with China contingent upon measurable improvements in China's human rights policy.

As China entered the World Trade Organization (WTO) in December 2001, the United States also offered extension of permanent Normal Trade Relations to China. The situation is very promising, but still challenges lie ahead. The U.S. government needs to do more to help China change its legal and political system to meet the challenges of its accession to the WTO. The wrenching social changes—including increased unemployment in large cities—caused by the opening of China's economy carry the risk of serious political instability. Besides, the current government and Communist Party leadership, which mixed with the politics of WTO implementation, could create systemic instability in China. If the United States the European Union, and Japan could provide assistance to China in restructuring its financial and legal systems, and in developing a public health infrastructure and systems for improved environmental protection, the possibility could be averted. Otherwise, foreign companies operating in, or contemplating entry into, China may experience undue uncertainties for the foreseeable future.[6]

The emergence of the Internet could also pose problems for Chinese trade relations. Though China seeks to free its markets in response to global pressure, particularly from the U.S., the Internet undermines China's general censorship policies. This dilemma was recently shown when China imprisoned a Chinese Internet entrepreneur for exchanging lists of e-mail addresses with a U.S. organization in the hope of growing his Web-based business.[7] Nonetheless, encouraged by reformist leaders, Internet use is growing explosively. In 1997, only 640,000 Chinese were connected. By April 2008, China's Internet users totaled 220 million individuals, surpassing the United States.[8] Today e-commerce has become a strong driver of China's market economy by expanding with annual sales rising at 40 percent. According to statistics from the Shanghai Modern Business Promoting Council, China's online transaction volume hit 1.7 trillion yuan ($243.55 billion) in 2007.[9] With the leading consumer marketplaces counting 50 million users, the value of daily online transactions for the first time surpassed the cash taken by major physical retailers in China, such as Wal-Mart.[10] Included in its plan for national economic and social development, China is vigorously promoting e-government, which includes a taxation management information system, a customs management information system, a financial management information system, an agricultural management information system, and a quality supervision management information system. E-commerce is on the development

---

[5]Sandie Robb, "Investors Eye Favorable Environment," *Foreign Affairs*, 84 (September/October 2005), p. 3.

[6]Andrew Batson, "China Needs Help Meeting Challenges of WTO-Academic," *Dow Jones Newswire*, June 28, 2002.

[7]Craig S. Smith, "China Imprisons Internet Entrepreneur," *Wall Street Journal* (January 21, 1999), p. A13.

[8]"China Vaults Past USA in Internet Users," *USA Today*, April 21, 2008.

[9]Hao Zhou, "First E-Business Specifications Go Public," *Chinadaily.com.cn*, May 14, 2008.

[10]Jack Ma, "E-commerce with Chinese Characteristics," *Economist.com*, http://www.economist.com/theworldin/displaystory.cfm?story_id=10125658, accessed August 30, 2008.

agenda and China is eager to expedite the application of information technology in such key areas as foreign trade, petrochemicals, metallurgy and machinery.[11]

International marketers must understand the fluid nature of the host country political climate in relation to the home country policies. Some countries are relatively stable over time; other countries experience different degrees of political volatility that make it difficult for international marketers to predict and plan ahead. Nonetheless, there are a few crucial political factors international executives should know that determine the nature of the host country's political climate.

**Structure of Government**

*Ideology.* One way to characterize the nature of government is by its political ideology, ranging from **communism** and socialism to capitalism. Under strict communism, the government owns and manages all businesses and no private ownership is allowed. As the recent breakup of the Soviet Union shows, the strict government control not only strip its people of private incentives to work but also is an inefficient mechanism to allocate scarce resources across the economy. On the other hand, **capitalism** refers to an economic system in which free enterprise is permitted and encouraged along with private ownership. In a capitalistic society, free-market transactions are considered to produce the most efficient allocation of scarce resources. However, capitalism is not without critics. Even the Wall Street financier, George Soros, has called attention to the threat that the values propagated by global laissez-faire capitalism poses to the very values on which open and democratic societies depend. Without social justice as the guiding principle of civilized life, life becomes a survival of the fittest.[12] For example, capitalism, if unfettered, may result in excessive production and excessive consumption, thereby causing severe air and water pollution in many parts of the world, as well as depleting the limited natural resources. Government roles would be limited to those functions that the private sector could not perform efficiently, such as defense, highway construction, pollution control, and other public services. An interesting example can be found in Japan. Although Japanese companies perfected an efficient just-in-time (JIT) delivery system, frequent shipments have caused increased traffic congestion and air pollution in Japan, and thus may not be as efficient in delivering social well-being.[13] Now the Japanese government is trying to regulate the use of JIT production and delivery systems. **Socialism** generally is considered a political system that falls in between pure communism and pure capitalism. A socialistic government advocates government ownership and control of some industries considered critical to the welfare of the nation.[14]

After the breakup of the Soviet Union, most Central and East European countries have converted to capitalistic ideology.[15] Similarly, China is in a transition stage, although some uncertainties still remain. There remain few countries that adhere to the extreme communist doctrine other than North Korea and Cuba. While many countries cherish capitalism and democracy, the extent of government intervention in the economy varies from country to country. (Both capitalistic and socialistic countries in which government planning and ownership play a major role are also referred to as **planned economies**).

*Political Parties.* The number of political parties also influences the level of political stability. A one-party regime does not exist outside the communist country. Most countries have a number of large and small political parties representing different views and value systems of their population. In a **single-party-dominant country**, government policies tend to be stable and predictable over time. Although such a government

---

[11]"Report on China's Economic and Social Development Plan," *Xinhua*, March 16, 2005.

[12]George Soros, *The Crisis of Global Capitalism*, New York: PublicAffairs, 1998.

[13]Kamran Moinzadeh, Ted Klastorin, and Emre Berk, "The Impact of Small Lot Ordering on Traffic Congestion in a Physical Distribution System," *IIE Transactions*, 29 (August 1997), pp. 671–79.

[14]Refer to an excellent classic treatise on capitalism, socialism, and communism by Joseph A. Schumpeter, *Capitalism, Socialism, and Democracy*, New York: Harper & Brothoers, 1947.

[15]Tom Diana, "Steady Economic Progress in Central and Eastern Europe," *Business Credit*, 107 (June 2005), pp. 54–57.

provides consistent policies, they do not always guarantee a favorable political environment for foreign companies operating in the country. A dominant party regime may maintain policies such as high tariff and non-tariff barriers, foreign direct investment restrictions, and foreign exchange controls, which reduce the operational flexibility of foreign companies. For example, in Mexico a few political parties have always existed, but one party, called the Institutional Revolutionary Party, had been dominant in the past seventy years. However, since 1994, Mexico's ruling party has lost its firm grip on its politics. Although the opening of the Mexican political system may eventually lead to a stronger democracy over time, it is believed that its economy will experience an unknown degree of political instability for the foreseeable future.[16]

The trauma followed by the collapse of one-party-dominant systems can be relatively large, as experienced by the breakup of the Soviet Union. In the early 1970s, PepsiCo had cultivated ties with Soviet leaders that led to a deal providing the Soviet Union and its East European allies with Pepsi concentrate and state-of-the-art bottling technology in return for the inside track to the huge unexploited soft-drink market within the Soviet Empire. However, when the Soviet Union collapsed in 1991, PepsiCo was devastated. Almost overnight, all the hard earned skills and nepotism that PepsiCo had developed for operating in a centralized command economy counted for nothing. Making matters worse, customers associated PepsiCo with the discredited former regime. Archrival Coca-Cola almost immediately launched a drive for market share. The results were striking. In Hungary, for example, PepsiCo's market share tumbled from 70 percent to 30 percent almost overnight.[17]

In a **dual-party system**, such as the United States and Britain, the parties are usually not divided by ideology but rather have different constituencies. For example, in the United States, the Democrats tend to identify with working-class people and assume a greater role for the federal government while the Republicans tend to support business interests and prefer a limited role for the federal government. Yet both parties are strong proponents of democracy. In such a dual-party system, the two parties tend to alternate their majority position over a relatively long period. In 1995, the Democrats finally relinquished control of Congress to the Republican majority after many years. We have since seen some sweeping changes in government policy, ranging from environmental protection to affirmative action, usually in support of business interests.[18]

The other extreme situation is a **multiple-party system** without any clear majority, found in Italy and more recently in Japan and Taiwan. The consistency of government policies may be compromised as a result. Since there is no dominant party, different parties with differing policy goals form a coalition government. The major problem with a coalition government is a lack of political stability and continuity, and this portends a high level of uncertainty in the business climate. Since, in Japan, career bureaucrats, who are not political appointees, used to be in virtual control of government policy development and execution, the changes in government leadership did not seem to pose any measurable policy change until recently. However, in recent years owing to Japan's prolonged recession, those non-political elite bureaucrats had lost clout, and instead the current prime minister, leading the ruling party, has initiated many economic and financial reforms for Japan's resurgence.[19]

Besides the party system, foreign businesses also have to pay attention to the local government structure. Some governments are very weak and hardly have any control at the local level. For example, Indonesia, whose government used to be very centralized and straightforward, now has been steadily releasing power to local communities. This means that foreign businesses now have to deal with local government and political system in each of its 32 provinces.[20]

---

[16] "Mexico: Money, the Machine and the Man," *Economist*, July 7, 2005, p. 30.

[17] Hugh D. Menzies, "Pepsico's Soviet Travails," *International Business*, November 1995, p. 42.

[18] "Shades of '94—But Cloudier," *CQ Weekly*, August 15, 2005, pp. 2230–238.

[19] "The Push for Freer Markets in Japan," *Wall Street Journal*, December 14, 2007, p. C5.

[20] John McBeth, "Power to The People," *Far Eastern Economic Review*, August 14, 2003, pp. 48–50.

## Government Policies and Regulations

It is the role of government to promote a country's interests in the international arena for various reasons and objectives. Some governments actively invest in certain industries that are considered important to national interests. Other governments protect fledgling industries in order to allow them to gain the experience and size necessary to compete internationally. In general, reasons for wanting to block or restrict trade are as follows:

1. National security
   - Ability to produce goods necessary to remain independent (e.g., self-sufficiency)
   - Not exporting goods that will help enemies or unfriendly nations
2. Developing new industries
   - Idea of nurturing nascent industries to strength in a protected market
3. Protecting declining industries
   - To maintain domestic employment for political stability

For example, Japan's active industrial policy by the Ministry of International Trade and Industry (MITI) in the 1960s and 1970s is well known for its past success and has also been adopted by newly industrialized countries (NICs), such as Singapore, South Korea, and Malaysia.[21] Governments use a variety of laws, policies, and programs to pursue their economic interests. More recently, the Baltic States of Estonia, Latvia, and Lithuania, controlled by the Soviet regime until the late 1980s, have liberalized their economies significantly by opening up their economies to international trade and foreign direct investment as well as treating foreign companies no differently than domestic companies. As a result of their rapid transition to open market economies, they were formally inducted into the European Union in 2004.[22]

This section focuses on describing those government programs, trade and investment laws, and macroeconomic policies that have an immediate and direct impact on the international business in a country. We will discuss laws regulating business behavior—such as antitrust laws and anti-bribery laws—in a subsequent section on international legal environments. Later sections of this chapter will discuss the legal systems that produce and enforce a country's laws.

***Incentives and Government Programs.*** Most countries use government loans, subsidies, or training programs to support export activities and specific domestic industries. These programs are important for host-country firms, as well as for firms considering production in one country for export to others. In the United States, the International Trade Administration (ITA) has a national network of district offices in every state, offering export promotion assistance to local businesses. Furthermore, in light of federal budget cuts and as a supplement to the ITA's trade promotion efforts, state governments have significantly increased their staff and budgets, not only for export assistance, particularly in nurturing small local businesses,[23] but also for attracting foreign direct investment to increase employment in their respective states.[24] Thus, the major objectives of any state government support are (1) job creation and (2) improving the state balance of trade (as in any country).

The state government's export promotion activities are more systematic, while its investment attraction activities are characterized by their case-by-case nature. Foreign

[21]Masaaki Kotabe, "The Roles of Japanese Industrial Policy for Export Success: A Theoretical Perspective," *Columbia Journal of World Business*, 20 (Fall 1985), pp. 59–64; Mark L. Clifford, "Can Malaysia Take That Next Big Step?" *Business Week* (February 26, 1996), pp. 96–106.

[22]"The External Sector: Capital Flows and Foreign Debt," *Country Profile. Estonia*, 2005, pp. 43–45.

[23]Masaaki Kotabe and Michael R. Czinkota, "State Government Promotion of Manufacturing Exports: A Gap Analysis," *Journal of International Business Studies*, 23 (Fourth Quarter 1992), pp. 637–58; and for the most recent comprehensive study, see Timothy J. Wilkinson, Bruce D. Keillor, and Michael d'Amico, "The Relationship between Export Promotion Spending and State Exports in the U.S.," *Journal of Global Marketing*, 18 (3/4), 2005, pp. 95–114.

[24]J. Myles Shaver, "Do Foreign-Owned and U.S.-Owned Establishments Exhibit the Same Location Pattern in U.S. Manufacturing Industries?" *Journal of International Business Studies*, 29, Third Quarter 1998, pp. 469–92.

**Products and Services for the World**

Chile

Courtesy ProChile. Reproduced with permission.

A government agency actively solicits foreign buyers by helping them find sales leads with local firms.

investment attraction activities generally consist of seminars, various audio-visual and printed promotional materials, and investment missions, among others. Of these, investment missions and various tax and other financial incentives appear to play the most important role in investment promotional efforts. Investment missions are generally made by government officials, particularly by the governor of the state, visiting with potential investors. One study has shown that whether or not they participate in foreign investment attraction activities, state governments that are active in export promotion tend to attract more foreign companies' direct investment in their states than those state governments that are not active.[25] For example, export-active states may be more politically favorable and receptive to foreign companies operating there. A well-known example is that to attract a Nissan plant, Tennessee spent $12 million for new roads to the facility, and provided a $7 million grant for training plant employees and a $10 million tax break to the Japanese company in 1985.[26] Similarly, Alabama provided a $253 million package of capital investments and tax breaks to lure Mercedes-Benz's sports utility vehicle production facility to the state in the early 1990s.[27] Similarly, to encourage Japanese automakers to produce in Thailand, the Thai government provides cheap labor, 8-year tax holiday, and virtually eliminated excise taxes on domestic pickup sales.[28] Since the mid 1980s, the Chinese government has offered preferential tax rates to attract foreign companies' investment in China. On average, the income tax rate for domestic companies is 33 per cent while foreign

---

[25]Masaaki Kotabe, "The Promotional Roles of the State Government and Japanese Manufacturing Direct Investment in the United States," *Journal of Business Research*, 27 (June 1993), pp. 131–46.

[26]"Tennessee's Pitch to Japan," *New York Times* (February 27, 1985), pp. D1, D6.

[27]"Tax Freedom Day Index Would Be Keen Indicator," *Orlando Sentinel* (May 8, 1994), p. D1.

[28]"In a World of Car Builders, Thailand Relies Heavily on a Pickup," *New York Times*, June 16, 2005.

companies pay half of that. Foreign manufacturers also often received "tax holidays," like two-year exemptions followed by three years in which their rates were cut in half. Statistics show that foreign companies used to get an annual tax break of approximately US$50 billion in China. But the tax honeymoon for foreign companies investing in China ended with the implementation of a new corporate income tax law from January 1 2008. In the new tax regime, the unified tax rate is set at 25 percent for both the Chinese and foreign firms, creating a competitive environment for both domestic and foreign investors. While putting an end to many preferential tax policies and incentives enjoyed by foreign firms, the new law retains some favorable terms for companies whose development is in line with the nation's strategic priorities, such as the 20 percent preferential rate for small enterprises with small profit margins and also a 15 percent rate for high-tech companies.[29]

Most governments subsidize certain industries directly. Direct government subsidies are an important international consideration. In Europe, Airbus Industries was established with joint government subsidies from the governments of Britain, France, Germany, and Spain in 1970 to build a European competitor in the jet aircraft industry once dominated by U.S. companies, including Boeing and McDonnell-Douglas-Lockheed. The United States is no exception. When threatened by Japanese competition in the semiconductor industry in the 1980s, the Reagan administration launched a Japanese-style government-industry joint industrial consortium known as SEMA-TECH (Semiconductor Manufacturing Technology) in 1987, with the federal government subsidizing half of its $200 million operating budget.[30] Thanks to SEMATECH, the U.S. semiconductor industry has finally recaptured the leading market share position by 1995, long lost to Japanese in the 1980s.

The point is to recognize how government support for particular industries or for exporting in general will affect which industries are competitive and which are not. International businesses can benefit by planning for and utilizing home-country and host-country government programs.

***Government Procurement.*** The ultimate government involvement in trade is when the government itself is the customer. It engages in commercial operations through the departments and agencies under its control. The U.S. government accounts for a quarter of the total U.S. consumption, so the government has become the largest single consuming entity in the United States. Thus, the government procurement policy has an enormous impact on international trade. In the United States, the Buy American Act gives a bidding edge to domestic suppliers, although the U.S. Congress has recently begun to open certain government procurements to goods and services from countries that are parties to various international trade agreements that the United States also belongs to.[31] For foreign suppliers to win a contract from a U.S. government agency, their products must contain at least 50 percent of U.S.-made parts, or they must undercut the closest comparable U.S. product by at least 6 percent.[32] This "buy domestic" policy orientation is not limited to the United States, but applies to all other nations. In other words, when a U.S. company tries to sell to any foreign government agency, it should always expect some sort of bidding disadvantage relative to local competitors.

---

[29]Jim Yardley, "China Moves to End Tax Breaks for Foreign Businesses," *International Herald Tribune*, March 8, 2007; "Tax Burdens Equalized for Chinese, Foreign Firms," *Beijing*, http://www.btmbeijing.com, April 15, 2007; and Bi Xiaoning, "Businesses Positive about Corporate Tax Law," *China Daily*, April 11, 2008.

[30]Due to the U.S. government's gradual budget cut, SEMATECH became a technology consortium funded solely by member companies in 1998.

[31]William T. Woods, "Federal Procurement: International Agreements Result in Waivers of Some U.S. Domestic Source Restrictions," GAO-05-188, *GAO Reports*, January 26, 2005, pp. 1–24.

[32]Robert Fryling, "Buy American Act: Help for United States Manufacturers," *Contract Management Magazine*, 42 (April 2002), pp. 42–43; and "Part 25.001: The Buy American Act," Federal Acquisitions Regulation, http://www.arnet.gov/far/current/html/Subpart%2025_1.html, accessed February 10, 2006.

***Trade Laws.*** National trade laws directly influence the environment for international business. Trade controls can be broken into two categories—economic trade controls and political trade controls. Economic trade controls are those trade restraints that are instituted for primarily economic reasons, such as to protect local jobs. Both **tariff** and **non-tariff** barriers (NTBs) work to impede imports that might compete with locally produced goods (See **Exhibit 5.1**). Tariffs tax imports directly, and also function as a form of income for the country that levies them. In industrialized countries today, average tariff rates on manufactured and mining products are about 5-6 percent. Tariff protection for agricultural commodities is higher than for manufactured products, both in industrial and in developing countries. But in industrialized countries the average tariff rate on agriculture is almost double the tariff for manufactured products. Tariffs on labor-intensive products also largely surpass the average for industrial goods. Compared to industrial products as a whole, labor-intensive products are again more protected in industrialized countries than in developing countries, by an estimated one-third.[33]

Non-tariff barriers include a wide variety of quotas, procedural rules for imports, and standards set upon import quality that have the effect of limiting imports or making importing more difficult. For example, European carmakers are facing challenges from non-tariff barriers in South Korea. Rather than adopting internationally harmonized standards, South Korea sets a series of complicated domestic regulations on noise, emissions, safety belts and other issues that have prevented many European firms from entering the market. In 2007, European carmakers only managed to sell 15,000 vehicles in South Korea, generating revenue of $650 million. In contrast, Korean automakers exported slightly more than 74,000 cars to Europe with revenue of $3,900 million.[34-]

**Embargoes** and **sanctions** are country-based political trade controls. Political trade restraints have become an accepted form of political influence in the international community. They are coercive or retaliatory trade measures often enacted unilaterally with the hopes of changing a foreign government or its policies without resorting to military force. Embargoes restrict all trade with a nation for political purposes. The United States maintains an economic embargo on Cuba today in an effort to change the country's political disposition. Sanctions are more narrowly defined trade restrictions, such as the U.S. government's threat in 1999 to impose retaliatory tariffs of 100 percent on hundreds of millions of dollars in European imports to compensate U.S. banana companies for their lost sales to Europe and the government's declaration in March 2008 about introduction of sanctions concerning of some foreign companies (such as Armenian Blue Airways and Iranian Mahan Airways) for illegal re-export of the American planes to Iran.[35]

A trade war waged by the U.S. government could make such seemingly unrelated items as Scottish cashmere sweaters, Pecorino cheese (but only the soft kind), German coffee makers, and French handbags scarce on American store shelves.[36] **Global Perspective 5-1** describes the relationships between the United States and the European Union in terms of government regulations and trade war currently under way.

**Export license requirements** are product-based trade controls. All exports officially require a specific export license from the Export Administration of the Department of Commerce. However, most products that are not sensitive to national security or are in short supply in the country may be sent to another country using only a general license. The application process for more sensitive products, including much high-technology exports, is quite extensive and can include review by numerous government agencies (See Chapter 16 for export control).

International businesses have a number of reasons to be concerned with trade restrictions. First, trade restrictions may completely block a company's ability to export

---

[33]*Global Economic Prospects and the Developing Countries 2002,* Washington, D.C.: World Bank, 2002 (see Chapter 2).

[34]Lawrence J. Speer, "Talks Aim to Ease Access to Korean Market," *Automotive News Europe*, May 12, 2008.

[35]"USA Enter Sanctions against Some Companies for their Assistance to Iran," http://www.world-terrorism.org/. March 23, 2008.

[36]"Trade Fight Spills Over into Handbags, Coffee Makers," *CNN Interactive*, www.cnn.com, March 3, 1999.

**EXHIBIT 5-1**
TARIFF AND NON-TARIFF BARRIERS

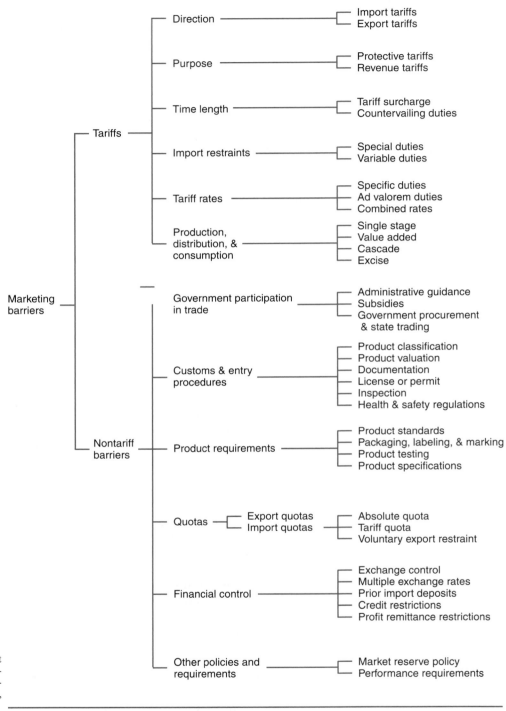

*Source:* Adapted from Sak Onkvist and John J. Shaw, "Marketing Barriers in International Trade," Business Horizons, 31, May–June 1988, p. 66.

to a country. Even if the company can export its goods, restrictions such as quotas or local modification requirements may make the product so expensive that an otherwise lucrative market is eliminated. Some companies attempt to benefit from import restrictions by establishing production facilities inside the foreign market country. For example, Brazil suddenly raised a tariff on imported cars from 20 percent to 70

◆ ◆ ◆ ◆ ◆ ◆ ◆ ◆ ◆ ◆ ◆ ◆ ◆ ◆ ◆ ◆ ◆ ◆ ◆ ◆ ◆ ◆ ◆ ◆ ◆ ◆ ◆ ◆ ◆ ◆ ◆ ◆ ◆ ◆

## $G$LOBAL PERSPECTIVE 5-1

### RELATIONSHIPS BETWEEN THE UNITED STATES AND THE
### EUROPEAN UNION: GOVERNMENT REGULATIONS AND TRADE WAR

American business has an enormous stake in the trading relationship with the EU. The EU is the United States' largest trading partner, and together they account for almost 40 percent of world trade and 60 percent of the world's gross national product. Importantly, this trade relationship directly supports a total of more than seven million jobs in the United States and the fifteen EU countries.

Over the last thirty years, as a result of a series of treaties agreed to by the member countries of the EU, the EU has won wide and growing powers to regulate business. In every area of economic activity, the EU has used these new powers to push through a determined harmonization program in an effort to unify marketplace standards throughout Europe. Harmonization has made selling to all 350 million western Europeans easier, as opposed to selling to each individual country within the EU.

Importantly for U.S. businesses, the EU is now in a much stronger position to punish American companies—and not with just trade sanctions, but also with domestic European legislation targeted at American companies.

*Sources*: John Grimley and Anthony Brown, "U.S.–EU Trading Relationships: The Stakes are Mounting," *Financial Executive*; 18, May 2002, pp. 21–22; and "Transatlantic Tiff," *Economist*, March 6, 2004, pp. 66–67.

For Americans, the EU is unlike any lawmaking body they are familiar with at home. A mixture of different political governance philosophies, and with a strong bureaucracy supporting the democratic voice of members of the European Parliament and national governments—but without the check upon centralization provided by the U.S. Supreme Court—the EU regulatory environment is unique, powerful and generally the first and last word on regulatory matters.

Trade wars between the United States and Europe are spreading. In 2004, the European Union EU imposed tariffs on $4 billion of U.S. the biggest authorized sanctions in the World Trade Organization's (WTO) history. These latest fines are over so-called Foreign Sales Corporation and Extraterritorial Income tax breaks for American exporters, which were ruled illegal by the WTO in two years earlier. Although the EU had notified the U.S. of its plans in 2003, the U.S. Congress has done next to nothing to stop the damage. As result, protectionist sentiment is running higher than ever in the United States. In another case, the WTO ruled that the EU could sue the United States for damages caused by its anti-dumping laws. In addition, there is yet a further dispute at the WTO over the United States' hormone-treated beef, which the EU wants labeled to protect its consumers.

---

percent in late 1994. As a result, foreign auto makers Fiat and Ford, with operating plants in Brazil, enjoyed a definite cost advantage over Chrysler, Toyota, Volvo, and others that exported cars to the country. Naturally, those latecomers decided to begin production in Brazil to avoid its hefty import tariffs. This is one illustration of strategic reasons why firms sometimes have plants in various countries rather than rely solely on exporting from home. In this manner those companies, domestic or foreign, already manufacturing in the market can access the desired market with little competition from external producers.

However, trade restrictions are not necessarily good, even for companies inside a protected country. Trade restrictions often block companies from purchasing needed inputs at competitive prices. For example, in 1992 the U.S. International Trade Commission levied an import tariff on the flat panel display screens used in laptop computers in response to a complaint that foreign companies were dumping the screens below cost on the U.S. market. Although local producers of computer screens benefited from the protection from competition, U.S. producers of laptop computers, which relied mostly on imported screens, could no longer compete. Many laptop producers were forced to ship their assembly plants overseas in order to stay in the market.

At a more macro level, if trade laws harm other countries, they are likely to invoke retaliation. For example, wrangling over the United States' inability to repeal the Byrd Amendment that the antidumping duties are channeled to U.S. steel companies that filed the antidumping charges against foreign steel producers, The Byrd Amendment literally encourages U.S. steel companies to file antidumping charges against foreign producers for their own interest, and The WTO ruled that the Byrd amendment violates international trade agreements. Canada is threatening to impose 100 percent duties on U.S.-made bicycles and a few hundred other American products, ranging from fish byproducts to plywood to skis to home exercise equipment. Brazil, Canada, Chile, the European Union, India, Japan, Mexico and South Korea apparently drew the same conclusion. They also promise to retaliate and target U.S. industries that assure that Congressmen feel their constituents' pain.[37] However, trade wars, if left unchecked, usually harm all countries by limiting the ability of competitive firms to export and generate the benefits created by specialization. One thing is clear—government trade laws have a complex and dynamic impact on the environment for international business (See **Global Perspective 5-2**).

---

## 𝒢LOBAL PERSPECTIVE 5-2

### WANT TO DO BUSINESS IN SOUTH ASIA?–ARE YOU READY FOR TRADE BARRIERS THERE?

In the era of globalization, many countries in South Asia have conducted a noticeable cut in tariff rates. However, this region is still highly protected as compared with other regional trade blocs. The non-tariff barriers, including anti-dumping and countervailing duties, quota, restrictions, packaging and labeling requirements, testing, quarantine and other certifications, are a common mode to restrict imports. This is especially true in India, which is known to have a larger number of such barriers compared to other South Asian countries.

There are 109 specific commodities, including food preservatives, additives, milk powder, infant milk foods, certain types of cement, household and similar electrical appliances, gas cylinders and multi-purpose dry cell batteries, that the Bureau of Indian Standards (BIS) must certify before goods are imported. In order to get this certificate, importers must pay a licensing fee of 0.2–1 percent of the value of certified goods.

For plant imports, such as almonds, pulses, fresh fruits and vegetables, India applied plant quarantine (regulation of import) order-2003 and its amendments without prior notification to the WTO SPS Committee. India has also implemented several sanitary restrictions that are not in consonance with the Office of International Epizootics (OIE) and CODEX (an international food standards organization) recommendations. India maintains a negative import list involving three categories: (1) prohibited items (i.e., tallow, fat, and roils of animal origin); (2) restricted items which require a non-automatic import license (e.g., livestock products, certain chemicals); and (3) "canalized" items (e.g., petroleum products, certain pharmaceuticals, and bulk grains) importable only by the government trading monopolies subject to cabinet approval on timing and quantity.

In addition to the applied customs rates, importers are required to pay another one percent customs handling fee and a two percent education assessment on all sales, a surcharge applied to almost all direct and indirect taxes. After these, the process does not end yet—during inter-state commerce, each state levies taxes adding further confusion to the tax system. What is worse, for the tariff, fees and additional tax

rates applied to imports, there is no single official publication that includes all information. Importers have to consult separate tariff and excise schedules as well as any applicable additional public notifications and notices, to determine current tariff and tax rates, the system of which lacks transparency.

This situation is further complicated due to extensive documentation required by the customs that hinders the free flow of trade and leads to frequent processing delays. Delay is mainly caused by complex tariff structure and multiple exemptions. The number of signatures in South Asia is 12 for export and 24 for import. In India, the number is as high as 22 for export and 27 for import.

For other South Asia countries, they also impose non-tariff barriers, although not as high and complicated as India sets. For example, Pakistan's Import Policy Order bans imports of certain items on religious, environmental, security and health grounds. Sri Lanka requires import licenses for over 300 items at the 6-digit level of the harmonized system mostly for health, environment and national security reasons. Importers have to pay a fee equal to 0.1 percent of the import price to receive an import license. There are 85 items that come under die Sri Lanka standard institutions (SLSI) mandatory import inspection schemes. Importers are required to obtain a clearance certificate from die SLSI to sell their goods.

Despite the South Asian Preferential Trade Agreement, the customs procedures at borders make intra-regional trade difficult and costly. Export and import in China or performers in ASEAN (Association of Southeast Asian Nations) states takes about 20 days to export and import. Of the South Asian countries, only Pakistan scores similarly. In India and Bangladesh, export-import time averages 34 days and 46 days, respectively. Besides, it costs less than $400 in the PRC and less than $500 in Malaysia to bring a standard 20-foot container across the border. Prices in South Asia range from about $800 in Sri Lanka to $1100 in Bangladesh.

Doubtlessly, high non-tariff barriers in South Asia have the potential of frustrating efforts for regional economic integration. In order to prosper the economy in this region through international business, the high trade barriers should be further removed.

*Source*: Jamil Nasir, "Trade Barriers in South Asia," *Economic Review*, 38 (August), 2007, pp. 62–63.

---

[37]"U.S. Bike Makers Caught in Trade War with Canada," *Bicycle Retailer & Industry News*, February 1, 2005, p. 1 and p. 43.

Trade war can have positive consequences, however, if it leads to freer trade instead of more restricted trade. The Association of South East Asian Nations (ASEAN) nations are slashing tariffs among themselves to compete with China. A pact to drop tariffs on goods traded within the 10-nation group to 5 percent or less now makes it possible for P&G to export to most of Asia out of its single remaining shampoo factory in Bangkok. Before the pact, P&G had to buy new production gear for separate plants in Thailand, Indonesia, and the Philippines.[38]

***Investment Regulations.*** International investments have been growing at a much faster pace than international trade. Many of these investments are being made by multinational corporations. Foreign direct investments are explained in terms of various market imperfections, including government imposed distortions, but governments also have a significant role in constructing barriers to foreign direct investment and portfolio flows. These barriers can broadly be characterized as ownership and financial controls.

**Ownership Controls.** Most countries feel that some assets belong to the public—there is a sense of "national ownership." In a highly nationalistic country, this sentiment could apply to the ownership of any company. In many countries, the natural resources (e.g., the land and mineral wealth) are viewed as part of the national wealth, not to be sold to foreigners. For example, Kuwait has a constitutional ban on foreign ownership of its oil reserves. Recently, there was a heated debate as to whether or not state-owned Kuwait Petroleum Corp. (KPC) had the right to sign agreements with foreign oil companies to produce local oil. The government argued that KPC was allowed under existing laws to forge foreign participation accords in return for cash incentives. But its efforts to advance the plan repeatedly came under attack by opposition members of parliament who argued that foreign companies' provision of cash incentives would amount to foreign direct investment, thus foreign control.[39] In a similar vein, Russia has decided to revive its ailing auto industry—which is rapidly losing market share to Western and Japanese imports and locally assembled foreign models—through direct state intervention. The Russian government seized control of General Motors' pioneering joint venture with Russia's largest automaker, OAO Avtovas in early 2006.[40]

The United States has very few restrictions on foreign ownership; however, for reasons of national security, limitations do exist. For example, the Federal Communications Commission limits the control of U.S. media companies to U.S. citizens only. This was one of the motivating factors for Rupert Murdoch to relinquish his Australian citizenship for U.S. citizenship in order to retain control of his media network, Fox Television. Similarly, the U.S. Shipping Act of 1916 limits noncitizen ownership of U.S. shipping lines. The Federal Aviation Act requires airlines to be U.S. citizens (defined as one where 75 percent of the voting rights of the firm are owned and controlled by U.S. citizens) in order to hold U.S. operating rights. The International Banking Act of 1978 limits interstate banking operations by foreign banks. Consequently, foreign banks cannot purchase or take over U.S. banks with interstate operations.

**Financial Controls.** Government-imposed restrictions can serve as strong barriers to foreign direct investments. Some common barriers include restrictions on profit remittances, and differential taxation and interest rates. Restrictions of profit remittances can serve as a disincentive to invest, since returns cannot be realized in the home currency of the parent company. Although government controls on profit remittance are drawbacks in attracting investment, some governments also use such restrictions as a way to encourage foreign companies to increase exports from the host country. For

---

[38]Michael Shar, "A New Front in the Free-Trade Wars," *Business Week*, June 3, 2002.

[39]Jeanne M. Perdue, "Kuwait Gets Green Light to Invite Majors," *Petroleum Engineer International*, 72 (September 1999), p. 7.

[40]"GM Venture in Russia Hits Snag Following Kremlin Involvement," *Wall Street Journal*, February 18, 2006, p. A7.

example, Zimbabwe permits higher profit remittance rates—up to 100 percent—to foreign companies operating in that country that export significantly.[41]

Various multinational companies have been able to exploit legal loopholes to circumvent this problem to some extent. Tactics include currency swaps, parallel loans, countertrade activities, and charging for management services, among others. Also, various countries treat operations of foreign companies differently from those of local companies. Two means through which local companies are supported are lower tax rates and lower interest rates for loans secured from local financial institutions. These differences can put foreign companies at a significant disadvantage relative to domestic companies in that particular market, and can also act as a deterrent to foreign direct investments.

***Macroeconomic Policies.*** Companies search internationally for stable growing markets where their profits will not be deteriorated by exchange loss or inflation. Government policies drive many economic factors such as the cost of capital, levels of economic growth, rates of inflation, and international exchange rates. Governments may directly determine the prime lending rate, or they may print or borrow the funds necessary to increase money supply. Governments may fix their currencies' exchange rates, or they may decide to allow the international currency market to determine their exchange rates. The monetary and exchange policies a government pursues will affect the stability of its currency—which is of critical concern to any company doing business abroad. Mexico kept the peso's exchange rate artificially high despite its increasing trade deficit in the early 1990s. One primary objective for such an exchange rate policy was to make it relatively easy for Mexico to import capital goods, such as machinery, from the United States for economic development. When Mexico's trade deficit rose to well over 8 percent of the country's GNP by 1994, Mexico could no longer hold on to an artificially high value of the peso and let it loose in December 1994. How serious was Mexico's trade deficit? Think, for a moment, that the United States had registered the large trade deficit of $172 billion in 1987, which once ushered in a doomsday prophecy of the decline of U.S. competitiveness. Yet, the U.S. trade deficit was no more than 3 percent of the country's GNP then! Now, as shown in Chapter 2, the U.S. trade deficit had constantly increased to $813 billion, or about 6 percent of U.S. GDP by 2008. As we discussed in Chapter 3, the U.S. trade deficit could not keep growing without a possibility of more ominous consequences than the current unprecedented recession since late 2008. Today, the United States is the world's largest debtor, with Japan being the largest creditor and China an increasingly important creditor to the United States. A sharp reversal in Japan's and China's appetite for U.S. treasury bonds could send U.S. interest rates soaring.[42] The U.S. government, too, needs to develop policies by which to reduce the country's trade deficit.

Government fiscal policies also strongly influence macroeconomic conditions. The types of taxes a government employs will influence whether a particular type of business is competitive within a country. For example, if a government lowers long-term capital gains taxes or allows accelerated depreciation of corporate capital assets, it will encourage investment in manufacturing facilities. The Japanese government has been known for its pro-business tax abatement and depreciation policies that helped develop the world's leading manufacturing industries in Japan, ranging from steel and shipbuilding in the 1960s and 1970s, to machine tools, automobiles, and consumer electronics in the 1970s and 1980s, and to semiconductor and semiconductor manufacturing equipment in the 1980s and 1990s.

Although a government can play a role in a thriving economy and accessible capital, a number of other factors also determine a country's political environment. Historical considerations, social and political pressures, and the interests of particular constituencies will affect the political environment in important ways. For example, during the early 1990s China was enjoying an unprecedented economic boom.

---

[41]Cris Chinaka, "Zimbabwe Announces Measures to Boost Investment," *Reuter Library Report* (April 27, 1993).

[42]"World Bank Warns Global Recovery Has Peaked," *Wall Street Journal*, April 7, 2005, p. A2.

However, companies that tried to take advantage of China's open market policy have met with mixed results.[43] When China joined the WTO in December 2001, it agreed to open up its financial industry, but only gradually. Foreign companies are not yet permitted to become majority owners. In banking, foreigners' stakes are limited to 15 percent, and it is not until 2006 can foreigners conduct local-currency business with Chinese citizens in banking.[44]

India, on the other hand, still has some restrictions on foreign investment over the years. One example is Press Note 18 that requires any investor with previous or existing joint ventures or technology agreements to seek approval from the Foreign Investment Promotion Board (FIPB) for new direct investments in the same or related field. Applicants must prove that the new proposal will not jeopardize the interest of the existing joint venture or technology partner. The Press Note 18 is intended to protect the interests of shareholders, public financial institutions and workers. Although many foreign investors complain about the policy, influential government officials do not want to abandon the guidelines because they consider their domestic industry not strong enough to face direct competition from foreign firms in selected sectors. Under the guidelines, recently Suzuki, a small Japanese automaker, has to include Maruti Udvog, its existing joint venture, in its plans to make new investments for a car assembly plant and a diesel engine plant. According to Suzuki, the governmental regulations have become a tool of the Indian partners to demand unrealistic and opportunistic exit valuations or to create more barriers for foreign competitors.[45]

## POLITICAL ENVIRONMENT—SOCIAL PRESSURES AND POLITICAL RISK

Foreign companies also have to consider social factors as part of the political environment of host countries. The political environment in every country is regularly changing. New social pressures can force governments to make new laws or to enforce old policies differently. Policies that supported international investment may change toward isolationism or nationalism. In order to adequately prepare for international business or investment, the environment in each target country should be analyzed to determine its level of economic and political risk and opportunity.

**Social Pressures and Special Interests**

Governments respond to pressures from various forces in a country, including the public at large, lobbyists for businesses, the church, non-governmental organizations (NGOs), and sometimes the personal interests of the members of the government. In order to assess the political stability of a country, it is critical to evaluate the importance of major forces on the government of the country. Many developing countries have undertaken significant liberalization programs during the 1980s and 1990s.[46] Although regularly promoted by the International Monetary Fund (IMF), the success of these programs during recent years must be attributed to a larger social acceptance of the potential benefits of necessary austerity measures. For example, one study has shown that the IMF's Structural Adjustment Program helped improve the economic efficiency of both domestic and foreign companies operating in Nigeria in the 1980s.[47] The benefits of liberalization extend beyond the borders of the countries involved. Consider the liberalization in Mexico, where the privatization of the state telephone company

[43]"To Enter or Not to Enter?" *Country Monitor*, January 28, 2002, p. 5.
[44]"Strings Attached," *Economist*, March 8, 2003, pp. 67–68.
[45]"Can They Let Go?" *Business India Intelligence*, October 16, 2004, pp. 1–2.
[46]Kate Gillespie and Hildy J. Teegen, "Market Liberalization and International Alliance Formation," *Columbia Journal of World Business*, 31 (Winter 1996), pp. 40–54.
[47]Sam C. Okoroafo and Masaaki Kotabe, "The IMF's Structural Adjustment Program and Its Impact on Firm Performance: A Case of Foreign and Domestic Firms in Nigeria," *Management International Review*, 33 (2) (1993), pp. 139–56.

(TelMex) led to large investments by Southwestern Bell. Similarly, private companies are moving rapidly to finance other large public projects. An international consortium composed of Mexico's Grupo Hermés, the United States' AES Corp., and the Japanese firm Nichimen constructed Mexico's first independent power-producing plant in Yucatán State.[48] While liberalization may provide unprecedented opportunities, the forces of special interests or the backlash of public sentiment may also cause governments to limit or curtail entirely certain international business operations.

Feelings of national interest can act as a deterrent to international business. For example, Carrefour, the world's No. 2 retailer from France, faced a boycott in China in April 2008 because of pro-Tibet protests in Paris and President Sarkozy's threat to shun Olympic ceremonies. Angry Chinese crowds gathered outside Chinese outlets of Carrefour to protest France's efforts to use the Beijing Olympics to pressure China on human rights and Tibet. Although Carrefour in reality did not have any involvement in politics regarding the related issues, it still suffered largely from it and faced the huge social pressures from Chinese people. Another striking example involves Dell Computer.[49] As a manifestation of nationalistic sentiment, there were regular complaints from Dell China customers over the display of the Taiwan flag on the Dell Taiwan website. Dell Computer tried to placate these customers in China via various visual interface designs back in 2002. During the last Taiwan presidential election in 2005, Chinese customers again lodged another massive complaint with Dell Computer over the flag issue. Executives at Dell Computer came to learn that political events often supersede meticulous business plans. As Dell Computer sees China as the main revenue growth in Asia, the company has finally decided to remove all flags from Dell Asia-Pacific websites immediately for fear of a potential boycott of Dell products in China. At the time of this writing, therefore, there are no flag displays for China, Taiwan, Korea, India, Singapore, Vietnam, and other Asian countries, except Dell Japan, which retained its own flag display since it is considered a separate business entity from the Asia-Pacific segment (due to maturity of its customer base and purchasing power). Of course, since Dell Computer is dealing with nationalistic sensitivities, it could be only a matter of time before Dell China customers will suddenly realize the Chinese flag not being displayed while Dell Japan still has its own flag display. Corporate diplomacy can indeed be very delicate. As one ex-Dell executive confides, "One can never foresee all possibilities, but as marketers, we always need to plan for such contingencies."[50]

Besides such outcries from local customers, large-scale strikes organized by labor union could equally harm businesses across national boundaries. In June 2002, thousands of passengers across Europe got left stranded as air traffic controllers went on strike. The strike was in protest at a plan for a continent-wide "single-sky" plan intended to reduce congestion and delays. Ninety percent of Air France's long-haul flights did not take off, Germany's Lufthansa airlines cancelled 130 of its 140 flights to and from France, and British Airways was operating only four of its usual 126 flights into France. Partial strikes in Greece, Hungary, Portugal, Spain, and Italy also halted some flights.[51]

Furthermore, in recent years, the emergence of nongovernmental organizations (NGOs) as organizational manifestations of broader social movements has dramatically altered the global political-economic landscape. NGOs are relatively informal organizations established by "concerned people" who participate in global value creation and governance. Sometimes, NGOs are anti-government or anti-MNCs, trying to address societal and environmental issues that they feel are unsatisfactorily addressed.[52] The

---

[48]"Mexico's Energy Infrastructure Expanding to Match Growth," *NAFTA Works* (February 1997), pp. 1–2.

[49]"France's Carrefour Feels China's Ire," *BusinessWeek.com*, April 22, 2008.

[50]This paragraph is based on the authors' personal discourse with Leon Z. Lee, an former executive at Dell Computer in charge of the company's global branding, Web globalization and intercultural relations, March 10, 2006.

[51]"Strike Cripples European Air Travel," *CNN News*, June 19, 2002.

[52]Hildy Teegen, Jonathan P. Doh, and Sushil Vachani, "The Importance of Nongovernmental Organizations (NGOs) in Global Governance and Value Creation: An International Business Research Agenda," *Journal of International Business Studies*, 35, November 2004, pp. 463–83.

◆ ◆ ◆ ◆ ◆ ◆ ◆ ◆ ◆ ◆ ◆ ◆ ◆ ◆ ◆ ◆ ◆ ◆ ◆ ◆ ◆ ◆ ◆ ◆ ◆ ◆ ◆ ◆ ◆ ◆ ◆ ◆

## $\mathscr{G}$LOBAL PERSPECTIVE 5-3

### SOCIAL PRESSURES AFFECTING GOVERNMENT AND CORPORATE POLICIES: A ROLE OF NGOS

The emergence of nongovernmental organizations (NGOs) as organizational manifestations of broader social movements has dramatically altered the global political-economic landscape. NGOs are relatively informal organizations established by "concerned people" who participate in global value creation and governance. Sometimes, NGOs are anti-government or anti-MNCs, trying to address societal and environmental issues that they feel are unsatisfactorily addressed. Take the Exxon case as an example.

Exxon, world's second-largest corporation, is building a 660-mile pipeline from the oil fields of Chad, in the geographic heart of Africa, to the coast of Cameroon. The pipeline, three feet under ground, will cut through forests and farmlands as it makes its way to the sea. Besides local governments to deal with, Exxon has to confront various NGOs for the environmental concerns. Under pressure for activists, Exxon has been forced to take on the unlikely role of development agency, human-right promoter, de facto local government, and even environmental watchdog.

Using the Internet and mass media as cudgels, NGOs such as Greenpeace, Human Rights Watch, and Friends of the Earth, have grown increasingly adept at singling out multinationals. The oil company offers a particularly ripe target. Companies like Exxon are big, which NGOs readily translate as "bad." Exxon has highly visible brands, making it vulnerable to boycotts at the pump. The oil company cannot choose where oil deposits are located, which means that it increasingly operates in countries with unsavory rulers, sensitive environments, and impoverished populations. And its power tends to dwarf that of its host countries. Exxon's 2001 revenues were $191.6 billion, compared with Chad's GDP of $1.4 billion.

The solution is a complex, four-way agreement between Exxon, the host governments, activists and the World Bank. In keeping with its mission of alleviating poverty, the World Bank would lend $93 million to the governments of Chad and Cameroon so they could participate as equity investors in the project. By standing between Exxon and its worst critics, and between Exxon and the troublesome host governments, the World Bank could serve as a moral buffer, providing Exxon with invaluable political insurance. While reassuring people on its skills and technology, Exxon has helped oversee a $1.5 million initiative in which the oil company has built schools, funded health clinics, dug wells, advised local entrepreneurs, fielded an AIDS-education van, and distributed 32,000 anti-malarial mosquito nets. It has also paid for prostitute focus groups, gorilla habitat studies, even ritual chicken sacrifices.

Between 1993 and 1999 there were already 145 meetings involving 250 NGOs and Exxon had agreed to 60 changes in the pipeline's route. It also promised to help create an environmental foundation, two national parks in Cameroon, and an "Indigenous Peoples Plan" for the Pygmies, local minorities in Africa. And Exxon will offer compensation to owners of every mango tree, bean plant and cotton field, on a plant's expectancy, annual yield, local fruit prices, and so forth.

To complicate matters for Exxon, the demands of Western NGOs often conflict directly with the wishes of locals. The NGOs want Cameroon's rain forests untouched; local farmers plead for Exxon to clear them with chain saws. The NGOs want roads routed around village; villagers sneak out at night to move road markers closer to their homes and stores, so that they will have more compensation money to improve their life.

It still remains a question whether the local Chad government could be trusted with Exxon's oil money. Although the World Bank will retain its right to cut off all loans and future aid to Chad, nothing can stop its leader to live high on the hog, pay his army, and say to heck with the other seven million people. Last time the $25 million was paid to Chad's President, he used $4.5 million to buy weapons.

With the "help" of NGOs, the World Bank, and chicken sacrifice, Exxon is practicing an unfamiliar way of doing business. If the experiment succeeds, observers say, it could rewrite the rulebook for how multinationals operate worldwide. The traditional way of doing business, getting the oil out of the ground without getting involved in politics, human rights, and the environment, just is not tenable anymore.

*Source:* Jerry Useem, "Exxon's African Adventure," *Fortune*, April 15, 2002, pp. 50–58.

Exxon case presented in **Global Perspective 5-3** vividly illustrates the social pressures from NGOs affecting government and corporate policies.

How should a manager evaluate the opportunities and risks a country presents? Obviously this depends upon too many factors to discuss them all. A manager should certainly consider the political history of the country, as well as the history of similar industries within the country. In the following section we will discuss a number of factors that international managers should consider when determining the economic and political risks associated with a country.

**Managing the Political Environment**

International managers must manage the political environment in which the international firm operates. This means, first and foremost, learning to follow the customs of the country in which the firm is operating. But managing the political environment also means knowing which facets of the foreign country must be carefully monitored, and which can be manipulated. If managed correctly, the political environment could become a marketing support system, rather than an inhibitor, for the foreign company.[53]

In order to make informed decisions, the marketing manager must understand the political factors of the country, and also must understand the national strategies and goals of the country. The political factors in a country include: the political stability, the predominant ideology toward business (and foreign business in particular), the roles that institutions have in the country (including the church, government agencies, and the legal systems), and the international links to other countries' legal and ideological structures.[54]

In order to be welcomed in a host country, the foreign firm has to offer some tangible benefits that the host government desires. Thus, it is critical that a manger recognize what the host country government's motivations and goals are. Most international business activities offer something to all parties involved. If the host country is actively pursuing job creation goals, then a foreign firm that can offer jobs has leverage for obtaining concessions against other problems. The manager will want to understand what national policies are being pursued, and what policy instruments the government typically uses to promote its interests (see **Exhibit 5-2**).

It is important to carefully assess the political power structure and mood in a country before making decisions regarding business operations. By evaluating various environmental factors (see **Exhibit 5-3**), marketing managers can arrive at a more thorough understanding of the likelihood of various problems or opportunities in a country. As shown in **Exhibit 5-4**, managers can also purchase or subscribe to country risk ratings provided by various risk analysis agencies such as the PRS Group's

## EXHIBIT 5-2
### GOVERNMENT POLICY AREAS AND INSTRUMENTS

| Policy Instruments | Policy Areas | | | | | |
|---|---|---|---|---|---|---|
| | *Monetary* | *Fiscal* | *Trade* | *Foreign Investment* | *Incomes* | *Sectoral* |
| Legal | • Banking reserve levels | • Tax rates<br>• Subsidies | • Government import controls | • Ownership laws | • Labor laws | • Land tenure laws |
| Administrative | • Loan guarantee<br>• Credit regulation | • Tax collection | • Import quotas<br>• Tariffs<br>• Exchange rates and controls | • Profit repatriation controls<br>• Investment approvals | • Price controls<br>• Wage controls | • Industry licensing<br>• Domestic content |
| Direct market operations | • Money creation | • Government purchases | • Government imports | • Government joint ventures | • Government wages | • State-owned enterprises |

*Source:* Adapted from James E. Austin, Managing in Developing Countries: Strategic Analysis and Operating Techniques (New York: Free Press, 1990), p. 89.

---

[53]Michael G. Harvey, Robert F. Lusch, and Branko Cavarkapa, *"A Marketing Mix for the 21st Century," Journal of Marketing Theory and Practice,* 4 (Fall 1996), pp. 1–15
[54]James E. Austin, *Managing in Developing Countries: Strategic Analysis and Operating Techniques* (New York: Free Press, 1990).

**EXHIBIT 5-3**
COUNTRY RISK ASSESSMENT CRITERIA

| Index Area | Criteria |
|---|---|
| Economic Risk | • GDP Per Capita<br>• Real Annual GDP Growth as Annual percent Change<br>• Annual Inflation Rate as Annual percent Change<br>• Budget Balance as percent of GDP<br>• Current Account as percent of GDP |
| Financial Risk | • Foreign Debt as percent of GDP<br>• Foreign Debt Service as percent of Exports of Goods and Services<br>• Current Account as percent of Exports of Goods and Services<br>• International Liquidity as Months of Import Cover<br>• Exchange Rate Stability as percent Change |
| Political Risk | • Government Stability<br>• Socioeconomic Conditions<br>• Investment Profile<br>• Internal Conflict<br>• External Conflict<br>• Corruption<br>• Military in Politics<br>• Religious Tensions<br>• Law and Order<br>• Ethnic Tensions<br>• Democratic Accountability<br>• Bureaucracy Quality |

*Source:* The PRS Group, *International Country Risk Guide*, http://www.prsgroup.com/, accessed July 20, 2009.

**EXHIBIT 5-4**
EXAMPLES OF COUNTRY RISK RATINGS (70 SELECTED COUNTRIES RANKED BY COMPOSITE OVERALL RATING, AS OF JULY 2008)

| Rank | Country | Composite Risk Measure | Economic Risk | Financial Risk | Political Risk |
|---|---|---|---|---|---|
| 1 | Norway | 91.8 | 88.5 | 47.5 | 47.5 |
| 3 | Brunei | 88.5 | 83.5 | 46.0 | 47.5 |
| 3 | Switzerland | 88.5 | 88.5 | 43.5 | 45.0 |
| 4 | Finland | 87.5 | 92.5 | 37.0 | 45.5 |
| 6 | Singapore | 87.0 | 84.5 | 43.5 | 46.0 |
| 6 | Sweden | 87.0 | 88.5 | 40.5 | 45.0 |
| 8 | Denmark | 86.0 | 86.0 | 43.0 | 43.0 |
| 8 | Germany | 86.0 | 86.5 | 42.0 | 43.5 |
| 9 | Netherlands | 85.5 | 86.0 | 41.0 | 44.0 |
| 11 | Canada | 85.0 | 86.0 | 42.0 | 42.0 |
| 11 | Kuwait | 85.0 | 77.5 | 44.5 | 48.0 |
| 12 | Austria | 84.8 | 88.0 | 38.0 | 43.5 |
| 13 | Botswana | 84.0 | 76.0 | 49.0 | 43.0 |
| 15 | Taiwan | 83.8 | 80.0 | 45.0 | 42.5 |
| 15 | United Arab Emirates | 83.8 | 79.0 | 42.0 | 46.5 |
| 17 | Belgium | 83.3 | 82.5 | 40.5 | 43.5 |
| 17 | Ireland | 83.3 | 89.5 | 38.0 | 39.0 |
| 18 | Bahrain | 82.0 | 72.5 | 42.0 | 49.5 |
| 19 | Japan | 81.8 | 77.5 | 46.0 | 40.0 |
| 20 | South Korea | 81.3 | 78.5 | 41.0 | 43.0 |
| 21 | Australia | 80.5 | 86.5 | 34.0 | 40.5 |
| 22 | Chile | 79.8 | 78.5 | 40.0 | 41.0 |
| 23 | Saudi Arabia | 79.5 | 68.5 | 45.0 | 45.5 |
| 24 | Malaysia | 79.3 | 73.5 | 43.0 | 42.0 |

*(Continued)*

**EXHIBIT 5-4**
(CONTINUED)

| Rank | Country | Composite Risk Measure | Economic Risk | Financial Risk | Political Risk |
|------|---------|------------------------|---------------|----------------|----------------|
| 25 | United Kingdom | 78.8 | 80.0 | 40.5 | 37.0 |
| 26 | China | 78.5 | 67.5 | 48.0 | 41.5 |
| 27 | France | 78.0 | 78.5 | 38.5 | 39.0 |
| 28 | New Zealand | 77.8 | 83.5 | 33.0 | 39.0 |
| 29 | Portugal | 77.5 | 83.0 | 36.5 | 35.5 |
| 30 | Italy | 77.3 | 80.5 | 37.0 | 37.0 |
| 32 | Mexico | 76.8 | 74.0 | 41.0 | 38.5 |
| 32 | Russia | 76.8 | 66.5 | 44.5 | 42.5 |
| 33 | United States | 76.5 | 81.0 | 32.0 | 40.0 |
| 34 | Poland | 76.3 | 80.5 | 34.5 | 37.5 |
| 35 | Slovenia | 75.8 | 77.5 | 35.5 | 38.5 |
| 36 | Spain | 75.5 | 78.5 | 35.0 | 37.5 |
| 37 | Costa Rica | 73.8 | 72.5 | 40.0 | 35.0 |
| 39 | Morocco | 73.5 | 70.5 | 40.5 | 36.0 |
| 39 | Peru | 73.5 | 62.5 | 43.0 | 41.5 |
| 40 | Kazakhstan | 73.3 | 75.5 | 36.0 | 35.0 |
| 41 | Croatia | 72.5 | 73.5 | 34.0 | 37.5 |
| 42 | Greece | 72.0 | 74.5 | 33.0 | 36.5 |
| 44 | Estonia | 71.8 | 76.0 | 32.5 | 35.0 |
| 44 | South Africa | 71.8 | 68.0 | 37.5 | 38.0 |
| 47 | Argentina | 71.5 | 66.0 | 38.0 | 39.0 |
| 47 | Hungary | 71.5 | 75.0 | 34.0 | 34.0 |
| 47 | Iran | 71.5 | 56.5 | 46.0 | 40.5 |
| 49 | Brazil | 71.0 | 66.5 | 37.5 | 38.0 |
| 49 | Israel | 71.0 | 61.5 | 38.0 | 42.5 |
| 50 | Philippines | 70.0 | 62.0 | 38.5 | 39.5 |
| 51 | Indonesia | 69.0 | 59.0 | 40.5 | 38.5 |
| 52 | Vietnam | 68.8 | 66.5 | 40.0 | 31.0 |
| 53 | Ghana | 68.5 | 67.0 | 38.5 | 31.5 |
| 54 | Thailand | 68.5 | 59.0 | 41.5 | 36.5 |
| 55 | Ukraine | 68.5 | 69.0 | 37.0 | 31.0 |
| 56 | Cuba | 67.8 | 58.0 | 40.0 | 37.5 |
| 57 | Armenia | 67.5 | 59.5 | 40.0 | 35.5 |
| 58 | India | 67.3 | 60.5 | 43.5 | 30.5 |
| 59 | Venezuela | 67.0 | 49.5 | 46.0 | 38.5 |
| 60 | Colombia | 65.3 | 58.5 | 36.0 | 36.0 |
| 61 | Nigeria | 64.8 | 43.5 | 46.5 | 39.5 |
| 62 | Turkey | 63.5 | 59.5 | 32.5 | 35.0 |
| 63 | Bangladesh | 62.8 | 50.0 | 40.0 | 35.5 |
| 64 | Nicaragua | 61.5 | 66.0 | 33.5 | 23.5 |
| 65 | Ethiopia | 59.5 | 49.5 | 39.5 | 30.0 |
| 66 | Lebanon | 58.5 | 57.0 | 31.5 | 28.5 |
| 67 | Sudan | 54.5 | 44.0 | 34.0 | 31.0 |
| 68 | Iraq | 53.0 | 36.0 | 36.0 | 34.0 |
| 69 | Zimbabwe | 40.5 | 41.0 | 23.5 | 16.5 |
| 70 | Somalia | 39.3 | 23.5 | 33.0 | 22.0 |

*Note:* Lower scores represent higher risk (highest risk = 1, lowest risk = 100)

*Source:* Compiled from the PRS Group, *International Country Risk Guide*, http://www.prsgroup.com/, accessed July 20, 2009.

International Country Risk Guide, the Economist Intelligence Unit (EIU), Business Environment Risk Intelligence (BERI), and Business Monitor International (BMI).

Regardless of categories employed in their risk ratings, there are three general types of risks involved in operating in a foreign country: risks associated with changes in company ownership, risks associated with changes in company operations, and risks associated with changes in transfers of goods and money. Changes in ownership structure are usually due to dramatic political changes, such as wars or coups d'état.

A company may face the expropriation or confiscation of its property, or it may face the nationalization of its industry. **Expropriation** refers to foreign government's takeover of company goods, land, or other assets, with compensation that tends to fall short of their market value. **Confiscation** is an outright takeover of assets without compensation. **Nationalization** refers to foreign government's takeover for the purpose of making the industry a government-run industry. In nationalization, companies usually receive some level of compensation for their losses.

To reduce risk of expropriation or confiscation of corporate assets overseas, many companies use joint ventures with local companies or adopt a domestication policy. Joint ventures with local companies imply shared activities and tend to reduce nationalistic sentiment against the company operating in a foreign country. **Domestication policy** (also known as **phase-out policy**) refers to a company gradually turning over management and operational responsibilities as well as ownership to local companies over time.

However, these risks have been reduced in recent years as many countries have realized the need for international support in order to receive the loans and investment they need to prosper. Consequently, the number of privatizations of once government-owned industries has increased in the last decade.[55] It is well known that government-owned companies generally do not measure up to the performance standard of private companies.[56]

Other changes in operating regulations can make production unprofitable. For example, local-content requirements may force a company to use inputs of higher cost or inferior quality, making its products uncompetitive. Price controls may set limits on the sales price for a company's goods that are too low to recover investments made. Restrictions on the number of foreign employees may force a company to train local citizens in techniques that require years of specialization.

Shifts in regulations on the transfer of goods and money can also dramatically affect the profitability of operating in a country. These changes include exchange rate restrictions or devaluations, input restrictions, and output price fixing. If a country is experiencing a shortage of foreign capital, it may limit the sale of foreign currencies to companies that need to buy some inputs from abroad or repatriate profits back home. Faced with such foreign exchange restrictions, companies have developed creative, if not optimal, means to deal with the foreign exchange restrictions. **Countertrade** is a frequently used method that involves trading of products without involving direct monetary payments. For example, in order to expand its operations in Russia, the Russian subsidiary of PepsiCo needed to import bottling equipment from the United States. However, the Russian government did not allow the company to exchange rubles for dollars, so it exported Russian vodka to the United States to earn enough dollars to import the needed equipment. As a result of the countertrade arrangement, PepsiCo is now considered the most widely available western consumer product in the Commonwealth of Independent States (ex-Soviet states). Firms that use countertrade are also shifting away from short-term marketing motives, such as disposing of surplus, obsolete, or perishable products, to long-term marketing motives such as establishing relationships with new partners, gaining entry to new or difficult markets, and accessing networks and expertise.[57]

---

[55]Douglas L. Bartley and Michael S. Minor, "Privatization in Eastern Europe: A Field Report," *Competitiveness Review*, 6 (2), 1996, pp. 31–43; and John Nellis, "Time to Rethink Privatization in Transition Economies," *Finance & Development*, 36 (June 1999), pp. 16–19.

[56]Lien-Ti Bei and Cian-Fong Shang, "Building Marketing Strategies for State-Owned Enterprises against Private Ones Based on the Perspectives of Customer Satisfaction and Service Quality," *Journal of Retailing & Consumer Services*, 13, January 2006, pp. 1–13.

[57]Dorothy Paun and Aviv Shoham, "Marketing Motives in International Countertrade: An Empirical Examination," *Journal of International Marketing*, 4 (3), 1996, pp. 29–47.

◆ ◆ ◆ ◆ ◆ ◆ ◆ ◆   TERRORISM AND THE WORLD ECONOMY

Terrorism used to be considered a random political risk of relatively insignificant proportions. However, it seems to have gradually escalated in the last decade or so.[58] It culminated on September 11, 2001 in New York City and Washington, D.C., when massive terrorist attacks occurred. No one can ever forget what happened that day in the United States. Americans and the rest of the world were stunned, not only by the terror attacks, but also by the vulnerability revealed. By attacking the World Trade Center and the Pentagon, the symbol of the financial and economic center and the military power, respectively, terrorists also disrupted the U.S. economy and affected the global market as well. The cost of the attack is hard to believe. An IMF study identified the direct loss as totaling about $21.4 billion, or about 0.25 percent of the U.S. GDP.[59] Other studies' estimates are much higher.[60] Short-term lost economic output was estimated as $47 billion and lost stock market wealth at $1.7 trillion.[61] At least 125,000 workers were laid off for 30 days or longer, and according to a Milken Institute study, Metropolitan areas in the U.S. lost as much as 1.6 million jobs in 2002 because of the attacks.[62] Long-term costs of security spending and anti-terrorist activities can also be significant.

The tighter security measures after September 11 affects international trade tremendously. Security check causes delays in shipments of goods and raising concerns among businesses that reply on just-in-time delivery. In the United States after the attack, because of the security check at the Canadian border, Ford Motor and General Motors experienced periodic parts shortages which delayed production for hours, steel makers slowed production, and office-supply stores in the New York area ran out of ink and paper.

Similarly, The Middle East crisis, with over hundreds of Israelis killed and thousands wounded, has had a big impact on Israel's economy and foreign investment. The Bank of Israel reported that Israel's balance of payments worsened by $1.9 billion in 2001 due to the deteriorating security situation, including a loss of $1.7 billion in tourism revenue. Because international investors are less willing to visit or make fact-finding trips to Israel, Israeli firms find it much more difficult to raise funds abroad. The whole economy shrank in 2001, with GDP falling by 0.6 percent, compared to a 6.4 percent increase in 2000.[63]

The worsened Middle East crisis, the September 11 terrorist attacks on the United States, and subsequently the Iraq war have caused tremendous concern about future oil supply for economic security. Since Arab oil supplies look shakier than ever, U.S. policy makers and oil companies are working on oil pipelines in Africa and other parts of Asia. An oil pipeline currently under construction from Baku through Georgia to the Turkish port of Ceyhan is a vital project for oil security.[64] Oil pipelines in some parts of Africa are also facing frequent attacks from terrorists. For example, actions of insurgents in recent years have led to a significant reduction of oil production in Nigeria. Thousands of foreign workers have been compelled to leave the country, and two oil-refining

---

[58]Masaaki Kotabe, "Global Security Risks and International Competitiveness," *Journal of International Management*, 11 (December 2005), pp. 453–56.

[59]International Monetary Fund, "How Has September 11 Influenced the Global Economy," *World Economic Outlook*, (December 2001), p. 16.

[60]Jim Saxton, "The Economic Costs of Terrorism Pose Policy Challenges," Joint Economic Committee Press Release, United States Congress, www.house.gov/jec/, May 1, 2002.

[61]Peter Navarro and Aron Spencer, "September 11, 2001: Assessing the Costs of Terrorism," *Milken Institute Review*, (Fourth Quarter 2001), p. 20.

[62]Ross Devol, et. al., "The Impact of September 11 on U.S. Metropolitan Areas," *Milken Institute Research Report*, (January 2002).

[63]"The Cost of Terrorism," *Jerusalem Post*, (March 24, 2002), p. 6.

[64]Background note: Georgia, U.S. Department of State, Bureau of European and Eurasian Affairs, February 2008.

factories have been closed. In the middle of 2007 regular attacks of insurgents had resulted in the large reduction of Nigeria oil export volume by 25 percent.[65]

Even two massive terrorist bombings in Bali, Indonesia on October 12, 2002 and on October 1, 2005 affected many nationalities ranging from Australia to South Africa and from Ecuador to Sweden. The majority of the dead in the first attack was Australians. Australians always thought that given their country's relatively geographically isolated location, they were immune to terrorism. Now even Australian firms as well as tourists have to think twice about where to invest and travel, respectively.[66] According to the new National Counterterrorism Center, there was a tremendous increase in terrorist attacks in 2004, with 651 significant strikes worldwide. The growing threat today is from the so-called "global jihad movement," a mixed group inspired, but not directed, by Osama bin Laden. This group, in particular, is carrying out most of the terrorist attacks against U.S. and allied interests.[67]

As recently as 2006, the U.S. government, sensitive about Middle Eastern terrorism, entered a heated dispute over port security issues resulting from the proposed purchase of five major U.S. commercial port operations by Dubai Ports World, a United Arab Emirates-owned company and one of the most globally efficient port operators.[68] Eventually, the U.S Congress introduced legislation to delay the sale. Clearly, economic efficiency cannot be pursued devoid of international politics.

Terrorist activities and local military skirmishes in various parts of the world disrupt not only international movement of supplies and merchandise but also international financial flow as well as tourism. They threaten the smooth functioning of international marketing activities we had taken for granted in the last thirty years. International marketers should be aware that global strategy based on coordination of various value-adding activities scattered around the world as envisioned in the 1980s and 90s may need to be replaced (at least on a case-by-case basis) by more locally- and regionally-based strategy that require increased levels of local procurement and local marketing for the sake of political correctness and local sensitivity.[69]

## INTERNATIONAL AGREEMENTS

◆ ◆ ◆ ◆ ◆ ◆ ◆

International politics has always been characterized by the predominance of strong ideological links, centered around, and dominated by, a relatively small number of large powers. After World War II, those ideological links were centered around the two contending superpowers: the United States and the former Soviet Union. Recently, however, the hierarchical structure of world politics has been challenged by two processes.

First, the true independence of previously colonial countries has led to a much larger set of nations playing relatively independently on the international stage, entering into contracts and relations with new political and economic partners. Second, the loosening of the tight bipolarity in world politics, combined with the relative decline of the United States as the economic superpower in the free world and the breakup of the Soviet Union that had once led the communist world, has created an increased level of ambiguity in geopolitical stability.[70]

While most nations guard their independence by maintaining the ability to produce critical products domestically, citizens around the world have learned to expect and

---

[65]"In Nigeria Insurgents Have Damaged Oil Pipeline and Have Killed 11 Militarians," http://www.world-terrorism.org/items/date/2008/05, accessed September 1, 2008.

[66]The Bomber Will Always Get Through," *Economist*, October 8, 2005, pp. 12–13.

[67]Lisa Stein, "The Week," *U.S. News & World Report*, May 9, 2005, pp. 14–18.

[68]"Big Problem, Dubai Deal or Not," *New York Times*, February 23, 2006.

[69]Masaaki Kotabe, "To Kill Two Birds with One Stone: Revisiting the Integration-Responsiveness Framework," in Michael Hitt and Joseph Cheng, ed., *Managing Transnational Firms*, New York: Elsevier, 2002, 59–69.

[70]Tom Nierop, *Systems and Regions in Global Politics—An Empirical Study of Diplomacy, International Organization and Trade, 1950–1991* (New York: Wiley, 1994).

demand the lifestyle that international trade provides. Thus, domestic politics cannot be isolated from international politics. Political actions in one country will eventually influence the actions of other countries. For example, Mexico's recent decision to devalue its currency caused U.S. exports to Mexico to decrease. If the industries that are harmed by the decrease in sales have enough political force, they might ask the U.S. government to pressure Mexico to invest in strengthening its currency or face trade repercussions.

Not only do nations react to each other's actions, they develop relationships that determine their future actions. They form networks for achieving mutual goals, and they develop political and trade histories and dependencies that influence their perceptions of the world. Thus, the international political environment is determined by a dynamic process of the interactions of players, all of whom are pursuing their own interests and working together for mutual interests. Coordination is required, for example, in order to establish and maintain a trade embargo as a viable alternative to military force. Similarly, coordination is required to avoid harmful currency devaluations or the financial insolvency of governments. The level at which governments rely on each other and are affected by each other's actions also leads to regular conflicts and tensions. Indeed, history has shown that a war—an ultimate form of international conflicts and tensions—is less likely to occur between the two countries, the more trade they engage in with each other.[71]

In the United States, the Congress, not the president, is in charge of international trade negotiations. As a legislative process, any decision-making on trade-related issues tends to be slow, and the U.S. government's inaction sometimes becomes a bottleneck to international trade negotiations. As a result, the U.S. government may lose credibility in such negotiations. If the Congress sees the benefit of faster trade negotiations, it may grant fast-track trade authority to the President. **Fast-track trade authority** gives the U.S. President a free hand in directly negotiating trade deals with foreign governments. Although ex-President Clinton did not get a fast-track trade authority, President George W. Bush was granted this authority in 2002.[72] Similarly, Mexico, whose trade volume with the United States and Canada has more than tripled since the implementation of NAFTA in 1994, considered granting president Vicente Fox fast track trade authority to impose a 40 percent tariff on fresh apples imported from the United States. Mexico accused the United States of selling the fruit at an unfair price, hurting domestic growers.[73]

The roles of the General Agreement on Tariffs and Trade (GATT) and the World Trade Organization that succeeded GATT in 1995 were explained earlier as part of the economic environment in Chapter 2. We limit our discussion to two major international agreements that have shaped and will reshape the political economies of the world.

**Group of Seven (G7), Group of Eight (G8), and Group of Eight plus Five (G8+5)**

The **G7** is an economic policy coordination group made up of political leaders from Canada, England, France, Germany, Italy, Japan, and the United States. The G7 began during the economic crises of the mid-1970s. The G7 countries continued to play a major role in world economy. For example, during a recent G7 meeting in Washington, D.C. in September 2005, soaring oil prices emerged as the topic dominating the discussion among finance ministers from the Group of Seven industrialized countries. The Bush administration called for measures that would increase oil supply and stem supply disruptions, while some in Europe called for measures to reduce consumption. There was a clear difference mirroring trans-Atlantic disputes over issues such as global warming. Other issues on the table at the meeting were debt relief for developing countries and the U.S. budget deficit.[74]

---

[71]Edward D. Mansfield, *Power, Trade, and War* (Princeton, NJ: Princeton University Press, 1994).

[72]"Fast-Trace Authority: Don't Underestimate its Clout," *Business Week*, August 12, 2002, p. 35.

[73]Ginger Thompson, "Mexico: Apple Dumping Duties," *New York Times*, August 10, 2002, p. 3.

[74]"Oil Likely to Be Focus of G-7 Meeting," *Wall Street Journal*, September 22, 2005, p. A8.

Russia joined the G7 in 1997, and the group consisting of the original G7 and Russia is known as the **G8**. Heads of state, senior economic ministers, and heads of central banks typically meet once a year to further economic coordination. G7 meetings have primarily dealt with financial and macroeconomic issues (such as the Asian and Latin American financial crisis), but since Russia's participation, the G8 has included some politically sensitive issues such as an effort to make arrangements for the reconstruction of Kosovo—and indeed of the Balkan states as a whole—after the Kosovo conflict. Recently, as a result of a remarkable economic and democratic transformation, Russia has demonstrated its potential to play a full and meaningful role in addressing the global problems with the seven industrialized nations. The Group of Eight industrialized nations, in a G8 summit meeting in Calgary, Canada in June 2002, agreed to have Russia become the group's president and host the summit meeting in 2006.[75]

Group of Eight (G8) leaders met at the Toyako Summit in Japan in July 2008 to tackle a number of impending issues including climate change, the food crisis, and oil supply stability.

In 2005, a new Group of Eight plus Five (G8+5) was formed when Tony Blair, then-Prime Minister of the United Kingdom, in his role as host of the 31st G8 summit at Gleneagles, Scotland, invited the leading emerging countries (Brazil, China, India, Mexico and South Africa) to join the talks. This enlargement aimed to form a stronger and more representative group that would inject fresh impetus into the trade talks at Doha, and the need to achieve a deeper cooperation on climate change. Following the 33rd G8 summit Heiligendamm 2007, German chancellor Angela Merkel announced the establishment of the "Heiligendamm Process," through which the full institution-alization of the permanent dialogue between the G8 countries and the 5 major emerging economies, which deals with the biggest challenges the global economy is facing today, would be implemented.[76]

The most recent 34th G8 summit was held in Hokkaido Tokyo, Japan, in July 2008. Although it was originally expected to find common ground on climate change, the global economy and a host of political crises, the leaders of the G8 actually rose to the challenges posed by the three Fs—food, fuel, and the financial credit crunch, and little effort was made to resolve the contradiction between calls for larger oil supplies and the promise of a low-carbon future.[77]

---

[75]"G8: Russia To Lead G8, Host Summit in 2006," *Dow Jones Newswire*, June 27, 2002.

[76]"Heiligendamm Process", GLOBE INTERNATIONAL, http://www.globeinternational.org/index.php, accessed September 1, 2008.

[77]"Key Agreements at G8 Summit," *Economic Times*, July 8, 2008; "The G8 Summit in Hokkaido: They Came, They Jawed, They Failed to Conquer," *Economist*, July 12, 2008, p. 44.

**Wassenaar Arrangement**

**Wassenaar Arrangement** was founded in 1995 is a multilateral export control agreement on conventional arms and dual-use goods and technologies. It is essentially a successor to the Cold-War era COCOM (the Coordinating Committee for Multilateral Controls). COCOM was founded in 1949 to stop the flow of Western technology to the former Soviet Union. Australia, Japan, and the NATO countries (except Iceland) are members. For example, even when U.S. franchises were already operating in the former Soviet Union, it was illegal to export personal computers for them to use! The initial emphasis of COCOM was on all technology products. Subsequently, the focus shifted to various types of dual-purpose hardware and software technology products —that is, products that could be used for civilian as well as military purposes. Two trends, however, started exerting pressure on the policies adopted by COCOM. First, technologies that had primarily military applications were increasingly finding more civilian applications. Satellites, computers, and telecommunication technologies were prime examples of this trend. Second, the trend of economic liberalization in the newly industrializing and developing countries put further competitive pressures on Western companies to share technologies that were until then privy to the Western world. U.S. firms were particularly adversely affected. Many U.S. companies, including the large telecommunications companies, complained to the government that the restrictions were outdated and that they were losing valuable contracts to competitors from countries without such restrictions.

In 1992, COCOM reevaluated its mission and loosened restrictions on exports of computers, telecommunications equipment, machine tools, and other materials that might assist the newly independent nations of Eastern Europe and the former Soviet Republics in their effort to develop market-driven economies. Due to the changed political and economic environment, the COCOM agreement was terminated in 1994 and replaced by the **Wassenaar Arrangement** of 1995. However, the spirit of the committee still lives on. The new group of 40 countries includes not only the original COCOM members but also Russia and a few other ex-Soviet republics. Unlike COCOM, recommendations by the group to restrict sensitive exports to specified countries are not binding on the members. Two issues of primary importance for being considered within this multilateral system are nuclear technologies and missile (especially ballistic missile) technologies. Today, the United States and some other industrialized countries forbid the export of such generally available technology as software for encoding electronic messages and semiconductor manufacturing equipment. For example, in 2000, the Japanese government imposed an export control on Sony's PlayStation 2 (PS2) electronic game console. PS2's 128-bit central microprocessor developed by Sony and Toshiba has twice the raw number-crunching power of Intel's most advanced Pentium chip used in professional desktop computers. When coupled with a video camera, PS2 could make an ideal missile-guidance system! The biblical prophesy promising peace to those who turn their swords to ploughshares seems very optimistic in today's world of dual-usage technologies, known as DUTs. Such provocations led the Japanese government to designate the machine a "general-purpose product related to conventional weapons". Under Japan's Foreign Exchange and Foreign Trade Control Law, this requires anyone wishing to take more than 50,000 yen (a little more than $400) worth of such equipment out of Japan to get permission from the Ministry of Economy, Trade and Industry. Violators trying to sneak loads of PS2s abroad could face up to five years in jail.[78] Now think for a moment: Sony's PlayStation 3 (PS3) introduced in 2006, is several times more powerful than PS2, and is capable of surpassing 250 gigaflops per second, rivaling the best mid-1990s supercomputer.[79]

---

[78]"War Games," *Economist*, April 22, 2000, p. 60; and Richard Re, "Playstation2 Detonation," *Harvard International Review*, 25 (Fall 2003), pp. 46–50.
[79]"Super Cell," *Forbes*, February 14, 2005, p. 46.

# INTERNATIONAL LAW AND LOCAL LEGAL ENVIRONMENT ◆ ◆ ◆ ◆ ◆ ◆ ◆

International marketing managers should understand two legal environments—the legal environment in each country in which they do business, and the more general international legal environment. At a macro level, international law and the bodies that evaluate it affect high-level international disputes and influence the form of lower-level arbitration and decisions. Local laws and legal systems directly determine the legal procedures for doing business in a foreign country. Local laws also determine the settlement of most international business conflicts—the country whose laws are used is determined by the jurisdiction for the contract.

**International law**, or "the law of nations," may be defined as a body of rules that is binding on states and other international persons in their mutual relations. Most nations and international bodies have voluntarily agreed to subjugate themselves to some level of constraint for the purpose of living in a world in which order, and not chaos, is the governing principle. In short, international law represents "gentlemen's agreements" among countries.

**International Law**

Although, technically speaking, there is no enforceable body of international law,[80] international customs, or treaties, and court decisions establish a defined international legal environment. International bodies and policies exist for arbitrating cases that cannot be settled fairly in any given country.

International law comes from three main sources—**customs**, international **treaties**, and national and international **court decisions**. Customs are usages or practices that have become so firmly accepted that they become rules of law. For example, nations have historically claimed sovereignty over the resources in their offshore continental shelves. This historical practice has developed into a consensus that amounts to an international law. Custom-based laws develop slowly.

Treaties and international contracts represent formal agreements among nations or firms that set down rules and obligations to govern their mutual relationships. Treaties and contracts are only binding on those who are members to them, but if a great number of treaties or contracts share similar stipulations, these may take on the character of a customer-based law or a general rule.

National courts often make rulings in cases that apply to international issues. When these rulings offer an unusually useful insight into the settlement of international cases, or when they develop into a series of interpretations consistent with other nations' courts, then national rulings may be accepted as international laws. If the issue of conflict is one where a national court is not acceptable to one or both parties, international courts and tribunals may rule. International tribunals may be turned to for **arbitration** if the parties agree to let the case be tried. The International Court of Justice was established by the United Nations to settle international conflicts between nations, not between individual parties (such as firms) across national boundaries. However it must be again noted that international court rulings do not establish precedent, as they might in the United States, but rather, apply only to the case at hand.

Legal systems and the laws they create differ dramatically in countries around the world. Many legal systems do not follow the common law system followed in the United States. We discuss a number of different legal systems and the types of laws that govern contracts and business in each system. We also discuss the issue of jurisdiction, which determines the critical issue of what courts, and what laws, are used in deciding a legal question. For most business issues, international law is primarily a question of which

**Local Legal Systems and Laws**

---

[80]The government of a sovereign nation stipulates its laws with policing authority. Since no supra-national government exists, no supra-national (i.e., international) laws are binding. Although the United Nations is the most comprehensive political body, made up of more than a hundred member nations, it is not a sovereign state, and therefore, does not have enforceable laws that the member nations have to abide by other than voluntarily.

national laws apply and how to apply them to cases involving international contracts, shipping, or parties.

The laws that govern behavior within a country, as well as the laws that govern the resolution of international contractual disputes, are primarily local, or municipal, laws. Foreign subsidiaries and expatriate employees live within the legal bounds of their host countries' legal systems. Although U.S. embassy property is considered U.S. territory no matter where it is located, companies and their employees must live within the local country laws. The inability of the U.S. government in 1994 to change the Singapore government's punishment by caning of Michael Fay, an American teenager charged of vandalism there, illustrates a clear example of the sovereignty of each country's laws.[81] The international marketing manager must be aware of the laws that will govern all business decisions and contracts.

***Business Practices and the Legal System.*** Businesses face a myriad of legal issues every day. Questions relating to such issues as pricing policies and production practices must be clearly answered in order to avoid legal rapprochement and punishment. Choices relating to legal industry constraints and various regulations on product specifications, promotional activities, and distribution must be understood in order to function efficiently and profitably. Legal systems in each country deal with these questions differently. For a brief summary of legal issues facing companies, see **Exhibit 5-5**.

For example, in many parts of the world, automobiles with engines larger than a 2,000 cc displacement, face a much stiffer commodity tax than those with smaller engines. In Germany, there is a Rabattgesetz, or rebate law, that businesses cannot give special prices to select customers. This law also prevents retailers from discounting more than 3 percent from an advertised price. This makes it extremely difficult for e-commerce retailers, especially auction sites. Other German laws prevent online shops like Amazon.com from discounting book prices and block sales of prescription drugs and health products online.[82] In some countries it is illegal to mention a competitor's

**EXHIBIT 5-5**
LEGAL ISSUES FACING THE COMPANY

| Type of Decision | Issue |
|---|---|
| Pricing decisions | Price fixing<br>Deceptive pricing<br>Trade discount |
| Packaging decisions | Pollution regulations<br>Fair packaging and labeling |
| Product decisions | Patent protection<br>Warranty requirements<br>Product safety |
| Competitive decisions | Barriers to entry<br>Anticompetitive collusion |
| Selling decisions | Bribery<br>Stealing trade secrets |
| Production decisions | Wages and benefits<br>Health and safety requirements |
| Channel decisions | Dealers' rights<br>Exclusive territorial distributorships |

*Source:* Adapted from Kotler, Philip and Gary Armstrong, *Principles of Marketing*, 8th ed. (Englewood Cliffs, N.J.: Prentice Hall), 1998.

---

[81]"Singapore's Prime Minister Denounces Western Society," *Wall Street Journal* (August 22, 1994), p. A8.

[82]Neal E. Boudette, "Germany's Primus Online Faces Legal Challenges," *Wall Street Journal*, January 6, 2000, p. A17.

name in an advertisement. In some countries that follow Islamic law, it is even illegal to borrow money or charge an interest! However, businesses need financial resources to grow; thus they must learn how to acquire the resources they need within the legal limits established by the country in which they are operating. For example, in Pakistan, importers and exporters of raw materials rely on a technique that is known as *murabaha* to avoid the ban on interest. In this arrangement, a bank buys goods and sells them to a customer who then pays the bank at a future date and at a markup agreed upon by the bank and its customer. In Indonesia, credit card companies such as Visa and Master-Card receive collateral assets, such jewelry and cattle, which they can sell, from card users instead of charging interest.[83]

In recent years, some countries have started raising legal requirements for environmental protection. In Japan, the famed just-in-time delivery system, such as the one practiced by Toyota and 7-Eleven Japan, has been criticized as causing traffic congestion and air pollution. Laws are being considered to reduce the just-in-time practices.[84] **Green marketing** has become fashionable in an increasing number of countries. It is marketers' reaction to governments' and concerned citizens' increased call for reduction of unnecessary packaging materials and increased recycling and recyclability of materials used in the products. Recent developments in the European Union threaten to utilize environmental standards to control internal and external trade in consumer products. In many parts of Asia, consumer awareness and appreciation of environmental protection is also making green issues a crucial part of firm's marketing strategy.[85] Marketers who do not conform may be restricted from participation. Meanwhile, those marketers who do meet the requirements enjoy the benefits of improved product development capabilities, although such capabilities may not automatically translate into improved market share.[86]

***Regulations on E-Commerce.*** Local business laws also affect the use of the Internet. While there are no measurable restrictions for e-commerce in the United States, it is not the case in foreign countries. For example, in Germany, there are strict regulations over providing "digital signatures" to ensure security when making purchases over the Internet.[87] Likewise, France has regulated that the use of "cookies," software or hardware that identifies the user, should only be allowed when consent is granted.[88] Britain has a set of e-commerce laws designed to protect consumers. Interestingly, however, one study shows that almost half of the UK's top 50 retailers are flouting these laws. For example, one website failed to contain an appropriate data protection consent form. Another website informed users that their personal details would be passed onto other firms unless they sent an e-mail opting out. Both are in direct violation of the British laws. With so much business being done over the Internet, it is disconcerting that major retailers are not meeting the letter and the spirit of the laws.[89]

---

[83]Clement M. Henry, ed., "Special Issue: Islamic Banking," *Thunderbird International Business Review*, 41 (July/August and September/October 1999); Ahmed Al Janahi and David Weir, "How Islamic Banks Deal with Problem Business Situations: Islamic Banking as a Potential Model for Emerging Markets," *Thunderbird International Business Review*, 47 (July/August 2005), pp. 429–45. For broader regulatory issues on Islamic finance, an excellent treatise is found in Mohammed El Qorchi, "Islamic Finance Gears Up: While Gaining Ground, the Industry Faces Unique Regulatory Challenges," *Finance and Development*, 42 (December 2005), pp. 46–49.

[84]Eiji Shiomi, Hiroshi Nomura, Garland Chow, and Katsuhiro Niiro, "Physical Distribution and Freight Transportation in the Tokyo Metropolitan Area," *Logistics and Transportation Review*, 29 (December 1993), pp. 335–43.

[85]"Green Marketing Makes its Asian Debut," *Media: Asia's Media & Marketing Newspaper*, April 3, 2008, p. 22.

[86]William E. Baker and James M. Sinkula, "Environmental Marketing Strategy and Firm Performance: Effects on New Product Performance and Market Share," *Journal of the Academy of Marketing Science*, 33 (Fall 2005), pp. 461–75.

[87]"Germany Moves Digital Signatures to Next Level," *Journal of Internet Law*, February 2002, p. 23.

[88]John Leyden, "Online Data Protection Incites Worry," *Network News*, May 5, 1999, p. 4.

[89]"Half of Top 50 UK Retailers are Breaking Online Trading Laws," *Computer Weekly*, February 13, 2003, p. 18.

### Types of Legal Systems.

Four principal legal "systems" are used in the majority of counties: common law systems, code law systems, and Islamic law systems. **Common law** systems base the interpretation of law on prior court rulings—that is, legal precedents and customs of the time. The majority of the states in the United States follow common law systems (Louisiana is an exception). **Code (written) law** systems rely on statutes and codes for the interpretation of the law. In essence, there is very little "interpretation" in a code law system—the law must be detailed enough to prescribe appropriate and inappropriate actions. The majority of the world's governments rely on some form of code law system. **Islamic law (Sharia)** systems rely on the legal interpretation of the Koran and the words of Mohammed. Unlike common and code law systems, which hold that law should be man-made and can be improved through time, Islamic legal systems hold that God established a "natural law" that embodies all justice. Finally, **socialist laws**, developed in the ex-Soviet Union after the Russian Revolution of 1917 and later assimilated by other communist states, are distinguished from other legal systems by the influence of state ownership of the means of production, the pervasive influence of the Communist Party, and the ties between the legal system and national central planning. Since the breakup of the Soviet Union, socialist laws have mostly faded from world political systems, except in countries such as Cuba and North Korea.

### Examples of Different Laws.

Legal systems address both criminal and civil law. Criminal law addresses stealing and other illegal activities. **Civil law** addresses the enforcement of contracts and other procedural guidelines. Civil laws regulating business contracts and transactions are usually called **commercial law**. International businesses are generally more concerned with differences in commercial laws across different countries. For example, who is responsible if a shipper delivers goods that are not up to standards and the contract fails to address the issue? What if the ship on which goods are being transported is lost at sea? What if goods arrive so late as to be worthless? What if a government limits foreign participation in a construction project after a foreign company has spent millions of dollars designing the project?

Sometimes the boundary between criminal and civil law will also be different across countries. For example, are the officers of a company liable for actions that take place while they are "on duty"? When a chemical tank leak in Bhopal, India, killed more than 3,000 Indian citizens in 1984, it was not immediately clear whether the officers of Union Carbide were criminally liable. Since then, some 20,000 people have died from the contamination. It was seven years later in 1991 that the Bhopal court finally issued an arrest warrant for the former CEO of Union Carbide, now living in the United States. Subsequently, in 2001 Dow Chemical acquired Union Carbide. In that same year, the same court in Bhopal rejected an attempt by the Indian government to reduce homicide charges to negligence and stepped up demands that the U.S. extradite the former Union Carbide CEO to stand trial. The issue still lingers on to this day.[90]

### Cultural Values and Legal Systems.

In Japan, legal confrontations are very rare. As shown in **Exhibit 5-6**, Japan's population of lawyers is low, which makes it difficult to obtain evidence from legal opponents. Also, rules against class-action suits and contingency-fee arrangements make it difficult to bring suit against a person or company. There are disadvantages to Japan's system, but it supports the cultural value of building long-term business ties based on trust.

In the United States, there is a strong belief in the use of explicit contracts and a reliance on the legal system to resolve problems in business. In other countries, such as China, a businessperson who tries to cover all possible problems or contingencies in a

**EXHIBIT 5-6**

THE NUMBER OF LAWYERS PER 100,000 RESIDENTS

| | |
|---|---|
| United States | 370.4 |
| Britain | 175.4 |
| Germany | 158.7 |
| France | 66.7 |
| Japan | 16.9 |

*Source:* Compiled from "Panel Eyes 3-Fold Increase in Legal Professionals by 2020," *Japan Economic Newswire,* February 3, 2001.

---

[90] "Dow Chemical: Liable for Bhopal?" *Business Week,* June 9, 2008, pp. 61–62.

contract may be viewed as untrustworthy. Chinese culture values relationships (known as *guanxi*) and therefore relies more heavily on trust and verbal contracts than does U.S. culture.[91] In Brazil, however, there is a value system different from both the United States' explicit contractual agreement and China's mutual trust and verbal contract. The Brazilian value system is known as *Jeitinho*, in which people believe that they can always find a solution outside the legal contract on a case-by-case basis.[92] If a culture does not respect the value of following through on an obligation, no legal system, whether written or verbal, will afford enough protection to make doing business easy.

**Jurisdiction**

Because there is no body of international law in the strictly legalistic sense, the key to evaluating an international contract is by determining which country's laws will apply, and where any conflicts will be resolved.

*Planning Ahead.* By far the easiest way to assure what laws will apply in a contract is to clearly state the applicable law in the contract. If both a home country producer and a foreign distributor agree that the producer's national laws of contracts will apply to a contract for the sale of goods, then both can operate with a similar understanding of the legal requirements they face. Similarly, to assure a venue that will interpret these laws in an expected manner, international contracts should stipulate the location of the court or arbitration system that will be relied upon for resolving conflicts that arise.

If contacts fail to provide for the jurisdiction of the contract, it is not so clear which laws apply. Courts may use the laws where the contract is made. Alternatively, courts may apply the laws where the contract is fulfilled.

*Arbitration and Enforcement.* Due to the differences in international legal systems, and the difficulty and length of litigating over a conflict, many international contracts rely on a pre-arranged system of arbitration for settling any conflict. Arbitration may be by a neutral party, and both parties agree to accept any rulings.

However if one of the parties does not fulfill its contracted requirements and does not respond to or accept arbitration, there is little the injured party can do. There is no "international police" to force a foreign company to pay damages.[93]

## ISSUES TRANSCENDING NATIONAL BOUNDARIES

◆ ◆ ◆ ◆ ◆ ◆ ◆

**ISO 9000 and 14000**

In a bid to establish common product standards for quality management, so as to obviate their misuse to hinder the exchange of goods and services worldwide, the International Standards Organization (based in Geneva, Switzerland) has instituted a set of process standards. Firms who conform to these standards are certified and registered with International Standards Organizations. This common standard is designated **ISO 9000**. The ISO 9000 series was developed by its Technical Committee on Quality Assurance and Quality Management between 1979 and 1986 and was published in 1987. The series has been adopted widely by companies in the United States. The adoption of the ISO 9000 standards by member countries of the European Union has spurred widespread interest in companies worldwide to obtain this certification if they intend to trade with the European Union.

One of the reasons for the spurt of interest in ISO 9000 is the decision by the European Union to adopt ISO standards; the other main reason is the acknowledgment of the importance of quality by companies worldwide. It must be highlighted that ISO

---

[91]See, for example, Don Y. Lee and Philip L. Dawes, "Guanxi, Trust, and Long-Term Orientation in Chinese Business Markets," *Journal of International Marketing*, 13 (2), 2005, pp. 28–56; and Yi Liu, Yuan Li, Lei Tao, Ying Wang, "Relationship Stability, Trust and Relational Risk in Marketing Channels: Evidence from China," *Industrial Marketing Management*, 37 (June), 2008, pp. 432–46.

[92]Fernanda Duarte, "Exploring the Interpersonal Transaction of the Brazilian Jeitinho in Bureaucratic Contexts," *Organization*, 13 (July), 2006, pp. 509–27.

[93]Gerald Aksen, "Reflections of an International Arbitrator," *Arbitration International*, 23 (2), 2007, pp. 255–59.

9000 is not only concerned with standardized systems and procedures for manufacturing, but for all the activities of firms. These activities include management responsibility, quality systems, contract reviews, design control, document control, purchasing, product identification and tracing, (manufacturing) process control, inspection and testing, control of nonconforming products and necessary corrective actions, handling, storage, packaging and delivering, recordkeeping, internal quality audits, training, and servicing.

With the growing adoption of the ISO 9000 standards by firms worldwide, an ISO 9000 certification has become an essential marketing tool for firms. Firms that have it will be able to convince prospective buyers of their ability to maintain strict quality requirements. Firms that do not have ISO 9000 certification will increasingly be at a disadvantage relative to other competitors, not only in Europe but also in most parts of the world.

Over the past decade, the need to pursue "sustainable development" has been at the center of discussion of environmental issues and economic development. Attainment of sustainable development was articulated as a goal in 1987 by the World Commission on the Environment and Development (World Commission), a body established by the United Nations. The World Commission defined sustainable development as development that "meets the needs of the present without compromising the ability of future generations to meet their own needs." Sustainable development was the focus of discussion at the United Nations Conference on the Environment and Development held in Rio de Janeiro in 1992, and its attainment was articulated as a goal in the Environmental Side Agreement to the North American Free Trade Agreement (NAFTA). In 1996, the International Organization for Standardization (ISO) named the attainment of sustainable development as a major goal in its new ISO 14000 Series Environmental Management Standards. The ISO 9000 standards is a forerunner to and served as a model for the ISO 14000 series.

The **ISO 14000** standards are receiving significant amounts of attention from business managers and their legal and economic advisors. Business managers view ISO 14000 as a market-driven approach to environmental protection that provides an alternative to "command and control" regulation by government. Businesses view implementation of ISO 14000 as a means to "self-regulate," thereby minimizing their exposure to surveillance and sanctions by the United States Environmental Protection Agency and its state-level counterparts. For example, ISO 14000 is already strengthening chemical companies' relations with plant communities by providing third-party audits of a plant's environmental systems. It is an efficient way to show the community that companies are making environmental improvements. Therefore, any person or organization interested in environmental protection or business management should become familiar with the provisions and potential ramifications of ISO 14000.[94]

## Intellectual Property Protection

Intellectual property refers to "a broad collection of innovations relating to things such as works of authorship, inventions, trademarks, designs and trade secrets."[95] Intellectual property rights broadly include patents, trademarks, trade secrets, and copyrights. These ideas typically involve large investments in creative and investigative work to create the product, but fairly low costs of manufacturing. As such they are amenable to being duplicated readily by imitators. Imitation reduces the potential returns that would have accrued to the innovator, thereby limiting its ability to appropriate the large investments made. With increasing movements of goods and services across borders,

---

[94]V. Kanti Prasad and G. M. Naidu, "Perspectives and Preparedness Regarding ISO-9000 International Quality Standards," *Journal of International Marketing*, 2 (2), 1994, pp. 81–98; and Morgan P. Miles, Linda S. Munilla, Gregory R. Russell, "Marketing and Environmental Registration/Certification: What Industrial Marketers Should Understand About ISO 14000," *Industrial Marketing Management*, 26 (July), 1997, pp. 363–70.

[95]Subhash C. Jain, "Intellectual Property Rights and International Business," in Masaaki Kotabe and Preet S. Aukakh, ed., *Emerging Issues in International Business Research*, Northampton, MA: Edward Elgar Publishing, 2002, pp. 37–64.

the potential loss of revenues to innovator firms, most of which reside in industrialized countries, is significant.

Few topics in international business have attracted as much attention and discussion in recent years as intellectual property rights.[96] In 2007, the Organization for Economic Cooperation and Development (OECD) released a report estimating the annual value of the international, physical trade of counterfeited consumer products at approximately $200 billion. This equals around 2 percent of the entire world trade and exceeds the GDP of 150 countries.[97] Apart from hurting legitimate businesses and trade, intellectual property infringement leads to the loss of government tax revenue.

Piracy is most rampant in software industry. For example, according to the Business Software Alliance, a global anti-piracy watchdog group, 35 percent of the software installed in 2006 on personal computers (PCs) worldwide was obtained illegally, amounting to nearly $40 billion in global losses due to software piracy. In percentage terms, Central/Eastern Europe topped the piracy rate at 68 percent of all software used, followed by Latin America at 66 percent, Middle East/Africa at 60 percent, Asia Pacific at 50 percent, the European Union at 36 percent, and North America at 22 percent.[98] More concerning is the counterfeiting of medicines, which threatens public safety and poses a growing threat around the world. Between 2000 and 2006, the Food and Drug Administration saw an eightfold increase in the number of new counterfeit drugs cases. In developing countries with weak regulatory systems, approximately 10 percent to 30 percent of all medicines could be counterfeit. Worldwide sales of counterfeit drugs are forecast to reach $75 billion by 2010.[99]

Various anti-counterfeiting tools and technologies are developed by firms to aid others' anti-counterfeiting efforts, or to enhance their own. Hewlett-Packard's Specialty Printing Systems, for instance, has expanded its offerings to the pharmaceutical industry with the introduction of a new ink cartridge that allows individual capsules or tablets to be marked. Eastman Kodak Co. developed a Traceless System for anti-counterfeiting on its branded rechargeable lithium-ion digital camera batteries supplied by Sanyo Electric. With "forensically undetectable" markers put on printed materials, product packaging or product components, the system can help fighting against counterfeiting as only handheld Kodak readers can detect the markers. Also among the firms deploying this anti-counterfeiting technology are DonRuss Playoff and Liz Claiborne. However, in spite of anti-counterfeiting tools and technologies, litigation, as well as legislation that we will discuss later in this section, piracy is still rampant around the world.[100]

Now with the convenient online access, it is even more difficult to ensure that copyright rules are not violated in the cyberspace. Recently, Google's books online was criticized by American publishing organizations for breaching copyright laws.[101] Google aims to put 15-million volumes online from four top U.S. libraries by 2015—the libraries of Stanford, Michigan, and Harvard Universities, and of the New York Public Library. The critics worry that if the people can read a book online for free they would not bother purchasing it. As easy as a click to download music online to listen to offline, a recent court ruling clearly states that even though the copyright of music has lapsed, reproducing and distributing the music is a breach to the copyright law. New York's highest court found Naxos guilty of illegally releasing

---

[96]Clifford J. Shultz III and Bill Saporito, "Protecting Intellectual Property: Strategies and Recommendations to Deter Counterfeiting and Brand Piracy in Global Markets," *Columbia Journal of World Business*, 31 (Spring 1996), pp. 19–27.

[97]Andreas Geiger, "A View From Europe: The High Price of Counterfeiting, and Getting Real about Enforcement," *theHill.com*, April 30, 2008.

[98]*2007 Global Piracy Study*, Business Software Alliance, http://www.bsa.org/, accessed September 20, 2008.

[99]Drew Buono, "Counterfeit Drugs a Growing Worldwide Danger," *Drug Store News*, June 23, 2008, pp. 60–62.

[100]Jill Jusko, "Counterfeiters Be Gone," *Industry Week*, July 2008, pp. 67–68.

[101]A settlement agreement was reached in 2008. If interested, see http://books.google.com/booksrightsholders/agreement-contents.html.

classical recordings by (the late) Yehudi Menuhin and others, because such recordings were still covered by the common law.[102]

Counterfeiting is not restricted to poor countries, either. Milan, Italy, for example, is a leading producer of counterfeit luxury products; the U.S. state of Florida is an international haven for fake aircraft parts; and Switzerland is a big player in pharmaceutical counterfeits production with almost 40 percent of fake medicines seized by the EU. According to the analyst, there is a globalized trend of counterfeiting, like manufacturing. Increasingly, all countries of the World Trade Organization (WTO) are required to implement **Trade Related Aspects of Intellectual Property Rights (TRIPS)** to execute intellectual property protection and companies are joining together to fight against the violations.[103] Revisit Chapter 2 for TRIPS.

***Patent.*** A patent, if granted, offers a patent holder a legal monopoly status on the patented technology and/or process for a certain extended period (usually 15-21 years depending on a country). Patent laws in the United States and Japan provide an example of the differences in laws across countries and their implications for corporations.[104] The most significant difference between the two countries is on the **"first-to-file"** and **"first-to-invent"** principles. While most countries follow the "first-to-file" principle, only the United States (along with the Philippines) follows the "first-to-invent" principle. In the majority of countries, the patent is granted to the first person filing an application for the patent. In the United States, however, the patent is granted to the person who first invented the product or technology. Any patents granted prior to the filing of the patent application by the "real" inventor would be reversed in order to protect rights of the inventor. The difference between the two principles is no small matter. See **Global Perspective 5-4** for far-reaching implications.[105]

The marketing implications of this difference for U.S. companies as well as foreign companies are significant. To protect any new proprietary technologies, U.S. companies must ensure that their inventions are protected abroad through formal patent applications being filed in various countries, especially the major foreign markets and the markets of competitors and potential competitors. For foreign companies operating in the United States, the implications are that they must be extremely careful in introducing any technologies that have been invented in the United States. A "first-to-file" mentality could result in hasty patent applications and significant financial burden in the form of lawsuits that could be filed by competitors that claim to have invented the technology earlier.

In some extreme situation, governments have broken patent law for public health reasons. For example, Brazil's government, after signing intellectual property protection agreement, announced in August 2001 its plans to break a patent for a drug used to treat AIDS despite the international patent held by Roche, the drug's Swiss-based pharmaceutical company. Federal officials said they were unsuccessful in talks with Roche to lower the prices the country paid for nelfinavir, a drug blocking the HIV virus from replicating itself and infecting new cells.[106] The Brazilian government is not the only one to grab a company's patent rights in the interest of public health. Scared by the

---

[102]"Court Secures Classical Copyright," *BBC News*, http://news.bbc.co.uk/2/hi/entertainment/4415829.stm, April 6, 2005.

[103]"Imitating property is theft," May 15, 2003, p. 52; Quality Brands Protection Committee, Chinese Association of Enterprise with Foreign Investment, http://www.qbpc.org.cn/en/about/about/factsheet, accessed February 10, 2006. http://news.bbc.co.uk/2/hi/business/4123319.stm; and Drew Buono, "Counterfeit Drugs a Growing Worldwide Danger," *Drug Store News*, June 23, 2008, pp. 60–62.

[104]Masaaki Kotabe, "A Comparative Study of U.S. and Japanese Patent Systems," *Journal of International Business Studies*, 23 (First Quarter 1992), pp. 147–168.

[105]Forty-one nations, including the United States, the European Union, and Japan, reached a basic agreement to draft a treaty for standardizing the patent approval process based on the first-to-file principle in September 2006. If it goes smoothly, the treaty could be adopted as early as 2007. See "Japan, U.S., Others Agree to Craft 1st-to-File Patent Pact," *NikkeiNet Interactive*, http://www.nni.nikkei.co.jp, September 26, 2006.

[106]"Brazil to Break Patent, Make AIDS Drug," *CNN.com*, http://www.cnn.com/2001/WORLD/americas/08/23/aids.drug0730/index.html, August 23 2001.

## $\mathcal{G}$LOBAL PERSPECTIVE 5-4

## TWO WORLDS APART: THE "FIRST-TO-INVENT" PRINCIPLE VERSUS THE "FIRST-TO-FILE" PRINCIPLE

A diplomatic conference to discuss the initial draft of patent harmonization treaty was convened by the World Intellectual Property Organization (WIPO) in May 2002. Most neutral observers would suggest that U.S. domestic politics is one principal impediment to the conference's success. In the United States, the *first* to *invent* wins the patent, while in the rest of the world a patent is awarded to the *first* to *file* an application. The conference examined the virtue of the U.S. "first-to-invent" principle vis-à-vis the "first-to-file" principle espoused in the rest of the world. The conference's recommendation involved changing the law to award patents to the "first to file" instead of to the "first to invent," which has guided the awarding of U.S. patents since Thomas Jefferson looked at the first ones filed in 1790.

Under current U.S. law, an individual applicant for a patent must prove that he had the idea first, not simply that he won the race to the courthouse. He can assert his priority to the invention at any time; he is entitled to a patent if thereafter he has not "suppressed, abandoned, or concealed" the invention. The U.S. system was established to protect the inventor who lacks the resources to keep up a stream of patent applications merely to invoke their priority. Not surprisingly, the system is championed today by resource-poor universities and independent inventors.

Supporters of the "first-to-file" system, largely lawyers and corporations, argue that it would better serve the public because it is simpler and conforms to the systems in the rest of the world. Moreover, it would spur inventors to file for patents earlier and to disclose their inventions sooner, thus speeding the progression from idea to finished product. Many supporters also note that most U.S. companies are equipped to act on a first-to-file basis, since they typically apply for patents as soon as inventions are produced. With the adoption of the first-to-file system, this date would also affect patent rights

abroad, and thus provide greater reliability for U.S. patents worldwide.

Many are apprehensive about such a change. The principal objection to the first-to-file system is that it fosters premature, sketchy disclosure in hastily filed applications, letting the courts work things out later. Although unlikely, it leaves open the possibility of someone stealing the profits of an invention from the true inventor by beating him to the courthouse steps. In the end, the Patent Office could be deluged with applications filed for defensive purposes, as is the case in Japan where this phenomenon is called "patent flooding."

Sensitive to these criticisms, the commission recommended several other reforms to ensure fairness in implementing the "first-to-file" proposal. These reforms include issuing a provisional patent application at reduced cost while the patent itself is undergoing examination, and establishing a grace period for public disclosure without affecting patentability. Most importantly, the commission suggested adopting the rule of "prior-use right," allowing users of inventions to continue their use under certain conditions, even after a patent on the invention is obtained by another party.

The effect of "first to file" vs. "first to invent" may be best illustrated by the case of the laser, a discovery generally credited to physicist Charles Townes, who won a Nobel Prize for elucidating the principle of the maser, the theoretical father of the laser. Townes owned the patent on the device. Years later, Gordon Gould, a former graduate student at Columbia University, where Townes taught physics, proved by contemporary notebooks and other means that he had developed the idea long before Townes patented it in 1958.

Gould could not have brought his case to the courts in foreign countries that give priority to the first to file. In the United States, however, the court accepted Gould's evidence of priority and awarded him the basic patents to the laser in 1977 and 1979, ruling that Townes and his employer, at the time AT&T Co., had infringed on Gould's idea. Patlex Corp., of which Gould is a director, now collects fees from laser users throughout the world.

*Source:* Lee Edson, "Patent Wars," *Across the Board*, 30, April 1993, pp. 24–29; and Q. Todd Dickinson, "Harmony and Controversy," *IP Worldwide*, September 2002, pp. 22–24.

---

anthrax outbreaks in the United States, Canada's health ministry decided that public health came first. It commissioned a generic drug company to make a million doses of ciprofloxacin, a drug used to treat one of the nastier forms of the disease whose patent belongs to German drug giant Bayer.[107]

***Copyright.*** Copyrights protect original literary, dramatic, musical, artistic, and certain other intellectual works. Copyright protection lasts 50 years in the European Union countries and Japan, compared with 95 years in the United States.[108] The

---

[107]"Patent Problems Pending," *Economist*, October 27, 2001, p. 14.

[108]"Copyright Revisions Have Japan's Majors Jumping into the Vaults," *Billboard*, April 18, 1998, p. 52; and "Companies in U.S. Sing Blues As Europe Reprises 50's Hits," *New York Times*, January 3, 2003, Late Edition, p. A1.

difference in the lengths of period of copyright protection could cause tremendous price differences between countries for those products whose copyrights expired in the EU or Japan but are still effective in the United States. This issue will be discussed in detail in the "Gray Markets" section of Chapter 17.

A computer program is also considered a literary work and is protected by copyright. A copyright provides its owner the exclusive right to reproduce and distribute the material or perform or display it publicly, although limited reproduction of copyrighted works by others may be permitted for fair use purposes. In the United States, the use of the copyright notice does not require advance permission, or registration with, the Copyright Office. In fact, many countries offer copyright protection without registration, while others offer little or no protection for the works of foreign nationals.[109]

In the United States, the **Digital Millennium Copyright Act** (DMCA) was passed in 1998 to address a growing struggle in the cyberspace between industries supplying digital content and those arguing against strict enforcement of copyright on the Internet. The DMCA bans any efforts to bypass software that protects copyrighted digital files. Similar laws have been passed in other countries as well. For example, selling "mod" (modification) chips, a device used to play copied games, tinkering with a game console to play legally and illegally copied software, is a practice that has turned into a legal landmine for the video game sector. In 2004, Sony filed a lawsuit against David Ball, a British national, in Britain's High Court for selling thousands of mod chips called Messiah 2 for Sony's PlayStation 2 games consoles. He also published information explaining how to install the chips in PlayStation 2 consoles. He was found guilty of violating all counts of UK copyright law.[110]

*Trademark.* A trademark is a word, symbol, or device that identifies the source of goods and may serve as an index of quality. It is used primarily to differentiate or distinguish a product or service from another. Trademark laws are used to prevent others from offering a product or service with a confusingly similar mark. In the United States, registration is not mandatory, since "prior use" technically determines the rightful owner of a trademark. However, because determining who used the trademark prior to anyone else is difficult and subject to lawsuits, trademark registration is highly recommended. In most foreign countries, registration is mandatory for a trademark to be protected. In this sense, the legal principle that applies to trademarks is similar to the one that applies to patents: the "first-to-use" principle in the United States and the "first-to-file" principle in most other countries. Therefore, if companies are expected to do business overseas, their trademarks should be registered in every country in which protection is desired (see **Global Perspective 5-5** for the extent to which U.S. firms could legally protect their own copyright and trademark used by other firms abroad).

*Trade Secret.* A trade secret is another means of protecting intellectual property and fundamentally differs from patent, copyright, and trademark in that protection is sought without registration. Therefore, it is not legally protected. However, it can be protected in the courts if the company can prove that it took all precautions to protect the idea from its competitors and that infringement occurred illegally by way of espionage or hiring employees with crucial working knowledge.

**International Treaties for Intellectual Property Protection**

Although patent and copyright laws have been in place in many countries for well over a hundred years, laws on trademarks and trade secrets are of relatively recent vintage, having been instituted in the late nineteenth century and beginning of the twentieth century.[111] The laws are essentially national so there are many

---

[109]Subhash C. Jain, "Intellectual Property Rights and International Business," in Masaaki Kotabe and Preet S. Aukakh, ed., *Emerging Issues in International Business Research*, Northampton, MA: Edward Elgar Publishing, 2002, pp. 37–64.

[110]"Game Over for Mod Chip Dealer," *Managing Intellectual Property*; September 2004, pp. 113–14.

[111]Bruce A. Lehman, "Intellectual Property: America's Competitive Advantage in the 21st Century," *Columbia Journal of World Business*, 31 (Spring 1996), pp. 8–9.

### GLOBAL PERSPECTIVE 5-5

## COULD U.S. FIRMS ALWAYS PROTECT THEIR OWN COPYRIGHT AND TRADEMARK USED BY OTHER FIRMS ABROAD? THE ANSWER IS CLEARLY NO!

Infringement of intellectual property rights is not confined to the United States. Inadequate protection of intellectual property rights in foreign countries could also result in copyrights and trademarks illegally used abroad making their way back to the United States. In many industrialized countries, it is possible to stem illegally used copyrights and trademarks from entering the home country. For example, in the United States, the U.S. Customs Service provides protection to copyrights and trademarks.

Prior to receiving U.S. Customs protection, copyrights and trademarks have to be registered first with the U.S. Copyright Office and the U.S. Patent and Trademark Office, respectively. Then for U.S. Customs protection, each copyright and trademark must be recorded at the U.S. Customs Service Office. The fee is $190. Although there are no standard application forms, the application requirements for recording a copyright and a trademark are listed in Section 133.1–133.7 of the U.S. Customs regulations. An application should include the following information: (1) a certified status copy and five photocopies of the copyright or trademark registration, (2) the name of its legal owner, (3) the business address of the legal owner, (4) the states or countries in which the business of the legal owner is incorporated or otherwise conducted,(5) a list of the names and addresses of all foreign persons or companies authorized or licensed to use the copyright or trademark to be protected, (6) a list of the names and addresses of authorized manufacturers of goods, and (7) a list of all places in which goods using the copyright or bearing the trademark are legally manufactured. Although it is not necessary to submit a separate application for protection of each copyright or trademark, the filing fee of $190 still applies to each and every copyright or trademark being recorded with the Customs Service. Additional information can be obtained by contacting the U.S. Customs Service at the Intellectual Property Rights Branch, Franklin Court, 1301 Constitution Avenue, N.W., Washington, D.C. (Ph. 202-482-6960).

Unfortunately, the U.S. Patent and Trademark Office has little or no legal recourse when it comes to U.S. copyrights or trademarks used by foreign companies outside the United States. For example, in Brazil, America Online's famous "aol.com" domain is legally owned by StarMedia Network, a small Internet services Brazilian company in the fast-growing Latin American market. America Online (AOL) had sued StarMedia Network alleging trademark infringement and contested the Brazilian provider's use of the domain name "aol.com.br." However, the Brazilian court ruled in May 1999 that since Brazil's America Online registered the name first, it would not have to surrender the domain name to its US rival. As a result of the Brazilian court's ruling in favor of StarMedia Network, its shares rose 74 percent in its first day of trading. AOL was then forced to market its Brazilian services under "br.aol.com".

Although no other news leaked on a possible out-of-court settlement on StarMedia's "aol.com.br" versus AOL's "br.aol.com," recent news articles suggest that AOL may have eventually purchased the right to use "aol.com.br" for an undisclosed sum of money (which would not come cheap).

The decision may touch off concerns about international cybersquatting as many Internet dotcom companies begin to launch overseas operations, only to find that country-level version of the domain name is already registered. For example, the AOL domain had been registered in about 60 countries in addition to Brazil, and not all of these registrations were madeby the American company.

*Source:* Maxine Lans Retsky, "Curbing Foreign Infringement," Marketing News (March 31, 1997), p. 10; "Brazilian ISP Prevails in AOL Lawsuit," a news report provided by "LatPro.com ejs@LatPro.com, May 31, 1999; "No Free Ride," *Latin Trade*, May 2001, p. 54; and "AOL Latin America Launches Upgraded Wireless E-Mail in Brazil, Mexico and Argentina," *World IT Report*, February 17, 2002, p. N.

---

international treaties to help provide intellectual property protection across national boundaries. Some of the most important treaties are the Paris Convention, Patent Cooperation Treaty, Patent Law Treaty, European Patent Convention, and Berne Convention.

***Paris Convention.*** The Paris Convention for the Protection of Industrial Property was established in 1883, and the number of signatory countries currently stands at 140. It is designed to provide "domestic" treatment to protect patent and trademark applications filed in other countries. Operationally, the convention establishes rights of priority that stipulate that once an application for protection is filed in one member country, the applicant has twelve months to file in any other signatory countries, which should consider such an application as if it were filed on the same date as the original application.[112] It also means that if an applicant does not file for protection in other signatory countries within a grace period of twelve months of original filing in one country, legal protection could not be provided. In most countries, other than the United States, the "first-to-file" principle is used for intellectual property protection. Lack of filing within a grace period in all other countries in which protection is desired could mean a loss of market opportunities to a competitor who filed for protection of either an identical or a similar type of intellectual property. The two new treaties, explained below, are further attempts to make international patent application as easy as domestic patent application.

***Patent Cooperation Treaty.*** The Patent Cooperation Treaty (PCT) was established in 1970, amended in 1979 and modified in 1984. It is open to any signatory member country to the Paris Convention. The PCT makes it possible to seek patent protection for an invention simultaneously in each of a large number of countries by filing an "international" patent application. The patent applicant can file an international patent application with his or her national patent office, which will act as a PCT "Receiving" Office, or with the International Bureau of World Intellectual Property Organization (WIPO) in Geneva. If the applicant is a national or resident of a contracting State that is party to the European Patent Convention, the Harare Protocol on Patents and Industrial Designs (Harare Protocol) or the Eurasian Patent Convention, the international application may also be filed with the European Patent Office (EPO), the African Regional Industrial Property Organization (ARIPO) or the Eurasian Patent Office (EAPO), respectively.[113]

***Patent Law Treaty.*** The Patent Law Treaty (PLT), adopted in Geneva in June 2000, comes as the result of a World Intellectual Property Organization (WIPO) initiative. Its aim is to harmonize the formal requirements set by patent offices for granting patents, and to streamline the procedures for obtaining and maintaining a patent. Initially, PLT will apply to all European Union countries, the United States, Japan, Canada, and Australia. Eventually it will include virtually all countries in the world. While the PLT is only concerned with patent formalities, many of the provisions will prove extremely useful when the PLT comes into force for a large number of states, providing speedier and less costly procedures for years to come.[114]

***European Patent Convention.*** The European Patent Convention is a treaty among 25 European countries (as of January 1, 2003) setting up a common patent office, the European Patent Office, headquartered in Munich, Germany, which examines patent applications designated for any of those countries under a common patent procedure and issues a European patent valid in all of the countries designated. The European Patent Office represents the most efficient way of obtaining protection in these countries if a patent applicant desires protection in two or more of the countries. The European Patent Convention is a party to the Paris Convention, and thus recognizes the filing date of an application by anyone in any signatory country as its own priority date if an application is filed within one year of the original filing date. The European Patent Office receives the application in English. The application will be published 18 months after the filing, consistent with the "first-to-file" principle. Once a patent is approved, registrations in, and translations into the language of, each designated country will be required. The European Patent Convention does not supersede any signatories' pre-existing national patent system. Patent applicants still

---

[112]World Intellectual Property Organization, *Paris Convention for the Protection of Industrial Property*, http://www .wipo.int/treaties/en/ip/paris/, accessed February 20, 2006.
[113]World Intellectual Property Organization, *International Protection of Industrial Property-Patent Cooperation Treaty*, http://www.wipo.int/pct/en/treaty/about.htm, accessed February 20, 2006.
[114]Q. Todd Dickinson, "Harmony and Controversy," *IP Worldwide*, September 2002, pp. 22–24.

**EXHIBIT 5-7**
RATINGS FOR THE LEVEL OF INTELLECTUAL PROPERTY PROTECTION IN
VARIOUS COUNTRIES (MINIMUM = 0 . . . 10 = MAXIMUM)

| Country | Patents | Copyrights | Trademarks | Trade Secrets |
|---------|---------|------------|------------|---------------|
| Argentina | 3.8 | 5.7 | 7.1 | 4.4 |
| Brazil | 3.3 | 5.2 | 3.3 | 3.3 |
| Canada | 8.1 | 7.7 | 9.0 | 7.8 |
| Chile | 5.7 | 5.7 | 7.6 | 7.8 |
| China | 2.4 | 2.9 | 6.2 | 3.3 |
| Germany | 8.6 | 8.6 | 9.0 | 10.0 |
| India | 3.3 | 5.7 | 3.8 | 3.3 |
| Israel | 7.1 | 7.1 | 8.6 | 8.9 |
| Mexico | 3.3 | 7.6 | 3.8 | 3.3 |
| New Zealand | 7.1 | 8.1 | 9.5 | 7.8 |
| Philippines | 7.1 | 6.2 | 7.6 | 7.8 |
| Singapore | 7.1 | 6.7 | 8.6 | 5.6 |
| South Korea | 3.3 | 4.8 | 3.8 | 3.3 |
| Thailand | 2.4 | 4.8 | 6.7 | 5.6 |
| United States | 9.0 | 8.1 | 9.0 | 7.8 |

*Source:* Adapted from Belay Seyoum, "The Impact of Intellectual Property Rights on Foreign Direct Investment," *Columbia Journal of World Business*, 31 (Spring 1996), p. 56.

should file and obtain separate national patents, if they would prefer national treatment (favored over pan-European treatment by individual national courts).[115]

***Berne Convention.*** The Berne Convention for the Protection of Literary and Artistic Works is the oldest and most comprehensive international copyright treaty. This treaty provides reciprocal copyright protection in each of the fifteen signatory countries. Similar to the Paris Convention, it establishes the principle of national treatment and provides protection without formal registration. The United States did not join the Berne Convention until 1989.[116]

Although there are separate laws to protect the various kinds of intellectual property, there appears to be a strong correlation between the levels of intellectual property in various countries. Exhibit provides some of the results of a 1996 academic study based on survey questionnaires administered to experts/practitioners in the various countries.

A feature that corporations as well as individual managers have to deal with is the growing importance of intellectual property as a significant form of competitive advantage. The laws to deal with this issue are neither uniform across countries, nor are they extended across national boundaries (outside of the government pressure). Even if they are similar, the implementation levels vary significantly. Essentially, protection of intellectual property requires registration in all the countries in which a firm plans to do business. Managers need to be cognizant of this and take proactive measures to counteract any infringements.

The most recent development in international copyright protection is the WIPO Copyright Treaty, which entered into force in March 2002, addressing the copyright protection in the Internet era. This treaty updates and supplements the Berne Convention by protecting the rights of authors of literary and artistic works distributed within the digital environment. The treaty clarifies that the traditional right of reproduction continues to apply in the digital environment and confers a right holder's right to control on-demand delivery of works to individuals.[117]

---

[115]Martin Grund and Stacy J. Farmer, "The ABCs of the EPC 2000," *Managing Intellectual Property*, April 2008, pp. 85–88.

[116]Nancy R. Wesberg, "Canadian Signal Piracy Revisited in Light of United States Ratification of the Free Trade Agreement and the Berne Convention: Is This a Blueprint for Global Intellectual Property Protection?" *Syracuse Journal of International Law & Commerce*, 16 (Fall 1989), 169–205.

[117]Amanda R. Evansburg, Mark J. Fiore, Brooke Welch, Lusan Chua, and Phyllis Eremitaggio, "Recent Accessions to WIPO Treaties," *Intellectual Property & Technology Law Journal*, 16 (August 2004), p. 23.

*Further Developments.*   In 2007 a select handful of the wealthiest countries began a treaty-making process to create a new global standard for intellectual property rights enforcement, the Anti-Counterfeiting Trade Agreement (ACTA). ACTA is spearheaded by the United States, the European Commission, Japan, and Switzerland—those countries with the largest intellectual property industries. Other countries invited to participate in ACTA's negotiation process are Canada, Australia, Korea, Mexico, and New Zealand. Noticeably absent from ACTA's negotiations are leaders from developing countries who hold national policy priorities that differ from the international intellectual property industry.[118]

At the 34th G8 summit held by Japan in July 2008, the eight leaders in their document on the "World Economy" called for finalizing negotiations of the much-debated ACTA by the end of the year. The summit also declared patent harmonization a topic of high importance, asking for accelerated discussions of the Substantive Patent Law Treaty (SPLT), a proposed international patent law treaty aimed at harmonizing substantive points of patent law. In contrast with the Patent Law Treaty which only relates to formalities, the SPLT aims at going far beyond formalities to harmonize substantive requirements such as novelty, inventive step and non-obviousness, industrial applicability and utility, as well as sufficient disclosure, unity of invention, or claim drafting and interpretation.[119]

## Antitrust Laws of the United States

The antitrust laws of the United States[120] need to be highlighted as the U.S. government makes extraterritorial applications of its antitrust laws, affecting both U.S. and foreign businesses not only in the United States but also in foreign countries. The U.S. antitrust laws have their foundation in the Sherman Antitrust Act of 1890, the Clayton Act of 1914, the Federal Trade Commission Act of 1914, and the Robinson Patman Act of 1936. U.S. antitrust laws have been, from the beginning, concerned with maximizing consumer welfare through the prevention of arrangements that increase market power without concurrently increasing social welfare through reduced costs or increased efficiency.

The Sherman Act specifically forbade every contract, combination, or conspiracy to restrain free and open trade, but it was soon argued that the law was intended to punish only unreasonable restraints. In the *Standard Oil* case of 1911, the courts ruled that an act must be an unreasonable restraint of trade for the Sherman Act to apply. Toward this end, a distinction developed between (1) cases in which a rule of reason should apply, and (2) cases considered to be *per se* violations of the law.

The Clayton Act strengthened the U.S. antitrust arsenal by prohibiting trade practices that were not covered by the Sherman Act. It outlawed exclusive dealing and price discrimination. Both are subject to the rule of reason—that is, they are unlawful only if the effect may be to substantially lessen competition. This concept even applies to "any imaginary threat to competition, no matter how shadowy and insubstantial" as being reasonably probable of restraining trade.[121]

Concurrent with the enactment of the Clayton Act, Congress created the Federal Trade Commission (FTC) and empowered it to enjoin unfair methods of competition in commerce. Prior to the FTC, violations of antitrust laws were the jurisdiction of the Antitrust Division of the Justice Department. Since 1914, the organizations have pursued dual enforcement of the antitrust laws with considerable, though some argue inefficient, overlap. The Justice Department focuses largely on criminal price-fixing

---

[118]"The Anti-Counterfeiting Trade Agreement (ACTA)," *IP Justice*, http://ipjustice.org/, accessed September 10, 2008.

[119]William New, "G8 Governments Want ACTA Finalized This Year, SPLT Talks Accelerated," Intellectual Property Watch, http://www.ip-watch.org/, July 9, 2008; and "Substantive Patent Law Harmonization," World Intellectual Property Organization, http://www.wipo.int/patent-law/en/harmonization.htm, accessed February 28, 2009.

[120]This section draws from Masaaki Kotabe and Kent W. Wheiler, *Anticompetitive Practices in Japan: Their Impact on the Performance of Foreign Firms* (Westport, CT: Praeger Publishers, 1996).

[121]Robert H. Bork, *The Antitrust Paradox* (New York: Basic Books, 1978), p. 48.

and merger review. The FTC, which does not handle criminal cases, concentrates about 60 percent of its total resources on merger review.

The U.S. antitrust laws were originally aimed at domestic monopolies and cartels, although the act expressly extends coverage to commerce with foreign nations. In the 1940s, the prosecution of Alcoa (*United States vs. Aluminum Company of America*, 148 F. 2d 416 1945) resulted in a clear extension of U.S. antitrust laws to activities of foreign companies, even if those actions occur entirely outside the United States as long as they have a substantial and adverse effect on the foreign or domestic commerce and trade of the United States.

Successful extraterritorial enforcement, however, depends on effective jurisdictional reach. Detecting, proving, and punishing collusion and conspiracy to restrain trade among foreign companies is extremely difficult. From gathering evidence to carrying out retribution, the complexity of nearly every aspect of antitrust litigation is compounded when prosecuting a foreign entity. Issues of foreign sovereignty and diplomacy also complicate extraterritorial antitrust enforcement. If a foreign entity's actions are *required* by their own government, that entity is exempt from prosecution under U.S. law. Prior to the 1990s and the demise of the Soviet Union, U.S. trade and economic matters were typically a lower priority to defense and foreign policy concerns. This was particularly true with Japan. In nearly every major trade dispute over steel, textiles, televisions, semiconductors, automobiles, and so on, the Departments of State and Defense opposed and impeded retaliation against Japanese companies for violations of U.S. antitrust laws. A strong alliance with Japan and the strategic geographic military locations the alliance provided were deemed to be of more importance than unrestricted trade. This arrangement helped Japanese companies improve their competitive position.

The extraterritorial application of U.S. antitrust laws has recently been subject to considerably more debate. In 1977 the Antitrust Division of the Justice Department issued its *Antitrust Guidelines for International Operations*, which, consistent with the precedent established in the Alcoa case, reaffirmed that U.S. antitrust laws could be applied to an overseas transaction if there were a direct, substantial, and foreseeable effect on the commerce of the United States. The Foreign Trade Antitrust Improvements Act of 1982 again reiterated this jurisdiction. There has been controversy, however, over the degree of U.S. commerce to which jurisdiction extends.

The 1977 Justice *Guidelines* suggested that foreign anticompetitive conduct injuring U.S. commerce raises antitrust concerns when either U.S. consumers or U.S. exporters are harmed. In a 1988 revision of the *Guidelines*, the reference to exporters was omitted. Later, in 1992, U.S. Attorney General William Barr announced that Justice would take enforcement action against conduct occurring overseas if it unfairly restricts U.S. exports, arguing that anticompetitive behavior of foreign companies that inhibits U.S. exports thereby reduces the economies of scale for U.S. producers and indirectly affects U.S. consumers through higher prices than might otherwise be possible.

Critics argue that comity concerns and the difficulties in gathering evidence and building a case around conduct occurring wholly within a foreign country make it unrealistic for the Justice Department to attempt such an extraterritorial application of U.S. laws. Perhaps the gravest concern, however, is that the policy may lead to prosecution of foreign business methods that actually promote U.S. consumer welfare, for it is predominantly believed in the U.S. economic and legal community that antitrust laws should be concerned solely with protecting consumer welfare. U.S. public opinion has also traditionally and strongly supported the government's role as the champion of consumer rights against commercial interests. U.S. antitrust laws have always reflected this grassroots backing. Such a tradition has not existed in Japan, and the development of antitrust laws there has been quite different.

Fully cognizant that there were many small- and medium-size firms with exportable products that were not currently exporting, in 1982, the U.S. Congress passed the Export Trading Company legislation (ETC Act), which exempted these firms from antitrust laws, to encourage them to improve their export performance by joining forces. Patterned after practices in Germany and Japan, the ETC Act also permits banks to own and operate export trading companies (ETCs) so that the export trading companies will have better access to capital resources, as well as market information through their banks.[122] As a result, the ETC Act assists in the formation of shippers' associations to reduce costs and increase efficiency, covers technology–licensing agreements with foreign firms, and facilitates contact between producers interested in exporting and organizations offering export trade services. However, those trading companies are not allowed to join forces in their importing businesses, hence they are called export trading companies. In reality, many manufacturing companies import raw materials and in-process components from abroad and export finished products using those imported materials. Japanese trading companies handle both exports and imports, and have many manufacturing companies as captive customers for both exports and imports. However, in the United States, those trading companies certified as ETCs under the ETC Act may not fully exploit economies of scale in their operations, as they cannot collectively handle manufacturing firms' imports.

## Antitrust Laws of the European Union

Besides the United States' antitrust forces, other countries have an organization that settles antitrust cases. The European Union (EU) is no exception. While the EU does not apply its antitrust laws extraterritorially outside the region, its laws are applied not only to EU-member country companies but also to foreign companies as long as their corporate action has antitrust implications within the EU community.

In 2000, the European Commission indicated that it was prepared to block the merger of EMI Group and Time Warner, Inc. unless they came up with concrete proposals to allay concerns that the size of the joint venture will allow it to limit access to its copyrights and raise prices. In September 2000, in an effort to save their proposed music join venture Warner-EMI, which would be by far the largest music publisher, the two companies submitted to the European Commission a new set of antitrust remedies involving sales of music labels and copyrights. They also offered to sell several catalogs of songs to reduce their huge market shares in music publishing.[123] Similarly, Microsoft faces a tough time in Europe although it prevailed in the United States against the government's efforts to unbundle its code. In 2004, the European regulators forced the company to remove the Media Player software from its Windows operating system. The EU also requested the company to release more of its Windows code to competitors. Further, the EU can levy fines of up to 10 percent, roughly $3.2 billion, of the company's revenue.[124]

To do business in Europe, foreign companies must comply with EU antitrust law, just as European companies must abide by U.S. antitrust law to do business in the United States. In 2001, the European Union formally blocked General Electric's $43-billion purchase of Honeywell International—the first time a proposed merger between two U.S. companies has been prevented solely by European regulators. The veto by the EU's 20-member executive commission was widely expected after the U.S. companies failed to allay European fears that the deal would create an unfairly dominant position in markets for jetliner engine and avionics. The deal had already secured regulatory approval from U.S. antitrust authorities but was blocked by EU.[125]

## U.S. Foreign Corrupt Practices Act of 1977

Among the many corrupt practices that international marketers face, bribery is considered the most endemic and murky aspect of conducting business abroad.

[122]Charles E. Cobb, Jr., John E. Stiner, "Export Trading Companies: Five Years of Bringing U.S. Exporters Together: The Future of the Export Trading Company Act," *Business America*, 10 (October 12, 1987), pp. 2–9.
[123]Philip Shishkin and Martin Peers, "EMI Group and Time Warner Submit Concessions to Allay Antitrust Worries," *Wall Street Journal*, September 20, 2000.
[124]"Microsoft Detaches Windows from Media Player in Europe," *Wall Street Journal*, January 25, 2005, p. B3.
[125]Syed Tariq Anwar, "EU's Competition Policy and the GE-Honeywell Merger Fiasco: Transatlantic Divergence and Consumer and Regulatory Issues," *Thunderbird International Business Review*, 47 (September/October 2005), pp. 601–26.

However, special care must be taken to identify and accommodate the differences between international markets and those in the United States. Laws may vary widely from country to country, and these laws may on occasion conflict with one another, although international organizations such as the International Monetary Fund, the Organization of Economic Cooperation and Development (OECD), have increased global efforts to combat corrupt business practices.[126] Several countries in the Asia-Pacific Economic Cooperation (APEC) also joined the OECD Convention criminalizing foreign commercial bribery in 1997.[127] Bribery is a means for one party to get from another party (at the cost of a third party) some special treatment that would otherwise not normally be obtainable. However, what constitutes bribery may also differ, depending on local customs and practices.

In order to create the level playing field for U.S. companies to do business abroad and to establish a high ethical standard to be followed by foreign countries, the United States passed the **Foreign Corrupt Practices Act** (FCPA) in 1977. The FCPA was designed to prohibit the payment of any money or anything of value to a foreign official, foreign political party, or any candidate for foreign political office for purposes of obtaining, retaining, or directing business. For example, in 2005, Monsanto Chemical was fined $1.5 million for violating the FCPA by making illegal cash payment to a senior Indonesian Ministry of Environment official a few years earlier.[128] The long arm of the U.S. law even reaches into the offices of Germany's most important company, Siemens. Because its shares are listed on the New York Stock Exchange and it has extensive operations in the United States, Siemens is subject to the FCPA. Siemens or its employees face accusations that they used bribes to sell medical equipment in China and Indonesia, close deals to provide sell telecom gear to the Hungarian and Norwegian armed forces, and win a power plant contract in Serbia, to name a few examples. Munich prosecutors, who uncovered evidence that Siemens used bribes to land contracts around the globe, have already extracted $290 million in fines. With $1.9 billion in questionable payments made to outsiders by the company from 2000 to 2006, Siemens is the biggest FCPA case—foreign or domestic—of all time. And the U.S. authorities see the Siemens case as a splendid opportunity to show they are serious about pursuing foreign companies that violate U.S. anti-corruption laws.[129] The FCPA sets a high ethical standard for U.S. firms doing business abroad, but it basically cannot keep foreign firms (in spite of the rare example of its reaching into Siemens mentioned above) from engaging bribery and other anticompetitive acts in foreign countries.

The FCPA, although silent on the subject, does not prohibit so called "facilitating" or "grease" payments, such as small payments to lower-level officials for expediting shipments through customs or placing a transoceanic telephone call, securing required permits, or obtaining adequate police protection—transactions that simply facilitate the proper performance of duties. These small payments are considered comparable to tips left for waiters. While some companies find such payments morally objectionable and operate without paying them, other companies do not prohibit such payments but require that employees seek advice in advance from their corporate legal counsel in cases where facilitating payments may be involved.[130]

The FCPA does not prohibit bribery payments to nongovernmental personnel, however. Nor does the United States have laws regulating other forms of payment that approach extortion. What constitutes bribery or extortion also becomes less transparent, and international marketers' ethical dilemma increases (see **Global Perspective 5-6**). From an ethical point of view, the major questions that must be answered are:

---

[126]Carolyn Hotchkiss, "The Sleeping Dog Stirs: New Signs of Life in Efforts to End Corruption in International Business," *Journal of Public Policy & Marketing*, 17 (Spring 1998), pp. 108–15.

[127]Madeleine K. Albright, "APEC: Facing the Challenge," *U.S. Department of State Dispatch*, 8 (December 1997), pp. 3–5.

[128]"Bribe Costs Monsanto $1.5 million," *Chemical & Engineering News*, January 17, 2005, p. 28.

[129]Jack Ewing, "Siemens Braces for a Slap from Uncle Sam," *BusinessWeek.com*, November 15, 2007.

[130]Mary Jane Sheffet, "The Foreign Corrupt Practices Act and the Omnibus Trade and Competition Act of 1988: Did They Change Corporate Behavior?" *Journal of Public Policy and Marketing*, 14 (Fall 1995), pp. 290–300.

✦ ✦ ✦ ✦ ✦ ✦ ✦ ✦ ✦ ✦ ✦ ✦ ✦ ✦ ✦ ✦ ✦ ✦ ✦ ✦ ✦ ✦ ✦ ✦ ✦ ✦ ✦ ✦ ✦ ✦ ✦

# $\mathcal{G}$LOBAL PERSPECTIVE 5-6

## CULTURAL RELATIVISM/ACCOMMODATION—SELLING OUT?

The following is an excerpt from an anonymous source circulating via e-mail on the GINLIST:

Cultural accommodation is an essential element in successful international and cross-cultural relationships. The question faced by the U.S. multinationals is whether to follow the advice, "When in Rome, do as the Romans do." Foreign firms operating in the U.S. are faced with a similar question, "When in America, should you do as the Americans do?" How far does an individual or a company go to accommodate cultural differences before they sell themselves out? . . . I will attempt to answer this question by looking at issues involving my personal core values, bribery and gift giving, and how these relate to the definitions presented. I will also discuss trust and credibility and how these qualities relate to the subject and present a case for marketplace morality. I will conclude by presenting what I feel is the answer to the question posed above.

The primary issue . . . is one of cultural relativism and its place in cross-cultural encounters. Cultural relativism is a philosophical position which states that ethics is a function of culture. . . . Ethical relativism is the belief that nothing is objectively right or wrong, and that the definition of right or wrong depends on the prevailing view of a particular individual, culture, or historical period.

Cultural or ethical relativists will find themselves in a constant state of conflict within their own society. By definition, it would be impossible to reach an agreement on ethical rights and wrongs for the society. An ethical relativist believes that whatever an individual (any individual) believes to be right or wrong is in fact correct. The only cultural norm would be one of chaos since it would be impossible to hold anyone accountable to a prevailing or arbitrary ethos due to the accepted fact that all is relative and all is correct by definition.

As an example, imagine trying to hold Hitler's Nazi government accountable for their crimes during World War II from this perspective. If ethics is relative and that right and wrong are defined by the prevailing view of a particular individual, culture, or historical period, then Hitler's policies of racial purification were ethically correct. However, according to my ethical beliefs (and those of the world's representatives who presided over the Nuremburg Trials), that conclusion is completely unacceptable. There are some things that are moral and ethical absolutes. . . .

As we adapt to the differences in cultures, each individual and culture must still determine where the line is (which defines) the clear violations of moral absolutes. In pursuing this objective, understanding who we are and what we stand for are essential in identifying the sell-out point. We must come to terms with our core values and how they match up with both the company ethos and that of the host and home countries. . . .

*Source:* An anonymous source, distributed via e-mail on GINLIST, October 11, 1994.

It is interesting to note the Catch 22 that an international company can find itself in on this subject. In reference to China, if the company tries to avoid the appearance of a bribe by not participating in a culture's gift giving custom and just say "thanks," they may be seen as using the "verbal thanks as getting out of their obligation." The international manager must not only understand and respect the cultural subtleties, but know how to find the limits of the ethical behavior. One specific limit put in place by the U.S. Government is the Foreign Corrupt Practices Act (FCPA). This Act was passed in reaction to a "rash of controversial payments to foreign officials by American business in the 1970s." The Act specifically calls for "substantial fines for both corporations and individual corporate officers who engage in the bribery of foreign government officials."

U.S. firms are restricted from bribing; however, many companies in other countries engage in this practice routinely. American firms allege that restricting them from this practice puts them at a serious disadvantage to other nations' firms. In the short term, this may be true. Consider what would happen if every firm bribed. The cost of a project would be driven up so high that the country itself could no longer afford it. The bribe is not free and is always paid either by a higher contract price or through shortcuts in quality and material which may result in serious social costs. Consider a freeway overpass or a bridge not built to adequate safety standards or with poor quality materials. The result could be a collapsed bridge, resulting in loss of both life and property. The bribe also undermines the competitive process so that the purchaser pays more than the competitive price and erodes the trust in the public officials and the firm.

Is there a morality separate from the individual and from the culture? . . . A multinational corporation doing business in societies with differing moral norms must subscribe to a morality of the marketplace which is based on trust and credibility. Violating such norms would be self-defeating. Companies engaging in business practices that result in a loss of trust or credibility will eventually lose their share of the market . . .

A person who approaches the world from a cultural relativist perspective will change his or her position and standards depending on the prevailing view of the culture or sub-culture that person is in. Trust and credibility can neither be built nor retained from such a position. International or domestic businessmen want to know who they are dealing with. They want to know if they can trust the person and/or company they are about to join together with. . . .

Where is the line drawn that separates accommodation from selling out? In a large part it depends on the individual's value system, since what they're selling out on is really their own core values, trust, and credibility. There are moral absolutes, which, if violated, are always examples of stepping across the line.

1. Does such an act involve unfairness to anyone or violate anyone's right?
2. Must such an act be kept secret, such that it cannot be reported as a business expense?
3. Is such an act truly necessary in order to carry on business?

Unless the first two questions are answered in the negative and the third is answered in the positive, such an act is generally deemed unethical.[131] It is advised that multinational firms maintain good "corporate citizenship" wherever they do business, since long-term benefits tend to outweigh the short-term benefit gained from bribes for the same reasons just mentioned—for example, corporate contributions to humanitarian and environmental causes, such as the Save the Rain Forest project in Brazil, and moral stands on oppressive governments, such as two European brewers, Carlsberg and Heineken, pulling out from Burma to protest this Asian country's dictatorship regime.[132]

## SUMMARY ◆ ◆ ◆ ◆ ◆ ◆ ◆ ◆ ◆ ◆ ◆ ◆ ◆ ◆ ◆ ◆ ◆ ◆ ◆ ◆ ◆ ◆ ◆ ◆ ◆ ◆ ◆ ◆ ◆

When doing business across national boundaries, international marketers almost always face what is perceived to be political and legal barriers. It is because that government policies and laws can be very different from country to country. In most cases, a foreign company has to accept a host country's government policies and laws, as they are usually outside its control. Some large multinational firms, if backed by their home country government, may sometimes influence the host country's policies and laws. However, such an extraterritorial interference may have negative consequences in the long run for a short-term gain.

Despite various international agreements brought about by such international organizations as WTO, G8, and COCOM, which collectively strive toward freer and more equitable world trade, every nation is sovereign and maintains its special interests, which may occasionally clash with those of the international agreements. Although the world has been moving toward a freer trade and investment environment, the road has not necessarily been smooth. When considering entry or market expansion in foreign countries, their country risks need to be assessed. Multinational firms need to be aware of political risks arising from unstable political parties and government structure, changes in government programs, and social pressures and special interest groups in a host country. Political risks are further compounded by economic and financial risks. When disputes arise across national boundaries, they will most likely have to be settled in one country. Therefore, careful planning for establishing the jurisdictional clause in the contract is needed before the contract is entered into.

Although government policies and the laws of a country usually affect business transactions involving that country, increased business activities transcending national boundaries have tested the territoriality of some policies and laws of a country. The United States frequently applies its laws, such as antitrust laws and the Foreign Corrupt Practices Act, outside its political boundary to the extent that U.S. businesses are affected or to the extent that its legal value system can be extended. On the other hand, despite the importance of intellectual property in international business, protection of intellectual property in foreign countries is granted essentially by registration in those countries. International marketing managers should be aware that usually, domestic protection cannot be extended beyond their national boundary.

## KEY TERMS ◆ ◆ ◆ ◆ ◆ ◆ ◆ ◆ ◆ ◆ ◆ ◆ ◆ ◆ ◆ ◆ ◆ ◆ ◆ ◆ ◆ ◆ ◆ ◆ ◆ ◆ ◆ ◆ ◆ ◆

| | | | |
|---|---|---|---|
| Fast-track trade authority | Multilateral Controls), see also Wassenaar Arrangement | Domestication (phase-out) policy | Green marketing |
| "First-to-File" patent principle | | European Patent Convention | Home country |
| "First-to-Invent" patent principle | Code (written) law | Export license | Host country |
| Berne Convention | Commercial law | Expropriation | Islamic law |
| Capitalism | Common law | Foreign Corrupt Practices Act of 1977 | ISO 9000 |
| Civil law | Confiscation | G7 | ISO 14000 |
| COCOM (The Coordinating Committee for | Copyright | G8 | Nationalization |
| | Countertrade | G8+5 | Non-tariff barriers |
| | | | Paris Convention |

---

[131]Richard T. De George, *Business Ethics*, 4th ed. (Englewood Cliffs, N.J.: Prentice Hall, 1995), pp. 511–12.

[132]"Brewer Decides to Pull Out of Its Business in Burma," *Wall Street Journal*, July 12, 1996, p. A8A.

| | | | |
|---|---|---|---|
| Patent Cooperation Treaty | Socialist law | Trademark | Wassenaar Arrangement |
| Patent Law Treaty | Tariffs | Trade Related Aspects of | |
| Sharia, see Islamic law | Trade secret | Intellectual Property | |
| | | Rights (TRIPS) treaties | |

## REVIEW QUESTIONS

1. Describe with examples the role of governments in promoting national interests pertaining to business activities.

2. What different types of trade controls influence international business? What are their intended objectives?

3. How do host country macroeconomic and fiscal policies affect foreign company operations?

4. What are the factors that international managers should consider in determining the economic and political risks associated with a country?

5. International law is derived from three sources. What are these three? Compare and contrast them.

6. Briefly describe the various types of local legal systems. How do differences in these legal systems affect international business?

7. Enumerate some of the legal issues that international business managers need to take cognizance of in host countries.

8. Describe the various types of barriers to international trade and investment.

## DISCUSSION QUESTIONS

1. The term, bribery, sounds bad. How about kickbacks, tips, contingency fees, consultation fees, etc? Terms vary, objectives to be accomplished by not-so-easy-to-define payments vary, and to whom such payments are made varies. Personal income levels vary from country to country, and thus the level of financial incentive provided by such payments vary. Also, as you learned from Chapter 4, cultural value systems vary; thus the degree of legality, or social acceptability, varies for such payments. In general, "facilitating" payments–legal or illegal aside–tend to be used more often in countries characterized by high levels of power distance, uncertainty avoidance, and collectivism than in other countries. As debated also in **Global Perspective 5-6**, could there be some things that are moral and ethical absolutes when it comes to payment of money to someone in the third party to influence and/or facilitate business transactions in your favor? How about the U.S. standard, as stipulated in the Foreign Corrupt Practices Act of 1977? The United States is a country characterized as having low levels of power distance and uncertainty avoidance and a high level of individualism—the opposite of those countries indicated above. Discuss how you would like to address this issue.

2. Various foreign companies operating in Russia, especially in the oil and gas exploration business, have had to face the vagaries of Russian legislation, which changes frequently, making it difficult to plan activities. Besides being heavily taxed, foreign firms have had to face a change in export duties of crude oil over a dozen times in the past few years. Yet most companies continue to negotiate for making investments worth billions of dollars. Discuss some of the possible reasons for the actions of these companies. Companies take various steps to manage political risk. If you were representing a company negotiating investments in Russia, what steps would you take to manage (and/or reduce) the political risk associated with these investments?

3. The following examples highlight the impact of differences in laws and social norms on various aspects of the marketing program. What are the implications of such differences for

using standardized product or advertising strategies (or using standardized advertising themes)?

a. Pepsi International's humorous global ad campaign fronted by model Cindy Crawford, which includes the use of a Coke can, will not be seen in Germany because German regulations forbid the use of comparative advertising.

b. Advertising laws in China have restricted the use of Budweiser posters, featuring young attractive women in Budweiser swimsuits, by Anheuser-Busch to bars and stores with adult clientele only. Furthermore, when Anheuser-Busch wanted models to wear swimsuits for a beer festival, the mothers of the models used insisted on the girls wearing T-shirts beneath the swimsuits.

c. An Austin, Texas-based designer of computer games wants to market a game that involves humans fighting against aliens from different planets. One aspect of the game is that if the humans are shot, blood is shown to come out of their bodies. German laws, however, do not permit any depiction of red blood in computer games. The company wants to market this game in Germany, which is a huge market. One suggestion the company is working on is the use of an alternate color to depict human blood. However, it risks the prospect of making the game less realistic—"What would children make out of green liquid coming out of the human figure on being shot?"

4. KFC, a fast-food operator, faced immense resistance from some politically active consumer groups when it opened its operations in India. One group proclaimed that opening KFC outlets in the country would propagate a "junk-food" culture. Others proclaimed that this was "the return of imperialistic powers" and was an attempt to "Westernize the eating habits" of Indians. Overzealous local authorities in the city of Bangalore used a city law restricting the use of MSG (a food additive used in the chicken served by KFC) over a certain amount as a

pretext for temporarily closing down the outlet, despite the fact that the authorities did not even have the equipment to measure the MSG content in the proportions stated in the law. In the capital city of New Delhi, a KFC outlet was temporarily closed down because the food inspector found a "house-fly" in the restaurant. While both of these issues got resolved through hectic consultations with these consumer groups and through legal orders issued protecting the interests of the outlets, they do reflect how political and social concerns of even a small segment of the population can adversely affect the operations of companies in foreign markets. If you were the country manager of KFC in India, what steps would you have taken to avoid these problems?

5.  The entertainment industry has been warring for years to combat computers and the Internet to copy and transmit music and movies. The biggest winner has been consumers who pay very little or nothing to get their favorite movies due largely to the Internet sector's innovations. There are over 12,000 cases with the entertainment industry suing individual users. Recently, The U.S. Supreme Court ruled in favor of copyright holders and against two companies that distribute peer-to-peer (P2P) software, which allows users to share files online with others. Tens of millions of Internet users regularly use P2P to exchange music and, to a lesser extent, films. It seems that with continuous technology introduction, free downloads will continue to increase. The real challenge for content providers is to use new technology to create value for customers and to make those who fail to use legitimate content feel bad about it. Do you think entertainment companies should craft ways to use innovative technology to realize their wares in ways that will also allow copyright to be protected? Since the Internet has no virtual borders, what should entertainment companies do to secure their global market, especially in those countries that have weak intellectual property protection?

6.  An extension of the antitrust laws into the arena of international trade has taken the form of anti-dumping laws, which have been enacted by most Western countries, and which are increasingly being enacted by developing countries. On the surface, most of the anti-dumping laws across the various countries seem to be similar to each other. However, since much of the content of these laws is open to interpretation, the results of these laws could vary significantly. The bottom line for the initiation of any anti-dumping investigation is that if a foreign manufacturer gets an "undue" advantage while selling its products (either through pricing its products higher in other protected markets or through government subsidies) in another country relative to the domestic manufacturer and hurts the domestic industry, the company is resorting to unfair competition and should be penalized for it. While large firms are relatively more aware of the nuances of anti-dumping laws, and have the resources, especially legal ones, to deal with this issue, it is the smaller firms, which often depend on governmental export assistance in various forms, that are the most susceptible to being penalized.

One of your friends is planning to start exporting an industrial product to various countries in Europe. To help finance his export endeavor, he plans to utilize concessional export credit provided by the U.S. government to small exporters. This product is highly specialized, and caters to an extremely small niche market. Europe is a large market for this product. There are only two other manufacturers of this product, both based in Europe. One of these manufacturers is a $100-million company, which manufactures various other products besides the product in question. What would be your advice to your friend in terms of the significance of antidumping laws? What specific steps, if any, would you encourage your friend to take, especially in context of his limited financial resources?

7.  Unfortunately, intellectual property law cannot protect the business everywhere. For example, there is a flood of cheap imitations of Japanese motorcycles on the Chinese market, and Honda Motor finally had to release in China a line of inexpensive 125cc motorcycles in 2002, even though manufacturing motorcycles at such low prices will mean a drastic change in Honda's normal policy of making high-priced, high-quality products. By some estimates, 7 million out of 10 million motorcycles produced in China every year are imitations. Do you think all companies should lower their prices to protect themselves from local imitations and fake products? What kind of suggestions would you make to a high-end brand manager if the brand were going to a developing country with less strict government controls on imitation products?

## SHORT CASES

# CASE 5-1

## COCA-COLA IN INDIA

Coca Cola has had a glorious past selling cola all over the world. In fact, the "Coke" brand is one of the most well-known in the world and it carries with it an image of American culture. But Coke's experience in the emerging Indian market has always been especially challenging due to the protectionist political and legal environment.

Today, the Indian economy is gradually opening its doors to foreign companies in various industrial sectors. But when Coke first stepped into the Indian market, it acquired a significant market share and was a popular drink in the market. It was then forced to exit India in 1977 when the government at that time demanded that Coca-Cola reduce its stake in its wholly owned Indian subsidiary to 40 percent. Since then, India has revised its attitude toward foreign investment in a major way and Coca-Cola once again entered India in 1994 after staying away from this largely populated and thus attractive market for many years. This time around, though, Coca-Cola fully owns its subsidiary and when it returned to the Indian market, it also acquired some local cola and soft drinks brands, including Thumbs Up, which had over 59 percent market share and a great distribution network. Coca-Cola's biggest rival, Pepsi had already carved its niche in the market with more than 25 percent market share.

While things went smoothly for a while after Coke's re-entry into India, it soon started run-ins with the regional political bodies. Coca-Cola had set up a $12 million plant in Plachimada, a rural town in the southern state of Kerala in India in 2000. But four years later, in 2004, the company had to shut it down, at least temporarily to begin with. The start of 2002 witnessed the anti-Coke 'Coca Cola, Quit Plachimada, Quit India' movement. It began when people who were living close to the plant noticed that water in their wells was drying up or becoming polluted, acidic and therefore not drinkable. Never having faced this water situation before, all fingers pointed toward the newly established Coke plant, which extracted considerable quantities of ground water on a daily basis for its operations. A small local protest that started off with less than a hundred people, exploded into a nationwide agitation. Soon, social activists and nationalists, who were against foreign firms and privatization, joined in. Before long, the campaign against Coca-Cola had found supporters from all over the world including the U.S., Sweden and France.

*Source:* Mark Thomas, "If Water Has Become a Scarce Resource, then the Americans Will Invade Wales and the PM Will Defend Them by Insisting that Wales Could Launch a Water-Borne Chemical Attack," *New Statesman,* February 16, 2004, p. 14; Terrence H. Witkowski, "Antiglobal Challenges to Marketing in Developing Countries: Exploring the Ideological Divide," *Journal of Public Policy & Marketing,* 24 (Spring 2005), pp. 7–23; and "Coke In India: A Not-So-Silent Spring," *Corporate Accountability International,* http://www.stopcorporateabuse.org/cms/page1764.cfm, June 2008.

The local political body in the area, known as the Panchayat, which had initially laid out the red carpet for the Coca-Cola plant refused to renew HCCBPL's (Hindustan Coca Cola Beverages Private Limited) license in 2003. The state government also chipped in and joined the dispute. Eager to fight back, Coca-Cola approached the High Court in India, but the court ruled that water, being common property, could not be excessively used by one body. By the year 2004, the controversy had erupted to such an extent that Kerala state government ordered that the company stop using the ground water. Shortly thereafter, Coca Cola was forced to suspend production at the plant.

As a result of this incident and other incidents in India where researchers found that its beverages contained high levels of pesticides that were potentially harmful to human beings, Coca-Cola lost millions in the Indian market. In September 2003, a legal notice was issued to the company's headquarters in Atlanta, the U.S. by the Joint Parliamentary Committee in India asking the company to immediately suspend sales in India or then it would sue the company for $10 billion for selling dangerous drinks. A similar notice was given to Pepsi as well. They were also expected to recall any already sold products. Coca-Cola overcame this particular setback eventually but it did not in any way make its survival in the Indian market any easier. Its new product launches in India such as the vanilla flavored Coke drink and others such as its energy drink Shock proved to be debacles. However, Coca-Cola is not giving up in India this time. It is hanging on with the hope that some day it will be able to win over the world's second largest population. Coca-Cola has responded to growing protests against it in India through a variety of corporate social responsibility initiatives, including the much-hyped Every Drop Counts campaign launched in 2007.

**USEFUL TWO VIDEO CLIPS MAY BE VIEWED AT WWW.UTUBE.COM:**

1. Coca-Cola responsible for water depletion in India http://www.youtube.com/watch?v=U8OA_M-sMnw

2. Indians Protest Coca Cola Plant http://www.youtube.com/watch?v=wyFsodVUd-o&feature=related

**DISCUSSION QUESTIONS**

1. What should Coca-Cola do to appease the Indian government and ensure its survival in the market?

2. What effect will this case have on Coca-Cola's operations in India?

3. What lesson does this case have for other multinationals that want to enter the Indian market?

# CASE 5-2

## CAN I GET A BUD, PLEASE? WHICH BUD? CZECH OR AMERICAN?

The growing power of the European Union (EU) in recent times is proving beneficial to European firms but it is rubbing global trade bodies and a lot of U.S. multinational firms the wrong way. One U.S. firm that is particularly disconcerted is brewer Anheuser Busch. The reason being the recent (May 5, 2005) Protected Geographical Indication (PGI) status granted to a Czech beer brand, Budweiser Budvar by the EU. Anheuser-Busch claims the Czech product is making its way in international markets using Anheuser-Busch's original beer brand name Budweiser or 'Bud' as it is widely known. The Czech Republic is one of the EU's newest members, having entered the EU in May 2004.

The EU has reserved the PGI status for those products that can be identified by virtue of their place of origin and the indigenous process of manufacturing these products. There is a prestigious group of brands that enjoy this status and it includes German beer product Kolsh originating from the North Western part of Germany, Gruyere cheese from Switzerland and the well-known Cognac. There is another category of products that are assigned the title of Protected Designations of Origin (PDO) by the EU regulation 2081/92. Although the EU believes that this classification is what needs to be done to protect the identity of its region's popular products, the U.S. and even the World Trade Organization contend that this is just one more political weapon in the hands of the often protectionist EU countries against free trade. Furthermore, the Czech Republic is a new addition to the EU and compared to the other countries, is much smaller in size and bargaining power within the EU. According to this regulation, PGI products cannot be made or packaged anywhere except in their own region, after which they are named. In case of Budweiser Budvar beer, for example, it cannot be brewed or packaged anywhere except in its own specific region. If the company, in the future, decided to relocate to another region, its status would be likely to be revoked. For example, when UK-based Scottish & Newcastle closed down its oldest brewing plant in Newcastle due to a move to rationalize its operations, it was compelled to apply for its brand name Newcastle Brown to be revoked because it could no longer enjoy the PGI status.

Budejovicky Budvar (Budvar), which has brewed its beer in the Czech town of Ceske Budejovice (also known as Budweis) near Prague since before the beginning of the 20th century, has to be sold in the U.S. and some other regions outside of the EU as CzechVar. Budvar claims that it has been using its brand names. Including Budweiser, since times unmemorable, although Anheuser-Busch contends that it has used the same brand names since its establishment in 1876, several years before Budvar came into existence. Budvar argues that it has the sole right to the brand name due to the association with the region and the EU ruling merely brings additional support for this assertion.

Whereas in their early years of international operation, the two firms managed to carve out their areas and remain sellers in those markets, in recent times, global competition has heated up not only in technology intensive industries but also in the brewing industry and hence the firms found themselves stepping on each others' toes, thus initiating an intense struggle for market dominance. However, Anheuser-Busch's marketing issues with Budvar go back to 1906 when Budvar first entered the U.S. market, and extend to 40 different countries where the two firms and their respective brands, Budvar and Anheuser-Busch's Budweiser are embroiled in legal battles, making it a truly global marketing crusade for the same brand names, Bud, Budweiser and Budvar. Although Anheuser-Busch is larger and therefore assumed to be more powerful than the smaller Czech company, Budweiser has been losing out to Budvar in many of its markets. Anheuser-Busch brought action against Budvar using its trade name Budweiser in different international markets. To make it worse, the Czechs are winning some of the legal cases as well, the most recent one being Budvar's win in Cambodia and some years back in Switzerland, where Anheuser-Busch was prevented from marketing its products under the Budweiser brand names. Budvar lost its case against Anheuser-Busch in France a few years back. A surprising outcome of the legal case was in the UK where the court allowed both firms to market their products with the same brand names.

Industry experts contend that Budvar has a unique global marketing strategy in place, whereby it can piggyback on the free publicity gained for it by its dispute with Anheuser-Busch. The coveted PGI status is going to be a useful add-on to its marketing strategy because it is believed that consumers will now desire the beer for its authenticity and association with the Czech Republic and therefore perceive more value in purchase of the product. In order to emphasize its newfound eminence, Budvar is planning to stick blue and gold seals on its beer products. Budvar's latest twist to its marketing strategy is to promote its beer as a finer quality brew based on provenance, which some believe will take it a long way in sales irrespective of whether it wins in the courts or not. This is in contrast to Anheuser-Busch's strategy in global markets to promote its Budweiser brands as more of familiar, general brand.

The trademark war between Budvar and Anheuser-Busch has been going on for decades and given that neither company is ready to back down, the battle will probably go on for another few decades as both firms enter new markets and try to acquire market share.

### DISCUSSION QUESTIONS

**1.** How important is it for Anheuser-Busch to market its products under their original brand names in different countries?

**2.** If you were asked to be the judge in this case, whom would you side with and why?

**3.** Since the legal battle between Anheuser Busch and Budvar seems to be never ending, how could the firms possibly settle this matter outside of court?

**4.** What alternative strategies could both firms adopt in foreign markets in which both of them compete?

*Source:* James Curtis, "Provenance or Protectionism?" *Marketing,* May 11, 2005, p. 16; and various other sources.

# CASE 5-3

## HOW TWO COMPANIES HANDLED A POLITICALLY SENSITIVE CRISIS SITUATION

Burger King and McDonald's recently experienced crises in politically sensitive areas of the world. The following is how those two global hamburger chains handled the similar volatile political situations.

### BURGER KING

In the face of a boycott threat by Arab and Muslim groups in late 1999, Burger King Corp. decided to revoke a franchise agreement for a restaurant in the Israeli-occupied West Bank. Burger King maintained that the decision to cancel the agreement with its Israeli franchisee, Rikamor Ltd., was the result of Rikamor's breach of contract. Rikamor told Burger King that the restaurant would be located in Israel proper, not the disputed West Bank. Rikamor has been asked to remove the Burger King name from the restaurant, although the chain has no power to force the restaurant to close. A statement released by Burger King said it had made it clear that it "would not approve Rikamor opening restaurants in the West Bank at this sensitive time in the peace process." Now backed by Jewish settlers who long for brand-name legitimacy, Burger King's Israeli franchisee swore to fight the fast food giant's break with a branch in a West Bank Jewish settlement. Angry Israeli settlers called for a worldwide boycott of Burger King restaurants and a halt to Israeli-Palestinian peace talks, after the chain canceled its franchise in Maale Adumim, a Jewish settlement near Jerusalem. Burger King said its decision was purely commercial and that it does not take sides in the Arab-Israeli peace process. Israel captured the West Bank in 1967, and Jewish settlements, located throughout the territory, are at the center of the Middle East conflict. Palestinians say the West Bank settlements are illegal.

### MCDONALD'S

At the outset of the NATO's air war against Yugoslavia (now known as Serbia-Montenegro) during the Kosovo Crisis in 1999, McDonald's, as a quintessential American trademark, was forced to temporarily close its 15 restaurants in Yugoslavia due to vandalism by angry Serbian mobs. But when local managers re-opened the doors shortly after, they accomplished an extraordinary comeback using an unusual marketing strategy. They put McDonald's U.S. citizenship on the back burner. To help overcome animosity toward an American icon, the local restaurants promoted the McCountry, a domestic pork burger with paprika garnish. As a national flourish to evoke Serbian identity and pride, they produced posters and lapel buttons showing the golden arches topped with a traditional Serbian cap called the sajkaca. They also handed out free cheeseburgers at anti-NATO rallies. The basement of one restaurant in the Serbian capital even served as a bomb shelter. Now that the NATO-led war against Yugoslavia is over, many Serbians do not associate McDonald's with the United States but rather as their own.

Different companies may have different corporate philosophies. If you had been in charge of international operations for either Burger King or McDonald's, how would you have addressed these political crises?

---

# FURTHER READING

Anwar, Syed Tariq. "EU's Competition Policy and the GE-Honeywell Merger Fiasco: Transatlantic Divergence and Consumer and Regulatory Issues." *Thunderbird International Business Review*, 47 (September/October 2005): 601–26.

Cragg, Wesley and William Woof. "The U.S. Foreign Corrupt Practices Act: A Study of Its Effectiveness." *Business & Society Review*, 107 (Spring 2002): 98–144.

Doh, Jonathan and Terrence Guay. "The Changing Global Political and Institutional Environment" in Masaaki Kotabe and Kristiaan Helsen,ed., *The SAGE Handbook of International Marketing*, London: Sage Publications, 2009, pp. 36–54.

Duina, Francesco G. *Harmonizing Europe: Nation-States within the Common Market*, Albany, NY: State University of New York Press, 1999.

Erevelles, M. Sunil, Veronica Horton, and Ana Marinova. "The Triadic Model: A Comprehensive Framework for Managing Country Risk." *Marketing Management Journal*, 15 (Fall 2005): 1–17.

Gu, Flora F, Kineta Hung, David K. Tse. "When Does Guanxi Matter? — Issues of Capitalization and Its Dark Sides." *Journal of Marketing*, 72 (July 2008): 12–28.

Hoffmann, Stanley. "Clash of Globalizations." *Foreign Affairs*, 81 (July/August 2002): 104–15.

Gillespie, Kate. "Smuggling and the Global Firm." *Journal of International Management*, 9(3), 2003: 317–33.

Gillespie, Kate, Kishore Krishna, and Susan Jarvis. "Protecting Global Brands: Toward a Global Norm." *Journal of International Marketing*, 10 (Issue 2, 2002): 99–112.

Jain, Subhash and Robert Bird. "Marketing and the Global Legal Environment" in Masaaki Kotabe and Kristiaan Helsen,ed. *The SAGE Handbook of International Marketing*, London: Sage Publications, 2009, pp. 55–70.

Kotabe, Masaaki. "Special Issue: Global Security Risks and International Competitiveness." *Journal of International Management*, 11 (December 2005).

Naidu, G. M., V. Kanti Prasad, and Arno Kleimenhagen. "Purchasing's Preparedness for ISO 9000 International

Quality Standards." *International Journal of Purchasing & Materials Management*, 32 (Fall 1996): 46–53.

Redding, Gordon. "The Thick Description and Comparison of Societal Systems of Capitalism." *Journal of International Business Studies*, 36 (March 2005): 123–55.

Rugman, Alan, John Kirton, and Julie Soloway. *Environmental Regulations and Corporate Strategy: A NAFTA Perspective.* Oxford, England: Oxford University Press, 1999.

Unruh, Gregory. "Should You Manage Ethics or Corruption?" *Thunderbird International Business Review*, 50 (September/ October 2008): 287–94.

Witkowski, Terrence H. "Antiglobal Challenges to Marketing in Developing Countries: Exploring the Ideological Divide." *Journal of Public Policy & Marketing*, 24 (Spring 2005): 7–23.

# GLOBAL MARKETING RESEARCH  6

## CHAPTER OVERVIEW

1. RESEARCH PROBLEM FORMULATION

2. SECONDARY GLOBAL MARKETING RESEARCH

3. PRIMARY GLOBAL MARKETING RESEARCH

4. LEVERAGING THE INTERNET FOR GLOBAL MARKET RESEARCH STUDIES

5. MARKET SIZE ASSESSMENT

6. NEW MARKET INFORMATION TECHNOLOGIES

7. MANAGING GLOBAL MARKETING RESEARCH

Oreo cookies, the iconic American cookie brand, were first introduced in China in 1996, more than eighty years after the U.S. launch. In 2005, as sales of Oreos in China had been flat for five years, Kraft decided to refashion the Oreo for the China market. Up to then Kraft was simply selling the U.S. version of Oreos. To guide the makeover, Kraft initiated a huge market research project. Kraft learned that Oreos were far too sweet for Chinese consumers. The company tested out twenty prototypes of reduced-sugar Oreos before arriving at the right formulation. Another finding was that a package of 14 Oreos priced at five yuan (about seventy cents) was too expensive for many Chinese. Kraft launched smaller-sized packages for just two yuan. However, the most radical change was the shape of the cookies. Kraft's researchers found out that sales of wafer cookies were increasing much faster than traditional round cookies. Therefore, in 2006 Kraft introduced a new version of the Oreo: a long, narrow, layered stack of crispy wafer filled with vanilla and chocolate cream, all coated with chocolate (see **Exhibit 6-1**). The new Oreos were so successful that Kraft decided to sell them in other Asian markets, in Australia, and in Canada.[1]

The Kraft story highlights the potentially huge benefits of market research in foreign markets. Given the complexity of the global marketplace, solid marketing research is critical for a host of global marketing decisions. Skipping the research phase

---
[1]"Kraft Reinvents Iconic Oreo to Win in China," *The Wall Street Journal*, May 1, 2008, p. 28.

**EXHIBIT 6-1**
OREO WAFER STICKS—PRODUCT DEVELOPED BASED ON KRAFT'S MARKET
RESEARCH IN CHINA

*Courtesy Kristiaan Helsen*

in the international marketing decision process can often prove a costly mistake. The following anecdotes illustrate that even marketing behemoths such as Wal-Mart and Procter & Gamble sometimes fail to live up to the "Test, Test, Test" maxim:

• When Wal-Mart first entered the Argentine market, its meat counters featured T-bone steaks—not the rib strips and tail rumps that Argentines prefer. Jewelry counters displayed emeralds, sapphires, and diamonds. Argentine women, however, prefer wearing gold and silver. The hardware departments had tools and appliances for 110-volt electric power, while the standard throughout Argentina is 220-volt.[2]

• In Japan, Procter & Gamble stumbled into a cultural minefield by showing a Camay commercial that featured a man walking into the bathroom while his spouse was taking a bath. This spot raised eyebrows in Japan, where a husband is not supposed to impose on his wife's privacy in the bathroom. A Japanese ad campaign for its all-temperature Cheer laundry detergent brand mistakenly assumed that Japanese housewives wash clothes in different temperatures. Japanese women do their laundry in tap water or leftover bath water.[3]

• In China, Toyota was forced to withdraw an ad showing Chinese stone lions bowing in respect to a Prado Land Cruiser sport-utility vehicle. The ad campaign was intended to reflect Prado's imposing presence when driving in the city. The campaign struck a historic nerve for some Chinese consumers because, as some consumer critics pointed

---

[2]"Wal-Mart Learns a Hard Lesson," *International Herald Tribune*, December 6, 1999, p. 15.

[3]Alecia Swasy, *Soap Opera. The Inside Story of Procter & Gamble* (New York: Random House, 1993), p. 268.

out, the lions bore a close resemblance to those flanking the Marco Polo Bridge, the site near Beijing of the opening battle in Japan's 1937 invasion of China.[4]

Most of such cultural blunders stem from inadequate marketing research. Market research assists the global marketing manager in two ways:[5] (1) to make better decisions that recognize cross-country similarities and differences and (2) to gain support from the local subsidiaries for proposed marketing decisions.

To some degree, the procedures and methods that are followed in conducting global marketing research are close to those used in standard domestic research. Most of the marketing research tricks-of-the-trade available for the domestic market scene (e.g., questionnaire design, focus group research, multivariate techniques such as cluster analysis, conjoint measurement) can be employed fruitfully in the global marketplace. Also, the typical sequence of a multicountry market research process follows the familiar pattern used in domestic marketing research. In particular, the steps to be followed to conduct global market research are:

1. Define the research problem(s).

2. Develop a research design.

3. Determine information needs.

4. Collect the data (secondary and primary).

5. Analyze the data and interpret the results.

6. Report and present the findings of the study.

A typical example of a multicountry market research project is summarized in **Exhibit 6-2**. At each of these six steps, special problems may arise when the research activity takes place in foreign markets. The major challenges that global marketing researchers need to confront are:[6]

### EXHIBIT 6-2

A MULTICOUNTRY MARKETING RESEARCH PROJECT AT ELI LILLY: ESTIMATING THE MARKET POTENTIAL FOR A PRESCRIPTION WEIGHT LOSS PRODUCT

- **Research Problem:**
  Estimate the dollar potential for a prescription weight-loss product in the U.K., Spain, Italy, and Germany.
- **Research Hypothesis:**
  Patients would be willing to pay a premium price for the product even without reimbursement by the government.
- **Secondary Data Research:**
  - Market share of a similar product (Isomeride).
  - Incidence of overweight and obesity in Europe.[7]
- **Primary Data Research:**
  - Sample size: 350 physicians from the U.K., Italy, Spain, and Germany.
  - Sampling procedure: random selection from a high-prescribers doctor list based on company data.
  - Data Collected:
    (1) Diary kept by physicians for 2 weeks.
    (2) Questionnaires completed by patients who were judged to be prospect for the product by physician.
    (3) Pricing study done based on 30 additional phone interviews with physicians in the U.K., Italy and Spain to measure price sensitivity.

*Source:* Based on: William V. Lawson, "The "Heavyweights" — Forecasting the obesity market in Europe for a new compound," *Marketing and Research Today,* November 1995, pp. 270–74.

---

[4]"Cultural Pitfalls Tarnish Some Ads in China," *Asian Wall Street Journal,* January 19, 2004, p. A8.

[5]Kamran Kashani, "Beware the Pitfalls of Global Marketing," *Harvard Business Review,* Sept.–Oct. 1989, p. 97.

[6]Susan P. Douglas and C. Samuel Craig, *International Marketing Research,* Englewood Cliffs, NJ: Prentice-Hall, 1983.

[7]Overweight: people whose body-weight is 25–29 percent over the recommended weight; obese: people whose body-weight is more than 30 percent over their ideal weight.

1. Complexity of research design due to environmental differences.
2. Lack and inaccuracy of secondary data.
3. Time and cost requirements to collect primary data.
4. Coordination of multicountry research efforts.
5. Difficulty in establishing comparability across multicountry studies.

In this chapter, you will learn about the major issues that complicate cross-country research. We also suggest ways to cope with these roadblocks. We then describe several techniques that are useful for market demand assessment. Next we discuss how the Internet can support global market research studies. During the last two decades new market information technologies have emerged. We discuss the impact of these technological advances on marketing research. Finally, we consider several issues that concern the management of global market research.

---

## RESEARCH PROBLEM FORMULATION       ◆ ◆ ◆ ◆ ◆ ◆ ◆

Any research begins with a precise definition of the research problem(s) to be addressed. The cliché of a well-defined problem being a half-solved problem definitely applies in a global setting. Fancy data-analytical tools will not compensate for wrong problem definitions. Once the nature of the research problem becomes clear, the research problem needs to be translated in specific research questions. The scope of market research questions extends to both strategic and tactical marketing decisions. For example, a product positioning study carried out for BMW in the European market centered on the following three issues:

1. What does the motorist in the country concerned, demand of his/her car?
2. What does s/he believe s/he is getting from various brands?
3. What does that imply with regard to positioning the BMW brand across borders?[8]

In an international context, the marketing research problem formulation is hindered by the self-reference criterion, that is, people's habit to fall back on their own cultural norms and values (see Chapter 4). This tendency could lead to wrong or narrow problem definitions. In a multicountry research process, the self-reference criterion also makes finding a consensus between headquarters and local staff an immensely formidable task. To avoid such mishaps, market researchers must try to view the research problem from the cultural perspective of the foreign players and isolate the influence of the self-reference criterion. At any rate, local subsidiaries should be consulted at every step of the research process if the study will affect their operations, including the first step of the problem definition.

A major difficulty in formulating the research problem is the lack of familiarity with the foreign environment. This may lead to making false assumptions, misdefining the research problem(s), and, ultimately, misleading conclusions about the foreign market(s). To reduce part of the uncertainty, some exploratory research at the early stage of the research process is often very fruitful. A useful vehicle for such preliminary research is an **omnibus survey**.[9] Omnibus surveys are regularly scheduled surveys that are conducted by research agencies (e.g., ACNielsen) with questions from multiple clients. The surveys are administered to a very large sample of consumers, usually a panel created by the agency. The questionnaire contains a plethora of questions on a variety of topics. Each research client can include one or more questions in the survey while sharing demographic information about respondents with the other clients. The

---

[8]Horst Kern, Hans-Christian Wagner, and Roswitha Hassis, "European Aspects of a Global Brand: The BMW Case," *Marketing and Research Today*, February 1990, pp. 47–57.
[9]David A. Aaker, V. Kumar, and George S. Day, *Marketing Research* (New York: John Wiley & Sons, Inc., 1998), p. 237.

prime benefit of an omnibus survey is its cost, as the subscribers to the survey share the expenses. Surveys are typically priced on a per-question basis. Another selling point is speed; results are quickly available, sometimes within a week when the omnibus is run on a weekly basis. A major disadvantage is that only a limited amount of company-relevant information is obtainable through an omnibus. Also, the panel is not always representative of the firm's target market profile although the client can sometimes select from a target market rather than sample from all respondents.

Still, an omnibus survey is probably the most economical way to gather preliminary information on target markets. An omnibus is particularly suitable when you need to ask a few simple questions across a large sample of respondents. Findings from an omnibus can assist managers and researchers in fine-tuning the research problem(s) to be tackled. An omnibus is also an option to gauge the market potential for your product in the foreign market when you have only a limited budget. Omnibuses conducted on a regular basis can also be useful as a tracking tool to spot changes in consumer attitudes or behaviors. **Exhibit 6-3** presents the key features of ACNielsen's China omnibus.

Once the research issues have been stated, management needs to determine the information needs. Some of the information will be readily available within the company or in publicly available sources. Other information will need to be collected from scratch.

### EXHIBIT 6-3
ACNIELSEN CHINA OMNIBUS

**Geographical Coverage:**
  (a) Key cities: Guangzhou, Shanghai, Beijing
  (b) 7 other cities: Chengdu, Fuzhou, Hangzhou, Nanjing, Shenyang, Tianjin, Wuhan

**Timing:**
  Four rounds

**Sample Size:**
  500 interviews in each city

**Sampling Procedure:**
  Random probability sampling with face-to-face interviews

**Deliverables:**
  — Self-explanatory charts and computer tables.
  — Demographics (including, gender, age, education, marital data, household size, household purchase decision maker, household head, occupation, nature of work unit, monthly household income) tabulated against proprietary questions.

**Examples of Omnibus Questions:**
  — Do you use X?
  — How often do you use X?
  — What do you like/dislike about X?
  — How much did you pay for X?
  — Have you seen any ad for Y?

**Cost:**
Total cost depends on:

  (a) Number of questions
  (b) Nature of question: open-ended versus close-ended
  (c) Sample size
  (d) Number of cities

Fee per person is USD1.00 or less (sample size) with setup cost of USD2,000 for any project under USD10,000. For instance, a project covering two cities and a sample size of 1,000 subjects will cost USD3,000.

*Source:* Based on information provided by ACNielsen (China).

# SECONDARY GLOBAL MARKETING RESEARCH    ◆ ◆ ◆ ◆ ◆ ◆ ◆

Assessing the information needs is the next step after the research problem definition. Some pieces of information will already be available. That type of information is referred to as **secondary data**. When the information is not useful, or simply does not exist, the firm will need to collect the data. **Primary data** are data collected specifically for the purpose of the research study. Researchers will first explore secondary data resources, since that kind of information is usually much cheaper and less time consuming to gather than primary data. Both forms of data collection entail numerous issues in an international marketing setting. We first discuss the major problems concerning secondary data research.

Market researchers in developed countries have access to a wealth of data that are gathered by government and private agencies. Unfortunately, the equivalents of such databases often are missing outside the developed world. Even when the information is available, it may be hard to track down. A starting point for data collection is the internet or a computerized service such as Lexis/Nexis (http://www.lexisnexis.com) that provides real-time online access to information resources based on user-provided keywords. **Exhibit 6-4** shows the wide variety of secondary data resources that are available to

**Secondary Data Sources**

## EXHIBIT 6-4
### RESOURCES FOR SECONDARY DATA

**International Trade**
- *Yearbook of International Trade Statistics* (United Nations)
- *US Imports* (U.S. Bureau of the Census)
- *US Exports* (U.S. Bureau of the Census)
- *Exporters' Encyclopaedia* (Dun and Bradstreet)

**Country Information (Socioeconomic & Political Conditions)**
- *Yearbook of Industrial Statistics* (United Nations)
- *Statistical Yearbook* (United Nations; Updated by *Monthly Bulletin of Statistics*)
- *OECD Economic Survey*
- *The World Competitiveness Yearbook* (IMD)
- *Country Reports* (The Economist Intelligence Unit)
- *Demographic Yearbook* (United Nations)
- *Statistical Yearbook* (United Nations)
- *UNESCO Statistical Yearbook*
- *CIA World Fact Book* (www.cia.gov/cia/publications/factbook)
- www.countrydata.com (PRS Group)

**International Marketing**
- Euromonitor publications (www.euromonitor.com): *European Marketing Data and Statistics*, *International Marketing Data and Statistics*, *Consumer Europe*, and *European Advertising Marketing and Media Data*
- *Advertising Age* (www.adage.com)
- *FINDEX: The Worldwide Directory of Market Research Reports, Studies & Surveys* (Cambridge Information Group Directories)

**Chambers of Commerce**
- www.worldchambers.com/chambers.html

**Directories of Foreign Firms**
- *D & B Europa* (Dun & Bradstreet)
- *Directory of American Firms Operating in Foreign Countries* (World Trade Academy Press)
- *Directory of Foreign Firms Operating in the United States* (World Trade Academy Press)
- *Europe's 15,000 Largest Companies* (E L C Publishing)
- *International Directory of Importers: Europe* (Interdata)
- *Mailing Lists of Worldwide Importing Firms* (Interdata)
- *Moody's International Manual* (Moody's Investors Service)
- *Principal International Businesses; The World Marketing Directory* (Dun & Bradstreet)

global market researchers. Also, a wealth of international business resources can be accessed via the internet. One of the most comprehensive resources is the National Trade Data Bank (NTDB), maintained by the U.S. Department of Commerce (http://www.stat-usa.gov).[10] The NTDB includes market research reports, information on export opportunities, how-to-market guides, and so forth. One of the nice features is a search engine that allows users to retrieve any information that is available on the NTDB for a given topic. Another very valuable online resource for global business intelligence is global-EDGE (http://globaledge.msu.edu) created by the International Business Center at Michigan State University. This resource is an extremely well-organized directory that provides linkages to hundreds of online international business resources on the internet.

Obviously, researchers can also tap information resources available within the company. Many companies have their own libraries that provide valuable data sources. Large companies typically compile enormous databanks on their operations. Government publications sometimes offer information on overseas markets. In the United States, the U.S. Department of Commerce offers detailed country reports and industry surveys. Many countries have a network of government sponsored commercial delegations (e.g., Chambers of Commerce, the Japanese External Trade Organization[11] — www.jetro.go.jp). These agencies will often provide valuable information to firms that desire to do business in their country, despite the fact that the main charter of most of these agencies is to assist homegrown companies in the foreign market.

Besides government offices, international agencies such as the World Bank, the Organization for Economic Cooperation and Development (OECD), the International Monetary Fund (IMF), and the United Nations gather a humongous amount of data. Reports published by these organizations are especially useful for demographic and economic information. Given that most of these documents report information across multiple years, their data can be used to examine trends in socioeconomic indicators. Unfortunately, reports published by such international agencies cover only their member states.

Several companies specialize in producing business-related information. Such information is usually far more expensive than government-based data. However, this sort of information often has more direct relevance for companies. Two prominent examples are The Economist Intelligence Unit (E.I.U.) and Euromonitor. Some of the most useful resources put together by the E.I.U. (http://www.eiu.com) are the country reports that appear on a quarterly basis. These country reports give a detailed update on the major political and economic trends in the countries covered. Euromonitor publishes several reports that are extremely useful to global marketers. Two well-known reports are the *European Marketing Data and Statistics* and *International Marketing Data and Statistics*, annual volumes covering Europe and the global market-place outside Europe, respectively. Euromonitor's databases are also accessible online on a subscription basis (www.euromonitor.com).

Another form of secondary data sources are syndicated datasets sold by market research companies such as ACNielsen (www.acnielsen.com) and Taylor Nelson Sofres (www.tns-global.com). These firms acquire datasets that cover purchase transactions from retail outlets whose cash registers are equipped with optical scanning equipment. Until about a decade ago, such data sources were only available in the United States. Optical scanners are now well entrenched in most Western countries. Both giants in the syndicated data business, ACNielsen and Taylor Nelson Sofres, have a major international presence now.

As firms move from government publications to syndicated data, the richness of the information increases enormously. At the same time, the cost of collecting and processing data goes up. Just as in a domestic marketing context, firms planning research in the global marketplace have to decide on the value added of additional information and make the appropriate trade-offs.

---

[10] The National Trade Data Bank information is also available on CD-ROM.

[11] JETRO.

In the global market scene, some of the information sought by market researchers does not exist. When data are missing, the researcher needs to infer the data by using proxy variables or values from previous periods. Even if the datasets are complete, the researcher will usually encounter many problems:

***Accuracy of Data.*** The accuracy of secondary data is often questionable, for various reasons. The definition used for certain indicators often differs across countries. The quality of information may also be compromised by the mechanisms that were used to collect it. Most developed countries use sophisticated procedures to assemble data. Due to the lack of resources and skills, many developing countries have to rely on rather primitive mechanisms to collect data. The purpose for which the data were collected could affect their accuracy. International trade statistics do not cover cross-border smuggling activities. Such transactions are, in some cases, far more significant than legitimate trade.

***Age of Data.*** The desired information may be available but outdated. Many countries collect economic activity information on a far less frequent basis than the United States. The frequency of census-taking also varies from country to country. In many developed countries (e.g., Italy, Spain, Poland, United States) a census is carried out every ten years. In many emerging markets, census-taking seldom takes place. In Saudi Arabia, for instance, the census has been taken only four times since the foundation of the kingdom. Lebanon has not conducted a census since 1932.

***Reliability over Time.*** Often companies are interested in historical patterns of certain variables to spot underlying trends. Such trends might indicate whether a market opportunity opens up or whether a market is becoming saturated. To track trends, the researcher has to know to what degree the data are measured consistently over time. Sudden changes in the definition of economic indicators are not uncommon. Juggling with economic variable measures is especially likely for variables that have political ramifications, such as unemployment and inflation statistics. For instance, government authorities may adjust the basket of goods used to measure inflation to produce more favorable numbers. One notable example is Argentina. In June 2008, the country's monetary policymakers introduced a new consumer price index to doctor the official inflation rate. According to the new inflation measurement procedure, a product is removed from the index when its price rises too sharply.[12] Market researchers should be aware of such practices and, if necessary, make the appropriate corrections.

***Comparability of Data.*** Cross-country research often demands a comparison of indicators across countries. Different sources on a given item often produce contradictory information. The issue then is how to reconcile these differences. One way to handle contradictory information is to **triangulate**, that is, to obtain information on the same item from at least three different sources and speculate on possible reasons behind these differences.[13] For instance, suppose you want to collect information on the import penetration of wine as a percentage of total consumption in various European countries. Triangulation might show that some of the figures you collected are based on value, while others are based on volume. It might also reveal that some sources include champagne but others do not.

Comparability can also be hindered by the lack of **functional** or **conceptual** **equivalence**.[14] **Functional equivalence** refers to the degree to which similar activities

[12]"Hocus-pocus," *The Economist*, http://www.economist.com, June 12, 2008.

[13]S.C. Williams, "Researching Markets in Japan – A Methodological Case Study," *Journal of International Marketing*, 4, no. 2, 1996, pp. 87–93.

[14]Michael R. Mullen, "Diagnosing Measurement Equivalence in Cross-National Research," *Journal of International Business Studies*, 26 (3), 1995, pp. 573–596.

or products in different countries fulfill similar functions. Many products perform very different functions in different markets. In the United States bicycles are used primarily for leisure. In countries such as the Netherlands and China, bicycles are a major means of transportation. Absence of conceptual equivalence is another factor that undermines comparability. **Conceptual equivalence** reflects the degree to which a given concept has the same meaning in different environments. Many concepts have totally different meanings or may simply not exist in certain countries. The concept of "equal rights" for women is unfamiliar in many Muslim societies. Likewise, the notion of "intellectual property" is often hard to grasp in some cultures. Often, what one culture sees as obvious the other does not.

The comparison of money-based indicators (e.g., income figures, consumer expenditures, international trade statistics) is hampered by the need to convert such figures into a common currency. The key issues are what currency to use and at what exchange rate (beginning of the year, year-end, or year-average). A further complication is that exchange rates do not always reflect the relative buying power between countries. As a result, comparing economic indicators using market exchange rates can be very misleading.

***Lumping of Data.*** Official data sources often group statistics on certain variables in very broad categories. This compromises the usefulness and the interpretation of such data for international market researchers. Managers should check what is included in certain categories.[15]

Given the hurdles posed by secondary data, it is important to verify the quality of collected information. To assess the quality of data, the researcher should seek answers to the following checklist:

1. When were the data collected? Over what time frame?
2. How were the data collected?
3. Have the variables been redefined over time?
4. Who collected the data?
5. For what purpose were the data gathered?

Of course, satisfactory answers to any of these questions may not ensure total peace of mind. Researchers and managers should always be on guard regarding the quality of secondary data.

---

## ◆ ◆ ◆ ◆ ◆ ◆ ◆ ◆  PRIMARY GLOBAL MARKETING RESEARCH

Seldom do secondary data prove sufficient for international market research studies. The next step in the research process is to collect primary data specifically for the purpose of the research project. Primary data can be collected in several ways: (1) focus groups, (2) survey research, (3) observational research, and (4) test markets. In this section we will concentrate the first three approaches. The last one, test marketing, is discussed in Chapter 11 on global new product development. Global Perspective 6-1 shows the important role of primary market research for multinational companies like L'Oréal.

**Focus Groups**     Before embarking on large-scale quantitative market research projects, most firms will conduct exploratory research. One of the most popular tools at this stage is the focus group. A **focus group** is a loosely structured free-flowing discussion among a small group (eight to twelve people) of target customers facilitated by a professional moderator. Focus groups can be used for many different purposes: to generate

---

[15]S.C. Williams, "Researching Markets in Japan," p. 90.

## $\mathcal{G}$LOBAL PERSPECTIVE 6-1

### GLOBAL MARKET RESEARCH IN THE WORLD OF BEAUTY

Research is an essential weapon in the global cosmetics and grooming market, worth around $231 billion in 2005. L'Oréal, a leading French cosmetics maker, spent €507 million ($608 million) on research in 2005, more than 3 percent of its sales revenues. The company has a network of 14 research centers spanning the globe. In 2003, the company opened a multi-million dollar R&D lab in Chicago. The Chicago facility boasts being the first lab that focuses on the beauty needs of people of color.

Differences clearly exist in the world of beauty. In Japan, women apply mascara with an average of one hundred brush strokes, compared to fifty strokes for European women. South Korean women use no less than 9 to 12 products for their morning grooming routine. In France, L'Oréal researchers created an "atlas for the human hair" based on a study of the hair of test subjects from the Paris region and Chinese cities. Differences between ethnic groups were found in hair-growth rates, development of grayness, and hair density.

*Sources:* www.loreal.com, accessed February 18, 2006; "The World of Beauty: Skin Deep, But So Very Personal," *International Herald Tribune* (February 4–5, 2006): 13–14; "Battle for the Face of China," *Fortune* (December 12, 2005): 156–62.

China is one of L'Oréal's strategically most critical markets. L'Oréal translates its name into Putongua as "Olayia" meaning "elegance from Europe." Thirty percent of its products are adapted for the China market. Sales in China generated revenue of around $240m in 2004. In 2005 L'Oréal opened an R&D center in Shanghai. The facility occupies a 32,000 square-foot (about 3,200 square-meter) area in Pudong, Shanghai's industrial center, and is stocked with pigments, oils, and waxes. Microscopes and chromometers measure the effectiveness of skin-whitening creams. Two-way mirrors allow researchers to observe the way Chinese women apply makeup. The lab also tests the effectiveness of Chinese herbs, roots, and flowers for the skin and hair.

Each year, L'Oréal interviews 35,000 women in China to learn about their tastes. Its researchers discovered a Shanghai woman whose hair is four meters (13 feet) long. The subject is now under contract as a test case to study the impact of aging on hair fiber. L'Oréal researchers also make house calls to get a picture of Chinese women's grooming habits. From these home visits, L'Oréal found out that many Chinese wash themselves and shampoo over a bowl of water to conserve water in places with water supply shortages. Spurred by this finding, L'Oréal developed a new shampoo that allows easy suds rinsing.

---

information to guide the quantitative research projects, to uncover new product opportunities, to test out new product concepts, and so forth.[16] Early 2008 focus groups in Stockholm, Tokyo, Zürich, and London were introduced to and asked to comment on digital Sony e-readers and prototype color e-paper displays, less than a millimeter thick. The global focus group test allowed newspaper publishers to identify common drivers and barriers in consumer expectations as well as regional differences.[17]

The rules for designing and running focus groups in a domestic marketing setting, apply to global market research projects as well.[18] Hiring well-trained moderators is critical in conducting focus groups for international market research. Moderators should be familiar with the local language and social interaction patterns. In some countries the focus group moderator should be of the same gender as the participants. Cultural sensitivity is an absolute must with focus groups. Japanese consumers tend to be much more hesitant to criticize new product ideas than their Western counterparts.[19] Also, many Asian societies like Japan are highly collective ("Confucian"). Strangers outside the group are excluded. As a result, getting the desired group dynamics for

---

[16]One of the authors recently participated in a focus group for Cathay Pacific, a Hong Kong based airline. The focus group discussion covered topics such as the launch of a new lounge, Cathay's website, and its in-flight magazine.

[17]http://www.biz-community.com/Article/196/16/25598.html, accessed on January 19, 2009.

[18]See, for example, Thomas C. Kinnear and James R. Taylor, *Marketing Research*, New York, NY: McGraw-Hill, Inc., 1996, Chapter 10.

[19]David B. Montgomery, "Understanding the Japanese as customers, competitors, and collaborators," *Japan and the World Economy*, vol. 3, no. 1, 1991, pp. 61–91.

focus groups within such cultures is often very hard. To stimulate group dynamics, the following steps should be taken:[20]

- Be precise in recruitment to ensure group homogeneity and ease of bonding.
- Hire moderators who are able to develop group dynamics quickly through warm-ups, humor, group-playing.
- Hire moderators who can spot and challenge "consensus"-claimed behaviors and attitudes.

When analyzing and interpreting focus group findings, market researchers should also concentrate on the nonverbal cues (e.g., gestures, voice intonations).[21] Information provided by these nonverbal cues is often as important as the verbal content of the focus groups.

## Survey Methods for Cross-Cultural Marketing Research

Questionnaires are the most common vehicle to gather primary data in marketing research. Survey research begins with the design of a questionnaire. The next step is to develop a sampling plan to collect the data. Once these two tasks have been accomplished, the researcher moves to the next phase, the physical collection of information to the questionnaires. Each stage may lead to major headaches.

### Questionnaire Design.

By far the most popular instrument to gather primary data is the questionnaire. Preparing questionnaires for global market research poses tremendous challenges. As in domestic marketing, care should be exercised with the wording and the sequencing of the questions. With multicountry projects, further care is needed to assure comparability of survey-based results across frontiers. Measurement issues in cross-country research center around this question: "Are the phenomena in countries A and B measured in the same way?" Absence of measurement equivalence will render cross-country comparisons meaningless. Earlier we discussed the need for conceptual and functional equivalence of secondary data. The same requirements apply to primary data in order to avoid cultural biases. Cross-country survey research needs to fulfill two further criteria: **translation** and **scalar equivalence**.

The first aspect deals with the translation of the instrument from one language into another one. Cross-cultural research, even within the same country or parent language (e.g., English, Spanish), demands adequate translations from the master questionnaire into other languages. Careless translations of questionnaires can lead to embarrassing mistakes. Good translations are hard to accomplish. Several methods exist to minimize translation errors. Two procedures often used to avoid sloppy translations are back-translation and parallel translation. **Back-translation** is a two-phase process. Suppose a company wants to translate a questionnaire from English into Arab. In the first step, the master questionnaire is translated into Arab by a (bilingual) translator whose native language is Arab, the target language. In the second stage, another bilingual interpreter whose native language is English, the base language, translates the Arab version back into English. This version is then compared with the original survey to uncover any bugs or translation errors. The process is repeated until an acceptable degree of convergence is achieved. **Parallel translation** consists of using multiple interpreters who translate the same questionnaire independently. A committee of translators compares alternative versions and differences are reconciled.

Most surveys typically have a battery of questions or "Agree/Disagree" statements with a scale (e.g., 7-point) to record responses. To make the findings of cross-country market research projects meaningful, it is paramount to pursue **scalar equivalence**:

---

[20]Chris Robinson, "Asian culture: the marketing consequences," *Journal of the Market Research Society*, 38, no. 1, 1996, pp. 55–62.

[21]Naresh K. Malhotra, James Agarwal, and Mark Peterson, "Methodological issues in cross-cultural marketing research. A state-of-the-art review," *International Marketing Review*, 13, no. 5, 1996, pp. 7–43.

scores from subjects of different countries should have the same meaning and interpretation.[22] The standard format of scales used in survey research differs across countries. Keep in mind that high scores in one country are not necessarily high scores elsewhere. Latin Americans, for example, tend to use the high end of the scale. An unenthusiastic respondent may still give your company a "7" or an "8" score. Asians, on the other hand, tend to use the middle of the scale.[23]

In some cases, you may also need to adjust the anchors of the scale. One market research study that measured attitudes of Japanese managers adopted scales that included "definitely true," "somewhat true," and "not all true." A pre-test of the survey showed that the Japanese respondents had trouble with the concept of "agree/disagree."[24] To make cross-country comparisons meaningful, it is advisable to adjust responses in each country by, for instance, taking deviations from country-averages on any given question. By the same token, in some societies people are cued to view "1" as best and the other endpoint of the scale as worst, while in others "1" is considered the worst, regardless of how the scale is designated.

Survey research in developing nations is further compounded by low levels of education. Specially designed visual scales like the Funny Faces scale (see **Exhibit 6-5**) are sometimes used to cope with illiteracy. In developing countries, market researchers should also try to reduce the verbal content and use visual aids. In countries that are unfamiliar with survey research, it is advisable to avoid lengthy questionnaires or open-ended questions.[25]

Regardless of whether the survey is to be administered in Paris, Texas, or Paris, France, it is absolutely imperative to pre-test the questionnaire. Pre-testing is the only foolproof way to debug the questionnaire and spot embarrassing, and often expensive, mistakes. Speed is often critical when collecting data. However, rushing into the field without a thorough pre-test of the questionnaire is a highly risky endeavor.

***Sampling Plan.*** To collect data, the researcher has to draw a sample from the target population. A sampling plan basically centers around three issues:[26]

1. Who should be surveyed? What is our target population (**sampling unit**)?

2. How many people should be surveyed (**sample size**)?

3. How should prospective respondents be chosen from the target population (**sampling procedure**)?

Decisions on each of these issues will be driven by balancing costs, desired reliability, and time requirements. In multicountry research, firms also need to decide what countries should be researched. There are two broad approaches. The first approach starts off with a large-scale exploratory research project covering many countries. This step might take the form of an omnibus survey. The alternative approach focuses on a few key countries. To choose these countries, a firm might group countries (e.g., along sociocultural indicators) and pick one or two representative members from each cluster. Depending on the findings coming from this first pool of countries, the research process is extended to cover other countries of interest.

The preparation of a sampling plan for multicountry research is often a daunting task. When drawing a sample, the researcher needs a sampling frame, that is, a listing of the target population (e.g., a telephone directory). In many countries, such listings simply do not exist or may be very inadequate. The proportion of individuals meeting

**EXHIBIT 6-5**
THE FUNNY FACES SCALE

Very happy

Happy

Not happy but also not unhappy

Unhappy

Very unhappy

*Source:* C.K. Corder, "Problems and Pit-falls in Conducting Marketing Research in Africa," in Betsy Gelb, ed., *Marketing Expansion in a Shrinking World.* Proceedings of American Marketing Association Business Conference (Chicago: AMA, 1978), pp. 86–90.

---

[22]Naresh K. Malhotra, James Agarwal, and Mark Peterson, "Methodological issues in cross-cultural marketing research. A state-of-the-art review," *International Marketing Review*, p. 15.

[23]Jennifer Mitchell, "Reaching across borders," *Marketing News* (May 10, 1999), p. 19.

[24]Jean L. Johnson, Tomoaki Sakano, Joseph A. Cote, and Naoto Onzo, "The Exercise of Interfirm Power and Its Repercussions in U.S.-Japanese Channel Relationships," *Journal of Marketing*, vol. 57, no. 2, April 1993, pp. 1–10.

[25]Kaynak Erderer, *Marketing in the Third World*, New York: Praeger, 1982, Chapter 4.

[26]See, for example, Naresh K. Malhotra, *Marketing Research. An Applied Orientation*, Englewood-Cliffs, NJ: Prentice Hall, 1993, Chapter 13.

the criteria of the target population could vary considerably. This forces the researcher to be flexible with the sampling methods employed in different countries.[27]

Computing the desired sample size in cross-country market research often becomes at best guesswork because the necessary pieces of information are missing. Desired sample sizes may also vary across cultures. Typically, heterogeneous cultures (e.g., India) demand bigger samples than homogeneous cultures (e.g., South Korea, Thailand).[28] This is due to the fact that diverse cultures typically have much more variance in the traits to be measured than homogeneous ones.

Most researchers prefer some form of probabilistic sampling that enables them to make statistical inferences about the collected data. The absence of sampling frames and various cultural hurdles (e.g., inapproachability of women in Muslim societies) make a non-probabilistic sampling procedure such as convenience sampling, the only alternative, especially in developing countries.

***Contact Method.*** After preparing a sampling plan, you need to decide how to contact prospective subjects for the survey. The most common choices are mail, telephone, or person-to-person interviews (e.g., shopping mall intercepts). These days the internet has also become a viable alternative. Several factors explain why some methods prevail in some countries and are barely used elsewhere. Cultural norms often rule out certain data collection methods. Germans tend to show greater resistance to telephone interviewing than other Europeans.[29] In several countries, landline phones are in decline. In Finland, for instance, about 50 percent of the homes are mobile phone only.[30] Daytime phone calls will not work in Saudi Arabia, since social norms dictate that housewives do not respond to calls from strangers.[31] Cost differentials will also make some methods preferable over others. **Exhibit 6-6** shows a market research cost

**EXHIBIT 6-6**
ESOMAR 2007 MARKET RESEARCH
PRICE STUDY

| Rank | Country | Index |
|------|---------|-------|
| 1 | Ireland | 224 |
| 2 | USA | 220 |
| 3 | France | 204 |
| 4 | UK | 202 |
| 5 | Belgium | 185 |
| 6 | Germany | 181 |
| 7 | Switzerland | 179 |
| 8 | Japan | 176 |
| 9 | Finland | 173 |
| 10 | Sweden | 170 |
| 54 | Peru | 59 |
| 55 | Cyprus | 58 |
| 56 | Ecuador | 57 |
| 56 | Ukraine | 57 |
| 58 | Egypt | 56 |
| 59 | Panama | 54 |
| 60 | Guatemala | 52 |
| 61 | Bulgaria | 46 |
| 62 | Macedonia | 41 |
| 63 | Pakistan | 35 |

*Source:* Compiled from data presented at http://www.b2binternational.com/b2b-blog/2007/11/15/market-research-prices-a-global-comparison-part-i/

---

[27]D. N. Aldridge, "Multicountry Research," in *Applied Marketing and Social Research*, U. Bradley, Ed., 2nd Edition, New York: John Wiley, 1987, pp. 364–65.

[28]N. K. Malhotra, et al., "Methodological issues," p. 27.

[29]D. N. Aldridge, "Multicountry Research," p. 365.

[30]http://www.b2binternational.com/b2b-blog/2007/11/15/market-research-prices-a-global-comparison-part-i/, accessed January 16, 2009.

[31]Secil Tuncalp, "The Marketing Research Scene in Saudi Arabia," p. 19.

comparison based on a survey conducted by ESOMAR in 2007. The index is a composite score that was calculated using a representative quantitative and qualitative study, where an index value of 100 represents the midpoint. Note that a market research project done in the United States is more than six times as expensive as a similar study conducted in Pakistan.

In many emerging markets, the lack of a well-developed marketing research infrastructure is a major hurdle to conduct market research studies. Lack of decent phone service in many emerging countries creates a challenge for phone surveys. Using the internet to collect questionnaire data can also be hindered due to the lack of internet access or low levels of technological literacy. In the wake of cost differences and various obstacles, researchers are often forced to use multiple data collection modes to conduct a global research project.

***Collect the Information.*** Once the design of your questionnaire and your sampling plan are completed, you need to collect the data in the field. This field will be covered with "landmines," some of them fairly visible, others invisible. Primary data collection may be hindered by respondent- and/or interviewer-related biases.

Probably the most severe problem is nonresponse due to a reluctance to talk with strangers, fears about confidentiality, or other cultural biases. In many cultures, the only way to cope with nonresponse is to account for it when determining sample sizes. In China, surveys that are sanctioned by the local authorities will lead to a higher response rate.[32]

**Courtesy bias** refers to a desire to be polite towards the other person. This bias is fairly common in Asia and the Middle East.[33] The subject feels obliged to give responses that hopefully will please the interviewer. Another snag in survey research are biases towards **yea-** or **nay-saying**. In some countries, responses may reflect a **social desirability bias** where the subject attempts to impress the interviewer or reflect a certain social status in his responses. Topics such as income or sex are simply taboo in some regions. Unfortunately, there are no magic bullets to handle these and other biases. Measures such as careful wording and thorough pre-testing of the survey and adequate training of the interviewer, will minimize the incidence of such biases. In some cases, it is worthwhile to incorporate questions that measure tendencies such as social desirability. Another option for handling cultural biases is to transform the data first before analyzing them. For instance, one common practice is to convert response ratings or scores to questions into rankings.

House-to-house or shopping mall survey responses could also be scrambled by interviewer related biases. Availability of skilled interviewers can be a major bottleneck in cross-country research, especially in emerging markets. Lack of supervision or low salaries will tempt interviewers in some countries to cut corners by filling out surveys themselves or ignoring the proper sampling procedure. In many cultures, it is advisable to match interviewers to interviewees. Disparities in cultural backgrounds may lead to misunderstandings.[34] In some societies (e.g., Latin America), local people regard survey-takers with suspicion.[35] Obviously, adequate recruiting, training and supervision of interviewers will lessen interviewer-related biases in survey research. In countries where survey research is still in an early stage and researchers have little expertise, questionnaires should not be overly complex.[36] When developing a survey instrument like a questionnaire for a global market research project, it is also helpful to have **redundancy**: Ask the same question in different ways and in various parts of the questionnaire. That way, the researcher can crosscheck the validity of the responses.[37]

[32]Henry C. Steele, "Marketing Research in China," p. 160.

[33]Erdener Kaynak, *Marketing in the Third World*, p. 171.

[34]D. N. Aldridge, "Multicountry Research," p. 371.

[35]S. P. Douglas and C. S. Craig, *International Marketing Research*, p. 227.

[36]J. Stafford and N. Upmeyer, "Product Shortages," p. 40.

[37]Naghi Namakforoosh, "Data collection methods hold key to research in Mexico," *Marketing News*, Aug. 29, 1994, p. 28.

## 𝒢LOBAL PERSPECTIVE 6-2

### NOKIA'S USE OF ETHNOGRAPHIC RESEARCH

Nokia Design is a group of 250 people (psychologists, industrial designers, anthropologists) worldwide that uses human-behavioral research to get insights useful for the design of new mobile phones. Research questions may focus on current behaviors (e.g., "how are early adopters of mobile TV using mobile TV?") or areas where growth is likely in the medium- or long-term.

The process starts with a team of anthropologists and psychologists. These researchers will spend time with local people to better understand how they behave and communicate. Insights gathered from ethnographic research assist Nokia in spotting new behavior patterns and can then be brought into the design process. Nokia also has an advanced design team that looks five to fifteen years out, trying to predict mega-trends in society.

One study looked into how people share objects. For the study, Nokia picked two cultures, Indonesia and Uganda. For

*Sources:* "Nokia's Global Design Sense," http://www.businessweek.com/print/innovate/content/aug2007/id20070810_686743.htm, accessed July 31, 2008 and ""Nokia's Design Research for Everyone," http://www.businessweek.com/innovate/content/mar2007/id20070314_689707.htm?chan=search, accessed July 31, 2008.

the Uganda project, Nokia's researchers wanted to spend time in the capital Kampala, in a remote fishing village, and in villages with no mobile connectivity. The study typically lasted ten to twelve days with a research team that included two or three Nokia people, one or two local guides, and up to six local university students. At each site, Nokia's researchers observed and interviewed around thirty local people.

One surprising finding that emerged from Nokia's research in emerging markets is the challenge of the basic assumption that a mobile phone is owned and used by a single person. Due to the cost barrier, mobile phones in emerging market communities are often shared. As a result, Nokia designed phones (Nokia 1200 and Nokia 1208) with shared use as the top priority. The phones include a shared address book so that users can save their own contacts separately from others and a call tracker that allows people to preset a time or cost limit on each call. Other features include a keypad to protect the phone from dust, a special grip to cope with hot weather conditions, a one-touch flashlight (in case of power outages), and a demo mode to quickly learn how to use a phone.

---

**Observational Research**    Besides traditional survey research methods companies also increasingly rely on less conventional observation-based methods such as **ethnographic research**. With this research approach, field workers (usually cultural anthropologists) embed themselves in the local communities that they are studying. The basic notion is to gather useful information by participating in the everyday life of the people being studied. Part of the data collection exercise often involves videotaping participating consumers in purchase or consumption settings. Techniques such as picture completion or collages are often useful when studying the behavior or feelings of young children.[38]**Global Perspective 6-2** describes how Nokia uses ethnographic research studies to design new mobile phones.

---

## ◆◆◆◆◆◆◆◆ LEVERAGING THE INTERNET FOR GLOBAL MARKET RESEARCH STUDIES

The internet has opened up new avenues for gathering market intelligence about consumers and competitors worldwide. It is without doubt one of the richest and least expensive resources of secondary data available. One shortcoming is the sheer wealth of data that has led to an embarrassment of riches: How does one separate out the useful from the useless information? Where can one find the most reliable information? Advances in search-engine technology will hopefully provide ample solutions.

In terms of primary research, the internet has created stunning possibilities. The lower cost of online survey is clearly a major driver behind the rise of online global market research. ESOMAR's 2007 global market research cost study found that online research

---

[38]C. Samuel Craig and Susan P. Douglas, "Conducting International Marketing Research in the 21st Century," *International Marketing Review* 18, No. 1 (2001): 80–90.

**EXHIBIT 6-7**
PROS AND CONS OF THE INTERNET AS A TOOL FOR GLOBAL
MARKETING RESEARCH

**Pros:**

- Large samples are possible in small amount of time.
- Global access of the internet.
- Cost—in most cases, on-line surveys can be done much more cheaply than using other methods—also costs are largely scale-independent in the sense that large scale surveys do not demand far bigger resources than small surveys
- Anonymity—can be helpful for sensitive topics.
- Data analysis—data can be directly loaded into statistical tools and databases, saving time and resources.
- Short response times.

**Cons:**

- Infrastructure—in many countries, access to the internet is still fairly limited.
- Sample representativeness—for random website surveys and e-mail surveys, representativeness can be a major issue. Likewise, there is also the risk of a self-selection bias.
- Time necessary to download pages (for website surveys)
- Technological problems such as incorrect e-mail addresses, poor connections.
- Low response rates—response rates can be fairly low; respondents may quit halfway.
- Multiple responses from same respondent.

*Sources:* Jonathan Dodd, "Market research on the Internet—threat or opportunity?" *Marketing and Research Today* (February 1998), pp. 60–67; Cheryl Harris, "Developing online market research methods and tools—Considering theorizing interactivity: models and cases," *Marketing and Research Today* (November 1997), pp. 267–73; and Janet Ilieva, Steve Baron, and Nigel M. Healey, "Online Surveys in Marketing Research: Pros and Cons," *International Journal of Market Research*, vol. 44 (Quarter 3, 2002), pp. 361–76.

was 33 percent cheaper than phone-based research. The same study also showed that online research costs are still declining in many countries such as Australia, Japan, and the United Kingdom.[39] Another major advantage is that marketers can get instant feedback on new product concepts or advertising concepts. Measurement tools that are especially useful in global market research include the following:

- **Online surveys.** For online survey research, three types of methods exist: (1) e-mail surveys, (2) website surveys, and (3) panel website surveys.[40] E-mail surveys are self-administered questionnaires that are sent as an attachment to e-mails to be completed by the addressee. With random website surveys, visitors to a site are asked to fill out a questionnaire. They are directed to the web page on which the survey is posted. Another variant is the pop-up survey that pops up in a new window while the user is browsing a website. These surveys are useful when the target audience is wide. Panel website surveys rely on a panel of respondents where each panel member has an e-mail address. When eligible for a survey, panel members are contacted via e-mail and asked to complete a survey that is accessible only via a password. The different forms have their advantages and disadvantages. Web-based surveys allow a better display of the questionnaire than an e-mail survey. However, e-mail surveys enable better control over who can participate. **Exhibit 6-7** summarizes the pros and cons of using on-line surveys in international marketing research. In many countries, especially those with low internet penetration, getting adequate sample representativeness of the target population is a major hurdle. To remedy this problem, global market research projects can rely on a multimode approach (e.g., web and phone interview combined with internet surveys).[41] Over time, as technology and internet access improve, the appeal of online surveys is expected to grow.

- **Bulletin boards and chat groups.** Online bulletin boards are virtual corkboards where visitors can post questions, responses, and comments. Chat groups are virtual discussion groups that hold online conversations on a topic of their choice. Companies can monitor and participate in bulletin board and chat group discussions in many countries simultaneously.

---

[39]http://www.b2binternational.com/b2b-blog/2007/11/19/market-research-prices-a-global-comparison-part-ii/, accessed on January 16, 2009.

[40]Jonathan Dodd, "Market research on the Internet—threat or opportunity?" *Marketing and Research Today*, (February 1998), pp. 60–66.

[41]Janet Ilieva, Steve Baron, and Nigel M. Healey, "Online Surveys in Marketing Research: Pros and Cons," *International Journal of Market Research*, 44 (Quarter 3) (2002), pp. 361–76.

- **Web visitor tracking.** Servers automatically collect a tremendous amount of information on the surfing behavior of visitors such as the amount of time spent on each page. Marketers can access and analyze this information to see, for instance, how observed patterns relate to purchase transactions.

- **Online (virtual) panels.** An **online panel** is a group of pre-screened respondents who have voluntarily agreed to participate in various online research studies. Prior to joining the online panel, respondents usually complete fill out a profiling questionnaire that gathers information on their demographics, lifestyles, interests, and so forth. Several global market research companies have set up online panels in scores of countries that can be used to collect data for multicountry market research projects for their clients. One of the largest panels is the Harris Poll Online Panel, which has over six million members from over 125 countries.[42]

- **Focus groups.** An online focus group is set up by selecting participants who meet certain criteria. Subjects are told which chat room to enter and when. They are run like ordinary focus groups. Not only can they be administered worldwide, but transcripts of the group discussions are immediately available.

Although online research can produce high-quality market intelligence, it is important that one is aware of its shortcomings. Sample representativeness could be a major issue when internet users are not representative of the target population as a whole. This is especially a concern in countries where internet access is still low. When a sample is to be drawn, online research could be hampered through incorrect or outdated e-mail addresses.

With some of the research methods described (e.g., website surveys), there could also be a self-selection bias. Website visitors might also fill out the same questionnaire multiple times. It is also difficult to find out whether or not respondents are honest. Identity validation can also be an issue, especially when multiple people use the same e-mail address. Despite these limitations, the internet offers some clear advantages for running international market research projects. **Exhibit 6-8** describes the research methodology used by Durex to conduct its annual global "Sexual Wellbeing" survey online.

**EXHIBIT 6-8**
RESEARCH METHODOLOGY BEHIND THE DUREX "SEXUAL WELLBEING" SURVEY

1. **Timing:** August–September 2006.

2. **Research objectives:** To gain global consumer insight into sexual wellbeing and its importance in overall wellbeing; understanding what makes up sexual wellbeing and the importance of each of its attributes; current levels of satisfaction.

3. **Sample size:** Around 26,000 people in 26 countries (Australia, Austria, Brazil, Canada, China, France, Germany, Greece, Hong Kong, Italy, Japan, India, Malaysia, Mexico, Netherlands, New Zealand, Nigeria, Poland, Russia, Singapore, Spain, South Africa, Switzerland, Thailand, United Kingdom, and the United States).

4. **Contact method:** Online with the assistance of the Harris Interactive market research agency. However, for Nigeria, a face-to-face/self completion approach was used due to low use of internet and telephone in this country.

5. **Sampling approach:** Random samples of participants aged 16+ or 18+ were sent an e-mail invitation. Samples were drawn from Harris Interactive's internet panel.

6. **Questionnaire design:** A literature review was undertaken, followed by a series of workshops in local markets to ensure that the survey was culturally relevant. Once a draft was prepared, a two-phase pilot study was run to make sure respondents understood the questionnaire and found it easy to complete. The final draft was also reviewed by field experts.

*Source:* http://www.durex.com/ en-GB/SexualWellbeingSurvey accessed on August 1, 2008.

---

[42]www.harrisinteractive.com, accessed on January 19, 2009.

## MARKET SIZE ASSESSMENT ◆ ◆ ◆ ◆ ◆ ◆ ◆

When deciding whether to enter a particular country, one of the key drivers is the market potential. In most developed countries, a fairly accurate estimate of the market size for any particular product is easily obtainable. For many frequently purchased consumer goods, information suppliers like ACNielsen are able to give an up-to-date estimate of category volume and market shares based on scanning technology. Such information, however, does not come cheap. Before investing a substantial amount of money, you might consider less costly ways to estimate market demand. For many industries and developing countries, information on market demand is simply not readily available. Under such circumstances, there is a need to come up with a market size estimate, using "simple" ingredients.

Below we introduce four methods that can be fruitfully employed to assess the size of the market for any given product. All of these procedures can be used when very little data are available and/or the quality of the data is dismal, such as is typically the case for many emerging markets. All four methods allow you to make a reasonable guesstimate of the market potential without necessitating intensive data-collection efforts. Market size estimates thus derived prove useful for country selection at the early stage. Countries that do not appear to be viable opportunities are weeded out. After this preliminary screening stage, richer data regarding market size and other indicators are collected for the countries that remain in the pool.

**Method of Analogy**

The first technique, the **analogy method**, starts by picking a country that is at the same stage of economic development as the country of interest and for which the market size is known. The method is based on the premise that the relationship between the demand for a product and a particular indicator, for instance, the demand for a related product, is similar in both countries.

Let us illustrate the method with a brief example. Suppose that a consumer electronics company wants to estimate the market size for DVD players in the Ukraine. For the base country, it picks a neighboring Central European country, say Poland, for which the firm possesses information on the sales of DVD players. It also needs to choose a proxy variable that correlates highly with the demand for DVD players. One reasonable candidate is the number of color televisions in use. So, in this example, we assume that the ratio of DVD-player sales to color TV ownership in the Ukraine and Poland is roughly equivalent:

$$\frac{\text{DVD Player Demand}_{\text{Ukraine}}}{\text{Color TVs in Use}_{\text{Ukraine}}} = \frac{\text{DVD Player Demand}_{\text{Poland}}}{\text{Color TVs in Use}_{\text{Poland}}}$$

Because the company is interested in the demand for DVD players, it can derive an estimate based on the following relationship:

$$\text{DVD Player Demand}_{\text{Ukraine}} = \frac{\text{Color TVs in Use}_{\text{Ukraine}} * \text{DVD Player Demand}_{\text{Poland}}}{\text{Color TVs in Use}_{\text{Poland}}}$$

For this specific example, we collected the following bits of information (2001 figures):

| | Sales | |
|---|---|---|
| | Color TV (000s) | DVD Players (000s) |
| Poland | 14,722.64 | 69.17 |
| Ukraine | 15,626.15 | ??? |

Plugging in those numbers, we get:

$$\text{Estimate DVD Player Demand}_{\text{Ukraine}} \text{ (Annual Retail Sales)}$$

$$= 15,626.15 * \frac{69.17}{14,722.64} = 73.4$$

The critical part is finding a comparable country and a good surrogate measure (in this case, the number of color television sets in use). In some cases, the analogy exists between different time periods. For example, the stage of economic development in country A ten years back could be similar to the current state of the economy in country B. In the same fashion as illustrated above, we can derive an estimate for the product demand in country B, but this time we would apply the ratio between product demand and the surrogate measure in country A that existed ten years ago:

$$M_B^{2010} = X_B^{2010} * (M_A^{2000}/X_A^{2000})$$

where

$M$ = the market size for the product of interest
$X$ = the surrogate measure

This variant is sometimes referred to as the **longitudinal method of analogy**. Use of either approach produces misleading estimates whenever:[43]

1. Consumption patterns are not comparable across countries due to strong cultural disparities.

2. Other factors (competition, trade barriers) cause actual sales to differ from potential sales.

3. Technological advances allow use of product innovations in a country at an earlier stage of economic development ("leapfrogging").

McDonald's uses a variation of the analogy method to derive market size estimates:[44]

$$\frac{\text{Population of Country X}}{\text{No. of People per McDonald's in United States }(21,629)} \times \frac{\text{Per Capita Income of Country X}}{\text{Per Capita Income in United States }(\$41,800)} = \begin{array}{c}\text{Potential} \\ \text{Penetration} \\ \text{in Country X}\end{array}$$

This method is illustrated in **Exhibit 6-9**, which contrasts the number of restaurants McDonald's could build with its current (2004) number of outlets for a sample of countries.[45] As a benchmark, we also included the 1996 numbers. Currently, McDonald's has around 31,000 restaurants in 121 countries and territories, out of which about 55 percent are located outside the United States.[46] Interestingly, in several countries McDonald's appears to have saturated the market. Examples include Canada and Australia. However, in quite a few other countries, the fast-food chain still has a lot of mileage. Not surprisingly, China provides the biggest opportunity.

**Trade Audit**  An alternative way to derive market size estimates is based on local production and import and export figures for the product of interest. A **trade audit** uses a straightforward logic: Take the local production figures, add imports, and subtract exports:

$$\text{Market Size in Country A} = \text{Local Production} + \text{Imports} - \text{Exports}$$

---

[43]Lyn S. Amine and S. Tamer Cavusgil, "Demand Estimation in Developing Country Environment: Difficulties, Techniques and Examples," *Journal of the Market Research Society*, 28, no. 1, pp. 43–65.

[44]"How Many McDonald's Can He Build," *Fortune* (October 17, 1994), p. 104. Population and per capita income based on estimates reported in http://www.cia.gov/cia/publications/factbook/, accessed on February 22, 2006.

[45]For a complete listing, see http://www.mcdonalds.com/corp/invest/pub/2004InteractiveFinancialHighlights.html.

[46]http://www.mcdonalds.com/corp/invest/pub/Interactive_Charts.html, accessed on January 13, 2009.

**EXHIBIT 6-9**
MARKET POTENTIAL ESTIMATES FOR MCDONALD'S

| Country | Current Number of Restaurants (2004) | 1996 Number of Restaurants | Market Potential |
|---|---|---|---|
| Japan | 3,774 | 2,004 | 4,284 |
| Canada | 1,362 | 992 | 1,190 |
| Germany | 1,262 | 743 | 2,707 |
| UK | 1,249 | 737 | 2,064 |
| France | 1,034 | 540 | 2,004 |
| Australia | 729 | 608 | 711 |
| China | 639 | 117 | 8,958 |
| Brazil | 549 | 214 | 1,750 |
| Taiwan | 346 | 163 | 676 |
| Spain | 345 | 121 | 1,118 |
| South Korea | 337 | 77 | 1,087 |
| Italy | 331 | 147 | 1,819 |
| Mexico | 304 | 112 | 1,175 |
| Sweden | 244 | 129 | 295 |
| Philippines | 242 | 113 | 495 |
| Netherlands | 227 | 151 | 553 |
| Hong Kong | 211 | 125 | 281 |
| Poland | 207 | 65 | 542 |
| Argentina | 186 | 88 | 594 |
| Malaysia | 164 | 129 (1999) | 275 |

*Sources:* "How Many McDonald's Can He Build?" Fortune, October 17, 1994, p. 104; *World Factbook 2005*; and http://www.mcdonalds.com/corp/invest/pub/2004InteractiveFinancial Highlights.html, *CIA* accessed on February 22, 2006

Strictly speaking, one should also make adjustments for inventory levels. While the procedure is commonsensical, the hard part is finding the input data. For many emerging markets (and even developed countries), such data are missing, inaccurate, outdated or collected at a very aggregate level in categories that are often far too broad for the company's purposes.

The **chain ratio method** starts with a very rough base number as an estimate for the market size (e.g., the entire population of the country). This base estimate is systematically fine-tuned by applying a string ("chain") of percentages to come up with the most meaningful estimate for total market potential.

**Chain Ratio Method**

To illustrate the procedure, let us look at the potential market size in Japan for Nicorette gum, a nicotine substitute marketed by GlaxoSmithKline. Japan's total population is 127 million. In 2002, Japan's smoking rate was around 31 percent.[47] Nicorette's target is adult smokers. The 15- to 64-year-old age group is about 67.5 percent of Japan's total population.[48] With the chain ratio method, we can then derive a rough estimate for Nicorette's market potential in Japan as follows:

| Japan | |
|---|---|
| Base Number | |
| Total Population: | 127 MM people |
| Adult population (15–64) | 85.6 MM = 0.675 × 127 MM |
| Adult smokers | 26.5 MM = 0.31 × 85.6 MM |

Obviously, given further information, we can refine this market-size estimate much further. In this case, the company also learned via surveys that 64 percent of adult smokers in Japan would like to quit or cut smoking and 25 percent of them would like to quit immediately.[49] So, Nicorette's market size potential would be approximately 4.2 million smokers (= 0.25 × 0.64 × 26.5 MM adult smokers).

---

[47]http://www.jointogether.org/sa/news/summaries/reader/0,1854,554957,00.html.

[48]http://www.cia.gov/cia/publications/factbook/geos/ja.html#People.

[49]"Stubbing Out Japan's Taboo Smoking Habit," *Ad Age Global* (November 2001), p. 23

## Cross-Sectional Regression Analysis

Statistical techniques such as cross-sectional regression can be used to produce market size estimates. With regression analysis, the variable of interest (in our case "market size") is related to a set of predictor variables. To apply regression, you would first choose a set of indicators that are closely related to demand for the product of interest. You would then collect data on these variables and market size figures for a set of countries (the cross-section) where the product has already been introduced. Given these data, you can then fit a regression that will allow you to predict the market size in countries in your consideration pool.[50]

Again, let us illustrate the procedure with a simple example. Suppose a consumer electronics firm XYZ based in Europe is considering selling DVD players in the Balkan region or the Near East. Five countries are on its shortlist: Croatia, Greece, Israel, Romania, and Turkey. The company has gathered information on the annual sales figures of DVD players in several (mostly Western) European countries. As predictor variables, the firm chose two indicators: per capita GDP (on a purchasing power parity basis) and the number of color TV sets in use. It collected data on these two measures and the (2001) sales of DVD players in fifteen European countries.[51] Using these data as inputs, it came up with the following regression model:

$$\text{Annual Unit Sales DVD Players} = -13.3 + 2.43 \times \text{Per Capita Income} + 1.25 \times \text{Number of Color TVs in Use}^{[52]}$$

Based on this regression, we are now able to predict the yearly unit sales of DVD players in the five countries being considered. We plug in the income and number of color TV sets for the respective countries in this equation, with the following results:[53]

| | |
|---|---|
| Croatia | 3,639 |
| Greece | 55,403 |
| Israel | 36,774 |
| Romania | 5,943 |
| Turkey | 34,345 |

Clearly, at least from a unit sales perspective, Greece seems to be the most promising market. Runner-up countries are Israel and Turkey.

When applying regression to produce a market size estimate, you should be careful in interpreting the results. For instance, caution is warranted whenever the range of one of the predictors for the countries of interest is outside the range of the countries used to calibrate the regression. Having said this, regression is probably one of the handiest tools to estimate market sizes, keeping in mind its constraints.

The methods we just described are not the only procedures you can use. Other, more sophisticated, procedures exist. Finally, some words of advice. Look at the three estimates for the size of the wallpaper market (in terms of number of rolls) in Morocco, based on different market-size estimation techniques:[54]

| | |
|---|---|
| Chain Ratio Method: | 484,000 |
| Method by Analogy: | 1,245,000 |
| Trade Audit: | 90,500 |

---

[50]For further details, see, for example, David A. Aaker, V. Kumar, and George S. Day, *Marketing Research*, New York, NY: John Wiley & Sons, 1995, Chapter 18.

[51]Our source for the data is http://www.euromonitor.com.

[52]The $R^2$ equals 0.92; t-statistics are 8.1 and 8.7 for "Per Capita Income" and "Number of Color TVs" respectively. Note that we transformed the data by taking logarithms first.

[53]GDP per capita figures (2001) are: Croatia $8,300; Greece $17,900; Israel $20,000; Romania $6,800; Turkey $6,700. Number of color TV sets in use figures (2001, in thousands) are: Croatia 1,955; Greece 3,948; Israel 2,088; Turkey 17,262.

[54]Lyn S. Amine and S. Tamer Cavusgil, "Demand Estimation in a Developing Country," Table 4.

You immediately notice a wide gap among the different methods. Such discrepancies are not uncommon. When using market size estimates, keep the following rules in mind:

1. Whenever feasible, use several different methods that possibly rely on different data inputs.

2. Do not be misled by the numbers. Make sure you know the reasoning behind them.

3. Do not be misled by fancy methods. At some point, increased sophistication will lead to diminishing returns (in terms of accuracy of your estimates), not to mention negative returns. Simple back-of-the-envelope calculations are often a good start.

4. When many assumptions are to be made, do a sensitivity analysis by asking what-if questions. See how sensitive the estimates are to changes in your underlying assumptions.

5. Look for interval estimates with a lower and upper limit rather than for point estimates. The range indicates the precision of the estimates.[55] The limits can later be used for market simulation exercises to see what might happen to the company's bottom line under various scenarios.

## NEW MARKET INFORMATION TECHNOLOGIES      ◆ ◆ ◆ ◆ ◆ ◆ ◆

These days almost all packaged consumer goods come with a bar code. For each purchase transaction, scanner data are gathered at the cash registers of stores that are equipped with laser scanning technology. The emergence of scanner data, coupled with rapid developments in computer hardware (e.g., workstations) and software has led to a revolution in market research. Although most of the early advances in this information revolution took place in the United States, Europe, and Japan rapidly followed suit. Scanning technology has spurred several sorts of databases. The major ones include:[56]

• **Point-of-sale (POS) store scanner data.** Companies like ACNielsen, Taylor Nelson Sofres (TNS), and Information Resources (IRI) obtain sales movement data from the checkout scanner tapes of retail outlets. These data are processed to provide instant information on weekly sales movements and market shares of individual brands, sizes and product variants. Shifts in sales volume and market shares can be related to changes in the store environment (retail prices, display, and/or feature activity) and competitive moves. In the past, tracking of sales was based on store audits or warehouse withdrawal. The advantage of POS scanner data over these traditional ways of data gathering is obvious: far better data quality.[57] The data are collected on a weekly basis instead of bimonthly. Further, they are gathered at a very detailed UPC[58]-level, not just the brand level.

• **Consumer panel data.** Market research companies such as ACNielsen and TNS have consumer panels that record their purchases. There are two approaches to collect household level data. Under the first approach, panel members present an ID card when checking out at the cash register. That information is entered each time the household shops. The alternative approach relies on at-home scanning. On returning from each shopping trip, the panel member scans the items bought. ACNielsen's Homescan panel is an example of the latter. ACNielsen runs Homescan panels in 28 countries, monitoring the purchase behavior of over 300,000 households. In February

---

[55]Referred to as a "confidence interval" by statisticians.

[56]See, for example, Del I. Hawkins and Donald S. Tull, *Essentials of Marketing Research*, New York, NY: Macmillan Publishing Company, 1994, pp. 115–21.

[57]Gerry Eskin, "POS scanner data: The state of the art, in Europe and the world," *Marketing and Research Today*, May 1994, pp. 107–17.

[58]Universal Product Code.

2008, ACNielsen set up a Homescan consumer purchase panel with over 40,000 households in China.[59]

• **Single-source data.** Such data are continuous data that combine for any given household member TV viewing behavior with purchase transaction (product description, price, promotion, etc.) information. TV viewing behavior is tracked at the panel member's home via so-called Peoplemeters. The TV audience measurement system usually requires cooperation of the panel member. Each time the family member watches a program, he or she has to push a button to identify him/herself. More advanced systems involve a camera that records which members of the household are watching TV. Single-source data allow companies to measure, among other things, the effectiveness of their advertising policy.

Household level scanning data are collected now in most developed countries by research firms such as ACNielsen and GfK. Companies like Nestlé also put together their own databases. These innovations in marketing decision support systems have spurred several major developments in the marketing area:

• **Shift from mass to micro marketing.**[60] Better knowledge on shopping and viewing behavior has moved the focus from mass marketing to the individual. New information technologies enable firms to tailor their pricing, product line, advertising and promotion strategies to particular neighborhoods or even individuals. Database marketing gives companies an opportunity to enter into direct contact with their customers. Nestlé's strategy for its Buitoni pasta brand offers a good example of the power of database marketing in a pan-European context. In the United Kingdom, Nestlé built up a database of people who had requested a free recipe booklet. The next step was the launch of a Casa Buitoni Club. Members of the club receive a magazine and opportunities to win a trip for cooking instruction. The goal of the strategy is to build up a long-term commitment to the Buitoni brand.[61] Likewise, in Malaysia Nestlé built up a database with information on consumption patterns, lifestyle, religion, race, and feelings about specific brands. By building up its database knowledge, Nestlé hopes to do a better job in target marketing and adapting its products to the local market.[62]

• **Continuous monitoring of brand sales/market share movements.** Sales measurement based on scanner data are more accurate and timely than, for instance, data from store audits. In Japan, thousands of new products are launched continuously. Accurate tracking information on new brand shares and incumbent brand shares is crucial information for manufacturers and retailers alike.[63]

• **Scanning data are used by manufacturers to support marketing decisions.** Initially, most scanning data were simply used as tracking devices. This has changed now. Scanning data are increasingly used for tactical decision support. The databases are used to assist all sorts of decisions in inventory management, consumer/trade promotions, pricing, shelf space allocation, and media advertising. Scanning data are also increasingly used for category management.

• **Scanning data are used to provide merchandising support to retailers.** Many manufacturers also employ information distilled from scanning data to help out retailers with merchandising programs (e.g., in-store displays). Such support helps to build up a long-term relationship with retailers. Scanning data help manufacturers to show the "hard facts" to their distributors.

---

[59]http://www.nielsen.com/media/2008/pr_080221.html, accessed October 30, 2008.

[60]David J. Curry, *The New Marketing Research Systems. How to Use Strategic Database Information for Better Marketing Decisions*, New York, NY: John Wiley & Sons, 1994.

[61]Stan Rapp and Thomas L. Collins, *Beyond Maxi-Marketing: The New Power of Caring and Sharing*, New York, NY: McGraw-Hill, 1994.

[62]"Nestlé builds database in Asia with direct mail," *Ad Age International* (January 1998), p. 34.

[63]H. Katahira and S. Yagi, "Marketing Information Technologies in Japan," p. 310.

Richer market information should help global marketers to improve marketing decisions that have cross-border ramifications. Scanning data from the pan-European region allows marketers to gauge the effectiveness of pan-European advertising campaigns, branding decisions, distribution strategies, and so forth. The information can also be used to monitor competitors' activities. With the emergence of consumer panel data, marketers are able to spot similarities and differences in cross-border consumer behavior. In short, the consequences of new market research systems are dramatic. Several environmental forces (e.g., single European market, cultural trends) promote the so-called "global village" or "flat world" phenomenon with a convergence in tastes, preferences leading to universal segments. On the other hand, the new information technologies will ultimately allow marketers to enter into one-to-one relationships with their individual customers.

Despite the promises of scanner databases, their full potential is not yet exploited in many countries. Many users still simply view scanner data as an instrument to track market shares. Two factors are behind this state of affairs. One reason is the conservatism of the users of the data. Another factor is the attitude of local retailers toward data access. In countries like the United Kingdom, retailers are reluctant to release their data because they fear that by doing so they might inform their competition. Rivals are not just other retailers but in many cases the manufacturers who compete with the retailer's store brands.

State-of-the-art marketing research tools are also being developed to track the effectiveness of newer marketing mix media vehicles such as the Internet. For instance, the WebAudit is a package designed by ACNielsen Australia that allows subscribers to evaluate the performance of their website. Subscribers to the service receive information on user profiles by region, most requested pages, most downloaded files, and so on. The ultimate goal is to establish a "Nielsen rating" for websites similar to the ratings ACNielsen currently provides for television programming.[64]

Advances in computer technology have also spurred new data collection techniques such as computer-assisted telephone interviewing (CATI) and computer-assisted personal interviewing (CAPI). Benefits derived from such tools include: speed, accuracy, and the ability to steer data collection based on the response. In international marketing research, another material advantage of these techniques is that they can be used to centrally administer and organize data collection from international samples.[65]

## MANAGING GLOBAL MARKETING RESEARCH

◆ ◆ ◆ ◆ ◆ ◆ ◆

Global marketing research projects have to cater to the needs of various interest groups: global and regional headquarters, local subsidiaries. Different requirements will lead to tension among the stakeholders. In this section we center on two highly important issues in managing global marketing research: (1) who should conduct the research project, and (2) coordination of global marketing research projects.

Even companies with in-house expertise will often employ local research agencies to assist with a multicountry research project. The choice of a research agency to run a multicountry research project is made centrally by headquarters or locally by regional headquarters or country affiliates. Reliance on local research firms is an absolute must in countries such as China, both to be close to the market and to get around government red tape.[66] Local agencies may also have a network of contacts that give access to secondary data sources. Whatever the motive for using a local research agency, selection of an agency should be made based on careful scrutiny and screening of possible candidates. The first step is to see what sorts of research support services are

**Selecting a Research Agency**

---

[64]"Benchmark standards for worldwide web sites," *AC Nielsen SRG News*, October 1996, p. 3.

[65]C. Samuel Craig and Susan P. Douglas, "Conducting International Marketing Research."

[66]H. C. Steele, "Marketing Research in China," p. 158.

available to conduct the research project. Each year *Marketing News* (an American Marketing Association publication) puts together a directory of international marketing research firms (www.marketingpower.com/ama_custom_honomichl25.php).

Several considerations enter the agency selection decision. Agencies that are partners or subsidiaries of global research firms are especially useful when there is a strong need for coordination of multicountry research efforts. The agency's level of expertise is the main ingredient in the screening process: What are the qualifications of its staff and its field-workers? The agency's track record is also a key factor: How long has it been in business? What types of research problems has it handled? What experience does the agency have in tackling a particular type of research problem(s)? For what clients has it worked? In some cases, it is worthwhile to contact previous or current clients and explore their feelings about the prospective research supplier.

When cross-border coordination is an issue, companies should also examine the willingness of the agency to be flexible and be a good team player. Communication skills are another important issue. When secrecy is required, it is necessary to examine whether the candidate has any possible conflicts of interest. Has the agency any ties with (potential) competitors? Does it have a good reputation in keeping matters confidential? Again, a background check with previous clients could provide the answer.

Cost is clearly a crucial input in the selection decision. Global research is usually much more expensive than research done in the United States.[67] The infrastructure available in the United States to do market research is far more economical than in most other parts of the world. However, there are other costs associated with global research that are not incurred with domestic research. Such cost items include the cost of multiple translations, multicountry coordination, and long-distance project management.

Quality standards can vary a lot. One golden rule needs to be observed though: Beware of agencies that promise the world at a bargain price. Inaccurate and misleading information will almost certainly lead to disastrous decisions.

## Coordination of Multicountry Research

Multicountry research projects demand careful coordination of the research efforts undertaken in the different markets. The benefits of coordination are manifold.[68] Coordination facilitates cross-country comparison of results whenever such comparisons are crucial. It also can have benefits of timeliness, cost, centralization of communication and quality control. Coordination brings up two central issues: (1) who should do the coordinating? and (2) what should be the degree of coordination? In some cases, coordination is implemented by the research agency that is hired to run the project. When markets differ a lot or when researchers vary from country to country, the company itself will prefer to coordinate the project.[69]

The degree of coordination centers on the conflicting demands of various users of marketing research: global (or regional) headquarters and local subsidiaries. Headquarters favor standardized data collection, sampling procedures, and survey instruments. Local user groups prefer country-customized research designs that recognize the peculiarities of their local environment. This conflict is referred to as the *emic versus etic dilemma.*[70] The **emic** school focuses on the peculiarities of each country. Attitudinal phenomena and values are so unique in each country that they can only be tapped via culture-specific measures. The other school of thought, the **etic** approach, emphasizes universal behavioral and attitudinal traits. To gauge such phenomena requires culturally unbiased measures. For instance, for many goods and services, there appears to be convergence in consumer preferences across cultures. Therefore, consumer preferences could be studied from an etic angle. Buying motivations behind those preferences,

---

[67]Brad Frevert, "Is Global Research Different?" *Marketing Research* (Spring 2000), pp. 49–51.

[68]D. N. Aldridge, "Multicountry Research," p. 361.

[69]"Multicountry research: should you do your own coordinating?" *Industrial Marketing Digest*, pp. 79–82.

[70]S. P. Douglas and C.S Craig, *International Marketing Research*, pp. 132–37.

however, often differ substantially across cultures. Hence, a cross-country project that looks into buying motivations is likely to require an emic approach.[71]

In cross-cultural market research, the need for comparability favors the *etic paradigm* with an emphasis on the cross-border similarities and parallels. Nevertheless, to make the research study useful and acceptable to local users, companies need to recognize the peculiarities of local cultures. So, ideally, survey instruments that are developed for cross-country market research projects should encompass both approaches—emic *and* etic.[72] There are several approaches to balance these conflicting demands. In a pan-European positioning study conducted for BMW, coordination was accomplished via the following measures:[73]

1. All relevant parties (users at headquarters and local subsidiaries) were included from the outset in planning the research project.

2. All parties contributed in funding the study.

3. Hypotheses and objectives were deemed to be binding at later stages of the project.

4. Data collection went through two stages. First, responses to a country-specific pool of psychographic statements were collected. The final data collection in the second stage used a mostly standardized survey instrument containing a few statements that were country-customized (based on findings from the first run).

The key lessons of the BMW-example are twofold. First, *coordination* means that all parties (i.e., user groups) should get involved. Neglected parties will have little incentive to accept the results of the research project. Second, multicountry research should allow some leeway for country peculiarities. For instance, questionnaires should not be over standardized but may include some country-specific items. This is especially important for collecting so-called "soft" data (e.g., lifestyle/attitude statements).

---

[71]Malhotra, Agarwal, and Peterson, p. 12.

[72]N. K. Malhotra, J. Agarwal, and M. Peterson, "Methodological issues," p. 12.

[73]H. Kern, H.-C. Wagner, and R. Hassis, "European Aspects of a Global Brand," pp. 49–50.

# SUMMARY   ◆ ◆ ◆ ◆ ◆ ◆ ◆ ◆ ◆ ◆ ◆ ◆ ◆ ◆ ◆ ◆ ◆ ◆ ◆ ◆ ◆ ◆ ◆ ◆ ◆ ◆ ◆ ◆ ◆

Whenever you drive to an unknown destination, you probably use a road map, ask for instructions to get there, and carefully examine the road signals. If not, you risk getting lost. By the same token, whenever you need to make marketing decisions in the global marketplace, market intelligence will guide you in these endeavors. Shoddy information invariably leads to shoddy decision-making; good information facilitates solid decision-making. In this day and age, having timely and adequate market intelligence also provides a competitive advantage. This does not mean that global marketers should do research at any cost. As always, examining the costs and the value added of having more information at each step is important. Usually it is not difficult to figure out the costs of gathering market intelligence. The hard part is the benefit component. Views on the benefits and role of market research sometimes differ between cultures. Global Perspective 6-3 highlights the peculiarities of Japanese firms' approach to marketing research. What can marketers do to boost the payoffs of their global marketing research efforts? As always, there are no simple solutions.

The complexities of the global marketplace are stunning. They pose a continuous challenge to market researchers. Hurdles are faced in gathering secondary and primary data.

Not all challenges will be met successfully. Mistakes are easily made. One American toiletries manufacturer conducted its market research in (English-speaking) Toronto for a bar soap to be launched in (French-speaking) Québec. The whole venture became a sad soap opera with a tragic ending.[74]

In this chapter we discussed the intricacies in developing and implementing a market research project in a cross-national setting. We also reviewed several techniques that prove useful to estimate the market size whenever few or only poor quality data are at your disposal.

To make cross-country comparisons meaningful, companies need to adequately manage and coordinate their market research projects with a global scope. Inputs from local users of the research are desirable for several reasons. When the locals feel that they were treated like stepchildren, it will be hard to "sell" the findings of the research project. As a result, getting their support for policies based on the study's conclusions becomes a formidable task. Local feedback also becomes necessary to uncover country-specific peculiarities that cannot be tapped with over standardized measurement instruments.

---

[74]Sandra Vandermerwe, "Colgate-Palmolive: Cleopatra," Case Study, Lausanne: IMD, 1990.

◆ ◆ ◆ ◆ ◆ ◆ ◆ ◆ ◆ ◆ ◆ ◆ ◆ ◆ ◆ ◆ ◆ ◆ ◆ ◆ ◆ ◆ ◆ ◆ ◆ ◆ ◆ ◆ ◆ ◆ ◆ ◆ ◆ ◆ ◆ ◆

### 𝒢LOBAL PERSPECTIVE 6-3

#### HOW DOES JAPANESE MARKET RESEARCH DIFFER?

There is a philosophical difference in the role of marketing research between U.S./European and Japanese executives. Marketing researchers in the United States (and also to some extent within Europe) believe that various dimensions of consumer attitudes and behaviors can be measured with statistical tools. Japanese marketing researchers, however, believe that those tools are not sufficient enough to gauge the vagrant nature of consumer attitudes. As a result, Japanese marketing researchers rely far less on statistical techniques than their U.S. counterparts.

Toru Nishikawa, marketing manager at Hitachi, lists five reasons against "scientific" market research in the area of new product development:

1. Indifference of respondents. Careless random sampling leads to mistaken judgments, because some people are indifferent towards the product in question.

2. Absence of responsibility. The consumer is most sincere when spending, not when s/he is talking.

3. Conservative attitudes. Ordinary consumers are conservative and tend to react negatively to new product ideas.

*Sources:* Michael R. Czinkota and Masaaki Kotabe, "Product Development the Japanese Way," *Journal of Business Strategy*, 11, Nov./ Dec. 1990, pp. 31–36 and Johny K. Johansson and Ikujiro Nonaka, *Relentless: The Japanese Way of Marketing*, New York, NY: Harper Business, 1996.

4. Vanity. It is part of human nature to exaggerate and put on a good appearance.

5. Insufficient information. The research results depend on information about product characteristics given to survey participants.

Japanese firms prefer more down-to-earth methods of information gathering. Instead of administering surveys, Japanese market researchers will go into the field and observe how consumers use the product. For example, Toyota sent a group of engineers and designers to Southern California to observe how women get into and operate their cars. They found that women with long fingernails have trouble opening the door and handling various knobs on the dashboard. Consequently, Toyota altered some of their automobiles' exterior and interior designs.

Hands-on market research does not negate the importance of conventional marketing research. In fact, scores of Japanese firms assign more people to information gathering and analysis than U.S. firms. What is unique about Japanese market research is that Japanese research teams include both product engineers and sales and marketing representatives. Engineers gain insights from talking with prospective customers as much as their marketing peers. They can directly incorporate user comments into product specifications.

## KEY TERMS ◆ ◆ ◆ ◆ ◆ ◆ ◆ ◆ ◆ ◆ ◆ ◆ ◆ ◆ ◆ ◆ ◆ ◆ ◆ ◆

| | | | |
|---|---|---|---|
| analogy method | courtesy bias | functional equivalence | social desirability bias |
| back-translation | emic | omnibus survey | translation equivalence |
| chain ratio method | etic | parallel translation | triangulate |
| conceptual equivalence | ethnographic research | scalar equivalence | |

## REVIEW QUESTIONS ◆ ◆ ◆ ◆ ◆ ◆ ◆ ◆ ◆ ◆ ◆ ◆ ◆ ◆ ◆ ◆ ◆ ◆

1. What are the major benefits and limitations of omnibus surveys?

2. What is the notion of "triangulation" in global market research?

3. Discuss the major issues in running focus group discussions in an international context.

4. Discuss why market size estimates may differ depending on the method being used. How can such differences be reconciled?

5. Contrast the emic versus the etic approach in international marketing research.

# DISCUSSION QUESTIONS ✦ ✦ ✦ ✦ ✦ ✦ ✦ ✦ ✦ ✦ ✦ ✦ ✦ ✦ ✦ ✦ ✦ ✦ ✦ ✦

**1.** Chapter 6 suggests two ways to select countries for multi-country market research projects: (1) start with a preliminary research in each one of them or (2) cluster the countries and pick one representative member from each cluster. Under what circumstances would you prefer one option over the other?

**2.** Refer to Exhibit 6-9, which presents McDonald's market potential based on the formula given on page 211.

   a. Using the same formula, estimate what McDonald's market potential would be for the following Pacific-Rim countries: India, Indonesia, Malaysia, Myanmar, the Philippines, Singapore, and Thailand.

   b. What factors are missing in the formula that McDonald's uses?

**3.** In most cases, standard data collection methods are still mail, phone, or personal interviewing. Tokyu Agency, Tokyo, a Japanese ad agency, has started using the Internet to find out how Japanese youngsters spend their money and what their views are on various issues (e.g., environment). What opportunities does the Internet offer as a data-gathering tool in international market research? What are its merits and disadvantages in this regard?

**4.** Company Euronappy sells disposable diapers in Europe. It would like to expand into the Middle East. After some preliminary market research, four countries put on the short list, namely: Bahrain, Kuwait, Saudi Arabia, and the United Arab Emirates (UAE). Given its limited resources, the company can only enter two of these countries. Your assignment is to come up with a market size estimate for each one of them so that Euronappy can decide which one to enter. You decide to run a regression using data from Euronappy's European market. Three variables are presumed to predict the sales of disposable diapers: population size, per capita GDP, and the birth rate. Data were collected on all three variables (source: http://www.cia.gov/cia/publications/factbook/) for the 19 European countries where Euronappy operates. However, the birth rate did not seem to be a factor. The estimated regression model is:

$$Y = -630.6 + 0.015 X_1 + 47.15 X_2$$
$Y$ = annual sales of diapers in millions of units
$X_1$ = population in thousands
$X_2$ = per capita Gross Domestic Product (GDP–Purchasing Power Parity Basis) in thousands US$.

   a. Collect data on the population and per capita GDP for the four countries on the list (Bahrain, Kuwait, Saudi Arabia, and the UAE).

   b. Now use the estimated regression model to predict the yearly sales of disposable diapers for these four countries. Which of these two would you choose?

   c. Suppose the company is also looking at North Africa, in particular: Egypt, Morocco, and Tunisia. Would you advise them to use the same estimated regression model? Why, or why not?

**5.** Clarion Marketing and Communications, a Connecticut-based marketing research firm, recently launched Global Focus, a technique that allows companies to run focus groups in different countries that interact with each other. The focus groups are held in videoconference centers in the different cities (e.g., one in New York, one in London) with a moderator in each location. Do you see a need for "global focus groups"? Why? (or why not?) What are potential benefits? Concerns?

**6.** Imagine that Nokia plans to expand its market in South America. Use the chain-ratio method to come up with market size estimates for cellular phones in the following four countries: Argentina, Brazil, Chile, and Peru.

**7.** When developing a survey instrument for a cross-country study, market researchers often need to construct a scale (e.g., a 7-point disagree/agree scale). What are the major items that one should be concerned about when building such scales?

**8.** Download the Durex Global Sex Survey (GSS) (http://www.durex.com/cm/gss2005results.asp). The survey was conducted online via the durex.com website. Durex claims that their survey is the largest sexual health research project of its kind in the world. More than 317,000 people took part from 41 countries.

   a. What do you envision as the main challenges in developing and conducting a survey like the GSS?

   b. The survey was conducted online. What are the key benefits of doing this online compared to more traditional survey methods? What are the possible drawbacks?

   c. How would this survey benefit SSL, the British company that owns the Durex brand in formulating their marketing strategy (another big brand the company owns is the Scholl footwear brand)? Do you see other possible payoffs?

# FURTHER READING ✦ ✦ ✦ ✦ ✦ ✦ ✦ ✦ ✦ ✦ ✦ ✦ ✦ ✦ ✦ ✦ ✦ ✦ ✦ ✦

Aldridge, D. N., "Multicountry Research," in *Applied Marketing and Social Research*, U. Bradley, Ed., 2nd Edition, New York, NY: John Wiley & Sons, 1987.

Amine, S. Lyn and S. Tamer Cavusgil, "Demand Estimation in a Developing Country Environment: Difficulties, Techniques and Examples," *Journal of the Market Research Society*, vol. 28, no. 1, pp. 43–65.

Craig, C. Samuel and Susan P. Douglas. "Conducting International Marketing Research." *International Marketing Review* 18, No. 1 (2001): 80–90.

Davis, Tim R.V. and Robert B. Young. "International Marketing Research: A Management Briefing." *Business Horizons,* 45(2): 31–38.

Eskin, Gerry, "POS scanner data: The state of the art, in Europe and the world," *Marketing and Research Today,* May 1994, pp. 107–17.

Hibbert, Edgar, "Researching international markets—How can we ensure validity of results?" *Marketing and Research Today,* November 1993, pp. 222–28.

Johansson, K. Johny and Ikujiro Nonaka, "Market research the Japanese way," *Harvard Business Review,* May-June 1987, pp. 16–22.

Kumar, V. *International Marketing Research.* Upper Saddle River, NJ: Prentice Hall, 2000.

"Researching International Markets: Philosophical and Methodological Issues," in *The Sage Handbook of International Marketing,* eds. M. Kotabe and K Helsen (London: Sage Publications, 2009).

Malhotra, Naresh K., James Agarwal, and Mark Peterson, "Methodological issues in cross-cultural marketing research. A. state-of-the-art review," *International Marketing Review,* vol. 13, no. 5, 1996, pp. 7–43.

Schroiff, Hans-Willi. "Creating Competitive Intellectual Capital," *Marketing and Research Today* (November 1998): 148–56.

Steele, Henry C., "Marketing Research in China: The Hong Kong Connection," *Marketing and Research Today,* August, 1990, pp. 155–64.

Tuncalp, Secil, "The Marketing Research Scene in Saudi Arabia," *European Journal of Marketing,* vol. 22, no.5, 1988, pp. 15–22.

Williams, S. C., "Researching Markets in Japan—A Methodological Case Study," *Journal of International Marketing,* vol. 4, no. 2, 1996, pp. 87–93.

# GLOBAL SEGMENTATION AND POSITIONING

HAPTER OVERVIEW

1. REASONS FOR INTERNATIONAL MARKET SEGMENTATION

2. INTERNATIONAL MARKET SEGMENTATION APPROACHES

3. SEGMENTATION SCENARIOS

4. BASES FOR INTERNATIONAL MARKET SEGMENTATION

5. INTERNATIONAL POSITIONING STRATEGIES

6. GLOBAL, FOREIGN, AND LOCAL CONSUMER CULTURE POSITIONING

Early February 2009 Lenovo, the Chinese computer maker that vaulted onto the international stage four years earlier by buying the personal computers divisions of IBM, reported a loss of $97 million for the fiscal quarter ending Dec. 31, 2008. PC shipments were down 5 percent while revenue dropped 20 percent compared to the year-earlier quarter. To overhaul its business, Lenovo announced that it would refocus on China and other emerging markets. Lenovo's management also would concentrate on consumers rather than the big corporate customers, the mainstay of the former IBM PC business.[1]

Few companies can be all things to all people. Instead of competing across the board, most companies will identify and target the most attractive market segments that they can serve effectively. Variation in customer needs is the primary motive for market segmentation. When consumer preferences vary, marketers can design a marketing mix program that is tailored toward the needs of the specific segments that the firm targets. Marketers select one or more segmentation bases (e.g., age, lifestyle) and slice up their prospective customer base according to the chosen criteria. Marketing programs are then developed that are in tune with the particular needs of each of the segments that the company wants to serve.

In global marketing, market segmentation becomes especially critical, given the sometimes incredibly wide divergence in cross-border consumer needs and preferences. In this chapter, we first focus on the motivations for international market segmentation. Given information on the segmentation criteria you plan to use, you can take several

---

[1] "Lenovo Refocuses on China," *The Wall Street Journal Asia*, February 6–8, 2009, pp. 1, 15.

country segmentation approaches. We describe in detail several possible segmentation scenarios. We then consider several bases that marketers might consider for country segmentation. Once the company has chosen its target segments, management needs to determine a competitive positioning strategy for its products. The final sections focus on different international positioning strategies that companies can pursue.

◆ ◆ ◆ ◆ ◆ ◆ ◆ ◆     # REASONS FOR INTERNATIONAL MARKET SEGMENTATION

The goal of market segmentation is to break down the market for a product or a service into different groups of consumers who differ in their response to the firm's marketing mix program. That way, the firm can tailor its marketing mix to each individual segment, and, hence, do a better job in satisfying the needs of the target segments. This overall objective also applies in an international marketing context. In that sense, market segmentation is the logical outgrowth of the marketing concept.[2]

The requirements for effective market segmentation in a domestic marketing context also apply in international market segmentation. In particular, segments ideally should possess the following set of properties:[3]

1. *Identifiable.* The segments should be easy to define and to measure. This criterion is easily met for "objective" country traits such as socioeconomic variables (e.g., per capita income). However, the size of segments based on values or lifestyle indicators is typically much harder to gauge.

2. *Sizable.* The segments should be large enough to be worth going after. Note that modern technologies such as flexible manufacturing enable companies to relax this criterion. In fact, many segments that might be considered too small in a single-country context become attractive once they are lumped together across borders.

3. *Accessible.* The segments should also be easy to reach through promotional and distributional efforts. Differences in the quality of the distribution (e.g., road conditions, storage facilities) and media infrastructure (e.g., Internet penetration) imply that a given segment might be hard to reach in some countries and easy to target in other marketplaces.

4. *Stability.* If target markets change their composition or behavior over time, marketing efforts devised for these targets are less likely to succeed.

5. *Responsive.* For market segmentation to be meaningful, it is important that the segments respond differently from each other to differentiated marketing mixes.

6. *Actionable.* Segments are actionable if the marketing mix necessary to address their needs is consistent with the goals and the core competencies of the company.

Let us consider now the major reasons why international marketers implement international market segmentation.

**Country Screening**    Companies usually do a preliminary screening of countries before identifying attractive market opportunities for their product or service. For preliminary screening, market analysts rely on a few indicators for which information can easily be gathered from secondary data sources. At this stage, the international market analyst might classify countries in two or three piles. Countries that meet all criteria will be grouped in the "Go" pile for further consideration at the next stage. Countries that fail to meet most of the criteria will enter the "No Go" pile. The third set of countries meet some of the criteria but not all of them. They may become of interest in the future but probably not in the short term.

---

[2]Yoram Wind and Susan P. Douglas, "International Market Segmentation," *European Journal of Marketing*, vol. 6, no. 1, 1972, pp. 17–25.

[3]Michel Wedel and Wagner A. Kamakura, *Market Segmentation. Conceptual and Methodological Foundations* (Boston: Kluwer Academic Publishers, 1998), Chapters 1 and 2.

Companies will use different sets of criteria to screen countries, depending on the nature of the product. Cultural similarity to the domestic market is one criterion on which companies often rely. Other popular screening criteria include market attractiveness in terms of economic prosperity (e.g., per capita GNP), geographic proximity and the country's economic infrastructure.[4]

Country segmentation also plays a role in global marketing research. Companies increasingly make an effort to design products or services that meet the needs of customers in different countries. Certain features might need to be added or altered, but the core product is largely common across countries. Other aspects of the marketing mix program such as the communication strategy might also be similar. The benefits of a standardization approach often outweigh the possible drawbacks. Still, to successfully adopt this approach, companies need to do sufficient market research. Given the sheer number of countries in which many companies operate, doing market research in each one of them is often inefficient. Especially at the early stage, companies are likely to focus on a select few countries. The key question, then, is which countries to choose. One approach is to start grouping prospective markets into clusters of homogeneous countries. Out of each group, one prototypical member is chosen. Research efforts will be concentrated on each of the key members, at least initially. Presumably, research findings for the selected key member countries can then be projected to other countries belonging to its cluster. For example, Heineken chose four countries to do market research for Buckler, a non-alcoholic beer: the Netherlands, Spain, the United States, and France. The Dutch brewer wanted to assess the market appeal of Buckler and the feasibility of a pan-European marketing strategy consisting of a roughly common targeting, positioning, and marketing mix strategy across the continent.[5]

**Global Marketing Research**

When a product or service does well in one country, firms often hope to replicate their success story in other countries. The strategic logic is to launch the product in countries that in some regards are highly similar to the country where the product has already been introduced.[6] For example, Cadbury-Schweppes was very confident about launching Schweppes tonic water in Brazil, given that the beverage was well accepted in culturally similar countries such as Mexico.

**Entry Decisions**

It is important, though, to realize that a host of factors make or break the success of a new product launch. Tabasco sauce is very popular in many Asian countries like Japan with a strong liking for spicy dishes. Hence, McIlhenny, the Louisiana-based maker of Tabasco sauce, might view entering Vietnam and India, two of the emerging markets in Asia with a palate for hot food, as the logical next step for its expansion strategy in Asia. Other factors, however, such as buying power, import restrictions, or the shoddy state of the distribution and media infrastructure could lessen the appeal of these markets.

Segmentation decisions are also instrumental in setting the company's product positioning strategy. Once the firm has selected the target segments, management needs to develop a positioning strategy to embrace the chosen segments. Basically, the company must decide on how it wants to position its products or services in the mind of the prospective target customers. Environmental changes or shifting consumer preferences often force a firm to rethink its positioning strategy. Cathay Pacific's repositioning strategy in the mid-1990s is a good example. The Hong Kong-based airline carrier realized that its product offerings failed to adequately meet the needs of its Asian clients, who represent 80 percent of its customer base. To better satisfy this target segment, the airline repositioned itself in the fall of 1994 to become the preferred airline among Asian travelers. To that end, Cathay

**Positioning Strategy**

---

[4]Debanjan Mitra and Peter N. Golder, "Whose Culture Matters? Near-Market Knowledge and Its Impact on Foreign Market Entry Timing," *Journal of Marketing Research*, 39 (August 2002), pp. 350–65.

[5]Sandra Vandermerwe, "Heineken NV: Buckler Nonalcoholic Beer," Case Study, International Institute for Management Development, Switzerland, 1991.

[6]Johny K. Johansson and Reza Moinpour, "Objective and Perceived Similarity for Pacific-Rim Countries," *Columbia Journal of World Business*, Winter 1977, pp. 65–76.

**EXHIBIT 7-1**
MARKET CLUSTERING APPROACH FOR INSTANT COFFEE

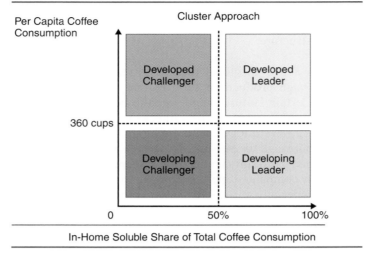

wanted to project an Asian personality with a personal touch. Cathay now offers a wide variety of Asian meals and entertainment. Other measures include a new logo (by some people referred to as a shark-fin), new colors, repainted exteriors, and redesigned cabins and ticket counters. To communicate these changes to the public, Cathay launched a heavy advertising campaign with the slogan "The Heart of Asia."[7]

**Resource Allocation**

Market segmentation will also be useful in deciding how to allocate the company's scarce marketing resources across different countries. **Exhibit 7-1** shows how Nestlé clusters countries using two criteria for Nescafé, its instant coffee brand: per capita coffee consumption and the market share of in-home soluble coffee of overall coffee consumption. Countries where the share of instant coffee is more than 50 percent are classified as *leader* markets; countries where R&G coffee[8] is dominant are classified as *challenger* markets. Developed markets are those with an annual per capita consumption of more than 360 cups. Countries below the 360-cups cutoff are developing markets from Nestlé's perspective. A representation such as the one shown in Exhibit 7-1 offers guidance for an MNC in formulating its strategic objectives and allocating resources across groups of countries in a given region or worldwide. For instance, Nestlé's managers could decide to concentrate marketing resources in countries that have a low market share but a high per capita consumption to bolster their firm's market share. Alternatively, resources could be allocated to countries where the firm has a strong competitive position but still fairly low coffee consumption. At the same time, managers would probably ponder cutting resources in markets with low coffee consumption and where Nestlé's market share is weak.

**Marketing Mix Policy**

In domestic marketing, segmentation and positioning decisions dictate a firm's marketing mix policy. By the same token, country segmentation guides the global marketer's mix decisions. A persistent problem faced by international marketers is how to strike the balance between standardization and customization. International market segmentation could shed some light on this issue. Countries belonging to the same segment might lend themselves to a standardized marketing mix strategy. The same product design, an identical pricing policy, similar advertising messages and media, and the same distribution channels could be used in these markets. Of course, marketers need to be very careful when

---

[7]John Pies, former Cathay Pacific executive, private communication.
[8]Roast and ground.

contemplating such moves. There should be a clear linkage between the segmentation bases and the target customers' responsiveness to any of these marketing mix instruments.

Usually, it is very difficult to establish a linkage between market segments and all four elements of the marketing mix. For instance, countries with an underdeveloped phone infrastructure (e.g., India, China, sub-Saharan Africa) are typically prime candidates for mobile phone technologies. However, many of these countries dramatically differ in terms of their price sensitivities given the wide gaps in buying power. Therefore, treating them as one group as far as the pricing policy goes might lead to disastrous consequences. The marketing team behind the Johnnie Walker scotch brand developed a schema classifying countries as "mature" (Western countries and Japan), "developing" (e.g., Spain, Portugal, Mexico, South Korea), or "emerging" (e.g., Brazil, Thailand, Russia, China). Each country group is characterized by different market conditions. For instance, Johnnie Walker faces rising costs of doing business (due to duties increases, product piracy) in "developing" countries and gray-channel situations in "emerging" markets.[9] Depending on the prevailing conditions, different marketing strategies are called for.

## INTERNATIONAL MARKET SEGMENTATION APPROACHES ◆ ◆ ◆ ◆ ◆ ◆ ◆

Global marketers approach the segmentation process from different angles. A very common international segmentation procedure classifies prospect countries geographically on a single dimension (e.g., per capita Gross National Product) or on a set of multiple socioeconomic, political, and cultural criteria available from secondary data sources (e.g., the World Bank, UNESCO, OECD). This is known as **country-as-segments** or **aggregate segmentation**. In **Exhibit 7-2**, you can see how the Swiss

**EXHIBIT 7-2**
NESTLÉ'S GEOGRAPHIC SEGMENTATION OF THE AMERICAS

*Source:* Nestle

---

[9]Amitava Chattopadhyay (2006), "Building the Johnnie Walker Brand," INSEAD Case Study # 506-212-1.

**EXHIBIT 7-3**
MACRO-LEVEL COUNTRY CHARACTERISTICS

| Construct | Items |
|---|---|
| 1. Aggregate production and transportation (mobility) | Number of air passengers/km<br>Air cargo (ton/km)<br>Number of newspapers<br>Population<br>Cars per capita<br>Gasoline consumption per capita<br>Electricity production |
| 2. Health | Life expectancy<br>Physicians per capita<br>Political stability |
| 3. Trade | Imports/GNP<br>Exports/GNP |
| 4. Lifestyle | GDP per capita<br>Phones per capita<br>Electricity consumption per capita |
| 5. Cosmopolitanism | Foreign visitors per capita<br>Tourist expenditures per capita<br>Tourist receipts per capita |
| 6. Miscellaneous | Consumer price index<br>Newspaper circulation<br>Hospital beds<br>Education expenditures/<br>   Government budget<br>Graduate education in population<br>   per capita |

*Source:* Kristiaan Helsen, Kamel Jedidi, and Wayne S. DeSarbo, "A New Approach to Country Segmentation Utilizing Multinational Diffusion Patterns," *Journal of Marketing*, 57, (5), October 1993 p. 64. Reprinted with permission from the *Journal of Marketing*, published by the American Marketing Association.

consumer conglomerate Nestlé geographically segments the Americas. While it treats some countries as stand-alone segments (e.g., Brazil, Canada, the United States), it groups others with neighboring countries. **Exhibit 7-3** presents a list of various general country characteristics that analysts might consider for classifying countries in distinct segments. When there are numerous country traits, the segmentation variables are usually first collapsed into a smaller set of dimensions using data reduction techniques such as factor analysis. The countries under consideration are then classified into homogeneous groups using statistical algorithms such as cluster analysis (see the Appendix for a brief overview of some of these techniques).

The country-as-segments approach has some major flaws. From a global marketer's perspective, the managerial relevance of geographic segments is often questionable. Country boundaries rarely define differences in consumer response to marketing strategies. Furthermore, it is seldom clear what variables should be included in deriving the geographic segments.

An alternative approach is **disaggregate international consumer segmentation**. Here, the focus is the individual consumer. Just as with domestic marketing, one or more segmentation bases (e.g., lifestyle, demographic, values) are chosen. Consumer segments are then identified in terms of consumer similarities with respect to the chosen bases. The key problem here is that targeting a consumer segment that is geographically dispersed can become a logistical nightmare.

To address the shortcomings of the previous two approaches, **two-stage international segmentation** can offer solace.[10] The first step—**macro-segmentation**—is the classification of countries into different groups. The second phase—**micro-segmentation**—consists of segmenting consumers for each country-cluster identified in the first step. In the first macro-level stage, countries are grouped on general segmentation bases. Some bases

---

[10]J.-B.E.M. Steenkamp and F. Ter Hofstede, "International Market Segmentation: Issues and Perspectives," *International Journal of Research in Marketing* (September 2002), pp. 185–214.

are independent of the product or service for which the segmentation is being done. They can be observable (e.g., demographic, socioeconomic, cultural) or unobservable (e.g., lifestyle, values, personality) traits. This first step also enables the manager to screen out countries that are unacceptable (e.g., because of high political risk or low buying power) or do not fit the company's objectives. The second micro-level phase is similar to standard segmentation within a given country except that most consumer segments overlap across countries rather than being restricted to one particular country. The candidate micro-level segmentation criteria are similar to the segmentation bases considered for standard market segmentation: demographics (e.g., age, gender, family life-cycle stage), socio-economic measures (e.g., per capita income, social class), lifestyle, values, and benefits sought. The particular bases selected depend on the nature of the goal of the segmentation. Benefit segmentation, for example, is preferred when assessing new product ideas. These disaggregate data then form the ingredients for identifying cross-national segment of consumers within the geographic segment(s) chosen. Two-stage segmentation has several benefits. First, compared to purely geographic country-level aggregation, the segments will be more responsive to marketing efforts. The segments are also more in tune with a market-orientation perspective as they focus on consumer needs rather than simply macro-level socioeconomic or cultural variables. Second, as opposed to dis-aggregate consumer segmentation, the derived segments will be more accessible.[11]

## SEGMENTATION SCENARIOS

When a firm segments foreign markets, different scenarios may arise. A common phenomenon is illustrated in **Exhibit 7-4** where we have one universal segment (A) and the other segments are either unique to a particular country or exist in only two of the three countries. Note also that the size of the different segments varies depending on the country.

One possibility is that you uncover so-called **universal** or **global segments**. These are segments that transcend national boundaries. They are universal in the sense that customers belonging to such segments have common needs. Note that this segment could also be a universal niche. A *niche* is commonly defined as a more narrowly defined group of consumers who seek a very special bundle of benefits. Examples of possible universal segments that are emerging include the global youth, international

**EXHIBIT 7-4**
DIFFERENT SEGMENT SCENARIOS

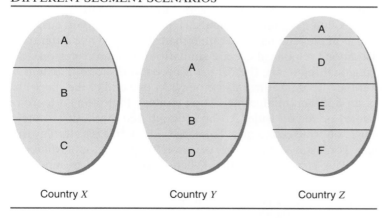

Country X    Country Y    Country Z

---

[11]There are other segmentation approaches that allow for cross-border segments with spatial contiguity. One interesting methodology is outlined in F. Ter Hofstede, M. Wedel, and J.-B.E.M. Steenkamp, "Identifying Spatial Segments in International Markets," *Marketing Science*, 21 (Spring 2002), pp. 160–77.

business travelers, and the global elite. One study done at Harvard University looked at consumers' attitudes toward global brands. Based on a survey done with 1,800 respondents in twelve countries the authors derived the following seven global segments:

- *Global climbers (23.3%).* These people are extremely conscious of and attracted to brands that exude global status. They are unimpressed by brands that are linked with countries that have a strong quality reputation for specific products.
- *Civic libertarians (21.5%).* This group puts heavy emphasis on social responsibility. They are not impressed by brands that are produced in countries with a high reputation in the product category.
- *Multinational fans (15.5%).* This segment ranks highest on the influence of reputation and global status on brand preference.
- *Antiglobalists (13.1%).* These people are strongly against brands that express American values and are very cynical about the ethics of companies that own global brands.
- *Global citizens (10.1%).* This segment values social responsibility.
- *Global agnostics (7.6%).* These consumers value global brands just as any other brand without using the global dimension as a cue.
- *Pro-West (7.6%).* These people have a high esteem for American values. Their brand preferences are highly influenced by global status.[12]

How similar customer needs are clearly depends on the product category.[13] Axe,[14] Unilever's brand of male grooming products, shows how one company can successfully market its products to a global segment, in this case the global youth. To grab exposure among web-savvy young males worldwide, Unilever developed clever digital marketing ideas around the fragrance. For instance, Axe's marketing team created a series of online games and videos (http://www.theaxeeffect.com/flash.html) showing the "Axe effect"—women chasing men who used the deodorant.[15] Redd's, a beer-like brand sold by SABMiller, is an example of a product that is targeted toward a universal segment. The brew, an "apple-infused malt beverage, with a citrus flavor," is aimed specifically at women, a segment that traditionally has been neglected by beer companies. Redd's is sold in packages of five or ten bottles, rather than six- or twelve-packs for typical beer brand. The packs are shaped like a woman's handbag. The brand was first introduced in South Africa and Eastern Europe and then also launched in Latin America.[16]

Commonality of consumer needs is high for high-tech consumer durables and travel-related products (e.g., credit cards, airlines). At the other end of the spectrum are food products, where customer needs tend to be very localized. Apart from global segments, you may also encounter **regional segments**. Here the similarity in customer needs and preferences exists at the regional level rather than globally. While differences in consumer needs exist among regions, there are similarities within the region.

With universal or regional segments, the firm still needs to decide the extent to which it wants to differentiate its marketing mix strategy. At one end of the spectrum, management can adopt an undifferentiated marketing strategy that offers a more or less uniform package world or region wide. An undifferentiated marketing strategy allows the firm to capitalize on scale economies. To a large extent, this is a strategy that suits high-tech companies. For instance, the corporate advertising director of Microsoft remarked in a forum: "The character of the [Microsoft] product is universal.

---

[12]Douglas B. Holt, John A. Quelch, and Earl L. Taylor, "Managing the Global Brand. A Typology of Consumer Perceptions," in *The Global Market*, eds. John Quelch and Rohit Deshpande. (Boston, MA: Harvard Business School Press, 2004), pp. 180–201.

[13]George S. Yip, *Total Global Strategy* (Englewood Cliffs, NJ: Prentice Hall, 1995), pp. 30–32.

[14]The brand is named Lynx in Australia, Ireland, New Zealand, and the United Kingdom.

[15]"Children of the Web," *Business Week*, July 2, 2007, pp. 51–58.

[16]"Five-packs for Latinas," *International Herald Tribune*, October 15, 2007, pp. 12–13.

Technology is an English-based thing, so there's a lot of willingness to embrace Western companies."[17] At the other end of the spectrum are firms that tailor their marketing strategy to local markets. Although consumer needs and preferences may be similar, differentiation of positioning and other marketing mix elements might be necessary to cope with variations in local market conditions. A differentiated strategy allows the company to stay better in tune with the local market and to be more flexible.

**Unique (diverse) segments** are the norm when gaps in cross-country customer needs and preferences are so substantial that it becomes very hard to derive meaningful cross-border segments. Under such a scenario, marketing mix programs must be localized to meet local consumer needs. Rather than going after one common cross-border segment, management picks the most attractive target markets in each individual market. A case in point is the Canon AE-1 camera. When Canon launched this camera, it developed three different marketing programs: one for Japan, one for the United States, and one for Europe. In Japan, Canon targeted young replacement buyers. In the United States, it concentrated on upscale, first-time buyers of 35mm single-lens reflex cameras. In Germany, Canon focused on older and technologically more sophisticated replacement buyers.[18] Jack Daniel's, the Tennessee-based whiskey brand, also pursues diverse target markets. In Australia and New Zealand, the beverage brand pursues young, hip, social drinkers. In China, where a bottle of Jack Daniel's costs $30 or more—double its U.S. price—the target is the 30- to 40-year old urban professional who earns $1,000 a month working for a joint-venture company.[19]

In most instances, there is a mixture of universal, regional, and country-specific market segments. One final comment to be made here is that markets differ a great deal in terms of their degree of segmentation. Gaps in the degree of segmentation are most visible when contrasting the market structure in a developed country with the one in an emerging market. For most consumer goods, the market structure for a category in the emerging market is often pretty unsophisticated: premium versus economy. Developed countries, on the other hand, have typically many more segments and niches. This is to a large extent due to differences in the degree of market development. Early on in the product life cycle, the market is still relatively undersegmented. As consumers grow more sophisticated and demanding and as the category develops, new segments and niches emerge.

---

## BASES FOR INTERNATIONAL MARKET SEGMENTATION ◆ ◆ ◆ ◆ ◆ ◆ ◆

The first step in doing international market segmentation is deciding which criteria to use in the task. Just as in a domestic marketing context, the marketing analyst faces an embarrassment of riches. Literally hundreds of country characteristics could be used as inputs. In a sense, you can pick and choose the variables that you want. However, for the segmentation to be meaningful, the market segments and the response variable(s) the company is interested in should have a linkage. Usually it is not a trivial exercise to figure out a priori which of the variables will contribute to the segmentation. Instead, the marketing analyst will need to do some experimentation to find a proper set of segmentation variables. Furthermore, information on several segmentation criteria is typically missing, inaccurate, or outdated for some of the countries to be segmented.

We now briefly discuss different types of country variables that are most commonly used for country segmentation purposes. Most of these criteria can be used for the two segmentation approaches that we discussed earlier. For instance, one could use a

---

[17]"U.S. Multinationals," *Advertising Age International* (June 1999), p. 41.

[18]Hirotaka Takeuchi and Michael E. Porter, "Three Roles of International Marketing in Global Strategy," in *Competition in Global Industries*, ed. M. E. Porter (Boston, Mass.: Harvard Business School Press, 1986), pp. 139–40.

[19]"Jack Daniel's goes down smooth in Australia, New Zealand, China," *Ad Age International* (September 1997), pp. i38–i39.

socioeconomic variable such as per-capita income as a segmentation base to group countries. However, one could also use the income dimension to segment consumers within country first and then derive regional or global segments (e.g., pan-Asian middle class).

**Demographics**     Demographic variables are among the most popular segmentation criteria. One reason for their popularity is that they are very easy to measure (recall the "measurability" requirement for effective market segmentation). Moreover, information on population variables is mostly reasonably accurate and readily available.

As part of its 2007 Global HABIT study, Hakuhodo, one of Japan's largest ad agencies, conducted a segmentation study of Asian women. The study revealed five distinct clusters (the percentages indicate the share of each segment of the entire sample):

1. *Socially conscious (8.2%)*. These women tend to be autonomous and community oriented, active at both home and work, and aspire to make a meaningful contribution to the betterment of society. Family and work are both important. Most common in Hong Kong.

2. *My small world (26.3%)*. What is important for women in this cluster are relationships with family and others close to them. Their attitudes are conservative; they prefer traditional gender roles. A happy family is the primary goal. Most common in Manila and Jakarta.

3. *Happy as I am (26.0%)*. These women are satisfied with their life; they want enough money to maintain their current lifestyle. They like taking it easy but worry a little about how other people see them. Most common in Shanghai, Seoul, and Bangkok.

4. *I want more (26.2%)*. To these women life enjoying life matters more than work. Loving newness and fun, they want a stylish lifestyle. They like to try new things. Fashion is a way of expressing themselves. Very common in Taipei and Hong Kong.

5. *Look at me (13.2%)*. These women are status hungry. They want to be the center of attention. They are ambitious, concerned about their appearance, and want to be seen as leaders. Most common in Mumbai and Seoul.

**Exhibit 7-5** shows the clusters for three of the cities where the study was run.

One segment that marketers often overlook is the elderly. In industrialized countries, the over-60 age segment is expected to rise to a third of the population (over two-fifths in Japan) from 20 percent now. Many of these people are more prosperous and healthier than ever before. Countries with an aging population clearly offer market opportunities for consumer goods and services that cater to the elderly. To gain a foothold within this target market, it is critical to understand the subtleties of marketing to the over-60 group, especially in youth-obsessed cultures. Gerber's launch of a baby-food like product line called Senior Citizen proved to be a failure because older shoppers have no desire to vividly show their age.[20] Unilever's low-fat pro.activ sub-brand margarine spread,[21] however, was a major success. The pro.activ addresses the need for a heart-friendly margarine among aging consumers. Pro.activ was proven to lower cholesterol levels. As a result, Unilever was able to establish agreements with insurance companies in France and the Netherlands to offer discounts to their insurance customers for consuming pro.activ products.[22]

By the same token, countries with high birth rates have similar buying patterns. Examples of goods and services with high potential in such countries include baby food

---

[20]"Over 60 and Overlooked," *The Economist* (August 10, 2002), pp. 51–52.

[21]Pro-activ is a sub-brand of Unilever's Becel/Flora margarine brand. In the United States the product is sold under the Promise brand name.

[22]http://www.functionalingredientsmag.com/ASP/articleLoader.asp?catId=404&path=D:\vol\NewHope\FFN\Live\FFNSite\Content\Issue\51\887.html&strSource=

## EXHIBIT 7-5
## MARKET SEGMENTATION OF ASIAN WOMEN

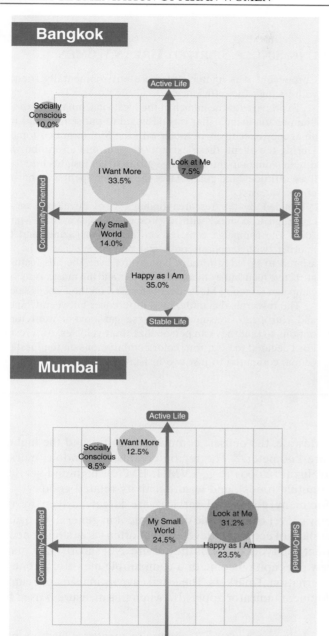

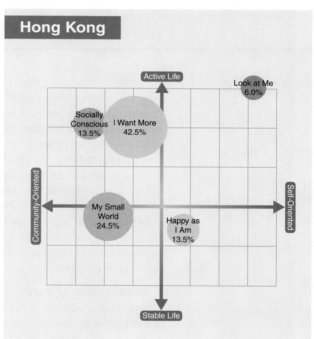

*Source:* Hakuhodo Global HABIT 2008 Survey

and clothing, toys, prenatal care services, and birth-control devices. **Global Perspective 7-1** discusses how the Ford targets young, single women in China with the new Fiesta.

Satellite photos taken of the European continent at night show a blue curve of light that stretches from Manchester, Britain, through the Rhineland down to northern Italy. French journalists labeled this area the *blue banana* ("banane bleue"). It has the largest

**Socioeconomic Variables**

## GLOBAL PERSPECTIVE 7-1

### FORD FIESTA IN CHINA—TARGETING "MEI" OR YOUNG, SINGLE, SPIRITED, URBAN WOMEN

Critical to the success of the Ford's marketing strategy in China is "Mei" (meaning beautiful in Chinese). Mei represents the twenty-something, single urban, college-educated female, who earns $880 to $1,500 a month and plans to buy her first car. This is Ford's target market for the rollout of the new Fiesta in China. China's car market is the second biggest in the world (behind the United States). Yet, although passenger-vehicle sales rose almost 7 percent in 2008, sales of Ford brand cars dropped 10 percent. Ford hopes that the new Fiesta will halt the sales decline.

The new Ford Fiesta is the first of Ford's global car strategy that centers on the idea of selling car models worldwide in order to save on development costs and gain economies of scale. The new model was first revealed at the 2008 Geneva car show. Ford planned to launch the car first in Asia in 2009, then in Europe, and ultimately in North America. The new Fiesta has the same size as the old small-car Fiesta that was sold in

*Source:* "Ford's Fortunes in China Depend on 'Mei'," *The Wall Street Journal Asia*, February 10, 2009, p. 16 and "2009 Ford Fiesta—Auto Shows," www.caranddriver.com, accessed on February 10, 2009.

Europe but it is lighter and more environmentally friendly with its high-fuel efficiency.

To prepare for the launch of the Fiesta in China, Ford ran an "immersion event" that was designed to put senior Ford and ad agency executives in touch with the Mei target customers. During the event, these executives spent one afternoon with fifteen women in the Fiesta age group to get insights into their lives, attitudes, and goals. All of the women spent a lot of time on the internet.

Guided by the research findings, Ford developed an ad campaign to connect with its prospects that started in March 2009. The campaign centered on lifestyle magazines and the internet, with emphasis on social networking sites. The ads aspired to be edgy without being offensive. The ads featured attractive men and women, bright colors and hip music. A second campaign targeting Mei's parents focused on the Fiesta's safety.

The research also underlined differences between Chinese and European consumers: Chinese car buyers want more options so that they can personalize their vehicles. As a result, Ford decided to offer four color combinations on the Fiesta in China, compared to just two in Europe.

---

concentration of big cities worldwide, the densest commercial traffic, and the highest production capacity per square kilometer.[23] The region creates tremendous market opportunities to marketers of luxury goods (e.g., LVMH, BMW), high-end services (e.g., resorts, internet access, mutual funds), and leisure-activity-related goods.

Consumption patterns for many goods and services are largely driven by the consumer wealth or the country's level of economic development in general. Consumers from countries at the same stage of economic development often show similar needs in terms of the per capita amount and types of goods they desire. Not surprisingly, many consumer good marketers view per capita income or a comparable measure as one of the key criteria in grouping international markets. The usual caveats in using per capita income as an economic development indicator apply also when this measure is used for country segmentation:[24]

- *Monetization of transactions within a country.* To compare measures such as per-capita GNP across countries, figures based on a local currency need to be translated into a common currency (e.g., the U.S. dollar or the euro). However, official exchange rates seldom reflect the true buying power of a currency. So, income figures based on GNP or GDP do not really tell you how much a household in a given country is able to buy.

- *Gray and black sectors of the economy.* National income figures only record transactions that arise in the legitimate sector of a country's economy. Many countries have a sizable *gray* sector, consisting of largely untaxed (or under-taxed) exchanges that often involve barter transactions. In cities in the developing world, many professors make ends

---

[23]http://www.msnbc.com/news/844728.asp.

[24]Vern Terpstra and Kenneth David, *The Cultural Environment of International Business*, Cincinnati, OH: South-Western Publishing Co., 1991.

meet by driving a taxi. In exchange for a dental checkup, a television repairman might fix the dentist's television set. Many communities also thrive on a substantial *black* sector, involving transactions that are outright illegal. Examples of such activities include the drug trade, smuggling, racketeering, gambling, and prostitution.

• *Income disparities.* Quantities such as the per capita GNP only tell part of the story. Such measures are misleading in countries with wide income inequalities such as Bolivia where the richest 10 percent of the population gets 47 percent share of the country's income, while the poorest 10 percent gets a mere 0.3 percent.[25]

To protect against these shortcomings of standard "per-capita income" segmentation exercises, marketers can employ other metrics to group consumers in terms of their buying power.[26] One alternative is to use the PPP (purchasing power parity) as a criterion. PPP reflects how much a household in each country has to spend (in U.S. dollars equivalent) to buy a standard basket of goods. PPP estimates can be found in the *World Bank Atlas* published annually by the World Bank and in the *CIA World Factbook*, which is also accessible online (http://www.cia.gov/cia/publications/factbook/).

Another alternative to analyze buying power in a set of countries is via a **socio-economic strata (SES) analysis**. For instance, Strategy Research Corporation applied an SES-analysis for Latin American households using measures like the number of consumer durables in the household, education level. Each country was stratified into five socio-economic segments, each one designated with a letter: upper class (A), middle-to-upper class (B), middle-class (C), lower class (D), and poverty level (E). **Exhibit 7-6** shows how

## EXHIBIT 7-6
### SABMILLER'S MARKET SEGMENTATION OF PERU'S BEER MARKET

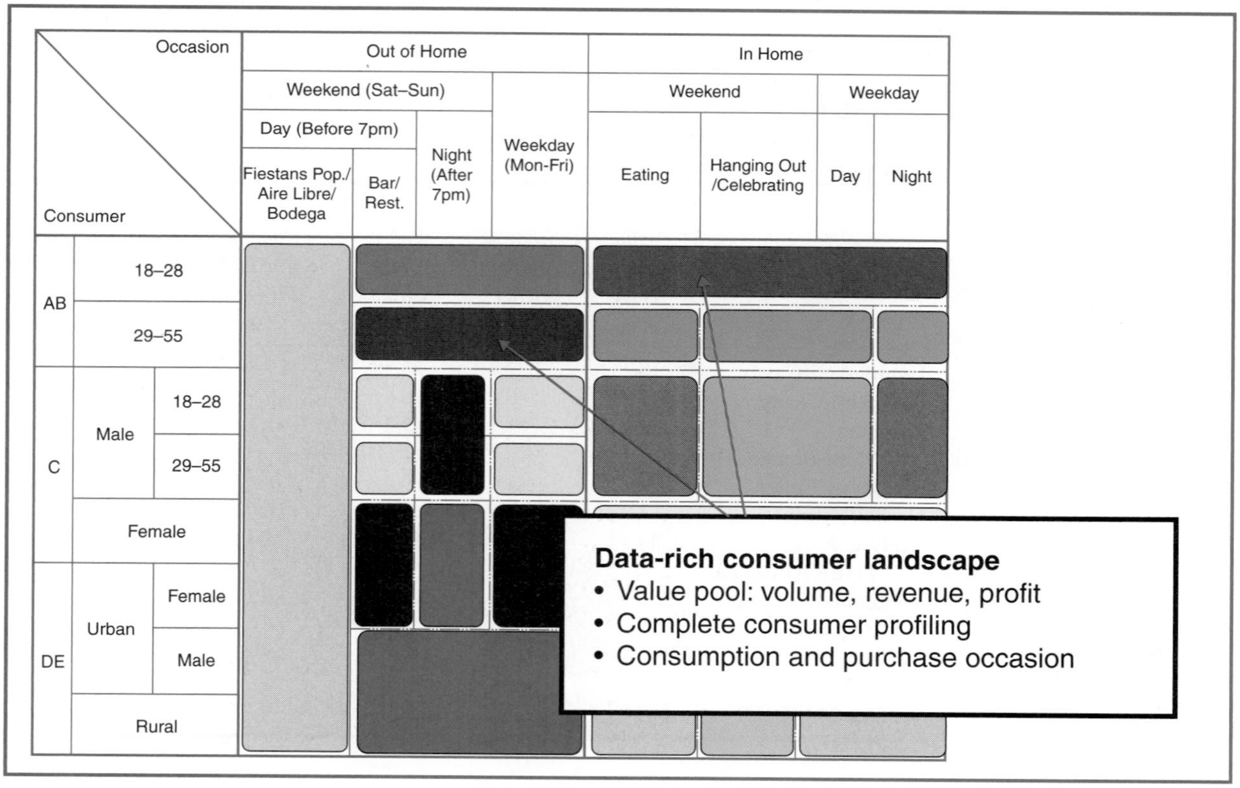

*Source:* SABMiller

---

[25]https://www.cia.gov/library/publications/the-world-factbook/, accessed on January 26, 2009.
[26]Chip Walker, "The Global Middle Class," *American Demographics*, September 1995, pp. 40–46.

SABMiller, one of the world's biggest beer brewers, uses SES analysis to segment the beer market in Peru.

Other schemes broaden the notion of a country's level of development by going beyond standard of living measures. One popular classification schema is based on the Human Development Index (HDI), which is released every year by the United Nations (see http://hdr.undp.org/en/). It covers 177 UN member countries and territories. HDI widens the notion of economic development by looking at a country's achievements in three areas: life expectancy at birth (a long and healthy life), knowledge (e.g., adult literacy), and a decent standard of living (per capita in PPP). The 2007/08 report classified 70 countries as having achieved a high level of economic development (HDI of 0.80 or above), 85 as medium (HDI of 0.5-0.799), and 22 as low (HDI of less than 0.50). The highest scorers were Norway (HDI of 0.968), Iceland (0.968),[27] and Australia (0.962). At the bottom of the table were Guinea-Bissau (0.374), Burkina Faso (0.370), and Sierra Leone (0.336).[28]

**Behavior-Based Segmentation**

As with domestic marketing, segments can also be formed based on behavioral response variables. Behavioral segmentation criteria include degree of brand/supplier loyalty, usage rate (based on per capita consumption), product penetration (that is, the percentage of the target market that uses the product or the brand), and benefits sought after. Just as in domestic marketing, benefit segmentation is often used in global marketing for product positioning, product design or product adaptation purposes. While benefit segments overlap different countries, their relative size often differs in each market. **Exhibit 7-7** shows the proportionate size and growth rate of benefit segments in the toothpaste category in three countries: the United States, Mexico, and China.

**EXHIBIT 7-7**
BENEFIT SEGMENTS OF TOOTHPASTE MARKET IN THE USA, CHINA, AND MEXICO

| | Value Share USA 2004 | % Change Share in USA vs. 2000 | Value Share China 2004 | % Change Share in China vs. 2000 | Value Share Mexico 2004 | % Change Share in Mexico vs. 2000 |
|---|---|---|---|---|---|---|
| Family Anti-Cavity | 18.3% | −22.7 | 28.5% | −29.8 | 64.8% | −1.9 |
| Kids Anti-Cavity | 3.7 | −0.1 | 0.6 | +0.5 | 1.2 | +0.1 |
| Premium Multi-Benefitx | 18.8 | +1.5 | 2.2 | −1.1 | 12.1 | +1.5 |
| Sensitivity Relief | 7.7 | +1.0 | 0.4 | −8.5 | 3.3 | −0.9 |
| Herbal/Natural | 1.9 | +1.9 | 15.8 | +10.1 | 2.0 | +2.0 |
| TOTAL THERAPEUTIC | 53.4 | −19.3 | 82.9 | −6.4 | 87.3 | +2.6 |
| Whitening | 30.3 | +16.4 | 8.9 | +3.8 | 2.7 | −2.2 |
| Freshening | 16.3 | +2.9 | 8.2 | +2.6 | 10.0 | −0.4 |
| TOTAL COSMETIC | 46.4 | +19.3 | 17.1 | +6.4 | 12.7 | −2.6 |
| TOTAL MARKET | 100.0 | | 100.0 | | 100.0 | |

*Source:* Compiled from Exhibits 2B, 7A, and 14 in John A. Quelch and Jacquie Labatt-Randle, "Colgate Max Fresh: Global Brand Roll-Out," Harvard Business School Case Study, 9-508-009, 2007.

[27]Given that Iceland's economy tanked in 2008 the next listing will probably show a much lower HDI.
[28]In fact, all of the low-HDI countries were African.

Marketers can group consumers according to their lifestyle (i.e., their attitudes, opinions, and core values). Lifestyle (psychographic) segmentation is especially popular in advertising circles. Many lifestyle segmentation schemes are very general and not related to a specific product category. Others are derived for a specific product or service area. Distinctions can also be made between whether a given typology was prepared for a specific country or a given region.

**Lifestyle**

An example of the general-type lifestyle segmentation approach is GfK Roper Consulting's *Valuescope* model. Each year, the market research company conducts 30,000 interviews around the world to monitor consumer values. Based on the responses, Valuescope identified seven values segments:

1. *Achievers* place high importance on obtaining and showing social status. They put their own interests ahead of others'.

2. *Traditionals* believe that their inherited way of life is the best and does not need any changes. Religious beliefs and cultural traditions rule their lives.

3. *Survivors* try to always give their best effort while being modest. They are not looking for a lot of money, just enough to eke out a living. They want to keep their life as simple and uncluttered as possible.

4. *Nurturers* place high value on maintaining long-term commitment to friends and family. In building relationships with friends and relatives, they find it important to be sincere and to have integrity.

5. *Hedonists* need instant gratification. They are always looking for new experiences. They need to feel young and want to have a good time.

6. *Socialrationals* view the world as a large and diverse place where differences should be respected. They value open-mindedness and try to save the world because they feel it is sensible to do so.

7. *Self-directeds* value freedom of action and thought so they can choose their own goals and achieve them.[29]

Lifestyle segmentation has been applied for the positioning of new brands, repositioning of existing ones, identifying new product opportunities, and developing brand personalities.[30] Practitioners and academics alike have raised concerns about the use of lifestyle segmentation:

• Values are too general to relate to consumption patterns or brand choice behavior within a specific product category. As a result, lifestyle segmentation is not very useful as a tool to make predictions about consumers' buying responsiveness. Obviously, this criticism only applies to the general value schemes.

• Value-based segmentation schemes are not always "actionable." Remember that one of the requirements for effective segmentation is actionability. Lifestyle groupings do not offer much guidance in terms of what marketing actions should be taken. Also, many of the typologies have too many different types to be useful for practical purposes.

• Value segments are not stable because values typically change over time.

• Their international applicability is quite limited because lifestyles, even within the same region, often vary from country to country.[31]

Aside from the criteria discussed here, many other dimensions could form the basis for segmentation. The proper criteria largely depend on the nature of the product and the objectives of the segmentation exercise.

---

[29]http://www.gfknop.com/customresearch-uk/expertise/consumertrends/valuescope/index.en.html.

[30]Marieke de Mooij, *Advertising Worldwide*, 2nd edition, Prentice Hall, 1994.

[31]Peter Sampson, "People are People the World over: The Case for Psychological Market Segmentation," *Marketing and Research Today*, November 1992, pp. 236–44.

◆ ◆ ◆ ◆ ◆ ◆ ◆ ◆   INTERNATIONAL POSITIONING STRATEGIES

Segmenting international markets is only part of the game. Once the multinational company has segmented its foreign markets, the firm needs to decide which target markets to pursue and what positioning strategy to use to appeal to the chosen segments. Some marketing scholars refer to positioning as the fifth *P* in the marketing mix in addition to product, price, promotion, and place. Developing a positioning theme involves the quest for a unique selling proposition (USP). In the global marketing scene, the positioning question boils down to a battle for the mind of your target customers, located not only within a certain country but also in some cases across the globe. The global positioning statement for the American beer brand Budweiser is shown in **Exhibit 7-8**. The formulation of a positioning strategy—be it local or global—moves along a sequence of steps:

1. Identify a relevant set of competing products or brands. What is the competitive frame?
2. Determine current perceptions held by consumers about your product/brand and the competition.
3. Develop possible positioning themes.
4. Screen the positioning alternatives and select the most appealing one.
5. Develop a marketing mix strategy that will implement the chosen positioning strategy.
6. Over time, monitor the effectiveness of your positioning strategy. If it is not working, check whether its failure is due to bad execution or an ill-conceived strategy.

**Uniform versus Localized Positioning Strategies**

Obviously, for global marketers, a key question is to what degree a uniform positioning strategy can be used. Clearly, one key driver here is the target market decision. Roughly speaking, MNCs have two choices: target a universal segment across countries or pursue different segments in the different markets. When focusing on a uniform segment, management needs to decide whether to use the same positioning worldwide or positioning themes that are tailored to individual markets. If the firm decides to opt for different segments on a country-by-country basis, the norm is to customize also the positioning appeals. **Exhibit 7-9** gives an overview of the different strategic options.

When target customers are very similar worldwide, sharing common core values and showing similar buying patterns, a uniform positioning strategy will probably work. By adopting a common positioning theme, the company can project a shared, consistent brand or corporate image worldwide. The need to have a consistent image is especially urgent for brands that have worldwide exposure and visibility. A few years ago, Samsung, a major South Korean consumer electronics manufacturer, announced its

**EXHIBIT 7-8**
BUDWEISER GLOBAL POSITIONING

Budweiser maintains its leadership positioning in the global beer industry by consistently being a brand that is:

- Refreshingly different from local brands, with its clean, crisp taste and high drinkability;
- A premium-quality beer, made using an all-natural process and ingredients;
- Global in stature, representing heritage, quality, and U.S. roots;
- Well-known as a world-class sponsor of sports and entertainment events;
- The world's best-selling beer.

*Source:* www.anheuser-busch.com

**EXHIBIT 7-9**
GLOBAL POSITIONING AND SEGMENTATION
STRATEGIES

|  | Universal Segment | Different Segments (case-by-case) |
|---|---|---|
| Uniform Positioning Strategy | ① | ② |
| Different Positioning Strategies | ③ | ④ |

intent to obtain the world number-one position in all its main product markets by 2005. To achieve this goal, it positioned its brand as being at the leading edge of digital technology, using an aggressive advertising campaign and developing a whole range of nifty, digital products (e.g., interactive televisions, DVD players, third-generation mobile phones).[32] Having the same positioning theme also enables the firm to make use of global media. Samsung, for instance, sponsors highly visible, global sports events such as the 2008 Summer Beijing Olympics and teams such as Chelsea FC, a top tier English soccer team.

Many firms position a brand that is *mainstream* in its home market as a premium brand in their overseas markets, thereby targeting a narrower segment that is willing to pay a premium for imports. By moving upscale in the host country, the company can support the higher costs of doing business there. A case in point is Pizza Hut. In the United States, Pizza Hut is a fading fast-food brand. In China and other overseas markets, however, Pizza Hut has found a new life as a fashionable casual-dining restaurant. Pizza Hut was the first restaurant chain to introduce pizza in China in 1990.[33] Yum! China, the owner of Pizza Hut, now has more than 500 restaurants in China and is still growing there.[34] Likewise, Burberry's, the British clothing brand, has lost some of its cachet in Britain especially after it became the outfit of choice for soccer hooligans and "chavs."[35] Yet, in spite of its woes in the home market, Burberry's has been able to maintain an upscale image in Asia. Other examples of brands that are mainstream in their home market but have a premium image in the international marketplace are Heineken, Levi's, and Budweiser. This strategy is especially effective in product categories where the local brands already are very well entrenched (like beer in most countries) and imported brands have a potential to leverage the cachet of being "imported." Local brands usually enjoy a pioneering advantage by the fact of being the first one in the market. Therefore, instead of competing head-on with the local competition, foreign brands (despite the fact that they are a mainstream brand in their home market) are mostly better off by targeting the upscale segment. Though smaller in numbers, this segment is willing to pay a substantial premium price. Note that

---

[32]"Koreans Aim to Create a Sharp Image," *Financial Times* (December 28, 2001), p. 14.

[33]"Brands: Moving Overseas to Move Upmarket," *Business Week*, published September 18, 2008, http://www.businessweek.com/magazine/content/08_39/b4101060110428.htm?chan=magazine+channel_special+report, accessed October 31, 2008.

[34]http://www.yum.com/about/china.asp, accessed on October 31, 2008.

[35]"Chavs" refers to an underclass of British society known for its aggressive and vulgar behavior, similar to "white trash" in the United States; http://en.wikipedia.org/wiki/Chav, accessed October 31, 2008. Note that their Burberry's gear is usually counterfeit.

# GLOBAL PERSPECTIVE 7-2

## SELLING THE ENERGY DRINK THAT GIVES YOU WINGS

Dietrich Mateschitz discovered Red Bull, the infamous energy drink, in Bangkok when he was marketing director for Blendax, a German toothpaste brand. Every time he was on his way from the airport in Bangkok he would buy a bottle: "One glass and the jet lag was gone." In fact, he loved the product so much that in 1984 he joined forces with two Thai partners, a father-and-son team, to turn the product into a global brand. They tinkered with the tonic's formula, carbonated it, and translated the Thai words *Krating Daeng* into English—Red Bull. The ingredients: taurine, an amino acid; glucuronolactone, a substance found in the body; and caffeine. The brew went on sale in Austria, Mr. Mateschitz' home country, in 1987. Red Bull was launched in Germany in 1994 and in the United Kingdom in 1993. By 2002, Red Bull had become a global cult drink selling 1.6 billion cans in 62 countries.

Initially, nightclubs and discos were not very keen on taking on the product. Instead, Mr. Mateschitz relied on traditional retail outlets and gas stations. Little by little, Red Bull gained a following among extreme sports enthusiasts, such as snowboarders and windsurfers, because of its alleged potency. Red Bull cultivates an image of being a tonic that makes old-age soft drinks look tame by comparison. According to some critics its potency is so big that it might in fact be dangerous. In the Swedish press, three deaths were linked to the consumption of Red Bull. In fact, France and Denmark do not allow the brand to be sold.

*Sources:* "Selling Energy," *The Economist* (May 11, 2002), p. 62; "Red Bull Rethinks Brand Image for Asia," *Media* (October 18, 2002), p. 26; "Extreme Sports and Clubbers Fuel Energetic Rise," *Financial Times* (November 23, 2001), p. 10; "Red Bull Puts Cash on Lifting Category," *Media* (October 4, 2002), p. 1.

Red Bull reinforces its edgy image by sponsoring extreme sports (e.g., a mountain-bike race down a German salt mine) and the Arrows Formula One (F1) team. The F1 sponsorship also gives Red Bull global exposure. To a large degree Red Bull's success is due to the consistent image that has been nurtured over the years through clever marketing activities. Since its launch in Austria, Red Bull has used the same communication strategy and the same tone of voice. It is touted as "the energy drink that gives you wings." Red Bull has largely ignored mass marketing. The only advertising is a series of whimsical TV cartoons. Instead Red Bull relies a great deal on event marketing and sponsorships. For instance, the company sponsors an annual *Flugtag*, where contestants build their own flying machines and leap off a parapet.

In most Western countries, Red Bull is pitched at nightclub goers who mix the tonic with alcohol, giving users the energy to party through the night. In several Asian countries, though, a different imaging strategy is needed. For starters, it is sold in a bottle, rather than a can—to tout a health drink image. In Malaysia, the majority of the population is Muslim. Hence, a bar focus would be unacceptable. Instead, the goal is to project Red Bull as an energy drink that can be consumed on its own. Just as in the West, sports sponsorship is a key activity although the focus is on more traditional motor sports such as motorcycle races and 4-wheel drive competitions. Target audiences include students, drivers, and athletes, with the main distribution channel being convenience stores. In Thailand, the home of the original Red Bull recipe, a new Red Bull product was created to differentiate between two distinct target markets. The original tonic is promoted as a pick-me-up for taxi drivers and blue-collar workers. Red Bull Extra, the new line extension, targets trendy teens and bar-goers. To capture their imagination, the brand uses sponsorships of extreme sports events and concerts.

such positioning strategies are not always successful. Gap, the U.S. casual clothing brand, failed to reinvent itself as a premium brand in Germany. Consumers' image of the brand may also deteriorate over time. A good example is the experience of General Motors China. Initially, GM China was pretty successful in positioning the Buick brand as a prestigious car in China even though the car marque had a dismal reputation in the United States. However, lately, Buick's esteem has dropped in the mind of Chinese car buyers. **Global Perspective 7-2** highlights some of the positioning customizations that were made for the energy drink Red Bull.

While a uniform positioning theme may be desirable, it is often very hard to come up with a good positioning theme that appeals in various markets. Universal themes often run the risk of being bland and not very inspired. Very rarely do positioning themes "travel." Instead, management usually modifies or localizes them. Appeals that work in one culture do not necessarily work in others. Differences in cultural characteristics, buying power, competitive climate, and the product life cycle stage force firms to tailor their positioning platform. Land Rover is an example of a brand where a global positioning strategy is hard to implement.[36] One of the core brand values that Land Rover has cultivated over the years in Europe is "authenticity." This core value is based on Land Rover's heritage of fifty-plus years as a 4 × 4-brand in Europe. The North American market, which Land Rover only entered in the 1980s, presents a different picture. There, Jeep, the Chrysler 4 × 4-brand, is perceived as the authentic, original four-wheel drive vehicle. Hence, Land Rover would have a formidable task creating the same image of "authenticity" in North America as it successfully did in Europe.

Universal positioning appeals are positioning themes that appeal to consumers anywhere in the world, regardless of their cultural background. Remember that positioning themes can be developed at different levels:

**Universal Positioning Appeals**

- Specific product features/attributes
- Product benefits (rational or emotional), solutions for problems
- User category
- User application
- Heritage
- Lifestyle

Products that offer benefits or features that are universally important would meet the criterion of a universal benefit/feature positioning appeal. In business-to-business markets, where buying behavior is often somewhat less culture-bound than for consumer goods, this is often true. Thus, a promise of superior quality, performance, or productivity for industrial products is one example of a positioning pitch with a universal ring. Benefit- or feature-based positioning can be universal for consumer goods when the core benefit is common worldwide. Superior quality or performance appeals for durables like television sets (superior picture quality), washing machines (cleaning performance), and so forth. However, for products where buying motivations are very culture-bound (for instance, most food and beverage products), coming up with a universal benefit- or feature-related appeal is a much harder task.

A special case where universal positioning clearly makes sense is the "global citizen" theme often used with corporate image strategies. Here the positioning strategy stresses a global leadership and/or global presence benefit. This strategy is often successfully used in industries where having a global presence is a major plus (e.g., credit cards, banking, insurance, telecommunications). **Global Perspective 7-3** discusses Swiss banking firm UBS's universal positioning "You and Us" campaign.

When positioning the product to a specific user category, a uniform approach will often succeed when the user-group shares common characteristics. Avon's "Let's Talk" campaign attests to this rule. The campaign, launched in 26 countries in 2000, was designed to reflect Avon's corporate mission of being a "company for women." To project this positioning, the global campaign highlighted Avon's wide range of beauty products and the company's unique network of 2.8 million sales reps, which facilitates one-on-one customer relationships.[37] Likewise, the global positioning used by Kotex, Kimberly-Clark's feminine protection pad brand, turned out to be highly effective in leveraging a common need among the global women segment. Kotex was positioned as the brand "that is designed to fit and feel better for your body, to help you feel better, more like yourself."[38] Examples where uniform positioning is likely to be futile are appeals that center on the "liberated women" group (e.g., Virginia Slims cigarettes: "You've come a long way, baby"), which is still a very culture-bound phenomenon.

Emotional appeals (e.g., lifestyle positioning) are usually difficult to translate into a universal theme. Values tend to be very culture bound. The trick is to come up with an

---

[36]Nick Bull and Martin Oxley, "The search for focus—brand values across Europe," *Marketing and Research Today* (November 1996), pp. 239–47.
[37]"Avon 'Talks' Globally to Women," *Ad Age Global* (October 2001), p. 43.
[38]"Kotex Wins a Game of Catch-Up," *Ad Age Global* (October 2001), p. 43.

### *G*LOBAL PERSPECTIVE 7-3

#### UBS—THE CONCEPT OF "TWO-NESS"

The wealth management group UBS was formed in 1998 by the merger of two major Swiss banks. It has expanded globally often through acquisitions (e.g., Paine Webber and Warburg in the United States) and now maintains a presence in over fifty countries. Brands that grow by acquiring existing firms face the task of establishing a clear brand identity both internally (employees) and externally (customers). In February 2004, UBS set out to establish a single consistent brand identity across all markets. This led to the "You and Us" advertising campaign. The campaign has two major targets: the high net-worth individual and corporate customers. The focus is the intimacy and strength of UBS's client relationships, backed by the bank's resources. Bernhard Eggli, head of brand management at UBS, noted: "What we found during research is that there's a lot of similarity in terms of the expectations that our client segments have for their preferred financial services

*Sources*: http://www.ubs.com/1/e/about/brand.html and http://www.brandchannel.com/features_effect.asp?pf_id=273.

provider, which made it possible for us to move to a single brand. The underlying brand promise works across the globe; the challenge is to find the right execution."

A key task to deliver the universal positioning for the campaign was finding a tagline with global appeal that conveyed UBS's identity. After conducting market research, UBS decided to leave the You and Us tagline in English. "In the attempt to translate the tagline in English, what we have found is that you are losing the simplicity and, to a certain extent, the charm of the tagline," observed Eggli. To underscore the positioning theme, the campaign used images of "two-ness"—two chairs, two cups of coffee, two people, and so on. These images symbolized the intimate relationship between the client and the UBS advisor. To cast actors for the campaign, people were chosen in pairs rather than individually. Background images—skyscrapers, offices—were chosen to reinforce the message that a UBS advisor has the support of a large, powerful institution that can mobilize global resource on behalf of the customer.

---

emotional appeal that has universal characteristics and—at the same time—does not sound dull. One lifestyle survey found that "protecting the family" was seen as a top value in twenty-two countries, including the United States.[39] So, appeals based on family values might be prospective candidates.

◆ ◆ ◆ ◆ ◆ ◆ ◆ ◆ ## GLOBAL, FOREIGN, AND LOCAL CONSUMER CULTURE POSITIONING[40]

Brand managers can position their brand as symbolic of a global consumer culture, a "foreign" culture, or a local culture. The first strategy can be described as **global consumer culture positioning** (GCCP). This strategy tries to project the brand as a symbol of a given global consumer culture. Thereby, buying the brand reinforces the consumer's feeling of being part of a global segment. It also fosters the buyer's self-image as being cosmopolitan, modern, and knowledgeable. Examples of brands that successfully use this strategy are Sony ("My First Sony") and Nike ("Just Do It").

At the other extreme is the **local consumer culture positioning** (LCCP) strategy. Despite the fact that the brand may be global, it is portrayed as an intrinsic part of the local culture. It is depicted as being consumed by local people, and, if applicable, manufactured by locals using local supplies or ingredients. Such brands have achieved a **multi-local status**. A good example is Singer, the maker of sewing

---

[39]Tom Miller, "Global segments from 'Strivers' to 'Creatives'," *Marketing News* (July 20, 1998), p. 11.

[40]Based on Dana L. Alden, Jan-Benedict E.M. Steenkamp, and Rajeev Batra, "Brand Positioning Through Advertising in Asia, North America, and Europe: The Role of Global Consumer Culture," *Journal of Marketing*, 63 (January 1999), pp. 75–87.

machines. Singer was seen as German in Germany, British in the UK, and American in the United States. In fact, during Word War II, German aviators avoided bombing Singer's European factories thinking they were German-owned.[41] When Mercedes launched its mid-price E-class model in Japan, its ad campaign used Japanese scenery and images. The local imagery was underscored with the tagline: "Mercedes and a beautiful country."[42]

A third strategy is **foreign consumer culture positioning** (FCCP). Here, the goal is to build up a brand mystique around a specific foreign culture, usually one that has highly positive connotations for the product (e.g., Switzerland for watches, Germany for household appliances). In China U.S. jeans maker Lee targets the children of rich Chinese families and young and upcoming executives. In the past, Lee was perceived as a Chinese company based in the U.S. (Li is a very common family name in China). At the same time, a market research study showed that the Chinese associate jeans with cowboys, the Wild West, freedom, and passion. As a result, the company decided to position Lee jeans as an expensive brand[43] with an American heritage. Lee's U.S. roots are highlighted in print materials with the line: "Founded Kansas, USA, 1889."[44] Other American brands such as Nike, Timberland, Cadillac, and Budweiser have been able to position themselves very strongly in their foreign markets as authentic pieces of Americana.

Which positioning strategy is most suitable depends on several factors. One important determinant is obviously your target market. When target consumers share core values, attitudes, and aspirations, using a GCCP strategy could be effective. Another driver is the product category. Products that satisfy universal needs and are used in a similar manner worldwide lend themselves more to a GCCP-type approach. High-tech consumer brands (e.g., Siemens, Nokia, Sony) that symbolize modernism and internationalism would qualify. A third factor is the positioning approach used by the local competition. If every player in the local market is using a GCCP strategy, you might be able to break more easily through the clutter by going for an LCCP strategy (or vice versa). A final factor is the level of economic development. In emerging markets that are still in an early stage of economic development, a GCCP approach might be more beneficial than LCCP. In these markets, a brand with a global image enhances the owner's self-image and status.

Sometimes local brands fight it out with global brands by using a GCCP or FCCP strategy. For instance, Brand, a local Dutch beer, uses a U.S. setting and the English language in its advertising. Some brands also use a hybrid approach, by combining ingredients of each of the three strategies. A good example of this approach is the positioning of HSBC, Europe's largest bank, as the "world's local bank." McDonald's is portrayed as a global, cosmopolitan fast-food brand (GCCP) but also as an authentic piece of Americana (FCCP). At the same time, in many countries, McDonald's often highlights its local roots, stressing the fact that it provides local jobs, uses local ingredients, and so forth (LCCP). The fast-food chain localizes its menu, selling salmon sandwiches in Norway, McTeriyaki burgers in Japan, McShawarma and McKebab in Israel, Samurai Pork burgers in Thailand, and so forth. **Exhibit 7-10** shows how McDonald's New Zealand promotes the fact that it sources most of its ingredients from local farmers and other suppliers to the tune of over NZ$100 million.[45] According to one story, Japanese Boy Scouts were pleasantly surprised to find a McDonald's restaurant in Chicago.[46]

---

[41] http://www.brandchannel.com/features_effect.asp?pf_id=261.

[42] "Mercedes-Benz Japan drifts down to earth alongside economy," *Ad Age International* (October 1997), p. 36.

[43] A pair of Lee jeans typically retails for $79, about one third of the average monthly salary in big Chinese cities.

[44] "Lee Plays Up US Roots To Target China's Elite," *Media* (May 17, 2002), p. 10.

[45] Around US$51.75 million.

[46] Emiko Ohnuki-Tierney, "McDonald's in Japan," in James L. Watson, *Golden Arches East. McDonald's in East Asia* (Stanford, CA: Stanford University Press, 1997), pp. 161–82.

**EXHIBIT 7-10**
MCDONALD'S PROMOTING ITS LOCAL COMMUNITY SUPPORT IN
NEW ZEALAND

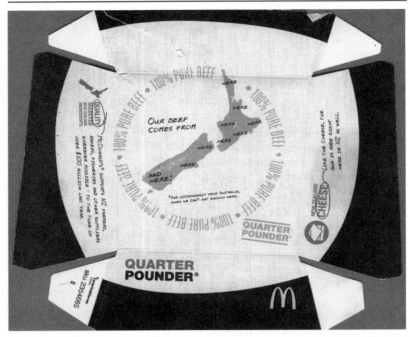

Courtesy of Kristiaan Helsen.

## SUMMARY ◆ ◆ ◆ ◆ ◆ ◆ ◆ ◆ ◆ ◆ ◆ ◆ ◆ ◆ ◆ ◆ ◆ ◆ ◆ ◆ ◆ ◆ ◆ ◆ ◆ ◆ ◆ ◆ ◆

A common theme in many writings on global marketing is the growing convergence of consumer needs.[47] Colorful phrases have been used to describe this phenomenon such as "global village," "global mall," "crystallization of the world as a single place," just to mention a few. This phenomenon of increasing globalization is especially visible for many upscale consumer goods and a variety of business-to-business goods and services that are bought by multinational customers. One director of a global marketing research firm even went so far as to state that "marketers make too much of cultural differences."[48] She supports her claim by two reasons. First, technology has given consumers worldwide the same reference points. People see the same TV ads, share similar life experiences, and they are exposed to the same products and services. Second, technology has also given us common aspirations. According to this school of thought, cultures do differ but these differences do not have any meaningful impact on people's buying behavior.

In the other camp are people like Nicholas Trivisonno, the former CEO of ACNielsen, who notes: "There is no global consumer. Each country and the consumer in each country has different attitudes and different behaviors, tastes, spending patterns."[49] The truth of the matter is somewhere in between these two extreme opinions. Without proper segmentation of your international markets, it is hard to establish whether the "global consumer" segment is myth or reality.

Global marketers have a continuum of choices to segment their customer base. At one end of the spectrum, the firm might pursue a "universal" segment. Essentially the same product is offered, using a common positioning theme. Most likely there are a few, mostly minor, adaptations of the marketing mix program to recognize cross-border differences. At the other end, the firm might consider treating individual countries on a case-by-case basis. In some circumstances, marketers might be able to offer the same product in each country, provided that the positioning is customized. However, typically, the product will need to be modified or designed for each country separately. In between these two extremes, there are bound to be many other possibilities.

By the same token, your positioning strategy can take different directions. Going after a uniform segment, you can adopt a universal positioning theme or themes that are custom-made. Universal appeals do have benefits. Companies

[47]Theodore Levitt, "The Globalization of Markets," *Harvard Business Review*, 61, May–June 1983, pp. 92–102.

[48]Luanne Flikkema, "Global marketing's myth: Differences don't matter," *Marketing News* (July 20, 1998), p. 4.

[49]"The global consumer myth," *The Financial Times*, (April 23, 1991), p. 21.

such as UBS, Intel, and Visa have been able to successfully project a uniform, consistent global image. Universal positioning allows the firm to develop a common communication strategy using global or pan-regional media channels. Unfortunately, coming up with a universal message that is appealing and not bland is often asking too much.

## KEY TERMS ◆ ◆ ◆ ◆ ◆ ◆ ◆ ◆ ◆ ◆ ◆ ◆ ◆ ◆ ◆ ◆ ◆

Diverse (Unique) segments
Foreign culture consumer positioning

Global consumer culture positioning
Local consumer culture positioning

Multi-local status
Socioeconomic strata (SES) analysis

Uniform (Localized) positioning
Universal positioning appeal
Universal (Global) segments

## REVIEW QUESTIONS ◆ ◆ ◆ ◆ ◆ ◆ ◆ ◆ ◆ ◆ ◆ ◆ ◆ ◆ ◆ ◆ ◆ ◆ ◆

1. Under what conditions should companies pursue universal market segments?

2. What are the major issues in using per capita GDP or GNP as a country segmentation criterion?

3. Discuss the weaknesses of lifestyle based segmentation schemes. For what kind of applications would lifestyle segmentation be appropriate?

4. Sometimes local brands use a global consumer culture positioning approach. Explain.

## DISCUSSION QUESTIONS ◆ ◆ ◆ ◆ ◆ ◆ ◆ ◆ ◆ ◆ ◆ ◆ ◆ ◆ ◆ ◆ ◆

1. Peter Sampson, a managing director of Burke Marketing Research, points out that "lifestyle and value-based segmentations are too general to be of great use in category specific studies . . . their international application is too limited as lifestyles vary internationally." Do you agree or disagree with his comment?

2. Fiat, the Italian carmaker (www.fiat.com), is looking to sell vehicles in Singapore again after it left the market in 2001. Singapore's car market is small and very competitive. Fiat sold only 68 cars in Singapore in 1968 and just 5 in 2000 before it pulled out of the market. Fiat's competitors in the small-car segment include cheaper Japanese and Korean firms that spend heavily on advertising. Fiat also must overcome the image that its cars are not suitable for local driving conditions. For instance, Fiat failed to offer a "tropicalization pack" for the Punto. Such a pack includes an air-conditioning system customized to Singapore's tropical climate. Given Fiat's marketing challenges, what positioning would you prescribe for the car marque in Singapore?

3. In a host of emerging markets (e.g., India, Brazil, Thailand), 50+ percent of the population is under 25 years old. One marketer observes: "teenagers are teenagers everywhere and they tend to emulate U.S. teenagers" (*Advertising Age International*, October 17, 1994, p. I-15). Is there a global teenager segment? Do teenagers in, say, Beijing really tend to emulate L.A. teenagers? Discuss.

4. Assignment (advanced). Select a particular consumption product (e.g., ice-cream). Try to come up with at least two variables that you believe might be related to the per-capita demand for the chosen product. Collect data on the per-capita consumption levels for your chosen product and the selected variables for several countries. Segment the countries using e.g., cluster analysis (SAS users might consider PROC FASTCLUS). Derive two- and three-cluster solutions. Discuss your findings.

5. Browse through a recent issue of *The Economist*. As you may know, *The Economist* has regional editions. Most of the ads target an international audience (regional or global). Pick four ads and carefully examine each one of them. Who is being targeted in each print ad? What sort of positioning is being used?

6. One phenomenon in scores of emerging markets is a rising middle class. In a recent *Ad Age International* article (October 17, 1994) on the global middle class, one analyst referred to this phenomenon as the *Twinkie-ization* of the world (Twinkie being the brand name of a popular snack in the United States): "It's the little things that are treats and don't cost much and feel like a luxury." What are these "little things"? Do you agree with this statement?

# SHORT CASES

ASE 7-1

## COACH — SELLING HANDBAGS OVERSEAS

Coach, Inc. is an American luxury leather goods company primarily known for ladies' handbags. The company started in 1941 as a family-run workshop based in a Manhattan loft. Now greatly expanded, the company aspires to maintain high standards for materials and craftsmanship. In 2008, faced with a severe economic slowdown in its core U.S. market, Coach decided to expand its drive into Asia. A key market in this expansion drive is China. According to Ernst & Young, China bought more than $2 billion worth of upscale products in 2008. This figure could rise to $11.5 billion by 2015. By the end of 2006, the country boasted 345,000 U.S. dollar millionaires, one third of whom were women. Coach expects China will make up over 4 percent of its sales by 2013 as it expands into a hundred cities. It also announced plans to acquire its own retail businesses in Greater China from current distributor ImagineX to boost its market presence. Coach plans to increase the number of stores there from 25 in 2008 to 80 by 2013. The stores will include flagship and stand-alone stores, as well as factory outlets.

Coach hopes to be able to replicate in China what it did in Japan (see Table) by increasing its market share from just 3 percent in 2008 (compared to 30 percent for Louis Vuitton) to 10 percent by 2013. Franfort explained how Coach could grab shares from its European competitors in Japan: "Many Japanese women told us they would rather spend 60,000 yen ($578) for a Coach bag and spend the other 60,000 yen that they would save by not buying a European luxury brand and use it to go to Thailand." Coach especially appeals to women under age 35. Older Japanese women prefer carrying European luxury brands as a status symbol.

### Handbag Market Shares in Japan

| Company | 2000 | 2008 |
|---|---|---|
| Louis Vuitton | 33% | 27% |
| Coach | 2% | 12% |
| Prada | >10% | <10% |
| Gucci | >10% | <10% |

*Source:* "Coach bets Chinese open the purse strings," *Wall Street Journal*

CEO Lew Frankfort states that Coach's competitive advantage over other luxury leather goods companies such as Louis Vuitton is that "We offer a well-made and stylish product . . . at less than half the price point of our European competitors.".[50] Coach handbags retail for $1,100, although many models are much cheaper. To keep the brand more accessible than its European luxury rival brands, Coach makes its product in lower-cost countries while sourcing its raw materials from high-quality mills and tanneries. As a result, Coach's labor costs are a fraction of its European competitors' costs.

## COACH FLAGSHIP STORE IN HONG KONG

Courtesy of Kristiaan Helsen

Coach's primary focus is on the female consumer because "she tends to be brand-loyal, will go shopping whether the stock market declines or not, and if she has a bad day at the office she may buy herself a Coach bag, where a man would have a double-scotch."

Describing the difference between the Chinese and U.S. consumer, Frankfort said: "In China, there's a luxury consumer that represents perhaps 0.05 percent of the population — very small but with enormous purchasing power. That's not our primary target. Our target is the emerging middle class who have gone to university and are now getting 30 to 40 percent [pay] increases a year . . . These women are trading up and investing in plasma TVs and laptop computers and Coach bags. They are looking for ways to broaden their life and Coach is one way . . . . There are some consumers who are extremely wealthy, and hopefully our limited-edition product will attract them, but they are not our primary thrust."[51] The next frontier

*Source:* "Handbag Brand Coach Plans Major Expansion in China," http://www.iht.com/articles/2008/05/29/style/coach.php; www.coach.com; "Coach Bets Chinese Open the Purse Strings," *Wall Street Journal Asia,* May 30-June 1, 2008, p. 28.

---

[50]"Handbag Brand Coach Plans Major Expansion in China," http://www.iht.com/bin/printfriendly.php?id=13302728.

[51]"Coach Bets Chinese Open the Purse Strings," *Wall Street Journal Asia*, (May 30–June 1, 2008), p. 28.

would be India, though for the time being that market is on the back burner because of infrastructure problems.

## DISCUSSION QUESTIONS

1. Will Coach be able to replicate its Japan success story in China? Why was the firm successful in Japan?

2. Reflect on Coach's targeting strategy. What are the alternatives? Coach decided to focus on the emerging middle class—do you agree?

3. Around the time that Coach announced its Asia expansion drive the global economy entered into a deep recession. To what extent would the recession affect Coach's strategy in Asia (primarily Japan and China)? Would Coach need to revisit its plans? If so how?

ASE 7-2

## CROCS: LOVE THEM, HATE THEM

In the demi-monde of footwear, the term *croc* once stood for the reptile skin used in elegant footwear. Today, it's synonymous with an entirely different (and altogether vegetarian) phenomenon. In just a few years, the shoes known as "Crocs" have spread around the world.

In June 2002, entrepreneur George Boedecker used a company he had previously formed called Western Brands to start up a shoe company that eventually became known as Crocs, Inc.[52] Earlier that same year Boedecker had been approached by a Canadian firm, Foam Creations, to distribute a newly developed shoe. The peculiar new shoe was made from a proprietary foam resin called "Croslite." The shoes are called Crocs because they resemble a crocodile's snout. Initially, the shoe was marketed as a lightweight boating and outdoor footwear that featured slip-resistant and non-marking soles. The first model, the Crocs *Beach*, was unveiled in November 2002 at the Ft. Lauderdale Boat show and the 200 initial pairs sold out immediately. Word of mouth spread. Early adopters were mostly people who spent a lot of time on their feet such as restaurant workers, nurses, and doctors. The Crocs epidemic soon engulfed the world as millions rushed to jump on the Crocs bandwagon. Celebrities such as George W. Bush and Jack Nicholson have been spotted wearing the shoes. Crocs wearers are almost evangelical about the shoes' comfort. Crocs shoes have been awarded the American Podiatric Medical Association (www.apma.org) Seal of Acceptance. The AMPA took special note of the fact that Croslite "warms and softens with body heat and molds to the users' feet, while remaining extremely lightweight."

Crocs capitalized on several strengths.[53] Kids like their brightness, squishiness, and the holes in the front in which charms can be placed. Parents like that the shoes are waterproof, odor-free, and washer-safe. The Croc fad also benefits from the appropriation of an ethnic look: the Dutch clog. Ugly is acceptable especially when it is imported (not unlike Australian Ugg boots). In *Rolling Stone* Crocs even ran ads proclaiming "Ugly can be beautiful." The anti-bourgeois quality of the shoes also has a certain appeal: Crocs are a bottom-up

© Ron Sachs/CNP/©Corbis

brand, embraced by ordinary people. They represent a kind of rebellion.

By June 2004, Crocs was able to acquire Foam Creations to secure its manufacturing operations and the patent to the foam resin material that its shoes were made from. In October 2006 Crocs also bought Jibbitz, a manufacturer of accessories that snap into the holes of Crocs. The Crocs franchise then continued to grow in 2007 as its product line expanded to over 250 styles and retail points mushroomed to 200 worldwide markets in Europe and Asia. CEO Ronald Snyder delivered a stunning

---

[52]www.crocs.com.
[53]http://www.slate.com/id/2170301/.

report card in 2007 of 139 percent growth and US$847 million sales revenues, up from US$355 million in 2006.

While many regard the shoes as comfortable and colorfully decorated, the popularity of Crocs has also led to the inevitable backlash. Many people regard Crocs as a fashion disaster or even a disease. Crocs have been lampooned as "clown shoes" or even worse. A *Washington Post* article described the Crocs criticism as follows: "Nor is the fashion world enamored of Crocs. Though their maker touts their "ultra-hip Italian styling," lots of folks find them hideous."[54] One British journalist who had seen the shoes in South Africa described them as "something crafted from a car tyre in a poverty-stricken local township and sold on street corners."[55] Two college students based in Halifax, Nova Scotia, set up a website called www.ihatecrocs.com with anti-Crocs rants and videos of the shoes being burned or shredded. Crocs ranked No. 6 on Maxim's "10 Worst Things to Happen to Men in 2007" listing.[56]

Probably even more worrisome are growing negative reports on the shoes' safety. Several wearers, mostly children, suffered injuries after their shoes got entrapped in escalators. The U.S. Consumer Product Safety Commission has documented 77 soft shoe entrapments on escalators since January 2006 and issued a warning in May 2008. One family of a child whose foot was maimed in an escalator accident at the Atlanta airport is suing Crocs for failure to put safety features in the soft-holed shoes.[57] The company maintains that the safe design and maintenance of escalators is the real issue. Yet it put warning tags on its footwear. Japan's Trade Ministry is looking into several reports of people damaging toenails on Jibbitz

accessories fixed to Crocs sandals. Following the incidents, Crocs Asia warned on its website that children should not wear oversized Crocs. "Jibbitz attached near the toes could harm toes or toenails," said the company on its Japanese website.[58] In April 2008, Japanese and Philippine authorities asked the firm to consider changing the footwear's design because of escalator incidents in their countries. Crocs promised to insert safety tags.

In recent days the allure of Crocs seems to be fading, at least in the United States. In 2008 U.S. retailers cut back on orders as U.S. consumers spend less in the wake of the weak economy. One retail analyst pointed out that the Crocs brand is not strong enough to command prices four times those of imitations. At Nordstrom stores, Crocs sell for $24.95 to $69.95 each compared to as little as $5 for similar clogs on Wal-Mart's website. Luckily for the company, international demand is still rising: sales in the second quarter of 2008 rose 13 percent in Europe and 65 percent in Asia. One retail consultant noted: "It's a fad, not an essential basic in the consumer's wardrobe . . . with the weak economy, consumers may not be interested in new Crocs this year."[59]

## DISCUSSION QUESTIONS

**1.** Explain why a "heinous synthetic shoe" (as described in a *Slate* article) conquered the world?

**2.** Sales in the United States are declining. Do you expect that Crocs will also lose momentum in the international markets and why? Is the phenomenon indeed just a fad?

**3.** One BBDO ad executive claimed that "Crocs may have been successful, but it has never been a brand. The name itself is well established but the equities are missing." Do you agree?

**4.** How would you target/position the Crocs brand in the international market (say Asia)?

[54]http://www.washingtonpost.com/wp-dyn/content/article/2006/07/31/AR2006073100890_pf.html.

[55]http://www.dailymail.co.uk/femail/article-470904/Curse-Crocs-Why-middle-aged-men-wear-ugliest-shoes-invented.html.

[56]http://www.maxim.com/The10bestandworstthingstohappentome-nin2007/articles/2/10316.aspx.

[57]http://www.foxnews.com/story/0,2933,419962,00.html.

[58]http://www.just-style.com/article.aspx?id=101631.

[59]http://www.rockymountainnews.com/news/2008/jul/25/crocs-shares-sink-grim-sales-news/

# FURTHER READING ◆ ◆ ◆ ◆ ◆ ◆ ◆ ◆ ◆ ◆ ◆ ◆ ◆ ◆ ◆ ◆ ◆ ◆ ◆

Alden, Dana L., Jan-Benedict E.M. Steenkamp, and Rajeev Batra, "Brand Positioning Through Advertising in Asia, North America, and Europe: The Role of Global Consumer Culture," *Journal of Marketing*, 63(1) (January 1999), pp. 75–87.

Hassan, Salah S. and Lea P. Katsanis, "Identification of Global Consumer Segments," *Journal of International Consumer Marketing*, vol. 3, no. 2, 1991, pp. 11–28.

Hinton, Graham and Jane Hourigan, "The Golden Circles: Marketing in the New Europe," *Journal of European Business*, vol. 1, no. 6, July/August 1990, pp. 5–30.

Johansson, Johny K. and Reza Moinpour, "Objective and Perceived Similarity for Pacific-Rim Countries," *Columbia Journal of World Business*, Winter 1977, pp. 65–76.

Kale, Sudhir, "Grouping Euroconsumers: A Culture-Based Clustering Approach," *Journal of International Marketing*, vol. 3, no. 3, 1995, pp. 35–48.

Kale, Sudhir and D. Sudharshan, "A Strategic Approach to International Segmentation," *International Marketing Review*, Summer 1987, pp. 60–70.

Sampson, Peter, "People are people the world over: the case for psychological segmentation," *Marketing and Research Today*, November 1992, pp. 236–44.

Steenkamp, Jan-Benedict E. and F. Ter Hofstede. "International Market Segmentation: Issues and Perspectives." *International Journal of Research in Marketing*, 19(September 2002): 185–213.

Ter Hofstede, Frenkel, Jan-Benedict E. Steenkamp, and Michel Wedel, "International Market Segmentation Based on Consumer-Product Relations," *Journal of Marketing Research*, 36(1) (February 1999), pp. 1–17.

Ter Hofstede, F., M. Wedel, and J.-B.E.M. Steenkamp. "Identifying Spatial Segments in International Markets." *Marketing Science*, 21 (Spring 2002): 160–77.

# APPENDIX ◆ ◆ ◆ ◆ ◆ ◆ ◆ ◆ ◆ ◆ ◆ ◆ ◆ ◆ ◆ ◆ ◆ ◆ ◆ ◆ ◆ ◆ ◆ ◆ ◆ ◆ ◆

In this appendix we give an overview of segmentation tools that can be used to do a country segmentation. A huge variety of segmentation methodologies have been developed in the marketing literature. Many of these techniques are quite sophisticated. We will just give you the flavor of two of the most popular tools without going through all the technical nitty-gritty.

When only one segmentation variable is used, classifying countries in distinct groups is quite straightforward. You could simply compute the mean (or median) and split countries into two groups based on the value (above or below) on the criterion variable compared to the mean (or median). When more than two groups need to be formed, one can use other quantiles. Things become a bit more complicated when you plan to use multiple country segmentation variables. Typically, the goal of market segmentation is to relate, in some manner, a battery of descriptive variables about the countries to one or more behavioral response variables:

$$Response = F(Descriptor_1, Descriptor_2, Descriptor_3, \dots)$$

For instance, the response variable might be the per-capita consumption of a given product. The descriptor variables could be the stage in the product life cycle, per-capita GNP, literacy level, and so on. We now describe two methods that can help you in achieving this goal: cluster analysis and regression.

***Cluster Analysis.*** *Cluster analysis* is an umbrella term that embraces a collection of statistical procedures for dividing objects into groups (*clusters*). The grouping is done in such a manner that members belonging to the same group are very similar to one another but quite distinct from members of other groups.

Suppose information was collected for a set of countries on two variables, X and Y. The countries are plotted in **Exhibit 7-11**. Each dot corresponds to a country. In this case, the clusters are quite obvious. Just by eyeballing the graph, you can distinguish two clear-cut clusters, namely

## EXHIBIT 7-11
PRINCIPLES OF CLUSTER ANALYSIS

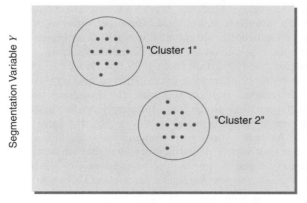

## EXHIBIT 7-12
PLOT OF CONCENTRATION VERSUS CATEGORY GROWTH CHOCOLATE MARKET

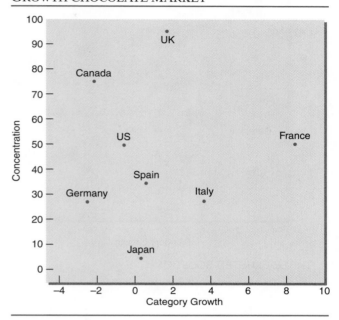

"Cluster 1" and "Cluster 2." Unfortunately, in real-world applications, clustering is seldom so easy. Consider **Exhibit 7-12**. This exhibit plots the values of chocolate volume growth rate and market concentration[60] in eight countries. For this example, it is far less obvious how many clusters there are, let alone how they are composed. In addition, most country segmentations involve many more than two criteria.

Luckily there are many statistical algorithms available that will do the job for you. The basic notion is to group countries together that are "similar" in value for the segmentation bases of interest. Similarity measures come under many guises. The most popular way is to use some type of distance measure:

$$Distance_{country\ A\ vs.\ B} = (X_{country\ A} - X_{country\ B})^2$$
$$+ (Y_{country\ A} - Y_{country\ B})^2$$

where X and Y are the segmentation variables. These distances[61] would be computed for each pair of countries in the set. The clustering algorithm takes these distances and uses them as inputs to generate the desired number of country groupings. Most "canned" statistical software packages (e.g., SAS, SPPS-X) have at least one procedure that allows you to run a cluster analysis. **Exhibit 7-13** provides the two- and three-cluster solutions for the chocolate market example.

---

[60]Measured via the combined market shares of the three largest competitors—Cadbury, Mars, and Nestlé.

[61]Strictly speaking, these are "squared" distances.

## EXHIBIT 7-13
### CLUSTER ANALYSIS

**TWO-CLUSTER SOLUTION**

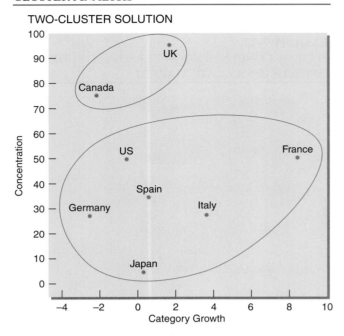

**THREE-CLUSTER SOLUTION**

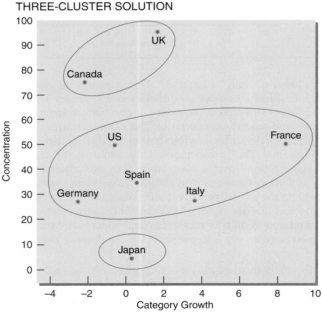

***Regression.*** Alternatively, you might consider using regression analysis to classify countries. In regression, one assumes that there exists a relationship between a response variable, Y, and one or more so-called predictor variables, $X_1$, $X_2$ and so on:

$$Y = a + b_1 X_1 + b_2 X_2 + b_3 X_3 + \ldots$$

The first term, a, is the intercept. It corresponds to the predicted value of Y when all the Xs are equal to 0. The other parameters, the bs, are the slope coefficients. For example, $b_1$

tells you what the predicted change in Y will be for a unit change in $X_1$.

In our context, the dependent variable, Y, would be a behavioral response variable (e.g., per-capita consumption) and the predictor variables would be a collection of country characteristics that are presumed to be related to the response measure. For given values of the parameters, you can compute the predicted Y-values, Y. Very seldom, these predicted values will match the observed Ys. The goal of regression is to find estimates for the intercept, *a*, and the slope coefficients, the *b*s, that provide the "best" fit by minimizing the prediction errors, Y – Y, between the predicted and observed values of Y. The most common regression procedure, ordinary least squares (OLS), minimizes the sum of the squared differences of these prediction errors.

For each of the parameter estimates, the regression analysis will also produce a standard error. Dividing the parameter estimate by the standard error yields the t-ratio. This ratio tells you whether or not the predictor variable has a "significant" (statistically speaking) relationship with the dependent variable. As a rule of thumb, a t-ratio (in absolute value) larger than 2.0 would indicate a significant effect of the predictor variable on the response variable. The overall goodness of fit is captured via the $R^2$-statistic. The higher the $R^2$ value, the better the ability of your regression model to predict your data.

To illustrate the use of regression analysis as a segmentation tool, let us look at a numerical example. Consider a microwave oven maker who wants to explore market opportunities in the European market. Data were collected for several European countries on the penetration of microwave ovens (as percentage of households owning a microwave). Data were also gathered on three potential segmentation variables: income (per-capita GDP), participation of women in the labor force, and per-capita consumption of frozen foods.[62] Using these data as inputs, the following results were obtained (t-ratios between parentheses):

MICROWAVE OWNERSHIP =

−76.7 −0.5 FROZEN FOOD + 2.7 WOMEN −0.03 PER CAP GDP
(−2.2) (−1.3)                   (2.9)            (−0.04)

$R^2 = 0.52$

Note that, apparently, the only meaningful segmentation base is the participation of women in the labor force: microwave ownership increases with the proportion of women in the labor force. Since the microwave is a timesaving appliance, this result intuitively makes sense. The other variables appear to have (statistically speaking) not much of an impact on the adoption of microwave ovens. Somewhat surprisingly, high consumption of frozen foods does not lead to an increased ownership of microwave ovens. There is also no relationship with income. Thus, in this case, the European marketing manager could group countries simply on the basis of the degree of participation of women in the labor force.

Aside from these two commonplace tools, there are many other multivariate statistical procedures that can be used to do country segmentation analysis (e.g., latent class analysis, discriminant analysis, Automatic Interaction Detection).

---

[62]The data for this example were collected from the *European Marketing Data and Statistics 1992*, London: Euromonitor.

# GLOBAL MARKETING STRATEGIES

## CHAPTER OVERVIEW

1. INFORMATION TECHNOLOGY AND GLOBAL COMPETITION

2. GLOBAL STRATEGY

3. GLOBAL MARKETING STRATEGY

4. R&D, OPERATIONS, AND MARKETING INTERFACES

5. REGIONALIZATION OF GLOBAL MARKETING STRATEGY

6. COMPETITIVE ANALYSIS

On a political map, country borders are clear as ever. But on a competitive map, financial, trading, and industrial activities across national boundaries have rendered those political borders increasingly irrelevant. Of all the forces chipping away at those boundaries, perhaps the most important are the emergence of regional trading blocs (e.g., NAFTA, the European Union, and MERCOSUR), technology developments (particularly in the IT area), and the flow of information.

Today people can see for themselves what tastes and preferences are like in other countries. For instance, people in India watching CNN and Star TV now know instantaneously what is happening in the rest of the world. A farmer in a remote village in Rajasthan in India asks the local vendor for Surf (the detergent manufactured by Unilever) because he has seen a commercial on TV. More than 10 million Japanese traveling abroad every year are exposed to larger-sized homes and much lower consumer prices abroad than at home. Such information access creates demand that would not have existed before.

The availability and explosion of information technology such as telecommunications has forever changed the nature of global competition. Geographical boundaries and distance have become less a constraint in designing strategies for the global market. The other side of the coin is that not only firms that compete internationally but also those whose primary market is home-based will be significantly affected by competition from around the world.

The firm is essentially a collection of activities that are performed to design, procure materials, produce, market, deliver, and support its product. This set of interrelated corporate activities is called the **value chain**. In this chapter, we explain the nature of global competition and examine various ways to gain competitive advantage along the value chain for the firm facing global competition.

◆ ◆ ◆ ◆ ◆ ◆ ◆ ◆ # INFORMATION TECHNOLOGY AND GLOBAL COMPETITION

The development of transportation technology, including jet air transportation, cold storage containers, and large ocean carriers, changed the nature of world trade in the fifty years after the Second World War. Since the 1980s, the explosion of information technology, particularly telecommunications, and more recently, electronic commerce (e-commerce), has forever changed the nature of competition around the world. Geographical distance has become increasingly less relevant in designing global strategy.

**Real-Time Management**

Information that managers have about the state of the firm's operations is almost in real time. Routinely, the chief executive officer of a firm can know the previous day's sales down to a penny, and can be alerted to events and trends now instead of in several months, when it may be too late to do anything about them.

In the mid-1990s, Volvo faced a classic supply chain dilemma. For whatever reason—perhaps just capricious consumer tastes—halfway through the year the company found itself with an excess inventory of green cars. The sales and marketing team responded appropriately by developing an aggressive program of deals, discounts, and rebates to push green vehicles through the distribution channel. The program worked well, and green Volvos began to move out off dealer lots. However, back at the factory, manufacturing planners also noted the surge in sales of green cars. Unfortunately, they were unaware of the big push taking place on the sales and marketing side and assumed that customers had suddenly developed a preference for the color green. So they responded by increasing production of green cars. The company soon found itself caught in a feedback loop that resulted in an even bigger surplus of green Volvos at end of the year. This story is typical of the kind of disconnect that is far too common in manufacturing companies, especially those that rely on multi-tier distribution. And that inability or failure to share real-time data or knowledge with partners can result in erroneous assumptions and costly errors in decision-making. In order to avoid the problem from happening, companies need to use information technology to link all parts of the organization into a real-time enterprise.[1]

Top retailers such as Wal-Mart and Toys 'R' Us get information from their stores around the world every two hours via telecommunications. Industry analysts say that former leader K-Mart fell behind due to its delay in installing point-of-sale information technology, which would have enabled it to get faster and more accurate information on inventories and shelf movement of products.[2] Such access is now possible because advances in electronic storage and transmission technology have made it possible to store twenty-six volumes of *Encyclopedia Britannica* on a single chip and transmit that material in a second; these figures are expected to improve by a factor of ten by the end of the decade.

The combination of information technology, access tools, and telecommunication has squeezed out a huge chunk of organizational slack from corporate operations that were previously inherent due to the slow and circuitous nature of information flow within the firm, with holdups due to human "switches." Ordering and purchasing components, which was once a cumbersome, time-consuming process, is now done by Electronic Data Interchange (EDI), reducing the time involved in such transactions from weeks to days and eliminating a considerable amount of paperwork. Levi-Strauss uses LeviLink, an EDI service for handling all aspects of order and delivery. Customers

---

[1]"Does Everyone Have the Same View in Your Supply Chain?" *Frontline Solutions*, 3 (July 2002), pp. 27–30.
[2]Julia King, "OLAP Gains Fans among Data-Hungry Firms," *Computerworld*, 30 (January 8, 1996), pp. 43, 48.

can even place small orders as needed, say, every week, and goods are delivered within two days. One of Levi-Strauss' customers, Design p.l.c., with a chain of sixty stores, was able to entirely eliminate its warehouses, which were used as a buffer to deal with the long lead times between order and delivery.[3]

Sales representatives on field calls who were previously, in effect, tied to the regional or central headquarters due to lack of product information and limited authority, are now able to act independently in the field, because laptop computers, faxes, and satellite uplinks enable instant access to data from the company's central database. Changes in prices due to discounts can now be cleared online from the necessary authority. This reduces reaction time for the sales representative and increases productivity. Monitoring problems for the firm are also reduced, as is paperwork.

**Online Communication**

Multiple design sites around the world in different time zones can now work sequentially on the same problem. A laboratory in California can close its day at 5pm local time when the design center in Japan is just opening the next day. That center continues work on the design problem and hands it over to London at the end of its day, which continues the work and hands over the cumulated work of Japan and London back to California. Finally, the use of telecommunications improves internal efficiency of the firm in other ways. For instance, when Microsoft came up with an upgrade on one of its applications that required some customer education, a customer, using video conferencing on its global information network, arranged a single presentation for the relevant personnel, dispersed across the world, obviating travel and multiple presentations.

Since the 1990s we have seen the explosive growth of e-commerce on the Internet, beginning from the United States. In 1995, only 4 percent of Americans used the Internet every day. In December 2007, the figure was 74 percent and still growing fast.[4] As mentioned in Chapter 1, the total global e-commerce turnover in 2006 hit $12.8 trillion, taking up 18 percent in the global trade of commodities. Developed countries led by the United States are still leading players in this field, while developing countries like China are emerging, becoming an important force in the global e-commerce market.[5] The number of Internet users reached 1.6 billion by March 2009, which amounts to 3.4 times of that of 2000. According to Internet World Stat, 41.2 percent of the Internet users come from Asia, followed by 24.6 percent and 15.7 percent from Europe and North America, respectively. Although Middle East and Africa constitute only 6.3 per cent of the Internet users, these two regions rank the top two with the usage growth of well over 1,000 percent respectively between 2000 and 2008. In the same period, the Internet usage in Asia and Latin America/Caribbean grew by 475 percent and 861 percent.[6]

**Electronic Commerce (E-Commerce)**

There is no other marketing channel than e-commerce where revenues are growing at this pace. There is no other way a business can grow unimpeded by the need to build commercial space and hire sales staff. While traditional mass-retailers, such as Wal-Mart in the United States, Carrefour in France, and Metro in Germany, will not disappear any time soon, the Internet has fundamentally changed customers' expectations about convenience, speed, comparability, price, and service. Even the traditional mass retailers are benefiting from e-commerce. In 2007, traditional chain retailers accounted for 39.9 percent of online sales among top 500 retailers, with a growing rate of 18 percent.[7] For example, Wal-Mart, the largest U.S. company, with annual sales of $375 billion, even creatively tried hiring TV stars so as to increase its online sales. It has

---

[3]Sidney Hill, Jr., "The Race for Profits," *Manufacturing Systems*, 16 (May 1998), pp. II–IV+.

[4]Internet usage statistics for the Americas, http://www.internetworldstats.com, accessed August 1, 2009.

[5]*2006-2007 Annual Report on the Development of Global E-Commerce Industry*, http://market.ccidnet.com/pub/report/show_17192.html, accessed August 1, 2009.

[6]http://www.internetworldstats.com, accessed August 1, 2009.

[7]"Chain Stores Ignore Online Retailing at Their Own Peril," InternetRetailer.com, http://www.internetretailer.com/, June 12, 2008.

been expanding its online section abroad. As a crucial part of the U.S. retailer's growth strategy in Brazil, the retail giant declared in April 2008 to branch out into electronic commerce in this Latin America's largest country, where it plans to invest $723 million to keep up with fast-growing consumer demand.[8] Likewise, Dell Computer rocketed to the top of the personal computer business in the United States by selling directly to consumers online. As commented by Mike George, the chief marketing officer and general manager of its consumer business unit, "if Dell changes prices on its website, its customers' buying patterns change literally within a minute." Many consumers are well-researched and knowledgeable about their prospective purchase from the Internet before they arrive at a showroom or a retail store.[9] Those new expectations will reverberate throughout the world, affecting every business, domestic or global, in many ways.

Marketing beyond the home country has always been hampered by geographical distance and the lack of sufficient information about foreign markets, although transportation and communications technology has reduced, if not eliminated, many difficulties of doing business across the national boundary. Now as a result of an explosive growth of e-commerce on the Internet, those difficulties are increasingly becoming a thing of the past. In other words, product life cycle is becoming shorter and shorter. E-commerce breaks every business free of the concept of geographic distance. No longer will geography bind a company's aspirations or the scope of its market. Traditional bookstores used to be constrained to certain geographical areas—probably within a few miles in radius of their physical locations. Now Amazon.com and BarnesandNoble.com can reach any place on earth whether you are in Amsterdam or Seoul as long as you have access to the Internet. For every early e-commerce mover to eliminate the geographic boundaries of its business, there will be dozens of companies that lose their local monopolies to footloose online businesses.

Although Japan was somewhat slower in adopting personal computers than the United States, the Internet has also taken off in the world's second largest economy. For example, Dell Computer and other U.S. computer manufacturers arguably were the first to market their products directly to Japanese consumers over the Internet. Dell Computer Japan reported that 75 percent of the total number of computers it sold to individual buyers was bought online in Japan. Rakuten Ichiba, Japan's largest Internet shopping site with more than 71,000 registered businesses, selling 37 million product items.[10] Sales grew from $26 million in 2000 to $1.77 billion in 2007, and net profits reached $304 million in 2007.[11]

Even the same explosive Internet growth is being experienced in countries that are still catching up technologically to countries such as the United States and Japan. For example, China has already become one of the world's largest Internet markets. The Internet community in China increased by more than 12 times within the ten years from 2000 to 2009, soaring from just 22.5 million users in 1997 to 298 million by March 2009.[12] Some large portals in China, such as Netease, Sina, Sohu, and Tom, have been making a healthy profit since 2003. Online gaming is fast growing and is one of the three largest moneymakers for Internet companies, with the other two being e-finance and e-education. Unlike other high Internet usage countries, the majority of gamers play at the Internet cafés in China, rather than at home, and it is estimated that China has 350,000 Internet cafés. China's largest e-game operator, Shanda Interactive Entertainment Limited, grows by operating licensed South Korean online games and has accumulated a huge amount of wealth within a few years. As of December 2007, Shanda

[8] "Wal-Mart 2008 Financial Review," Wal-Mart Stores 2008 Annual Report; "Increase Online Sales: Wal-Mart. com's Creative Talent," http://fashion-fox.com/increase-online-sales-wal-martcoms-creative-talent/, January 14, 2008; and "Wal-Mart Eyes e-Commerce in Fast-Growing Brazil," http://www.freshplaza.com/, accessed September 15, 2008.

[9] "Crowned at Last," *Economist*, April 2, 2005, pp. 3–6.

[10] Rakuten Ichiba, http://www.rakuten.co.jp/, accessed August 1, 2009.

[11] Rakuten Ichiba, Annual Report 2007, downloaded from http://www.rakuten.co.jp/, August 1, 2009.

[12] http://www.internetworldstats.com, accdessed August 1, 2009.

has over 600 million registered accounts for all its contents. In the first quarter of 2008, Shanda reported net revenues of 779.8 million yuan (US$111.1 million), representing an increase of 46.5 percent from 532.3 million yuan in the first quarter of 2007.[13] Now the company is shifting its business focus from the computer platform to the TV platform—including games, music, and literature—through a set-top box to penetrate those 340 million households that have already own a television.

**E-Company**

The ultimate effect of information networks within the multinational firm is expected to be on the nature of its organizational structure. As information flows faster across the organization and the number of "filtering" points between the source of information (e.g., point-of-sale information or market and industry analysis) and the user of the information (e.g., the brand manager or the chief executive officer) decreases, the nature of the organization chart in the multinational firm changes drastically. An increasing number of multinational firms have begun to use internal Web servers on the Internet to facilitate communications and transactions among employees, suppliers, independent contractors, and distributors.[14]

Many companies today realize the key to this change is e-business. Siemens, for example, spent 1 billion to turn itself into an e-company. Siemens is enabling itself to connect the different parts of its far-flung empire into a more coherent whole. In practice, Siemens plans to utilize its information technology to enhance knowledge management, online purchasing, change the company's value chain, and to efficiently deal with its customers. Now customers can click on "Buy from Siemens" on the company's home page and place orders. Inevitably, Siemens demand chain is going smoothly from customers, through Siemens, and then to its suppliers.[15] Similarly, an assembly-line worker in a Procter & Gamble plant knows from his computer that stores have been selling a particular brand of facial cream more briskly than anticipated. Having this information, he can change production scheduling on his own by giving the computer necessary instructions to cut down on some other brands and to increase the production of the brand in question. The foreperson and the section manager of a conventional plant are no longer required.

**Faster Product Diffusion**

The obvious impact of information technology is the more rapid dispersion of technology and the shorter product life cycles in global markets than ever before. It suggests that the former country-by-country sequential approach to entering markets throughout the world, described in the international product cycle model in Chapter 1, is increasingly untenable.

This trend is already reflected in many product markets. The diffusion lag for color television between the United States on one hand and Japan and Europe on the other was six years. With compact discs the household penetration rates had come down to one year. For Pentium-based computers, Taiwan, India, Japan, and U.S.-based companies released computers at about the same time in their respective national markets. Thus, a firm selling personal computers would have to launch a new product on a worldwide basis in order not to fall behind in the global sweepstakes.[16] This issue will be further discussed later when we discuss new product development in Chapter 10.

**Global Citizenship**

Another important contributing factor in the globalization of markets is the spread of English as the language of international business. The transformation of the European Union into a monetary union has already taken place with the introduction of the euro

---

[13]Shanda, http://www.snda.com/.

[14]John A. Quelch and Lisa R. Klein, "The Internet and International Marketing," *Sloan Management Review*, 37 (Spring 1996), pp. 60–75.

[15]Herbert Heinzel, "Siemens—The e-Company: In its Quest to Become an e-Business Company, Siemens is Pursuing a Comprehensive Approach that Goes Far Beyond the Mere Selling of Products over the Internet," *Supply Chain Management Review*, March 2002.

[16]Shlomo Kalish, Vijay Mahajan, and Eitan Muller, "Waterfall and Sprinkler New-Product Strategies in Competitive Global Markets," *International Journal of Research in Marketing*, 12 (July 1995), pp. 105–19.

as its common currency. Global citizenship is no longer just a phrase in the lexicon of futurologists. It has already become every bit as concrete and measurable as changes in GNP and trade flows. In fact, conventional measures of trade flows may have outlived their usefulness, as we will discuss later.

The global environment thus demands a strategy that encompasses numerous national boundaries and tastes, and that integrates a firm's operations across the national borders. This strategy is truly global in nature and has gone beyond the home-country-focused ethnocentric orientation or the multicountry focused polycentric orientation of many multinational firms in the middle of the twentieth century. The firm thus needs to adopt a geocentric orientation that views the entire world as a potential market and integrates firm activities on a global basis.[17]

## ♦♦♦♦♦♦♦♦  GLOBAL STRATEGY

The acid test of a well-managed company is being able to conceive, develop, and implement an effective global strategy. A **global strategy** is to array the competitive advantages arising from location, world-scale economies, or global brand distribution, namely, by building a global presence, defending domestic dominance, and overcoming country-by-country fragmentation. Because of its inherent difficulties, global strategy development presents one of the stiffest challenges for managers today. Companies that operate on a global scale need to integrate their worldwide strategy, in contrast to the earlier multinational or multidomestic approach. The earlier strategies would be categorized more truly as multidomestic strategies rather than as global strategies. In the section below, we approach the issue of global strategy through four conceptualizations: 1) global industry, 2) competitive industry structure, 3) competitive advantage, 4) hypercompetition, and 5)interdependency.

**Global Industry**    The first conceptualization is that of a **global industry**.[18] Global industries are defined as *those where a firm's competitive position in one country is affected by its position in other countries, and vice versa.* Therefore, we are talking about not just a collection of domestic industries, but also a series of interlinked domestic industries in which rivals compete against one another on a truly worldwide basis. For instance, 25 years after Honda began making cars in the first Japanese transplant in Marysville, Ohio, the automaker is increasingly relying on the U.S. market. It had boosted its North American production capacity 40 percent by 2006. Today, more than half the passenger sedans sold in the United States are import brands, and more than half the vehicles sporting foreign nameplates are made in the United States. It is foreign players that are reinvigorating America's automobile business and turning the United States into the center of a global industry.[19]

Therefore, the first question that faces managers is the extent of globalization of their industry. Assuming that the firm's activities are indeed global or that the firm wishes to grow toward global operations and markets, managers must design and implement a global strategy. This is because virtually every industry has global or potentially global aspects—some industries have more aspects that are global and more intensely so. Indeed, a case has been made that the globalization of markets has already been achieved, that consumer tastes around the world have converged, and that the global firm attempts, unceasingly, to drive consumer tastes toward convergence.[20] Four major forces determining the globalization potential of industry are presented in **Exhibit 8-1**.

---

[17]Shaoming Zou and S. Tamer Cavusgil, "The GMS: A Broad Conceptualization of Global Marketing Strategy and Its Effect on Firm Performance," *Journal of Marketing*, 66 (October 2002), pp. 40–56.

[18]Michael E. Porter, ed., Competition in Global Industries (Boston, Mass.: Harvard University Press, 1986).

[19]"Autos: A New Industry," *Business Week*, July 15, 2002, p. 98–104.

[20]Theodore Levitt, "The Globalization of Markets," *Harvard Business Review*, 61 (May-June 1983), pp. 92–102.

## EXHIBIT 8-1
### INDUSTRY GLOBALIZATION DRIVERS

### Market Forces

*Market forces* depend on the nature of customer behavior and the structure of channels of distribution. Some common market forces are:

- Per-capita income converging among industrialized nations

- Emergence of rich consumers in emerging markets such as China and India

- Convergence of lifestyles and tastes (e.g., McDonald's in Moscow and Stolichnaya vodka in America)

- Revolution in information and communication technologies (e.g., personal computer, fax machines, and the Internet)

- Increased international travel creating global consumers knowledgeable of products from many countries

- Organizations beginning to behave as global customers

- Growth of global and regional channels (e.g., America's Wal-Mart, France's Carrefour/ Promodès, Germany's Metro, and Japan's 7-Eleven)

- Establishment of world brands (e.g., Coca-Cola, Microsoft, Toyota, and Nestlé)

- Push to develop global advertising (e.g., Saatchi and Saatchi's commercials for British Airways)

- Spread of global and regional media (e.g., CNN, MTV, Star TV in India)

### Cost Forces

*Cost forces* depend on the economics of the business. These forces particularly affect production location decisions, as well as global market participation and global product development decisions. Some of these cost forces are:

- Push for economies of scale and scope, further aided by flexible manufacturing

- Accelerating technological innovations

- Advances in transportation (e.g., FedEx, UPS, DHL, and Yamato Transport)

- Emergence of newly industrializing countries with productive capabilities and low labor costs (e.g., China, India, and many Eastern European countries)

- High product development costs relative to shortened product life cycle

### Government Forces

Rules set by national governments can affect the use of global strategic decision-making. Some of these rules/policies include:

- Reduction of tariff and non-tariff barriers

- Creation of trading blocs (e.g., European Union, North American Free Trade Agreement, and MERCOSUR—a common market in South America)

*(continued)*

**EXHIBIT 8-1**

*(CONTINUED)*

- Establishment of world trading regulations (e.g., World Trade Organization and its various policies)

- Deregulation of many industries

- Privatization in previously state-dominated economies in Latin America

- Shift to open market economies from closed communist systems in China, Eastern Europe, and the former Soviet Union

**Competitive Forces**

*Competitive forces* raise the globalization potential of their industry and spur the need for a response on the global strategy levels. The common competitive forces include:

- Increase in world trade

- More countries becoming key competitive battlegrounds (e.g., Japan, Korea, China, India, and Brazil)

- Increased ownership of corporations by foreign investors

- Globalization of financial markets (e.g., listing of corporations on multiple stock exchanges and issuing debt in multiple currencies)

- Rise of new competitors intent on becoming global competitors (e.g., Japanese firms in the 1970s, Korean firms in the 1980s, Taiwanese firms in the 1990s, Chinese and Indian firms in the 2000s, and probably Russian firms in the 2010s)

- Rise of "born global" Internet and other companies

- Growth of global networks making countries interdependent in particular industries (e.g., electronics and aircraft manufacturing)

- More companies becoming geocentric rather than ethnocentric (e.g., Stanley Works, a traditional U.S. company, moved its production offshore; Uniden, a Japanese telecommunications equipment manufacturer has never manufactured in Japan)

- Increased formation of global strategic alliances

*Source:* Adapted from George S. Yip, *Total Global Strategy II* (Upper Saddle River, N.J.: Prentice Hall, 2003, pp. 10–12.

The implications of a distinction between multidomestic and global strategy are quite profound. In a multidomestic strategy, a firm manages its international activities like a portfolio. Its subsidiaries or other operations around the world each control all the important activities necessary to maximize their returns in their area of operation independent of the activities of other subsidiaries in the firm. The subsidiaries enjoy a large degree of autonomy, and the firm's activities in each of its national markets are determined by the competitive conditions in that national market. In contrast, a global strategy integrates the activities of a firm on a worldwide basis to capture the linkages among countries and to treat the entire world as a single, borderless market. This requires more than the transferring of intangible assets between countries.

In effect, the firm that truly operationalizes a global strategy is a geocentrically oriented firm. It considers the whole world as its arena of operation, and its managers maintain equidistance from all markets and develop a system with which to satisfy its needs for both global integration for economies of scale and scope *and* responsiveness to different market needs and conditions in various parts of the world (to be discussed in Chapter 15 in the context of sourcing strategy). In a way, the geocentric firm tries to "kill two birds with one stone."[21] Such a firm tends to centralize some resources at home, some abroad, and distributes others among its many national

---

[21]Masaaki Kotabe, "To Kill Two Birds with One Stone: Revisiting the Integration-Responsiveness Framework," in Michael Hitt and Joseph Cheng, ed., *Managing Transnational Firms*, New York: Elsevier, 2002, 59–69.

## GLOBAL PERSPECTIVE 8-1

### GLOBALIZING THE MULTIDOMESTIC CORPORATE CULTURE

At Unilever, three main groups used to be involved in strategic management: operating companies, management groups that oversee them, and the corporation as a whole. To be a successful global company, the strategies at different levels needed to interrelate, considering bottom-up and top-down approaches. The dilemma is to find the right equilibrium between instructions from the top and inputs from the bottom in order not to stifle management creativity at the bottom as well as to provide sufficient direction to achieve the interests of all the corporation's stakeholders.

The company's culture and philosophy influence this equilibrium. Unilever, for example, used to be highly decentralized, with individual operating companies, with their own identity, linked by a common corporate culture and some common services such as research, finance, and management development. After having experimented with various organizational structures to encourage global strategic management, Unilever has adopted a full-time Corporate Development board member, who is on staff with an advisory role, free from major line responsibilities.

In 2005, Unilever Chief Executive Patrick Cescau kicked off an ambitious restructuring program. He ditched under-performing brands, divested Unilever's frozen-foods business,

*Source*: Kerry Capell, "Unilever Lathers Up," BusinessWeek.com, February 15, 2008.

and stripped out layers of bureaucracy, including half the ranks of top management, which had for years kept the company lagging behind fleeter-footed rivals. Under Cescau's "One Unilever" plan, unnecessary complexity was removed. Brands now rely on one formulation, one packaging design, and one marketing strategy, instead of the fragmented approach of the past. Local managers no longer run the autonomous fiefdoms where they were responsible for everything from marketing and sales to running factories and back-office operations. Instead, these functions have been largely centralized, eliminating duplication and allowing for faster decision-making and global economies of scale. Equally important, emerging markets, where Unilever historically has been strong, were made a higher priority. To ensure products meet the needs of local consumers around the world, nearly one-third of the company's home and personal products brand development resources now are based in the developing world.

The changes are paying off. Unilever posted its best annual results in five years on February 7 2008, with sales up 5.5 percent, to $15 billion, and net profits of nearly $8 billion. "The transformation of Unilever continues apace," Cescau says. Unilever's London-traded shares are up 12 percent since a year ago. What's more, developing markets now account for nearly 45 percent of revenues, up from 38 percent in 2005.

---

operations, resulting in a complex configuration of assets and capabilities on a global basis.[22]

This is in contrast to an ethnocentric orientation, where managers operate under the dominant influence of home country practices, or a polycentric orientation, where managers of individual subsidiaries operate independently of each other—the polycentric manager in practice leads to a multidomestic orientation, which prevents integration and optimization on a global basis. Until the early 1980s the global operations of Unilever were a good example of a multidomestic approach. Unilever's various country operations were largely independent of each other, with headquarters restricting itself to data collection and helping out subsidiaries when required. As presented in **Global Perspective 8-1**, Unilever has started adding some geocentric dimensions to its global strategy.

*Competitive industry structure* is the second conceptualization that is useful in understanding the nature of global strategy. A conceptual framework that portrays the multidimensional nature of competitive industry structure is presented in **Exhibit 8-2**. It identifies the key structural factors that determine the strength of competitive forces within an industry and consequently industry profitability. Competition is not limited to the firms in the same industry. If firms in an industry collectively have insufficient

**Competitive Industry Structure**

---

[22]Christopher A. Bartlett and Sumantra Ghoshal, *Managing Across Borders*. Boston, MA: Harvard Business School Press, 1989; and for an empirical study, see, for example, Andreas F. Grein, C. Samuel Craig, Hirokazu Takada, "Integration and Responsiveness: Marketing Strategies of Japanese and European Automobile Manufacturers," *Journal of International Marketing*, vol. 9, no. 2, 2001, pp. 19-50.

**EXHIBIT 8-2**
NATURE OF COMPETITIVE INDUSTRY STRUCTURE

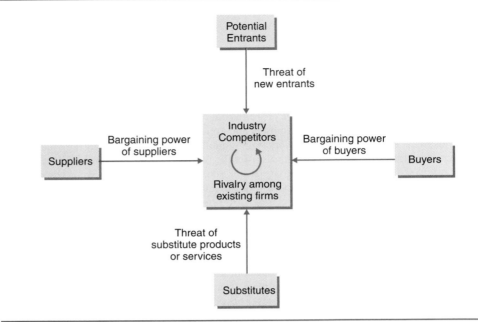

*Source:* Reprinted with the permission of the Free Press, a division of Simon & Schuster from COMPETITIVE STRATEGY: Techniques for Analyzing Industries and Competitors by Michael E. Porter, p. 4. Copyright © 1980 by The Free Press.

capacity to fulfill demand, the incentive is high for new market entrants. However, such entrants need to consider the time and investment it takes to develop new or additional capacity, the likelihood of such capacity being developed by existing competitors, and the possibility of changes in customer demand over time. Indirect competition also comes from suppliers and customers, as well as substitute products or services.

1. **Industry competitors** determine the rivalry among existing firms.

2. **Potential entrants** may change the rule of competition but can be deterred by entry barriers. For example, Shanghai Jahwa Co., Ltd., its predecessor founded in 1898, became the largest cosmetics and personal care products company in China by 1990.[23] Shanghai Jahwa owns such successful brands as Maxam, Liushen, Ruby, and G.L.F, among others, and is making gradual inroads into markets outside China. Although not yet known to the Western world, its brands may some day pose a major competitive threat to Clinique, Estée Lauder, Lancôme, Maxfactor, and other well-known brands and may change the nature of competition in the cosmetics and personal care products industry.

3. The **bargaining power of suppliers** can change the structure of industries. Intel has become a dominant producer of microprocessors for personal computers. Its enormous bargaining power has caused many PC manufacturers to operate on wafer-thin profit margins, making the PC industry extremely competitive.

4. The **bargaining power of buyers** may affect the firm's profitability. It is particularly the case when governments try to get price and delivery concessions from foreign firms. Similarly, Nestlé, whose subsidiaries used to make independent decisions on cocoa purchase, has centralized its procurement decision at its headquarters to take advantage of its consolidated bargaining power over cocoa producers around the world. Given its bargaining power, Nestlé has further completed a trial of a ground-breaking supply chain project that allows suppliers to view its production

---

[23]Based on the first author's visit to Shanghai Jahwa based in Shanghai, China, August 2002.

information and ensure it can meet fluctuations in demand for its products by removing about 20 percent of excess stock from its supply chain.[24]

5. The **threat of substitute products or services** can restructure the entire industry above and beyond the existing competitive structure. For example, a recent *Economist* article alerted that PlayStation 2, the successor to Sony's best-selling PlayStation, a computer game console, introduced in 2000, contained a 128-bit microprocessor having twice the raw number-crunching power of Intel's most advanced Pentium chip and that could play DVD movies, decode digital TV, and surf the Internet, for less than $400.[25] Now imagine Sony's PlayStation 3 introduced in 2006, is several times more powerful than PS2, and is capable of surpassing 250 gigaflops per second, rivaling the best mid-1990s supercomputer; it may even challenge the Microsoft-Intel PC standard.[26]

*Competitive advantage* is a third conceptualization that is of use in developing and understanding a strategy on a global scale. Companies may adopt different strategies for different competitive advantage. The firm has a competitive advantage when it is able to deliver the same benefits as competitors but eat a lower cost, or deliver benefits that exceed those of competing products. Thus, a competitive advantage enables the firm to create superior value for its customers and superior profits for itself.[27] Simply stated, competitive advantage is a temporary monopoly period that a firm can enjoy over its competitors. To prolong such a monopolistic period, the firm strives to develop a strategy that would be difficult for its competitors to imitate.

**Competitive Advantage**

The firm that builds its competitive advantage on economies of scale is known as one using a **cost leadership** strategy. Customized flexible manufacturing as a result of CAD/CAM (computer-aided design and computer-aided manufacturing) technology has shown some progress. However, it proved to be more difficult operationally than was thought, so economies of scale still remain the main feature of market competition. The theory is that the greater the economies of scale, the greater the benefits to those firms with a larger market share. As a result, many firms try to jockey for larger market shares than their competitors. Economies of scale come about because larger plants are more efficient to run, and their per-unit cost of production is less as overhead costs are allocated across large volumes of production. Further economies of scale also result from learning effects: the firm learns more efficient methods of production with increasing cumulative experience in production over time. All of these effects tend to intensify competition. Once a high level of economies of scale is achieved, it provides the firm strong barriers against new entrants to the market. In the 1970s and early 1980s, many Japanese companies became cost leaders in such industries as automobiles and consumer electronics. However, there is no guarantee that cost leadership will last. Also, the cost leadership strategy does not necessarily apply to all markets. According to a recent study, implementation of a cost-leadership strategy by developed-country multinational companies (MNCs) actually is rarely effective in emerging markets. In order to achieve high performance, therefore, MNCs that benefit from cost leadership strategy may try using different strategies in different markets instead of a single generic strategy globally.[28]

Until flexible manufacturing and customized production becomes fully operational, cost leaders may be vulnerable to firms that use a **product differentiation** strategy to better serve the exact needs of customers. Although one could argue that lower cost will attract customers away from other market segments, some customers are willing to pay a premium price for unique product features that they desire. Uniqueness

[24]Nestlé Links SAP Systems to Allow Suppliers to View Production Data," *Computer Weekly*, October 21, 2003, p. 8.

[25]"War Games," *Economist*, April 22, 2000, p. 60.

[26]"Super Cell," *Forbes*, February 14, 2005, p. 46.

[27]Michael E. Porter, *Competitive Advantage: Techniques for Analyzing Industries and Competitors*, New York: The Free Press, 1980.

[28]Daniel W. Baack and David J. Boggs, "The Difficulties in Using a Cost Leadership Strategy in Emerging Markets," *International Journal of Emerging Markets*, 3, April 2008, pp. 125–39.

may come in the form of comfort, product performance, and aesthetics, as well as status symbol and exclusivity. Despite the Japanese juggernaut in the automobile industry (primarily in the North American and Asian markets) in the 1970s and 1980s, BMW of Germany and Volvo of Sweden (currently under Ford's ownership), for example, managed to maintain their competitive strengths in the high-end segments of the automobile market. Indeed, Japanese carmakers have struggled for years to make a dent in the European market, and they are finally seeing a turnaround after releasing a spate of new models' that European drivers want to buy—small cars with spacious cabins—the type that European firms have yet to make, such as Honda's Jazz (known as the Fit in Japan), Toyota's Yaris (known as the Vitz in Japan), and Mazda's Mazda 6 (known as the Atenza in Japan).[29] While high oil prices are causing pain for U.S. carmakers such as GM and Ford, U.S. consumers welcome small Japanese cars. In May 2008, for example, the sales of Toyota's Camry and Corolla for the first time exceeded Ford's F-150 pick-up, one of the America's traditional favorite vehicles.[30]

Smaller companies may pursue a limited differentiation strategy by keeping a niche in the market. Firms using a **niche** strategy focus exclusively on a highly specialized segment of the market and try to achieve a dominant position in that segment. Again in the automobile industry, Porsche and Saab maintain their competitive strengths in the high-power sports car enthusiast segment. However, particularly in an era of global competition, niche players may be vulnerable to large-scale operators due to sheer economies of scale needed to compete on a global scale.

***First-Mover Advantage versus First-Mover Disadvantage.*** For many firms, technology is the key to success in markets where significant advances in product performance are expected. A firm uses its technological leadership for rapid innovation and introduction of new products. The timing of such introductions in the global marketplace is an integral part of the firm's strategy. However, the dispersion of technological expertise means that any technological advantage is temporary, so the firm should not rest on its laurels. The firm needs to move on to its next source of temporary advantage to remain ahead. In the process, firms that are able to continue creating a series of temporary advantages are the ones that survive and thrive. Technology, marketing skills, and other assets that a firm possesses become its weapons to gain advantages in time over its competitors. The firm now attempts to be among the pioneers, or first-movers, in the market for the product categories that it operates in.[31] Sony offers an excellent example of a company in constant pursuit of first-mover advantage with Trinitron color television, Betamax video recorder, Walkman, 8mm video recorder, DVD (digital video disc), and Blue-ray disc technology, although not all of its products, such as MiniDisc, succeeded in the market. Another interesting example in the IT era is Friendster, a Mountain View, California-based social networking site, which was one of the initial social networking sites to launch in 2003; it has been growing its Asian subscriber base since the first "connections" from the region were made in 2004. Due to its first-mover advantage in the Asian region, Friendster is getting 36 million monthly unique visitors from Asia, out of the overall 40 million globally—it was accessible ahead of its biggest competitor, Facebook, which opened its doors to global access later in 2006.[32]

Indeed, there could even be some first-mover disadvantages.[33] Citigroup's recent case vividly raises the possibility of first-mover disadvantages. To establish its foothold

---

[29]Japanese Carmakers Make European Dent," *Japan Times Online*, http://www.japantimes.co.jp/, December 31, 2002.

[30]"Crisis? What Oil Crisis?," *Economist*, June 7, 2008, pp. 73–74.

[31]Gerard J. Tellis and Peter N. Golder, "First to Market, First to Fail?: Real Causes of Enduring Market Leadership," *Sloan Management Review*, 37 (Winter 1996), pp. 65–75;); and Richard Makadok, "Can First-Mover and Early-Mover Advantages be Sustained in an Industry with Low Barriers to Entry/Imitation?" *Strategic Management Journal*, 19 (July 1998), pp. 683–96.

[32]Victoria Ho, "Friendster Looks to Expand Asian Base," *BusinessWeek.com*, June 26, 2008,

[33]Marvin B. Lieberman and David B. Montgomery, "First-Mover (Dis)advantages: Retrospective and Link with the Resource-Based View," *Strategic Management Journal*, 19 (December 1998), pp. 1111–125.

in the growing Chinese economy, Citigroup recently entered into an alliance with Shanghai Pudong Development Bank in China targeting the country's credit card market. About 10 million cards with revolving credit have already been issued in China. Some experts argue that Chinese credit services would be risky for first-mover companies given that the country has no nationwide credit-rating system and lacks adequate risk-management technology.[34]

In general, stable markets favor the first-mover strategy while market and technology turbulence favor the follower strategy. Followers have the benefit of hindsight to determine more preciously the timing, form, and scale of their market entry. It is therefore important for the firm to clearly assess the key success factors and the resulting likelihood of success for achieving the ultimate targeted position in the highly competitive global business environment.[35]

A firm's competitive advantage lies in its capability to effectively anticipate, react to, and lead change continuously and even rhythmically over time. Firms should "probe" into the unknown by making many small steps to explore their environments. These probes could take the form of a number of new product introductions that are "small, fast, and cheap," and can be supplemented by using experts to contemplate the future, making strategic alliances to explore new technologies, and holding meetings where the future is discussed by management. To compete on the edge, firms need to understand that:

1. Advantage is temporary. In other words, firms need to have a strong focus on continuously generating new sources of advantages.

2. Strategy is diverse, emergent, and complicated. It is crucial to rely on diverse strategic moves.

3. Reinvention is the goal. It is how firms keep pace with a rapidly changing marketplace.

4. Live in the present, stretch out the past, and reach into the future. Successful firms launch more experimental products and services than others while they exploit previous experiences and try to extend them to new opportunities.

5. Grow the strategy and drive strategy from the business level. It is important for managers to pay attention to the timing and order in which strategy is grown and agile moves are made at the business level.

6. To maintain sustainable power in fast-paced, competitive and unpredictable environments, senior management needs to recognize patterns in firms' development and articulate semi-coherent strategic direction.[36]

With these strategic flexibilities in mind, we could think of two primary approaches to gaining competitive advantage. The *competitor-focused* approaches involve comparison with the competitor on costs, prices, technology, market share, profitability, and other related activities. Such an approach may lead to a preoccupation with some activities, and the firm may lose sight of its customers and various constituents. *Customer-focused* approaches to gaining competitive advantage emanate from an analysis of customer benefits to be delivered. In practice, finding the proper links between required customer benefits and the activities and variables controlled by management is needed. Besides, there is evidence to suggest that listening too closely to customer requirements may cause a firm to miss the bus on innovations because current customers might not want innovations that require them to change how they operate.[37]

---

[34]"Risks in Credit Card Business," *China Daily*, January 10, 2005.

[35]Dean Shepherd and Mark Shanley, *New Venture Strategy: Timing, Environmental Uncertainty and Performance*, Thousand Oaks, CA: Sage publications, 1998.

[36]Shona L. Brown and Kathleen M. Eisenhardt, *Competing on the Edge*, Boston, MA: Harvard Business Press, 1998.

[37]See, for example, John P. Workman, Jr. "Marketing's Limited Role in New Product Development in One Computer Systems Firm," *Journal of Marketing Research*, 30 (November 1993), pp. 405–21.

***Competitor-Focused Approach.*** Black & Decker, a U.S.-based manufacturer of hand tools, switched to a global strategy using its strengths in the arenas of cost and quality and timing and know-how. In the 1980s Black & Decker's position was threatened by a powerful Japanese competitor, Makita. Makita's strategy of producing and marketing globally standardized products worldwide made it into a low-cost producer and enabled it to steadily increase its world market share. Within the company, Black & Decker's international fiefdoms combined with nationalist chauvinism to stifle coordination in product development and new product introductions, resulting in lost opportunities.

Then, responding to the increased competitive pressure, Black & Decker moved decisively toward globalization. It embarked on a program to coordinate new product development worldwide in order to develop core-standardized products that could be marketed globally with minimum modification. The streamlining of R&D also offered scale economies and less duplication of effort—and new products could be introduced faster. Its increased emphasis on design made it into a global leader in design management. It consolidated its advertising into two agencies worldwide in an attempt to give a more consistent image worldwide. Black & Decker also strengthened the functional organization by giving the functional manager a larger role in coordinating with the country management. Finally, Black & Decker purchased General Electric's small appliance division to achieve world-scale economies in manufacturing, distribution, and marketing. The global strategy initially faced skepticism and resistance from country managers at Black & Decker. The chief executive officer took a visible leadership role and made some management changes to start moving the company toward globalization. These changes in strategy helped Black & Decker increase revenues and profits by as much as 50 percent in the 1990s.[38] In order to meet further cost competition, Black & Decker's new global restructuring project plans to reduce manufacturing costs by transferring additional power tool production from the United States and England to low-cost facilities in Mexico, China, and a new leased facility in the Czech Republic and by sourcing more manufactured items from third parties where cost advantages are available and quality can be assured. Its global restructuring plan resulted in global sales increase of 20 percent to record $5.4 billion and increased earnings of 36 percent to $5.40 per share in 2005.[39]

A word of caution is in order. Although a company's financial resources provides durability for its strategy, regulatory and other barriers could prove to be overwhelming even in a very promising market such as China. As presented in **Global Perspective 8-2**, AOL/Time Warner's expansion into China illustrates this difficulty.

***Customer-Focused Approach.*** Estée Lauder is one good corporate example that superbly used cost and quality, timing and know-how, strongholds, and financial resources to its advantage. Estée Lauder has grown from a small, woman-owned cosmetics business to become one of the world's leading manufacturers and marketers of quality skin care, makeup, fragrance, and hair-care products. Its brands include Estée Lauder, Aramis, Clinique, Prescriptives, Origins, M·A·C, La Mer, Bobbi Brown, and Tommy Hilfiger, among others.

How did Estée Lauder accomplish such a feat? The answer lies in its ability to reach consumers in nearly every corner of the world, in its internal strengths, and in the diversity of its portfolio of brands. Since the beginning of its international operations, the company has always conducted in-depth research to determine the feasibility and compatibility of its products with each particular market, which has led to its high-quality image. Another reason for the company's success lies in its focus on global expansion before its competitors. Estée Lauder's international operations commenced in 1960. Because of its strong visibility in Europe, it served as a springboard to other

---

[38]Black & Decker, various annual reports.

[39]Black & Decker, Investor Relations, http://www.corporate-ir.net/ireye/ir_site.zhtml?ticker=BDK&script=2100, accessed December 10, 2005.

## GLOBAL PERSPECTIVE 8-2

### "ROME" COULD NOT BE BUILT IN A DAY . . . EVEN BY AOL/TIME WARNER IN CHINA

AOL, a Time Warner company, made a foray into China in 2001. AOL partnered with Lenovo (previously known as Legend), China's largest computer maker, to tackle the world's most promising Internet-service market; and became the first foreign broadcaster allowed onto a Chinese cable-TV service. However, AOL realized that it would take years and years to turn a profit. In China, any vendor or operator that wants to come into the Internet space needs deep pockets to last at least five years or more for anything to happen. It takes so many regulatory hurdles to just get approval to start offering Internet service in China. Furthermore, because China has a lot of competition, the margins have come down so much and Internet-service providers cannot become profitable instantly. But AOL could not wait for that long. Because of its continued losses in Japan, AOL just closed its Japanese venture. AOL's new portal had many problems. It is not even as good as similar services from money-losing portals like sina.com or sohu.com. Furthermore, Lenovo is essentially a hardware company without much experience in telecom operations. Thus, this partnership lacked a distribution channel for AOL services. As a result, the business failed to go anywhere, and Lenovo finally pulled out of its legacy relationship with Time Warner in 2004. So far, the only places where Internet-service providers make money are in protected markets like South Korea or Taiwan, or where a firm blows out its competition early, as AOL did in the United States. In competitive markets such as Hong Kong, Singapore, and China, price competition for basic services tends to leave everyone unprofitable.

Recently, AOL has been preparing to flex its mobile muscles. This includes its section in China as well—while AOL has revealed its wireless aspirations by hiring a telecommunications executive, former AT&T vice-president John Burbank, as new chief marketing officer for all of AOL, and listing 14 mobile-related jobs in the U.S., the careers section of AOL's corporate site currently registers even nine more, that is, 23 such jobs in China.

As for television, AOL and other foreign broadcasters still face many regulatory obstacles. Though CCTV has been granted "landing rights," it can only reach a very small part of Guangdong province, and its competitors include established programmers like Hong Kong's TVB and ATV. Meanwhile, AOL's other channels also have problems. Warner Music faces piracy issues that about 95 percent of all music and movie CDs in China are pirated; Time's two flagship news publications—Time and Fortune—officially only sell fewer than 2,000 copies each in China, although *Fortune China* published through a licensee is helping establish the brand name. As for movies, China promises to double the number of overseas films it allows to be released each year, but that still means only 20 films, distributed among all of the world's film studios, the potentials are not good enough for Time Warner. All these obstacles take a long time to improve, which means that Time Warner needs to have the patience and financial resources as well as a strong commitment in the China market, hoping that it will be the first player once China opens its door to foreign media companies.

*Sources:* Ben Dolvens and Alkman Granitsas, "Media—Don't Hold your Breath," *Far Eastern Economic Review,* www.feer.com, May 02, 2002; "Lenovo Reaches for New Direction," CRN, http://www.crn.com, December 3, 2004; and Olga Kharif, "AOL's Mobile Ambitions," *BusinessWeek.com*, September 26, 2007.

European markets. Shortly thereafter, the company made its foray with the Estée Lauder brand into new markets in the Americas, Europe, and Asia. In the late 1960s the Aramis and Clinique brands were founded and a manufacturing facility was established in Belgium. In the 1970s, Clinique was introduced overseas and Estée Lauder began to explore new opportunities in the former Soviet Union. During the 1980s, the company made considerable progress in reaching markets that were still out of reach for many American companies. For example, in 1989 Estée Lauder was the first American cosmetic company to enter the former Soviet Union when it opened a perfumery in Moscow. The same year, it established its first freestanding beauty boutique in Budapest, Hungary. In 1990s the firm moved further into untapped markets such as China. Recently, Clinique established a presence in Vietnam. The company is focusing further on China and the rest of Asia. In addition, there are still many opportunities in Europe. The company will continue to look to Latin America for expansion but with caution, due to economic circumstances and political instability. One more reason for the company's success is its use of financial resources to further strengthen brand value. Since 1989, the firm has opened some of its freestanding stores overseas because it could not find the right channels of distribution to maintain the brand's standards.

Estée Lauder has built strong brand equity all over the world with each brand having a single, global image. The company's philosophy of never compromising brand equity has guided it in its selection of the appropriate channels of distribution overseas. In the United States and overseas, products are sold through limited distribution channels to uphold the particular images of each brand.

At the same time, Estée Lauder has successfully responded to the needs of different markets. In Asia, for example, a system of products was developed to whiten the skin. This ability to adapt and create products to specific market needs has contributed greatly to the company's ability to enter new markets. Estée Lauder's global strategies have paid off. In 2001, 61 percent of net sales came from the Americas, 26 percent from Europe, the Middle East, and Africa, and 13 percent from Asia/Pacific countries. For the past five years, international sales have increased almost 10 percent annually. Estée Lauder currently has manufacturing facilities in the United Sates, Canada, Belgium, Switzerland, and the United Kingdom, and research and development laboratories in the United States, Canada, Belgium, and Japan.[40]

## Hypercompetition

*Hypercompetition*, a fourth conceptualization, refers to the fact that all firms are faced with a form of aggressive competition that is tougher than oligopolistic or monopolistic competition, but is not perfect competition where the firm is atomistic and cannot influence the market at all. This form of competition is pervasive not just in fast-moving high-technology industries like computers and deregulated industries like airlines, but also in industries that have traditionally been considered more sedate, like processed foods. The central thesis of this argument is that no type of competitive advantage can last—it is bound to erode.

In any given industry, firms jockey among themselves for better competitive position, given a set of customers and buyers, the threat of substitutes, and the barriers to entry in that industry. However, the earlier arguments represent the description of a situation without any temporal dimension; there is no indication as to how a firm should act to change the situation to its advantage. For instance, it is not clear how tomorrow's competitor can differ from today's. A new competitor can emerge from a completely different industry given the convergence of industries. Ricoh, once a low-cost facsimile and copier maker, has now come up with a product that records moving images digitally, which is what a camcorder and a movie camera do using different technologies. This development potentially pits Ricoh as a direct competitor to camcorder and movie camera makers, emphasizing differentiation by providing unique technical features—something not possible ten or twenty years ago.

Such a shift in competition is referred to as *creative destruction*. This view of competition assumes continuous change, where the firm's focus is on disrupting the market. In a hypercompetitive environment, a firm competes on the basis of price; quality, timing, and know-how; creating strongholds in the markets it operates in (this is akin to entry barriers); and the financial resources to outlast its competitors.[41]

## Interdependency

A fifth aspect of global strategy is *interdependency* of modern companies. Recent research has shown that the number of technologies used in a variety of products in numerous industries is rising.[42] Because access to resources limit how many distinctive competencies a firm can gain, firms must draw on outside technologies to be able to build a state-of-the-art product. Since most firms operating globally are limited by a lack of all required technologies, it follows that for firms to make optimal use of outside technologies, a degree of components standardization is required. Such standardization would enable different firms to develop different end products, using, in a large

---

[40]Anastasia Xenias, "The Sweet Smell of Success: Estée Lauder Honored at World Trade Week Event," *Export America*, May 2002 (print version), or to be accessed at http://www.trade.gov/exportamerica/.

[41]Richard D'Aveni, *Hypercompetition: Managing the Dynamics of Strategic Maneuvering* (New York: The Free Press, 1994).

[42]Aldor Lanctot and K. Scott Swan, "Technology Acquisition Strategy in an Internationally Competitive Environment," *Journal of International Management*, 6 (Autumn 2000), pp. 187–215.

measure, the same components.[43] Research findings do indicate that technology intensity—that is, the degree of R&D expenditure a firm incurs as a proportion of sales—is a primary determinant of cross-border firm integration.[44]

The computer industry is a good instance of a case where firms use components from various sources. HP/Compaq, Dell, and Acer all use semiconductor chips from Intel, AMD, or Cyrix, hard drives from Seagate Western Digital, Maxtor, or Hitachi, and software from Microsoft. The final product—in this case, the personal computer—carries some individual idiosyncrasies of Compaq, Dell, or Acer, but at least some of the components are common and, indeed, are portable across the products of the three companies.

In the international context, governments also tend to play a larger role and may, directly or indirectly, affect parts of the firm's strategy. Tariff and non-tariff barriers such as voluntary export restraints and restrictive customs procedures could change cost structures so that a firm could need to change its production and sourcing decisions. It is possible, however, that with the end of the Cold War and the spread of capitalism to previously socialist economies, such factors may decrease in importance. As presented in Chapter 2, the creation of the World Trade Organization in 1995, which launched the Doha Round of trade negotiations in 2001, is an encouraging sign because it leads to greater harmonization of tariff rules and less freedom for national governments to make arbitrary changes in tariff and non-tariff barriers and in intellectual property laws.

## GLOBAL MARKETING STRATEGY                    ◆ ◆ ◆ ◆ ◆ ◆ ◆

Multinational companies increasingly use global marketing and have been highly successful—for example, Nestlé with its common brand name applied to many products in all countries, Coca Cola with its global advertising themes, Xerox with its global leasing policies, and Dell Computer's "sell-direct" strategy. But global marketing is not about standardizing the marketing process on a global basis. Although every element of the marketing process—product design, product and brand positioning, brand name, packaging, pricing, advertising strategy and execution, promotion and distribution—may be a candidate for standardization, standardization is one part of a global marketing strategy and it may or may not be used by a company, depending on the mix of the product-market conditions, stage of market development, and the inclinations of the multinational firm's management. For instance, a marketing element can be global without being 100 percent uniform in content or coverage. **Exhibit 8-3** illustrates a possible pattern.

Let us take an instance from **Exhibit 8-3** and look at distribution with a magnitude of less than 50 percent on both coverage of world market and extent of uniform content. If we assume that the firm in question (represented in the diagram) does not have a manufacturing facility in each of the markets it serves, then to the extent that various markets have a uniform content, and presumably similar operations, there is a requirement for coordination with manufacturing facilities elsewhere in the firm's global network. Also, where content is not uniform, any change requirements for the non-uniform content of distribution require corresponding changes in the product and/or packaging. Thus, a global marketing strategy requires more intimate linkages with a firm's other functions, such as research and development, manufacturing, and finance.[45]

In other words, a global marketing strategy is but one component of a global strategy. For an analogy, you may think of a just-in-time inventory and manufacturing

[43]Masaaki Kotabe, Arvind Sahay, and Preet S. Aulakh, "Emerging Roles of Technology Licensing in Development of Global Product Strategy: A Conceptual Framework and Research Propositions," *Journal of Marketing*, 60 (January 1996), pp. 73–88.

[44]Stephen Kobrin, "An Empirical Analysis of the Determinants of Global Integration," *Strategic Management Journal*, 12 (1991), pp. 17–31.

[45]Masaaki Kotabe, *Global Sourcing Strategy: R&D, Manufacturing, and Marketing Interfaces* (New York: Quorum Books, 1992).

**EXHIBIT 8-3**
VARIATION IN CONTENT AND COVERAGE OF GLOBAL MARKETING.

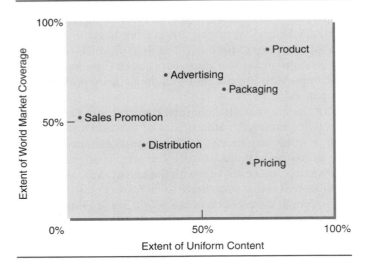

*Source:* Adapted from George S. Yip, *Total Global Strategy: Managing for Worldwide Competitive Advantage* (Englewood Cliffs, NJ: Prentice Hall, 1992), p. 136.

system that works for a single manufacturing facility to optimize production. Extend this concept now to finance and marketing, and include all subsidiaries of the firm across the world as well. One can imagine the magnitude and complexity of the task when a manager is attempting to develop and implement a global strategy. One implication is that without a global strategy for R&D, manufacturing, and finance that meshes with the various requirements of its global marketing strategy, a firm cannot best implement that global marketing strategy.

**Benefits of Global Marketing**

Global marketing strategy can achieve one or more of four major categories of potential globalization benefits: cost reduction, improved quality of products and programs, enhanced customer preference, and increased competitive advantage.[46] General Motors and Ford approach global marketing somewhat differently; such a strategic difference suggests that the two U.S. automakers are in search of different benefits of global marketing (see **Case Study 8-1**).

***Cost Reduction.*** This arises from savings in both workforce and materials. When multiple national marketing functions are consolidated, personnel outlays are reduced through avoidance of duplicating activities. Costs are also saved in producing global advertisements and commercials and producing promotional materials and packaging. Savings from standardized packaging include reduction in inventory costs. With typical inventory carrying costs at 20 percent of sales, any reduction in inventory can significantly affect profitability. With the availability of a global span of coverage by various forms of modern communication media, multicountry campaigns capitalizing on countries' common features would also reduce advertising costs considerably. ExxonMobil's "Put a Tiger in Your Tank" campaign (and the Tiger in many other forms) offers a good example of a campaign that used the same theme across much of the world, taking advantage of the fact that the tiger is almost universally associated with power and grace.[47]

---

[46]George S. Yip, Total *Global Strategy: Managing for Worldwide Competitive Advantage* (Englewood Cliffs, N.J.: Prentice Hall, 1992), pp. 21–23.

[47]If interested in the history of the Esso (ExxonMobil) tiger, probably one of the most recognized mascots in the world in the last 100 years, read "Tiger History," at ExxonMobil's website <http://www2.exxonmobil.com/Corporate/About/History/Corp_A_H_Tiger.asp>, accessed January 20, 2006.

Owning a website on the Internet for marketing to consumers is another way to reduce costs of conducting global marketing. It benefits both consumers, who can order to their own specifications everything from cars to swimsuits, and manufacturers in helping avoid inventory buildups. It also allows companies to have direct contact with consumers from different parts of the world, giving them deeper insight into market trends at a fraction of the cost incurred in traditional marketing. Cost savings can also translate into increased program effectiveness by allowing more money and resources into a smaller number of more focused programs. Disney, for example, is trying to break out of its traditional marketing methods with some alternative media. Now the company is launching a multi-player online game—Virtual Magic Kingdom—intended to drive kids to Disney resorts.[48]

***Improved Products and Program Effectiveness.*** This may often be the greatest advantage of a global marketing strategy. Good ideas are relatively scarce in the business arena. So a globalization program that overcomes local objections to allow the spread of a good marketing idea can often raise the effectiveness of the program when measured on a worldwide basis. Traditionally, R&D has been concentrated in the headquarters country of a global company. This has sometimes circumscribed a possible synergy from amalgamation of good ideas from around the world.

Procter & Gamble has solved this problem by setting up major R&D facilities in each of its major markets in the Triad—North America, Japan, and Western Europe—and by putting together the pertinent findings from each of the laboratories. As in the saying, "necessity is the mother of invention," different needs in different parts of the world may lead to different inventions. For example, Procter & Gamble's Liquid Tide laundry detergent was an innovative product developed in an innovative way by taking advantage of both the company's technical abilities and various market requirements in the key markets around the world. Germans had been extremely concerned about polluting rivers with phosphate, a key whitening ingredient in the traditional detergent. To meet the German customer demand, Procter & Gamble in Germany had developed fatty acid to replace phosphate in the detergent. Similarly, Procter & Gamble Japan had developed surfactant to get off grease effectively in tepid water that Japanese use in washing their clothes. In the United States, Procter & Gamble in Cincinnati, Ohio, had independently developed "builder" to keep dirt from settling on clothes. Putting all these three innovations together, the company introduced Liquid Tide and its sister products (e.g., Ariel) around the world.

Three benefits followed from this multiple R&D location strategy. By being able to integrate required product attributes from three separate markets, P & G was able to introduce a much better product than would otherwise be possible and increase its chances of success. Second, its development costs were spread over a much larger market—a market that was more inclined to receive the product favorably because of the incorporation of the product features described. Third, it increased the sources from which product ideas are available to it. Thus, not only does P & G have immediate returns, but also it has secured for itself a reliable resource base of future products.

***Enhanced Customer Preference.*** Awareness and recall of a product on a worldwide basis increase its value. A global marketing strategy helps build recognition that can enhance customer preferences through reinforcement. With the rise in the availability of information from a variety of sources across the world and the rise in travel across national borders, more and more people are being exposed to messages in different countries. So a uniform marketing message, whether communicated through a brand name, packaging, or advertisement reinforces the awareness, knowledge, and attitudes of people toward the product or service. Pepsi has a consistent theme in its marketing communication across the world—that of youthfulness and fun as a part of the experience of drinking Pepsi anywhere in the world.

---

[48]Disney's Virtual Magic Kingdom, http://vmk.disney.go.com/.

*Increased Competitive Advantage.*  By focusing resources into a smaller number of programs, global strategies magnify the competitive power of the programs. Although larger competitors might have the resources to develop different high-quality programs for each country, smaller firms might not. Using a focused global marketing strategy could allow the smaller firm to compete with a larger competitor in a more effective manner. However, the most important benefit of a global strategy may be that the entire organization gets behind a single idea, thus increasing the chances of the success of the idea. Avis created a global campaign communicating the idea, "We are number two, therefore we try harder," not only to customers, but also to its employees. As a result the entire organization pulled together to deliver on a global promise, not just in marketing but also in all activities that directly or indirectly affected the company's interface with the customer.

Equally if not more important, are the benefits of market and competitive intelligence provided by the increased flow of information due to the worldwide coordination of activities. As the global firm meshes the different parts of the organization into the framework of a focused strategy, information flow through the organization improves and enables the functioning of the strategy. A byproduct is that the organization as a whole becomes much better informed about itself and about the activities of its competitors in markets across the world. Access to more and timely information results in the organization being more prepared and able to respond to signals from the marketplace.

## Limits to Global Marketing

Although national boundaries have begun losing their significance both as a psychological and as a physical barrier to international business, the diversity of local environments, particularly cultural, political, and legal environments, still plays an important role not as a facilitator, but rather as an inhibitor, of optimal global marketing strategy development. Indeed, we still debate the very issue raised more than thirty years ago: counteracting forces of "unification versus fragmentation" in developing operational strategies along the value chain. As early as 1969, John Fayerweather wrote emphatically:

> What fundamental effects does (the existence of many national borders) have on the strategy of the multinational firm? Although many effects can be itemized, one central theme recurs; that is, their tendency to push the firm toward adaptation to the diversity of local environments which leads toward fragmentation of operations. But there is a natural tendency in a single firm toward integration and uniformity that is basically at odds with fragmentation. Thus the central issue . . . is the conflict between unification and fragmentation—a close-knit operational strategy with similar foreign units versus a loosely related, highly variegated family of activities.[49]

Many authors have since revisited the same counteracting forces in such terms as "standardization versus adaptation" (1960s), "globalization versus localization" (1970s), "global integration versus local responsiveness" (1980s), and most recently, "scale versus sensitivity" (1990s). Today, we may even add another variant, "online scale versus offline market sensitivity." Basically, the left-side concept (i.e., unification, standardization, globalization, global integration, scale, and online scale) refers to a *supply-side* argument in favor of the benefit of economies of scale and scope, while the right-side concept (i.e., fragmentation, adaptation, localization, local responsiveness, sensitivity, and offline market sensitivity) refers to a *demand-side* argument addressing the existence of market differences and the importance of catering to the differing market needs and conditions. Terms have changed, but the quintessence of the strategic dilemma that those multinational firms face today has not changed and will probably remain unchanged for years to come.[50]

---

[49]John Fayerweather, *International Business Management: Conceptual Framework* (New York: McGraw-Hill, 1969), pp. 133–34.
[50]Masaaki Kotabe, "To Kill Two Birds with One Stone: Revisiting the Integration-Responsiveness Framework," in Michael Hitt and Joseph Cheng, ed., *Managing Transnational Firms*, New York: Elsevier, 2002, 59–69.

Now the question is, to what extent can successful multinational firms circumvent the impact of local environmental diversity? In some industries, product standardization may result in a product that satisfies customers nowhere. For processed foods, for example, national tastes and consumption patterns differ sufficiently to make standardization counterproductive. In Latin America, a variety of canned spicy peppers, such as jalapeño peppers, is a national staple in Mexico, but is virtually unheard of in Brazil and Chile. Obviously, firms cannot lump together the whole of Latin America into one regional market for condiments.

The Internet is global in nature and so are the websites. Being on the Web arguably translates into reaching customers in many corners of the world from day one. However, it does not mean that e-commerce can be developed without any need for local and regional adaptation. To effectively target and reach the global consumers online, many companies still need to approach them in their languages, conforming to their cultural value systems.[51] Indeed, one recent study clearly shows that local websites of India, China, Japan, and the United States not only reflect cultural values of the country of their origin, but also differ significantly from each other on cultural dimensions.[52]

On the other hand, Merck, the world's second largest pharmaceutical company, faces a different kind of problem with global marketing. The company can market the same products around the world for various ailments, but cultural and political differences make it very difficult to approach different markets in a similar way. Merck, which operates internationally as MSD, has to increase public awareness of health care issues in Mexico, Central America, and much of South America by bringing top journalists from these countries together on a regular basis to meet with health care experts ranging from physicians to government officials. The company is trying to change the way it does business in the Pacific Rim. It used to operate through local distributors and licensees without learning the local quirks of pharmaceutical business. Now, the company is creating subsidiaries in nearly all main Asian countries, including Korea, China, the Philippines, Taiwan, Singapore, and Malaysia, to learn what goes on inside those markets. In Eastern Europe, Merck is starting from scratch, because its entry had been previously barred under the region's strict communist control. For example, in Hungary, the company devoted its initial investment to establishing resource centers that are affiliated with local hospitals and universities in order to create a special image for Merck.[53]

Even in supposedly similar cultures, there can be huge differences in what are effective marketing campaigns. The Body Shop found this out when it took a successful ad campaign in Britain and brought it to the United States, assuming it would have the same appeal. The ad showed the naked buttocks of three men and completely misfired in the U.S. market. In the words of Body Shop founder Anita Roddick, "We thought it was funny and witty here, but women in New Hampshire fainted."[54]

However, despite such cultural and political constraints in the markets, Nestlé, for example, has managed to integrate procurement functions to gain bargaining power in purchasing common ingredients such as cocoa and sugar. In other industries, such as computers and telecommunications, consumption patterns are in the process of being established and the associated cultural constraint is getting less prominent. Also, the simultaneous launch of most products in these categories across the world precludes large differences. For these products, governments frequently attempt to exert national control over technological development, the products or the production process.[55]

[51]E. James Randall and L. Jean Harrison-Walker, "If You Build It, Will They Come? Barriers to International e-Marketing," *Journal of Marketing Theory & Practice*, 10 (Spring 2002), pp. 12–21.

[52]Nitish Singh, Hongxin Zhao, and Xiaorui Hu, "Analyzing the Cultural Content of Web Sites: A Cross-National Comparison of China, India, Japan, and US," *International Marketing Review*, 22 (2), 2005, pp. 129–45.

[53]Fannie Weinstein, "Drug Interaction: Merck Establishes Itself, Country by Country, in Emerging Markets," *Profiles*, (September 1996), pp. 35–39; and Richard T. Clark, <ED:the following title is not readable due to this "picture">"Added Standing Behind Our Core Values," *Vital Speeches of the Day*, January 15, 2006, pp. 220–24.

[54]Ernest Beck, "Body Shop Gets a Makeover to Cut Costs," *Wall Street Journal*, (January 27, 1999), p.A18.

[55]C. K. Prahalad and Yves L. Doz, *The Multinational Mission* (New York: The Free Press, 1987).

**EXHIBIT 8-4**

DEGREE OF STANDARDIZABILITY OF PRODUCTS IN WORLD MARKETS

Local ← → Universal

| Factors Limiting Universality | Culture/Habits | Design Taste | Language | Size/Package | Technical System | User/Application | None |
|---|---|---|---|---|---|---|---|
| Example | • Fish sausage<br>• Root beer<br>• Boxer shorts<br>• Rice cooker | • Furniture<br>• Refrigerator<br>• Processed food | • Word processor<br>• Computer | • Textile<br>• Automotive (seat size)<br>• Soft drinks | • Color TV (PAL system in European voltage) | • Portable radio/cassette player (youths in U.S.)<br>• White-liqueur (young females in Japan) | • Watch<br>• Motorcycle<br>• Petrochemical products<br>• Piano<br>• Money (capital market) |

Key functions:
- Marketing concept
- Technology
- Product application
- Product concept

Legend: ☐ Must modify locally  ■ Could be shared globally

*Source:* Reprinted with the permission of The Free Press, a Division of Simon & Schuster Adult Publishing Group, from *Triad Power: The Coming Shape of Global Competition* by Kenichi Ohmae, p. 193. Copyright © 1985 by Kenichi Ohmae and McKinsey & Company, Inc.

However, while it is the multinational firms that are the vehicle through which technology, production and economic activity in general are integrated across borders, *it is the underlying technology and economic activity that should be globally exploited for economies of scale.* National markets, regardless of how they are organized economically, are no longer enough to support the development of technology in many industries. See **Exhibit 8-4** for some generalizations about the degree of product standardization around the world.

◆ ◆ ◆ ◆ ◆ ◆ ◆ ◆ ◆  **R&D, OPERATIONS, AND MARKETING INTERFACES**

Marketing managers cannot develop a successful marketing strategy without understanding how other functional areas, such as R&D and operations, influence the degree of their marketing decision-making as well as how those functions may be influenced by them. In this section, we focus on the three most important interrelated activities in the value chain: R&D (e.g., technology development, product design, and engineering), operations (e.g., manufacturing), and marketing activities. Marketing managers should understand and appreciate the important roles that product designers, engineers, production managers, and purchasing managers, among others, play in marketing decision making. Marketing decisions cannot be made in the absence of these people.[56] Management of the interfaces, or linkages, among these value-adding activities is a crucial determinant of a company's competitive advantage. A recent study also shows

---

[56]David B. Montgomery and Frederick E. Webster, Jr., "Marketing's Interfunctional Interfaces: The MSI Workshop on Management of Corporate Fault Zones," *Journal of Market Focused Management*, 2, 1997, pp. 7–26.

**EXHIBIT 8-5**
INTERFACES AMONG R&D, OPERATIONS, AND MARKETING

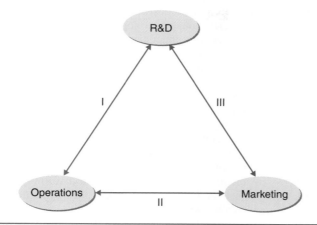

I. R&D/MANUFACTURING INTERFACE
  • Product innovation
  • Designing for manufacturability
  • Manufacturing process innovation
  • Components sourcing

II. OPERATIONS/MARKETING INTERFACE
  • Product and component standardization
  • Product modification

III. MARKETING/R&D INTERFACE
  • New product development
  • Product positioning

that marketing not only plays a pivotal role but also affects firm performance more than R&D and operations.[57] See **Exhibit 8-5** for an outline of a basic framework of management of R&D, operations, and marketing interfaces. Undoubtedly, these value-adding activities should be examined as holistically as possible, by linking the boundaries of these primary activities. As presented in Global Perspective 8-3, linking R&D and operations with marketing provides enormous direct and indirect benefits to companies operating in a highly competitive environment.

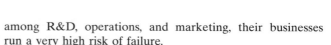

### 𝒢LOBAL PERSPECTIVE 8-3

#### POWER OF GOOD LINKAGE MANAGEMENT

In today's world of global competition and high-speed product development, linkage among R&D, operations and marketing is more vital to successful business than ever before. Delivering a competitive product to the market at the right time, with the right specifications and feature benefits, all at a manufacturing cost that allows for profit is one tough assignment. Add to this the global complexity of marketing, R&D, and operations not being co-located in the same place, competing in an environment where world-class product-development time is under 50 weeks, and you have a challenge that few companies are dealing with appropriately today.

International marketing executives can no longer have the luxury of time to consider R&D and manufacturing as activities remotely related and remotely relevant to them. They have to deal with all of this complexity and be fully aware that without adequate understanding of the linkages necessary among R&D, operations, and marketing, their businesses run a very high risk of failure.

John A. Bermingham, who has worked as executive vice president at Sony Corporation of America, president and CEO of AT&T Smart Cards Systems, and most recently as president and CEO of Rolodex Corporation, has a keen appreciation of how important and beneficial it is to manage linkages among R&D, operations, and marketing activities on a global basis. He offers the following advice:

•  When marketing determines a product need, the very first thing that marketing managers must do is to bring R&D and manufacturing together to establish a powerful linkage for the duration of the project. Marketing should also include finance, sales, and operations in this project, but the key linkage for the purpose of the product development is among marketing, R&D and manufacturing.

*(continued)*

---

[57]Alexander Krasnikov and Staish Jayachandran, "The Relative Impact of Marketing, Research-and-Development, and Operations Capabilities on Firm Performance," *Journal of Marketing*, 72, (July 2008), pp. 1–11.

According to John Bermingham, good linkage management has many benefits for these teams.

- A powerful linkage develops the requisite personal/business relationship needed among the three groups that allows for the understanding and empathy for each other's responsibilities. These relationships cannot be fostered via faxes and teleconferences. They need to be developed on a face-to-face basis as well as throughout the project, especially if the marketing, R&D and manufacturing teams are in different countries.

- A powerful linkage is necessary to ensure that issues are on top of the table at the beginning of the project and also as they develop throughout the project. Marketing must ensure that R&D and manufacturing are aware of the marketing strategy, competitive environment, and global implications. Any situations arising during the project must be discussed openly and positively with mutual understanding and with decisions being made to minimize impairment to the project, and with full understanding among the teams.

- A powerful linkage allows for speed. When you consider that world-class product development time is less than

50 weeks, and some say it will be less than forty weeks in the not too distant future, a powerful linkage is imperative. Teams must be working a series parallel effort. Some things have to happen before others, but others can be accomplished simultaneously. Only linkage makes this possible.

- A powerful linkage develops a high sense of urgency. Teams really begin to understand how important speed is in this type of environment when they go past understanding their own needs and problems and begin to understand the needs and problems of the other linked teams. Hence, urgency surrounds everything that these linked teams set out to accomplish. They see their linkage to the others and want to meet the needs of the entire team.

- A powerful linkage fosters mutual ownership individually and collectively. It is very important that there be individual ownership in the project, but it is just as important that the teams understand and accept collective ownership in the project. A tight linkage across the teams develops this collective ownership.

- A powerful linkage develops a true team environment that is essential and obligatory for success. Therefore, one of the most important roles for today and for the future for R&D and manufacturing in global marketing management is to ensure that these powerful linkages are established and strengthened.

*Source*: John A. Bermingham, "Executive Insights: Roles of R&D and Manufacturing in Global Marketing Management," *Journal of International Marketing*, 4 (4) (1996), pp. 75–84.

## R&D/Operations Interface

Technology is broadly defined as know-how. It can be classified based on the nature of know-how composed of product technology (the set of ideas embodied in the product) and process technology (the set of ideas involved in the manufacture of the product or the steps necessary to combine new materials to produce a finished product). However, executives tend to focus solely on product-related technology as the driving force of the company's competitiveness. Product technology alone may not provide the company a long-term competitive edge over competition unless it is matched with sufficient manufacturing capabilities.[58]

Consider the automobile industry as an example. R&D is critical today for automakers because manufacturers are under tremendous pressure to provide more innovative products. Customers continue to raise the bar with respect to styling, quality, reliability, and safety. At the same time, manufacturers face difficult technical challenges on the energy and environmental front. They must make continual improvements in vehicle fuel economy and reductions in tailpipe emissions everywhere in the world. Although more improvement can be squeezed out of the conventional internal combustion engine, manufacturers are looking ahead to hybrid vehicle technology and, ultimately, to a hydrogen-based fuel-cell vehicle. The development costs and infrastructure changes necessary to take the step to fuel cell technology are staggering, so it makes sense for auto manufacturers to team up and share knowledge in order to move the industry as a whole ahead faster.

To reduce the R&D costs, General Motors is working with its alliance partners on more than 50 joint technology development projects ranging from pedestrian protection and 42-volt electrical architecture to all-wheel drive and clean diesel engines. Besides cooperating with other manufacturers, GM has formed research partnerships

[58]Bruce R. Guile and Harvey Brooks, ed., *Technology and Global Industry: Companies and Nations in the World Economy* (Washington, D.C.: National Academy Press, 1987).

with suppliers, universities, and governmental agencies. These research alliances cover such areas as advanced internal combustion engine development, fuel cell technology, advanced chassis systems, and electronics and communications systems. They are truly global, involving companies and universities in Canada, Europe, Japan, China, and the Middle East.

By pulling together the talents and resources from this global R&D network, GM has been able to reduce redundancy, accelerate ongoing development, and jump-start new development. Of course, to launch such collaboration successfully requires that the companies involved overcome differences in culture, language, business practices, engineering, and manufacturing approaches.[59] This example suggests that manufacturing processes should also be innovative. To facilitate the transferability of new product innovations to manufacturing, a team of product designers and engineers should strive to design components such that they are conducive to manufacturing without the requirement of undue retooling. Low levels of retooling requirements and interchangeability of components are necessary conditions for efficient sourcing strategy on a global scale. If different equipment and components are used in various manufacturing plants, it is extremely difficult to establish a highly coordinated sourcing plan on a global basis.

A continual conflict exists between manufacturing operations and marketing divisions. It is to the manufacturing division's advantage if all products and components are standardized to facilitate standardized, low-cost production. The marketing division, however, is more interested in satisfying the diverse needs of customers, requiring broad product lines and frequent product modifications, which add cost to manufacturing. How have successful companies coped with this dilemma?

**Operations/ Marketing Interface**

Recently, an increasing amount of interest has been shown in the strategic linkages between product policy and manufacturing long ignored in traditional considerations of global strategy development. With aggressive competition from multinational companies emphasizing corporate product policy and concomitant manufacturing, many companies have realized that product innovations alone cannot sustain their long-term competitive position without an effective product policy linking product and manufacturing process innovations. The strategic issue, then, is how to design a robust product or components with sufficient versatility built in across uses, technology, and situations.[60]

Four different ways of developing a global product policy are generally considered an effective means to streamline manufacturing operations, thus lowering manufacturing cost, without sacrificing marketing flexibility: (1) core components standardization, (2) product design families, (3) universal product with all features, and (4) universal product with different positioning. [61]

***Core Components Standardization.*** Successful global product policy mandates the development of universal products, or products that require no more than a cosmetic change for adaptation to differing local needs and use conditions. A few examples illustrate the point. Seiko, a Japanese watchmaker, offers a wide range of designs and models, but they are based on only a handful of different operating mechanisms. Similarly, the best-performing German machine tool-making companies have a narrower range of products, use up to 50 percent fewer parts than their less successful rivals, and

---

[59]Larry J. Howell and Jamie C. Hsu, "Globalization within the Auto Industry," *Research Technology Management*, 45 (July/August 2002), pp. 43-49.

[60]K. Scott Swan, Masaaki Kotabe, and Brent Allred, "Exploring Robust Design Capabilities, Their Role in Creating Global Products, and Their Relationship to Firm Performance," *Journal of Product Innovation Management*, 22 (March 2005), pp. 144–64.

[61]Hirotaka Takeuchi and Michael E. Porter, "Three Roles of International Marketing in Global Strategy," in Michael E. Porter, ed. *Competition in Global Industries*, (Boston, MA: Harvard Business School Press, 1986), pp. 111–46.

make continual, incremental product and design improvements with new developments passed rapidly on to customers.

***Product Design Families.***   A variant of core components standardization involves product design families. It is also possible for companies marketing an extremely wide range of products due to cultural differences in product-use patterns around the world to reap economies of scale benefits. For example, Toyota offers several car models based on a similar family design concept, ranging from Lexus models to Toyota Avalons, Camrys, and Corollas. Many of the Lexus features well received by customers have been adopted into the Toyota lines with just a few minor modifications (mostly downsizing). In the process, Toyota has been able to cut product development costs and meet the needs of different market segments. Similarly, Electrolux, a Swedish appliance manufacturer, has adopted the concept of "design families," offering different products under four different brand names, but using the same basic designs. A key to such product design standardization lies in standardizing components, including motors, pumps, and compressors. Thus, two Electrolux subsidiaries, White Consolidated in the United States and Zanussi in Italy, have the main responsibility for component production within the group for worldwide application.

***Universal Product with All Features.***   As just noted, competitive advantage can be achieved by standardizing core components and/or product design families. One variant of components and product standardization is to develop a universal product with all features demanded anywhere in the world. Japan's Canon has done so successfully with its AE-1 cameras and newer models. After extensive market analyses around the world, Canon identified a set of common features customers wanted in a camera, including good picture quality, ease of operation with automatic features, technical sophistication, professional looks, and reasonable price. To develop such cameras, the company introduced a few breakthroughs in camera design and manufacturing, such as an electronic integrated circuitry brain to control camera operations, modularized production, and standardization and reduction of parts.

***Universal Product with Different Positioning.***   Alternatively, a universal product can be developed with different market segments in mind. Thus, a universal product can be positioned differently in different markets. This is where marketing promotion plays a major role to accomplish such a feat. Product and/or components standardization, however, does not necessarily imply either production standardization or a narrow product line. For example, Japanese automobile manufacturers have gradually stretched out their product line offerings, while marketing them with little adaptation in many parts of the world. This strategy requires manufacturing flexibility. The crux of global product or component standardization, instead, calls for proactive identification of homogeneous segments around the world, and is different from the concept of marketing abroad a product originally developed for the home market. A proactive approach to product policy has gained momentum in recent years as it is made possible by intermarket segmentation.[62] In addition to clustering countries and identifying homogeneous segments in different countries, targeting different segments in different countries with the same products is another way to maintain a product policy of standardization.

For example, Honda marketed almost identical Accord cars around the world by positioning them differently in the minds of consumers from country to country. Accord has been promoted as a family sedan in Japan, a relatively inexpensive sports car in Germany, and a reliable commuter car in the United States. In recent years, however, Honda has begun developing some regional variations of the Accord. Through a flexible global platform, Honda now offers Accords of different widths, heights, and lengths in the United States, Europe, and Japan. In addition, from the same platform, a minivan, a sport utility vehicle (SUV), and two Acura luxury cars have been developed. From a practical

---

[62]Theodore Levitt, "The Globalization of Markets," *Harvard Business Review*, 61 (May-June 1983), pp. 92–102.

standpoint, the platform is the most expensive and time-consuming component to develop. The global platform allows Honda to reduce the costs of bringing the three distinct Accords to market by 20 percent, resulting in a $1,200 savings per car. Honda clearly adheres to a policy of core component standardization so that at least 50 percent of the components, including the chassis and transmission, are shared across the variations of the Accord.[63]

**Marketing/R&D Interface**

Both R&D and manufacturing activities are technically outside the marketing manager's responsibility. However, the marketing manager's knowledge of consumers' needs is indispensable in product development. Without a good understanding of the consumers' needs, product designers and engineers are prone to impose their technical specifications on the product rather than fitting them to what consumers want. After all, consumers, not product designers or engineers, have the final say in deciding whether or not to buy the product.

Japanese companies, in particular, excel in management of the marketing/R&D interface.[64] Indeed, their source of competitive advantage often lies in marketing and R&D divisions' willingness to coordinate their respective activities concurrently. In a traditional product development, either a new product was developed and pushed down from the R&D division to the manufacturing and marketing divisions for sales, or a new product idea was pushed up from the marketing division to the R&D division for development. This top-down or bottom-up new product development takes too much time in an era of global competition, in which a short product development cycle is crucial to meet constant competitive pressure from new products introduced by rival companies around the world.

R&D and marketing divisions of Japanese companies are always on the lookout for the use of emerging technologies initially in existing products to satisfy customer needs better than their own existing and their competitors' products. This affords them an opportunity to gain experience, debug technological glitches, reduce costs, boost performance, and adapt designs for worldwide customer use. As a result, they have been able to increase the speed of new product introductions, meet the competitive demands of a rapidly changing marketplace, and capture market share.

In other words, *the marketplace becomes a virtual R&D laboratory for Japanese companies to gain production and marketing experience, as well as to perfect technology.* This requires close contact with customers, whose inputs help Japanese companies improve upon their products on an ongoing basis. In the process, they introduce new products one after another.

Another example worth noting is the exploitation of the so-called "fuzzy" logic by Hitachi and others.[65] When fuzzy logic was conceived in the mid-1960s by Lotfi A. Zadeh, a computer science professor at the University of California at Berkeley, nobody other than several Japanese companies paid serious heed to its potential application in ordinary products. The fuzzy logic allows computers to deal with shades of gray or something vague between 0 and 1—no small feat in a world of the binary computers. Today, Hitachi, Panasonic, Mitsubishi, Sony, and Nissan Motors, among others, use fuzzy logic in their products. For example, Hitachi introduced a "fuzzy" train that automatically accelerates and brakes so smoothly that no one reaches for the hanging straps. Panasonic began marketing a "fuzzy" washing machine with only one start button that automatically judges the size and dirtiness of the load and decides the optimum cycle times, amount of detergent needed, and water level. Sony introduced a palm-size computer capable of recognizing written Japanese, with a fuzzy circuit to iron out the inconsistencies in different writing styles. Now fuzzy circuits are put into the autofocus mechanisms of video cameras to get constantly clear pictures. Fuzzy chips

---

[63]"Can Honda Build a World Car," *Business Week,* September 8, 1997, pp. 100–108; and "The Also-Rans," *Economist,* February 21, 2004, pp. 61–62.

[64]X. Michael Song and Mark E. Parry, "A Cross-National Comparative Study of New Product Development Processes: Japan and the United States," *Journal of Marketing,* 61 (April 1997), pp. 1–18.

[65]Larry Armstrong, "Why 'Fuzzy Logic' Beats Black-or-White Thinking," *Business Week* (May 21, 1990), pp. 92–93.

have already been incorporated into a wide range of products in Japan, yet virtually unheard of in the rest of the world.[66]

The continual introduction of newer and better-designed products also brings a greater likelihood of market success.[67] Ideal products often require a giant leap in technology and product development, and naturally are subject to a much higher risk of consumer rejection. The Japanese approach of incrementalism not only allows for continual improvement and a stream of new products, but also permits quicker consumer adoption. Consumers are likely to accept improved products more quickly than very different products, because the former are more compatible with the existing patterns of product use and lifestyles. Indeed, a recent research reinforces the importance of information sharing between R&D and marketing departments as a way to reduce uncertainty in the highly volatile environment of new product development, whether it is in Japan, China, or the United States.[68]

## ◆◆◆◆◆◆◆◆ REGIONALIZATION OF GLOBAL MARKETING STRATEGY

Some firms, such as General Motors, may have difficulty in organizing, or may not be willing to organize, operations to maximize flexibility and encourage integration across national borders. Beyond various cultural, political, and economic differences across national borders, organizational realities also impair the ability of multinational firms to pursue global marketing strategies. Not surprisingly, integration has often been opposed by foreign subsidiaries eager to protect their historical relative independence from their parent companies.

In finding a balance between the need for greater integration and the need to exploit existing resources more effectively, many companies have begun to explore the use of regional strategies in Europe, North America, and the Pacific Rim. Regional strategies can be defined as the cross-subsidization of market share battles in pursuit of regional production, branding, and distribution advantages.[69] Regional strategies in Europe and North America have been encouraged by the economic, political, and social pressures resulting from the development of regional trading blocs, such as European Union, North American Free Trade Agreement (NAFTA), and Southern Common Market (MERCOSUR).[70]

Regional trading blocs have had two favorable effects. First, the volatility of foreign exchange rates within a bloc seems to be reduced.[71] Second, with the growing level of macroeconomic integration with regions, the trend is also toward greater harmonization of product and industry standards, pollution and safety standards, and environmental standards, among other things.[72] These regional commonalities further encourage firms to develop marketing strategies on a regional basis.[73] Global

[66]Robert J. Crawford, "Reinterpreting the Japanese Economic Miracle," *Harvard Business Review,* 76 (January/February 1998), pp. 179–84.

[67]Michael R. Czinkota and Masaaki Kotabe, "Product Development the Japanese Way," *Journal of Business Strategy,* 11 (November/December 1990), pp. 31–36.

[68]X. Michael Song and R. Jeffrey Thieme, "A Cross-National Investigation of the R&D–Marketing Interface in the Product Innovation Process," *Industrial Marketing Management,* 35 (April 2006), pp. 308–22.

[69]Allen J. Morrison and Kendall Roth, "The Regional Solution: An Alternative to Globalization," Transnational Corporations, 1 (August 1, 1992), pp. 37–55; and Gerald Millet, "Global Marketing and Regionalization—Worlds Apart?" *Pharmaceutical Executive,* 17 (August 1997), pp. 78–81.

[70]Alan M. Rugman, "Regional Strategy and the Demise of Globalization," *Journal of International Management,* 9 (4), 2003, pp. 409–17.

[71]Alan David MacCormack, Lawrence James Newmann, and Donald B. Rosenfield, "The New Dynamics of Global Manufacturing Site Location," *Sloan Management Review,* 35 (Summer 1994), pp. 69–80; and Masaaki Kotabe, "To Kill Two Birds with One Stone: Revisiting the Integration-Responsiveness Framework," in Michael Hitt and Joseph Cheng, ed., *Managing Transnational Firms,* New York: Elsevier, 2002, pp. 59–69.

[72]Edmund W. Beaty, "Standard Regionalization: A Threat to Internetworking?" *Telecommunications,* Americas Edition, 27 (May 1993), pp. 48–51.

[73]Maneesh Chandra, "The Regionalization of Global Strategy," A paper presented at 1997 Academy of International Business Annual Meeting, Monterrey, Mexico, October 8–12, 1997.

marketing strategy cannot be developed without considering competitive and other market forces from different regions around the world. To face those regional forces proactively, three additional strategies need to be considered at the firm level. These are cross subsidization of markets, identification of weak market segments, and the lead market concept.[74] See also **Global Perspective 8-4** for an example of global

## GLOBAL PERSPECTIVE 8-4

### SONY, MICROSOFT, AND NINTENDO BATTLING FOR GLOBAL DOMINANCE IN THE VIDEO GAME INDUSTRY

Back in 1995, Sony revolutionized the video game industry when it launched the PlayStation console. The consumer electronics behemoth set a new standard by tapping CD-technology in the design of game consoles. Sony was a relative latecomer in the industry. Sony's main rivals Sega and Nintendo had popularized the cartridge for gaming consoles. However, CD-technology was perceived as technologically superior to cartridge. CDs could hold up to 650 megabytes of data compared to only 16 megabytes storage capacity for cartridge-based consoles. CDs also yielded higher margins to third-party developers, one of the main reasons why they were attracted to the Sony PlayStation platform. CDs were also a less expensive medium, selling for $35 in retail outlets while Nintendo games were in the $75 price range. When Sony therefore adopted CD technology, the firm created the impression that the PlayStation would become the wave of the future in the videogame industry. Nintendo steadfastly refused to adopt this new technology even when it released its 64-bit N64. Nintendo's lack of enthusiasm for the CD-platform was mainly due to the fact that it *owned* the cartridge technology and, therefore, was reluctant to abandon this platform. Nintendo's slow response in the wake of new technologies proved to be a recipe for disaster.

Five years later in 2000, the second generation of PlayStation, known as PlayStation 2 (PS2), which Sony introduced instantly became dominant in the global gaming market. PS2 is the first video game system to use the Digital Video Disc (DVD) format. The DVD platform allows the PS2 to hold much more information than rival video game systems. Another solid feature of PS2 is that it is able to play most of the original PlayStation games. Due to the blockbuster success of the first generation PS, PS2 penetrated the video game market very easily.

The good times for the video game industry do not last forever. According to analysts, 2002 was the peak of the cycle

and the market cooled of gradually till the seventh generation of consoles began appearing since late 2005 when Microsoft Xbox 360 was introduced. On November 11, 2006, Sony launched PlayStation 3 (PS3), the successor to the PlayStation 2 as part of the PlayStation series. Eight days later, the Wii, the fifth home video game console by Nintendo, was released as the direct successor to the Nintendo GameCube.

In the competition of the seventh generation video game consoles, Nintendo is definitely the winner, with its units sales of 24.5 million which is much larger than the ever-champion Sony's 12.8 million of PS3 and Microsoft's 19 million of Xbox 360. The key for its success lies in its broader demographic target, which benefits from the console's distinguishing feature, the wireless controller known as the Wii Remote. The remote can be used as a handheld pointing device and detect movement in three dimensions, resulting in a revolution of the way playing video games. Another significant feather is Wii-Connect24, which enables it to receive messages and updates over the Internet while in standby mode. Its low price of $249 is also an important reason for its popularity.

The Sony-Microsoft-Nintendo competition is being played out globally and particularly in the Triad regions of North America, Japan, and Europe. The following table shows the launch dates and the sales volumes for Sony PS2, Microsoft Xbox, and Nintendo GameCube.

| | **Launch Date** | | |
|---|---|---|---|
| | *Sony PlayStation 3* | *Microsoft Xbox* | *Nintendo Wii* |
| Japan | **November 11, 2006** | December 10, 2005 | December 2, 2006 |
| United States | November 17, 2006 | **November 22, 2005** | **November 19, 2006** |
| Europe (U.K.) | March 23, 2007 | December 2, 2005 | December 8, 2006 |
| **Unit Sales since Launch** | 12.8 million (as of March 31, 2008) | 19 million (as of April 25, 2008) | 24.5 million (as of March 31 2008) |

*Sources*: "Sony's PS3 Problems Cast a Long Shadow," *BusinessWeek.com*, May 16, 2007; "How the Wii Is Winning," *BusinessWeek.com*, September 12, 2007; "Bringing PlayStation Back to Basics," *BusinessWeek.com*, September 24, 2007; and "More Delays for PlayStation," *BusinessWeek.com*, April 22, 2008.

---

[74]Gary Hamel and C.K. Prahalad, "Do You Really Have a Global Strategy?" *Harvard Business Review* (July–August 1985), pp. 139–48.

competition among Sony PlayStation, Microsoft Xbox, and Nintendo GameCube employing these three strategies on an ongoing basis.

## Cross-Subsidization of Markets

**Cross-subsidization of markets** refers to multinational firms using profits gained in a market where they have a strong competitive position to beef up their competitive position in a market where they are struggling to gain foothold. For example, Michelin used its strong profit base in Europe to attack the home market of Goodyear in the United States. Reducing prices in its home market (by Goodyear) would have meant that Goodyear would have reduced its own profits from its largest and most profitable market without substantially affecting Michelin's bottom line, because Michelin would have exposed only a small portion of its worldwide business by competing with Goodyear in the United States. Goodyear chose to strike back by expanding operations and reducing prices in Europe.

Kodak's ongoing rivalry with Fuji in the photographic film market provides another example of the importance of not permitting a global competitor unhindered operation in its home market. Kodak did not have a presence in Japan until the early 1980s. In this omission, Kodak was making the same mistake that many other Western companies have done—avoiding Japan as unattractive on a stand-alone basis, while not seeing its strategic importance as the home base of a global competitor and a source of ideas.[75]

## Identification of Weak Market Segments

The second strategy that firms should always keep an open eye for is the identification of **weak market segments** not covered by a firm in its home market. Japanese TV makers used small-screen portable TVs to get a foot in the door of the large U.S. market for TVs. RCA and Zenith did not think this segment attractive enough to go after. Another classic example is Honda's entry into the U.S. motorcycle market in the 1960s. Honda offered small, lightweight machines that looked safe and cute, attracting families and an emerging leisure class with an advertising campaign, "You can meet the nicest people on a Honda." Prior to Honda's entry, the U.S. motorcycle market was characterized by the police, military personnel, aficionados, and scofflaws like Hell's Angels and Devil's Disciples. Honda broke away from the existing paradigms about motorcycles and the motorcycle market, and successfully differentiated itself by covering niches that did not exist before.[76] Once the Japanese companies were established in the small niche they had a base to expand on to larger and more profitable product lines. More recently in 1997, Labatt International of Canada took advantage of freer trading relationships under NAFTA and awakened Canadian consumers to things Mexican by importing a Mexican beer, Sol, brewed by Cerveceria Cuauhtemoc Moctezuma, to fill a newly found market segment in Canada. Thus, firms should avoid pegging their competitive advantage entirely on one market segment in their home market.

What directions can this lead to in terms of a global product strategy—or a worldwide distribution, pricing, or promotion strategy? We discuss some aspects of a global product strategy for an automobile company. Suppose market data tell the managers that four dozen different models are required if the company desires to design separate cars for each distinct segment of the Triad market, but the company has neither the financial nor the technological resources to make so many product designs. Also, no single global car will solve the problems for the entire world. The United States, Japan, and Europe are different markets, with different mixes of needs and preferences. Japan requires right-hand drive cars with frequent inspections, while many parts of Europe need smaller cars as compared to the United States. The option of

---

[75]Yoshi Tsurumi and Hiroki Tsurumi, "Fujifilm-Kodak Duopolistic Competition in Japan and the United States," *Journal of International Business Studies*, 30 (4th Quarter 1999), pp. 813–30.

[76]Richard P. Rumelt, "The Many Faces of Honda," *California Management Review*, 38 (Summer 1996), pp. 103–11; and Richard D. Pascale, "Reflections on Honda," *California Management Review*, 38 (Summer 1996), pp. 112–17.

leaving out a Triad market would not be a good one. The company needs to be present in, at least, all of these three markets with good products.

The solution may be to look at the main requirements of each lead market in turn. A **lead market** is a market where unique local competition is nurturing product and service standards to be adopted by the rest of the world over time. A classic case is facsimile (fax) technology. Siemens in Germany had developed a considerable technological advantage in fax technology in the 1970s. However, because of lukewarm reaction from its domestic market, the German company abandoned the fax and concentrated on improving the telex system. In the meantime, sensing a strong demand for this technology, Japanese companies invested continuously in fax technology and introduced a stream of improved and affordable fax machines in Japan and abroad. Backed by the strength of the local markets, the Japanese bandwagon, led by Sharp and Ricoh, spread over to the rest of the world, displacing the telex system eventually. In retrospect, Siemens should have introduced fax machines in Japan as the lead market instead.[77]

> **Use of the "Lead Market" Concept**

Another example is wireless financial services. Although many U.S. banks are globally competitive, banks in Europe and Asia have already surpassed those in the United States when it comes to offering such services. According to a recent TowerGroup report, over 90 percent of the estimated 10 million users of wireless financial services are in the Asia-Pacific region and in Western Europe. The United States is far behind this trend.[78] There are several reasons, some technological and some cultural. A technological one involves digital phones. Although the push toward smart digital phones that can use the Web and e-mail has started, only one person in five in the United States has digital devices of any kind. Analog phones still account for a majority of cell phones in the United States. Digital has caught on earlier in Europe, where 40 percent of people have some sort of wireless digital device. Asia is not far behind. In Scandinavia and Japan, more than half the population has digital devices. In addition, Europe has one generally accepted standard for mobile phones—the Global System for Mobile Communications that allows for short, two-way messages. The United States has a hodgepodge of competing technologies, making it expensive for financial institutions to reach a broad range of customers. Europe and Japan could serve as lead markets or better learning grounds for U.S. financial institutions to be able to compete in the U.S. market down the road.

Emerging markets could also increasingly serve as potential lead markets. One such interesting example is Mahindra & Mahindra, a major Indian tractor manufacturer, began marketing in 2002 its basic tractors in a so-called recreational farmers market segment in the United States that U.S. tractor manufacturers had largely ignored. Deere & Co., a U.S. company known for its heavy-duty farm equipment and large construction gear Deere opened its R&D facility in Pune, India in 2001 to develop farm equipment suitable for the Indian market. Deere tractors marketed in India were so basic that the U.S. company had never even contemplated selling them in the United States until Mahindra's entry into the recreational farmers market. Now Deere, taking a cue from Mahindra, started marketing a slightly modified version with softer seats and higher horsepower of the Indian line of tractors to hobbyists and bargain hunters in the United States. As a result, India is fast becoming a lead market for developing stripped-down tractors for India and other emerging markets, which double as recreational tractors for hobbyists in the United States.[79]

As indicated earlier, this is a strategic response to the emergence of lead countries as a market globalization driver. Each can be a lead country model—a product carefully tailored to meet distinct individual needs. With a short list of lead country models in

---

[77]Marian Beise and Thomas Cleff, "Assessing the Lead Market Potential of Countries for Innovation Projects," *Journal of International Management*, 10 (October 2004), pp. 453–77.

[78]"Wireless Financial Services: Batteries Running Low," *American Banker*, July 23, 2002, p. 6A; and "Remember Wireless Financial Services? They Never Went Away," *Securities Industry News*, June 16, 2003, p. 38.

[79]"John Deere's Farm Team," *Fortune,* April 14, 2008, pp. 121–26.

hand, minor modifications may enable a fair amount of sales in other Triad markets and elsewhere. This will halve the number of basic models required to cover the global markets and, at the same time, cover a major proportion of sales with cars designed for major markets. Additional model types could be developed through adaptation of the lead country models for specific segments. This approach in each of the largest core markets permits development of a pool of supplemental designs that can be adapted to local preferences.

In line with our earlier example of Procter & Gamble, it is not necessary that the design and manufacture of a lead country model be restricted to one R&D and manufacturing facility. Ford has now integrated the design and manufacturing process on a global basis. It has design centers at Dearborn in the United States, England, Italy, and Japan, which are connected by a satellite uplink. Designers using fast workstations and massively parallel computers simulate a complete model and the working of the model for various conditions. Separate parts of the car are simulated at different facilities. Thereafter, the complete design for a lead country is integrated in the facility assigned for the purpose. For instance, the complete design for the new Ford Mustang was put together in Dearborn, but it incorporated some significant changes in body design that were made in England based on designs of Jaguar, which Ford had acquired. Similarly, different components of an automobile may be sourced from different parts of the global network of the firm or even from outside the firm. As firms move toward concentrating on developing expertise in a few core competencies,[80] they are increasingly outsourcing many of the components required for the total product system that constitutes the automobile.

This increase in outsourcing raises another question for firms that practice it. How can firms ensure uninterrupted flow of components when the component makers are independent companies? The answer to this question and the set of issues that it raises takes us into the area of cooperation between firms and strategic alliances, which will be discussed in Chapter 9.

**Marketing Strategies for Emerging Markets**

As stated earlier in Chapters 1 and 2, one salient aspect of the globalization of markets is the importance of the emerging markets, known as ten Big Emerging Markets (BEMs) including China, India, Indonesia, Russia, and Brazil. As multinational companies from North America, Western Europe, and Japan search for growth, they have no choice but to compete in those big emerging markets despite the uncertainty and the difficulty of doing business there. A vast consumer base of hundreds of millions of people—the middle class market, in particular—is developing rapidly. When marketing managers working in the developed countries hear about the emerging middle class markets in China or Brazil, they tend to think in terms of the middle class in the United Sates or Western Europe. In the United States, people who earn an annual income of between $35,000 and $75,000 are generally considered middle class.[81] In China and Brazil, people who have the purchasing power equivalent of $20,000 or more constitute only 2 and 9 percent of their respective populations and are considered upper class. In these emerging countries, people with the purchasing power equivalent of $5,000–$20,000 (and most of them in the $5,000–10,000 equivalent bracket) are considered middle class and constitute a little more than 25 percent of the population. Indeed, the vast majority (67 percent of the population) in China and Brazil are in the low-income class with the purchasing power equivalent of less than $5,000. Obviously, the concept of the middle class market segment differs greatly between developed and emerging countries, and so does what they can afford to purchase.[82]

---

[80]C. K. Prahalad and Gary Hamel, "The Core Competence of the Corporation," *Harvard Business Review*, 68 (May–June 1990), pp. 79–91.

[81]"The Billionaire Next Door," *Forbes*, October 11, 1999, pp. 50–62.

[82]C. K. Prahalad and Kenneth Lieberthal, "The End of Corporate Imperialism," *Harvard Business Review*, 76 (July–August 1998), pp. 69–79.

Consumers in big emerging markets are increasingly aware of global products and global standards, but they often are unwilling—and sometimes unable—to pay global prices. Even when those consumers appear to want the same products as sold elsewhere, some modification in marketing strategy is necessary to reflect differences in product, pricing, promotion, and distribution. Some unnecessary frills may need to be removed from the product to reduce price, yet maintaining its functional performance; and packaging may need to be strengthened as the distribution problems, such as poor road conditions and dusty air, in emerging markets hamper smooth handling. Promotion may need to be adapted to address local tastes and preferences. As these emerging markets improve their economic standing in the world economy, they tend to assert their local tastes and preferences over existing global products. Further, access to local distribution channels is often critical to success in emerging markets because it is difficult and expensive for multinational companies from developed countries to understand local customs and a labyrinthine network of a myriad of distributors in the existing channel.

If a vote were taken for the foreign company that has changed most in the Chinese market, the winner might be Amway, the U.S.-based direct sales company. It had to re-engineer its China network when its original method was virtually outlawed by China as unsuitable to national characteristics. It owns and runs some 200 retail outlets in China in 2008, but when it arrived in China in the early 1990s, it had none. It is churning out advertising campaigns featuring some of the world's most well-known athletes, while for most part of its history, its only marketing strategy was to depend on word of mouth. When it comes to pricing globally, Amway keeps a different price policy based on the local conditions of each country or regional market. In Southeast Asian markets, where currency levels are more fluid, prices are adjusted every couple of years. In China, raising prices seemed unavoidable in 2008 too as Amway needed to offset the inflation in almost every aspect of business - from labor to materials there.[83]

Despite these operational complexities, many foreign companies are actually making BEMs as corporate priority. Take two retail giants for example. Many of us tend to think that Wal-Mart is one of the most global. However, only 10 percent of its sales are generated outside its core NAFTA market, compared to Carrefour, which generates more than 20 percent of sales outside Europe. What is more, in the all-important emerging markets of China, South America and the Pacific Rim, Carrefour outpaces Wal-Mart in actual revenue. Take China, the land of a billion-plus consumers, as an example. Carrefour is the first foreign retailer tapping into the attractive Chinese market in 1997. By 2005, Carrefour had opened 62 stores and was planning to open between 12 and 15 new hypermarkets each year, with one-third of them located in central and western areas of China. Wal-Mart, with more than 5,000 stores worldwide, is catching up with Carrefour for its 46th store in China. In 2004, Carrefour generated sales revenues of $2 billion, whereas Wal-Mart had a sales revenue of $0.94 billion, or slightly less than half of Carrefour's revenue.[84] Wal-Mart needed to expand the number of outlets quickly in order to lower costs and capitalize on the growing affluence among China's urban customers before Carrefour and other rivals get a chance to further establish themselves. Being No. 2 risks being doomed for failure, as Wal-Mart learned to its cost in South Korea when it sold its eight-year-old operation there to the domestic market leader, Shinsegae, in May 2006. Wal-Mart has recently raised the stakes in China by acquiring Trust-Mart, the top retail chain of 100 stores that sell everything from food to electronics in the country, for about $1 billion. Despite Trust-Mart's reputation for mediocre management, Wal-Mart would gain massive scale through the acquisition for it to more than double its retail presence. By purchasing an entire chain rather than opening new stores, Wal-Mart will be able to bypass cumbersome Chinese

---

[83]You Nuo, "Amway's Way," *ChinaDaily.com*, May 12, 2008.

[84]"Boost for Foreign Retailers," *SPC Asia*, March 2005, p. 4; and "Wal-Mart Aims for 12–15 New China Stores in 2005," *China Daily*, May 18, 2005.

red tape: each city has its own requirements for new stores. By acquiring existing stores, Wal-Mart can avoid the complexities of land acquisition.[85]

European companies like Unilever have also broadened the scope of their market by addressing these issues and also competing for the low-income classes. In Indonesia, Unilever does brisk business by selling inexpensive, smaller-size products, that are affordable to everyone, and available anywhere. For instance, it sells Lifebuoy soap with the motto: "With a price you can afford." Unilever's subsidiary in India, Hindustan Lever, approaches the market as one giant rural market. It uses small, cheap packaging, bright signage, and all sorts of local distributors. In fact, Unilever has been so successful and profitable in Indonesia that its biggest rival, P & G, is now trying to follow suit.

Local companies from those emerging markets are also honing their competitive advantage by offering better customer service than foreign multinationals can provide. They can compete with established multinationals from developed countries either by entrenching themselves in their domestic or regional markets or by extending their unique homegrown capabilities abroad. For example, Honda, which sells its scooters, motorcycles, and cars worldwide on the strength of its superior technology, quality, and brand appeal, entered the Indian market. Competing head-on with Honda's strength would be a futile effort for Indian competitors. Instead, Bajaj, an Indian scooter manufacturer, decided to emphasize its line of cheap, rugged scooters through an extensive distribution system and a ubiquitous service network of roadside-mechanic stalls. Although Bajaj could not compete with Honda on technology, it has been able to stall Honda's inroads by catering to consumers who looked for low-cost, durable machines. Similarly, Jollibee Foods, a family-owned fast-food company in the Philippines, overcame an onslaught from McDonald's in its home market by not only upgrading service and delivery standards but also developing rival menus customized to local Filipino tastes. In additional to noodle and rice meals made with fish, Jollibee developed a hamburger seasoned with garlic and soy sauce, capturing more than half of the fast-food business in the Philippines. Using similar recipes, this Filipino company has now established dozens of restaurants in neighboring markets and beyond, including Hong Kong, the Middle East, and as far as California.[86]

In an era when manufacturing, customer service, and increasingly, the bulk of new sales are coming from Asia, a growing number of U.S. and European companies are starting to look east to India, China, and other emerging markets for their next generation of board leadership. Goldman Sachs, which is investing in Indian industry, named steel magnate Lakshmi Mittal a director on June 29, 2008. Finland's Nokia, the largest seller of mobile phones to India, added Lalita Gupte, chair of Mumbai's ICICI Venture Funds (IBN), to its board in May 2007. And Infosys Technologies co-founder N. R. Narayana Murthy joined the board of Dutch consumer products maker Unilever in 2007. Novartis, Procter & Gamble, and Deere are among the handful of other U.S. and European companies that have recruited Chinese and Indian natives to their boards. Given demand by an emerging middle class of consumers in India, China, and the Middle East for laptops and cell phones—as well as the need for those countries' industries to modernize their computer systems—technology companies, such as Hewlett-Packard, IBM, and Cisco Systems, are natural candidates to diversify their boards. Directors who hail from emerging markets can stand toe to toe with management on decisions about how to proceed in Asia, help the Western companies gauge the impact of decisions made in home countries on customers in host counterparts, and make more fit marketing strategies to make the companies be more compelling to customers in these fast growing regions.[87]

---

[85]"Wal-Mart Trumps Carrefour in China," *Forbes.com*, October 16, 2006.

[86]Niraj Dawar and Tony Frost, "Competing with giants. Survival strategies for local companies in emerging markets," *Harvard Business Review*, 77 (March-April 1999), pp. 119–29; and "Fast Food from Asia," *U.S. News & World Report*, February 26, 2001, p. 48.

[87]"For Corporate Boards, a Global Search," *BusinessWeek.com*, July 21, 2008.

# COMPETITIVE ANALYSIS

◆ ◆ ◆ ◆ ◆ ◆ ◆

As we have discussed so far, a firm needs to broaden the sources of competitive advantage relentlessly over time. However, careful assessment of a firm's current competitive position is also required. One particularly useful technique in analyzing a firm's competitive position relative to its competitors is referred to as **SWOT (Strengths, Weaknesses, Opportunities, and Threats) analysis**. A SWOT analysis divides the information into two main categories (*internal factors* and *external factors*) and then further into positive aspects (*strengths* and *opportunities*) and negative aspects (*weaknesses* and *threats*). The framework for a SWOT analysis is illustrated in **Exhibit 8-6**. The internal factors that may be viewed as strengths or weaknesses depend on their impact on the firm's positions; that is, they may represent strength for one firm but weakness, in relative terms, for another. They include all of the marketing mix (product, price, promotion, and distribution strategy); as well as personnel and finance. The external factors, which again may be threats to one firm and opportunities to another, include technological changes, legislation, sociocultural changes, and changes in the marketplace or competitive position.

Based on this SWOT framework, marketing executives can construct alternative strategies. For example, an S*O strategy may be conceived to maximize both the company's strengths and market opportunities. Similarly, an S*T strategy may be considered in such a way as to maximize the company's strengths and minimize external threats. Thus, a SWOT analysis helps marketing executives identify a wide range of alternative strategies to think about.

You should note, however, that SWOT is just one aid to categorization; it is not the only technique. One drawback of SWOT is that it tends to persuade companies to compile lists rather than think about what is really important to their business. It also presents the resulting lists uncritically, without clear prioritization, so that, for example, weak opportunities may appear to balance strong threats. Furthermore, using the company's strengths against its competitors' weaknesses may work once or twice but not over several dynamic strategic interactions, as its approach becomes predictable and competitors begin to learn and outsmart it.

**EXHIBIT 8-6**
SWOT ANALYSIS

SWOT Analysis

| Internal Factors / External Factors | Strengths | Weakness |
|---|---|---|
| | Brand Name, Human Resources, Management Know-How, Technology, Advertising, etc. | Price, Lack of Financal Resources, Long Product Development Cycle, Dependence on Independent Distributors, etc. |
| **Opportunities** Growth market Favorable investment Environment, deregulation, stable exchange rate, patent protection, etc. | **S*O Strategy** Develop a strategy to maximize strengths and maximize opportunities | **W*O Strategy** Develop a strategy to minimize weaknesses and maximize opportunities |
| **Threats** New entrants, change in consumer preference, new Environmental protection laws, local content requirement, etc. | **S*T Strategy** Develop a strategy to maximize strengths and minimize threats | **W*T Strategy** Develop a strategy to minimize weaknesses and minimize threats |

The aim of any SWOT analysis should be to isolate the key issues that will be important to the future of the firm and that subsequent marketing strategy will address.

## SUMMARY

Market-oriented firms, facing increased competitiveness in world markets, find it essential to assume a global perspective in designing and implementing their marketing strategies. Cost containment, rising technology costs and the dispersal of technology, a greater number of global competitors in many industries, and the advent of hypercompetition in many markets mean that international business practices need to undergo continuous refinement in order to keep them aligned with company goals. The explosive growth of e-commerce has added urgency to competitive analysis involving not only established multinational firms but also an increasing number of entrepreneurial start-ups leapfrogging geographical constraints via the Internet.

Strategic planning and the integration of the global activities into one coherent whole needs to be implemented for a firm to maximize its activities and for the firm to remain a viable player in international markets. In doing so, the multinational firm needs to mesh in information technology and telecommunications with its global operations in order to make relevant data available to managers in real time. In the end, a global strategy of any kind has to resolve a number of apparent contradictions. Firms have to respond to national needs yet seek to exploit know-how on a worldwide basis, while at all times striving to produce and distribute goods and services globally as efficiently as possible.

In recent years, however, as a result of the formation of regional trading blocs, an increasing number of companies have begun to organize their marketing strategies on a regional basis by exploiting emerging regional similarities. Globally minded, proactive firms increasingly exploit their competitive position in some regions by funneling abundant resources and regionally successful marketing programs to other regions where they do not necessarily occupy a strong market position. SWOT analysis helps isolate the key issues that will be important to a firm's competitiveness and that its subsequent marketing strategy will address.

## KEY TERMS

Bargaining power of buyers
Bargaining power of suppliers
Cost leadership
Cross-subsidization of markets
E-company
First-mover (dis)advantage

Global citizenship
Global industry
Global marketing strategy
Global strategy
Hypercompetition
Interdependency

Interfaces
Lead market
Niche
Potential entrant
Product differentiation
Regionalization

Substitute product (or service), threat of
SWOT (Strengths, Weaknesses, Opportunities, Threats) analysis

## REVIEW QUESTIONS

1. How are the developments in information technology impacting firms' global strategies?

2. What are the various factors/forces/drivers that determine the globalization potential of industries? How do global industries differ from multidomestic industries?

3. What do you understand by the term hypercompetition? What, according to hypercompetition, are the various arenas of competition?

4. How are the concepts interdependency and standardization related? What are the implications for global strategy?

5. How is a global marketing strategy distinct from standardization?

6. What are the benefits and limitations of global marketing strategies?

7. How do regional and global strategies differ? What are some advantages and disadvantages of a regional strategy?

## DISCUSSION QUESTIONS

1. Food habits have been known to vary considerably across countries and regions. Would you describe the food industry as primarily multidomestic or global in nature? Use the fast-food chain McDonald's as a case example to explain your answer. Note that while there are certain similarities in all of the McDonald's outlets around the world, there are differences,

especially in the menu, in various countries. Can the McDonald's example be generalized across the food industry?

**2.** In the summer of 1995, Procter & Gamble, the U.S. multinational giant, modified its global operational structure. Its new structure would include a top-tier management team consisting of four vice-presidents, each representing a particular region, namely North America, Europe (and also to include the Middle East and Africa), Asia (and Pacific Rim), and Latin America. One of the main reasons cited for this organizational change was the elimination of duties and regulations that now allows P&G to distribute its products to foreign consumers cheaper and quicker. While acknowledging that over 50 percent of the company's sales come from North America, and so, too, a bulk of its profits, the top management mentioned that it took care not to emphasize a particular region over the other. But competing globally with mature brands in saturated markets posed continued challenges. In 1999, a belt-tightening initiative called Organization 2005 was launched. Since then, a host of marginal and mature brands have been eliminated and a quarter of P&G's brand managers have left the company. Yet, there is no doubt that most of the company's new products originated in the United States. Few dominant products and brands have been originated from its foreign subsidiaries. There are, however, examples of brands, such as Tide that involved the cross-fertilization of ideas and technologies from its operations around the world.

Based on the facts provided, and any popular press information about P & G you have been exposed to, what would you consider to be P & G's predominant international strategy—global (integrated on a worldwide basis), regional (integrated on a regional level), ethnocentric (predominantly influenced by its operations in North America), or polycentric (primarily independent and autonomous functioning of its international subsidiaries)?

**3.** Since the early 1980s, the benefits of globalization have been acknowledged by researchers in academia and by business practitioners. However, practitioners have continually indicated the constraints on human management resources in actually implementing global strategies—to implement a global strategy, you need globally thinking managers. In your opinion, are business schools making progress in developing more global managers? Are corporations doing a good job of training their managers to think globally? What are the deficiencies? What are some of the steps that you would recommend to business schools as well as corporations in order to promote the development of executives who think globally?

**4.** One of the many advantages of globalization suggested is economy of scale and scope. There is, however, a counterargument to this advantage. Mass customization production techniques could lead to erosion of scale and scope economies with the added advantage of being able to customize products, if not for individual customers, definitely for individual markets. Discuss the strengths and weaknesses of this counterargument.

**5.** In today's highly competitive business environment, it is the disrupters rather than the disrupted that prolong their competitive advantage. Market disruption takes place a lot faster online than in the retail world. Today, "to Google" is a verb, while the words "Friends Reunited," Britain's most valuable online brand, often appear in newspaper headlines. What we witness is that successful firms are those that reinvent themselves continually and have an open mind about the future. Recently, China's leading Internet search engine, Baidu.com, was listed on America's NASDAQ exchange and became the largest first-day gain since the dotcom bubble with 354 percent stock increase and worth nearly $4 billion. As one of the world's largest Internet markets, China had roughly 94 million Internet users in 2004. Some large portals in China such as Netease, Sina, Sohu and Tom, have been making a healthy profit since 2003. Yahoo and Google also have established their presence in China. At the same time, they are facing intense competition from domestic rivals. Should U.S. companies adjust their marketing strategies in China? Should they approach the largest market with regional or global strategies? What are some of the advantages and disadvantages of different marketing strategies?

**6.** In East Asia, many of online games rely on a business model that is different from the way the video-games industry works in the West. Rather than selling games as shrink-wrapped retail products which can then be played on a PC or games console, the Asian industry often gives away the software as a free download and lets users play for nothing. Revenue comes instead from small payments made by more avid players to buy extras for their in-game characters, from weapons to haircuts. In this way, a minority of paying customers subsidizes the game for everyone else. Based on the fact above, discuss the implications for video game firms from the West to market their products in East Asia. Is it possible to apply this model to the West markets? Why or why not?

# SHORT CASES

## CASE 8-1

### GM AND FORD'S PURSUIT OF DIFFERENT BENEFITS FROM GLOBAL MARKETING

#### GLOBAL MARKETING THOUGHT: 1991–2000

Ford and General Motors approach globalization differently. In its quest for a "world car," Ford developed the so-called Ford 2000 program by creating five new vehicle centers—four in the United States and one in Europe—each responsible for designing and developing a different type of car worldwide. Ford's plan was put to test when it built a midsize world car in 1993 known as the Mondeo in Europe and the Ford Contour in North America. Its plan was to manufacture 700,000 cars a year in Europe and North America for nearly a decade with only a "refreshing" after four or five years. Ford executives say they can no longer afford to duplicate efforts and they want to emulate the Japanese, who develop cars that with minor variations can be sold around the world. While the Mondeo/Contour sold 642,000 units in the first two years in Europe, it had disappointing sales in the United States, attributed to its comparably higher price relative to the car's predecessors. Successful product development efforts require that the company avoid two problems that can arise from pursuing global design. First, the high cost of designing products or components that are acceptable in many settings could negatively affect efficiency. Second, the product, in this case a "world car," may be low cost but meet the lowest common denominator of taste in all countries.

Alternatively, General Motors took a more regional tack by retaining strong regional operations that develop distinctly different cars for their own. If a car has a strong crossover potential, engineers and marketers cross the Atlantic to suggest customization. Thus, Cadillac got an Americanized version of the Opel Omega small luxury sedan developed by GM's Opel subsidiary in Germany. GM managers contend that ad hoc efforts are cheaper and more flexible. One senior executive at Ford of Europe countered that "doing two conventional car programs would have cost substantially more than doing one global program. If we did it again, we could do it in 3½ years."

*Sources:* Larry J. Howell and Jamie C. Hsu, "Globalization within the Auto Industry," *Research Technology Management,* 45, July/August 2002, pp. 43–49; "Where Are the Hot Cars?" *Business Week,* June 24, 2002, pp. 66–67; "Small Carmakers Rise in Large China Market," *China Daily,* June 3, 2005; Jill Jusko, "Counterfeiters Be Gone," "Can Global Automakers Learn From Their Mistakes?" *BusinessWeek.com,* June 16, 2008; "Autos: China Auto Sales Up 17 percent in First Half Year," *ChinaDialy.com,* July 10, 2008; and "Autos: GM, Ford: China H1 Sales Up Steadily," *ChinaDialy.com,* July 9, 2008.

The two automakers' contrasting product development and marketing programs in the 1990s illustrate the traditionally viewed tradeoffs of efficiency and effectiveness, global standardization versus customization, market segmentation versus product differentiation, and product orientation versus customer orientation. These debates are framed by the tension between bending demand to the will of supply (i.e., driving the market) versus adjusting to market demand (i.e., driven by the market).

It is difficult to conclude that one strategy is always better than the other. One has to be reminded that while the Ford Mondeo/Contour project cost $6 billion and took six years to develop, potential cost savings from the global strategy could also be enormous for years to come. On the other hand, GM's regional strategy could also make sense if regional taste differences remain so large that a Ford-style global strategy could, indeed, end up producing a "blandmobile" that hits the lowest common denominator of taste in different markets.

Which was a winning strategy in the 1990s? Ford's ex-president, Jacques Nasser, wanted to keep the efficiencies generated from central thinking about design and production. But he wanted to reintroduce the market focus in regions across the globe that will give Ford stronger brands and more appealing products. The Ford 2000 was a good idea carried a bit too far. Ford Contour was discontinued from the U.S. market in 2001. Ford is now trying to redefine the Ford 2000 program with a heightened emphasis on the company's brands and to give the various regional and brand units more autonomy.

#### GLOBAL MARKETING THOUGHT: 2001–PRESENT

The automobile industry today is a growth industry in emerging markets. Only about 12 percent of the earth's 6 billion people enjoy the benefits of vehicle ownership, and industry growth remains positive at about 20 percent per decade, with the potential for global annual sales of 65 to 70 million vehicles by 2010. Most of this expansion will occur in emerging markets such as China, India, Russia, and Brazil.

General Motors' strategy in China and other Asian markets is very aggressive. Alliances have been the key to its marketing strategies. For example, GM acquired the majority of Korea's Daewoo Motor Company's automotive assets in 2002. While GM has 100 percent equity ownership of some of its key units—such as Opel and Saab—the company has used an approach that is more akin to a "loose confederation" in joining recently with other partners such as Suzuki, Fuji, and Fiat. GM has a minority equity stake in each of these companies. In addition, GM has major joint ventures in both

China and Russia. GM's alliance strategy and its initiatives to develop new markets are key elements in the company's approach to globalization. Alliances afford the opportunity for component and architecture sharing as well as the reduction in R&D costs that will be critical for manufacturers looking ahead to hybrid vehicle technology and, ultimately, hydrogen-based fuel-cell vehicles. By pulling together the talents and resources from its global R&D network, GM has been able to reduce redundancy, accelerate ongoing development and jump-start new development. Nevertheless, globalization entails risks from many quarters: economics, political forces, energy, and national differences in social and cultural norms. Consequently, GM is now focusing on the recruitment and empowerment of an international executive team, which will help accelerate the globalization process. For example, in Australia, GM operates through a subsidiary Holden, and it is closely integrated into GM's' global manufacturing strategies.

Ford's current strategy is to focus on its luxury brands. Now it owns Aston Martin and Volvo and has hired BMW guru Wolfgang Reitzle to run the duo though its new Premier Automotive Group (PAG), which brings together Aston Martin and Volvo with the American premium brand Lincoln. Since the mid-1990s, Ford Motor has plowed much of its bountiful profits from sports utility vehicles (SUVs) and trucks into a heady expansion of e-commerce ventures and luxury car brands. As a result, little attention has been paid to the development of mass-market cars and trucks. Ford still does not have the financial resources to implement a regional strategy as GM has done. Ford's global business lost US$5.4 billion in 2001. Consequently, the world's second largest carmaker is restructuring. Five plants are to be closed around the world, while four models, including the Escort, will be discontinued. In Latin America, a recent automotive trade accord between Brazil and Mexico is fostering integration between Ford's two main industrial bases in Latin America. Meanwhile, the company's operations in Argentina and Brazil—which were becoming an integrated business—are coming apart.

Recently, both GM and Ford reported decreased demand for their vehicles, especially their trucks and SUVs largely due to soaring oil price. Today, GM's and Ford's share prices have suffered an 81 percent and an 83 percent drop, respectively.

Toyota surpassed Ford in terms of overall sales to become the No. 2 seller in 2006 and become No. 1 in the world in 2008. GM's big sedans, Buick, which used to dominate the Chinese car market, are showing sluggish business in China. In the promising growing economy, car demand in China is shifting away from large sedans long favored by government officials to economy models demanded by families. GM faces harsh competition from both homegrown and Korean and Japanese automakers. According to China Association of Automobile Manufacturers, between January and June 2008, the country sold 3.61 million passenger motor vehicles, a growth of 17.1 percent over the same period in the previous year. The growth rate, however, was 5.2 percentage points lower than the 22.3 percent level recorded in the same period last year, although GM and Ford also reported strong first-half growth in this world's No. 2 car market. GM posted a 12.7 percent gain in first-half 2008 China sales while Ford sold 21 percent more vehicles over the same period, they are at the same time facing harsh competition from both homegrown and Korean and Japanese automakers. For example, Japan's Honda's sales in China rose 21.3 percent during the same period.

Although we cannot say that General Motors' strategy is genuinely better than Ford's, one thing is clear. General Motors has pursued the benefits of global marketing strategy methodically over time, whereas Ford seems to have been swayed more or less by "fads" of global marketing strategy. Although the recent global recession has caused an unprecedented retrenching not only for General Motors (now emerging from its recent bankruptcy) and Ford but also for the the whole auto industry including a seemingly invincible Toyota, GM-Ford rivalry is likely to continue. One thing is clear, however. Both U.S. automakers will continue to struggle in the face of competition from Japanese, Korean, and even Chinese automakers.

## DISCUSSION QUESTIONS

**1.** Discuss what is missing in GM's and Ford's global strategy.

**2.** Evaluate GM's going eco-friendly in China and discuss the possible global strategy for GM and Ford in an era of oil shortage.

ASE 8-2

### P&G: WE'RE ALSO CHINESE

It is common knowledge that having dominated the Triad region comprising of North America, Europe, and Japan for the better half of the last century, multinationals firms (MNCs)

*Sources:* Jacques Penhirin, "Understanding the Chinese Consumer," *McKinsey Quarterly*, 2004 Special Edition, p. 46; "Scrambling To Bring Crest To The Masses In China," *Business Week*, June 25, 2007, pp. 72–73; and "Emerging Markets Key to P&G Growth Plans," *Financial Times*, June 25, 2008.

turned their heads toward emerging economies like China, India, and other Asian economies, which are no longer just sources of cheap labor for MNC operations but are also large consumer bases. China, with the largest national population in the world, just became part of the World Trade Organization and therefore even more attractive to Western multinationals.

However, as MNCs are aware, doing business in China is not simple even though the economy is more open to foreign firms now than it has ever been. Local Chinese firms are growing rapidly and therefore pose a significant threat to foreign firms that are often unable to provide goods at competitive prices the way the local firms can. Today, more MNCs are finding success in the unique Chinese market than they used to. But they have learned the formula to success the hard way.

Take the example of American consumer products giant Proctor & Gamble (P&G) that first set up shop in China in 1998 through a joint venture with a local partner, Hutchison Whampoa. Eventually P&G bought out the remaining stake in the venture. P&G's brands like Tide detergent, Crest toothpaste, and skin-care product Oil of Olay made their place in homes in over 75 different countries worldwide and P&G's *modus operandi* included marketing its products as quality goods at profitable prices. When the company started selling its products in China, it soon discovered that its tried and tested global marketing strategy would not work the same way it had in other markets for a variety of reasons.

A developing market like China is characterized by huge disparity in income levels between the wealthy and the not so wealthy. Another glaring feature is the diversity in consumer needs based on whether it is a rural, urban, semi-urban area. These differences are further enhanced by the variety of outlets for sale of consumer goods ranging from large-scale foreign stores like French retailer Carrefour to local Chinese retailers and independent small stores. Therefore, for a company to succeed in China would mean offering a wide variety of products at reasonable prices. And succeed P&G did!

After entering the Chinese market, P&G soon figured out that selling its premium priced products would not help it achieve a significant market share let alone grant it the status of market leader, like many of its brands enjoyed in other foreign markets. Therefore, the company planned out a detailed marketing strategy specifically for the Chinese market. An important feature of strategic implementation was the three-tiered market system, whereby P&G divided the Chinese market up into three segments. According to Laurent Philippe, head of P&G's Greater China region, "Because we aspire to leadership, we need to compete in more than the premium segment. We need to compete at least in the middle segment as well. In volume terms, you can segment our categories into three price tiers: the top tier is 15 percent of the volume in units, the middle tier is 30 percent, and the bottom tier is 55 percent. The split in value, or revenue, is a little bit different: it is 30 percent in premium, 40 percent in the mid-priced segment, and only 30 percent in the low-end segment. This segmentation, by the way, is not mechanical; it is consumer driven." The main objective behind the company's marketing efforts in China was to promote their global products sold in China as Chinese brands so that consumers could identify with these products. And this strategy proved to be important given that P&G's competitors in the market include not only other foreign firms but also indigenous Chinese ones.

So, how did the company manage to successfully implement this strategy? Well, in the words of Philippe, "You cannot just take a global technology and make it cheaper by simply removing or replacing certain ingredients. The cost gap is too big. So we are now using our research-and-development capabilities to create different value offerings superior to those of the local competitors but at an equal or even lower manufacturing cost. These products are designed from the outset to meet certain cost, and therefore pricing, targets." P&G realized that low-income consumers in China often purchase single serve packets of shampoo, detergent, etc. and it soon began offering some of its products in these sizes. The company is using local resources to achieve its goals. Research and development for the Chinese market is done in Beijing at the Beijing Technical Center and it makes use of local ingredients desired by consumers.

P&G is also sending its advance staff into as many out-of-the-way villages as it can to get a feel for what rural Chinese want to buy and how much they are willing to spend. Just as it has done for years in the cities, P&G's teams of so-called customer research managers descend on villages, often moving in with families for a few days. They have discovered that while low prices surely help sales, it is equally important to develop products that follow cultural traditions. Urban Chinese are happy to pay more than $1 each for tubes of Crest toothpaste with exotic flavors such as Icy Mountain Spring and Morning Lotus Fragrance. However, those living in the countryside are apt to prefer 50-cent Crest Salt White, since many rural Chinese believe that salt whitens teeth. P&G applies similar segmenting strategies to its Olay moisturizing cream, Tide detergent, Rejoice shampoo, and Pampers diapers.

With more than $2.5 billion of annual sales, P&G has become the biggest consumer goods company in China today.

## DISCUSSION QUESTIONS

**1.** How does China's entry into WTO affect multinational firms' outlook toward China and their future investment in the country?

**2.** What are the drawbacks of P&G's strategy for the Chinese market?

**3.** What other marketing strategy could P&G have adopted for the Chinese market as an alternative to the tier system one?

# FURTHER READING ◆ ◆ ◆ ◆ ◆ ◆ ◆ ◆ ◆ ◆ ◆ ◆ ◆ ◆ ◆ ◆ ◆ ◆ ◆ ◆ ◆ ◆ ◆

Alden, Dana L., Jan-Benedict E.M. Steenkamp, and Rajeev Batra, "Consumer Attitudes toward Marketplace Globalization: Structure, Antecedents and Consequences," *International Journal of Research in Marketing*, 23, (September 2006): 227–39.

Bakhtiari, S. and N. Daneshvar, "The Challenges of Globalization and Regionalization for Developing Countries," *Journal of International Marketing & Marketing Research*, 26 (June 2001): 91–98.

Dawar, Niraj and Tony Frost, "Competing with Giants. Survival Strategies for Local Companies in Emerging Markets," *Harvard Business Review*, 77 (March-April 1999): 119–29.

Griffith, David A. and Michael G. Harvey, "A Resource Perspective of Global Dynamic Capabilities," *Journal of International Business Studies*, 32 (Third Quarter 2001): 597–606.

Grund, Michael, Oliver Heil, and Mark Elsner, "Global Competitive Marketing Strategy," in Masaaki Kotabe and

Kristiaan Helsen ed., *The SAGE Handbook of International Marketing*, London: Sage Publications, 2009, pp. 263–87.

Javalgi, Rajshekhar G., Patricia R. Todd, and Robert F. Scherer, "The Dynamics of Global E-Commerce: An Organizational Ecology Perspective," *International Marketing Review*, 22(4), 2005: 420–35.

Johnson, Joseph and Gerard J. Tellis, "Drivers of Success for Market Entry into China and India," *Journal of Marketing*, 72 (May 2008): 1–13.

Khanna, Tarun, Krishna G. Palepu, Jayant Sinha, Andy Klump, Niraj Kaji, Luis Sanchez, and Max Yacoub, "Strategies That Fit Emerging Markets," *Harvard Business Review*, 83 (June 2005): 63–76.

Laanti, Riku, Mika Gabrielsson, and Peter Gabrielsson, "The Globalization Strategies of Business-to-Business Born Global Firms in the Wireless Technology Industry," *Industrial Marketing Management*, 36 (November 2007): 1104–117.

Leamer, Edward E. and Michael Storper, "The Economic Geography of the Internet Age," *Journal of International Business Studies*, 32 (Fourth Quarter 2001): 641–65.

Lovelock, Christopher H., and George S. Yip. "Developing Global Strategies for Service Businesses." *California Management Review*, 38 (Winter 1996): 64–86.

Melewar, T. C. and Caroline Stead, "The Impact of Information Technology on Global Marketing Strategies," *Journal of General Management*, 27 (Summer 2002): 29–40.

Nakata, Cheryl and K. Sivakumar "Instituting the marketing concept in a multinational setting: The role of national culture," *Journal of the Academy of Marketing Science*, 29 (Summer 2001), 255–75.

Samiee, Saeed, "Global Marketing Effectiveness via Alliances and Electronic Commerce in Business-to-Business Markets," *Industrial Marketing Management*, 37 (January 2008): 3–8.

Townsend, Janell D., Sengun Yeniyurt, Z. Seyda Deligonul, and S. Tamer Cavusgil, "Exploring the Marketing Program Antecedents of Performance in a Global Company," *Journal of International Marketing*, 12(4), 2004: 1–24.

Zou, Shaoming and S. Tamer Cavusgil, "The GMS: A Broad Conceptualization of Global Marketing Strategy and Its Effect on Firm Performance," *Journal of Marketing*, 66 (October 2002): 40–56.

# GLOBAL MARKET ENTRY STRATEGIES

**9**

## CHAPTER OVERVIEW

Orange, France Telecom's mobile phone unit, was supposed to offer the marketing savvy and technological expertise.[1] TelecomAsia, at the time a Thai fixed-line phone operator, would leverage its local market knowledge and connections. Together, the two partners expected to conquer Thailand's booming mobile phone market. Alas, the honeymoon was short-lived. The joint venture partners split after merely two years. The relationship was troubled by different competing strategic visions. Orange managers wanted to expand the business with a low-price strategy to build up a broad customer base. TelecomAsia managers, however, preferred to push more multimedia options to attract higher-margin subscribers. TelecomAsia agreed to buy Orange's 39 percent stake. Orange left Thailand and TelecomAsia relaunched its mobile service under a new brand, True. True's president commented: "I learned a lot, I hope they learned too, about how important it is for a local partner to take the lead in the marketing area."

---

[1] "Thailand's Rocky Road," *Far Eastern Economic Review*, September 23, 2004, pp. 39–40.

Making the "right" entry decisions heavily impacts the company's performance in global markets. Granted, other strategic marketing mix decisions also play a big role. A major difference here is that many of these other decisions can easily be corrected, sometimes even overnight (e.g., pricing decisions), while entry decisions are far more difficult to redress.

We can hardly overstate the need for a solid market entry strategy. Entry decisions heavily influence the firm's other marketing mix decisions. Several interlocking decisions need to be made. The firm must decide on: (1) the target product/market, (2) the corporate objectives for these target markets, (3) the mode of entry, (4) the time of entry, (5) a marketing mix plan, and (6) a control system to monitor the performance in the entered market.[2] This chapter covers the major decisions that constitute market entry strategies. It starts with the target market selection decision. We then consider the different criteria that will impact the entry mode choice. Following that, we will concentrate on the various entry strategy options that MNCs might look at. Each of these will be described in some detail and evaluated. We will then focus on cross-border strategic alliances. The final two questions that we consider deal with timing-of-entry and divestment decisions.

## TARGET MARKET SELECTION

◆ ◆ ◆ ◆ ◆ ◆ ◆

A crucial step in developing a global expansion strategy is the selection of potential target markets. Companies adopt many different approaches to pick target markets. A flowchart for one of the more elaborate approaches is given in **Exhibit 9-1**.

To identify market opportunities for a given product (or service) the international marketer usually starts off with a large pool of candidate countries (say, all central European countries). To narrow down this pool of countries, the company will typically do a preliminary screening. The goal of this exercise is twofold: you want to minimize the mistakes of (1) ignoring countries that offer viable opportunities for your product, and (2) wasting time on countries that offer no or little potential. Those countries that make the grade are scrutinized further to determine the final set of target countries. The following describes a four-step procedure that a firm can employ for the initial screening process.

**Step 1.** *Indicator selection and data collection.* First, the company needs to identify a set of socioeconomic and political indicators it believes are critical. The indicators that a company selects are to a large degree driven by the strategic objectives spelled out in the company's global mission. Colgate-Palmolive views per capita purchasing power as a major driver behind market opportunities.[3] Starbucks looks at economic indicators, the size of the population, and whether the company can locate good joint-venture partners.[4] When choosing markets for a particular product, indicators will also depend on the nature of the product. P&G chose Malaysia and Singapore as the first markets in Asia (ex-Japan) for the rollout of Febreze, a fabric odor remover.[5] Not only were both markets known for "home-proud" consumers but people there also tend to furnish their homes heavily with fabrics. A company might also decide to enter a particular country that is considered as a *trendsetter* in the industry. Kodak, for example, re-entered the digital camera market in Japan precisely for that reason. As the president of Kodak Japan put it, "what happens in Japan eventually happens in the rest of world."[6]

Information on socioeconomic and political country indicators can easily be gathered from publicly available data sources (see Chapter 6). Typically,

[2]Franklin R. Root, *Entry Strategies for International Markets*, New York: Lexington Books, 1994, p. 23.

[3]"Tangney is bullish on L. America," *Advertising Age International*, May 17, 1993, p. I–23.

[4]"Coffee Talk," *Asia Inc*, March 2005, pp. 16–17.

[5]"Grey Showers Febreze over Southeast Asia," *Ad Age Global* (May 2002), p. 18.

[6]"Kodak Sets for Gamble on Re-entry to Japan," *Financial Times* (December 15, 2004), p. 21.

**EXHIBIT 9-1**
A LOGICAL FLOWCHART OF THE ENTRY DECISION PROCESS

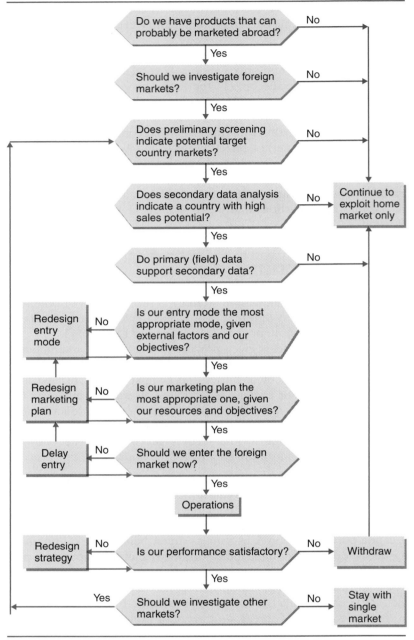

countries that do well on one indicator (say, market size) rate poorly on other indicators (say, market growth). For instance, India's beer market is growing rapidly at 14 percent a year but its per capita consumption of one liter per year is still a small fraction of the world average of 22 liters.[7] Somehow, the company needs to combine its information to establish an overall measure of market attractiveness for these candidate markets.

**Step 2.** *Determine the importance of country indicators.* The second step is to determine the importance weights of each of the different country indicators identified in the previous step. One common method is the "constant-sum"

---

[7]"SABMiller in Battle to Take Lid off India's Beer Market," *Financial Times,* December 30, 2008, p. 12.

**EXHIBIT 9-2**
METHOD FOR PRESCREENING MARKET OPPORTUNITIES: EXAMPLE

| Country | Per capita Income | Population | Competition | Political Risk | Score |
|---|---|---|---|---|---|
| A | 50 | 25 | 30 | 40 | 3400* |
| B | 20 | 50 | 40 | 10 | 3600 |
| C | 60 | 30 | 10 | 70 | 3650 |
| D | 20 | 20 | 70 | 80 | 3850 |
| Weight | 25 | 40 | 25 | 10 | |

$^*(25 \times 50) + (40 \times 25) + (25 \times 30)$
$+ (10 \times 40) = 3400$

allocation technique. This method simply allocates 100 points across the set of indicators according to their importance in achieving the company's goals (e.g., market share), so, the more critical the indicator, the higher the number of points it is assigned. The total number of points should add up to 100.

**Step 3.** *Rate the countries in the pool on each indicator.* Next, each country in the pool is assigned a score on each of the indicators. For instance, you could use a 10-point scale (0 meaning very unfavorable; 100 meaning very favorable). The better the country does on a particular indicator, the higher the score.

**Step 4.** *Compute overall score for each country.* The final step is to derive an overall score for each prospect country. To that end, the weighted scores that the country obtained on each indicator in the previous step are simply summed. The weights are the importance weights that were assigned to the indicators in the second step. Countries with the highest overall scores are the ones that are most attractive. An example of this four-step procedure is given in **Exhibit 9-2**.

Sometimes, the company may desire to weed out countries that do not meet a cut-off for criteria that are of paramount importance to the company. For instance, Wrigley, the U.S. chewing gum maker, was not interested in Latin America until recently because many of the local governments imposed ownership restrictions.[8] In that case, the four-step procedure should be done only for the countries that stay in the pool.

Other far more sophisticated methods exist to screen target markets. Kumar and colleagues, for example, developed a screening methodology that incorporates multiple objectives a firm could have (instead of just one), resource constraints, and its market expansion strategy.[9] One procedure, which is a bit more sophisticated than the method described here, is described in the appendix.

Over time, companies sometimes must fine-tune their market selection strategy. Grolsch, the Dutch premium beer brewer, used to export to emerging markets like China and Brazil. In the wake of flagging profits, Grolsch[10] decided to focus on mature beer markets where buying power is high and the premium segment is growing. Markets that meet those criteria include the United States, the United Kingdom, Canada, Australia, and continental Europe.[11] **Exhibit 9-3** shows the market opportunity matrix for the Asia-Pacific division of Henkel, a German conglomerate. The shaded area highlights the countries that look most promising from Henkel's perspective.

---

[8]"Guanxi spoken here," *Forbes*, November 8, 1993, pp. 208–10.

[9]V. Kumar, A. Stam and E. A. Joachimsthaler, "An interactive multicriteria approach to identifying potential foreign markets," *Journal of International Marketing*, vol. 2, no. 1, 1994, pp. 29–52; see also Lloyd C. Russow and Sam C. Okoroafo, "On the way towards developing a global screening model," *International Marketing Review*, vol. 13, no. 1, 1996, pp. 46–64.

[10]In November 2007, SABMiller, one of the world's largest brewers, offered €816 million to buy Grolsch. The takeover was completed in March 2008.

[11]"Grolsch targets mature markets," *Financial Times* (February 10, 1999), p. 20.

**EXHIBIT 9-3**
OPPORTUNITY MATRIX FOR HENKEL IN ASIA PACIFIC

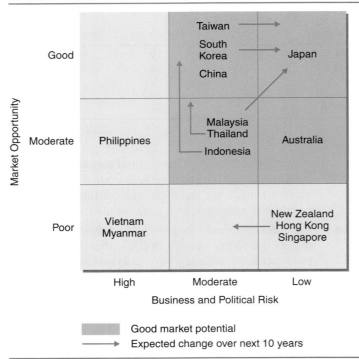

*Source:* Reprinted from Hellmut Schütte, "Henkel's Strategy for Asia Pacific," *Long Range Planning*, 28 (1), p. 98. Copyright 1995, with kind permission from Elsevier Science Ltd., The Boulevard, Langford Lane, Kidlington OX51GB, UK.

◆ ◆ ◆ ◆ ◆ ◆ ◆ ◆    **CHOOSING THE MODE OF ENTRY**

**Decision Criteria for Mode of Entry**

Several decision criteria will influence the choice of entry mode. Roughly speaking, two classes of decision criteria can be distinguished: internal (firm-specific) criteria and external (environment-specific) criteria. Let us first consider the major external criteria.

*Market Size and Growth.*   In many instances, the key determinant of entry choice decisions is the size of the market. Large markets justify major resource commitments in the form of joint ventures or wholly owned subsidiaries. Market potential can relate to the current size of the market. However, future market potential as measured via the growth rate is often even more critical, especially when the target markets include emerging markets.

*Risk.*   Another major concern when choosing entry modes is the risk factor. The role of risk in global marketing is discussed in Chapter 5. Risk relates to the instability in the political and economic environment that may impact the company's business prospects. Generally speaking, the greater the risk factor, the less eager companies are to make major resource commitments to the country (or region) concerned. Obviously, the level of country risk changes over time. In Bolivia, for example, the election of Evo Morales, a left-leaning indigenous former coca farmer, created enormous uncertainty for foreign investors in that country.[12] Many companies opt to start their presence with a liaison office in markets that are high-risk but, at the same time, look very appealing because of their size or growth potential. For instance, MetLife, the insurance company, opened

---

[12]http://lapaz.usembassy.gov/commercial/2005InvestClimateStat.pdf.

a liaison office in Shanghai and Beijing while it was waiting for permission from the Chinese government to start operations. A liaison office functions as a low-cost listening post to gather market intelligence and establish contacts with potential distributors and/ or clients.

***Government Regulations (Openness).***   Government regulations are also a major consideration in entry mode choices. In scores of countries, government regulations heavily constrain the set of available options. A good example is the regulation of the airline industry in the United States: airlines are classified as "strategic assets" and as a result foreign airlines cannot acquire majority ownership of U.S. carriers.[13] Trade barriers of all different kinds restrict the entry choice decision. In the car industry, local content requirements in countries such as France and Italy played a major role behind the decision of Japanese carmakers like Toyota and Nissan to build up a local manufacturing presence in Europe.

***Competitive Environment.***   The nature of the competitive situation in the local market is another driver. The dominance of Kellogg Co. as a global player in the ready-to-eat cereal market was a key motivation for the creation in the early 1990s of Cereal Partners Worldwide, a joint venture between Nestlé and General Mills. The partnership gained some market share (compared to the combined share of Nestlé and General Mills prior to the linkup) in some of the markets, though mostly at the expense of lesser players like Quaker Oats and Ralston Purina. By the same token, the acquisition by SABMiller, one of the world's largest beer brewers, of Colombia-based Bavaria in a $7.8 billion deal brought the company near-monopoly control in four South American countries: Peru, Colombia, Ecuador, and Panama.[14]

***Cultural Distance.***   Some scholars argue that the cultural distance between countries also has an impact on entry mode choice decisions. Opinions about the nature of the relationship differ. Some argue that through higher percentages of equity ownership, MNCs are able to bridge differences in cultural values and institutions. Others note that by relying on joint ventures instead of wholly owned subsidiaries MNCs are able to lower their risk exposure in culturally distant markets. A comprehensive analysis of a wide range of studies in the literature found no clear-cut evidence in favor of either argument.[15]

***Local Infrastructure.***   The physical infrastructure of a market refers to the country's distribution system, transportation network and communication system. In general, the poorer the local infrastructure, the more reluctant the company is to commit major resources (monetary or human).

The combination of all these factors determines the overall market attractiveness of the countries being considered. Markets can be classified in five types of countries based on their respective market attractiveness:[16]

- *Platform* countries that can be used to gather intelligence and establish a network. Examples include Singapore and Hong Kong.
- *Emerging* countries in which the major goal is to build up an initial presence, for instance, via a liaison office. Vietnam and the Philippines are examples.

---

[13]http://www.businessweek.com/debateroom/archives/2008/04/lift_us_airline.html.

[14]"SABMiller to Raise its Glass to Loyalty," *Financial Times*, July 25, 2005, p. 16.

[15]Laszlo Tihanyi, David A. Griffith, and Craig J. Russell, "The Effect of Cultural Distance on Entry Mode Choice, International Diversification, and MNE Performance: A Meta-Analysis," *Journal of International Business Studies* 36 (2005): 270–83.

[16]Philippe Lasserre, "Corporate strategies for the Asia Pacific region," *Long Range Planning*, vol. 28, no. 1, 1995, pp. 13–30.

**EXHIBIT 9-4**
ENTRY MODES AND MARKET DEVELOPMENT

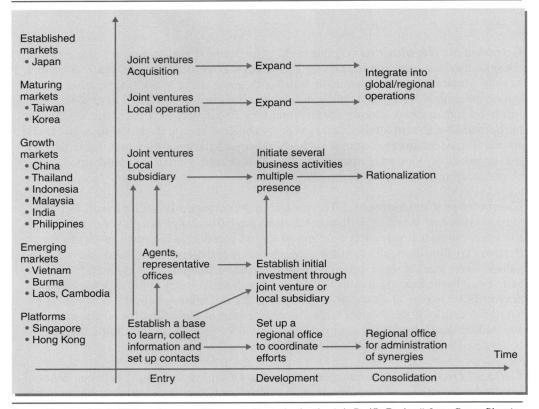

*Source:* Reprinted from Philippe Lasserre, "Corporate Strategies for the Asia Pacific Region," *Long Range Planning* 28 (1), p. 21. Copyright 1995, with kind permission from Elsevier Science Ltd., The Boulevard, Langford Lane, Kidlington OX5 1GB UK.

- *Growth* countries offer early mover advantages that often push companies to build a significant presence to capitalize on future market opportunities as in China and India.
- *Maturing* and *established* countries like South Korea, Taiwan and Japan. These countries have far fewer growth prospects than the other types of markets. Often local competitors are well entrenched. On the other hand, these markets have a sizable middle class and solid infrastructure. The prime task here is to look for ways to further develop the market via strategic alliances, major investments or acquisitions of local or smaller foreign players. A case in point is General Electric, the U.S. conglomerate. In the hope of achieving big profits in Europe, GE has invested more than $10 billion from 1989 through 1996, half of it for building new plants and half for almost 50 acquisitions despite the fact that Europe is a fairly mature market.[17]

Different types of countries require different expansion paths although deviations cannot be ruled out (see **Exhibit 9-4**).

We now give an overview of the key internal criteria.

***Company Objectives.*** Corporate objectives are a key influence in choosing entry modes. Firms that have limited aspirations will typically prefer entry options that entail a minimum amount of commitment (e.g., licensing). Proactive companies with ambitious strategic objectives, on the other hand, will usually pick entry modes that give

---

[17]"If Europe's dead, why is GE investing billions there?" *Fortune*, September 9, 1996.

them the flexibility and control they need to achieve their goals. InBev, a Belgo-Brazilian beverage company, needed a strong foothold in the U.S. market to become the leading beer brewer worldwide. In June 2008, InBev made an offer for Anheuser-Busch, which accepted the offer a month later after InBev raised the offer price.[18] By merging the two firms, InBev's CEO Carlos Brito hopes to create a "stronger, more competitive global company with an unrivaled worldwide brand portfolio and distribution network."[19]

***Need for Control.*** Most MNCs would like to possess a certain amount of control over their foreign operations. Control may be desirable for any element of the marketing mix plan: positioning, pricing, advertising, the way the product is distributed, and so forth. Caterpillar, for instance, prefers to stay in complete control of its overseas operations to protect its proprietary know-how. For that reason, Caterpillar avoids joint ventures.[20] To a large degree, the level of control is strongly correlated with the amount of resource commitment: the smaller the commitment, the lower the control. Most firms face a trade-off between the degree of control over their foreign operations and the level of resource commitment they are willing to make.

***Internal Resources, Assets and Capabilities.*** Companies with tight resources (human and/or financial) or limited assets are constrained to low-commitment entry modes such as exporting and licensing that are not too demanding on their resources. Even large companies should carefully consider how to allocate their resources between their different markets, including the home-market. In some cases, major resource commitments to a given target market might be premature given the amount of risk. On the other hand, if a firm is overly reluctant to commit resources, it could miss the boat by sacrificing major market opportunities. Internal competencies also influence the choice-of-entry strategy. When the firm lacks certain skills that are critical for the success of its global expansion strategy, it can try to fill the gap by forming a strategic alliance.

***Flexibility.*** An entry mode that looks very appealing today is not necessarily attractive 5 or 10 years down the road. The host country environment changes constantly. New market segments emerge. Local customers become more demanding or more price conscious. Their preferences may change over time. Local competitors become more sophisticated. To cope with these environmental changes, global players need a certain amount of flexibility. The flexibility offered by the different entry mode alternatives varies a great deal. Given their very nature, contractual arrangements like joint ventures or licensing tend to provide very little flexibility. When major exit barriers exist, wholly owned subsidiaries are hard to divest and, therefore offer very little flexibility compared to other entry alternatives.

Although some of the factors listed above favor high-control entry modes, other criteria suggest a low-control mode. The different entry modes can be classified according to the degree of control they offer to the entrant from low-control (e.g., indirect exporting, licensing) to high-control modes (e.g., wholly owned subsidiary). To some extent, the appropriate entry-mode decision boils down to the issue of how much control is desirable. Ideally, the entrant would like to have as much control as possible. However, entry modes that offer a large degree of control also impose substantial resource commitments and huge amounts of risk. Therefore, the entrant faces a tradeoff between the benefits of increased control and the costs of resource commitment and risk.

**Mode-of-Entry Choice — Two Opposing Paradigms: A Transaction-Costs versus Resource-Based View**

---

[18]After the merger the company was renamed Anheuser-Busch Inbev.

[19]"InBev Bags Anheuser-Busch," *Forbes*, http://www.forbes.com/, accessed August 22, 2008.

[20]"Engine Makers Take Different Routes," *Financial Times* (July 14, 1998), p. 11.

***Transaction-Cost Economics (TCE).*** One useful framework to resolve this conundrum is the so-called **transaction-cost economics (TCE)** perspective. A given task can be looked at as a "make-or-buy" decision: either the firm sources the task out to third party agents or partners (low-control modes such as exporting) or it does the job internally (high control modes such as foreign direct investment). TCE argues that the desirable governance structure (high- versus low-control mode) depends on the comparative transaction costs, that is, the cost of running the operation.

In the context of entry mode choice, the TCE perspective treats each entry as a "transaction."[21] The TCE approach begins with the premise that markets are competitive. Therefore, market pressure minimizes the need for control. Under this utopian scenario, low-control modes such as exporting are preferable because the competitive pressures force the outside partner to comply with its contractual duties. When the market mechanism fails, high-control entry modes become more desirable. From the TCE angle, market failure typically happens when **transaction-specific assets** become valuable. These are assets that are valuable for only a very narrow range of applications. Examples include brand equity, proprietary technology, and know-how. When these types of assets become very important, the firm might be better off to adopt a high-control entry mode in order to safeguard these assets against opportunistic behaviors of its managers and uncertainty.[22]

***Resource-Based View (RBV).*** The **resource-based view (RBV)** is based on the premise that possessing resources is not sufficient to create a competitive advantage: a firm also needs to be organized to take full advantage of its resources. RBV suggests that an entry should be considered in the context of the overall strategic posture of the firm.[23] According to this paradigm, firms with imperfectly imitable resource-based competitive advantages prefer to expand through wholly owned subsidiaries for two reasons. First, through wholly owned entry modes, the firm is better able to protect the value of its resource-based advantages against value erosion (e.g., patent theft). Second, by having a wholly owned subsidiary, the firm can capture and transfer knowledge between the parent and the foreign unit more efficiently.[24] There are three differences between the TCE and RBV perspectives.[25] First, the two theories differ in how they predict different entry modes. Whereas TCE predicts high-control entry modes because of opportunistic behavior of the firm's partner (e.g., licensee), the RBV attributes market failures to other mechanisms: when the multinational has superior capabilities in deploying its know-how and the prospective partner (e.g., licensee) faces challenges in efficiently acquiring and integrating that knowledge the MNC will prefer high-control entities.[26] Second, while TCE focuses on entries as a one-time event, RBV looks at a sequence of entries as a dynamic process where the MNC is able to learn from and build on its previous entry experience. The third difference relates to the firm-specific advantages: whereas TCE focuses on their exploitation the RBV stresses both their exploitation and development. The RBV states that market entries are not only "pushed" by the resources held by the MNC, but that the target entry could also help the MNC in developing new advantages.

[21] Erin Anderson and Hubert Gatignon, "Modes of Foreign Entry: A Transaction Cost Analysis and Propositions," *Journal of International Business Studies*, 11 (Fall 1986), pp. 1–25.

[22] For a good overview of entry mode choice studies that incorporate the TCA paradigm, see Hongxin Zhao, Yadong Luo, and Taewon Suh, "Transaction Cost Determinants and Ownership-Based Entry Mode Choice: A Meta-Analytical Review," *Journal of International Business Studies* 35 (2004): 524–44.

[23] C. Hill, P. Hwang, and W.C. Kim, "An Eclectic Theory of the Choice of International Entry," *Strategic Management Journal*, 9 (1990), pp. 93–104.

[24] Keith D. Brouthers, Lance Eliot Brouthers, and Steve Werner, "Resource-based Advantages in an International Context," *Journal of Management*, 34 (April 2008), pp. 189–217.

[25] Mike W. Peng, "The Resource-based View and International Business," *Journal of Management*, 27, (6) 2001, pp. 803–29.

[26] A. Madhok, "Cost, Value and Foreign Market Entry Mode: The Transaction and the Firm," *Strategic Management Journal*, 18, (1) 1997, pp. 39–61.

An empirical study of entry decisions made by the 180 largest MNCs over a fifteen-year period found that MNCs are most likely to enter with wholly owned subsidiaries when one of the following conditions holds:[27]

- The entry involves an R&D-intensive line of business
- The entry involves an advertising-intensive line of business (high brand-equity)
- The MNC has accumulated a substantial amount of experience with foreign entries

On the other hand, MNCs are most likely to prefer a partnership when one of these holds:

- The entry is in a highly risky country
- The entry is in a socioculturally distant country
- There are legal restrictions on foreign ownership of assets.

## EXPORTING

♦ ♦ ♦ ♦ ♦ ♦ ♦

Most companies start their international expansion by exporting. For many small businesses, exporting is very often the sole alternative for selling their goods in foreign markets. A fair number of Fortune 500 companies, such as Boeing and Caterpillar also generate a major part of their global revenues via export sales.

Chapter 17 discusses in detail export and import management matters. In this chapter we will give you a snapshot overview of exporting as an entry mode. Companies that plan to engage in exporting have a choice between three broad options: indirect, cooperative, and direct exporting. **Indirect exporting** means that the firm uses a middleman based in its home market to handle the exporting. With **cooperative exporting**, the firm enters into an agreement with another company (local or foreign) where the partner will use its distribution network to sell the exporter's goods. **Direct exporting** means that the company sets up its own export organization and relies on a middleman based in a foreign market (e.g., a foreign distributor).

*Indirect Exporting.*    Indirect exporting happens when the firm decides to sell its products in the foreign market through independent intermediaries. An **export merchant** is a trading company that will buy the firm's goods outright and then resell them in the foreign markets. The exporter merchant usually specializes in a particular line of products and/or in a certain geographical region. An **export agent** is a trading company that acts for local manufacturers, usually representing a number of non-competing manufacturers. They seek and negotiate foreign purchases. In return for obtaining an export order, the export agent receives a commission. Unlike the export merchant, the agent does not become the owner of the goods and therefore does not assume the risk of not being able to sell profitably overseas. The use of an **export management company (EMC)** is very popular among small businesses. An EMC is an independent firm that acts as the exclusive export sales department for non-competing manufacturers. EMCs come in all shapes and sizes. Some act as an agent, soliciting orders in foreign markets in the name of the manufacturer. Other EMCs act as a distributor on a "buy-sell" basis: the EMC buys from the firm at a set price and resells to the foreign customers at prices set by the EMC. Indirect exporting offers several advantages to the exporting company compared to other entry modes. The firm gets instant foreign market expertise. The indirect exporters are professionals. They can handle all the details involved in processing exporting orders. They also can appraise market opportunities for the manufacturer. Other strengths are their know-how in selecting agents and/or distributors and management of the distribution network. Often very little risk is involved.

---

[27]Hubert Gatignon and Erin Anderson, "The multinational corporation's degree of control over foreign subsidiaries: an empirical test of a transaction cost explanation," *Journal of Law, Economics, and, Organization*, vol. 4, no. 2, Fall 1988, pp. 305–36.

Generally speaking, no major resource commitments are required. When the middlemen's profits are based on how successfully they export, they are motivated to do a good job.

Indirect exporting has some downsides. The company has little or no control over the way its product is marketed in the foreign country. Lack of adequate sales support, wrong pricing decisions, or poor distribution channels will inevitably lead to poor sales. Ill-fated marketing mix decisions made by the intermediary could also damage the company's corporate or brand image. The middleman may have very limited experience with handling the company's product line. Also, as they are often relatively small, they may have limited resources to handle tasks such as warehousing or providing credit financing to foreign customers. Often intermediaries will focus their efforts on those products that maximize their profits. As a result, they might not support new product lines or products with low short-term profit potential.

Given the low commitment required, indirect exporting is often seen as a good beach-head strategy for "testing" the international waters: Once the demand for the product takes off, the manufacturer can switch to another, more proactive, entry mode. The decision to develop an export business via an independent middleman centers around three basic questions:[28]

1. Does the firm have the time and know-how to enter export markets?
2. Does the firm have money and/or specialized personnel needed to develop an export business?
3. Is the foreign business growing at a satisfactory rate?

If the answer to any of these questions is negative then manufacturers should seriously consider relying on specialized export firms.

***Cooperative Exporting.***   Companies that are unwilling to commit the resources to set up their own distribution organization but still want to have some control over their foreign operations should consider cooperative exporting. One of the most popular forms of cooperative exporting is **piggyback exporting**. With piggybacking, the company uses the overseas distribution network of another company (local or foreign) for selling its goods in the foreign market. Wrigley, the U.S. chewing gum company,[29] entered India by piggybacking on Parrys, a local confectionery firm. Through this tie-up, Wrigley could plug into Parrys' distribution network, thereby providing Wrigley immediate access to 250,000 retail outlets. The two major attractions that Parrys' network offered to Wrigley was the overlap in product category and the size of the distribution network.

The quality of the distribution network can also play a role. Gillette tied up with Bangalore based TTK, an Indian manufacturer of pressure cookers and kitchenware for the distribution of Braun products, despite the fact that Gillette has its own distribution network in India. Gillette needed department store-type outlets for its Braun product range, precisely the type of distribution channels that TTK uses for the distribution of its merchandise.[30]

***Direct Exporting.***   Under direct exporting, the firm sets up its own exporting department and sells its products via a middleman located in the foreign market. Once the international sales potential becomes substantial, direct exporting often looks far more appealing than indirect exporting. To some degree, the choice between indirect and direct exporting is a "make-or-buy" decision: should the company perform the export task, or is it better off sourcing the task out to outsiders? Compared to the indirect approach, direct exporting has a number of pluses. The exporter has far more

[28]http://www.powerhomebiz.com/vol7/export.htm.

[29]In 2008 Mars acquired Wrigley via a stock offer of around $23 billion.

[30]"India—Distribution Overview," IMI960321, U.S. Department of Commerce, International Trade Administration.

control over its international operations. Hence, the sales potential (and profit) is often times much more significant than under indirect exporting. It also allows the company to build up its own network in the foreign market and get better market feedback.

There is a price to be paid, though. Given that the responsibility for the exporting tasks is now in the hands of the company, the demands on resources—human and financial—are much more intense than with indirect exporting. Besides the marketing mix tasks, these tasks involve choosing target markets, identifying and selecting representatives in the foreign market, and scores of logistical functions (e.g., documentation, insurance, shipping, packaging).

## LICENSING

◆ ◆ ◆ ◆ ◆ ◆ ◆

Companies can also penetrate foreign markets via a licensing strategy. **Licensing** is a contractual transaction where the firm—the **licensor**—offers some proprietary assets to a foreign company—the **licensee**—in exchange for royalty fees. Examples of assets that can be part of a licensing agreement include trademarks, technology know-how, production processes, and patents. Royalty rates range from one-eight of 1 percent to 15 percent of sales revenue.[31] For instance, Oriental Land Company owns and operates Tokyo Disneyland under license from Disney. In return for being able to use the Disney name, Oriental Land Company pays royalties to Disney. In high-tech industries, companies often enter **cross-licensing** agreements. Under such agreement, parties mutually share patents without exchange of licensing fees when the patents involved are nearly equal in value. One big practitioner of cross-licensing is Microsoft. In August 2008, for instance, Microsoft and Nikon inked a patent cross-licensing agreement that covers digital cameras and other consumer products. The agreement enables both parties to innovate with each other's technologies.[32] Kodak and Nokia entered into a similar cross-patent agreement in October 2008 through which each company would get access to the other's intellectual property portfolio.[33]

**Benefits**

For many companies, licensing has proven to be a very profitable means for penetrating foreign markets. In most cases, licensing is not very demanding on the company's resources. Therefore, it is especially appealing to small companies that lack the resources and the wherewithal to invest in foreign facilities. Compared to exporting, another low-commitment entry mode, licensing allows the licensor to navigate around import barriers or get access to markets that are completely closed to imports. For instance, several foreign tobacco companies in China used licensing agreements to avoid the high import tax levied on imported cigarettes.[34] Local governments may also favor licensing over other entry modes.

Companies that use licensing as part of their global expansion strategy lower their exposure to political or economic instabilities in their foreign markets. The only volatilies that the licensor faces are the ups and downs in the royalty income stream. Other risks are absorbed by the licensee.

In high-tech industries, technology licensing has two more appeals. In highly competitive environments, rapid penetration of global markets allows the licensor to define the leading technology standard and to rapidly amortize R & D expenditures.[35] Research in Motion (RIM), the Canadian maker of the BlackBerry device, has entered numerous software-licensing agreements with competitors such as Nokia and

---

[31]"Licensing may be quickest route to foreign markets," *Wall Street Journal*, September 14, 1990, Sec. B, p. 2.

[32]http://www.microsoft.com/Presspass/press/2008/aug08/08-27MSNikonPatentPR.mspx.

[33]http://www.kodak.com/eknec/PageQuerier.jhtml?pq-path=2709&pq-locale=en_US&gpcid=0900688a809cc514.

[34]"Smoke signals point to China market opening," *South China Sunday Post*, October 6, 1996, p. 5.

[35]M. Kotabe, A. Sahay, and P.S. Aulakh, "Emerging role of technology licensing in the development of a global product strategy: conceptual framework and research propositions," *Journal of Marketing*, vol. 60, no. 1, January 1996, pp. 73–88.

Palm to establish its software architecture as the platform of choice for wireless communication tools.

**Caveats** Licensing comes with some caveats, though. Revenues coming from a licensing agreement could be dwarfed by the potential income that other entry modes such as exporting could have generated. Another possible disadvantage is that the licensee may not be fully committed to the licensor's product or technology. Lack of enthusiasm on the part of the licensee will greatly limit the sales potential of the licensed product. When the licensing agreement involves a trademark, there is the further risk that misguided moves made by the licensee tarnish the trademark covered by the agreement. Other risks include the risk of not getting paid, failure to produce in a timely manner or the desired volume, and loss of control of the marketing of the product.[36]

The biggest danger is the risk of opportunism. A licensing arrangement could nurture a future competitor: Today's comrade-in-arms often becomes tomorrow's rival. The licensee can leverage the skills it acquires during the licensing period once the agreement expires. **Global Perspective 9-1** chronicles the mishaps that Borden went through when its relationship with Meiji Milk, its licensee in Japan, turned sour.

Companies can make several moves to protect themselves against the risks of licensing arrangements.[37] If possible, the company should seek patent or trademark protection abroad. A thorough profitability analysis of a licensing proposal is an absolute must. Such an analysis must identify all the costs that the venture ensues, including the opportunity costs that stem from revenues that need to be sacrificed. Careful selection of prospective licensees is extremely important. Once a partner has been chosen, the negotiation process starts, which, if successful, will lead to a licensing

## *G*LOBAL PERSPECTIVE 9-1

### THE BORDEN-MEIJI MILK SAGA: THE MELTDOWN OF LADY BORDEN

When Borden, the U.S. multinational food company, entered Japan in 1971, it decided to tie up through a licensing arrangement with Meiji Milk. Borden's licensing agreement with Meiji Milk, Japan's leading dairy company, was the envy of many companies. Borden could benefit from Meiji Milk's vast distribution network. Meiji Milk, in turn, was able to acquire the expertise to manufacture various kinds of dairy products. The partnership also developed the premium ice cream market in Japan with its Lady Borden brand.

But the venture was not a fairy tale. Other brands entered the market and Lady Borden's market share started to flounder. As a result Borden wanted to dissolve its partnership with Meiji Milk, marketing Lady Borden on its own. Borden

*Sources:* "Borden's breakup with Meiji Milk shows how a Japanese partnership can curdle," *The Wall Street Journal*, February 21, 1991, pp. B1, B4; and, "Borden's hopes melt in Japanese market," *Advertising Age*, July 18, 1994, p. 38.

wanted to have more control over the marketing of its products in Japan so that it could respond more rapidly to the competitive challenges. Meiji Milk retaliated by rolling out two ice cream brands of its own, one of which, Lady Breuges, was in direct competition with Lady Borden. When Borden cut its ties with Meiji Milk, it also lost access to Meiji Milk's distribution channels. The company hoped that brand clout would pull Japanese customers to the Lady Borden brand. The pull of the Borden brand name did not make up for the loss of Meiji Milk's distribution muscle.

In June 1994, Borden, in a desperate move, licensed its trademarks and formulations for the Lady Borden brand to the confectionery maker Lotte Co. When Borden broke up with Meiji Milk in 1991, its share of Japan's premium ice cream market was around 50 percent. Three years later, when a Japanese newspaper compiled a score chart of the ice cream market, Meiji had 12 percent while Borden's share was so negligible that it didn't make the list.

---

[36]Sandra Mottner and James P. Johnson, "Motivations and Risks in International Licensing: A Review and Implications for Licensing to Transitional and Emerging Economies," *Journal of World Business*, 35 (2) (2000), pp. 171–87.

[37]Franklin R. Root, *Entry Strategies for International Markets*, Chapter 5.

contract. The contract will cover parameters such as the technology package, use conditions (including territorial rights and performance requirements), compensation, and provisions for the settlement of disputes.

## FRANCHISING

♦ ♦ ♦ ♦ ♦ ♦ ♦

Scores of service industry companies use franchising as a means for capturing opportunities in the global marketplace. For instance, of the 35,000-plus Yum! Brands restaurants,[38] more than two-thirds (24,297) are franchised.[39] The internationalization efforts of ten well-known franchise companies are summarized in **Exhibit 9-5**. Franchising is to some degree a "cousin" of licensing: It is an arrangement whereby the **franchisor** gives the **franchisee** the right to use the franchisor's trade names, trademarks,

**EXHIBIT 9-5**
INTERNATIONALIZATION EFFORTS OF TEN WELL-KNOWN FRANCHISE COMPANIES

| Company | Industry | Year Established | Year of First Franchise | Year First International Franchise | No. of Operating Units | No. of Countries |
|---|---|---|---|---|---|---|
| General Nutrition Centers | Vitamins retailing | 1935 | 1988 | 1991 | USA: 2954 CAN: 18 RoW: 227[1] | 27 |
| Mrs. Fields | Cookies | 1977 | 1990 | 1992 | USA: 849 CAN: 11 RoW: 60 | 12 |
| Uniglobe Travel | Travel Agencies | 1980 | 1981 | 1991 | USA: 856 CAN: 192 RoW: 87 | 15 |
| Subway | Sandwiches | 1965 | 1974 | 1984 | USA: 11452 CAN: 1259 RoW: 693 | 70+ |
| Computertots | Computer education | 1983 | 1989 | 1994 | USA: 132 CAN: 0 RoW: 92 | 12 |
| Midas | Automotive Services | 1956 | 1956 | 1968 | USA: 1898 CAN: 246 RoW: 561 | NA |
| Mailboxes Etc. | Business Support | 1980 | 1981 | 1988 | USA: 2971 CAN: 209 RoW: 377 | 70+ |
| Sir Speedy | Print & Copying Services | 1968 | 1968 | 1984 | USA: 1372 CAN: 9 RoW: 49 | 23 |
| Ponderosa | Steakhouse | 1965 | 1966 | 1985 | USA: 506 CAN: 8 RoW: 40 | NA |
| World Gym Fitness | Fitness | 1977 | 1985 | 1985 | USA: 276 CAN: 3 RoW: 9 | NA |

*Source:* www.franchiseintl.com.
[1]RoW = Rest of the World.

---

[38]Yum Brands! restaurant brands in the global arena are primarily Pizza Hut and KFC. The three remaining brands—Taco Bell, Long John Silver's, and A&W—are primarily U.S.-based and have a very marginal presence globally. In 2008 Yum! announced plans to also turn Taco Bell into a global brand.
[39]http://www.yum.com/investors/media/units_ww.pdf.

business models, and/or know-how in a given territory for a specific time period, normally 10 years.[40] In exchange, the franchisor gets royalty payments and other fees. The package could include the marketing plan, operating manuals, standards, training, and quality monitoring.

To snap up opportunities in foreign markets, the method of choice is often **master franchising**. With this system, the franchisor gives a master franchise to a local entrepreneur, who will, in turn, sell local franchises within his territory. The territory could be a certain region within a country or a group of countries (e.g., Greater China). Usually, the master franchise holder agrees to establish a certain number of outlets over a given time horizon.

**Benefits**    The benefits of franchising are clear. First and foremost, companies can capitalize on a winning business formula by expanding overseas with a minimum of investment. Just as with licensing, political risks for the rights-owner are very limited. Further, since the franchisees' profits are directly tied to their efforts, franchisees are usually highly motivated. Finally, the franchisor can also capitalize on the local franchisees' knowledge of the local marketplace. They usually have a much better understanding of local customs and laws than the foreign firm.

**Caveats**    Franchising carries some risks, though. Just like in the case of licensing, the franchisor's income stream is only a fraction of what it would be if the company held an equity stake in the foreign ventures. Firms with little or no name recognition typically face a major challenge finding interested partners in the foreign market. Finding suitable franchisees or a master franchisee can be a stumbling block in many markets. In many countries, the concept of franchising as a business model is barely understood.[41] A major concern is the lack of control over the franchisees' operations. Dissatisfied with the performance of its franchisees in Mexico and Brazil, Blockbuster Video changed tracks in 1995. The entertainment company decided to set up joint ventures and equity relations in Mexico and Brazil to replace the franchising arrangements held there, thereby getting more control and oversight.[42] Given the largely intangible nature of many franchising systems, cultural hurdles can also create problems. In fact, a recent study showed that cultural and physical proximity are the two most popular criteria used by companies for picking international markets in franchising.[43] **Exhibit 9-6** offers an overview of the key specifications of an international franchise agreement with Papa John's, the third largest pizza company in the world.

**EXHIBIT 9-6**
INTERNATIONAL FRANCHISING WITH PAPA JOHN'S (PJ)

**Franchise Support**

- *Training.* PJ provides training and development solutions and assistance with the development of trainers and training solutions.
- *Restaurant openings.* PJ offers assistance with determining the ideal site, review of market trade areas and site criteria, the build-out of the restaurant, and ordering of equipment.
- *Operations.* The company assists the franchisee with creating strategies and tactics to improve the operations, market penetration, and human resources development.
- *Food and supply chain.* PJ develops partnerships with suppliers in each country to ensure that international franchisees receive the highest-quality ingredients and supplies at the best possible prices.

*(continued)*

---

[40]Albert Kong, "How to Evaluate a Franchise," *Economic Bulletin*, (October 1998), pp. 18–20.

[41]Colin McCosker, "Trends and Opportunities in Franchising," *Economic Bulletin,* (October 1998), pp. 14–17.

[42]"Blockbuster's fast-forward," *Advertising Age International*, September 18, 1995, p. I-32.

[43]John F. Preble and Richard C. Hoffman, "Franchising systems around the globe: A status report," *Journal of Small Business Management*, April 1995, pp. 80–88.

- *Marketing.* PJ offers assistance in menu creation, long-term strategic planning, grand openings, and other marketing programs.
- *Information services.* The firm's information services department offers knowledge and tools to international franchisees to manage their operations.
- *Quality management.* PJ has three teams that support Research & Development, Quality Assurance, and Quality Control worldwide.

**Length of Contract**

- The initial term is ten years, with an option to renew for an additional 10-year term if certain criteria are met.

**Franchise Fee**

- US$25,000

**Ongoing Fees**

- Royalty fee of 5 percent of net sales is due monthly.

*Source:* http://company.papajohns.com/franchise_opps/franchise_int.shtm.

## CONTRACT MANUFACTURING (OUTSOURCING)

◆ ◆ ◆ ◆ ◆ ◆ ◆

With **contract manufacturing** (also known as **outsourcing**), the company arranges with a local firm to manufacture or assemble parts of the product or even the entire product. The marketing of the products is still the responsibility of the international firm.

Countless companies have become very successful by specializing in contract manufacturing. Flextronics, headquartered in Singapore, is one of the leading contract manufacturers with FY08 revenues of more than $33.6 billion.[44] The company helps its customers to design, build, ship, and service electronics products through its network of facilities in over thirty countries.[45] Its client list includes mostly electronics firms such as Sony Ericsson, Microsoft, Hewlett-Packard, and Nortel.[46] However, in 2006 the Danish toymaker Lego also decided to outsource most of its production to Flextronics as part of restructuring its supply chain.[47]

**Benefits**

Cost savings is the prime motivation behind contract manufacturing. Significant cost savings can be achieved for labor-intensive production processes by sourcing the product in a low-wage country. Typically, the countries of choice are places that have a substantial comparative labor cost advantage. Labor cost savings are not the only factor. Savings can also be achieved via taxation benefits, lower energy costs, raw materials costs, or overhead.

Some of the benefits listed for the previous entry modes also apply here. Subcontracting leads to a small amount of exposure to political and economic risks for the international firm. It also allows the company to focus on its core competencies (e.g., design, marketing prowess) and leave the manufacturing side to others. Other benefits include flexibility, access to external expertise, and less demand on the firm's resources (capital, staff).

**Caveats**

Contract manufacturing does have drawbacks, however. Clearly, the "nurture-a-future-competitor" concern raised for licensing and franchising also applies here. Consider what happened to Schwinn, the U.S. bicycle company.[48] Schwinn used to source about

---

[44] www.flextronics.com.

[45] Contract manufacturing in the electronics industry is often referred to as Electronics Manufacturing Services (EMS).

[46] http://www.ventureoutsource.com/contract-manufacturing/industry-pulse/2008/dissecting-the-new-flextronics, accessed on September 1, 2008.

[47] "Billionaire's Lego Farms Out to Flextronics," *Forbes,* http://www.forbes.com, accessed January 29, 2009.

[48] "Giant Grows, Peddling Its Own Brand," *Asian Wall Street Journal* (January 2, 2003), p. A5.

80 percent of its bikes from Giant Manufacturing, a Taiwanese company. When Schwinn switched suppliers, Giant, which had until then been a pure contract manufacturer, decided to create high-end bicycles under its own brand name. Giant is now the largest bike maker in the world, selling its bikes in around fifty countries. It has become the second-biggest brand of high-end bicycles in the United States. Schwinn, meanwhile, filed for bankruptcy and was sold to Pacific Cycle at a bankruptcy auction in 2001.[49] Because of such risk, many companies prefer to make high-value items or products that involve proprietary design features in-house. Contract manufacturers themselves often make products under their own brand, which usually leads to a conflict of interest with their customers. Acer, a Taiwanese computer maker, wrestled with such issues.[50] In 2000, business from products made for other global computer firms generated $1.8 billion revenue compared with about $1.2 billion revenue from its own-brand products. The key concern for many of Acer's clients was that by giving Acer business, they were subsidizing Acer's own-brand products, which were often similar but much less expensive. Acer's solution for this predicament was to split up the company. Giant, the Taiwanese bicycle maker mentioned earlier, addressed its customers' concerns by reassuring their clients that the firm would never launch cheap knockoffs of their products.

Contract manufacturing also offers less flexibility to respond to sudden market demand changes. Sony Ericsson Mobile Communications, which heavily relies on contracting for the manufacturing of its cellular phones, lost potential sales when its first color-screen model quickly sold out in Europe. Nokia, on the other hand, makes most of its products in-house. When it faced a last-minute glitch for the rollout of its first color-screen model, it plugged the gap by increasing the output of an existing model by 50 percent, using its plants in Finland, Germany, and China.[51]

A fixation with low-labor costs can often have painful consequences. Low-labor cost countries typically have very low labor productivity. Some of these countries, such as India and South Korea, also have a long tradition of bad labor relations. Too much reliance on low-cost labor could also create a backlash in the company's home-market among its employees and customers. Monitoring of quality and production levels is a must, especially during the start-up phase when "teething problems" are not uncommon.

When screening foreign subcontractors, the ideal candidate should meet the following criteria:[52]

- Be flexible and geared toward just-in-time delivery.
- Be able to meet quality standards and implement total quality management (TQM).
- Have solid financial footing.
- Be able to integrate with the company's business.
- Have contingency plans to handle sudden changes in demand.

## ◆ ◆ ◆ ◆ ◆ ◆ ◆ ◆   EXPANDING THROUGH JOINT VENTURES

For many MNCs who want to expand their global operations, joint ventures prove to be the most viable way to enter foreign markets, especially emerging markets. With a joint venture, the foreign company agrees to share equity and other resources with other partners to establish a new entity in the host country. The partners typically are local companies, but they can also be local government authorities, other foreign companies, or a mixture of local and foreign players. Depending on the equity stake, three forms of

---

[49]Pacific Cycle was in turn acquired by Dorel Industries in 2004.
[50]"Reinventing Acer," *Far Eastern Economic Review* (May 24, 2001), pp. 38–43.
[51]"Nokia Defies Odds and Thrives," *Asian Wall Street Journal* (January 6, 2003), pp. A1, A9.
[52]E. P. Hibbert, "Global make-or-buy decisions," *Industrial Marketing Management*, vol. 22, 1993, pp. 67–77.

partnerships can be distinguished: majority (more than 50 percent ownership), fifty-fifty and minority (50 percent or less ownership) ventures. Huge infrastructure or high-tech projects that demand a large amount of expertise and money often involve multiple foreign and local partners. Another distinction is between cooperative and equity joint ventures. A **cooperative joint venture** is an agreement for the partners to collaborate but does not involve any equity investments. For instance, one partner might contribute manufacturing technology whereas the other partner provides access to distribution channels. Cooperative joint ventures are quite common for partnerships between well-heeled multinational companies and local players in emerging markets. A good example of the collaborative approach is Cisco's sales strategy in Asia. Instead of investing in its own sales force, Cisco builds up partnerships with hardware vendors (e.g., IBM), consulting firms (e.g., KPMG), or systems integrators (e.g., Singapore-based Datacraft). These partners in essence act as front people for Cisco. They are the ones that sell and install Cisco's routers and switches.[53] An **equity joint venture** goes one step further. It is an arrangement in which the partners agree to raise capital in proportion to the equity stakes agreed upon.

A major advantage of joint ventures compared to lesser forms of resource commitment such as licensing is the return potential. With licensing, for instance, the company solely gets royalty payments instead of a share of the profits. Joint ventures also entail much more control over the operations than most of the previous entry modes discussed so far. MNCs that like to maximize their degree of control prefer full ownership. However, in many instances, local governments discourage or even forbid wholly owned ventures in certain industries. Under such circumstances, partnerships (joint ventures) are a second-best or temporary solution.

**Benefits**

Apart from the benefits listed above, the **synergy** argument is another compelling reason for setting up a joint venture. Partnerships not only mean a sharing of capital and risk. Other possible contributions brought in by the local partner include: land, raw materials, expertise on the local environment (culture, legal, political), access to a distribution network, personal contacts with suppliers, relations with government officials. Combined with the foreign partner's skills and resources, these inputs offer the key to a successful market entry. The Sony Ericsson partnership offers an excellent example. The tie-up combined Ericsson's technology prowess and strong links to wireless operators with Sony's marketing skills and expertise in consumer electronics. Each partner stood to gain from helping the other grow in regions where it was weak: Japan for Ericsson and Europe for Sony.[54]

For many MNCs, lack of full control is the biggest shortcoming of joint ventures. There are a number of ways for the MNC to gain more leverage. The most obvious way is via a majority equity stake. However, government restrictions often rule this option out. Even when for some reason majority ownership is not a viable alternative, MNCs have other means at their disposal to exercise control over the joint venture. MNCs could deploy expatriates in key line positions, thereby controlling financial, marketing and other critical operations of the venture. MNCs could also offer various types of outside support services to back up their weaker joint ventures in areas such as marketing, personnel training, quality control, and customer service.[55]

**Caveats**

As with licensing agreements, the foreign firm runs the risk that the partner could become a future competitor. Scores of China's most successful domestic companies started off as partners of multinationals. A case in point is Eastcom, a state-owned Chinese manufacturer and distributor of telecom equipment. After a 10-year-old

---

[53]"Cisco's Asian Gambit," *Fortune* (January 10, 2000), pp. 52–54.
[54]"Sony Ericsson: 'In Big Bloody Trouble'," *Business Week (Asian Edition)*, (November 4, 2002), pp. 54–55.
[55]Johannes Meier, Javier Perez and Jonathan R. Woetzel (1995), "Solving the puzzle—MNCs in China," *The McKinsey Quarterly*, No. 2, pp. 20–33.

**EXHIBIT 9-7**
CONFLICTING OBJECTIVE IN CHINESE JOINT VENTURES

|  | Foreign Partner | Chinese Partner |
|---|---|---|
| Planning | Retain business flexibility | Maintain congruency between the venture and the state economic plan |
| Contracts | Unambiguous, detailed, and enforceable | Ambiguous, brief, and adaptable |
| Negotiations | Sequential, issue by issue | Holistic and heuristic |
| Staffing | Maximize productivity; fewest people per given output level | Employ maximum number of local people |
| Technology | Match technical sophistication to the organization and its environment | Gain access to the most advanced technology as quickly as possible |
| Profits | Maximize in long term; repatriate over time | Reinvest for future modernization; maintain foreign exchange reserves |
| Inputs | Minimize unpredictability and poor quality of supplies | Promote domestic sourcing |
| Process | Stress high quality | Stress high quantity |
| Outputs | Access and develop domestic market | Export to generate foreign currency |
| Control | Reduce political and economic controls on decision making | Accept technology and capital but preclude foreign authority infringement on sovereignty and ideology |

*Source:* Reprinted from M. G. Martinsons and C.-S. Tsong, "Successful Joint Ventures in the Heart of the Dragon," Long Range Planning, 28 (5), p. 5. Copyright 1995, with kind permission from Elsevier Science Ltd., The Boulevard, Langford Lane, Kidlington OX5 1GB UK.

collaboration with Motorola, the company launched its own digital cell phone, undercutting Motorola's StarTAC model by $120.[56]

Lack of trust and mutual conflicts turn numerous international joint ventures into a marriage from hell. Conflicts could arise over matters such as strategies, resource allocation, transfer pricing, ownerships of critical assets like technologies and brand names. In many cases, the seeds for trouble exist from the very beginning of the joint venture. **Exhibit 9-7** contrasts the mutually conflicting objectives that the foreign partner and the local Chinese partner may hold when setting up a joint venture in China. Cultural strains between partners often spur mistrust and mutual conflict, making a bad situation even worse. Autolatina, a joint venture set up by Ford Motor Co. and Volkswagen AG in Latin America, was dissolved after 7 years in spite of the fact that it remained profitable to the very end. Cultural differences between the German and American managers were a major factor. One participating executive noted that "there were good intentions behind Autolatina's formation but they never really overcame the VW-Ford culture shock."[57]

When trouble undermines the joint venture, the partners can try to resolve the conflict via mechanisms built in the agreement. If a mutually acceptable resolution is not achievable, the joint venture is scaled back or dissolved. For instance, a joint venture between Unilever and AKI in South Korea broke up after seven years following disagreements over brand strategies for new products, resource allocation, advertising support, and brand ownership.[58] **Global Perspective 9-2** chronicles a partnership between Danone, the French beverage maker, and the Chinese Wahaha Group that involved a very bitter dispute.

**Drivers Behind Successful International Joint Ventures**

There are no magic ingredients to foster the stability of joint ventures. Still, some important lessons can be drawn from academic research of international joint ventures.

***Pick the Right Partner.*** Most joint venture marriages prosper by choosing a suitable partner. That means that the MNC should invest the time in identifying

---

[56]"The Local Cell-Phone Boys Get Tough," *Business Week (Asian Edition)*, (September 20, 1999), p. 24.
[57]"Why Ford, VW's Latin marriage succumbed to 7-year itch," *Advertising Age International*, March 20, 1995, p. I–22.
[58]"How Unilever's South Korean partnership fell apart," *Advertising Age*, August 31, 1992, pp. 3, 39.

# $\mathcal{G}$LOBAL PERSPECTIVE 9-2

## THE WAHAHA/DANONE JOINT VENTURE BRAWL

The Wahaha Joint Venture Company is a China based joint venture that was established between the Hangzhou Wahaha Group and Danone, the French food and beverage conglomerate. Since forming their joint venture in 1996, the partners have set up 39 companies in which Danone owns 51 percent each. The partnership was hailed as a "showcase" joint venture by *Forbes* magazine. Wahaha's bottled water, iced tea, and juices make up around 15 percent of the Chinese beverage market. The Wahaha brand is now a household name in China. Unfortunately, the honeymoon period has become a dim memory for both partners.

When Danone entered the joint venture, it left most of the day-to-day running in the hands of Wahaha's longtime chairman, Zong Qinghou, one of China's wealthiest businessmen. Zong was known for a brash management style. At the same time, Zong's entrepreneurial instinct was a key factor behind the success of the Wahaha brand.

In 2005, Danone noticed something odd with the financial figures coming from the joint venture. After a lengthy investigation, Danone suspected that Zong was setting up copycat operations outside the joint venture that were mimicking the joint venture and siphoning off revenues. Danone demanded a 51 percent stake in these non-joint venture companies. After months of negotiations, the two joint venture partners failed to settle their differences. In April 2007, Danone issued a statement saying that Zong was in breach of the joint venture agreement. The firm alleged that Zong was illegally selling similar products under the Wahaha brand name outside of the joint venture. Also, dealers who sold these products were apparently asked to set up new bank accounts for their payments.

The dispute partly centers on the issue of who owns the rights to use the Wahaha brand name. In the initial 1996 joint venture

agreement, the Wahaha Group agreed to transfer the trademark to the partnership. However, when the dispute started, the Wahaha Group claimed that the government authorities of Hangzhou, the group's hometown, had rejected this transfer agreement. In essence, Wahaha was claiming that the brand name was never really controlled by the joint venture.

Soon the dispute between the two partners became a full-blown brawl leading to ugly legal battles. The two partners filed a string of lawsuits and complaints against each other under Chinese and foreign jurisdictions (some of the external companies were registered overseas). Danone filed for arbitration in Stockholm in May 2007. One month later, Danone also launched a lawsuit against a Wahaha subsidiary in Los Angeles claiming $100 million in damages. Wahaha lodged suits in Shenyang and Jilin against Danone executives. Zong also fought back in the public domain. He posted a letter on the internet claiming that Danone officials had been fully aware of the outside companies and wanted to acquire them cheaply. A Hangzhou Arbitration Committee also ruled in favor of the Wahaha Group on a technicality. Local distributors and employees strongly came out in support of Zong, even calling for a boycott of Danone products. In December 2007, following a China visit by French President Sarkozy, Danone and Wahaha agreed to suspend all lawsuits and begin talks. So far, negotiations at allowing one side to buy out the other have failed. The dispute also took on a personal dimension when Danone helped the US tax authorities with a tax evasion investigation of Mr. Zong. The firm also tried to undermine Zong's claim that he was protecting the Wahaha brand heritage from foreign interference by pointing out the fact that Zong holds a U.S. green card. Each side claimed it remains committed to a successful Wahaha business and the products continue to be popular. Yet, both sides play down the likelihood of a friendly settlement. Mr. Zong is seeking a "divorce." One hurdle though is that the two sides differ in valuing the ventures.

Several drivers led to the breakdown of this lucrative partnership. Conflicts about marketing strategies and goals played a major role. Zong resented the fact that Danone was just collecting the money and restricted him from investing to expand the business. He also claimed that Danone reneged on their joint venture agreement by entering joint ventures with other related businesses (e.g., Huiyuan juice). Danone's lack of supervision of the joint venture also contributed a great deal. Although Danone owned 51 percent, it became little involved in Mr. Zong's operations, an arrangement that seemed to work for years.

*Sources:* "For Danone, China Risk Escalates in Nasty Brawl," *International Herald Tribune,* June 13, 2007, pp. 1, 12; "Danone Blow in China Brand Dispute," *Financial Times,* Dec. 11, 2007, p. 21; "Danone Dealt Setback in Battle with Wahaha," http://www.iht.com/articles/2008/07/14/business/danone.php, accessed September, 4, 2008; "Chinese Partners Mature, Rocking JV Status Quo," http://www.reuters.com/article/reutersEdge/idUSPEK22401820070618, accessed September, 4, 2008; "Danone, Wahaha Agree to End Confrontation, Resume Talks," http://www.chinadaily.com.cn/bizchina/wahaha.html, accessed on September 4, 2008; "Danone, Wahaha Look Likely to Part Ways," *The Wall Street* Journal, July 28, 2008, p. 4; and "Exit from Chinese Ventures not Always so Smooth for Danone," *Financial Times,* September 4, 2008, p. 14.

proper candidates. A careful screening of the joint venture partner is an absolute necessity. One issue is that it is not easy to sketch a profile of the "ideal" partner. The presence of complementary skills and resources that lead to synergies is one characteristic of successful joint ventures. Prospective partners should also have compatible goals. **Exhibit 9-8** lists the attributes that Starbucks requires.

**EXHIBIT 9-8**
STARBUCKS COFFEE'S CRITERIA IN SELECTING PARTNERS

- Shared values and corporate culture
- Strategic fit
- Seasoned operator of small-box, multi-unit retail
- Sufficient financial and human resources
- Involved and committed top management
- Real estate knowledge and access
- Local business leader
- Strong track record developing new ventures
- Experience managing licensed & premium brands and concepts
- Leverageable infrastructure
- Food & beverage experience

*Source: http://www.starbucks.com/aboutus/international.asp*, accessed January 30, 2009.

Some evidence indicates that partners should be similar in terms of size and resources. Partners with whom the MNC has built up an existing relationship (e.g., distributors, customers, suppliers) also facilitate a strong relationship.[59] The more balanced the contributions by the partners, the more trust and the more harmonious the relationship.[60] One issue that latecomers in a market often face is that the "best" partners have already been snapped up. Note, however, that the same issue arises with acquisition strategies. One study on joint venture performance in China offers five guidelines for partner selection.[61] First, integrate partner selection with your strategic goals. Second, obtain as much information as possible about the candidate (e.g., company brochures, business license). Third, visit the site. Fourth, check whether or not the potential partner shares your investment objective. And, finally, do not put too much emphasis on the role of *guanxi* (relationships).

***Establish Clear Objectives for the Joint Venture from the Very Beginning.***[62] It is important to clearly spell out the objectives of the joint venture from day one. Partners should know what their respective contributions and responsibilities are before signing the contract.[63] They should also know what to expect from the partnership.

***Bridge Cultural Gaps.***  Many joint venture disputes stem from cultural differences between the local and foreign partners. Much agony and frustration can be avoided when the foreign investor makes an attempt to bridge cultural differences. For instance, when setting up joint ventures in China, having an ethnic Chinese or an "old China hand" as a middleman often helps a great deal. The problem is that knowledgeable people who share the perspectives of both cultures are often very hard to find.[64]

***Top Managerial Commitment and Respect.***  Short of a strong commitment from the parent companies' top management, most international joint ventures are doomed to become a failure. The companies should be willing to assign their best managerial talent to the joint venture. Venture managers should also have complete access to and support from their respective parent companies.[65]

---

[59]Karen J. Hladik, "R&D and International Joint Ventures," in *Cooperative Forms of Transnational Corporation Activity*, edited by P. J. Buckley, London: Routledge, 1994.

[60]Akmal S. Hyder and Pervez N. Ghauri, "Managing International Joint Venture Relationships," *Industrial Marketing Management*, 29 (2000), pp. 205–18.

[61]Yadong Luo, "Joint Venture Success in China: How Should We Select a Good Partner," *Journal of World Business*, 32 (2) (1998), pp. 145–66.

[62]Dominique Turpin (1993), "Strategic alliances with Japanese firms: Myths and realities," *Long Range Planning*, vol. 26, no. 4, pp. 11–16.

[63]Maris G. Martinsons and Choo-sin Tseng, (1995) "Successful joint ventures in the heart of the dragon," *Long Range Planning*, vol. 28, no. 5, pp. 45–58.

[64]M.G. Martinsons and C.-S. Tseng (1995), "Successful joint ventures in the heart of the dragon," p. 56.

[65]D. Turpin, "Strategic alliances with Japanese firms: myths and realities," p. 15.

## GLOBAL PERSPECTIVE 9-3

### STARBUCKS IN CHINA: A COMBINATION OF GOOD PARTNERS & FLEXIBILITY

Since the first Starbucks outlet in (mainland) China opened in Beijing in 1999, Starbucks has become one of the most popular brands among Chinese white-collar workers in the 25–40 year-old segment. Like many Western retailers, Starbucks sees China as a key growth opportunity due to its fast-growing economy and the sheer size of its population.

To lower the risks of overseas expansion, Starbucks uses different types of ownership structures. It either designates a local developer to use the Starbucks brand or sets up a joint venture. Starbucks entered the China market with different partners in three regions.

For northern China, Starbucks authorized Beijing Meida Coffee to establish its brand. This firm is 90 percent owned by a Hong Kong-based company. A leading Chinese dairy held the remaining shares. For Shanghai and eastern China's Jiangsu and Zhejian provinces, Starbucks set up a joint venture with the Taiwan-based Uni-President Group. Initially, Starbucks only held a 5 percent stake. However, in 2003 Starbucks raised its stake to 50 percent after paying $21.3 million to its partner. A similar arrangement existed for southern China region (plus Hong Kong and Macau), which Starbucks entered through a joint venture with Maxim's, a Hong Kong-based catering conglomerate. Also here, Starbucks raised its stake from an initial 5 percent to 51 percent in 2005.

*Sources:* www.starbucks.com, accessed February 2, 2009; "Starbucks Soars in China," http://www.atimes.com/atimes/China_Business/HF15Cb06.html; "Starbucks Sees no Slowdown in China," http://uk.reuters.com/article/consumerproducts-SP/idUKPEK1296020090113?sp=true; "Starbucks to Boost China Investment After Closing U.S. Stores," http://www.bloomberg.com/apps/news?pid=20601082&sid=aOowxTtMI8jY&refer=canada#; "China Central to Starbucks Growth," news.bbc.co.uk, accessed on February 2, 2009; and "China's Next Export: Starbucks Coffee," http://www.chinadaily.com.cn/china/2009-01/14/content_7397643.htm.

Describing its growth model in China, Howard Schultz, the Starbucks CEO, said: "The Starbucks growth model has been successful with many different types of ownership structures. From time to time we revise those ownership structures because of strategic opportunities. China is no different from many other markets around the world. In 1999, we didn't have the infrastructure that we have today in China. Now we are more prepared and more capable of doing things. That might mean, over time some changes in equity."[66]

Even when the firm announced plans in 2008 to close 600 U.S. outlets its expansion drive in China continued. By 2009 Starbucks had more than 350 stores in 26 cities in China. Wang Jinlong, the company's Greater China president, declared: "We still have a long way to go. We'll continue to expand. The number of stores will not be in the hundreds, but in the thousands."[67] The retailer plans to expand in big cities such as Beijing and Shanghai, as well as smaller ones like Wuhan. Apart from adding stores, Starbucks also launched a new blend of coffee sourced in China's southwestern province of Yunnan. The launch of this new coffee blend, labeled "South of the Clouds," took three years. "Our intention is to work with the officials and the farmers in Yunnan province to bring Chinese coffee not (only) to China, but Chinese coffee to the world. Ultimately I'd love to see our coffees from China feature on the shelves of every of one of our stores in 49 countries around the world," stated Marin Coles, president of Starbucks Coffee International.[68]

[66]"Starbucks Soars in China," http://www.atimes.com/atimes/China_Business/HF15Cb06.html.

[67]"Starbucks to Boost China Investment After Closing U.S. Stores," http://www.bloomberg.com/apps/news?pid=20601082&sid=aOowxTtMI8jY&refer=canada#.

[68]"China's Next Export: Starbucks Coffee," http://www.chinadaily.com.cn/china/2009-01/14/content_7397643.htm.

***Incremental Approach Works Best.*** Rather than being overambitious, an incremental approach towards setting up the international joint venture appears to be much more effective. The partnership starts on a small scale. Gradually, the scope of the joint venture is broadened by adding other responsibilities and activities to the joint venture's charter. The foreign partner often starts off with a minority stake and gradually increases its stake in the joint venture. A case in point is Starbucks' expansion strategy in China as described in **Global Perspective 9-3**.

A study by a team of McKinsey consultants also advises the parents to create a launch team during the launch phase—beginning with the signing of a memorandum of understanding and continuing through the first 100 days of operation.[69] The launch team should address the four key joint venture challenges:

[69]James Bamford, David Ernst, and David G. Fubini, "Launching a World-Class Joint Venture," *Harvard Business Review* 82, February (2004): 90–101.

1. Build and maintain *strategic alignment* across the separate corporate entities, each of which has its own goals, market pressures, and shareholders.

2. Create a *governance* system that promotes shared decision-making and oversight between the parent companies.

3. Manage the *economic interdependencies* between the corporate parents and the joint venture (e.g., compensation of each parent for its contributions).

4. Build the *organization* for the joint venture (e.g., staffing positions, assigning responsibilities).

## ♦ ♦ ♦ ♦ ♦ ♦ ♦ ♦ ♦   WHOLLY OWNED SUBSIDIARIES

In September 2008, Coca-Cola offered $2.4 billion in cash to buy China Huiyuan Juice Group. At the time, this was the largest takeover offer ever made by a foreign company to buy a Chinese company. Muthar Kent, Coke's CEO, stated that the acquisition would "provide a unique opportunity to strengthen our business in China, especially since the juice segment is so dynamic and fast growing."[70] In March 2009, the Chinese government rejected the takeover bid due to fears that the acquisition could harm Coca-Cola's smaller competitors and raise consumer prices.[71] If the bid had been approved by the Chinese government,[72] it would have more than doubled Coca-Cola's market share in China's fruit juice market to around 20 percent.[73] Multinational companies often prefer to enter new markets with 100 percent ownership. Ownership strategies in foreign markets can essentially take two routes: **acquisitions** where the MNC buys up existing companies, or **greenfield operations** that are started from scratch. As with the other entry modes, full ownership entry entails certain benefits to the MNC but also carries risks.

**Benefits**   Wholly owned subsidiaries give MNCs full control of their operations. It is often the ideal solution for companies that do not want to be saddled with all the risks and anxieties associated with other entry modes such as joint venturing. Full ownership means that all the profits go to the company. Fully owned enterprises allow the foreign investor to manage and control its own processes and tasks in terms of marketing, production, logistics and sourcing decisions. Setting up fully owned subsidiaries also sends a strong commitment signal to the local market. In some markets—China, for example—wholly owned subsidiaries can be erected much faster than joint ventures with local companies that may consume years of negotiations before their final take-off.[74] The latter point is especially important when there are substantial advantages of being an early entrant in the target market.

**Caveats**   Despite the advantages of 100 percent ownership, many MNCs are quite reluctant to choose this particular mode of entry. The risks of full ownership cannot be easily discounted. Complete ownership means that the parent company will have to carry the full burden of possible losses. Developing a foreign presence without the support of a third party is also very demanding on the firm's resources. Obviously, apart of the market-related risks, substantial political risks (e.g., expropriation, nationalization) and economic risks (e.g., currency devaluation) must be factored in.

Companies that enter via a wholly owned enterprise are sometimes also perceived as a threat to the cultural and/or economic sovereignty of the host country. When InBev, the Brazilian/Belgian brewer, made a $46.3 billion unsolicited takeover bid for

---

[70]"Coke Eyes Record China Deal," *Financial Times*, (September 4, 2008), p. 13.

[71]"Beijing Thwarts Coke's Takeover Bid," online.wsj.com, accessed on July 20, 2009.

[72]Even though Huiyuan Juice is a private company, the deal still had to be approved by the Chinese government.

[73]"Coke to Squeeze More From China," *Financial Times*, (September 4, 2008), p. 14.

[74]Wilfried Vanhonacker, "Entering China: An Unconventional Approach," *Harvard Business Review*, March–April 1997.

Anheuser-Busch, the leading American beer brewer, several U.S. politicians and journalists were dismayed. Barack Obama, the 2008 Democratic presidential candidate and ultimate victor, stated at a press conference in St. Louis, headquarters of Anheuser-Busch, "I do think it would be a shame if Bud is foreign-owned. I think we should be able to find an American company that is interested in purchasing Anheuser-Busch."[75] Likewise, during the 2008 Italian elections campaign, when Alitalia, Italy's beleaguered airline, was approached by Air France-KLM, Berlusconi promised to keep the airline out of foreign hands.[76] In January 2009, however, Alitalia decided to sell a 25 percent stake of the company to Air France-KLM.[77] One way to address hostility to foreign acquisitions in the host country is via "localizing" the firm's presence in the foreign market by hiring local managers, sourcing locally, developing local brands, sponsoring local sports or cultural events and so forth.[78]

Companies such as Sara Lee have built up strong global competitive positions via cleverly planned and finely executed acquisition strategies. MNCs choose acquisition entry to expand globally for a number of reasons. First and foremost, when contrasted with greenfield operations, acquisitions provide a rapid means to get access to the local market. For relative latecomers in an industry, acquisitions are also a viable option to obtain well-established brand names, instant access to distribution outlets, or technology. Cadbury Schweppes $4.2 billion purchase in 2003 of Adams, Pfizer's candy business, illustrates the advantages of the acquisition entry mode. By acquiring the business, Cadbury was able to pick up several leading candy and chewing gum brands including Trident, Chiclets, Certs and Halls lozenges. The Adams purchase also bolstered Cadbury's position in the fast growing candy markets in the United States and Latin America. In recent years, some of the South Korean *chaebols* have used acquisition entries in foreign markets to gain a foothold in high-tech industries. Highly visible examples include Samsung's acquisition of the American computer maker AST and LG Electronics' take-over of Zenith. LG would have had to invest more than $1 billion to build up a strong global TV brand from scratch.[79] Cash-rich Chinese companies are also trying to gain a foothold in overseas markets by buying up foreign firms. These efforts have not always been successful. Huawei, the Chinese telecom equipment maker, had to drop its bid to buy a major stake in 3Com when U.S. lawmakers raised alarms concerned about Huawei's alleged ties with the People's Liberation Army.[80] **Global Perspective 9-4** discusses the acquisition of IBM's PC division by Lenovo, the Chinese computer behemoth.

Expansion via acquisitions or mergers carries substantial risks, however. Differences in the corporate culture of the two companies between managers are often extremely hard to bridge. A well-publicized example of a company that has been plagued with corporate culture disease is Alcatel-Lucent, the telecommunications equipment group that resulted from the 2006 merger of Alcatel and Lucent. Since its creation, the group has been hampered by cultural differences between the American and French arms. As one analyst observed: ". . . Alcatel-Lucent was a merger that sounded good in a PowerPoint presentation. But there have been a lot of serious integration challenges, including cultural issues, that were underestimated and still linger."[81]

**Acquisitions and Mergers**

---

[75]http://www.flex-news-food.com/pages/17605/Anheuser-Busch/InBev/obama-says-shame-anheuser-busch-sold-inbev.html; ultimately the deal went through and Inbev was renamed Anheuser Busch-InBev.

[76]"Berlusconi: Alitalia's White Knight?" http://www.forbes.com/2008/03/20/berlusconi-alitalia-italy-face-cx_vr_0320autofacescan01.html.

[77]"Air France-KLM Buys Stake in Alitalia," http://edition.cnn.com/2009/BUSINESS/01/13/alitalia.air.france.klm/index.html.

[78]W. Vanhonacker, "Entering China: An Unconventional Approach."

[79]"Guess who's betting on America's high-tech losers," *Fortune*, October 28, 1996.

[80]http://www.businessweek.com/globalbiz/blog/eyeonasia/archives/2008/02/huaweis_3com_de.html.

[81]"Culture Clash Hits Home at Alcatel-Lucent," http://www.iht.com/bin/printfriendly.php?id=14867263.

## $\mathcal{G}$LOBAL PERSPECTIVE 9-4

### THE LENOVO/IBM DEAL – A WINNING COMBINATION?

The $1.75 billion acquisition of IBM's personal computer business by Lenovo, the Chinese PC maker, marked the dawn of a new era. The cross-border deal gave Lenovo much more than Big Blue's PC business. Lenovo became the first state-controlled Chinese firm to acquire an iconic global brand. "If anyone still harboured any doubts that Chinese corporates were serious players on the global M&A stage those have now totally been dispelled," said Colin Banfield at CSFB.

The talks behind the deal took 18 months. By bringing together China's largest PC maker and IBM's PC division, Lenovo executives hoped they could create a formidable force to challenge the dominance of Hewlett-Packard and Dell, the market leaders. Lenovo estimated that it could save $200m a year by component cost savings. Lenovo would own IBM's Think trademark and IBM would become Lenovo's "preferred supplier" as part of the deal.

*Sources:* ""IBM Brand Loyalty Holds Key for Lenovo," *Financial Times*, December 9, 2004, p. 16; "Deal Divides Opinion Over Future Trends," *Financial Times*, December 9, 2004, p. 16; "Your Rules and My Processes," *Financial Times*, November 10, 2005, p. 10; "Quick-fire Lessons in Globalisation," *Financial Times*, November 11, 2005, p. 8; http://www.businessweek.com/technology/content/dec2005/tc20051221_376268.htm.

The growth plan spelled out for "new" Lenovo had three key elements: developing the ThinkPad notebook computer franchise, expanding into emerging markets such as India, Brazil, and Russia, and introducing Lenovo-branded PCs for small business owners in the United States and Europe.

Many observers were skeptical about blending the two very diverse corporate cultures. The focus at the "old" Lenovo was on rules. All employees were expected to clock in and clock out. Employees were forbidden to turn up late for meetings. Where Lenovo had rules, IBM had processes: regular meetings, conference calls, and milestones to keep projects on track. To the Chinese, the focus on processes could be as alien as the emphasis on rules for former IBM staff. Another cultural gap stems from conversational style differences: Americans like to talk; Chinese like to listen. Still, the enthusiasm is not lacking. The working language for the new Lenovo is English as hardly anyone from the IBM side speaks Chinese. Lenovo shifted its official headquarters from Beijing to Purchase, N.Y. Steven Ward, formerly head of IBM's PC division, became Lenovo's new CEO. Ward was replaced in December 2005 by William Amelio, who had been charge of the Asia-Pacific division of Dell, Lenovo's main competitor. With the new CEO, Lenovo was hoping to plug a gap in China, its home-market. Lenovo had a 32 percent market share in 2005 but was not strong among corporate buyers.

---

The assets of the acquisition do not always live up to the expectations of the acquiring company. Outdated plants, tarnished brand names or an unmotivated workforce are only a few of the many possible disappointments that the acquiring company could face. The local government might also attach certain conditions to the acquisition or expectations in terms of job creation. Failure to live up to such expectations could tarnish the image of the MNC in the host country. In 2005, BenQ, the Taiwanese consumer electronics firm, acquired the mobile phone division of Siemens in the hope of creating a leading brand in the category. Unfortunately, the German branch proved to be an albatross for BenQ, which decided to discontinue manufacturing phones in Germany. This move created a lot of bad feelings among German stakeholders (unions, government) with the suspicion that BenQ only bought the Siemens mobile business for its patents.[82] A careful screening and assessment of takeover candidates can avoid a lot of heartburn on the part of the acquiring company.

As mentioned earlier, open hostility toward foreign companies can also complicate acquisition plans. A joint $10.5 billion bid by Cadbury and Nestlé to buy Hershey Foods, the U.S. chocolate maker, got derailed in part of strong opposition against a "foreign takeover" from the local community. Another drawback is that acquisition entry can be a very costly global expansion strategy. Good prospects are usually unwilling to sell themselves. If they are, they do not come cheap. For instance, the $2.4 billion takeover offer that Coca-Cola made in 2008 for China's Huiyuan Juice Group was worth 35 times the Chinese firm's forecast 2009 earnings.[83] Other foreign or local

---

[82]"Siemens Strikes Back," http://www.spiegel.de/international/0,1518,440409,00.html.
[83]"All the Juice in China," *Financial Times*, September 4, 2008, p. 12.

companies are typically interested too, and the result is often a painful bidding war. The costs and strains of integrating the acquisition with the company can also be a substantial burden.

Acquisition strategies are not always feasible. Good prospects may already have been nabbed by the company's competitors. In many emerging markets, acceptable acquisition candidates often are simply not available. Overhauling the facilities of possible candidates is sometimes much more costly than building an operation from scratch. In the wake of these downsides, companies often prefer to enter foreign markets through greenfield operations that are established from scratch. Greenfield operations offer the company more flexibility than acquisitions in areas such as human resources, suppliers, logistics, plant layout, or manufacturing technology. Greenfield investments also avoid the costs of integrating the acquisition into the parent company.[84] Another motivation is the package of goodies (e.g., tax holidays) that host governments sometimes offer to whet the appetite of foreign investors. A major disadvantage, though, of greenfield operations is that they require enormous investments of time and capital.

**Greenfield Operations**

## STRATEGIC ALLIANCES

◆ ◆ ◆ ◆ ◆ ◆ ◆

A distinctive feature of the activities of global corporations today is that they are using cooperative relationships such as licensing, joint ventures, R&D partnerships, and informal arrangements—all under the rubric of alliances of various forms—on an increasing scale. More formally, a **strategic alliance** can be described as *a coalition of two or more organizations to achieve strategically significant goals that are mutually beneficial.*[85] The business press reports like clockwork the birth of strategic alliances in various kinds of industries. Eye-catching are especially those partnerships between firms that have been archenemies for ages. A principal reason for the increase in cooperative relationships is that firms today no longer have the capacity of a General Motors of the 1940s, which developed all its technologies in-house. As a result, firms, especially those operating in technology intensive industries, may not be at the forefront of all the required critical technologies.[86]

Strategic alliances come in all shapes. At one extreme, alliances can be based on a simple licensing agreement between two partners. At the other extreme, they can consist of a thick web of ties. The nature of alliances also varies depending on the skills brought in by the partners. A first category, very common in high-tech industries, is based on technology swaps. Given the skyrocketing costs of new product development, strategic alliances offer a means to companies to pool their resources and learn from one another. Such alliances must be struck from a position of strength. Bargaining chips might be patents that the company holds. A second type of cross-border alliances involves marketing-based assets and resources such as access to distribution channels or trademarks. A case in point is the partnership established by Coca-Cola and Nestlé to market ready-to-drink coffees and teas under the Nescafé and Nestea brand names. This deal allowed the two partners to combine a well-established brand name with access to a vast proven distribution network. In India, Huggies, Kimberly-Clark's diapers, are manufactured and distributed through an alliance with Hindustan Lever, the local unit of Unilever, whose powerful distribution network covers 400,000 retail outlets. A third category of alliances is situated in the operations and logistics area. In their relentless search for scale economies for operations/logistics activities, companies

**Types of Strategic Alliances**

[84]Jiatao Li (1995), "Foreign entry and survival: effects of strategic choices on performance in international markets," *Strategic Management Journal*, vol. 16, pp. 333–51.

[85]Edwin A. Murray, Jr. and John F. Mahon (1993), "Strategic alliances: Gateway to the new Europe?" *Long Range Planning*, August, pp. 102–11.

[86]Noel Capon and Rashi Glazer (1987), "Marketing and Technology: A Strategic Co-alignment," *Journal of Marketing*, 51(July), 1–14.

Source: Reprinted from P. Lorange, J. Roos, and P. S. Brønn, "Building Successful Strategic Alliances," *Long Range Planning*, 25 (6), 1992, p. 10. Copyright 1992, with kind permission from Elsevier Science Ltd., The Boulevard, Langford Lane, Kidlington OX51GB, UK.

**EXHIBIT 9-9**
GENERIC MOTIVES FOR STRATEGIC ALLIANCES

| | | Business Market Position | |
|---|---|---|---|
| | | Leader | Follower |
| Strategic Importance in Parent's Portfolio | Core | Defend | Catch Up |
| | Peripheral | Remain | Restructure |

may decide to join forces by setting up a partnership. Finally, operations-based alliances are driven by a desire to transfer manufacturing know-how. A classic example is the NUMMI joint venture set up by Toyota and General Motors to swap car-manufacturing expertise.

**The Logic behind Strategic Alliances**

The strategic pay-offs of cross-border alliances are alluring, especially in high-tech industries. Lorange and colleagues[87] suggest that there are four generic reasons for forming strategic alliances: defense, catch-up, remain, or restructure (see **Exhibit 9-9**). Their scheme centers around two dimensions: the strategic importance of the business unit to the parent company and the competitive position of the business.

- *Defend.* Companies create alliances for their core businesses to defend their leadership position. Basically, the underlying goal is to sustain the firm's leadership position by learning new skills, getting access to new markets, developing new technologies, or finessing other capabilities that help the company to reinforce its competitive advantage(s).[88]

- *Catch-Up.* Firms may also shape strategic alliances to catch up. This happens when companies create an alliance to shore a core business in which they do not have a leadership position. Nestlé and General Mills launched Cereal Partners Worldwide to attack Kellogg's dominance in the global cereal market. Likewise, Pepsi and General Mills, two of the weaker players in the European snack food business, set up a joint venture for their snack food business to compete more effectively in the European market.

- *Remain.* Firms might also enter a strategic alliance to simply remain in a business. This might occur for business divisions where the firm has established a leadership position but which only play a peripheral role in the company's business portfolio. That way, the alliance enables the company to get the maximum efficiency out of its position.

- *Restructure.* Lastly, a firm might also view alliances as a vehicle to restructure a business that is not core and in which it has no leadership position. The ultimate intent here is that one partner uses the alliance to rejuvenate the business, thereby turning the business unit in a "presentable bride," so to speak. Usually, one of the other partners in the alliance ends up acquiring of the business unit.

**Cross-Border Alliances that Succeed**

The recipe for a successful strategic alliance will probably never be written. Still, a number of studies done by consulting agencies and academic scholars have uncovered several findings on what distinguishes enduring cross-border alliances from the

---

[87]Peter Lorange, Johan Roos and Peggy S. Brønn (1992), "Building successful strategic alliances," *Long Range Planning*, vol. 25, no. 6, pp. 10–17.

[88]See also David Lei and John W. Slocum, Jr. (1992), "Global strategy, competence-building and strategic alliances," *California Management Review*, Fall, pp. 81–97.

floundering ones. An analysis of cross-border alliances done by McKinsey came up with the following recommendations:[89]

- *Alliances between strong and weak partners seldom work.* Building up ties with partners that are weak is a recipe for disaster. The weak partner becomes a drag on the competitiveness of the partnership. As a senior Hewlett-Packard executive put it: "One should go for the best possible partners—leaders in their field, not followers."[90]

- *Autonomy and flexibility.* These are two key ingredients for successful partnerships. Autonomy might mean that the alliance has its own management team and its own board of directors. This speeds up the decision-making process. Autonomy also makes it easier to resolve conflicts that arise. To cope with environmental changes over time, flexibility is essential. Market needs change, new technologies emerge, and competitive forces regroup. Being flexible, alliances can more easily adapt to these changes by revising their objectives, the charter of the venture, or other aspects of the alliance.

- *Equal ownership.* In 50-50 ownerships, the partners are equally concerned about the other's success. Both partners should contribute equally to the alliance.[91] Thereby, all partners will be in a win-win situation where the gains are equally distributed. However, 50-50 joint ventures between partners from developed countries and developing countries are more likely to get bogged down in decision-making deadlocks. One recent study of equity joint ventures in China found that partnerships with minority foreign equity holding run much more smoothly than other equity sharing arrangements. Indeed, 50-50 partnerships ran into all sorts of internal managerial problems including difficulties in joint decision-making and coordination with local managers. Majority foreign equity ventures had fewer internal problems but encountered many external issues such as lack of local sourcing and high dependence on imported materials.[92] So, in spite of the findings of the McKinsey study, the ownership question—50/50 versus majority stake—remains murky.

We would like to add a few more success factors to these. Stable alliances have the commitment and support of the top of the parents' organization. Strong alliance managers are key to success.[93] Alliances between partners that are related (in terms of products, markets, and/or technologies) or have similar cultures, assets sizes and venturing experiencing levels tend to be much more viable.[94] Furthermore, successful alliances tend to start on a narrow basis and broaden over time. A partnership between Corning, the U.S. glassmaker, and Samsung, the Korean electronics firm, started with one plant making television tubes in South Korea. Over time, the partnership broadened its scope, covering much of East Asia. Finally, a shared vision on the goals and the mutual benefits is the hallmark of viable alliances.

## TIMING OF ENTRY

◆ ◆ ◆ ◆ ◆ ◆ ◆

International market entry decisions also cover the timing-of-entry question: when should the firm enter a foreign market? Numerous firms have been burnt badly by entering markets too early. Ikea's first foray in Japan in 1974 was a complete fiasco.[95]

---

[89]Joel Bleeke and David Ernst (1991), "The way to win in cross-border alliances," *Harvard Business Review*, Nov.–Dec., pp. 127–35.

[90]"When Even a Rival Can Be a Best Friend," *Financial Times* (October 22, 1997), p. 12.

[91]Godfrey Devlin and Mark Bleackley (1988), "Strategic alliances—guidelines for success," *Long Range Planning*, vol. 21, no. 5, pp. 18–23.

[92]Yigang Pan and Wilfried R. Vanhonacker, 1994, "Equity sharing arrangements and joint venture operation in the People's Republic of China," Working Paper, February, Hong Kong University of Science & Technology.

[93]Godfrey Devlin and Mark Bleackley (1988), "Strategic alliances—guidelines for success," *Long Range Planning*, vol. 21, no. 5, pp. 18–23.

[94]Kathryn R. Harrigan (1988), "Strategic alliances and partner asymmetries," in *Cooperative Strategies in International Business*, F.J. Contractor and P. Lorange, eds., Lexington, MA: Lexington Books.

[95]http://www.businessweek.com/magazine/content/05_46/b3959001.htm.

**EXHIBIT 9-10**
TIMELINE OF WAL-MART'S INTERNATIONAL EXPANSION

| Market | Retail Units (as of Dec 31, 2008) | Date of Entry | Date of Exit |
|---|---|---|---|
| Mexico | 1,201 | Nov 1991 | |
| Puerto Rico | 56 | Aug 1992 | |
| Canada | 310 | Nov 1994 | |
| Brazil | 349 | May 1995 | |
| Argentina | 28 | Aug 1995 | |
| China | 225 | Aug 1996 | |
| South Korea | 16 | 1998 | 2006 |
| Germany | 85 | 1998 | 2006 |
| United Kingdom | 358 | Jul 1999 | |
| Japan | 387 | Mar 2002 | |
| Costa Rica | 164 | Sep 2005 | |
| El Salvador | 77 | Sep 2005 | |
| Guatemala | 160 | Sep 2005 | |
| Honduras | 50 | Sep 2005 | |
| Nicaragua | 51 | Sep 2005 | |
| India (cash-and-carry) | | Aug 2007 | |

Source: www.walmartstores.com/factsnews/

The Swedish furniture retailer hastily withdrew from Japan after realizing that Japanese consumers were not yet ready for the concept of self-assembly and preferred high quality over low prices. Ikea re-entered Japan in late 2005, but this time offering assembly services and home delivery.

**Exhibit 9-10** shows the timeline of Wal-Mart's international expansion strategy. Note that the gap was almost thirty years between the foundation of Wal-Mart by Sam Walton in 1962 and the retailer's first international operation in Mexico (1991). Since, then Wal-Mart has expanded very aggressively. Initially, Wal-Mart concentrated mostly on markets in the Americas. It is only toward the end of the 1990s that the retailer shifted its attention toward Europe and the Asia-Pacific region. As of 2009, Wal-Mart had about 3,100 stores in 13 countries outside the United States. It also operates a cash-and-carry wholesale operation in India through a joint-venture with Bharti Enterprises, an Indian conglomerate.[96]

Timing decisions also arise for the global launch of new products or services. Microsoft launched the Xbox videogame console first in its home-market (Fall 2001), next in Japan (February 2002), and then in Europe (March/April 2002). However, products are not always pioneered in the company's home market. A case in point is the Volkswagen New Beetle, which was first rolled out in the United States and later in Germany. Likewise, Toyota's luxury car marque Lexus was launched in July 2005 in Japan, more than 15 years after its 1989 debut in the United States. Qoo, a Coca-Cola children's fruit drink, was first rolled out in Japan in 1999. It was then introduced rapidly in other Asian markets (Korea, Singapore, China, Thailand, and Taiwan). In January 2003, Coke launched Qoo in Germany, the first European market.[97]

Research on international entry-timing decisions is scarce. One study examined the timing-of-entry decisions of U.S. Fortune 500 firms in China.[98] According to the study's findings, firms tend to enter China earlier:

- The higher the level of international experience;
- The larger the firm size;

---

[96]http://walmartstores.com/FactsNews/, accessed February 2, 2009.

[97]"Coca-Cola's Qoo to go to Germany," *Advertising Age* (December 16, 2002), p. 12.

[98]Vibah Gaba, Yigang Pan, and Gerardo R. Ungson, "Timing of Entry in International Markets: An Empirical Study of U.S. Fortune 500 Firms in China," *Journal of International Business Studies*, 33 (First Quarter 2002), pp. 39–55.

- The broader the scope of products and services;
- When competitors had already entered the market;
- The more favorable the risk (political, business) conditions; and
- When non-equity modes of entry (e.g., licensing, exporting, non-equity alliances) are chosen.

In general, companies that entered China relatively late often had an advantage over earlier entrants. A main reason is that latecomers face fewer restrictive business regulations than their predecessors. Companies now have much more flexible ways of setting up their joint ventures. In many industries, companies are now free to set up a wholly owned subsidiary instead of partnering with a Chinese company.[99] Still, some early entrants such as Yum! (the owner of KFC and Pizza Hut restaurants) and Procter & Gamble have been able to leave their competitors in the dust.

A second study looked at the entry-timing pattern for a sample of nineteen multi-national firms.[100] This study develops the concept of **near-market knowledge**. Near-market knowledge is defined as the knowledge (cultural, economic) generated in similar markets in which the MNC already operates. The study's key findings are fourfold, namely:

- Near-market knowledge has an important impact on foreign market entry timing. Near-market knowledge accumulated from successful foreign entries will lead to earlier entry in similar markets.
- Cultural similarity with the home market is not related to foreign market entry timing. Although cultural similarity with the domestic market may matter for initial foreign entry forays, it turns out not to be critical for later entries.
- Several economic attractiveness variables matter a great deal. Specifically, countries with wealthier consumers, larger economies, more developed infrastructure, and more easily accessible consumers are likely to be entered earlier.
- Economic factors are more crucial than cultural factors in entry timing decisions.

## EXIT STRATEGIES

◆ ◆ ◆ ◆ ◆ ◆ ◆

So far we have concentrated on international entry strategies. In this section we will concentrate on their flipside: exit (or divestment) strategies. Exits in global marketing are not uncommon. In 2001, Colgate-Palmolive sold its laundry detergent brands in Mexico to Henkel, its German competitor. Gateway radically overhauled its strategy in 2001 when it decided to discontinue its company-owned operations outside North America.[101] The personal computer maker closed down its manufacturing operations in Ireland and Malaysia. In 2006 Wal-Mart retreated twice in a row: the American mega-retailer first sold its stores in South Korea (see **Global Perspective 9-5**) and then, barely two months later, it also sold its German stores to Metro.[102] Similarly, Nokia, the world's largest mobile phone maker, decided to stop making phones for the Japanese market in 2008.

Decisions to exit or divest a foreign market are not taken lightly. Companies may have multiple good reasons to pull out of their foreign markets:

**Reasons for Exit**

- *Sustained losses.* Key markets are often entered with a long-term perspective. Most companies recognize that an immediate payback of their investments is not realistic and are willing to absorb losses for many years. Still, at some point, most companies have a limit to how long a period of losses they are willing to tolerate.

---

[99]"In China, It May Pay to Be Late," *Asian Wall Street Journal*, February 9, 2004, pp. A1, A6.

[100]Debanjan Mitra and Peter N. Golder, "Whose Culture Matters? Near-Market Knowledge and Its Impact on Foreign Market Entry Timing," *Journal of Marketing Research*, 39 (August 2002), pp. 350–65.

[101]http://www.gateway.com/about/news/2001report/01_annual_report.pdf.

[102]"Wal-Mart Gives Up Germany," July 29, 2006, http://www.iht.com/articles/2006/07/28/business/walmart.php.

❖ ❖ ❖ ❖ ❖ ❖ ❖ ❖ ❖ ❖ ❖ ❖ ❖ ❖ ❖ ❖ ❖ ❖ ❖ ❖ ❖ ❖ ❖ ❖ ❖ ❖ ❖ ❖ ❖ ❖ ❖ ❖ ❖ ❖

## $\mathcal{G}$LOBAL PERSPECTIVE 9-5

### WAL-MART LEAVES SOUTH KOREA

In May 2006, Wal-Mart announced that it had agreed to sell all sixteen of its South Korean stores to its biggest competitor there, Shinsegae. Wal-Mart is not the only outsider that fared poorly in South Korea. The French retailer Carrefour, the second-largest retailer worldwide after Wal-Mart, sold its 32 South Korean stores a month earlier. Wal-Mart arrived in Korea in 1998 by taking a majority stake in four supermarkets and six plots of land. It left Korea after grabbing a 3.8 percent market share and two years of huge losses. Wal-Mart had aimed to become one of Korea's three largest discount retailers.

Wal-Mart and Carrefour faced an uphill climb against local retailers. Both Wal-Mart and Carrefour were slow in broadening the scope of their operations. With a network of only sixteen stores (and just one in Seoul, Korea's capital), Wal-Mart failed to build up market share. Shinsegae, the discount store leader in Korea, adds on average 10 stores each year to its E-Mart chain. That network gives Shinsegae bargaining power with suppliers. Wal-Mart also fell short on the product mix by

*Sources:* "Lost in Cultural Translation," *International Herald Tribune,* May 26, 2006, p. 23; "Wal-Mart Exits Conglomerate-dominated Korea," *The Wall Street Journal,* May 23, 2006, p. 3; and "Wal-Mart Selling Stores and Leaving South Korea," http://www.nytimes.com, accessed on September 12, 2008.

misreading the tastes of local consumers. The frozen imported food it sold in bulk had limited appeal to local shoppers who prefer fresh products sold in smaller bundles. Shoppers also resented the subdued lighting and the height of the shelves. Koreans also prefer service over price. Another barrier was South Korea's chaebol system of interrelated companies that benefits local retailers who form part of the system. Such conglomerate connections help local retailers with costs and real estate.

In contrast to Wal-Mart and Carrefour, the British retailer Tesco is a remarkable case of succeeding in localizing. Tesco teamed up with Samsung Group to open its first store in 2000. Tesco holds an 89 percent stake in the partnership and pays royalties to use its partner's name—Samsung Tesco Home Plus. The latter was a clever move, as Koreans trust the Samsung name. Tesco also relied heavily on local managers and hired a Korean chief executive, which both Wal-Mart and Carrefour failed to do. Tesco planned to double its Korean network to 102 outlets by 2009. Martin Roll, an expert on Asian branding, notes that: "Asian consumers are showing a form of modernity and sophistication that would challenge even the most experienced brands. The retailers with local-market knowledge and distribution network will ultimately emerge as the winners."

---

- *Difficulty in cracking the market.* A company may also decide to pull the plug when it has difficulty to crack the market in the host country. This was the main reason why Nokia decided to stop making and selling mobile phones for the Japanese market in 2008. The Finnish mobile phone maker never had any luck into cracking open Japan's mobile phone market since entering the country in 2003. As a senior Nokia executive stated: "In the current global economic climate, we have concluded that the continuation of our investment in Japan-specific, localized products is no longer sustainable."[103] However, Nokia would still continue selling its luxury Vertu brand in Japan.

- *Volatility.* Companies often underestimate the risks of the host country's economic and political environment. Many multinationals have rushed into emerging markets lured by tempting prospects of huge populations with rising incomes. Unfortunately, countries with high growth potential often are very volatile. However, it is easy to ignore or downplay the risks associated with entering such markets, such as those stemming from exchange rate volatility, weak rule of law, political instability, economic risks, and inflation. Numerous multinational companies pulled out of Argentina and Indonesia in the wake of these countries' economic turmoil. As the then CEO of a major multinational wisecracked during an analyst meeting: "I wish we could just close Argentina."[104]

---

[103]http://news.zdnet.co.uk/hardware/0,1000000091,39564647,00.htm.
[104]"Submerged," *Advertising Age* (March 4, 2002), p. 14.

- *Premature entry.* As we discussed earlier, the entry-timing decision is a crucial matter. Entering a market too early can be an expensive mistake. Entries can be premature for reasons such as an underdeveloped marketing infrastructure (e.g., in terms of distribution, supplies), low buying power, and lack of strong local partners. Often exiting a market is the only sensible solution instead of hanging on.

- *Ethical reasons.* Companies that operate in countries such as Myanmar or Cuba with a questionable human rights record often get a lot of flak in other markets. The bad publicity engendered by human rights campaigners can tarnish the company's image. Rather than running the risk of ruining its reputation, the company may decide to pull out of the country. Heineken, for instance, decided to pull out of Myanmar in 1996 under pressure from a boycott of its products triggered by human rights activists.[105]

- *Intense competition.* Intense rivalry is often another strong reason for exiting a country. Markets that look appealing on paper usually attract lots of competitors. The outcome is often overcapacity, triggering price wars, and loss-loss situations for all players competing against one another. Rather than sustaining losses, the sensible thing to do is to exit the market, especially when rival players have competitive advantages that are difficult to overcome.

- *Resource reallocation.* A key element of marketing strategy formulation is resource allocation. A strategic review of foreign operations often leads to a shake-up of the company's country portfolio, spurring the MNC to reallocate its resources across markets. Of all emerging markets, only China has outgrown the United States in annual economic growth rate over the last three decades. This explains why several European companies such as Unilever, Nestlé, and Reckitt-Benckiser have shifted their focus to North America.[106] Poor results from global operations are often a symptom of overexpansion. For instance, following a review of the results of its global operations in 2002, McDonald's stated that it would concentrate on sales growth in existing restaurants. As a result, the fast-food giant announced that it would (1) close operations in three countries, (2) restructure its business in four other countries, and (3) close down 175 restaurants in about ten other countries.[107] More recently, in July 2008 Starbucks decided to close 61 Australian outlets (out of a total of 85)[108] as part of a global overhaul.[109]

**Risks of Exit**

Obviously, exiting a market is a decision that should be taken carefully. Just as there are barriers to entry, there are exit barriers that may delay or complicate an exit decision. Obstacles that compound divestment decisions include:

- *Fixed costs of exit.* Exiting a country often involves substantial fixed costs. In Europe, several countries have very strict labor laws that make exit very costly (e.g., severance payment packages). It is not uncommon for European governments to cry foul and sue a multinational company when the firm decides to shut down its operations. Long-term contracts that involve commitments such as sourcing raw materials or distributing products often involve major termination penalties.

- *Damage to corporate image.* A negative spillover of a divestment decision could also include damage to the firm's corporate image if plant closures lead to job losses. Nokia's decision to close down its manufacturing operations in Germany and shift them to more cost-friendly sites in Eastern Europe led to calls for a boycott of the firm's phones in Germany. Kurt Beck, the head at the time of the Social Democrats

---

[105]"Heineken Quits its Burmese Venture," http://query.nytimes.com/gst/fullpage.html?res=9C06E4D81139F932 A25754C0A960958260.

[106]"Western Aggression," *Advertising Age* (March 4, 2002), p. 14.

[107]http://www.mcdonalds.com/corporate/press/financial/2002/11082002/index.html.

[108]"Starbucks to Close 61 Australian Outlets," http://business.theage.com.au/business/starbucks-to-close-61-australian-outlets-20080729-3mkm.html.

[109]The company also announced the closure of 600 U.S. stores.

(SPD) told a local newspaper that "As far as I am concerned there will be no Nokia mobile phone in my house."[110]

- *Disposition of assets.* Assets that are highly specialized to the particular business or location for which they are being used also create an exit barrier.[111] The number of prospective buyers may be few and the price they are willing to pay for these assets will most likely be minimal. Hence, the liquidation value of such assets will be low. Sometimes, assets can be sold in markets where the industry is at an earlier stage in the product life cycle.

- *Signal to other markets.* Another concern is that exiting one country or region may send strong negative signals to other countries where the company operates. Exits may lead to job losses in the host country; customers risk losing after-sales service support; distributors stand to lose company support and might witness a significant drop in their business. Therefore, an exit in one country could create negative spillovers in other markets by raising red flags about the company's commitment to its foreign markets.

- *Long-term opportunities.* Although exit is sometimes the only sensible thing to do, firms should avoid shortsightedness. Volatility is a way of life in many emerging markets. Four years after the ruble devaluation in August 1998, the Russian economy made a spectacular recovery. The country became one of the fastest growing markets worldwide for many multinationals, including Procter & Gamble, L'Oréal, and Ikea.[112] Rather than closing shop, it is often better to pay a price in the short term and maintain a presence for the long haul. Exiting a country and re-entering it once the dust settles, comes at a price. Rival companies that stayed in the country will have an edge. Distributors and other prospective partners will be reluctant to enter into agreements. Consumers will be leery about buying the firm's products or services, especially when long-term relationships are involved.

## Guidelines

Growing through international expansion is not the right formula for all companies. The lure of emerging markets such as the BRIC countries[113] has titillated many marketing managers. Unfortunately, reality does not always live up to hype. Still, companies should handle exit decisions carefully. Here are a few guidelines that managers should ponder before making an exit decision:

- *Contemplate and assess all options to salvage the foreign business.* Exiting is painful— both for the company and other stakeholders (local employees, distributors, customers). Before making any moves, it is crucial to analyze why results are below expectations and to consider possible alternatives that might save the business. Original targets in terms of market share, return on investment, or payback period may have been too ambitious. Costs could be squeezed by, for instance, sourcing locally rather than importing materials or using local staff instead of expatriates. Repositioning or retargeting the business can offer a solution. NutraSweet's foray into China provides a good example. When NutraSweet's consumer division first entered the China market, it targeted the mass market. Sales were far below expectations. Instead of simply exiting the China market, which was one of the options being contemplated, NutraSweet decided to lower its sales targets, pursue the diabetics niche market, and position its brand as a medical product.

- *Incremental exit.* Short of a full exit, an intermediate option is an incremental exit strategy. Firms could "mothball" their operations and restart them when demand or

---

[110]"Germany Threatens Nokia Boycott," http://www.france24.com/france24Public/en/archives/news/business/20080122-Nokia-strike-boycott-germany-backlash-finnish-mobile-company.php.

[111]Michael E. Porter, *Competitive Strategy. Techniques for Analyzing Industries and Competitors*, New York: The Free Press, 1980.

[112]"To Russia With Love," *Business Week (Asian Edition)* (September 16, 2002), pp. 26–27.

[113]Brazil, Russia, India, and China.

cost conditions improve.[114] McDonald's restructured its presence in four countries by transferring ownership to licensees. Dial Corp. revamped its operations in Mexico by licensing its brands instead of selling them directly.

- *Migrate customers.* If exiting proves to be the optimal decision, one delicate matter is how to handle customers who depend on the company for after-sales service support and parts. Obviously, it is important that customers not be "orphaned." One solution is to migrate them to third parties. Gateway, for example, entered into contracts with third-party service providers to offer customer service support to its customers in the affected markets.

---

[114]David Besanko, David Dranove, and Mark Shanley, *Economics of Strategy* (New York: John Wiley & Sons, 2000), p. 338.

## SUMMARY ◆ ◆ ◆ ◆ ◆ ◆ ◆ ◆ ◆ ◆ ◆ ◆ ◆ ◆ ◆ ◆ ◆ ◆ ◆ ◆ ◆ ◆ ◆ ◆ ◆ ◆ ◆

Companies have a wide variety of entry strategy choices to implement their global expansion efforts. Each alternative has its pros and cons (see **Exhibit 9-11**). There is no shoe that one-size-fits-all solution. Many firms use a hodgepodge of entry modes. Starbucks, for instance, uses a combination of company-owned stores, licensing, and joint ventures.

Within the same industry, rivals often adopt different approaches to enter new markets. Cummins Engines, a leading U.S.-based diesel engine maker, uses a strategy based on joint ventures with outside groups—mostly customers but also competitors like Komatsu. Caterpillar, on the other hand, prefers to have total control over its new ventures, using acquisitions as a

**EXHIBIT 9-11**
ADVANTAGES AND DISADVANTAGES OF DIFFERENT MODES OF ENTRY

| Entry Mode | Advantages | Disadvantages |
|---|---|---|
| Indirect exporting | • Low commitment (in terms of resources)<br>• Low risk | • Lack of control<br>• Lack of contact with foreign market<br>• No learning experience<br>• Potential opportunity cost |
| Direct exporting | • More control (compared to indirect exporting)<br>• More sales push | • Need to build up export organization<br>• More demanding on resources |
| Licensing | • Little or no investment<br>• Rapid way to gain entry<br>• Means to bridge import barriers<br>• Low risk | • Lack of control<br>• Potential opportunity cost<br>• Need for quality control<br>• Risk of creating competitor<br>• Limits market development |
| Franchising | • Little or no investment<br>• Rapid way to gain entry<br>• Managerial motivation | • Need for quality control<br>• Lack of control<br>• Risk of creating competitor |
| Contract manufacturing | • Little or no investment<br>• Overcome import barriers<br>• Cost savings | • Need for quality control<br>• Risk of bad press (e.g., child labor)<br>• Diversion to gray and/or black markets |
| Joint venture | • Risk sharing<br>• Less demanding on resources (compared to wholly-owned)<br>• Potential of synergies (e.g., access to local distribution network) | • Risk of conflicts with partner(s)<br>• Lack of control<br>• Risk of creating competitor |
| Acquisition | • Full control<br>• Access to local assets (e.g., plants, distribution network, brand assets)<br>• Less competition | • Costly<br>• High risk<br>• Need to integrate differing national/corporate cultures<br>• Cultural clashes |
| Greenfield | • Full control<br>• Latest technologies<br>• No risk of cultural conflicts | • Costly<br>• Time consuming<br>• High political & financial risks |

route to expand overseas.[115] In the car industry, Ford likes to expand through acquisitions; General Motors prefers to rely on strategic alliances. Rick Wagoner, GM's chief executive, rationalizes the alliance strategy as follows: "Our alliance approach allows us to realize synergies faster than we could in a full buy-out situation. Alliances help us to grow in markets where we are underrepresented."[116] A company's expansion strategies can also vary across regions. Computer software company CA's expansion strategy in the United States was to buy up software companies and then integrate their software products with the rest of the firm. In Asia, the software maker has taken a different route. Instead, the firm expanded by forming joint ventures with local players.[117] In China, for instance, CA established six joint ventures, all with industry leaders. A key motivation was that the local government prefers partnerships for the software industry. CA claimed that it is in a much better position to compete with foreign and domestic vendors than if it had followed Microsoft's or Oracle's in-house approaches.[118]

Companies often adopt a phased entry strategy: they start off with a minimal-risk strategy; once the perceived risk declines they switch to a higher commitment mode, such as a wholly owned venture. Caterpillar, Inc., the U.S.-based manufacturer of earth-moving and construction equipment, entered the former Soviet bloc in 1992 via direct exporting to minimize its financial risk exposure. After sales took off,

Caterpillar upped the ante by establishing joint ventures with Russian and U.S. firms.[119]

As this chapter discussed, a broad range of variables impact the entry mode choice. The three major dimensions include the resource commitment the firm is willing to make, the amount of risk (political and market) the firm is willing to take, and the degree of control that is desirable.

To compete more effectively in the global arena, more and more companies use cross-border strategic alliances to build up their muscle. Depending on the strategic role and the competitive position of the business unit involved, the goal of the alliance could be to defend, strengthen, sustain, or restructure the strategic business unit (SBU). The benefits that the partners can derive from the synergies of the alliance often downplay the concerns the parent companies might have about the partnership. Still, the formation of the alliance should always be preceded by a meticulous analysis of questions like:[120]

- What are the mutual benefits for each partner?
- What learning can take place between firms?
- How can the parties complement each other to create joint capabilities?
- Are the partners equal in strength or is this the case of the "one-eyed guiding the blind"?

Satisfactory answers to these questions improve the chances of the cross-border alliance becoming a win-win situation for all partners involved.

---

[115]"Engine Makers Take Different Routes," *The Financial Times* (July 14, 1998), p. 11.
[116]"Carmakers Take Two Routes to Global Growth," *The Financial Times* (July 11, 2000), p. 29.
[117]"Integrating Into Asia," *Far Eastern Economic Review* (March 16, 2000), pp. 55–56.
[118]"Speak Nicely and Carry a Big Check," *Business China* (January 29, 2001), p. 12.

[119]Avraham Shama, "Entry Strategies of U.S. Firms to the Newly Independent States, Baltic States, and Eastern European Countries," *California Management Review*, vol. 37, no. 3, Spring 1995, pp. 90–109.
[120]Peter Lorange, Johan Roos and Peggy S. Bronn (1992), "Building successful strategic alliances," pp. 12–13.

## KEY TERMS ◆ ◆ ◆ ◆ ◆ ◆ ◆ ◆ ◆ ◆ ◆ ◆ ◆ ◆ ◆ ◆ ◆ ◆ ◆ ◆ ◆ ◆ ◆ ◆ ◆ ◆ ◆

| | | | |
|---|---|---|---|
| Acquisition and merger | Equity joint venture | Greenfield operation | Resource-based view (RBV) |
| Contract manufacturing | Export agent | Licensing | Strategic alliance |
| Cooperative exporting | Export management | Master franchising | Synergy |
| Cooperative joint venture | company (EMC) | Near-market knowledge | Transaction-cost economics |
| Cross-licensing | Export merchant | Outsourcing | (TCE) |
| Direct (indirect) exporting | Franchising | Piggyback exporting | |

## REVIEW QUESTIONS ◆ ◆ ◆ ◆ ◆ ◆ ◆ ◆ ◆ ◆ ◆ ◆ ◆ ◆ ◆ ◆ ◆ ◆ ◆ ◆ ◆ ◆ ◆

1. Why do some MNCs prefer to enter certain markets with a liaison office first?
2. What are the possible drawbacks of 50-50 joint ventures?
3. Draw up a list of the respective pros and cons of licensing.

4. What are the respective advantages and disadvantages of greenfield operations over acquisitions?
5. What mechanisms can firms use to protect themselves against ill-fated partnerships?

## DISCUSSION QUESTIONS ◆ ◆ ◆ ◆ ◆ ◆ ◆ ◆ ◆ ◆ ◆ ◆ ◆ ◆ ◆ ◆ ◆ ◆ ◆ ◆

1. NTT DoCoMo, which dominates Japan's mobile phone market, follows a somewhat unusual international expansion strategy. Its strategy is to take minority stakes rather than full control in a foreign mobile operator. The reason is that it prefers to acquire stakes up to a level that allows it to participate in management but respect the local company's

autonomy. DoCoMo claims that it can provide valuable technology expertise in mobile multimedia and 3G to its partners. Assess DoCoMo's expansion strategy.

2. Companies tend to begin their internationalization process in countries that are culturally very close. For instance, U.S-based companies would enter Canada and/or the United Kingdom first, before moving on to other countries. The so-called psychic distance between the United States and Canada (or Britain) is small given that these countries are supposedly very similar. A recent survey, however, found that only 22 percent of Canadian retailers felt that they were operating successfully in the United States. Explain why culturally close countries are not necessarily easy to manage.

3. Assignment. Check some recent issues of the *Wall Street Journal* and/or the *Financial Times*. Look for articles on cross-border strategic alliances. Pick one or two examples and find out more about the alliances you chose via a search on the Internet. Why were the alliances formed? What do the partners contribute to the alliance? What benefits do they anticipate? What concerns/issues were raised?

4. Helmut Maucher, former chairman of Nestlé was quoted saying: "I don't share the euphoria for alliances and joint ventures. First, very often they're an excuse, and an easy way out when people should do their own homework. Secondly, all joint ventures create additional difficulties—you share power and cultures, and decisions take longer." Comment.

5. **Exhibit 9-12** shows the timeline of Starbucks' global expansion. Discuss Starbuck's entry decisions. Do you see any patterns in its expansion strategy? Did the company over-expand in recent years especially given the turmoil the company experienced in 2008?

6. Ben Verwaayen, former chief executive of British Telecom (BT), was named as the new CEO of Alcatel-Lucent, the US/French telecommunications equipment group in September 2008. The merger that was completed in December 2006 was supposed to make the transatlantic group a world leader capable to compete with the likes of Nokia and Ericsson. Instead, the group has gone through a rocky marriage: the group reported a €1,102 million loss for the 2$^{nd}$ quarter of 2008 or €0.49 per share. A major reason for the wobbly merger has been the cultural differences between the French and American arms. The new CEO is an anglophile Dutchman who speaks fluent French. During his leadership at BT he built up a reputation as a turnaround artist. Can the new CEO end the culture clash at Alcatel-Lucent? What actions can incoming executives take to resolve internal strife in a global business? Is improved performance the best cure for cross-border chasms? Or should a new management team address cultural issues head-on?

**EXHIBIT 9-12**

TIMELINE INTERNATIONAL EXPANSION OF STARBUCKS COFFEE

| Year | Location |
|------|----------|
| 1971 | First location in Seattle |
| 1987 | Canada (Vancouver, British Columbia) |
| 1996 | Hawaii |
|      | Japan |
|      | Singapore |
| 1997 | Philippines |
| 1998 | Malaysia |
|      | New Zealand |
|      | Taiwan |
|      | Thailand |
| 1999 | China (Beijing) |
|      | Kuwait |
|      | Lebanon |
|      | South Korea |
| 2000 | Australia |
|      | Bahrain |
|      | China (Shanghai) |
|      | Dubai |
|      | Hong Kong |
|      | Qatar |
|      | Saudi Arabia |
| 2001 | Austria |
|      | Switzerland |
| 2002 | China (Shenzhen and Macau) |
|      | Germany |
|      | Greece |
|      | Indonesia |
|      | Mexico |
|      | Oman |
|      | Puerto Rico |
|      | Spain |
| 2003 | Chile |
|      | Cyprus |
|      | Peru |
|      | Turkey |
| 2004 | France |

*Source:* www.starbucks.com.

## SHORT CASES

ASE 9-1

### BENQ'S DEAL OF THE CENTURY?

Like other Taiwanese firm, BenQ has tried to escape the anonymity of contract manufacturing by promoting brands. The company's core products include flat-screen TV sets, notebooks, PC monitors, MP3 players, mobile phones, and other consumer electronics gadgets. Spun off from Acer in 2001, it took the name BenQ ("bringing enjoyment and quality to life"). The US$ 5.5 billion company wants to do more than churn out hardware with someone else's name on it. At present, 37 percent of BenQ's sales carry the BenQ brand name.

On June 7, 2005, BenQ, the Taiwanese consumer-electronics maker, suddenly became the world's fourth largest cellular-phone maker by acquiring the ailing handset division of Siemens AG, the German conglomerate. It looked like the bargain of the century. BenQ was getting the mobile handset business of Siemens for nothing—and the German company was even eating $430 million in costs surrounding the transaction. One Taipei-based brokerage analyst commented: "It's a deal too good to be true for BenQ. They get the whole business and a decent brand for free." BenQ would acquire the rights to the Siemens trademark for 18 months, and co-branding rights for five years. BenQ would also gain access to Siemens' intellectual property, including its CSM, GPRS and 3G patents. Further, Siemens agreed to buy 50 million euros of BenQ stock.

As a result of the deal, mobile phones would now become one of BenQ's core businesses. Armed with a renowned brand name, new technology, and access to Siemens' customer base in Europe and Latin America, BenQ aspired to become a major player in the mobile phone market. Martin Roll, the author of *Asian Brand Strategy*, commented, "Siemens brand equity will give BenQ a major push in its stride to gain credibility in the European and U.S. markets." Lee Kun-yao, BenQ's chairman, explained the reasoning behind the deal as follows: "In BenQ we come more from the enjoyment side and consumer side of technology . . . Siemens has a very strong heritage in German technologies."

Some skeptics raised major concerns, however. After grabbing the no. 4 slot and 9 percent market share in global handset sales in 2002, the Siemens unit slipped to no. 5 in 2005 with a share of just 5.5 percent. Siemens has provided no guarantees to BenQ about the profitability of the handset business. Market leaders Nokia, Motorola, and Samsung, which currently command 60 percent of the worldwide handset market, have been steadily pulling away from their smaller competitors. It is unclear how BenQ plans to turn the Siemens business unit

*Sources:* "BenQ May Be Getting What It Paid For," *Business Week*, June 20, 2005; "BenQ Must Capitalize on 'Fleeting Platform'," *Media*, July 29, 2005; "BenQ's Combined Brand in Handset Drive," *Financial Times*, January 18, 2006, p. 18; www.benq.com

around. In 2004, it incurred losses of $615 million on sales of $5.8 billion according to Merrill Lynch estimates. Siemens' efforts to squeeze costs were hampered by German trade unions, which had resisted relocations to lower-cost sites.

BenQ could use a lift. Vincent Chen, an analyst with CLSA Taipei, said that "Feedback on BenQ's products hasn't been great, and they've been late getting products to market." Kent Chan, an analyst with Citigroup Hong Kong, observed that: "The risk is that Siemens could wipe out BenQ profits in 2006." BenQ has little brand name recognition in Europe and in the United States. Its handset business was hit hard by a tumble in orders from Motorola, its biggest customers, after BenQ introduced its own brand name. BenQ has tried to make up for some of the Motorola loss with orders from the likes of Nokia and Kyocera, but its handset business is still smarting. BenQ's Q1 '05 profits tumbled by 90 percent to $9.7 million as its revenues fell 23 percent to $1 billion, compared with a year earlier.

The Siemens deal might solve some of its problems. BenQ planned to start using the Siemens name, then gradually introduce co-branded phones to build up the BenQ name in Europe and in the United States. The deal would also help BenQ gain access in new markets such as Latin America. Moreover, BenQ would inherit factories in Brazil and Germany and research facilities that have been working on next-generation products. "This kind of intellectual property is crucial to our success," noted BenQ president Sheaffer Lee.

BenQ and Siemens' combined market share dropped from 13.5 percent in the fourth quarter of 2004 to 9.8 percent in the third quarter of 2005. To reverse the fall, BenQ planned to focus on making handsets for 3G networks. It also sought to differentiate itself by using organic LED displays. Such displays are much brighter than standard LED screens, but wear out faster.

Still, BenQ's challenges seem tremendous. Professor Jagdish Sheth, co-author of "*The Rule of Three*," said that further consolidation of marginal players would be required for BenQ to succeed. BenQ will also inherit the labor troubles that plagued Siemens, taking over 3,700 workers in high-cost Germany. BenQ must honor labor contracts through 2006. For BenQ, making this the deal of the century will be a huge task.

### DISCUSSION QUESTIONS

1. How do you evaluate BenQ's acquisition deal of the Siemens handset unit? Is it indeed "too good to be true"? What are the pros and cons?

2. Where is BenQ vulnerable?

3. What strategic marketing recommendations would you make to BenQ's going forward?

## $\mathcal{C}$ASE 9-2

### CAN MCDONALD'S DE-THRONE THE COLONEL IN CHINA?

McDonald's opened its first restaurant in China in Shenzhen in 1990. McDonald's expansion since then has been rapid: it had 750 outlets by the end of 2005 and planned to have 1,000 restaurants by the time of the Beijing Summer Olympics in 2008, for which McDonald's is a sponsor. Contrary to KFC, which is opening outlets in second and third tier cities, McDonald's prefers to grow within the large cities. Tim Fenton, McDonald's executive in charge of Asian operation, says: "When you start to get out of the bigger cities you start to fragment your transportation infrastructure."

However, although McDonald's may be the undisputed fast food brand in the Western world, it is far behind Yum! Brands in China. Yum! Brands operates Pizza Hut (180 restaurants) and, most importantly, KFC. KFC has over 1,500 outlets in China and a broader geographic coverage than the Golden Arches. Yum! may have had a first-mover advantage: it was the first fast-food restaurant chain to enter China in 1987 (Pizza Hut was introduced in 1990). The fact that most Chinese consumers prefer chicken to beef also helped Yum! to build up a successful business in China. KFC has also a much more localized menu than McDonald's featuring items such as a "Dragon Twister," egg tarts, and congee. David Novak, Yum! Brands chief executive, predicts that KFC's China business is on track to become as big as McDonald's in the USA.

Still, McDonald's is not willing to cede China to the Colonel. One way that McDonald's is trying to narrow the gap is by adding drive-through restaurants. KFC was the first western fast-food chain to open a drive-through in China in 2002. McDonald's opened its first one in November 2005. The three it had by early 2006 were outperforming average volume of existing restaurants by 50–80 percent. The chain plans to open 12 to 15 drivethroughs every year for the coming three years. The company hopes to benefit from the rapid growth of car ownership.

McDonald's will also introduce menu changes. The company believes that there are three basic customer tiers: value-conscious diners; less price-sensitive diners loyal to the core menu items of Big Macs and fries; upper-level consumers who are willing to buy premium items. In China, McDonald's launched nine products priced at 60 US cents or less. It will also launch a rice burger, first introduced in Taiwan, targeted at higher spending consumers.

Clearly, McDonald's remains a brand to watch in China, in spite of the strides made by Colonel Sanders' KFC army. Fears triggered by bird flu might convince Chinese consumers to enjoy a Big Mac or rice burger instead of the Colonel's fried chicken. Nutritional concerns that have cast a shadow in developed markets are less of an issue in China. As Tim Fenton pointed out: China is obviously the biggest opportunity that we have going right now."

**DISCUSSION QUESTIONS**

**1.** Do you agree with the steps McDonald's plans to take to expand its business in China (adding drivethroughs, focus on big cities, localize menu)?

**2.** What other remedies would you prescribe if you were in Tim Fenton's shoes?

*Sources:* "Can McDonald's Steal Yum's China Crown?" *Media* (January 13, 2006): 15; and "McDonald's Drive Towards Big City Sales," *Financial Times* (February 22, 2006): 12.

## $\mathcal{C}$ASE 9-3

### FONTERRA ENGULFED IN CHINA'S TAINTED MILK CRISIS

Fonterra is a New Zealand dairy cooperative that is owned by 11,000 farmers. Its core business consists of exporting New Zealand dairy products across the globe. The cooperative accounts for more than a third of international dairy trade. With annual sales revenues of NZ$13.9 billion (around US$8.8 billion), Fonterra is the word's sixth largest dairy producer with

*Sources:* www.fonterra.com, accessed on October 10, 2008; "NZ Dairy raps China over secrecy; one brand is recalled in a first for the U.S. over the milk scandal," *The Wall Street Journal Asia*, Sept. 29, 2008: p. 2; http://www.economist.com/world/asia/displaystory.cfm?story_id= 12262271; http://en.wikipedia.org/wiki/Sanlu_Group, accessed on October 10, 2008; "Unknown risks of globalized food," *International Herald* Tribune, October 13, 2008: pp. 1, 6; and http://www.abc.net.au/news/stories/2008/09/24/2373501.htm.

brands such as Anchor and Anlene in its portfolio. As part of its mission to become a global business, Fonterra has established manufacturing sites and joint ventures in numerous countries.

In 2005 Fonterra paid $107 million to establish a 43 percent joint venture equity stake in Sanlu [literally *three deer*], a state-owned dairy food company based in Shijiazhuang, the capital city of Hebei province. Sanlu's milk powder brand had been China's leading brand in the category for many years. The group's 2007 turnover was ¥10 billion (around US$1.4 billion). Sanlu prided itself in its stringent quality control measures boasting that over 1,000 different tests were carried out before its products leave the factory. Posters at Sanlu's headquarters in Shijiazhuang proclaimed, "Quality and safety are the foundations of social harmony." The Sanlu Fonterra joint venture also gained much publicity in May 2008 when it donated $1.25 million worth of baby milk formula to infants orphaned or displaced by a devastating earthquake in Sichuan province.

In mid-July 2008 the government of Gansu province in Western China informed China's Ministry of Health about an unusual string of illnesses among infants caused by kidney stones. The infants had all consumed the same brand of Sanlu baby milk formula. Later investigations would point the finger to middlemen who collected milk from the farmers. Several of these middlemen had cheated by diluting their milk with water. To fool instruments used to measure protein content, melamine was added to the milk. Melamine, a white powder used to make plastics, was also the root cause behind the pet food poisoning that occurred a year earlier. The Chinese central government had boasted that it had reacted rapidly to the baby milk poisoning scandal. The chronology of events, however, suggested otherwise.

Sanlu's board told was informed about the melamine contamination at a board meeting on August 2nd though Beijing authorities claimed that Sanlu knew of reports of children becoming sick after drinking Sanlu formula as early as March. The following day Fonterra's China directors met with the local health officials in Shijiazhuang, Sanlu's hometown, and demanded a public recall. Instead, these officials advocated a "quiet" recall without any public disclosure. They cited the need for social stability. Some speculate that government officials were worried that the upcoming Beijing Olympics might be marred by a food scare. Fonterra accepted the compromise. Mr. Ferrier, Fonterra's CEO, said that the other option was to go public outside China to put pressure on the Chinese government. However, the company feared it would "lose control of the whole thing. At least we were effective in recalling the product." Sanlu withdrew over 10,000 tons of tainted milk powder from local stores. Still Fonterra felt that it was misled by local health officials who the company thought would have informed the central government. As the weeks passed the scandal was still kept under wraps. Finally, on September 5 Fonterra approached New Zealand's prime minister, Helen Clark, to prod the Beijing government to cope with the problem more urgently. Helen Clark alerted the Beijing government on the milk contamination by Fonterra. A few days later, on September 11, Sanlu announced a nationwide recall. Shortly after, the Ministry of Health gave its first press conference on the scandal and declared a national food-safety emergency. Though Sanlu was the focus of the scandal, traces of melamine were also found in many other dairy products produced in China, prompting the European Union and other governments to ban or recall products with Chinese milk ingredients. Eventually, the contamination caused kidney illnesses in 50,000 Chinese infants and led to at least four infant deaths.

The scandal clearly hurt Fonterra's profits and reputation. The company has been criticized by Helen Clark and others for not coming forward earlier. Fonterra executives maintained they had not made any mistakes. A Fonterra spokeswoman pointed out that: "Melamine is not something you would be reasonably expected to find in milk. We have only recently become aware of one dairy company in the world who routinely tests for melamine." Fonterra defended its decision to keep its information under wraps for so long. Andrew Ferrier, the company's chief executive, stated, "If you don't follow the rules of an individual market place then I think you are getting irresponsible." The company claimed that it tried to ensure a recall "as quickly as we could in the environment we were working in." The company was frustrated with the initial lack of public disclosure. Still Mr. Ferrier was concerned by allegations that Sanlu knew there was a problem for eight months: "If something did exist prior to that we're shocked that it did and we obviously feel that if people were aware of it, it should have gone to the [Sanlu] board." Fonterra does not regret investing in China but it acknowledges that the Sanlu brand could have been damaged beyond repair.

### DISCUSSION QUESTIONS

**1.** Fonterra waited 40 days (from August 2 until September 11) before going public with the information that its products in China were contaminated with melamine. Andrew Ferrier, its CEO, defended its response to the crisis and took what it regarded as the best action by working within the Chinese system. Do you agree? Where there any better alternative responses available to the company?

**2.** To what extent will the China milk contamination crisis hurt Fonterra's business?

**3.** What lessons are to be drawn from Fonterra's experience in China?

# FURTHER READING ◆ ◆ ◆ ◆ ◆ ◆ ◆ ◆ ◆ ◆ ◆ ◆ ◆ ◆ ◆ ◆ ◆ ◆ ◆ ◆ ◆ ◆ ◆

Anderson, Erin and Hubert Gatignon, "Modes of foreign entry: A transaction cost analysis and propositions," *Journal of International Business Studies*, vol. 11, Fall 1986, pp. 1–26.

Bamford, James, David Ernst, and David G. Fubini. "Launching a World-Class Joint Venture," *Harvard Business Review* 82 (February 2004): 90–101.

Bleeke, Joel and David Ernst, "The way to win in cross-border alliances," *Harvard Business Review*, Nov.–Dec. 1991, pp. 127–35.

Cavusgil, S. Tamer. "Measuring the Potential of Emerging Markets: An Indexing Approach." *Business Horizons*, 40 (January–February 1997): 87–91.

Devlin, Godfrey and Mark Bleackley, "Strategic alliances—guidelines for success," *Long Range Planning*, vol. 21, no. 5, pp. 18–23.

Gaba, Vibha, Yigang Pan, and Gerardo R. Ungson. "Timing of Entry in International Market: An Empirical Study of U.S. Fortune 500 Firms in China," *Journal of International Business Studies*, 33(1) (First Quarter 2002): 39–55.

Hyder, Akmal S. and Pervez N. Ghauri. "Managing International Joint Venture Relationships," *Industrial Marketing Management*, 29 (2000): 205–18.

Kumar, V., A. Stam and E. A. Joachimsthaler, "An interactive multicriteria approach to identifying potential foreign markets," *Journal of International Marketing*, vol. 2, no.1, 1994, pp. 29–52.

Lorange, Peter, Johan Roos and Peggy S. Brønn, "Building successful strategic alliances," *Long Range Planning*, vol. 25, no.6, pp. 10–17.

Martinsons, M. G. and C.-S. Tseng, "Successful joint ventures in the heart of the dragon," *Long Range Planning*, vol. 28, no. 5, pp. 45–58.

Mitra, Debanjan and Peter N. Golder. "Whose Culture Matters? Near-Market Knowledge and Its Impact on Foreign Market Entry Timing," *Journal of Marketing Research*, 39 (August 2002): 350–65.

Ostland, Gregory E. and S. Tamer Cavusgil, "Performance Issues in U.S.-China Joint Ventures," *California Management Review*, vol. 38, no.2, Winter 1996, pp. 106–30.

Preble, John F. and Richard C. Hoffman, "Franchising systems around the globe: A status report," *Journal of Small Business Management*, April 1995, pp. 80–88.

Root, Franklin R., *Entry Strategies for International Markets*, New York, NY: Lexington Books, 1994.

Shama, Avraham, "Entry Strategies of U.S. Firms to the Newly Independent States, Baltic States, and Eastern European Countries," *California Management Review*, vol. 37, no. 3, Spring 1995, pp. 90–109.

Tihanyi, Laszlo, David A. Griffith, and Craig J. Russell, "The Effect of Cultural Distance on Entry Mode Choice, International Diversification, and MNE Performance: A Meta-Analysis." *Journal of International Business Studies* 36 (2005): 270–83.

Turpin, Dominique, "Strategic alliances with Japanese firms: Myths and realities," *Long Range Planning*, vol. 28, no. 5, pp. 45–58.

Zhao, Hongxin, Yadong Luo, and Taewon Suh. "Transaction Cost Determinants and Ownership-Based Entry Mode Choice: A Meta-Analytical Review." *Journal of International Business Studies* 35 (2004): 524–44.

# APPENDIX ◆ ◆ ◆ ◆ ◆ ◆ ◆ ◆ ◆ ◆ ◆ ◆ ◆ ◆ ◆ ◆ ◆ ◆ ◆ ◆ ◆ ◆ ◆ ◆ ◆

**Alternative Country Screening Procedure.** When the product has already been launched in some regions, the firm might consider using a variant of the country screening procedure described in this chapter. The alternative method leverages the experience the firm gathered in its existing markets. It works as follows: Suppose the MNC currently does business in Europe and is now considering an expansion into Asia.

**Step 1.** *Collect historical data on European market*
Go back to your files and collect the historical data for the European markets on the indicators that you plan to use to assess the market opportunities for the Asian region. Let us refer to these pieces of information as $X_{iec}$, that is, the score of European country ec on indicator i.

**Step 2.** *Evaluate the MNC's post-entry performance in each of its existing European markets*
Assess the MNC's post-entry performance in each European country by assigning a success score (e.g., on a ten-point scale). If performance is measured on just one indicator, say, market-share achieved five years after entry, you could also simply use that indicator as a performance measure. Let us refer to the performance score for country ec as $S_{ec}$.

**Step 3.** *Derive weights for each of the country indicators*
The next step is to come up with importance weights for each of the country indicators. For this, you could run a cross-sectional regression using the European data gathered in the previous two steps. Our dependent variable is the post-entry success score ($S_{ec}$) while the predictor variables are the country indicators ($X_{iec}$):

$$S_{ec} = a + w_1 X_{1ec} + w_2 X_{2ec} + \ldots + w_I X_{Iec}$$
$$ec = 1, 2, \ldots, EC$$

By running a regression of the success scores, $S_{ec}$, on the predictor variables, $X_{iec}$ (i = 1, . . . , I), you can derive estimates for the importance weights of the different indicators.

**Step 4.** *Rate the Asian countries in the pool on each indicator*
Each of the Asian candidate markets in the pool is given a score on each of the indicators that are considered: $X_{iac}$.

**Step 5.** *Predict performance in prospect Asian countries*
Finally, predict the post-entry performance in the prospective Asian markets by using the weights estimated in the previous step and data collected on each of the indicators (the $X_{iac}$'s) for the Asian countries. For instance, the regression estimates might look like:

$$\text{Performance} = -0.7 + 6.0(\text{Market Size}) + 2.9(\text{Growth}) - 1(\text{Competition})$$

By plugging in the ratings (or actual values) for the Asian markets in this equation, you can then predict the MNC's performance in each of these countries.

# GLOBAL PRODUCT POLICY DECISIONS I: DEVELOPING NEW PRODUCTS FOR GLOBAL MARKETS

**10**

## CHAPTER OVERVIEW

1. GLOBAL PRODUCT STRATEGIES
2. STANDARDIZATION VERSUS CUSTOMIZATION
3. MULTINATIONAL DIFFUSION
4. DEVELOPING NEW PRODUCTS FOR GLOBAL MARKETS
5. TRULY GLOBAL PRODUCT DEVELOPMENT

A cornerstone of a global marketing mix program is the set of product policy decisions that multinational companies (MNCs) constantly need to formulate. The range of product policy questions that need to be tackled is bedazzling: What new products should be developed for what markets? What products should be added to, removed from, or modified for the product line in each of the countries in which the company operates? What brand names should be used? How should the product be packaged? serviced? and so forth. Clearly, product managers in charge of the product line of a multinational company have their work cut out for them.

Improper product policy decisions are easily made as the following anecdotes illustrate:

- *Ikea in the United States.*[1] Ikea's foray in the United States was plagued with teething problems. Stores were in poor locations. Ikea stubbornly refused to size its beds and kitchen cabinets to fit American sheets and appliances. Bookshelves were too small to hold a television set. Bath towels were too small and too thin. Customers bought vases to drink from, as glasses were too small. Sofas were too hard. Dining tables were too small to fit a turkey for Thanksgiving. Ikea's system of self-service and self-assembly puzzled Americans. Prices were too high. Ikea remedied the situation by adapting the product line, choosing new and bigger store locations, improving service, slashing prices. Some of the changes that Ikea made in the U.S. have since been introduced in Europe. For instance, U.S.-style softer sofas have become a great hit in Europe.

---

[1] www.brandchannel.com/features_effect.asp?pf_id=256 and www.businessweek.com/magazine/content/05_46/b3959001.htm.

# $\mathcal{G}$LOBAL PERSPECTIVE 10-1

## SELLING SATURNS IN JAPAN

Saturn, a unit of General Motors Corp., has been phenomenally popular in the United States with its refreshing approach to selling cars. The car's popularity in the U.S. market is due to its unique formula of customer-friendly retailing and no-haggle pricing. In light of its success story in the U.S., GM figured that Saturn might also do well in fiercely competitive Japan. The car premiered in Japan in April 1997. Saturn's launch strategy in Japan was to take on the local competition by competing as an everyday car. It installed right-hand drive steering and added features such as folding side mirrors. Saturn also established its own dealer network—a rather unusual move for car imports. Saturn's goal was to sign up twenty exclusive dealers who would only sell Saturns. It took the firm longer than expected to achieve its target. The car was priced at $14,000—competitive with local brands and cheaper than most other imports. Saturn also invested heavily in advertising to build brand recognition. Ads showed scenes of Saturn's headquarters in Tennessee and Japanese salespeople sporting Saturn's casual look.

Despite all the enthusiasm and GM's gung ho attitude, sales have been disappointing so far. In 1998, Saturn sold just 1,400

vehicles. Several factors seemed to be behind this setback. One was bad timing. When Saturn was introduced in Japan, the country was going through a deep economic slump. The launch date happened a few days after the government hiked the sales tax to 5 percent (from 3 percent), a move that weakened the car market overall. Sales of sedans—the only subcategory in which Saturn initially competed—were plunging around the launch time. Some analysts also felt that the Saturn strategy would not appeal to import-car buyers in Japan. The typical foreign-car buyer wants a car that makes him stand out of the crowd. Successful imports from the United States are quintessentially "American" cars like DaimlerChrysler's Jeep Cherokee and GM's Cadillac Seville. Setting up an own dealership network posed some challenges too. The economic recession meant that few potential dealers were willing to take the risk of selling a relatively unknown car model. Those who were interested had a hard time raising the money. With only twenty dealerships, potential customers may also have a hard time locating a dealer outlet.

Sales picked up a bit in 1999 with the launch of a three-door coupe model. In October 1998, Saturn announced that it plans to open eighty new stores over the coming five years. Saturn also set up an Internet showroom (www.saturn.co.jp) to better serve the needs of Internet savvy car-shoppers. However, GM finally pulled the plug after selling only 1,002 Saturn cars in 2001. Still, Saturn appears to have made some impact on the Japanese car market: Toyota adopted Saturn's no-haggle approach toward pricing at some of its dealerships in Japan.

*Sources*: "Saturn Signs 6 Firms to Sell Cars in Japan," *The Asian Wall Street Journal* (July 9, 1996), p. 6; "In Japan, Saturn Finds the Going Has Been Slow," *The Asian Wall Street Journal* (August 26, 1998), p. 1, 7; "Saturn in Japan Slows to Crawl," *Advertising Age International* (January 1998), p. 26; "Despite Problems in Japan, GM's Saturn Not Giving Up," *Dow Jones Business News* (April 14, 1999); "GM's Cruze Gets Lost In Japanese Market," *The Asian Wall Street Journal* (September 16, 2002), pp. A8, A10.

- *Procter & Gamble (P&G) in Australia.* Rather than manufacturing disposable diapers locally in Australia as Kimberly-Clark did, P&G decided to import them. The size of the Australian and New Zealand markets did not warrant local manufacturing according to P&G. Unfortunately, by using packaging designed for the Asian region with non-English labeling, P&G alienated its customers in Australia.[2]

- *U.S. carmakers in Japan.* Historically, U.S. car sales in Japan have been pretty dismal. Analysts have blamed import barriers and the fact that most U.S.-made cars were originally sold with the steering wheel on the left-hand side. There are other factors at play, though. Sales of Chrysler's Neon car during the first year of introduction in Japan were far below target. Japanese car buyers disliked the Neon's round curves; they preferred boxier designs. The sales of Ford's Taurus in Japan were also lackluster. Part of the problem was that, initially, the Taurus did not fit in Japanese parking spaces. In order for a car to be registered in Japan, the police needs to certify that it will fit in the customer's parking lot (see also **Global Perspective 10-1** on Saturn's marketing strategy in Japan).[3]

---

[2]"P&G puts nappies to rest in Australia," *Advertising Age International*, September 19, 1994, I–31.

[3]"Success Continues to Elude U.S. Car Makers in Japan," *The Asian Wall Street Journal*, January 10–11, 1997, pp. 1, 7.

These anecdotes amply show that even seasoned blue-chip companies commit the occasional "blunder" when making product decisions in the global marketplace. Apart from being amusing (at least for outsiders), product blunders can sometimes teach valuable lessons. This chapter focuses on new product development strategies for global markets. The first part of this chapter looks at the product strategic issues that MNCs face. The second part gives an overview of the new product development process in a global setting. Finally, we examine what it means to be a truly global innovator.

## ◆ ◆ ◆ ◆ ◆ ◆ ◆ ◆   GLOBAL PRODUCT STRATEGIES

Companies can pursue three global strategies to penetrate foreign markets.[4] Some firms simply adopt the same product or communication policy used in their home market as an **extension** of their homegrown product/communication strategies to their foreign markets. Other companies prefer to adapt their strategy to the local market-place. This strategy of **adaptation** enables the firm to cater to the needs and wants of its foreign customers. A third alternative is to adopt an **invention** strategy by which products are designed from scratch for the global market place. Using the extension/adaptation/invention framework for product and communications decision leads to five strategic options, as shown in **Exhibit 10-1**. Let us look at each one of these options in greater detail.

**Strategic Option 1: Product and Communication Extension—Dual Extension**

At one extreme, a company might choose to market a standardized product using a uniform communications strategy. Early entrants in the global arena often opt for this approach. Also, small companies with few resources typically prefer this option. For them, the potential payoffs of customized products and/or advertising campaigns usually do not justify the incremental costs of adaptation. Dual extension might also work when the company targets a "global" segment with similar needs. Blistex's marketing efforts for its namesake product in Europe is a typical example. The product, a lip balm, offers identical needs in each of the various European markets. Except for some minor modifications (e.g., labeling), the same product is sold in each country. In 1995, Blistex ran a uniform European advertising campaign, using identical positioning ("Care-to-Cure") and advertising themes across countries.[5]

Generally speaking, a standardized product policy coupled with a uniform communication strategy offers substantial savings coming from economies of scale. This strategy is basically product-driven rather than market-driven. The downside is that it is likely to alienate foreign customers, who might switch to a local or another foreign competing brand that is more in tune with their needs. In many industries, modern

**EXHIBIT 10-1**
GLOBAL EXPANSION STRATEGIES

*Source:* Warren J. Keegan, "Multinational Product Planning: Strategic Alternatives." Reprinted from *Journal of Marketing*, (January 1969), pp. 58–62, published by the American Marketing Association.

| Product Strategy | Function or Need Satisfied | Conditions of Product Use | Ability to Buy Product | Recommended Product Strategy | Recommended Communications Strategy |
|---|---|---|---|---|---|
| 1 | Same | Same | Yes | Extension | Extension |
| 2 | Different | Same | Yes | Extension | Adaptation |
| 3 | Same | Different | Yes | Adaptation | Extension |
| 4 | Different | Different | Yes | Adaptation | Adaptation |
| 5 | Same | — | No | Invention | Invention |

---

[4]Warren J. Keegan, "Multinational Product Planning: Strategic Alternatives," *Journal of Marketing*, 33, January 1969, 58–62.
[5]Mark Boersma, Supervisor International Operations, Blistex, Inc., Personal Communication.

production processes such as CAD/CAM[6] manufacturing technologies obviate the need for large production batch sizes.

Due to differences in the cultural or competitive environment, the same product oftenz is used to offer benefits or functions that dramatically differ from those in the home market. Such gaps between the foreign and home market drive companies to market the same product using customized advertising campaigns. Although it retains the scale economies on the manufacturing side, the firm sacrifices potential savings on the advertising front. Wrigley, the Chicago-based chewing gum company, is a typical practitioner of this approach. Most of the brands marketed in the United States are also sold in Wrigley's overseas markets. Wrigley strives for a uniformly superior quality product. To build up the chewing gum category, Wrigley sells its products at a stable and low price. Given that chewing gum is an impulse item,[7] Wrigley aims for mass distribution. The company sees an opportunity to sell its product at any place where money changes hands. Despite these similarities in Wrigley's product and distribution strategies, there are wide differences in its communication strategy. The benefits that are promoted in Wrigley's advertising campaigns vary from country to country. In the United States, Wrigley has capitalized on smoking regulations by promoting chewing gum as a substitute for smoking. In several European countries, Wrigley's advertising pitches the dental benefits of chewing gum. In the Far East, Wrigley promotes the benefit of facial fitness in its advertising campaigns.[8]

**Strategic Option 2: Product Extension — Communications Adaptation**

Alternatively, firms might adapt their product but market it using a standardized communications strategy. Local market circumstances often favor the case of product adaptation. Another reason for product adaptation could be the company's expansion strategy. Many companies add brands to their product portfolio via acquisitions of local companies. To leverage the existing brand equity enjoyed by the acquired brand, the local brand is often retained. Although these factors lead to product adaptation, similar core values and buying behaviors among consumers using the product might present an opening for a harmonized communications strategy. Within such a context, clever marketing ideas can be transferred from one country to another country, despite the product-related differences. For instance, a Taiwan-produced commercial for P&G's Pantene shampoo was successfully transferred with a few minor changes to Latin America.

**Strategic Option 3: Product Adaptation — Communications Extension**

Differences in *both* the cultural and physical environment across countries call for a dual adaptation strategy. Under such circumstances, adaptation of the company's product and communication strategy is the most viable option for international expansion.

Slim-Fast[9] adapts both product and advertising to comply with varying government regulations for weight-loss products. When Slim-Fast was first launched in Germany, its ads used a local celebrity. In Great Britain, testimonials for diet aids were not allowed to feature celebrities. Instead, the British introduction campaign centered around teachers, an opera singer, a disc jockey, and others. Also the product was adapted to the local markets. In the United Kingdom, banana became the most popular flavor but was not available in many other countries.[10]

**Strategic Option 4: Product and Communications Adaptation — Dual Adaptation**

Genuinely global marketers try to figure out how to create products with a global scope rather than just for a single country. Instead of simply adapting existing products or services to the local market conditions, their mindset is to zero in on global market opportunities. The product invention strategy consists of developing and launching products with a global mindset. Black & Decker is a good example of a company that

**Strategic Option 5: Product Invention**

---

[6]Computer-Aided-Design/Computer-Aided-Manufacturing.

[7]Impulse goods are products that are bought without any planning.

[8]Doug Barrie, former Group Vice-President International, Wm. Wrigley Jr., Personal Communication.

[9]In 2000 Unilever bought the Slim-Fast brand for $2.3 billion.

[10]"Slim-Fast beefs up in Europe," *Advertising Age International*, May 17, 1993, p. I-4.

adopts the product invention approach to global market expansion. It aims to bring out new products that cater towards common needs and opportunities around the world. To manage its global product development process, Black & Decker set up a Worldwide Household Board. This steering committee approves global plans, allocates resources, and gives direction and support, among other tasks. One of the product innovations that emerged from this global product planning approach is the SnakeLight Flexible Flashlight. The SnakeLight was first launched in North America, and then, six months later, in Europe, Latin America, and Australia. The product addresses a global need for portable lighting. The SnakeLight proved to be major hit around the world.[11]

Other companies increasingly adhere to the invention strategy. In the past, Procter & Gamble Europe was a patchwork of country-based operations, each with its own business. These days, P&G aims to develop products that appeal to the entire European region. Many other companies also recently jumped on the "produce globally, market locally" bandwagon. Not all of these efforts have been successful, though. The Ford Mondeo was part of the Ford 2000 project to put Ford's product development projects on a global basis. The car was among Ford's first efforts toward a world-car strategy. Developed in Europe, the car was sold in the United States as the Contour and Mercury Mystique sedan. Although the European version sold pretty well, the American versions were major fiascos.[12] American car buyers considered the models too small and too expensive given their size.[13] Ford hopes do a better job with the new small-car Fiesta that it rolled out in Asia, Europe, and the North America. The Fiesta was a best-selling car in Europe.[14] The updated Fiesta has the same size as its predecessor but is lighter through the use of lightweight, high-strength steel.[15] The Fiesta was developed and designed in Europe and is built in Spain, China, Germany, Thailand, and the United States.

## ◆ ◆ ◆ ◆ ◆ ◆ ◆ ◆   STANDARDIZATION VERSUS CUSTOMIZATION

Behr, headquartered in Stuttgart, Germany, is one of the leading manufacturers of radiators and air-conditioning systems for cars.[16] To adapt its products to satisfy tastes in local markets, the firm relies on a $6 million design lab at its headquarters in Germany. By blowing air at the vehicle at different wind speeds and changing the temperature, its lab can simulate driving conditions in any part of the world. Design is also influenced by local preferences: Germans prefer warm legs, Japanese like air being blown at their face, and Americans favor air that is directed over their entire bodies. Working closely with its carmaker customers and based on the lab findings, Behr is able to design air-conditioning units that give maximal comfort.

**Drivers Toward Standardization**

A recurrent theme in global marketing is whether companies should aim for a standardized or country-tailored product strategy. **Standardization** means offering a uniform product on a regional or worldwide basis. Minor alternations are usually made to meet local regulations or market conditions (for instance, voltage adjustments for electrical appliances). However, by and large, these changes only lead to minor cost increases. A uniform product policy capitalizes on the commonalities in customers' needs across countries. The goal is to minimize costs. These cost savings can then be passed through to the company's customers via low prices. With **customization**, on the other hand, management focuses on cross-border differences in the needs and wants of the firm's target customers. Under this regime, appropriate changes are made to match

---

[11]Don R. Garber, "How to Manage a Global Product Development Process," *Industrial Marketing Management*, 25, 1996, pp. 483–89.

[12]"The Revolution at Ford," *The Economist* (August 7, 1999), pp. 55–56.

[13]"The World Car Wears New Faces," *The New York Times* (April 10, 1998), p. 1.

[14]In fact the Fiesta nameplate dates back to 1976 and was sold in the U.S. from 1978 to 1980.

[15]http://www.caranddriver.com/news/auto_shows/2008_geneva_auto_show_auto_shows/production_debuts/2009_ford_fiesta_auto_shows+t-the_first_of_many_global_products+page-2.html.

[16]"One Size Fits All: Except for Local Preferences," http://www.ft.com, accessed on December 26, 2002.

local market conditions. While standardization has a product-driven orientation—lower your costs via mass-production—customization is inspired by a market-driven mindset—increase customer satisfaction by adapting your products to local needs.

Forces that favor a globalized product strategy include:

1. **Common customer needs.** For many product categories, consumer needs are very similar in different countries. The functions for which the product is used might be identical. Likewise, the usage conditions or the benefits sought might be similar. One example of a product that targets a global segment is Apple's iPhone. Since Apple launched iPhone in early 2007, Apple has sold about 13 million by October 2008.[17] Apart from offering the features and benefits that competing smart phones offer, the iPhone's emotional benefit of "coolness" is also a major reason for its popularity worldwide, especially among young audiences. Many product categories also show a gradual but steady convergence in consumer preferences. Growing similarities in consumer preferences have also been observed in the car industry.[18] The 2008 DuPont Automotive Color Popularity Report, for example, revealed that color preferences are converging around the world, but with subtle differentiation between markets (see also **Exhibit 10-2**).[19] White is a popular choice globally gaining

**EXHIBIT 10-2**
2008 AUTOMOTIVE COLOR POPULARITY

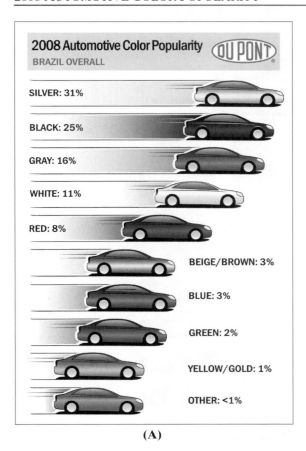

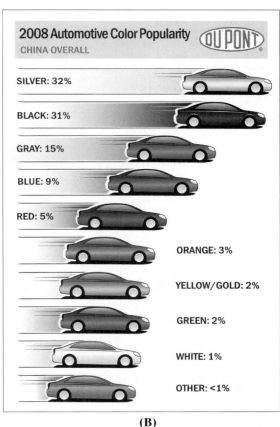

(A)                                        (B)

*(continued)*

---

[17]http://www.apple.com/pr/library/2008/10/21results.html.

[18]Takashi Hisatomi, "Global Marketing by the Nissan Motor Company Limited—A simultaneous market study of users' opinions and attitudes in Europe, USA and Japan," *Marketing and Research Today*, February 1991, pp. 56–61.

[19]http://vocuspr.vocus.com/VocusPR30/Newsroom/Query.aspx?SiteName=DupontNew&Entity=PRAsset&SF_PRAsset_PRAssetID_EQ= 111443&XSL=PressRelease&Cache=False.

**EXHIBIT 10-2**
(CONTINUED)

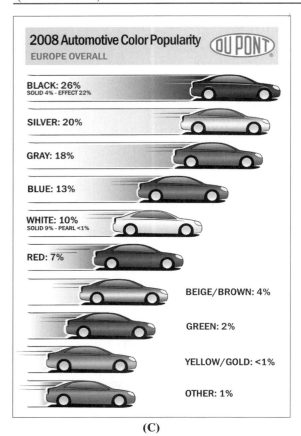

(C)

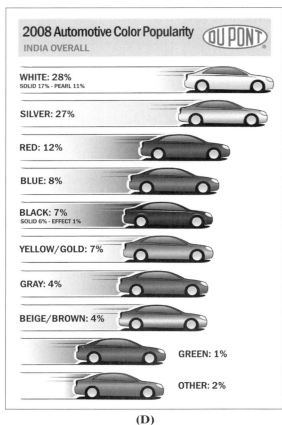

(D)

**2008 Automotive Color Popularity**
JAPAN OVERALL

WHITE: 32%
SOLID 8% - PEARL 24%

SILVER: 28%

BLACK: 13%
SOLID 8% - EFFECT 5%

BLUE: 7%

GRAY: 7%

RED: 3%

GREEN: 3%

BEIGE/BROWN: 2%

OTHER: 5%

(E)

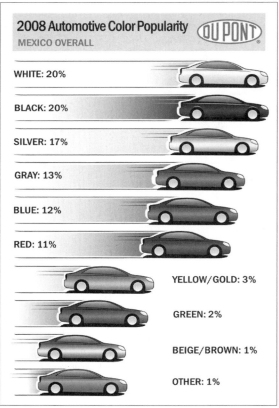

(F)

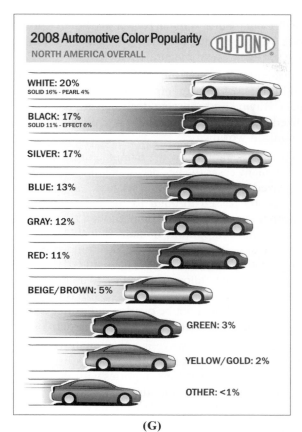

(G)

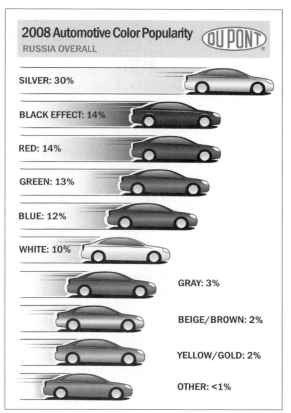

(H)

### 2008 Automotive Color Popularity — DUPONT
SOUTH KOREA OVERALL

SILVER: 50%

BLACK: 25%
SOLID 18% - EFFECT 7%

WHITE: 18%
SOLID 12% - PEARL 6%

GRAY: 3%

BLUE: 2%

RED: 1%

YELLOW/GOLD: 1%

OTHER: <1%

(I)

*Source:* DuPont Automotive Systems 2008 Global Color Popularity Report.

top spot in North America, India and Japan. Other popular choices include black (China, Mexico, and Europe) and silver (Brazil, China, Europe, India, Russia, and South Korea). One trend that the report observes is the growing popularity of blue worldwide, especially among consumers looking for more environmental themes.

2. **Global Customers.** In business-to-business marketing, the shift toward globalization means that a significant part of the business of many companies comes from MNCs that are essentially global customers. Buying and sourcing decisions are commonly centralized or at the least regionalized. As a result, such customers typically demand services or products that are harmonized worldwide.

3. **Scale Economies.** Cost savings from scale economies in the manufacturing and distribution of globalized products is in many cases the key driver behind standardization moves. Savings are also often realized because of sourcing efficiencies or lowered R&D expenditures. These savings can be passed through to the company's end-customers via lower prices. Scale economies offer global competitors a tremendous competitive advantage over local or regional competitors. In many industries though, the "economies of scale" rationale has lost some of its allure. Production procedures such as flexible manufacturing and just-in-time (JIT) production have shifted the focus from size to timeliness. CAD/CAM techniques allow companies to manufacture customized products in small batch sizes at reduced cost. Although size often leads to lower unit costs, the diseconomies of scale should not be overlooked. Bureaucratic bloat and employee dissatisfaction in large-scale operations often create hidden costs.[20]

4. **Time-to-Market.** In scores of industries, being innovative is not enough to be competitive. Companies must also seek ways to shorten the time to bring new product projects to the market. This is especially true for categories with shortening product life cycles. By centralizing research and consolidating new product development efforts on fewer projects, companies are often able to reduce the time-to-market cycle. For example, Procter & Gamble notes that a pan-European launch of liquid laundry detergents could be done in 10 percent of the time it took in the early 1980s, when marketing efforts were still very decentralized.[21] Likewise, the Swedish engineering group Alfa Laval has been able to speed its time-to-market by streamlining its global new product development process.[22]

5. **Regional market agreements.** The formation of regional market agreements such as the Single European Market encourages companies to launch regional (e.g., pan-European) products or redesign existing products as pan-regional brands. The legislation leading to the creation of the Single European Market in January 1993 sought to remove most barriers to trade within the European Union. It also provided for the harmonization of technical standards in many industries. These moves favor pan-European product strategies. Mars, for instance, now regards Europe as one giant market. It modified the brand names for several of its products, turning them into pan-European brands. Marathon in the United Kingdom became Snickers, the name used in Continental Europe. The Raider bar in Continental Europe was renamed Twix, the name used in the United Kingdom.[23]

**Two Alternatives— Modular and Core Product Approach**

Whether firms should strive for standardized or localized products is a bogus question. The issue should not be phrased as an either-or dilemma. Instead, product managers should look at it in terms of degree of globalization: What elements of my product policy should be tailored to the local market conditions? Which ones can I leave unchanged? At the same time, there are strategic options that allow firms to modify

---

[20]"Big is back. A survey of multinationals," *The Economist*, June 24, 1995, p. 4.

[21]Procter & Gamble, *Annual Report 1993*.

[22]http://www.alfalaval.com/about-us/investors/strategy-and-goals/research-and-development/Documents/Research_and_development.pdf.

[23]Dale Littler and Katrin Schlieper, "The development of the Eurobrand," *International Marketing Review*, vol. 12, no. 2, 1995, pp. 22–37.

their product while keeping most of the benefits flowing from a uniform product policy. Two of these product design policies are the **modular approach** and the **core-product** or **common platform approach**.[24]

### Modular Approach.

The first approach consists of developing a range of product parts that can be used worldwide. The parts can be assembled into numerous product configurations. Scale economies flow from the mass-production of more-or-less standard product components at a few sites. Vaillant, a French company that is Europe's biggest maker of heating boilers, exemplifies this approach. A wide variation in consumer tastes and building standards within the pan-European market means that Vaillant has to offer hundreds of different boiler models. However, lately, the firm has tried to minimize the costs of customization without narrowing customer offerings. The trick is to develop boilers that meet local requirements but with as many common features (e.g., burners, controls) as is doable.[25]

### Core-Product (Common Platform) Approach.

The core-product (common platform) approach starts with the design of a mostly uniform core-product or platform. Attachments are added to the core-product to match local market needs. Savings are achieved by reduced production and purchasing costs. At the same time companies adopting this approach have the flexibility that allows them to modify the product easily. The model design procedures of the French carmaker Renault exemplify this approach. More than 90 percent of Renault's sales revenues come from the European market. The body, engines, transmissions, and chassis of a given model are the same in the different markets. Minor changes, such as stronger heaters in Nordic countries or better air-conditioning for cars sold in Southern Europe, are easily implemented.[26] The common platform approach has emerged as a favored means for lots of other global carmakers.[27] Jaguar's S-Type marque shared a platform with Lincoln LS, Ford's other luxury brand. Volkswagen's Golf platform is also used for certain variants of Audi, Seat, and Skoda—some of the other brands that belong to Volkswagen's stable. Swedish Saab, owned by General Motors, uses platforms that were originally developed for Opel, GM's other European brand. **Global Perspective 10-2** describes how Deere and Electrolux use the core product approach in designing their products.

On the surface, the standardize-versus-customize conundrum could be settled via some straightforward cost-benefit type of analysis. In this section we introduce a very basic framework that allows you to look into the economics of the standardization/customization issue. The analytical tool that we discuss here in this section is known as **incremental break-even analysis (IBEA)**. The term sounds fancy but the thinking behind it is very straightforward. We illustrate the tool with a simple hypothetical example.

> **Back-of-the-envelope Calculations—Incremental Break-even Analysis (IBEA)**

Suppose a U.S.-based MNC developed a new yogurt drink. To keep matters simple, at this stage the company is planning to introduce the new beverage in two markets—its home market (say the United States) and the host market (say Brazil). The base case scenario is a uniform strategy for the two countries with just minor changes that are absolutely necessary (e.g., adding subtitles to the U.S. TV-commercial for Brazil, translating the bottle label from English into Portuguese). The other scenario is to adapt the marketing mix that was devised for the United States when launching the drink in Brazil. On the product front, adaptations proposed by the Brazilian country subsidiary include the flavors and the packaging. With regard to the communication strategy, the MNC ponders to develop an entirely new commercial for Brazil. To test

---

[24]Peter G. P. Walters and Brian Toyne, "Product modification and standardization in international markets: strategic options and facilitating policies," *Columbia Journal of World Business*, vol. 24, Winter 1989, pp. 37–44.

[25]"Fired up to gather new ideas," http://www.ft.com, accessed December 9, 2002.

[26]"Auto marketers gas up for world car drive," *Advertising Age International*, January 16, 1995, p. I–16.

[27]"A Platform for Choice," *The Financial Times* (June 28, 2000), p. 23.

◆ ◆ ◆ ◆ ◆ ◆ ◆ ◆ ◆ ◆ ◆ ◆ ◆ ◆ ◆ ◆ ◆ ◆ ◆ ◆ ◆ ◆ ◆ ◆ ◆ ◆ ◆ ◆ ◆ ◆ ◆ ◆

## $\mathcal{G}$LOBAL PERSPECTIVE 10-2

### TWO ILLUSTRATIONS OF THE COMMON PLATFORM APPROACH WITH GLOBAL PRODUCT DESIGN

#### DEERE

Deere is one of the world's biggest manufacturers of farm machinery. Deere's tractors worldwide are based on six "families" or platforms on which different elements (e.g., engines, gear boxes) can be fitted to suit needs in local markets. With that system, Deere can easily swap design ideas. For instance, some tractors made in Mannheim, Deere's European tractor plant, use a new gearbox designed in the United States. Likewise, some of the tractors made in the U.S.-plant contain a new axle suspension concept developed in the European site. The platform system allows Deere to meet customers' expectations worldwide while at the same time minimizing costs.

*Sources:* "Difficult furrow to plough," *The Financial Times* (March 9, 1999), p. 12; "Electrolux sees future in fewer, stronger brands," *The Financial Times* (February 20, 1999), p. 23.

#### ELECTROLUX

Electrolux has become the world's largest household appliance maker—owning more than forty different brands such as Electrolux, Frigidaire, Kelvinator, AEG, and Zanussi. In Europe alone, the firm sells 6,500 different types of oven. In February 1999, the Stockholm-based company announced plans to streamline its brand portfolio and to rationalize its product design process. The company aspires to move its broad product portfolio of 15,000 different product variants toward common product platforms and fewer brands. This move would result in lower purchasing and manufacturing costs. Electrolux plans to have common platforms in refrigerators and ovens, with customers able to choose particular features in different markets. Whether Electrolux will succeed is to be seen. When Whirlpool, its global rival, introduced a world washing machine, consumer response was lukewarm.

---

the flavors, the company would need to conduct a market research study in Brazil ($200,000). Developing a new ad campaign requires a $2 million outlay. The MNC would have to spend $1,500,000 for the new packaging manufacturing equipment. So the costs for making all the marketing mix adaptations for the Brazil launch are as follows:

| | |
|---|---|
| New ad campaign: | $2,000,000 |
| Flavors: | $500,000 |
| Packaging: | $1,500,000 |

Subtitling the existing U.S. commercial instead of creating an entirely new one would cost $300,000. Therefore, the total *incremental* cost of adapting the marketing mix for Brazil as opposed to a standardized one equals:

$$\$1,700,000^{28} + \$500,000 + \$1,500,000 = \$3,700,000$$

In this example, all the adaptation costs are fixed costs. In reality though, some of the adaptation costs could also be variable ones. The variable part of the packaging (or ingredients) costs, for example, could also be higher compared to the standardized packaging (or ingredients) costs. With standardization, the MNC can order its materials in bulk and, thereby, gains leverage to negotiate lower prices with its suppliers.

On the benefit side, adaptation may lead to higher sales volume. Also, consumers in the host market (in this case Brazil) may be willing to pay more for the customized product. In our example, a market research study shows that the drinks maker could charge $1.20 per bottle for the customized yogurt drink compared to just $1.00 for the standardized version. We assume that the variable cost is $0.70 per unit and is the same under both scenarios. From an economic angle, the key question facing the firm then is whether the extra costs of adaptation will be offset by the additional profits coming from

---

[28]That is, the cost of creating a new campaign (i.e., $2,000,000) minus the cost of subtitling the U.S. campaign (i.e., $300,000).

higher sales volume and the price premium. In other words, what will be the extra sales volume needed to justify the incremental costs of adapting the marketing mix for Brazil? To answer this question, the firm's marketing manager can do some simple back-of-the-envelope break-even type analysis. In particular, she could calculate at what sales level in Brazil the profits of both scenarios (customize versus standardize) are the same:

Profit in Brazil under standardization = [Price − Variable Cost] × Sales − Fixed Cost

Profit in Brazil under customization = [(Price + $\Delta$P) − (Variable Cost + $\Delta$VC)]

× Sales − Fixed Cost − Fixed Adaptation Costs

where $\Delta$P is the price premium that the firm can charge (in this example 20 cents = $1.20 − $1.00) for the adapted product in Brazil and $\Delta$VC is the difference in variable costs (here assumed to be zero) between the adapted and standardized product.

Therefore, the extra sales (i.e., incremental break even volume or IBEV) can be derived as follows:

Profit under customization = Profit under standardization

or:

[Price − Variable Cost] × Sales − Fixed Cost = [(Price + $\Delta$P) − (Variable Cost + $\Delta$VC)]

× Sales − Fixed Cost − Fixed Adaptation Costs

or simply rearranging the terms:

$$\text{Sales } (= \text{IBEV}) = \frac{\text{Fixed Adaptation Costs}}{[\text{Price} + \Delta\text{P}] - [\text{Variable Cost} + \Delta\text{VC}]}$$

Plugging in the numbers for our hypothetical example we get:

$$\text{IBEV} = \frac{\$3,700,000}{[\$1.00 + \$0.20] - [\$0.70 + \$0.00]}$$
$$= 7,400,000 \text{ units}$$

To put this figure in perspective, let us assume that annual sales in the category total 400 million bottles. Then, the extra market share needed to justify the proposed adaptations would be:

$$7.4 \text{ million}/400 \text{ million} = 1.85 \text{ percent}.$$

The tool can be used to do some simple simulations and answer what-if questions. For instance, if the firm decides only to adapt the television commercial but keep the product unchanged (i.e., same flavors; same packaging) then the required extra sales for Brazil would be:

IBEV = $1,700,000/[$1.20 − $0.70] = 3,400,000 units or 0.85 percent extra market share.

While these calculations can be insightful, they should not be treated as an oracle. Other less quantifiable costs should also be factored in. Imposing a uniform marketing mix strategy without much input from the local staff could create discontent and de-motivate marketing managers in the overseas country subsidiary. On the other hand, marketing mix adaptations proposed by the country subsidiary could delay the rollout of the new product in the host country.

The balancing act between standardization and adaptation is very tricky. One scholar[29] describes **overstandardization** as one of the five pitfalls that global marketers could run into. Too much standardization stifles initiative and experimentation at the local subsidiary level. However, one should not forget that there is also a risk of **overcustomization**. Part of the appeal of imported brands is often their *foreignness*. By adapting too much to the local market conditions, an import runs the risk of losing that

---

[29]Kamran Kashani, "Beware the pitfalls of global marketing," *Harvard Business Review*, September–October 1989.

cachet and simply becoming a me-too brand, barely differentiated from the local brands. Apparently, General Motors Corp. (GM) made such a mistake in Japan. In 2001, GM rolled out a new subcompact car in Japan called the Chevrolet Cruze, built by Suzuki, GM's affiliate. Seven months after the launch, GM had sold only 6,600 cars. One problem seems to have been that the Cruze was "too Japanese" (except for the price tag!). Despite GM's efforts to give the Cruze American looks, it was very similar to the Suzuki Swift, which was far cheaper (790,000 yen versus a starting price of 1.2 million yen for the Cruze), had the same engine size, and, contrary to the Cruze, came with a stereo system.[30,31]

## ◆ ◆ ◆ ◆ ◆ ◆ ◆ ◆   MULTINATIONAL DIFFUSION

The speed and pattern of market penetration for a given product innovation can differ enormously between markets. It is not uncommon that new products that were phenomenally successful in one country or region turn out to be flops in other markets. A good example is Microsoft's Xbox videogame console, which was first released in the United States in November 2001 and subsequently in Japan in February 2002 and Europe in March 2002. Although sales of Xbox were impressive in the United States, they were far below expectations in Japan and Europe. Seven months after the launch of Xbox in Japan, only 274,000 consoles had been shipped.[32] One reason for Xbox' failure to woo Japanese gamers is that Xbox games cater mainly to people who are used to personal computer games, which are far less popular in Japan than in the United States.[33] Obviously, the other reason is that Japan is the home-market of two of Xbox's big rivals, Sony and Nintendo. In this section we will introduce several concepts and insights from multinational new product diffusion research. These explain some of the differences in new product performance between different countries.

In general, three types of factors drive the adoption of new products: individual differences, personal influences, and product characteristics. Individuals differ in terms of their willingness to try out new products. Early adopters are eager to experiment with new ideas or products. Late adopters take a wait-and-see attitude. Early adopters differ from laggards in terms of socioeconomic traits (income, education, social status), personality, and communication behavior. A prominent role is also played by the influence of prior adopters. Word-of-mouth spread by previous adopters often has a much more significant impact on the adoption decision than non-personal factors such as media advertising. For many product categories, peer pressure will often determine whether (and when) a person will adopt the innovation. The third set of factors relates to the nature of the product itself. Five product characteristics are key:[34]

1. **Relative Advantage.** To what extent does the new product offer more perceived value to potential adopters than existing alternatives?

2. **Compatibility.** Is the product consistent with existing values and attitudes of the individuals in the social system? Are there any switching costs that people might incur if they decide to adopt the innovation?

3. **Complexity.** Is the product easy to understand? Easy to use?

4. **Triability.** Are prospects able to try out the product on a limited basis?

5. **Observability.** How easy is it for possible adopters to observe the results or benefits of the innovation? Can these benefits easily be communicated?

[30]"GM's Cruze Gets Lost In Japanese Market," *The Asian Wall Street Journal* (September 16, 2002), pp. A8, A10.

[31]At the Paris Motor Show in October 2008 GM revealed a new sedan also named Cruze. According to GM's announcement, Cruze is the "result of a development process harnessing GM's global expertise." It is the first of a new line of compact cars. GM planned to launch the Cruze in Europe in March 2009 (see http://media.gm.com/featured_vehicles/Chevy_Cruze.htm).

[32]"Microsoft Gives Xbox Serves, Games Big Push," *The Asian Wall Street Journal* (September 23, 2002), p. A9.

[33]"Microsoft Shows Slow Reactions," *The Financial Times* (March 12, 2002), p. 20.

[34]Thomas S. Robertson, *Innovative Behavior and Communication*, New York: Holt, Rinehart and Winston, 1971.

Aside from these variables there are several country characteristics that can be used to predict new product penetration patterns. Communication leading to the transfer of ideas tends to be easier when it happens between individuals who have a similar cultural mindset. Therefore, the adoption rate for new products in countries with a **homogeneous population** (e.g., Japan, South Korea, Thailand) is usually faster than in countries with a highly diverse culture. When a new product is launched at different time intervals, there will be **lead countries**, where it is introduced first, and **lag countries,** that are entered later. Generally, adoption rates seem to be higher in lag countries than in the lead country. Potential adopters in lag-countries have had more time to understand and evaluate the innovation's perceived attributes than their counterparts in the lead-country. Also, over time, the product's quality tends to improve and its price usually drops due to economies of scale.[35]

One research study that looked at the penetration patterns for consumer durables in Europe identified three more country characteristics that are relevant.[36] The first variable is **cosmopolitanism**. *Cosmopolitans* are people who look beyond their immediate social surroundings, while *locals* are oriented more toward their immediate social system. The more cosmopolitan the country's population, the higher its propensity for innovation. The second country trait is labeled **mobility**. Mobility is the ease with which member of a social system can move around and interact with other members. It is largely determined by the country's infrastructure. Mobility facilitates interpersonal communication, and, hence has a positive impact on the product's penetration in a given market. Finally, the **percentage of women in the labor force** impacts the spread of certain types of innovations. A higher participation rate of women in the work force means higher incomes and hence more spending power. Timesaving products (such as washing machines, dishwashers) appeal to working women. By the same token, time-consuming durables will be less valued in societies where working women form a substantial portion of the labor force.

Another study examined the diffusion of six products in 31 developing and developed countries across the world.[37] A key finding was that developing countries tend to experience a far slower adoption rate than developed countries. Average penetration potential for developing countries turned out to be about one-third (0.17 versus 0.52) of that for developed countries. Also, it took developing nations on average 18 percent longer (19.25 versus 16.33 years) to reach peak sales.

One useful metric to characterize the takeoff of new products is the **time-to-takeoff**, that is, the period from the launch of the new product in a particular country market to the takeoff.[38] Takeoff marks the turning point between the introduction and the growth stages of the product life cycle. A recent study[39] looked at the time-to-takeoff for sixteen new products in 31 countries. The mean time-to-takeoff (averaged across product categories) ranged from 5.4 years in Japan to 13.9 years in China and Vietnam (see **Exhibit 10-3**). Research done by Tellis and his colleagues offers the following insights:

1. Time-to-takeoff is declining over the years. For instance, time-to-takeoff for communication products dropped from 8.6 years for mobile phones to 3.4 years for broadband.

2. Country differences are strong. Newly developed countries (e.g., South Korea) in Asia show faster times-to-takeoff than established European countries (e.g., France).

[35]Hirokazu Takada and Dipak Jain, "Cross-National Analysis of Diffusion of Consumer Durable Goods in Pacific Rim Countries," *Journal of Marketing*, vol. 55, no. 2 (April 1991), pp. 48–54.

[36]Hubert Gatignon, Jehoshua Eliashberg, and Thomas S. Robertson, "Modeling Multinational Diffusion Patterns: An Efficient Methodology," *Marketing Science*, vol. 8, no. 3 (Summer 1989), pp. 231–47.

[37]Debabrata Talukdar, K. Sudhir, and Andrew Ainslie, "Investigating New Product Diffusion Across Products and Countries," *Marketing Science*, 21 (Winter 2002), pp. 97–144.

[38]Gerard J. Tellis, Stefan Stremersch, and Eden Yin, "The International Takeoff of New Products: The Role of Economics, Culture, and Country Innovativeness," *Marketing Science*, 22 (Spring 2003), pp. 188–208.

[39]Deepa Chandrasekaran and Gerard J. Tellis, "Global Takeoff of New Products: Culture, Wealth or Vanishing Differences?" *Marketing Science*, 27 (Sept.–Oct. 2008), pp. 844–60.

**EXHIBIT 10-3**
MEAN TIME-TO-TAKEOFF ACROSS PRODUCT
CATEGORIES WITHIN COUNTRY

| Country | Number of Categories | Mean Time-to-Takeoff (years) |
|---|---|---|
| Japan | 14 | 5.4 |
| Norway | 15 | 5.7 |
| Sweden | 15 | 6.1 |
| Netherlands | 16 | 6.1 |
| Denmark | 15 | 6.1 |
| United States | 14 | 6.2 |
| Switzerland | 15 | 6.3 |
| Belgium | 16 | 6.5 |
| Canada | 12 | 6.9 |
| South Korea | 12 | 7.2 |
| United Kingdom | 14 | 8.0 |
| France | 15 | 8.2 |
| Italy | 15 | 8.3 |
| Spain | 14 | 8.5 |
| Mexico | 11 | 8.7 |
| Brazil | 11 | 9.3 |
| Thailand | 12 | 10.2 |
| India | 14 | 12.4 |
| Philippines | 13 | 12.6 |
| Vietnam | 14 | 13.9 |
| China | 16 | 13.9 |

*Source:* Based on Deepa Chandrasekaran and Gerard J. Tellis, "Global Takeoff of New Products: Culture, Wealth or Vanishing Differences?" *Marketing* Science, 27 (September–October 2008), Table 3, p. 851.

Emerging markets (e.g., China, India, Philippines) still lag much behind other countries: 11 years versus 7 years time-to-takeoff.

3. Both economic development and cultural differences explain cross-country variations in time-to-takeoff. High levels of collectivism, power distance, and religiosity are associated with longer time-to-takeoffs.

4. Takeoff for "fun" products (e.g., CD player, mobile phone, digital camera) is much faster than for "work" products (e.g., kitchen appliances): 7 versus 12 years.

5. The probability of takeoff in a target country increases with previous takeoffs in other countries.[40]

◆ ◆ ◆ ◆ ◆ ◆ ◆ ◆ **DEVELOPING NEW PRODUCTS FOR GLOBAL MARKETS**

For most companies, new products are the bread-and-butter of their growth strategy. Unfortunately, developing new products is a time-consuming and costly endeavor, with tremendous challenges. The new product development process becomes especially a major headache for multinational organizations that try to coordinate the process on a regional or sometimes even worldwide basis. The steps to be followed in the global new product development (NPD) process are by-and-large very similar to domestic marketing situations. In this section, we will focus on the unique aspects that take place when innovation efforts are implemented on a global scope. **Global Perspective 10-3** describes the development of so-called vitamin-fortified beverages that target youngsters in developing nations.

**Identifying New Product Ideas**

Every new product starts with an idea. Sources for new product ideas are manifold. Companies can tap into any of the so-called 4 C's—*company, customers, competition*

---
[40]Ibid.

# THE *World* at a Glance

## CONTENTS

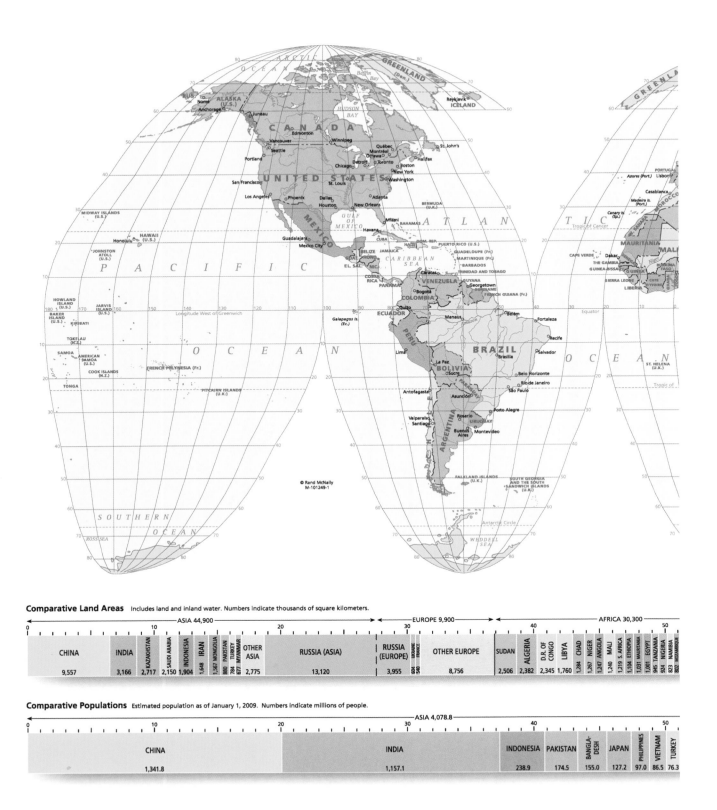

**Comparative Land Areas** Includes land and inland water. Numbers indicate thousands of square kilometers.

| | ASIA 44,900 | | | | | | | | | | | EUROPE 9,900 | | | | AFRICA 30,300 | | | | | | | | | | | | | | |
|---|---|---|---|---|---|---|---|---|---|---|---|---|---|---|---|---|---|---|---|---|---|---|---|---|---|---|---|---|---|---|
| CHINA | INDIA | KAZAKHSTAN | SAUDI ARABIA | INDONESIA | IRAN | MONGOLIA | PAKISTAN | TURKEY | MYANMAR | OTHER ASIA | RUSSIA (ASIA) | RUSSIA (EUROPE) | UKRAINE | FRANCE | OTHER EUROPE | SUDAN | ALGERIA | D.R. OF CONGO | LIBYA | CHAD | NIGER | ANGOLA | MALI | S. AFRICA | ETHIOPIA | MAURITANIA | EGYPT | TANZANIA | NIGERIA | NAMIBIA | MOZAMBIQUE |
| 9,557 | 3,166 | 2,717 | 2,150 | 1,904 | 1,648 | 1,567 | 880 | 784 | 677 | 2,775 | 13,120 | 3,955 | 604 | 549 | 8,756 | 2,506 | 2,382 | 2,345 | 1,760 | 1,284 | 1,267 | 1,247 | 1,240 | 1,219 | 1,104 | 1,031 | 1,001 | 945 | 924 | 823 | 802 |

**Comparative Populations** Estimated population as of January 1, 2009. Numbers indicate millions of people.

| | ASIA 4,078.8 | | | | | | | | |
|---|---|---|---|---|---|---|---|---|---|
| CHINA | INDIA | INDONESIA | PAKISTAN | BANGLA-DESH | JAPAN | PHILIPPINES | VIETNAM | TURKEY |
| 1,341.8 | 1,157.1 | 238.9 | 174.5 | 155.0 | 127.2 | 97.0 | 86.5 | 76.3 |

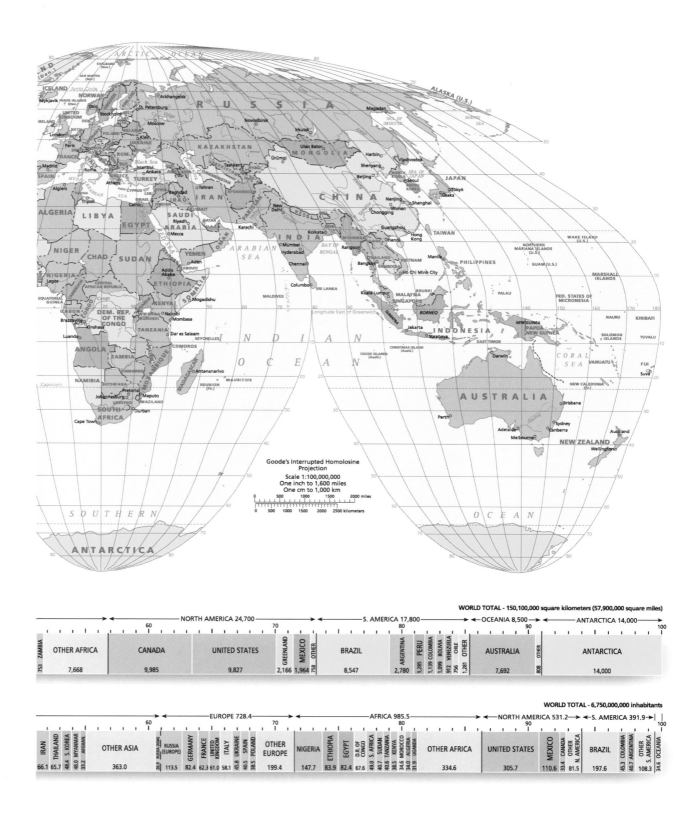

Goode's Interrupted Homolosine
Projection
Scale 1:100,000,000
One inch to 1,600 miles
One cm to 1,000 km

0   500   1000   1500   2000 miles

0   500   1000   1500   2000   2500 kilometers

**WORLD TOTAL - 150,100,000 square kilometers (57,900,000 square miles)**

| ← NORTH AMERICA 24,700 → | | | | | | ← S. AMERICA 17,800 → | | | | | | | ← OCEANIA 8,500 → | ← ANTARCTICA 14,000 → |
|---|---|---|---|---|---|---|---|---|---|---|---|---|---|---|

| ZAMBIA | OTHER AFRICA | CANADA | UNITED STATES | GREENLAND | MEXICO | OTHER | BRAZIL | ARGENTINA | PERU | COLOMBIA | BOLIVIA | VENEZUELA | CHILE | OTHER | AUSTRALIA | OTHER | ANTARCTICA |
|---|---|---|---|---|---|---|---|---|---|---|---|---|---|---|---|---|---|
| 753 | 7,668 | 9,985 | 9,827 | 2,166 | 1,964 | 758 | 8,547 | 2,780 | 1,285 | 1,139 | 1,099 | 912 | 756 | 1,281 | 7,692 | 808 | 14,000 |

**WORLD TOTAL - 6,750,000,000 inhabitants**

| ← EUROPE 728.4 → | | | | | | | | | | ← AFRICA 985.5 → | | | | | | | | | | ← NORTH AMERICA 531.2 → | ← S. AMERICA 391.9 → | |
|---|---|---|---|---|---|---|---|---|---|---|---|---|---|---|---|---|---|---|---|---|---|---|---|

| IRAN | THAILAND | S. KOREA | MYANMAR | AFGHAN. | OTHER ASIA | RUSSIA (ASIA) | RUSSIA (EUROPE) | GERMANY | FRANCE | UNITED KINGDOM | ITALY | UKRAINE | SPAIN | POLAND | OTHER EUROPE | NIGERIA | ETHIOPIA | EGYPT | D.R. OF CONGO | S. AFRICA | SUDAN | TANZANIA | KENYA | MOROCCO | ALGERIA | UGANDA | OTHER AFRICA | UNITED STATES | MEXICO | CANADA | OTHER N. AMERICA | BRAZIL | COLOMBIA | ARGENTINA | OTHER S. AMERICA | OCEANIA |
|---|---|---|---|---|---|---|---|---|---|---|---|---|---|---|---|---|---|---|---|---|---|---|---|---|---|---|---|---|---|---|---|---|---|---|---|---|
| 66.1 | 65.7 | 48.4 | 48.0 | 33.2 | 363.0 | 26.9 | 113.5 | 82.4 | 62.3 | 61.0 | 58.1 | 45.8 | 40.5 | 38.5 | 199.4 | 147.7 | 83.9 | 82.4 | 67.6 | 49.0 | 40.7 | 40.6 | 38.5 | 34.6 | 34.0 | 31.9 | 334.6 | 305.7 | 110.6 | 33.4 | 81.5 | 197.6 | 45.3 | 40.7 | 108.3 | 34.6 |

**M-3**

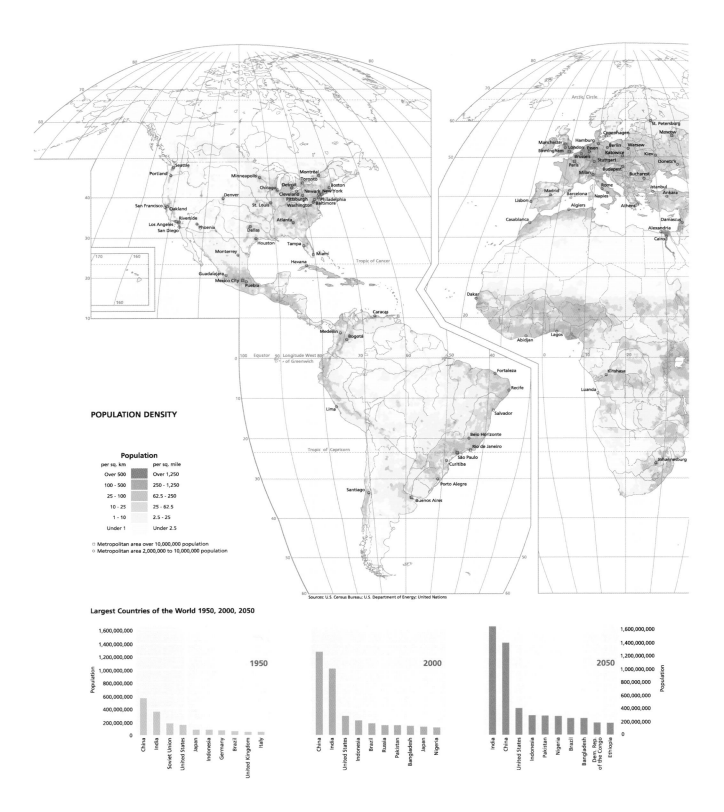

## POPULATION DENSITY

### Population

| per sq. km | per sq. mile |
|---|---|
| Over 500 | Over 1,250 |
| 100 - 500 | 250 - 1,250 |
| 25 - 100 | 62.5 - 250 |
| 10 - 25 | 25 - 62.5 |
| 1 - 10 | 2.5 - 25 |
| Under 1 | Under 2.5 |

□ Metropolitan area over 10,000,000 population
○ Metropolitan area 2,000,000 to 10,000,000 population

Sources: U.S. Census Bureau; U.S. Department of Energy; United Nations

### Largest Countries of the World 1950, 2000, 2050

**1950**

**2000**

**2050**

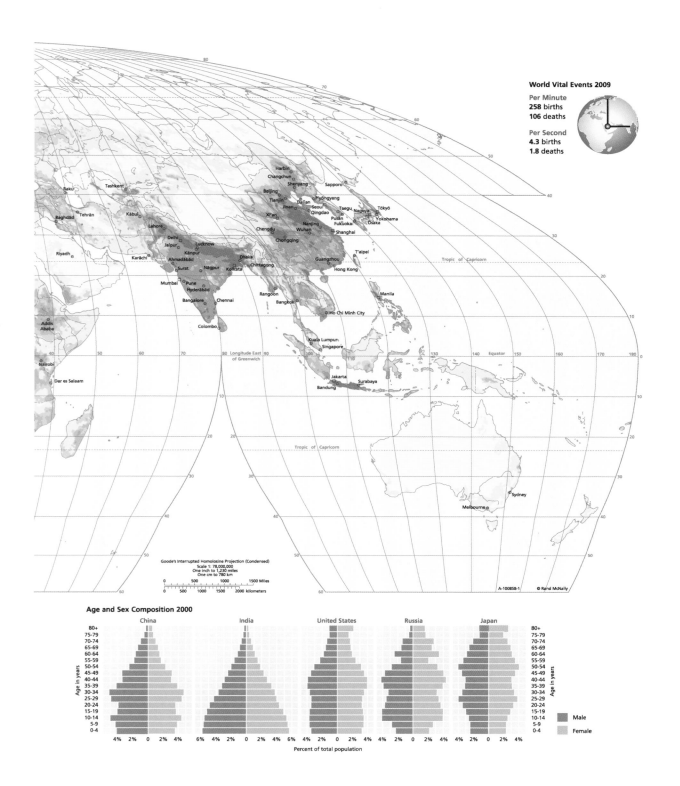

**World Vital Events 2009**

Per Minute
**258** births
**106** deaths

Per Second
**4.3** births
**1.8** deaths

Goode's Interrupted Homolosine Projection (Condensed)
Scale 1: 78,000,000
One inch to 1,230 miles
One cm to 780 km

| 0 | 500 | 1000 | 1500 Miles |

| 0 | 500 | 1000 | 1500 | 2000 kilometers |

A-100858-1    © Rand McNally

**Age and Sex Composition 2000**

China    India    United States    Russia    Japan

Age in years

80+
75-79
70-74
65-69
60-64
55-59
50-54
45-49
40-44
35-39
30-34
25-29
20-24
15-19
10-14
5-9
0-4

China: 4% 2% 0 2% 4%
India: 6% 4% 2% 0 2% 4% 6%
United States: 4% 2% 0 2% 4%
Russia: 4% 2% 0 2% 4%
Japan: 4% 2% 0 2% 4%

Percent of total population

■ Male
■ Female

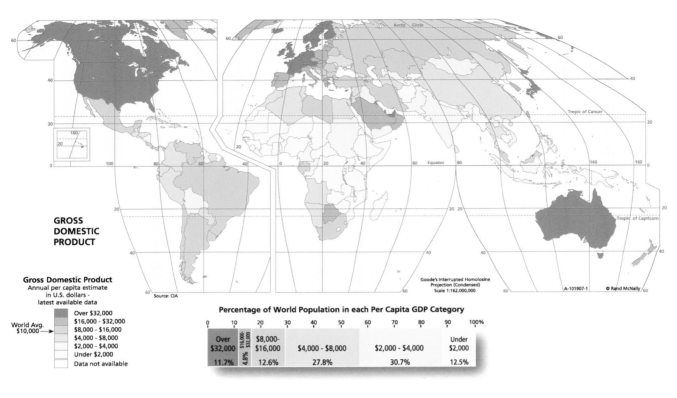

GROSS
DOMESTIC
PRODUCT

**Gross Domestic Product**
Annual per capita estimate
in U.S. dollars -
latest available data

Source: CIA

World Avg.
$10,000 →

Over $32,000
$16,000 - $32,000
$8,000 - $16,000
$4,000 - $8,000
$2,000 - $4,000
Under $2,000
Data not available

Goode's Interrupted Homolosine
Projection (Condensed)
Scale 1:162,000,000

A-101907-1    © Rand McNally

**Percentage of World Population in each Per Capita GDP Category**

| | | | | | | | | | | | |
|---|---|---|---|---|---|---|---|---|---|---|---|
| 0 | 10 | 20 | 30 | 40 | 50 | 60 | 70 | 80 | 90 | 100% | |

| Over $32,000 | $16,000-$32,000 | $8,000-$16,000 | $4,000 - $8,000 | $2,000 - $4,000 | Under $2,000 |
|---|---|---|---|---|---|
| 11.7% | 4.8% | 12.6% | 27.8% | 30.7% | 12.5% |

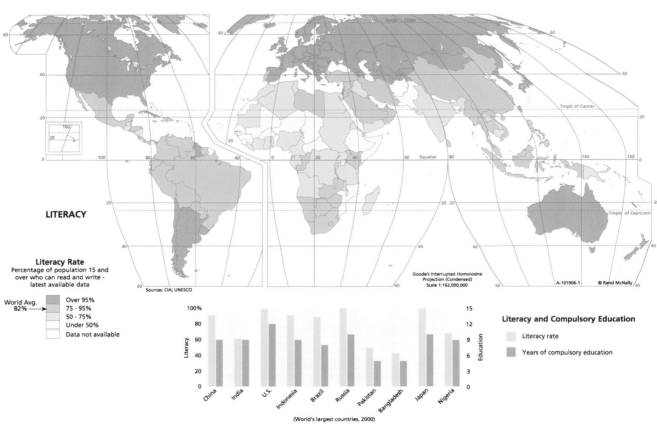

LITERACY

**Literacy Rate**
Percentage of population 15 and
over who can read and write -
latest available data

Sources: CIA; UNESCO

World Avg.
82% →

Over 95%
75 - 95%
50 - 75%
Under 50%
Data not available

Goode's Interrupted Homolosine
Projection (Condensed)
Scale 1:162,000,000

A-101906-1    © Rand McNally

**Literacy and Compulsory Education**

Literacy rate

Years of compulsory education

(World's largest countries, 2000)

China   India   U.S.   Indonesia   Brazil   Russia   Pakistan   Bangladesh   Japan   Nigeria

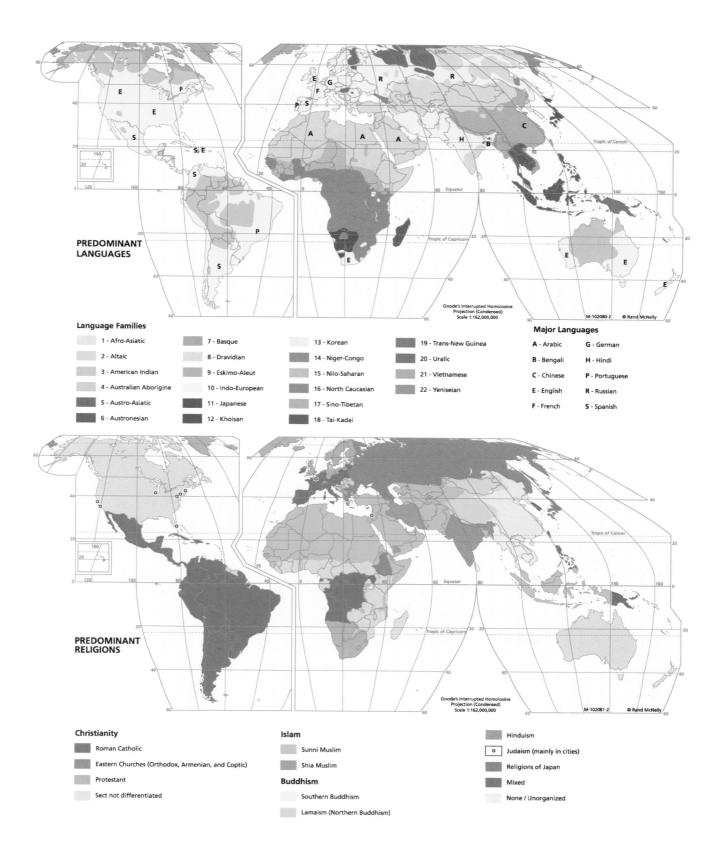

## PREDOMINANT LANGUAGES

**Language Families**

1 - Afro-Asiatic
2 - Altaic
3 - American Indian
4 - Australian Aborigine
5 - Austro-Asiatic
6 - Austronesian
7 - Basque
8 - Dravidian
9 - Eskimo-Aleut
10 - Indo-European
11 - Japanese
12 - Khoisan
13 - Korean
14 - Niger-Congo
15 - Nilo-Saharan
16 - North Caucasian
17 - Sino-Tibetan
18 - Tai-Kadai
19 - Trans-New Guinea
20 - Uralic
21 - Vietnamese
22 - Yeniseian

**Major Languages**

A - Arabic
B - Bengali
C - Chinese
E - English
F - French
G - German
H - Hindi
P - Portuguese
R - Russian
S - Spanish

Goode's Interrupted Homolosine
Projection (Condensed)
Scale 1:162,000,000

M-102080-2 © Rand McNally

## PREDOMINANT RELIGIONS

Goode's Interrupted Homolosine
Projection (Condensed)
Scale 1:162,000,000

M-102081-2 © Rand McNally

**Christianity**

Roman Catholic
Eastern Churches (Orthodox, Armenian, and Coptic)
Protestant
Sect not differentiated

**Islam**

Sunni Muslim
Shia Muslim

**Buddhism**

Southern Buddhism
Lamaism (Northern Buddhism)

Hinduism
Judaism (mainly in cities)
Religions of Japan
Mixed
None / Unorganized

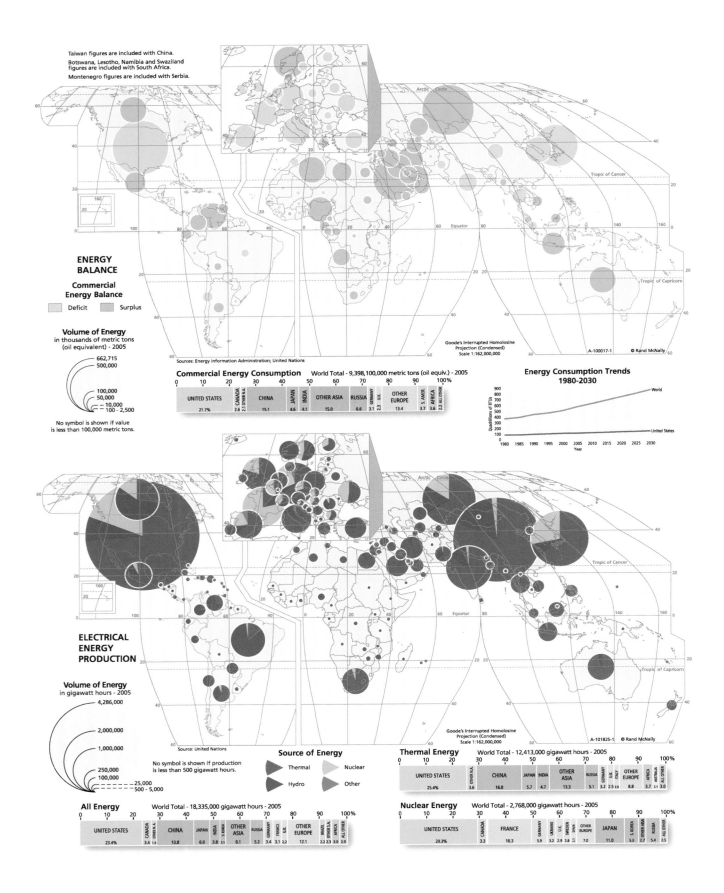

Taiwan figures are included with China.

Botswana, Lesotho, Namibia and Swaziland figures are included with South Africa.

Montenegro figures are included with Serbia.

**ENERGY BALANCE**

**Commercial Energy Balance**

Deficit   Surplus

**Volume of Energy**
in thousands of metric tons
(oil equivalent) - 2005

662,715
500,000
100,000
50,000
10,000
100 - 2,500

No symbol is shown if value is less than 100,000 metric tons.

Sources: Energy Information Administration; United Nations

Goode's Interrupted Homolosine Projection (Condensed)
Scale 1:162,000,000

A-100017-1   © Rand McNally

**Commercial Energy Consumption**   World Total - 9,398,100,000 metric tons (oil equiv.) - 2005

| UNITED STATES | CANADA | OTHER N.A. | CHINA | JAPAN | INDIA | OTHER ASIA | RUSSIA | GERMANY | U.K. | OTHER EUROPE | S. AMER. | AFRICA | ALL OTHER |
|---|---|---|---|---|---|---|---|---|---|---|---|---|---|
| 21.7% | 2.6 | 2.1 | 15.1 | 4.6 | 4.1 | 15.0 | 6.6 | 3.1 | 2.3 | 13.4 | 3.7 | 3.6 | 2.2 |

**Energy Consumption Trends 1980-2030**

World
United States

**ELECTRICAL ENERGY PRODUCTION**

**Volume of Energy**
in gigawatt hours - 2005

4,286,000
2,000,000
1,000,000
250,000
100,000
25,000
500 - 5,000

No symbol is shown if production is less than 500 gigawatt hours.

Source: United Nations

**Source of Energy**

Thermal   Nuclear
Hydro   Other

Goode's Interrupted Homolosine Projection (Condensed)
Scale 1:162,000,000

A-101825-1   © Rand McNally

**Thermal Energy**   World Total - 12,413,000 gigawatt hours - 2005

| UNITED STATES | OTHER N.A. | CHINA | JAPAN | INDIA | OTHER ASIA | RUSSIA | GERMANY | ITALY | OTHER EUROPE | AFRICA | ALL OTHER |
|---|---|---|---|---|---|---|---|---|---|---|---|
| 25.4% | 3.6 | 16.8 | 5.7 | 4.7 | 13.3 | 5.1 | 3.2 | 2.5 | 8.8 | 3.7 | 3.0 |

**All Energy**   World Total - 18,335,000 gigawatt hours - 2005

| UNITED STATES | CANADA | OTHER N.A. | CHINA | JAPAN | INDIA | S. KOREA | OTHER ASIA | RUSSIA | GERMANY | FRANCE | U.K. | OTHER EUROPE | BRAZIL | OTHER S.A. | AFRICA | ALL OTHER |
|---|---|---|---|---|---|---|---|---|---|---|---|---|---|---|---|---|
| 23.4% | 3.4 | 1.9 | 13.8 | 6.0 | 3.8 | 2.1 | 9.1 | 5.2 | 3.4 | 3.1 | 2.2 | 12.1 | 2.2 | 2.3 | 3.0 | 2.9 |

**Nuclear Energy**   World Total - 2,768,000 gigawatt hours - 2005

| UNITED STATES | CANADA | FRANCE | GERMANY | UKRAINE | U.K. | SWEDEN | SPAIN | OTHER EUROPE | JAPAN | S. KOREA | OTHER ASIA | RUSSIA | ALL OTHER |
|---|---|---|---|---|---|---|---|---|---|---|---|---|---|
| 29.3% | 3.3 | 16.3 | 5.9 | 3.2 | 2.9 | 2.6 | 2.1 | 7.0 | 11.0 | 5.3 | 2.7 | 5.4 | 2.5 |

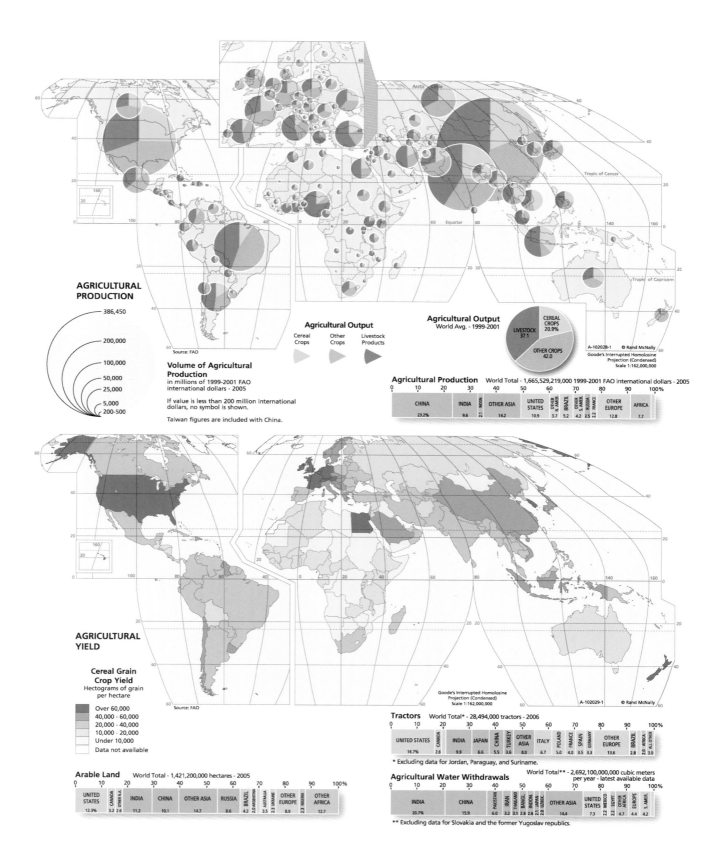

# AGRICULTURAL PRODUCTION

386,450
200,000
100,000
50,000
25,000
5,000
200-500

Source: FAO

**Volume of Agricultural Production**
in millions of 1999-2001 FAO international dollars - 2005

If value is less than 200 million international dollars, no symbol is shown.

Taiwan figures are included with China.

**Agricultural Output**

Cereal Crops | Other Crops | Livestock Products

**Agricultural Output**
World Avg. - 1999-2001

CEREAL CROPS 20.9%
LIVESTOCK 37.1
OTHER CROPS 42.0

A-102028-1 © Rand McNally
Goode's Interrupted Homolosine Projection (Condensed)
Scale 1:162,000,000

**Agricultural Production** World Total - 1,665,529,219,000 1999-2001 FAO international dollars - 2005

| 0 | 10 | 20 | 30 | 40 | 50 | 60 | 70 | 80 | 90 | 100% |
|---|---|---|---|---|---|---|---|---|---|---|

| CHINA | INDIA | INDON. | OTHER ASIA | UNITED STATES | OTHER N. AMER. | BRAZIL | OTHER S. AMER. | RUSSIA | FRANCE | OTHER EUROPE | AFRICA |
|---|---|---|---|---|---|---|---|---|---|---|---|
| 23.2% | 9.6 | 2.1 | 14.2 | 10.9 | 3.7 | 5.2 | 4.2 | 2.5 | 2.2 | 12.8 | 7.7 |

# AGRICULTURAL YIELD

**Cereal Grain Crop Yield**
Hectograms of grain per hectare

- Over 60,000
- 40,000 - 60,000
- 20,000 - 40,000
- 10,000 - 20,000
- Under 10,000
- Data not available

Source: FAO

Goode's Interrupted Homolosine Projection (Condensed)
Scale 1:162,000,000
A-102029-1 © Rand McNally

**Tractors** World Total* - 28,494,000 tractors - 2006

| 0 | 10 | 20 | 30 | 40 | 50 | 60 | 70 | 80 | 90 | 100% |
|---|---|---|---|---|---|---|---|---|---|---|

| UNITED STATES | CANADA | INDIA | JAPAN | CHINA | TURKEY | OTHER ASIA | ITALY | POLAND | FRANCE | SPAIN | GERMANY | OTHER EUROPE | BRAZIL | AFRICA | ALL OTHER |
|---|---|---|---|---|---|---|---|---|---|---|---|---|---|---|---|
| 16.7% | 2.6 | 9.9 | 6.6 | 5.5 | 3.6 | 8.0 | 6.7 | 5.0 | 4.0 | 3.5 | 3.3 | 13.6 | 2.0 | 2.0 | 3.0 |

*Excluding data for Jordan, Paraguay, and Suriname.

**Arable Land** World Total - 1,421,200,000 hectares - 2005

| 0 | 10 | 20 | 30 | 40 | 50 | 60 | 70 | 80 | 90 | 100% |
|---|---|---|---|---|---|---|---|---|---|---|---|

| UNITED STATES | CANADA | OTHER N.A. | INDIA | CHINA | OTHER ASIA | RUSSIA | BRAZIL | ARGENTINA | AUSTRALIA | UKRAINE | OTHER EUROPE | NIGERIA | OTHER AFRICA |
|---|---|---|---|---|---|---|---|---|---|---|---|---|---|
| 12.3% | 3.2 | 2.6 | 11.2 | 10.1 | 14.7 | 8.6 | 4.2 | 2.0 | 3.5 | 2.3 | 8.9 | 2.3 | 12.7 |

**Agricultural Water Withdrawals** World Total** - 2,692,100,000,000 cubic meters per year - latest available data

| 0 | 10 | 20 | 30 | 40 | 50 | 60 | 70 | 80 | 90 | 100% |
|---|---|---|---|---|---|---|---|---|---|---|---|

| INDIA | CHINA | PAKISTAN | IRAN | THAILAND | BANGL. | INDON. | JAPAN | UZBEK. | OTHER ASIA | UNITED STATES | MEXICO | OTHER AFRICA | EUROPE | S. AMER. |
|---|---|---|---|---|---|---|---|---|---|---|---|---|---|---|
| 20.7% | 15.9 | 6.0 | 3.2 | 3.1 | 2.8 | 2.8 | 2.0 | 2.3 | 14.4 | 7.3 | 2.2 | 4.7 | 4.4 | 4.2 |

**Excluding data for Slovakia and the former Yugoslav republics.

**M-9**

# COMMUNICATION NETWORK INFRASTRUCTURE

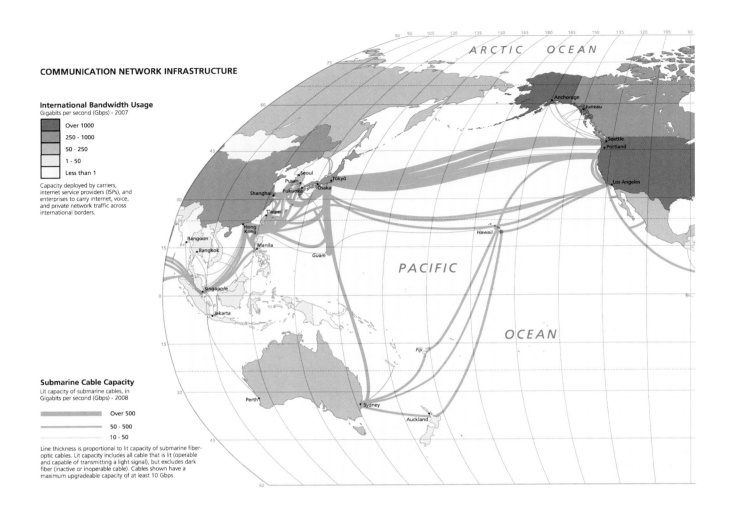

## International Bandwidth Usage

Gigabits per second (Gbps) - 2007

- Over 1000
- 250 - 1000
- 50 - 250
- 1 - 50
- Less than 1

Capacity deployed by carriers, internet service providers (ISPs), and enterprises to carry internet, voice, and private network traffic across international borders.

## Submarine Cable Capacity

Lit capacity of submarine cables, in Gigabits per second (Gbps) - 2008

- Over 500
- 50 - 500
- 10 - 50

Line thickness is proportional to lit capacity of submarine fiber-optic cables. Lit capacity includes all cable that is lit (operable and capable of transmitting a light signal), but excludes dark fiber (inactive or inoperable cable). Cables shown have a maximum upgradeable capacity of at least 10 Gbps.

# INTERNET CAPACITY

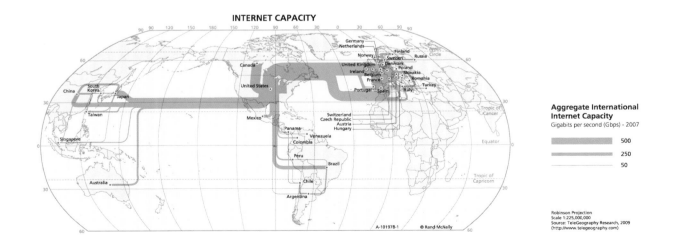

## Aggregate International Internet Capacity

Gigabits per second (Gbps) - 2007

- 500
- 250
- 50

Robinson Projection
Scale 1:225,000,000
Source: TeleGeography Research, 2009
(http://www.telegeography.com)

A-101978-1      © Rand McNally

### Submarine Cable Capacity by Route

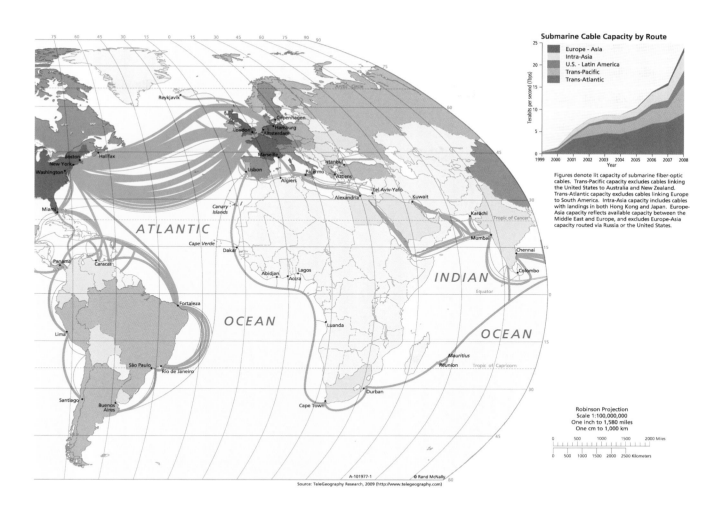

Figures denote lit capacity of submarine fiber-optic cables. Trans-Pacific capacity excludes cables linking the United States to Australia and New Zealand. Trans-Atlantic capacity excludes cables linking Europe to South America. Intra-Asia capacity includes cables with landings in both Hong Kong and Japan. Europe-Asia capacity reflects available capacity between the Middle East and Europe, and excludes Europe-Asia capacity routed via Russia or the United States.

Robinson Projection
Scale 1:100,000,000
One inch to 1,580 miles
One cm to 1,000 km

Source: TeleGeography Research, 2009 (http://www.telegeography.com)

## SHIPPING LANES

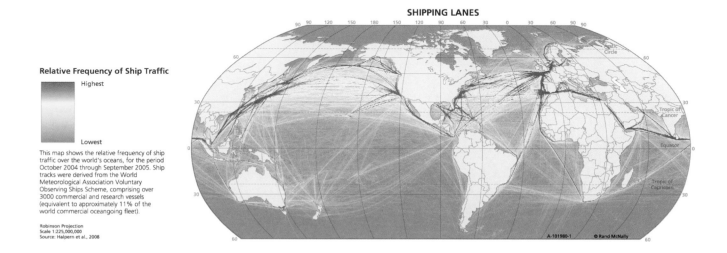

### Relative Frequency of Ship Traffic

Highest

Lowest

This map shows the relative frequency of ship traffic over the world's oceans, for the period October 2004 through September 2005. Ship tracks were derived from the World Meteorological Association Voluntary Observing Ships Scheme, comprising over 3000 commercial and research vessels (equivalent to approximately 11% of the world commercial oceangoing fleet).

Robinson Projection
Scale 1:225,000,000
Source: Halpern et al., 2008

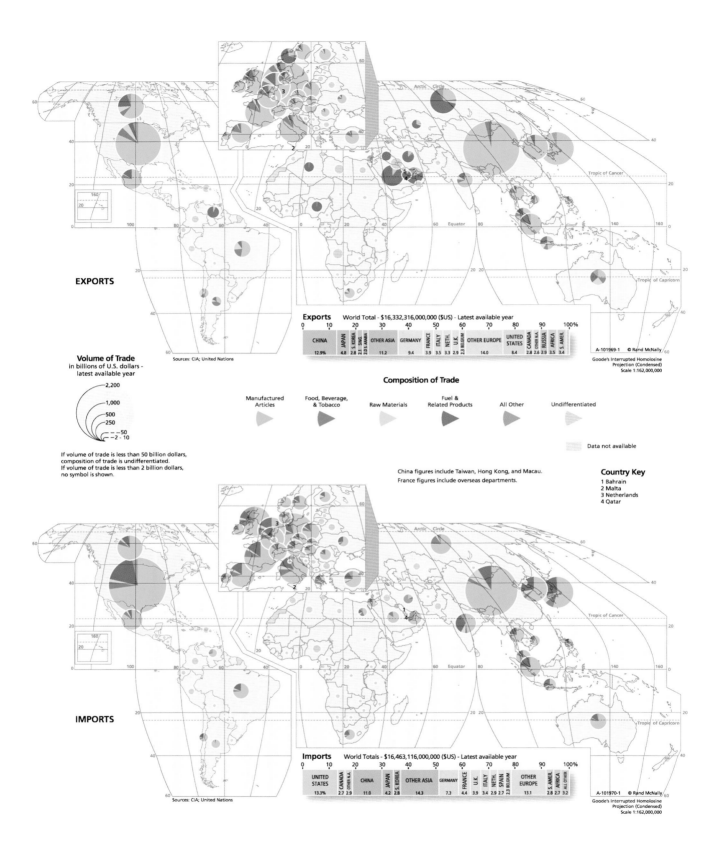

**EXPORTS**

**Volume of Trade**
in billions of U.S. dollars -
latest available year

- 2,200
- 1,000
- 500
- 250
- 50
- 2 - 10

If volume of trade is less than 50 billion dollars,
composition of trade is undifferentiated.
If volume of trade is less than 2 billion dollars,
no symbol is shown.

Sources: CIA; United Nations

**Exports** World Total - $16,332,316,000,000 ($US) - Latest available year

| | 0 | 10 | 20 | 30 | 40 | 50 | 60 | 70 | 80 | 90 | 100% |
|---|---|---|---|---|---|---|---|---|---|---|---|

| CHINA | JAPAN | S. KOREA | SING | 2.0 S. ARABIA | OTHER ASIA | GERMANY | FRANCE | ITALY | NETH. | U.K. | BELGIUM | OTHER EUROPE | UNITED STATES | CANADA | OTHER N.A. | RUSSIA | AFRICA | S. AMER. |
|---|---|---|---|---|---|---|---|---|---|---|---|---|---|---|---|---|---|---|
| 12.9% | 4.8 | 2.8 | 2.1 | | 11.2 | 9.4 | 3.9 | 3.5 | 3.3 | 2.9 | 2.3 | 14.0 | 8.4 | 2.8 | 2.6 | 2.9 | 3.5 | 3.4 |

A-101969-1  © Rand McNally

Goode's Interrupted Homolosine
Projection (Condensed)
Scale 1:162,000,000

**Composition of Trade**

Manufactured Articles | Food, Beverage, & Tobacco | Raw Materials | Fuel & Related Products | All Other | Undifferentiated

Data not available

China figures include Taiwan, Hong Kong, and Macau.
France figures include overseas departments.

**Country Key**
1 Bahrain
2 Malta
3 Netherlands
4 Qatar

**IMPORTS**

Sources: CIA; United Nations

**Imports** World Totals - $16,463,116,000,000 ($US) - Latest available year

| | 0 | 10 | 20 | 30 | 40 | 50 | 60 | 70 | 80 | 90 | 100% |
|---|---|---|---|---|---|---|---|---|---|---|---|

| UNITED STATES | CANADA | OTHER N.A. | CHINA | JAPAN | S. KOREA | OTHER ASIA | GERMANY | FRANCE | U.K. | ITALY | NETH. | SPAIN | BELGIUM | OTHER EUROPE | S. AMER. | AFRICA | ALL OTHER |
|---|---|---|---|---|---|---|---|---|---|---|---|---|---|---|---|---|---|
| 13.3% | 2.7 | 2.9 | 11.0 | 4.2 | 2.8 | 14.3 | 7.3 | 4.4 | 3.9 | 3.4 | 2.9 | 2.7 | 2.3 | 13.1 | 2.8 | 2.7 | 3.2 |

A-101970-1  © Rand McNally

Goode's Interrupted Homolosine
Projection (Condensed)
Scale 1:162,000,000

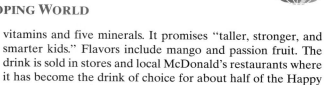

## 𝒢LOBAL PERSPECTIVE 10-3

### VITAMIN-FORTIFIED BEVERAGES FOR THE DEVELOPING WORLD

A shortage of essential vitamins and minerals such as vitamin A, iron, and zinc is believed to affect two billion children worldwide. The impact of such deficiencies on children's learning capabilities and health is huge. As vitamin pills are costly to distribute, one solution to combat this problem in the developing world is through fortification of foods and drinks with vitamins and minerals. Companies such as Procter & Gamble and Coca-Cola have recently launched vitamin-loaded beverages aimed at middle- and lower-middle-class families who—although not destitute—can hardly afford the most nutritious diets for their children.

Developing a fortified drink that is affordable, effective, and tasty is a triple challenge. Nutridelight, an orange-flavored powdered beverage, was launched by P&G in the Philippines in 1999. However, the product never became successful as it turned out to be too pricey. Another product, NutriStar, which P&G rolled out in Venezuela a couple of years later, appeared to be more promising. The powdered drink contains eight

vitamins and five minerals. It promises "taller, stronger, and smarter kids." Flavors include mango and passion fruit. The drink is sold in stores and local McDonald's restaurants where it has become the drink of choice for about half of the Happy Meals sold.

Coca-Cola tried to develop fortified drinks in the 1970s but did not succeed, as the technology was not advanced enough at that time. More recently, Coca-Cola set up Project Mission. A major goal of Project Mission is to extend relationships with local governments and schools. By becoming a good corporate citizen, Coca-Cola hopes to be able to advance its core brand in the long term. With the aid of pediatricians and health authorities, the soft drink maker experimented with different combinations of vitamins and minerals to come up with a fortified drink that maximizes both taste and effectiveness. Taste tests were run in countries such as South Africa and Botswana.

One result of these efforts is Kapo, which means "the best" in Spanish. The ready-to-drink fruit juice beverage is enriched with vitamins C, B1, and B6. It has been launched in Argentina, Brazil, Chile, Costa Rica, Ecuador, South Africa, Peru, and Turkey. In Peru, Kapo comes in three flavors—bubblegum, orange, and pineapple. Targeting children aged 8 to 12, Kapo is promoted as delicious, fun, and healthy.

*Sources:* "Coke launches Kapo range in Peru," www.adageglobal.com, accessed December 13, 2002; "New Fortified Drinks May Quench a Need," *The Asian Wall Street Journal* (November 28,2001), pp. 6, 8.

and *collaborators* (e.g., distribution channels, suppliers)—for creative new product ideas. Obviously, many successful new products originally started at the R&D labs. Other internal sources include salespeople, employees, and market researchers. Multinational companies often capitalize on their global know-how by transplanting new product ideas that were successful in one country to other markets. A good example of this practice is the Dockers line of casual slacks. This product was introduced in Japan by Levi Strauss Japan in 1985. The line became incredibly successful in Japan. As a result, Levi Strauss subsequently decided to launch the line also in the United States and Europe as well.[41]

A good source to spot new product ideas is the competition. The Global New Product Database (GNPD) set up by the Mintel International can be useful resource in this regard (http://www.gnpd.com/sinatra/gnpd/frontpage/). This database monitors new product introductions for 39 consumer packaged goods categories[42] in 48 countries worldwide. The service sends out regular e-mail alerts to its clients about products launched by competitors around the world.

These days many MNCs create organizational structures to foster global (or regional) product development. Unilever set up a network of worldwide innovation centers (ICs) for personal care and food products. Each IC unit consists of marketing, advertising agency, and technical people and is headed by the company chairman of the country subsidiary where the IC is based. The centers are responsible for developing product ideas and research, technology, and marketing expertise. Black & Decker sets

---

[41]"The Jeaning of Japan," *Business Tokyo*, February 1991, pp. 62–63.

[42]Food, drink, health & beauty care, pet care.

up business teams to develop global products. Each team is headed by a Product General Manager and has representatives from the various geographic regions. The charter of the teams is to develop new products with "the right degree of commonality and the right amount of local market uniqueness." Project leadership is assigned to that country or region that has a dominant category share position.[43]

**Screening**

Clearly not all new product ideas are winners. Once new product ideas have been identified, they need to be screened. The goal here is to weed out ideas with little potential. This filtering process can take the form of a formal scoring model. One example of a scoring model is NewProd, which was based on almost two hundred projects from a hundred companies.[44] Each of the projects was rated by managers on about 50 screening criteria and judged in terms of its commercial success. The model has been validated in North America, Scandinavia, and the Netherlands.[45] According to the NewProd model the most important success factor is product advantage (superiority to competing products, higher quality, and unique features), followed by a good fit between the project requirements and the company's resources/skills, and customer needs. Studies that interviewed Chinese[46] and Japanese[47] product managers reinforced the major role of product advantage in screening new product winners from losers. However, the study done in China also showed that:

1. Competitive activity was negatively correlated with new product success.

2. Being first in the market (pioneer entry) was an important success factor.

3. Product ideas derived from the market place were much more likely to be successful than ideas that came from technical work or in-house labs.

A large-scale research study conducted by researchers at the University of North-Carolina looked at the key drivers of first-year consumer acceptance of new packaged. The researchers analyzed a database that covered 301 new products launched in Germany, the U.K., France, and Spain. Some of the main findings include:

• Consumer acceptance is greater when the product is introduced by a brand with more market power (e.g., market support, distribution coverage, shelf space amount and quality) and when marketed as a brand extension.

• There is a U-shaped relation between newness and consumer acceptance. Products with incremental or major newness are more successful than products of medium newness.

• New product acceptance is also highly influenced by the competitive environment: it is higher in less concentrated, less heavily promoted, and less advertised categories and in categories with more intense innovation rivalry. Competitive conduct (e.g., price competition), however, is more important than competitive structure (e.g., market concentration). Further, the firm's brand reputation and product newness can buffer against negative competitive effects.

• Consumer characteristics also matter: acceptance is higher among consumers who are more predisposed to buy new products, younger consumers, and larger households.[48]

---

[43]Don R. Graber, "How to Manage a Global Product Development Process," *Industrial Marketing Management*, 25, 1996, pp. 483–89.

[44]Robert G. Cooper, "Selecting New Product Projects: Using the NewProd System," *Journal of Product Innovation Management*, vol. 2, no. 1, March 1985, pp. 34–44.

[45]Robert G. Cooper, "The NewProd system: the industry experience," *Journal of Product Innovation Management*, vol. 9, no. 2, June 1992, pp. 113–27.

[46]Mark E. Parry and X. Michael Song, "Identifying New Product Successes in China," *Journal of Product Innovation Management*, 11 (1994), pp. 15–30.

[47]X. Michael Song and Mark E. Parry, "What Separates Japanese New Product Winners from Losers," *Journal of Product Innovation Management*, 13 (1996), pp. 422–39.

[48]Katrijn Gielens and Jan-Benedict E.M. Steenkamp, "Drivers of Consumer Acceptance of New Packaged Goods: An Investigation Across Products and Countries," *International Journal of Research in Marketing*, 24, 2007, pp. 97–111.

Once the merits of a new product idea have been established in the previous stage, it must be translated into a **product concept**. A product concept is a fairly detailed description, verbally or sometimes visually, of the new product or service. To assess the appeal of the product concept, companies often rely on focus group discussions. Focus groups are a small group of prospective customers, typically with one moderator. The focus group members discuss the likes and dislikes of the proposed product and the current competing offerings. They also state their willingness to buy the new product if it were to be launched in the market (see Chapter 6 for a more detailed discussion of focus group research). Other more sophisticated tools exist to test out and further refine new product concepts. One such tool that has gained wide popularity in the last few decades is **conjoint analysis** (sometimes also referred to as *tradeoff analysis*).[49] The appendix in this chapter illustrates the use of conjoint analysis in global new product development with a hypothetical example.

Clearly, the results of product concept testing should be treated with the same amount of caution as the predictions of a fortune teller (if not even much more). Prior to launching Red Bull, Dietrich Mateschitz, the beverage brand's founder, tested out the concept: "People didn't believe the taste, the logo, the brand name . . . a disaster."[50]

**Concept Testing**

In many Western countries, test marketing of new products before the full-fledged rollout is the norm for most consumer goods industries. Test marketing is essentially a field experiment where the new product is marketed in a select set of cities to assess its sales potential and scores of other performance measures. In a sense, a test market is the dress rehearsal prior to the product launch (assuming the test market results support a "GO" decision). There are several reasons why companies would like to run a test market before the rollout. It allows them to make fairly accurate projections of the market share, sales volume, and penetration of the new product. In countries where household scanning panels are available, firms can also get insights into likely trial, repeat purchase, and usage rates for the product. Another boon of test marketing is that companies can contrast competing marketing mix strategies to decide which one is most promising in achieving the firm's objectives.

**Test Marketing**

Despite these merits, test markets also have several shortcomings. They are typically very time-consuming and costly. Apart from the direct costs of running the test markets, there is also the opportunity cost of lost sales that the company would have achieved during the test market period in case of a successful global rollout. Moreover, test market results can be misleading. It may be difficult to replicate test market conditions with the final rollout. For instance, certain communication options that were available in the test market cities are not always accessible in all of the final target markets. Finally, there is also a strategic concern: test markets might alert your competitors and thereby allow them to pre-empt you.

In light of these drawbacks, MNCs often prefer to skip the test market stage. Instead they use a market simulation or immediately launch the new product (one survey done in the 1990s indicated that pan-European financial institutions conducted test markets less than 20 percent of the time[51]). One alternative to test marketing is the laboratory test market. Prospective customers are contacted and shown commercials for the new item and existing competing brands. After the viewing, they are given a small amount of money and are invited to make a purchase in the product category in a simulated store setting ("lab"). Hopefully, some of the prospects will pick your new product. Those who purchase the new product take it home and consume it. Those who choose a competing brand are given a sample of the new product. After a couple of weeks the subjects are contacted again via the phone. They are asked to state their attitude toward the new item in terms of likes and dislikes, satisfaction, and whether they would be willing to buy the product again.

Such procedures, although relatively cheap, still give valuable insights about the likely trial and repeat buying rates, usage, and customer satisfaction for the new product,

---

[49]For a detailed discussion of conjoint analysis, see Chapter 22 in David A. Aaker, V. Kumar, and George S. Day, *Marketing Research* (New York: John Wiley & Sons, 2006).

[50]"Why Marketing Clashes with Management," *Advertising Age*, February 2, 2009, p. 19.

[51]Aliah Mohammed-Salleh and Chris Easingwood, "Why European financial institutions do not test-market new consumer products," *International Journal of Bank Marketing*, vol. 11, no. 3, 1993, pp. 23–27.

price sensitivities, and the effectiveness of sampling. The collected data are often used as inputs for a marketing computer simulation model to answer "what if" questions.

Another route that is often taken is to rely on the sales performance of the product in one country, the **lead market**, to project sales figures in other countries that are considered for a launching decision. In a sense, an entire country is used as one big test market. One practitioner of this approach is Colgate-Palmolive. For example, it used Thailand as a bellwether for the worldwide introduction of Nouriché, a treatment shampoo.[52] Thailand was chosen as a springboard because of the size and growth potential of its hair-care market. BMW used Australia as a global test market for a chain of BMW Lifestyle concept stores selling accessories (e.g., wallets, garments) under the BMW brand name. The concept is a way of keeping in touch with BMW customers to build a long-term relationship.[53] McCafé, McDonald's chain of upmarket coffee shops, is another good example. The first McCafé was launched in Australia in 1993. Restaurants with a McCafé generated 15 percent more revenue than regular ones. By 2003 McCafé had become the largest coffee shop brand in Australia and New Zealand. In light of the concept's success, the company introduced it in other countries around the world including the United States (2001) and Japan (2007). By 2008 there were 1,300 McCafé outlets worldwide.[54] Other recent instances of the use of an entire country as a test market are summarized in **Exhibit 10-4**.

Using a country as a test market for other markets raises several issues. How many countries should be selected? What countries should be used? To what degree can sales experience gleaned from one country be projected to other countries? Generally speaking, cross-cultural and other environmental differences (e.g., the competitive climate) turn cross-country projections into a risky venture. The practice is only recommendable when the new product targets cross-border segments.

**Timing of Entry: Waterfall versus Sprinkler Strategies**

A key element of a global or regional product launch strategy is the entry timing decision: When should you launch the new product in the target markets? Roughly speaking, there are two broad strategic options: the *waterfall* and the *sprinkler model* (see **Exhibit 10-5**).[55]

**EXHIBIT 10-4**
EXAMPLES OF TEST MARKET COUNTRIES

| Company | Product | Test Market Used | Geographic Coverage |
|---|---|---|---|
| Colgate-Palmolive | Nouriché (Shampoo) | Thailand | World |
| Unilever | Organics (Shampoo) | Thailand | World |
| Toyota | Toyota Soluna | Thailand | Asia |
| Coca-Cola | Coca-Cola Blak (Coffee-flavored cola) | France | World |
| Honda | Honda City | Thailand | Asia |
| Miller | Red Dog (Beer) | Canada | North-America |
| BMW | Concept Stores | Australia | World |
| Unilever | Dove Cream Shampoo | Taiwan | Asia |
| Procter & Gamble | Nutristar (Vitamin-packed Children Drinks) | Venezuela | Developing world |
| McDonald's | Golden Arch Hotel | Switzerland | Europe |
| KFC | Breakfast Menu | Singapore | World |
| Fiat | Palio | Brazil | World |
| Philip Morris Intl. | Marlboro Gold Edge | Poland | Central & Eastern Europe |
| Philip Morris Intl. | Marlboro Intense | Turkey | Europe |
| Microsoft | Search based advertising engine | France, Singapore | World |

[52]"Colgate tries Thai for global entry," *Advertising Age International*, May 16, 1994, p. I–22.

[53]"In Australia, BMW to Test New Concept in Dealerships: Branded Fashion Sales," *Advertising Age International* (March 8, 1999), p. 2.

[54]http://en.wikipedia.org/wiki/Mccafe, accessed on February 10, 2009.

[55]Riesenbeck, Hajo and Anthony Freeling, "How global are global brands?" *The McKinsey Quarterly*, No. 4, 1991, pp. 3–18.

**EXHIBIT 10-5**
WATERFALL VERSUS SPRINKLER MODELS

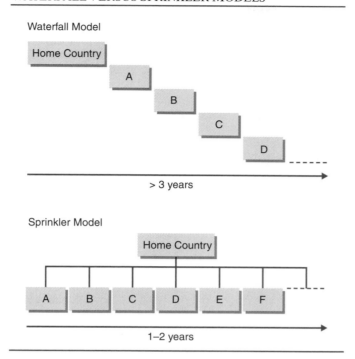

Waterfall Model

Home Country

A

B

C

D

> 3 years

Sprinkler Model

Home Country

A    B    C    D    E    F

1–2 years

The first option is the **global phased rollout** or **waterfall model**, where the company releases the new product stage-wise in its different country markets.[56] The typical pattern is to introduce the new product first in the company's home market. Next, the innovation is launched in other advanced markets. In the final phase, the multinational firm markets the product in less advanced countries. This whole process of geographic expansion may last several decades. The time span between the U.S. launch and the foreign launch was 22 years for McDonald's, 29 years for Wal-Mart, 25 years for Starbucks (outside North America), 20 years for Coca-Cola, and 35 years for Marlboro.[57] For other products, especially high-tech goods with short a product life cycle, the sequence happens over a much shorter time span. **Exhibits 10-6a and b** shows the rollout for two recently launched competing innovations in the game console industry, namely Microsoft's Xbox 360 and Sony's PlayStation 3.

The prime motive for the waterfall model is that adaptations of the marketing strategy for the host market can be very time-consuming. A phased rollout is also less demanding on the company resources. Other constraints such as the absence of good local partners may block a global rollout. Apple, for example, needed to negotiate partnership deals with local mobile phone service companies for the launch of its iPhone. These negotiations were not always successful. In China, for instance, Apple's negotiations with China Mobile, China's largest mobile service provider, broke down, leading to a significant delay of the iPhone launch in that market.[58] On the other hand, staggered rollouts are not always acceptable. In many industries—especially business-to-business markets—consumers worldwide do not want to be left behind. They all want to have access to the latest generation. A good example is what happened with the iPhone. Long before its official launch outside the United States, many Asian and European customers eager to get Apple's smart phone would buy an unauthorized

---

[56]Ohmae, Kenichi, "The triad world view," *Journal of Business Strategy*, 7, Spring 1985, 8–19.

[57]Numbers quoted in Riesenbeck and Freeling, "How global are global brands?."

[58]China Unicom, a smaller competitor of China Mobile, launched the iPhone in September 2009.

**EXHIBIT 10-6A**
ROLLOUT OF XBOX 360

| Launch Date Xbox 360 | Location |
|---|---|
| November 22, 2005 | Canada |
| | United States |
| December 2, 2005 | Eurozone |
| | Finland |
| | Ireland |
| | Latvia |
| | Norway |
| | Portugal |
| | Sweden |
| | United Kingdom |
| December 10, 2005 | Japan |
| February 2, 2006 | Colombia |
| | Mexico |
| February 24, 2006 | South Korea |
| March 16, 2006 | Hong Kong |
| | Singapore |
| | Taiwan |
| March 23, 2006 | Australia |
| | New Zealand |
| July 7, 2006 | Chile |
| September 25, 2006 | India |
| September 29, 2006 | South Africa |
| November 3, 2006 | Czech Republic |
| | Poland |
| December 1, 2006 | Brazil |
| February 10, 2007 | Russia |
| February 26, 2008 | Peru |

Source: http://en.wikipedia.org/wiki/Xbox_360_launch.

**EXHIBIT 10-6B**
ROLLOUT OF SONY PLAYSTATION 3

| Launch Date | Location |
|---|---|
| November 11, 2006 | Japan |
| November 17, 2006 | Canada |
| | Hong Kong |
| | Taiwan |
| | United States |
| March 7, 2007 | Singapore |
| March 22, 2007 | Saudi Arabia |
| | United Arab Emirates |
| March 23, 2007 | Australia |
| | Croatia |
| | Denmark |
| | Estonia |
| | Eurozone |
| | Iceland |
| | Latvia |
| | New Zealand |
| | Norway |
| | Pakistan |
| | Serbia |
| | South Africa |
| | Sweden |
| | Switzerland |
| April 20, 2007 | Russia |
| April 27, 2007 | India |
| August 20, 2008 | Mexico |
| August 2008 | Argentina |

Source: http://en.wikipedia.org/wiki/PlayStation_3_launch.

iPhone that was "unlocked" by a third party for a fee. Further, a phased rollout gives competitors time to catch up. For instance, the delay of the iPhone launch in the Asia-Pacific market allowed other smart phone makers such as Taiwan-based HTC to gain ample headway in pitching their smart phone models in the region as an acceptable alternative to iPhone.

The second timing decision option is the **sprinkler strategy** of simultaneous worldwide entry. Under this scenario, the global rollout takes place within a very narrow time-window. The growing prominence of universal segments and concerns about competitive pre-emption in the foreign markets are the two major factors behind this expansion approach.

The waterfall strategy of sequential entry is preferable over the sprinkler model when:[59]

1. The lifecycle of the product is relatively long.

2. Nonfavorable conditions govern the foreign market, such as:
   - Small market size (compared to the home market).
   - Slow growth.
   - High fixed costs of entry.

3. The host country market has a weak competitive climate because of such things as:
   - Very weak local competitors.
   - Competitors willing to cooperate.
   - No competitors.

---

[59]Shlomo Kalish, Vijay Mahajan and Eitan Muller, "Waterfall and sprinkler new-product strategies in competitive global markets," *International Journal of Research in Marketing*, 12, July 1995, pp. 105–19.

If a waterfall strategy is chosen, one important question is the sequence of countries to be entered: in which markets should the firm launch the product first and which ones later? Chandrasekaran and Tellis suggest the following two options:

- If a company wishes to launch the product in an innovative and large market, the best countries would be Japan or the United States.
- However, if a company wishes to test market the product in a small, highly innovative country, the best choices would be one of the Scandinavian countries, Switzerland or the Netherlands in Europe and South Korea in Asia.[60]

A research team at Erasmus University explored this issue by developing a model that captures the effect of global spillovers with new product introductions: consumers in one country could be influenced by consumers in other countries in their new product adoption decisions. The ideal country to enter first should have a fast time-to-takeoff, large market size, and strong influence on other countries. In Europe, good candidates that are highly influential include Germany and France. However, these two have a somewhat slower takeoff time compared to other European countries. The United Kingdom, on the other hand, shows a fast time-to-takeoff but has a modest spillover influence on other countries. Candidates with a slow takeoff and limited influence on other countries, but susceptible for foreign influences, are ideal for later entry. In Asia, countries such as Singapore, India, Pakistan, and China meet this profile.[61]

## TRULY GLOBAL PRODUCT DEVELOPMENT                    ◆ ◆ ◆ ◆ ◆ ◆ ◆

Scores of companies have research centers that are spread across the world. Unilever, for example, has a network of centers of excellence. However, these centers often concentrate on knowledge and technical expertise that is available in the countries or regions where they are located. Far fewer are those companies that have managed to set up a truly **global product development process** (GPD) that transcends local clusters. Such companies use a network of cross-functional product development teams spread across the globe. The benefits of GPD include greater engineering efficiency (through utilization of lower-cost resources), access to technical expertise that is distributed internationally, design of products for more global markets, and more flexible product development resource allocation (through use of outsourced staff).[62] Doz and his colleagues labeled such companies as **metanational innovators**.[63] Nokia is one example of a company that excelled as a metanational innovator. Nokia developed its first digital mobile phone from its R&D lab in the United Kingdom, not Finland. After observing consumer trends in Asia, Nokia tapped into design skills in Italy and California to turn the mobile phone into a fashion accessory. Nokia gained experience from Japan in miniaturization and improved user interface. Realizing the potential of mobile telephony to substitute fixed line communication in China and India, Nokia looked at Asia for skills to lower manufacturing costs.

The development of the ProLiant ML150 server by Hewlett-Packard provides another illustration of truly global innovation.[64] This server helps companies to manage customer databases and run e-mail systems. The initial idea was born in Singapore. After concept approval in Houston, concept design for the new server was done in

---

[60]Deepa Chandrasekaran and Gerard J. Tellis, "Global Takeoff of New Products: Culture, Wealth or Vanishing Differences?" *Marketing Science*, 27 (September–October 2008), pp. 844–60.

[61]Yvonne van Everdingen, Dennis Fok, and Stefan Stremersch, "Meeting Global Spillover in New Product Takeoff," Report No. 08-121, 2008, Marketing Science Institute.

[62]Steven D. Eppinger and Anil R. Chitkara, "The New Practice of Global Product Development," *MIT Sloan Management Review,* 47 (Summer 2006), pp. 22–30.

[63]Yves Doz, Jose Santos, and Peter Williamson, *From Global to Metanational: How Companies Win in the Knowledge Economy* (Boston: Harvard Business School Press, 2001) and www.metanational.net.

[64]"H-P Looks Beyond China," *Asian Wall Street Journal* (February 23, 2004), pp. A1, A7.

Singapore. Then HP picked a contractor in Taiwan to come up with the engineering design. Final assembly was made in four countries: Singapore, Australia, China, and India. In the past, design for high-end servers was done in the United States. However, by designing the ML150 in Asia, H-P could cut costs and make the new product more relevant to its Asian customers, the target market for this particular server.

To harvest the benefits of metanational innovation, a company must pursue three things:[65]

1. *Prospecting.* Find valuable new pockets of knowledge from around the world. For this to be effective, companies should keep an open mind on where knowledge can be found. For instance, while many view California as the hotbed for micro-electronics innovations, Israel and Singapore are also at the forefront in this area. Geographic proximity of the company's knowledge center to other firms or research institutions in the same industry should *not* be the key driver. Much more advantage can be derived from developing and nurturing relationships with potential pockets of knowledge, regardless of their location.[66]

2. *Assessing.* Decide on the optimal footprint, that is, the number and dispersion of knowledge sources. In terms of the number of knowledge sources, companies face a tradeoff between improved chances of developing a novel product and increased costs of integration. Often, the footprint evolves as the new product development process unfolds, especially for radical innovations.

3. *Mobilizing.* To harness the benefits of global innovation, companies must find ways to mobilize pockets of knowledge (e.g., technical blueprints, patents, equipment, market knowledge). The optimal strategy for mobilizing knowledge depends on the type (simple versus complex) and nature (technical versus market) of the knowledge involved. This leads to four possible scenarios as shown in **Exhibit 10-7**.

**EXHIBIT 10-7**
MOBILIZING KNOWLEDGE

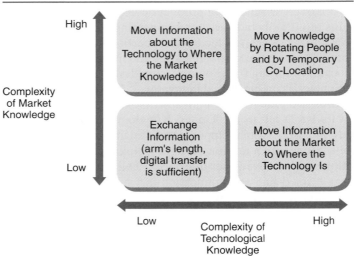

The optimum strategy for transferring knowledge depends on the complexity of both market knowledge (low versus high) and technological knowledge (low versus high).

[65] Jose Santos, Yves Doz, and Peter Williamson, "Is Your Innovation Process Global?" *MIT Sloan Management Review* 45 (Summer 2004): 31–37.
[66] See also Shankar Ganesan, Alan J. Malter, and Aric Rindfleisch, "Does Distance Still Matter? Geographic Proximity and New Product Development," *Journal of Marketing* 69 (October 2005): 44–60.

# SUMMARY

Global product policy decisions are tremendously important for the success of an MNC's global marketing strategies. In this chapter, the focus was on managing the new product development process in a global context. We first gave an overview of the different product strategy options that companies might pursue. Roughly speaking, a multinational company has three options: extension of the domestic strategy, adaptation of home-grown strategies, and invention by designing products that cater to the common needs of global customers. One of the major issues firms wrestle with is the standardization-versus-customization issue. By now, you should realize that this issue should not be stated in "either-or" terms. Instead, it is a matter of "degree": To what extent should we adapt (or if you want: standardize) our product strategy? We described the major forces that favor a globalized (or regionalized) product strategy. At the same time, there will always be forces that push your product strategy in the direction of customization.

Ideally, companies strike a neat balance between product standardization and adaptation. We described two product design approaches that enable a firm to capture the benefits of either option: the **modular** and the **core-product** approach. By adopting these approaches or their variants, firms minimize the risk of over-standardizing their product offerings while still grabbing the scale economies benefits that flow from a uniform product policy. We also demonstrated how you can use one market research tool—conjoint analysis—to make global product design decisions in practice.

The last part of this chapter highlighted the different stages in the new product development process. By and large, the pattern is similar to the steps followed in developing new products for the home market. However, there are a number of complicating factors that need to be handled: How do we coordinate global NPD efforts across different cultures? What mechanisms and communication channels can we use to stimulate idea exchanges? What alternatives do we have when certain steps of the NPD sequence are not do-able (e.g., test marketing)? Companies such as Nokia have configured innovation processes that are truly global. In the final section of this chapter, we looked at the characteristics of these so-called metanational innovators.

It is fitting to conclude this chapter with the insights of a seasoned practitioner. Don Graber, president of Worldwide Household Products at Black & Decker, offers the following set of guidelines on global product development:[67]

- Start with the consumer. Understand the commonalities and differences in regional needs.

- Do not try to make a product more global than it really is. A good, well-executed regional product is better than a "poorly executed" global product.

- Global business teams that are multifunctional and multigeographic are very helpful in supporting a global product program.

- Top managerial commitment and support is absolutely essential.

---

[67]Don R. Graber, "How to Manage a Global Product Development Process," *Industrial Marketing Management*, 25, 1996, pp. 483–89.

# KEY TERMS

| | | | |
|---|---|---|---|
| Adaptation | Invention | Sprinkler strategy | Waterfall strategy |
| Core-product approach | Global new product database (GNPD) | Overcustomization (Overstandardization) | |
| Customization | Lead (lag) country | Sprinkler strategy | |
| Extension | Metanational innovators | Standardization | |
| Incremental break-even analysis (IBEA) | Modular approach | Time-to-takeoff | |

# REVIEW QUESTIONS

1. Under what conditions is a dual extension strategy advisable? When is product invention more appropriate?

2. Explain the difference between the modular and core-product approaches.

3. Discuss the forces that favor a globalized product design strategy.

4. What could be the hidden costs of when adapting a product to be launched in a foreign market?

5. In what sense is the "standardize-versus-customize" question in global product design a bogus issue?

6. MNCs tend to move more and more towards a sprinkler strategy in terms of their global launch timing decisions. What forces lie behind this trend?

7. What are the major dangers in using an entire country as a "test market" for new products that are to be launched globally (or regionally)?

## DISCUSSION QUESTIONS ◆ ◆ ◆ ◆ ◆ ◆ ◆ ◆ ◆ ◆ ◆ ◆ ◆ ◆ ◆ ◆ ◆ ◆ ◆

1. Do you agree/disagree with the following statement recently made by John Dooner, chairman-CEO of McCann-Erickson Worldwide, a global advertising agency (*Advertising Age International*, September 1996, p. I-21):

"The old global view was that a centrally developed brand idea could be made relevant in just about any market, depending on how it was adapted. The reality of the new globalism is that a brand viewpoint that starts out being relevant in one market can become relevant in others, because of the nature of converging consumers. Creative ideas literally can come from anywhere, as long as there is a coordinated system for recognizing and disseminating these ideas. Countries that were once thought of as only being on the receiving end of global ideas can now also be the creators and exporters of these ideas."

2. Seagram Co. is well known for its high-end alcohol brands such as Martell and Chivas Regal. In May 2001, Seagram introduced a locally made whiskey, branded "30% High" in China. The brand name refers to the brand's 30 percent alcohol content and the alcohol high that comes with whiskey consumption. The target age group is 20–39 who cannot afford Seagram's more expensive brands such as Chivas. Priced at $4.75 per bottle it is more expensive than baijiu, the spirit made by local manufacturers. More than 100 million cases of baijiu are sold in China's biggest cities each year, compared to only 650,000 cases of imported spirits. At the launch, Seagram believed that "30% High" would work as it claimed that there was a market for a spirit with a sophisticated but affordable image. What obstacles do you see that Seagram might change with "30% High"? Presuming that "30% High" proves to be successful, can you think of other potential markets where there might be an opportunity for this new brand?

3. At a press conference in March 2008, Martin Wiederkorn, Volkswagen's chief executive, stated that: "In the coming years, we will make the VW group the world's most international carmaker. The days of the 'world car' are dead and buried. Our customers in China or India expect us, as a global player, to offer entirely different solutions than we do in the United States or Western Europe." ("VW Chief Kills 'World Car' Dream," *Financial Times*, March 14, 2008, p. 21). Do you agree or disagree? Why?

4. In the late 1990s McDonald's headquarters in Chicago decided to launch a "diversification" strategy to foster new ideas and concepts worldwide. One of the initiatives came from McDonald's Swiss branch. Urs Hammer, the then head of McDonald's Switzerland, proposed extending the brand into the hotel business by leveraging McDonald's image of cleanliness and fast, friendly service. With McDonald's strong global brand recognition, Hammer was convinced the project would be a success. In 2001 McDonald's opened two hotels, one in Zürich and one in Lully, under the name "Golden Arch Hotel" with room rates slightly about $100 a night. The hotels were positioned as four-star accommodations with cutting-edge in-room technology and unique, modern interior design. The hotels offered high-speed Internet access and an online booking system with special Internet rates. Beds featured distinctive arch-shaped headboards. The target markets encompassed business travelers during weekdays and young adults on weekends. What is your view about the selection of Switzerland as the first market for the Golden Arch Hotel concept? Do you see potential to extend the concept to other countries and if so which ones? (See also http://www.youtube.com/watch?v=FcD-Fn-LzU0.)

5. The Tata Nano car has been labeled the Model T for the 21st century. Selling for $2,500 it claims to be the world's cheapest car and could democratize car ownership in Indian and other emerging markets by fulfilling the dream of a lot of people in those countries who would like to own a car. Do you see potential for the Nano beyond India? Why or why not? If yes, what criteria would you use to select markets? Could Tata even launch the car in developed markets such as Hong Kong or Japan? Why or why not? For a visual impression of the Nano you could look at YouTube clips (see, for example, http://www.youtube.com/watch?v=wzuy3Aw0iDo).

6. What particular challenges do you see for companies introducing product categories that are truly new—recent examples include frozen yogurt (TCBY) and breakfast cereals (Kellogg's) in China; iced tea (Snapple) in Europe—into the foreign market? How might the marketing mix strategies used by the companies involved differ from the strategies used in the more developed markets?

# SHORT CASES

## CASE 10-1

### CASE 10-1: LEXUS IN EUROPE: A BUMPY RIDE

Lexus is the luxury car division of Japanese automaker Toyota. The foundations for the Lexus brand were laid in 1983 at a secret meeting of Toyota executives. At the meeting, Toyota's then chairman Eiji Toyoda posed the question: "Can we create a luxury vehicle to challenge the world's best?" Following the meeting, Toyota started a top-secret project, codenamed F1, which eventually led to the development of the Lexus LS 400. The LS 400 was revealed to the public in January 1989 at the Detroit Auto Show and debuted in the United States in September 1989. The LS 400 was widely praised in the automotive press for its silence, build quality, engine performance, high quality, and fuel economy. Lexus soon introduced other models including the RX 400h, the world's first hybrid luxury SUV. By 2007, Lexus's annual sales in the United States had risen to 329,177 units. For seven years in a row, Lexus has been the number one selling luxury brand in the world's largest automotive market.

In Europe, however, Lexus is struggling. Vehicle sales in 2007 were only 54,000 units in the region, less than one fifth of Lexus's U.S. sales volume. While Lexus fared well in the United Kingdom, sales in Germany, the home turf of BMW and Mercedes, have been dismal. One reason for the marque's poor reception in Europe could have been the design. According to Karl Schlicht, the brand's vice-president for Europe: "To Europeans, it looked very American—boxy and not enough

style, not enough design, not enough features." Lexus also offered only one diesel model, in spite of Europeans' liking for diesel cars. In 2007, Lexus changed the look of its cars in the hope of spurring sales. To differentiate from other luxury carmakers, Lexus decided to offer hybrid alternatives of several of its cars. It also announced plans to revamp its dealership network. Lexus is targeting 65,000 sales in Europe by 2010, still far below U.S. sales.

However, a new competitor is on the horizon: Infiniti. Infiniti, Nissan's luxury brand, prepared a Europe-wide launch for 2008. The launch pad is Russia—a "comparatively easy market"—where its cars were already available through grey-market imports. Nissan aims to sign up about fifteen business partners for dealerships and will replicate its U.S. retail environment, which it likens to a modern design hotel. Initially, it will only launch models with petrol engines. A diesel option will be added by 2010. An Infiniti spokesman noted, "The European market is the toughest in the world. We're going for a different angle: performance and fun to drive."

#### DISCUSSION QUESTIONS

1. Why did Lexus fail miserably in Europe?

2. Is there still hope for Lexus to recover in Europe? Are the changes announced for 2007 enough or is more drastic action needed?

3. Will Nissan's Infiniti luxury brand be more successful? Why or why not?

*Sources*: "Lexus Reveals Latest Model to Tempt Fussy European Drivers," *Financial Times*, March 6, 2007, p. 20 and http://en.wikipedia.org/wiki/Lexus.

## CASE 10-2

### CASE 10-2: PHILIP MORRIS INTERNATIONAL—THRIVING IN A HOSTILE WORLD

In March 2008, the Altria board approved the spin-off of Philip Morris International (PMI). This newly created entity is a leading international tobacco company with products sold in around 160 countries. It is also the world's third most profitable consumer goods company after Procter & Gamble and Nestlé. The change was supposed to free the tobacco giant's global business of legal and public-relations headaches in the United States.

The breakup should also make it easier for PMI to market a slate of new smoking concepts each targeted to different foreign markets. Ahead of the reorganization, Philip Morris streamlined the international new product decision-making process: local managers now have the "power to decide" which

new ideas may have legs in a particular region. PMI also overhauled its manufacturing: it halted imports from the U.S. sister company and, instead, now gets its entire supply from 42 manufacturing centers around the world.

While smoking rates in developed countries have steadily declined, they are still rising in many emerging markets such as Pakistan (up 42% since 2001), Ukraine (up 36%), and Argentina (up 18%). China, with 350 million smokers (50 million more than the U.S.), is a tremendous opportunity for PMI. One of the company's goals is to gain a foothold in China. For the time being, though, foreign tobacco companies such as PMI are limited to importing cigarettes for sale in China. Imports are subject to high import duties and stringent quotas. After lengthy years of negotiating, PMI reached a joint venture deal with CNTC (China National Tobacco Corporation). PMI hopes to develop CNTC as a key strategic partner. As part of the deal, Marlboro is manufactured and sold under license by CNTC in China. PMI also plans to market Chinese brands internationally, primarily in Central and Eastern Europe, and Latin America. PMI will adapt these Chinese brands to make them more appealing to non-Chinese smokers. Chinese smokers prefer full-tar brands while most Europeans and Latin Americans favor lower-tar brands. Chinese brands' packaging also tends to be too flashy for non-Chinese.

PMI also launched a slate of new products in markets around the world. For instance, to appeal to Southeast Asian consumers PMI launched Marlboro Mix 9, a sweet-smelling cigarette with twice the nicotine and tar of a conventional U.S. cigarette. Mix 9 debuted in Indonesia and was later introduced in other countries in the region. Other recent new Marlboro launches include *Marlboro Filter Plus* and *Marlboro Intense*. *Marlboro Filter Plus* (sold as *Marlboro Flavor Plus* in some countries) is PMI's most significant innovation in years. It has a unique multi-chamber filter and is sold in an original sliding pack. The brand is available at three tar levels (1 mg, 3 mg, and 6 mg) and generally retails at a premium.

### Market Share Levels (Sept. 2008) *Marlboro Filter Plus*

| | |
|---|---|
| Kuwait | 2.1% |
| Romania | 2.0% |
| Kazakhstan | 1.4% |
| Belarus | 0.6% |
| Moscow | 1.0% |
| Lithuania | 1.0% |

*Source*: www.philipmorrisinternational.com.

Another major global product launch for PMI in 2008 was the *Marlboro Intense* brand. This new product explores the concept of a rich, flavorful smoke in a shorter cigarette. It was first launched in Turkey and has since then been expanded to a wide range of EU markets (e.g., Belgium, Italy, Germany, Portugal). It achieved a 0.6 percent market share in September 2008.

To cope with smoking bans in mature markets PMI is developing the Heatbar, an odd-looking electronic device that resembles an electric toothbrush. This new device releases 90 percent less smoke than a normal cigarette. Smokers would

*Sources:* "Philip Morris Readies Aggressive Global Push," http://online.wsj.com/article/SB120156034185223519.html?mod=hpp_us_-pageone and www.philipmorrisinternational.com, accessed February 9, 2009.

be able to rent or buy the gadget. PMI has shown prototypes of the Heatbar to regulators in Australia, New Zealand, and the U.K., all countries with stringent anti-smoking regulations. Another recent new product is TBS ("Tobacco Block System"), which was first introduced in Germany. The tool targets smokers who prefer roll-your-own tobacco that is taxed significantly less than normal cigarettes. The TBS kit enables smokers to quickly roll their own cigarettes.

REUTERS/Dadang Tri/Landov LLC

To compete with low-priced smokes, PMI plans to launch new products with fancier packaging. One example is the *Marlboro Filter Plus* mentioned earlier. In 2008, PMI also test marketed a new more modern pack of *Marlboro Gold* in Austria, France, and Italy. Another critical market for PMI is Japan where continuous innovation is crucial. In the summer 2008, the firm launched *Marlboro Black Menthol* in Japan where smokers have a strong preference for menthol smokes.

In February 2009 PMI entered into a joint venture agreement with Swedish Match AB to commercialize Swedish Snus and other smoke-free tobacco products. Snus is a moist powdered tobacco product that is consumed by placing it beneath the upper lip for an extended time. Despite the fact that it does not affect the lungs as cigarettes do, the product is banned in most EU countries.

### DISCUSSION QUESTIONS

**1.** Some anti-tobacco critics sounded alarm bells about the PMI spin-off fearing that the cigarette maker now has more freedom to pursue sales growth in emerging markets by shielding the company from U.S. legal and regulatory issues. Do you agree with that concern?

**2.** The case discusses PMI's recent new product launches around the world. What is the major thrust of these innovations? Is PMI on the right track? Why or why not?

**3.** What else would you recommend PMI to do in the area of new product development?

# FURTHER READING ◆ ◆ ◆ ◆ ◆ ◆ ◆ ◆ ◆ ◆ ◆ ◆ ◆ ◆ ◆ ◆ ◆ ◆ ◆ ◆ ◆

Bose, Amit and Khushi Khanna, "The Little Emperor. A. case study of a new brand launch," *Marketing and Research Today*, November 1996, pp. 216–21.

Chandrasekaran, Deepa, and Gerard J. Tellis. "Global Takeoff of New Products: Culture, Wealth, or Vanishing Differences?" *Marketing Science*, 27(5), September-October 2008, pp. 844–60.

Duarte, Deborah and Nancy Snyder. "Facilitating Global Organizational Learning in New Product Development at Whirlpool Corporation," *Journal of Product Innovation Management*, 14(1997): 48–55.

Eppinger, Steven D., and Anil R. Chitkara. "The New Practice of Global Product Development." *MIT Sloan Management Review*, 47(Summer 2006), pp. 22–30.

Garber, Don, "How to Manage a Global Product Development Process," *Industrial Marketing Management*, 25, 1996, pp. 483–89.

Gielens, Katrijn, and Jan-Benedict E.M. Steenkamp. "Drivers of Consumer Acceptance of New Packaged Goods: An Investigation Across Products and Countries." *International Journal of Research in Marketing*, 24(2007), pp. 97–111.

Herbig, Paul A. and Fred Palumbo, "A Brief Examination of the Japanese Innovative Process: Part 2," *Marketing Intelligence & Planning*, 12(2), 1994, pp. 38–42.

Kalish, Shlomo, Vijay Mahajan, and Eitan Muller, "Waterfall and sprinkler new-product strategies in competitive global markets," *International Journal of Research in Marketing*, 12, July 1995, pp. 105–19.

Kleinschmidt, E. J., "A Comparative Analysis of New Product Programmes," *European Journal of Marketing*, 28(7), 1994, pp. 5–29.

Lynn, Michael and Betsy D. Gelb, "Identifying innovative national markets for technical consumer goods," *International Marketing Review*, 13(6), 1996, pp. 43–57.

Nakata, Cheryl and K. Sivakumar, "National Culture and New Product Development: An Integrative Review," *Journal of Marketing*, 60, January 1996, pp. 61–72.

Song, X. Michael and Mark E. Parry. "The Dimensions of Industrial New Product Success and Failure in State Enterprises in the People's Republic of China." *Journal of Product Innovation Management*, 11(2), 1994: 105–18.

Song, X. Michael and Mark E. Parry. "The Determinants of Japanese New Product Successes." *Journal of Marketing Research*, 34 (February 1997): 64–76.

Song, X. Michael and Mark E. Parry. "A Cross-National Comparative Study of New Product Development Processes: Japan and the United States." *Journal of Marketing*, 61 (April 1997): 1–18.

Song, X. Michael, C. Anthony Di Benedetto, and Yuzhen Lisa Zhao, "Pioneering Advantages in Manufacturing and Service Industries: Empirical Evidence From Nine Countries." *Strategic Management Journal*, 20(1999): 811–36.

Takada, Hirokazu and Dipak Jain, "Cross-National Analysis of Diffusion of Consumer Durable Goods in Pacific Rim Countries," *Journal of Marketing*, 55, April 1991, pp. 48–54.

Talukdar, Debabrata, K. Sudhir, and Andrew Ainslie. "Investigating New Product Diffusion Across Products and Countries." *Marketing Science*, 21(Winter 2002): 97–114.

Tellis, Gerard J., Stefan Stremersch, and Eden Yin. "The International Takeoff of New Products: The Role of Economics, Culture, and Country Innovativeness." *Marketing Science* 22(Spring 2003): 188–208.

# APPENDIX: USING CONJOINT ANALYSIS FOR CONCEPT TESTING IN GLOBAL NEW PRODUCT DEVELOPMENT ❖ ❖ ❖ ❖ ❖ ❖ ❖ ❖ ❖ ❖ ❖ ❖ ❖ ❖

In this appendix we discuss how international marketers can use conjoint analysis to test new product concepts. Most products and services can be considered as a bundle of product attributes. The starting premise of conjoint analysis is that people make trade-offs between the different product attributes when they evaluate alternatives (e.g., brands) from which they have to pick a choice. The purpose, then, of conjoint is to gain an understanding of the trade-offs that consumers make. The outcome of the exercise will be a set of "utilities" for each level of each attribute, derived at the individual household or consumer segment level. By summing these utilities for any a specific product concept, we can see how attractive that concept is to a particular consumer. The higher this utility score, the more attractive is the concept. This information allows the company to answer questions such as how much their customers are willing to pay extra for additional product features or superior performance. The tool can also be used to examine to what degree a firm should customize the products it plans to launch in the various target markets.

To illustrate the use of the conjoint for the design of products in an international setting, let us look at a hypothetical example. In what follows, we focus on the use of conjoint analysis in the context of global new product development.[68] Imagine that company XYZ considers selling satellite TV-dishes in two Southeast Asian countries, Thailand and Malaysia.

The first step is to determine the salient attributes for the product (or service). Exploratory market research (e.g., a focus group discussion) or managerial judgment can be used to figure out the most critical attributes. At the same time, we also need to consider the possible levels ("values") that each of the attributes can take. In our example (see **Exhibit 10-8**) four attributes are considered to be important: (1) the number of channels, (2) the purchase price,[69] (3) the installation cost, and (4) the size of the dish (in terms of inches). Each of the attributes has three possible levels. For instance, the diameter of the dish could be 18, 25, or 30 inches.

The next step is to construct product profiles by combining the various attribute levels. Each profile would represent a description of a hypothetical product. In most applications it is unrealistic to consider every possible combination since the

---

[68]Those of you who are interested in the technical background should consult Paul E. Green and Yoram Wind, "New ways to measure consumers' judgments," *Harvard Business Review*, vol. 53, 1975, pp. 107–17.

[69]In the example we assume that no middlemen will be used, so the retail price is the same as the ex-factory price.

**EXHIBIT 10-8**
SALIENT ATTRIBUTES AND
ATTRIBUTE LEVELS FOR SATELLITE
DISHES

| Product Attributes | Attribute Levels |
|---|---|
| Number of channels | (1) 30 |
| | (2) 50 |
| | (3) 100 |
| Selling price | (1) $500 |
| | (2) $600 |
| | (3) $700 |
| Installation fee | (1) Free |
| | (2) $100 |
| | (3) $200 |
| Size of dish | (1) 18″ |
| | (2) 25″ |
| | (3) 30″ |

**EXHIBIT 10-10**
RESULTS OF CONJOINT ANALYSIS FOR SATELLITE
DISHES

| Attributes | Thailand Segment I | Thailand Segment II | Malaysia Segment I | Malaysia Segment II |
|---|---|---|---|---|
| Number of Channels: | | | | |
| 30 | 0.0 | 0.0 | 0.0 | 0.0 |
| 50 | 1.5 | 3.4 | 1.4 | 1.8 |
| 100 | 3.2 | 5.6 | 3.0 | 2.5 |
| Purchase Price: | | | | |
| $500 | 0.0 | 0.0 | 0.0 | 0.0 |
| $600 | −3.2 | −1.5 | −2.8 | −2.5 |
| $700 | −4.6 | −2.0 | −4.8 | −3.0 |
| Installation: | | | | |
| Free | 0.0 | 0.0 | 0.0 | 0.0 |
| $100 | −1.5 | −0.2 | −1.4 | −1.0 |
| $200 | −1.8 | −0.4 | −2.1 | −1.7 |
| Size of Dish (Diameter): | | | | |
| 18″ | 0.0 | 0.0 | 0.0 | 0.0 |
| 25″ | −0.5 | −1.0 | −0.4 | −2.0 |
| 30″ | −0.8 | −1.5 | −1.0 | −5.0 |
| Size of Segment | 12,000 | 28,000 | 15,000 | 16,000 |

number of possibilities rapidly explodes. Instead, one uses an experimental design to come up with a small but manageable number of product profiles; this number varies from study to study. Obviously, the number of profiles will depend on the number of attributes and attribute levels, but also on other factors like the amount of information you want to collect. In most studies, the number of profiles ranges between 18 and 32. An example of such a profile is given in **Exhibit 10-9**.

After the profiles have been finalized, the company can go into the field and ask subjects to evaluate each concept. In each country several prospective target customers will be contacted. For instance, you might ask the respondent to rank the product profiles from most to least preferred. In addition, other data (e. g., demographics, lifestyle) are collected that often prove useful for benefit segmentation purposes.

Once you have collected the preference data, you need to analyze them using a statistical software package (e.g., SAS). The computer program will assign utilities to each attribute level based on the product evaluation judgment data that were gathered. Hypothetical results for our example are shown in **Exhibit 10-10**. Each country has two segments: a price-sensitive and quality-sensitive segment. The entries in the columns represent the utilities for the respective attribute levels. For instance, the utility of 100 channels in Thailand would be 5.6 for Segment II compared to 2.5 for Malaysia's performance Segment II. The results can be used to see which attributes matter most to each of the segments in the different target markets. The relative range of the utilities indicates the attribute importance weights. In this example, price is most

critical for Thai Segment I (utility range: 0 to -4.6), whereas the number of channels (utility range: 0 to 5.6) matters most for Thai Segment II. The technical nitty-gritty is less important here, but we would like you to get a flavor of how conjoint analysis can be used to settle product design issues in a global setting. Let us consider the standardization versus customization issue.

For the sake of simplicity, suppose that currently there is one incumbent competitor, ABC, in the satellite dish industry in Thailand and Malaysia. The ABC brand has the following features:

| | |
|---|---|
| Number of channels: | 30 |
| Selling price: | $500 |
| Installation fee: | Free |
| Size of dish: | 30″ |

XYZ is looking at two possibilities: (1) sell a standardized product (model XYZST) or (2) launch a customized product for each of the two markets (models XYZTH and XYZMA). The standardized product (XYZST) has the following profile:

| | |
|---|---|
| Number of channels: | 50 |
| Price: | $600 |
| Installation: | $100 |
| Size of dish: | 25″ |

The customized products would have the following characteristics:

| Attribute | Product XYZTH (Thailand) | Product XYZMA (Malaysia) |
|---|---|---|
| No. of Channels | 100 | 30 |
| Price | $700 | $700 |
| Installation | $200 | Free |
| Size of Dish | 25″ | 18″ |

**EXHIBIT 10-9**
EXAMPLE OF A PRODUCT
PROFILE

*Product Profile 18*

(1) Number of channels: 30
(2) Price: $500
(3) Installation fee: $100
(4) Size of dish: 25″

**EXHIBIT 10-11**
UTILITIES FOR RESPECTIVE ALTERNATIVES
DERIVED VIA CONJOINT STUDY

| Alternative | Thailand Segment I | Thailand Segment II | Malaysia Segment I | Malaysia Segment II |
|---|---|---|---|---|
| ABC (Competitor) | −0.8 | −1.5 | −1.0 | −5.0 |
| XYZST (Standardized) | −3.7[70] | 0.7 | −3.2 | −3.7 |
| XYZTH (Customized Thailand) | −4.0 | 2.2 | Not Offered | Not Offered |
| XYZMA (Customized Malaysia) | Not Offered | Not Offered | −4.8 | −3.0 |

In this example, the selling price for the uniform product is less than the price for the standardized product because of scale economies. By computing the overall utility for each of the alternatives we are able to estimate the market share that each product would grab in the two countries. This overall score is simply the sum of the utilities for the attribute levels. The respective utilities for the various product configurations are shown in **Exhibit 10-11**.

Assuming that each customer will pick the alternative that gives the highest overall utility, we can derive market share estimates in the two countries for the two product alternatives. For instance, we find that customers in Segment II would prefer the standardized dish to the competing model (as 0.7 > −1.5). On the other hand, Segment I in Thailand would pick ABC (since −3.7<−0.8). Hence, the market share for the standardized model (XYZST) in the Thai market would equal 70 percent: the number of households in the quality segment, 28,000 (see bottom row of Exhibit 10-11) divided by the entire market size for satellite dishes in Thailand, 40,000. In the same manner, we can compute XYZ's market share for the standardized model in Malaysia and for the customized models in the two countries:

---

[70]$1.5 + (−3.2) + (−1.5) + (−0.5) = −3.7.$

Market Share Standardized Product XYZST in Malaysia $= 51.6\%$ (16,000/31,000)

Market Share Customized Product XYZTH in Thailand $= 70\%$ (28,000/40,000)

Market Share Customized Product XYZMA in Malaysia $= 51.6\%$ (16,000/31,000)

In our example, the market share estimates for the two alternatives (standardized versus customized) end up being equal. Once we have cost estimates for the manufacturing and marketing of the different alternatives, we can estimate their expected profits. For instance, let us assume that the variable costs are equal (say, $400 per unit) but the fixed costs (combined across the two markets) differ: $5 million for the standardized product option as opposed to $10 million for the customized product option. Plugging in our market share estimates and these cost estimates, we can assess the profit potential of the various options:

Profits for standardized product approach (combined across the two countries):

$$(\text{Unit Sales Thailand} + \text{Unit Sales Malaysia})$$
$$(\text{Unit Contribution}) - \text{Fixed Costs}$$

or

$$(28{,}000 + 16{,}000) \times (\$600 + \$100 - \$400)$$
$$- \$5{,}000{,}000 = \$8.2 \text{ million}[71]$$

Profits for the customized product strategy:

$$(28{,}000) \times (\$700 + \$200 - \$400) + (16{,}000)$$
$$\times (\$700 + \$0 - \$400) - \$10{,}000{,}000 = \$8.8 \text{ million}.$$

Given the higher profit potential for the second alternative, launching two customized models (model XYZTH targeted toward Thailand and model XYZMA toward Malaysia) is clearly the winning option here. Obviously, in addition to the economics, other factors need to be considered before making a final decision.

---

[71]The unit contribution in this example is: selling price + installation fee − variable cost.

# GLOBAL PRODUCT POLICY DECISIONS II: MARKETING PRODUCTS AND SERVICES

## CHAPTER OVERVIEW

1. GLOBAL BRANDING STRATEGIES

2. MANAGEMENT OF MULTINATIONAL PRODUCT LINES

3. PRODUCT PIRACY

4. COUNTRY-OF-ORIGIN (COO) EFFECTS

5. GLOBAL MARKETING OF SERVICES

The detergent division of the German company Henkel has long been committed to a strategy of strong local brands. In Europe Henkel varies its laundry detergent strategy to address regional variations in laundry practices. Southern Europeans traditionally washed their clothes with lower temperatures than their northern counterparts. They prefer less powerful detergents, often used in combination with bleach. Northern Europeans favor powerful detergents and mostly dislike bleach in their laundry. Packaging preferences also differ. People in Northern Europe like compact products, while Southern consumers favor large boxes. To cope with all these variations, Henkel customizes its brand portfolio, positioning, and the product formulations. Henkel's flagship brand is Persil. However, Henkel did not own the Persil brand name in France[1]; it offered a similar product under the brand name Le Chat ("The Cat"). The positioning was also tweaked in different countries. For instance, Persil's whiteness positioning in Germany was replicated for Le Chat in France. In the Netherlands, Persil was positioned as an eco-friendly product. In Italy and Spain, Henkel had not introduced Persil for historical reasons. In Italy, consumers had a strong preference for blue detergents with a stain-fighting capability. This did not fit Persil's core value proposition ("whiteness with care"). Instead, Henkel entered Italy with Dixan, a performance brand. Henkel also entered Spain, another performance-oriented market, by acquiring Wipp, a strong local brand.[2] **Global Perspective 11-1** discusses further how Henkel deals with the challenges in the global market place.

---

[1]In France the Persil brand name is owned by Unilever.

[2]David Arnold, "Henkel KGaA: Detergents Division," Case Study, Boston: Harvard Business School, 2003.

◆ ◆ ◆ ◆ ◆ ◆ ◆ ◆ ◆ ◆ ◆ ◆ ◆ ◆ ◆ ◆ ◆ ◆ ◆ ◆ ◆ ◆ ◆ ◆ ◆ ◆ ◆ ◆ ◆ ◆ ◆ ◆ ◆

# *G*LOBAL PERSPECTIVE 11-1

## HENKEL: SQUARING LOCAL TASTES WITH GLOBAL ECONOMIES OF SCALE

Henkel, headquartered in Düsseldorf, Germany, is a leading German multinational with a presence in 125 countries. Its 2007 sales revenue was around €13 billion (±$17 billion). The company operates in three business areas: Laundry & home care (brands such as Persil, Dixan, Purex), cosmetics/toiletries (Dial, Fa, Schwarzkopf), and adhesives (Pritt, Loctite). In an interview with the *Financial Times*, Mr. Ulrich Lehner, Henkel's former chief executive, says that it would be nice to have one factory that could make a single global product, a central marketing department that could sell it everywhere using one brand name, packaging, and advertising campaign: "Realising economies of scale is every businessman's ambition." Still, truly global products are rare. The only Henkel brand that comes close is the Loctite glue. Usually, Henkel has to adapt the name or formulation of its products to local tastes.

A typical example is deodorants. In spring 2006 Henkel bought the Right Guard and other deodorant brands from Procter & Gamble for $275 million to gain a foothold in the U.S. market. Americans tend to prefer to suppress transpiration whereas continental Europeans like to conceal any odor without blocking sweating. Henkel's launch of its Fa personal care brand in 2000 in the United States was a failure. Similarly, there are also major differences in the laundry detergent market: U.S. washing machines tend to use more water at

*Sources:* www.henkel.com and "Brands that Stop at the Border," *Financial Times*, October 6, 2006, p. 10.

lower temperatures than European ones. As a result, Persil, Henkel's core detergent brand, would not have been suitable for the U.S. market. Instead of trying to roll out Persil in the United States, Henkel bought the Dial Group in 2003 to acquire Purex, the U.S. detergent brand. Mr. Lehner notes: "Abroad, we've grown more through acquisition than through the introduction of existing brands. Some of our competitors prefer to roll out their brands to other countries. You can, of course, try to push brands in a market if you have a lot of money."

Henkel's challenge is to balance between local insight and centralized economies of scale. Its answer is to bundle brands and products as "platforms" that ensure a degree of cost efficiency through scale in the sales or manufacturing area or even both. Henkel's strategy in eastern and central Europe illustrates this approach. The company bought up a range of local washing powders after the fall of the Berlin Wall. Henkel soon began standardizing the various powders and then steadily harmonized the packaging to lower costs and to reinforce the brand. As a result, Henkel brands such as Losk in Russia and Tursil in Turkey have similar product formulations and their brand names all tilt in bright red letters across the packet.

Like other global marketers, Henkel tries to transfer lessons learned in one market to other markets as it did with Purex, its U.S. washing powder: "It was the first time we did a value-for-money washing powder. We took elements of the Purex washing powders for emerging markets like China and Russia."

The challenges that Henkel addressed—global brand and product line management—are the focal issues in this chapter. Companies that brand their products have various options when they sell their goods in multiple countries. More and more companies see global (or at least regional) branding as a must. Nevertheless, quite a few firms still stick to local branding strategies. In between these two extreme alternatives, there are numerous variations. This chapter will consider and assess different branding approaches. Next, we shift our attention to the managing of an international product line. Multinational product line management entails issues such as: What product assortment should the company launch when it first enters a new market? How should the firm expand its multinational product line over time? What product lines should be added or dropped?

Another concern that global marketers face is the issue of product piracy. In this chapter we will suggest several approaches that can be employed to tackle counterfeiting. A lot of research has investigated the impact of country-of-origin effects on consumer attitudes towards a product. We will explore the major findings of this research stream and examine different strategies that firms can use to handle negative country-of-origin stereotypes. The balance of this chapter covers the unique problems of marketing services internationally. Services differ from tangible products in many respects. What these differences imply in terms of market opportunities, challenges and marketing strategies will be discussed in the last section.

♦ ♦ ♦ ♦ ♦ ♦ ♦ ♦    ## GLOBAL BRANDING STRATEGIES

For many firms the brands they own are their most valuable assets. A *brand* can be defined as "a name, term, sign, symbol, or combination of them which is intended to identify the goods and services of one seller or group of sellers and to differentiate them from those of competitors."[3] Linked to a brand name is a collection of assets and liabilities—the **brand equity** tied to the brand name. These include brand-name awareness, perceived quality, and any other associations invoked by the brand name in the customer's mind. The concerns that are to be addressed when building up and managing brand equity in a multinational setting include:[4]

- How do we strike the balance between a global brand that shuns cultural barriers and one that allows for local requirements?
- What aspects of the brand policy can be adapted to global use? Which ones should remain flexible?
- Which brands are destined to become "global" mega-brands? Which ones should be kept as "local" brands?
- How do you condense a multitude of local brands (like in the case of Sara Lee) into a smaller, more manageable number of global (or regional) brands?
- How do you execute the changeover from a local to a global brand?
- How do you build up a portfolio of global mega-brands?

Suffice it to say, there are no simple answers to these questions. In what follows, we will touch on the major issues regarding international branding.

**Global Branding**    Reflect on your most recent trip overseas and some of the shopping expeditions that you undertook. Several of the brand names that you saw there probably sounded quite familiar: McDonald's, Coca-Cola, Levi Strauss, Canon, Rolex. On the other hand, there were most likely some products that carried brand names that you had never heard of before or that were slight (or even drastic) variations of brand names with a more familiar ring. A key strategic issue that appears on international marketers' agenda is whether or not there should be a **global brand**. What conditions favor launching a product with a single brand name worldwide? The same logo? And perhaps even the same slogan? When is it more appropriate to keep brand names local? Between these two extremes are several other options. For instance, some companies use local brand names but at the same time put a corporate banner brand name on their products (e.g., "Findus by Nestlé").

**Exhibit 11-1** shows two listings of the most valuable brands in the world (in 2008); one put together by Interbrand and one by Milward Brown. The two research companies use somewhat different brand valuation methodologies, hence the sometimes dramatic differences between the two rankings.[5] Interbrand, for instance, assesses the profit stream likely to be generated by products carrying the brand name.[6] Note that both lists are heavily dominated by American brands. This is not too surprising since companies based in the United States have had much more experience with brand management than firms from other countries. It also reflects on the strength of the U.S. domestic market as a springboard for companies with global aspirations.[7]

A truly global brand is one that has a consistent identity with consumers across the world. This means the same product formulation, the same core benefits and value

---

[3]Philip H. Kotler, *Marketing Management*, Upper Saddle River, NJ: Prentice Hall, 2000.

[4]Jean-Noel Kapferer, *Strategic Brand Management. New Approaches to Creating and Evaluating Brand Equity*. London: Kogan Page, 1992.

[5]For instance, Google is worth $86 million according to Millward Brown as opposed to just $25.6 million based on Interbrand's method.

[6]You may notice that some major brands like Levi's and Lego appear to be missing. The reason is that Interbrand's calculation method relies on publicly available financial data. Privately-owned companies like Levi Strauss or Lego do not offer sufficient financial information.

[7]"Assessing a Name's Worth," *Financial Times* (June 22, 1999), p. 12.

## EXHIBIT 11-1
### WORLD'S MOST VALUABLE BRANDS (2008)

| Interbrand Ranking | BrandZ (Millward Brown) Ranking | Brand | 2008 Brand Value (in $millions) (Interbrand) | 2008 Brand Value (in $millions) (BrandZ) | Country of origin |
|---|---|---|---|---|---|
| 1 | 4 | Coca-Cola | 66,667 | 58,208 | USA |
| 2 | 6 | IBM | 59,031 | 55,335 | USA |
| 3 | 3 | Microsoft | 59,007 | 70,887 | USA |
| 4 | 2 | GE | 53,086 | 71,379 | USA |
| 5 | 9 | Nokia | 35,942 | 43,975 | Finland |
| 6 | 12 | Toyota | 34,050 | 35,134 | Japan |
| 7 | 27 | Intel | 31,261 | 22,027 | USA |
| 8 | 8 | McDonald's | 31,049 | 49,499 | USA |
| 9 | 23 | Disney | 29,251 | 23,705 | USA |
| 10 | 1 | Google | 25,590 | 86,057 | USA |
| 11 | 36 | Mercedes | 25,577 | 18,044 | Germany |
| 12 | 16 | HP | 23,509 | 29,278 | USA |
| 13 | 17 | BMW | 23,298 | 28,015 | Germany |
| 14 | 30 | Gillette | 22,069 | 21,523 | USA |
| 15 | 20 | American Express | 21,940 | 24,816 | USA |
| 16 | 19 | Louis Vuitton | 21,602 | 25,739 | France |
| 17 | 22 | Cisco | 21,306 | 24,101 | USA |
| 18 | 10 | Marlboro | 21,300 | 37,324 | USA |
| 19 | 15 | Citi | 20,174 | 30,318 | USA |
| 20 | 37 | Honda | 19,079 | 16,649 | Japan |
| 21 | 58 | Samsung | 17,689 | 11,870 | S. Korea |
| 22 | 66 | H&M | 13,840 | 11,182 | Sweden |
| 23 | 26 | Oracle | 13,831 | 23,208 | USA |
| 24 | 7 | Apple | 13,724 | 55,206 | USA |
| 25 | NA | Sony | 13,583 | NA | Japan |

*Source:* Adapted from http://bwnt.businessweek.com/interactive_reports/global_brand_2008/ and "Global Brands," *Financial Times* (April 21, 2008), Special Report Global Brands, p. 2.

proposition, the same positioning. Very few brands meet these strict criteria. Even a global marketing juggernaut like Procter & Gamble has only a few brands in its portfolio that can be described as truly global (e.g., Pringles, Pantene, Duracell, Gillette). Legal constraints often force the company to market a particular product under two or even more brand names. Lynx/Axe, Unilever's line of male grooming products, is a case in point. The Axe brand was launched in the early 1980s in France by Fabergé, a company bought by Unilever in 1989. In most countries the product is sold under the Axe brand name. However, in several countries such as the United Kingdom and Australia it is named Lynx as the Axe trademark belonged to another firm in these countries. For a similar reason, the Burger King fast food giant was forced to rename itself in Australia "Hungry Jack's" as the BK trademark was already registered by a take-away food shop in Adelaide.

What is the case for global branding? One advantage of having a global brand name is obvious: economies of scale. First and foremost, the development costs for products launched under the global brand name can be spread over large volumes. This is especially a bonus in high-tech industries (e.g., pharmaceuticals, computing, chemicals, automobiles) where multi-billion dollar R&D projects are the norm. Scale economies also arise in manufacturing, distribution (warehousing and shipping), and, possibly, promotion of a single-brand product. As we noted in the last chapter, computerized design and manufacturing processes allow companies to harvest the scale benefits of mass production while customizing the product to the needs of the local market. Even then, substantial scale advantages on the distribution and marketing front often strongly favor global branding.

Scale advantage is only one of the reasons for using a global brand name.[8] Part of the task of brand managers is building up brand awareness. By its very nature, a global brand

---

[8]David A. Aaker, *Managing Brand Equity. Capitalizing on the Value of a Brand Name.* New York: The Free Press, 1991.

has much more visibility than a local brand. Prospective customers who travel around may be exposed to the brand both in their home country and in many of the countries they visit. Therefore, it is typically far easier to build up brand awareness for a global brand than for a local brand. A global brand can also capitalize on the extensive media overlap that exists in many regions. Cable TV subscribers in Europe and many Asian countries have access to scores of channels from neighboring countries. Having a global brand that is being advertised on one (or more) of these channels can mean more bang for the bucks.

A further benefit is the prestige factor. Simply stated, the fact of being *global* adds to the allure of a brand: It signals that you have the resources to compete globally and the willpower and commitment to support the brand worldwide.[9] The prestige image of being global was also one of the motivations behind Lenovo's decision to develop a global brand: recognition as a global brand would boost the PC maker's image in China, its home market, and thereby create positive spillovers. Those global brands that can claim worldwide leadership in their product category have even more clout: Colgate, Intel, Marlboro, Coca-Cola, and Nike, to mention just a few.

In some cases global brands are also able to leverage the country association for the product: McDonald's is U.S. fast food, L'Oréal is French cosmetics, Swatch is a Swiss watch, Nissin Cup is Japanese noodles, and so on. Brown-Forman, the U.S. distiller, pitches Jack Daniel's, its flagship brand, as a U.S. label. In Romania, Brown-Forman set up a company-sponsored event in September 2004 to celebrate the birthday of Jack Daniel. Romanian actors entertained a crowd by dressing up as the Tennessee backwoodsman.[10] A desire to reflect its U.S. roots motivated Disney to change the name for its Paris theme park from Euro Disney to Disneyland Paris.[11] Of course, such positioning loses some of its appeal when your competition has the same heritage. For instance, Marlboro is a U.S. cigarette brand, but so are Camel and Salem. Further, strong ties between the brand and the home country could hurt the brand when relationships between the home and host country become strained. Anti-China protests in Paris during the 2008 Olympic torch relay enraged many Chinese people and triggered a widespread boycott of Carrefour stores in China.

French retailer Carrefour faced China boycott after pro-Tibet protests during the 2008 Olympic torch relay in Paris.

Courtesy of Kristaan Helsen

[9] David A. Aaker, *Building Strong Brands*. New York: The Free Press, 1996.

[10] "Drinking to the Dollar," *Forbes Global*, April 18, 2005: 34–38.

[11] "The kingdom inside a republic," *The Economist*, April 13, 1996, pp. 68–69.

One important question here is also how consumers value global brands. A 2002 study on this issue identified three key dimensions:[12]

1. **Quality signal.** Consumers perceive global brands as being high in quality. A company's global stature signals whether it excels on quality. Consumers often believe that global brands connote better quality and offer higher prestige.[13]

2. **Global myth.** Consumers look at global brands as cultural ideals. The global brand gives its customer a sense of belonging, of being part of something bigger.

3. **Social responsibility.** Consumers also expect global brands to have a special duty to address social issues, to act as good citizens. The playing field is not level. Global players such as Nike and Shell are often held up to higher standards than their smaller counterparts in terms of how they conduct business.[14]

The arguments for global branding listed so far sound very powerful. Note though that, like many other aspects of global marketing, the value of a brand, its *brand equity*, usually varies a great deal from country to country. A large-scale brand assessment study done by the advertising agency DDB Needham in Europe illustrates this point:[15] brand equity scores for Kodak ranged from 104 in Spain to 130 in the United Kingdom and Italy.[16] Cross-country gaps in brand equity may be due to any of the following factors:

1. **History.** By necessity, brands that have been around for a long time tend to have much more familiarity among consumers than latecomers. Usually, early entrants also will have a much more solid brand image if they have used a consistent positioning strategy over the years.

2. **Competitive climate.** The battlefield varies from country to country. In some countries the brand faces only a few competitors. In others the brand constantly has to break through the clutter and combat scores of competing brands that nibble away at its market share.

3. **Marketing support.** Especially in decentralized organizations, the communication strategy used to back up the brand can vary a great deal. Some country affiliates favor push strategies, using trade promotions and other incentives targeted toward distributors. Others might prefer a pull strategy and thus focus on the end consumers. It is not uncommon for the positioning theme used in the advertising messages to vary from country to country (see Chapter 7).

4. **Cultural receptivity to brands.** Another factor is the cultural receptivity towards brands. Brand receptivity is largely driven by risk aversion. Within Europe, countries such as Spain and Italy are much more receptive toward brand names than Germany or France.[17] One recent study looked at the role of brands as signals using survey and experimental data collected in seven countries on purchase behavior for orange juice and personal computers.[18] The study found that the impact of a brand's credibility as a signal of quality on consumers' brand choice is larger in high uncertainty avoidance and high-collectivist[19] cultures.[20]

---

[12]Douglas B. Holt, John A. Quelch, and Earl L. Taylor, "How Global Brands Compete," *Harvard Business Review*, 82 (September 2004), pp. 68–75.

[13]Jan-Benedict E.M. Steenkamp, Rajeev Batra, and Dan L. Alden, "How Perceived Brand Globalness Creates Brand Value," *Journal of International Business Studies* 34, 1 (January 2003): 53–65.

[14]"How Model Behavior Brings Market Power," *Financial Times* (August 23, 2004): 9.

[15]Jeri Moore, "Building brands across markets: cultural differences in brand relationships within the European Community," in *Brand Equity & Advertising: Advertising's Role in Building Strong Brands,* D. A. Aaker and A. L. Biel, eds., Hillsdale, NJ: Erlbaum Associates, 1993.

[16]The scores were derived via a multiplication formula: Brand Awareness X Brand Liking X Brand Perception.

[17]Jeri Moore, "Building brands across markets: cultural differences in brand relationships within the European Community."

[18]Brazil, Germany, India, Japan, Spain, Turkey, and the United States.

[19]Note though that the effect of collectivism was only found for orange juice.

[20]Tülin Erdem, Joffre Swait, and Ana Valenzuela, "Brand as Signals: A Cross-Country Validation Study," *Journal of Marketing Research*, 70, January 2006, pp. 34–49.

**5. Product category penetration.** A final factor is the salience of the product category in which the brand competes. Because of lifestyle differences, a given category will be established much more solidly in some countries than in others. In general, brand equity and product salience go together: The higher the product usage, the more solid will be the brand equity.

## Local Branding

Coca-Cola has four core brands in its brand portfolio (Coke, Sprite, Diet Coke, and Fanta). At the same time, it also owns numerous regional and local brands worldwide. In India, its biggest-selling cola is not Coke but Thums Up, a local brand that Coca-Cola acquired in 1993. In Japan, where carbonated soft drinks are less popular than most other countries, the ready-to-drink coffee brand Georgia is one of Coca-Cola's best-selling brands. Maytag Corp., the U.S. appliance maker, decided to sell its Chinese appliances using a local name, Rongshida, which comes from its Chinese partner, Hefei Rongshida. The Maytag name is virtually unknown in China. Furthermore, consumer research showed that American appliances were perceived as bulky and big by Chinese consumers. Therefore, rather than selling under the Maytag badge, the company preferred to leverage the image of a long-standing Chinese brand, even though it had come to be seen as somewhat dated.[21] Although the advantages of a global brand name are numerous, there could also be substantial benefits of using a local brand.

In some cases, a local brand becomes necessary because the name or a very similar name is already used within the country in another (or even the same) product category. Use of a global brand name may also be limited because someone already owns the right for the trademark in the foreign market. Going back to the example we introduced in this chapter, Henkel owns the Persil trademark in most European countries. However, the Persil trademark belongs to Unilever, Henkel's archrival, in the United Kingdom, France, and Ireland.

Cultural barriers also often justify local branding. Without localizing the brand name, the name might be hard to pronounce or may have undesirable associations in the local language. Pocari Sweat, a Japanese sport drink, which is promoted as an "Ion supply drink," never became popular in Ireland despite its strong appeal in Japan and several Asian countries. Its peculiar brand name could have been one explanation. Associations linked to the brand name often lose their relevance in the foreign market.[22] Brand names like Snuggle, Healthy Choice, Weight Watchers, or I Can't Believe It's Not Butter don't mean much in non-English-speaking foreign markets.

Courtesy of Kristiaan Helsen

A local linkage can also prove helpful in countries where patriotism and buy-local attitudes matter. Under such circumstances, the local brand name offers a cue that the company cares about local sensitivities. A case in point is the beer industry. Karel Vuursteen, a former chairman of Heineken, said: "There is strong local heritage in the [beer] industry. People identify with their local brewery, which makes beer different from detergents or electronic products."[23] In many emerging markets, once the novelty and curiosity value of Western brands wears off, consumers switch back to local brands. This is partly a matter of affordability. A can of Coca-Cola or a McDonald's Happy Meal is an expensive luxury in most developing countries.

---

[21]"Maytag Name Missing in China Ad Effort," *Ad Age Global* (May 2000), pp. 2, 11.
[22]Rajeev Batra, "The why, when, and how of global branding," in *Brand Equity and the Marketing Mix: Creating Customer Value,* Sanjay Sood, ed., Marketing Science Institute, Report No. 95-111, September 1995.
[23]"Time for another round," *The Financial Times* (June 21, 1999).

When choosing between the local and foreign product, consumers may also prefer the local alternative because of animosity toward the foreign country.[24] Ariel, P&G's laundry detergent, fell prey to boycott campaigns in the Middle East because of its alleged ties with Ariel Sharon, Israel's prime minister. Mecca Cola is a new soft drink that was launched by a French entrepreneur to cash in on anti-American sentiments in Europe and the Middle East. Its bottles bear the none-too subtle slogan "No more drinking stupid, drink with commitment."[25]

If the local brand name stems from an acquisition, keeping the local brand can be preferable to changing it into a global brand name. The brand equity built up over the years for the local brand can often be a tremendous asset. Thus, one motive for sticking with the local brand name is that the potential pay-offs from transforming it into a global brand name do not outweigh the equity that would have to be sacrificed. This reasoning lies behind Danone's branding strategy in China. The French food conglomerate expands in China by acquiring stakes in Chinese companies and continuing to sell their products under the local brand names.[26] For instance, after acquiring a controlling stake in Wahaha, Danone used the Wahaha brand and distribution network to enter the bottled water market. In 2002, Chinese brands accounted for 80 percent of Danone's sales in China. Another motive for keeping the local brand name could be the firm's strategic positioning goals: MNCs may aspire to cover the entire market by having brands positioned at all price points. Often the local brands are positioned at the bottom or medium end while the global brands cover the upper end of the market. Heinz, for example, sells two ketchup brands in Poland: the premium-priced Heinz core brand and Pudliszki, a Polish brand that Heinz acquired after the fall of the Berlin Wall.[27]

**Global or Local Branding?**

Philip Morris International (PMI) top-selling brand is Marlboro, which outsells its closest competitors by almost three times. It ranked 18th in the 2008 Interbrand global brand list with an estimated brand value of $21,300 million (see Exhibit 11-1). Apart from the core Marlboro brand, PMI has many other brands in its portfolio: 150 distinct brands and over 1,900 variants.[28] **Exhibit 11-2** shows some of these brands. As you can see, PMI has a mixture of global and local brands. Besides PMI, many other major multinationals have a portfolio of local, regional, and global brands. By now you probably realize that there are no simple answers to the global-versus-local brand dilemma. The **brand structure** or **brand portfolio** of a global marketer is the firm's current set of brands across countries, businesses, and product-markets.[29] There are basically four main types of branding approaches:[30]

- *Solo branding.* Each brand stands on its own, with a product or brand manager running it (e.g., Unilever, Procter & Gamble).
- *Hallmark branding.* The firm tags one brand, usually the corporate one, to all products and services, and does not use any sub-brands (e.g., most banks).
- *Family (umbrella) branding.* This is a hierarchy of brands that uses the corporate brand as an authority symbol and then has a number of sub-brands under the corporate badge (e.g., Sony PlayStation).

---

[24]Jill Gabrielle Klein, "Us Versus Them, or Us Versus Everyone? Delineating Consumer Aversion to Foreign Goods," *Journal of International Business Studies*, 33(2) (Second Quarter 2002), pp. 345–63.

[25]"Mecca Cola Challenges US Rival," on http://news.bbc.co.uk/2/hi/middle_east/2640259.stm.

[26]"China Market Finally Pays Off," *Asian Wall Street Journal* (January 9, 2003), pp. A1, A10.

[27]In fact, the Pudliszki brand is so popular in Poland that Heinz now also sells it in countries such as the United Kingdom with a large Polish community.

[28]www.philipmorrisinternational.com, accessed on February 10, 2009.

[29]Susan P. Douglas, C. Samuel Craig, and Edwin J. Nijssen, "Integrating Branding Strategy Across Markets: Building International Brand Architecture," *Journal of International Marketing*, 9(2) (2001), pp. 97–114.

[30]Lars Göran Johansson, "Electrolux Case Study: The Beginning of Branding as We Know It," in *Global Branding*. MSI Working Paper Series No. 00-114 (2000), pp. 29–31.

• *Extension branding.* The idea is to start with one product and then stretch the brand to other categories, as far as possible (e.g., luxury and fashion industries).

A firm's global brand structure is shaped by three types of factors: firm-based drivers, product-market drivers, and market dynamics.[31]

***Firm-Based drivers.*** The firm's administrative heritage, in particular its organizational structure is one key factor. Centralized firms are more likely to have global brands. Decentralized companies where country managers have a large degree of autonomy will have a mish-mash of local and global brands. Another important driver is the company's expansion strategy: does the firm mainly expand via acquisitions or via organic (that is, internal) growth? Ahold, a Dutch retailer, operates under 25 names worldwide (e.g., Superdiplo in Spain, Stop & Shop and Giant in the United States, and ICA in Sweden).[32] The company started expanding internationally in 1973 by buying established brands. Its policy ever since has been to maintain the local brands, governed by the mantra: "Everything the customer sees, we localize. Everything they don't see, we globalize."[33] Each chain has its own positioning and the store names and logos vary enormously across countries. This local branding strategy is driven by the belief that all retailing is local as shoppers develop a store loyalty to brands they have known for decades. Obviously, the importance of the firm's corporate identity also plays a major role. Lastly, product diversity is another important factor. For instance, Unilever's product range is far more diverse than Nokia's.

***Product-Market Drivers.*** The second set of brand portfolio drivers relate to product-market characteristics. Three drivers can be singled out here. The first driver is the nature and scope of the target market: how homogeneous are the segments? Are segments global, regional, or localized? The second factor is the degree of cultural embeddedness. Products with strong local preferences (e.g., many foods and beverages) are more likely to succeed as local brands. A final factor is the competitive market structure: Are the key players local, regional, or global competitors?

***Market Dynamics.*** The firm's brand structure is also shaped by the underlying market dynamics. The level of economic integration is the first important driver here. Economic integration typically leads to harmonization of regulations. It also often entails fewer barriers to trade and business transactions within the region. The second factor is the market infrastructure in terms of media and distribution channels (e.g., retailing). Finally, consumer mobility (e.g., travel) also plays an important role. With increased mobility, global brands stand to benefit from enhanced visibility.

Apart from the brand structure, the **brand architecture** is another important cornerstone of the firm's international branding strategy. The brand architecture guides the dynamics of the firm's brand portfolio. It spells out how brand names ought to be used at each level of the organization. In particular, the brand architecture establishes how new brands will be treated; to what extent umbrella brands are used to endorse product-level brands; to what degree strong brands will be extended to other product categories (brand extensions) and across country borders. This architecture has three key dimensions (see **Exhibit 11-3**): the level in the organization at which the brand is used, the geographic scope of the brand, and the product scope. Electrolux, the leading maker of kitchen, cleaning, and outdoor appliances, settled on the following guidelines:[34]

• Use the Electrolux brand name as the family brand standing for quality, leadership, and trust.

• Reduce the number of brands. Create bigger, stronger ones.

---

[31]Douglas, Craig, and Nijssen, pp. 100–105.
[32]"Ahold Promotes Its Many Brands," *Asian Wall Street Journal* (September 28, 2000), p. 26.
[33]"European Consumers Prefer Familiar Brands for Grocers," *Asian Wall Street Journal* (September 3, 2001), p. N7.
[34]"Electrolux Case Study," p. 30.

**EXHIBIT 11-3**

DIMENSIONS OF INTERNATIONAL BRAND ARCHITECTURE

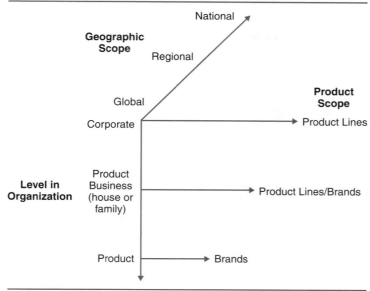

*Source:* Susan P. Douglas, C. Samuel Craig, and Edwin J. Nijssen, "Integrating Branding Strategy across Markets: Building International Brand Architecture," *Journal of International Marketing 9*, No. 2, 2001, pp. 97–114.

• Converge to worldwide, consistently positioned brands; both geographically and across product lines.

• Leave to the local manager the burden of proving that his or her local situation should be an exception to the worldwide strategy.

Nestlé provides another example of a company with a well-defined brand architecture. The Swiss food multinational owns nearly 8,000 different brands worldwide. **Exhibit 11-4** shows Nestlé's brand architecture. As you can see, Nestlé's brands are organized in a branding tree. At the root are ten worldwide corporate brands—brands like Carnation, Nestlé, and Perrier. The next level consists of 45 strategic brands that are managed at the strategic business unit level. Examples include KitKat, After Eight, and Smarties. Climbing further, you can spot the regional strategic brands, managed at the regional level. For instance, in the frozen food category, Nestlé markets the Stouffer's brand in America and Asia and the Findus brand in Europe. At the very top of the tree is a multitude of local brands (about 7,000) that are the responsibility of the local subsidiaries.

Although companies often feel driven to build up global brands, there are solid reasons to make an in-depth analysis before converting local brands into regional or global ones. In fact, local brands sometimes can have much more appeal among consumers than their global competing brands. This is especially true when there is not much benefit from being global.

David Aaker, an expert on branding, offers the following checklist for analyzing globalization propositions:[35]

1. What is the cost of creating and maintaining awareness and associations for a local brand versus a global one?

2. Are there significant economies of scale in the creation and running of a communication program globally (including advertising, public relations, sponsorships)?

3. Is there value to associations of a global brand or of a brand associated with the source country?

---

[35]David A. Aaker, *Managing Brand Equity.* New York: The Free Press, 1991.

**EXHIBIT 11-4**
NESTLÉ BRANDING TREE

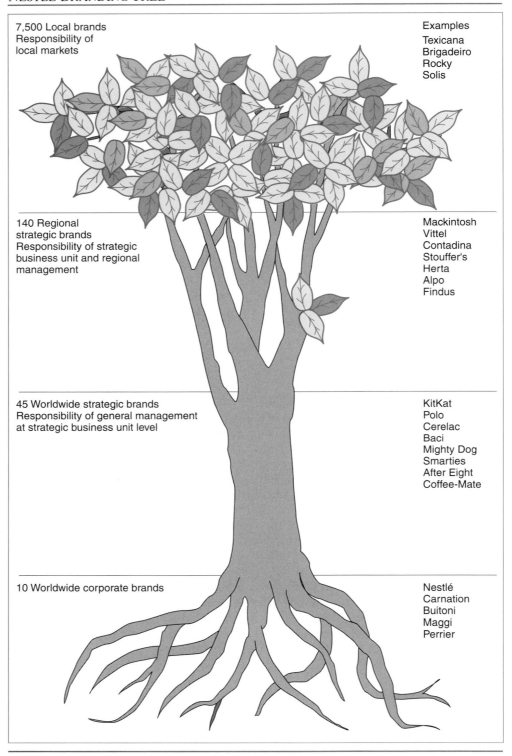

7,500 Local brands
Responsibility of
local markets

Examples
Texicana
Brigadeiro
Rocky
Solis

140 Regional
strategic brands
Responsibility of strategic
business unit and regional
management

Mackintosh
Vittel
Contadina
Stouffer's
Herta
Alpo
Findus

45 Worldwide strategic brands
Responsibility of general management
at strategic business unit level

KitKat
Polo
Cerelac
Baci
Mighty Dog
Smarties
After Eight
Coffee-Mate

10 Worldwide corporate brands

Nestlé
Carnation
Buitoni
Maggi
Perrier

*Source:* Reprinted with special permission from "*The McKinsey Quarterly,*" 2 (1996). Copyright © 1996 McKinsey & Company. All rights reserved.

4. What local associations will be generated by the global name? symbol? slogan? imagery?

5. Is it culturally and legally do-able to use the brand name, symbol, and slogan across the different countries?

6. What is the value of the awareness and associations that a regional brand might create?

One of P&G's most popular brands in Germany was a liquid dishwashing detergent named Fairy. Early 2000, the brand had a market share of nearly 12 percent. In the middle of 2000, P&G rechristened the brand using the Dawn global brand name. There was no change in the product formulation. The renamed brand's market share crashed. One year later, Dawn's share stood at 4.7 percent. While Fairy represented a trusted and well-known brand to German consumers, Dawn meant nothing.[36] This bond of trust had been broken with the renaming. It was estimated that P&G sustained a loss in turnover of $8 million. In the end, P&G decided to go back to the old Fairy name. P&G made the same kind of mistake in Austria when it replaced Bold with Dash.[37] Changing the brand name from a local to a global (or regional) brand name is not a trivial matter. Attachments to the existing brand name can be very deep and emotional.

**Brand-Name Changeover Strategies**

When the case for a transition from a local to a global brand name is made, the firm needs to decide on how to implement the changeover in practice. Four broad strategic options exist:[38] (1) *fade-in/fade-out*, (2) combine brands via *co-branding* or under one *umbrella brand*, (3) *transparent forewarning*, and (4) *summary axing.*

With **fade-in/fade-out**, the new global brand name is somehow tied with the existing local brand name. After a transition period, the old name is dropped. A typical example is the brand name change that Disney implemented for its Paris theme park. It first shrunk the *Euro* part in Euro Disney and added the word *land*. In October 1994 the word *Euro* was dropped altogether and the theme park is now branded as *Disneyland Paris.*[39]

The second route combines the "old" local brand and the global or regional brand in some manner. One tactic that is sometimes employed is to have the global brand as an umbrella or endorser brand. For example, Pedigree was launched in the late 1980s in France as "Pedigree by Pal." Another possibility is **dual branding (co-branding)**. During a transition period, the local and global brand names are kept so that consumers and the trade have sufficient time to absorb the new brand name. When Whirlpool acquired the white goods division of Philips, the company initially employed a dual branding strategy—Philips and Whirlpool. After a transition period, the Philips brand name was dropped. Likewise, Danone used co-branding in South Africa shortly after it bought a stake in the Clover company, South Africa's leading fresh dairy producer. Although Danone is a global brand, at the time the brand name was virtually unknown in South Africa. By using co-branding, Danone was able to leverage the huge brand equity that Clover had in South Africa as well as Clover's strong association with dairy products in the local consumer's mind.[40]

The third approach, transparent forewarning, alerts the customers about the brand name change. The forewarning is typically done via the communication program, in-store displays, and product packaging. A good example is the transition made by Mars in continental Europe for one of its best-selling candy bars. Up to 1991 the candy bar known

---

[36]Randall Frost, "Should Global Brands Trash Local Favorites," www.brandchannel.com, accessed on February 9, 2009.

[37]Jean-Noël Kapferer, *The New Strategic Brand Management,* London: Kogan Page, 2008.

[38]Trond Riiber Knudsen, Lars Finskud, Richard Törnblom, and Egil Hogna, "Brand Consolidation Makes a Lot of Economic Sense," *The McKinsey Quarterly,* 4 (1997), pp. 189–93.

[39]"The kingdom inside a republic," *The Economist,* April 13, 1996, p. 69.

[40]Russell Abratt and Patience Motlana, "Managing Co-Branding Strategies: Global Brands Into Local Markets," *Business Horizons,* (Sept.–Oct. 2002), pp. 43–50.

**EXHIBIT 11-5**
GERMAN PRINT AD FOR RAIDER/TWIX CHANGEOVER
(Translation: "From Raider becomes Twix—but everything else does not change!")

Twix® is a registered trademark of Mars, Incorporated and its affiliates. This trademark is used with permission. Mars, Incorporated is not associated with John Wiley and Sons, Inc. Advertisement printed with permission of Mars, Incorporated.

as Twix in the USA was sold under the Raider brand name in most of Europe. For various strategic reasons (e.g., economies of scale) Mars decided to drop the Raider name and replace it with the Twix brand name. Given that Raider had very strong brand equity in continental Europe (the second most popular candy bar after Mars), the changeover was not a trivial matter. Mars left no stone unturned in the countries affected by the change: Mars aired a high-impact television ad campaign starring David Bowie with strong emphasis on Twix pack-shots, it ran print-ads to signal the change (see **Exhibit 11-5**), it used in-store promotions to maximize visibility and awareness, and it also indicated the changeover on the Raider's wrappings with the words "known globally as Twix" during the transition period.[41]

Far less common is the fourth practice, summary axing, where the company simply drops the old brand name almost overnight and immediately replaces it with the global name. This is only appropriate when competitors are rapidly gaining global clout by building up global brands.

To manage the transition effectively, several rules should be respected.[42] First, it is critical to conduct consumer research prior to the brand name changeover to understand consumers' perceptions and gauge their response to any modifications (e.g., packaging, logo, brand name). When the brand name is changed gradually, one of the key concerns is the proper length for the transition period. When IBM sold its personal computer division to Lenovo, part of the deal was that Lenovo would have access to the IBM brand name up to five years. The IBM logo could only be used on Think-family products. When the IBM logo was shown in Lenovo ads, it could only be displayed on the product within the ad. However, ownership of the Think sub-brand (i.e., ThinkPad and ThinkCentre) would be permanent. The timeline agreed between Lenovo and IBM for usage of the IBM name had three phases:[43]

- *Phase 1 (first 18 months).* Current IBM branding to remain unchanged.
- *Phase 2 (second 40 months).* The IBM brand name must be less prominent and separate from the Think sub-brand.
- *Phase 3 (remaining 2 months).* IBM is more like an ingredient or endorsement brand.

In principle, the firm should allow sufficient time for the customers to absorb the name change. How long this process will take depends on the product and the strength of the image associated with the old brand name. For some product categories, the purchase cycle matters too. Sometimes the phase-out can be completed sooner than scheduled. Lenovo, for example, dropped the IBM name two years ahead of schedule.

---

[41] For further details and other examples, see *The New Strategic Brand Management*, London: Kogan Page, 2008.

[42] Marieke de Mooij, *Advertising Worldwide. Concepts, Theories, and Practice of International, Multinational and Global Advertising.* Upper Saddle River, NJ: Prentice Hall, 1994.

[43] John Quelch and Carin-Isabel Knoop, "Lenovo: Building a Global Brand," Case Study, Boston, MA: Harvard Business School, 2006.

It is also important that consumers who are exposed to the changeover messages associate the new brand name with the old one. One of the primary goals of Whirlpool's advertising campaign was to maintain awareness of the Philips brand name while building up association with Whirlpool.[44]

To avoid negative spillovers on the global brand name, companies should also ensure that the local products are up to standard before attaching the global brand name to them. Otherwise, the goodwill of the global brand name could be irreparably damaged. As a result, other products launched under the global brand name might be viewed with skepticism by consumers in the foreign market. Part of Whirlpool's geographic expansion in China involved a joint venture that makes air conditioners based on Japanese designs. The air conditioners, sold under a local brand name, Raybo, initially had about half the life expectancy of U.S.-made Whirlpool models. Whirlpool's president declared that his company would not put the Whirlpool name on the product until Raybo's quality problems were fixed.[45]

Finally, companies should monitor the marketplace's response to the brand name change with marketing research. Such tracking studies enable the firm to ensure that the changeover runs smoothly. They also assist firms in determining how long promotional programs that announce the name change should last. Whirlpool tracked brand recognition and buying preference of consumers on a weekly basis during the brand-change period. **Global Perspective 11-2** describes the efforts made by British oil company BP to implement a global corporate makeover.

## $\mathcal{G}$LOBAL PERSPECTIVE 11-2

### BEYOND PETROLEUM—BP AMOCO'S CORPORATE MAKEOVER

In July 2000, BP Amoco unveiled a global corporate makeover that included a new brand identity and revamped, high-technology service stations. BP spent $7 million of research and design funds to develop the global corporate makeover. The new "exploding sunflower" motif was named the Helios mark after the sun god of ancient Greece. The company ditched the shield logo, which BP had used for 70 years. BP declared: "Our new mark resembles a dynamic burst of energy; bright white at the core with radiant beams of yellow and green light. Our mark's interlocking parts represent the diversity of our people, products and services. Its radiance is a daily reminder of our aspirations and purpose . . . In a hundred countries across the globe, BP employees bring the world energy in the forms of light, warmth, and mobility."

Although the revamp happened worldwide, the impetus for the change came from BP's U.S. operations. The U.S. market

is home to about one-third of BP's 28,000 retail outlets worldwide. After its merger with Amoco and a major acquisition spree, BP owned four separate brands: BP, Amoco, ARCO, and Castrol. BP Amoco recognized the need for a new, unifying image. However, Arco's service station network on the West coast of the United States was not affected by the rebranding exercise as ARCO's existing business has a strong brand identity there.

One reason for the consolidation was the sense to bond BP employees around the world following the merger and acquisitions. However, another key factor was BP's desire to alter the public's perception of BP from a traditional "old economy" British oil company to a global "new economy" energy services group, taking BP into the "Beyond Petroleum" era.

Besides introducing a new logo, BP also upgraded its service stations. New high-tech service stations were rolled out with brightly lit fueling and parking areas. Some of stations are solar-powered and provide internet access to customers. BP spent $7 million on research and design.

*Sources:* "BP Amoco Unveils Corporate Makeover," *The Financial Times* (July 25, 2000), p. 26; "Oil Group Hopes Helios Will Bring Sunshine," *The Financial Times* (July 25, 2000), p. 26; "BP's Step Beyond Petroleum," *The Financial Times* (August 9, 2000), p. 19.

---

[44]Jan Willem Karel, "Brand Strategy Positions Products Worldwide," *The Journal of Business Strategy*, May/June 1991, pp. 16–19.

[45]"For Whirlpool, Asia is the new frontier," *The Wall Street Journal*, April 25, 1996, p. B1.

◆ ◆ ◆ ◆ ◆ ◆ ◆ ◆    ## MANAGEMENT OF MULTINATIONAL PRODUCT LINES

Most companies sell a wide assortment of products. The product assortment is usually described on two dimensions: the width and the length of the product mix. The first dimension—width—refers to the collection of different product lines marketed by the firm. For most companies, these product lines are closely related. Some companies, especially major multinationals, market a very broad array of product lines. Besides bakery products, Sara Lee also offers products in the following categories: beverages, meats, body care, air care, detergents, insecticides, and shoe care.[46] The second dimension—length—refers to the number of different items that the company sells within a given product line. Thus, the product mix for a particular multinational could vary along the width and/or length dimension across the different countries where the firm operates.

When comparing the product mix in the company's host and home markets, there are four possible scenarios. The product mix in the host country could be (1) an extension of the domestic line, (2) a subset of the home market's product line, (3) a mixture of local and non-local product lines, or (4) a completely localized product line.

Small firms with a narrow product assortment usually simply extend their domestic product line. Blistex, a small family-run U.S. company that makes primarily lip-care products, has a very limited range of product lines marketed in all of its foreign markets. On the other hand, larger companies that enter new markets carefully select a subset of their product mix. When Coca-Cola goes into a new market, the focus is obviously first on Coca-Cola. Once the flagship brand is well established, the next introduction is typically Fanta, the flavor line. Fanta is followed by Sprite and Diet Coke (or Coke Light). Once the infrastructure is in place, other product lines—including local ones—are added over a period of time.[47] Most MNCs have a product mix that is partly global (or regional) and partly local.

Several drivers impact the composition of a firm's international product line. We briefly discuss the key factors:

***Customer Preferences.*** In many product categories, consumer preferences vary from country to country. Especially for consumer-packaged goods, preferences are still very localized. To cater to distinctive customer needs, marketers may add certain items to the individual country's or region product line or fine-tune the line. A good example is Procter & Gamble's change of strategy for Pantene shampoo in the Asia-Pacific region.[48] Based on consumer research in key markets, P&G revamped the Pantene brand and created new monikers such as Smooth & Sleek, Hydrating Curls, and Vibrant Colors. However, for the Asia-Pacific region, P&G had to fine-tune this new global approach. "Curls" are not relevant for Asian consumers; few Asians understood the meaning of "sheer volume"; few were interested in changing their hair color. Therefore, P&G created new varieties of Pantene for the region such as Smooth & Silky, Volume & Fullness, and a Classic Clean range (Balance Clean, Lively Clean, and Anti-Dandruff) (see **Exhibit 11-6**). Following the revamp, Pantene's market share in Southeast Asia grew from 14 to 16 percent.

**Exhibit 11-7** lists some of the sandwiches that McDonald's introduced on its menu to cater toward local tastes. Japanese consumers' notorious desire for innovation forces consumer goods marketers in Japan to constantly come out with new product variants. As a result the product variety of many multinational consumer goods company in Japan is much broader than that in other countries. A good example is Nestlé's KitKat brand, which has become very popular in Japan, largely due to the similarity of the

---

[46]http://www.saralee.com/OurBrands/AllBrands.aspx, accessed on February 10, 2009.

[47]www.thecoca-colacompany.com/investors/Divester.html.

[48]"Pantene Shampoo is Reborn," *Ad Age Global* (May 2002), pp. 18–19.

**EXHIBIT 11-6**
PANTENE SHAMPOO BRANDS IN ASIA

Courtesy of Kristiaan Helsen

brand's name to the phrase *kitto katsu* ("you will surely win!"). To cater to its Japanese consumers yearning for novelty, Nestlé has launched an incredible range of flavors (many for a limited time only) including some rather unusual ones such as kiwi, maple syrup, strawberry, banana, green tea, cherry blossom, and cookies & milk (see **Exhibit 11-8**).[49]

**EXHIBIT 11-7**
HOW MCDONALD'S CUSTOMIZES ITS MENU

| Country | Sandwich | Description |
| --- | --- | --- |
| France | Croque McDo | A grilled ham and cheese sandwich on toast |
| India | Maharaja Mac | Two grilled chicken patties with smoke-flavored mayonnaise, onions, tomatoes and cheddar cheese |
| Taiwan | Rice Burger | Shredded beef between two rice patties |
| Japan | Teriyaki Burger | A chicken cutlet patty marinated in teriyaki sauce |
| Middle East | McArabia Sandwich | A marinated grilled chicken sandwich in flatbread |
| New Zealand | Kiwi Burger | A hamburger with a fried egg and a slice of pickled beet |
| Poland | McKielbasa | Kielbasa (Polish sausage) patty topped with ketchup, mustard, and onion. |
| Pakistan | Spicy McChicken | A chicken sandwich with chutney |
| Thailand | Samurai Pork Burger | A pork burger flavored with teriyaki sauce |
| South Korea | Bulgogi Burger | Pork patty marinated in soy-based sauce |
| Netherlands | McKroket | A deep fried roll containing beef ragout and potato |
| Greece | Greek Mac | A pita bread sandwich with two beef patties and some yoghurt |
| Israel | McShawarma | Shawarma served in flatbread |

*Source*: http://en.wikipedia.org/wiki/McDonald%27s_menu_items#Regional_dishes and "Big Mac's Local Flavor," *Fortune*, May 5, 2008, p. 85.

---

[49]http://www.breaktown.com/, accessed on February 12, 2009.

**EXHIBIT 11-8**
KIT KAT FLAVORS IN JAPAN

Courtesy of Kristaan Helsen

***Price Spectrum.*** In emerging markets, companies often compete across the price spectrum by offering premium and budget products. The upscale products are targeted toward wealthy consumers. Budget products are offered as entry-level or value products for other consumers. These low-end products often come in smaller sizes, more economical packaging, and/or cheaper formulations. Nestlé, for instance, launched 29 new ice cream brands in China in March 2005. Many of these were low- and mid-range priced value-for-money products selling for as little as 12¢.[50]

***Competitive Climate.*** Differences in the competitive environment often explain why a company offers certain product lines in some countries but not in others. A telling example is the canned soup industry. In the United States, the wet soup category is basically owned by Campbell Soup: the company has a nearly 70 percent share of the wet soup market.[51] Given the clout of the Campbell brand name, it is virtually impossible to penetrate the U.S. canned soup market. The picture is quite different in the United Kingdom where Campbell was a relative latecomer. In the United Kingdom, the Heinz soup range owns a 56 percent market share.[52] Coca-Cola's product line strategy in Japan is also driven to a large degree by the local rivalry in the Japanese beverage market. One of the pillars of Coke's Japan-marketing strategy is to improve on its rivals' products. As a result, Coke sells an incredible variety of beverages in Japan that are not available anywhere else (see **Exhibit 11-9**).

***Organizational Structure.*** Especially in MNCs that are organized on a country-by-country basis, product lines may evolve to a large degree independently in the different countries. The scope of the country manager's responsibility is increasingly being limited in many MNCs (see Chapter 17). Nevertheless, country managers still have a great deal of decision-making autonomy in many functional areas, including product policy.

---

[50]"Nestlé Hits Mainland with Cheap Ice Cream," *Advertising Age* (March 7, 2005): 12.

[51]http://www.campbellsoupcompany.com.

[52]http://www.heinz.com/2005annualreport/goodfood_uk.html.

**EXHIBIT 11-9**
COCA-COLA LOCAL BRANDS IN JAPAN

| Brand | Launch Year | Product Description |
|---|---|---|
| Ambasa | 1981 | Noncarbonated, lactic soft drink with familiar smooth taste for everyday use. |
| Calo | 1997 | "Functional" soft drink with cocoa taste; helps build healthy bones. |
| Georgia | 1975 | Authentic, real coffee drink with variety of flavors sourced from around the world. |
| Ko Cha Ka Den | 1992 | Line of blended teas. |
| Lactia | 1996 | Lactic, noncarbonated soft drink; offers healthy digestion and quick refreshment. |
| Perfect Water | 1997 | Mineral-balanced water; helps restore balance to daily life. |
| Real Gold | 1981 | Carbonated, herb-mix flavored drink; provides quick energy. |
| Saryusaisai | 1993 | Nonsugar Oolong tea drink. |
| Seiryusabo | 1994 | Green and barley tea drinks. |
| Shpla | 1996 | Citrus-flavored soft drink; helps overcome mental stress and dullness. |
| Vegitabeta | 1991 | Peach-flavored soft drink; helps maintain healthy balance. |

***History.***    Product lines often become part of an MNC's local product mix following geographic expansion efforts. Companies like Procter & Gamble, Heinz, and Sara Lee penetrate new and existing markets via acquisitions. Some of these acquisitions include product lines that are outside the MNC's core business. Rather than divesting these non-core businesses, a company often decides to keep them. As part of its growth strategy in Central Europe, Heinz acquired Kecskemeti Konzervgyar, a Hungarian canned food company. The company makes a broad range of food products, including baby food, ketchup, pickles—staple items for Heinz—but also products like jams and canned vegetables—items that are not really part of Heinz's core business lines.

Apart from the drivers mentioned above, there could be other idiosyncratic reasons that determine a firm's product line outside the home market. A case in point is Danone's cola business in China. When the Chinese government wanted to have a *local* cola to compete with the likes of Coca-Cola and Pepsi, Beijing approached Wahaha, a Chinese company controlled by Danone.[53] As a result, Danone now owns Future Cola, which has become the No. 3 cola brand in China, marketed as *the Chinese people's own cola*. China is also the only market where Danone sells soft drinks.

Global marketers need to decide for each market of interest which product lines should be offered and which ones are to be dropped. When markets are entered for the first time, market research can be very helpful for designing the initial product assortment. Market research is less useful for radically new products (e.g., frozen yogurt, electric vehicles) or newly emerging markets. In such situations, the company should consider using a "probing-and-learning" approach. Such a procedure has the following steps:

1. Start with a product line that has a minimum level of product variety.
2. Gradually adjust the amount of product variety over time by adding new items and dropping existing ones.
3. Analyze the incoming actual sales data and other market feedback.
4. Make the appropriate inferences.
5. If necessary, adjust the product line further.[54]

---

[53]"China Market Finally Pays Off," *Asian Wall Street Journal* (January 9, 2003), pp. A1, A10.

[54]Anirudh Dhebar, "Using Extensive, Dynamic Product Lines for Listening in on Evolving Demand," *European Management Journal*, vol. 13, no. 2, June 1995, pp. 187–92.

The gist of this procedure is to use the product line as a **listening post** for the new market to see what product items work best.

By and large, add/drop decisions should be driven by profit considerations. In the global marketing arena, it is crucial not just to look at profit ramifications within an individual country. Ideally, the profitability analysis should be done on a regional or even global basis. A good start is to analyze each individual country's product portfolio on a sales turnover basis. Product lines can be categorized as (1) core products, (2) niche items, (3) seasonal products, or (4) filler products.[55] *Core products* are the items that represent the bulk of the subsidiary's sales volume. *Niche products* appeal to small segments of the population, which might grow. *Seasonal products* have most of their sales during limited times of the year. Finally, *filler products* are items that account for only a small portion of the subsidiary's overall sales. These might include "dead-weight" items whose sales were always lackluster or prospective up-and-coming products. From a global perspective, a comparison of the product mix make-up across the various countries provides valuable insights. Such an analysis might provide answers to questions like:

- Could some of our "seasonal" products in country A be turned into "core" items in country B?
- Given our track record in country A, which ones of our filler products should be considered as up-and-coming in country B and which ones should be written off as dead-weight products?
- Is there a way to streamline our product assortment in country A by dropping some of the items and consolidating others, given our experience in country B?

## ◆◆◆◆◆◆◆◆ PRODUCT PIRACY

At the 2009 Shanghai auto show, one of the biggest events was the debut of the Geely Excellence (GE) made by Geely, one of China's leading carmakers. With its winged mascot and huge radiator grill, the GE has a close resemblance to the Rolls Royce Phantom (see **Exhibit 11-10**).[56] However, while a purchaser of the Phantom may have to fork out at least $1 million, the GE clone would set her back only about $60,000.[57] Geely denies any copycatting, but Rolls-Royce may consider legal action. **Product piracy** is one of the downsides that marketers with popular global brand names face. The World Customs Organization estimated that 7 percent of world merchandise trade (or $512 billion) in 2004 might have been bogus products.[58] Any aspect of the product is vulnerable to piracy, including: the brand name, the logo, the design, and the packaging. The impact on the victimized company's profits is twofold. Obviously, there are the losses stemming from lost sales revenues. The monetary losses due to piracy can be staggering. In China, Procter & Gamble estimates that 15 percent of the soaps and detergent goods carrying P&G brand names are fake, costing $150 million a year in foregone sales. Yamaha estimates that five out of six motorbikes and scooters in China bearing its brand name are fake.[59] Rampant piracy in countries such as China is for many companies also a reason not to enter these markets. Blockbuster, the world's largest video rental chain, scrapped plans to expand into China due to piracy issues.[60] A newly worrying trend is the increased export of fake products made in China. Counterfeiters also depress the MNC's profits indirectly. In many markets, MNCs often are forced to lower their prices in order to defend their market share against their counterfeit competitors.

---

[55]John A. Quelch and David Kenny, "Extend Profits, Not Product Lines, *Harvard Business Review*, Sept.–Oct. 1994, pp. 153–60.

[56]"A Rolls-Royce Knock-Off From China," www.nytimes.com, accessed on May 3, 2009.

[57]http://au.carbage.blogs.topgear.com/2009/04/28/geely-geely-good/.

[58]"The Global Counterfeit Industry . . . " *Business Week* (February 7, 2005): 48.

[59]"China's Fakes," *Business Week (Asian Edition)* (June 5, 2000), pp. 20–25.

[60]"Blockbuster's China Ambition Ended by Piracy," *Financial Times* (January 31/February 1, 2004): 1.

**EXHIBIT 11-10**
THE GEELY GE HAS BEEN BRANDED A KNOCK-OFF OF THE ROLLS-ROYCE PHANTOM

REUTERS/Nir Elias/Landov LLC

Even more worrisome than the monetary losses is the damage that pirated products could inflict to the brand name. Pirated products tend to be of poor quality. As a result, the piracy scourge often jeopardizes the brand's reputation built over the years. Such risks are especially big in emerging markets where consumers have only recently been exposed to premium branded products and counterfeits often outnumber the real thing by a significant factor.[61] In some categories, counterfeit products can also turn out to be downright dangerous to consumers. The World Health Organization estimates that 5 to

---

[61]"Business Faces Genuine Problem of Chinese Fakes," *Financial Times* (April 4, 2000), p. 6.

7 percent of medicines sold are copycat—with too few active ingredients, too many impurities, or labels that cover up expiration dates. Dodgy counterfeit aircraft or car parts can have fatal consequences. According to one study, 10 percent of car spare parts being sold in the EU were reckoned to be counterfeit. Forged aviation parts were the suspected cause of a 2001 American Airlines crash.

Several factors lie behind the rise of piracy in countries such as China. The spread of advanced technology (e.g., color copying machines, know-how stolen from multinationals by local partners) is one catalyst. Global supply chains also play a key role. Traders often use the web and unauthorized distributors to sell fakes around the world. China's weak rule of law and poor enforcement of existing legislation also contributes to the piracy spread. Finally, profits that can be made from piracy are huge. For instance, profit margins on fake Chinese-made car parts such as shock absorbers can reach 80 percent versus 15 percent for the genuine thing.[62]

**Strategic Options against Product Piracy**

MNCs have several strategic options at their disposal to combat counterfeiters. **Exhibit 11-11** lists some guidelines to protect intellectual property (IP) in China, which is the source of most of the world's counterfeit goods. Other major weapons at the disposal of MNCs are as follows:

***Lobbying Activities.*** Lobbying governments is one of the most common courses of action that firms use to protect themselves against counterfeiting. Lobbyists pursue different types of objectives. One goal is to toughen legislation and enforce existing laws in the foreign market. However, improved intellectual property rights (IPR) protection is more likely to become reality if one can draw support from local stakeholders. For instance, Chinese technology developers increasingly favor a tighter IPR system.[63] Another route is to lobby the home government to impose sanctions against countries that tolerate product piracy. Lastly, MNCs might also lobby their government to negotiate for better trademark protection in international treaties such as the WTO or bilateral trade agreements.

***Legal Action.*** Prosecuting counterfeiters is another alternative that companies can employ to fight product piracy. In China, two big foreign brands, Starbucks and Ferrero Rocher—recently won highly publicized IPR court cases. In the case of Starbucks,

---

**EXHIBIT 11-11**
GUIDELINES FOR IP PROTECTION IN CHINA

- *Educate your employees.* Employees are the source of most IP losses. IP is still a fairly new concept in China, so education of workforce on IP is very important. Concentrate on everyday examples.

- *Speedy patent and trademark registration.* Often a Chinese company already registered a patent or trademark in China to gain an edge against foreign competitors or to sell it back to the foreign firm at a lucrative price. It is important to also register Chinese language translations of the trademarks.

- *Keep up with best practices.* Information on best practices to protect IP in China is available through trade associations and chambers of commerce. An excellent resource to consult best practices is the website of the Quality Brands Protection Committee (QBPC): http://www.qbpc.org.cn/.

Source: "Protecting Intellectual Property in China," *The Wall Street Journal Asia*, March 10, 2008, p. R8.

- *Put a senior level executive in charge of IP security.* For effective IP protection, a senior level executive should be in charge of IP security across the firm.

- *Think globally to protect IP.* A company's strategy to combat IP infringement in China should be global as a leak anywhere could affect the firm's business anywhere in the world.

---

[62]"China's Piracy," pp. 22–23.
[63]Pitman B. Potter and Michel Oksenberg, "A Patchwork of IPR Protections," *The China Business Review* (Jan.–Feb. 1999), pp. 8–11.

Shanghai company Xingbake Café was using a logo and a name that when translated was similar to that of the global coffee giant. The court ordered Xingbake to pay Rmb500,000 (about $62,000) in damages to Starbucks. Similarly, the British drinks group Diageo successfully sued a local Chinese company that had copied the bottle design and packaging of Johnnie Walker Black Label whiskey.[64] In order to sue infringers, companies need to track them down first. In countries like China foreign firms can hire private agencies to help them with investigations of suspected infringers. Legal action has numerous downsides, though. A positive outcome in court is seldom guaranteed. The whole process is time-consuming and costly. Chinese courts and administrative bodies cope with more than 100,000 IP infringement cases per year. The percentage of judgments that are enforced is very low and for most companies winning a case in itself is a victory.[65] Court action can also generate negative publicity.[66] Microsoft's experience in China illustrates this point. When the company sued Yadu Group, a local humidifier maker, for pirating Microsoft products, the Chinese press had a field day bashing Microsoft for going after a local company. The case was dismissed because of a legal technicality. The only party that gained (apart from the lawyers involved) was the defendant whose brand awareness increased enormously because of all the publicity surrounding the case.[67]

***Customs.*** Firms can also ask customs for assistance by conducting seizures of infringing goods. In countries with huge trade flows like China, customs can only monitor a small proportion of traded goods for IP compliance. Customs officers will most likely attach low priority to items such as Beanie Babies or Hello Kitty dolls. However, courtesy calls can be very effective. IP owners could also pinpoint broader concerns to the customs officials such as risks to consumers of fake goods or to the reputation of the host country.[68]

***Product Policy Options.*** The third set of measures to cope with product piracy covers product policy actions. For instance, software manufacturers often protect their products by putting holograms on the product to discourage counterfeiters. Holograms are only effective when they are hard to copy. Microsoft learned that lesson the hard way when it found out that counterfeiters simply sold MS-DOS 5.0 knockoffs using counterfeit holograms.[69] In 2008 Microsoft initiated a highly controversial initiative to combat software piracy in markets such as China.[70] The firm sent out a security measure through a software update to millions of users of the Windows XP operating system. The update could turn the users' desktop wallpaper black if they were using pirated software.[71] LVMH, the owner of a wide variety of upscale liquor brands, redesigned its bottles to make it harder for copycatters to re-use LVMH bottles for their own brews.[72] Yamaha decided to combat China's counterfeiters by launching new motorcycle models at a similar price as the fake products.

***Distribution.*** Changes in the distribution strategy can offer partial solutions to piracy. When launching Windows XP in China, Microsoft struck a deal with four of China's leading PC makers to bundle the operating system into their computers. Pirated versions of Windows XP were on sale in China for less than $5 shortly after the product was launched in the United States.[73]

---

[64] "Chinese to Pay Damages over Diageo Designs," *Financial Times*, November 28, 2008, p. 17.

[65] "The Realities of Tackling Corporate Brand Theft in China," *Financial Times*, January 22, 2008, p. 2.

[66] "Counter Feats," *The China Business Review*, Nov./Dec. 1994, pp. 12–15.

[67] "Microsoft-Bashing Is Paying Off For Software Giant's Foes in China," *The Asian Wall Street Journal* (January 3, 2000), pp. 1, 4.

[68] Joseph T. Simone, "Countering Counterfeiters," *The China Business Review*, (Jan.–Feb. 1999), pp. 12–19.

[69] "Catching Counterfeits," *Security Management*, December 1994, p. 18.

[70] "Microsoft Stirs Up Pirates," *Wall Street Journal Asia*, October 23, 2008, p. 6.

[71] See also http://www.youtube.com/watch?v=xRsFvmo72_A.

[72] Mr. Joël Tiphonnet, former Vice-President LVMH Asia Pacific, personal communication.

[73] "Microsoft Victory in China Software Piracy Battle," *Financial Times* (December 7, 2001), p. 6.

***Pricing.*** Marketers can also fight counterfeiters on the price front. Microsoft China, for example, cut the price for its software drastically in October 2008 partly to outmaneuver software piracy competitors: the price for the home and student version of Microsoft Office was lowered from $102 to $30.[74]

***Communication Options.*** Companies also use their communication strategy to counter rip-offs. Through advertising or public relations campaigns, companies warn their target audience about the consequences of accepting counterfeit merchandise. In Japan, LVMH distributed a million leaflets at three airports. The goal of this campaign was to warn Japanese tourists that the importation of counterfeit products is against the law.[75] Anti-counterfeiting advertising campaigns that target end-consumers could also try to appeal to people's ethical judgments: a "good citizen" does not buy counterfeit goods.[76] The target of warning campaigns is not always the end-customer. Converse, the U.S. athletic shoemaker, ran a campaign in trade journals throughout Europe alerting retailers to the legal consequences of selling counterfeits.[77]

## ◆ ◆ ◆ ◆ ◆ ◆ ◆ ◆   COUNTRY-OF-ORIGIN (COO) EFFECTS

Two of the biggest cosmetics companies in the world are Japanese: Kao and Shiseido. While successful in Japan and other Asian countries, Kao and Shiseido have had a hard time penetrating the European and American markets. Apparently, part of the problem is that they are Japanese. In China, however, Shiseido has built up a loyal following. One senior marketing executive of the company observed that: "China and Japan are from the same Asian background, so people think Shiseido is a specialist in Asian skin treatment. They may think it is more suitable for them than Western products."[78] **Exhibit 11-12** shows some of the results of a survey that was done in six cities around the world by the Japanese advertising agency Hakuhodo. The figures show the percentage of respondents in each city who rated a product high quality given its origins. Clearly, Japanese products boast a high-quality image whereas Chinese products, and to a lesser extent Korean, possess a rather poor image. Consumers often rely on a product's **country-of-origin (COO)** as an important cue to assess its quality. This phenomenon

### EXHIBIT 11-12
QUALITY IMAGE OF PRODUCTS MADE IN VARIOUS COUNTRIES
(Percent (%) of respondents rate xxx products as being high quality)

| | Hong Kong | Taipei | Seoul | Bangkok | Shanghai | Moscow | Frankfurt |
|---|---|---|---|---|---|---|---|
| 1 | Japanese (86.4%) | Japanese (94.3%) | Japanese (29.6%) | Japanese (54.3%) | Japanese (49.6%) | Japanese (70.4%) | European (64.2%) |
| 2 | European (74.1%) | European (78.3%) | Korean (28.9%) | U.S. (45.8%) | U.S. (39.2%) | European (42.6%) | Japanese (38.6%) |
| 3 | U.S. (60.5%) | U.S. (61.0%) | U.S. (19.3%) | European (34.4%) | Chinese (33.6%) | U.S. (24.8%) | U.S. (24.2%) |
| 4 | Korean (38.0%) | Korean (28.3%) | European (11.8%) | Korean (20.3%) | European (26.9%) | Korean (15.4%) | Chinese (9.4%) |
| 5 | Chinese (6.0%) | Chinese (2.1%) | Chinese (2.5%) | Chinese (11.6%) | Korean (16.0%) | Chinese (1.0%) | Korean (7.9%) |

*Source:* Hakuhodo Global HABIT 2008 Survey.

---

[74]"Microsoft Stirs Up Pirates.

[75]"Modern day pirates a threat worldwide," *Advertising Age International*, March 20, 1995, pp. I–3, I–4.

[76]Alexander Nill and Clifford J. Shultz II, "The Scourge of Global Counterfeiting," *Business Horizons*, Nov.–Dec. 1996, pp. 37–42.

[77]"Converse jumps on counterfeit culprits with ad," *Marketing*, October 21, 1993, p. 11.

[78]"When Chinese Desire Transcends Politics," *Financial Times* (April 1, 2004): 9.

can be defined as "the overall perception consumers form of products from such a country, based on their prior perceptions of the country's production and marketing strengths and weaknesses."[79] In this section we explore country-of-origin effects and strategies to cope with them.

In most product categories, the country-of-origin has a major impact on consumer decision-making. Most of us prefer a bottle of French wine or champagne to a Chinese-made bottle, despite the huge price gap. Consumers hold cultural stereotypes about countries that will influence their product assessments. Academic research studies of COO-effects clearly show that the phenomenon is complex. Some of the key research findings follow:[80]

**Country-of-Origin (COO) Influences on Consumers**

- *Stability over time.* COO-effects are not stable; perceptions change over time.[81] Country images will change when consumer become more familiar with the country, the marketing practices behind the product improve over time, or when the product's actual quality improves. A classic example is Japanese-made cars where COO-effects took a 180 degree turn during the last couple of decades, from a very negative to a very positive country image.[82] A similar phenomenon happened more recently for Korean-made cars.

- *Design versus manufacturing.* Research also shows that both the country of design and the country of manufacturing/assembly play a role. Foreign companies can target patriotic consumers by becoming a local player in the host market. For instance, they might set up an assembly base in the country. At the same time, they can capitalize on their country-image to attract those customers who recognize the country's design image. For instance, Toyota pitched its Camry model as "The best car built in America."[83]

- *Consumer demographics.* Demographics make a difference. COO influences are particularly strong among the elderly,[84] less educated, and politically conservative consumers.[85] Consumer expertise also makes a difference: novices tend to use COO as a cue in evaluating a product under any circumstances, experts only rely upon COO stereotypes when product attribute information is ambiguous.[86]

- *Emotions.* One recent study indicates that emotions consumer experience prior to their product evaluations also play a role: angry consumers are more likely to use COO information in their product evaluations than sad consumers.[87]

---

[79]Martin S. Roth and Jean B. Romeo, "Matching Product Category and Country Image Perceptions: A Framework for Managing Country-of-Origin Effects," *Journal of International Business Studies*, 23, (Third Quarter 1992), pp. 477–97.

[80]For an excellent in-depth overview of the literature, see Duhairaj Maheswaran and Cathy Yi Chen, "Nation Equity: Country-of-Origin Effects and Globalization," in *The Sage Handbook of International Marketing* (Masaaki Kotabe and Kristiaan Helsen, eds.) (London: Sage Publications, 2009).

[81]Van R. Wood, John R. Darling, and Mark Siders (1999), "Consumer Desire To Buy and Use Products In International Markets: How to Capture It, How to Sustain It," *International Marketing Review*, Vol. 16(3), pp. 231–56.

[82]Akira Nagashima, "A Comparison of Japanese and US attitudes toward foreign products," *Journal of Marketing*, January 1970, pp. 68–74.

[83]Glen H. Brodowsky and J. Justin Tan, "Managing Country of Origin: Understanding How Country of Design and Country of Assembly Affect Product Evaluations and Attitudes Toward Purchase," in *American Marketing Association Summer Educators' Conference Proceedings*, Steven Brown and D. Sudharshan, eds., Chicago: American Marketing Association, 1999, pp. 307–20.

[84]Terence A. Shimp and Subhash Sharma, "Consumer ethnocentrism: Construction and validation of the CETSCALE," *Journal of Marketing Research*, vol. 24, August 1987, pp. 280–89.

[85]Thomas W. Anderson and William H. Cunningham, "Gauging foreign product promotion," *Journal of Advertising Research*, February 1972, pp. 29–34.

[86]Durairaj Maheswaran, "Country of origin as a Stereotype: Effects of Consumer Expertise and Attribute Strength on Product Evaluations," *Journal of Consumer Research*, vol. 21, September 1994, pp. 354–65.

[87]Durairaj Maheswaran and Cathy Yi Chen, "Nation Equity: Incidental Emotions in Country-of-origin Effects," *Journal of Consumer Research*, 33(3), pp. 370–76.

- *Culture.* Cultural orientations play a role. One study contrasted COO influences between members of an individualist (United States) and a collectivist culture (Japan).[88] The study's findings showed that individualists evaluated the home country product more favorably only when it was superior to the competition. Collectivists, however, rated the home country product higher regardless of product superiority.[89]

- *Brand name familiarity.* Consumers are likely to use the origin of a product as a cue when they are unfamiliar with the brand name carried by the product.[90]

- *Product category.* Finally, COO-effects depend upon the product category.[91] A 2008 study in fourteen cities[92] that surveyed consumers' opinions about Japanese products recorded high "good quality" scores for digital cameras (28.6%), white goods (28.5%), flat-screen TVs (25.8%), and cars (25.4%).[93] Scores were low for cosmetics (13.6%), skincare products (12.1%), facial cleanser (12.0%), and instant foods (9.7%).[94] As shown in **Exhibit 11-13**, there are four possible outcomes depending on (1) whether

**EXHIBIT 11-13**
PRODUCT-COUNTRY MATCHES AND MISMATCHES: EXAMPLES AND STRATEGIC IMPLICATIONS

| | | Country Image Dimensions | |
|---|---|---|---|
| | | *Positive* | *Negative* |
| **Dimensions as Product Features** — *Important* | | I Favorable Match<br>Examples:<br>• Japanese auto<br>• German watch<br><br>Strategic Implications:<br>• Brand name reflects COO<br>• Packaging includes COO information<br>• Promote brand's COO<br>• Attractive potential manufacturing site | II Unfavorable Match<br>Examples:<br>• Hungarian auto<br>• Mexican watch<br><br>Strategic Implications:<br>• Emphasize benefits other than COO<br>• Noncountry branding<br>• Joint venture with favorable match partner<br>• Communication campaign to enhance country image |
| **Dimensions as Product Features** — *Not Important* | | III Favorable Mismatch<br>Example:<br>• Japanese beer<br><br>Strategic Implications:<br>• Alter importance of product category image dimensions<br>• Promote COO as secondary benefit if compensatory choice process | IV Unfavorable Mismatch<br>Example:<br>• Hungarian beer<br><br>Strategic Implications:<br>• Ignore COO—such information not relevant |

*Source:* Martin S. Roth and Jean B. Romeo, "Matching Product Category and Country Image Perceptions: A Framework for Managing Country-of-Origin Effects," *Journal of International Business Studies*, Third Quarter 1992, p. 495.

[88]Zeynep Gürhan-Canli and Durairaj Maheswaran, "Cultural Variations in Country of Origin Effects," *Journal of Marketing Research*, 37 (August 2000), pp. 309–17.

[89]See also V. Swaminathan, K. L. Page, and S. Gürhan-Canli, "'My' Brand or 'Our' Brand: The Effects of Brand Relationship Dimensions and Self-construal on Brand Evaluations," *Journal of Consumer Research*, 34(2), pp. 248–59.

[90]Victor V. Cordell, "Effects of consumer preferences for foreign sourced products," *Journal of International Business Studies*, Second Quarter 1992, pp. 251–69.

[91]George Balabanis and Adamantios Diamantopoulos, "Domestic Country Bias, Country-of-Origin Effects, and Consumer Ethnocentrism: A Multidimensional Unfolding Approach," *Academy of Marketing Science Journal* 32 (Winter 2004): 80–95.

[92]Shanghai, Beijing, Hong Kong, Taipei, Seoul, Singapore, Bangkok, Jakarta, Kuala Lumpur, Manila, Ho Chi Minh City, Delhi, Mumbai, and Moscow.

[93]http://www.hakuhodo.jp/press/20090121.html.

[94]The scores refer to the percentage of respondents in the survey who agreed with the statement, "Japanese products are of good quality."

there is a match between the product and country and (2) whether or not the (mis-) match is favorable. For each combination, the exhibit also lists some of the strategic implications.

Before exploring strategic options to deal with COO, firms should conduct market research to investigate the extent and the impact of COO stereotypes for their particular product. Such studies would reveal whether the country-of-origin really matters to consumers and to what degree COO hurts or helps the product's evaluation. One useful technique makes use of a *dollar preference* scale. Participants are asked to indicate how much they are willing to pay for particular brand/country combinations.[95]

**Strategies to Cope with COO Stereotypes**

Country image stereotypes can either benefit or hurt a company's product. Evidently, when there is a favorable match between the country image and the desired product features, a firm could leverage this match by touting the origin of its product, provided its main competitors do not have the same (or better) origin. Our focus below is on strategies that can be used to counter negative COO stereotypes. The overview is organized along the four marketing mix elements:

***Product Policy.*** A common practice to cope with COO is to select a brand name that disguises the country-of-origin or even invokes a favorable COO.[96] It is probably no coincidence that two of the more successful apparel retailers based in Hong Kong have Italian-sounding names (Giordano and Bossini). Print ads for Finlandia vodka in the U.S. magazines highlight the linkage between the vodka's origin (*Vodka of Finland*) and its ingredients (*Made from pure glacial spring water, untouched, untainted, and unspoiled*). Another branding option to downplay negative COO feelings is to use private-label branding. One study that looked at COO influences on prices in the Philippines shows that marketers can overcome negative COO effects by developing brand equity.[97] Sheer innovation and a drive for superior quality will usually help firms to overcome COO biases in the long run. Skoda, the Czech carmaker, exemplifies this approach.[98] Car brands from Central and Eastern Europe such as Skoda used to be the butt of countless jokes.[99] However, Skoda managed to overcome its shoddy image with a relentless focus on quality. The brand ranks very highly now in quality surveys across Europe. Skoda's chief executive commented: "To fix brand image we needed to go for top quality. We can't allow failure, or the old image might come back."[100]

***Pricing.*** Selling the product at a relatively low price will attract value-conscious customers who are not very concerned about the brand's country-of-origin. Obviously, this strategy is only doable when the firm enjoys a cost advantage. At the other end of the pricing spectrum, firms could set a premium price to combat COO biases. This is especially effective for product categories in which price plays a role as a signal of quality (e.g., wines, cosmetics, clothing).

***Distribution.*** Alternatively, companies could influence consumer attitudes by using highly respected distribution channels. In the United Kingdom, Hungarian and Chilean wines are becoming increasingly popular. One reason for their success is the fact that they are sold in prestigious supermarket chains in Britain like Tesco.[101]

---

[95]Usually the respondents are also given an anchor point (e.g., "Amount above or below $10,000?"). For further details see: Johny K. Johansson and Israel D. Nebenzahl, "Multinational production: effect on brand value," *Journal of International Business Studies*, Fall 1986, pp. 101–26.)

[96]France Leclerc, Bernd H. Schmitt, and Laurette Dubé, "Foreign Branding and Its Effects on Product Perceptions and Attitudes," *Journal of Marketing Research*, vol. 31, May 1994, pp. 263–70.

[97]John Hulland, et al., "Country-of-Origin Effects on Sellers' Price Premiums," ibid.

[98]Skoda became a subsidiary of German carmaker Volkswagen in 1991.

[99]One gag went as follows: "Why do you need a rear-window defroster on a Skoda? To keep your hands warm when you're pushing it."

[100]"Skoda Means Quality. Really," *BusinessWeek*, October 1, 1997, p. 46.

[101]"Non-traditional nations pour into wine market," *Advertising Age International*, May 15, 1995, p. I–4.

*Communication.*    Lastly, the firm's communication strategy can be used to alter consumer's attitudes toward the product. Such strategies could pursue either of two broad objectives: (1) improve the country image or (2) bolster the brand image. The first goal, changing the country image, is less appealing since it could lead to "free-rider" problems. Efforts carried out by your company to change the country image would also benefit your competitors from the same country of manufacture, even though they don't spend a penny on the country-image campaign. For that reason, country-image-type campaigns are done mostly by industry associations or government agencies. For instance, in the United States, Chilean wines were promoted with wine tastings and a print advertising campaign with the tag line: "It's not just a wine. It's a country." The $2-3 million campaign was sponsored by ProChile, Chile's Ministry of Foreign Affairs' trade group.[102] Seagram UK, on the other hand, developed a strategy to build up the Paul Masson brand image when the California wine was first launched in the United Kingdom.[103]

◆ ◆ ◆ ◆ ◆ ◆ ◆ ◆    **GLOBAL MARKETING OF SERVICES**

Most of the discussion in this chapter so far has focused on the marketing of so-called tangible goods. However, as countries grow richer, services tend to become the dominant sector of their economy. In this section we will first focus on the challenges and opportunities that exist in the global service market. We will then offer a set of managerial guidelines that might prove fruitful to service marketers who plan to expand overseas.

**Challenges in Marketing Services Internationally**    Compared to marketers of *tangible* goods, *service* marketers face several unique hurdles on the road to international expansion. The major challenges include:

*Protectionism.*    Trade barriers to service marketers tend to be much more cumbersome than for their physical goods counterparts. Many parts of the world are littered with service trade barriers coming under many different guises. Most cumbersome are the non-tariff trade barriers, where the creative juices of government regulators know no boundaries. In the past, the service sector has been treated very stepmotherly in trade agreements. The rules of the GATT system, for instance, only applied to visible trade. Its successor, the World Trade Organization (WTO), now expands at least some of the GATT rules to the service sector.[104]

*Need for Geographic Proximity with Service Transactions.*    The human aspect in service delivery is much more critical than for the marketing of tangible goods. Services are *performed*. This performance feature of services has several consequences in the international domain. Most services cannot are difficult to trade internationally and require a physical presence of the service provider. Given the intrinsic need for people-to-people contact, cultural barriers in the global marketplace are much more prominent for service marketers than in other industries. Being in tune with the cultural values and norms of the local market is essential to be successful in most service industries. As a result, services are typically standardized far less than are tangible products.[105] At the same time, service companies usually aspire to provide a consistent quality image worldwide. Careful screening and training of personnel to assure consistent quality is extremely vital for international service firms. To foster the

---

[102]"Non-traditional nations pour into wine market," *Advertising Age International.*

[103]Paul E. Breach, "Building the Paul Masson Brand," *European Journal of Marketing*, vol. 23, no. 9, 1989, pp. 27–30.

[104]Joseph A. McKinney, "Changes in the World Trading System."

[105]B. Nicolaud, "Problems and Strategies in the International Marketing of Services," *European Journal of Marketing*, vol. 23, no. 6, pp. 55–66.

transfer of know-how between branches, many service companies set up communication channels such as regional councils.

The need for direct customer interface also means that service providers often need to have a local presence. This is especially the case with support services such as advertising, insurance, accounting, law firms, or overnight package delivery. In order not to lose MNC customer accounts, many support service companies are often obliged to follow in their clients' footsteps.

***Difficulties in Measuring Customer Satisfaction Overseas.***   Given the human element in services, monitoring consumer satisfaction is an absolute must for successful service marketing. The job of doing customer satisfaction studies in an international context is often frustrating. The hindrances to conducting market research surveys also apply here. In many countries, consumers are not used to sharing their opinions or suggestions. Instead of expressing their true opinions about the service, foreign respondents may simply state what they believe the company wants to hear (the "courtesy" bias).[106]

Despite the challenges described above, many international service industries offer enormous opportunities to savvy service marketers. The major ones are given here:

**Opportunities in the Global Service Industries**

***Deregulation of Service Industries.***   While protectionism is still rampant in many service industries, there is a steady improvement for international service providers in terms of deregulation. Some of the GATT rules that only applied to tangible goods are now extended to the international service trade under the new WTO regime. In scores of countries, government authorities have privatized services such as utilities (e.g., water, electricity), telecommunications, and mail delivery. The underlying thinking is that private firms can run these services more efficiently and have the resources to upgrade the infrastructure. Further, by shifting these services to the private sector, governments can allocate their resources to other areas (e.g., education, social welfare). Several individual countries are taking steps to lift restrictions targeting foreign service firms. Even sectors that were traditionally off-limits to foreigners are opening up now in scores of countries. India and the Philippines, for example, opened up their telephone industry to foreign companies.[107]

***Increasing Demand for Premium Services.***   Demand for premium quality services expands with increases in consumers' buying power. International service providers that are able to deliver a premium product often have an edge over their local competitors. There are two major factors behind this competitive advantage. One of the legacies of years of protectionism is that local service firms are typically unprepared for the hard laws of the marketplace. Notions such as customer orientation, consumer satisfaction, and service quality are marketing concepts that are especially hard to digest for local service firms that, until recently, did not face any serious competition. For example, local funeral companies in France invested very little in funeral homes. Prior to the de-monopolization of the industry, funeral business in France was basically a utility: firms bid for the right to offer funeral services to a municipality at fixed prices. Service Corp. International, a leading American funeral company, now plans to gain a foothold in France by selling premium products and upgraded facilities.[108] Despite Malaysia's highly protectionist banking laws, Citibank Malaysia has become one of the country's biggest mortgage lenders through a combination of savvy marketing, an assertive sales force, and a strong customer service orientation.[109]

---

[106]Gaye Kaufman, "Customer satisfaction studies overseas can be frustrating," *Marketing News,* August 29, 1994, p. 34.

[107]"Asia, at your service," *The Economist*, February 11, 1995, pp. 53–54.

[108]"Funereal prospects," *Forbes*, September 11, 1995, pp. 45–46.

[109]"Citibank Expands Niche In Malaysian Mortgages By Courting Customers," *Asian Wall Street Journal* (November 28, 2002), p. A5.

Global service firms can also leverage their "global know-how" base. A major strength for the likes of Federal Express, Wal-Mart, and AT&T is that they have a worldwide knowledge base into which they can tap instantly.

***Increased Value Consciousness.*** As customers worldwide have more alternatives to choose from and have become more sophisticated; they have also grown increasingly value conscious. Service companies that compete internationally also have clout on this front versus local service providers, since global service firms usually benefit from scale economies. Such savings can be passed through to their customers. McDonald's apparently saved around $2 million by centralizing the purchase of sesame seeds.[110] In Thailand, Makro, a large Dutch retailer, uses computerized inventory controls and bulk selling to undercut its local rivals.[111] Given the size of its business, Toys 'R' Us, the U.S. discount toy retailer, was able to set up its own direct import company in Japan, allowing the firm to deliver merchandise straight from the docks to its warehouses, thereby bypassing distributors' margins.[112]

**Global Service Marketing Strategies**

To compete in foreign markets, service firms resort to a plethora of different strategies.

***Capitalize on Cultural Forces in the Host Market.*** To bridge cultural gaps between the home and host market, service companies often customize the product to the local market. Successful service firms grab market share by spotting cultural opportunities and setting up a service product around these cultural forces.

***Standardize and Customize.*** As noted in the last chapter, one of the major challenges in global product design is striking the right balance between standardization and customization. By their very nature (service delivery at the point of consumption) most services do not need to wrestle with that issue. Both standardization and adaptation are doable. The core service product can easily be augmented with localized support service features that cater to local market conditions.[113]

***Central Role of Information Technologies (IT).*** Information technology forms a key pillar of global service strategies. Service firms add value for their customers by employing technology such as computers, intelligent terminals, and state-of-the-art telecommunications. Many service firms have established internet access to communicate with their customers and suppliers. IT is especially valued in markets that have a fairly underdeveloped infrastructure. Companies should also recognize the potential of realizing scale economies by centralizing their IT functions via "information hubs."[114] A case in point is HSBC, a leading British bank.[115] HSBC relies on 400 low-cost employees in Hyderabad, India, and Guangzhou, China, to industrialize its simple back-room operations on a global scale, freeing up its UK backrooms for more complicated tasks.

***Add Value by Differentiation.*** Services differ from tangible products by the fact that it is usually far easier to find differentiation possibilities. Service firms can appeal to their customers by offering benefits not provided by their competitors and/or lowering costs. Apart from monetary expenses, cost items include psychic costs (hassles), time costs (waiting time), and physical efforts.[116] Especially in markets where the service industry is still developing, multinational service firms can add value

---

[110]"Big Mac's counter attack," *The Economist,* November 13, 1993, pp. 71–72.

[111]"Asia, at your service," *The Economist,* February 11, 1995, pp. 53–54.

[112]"Revolution in toyland," *The Financial Times,* April 8, 1994, p. 9.

[113]Christopher H. Lovelock and George S. Yip, "Developing Global Strategies for Service Businesses," *California Management Review,* vol. 38, no. 2, Winter 1996, pp. 64–86.

[114]ibid.

[115]"Bull-terrier Banking," *Forbes Global* (July 24, 2000), pp. 36–38.

[116]"Services go international," *Marketing News,* March 14, 1994, pp. 14–15.

by providing premium products. AIG allows its customers in China to settle their bills by bank transfers. Local insurance companies required their customers to wait in line to pay the premiums in cash.

***Establish Global Service Networks.*** Service firms with a global customer base face the challenge of setting up a seamless global service network. One of the key questions is whether the company should set up the network on its own, or use outside partners. Given the huge investments required to develop a worldwide network, more and more companies are choosing the latter route. Trends of firms grouping together to establish global network can be observed service industries like airline travel (e.g., the Star Alliance, One World) and advertising.

## SUMMARY ◆ ◆ ◆ ◆ ◆ ◆ ◆ ◆ ◆ ◆ ◆ ◆ ◆ ◆ ◆ ◆ ◆ ◆ ◆ ◆ ◆ ◆ ◆ ◆ ◆ ◆ ◆ ◆

Mission statements in annual reports reflect the aspiration of countless companies to sell their products to consumers worldwide. This push toward global expansion raises many tricky questions on the product policy front. Mastering these global product issues will yield success and possibly even worldwide leadership.

Companies need to decide what branding strategies they plan to pursue to develop their overseas business. There is plenty of ammunition to build a case for global brands. At the same time, there are also many arguments that can be put forward in favor of other branding strategies. Developing a global branding strategy involves tackling questions such as:

• Which of the brands in our brand portfolio have the potential to be globalized?

• What is the best route towards globalizing our brands? Should we start by acquiring local brands, develop them into regional brands, and, ultimately, if the potential is there, into a "truly" global brand?

• What is the best way to implement the changeover from a local to a global (or regional) brand?

• How do we foster and sustain the consistency of our global brand image?

• What organizational mechanisms should we as a company use to coordinate our branding strategies across markets? Should coordination happen at the regional or global level?

The ultimate reward of mastering these issues successfully is regional, sometimes even worldwide, leadership in the marketplace.

## KEY TERMS ◆ ◆ ◆ ◆ ◆ ◆ ◆ ◆ ◆ ◆ ◆ ◆ ◆ ◆ ◆ ◆ ◆ ◆ ◆ ◆

| | | | |
|---|---|---|---|
| Brand architecture | Country-of-origin stereotype | Global brand | Transparent forewarning |
| Brand structure | Dual branding | Product piracy | Umbrella branding |
| Co-branding | Fade-in/fade-out | Summary axing | |

## REVIEW QUESTIONS ◆ ◆ ◆ ◆ ◆ ◆ ◆ ◆ ◆ ◆ ◆ ◆ ◆ ◆ ◆ ◆ ◆ ◆ ◆ ◆

**1.** For what types of product/service categories would you expect global brand names? For which ones would you anticipate localized names?

**2.** Why is the market share of private labels much higher in Europe than in Asia?

**3.** Explain why the strength of a global brand may vary enormously from country to country.

**4.** What factors should MNCs consider when implementing a brand-name facelift in their foreign markets?

**5.** Describe the key success factors behind private labels in Europe.

**6.** What strategies can MNCs adopt to cope with product piracy?

**7.** How does the marketing of global services differ from marketing tangible goods worldwide?

## DISCUSSION QUESTIONS ◆ ◆ ◆ ◆ ◆ ◆ ◆ ◆ ◆ ◆ ◆ ◆ ◆ ◆ ◆ ◆ ◆

**1.** Altoids, the "curiously strong" peppermint, has evoked its British heritage since its introduction in the United States in 1918. The mint's original recipe dates back to the reign of King George III. Wrigley (now part of Mars) bought the brand for $1.46 billion in 2004. In the U.S. market, Altoids' market share had slumped from 24.3 percent in 2003 to 20.6 percent in

November 2005. In late 2005, Wrigley announced plans to shut down the Altoids factory in Wales and shift production to Tennessee. Some observers worried that the move could be risky since a similar initiative damaged the image of the Löwenbräu beer brand in the 1970s. Wrigley disputed that this would also happen to Altoids. Do you agree? Is this a wise move? Why or why not?

**2.** Dr. Hans-Willi Schroiff, vice-president of market research at Henkel, a German company, made the following observation about P&G's multinational marketing strategy: "A strict globalization strategy like P&G's [will not be] successful if 'meaningful' local brands are corpses on the battlefield. It caused severe share looses for P&G here in Europe. Consumers do not switch to the global brand, but to another brand that looks more like 'home' to them." Comment on this statement. Do you agree or disagree (and why)?

**3.** In September 1999, Unilever announced that it would trim over one thousand brands. The company wants to focus on 400 of its current 1,600 brands, with a core group of so-called power brands that are known globally or region-wide (e.g., Magnum ice cream, Lipton tea, Vaseline skin cream). These 400 brands accounted for 90 percent of Unilever's 1998 sales revenues. The brands outside the core group will gradually lose marketing support, then ultimately sold, withdrawn, or consolidated into bigger brands. Discuss Unilever's decision. What do you as possible advantages? Disadvantages?

**4.** Software piracy in China is a huge problem for Microsoft. In 2008 Microsoft went on the offensive by sending a software update that could turn the desktop wallpaper black when a pirated Windows XP operating system was being used (http://www.youtube.com/watch?v=xRsFvmo72_A). Not surprisingly, this move stirred much controversy in China. Is this the right approach to combat piracy? What are the possible risks? Are there better ways to fight the problem, if so, how?

**5.** Most of the luxury watches have a Swiss-made label. Discuss strategies that a "Made in India" watch, aiming to target the premium segment in the Western world, might want to consider.

**6.** Nestlé, the Swiss food conglomerate, has created a Nestlé Seal of Guarantee that it puts on the back of some of its products (e.g., Maggi sauces). The Seal of Guarantee is not used for many of its other products like pet food and mineral water. What might be Nestlé's motivations for adding or dropping its Nestlé Seal of Guarantee stamp to the brand name?

**7.** The Rover Mini is a squat, boxy car that was designed in the late 1950s when the Suez Canal crisis prompted gas rationing in Europe (if you are not familiar with the car, check out its website: www.mini.co.uk). These days, the brand is owned by BMW. The Mini sells for between 1.8 million yen and 2.4 million yen. A Japanese model of the same size costs about half that. Yet the Mini has many takers. Rover rarely does TV ads; instead it relies on word of mouth. Despite the price tag and little advertising, Rover sells more Minis in Japan than anywhere else in the world. The car has been far more successful in Japan than most other imported car makes like GM's Saturn or DaimlerChrysler's Neon. What factors do you think explain the Rover Mini's success in Japan?

# SHORT CASES

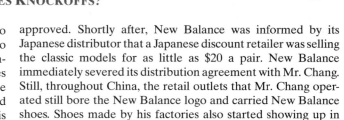

## CASE 11-1

### WHAT TO DO WHEN YOUR OWN SUPPLIER MAKES KNOCKOFFS?

China's cheap labor and high-quality manufacturing are two major reasons why scores of global brands have decided to source their products from China-based suppliers. Unfortunately, many firms are finding out that they sometimes pay a steep price for doing so. It is not uncommon that the China-based supplier starts selling knockoffs under your brand name. New Balance, the U.S. athletic-shoemaker, learned this the hard way. About 70 percent (meaning 35 million pairs a year) of New Balance's global output is made in China. One of the firm's key suppliers was a company headed by Mr. Chang, a Taiwanese businessman, whose factories made shoes for New Balance initially in Taiwan and later also in China. In 1995, New Balance made him the official sales and distribution partner for China. After a slow take-off, sales improved when Mr. Chang convinced New Balance to push lower-price, lower-tech classic-style shoe models for China. In 1998, sales in China were 57,000 pairs. However, New Balance became uneasy when, following a sales conference meeting, Mr. Chang made a pitch to sell 250,000 pairs. The reason for top management's worry was that selling so many classic-style shoes might tarnish its image as a maker of premium quality athletic shoes. Instead of getting a pat on the back, Mr. Chang was told to scale back the sales of classic shoes.

Shortly after the meeting, New Balance learned that Mr. Chang had bought materials to make 460,000 pairs. He also planned to make styles and colors that the company had never

*Source:* "What Happens When Knockoffs Are Made By Your Own Supplier?" *The Asian Wall Street Journal* (December 19, 2002), pp. A1, M8.

approved. Shortly after, New Balance was informed by its Japanese distributor that a Japanese discount retailer was selling the classic models for as little as $20 a pair. New Balance immediately severed its distribution agreement with Mr. Chang. Still, throughout China, the retail outlets that Mr. Chang operated still bore the New Balance logo and carried New Balance shoes. Shoes made by his factories also started showing up in stores in Switzerland, Italy, Spain, and Taiwan.

New Balance then approached China's State Administration for Industry and Commerce (AIC), the trademark and intellectual-property enforcement agency. This agency raided some of Mr. Chang's warehouses and confiscated 100,000 pairs. Besides New Balance shoes, they also found shoes branded Henkee, whose style and logo had a striking similarity with those of New Balance. However, a court in Shenzhen ruled against the company on the basis of a document in which New Balance had guaranteed that Mr. Chang's company could make its shoes until 2003. The company appealed but a favorable ruling is unlikely. As a result of this whole experience, New Balance cut down the number of factories in China to six and now monitors them more closely. It also started using more high-tech labels to better keep control of its own production. Still, the whole episode could easily happen again with any other suppliers, anywhere in the world.

### DISCUSSION QUESTIONS

1. How did New Balance's problem arise?
2. What strategic options can New Balance pursue to protect itself against episodes such as the one described in the case?

## CASE 11-2

### MATSUSHITA ELECTRIC TO CHANGE NAME TO PANASONIC CORPORATION

On January 10, 2008 Japanese electronics manufacturer Matsushita unveiled a radical re-branding initiative: it announced that the company would change its company name to *Panasonic Corporation* effective October 2008. The company would also unify its corporate brands to the *Panasonic* brand around

*Sources:* "Panasonic Eyes Unity in Brand Revamp," *Media*, October 16, 2008, p. 5; "Best Global Brands 2008," http://bwnt.businessweek.com/interactive_reports/global_brand_2008/; www.panasonic.co.jp, accessed on February 10, 2009; "Matsushita Electric to Change Name to Panasonic Corporation," http://panasonic.co.jp/corp/news/official.data/data.dir/en080110-6/en080110-6.html, accessed onFebruary 10, 2009.

the world. The *National* and *Technics* brands were to be dropped and replaced by the Panasonic brand, the highest profile brand marque. As the re-branded Panasonic, the company aspired to increase its revenue to 10 trillion yen ($101 billion) by 2010.

With the branding overhaul, the new Panasonic hopes to boost its brand image. In the 2008 Interbrand/*Business Week* Global Brand ranking, Panasonic ranked 78 (worth $4.3 million), far behind Samsung (ranked 21, valued at $17.7 million) and Sony (ranked 25 at $13.6 million). In 2008, half of the company's sales came from Japan. Panasonic hopes that the re-branding will also help the firm to expand in India and China.

It is also targeting Europe where it plans to introduce its three main appliance products—air conditioners, refrigerators, and washing machines. At present, Panasonic is primarily known as a TV manufacturer in its non-Asian markets.

By focusing on a single brand, marketing investments could be reduced, as only one brand needs to be promoted. Gregory Birge, a marketing consultant cautioned against the move: the phase-out of the National brand, which is recognized for its budget products in the U.S. market and Japan, risks weakening Panasonic's brand equity. In an interview with *Media* he states: "People who see National as cheap may come to see Panasonic as a cheap brand. If the company wants to switch it to Panasonic, it will need to change the product. But it's easier to lower the cost of a very expensive product."

## DISCUSSION QUESTIONS

**1.** What was the motivation behind the Panasonic brand overhaul?

**2.** Is the overhaul justified? What are the possible risks?

**3.** What does Panasonic need to do to make the changeover successful?

# $\mathcal{C}$ASE 11-3

## TATA MOTORS ACQUIRES THE JAGUAR ICON

On March 26, 2008 India's Tata Motors finalized a deal to acquire the Jaguar and Land Rover luxury brands from Ford for $2.3 billion. Tata Motors has built vehicles for more than 50 years, though mainly trucks. Earlier in 2008 Tata Motors had revealed plans to launch the Tata Nano, a budget $2,500 (*one lakh rupee*) compact city car. Tata Motors is part of the Tata Group, one of India's biggest conglomerates. Some of Tata's other businesses include luxury hotels (Taj Mahal in Mumbai, Pierre in New York), tea (Tetley), steel (Corus), insurance, and mobile phone service. The company is highly respected in India.

Not surprisingly, many people were very skeptical about the merits of the deal and questioned whether an Indian company was really the best steward for a luxury marque like Jaguar. Some speculated that the deal was motivated by Tata's desire to acquire iconic brands, almost like former colonials acquiring the trappings of the former empire. Jaguar had lost Ford $15 billion during Ford's 18-year ownership of the brand, and Jaguar's sales were in a steady decline. Jaguar sold 60,485 cars in 2007, a huge drop from 130,334 in 2002. Some industry analysts struggled to see what value Tata could add that had eluded Ford, and what synergies could arise between the selling of the $2,500 Nano and the prestigious Jaguar brand icon.

Some experts say that Ford never really understood how to fit the Jaguar brand in its portfolio and how to market it better. Ford's biggest blunder may have been undermining Jaguar's brand heritage with the launch of low-end models, the mid-range S-Type in 1998 and the compact executive X-Type in 2001. Ford discontinued both models in 2008.

*Sources:* "Maybe Tata, Jaguar/Land Rover Is Not Such An Odd Couple," *USA Today*, May 27, 2008; "A Used-car Bargain," *The Economist*, May 26, 2008; "Can Tata Turn Jaguar Into an Object of Desire?" *Media*, May 15, 2008, p. 18.

Tata has experience taking over global brands (e.g., Tetley Tea, Corus Steel). Its strategy has been to let each business run its own entity, with modest input from the home office. The purchase of Daewoo, the South Korean truck manufacturer, illustrates this strategy. After Tata bought the firm in 2004, Daewoo still operates mostly as a Korean business. Tata Motors has promised not to shift production from Jaguar's British factories. A key element of the deal is that Ford will continue to supply Jaguar with engines and components, as well as provide access to Ford's hybrid and low-emission power-train technology. The new owner plans to return the Jaguar marque to its premium heritage, eschewing volume models such as the X-Type. Ravi Kant, the chairman of Tata Motors said: "At this moment, our focus is on making sure we strengthen our position in the segments we are already and seeing that Jaguar and Land Rover go on to become not just a very cherished brand but a very profitable brand." (*USA Today*, May 27, 2008). The first step will be an update of the XJ-Type, Jaguar's flagship saloon. Tata also ponders the launch of a successor to the E-Type sports car of the 1960s. Tata hopes that the Jaguar's footprint will enable it to penetrate into Europe and the United States, markets where it is completely unknown at present.

## DISCUSSION QUESTIONS

**1.** Will the acquisition of the Jaguar marque be a smooth ride for Tata? Does the Tata/Jaguar deal make any sense? What are Tata's underlying motives for the acquisition?

**2.** What cultural issues do you think will crop up between Tata Motors and the new acquisition? How should Tata cope with these?

**3.** What are the marketing challenges that Tata will face? How do you think these should be tackled?

$\mathscr{C}$ASE 11-4

## L'OREAL CHINA—NURSING MININURSE BACK TO HEALTH

When L'Oréal bought Mininurse, a Chinese mass skincare brand, from Shenzhen firm Raystar Cosmetics in December 2003, the move was seen as a major coup for L'Oréal. Lindsay Owen-Jones, L'Oréal's CEO, commented: "This acquisition is an outstanding opportunity to speed up our growth in the Chinese market. It is a major step forward in L'Oréal's development in a market which is strategically important for the company." Paolo Gasparrini, president of L'Oréal China, added: "Aimed at women with a natural style, Mininurse complements our brand portfolio perfectly and enables us to move more quickly into the Chinese consumer skincare market." At the time of the deal, which took four years to negotiate, Mininurse was one of China's top-three skincare brands with a 5 percent market share. The Chinese cosmetics market is clearly booming. A little more than a decade ago, hardly any women used cosmetics. These days, the beauty industry in China is exploding. It was worth $7.25bn in 2004 and is expected to grow to $9.6bn by 2009. Some 90 million urban women spend at least 10 percent of their income on beauty products. Skincare products are now a major rage. They account for 40 percent of the market and are growing rapidly at an annual rate of 20 percent. L'Oréal's 2004 sales revenues were $350m, up 58 percent over the previous year. The firm markets 17 skincare and hair-care brands, mostly imports except for Mininurse and Yue-Sai, a skincare and make-up brand bought shortly after the Mininurse deal.

Mininurse, first launched in 1992, is one of China's best-known skincare brands with a 90 percent brand recognition. Recognition was even higher among Mininurse's target group of younger women: 96 percent. The brand had built up a solid distribution network of 280,000 outlets. With the deal, L'Oreal got access to the brand, its marketing network, and a manufacturing facility in Hubei province.

Soon after the deal, L'Oreal decided to co-brand Mininurse with Garnier, L'Oreal's global mass-market brand. Through Garnier R&D endorsement, L'Oreal essentially dressed Mininurse in international clothes. The Garnier name would bring international technology credentials and bolster Mininurse's brand equity. The firm ran an ad campaign to re-launch Mininurse. According to Publicis China, the ad agency behind the ad campaign, the goal was "to project to the consumer that Mininurse has changed—it's refreshed and revitalized as a brand . . . We needed to explain to people that this is a whole new phase in the delivery of the brand. What is new is that the Mininurse has the experience and backing of Laboratory Garnier." The face for the campaign was Tong Sun Jie, a Chinese actress. The re-launch was also communicated through Mininurse's website: www.mininursegarnier.com. It was believed that L'Oreal saw Mininurse as a platform to further develop its mass market Garnier range in China. Until the re-launch, Garnier's presence in China was mainly in the haircare segment.

However, Mininurse has been struggling lately. Market data showed that the brand's market share tumbled from 5.1 percent in October 2003, shortly before the deal, to 3.5 percent 2 years later (see Table). Was Mininurse worth the four-year wait? Can L'Oréal nurse the brand back to health? And, if so, what would be the proper health regime?

**Market Share for Moisturizer Brands in China**

| Brand | October 2003 | October 2005 |
|---|---|---|
| Da Bao | 12.1% | 11.0% |
| Long Li Qi | 3.9% | 5.4% |
| Mininurse | 5.1% | 3.5% |
| Tjoy | 2.1% | 4.1% |

*Source:* ACNielsen.

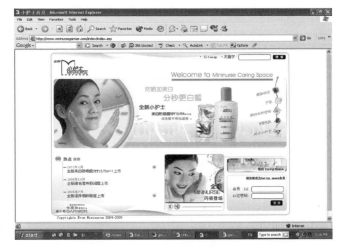

*Sources:* "New L'Oreal Label Touts Laboratory Garnier Back-Up," *Media* (June 4, 2004): 11; http://www.mininursegarnier.com/index/index.asp, accessed February 17, 2006; "China: Acquisition of Mininurse Brand," http://www.loreal-finance.com/pdf/dwd_pdf.asp, accessed February 17, 2006; "Who Is the Fairest of All," http://www.bjreview.com.cn, accessed February 17, 2006; "L'Oréal to Smooth Wrinkles for China Expansion," http://www1.cei.gov.cn, accessed February 17, 2006; "The Business of Beauty," http://www.sinomedia.netl, accessed February 17, 2006; "Mininurse Problems More than Skin Deep," *Media* (February 10, 2006): 17; "China Face-Off," *Fortune* (December 12, 2005): 28–34.

## DISCUSSION QUESTIONS

**1.** Was the Mininurse acquisition really worth the wait and the effort for L'Oréal?

**2.** What might have been the drivers behind Mininurse's market share drop? Was the Mininurse-Garnier co-branding a strategic mistake?

**3.** What is your prescription to revitalize Mininurse? Should L'Oreal discard the Garnier endorsement? Should the brand be repositioned?

# FURTHER READING

◆ ◆ ◆ ◆ ◆ ◆ ◆ ◆ ◆ ◆ ◆ ◆ ◆ ◆ ◆ ◆ ◆ ◆ ◆ ◆ ◆ ◆ ◆ ◆

Aaker, David A. and Erich Joachimsthaler, "The Lure of Global Branding," *Harvard Business Review,* Nov.–Dec. 1999, pp. 137–44.

Abratt, Russell and Patience Motlana. "Managing Co-Branding Strategies: Global Brands into Local Markets," *Business Horizons*, (Sept.–Oct. 2002): 43–50.

Cordell, Victor V., "Effects of Consumer Preferences for Foreign Sourced Products," *Journal of International Business Studies*, Second Quarter 1992, pp. 251–69.

Douglas, Susan P., C. Samuel Craig, and Edwin J. Nijssen, "Integrating Branding Strategy Across Markets: Building International Brand Architecture," *Journal of International Marketing*, 9(2) (2001): 97–114.

Erdem, Tülin, Joffre Swait, and Ana Valenzuela, "Brand as Signals: A Cross-Country Validation Study," *Journal of Marketing Research*, 70 (January 2006), pp. 34–49.

Ettenson, Richard, and Jonathan Knowles, "Merging the Brands and Branding the Merger," *MIT Sloan Management Review*, 47 (Summer 2006), pp. 39–49.

Holt, Douglas B., John A. Quelch, and Earl L. Taylor. "How Global Brands Compete." *Harvard Business Review* 82 (September 2004): 68–75.

Jain, Subhash C., "Problems in International Protection of Intellectual Property Rights," *Journal of International Marketing*, vol. 4, no. 1, 1996, pp. 9–32.

Leclerc, France, Bernd H. Schmitt, and Laurette Dubé, "Foreign Branding and Its Effects on Product Perceptions and Attitudes," *Journal of Marketing Research*, vol. 31, May 1994, pp. 263–70.

Lovelock, Christopher H. and George S. Yip, "Developing Global Strategies for Service Businesses," *California Management Review*, vol. 38, no. 2, Winter 1996, pp. 64–86.

Pagano, Camillo, "The Management of Global Brands," in *Brand Power*, P. Stobart, Ed., London: MacMillan Press, Ltd., 1994.

Partoyan, Garo, "Protecting Power Brands," in *Brand Power*, P. Stobart, Ed., London: MacMillan Press, Ltd., 1994.

Roth, Martin S. and Jean B. Romeo, "Matching Product Category and Country Image Perceptions: A Framework for Managing Country-of-Origin Effects," *Journal of International Business Studies*, Third Quarter 1992, pp. 477–97.

Shultz, C. and B. Saporito, "Protecting Intellectual Property: Strategies and Recommendations to Deter Counterfeiting and Brand Piracy in Global Markets," *Columbia Journal of World Business*, Spring 1996, pp. 18–28.

Steenkamp, Jan-Benedict E. M., Rajeev Batra, and Dana L. Alden. "How Perceived Brand Globalness Creates Brand Value," *Journal of International Business Studies* 34, 1 (January 2003): 53–65.

Tanaka, Hiroshi, "Branding in Japan," in *Brand Equity & Advertising: Advertising's Role in Building Strong Brands*, D. A. Aaker and A. L. Biel, Eds., Hillsdale, NJ: Erlbaum Associates, 1993.

# GLOBAL PRICING

## HAPTER OVERVIEW

1. DRIVERS OF FOREIGN MARKET PRICING

2. MANAGING PRICE ESCALATION

3. PRICING IN INFLATIONARY ENVIRONMENTS

4. GLOBAL PRICING AND CURRENCY FLUCTUATIONS

5. TRANSFER PRICING

6. GLOBAL PRICING AND ANTIDUMPING REGULATION

7. PRICE COORDINATION

8. COUNTERTRADE

Global pricing is one of the most critical and complex issues that global firms face. Price is the only marketing mix instrument that creates revenues. All other elements entail costs. Thus, a company's global pricing policy may make or break its overseas expansion efforts. Furthermore, a firm's pricing policy is inherently a highly cross-functional process based on inputs from the firm's finance, accounting, manufacturing, tax, and legal divisions. Predictably, the interests of one group (say, marketing) may clash with the objectives of another group (say, finance).

Multinationals also face the challenge of how to coordinate their pricing policy across different countries. A lack of coordination will create a parallel trade or gray market situation (see Chapter 15). With parallel imports, middlemen make a profit by shipping products from low priced countries to higher priced markets. These imports will compete with the high-priced equivalent products offered by legitimate distributors. Efforts to trim big price gaps between countries may be hampered by stonewalling attempts of local country managers or distribution channels.

This chapter will focus on global pricing strategies. After presenting an overview of the key drivers of foreign market pricing, we will discuss several strategic international pricing issues. The chapter concludes with a discussion of countertrade, which is a form of non-cash pricing.

**EXHIBIT 12-1**
RETAIL PRICE COMPARISON ACROSS CITIES
(Index = Recorded Price/Lowest Price × 100)

| Item | New York | Hong Kong | Seoul | Tokyo | Paris | London | Shanghai | Sydney | Date |
|---|---|---|---|---|---|---|---|---|---|
| Nikon D80 SLR Camera | 103.9 ($816) | **100.0** **($786)** | 105.2 ($827) | 114.9 ($903) | 167.4 ($1,316) | 129.9 ($1,021) | 107.6 ($846) | NA | March 2008 |
| Davidoff Cigar Cutter | 145.0 ($322) | 164.0 ($364) | **100.0** **($222)** | 202.7 ($450) | 137.3 ($305) | 124.3 ($276) | 164.4 ($365) | 154.9 ($344) | December 2008 |
| Listerine Mouthwash | 131.1 ($4.72) | 121.4 ($4.37) | **100.0** **($3.60)** | NA | 215.3 ($7.75) | 164.7 ($5.93) | NA | 150.3 ($5.41) | December 2008 |
| iRobot Vacuum Cleaner | **100.0** **($324)** | 182.4 ($591) | 115.7 ($375) | 232.7 ($754) | 130.9 ($424) | 109.6 ($355) | NA | 122.5 ($397) | October 2008 |
| Prada Nappa Gauffré Antik handbag | 111.8 ($2,915) | **100.0** **($2,607)** | 116.5 ($3,038) | 111.9 ($2,918) | NA | NA | 112.1 ($2,923) | 113.0 ($2,945) | November 2006 |
| TaylorMade Golf Club | 127.8 ($216) | **100.0** **($169)** | NA | 174.0 ($294) | NA | NA | NA | 140.0 ($236) | November 2006 |
| Jack Daniel's 750 ml Whiskey | 106.0 ($25.46) | 156.4 ($37.55) | 200.0 ($47.96) | 126.0* ($30.26) | **100.0*** **($24.01)** | 141.3* ($33.94) | NA | NA | November 2006 |
| Sonicare Toothbrush | 107.1 ($120) | **100.0** **($112)** | 108.9 ($122) | 103.6 ($116) | 139.3 ($156) | 158.9 ($178) | 156.2 ($175) | NA | September 2008 |
| BlackBerry Bold 9000 | **100.0** **($571)** | 115.1 ($657) | 116.7 ($666) | NA | 114.9 ($656) | 128.7 ($735) | NA | 132.0 ($754) | April 2009 |
| Brita Marella Jug | NA | 222.0 ($46.16) | 231.5 ($48.13) | 207.7 ($43.19) | 121.6 ($25.29) | 108.4 ($22.54) | NA | **100.0** **($20.79)** | November 2008 |

*700 ml

Source: Based on various issues of the Weekend Journal of the *Wall Street Journal* ("Arbitrage")

◆ ◆ ◆ ◆ ◆ ◆ ◆ ◆ **DRIVERS OF FOREIGN MARKET PRICING**

In December 2008, the retail price recorded for a 500 ml bottle of Listerine mouthwash was $3.60 (4,720 won) in Seoul, $4.72 in New York, and $11.27 (€8) in Rome; for a Davidoff cigar cutter was $222 (323,000 won) in Seoul, $322 in New York, and $727 (25,900 baht) in Bangkok.[1] Even within the same geographic area such as the pan-European market, wide cross-border price differences are quite common. **Exhibit 12-1** shows retail price variations for a sample of other products around the world. What lies behind these enormous price variations? A hodgepodge of factors governs global pricing decisions. Some of the drivers are related to the 4 Cs: *Company* (costs, company goals), *Customers* (price sensitivity, segments, consumer preferences), *Competition* (market structure, intensity), and *Channels*. Aside from these, in many countries, multinationals' pricing decisions are often influenced by government policies (price controls, taxes, import duties). We now consider the main drivers that may affect global pricing.

**Company Goals**   When developing a pricing strategy for its global markets, the firm needs to decide what it wants to accomplish with its strategy. These goals might include maximizing current profits, penetrating the market, projecting a premium image, and so forth. According to one study,[2] the most important pricing objectives of companies doing business in the

---

[1] Price data compiled from December 2008 issues in the "Arbitrage" section of the weekend edition of *Wall Street Journal*. Prices include taxes.

[2] S. Samiee, "Pricing in Marketing Strategies of U.S.- and Foreign-Based Companies," *Journal of Business Research*, vol. 15, 1987, pp. 17–30.

United States (including foreign-based firms) are (1) to achieve a satisfactory return on investment, (2) to maintain market share, and (3) to meet a specified profit goal (in that order). Company objectives will vary from market to market, especially in multinationals with a large degree of local autonomy. New Balance, the U.S.-based maker of high-tech running shoes, sells its shoes in France as haute couture items rather than simply athletic shoes (as it does in the United States for instance). To beef up the premium image, the price in France is almost twice the U.S.-price.[3] Company goals are likely to change over time. Initially, when a firm enters a country, it often sets a relatively low price (compared to other countries) to penetrate the market. Once the firm is well entrenched, it may shift its objectives and bring them in line with the goals pursued in other countries.

Company costs figure prominently in the pricing decision. Costs set the floor: the company wants to set at least a price that will cover all costs needed to make and sell its products. Cost differentials between countries can lead to wide price gaps. It is important that management considers all relevant costs of manufacturing, marketing and distributing the product. Company costs consist of two parts: variable costs, which change with sales volume, and fixed costs (e.g., overheads) that do not vary.

**Company Costs**

Export pricing policies differ depending on the way costs are treated.[4] Three basic options exist for setting export prices: (1) rigid cost-plus pricing, (2) flexible cost-plus pricing, and (3) dynamic incremental pricing.[5] With **rigid cost-plus pricing**, the export price is set by adding all costs accrued in selling the product to the international market and a gross margin. The second option, **flexible cost-plus pricing**, closely resembles the first method but adjusts prices to market conditions in the host market (e.g., level of competition). The final method, **flexible cost-plus pricing**, arrives at a price after removing domestic fixed costs. The premise is that these costs have to be borne anyway, as they are *sunk costs*, regardless of whether or not the goods are exported. Only variable costs generated by the exporting efforts and a portion of the overhead load (the "incremental" costs) should be recuperated. Examples of exporting-related incremental costs include manufacturing costs, shipping expenses, insurance, and overseas promotional costs. Although the last approach is more suitable from an economic perspective, it comes with certain risks. In the export market, situations where the export list price is far below the domestic price could trigger accusations of dumping, as discussed later.

When demand is highly price sensitive, the company needs to consider how it can reduce costs from a global perspective. Manufacturing scale economies provide an incentive to standardize product offerings or to consolidate manufacturing facilities. In some markets, logistics costs can be trimmed by centralizing distribution centers or warehouse facilities. By the same token, significant marketing costs may prompt a multinational operating in Europe to develop pan-European advertising campaigns. In many developing countries, high price sensitivity is a big hurdle. Hindustan Lever, Unilever's India subsidiary, spends a large amount of its R&D money on developing new technologies to lower production costs. Companies operating in these countries typically try to source mainly from local suppliers. McDonald's India imports only potato chips; all other ingredients are sourced locally. However, the company has set up a potato research unit to improve the quality of Indian potatoes.[6] Kellogg, on the other hand, entered India with costly packaging (seven-ply cartons, foil pouches, five colors), and expensive advertising. A local competitor, Champion, piggybacked on Kellogg's marketing efforts and conquered the breakfast cereal market with products at one-fifth of Kellogg's price.[7]

[3] "The Road to Richesse," *Sales & Marketing Management* (November 1999), pp. 89–96.

[4] S. Tamer Cavusgil, "Unraveling the Mystique of Export Pricing," *Business Horizons*, vol. 31, May–June 1988, pp. 54–63.

[5] See for instance, Kristiaan Helsen, "Pricing in the Global Marketplace," in *The SAGE Handbook of International Marketing*, M. Kotabe and K. Helsen (eds.) (London: SAGE Publications, 2009).

[6] "Hard Sell to a Billion Consumers," *Financial Times* (April 25, 2002), p. 14.

[7] "Slim Pickings for the Global Brand in India," *Financial Times* (October 11, 2000), p. 14.

**Customer Demand**     Whereas costs set a floor, the consumers' willingness to pay for your product set a ceiling to the price. Consumer demand is function of buying power, tastes, habits and substitutes. These demand conditions will vary from country to country. Buying power is a key consideration in pricing decisions. Countries with low per-capita incomes pose a dilemma. Consumers in such countries are far more price-sensitive than in developed markets. Therefore, price premiums are often a major hurdle for most consumers in these markets. Foreign companies targeting the masses in emerging markets such as China or India offer cheaper products with lower costs by changing the product formula, packaging or size. One risk here is brand dilution, where a premium brand loses its cachet when a large number of consumers start using it. Another danger is cannibalization. This occurs when high-income customers switch to the cheaper products in the firm's product line. The marketing of Procter & Gamble's Crest toothpaste in China illustrates how companies can manage these issues. To lure the Chinese middle classes, P&G changed the brand's formulation and packaging to emphasize cavity prevention, a generic benefit. The whitening benefit was reserved for premium Crest products.[8] In Egypt, one of the moves that P&G undertook to revitalize the sales of Ariel, its high suds laundry detergent brand, was to downsize the package size from 200 grams to 150 grams, thereby lowering the cash outlay for ordinary consumers.[9]

Another strategic option is to be a niche player by charging prices in the same range as Western prices and target the upper-end of the foreign market. Marketers such as Starbucks and Häagen-Dazs follow this option in their global strategy. Starbucks charges by and large the same price worldwide, whether its coffee is sold in wealthy Western markets or poorer countries such as Thailand or China. A third option is to have a portfolio of products that cater to different income tiers. Hindustan Lever, Unilever's India subsidiary, dominates many consumer goods categories by following this road. One final option—which seldom works—is to sell older versions of the product at a lower price in markets with low buying power. For instance, in India, Daimler sold older Mercedes models; United Distillers sold passé brands such as Vat 69. Such a pricing strategy can backfire as it manifests a certain amount of arrogance toward the local population.[10]

Typically, the nature of demand will change over time. In countries that were entered recently, the firm may need to stimulate trial via discounting or a penetration pricing strategy. In more mature markets, the lion's share of customers will be repeat-buyers. Once brand loyalty has been established, price will play less of a role as a purchase criterion, and the firm may be able to afford the luxury of a premium pricing strategy. Obviously, the success of such a pricing strategy will hinge on the company's ability to differentiate its product from the competition.

Cultural symbolism can also influence pricing decisions. In Chinese cultures, the number "8" has an auspicious meaning as the word for "eight" (bā) sounds similar to the Chinese word for "wealth" (fā). As a result, special price offers in Chinese cultures often end with at least one 8 digit (see **Exhibit 12-2**). For instance, Bank of China, the world's third largest bank, set a mortgage arrangement fee of £888 when it started offering mortgages to British house buyers. However, it switched to the more recognizable figure of £995.[11]

**Competition**     Competition is another key factor in global pricing. Differences in the competitive situation across countries will usually lead to cross-border price differentials. The competitive situation may vary for a number of reasons. First, the number of competitors typically differs from country to country. In some countries, the firm faces very few

---

[8]"The Right Way to Appeal to the Masses," *Financial Times* (September 15, 2004): 10.

[9]Mahmoud Aboul-Fath and Loula Zaklama, "Ariel High Suds detergent in Egypt—A case study," *Marketing and Research Today*, May 1992, pp. 130–35.

[10]"Slim Pickings for the Global Brand in India," *Financial Times* (October 11, 2000), p. 14.

[11]"Bank of China Offers Mortgages to UK Borrowers," http://www.ft.com, accessed on July 29, 2009.

**EXHIBIT 12-2**
PRICE PROMOTIONS IN CHINESE CULTURES WITH END-8 PRICES

Courtesy of Kristiaan Helsen

competitors (or even enjoys a monopoly position), whereas in others, the company has to combat numerous competing brands. Also, the nature of competition will differ: global versus local players, private firms versus state-owned companies. Even when local companies are not state-owned, they often are viewed as "national champions" and treated accordingly by their local governments. Such a status entails subsidies or other goodies (e.g., cheap loans) that enable them to undercut their competitors. In some markets, firms have to compete with a knock-off version of their own product. The presence of counterfeit products could force the firm to lower its price in such markets. Microsoft, for instance, slashed the Chinese price of its MS Office software suite by more than 70 percent from Rmb699 to Rmb199 ($29) in 2008 to encourage consumers to purchase genuine software instead of pirated software. The piracy rate for personal computer software in China was estimated to be more than 80 percent in 2007.[12]

In developing countries, especially in rural areas, the nature of competition can also vary. An Indian villager is not just choosing between a bottle of Coca-Cola and Pepsi but also between buying one soft drink, a disposable razor or a tube of toothpaste.

The role of competition can be illustrated by taking a look at the pharmaceutical industry. The data in **Exhibit 12-3** show the average quarterly volume sales and selling price (charged by manufacturers) for three antidepressants (Prozac, Zoloft, Paxil) marketed in the United States, the UK, France, Italy, and Germany. Looking at the

---

[12]"Microsoft Aims to Undercut Chinese Pirates," *Financial Times*, September 24, 2008, p. 22.

**EXHIBIT 12-3**

AVERAGE QUARTERLY SALES & EX-FACTORY SELLING PRICES OF
ANTIDEPRESSANTS (1988, Q1–1999, Q1)

| Brand | Manufacturer | United States | Germany | Italy | UK | France |
|-------|--------------|---------------|---------|-------|------|--------|
| Prozac | Eli | Lilly | | | | |
| Sales | (U.S.) | 162.13 | 2.47 | 3.65 | 18.88 | 32.92 |
| Price | | 1.62 | 1.48 | 0.99 | 1.18 | 0.84 |
| Zoloft | Pfizer (U.S.) | | | | | |
| Sales | | 140.05 | 1.99 | 1.77 | 7.3 | 9.47 |
| Price | | 1.59 | 1.0 | 0.92 | 1.4 | 0.70 |
| Paxil | GSK (U.K.) | | | | | |
| Sales | | 110.46 | 1.66 | 4.04 | 16.70 | 21.94 |
| Price | | 1.59 | 1.48 | 1.20 | 1.26 | 0.65 |

*Source:* Based on Table 1 (p. 73) of Pradeep K. Chintagunta and Ramarao Desiraju, "Strategic Pricing and Detailing Behavior in International Markets," *Marketing Science* 24 (Winter 2005).

data, you can see that Prozac (from Eli Lilly based in the United States) charges a higher price than Paxil (from GlaxoSmithKline in the UK). However, the reverse is the case in the United Kingdom. An in-depth analysis of this particular industry found that pharmaceutical companies tend to behave much more aggressively toward their competitors in the home market as opposed to foreign markets.[13]

In many markets, legitimate distributors of global brands need to compete with smugglers. Smuggling operations put downward pressure on the price of the affected product. The strength of private labels (store brands) is another important driver. In countries where store brands are well entrenched, companies are forced to accept lower margins than elsewhere.

A company's competitive position typically varies across countries. Companies will be price leaders in some countries and price takers in other countries. Heinz's policy is to cut prices in markets where it is not the leading brand.[14] Finally, the rules of the game usually differ. Non-price competition (e.g., advertising, channel coverage) may be preferable in some countries. Elsewhere, price combats are a way of life. For example, in Western countries, a price war is to be avoided at all cost. In contrast, Chinese companies often see a price war as a strategic weapon to grab market dominance, as illustrated in **Global Perspective 12-1**.

**Distribution Channels**

Another driver behind global pricing is the distribution channel. The pressure exercised by channels can take many forms. Variations in trade margins and the length of the channels will influence the ex-factory price charged by the company. The balance of power between manufacturers and their distributors is another factor behind pricing practices. Countries such as France and the United Kingdom are characterized by large retailers who are able to order in bulk and to bargain for huge discounts with manufacturers. In the pan-European market, several smaller retailers have formed cross-border co-ops to strengthen their negotiation position with their common suppliers. The power of large-scale retailers in Europe is vividly illustrated by the hurdles that several manufacturers faced in implementing every-day-low-pricing (EDLP). With EDLP, the manufacturer offers consistently lower prices to the retailer (and the ultimate shopper) instead of promotional price discounts and trade promotions.[15] Several German supermarket chains de-listed P&G brands like Ariel, Vizir, and Lenor detergent products, Bess toilet tissue

---

[13]Pradeep K. Chintagunta and Ramarao Desiraju, "Strategic Pricing and Detailing Behavior in International Markets," *Marketing Science* 24 (Winter 2005): 67–80.

[14]"Counting costs of dual pricing," *Financial Times*, July 9, 1990, p. 4.

[15]Trade promotions are promotions where the manufacturer offers monetary incentives to the channel (e.g., wholesalers, retailers) as a reward for activities (e.g., in-store displays, price discounts, advertising the manufacturer's product) that will stimulate the sales of the product. The most common trade promotion tools include off-invoice allowances (discount off the list price on the invoice) and extra cases of merchandise for channels who order a minimum amount.

## GLOBAL PERSPECTIVE 12-1

### PRICE WARFARE IN CHINA'S COLOR TV MARKET

China's color TV industry was highly fragmented in early 1996, with more than 130 manufacturers. Of there, only 12 had annual sales of over 500,000 units. Among these, each player sold less than 120,000 units per year. As a result, very few manufacturers could enjoy economies of scale. A vast majority of these companies were owned by local governments. As a result, there was very little room to achieve scale economies through merger and acquisitions or market entry. At the time, China's TV market was a two-tier market with local brands at the low-end and foreign brands such as Sony serving the top-end of the market with a 20 percent price premium over local brands.

Among the Chinese producers, Changhong was at the time the largest and most cost efficient manufacturer, with a capacity that was at least double of the next biggest one. Being the largest producer of many key TV components (e.g., plastic injections, remote controls), the firm was also highly vertically integrated. In spite of its dominance, Changhong was very concerned about its long-term future. The company's success had made it a target of foreign competitors. Changhong had to find a way to shore up its competitive position. Based on inputs from pricing experts and market surveys the firm

*Source:* Z. John Zhang and Dongsheng Zhou, "The Art of Price War: A Perspective from China," Working Paper, The Wharton School of the University of Pennsylvania, 2006.

decided that the best means to bolster its market share would be a price war. Several reasons were behind their thinking. First, a price war would squeeze out small, less efficient domestic players. Second, a price war would also enable Changhong to tackle its foreign (mainly Japanese) rivals. If they followed suit and lowered their prices, they might cheapen their brand image and hurt their profit margin. Further, any drastic price cut would require approval from headquarters, which could be a very time-consuming ordeal. Finally, a price war could also capitalize on Changhong's huge inventory and its integrated supply chain. On March 16, 1996, Changhong triggered a price war by announcing a discount of 8 percent to 18 percent for all its 17-inch to 29-inch color TVs. The war evolved largely according to plan. The four biggest domestic players did not follow suit until June 6, 1996. Three reasons were behind their slow response: (1) surprise, (2) the fragmented nature of the Chinese TV market, and (3) thin profit margins. Foreign brands decided to sit on the fence and focus on quality, not on price.

The price war drastically changed the competitive landscape in China's TV market. A few months after the price war, Changhong's market share had increased from 16.7 percent to 31.6 percent. The market share of small domestic brands tumbled. The Japanese players' market share also declined drastically.

---

when P&G introduced EDLP in Germany in early 1996.[16] Likewise, Delhaize,[17] a large Belgian grocery chain, removed about 300 Unilever products from its stores claiming that they were priced too high. The banished products included major brands such as Dove soap and Axe deodorant.[18]

Large cross-country price gaps open up arbitrage opportunities that lead to **parallel imports (gray markets)** from low-price countries to high-price ones. These parallel imports are commonly handled by unauthorized distributors at the expense of legitimate trade channels. To curtail parallel trade, firms can consider narrowing cross-border price disparities. Thus, pre-emption of cross-border bargain hunting is often times a strong motivation behind a company's pricing practices.

Even after the launch of the euro, car prices in the European Union can still vary by up to 50 percent. One of the main reasons for these car price disparities is the sales tax rate for new cars. These vary from as low as 15 percent in Luxembourg up to 213 percent in Denmark. This taxation gap also has an impact on pre-tax car prices. In fact, most carmakers in Europe subsidize the pre-tax prices in high-tax countries by charging more in low-tax countries.[19]

**Government Policies**

---

[16]"Heat's on value pricing," *Advertising Age International*, January 1997, pp. I–21, I–22.

[17]Delhaize also operates 1,500 stores in the United States, including the Food Lion chain.

[18]"Belgian Grocer Battles Unilever on Pricing," *The Wall Street Journal Asia*, February 12, 2009, p. 16.

[19]"Car price disparities highlighted," *Financial Times* (January 7, 1999), p. 2.

Government policies can have a direct or indirect impact on pricing policies. Factors that have a direct impact include sales tax rates (e.g., value added taxes), tariffs, and price controls. Sometimes government interference is very blatant. The Chinese government sets minimum prices in scores of industries. The goal is to stamp out price wars and protect the Chinese economy against deflation pressures. Firms that ignore the pricing rules are slapped with hefty fines.[20]

An increase in the sales tax rate will usually lower overall demand. However, in some cases taxes may selectively affect imports. For instance, in the late 1980s, the U.S. government introduced a 10-percent luxury tax on the part of a car's price that exceeds $30,000. This luxury tax primarily affected the price of luxury import cars since few U.S.-made luxury cars sell for more than the $30,000 threshold. Tariffs obviously will inflate the retail price of imports. Another concern is price controls. These affect either the whole economy (for instance, in high-inflation countries) or selective industries. In many countries, a substantial part of the health care costs are borne by the government. Prices for reimbursable drugs are negotiated between the government authorities and the pharmaceutical company. Many pharmaceutical companies face the dilemma of accepting lower prices for their drugs or having their drugs registered on a negative list, which contains drugs that the government will not reimburse.[21] Furthermore, several governments heavily encourage the prescription of generics or stimulate parallel imports from low-price countries to put price pressure on drug companies. In the European Union, governments increasingly benchmark their prices against other member states and adjust them if necessary.[22] To sustain higher prices, manufacturers often launch new drugs in high-price markets first so that prices in these countries can be used as reference points.[23]

Aside from direct intervention, government policies can have an indirect impact on pricing decisions. For instance, huge government deficits spur interest rates (cost of capital), currency volatility, and inflation. The interplay of these factors will affect the product cost. Inflation might also impact labor costs in those countries (e.g., Belgium, Brazil) that have a wage indexation system. Such a system adjusts wages for increases in the cost of living.

Earlier we pinpointed the main factors that will drive global pricing decisions. We now highlight the key managerial issues in global pricing.

## ◆ ◆ ◆ ◆ ◆ ◆ ◆ ◆ ◆   MANAGING PRICE ESCALATION

Exporting involves more steps and substantially higher risks than simply selling goods in the home market. To cover the incremental costs (e.g., shipping, insurance, tariffs, margins of various intermediaries), the final foreign retail price will often be much higher than the domestic retail price. This phenomenon is known as **price escalation**. Price escalation raises two questions that management needs to confront: (1) Will our foreign customers be willing to pay the inflated price for our product ("sticker shock")? And (2) will this price make our product less competitive? If the answer is negative, the exporter needs to decide how to cope with price escalation.

There are two broad approaches to deal with price escalation: (1) find ways to cut the export price, or (2) position the product as a (super) premium brand. Several options exist to lower the export price:[24]

1. **Rearrange the distribution channel.** Channels are often largely responsible for price escalation, either due to the length of the channel (number of layers between

---

[20]"So Much for Competition," *Business Week (Asian edition),* (November 30, 1998), pp. 22–23.

[21]Some countries have a "positive" list of drugs from which physicians can prescribe.

[22]Neil Turner, "European Pricing Squeeze," *Pharmaceutical Executive,* (October 2002), pp. 84–91.

[23]David Hanlon and David Luery, "The Role of Pricing Research in Assessing the Commercial Potential of New Drugs in Development," *International Journal of Market Research,* 44(4) (2002), pp. 423–47.

[24]S. Tamer Cavusgil, "Unraveling the Mystique of Export Pricing," *Business Horizons,* May–June 1988, p. 56.

manufacturer and end-user) or because of exorbitant margins. In some circumstances, it is possible to shorten the channel. Alternatively, firms could look into channel arrangements that provide cost efficiencies. In recent years, several U.S. companies have decided to penetrate the Japanese consumer market through direct marketing (e.g., catalog sales, telemarketing, selling through the internet). This allows them to bypass the notorious Japanese distribution infrastructure and become more price-competitive.

2. **Eliminate costly features (or make them optional).** Several exporters have addressed the price escalation issue by offering no-frills versions of their product. Rather than having to purchase the entire bundle, customers can buy the core product and then decide whether or not they want to pay extra for optional features.

3. **Downsize the product.** Another route to dampen sticker shock is downsizing the product by offering a smaller version of the product or a lesser count.[25] This option is only desirable when consumers are not aware of cross-border volume differences. To that end, manufacturers may decide to go for a local branding strategy.

4. **Assemble or manufacture the product in foreign markets.** A more extreme option is to assemble or even manufacture the entire product in foreign markets (not necessarily the export market). Closer proximity to the export market will lower transportation costs. To lessen import duties for goods sold within European Union markets, numerous firms have decided to set up assembly operations in EU member states.

5. **Adapt the product to escape tariffs or tax levies.** Finally, a company could also modify its export product to bring it into a different tariff or tax bracket. When the United States levied a new 10 percent tax on over $30,000 luxury cars, Land Rover increased the maximum weight of Range Rover models sold in America to 6,019 pounds. As a result, the Range Rover was classified as a truck (not subject to the 10 percent luxury tax) rather than a luxury car.

These measures represent different ways to counter price escalation. Alternatively, an exporter could exploit the price escalation situation and go for a premium positioning strategy. LEGO, the Danish toymaker, sells building block sets in India that are priced between $6 and $223, far more than most other toys that Indian parents can purchase. To justify the premium price, LEGO uses a marketing strategy that targets middle-class parents and stresses the educational value of LEGO toys.[26] Of course, for this strategy to work, other elements of the export marketing-mix should be in tandem with the premium positioning. In Europe and Japan, Levi Strauss sells its jeans mainly in upscale boutiques rather than in department stores.[27]

## PRICING IN INFLATIONARY ENVIRONMENTS ◆ ◆ ◆ ◆ ◆ ◆ ◆ ◆

When McDonald's opened its doors in January 1990, a Big Mac meal (including fries and a soft drink) in Moscow cost 6 rubles. Three years later, the same meal cost 1,100 rubles.[28] Rampant inflation is a major obstacle to doing business in many countries. Moreover, high inflation rates are usually coupled with highly volatile exchange rate movements. In such environments, price setting and stringent cost control become extremely crucial. Not surprisingly, in such markets, companies' financial divisions are often far more important than other departments.[29]

---

[25]Loyal Coca-Cola cross-border travelers may have noticed can-size differences of their favorite tipple. For instance, for Diet Coke, can sizes range from 325 ml (e.g., Malaysia, Thailand) up to 355 ml (U.S.A.). See http://xoomer.virgilio.it/davide.andreani/Cokesize.htm for a complete listing of Coke can sizes around the world.

[26]"LEGO building its way to China," *Advertising Age International*, March 20, 1995, p. I–29.

[27]"The Levi straddle," *Forbes*, January 17, 1994, p. 44.

[28]"Inflation bits Russians, who still bite into Big Mac," *Advertising Age International*, March 15, 1993, pp. I–3, I–23.

[29]"A rollercoaster out of control," *The Financial Times*, February 22, 1993.

There are several alternative ways to safeguard against inflation

1. **Modify components, ingredients, parts and/or packaging materials.** Some ingredients are subject to lower inflation rates than others. This might justify a change in the ingredient mix. Of course, before implementing such a move, the firm should consider all its consequences (e.g., consumer response, impact on shelf life of the product).

2. **Source materials from low-cost suppliers.** Supply management plays a central role in high inflation environments. A first step is to screen suppliers and determine which ones would be most cost efficient without cutting corners. If feasible, materials could be imported from low-inflation countries. Note, however, that high inflation rates are coupled with a weakening currency. This will push up the price of imports.

3. **Shorten credit terms.** In some cases, profits can be realized by juggling the terms of payment. For instance, a firm that is able to collect cash from its customers within fifteen days, but has one month to pay its suppliers, can invest its money during the 15-day grace period. Thus, firms strive to push up the lead time in paying their suppliers. At the same time, they also try to shorten the time to collect from their clients.[30]

4. **Include escalator clauses in long-term contracts.** Many business-to-business marketing situations involve long-term contracts (e.g., leasing arrangements). To hedge their position against inflation, the parties will include escalator clauses that will provide the necessary protection.

5. **Quote prices in a stable currency.** To handle high inflation, companies often quote prices in a stable currency such as the U.S. dollar or the euro.

6. **Pursue rapid inventory turnovers.** High inflation also mandates rapid inventory turnarounds. As a result, information technologies (e.g., scanning techniques, computerized inventory tracking) that facilitate rapid inventory turnovers or even just-in-time delivery will yield a competitive advantage.

7. **Draw lessons from other countries.** Operations in countries with a long history of inflation offer valuable lessons for ventures in other high-inflation countries. Cross-fertilization by drawing from experience in other high inflation markets often helps. Some companies—McDonald's[31] and Otis Elevator International,[32] for example— have relied on expatriate managers from Latin America to cope with inflation in the former Soviet Union. One of the lessons drawn from Brazil was that McDonald's negotiates a separate inflation rate with each supplier. These rates are then used for monthly realignments, instead of the government's published inflation figures.

To combat hyperinflation, governments occasionally impose price controls (usually coupled with a wage freeze). For instance, Brazil went through five price freezes over a six-year interval. Such temporary price caps could be selective, targeting certain products, but, in extreme circumstances, they will apply across-the-board to all consumer goods. Price freezes have proven to be very ineffective to dampen inflation—witness the experience of Brazil. Often, expectations of an imminent price freeze start off a rumor mill that will spur companies to implement substantial price increases, thereby setting off a vicious cycle. One consequence of price controls is that goods are diverted to the black market or smuggled overseas, leading to shortages in the regular market.

Companies faced with price controls can consider several action courses:

1. **Adapt the product line.** To reduce exposure to a government imposed price freeze, companies diversify into product lines that are relatively free of price controls.[33] Of

---

[30]"A rollercoaster out of control," *Financial Times*, February 22, 1993.

[31]"Inflation lessons over a Big Mac," *Financial Times*, February 22, 1993.

[32]"Russians up and down," *Financial Times*, October 18, 1993, p. 12.

[33]Venkatakrishna V. Bellur, Radharao Chaganti, Rajeswararao Chaganti, and Saraswati P. Singh, "Strategic Adaptations to Price Controls: The Case of the Indian Drug Industry," *Journal of the Academy of Marketing Science*, vol. 13, no. 1, Winter 1985, pp. 143–59.

course, before embarking on such a changeover, the firm has to examine the long-term ramifications. Modifying the product line could imply loss of economies of scale, an increase in overheads, and adverse reactions from the company's customer base.

2. **Shift target segments or markets.** A more drastic move is to shift the firm's target segment. For instance, price controls often apply to consumer food products but not to animal-related products. So, a maker of corn-based consumer products might consider a shift from breakfast cereals to chicken-feed products. Again, such action should be preceded by a thorough analysis of its strategic implications. Alternatively, a firm might consider using its operations in the high-inflation country as an export base for countries that are not subject to price controls.

3. **Launch new products or variants of existing products.** If price controls are selective, a company can navigate around them by systematically launching new products or modifying existing ones. Faced with price controls in Zimbabwe, bakers added raisins to their dough and called it "raisin bread," thereby, at least momentarily, escaping the price control for bread.[34] Also here, the firm should consider the overall picture by answering questions such as: Will there be a demand for these products? What are the implications in terms of manufacturing economies? Inventory management? How will the trade react? Furthermore, if these products are not yet available elsewhere, this option is merely a long-term solution.

4. **Negotiate with the government.** In some cases, firms are able to negotiate for permission to adjust their prices. Lobbying can be done individually, but is more likely to be successful on an industry-wide basis.

5. **Predict incidence of price controls.** Some countries have a history of price freeze programs. Given historical information on the occurrence of price controls and other economic variables, econometric models can be constructed to forecast the likelihood of price controls. Managers can use that information to see whether or not price adjustments are warranted, given the likelihood of an imminent price freeze.[35]

A drastic action course is simply to leave the country. Many consumer goods companies have chosen this option when they exited their South-American markets during the 1980s. However, companies that hang on and learn to manage a high-inflation environment will be able carry over their expertise to other countries. Further, they will enjoy a competitive advantage (due to entry barriers such as brand loyalty, channel and supplier ties) versus companies that reenter these markets once inflation has been suppressed.

# GLOBAL PRICING AND CURRENCY FLUCTUATIONS

In May 1992, two of the most expensive car markets in the European Union were Spain and Italy. One year later, Italy and Spain were the two lowest priced markets.[36] Currency volatility within the European Union was mostly responsible for these car price reversals. With a few exceptions (e.g., some Caribbean islands, Ecuador), most countries have their own currency. Exchange rates reflect how much one currency is worth in terms of another currency. Due to the interplay of a variety of economic and political factors, exchange rates continuously float up- or downward. Even membership to a monetary union does not guarantee exchange rate stability. Given the sometimes-dramatic exchange rate movements, setting prices in a floating exchange rate world poses a tremendous challenge.[37] **Exhibit 12-4** lists several exporter strategies under varying currency regimes.

[34]"The Zimbabwean Model," *The Economist* (November 30, 2002), p. 72.

[35]James K. Weekly, "Pricing in Foreign Markets: Pitfalls and Opportunities," *Industrial Marketing Management*, vol. 21, 1992, pp. 173–79.

[36]"Fluctuating exchange rates main factor in European car price comparisons," *Financial Times*, July 5, 1993.

[37]Llewlyn Clague and Rena Grossfield, "Export Pricing in a Floating Rate World," *Columbia Journal of World Business*, Winter 1974, pp. 17–22.

**EXHIBIT 12-4**
EXPORTER STRATEGIES UNDER VARYING CURRENCY CONDITIONS

| When Domestic Currency is WEAK ... | When Domestic Currency is STRONG ... |
|---|---|
| • Stress price benefits | • Engage in nonprice competition by improving quality, delivery, and aftersale service |
| • Costly features expand product line and add more | • Improve productivity and engage in vigorous cost reduction |
| • Shift sourcing and manufacturing to domestic market | • Shift sourcing and manufacturing overseas. |
| • Exploit export opportunities in all markets | • Give priority to exports to relatively strong-currency countries |
| • Conduct conventional cash-for-goods trade | • Deal in countertrade with weak-currency countries |
| • Use full-costing approach but use marginal-cost pricing to penetrate new/competitive markets | • Trim profit margins and use marginal-cost pricing |
| • Speed repatriation of foreign-earned income and collections | • Keep the foreign-earned income in host country, slow collections |
| • Minimize expenditures in local, host-country currency | • Maximize expenditure in local, host-country currency |
| • Buy needed services (advertising, insurance, transportation, etc.) in domestic market | • Buy needed services abroad and pay for them in local currency |
| • Minimize local borrowing | • Borrow money needed for expansion in local market |
| • Bill foreign customers in domestic currency | • Bill foreign customers in their own currency |

*Source:* S. Tamer Cavusgil, "Unraveling the Mystique of Export Pricing," reprinted from *Business Horizons* (May–June 1988). Copyright 1988 by the Foundation for the School of Business at Indiana University. Used with permission.

**Currency Gain/Loss Pass Through**

Two major managerial pricing issues result from currency movements: (1) How much of an exchange rate gain (loss) should be passed through to our customers? and (2) In what currency should we quote our prices? Let us first address the **pass-through** issue. Consider the predicament of American companies exporting to Japan. In principle, a weakening of the U.S. dollar versus the Japanese yen will strengthen the competitive position of U.S.-based exporters in Japan. A weak dollar allows U.S.-based firms to lower the yen-price of American goods exported to Japan. This enables American exporters to steal market share away from the local Japanese competitors without sacrificing profits. By the same token, a stronger U.S. dollar will undermine the competitive position of American exporters. When the dollar appreciates versus the yen, we have the mirror picture of the previous situation: the retail price in yen of American exports goes up. As a result, American exporters might lose market share if they leave their ex-factory prices unchanged. To maintain their competitive edge, they may be forced to lower their ex-factory dollar prices. Of course, the ultimate impact on the exporter's competitive position will also depend on the impact of currency movement on the exporter's costs and the nature of the competition in the Japanese market. The benefits of a weaker dollar could be washed out when many parts are imported from Japan, since the weaker dollar will make these parts more expensive. When most of the competitors are U.S.-based manufacturers, changes in the dollar's exchange rate might not matter.

Let us illustrate these points with a numerical example. Consider the situation in **Exhibit 12-5**, which looks at the dilemmas that a hypothetical U.S.-based exporter to Japan faces when the exchange rate between the U.S. dollar and the Japanese yen changes. In the example we assume a simple linear demand schedule:

Demand (in units) in Japanese export market = 2,000 − 50 × yen price.

We also make an admittedly dubious assumption: our exporter does not face any costs (in other words, total revenues equal total profits). Initially, one U.S. dollar equals 100

**EXHIBIT 12-5**
A NUMERICAL ILLUSTRATION OF PASS THROUGH AND LOCAL CURRENCY
STABILITY

*Demand in Japan (Units) = 2000 − 50 × Price (in Yen)*
*Costs = $0.0*

Panel A: 100% Pass Through

| Exchange Rate | Unit Price in US$ | Unit Price in Yen* | Units Sold | US$ Revenue* |
|---|---|---|---|---|
| 100 yen = $1 | $30,000 | 3.0 | 1,850 | $55.50 |
| 130 yen = $1 | 30,000 | 3.9 | 1,805 | 54.15 |
| 70 yen = $1 | 30,000 | 2.1 | 1,895 | 56.85 |

*Panel B: Local Currency Price Stability (in millions except units sold)*

| Exchange Rate | Unit Price in US$ | Unit Price in Yen* | Units Sold | US$ Revenue* | Revenue Gain(Loss) vs. 100% PT* |
|---|---|---|---|---|---|
| 100 yen = $1 | $30,000 | 3.0 | 1,850 | $55.50 | $0.00 |
| 130 yen = $1 | 23,077 | 3.0 | 1,850 | 42.69 | (11.45) |
| 70 yen = $1 | 42,857 | 3.0 | 1,850 | 79.28 | 22.45 |

*In millions.

*Note:* The dollar appreciation measures the movement of the U.S. producer price index relative to the Japanese and German producer price indices converted into dollars by the nominal exchange rate. The real retail price change measures the movement of the dollar retail price of specific auto models relative to the retail unit value of all domestically produced cars.

*Source:* Reprinted from Joseph A. Gagnon and Michael M. Knetter, "Markup Adjustment and Exchange Rate Fluctuations: Evidence from Panel Data on Automobile Exports," *Journal of International Money and Finance* 14 (2), p. 304. Copyright 1995, with kind permission from Elsevier Science Ltd., Langford Lane, Kidlington OX5 IGB, UK.

yen, and the firm's total export revenue is $55.5 million. Suppose now that the U.S. dollar has strengthened by 30 percent versus the Japanese yen, moving from an exchange rate of 100 yen to 1 US$ to a 130-to-1 exchange rate (row 2 in Exhibit 12-5). If the US$ ex-factory price remains the same (i.e., $30,000), Japanese consumers will face a 30-percent price increase. Total demand decreases (from 1,850 units to 1,805 units), and US$ revenue goes down by $1.35 m. Our American exporter faces the problem of whether or not to pass through exchange rate losses, and if so, how much, of the loss he should absorb. If our exporter does not lower the U.S. dollar ex-factory price, he is likely to lose market share to his Japanese (and/or European) competitors in Japan. Thus, to sustain its competitive position, the U.S.-based manufacturer would be forced to lower its ex-factory price. In this situation, American exporters face the trade-off between sacrificing short-term profits (maintaining price) and sustaining long-term market share in export markets (cutting ex-factory price). For example, in the extreme case, the U.S. firm might consider sustaining the yen-based retail price (i.e., 3 million yen). In that case, US$ revenues would go down by $11.45 million.

Generally speaking, the appropriate action will depend on four factors, namely: (1) customers' price sensitivity, (2) the size of the export market, (3) the impact of the dollar appreciation on the firm's cost structure, (4) the amount of competition in the export market, and (5) the firm's strategic orientation. The higher consumers' price sensitivity in the export market, the stronger the case for lowering the ex-factory price. One route to lower price sensitivity is by investing in brand equity. High brand equity provides a buffer to global price competition. With vast markets such as the United States, firms are usually more inclined to absorb currency losses than with smaller countries. A decline in costs resulting from the strengthening of the U.S. dollar (e.g., when many parts are imported from Japan) broadens the price adjustment latitude. The

**EXHIBIT 12-6**
RETAIL PRICE CHANGES DURING DOLLAR APPRECIATIONS:
JAPANESE AND GERMAN EXPORTS TO THE U.S. MARKET

| Model | Real Dollar Appreciation | Real Retail Price Change in U.S. Market |
|---|---|---|
| Honda Civic 2-Dr. Sedan | 39% | −7% |
| Datsun 200 SX 2-Dr. | 39 | −10 |
| Toyota Cressida 4-Dr. | 39 | 6 |
| BMW 320i 2-Dr. | 42 | −8 |
| BMW 733i 4-Dr. | 42 | −17 |
| Mercedes 300 TD Sta. Wgn. | 42 | −39 |

more intense the competition in the export market, the stronger the pressure to cut prices. The fourth factor is the firm's strategic orientation. Firms could be market-share oriented or focus on short-term profits. Naturally, market-share oriented firms would tend to pass through less of the cost increase than their financial performance-oriented counterparts.[38] The bottom row of Exhibit 12-4 shows what happens when the U.S. dollar weakens by 30 percent. In that case we have the mirror picture of the previous scenario.

American exporters might lower their markups much higher in price-conscious export markets than in price-insensitive markets. This type of destination-specific adjustment of markup in response to exchange-rate movement is referred to as **pricing-to-market (PTM)**. PTM behaviors differ across source countries. One study of export pricing adjustments in the U.S. automobile market contrasted pricing decisions of Japanese and German exporters over periods where both the Japanese yen and the German mark depreciated against the U.S. dollar.[39] The results of the study showed that there was much more pass-through (and less PTM) by German exporters than by their Japanese rivals (see **Exhibit 12-6**).

Playing the PTM game carries certain risks. Frequent adjustments of prices in response to currency movements will distress local channels and customers. When local currency prices move up, foreign customers may express their disapproval by switching to other brands. On the other hand, when prices go down, it will often be hard to raise prices in the future. Therefore, often, the preferred strategy is to adjust mark-ups in such a way that local currency prices remain fairly stable. This special form of PTM has been referred to as **local-currency price stability (LCPS)** where markups are adjusted to stabilize prices in the buyer's currency.[40] A case in point is Heineken's pricing policy in the United States. In the three-year period since January 2002, the U.S. dollar lost about a third of its value against the euro. However, the U.S. wholesale price of Heineken and Amstel Light had been increased just twice during the same period, each time by a tiny 2.5 percent. U.S. beer drinkers' gain was Heineken's pain. According to analysts Heineken's annual operating profit from the United States must have fallen from €357 m to €119 m between 2002 and 2006.[41] The bottom panel of Exhibit 12-5 reports the revenue losses or gains of an exporter who maintains LCPS. To pass through exchange rate gains from U.S. dollar devaluations, U.S.-based exporters could resort to

[38]Terry Clark, Masaaki Kotabe, and Dan Rajaratnam, "Exchange Rate Pass-Through and International Pricing Strategy: A Conceptual Framework and Research Propositions," *Journal of International Business Studies*, 30 (Second Quarter 1999), pp. 249–68.
[39]Joseph A. Gagnon and Michael M. Knetter, "Markup adjustment and exchange rate fluctuations: evidence from panel data on automobile exports," *Journal of International Money and Finance*, vol. 14, no. 2, 1995, pp. 289–310.
[40]Michael M. Knetter, "International Comparisons of Pricing-to-Market Behavior," *American Economic Review*, vol. 83, no. 3, pp. 473–486.
[41]"Taking the Hit: European Exporters Find the Dollar's Weakness is Hard to Counter," *Financial Times* (May 3, 2005): 11.

temporary price promotions or other incentives (e.g., trade deals) rather than a permanent cut of the local currency regular price.

Another pricing concern that ensues from floating exchange rates centers on which currency unit is to be used in international business transactions. Sellers and buyers usually prefer a quote in their domestic currency. That way, the other party will have to bear currency risks. The decision largely depends on the balance of power between the supplier and the customer. Whoever yields will need to cover currency exposure risk through hedging transactions on the forward exchange market. A survey of currency choice practices of Swedish, Finish, and American firms found that firms using foreign currencies have higher export volumes and transaction values than exporters using their home currency. However, profit margins suffer.[42] Some firms decide to use a common currency for all their business transactions, world- or region-wide. In the wake of the euro, companies such as Siemens are switching to a euro-regime both for their internal (e.g., transfer pricing) and external (suppliers and distributors) transactions.

**Currency Quotation**

---

# TRANSFER PRICING

◆ ◆ ◆ ◆ ◆ ◆ ◆

Most large multinational corporations have a network of subsidiaries spread across the globe. Sales transactions between related entities of the same company can be quite substantial, involving trade of raw materials, components, finished goods, or services. **Transfer prices** are prices charged for such transactions. Transfer pricing decisions in an international context need to balance off the interests of a broad range of stakeholders: (1) parent company, (2) local country managers, (3) host government(s), (4) domestic government, and (5) joint venture partner(s) when the transaction involves a partnership. Not surprisingly, reconciling the conflicting interests of these various parties can be a mind-boggling juggling act.

A number of studies have examined the key drivers behind transfer pricing decisions. One survey of U.S.-based multinationals found that transfer pricing policies were primarily influenced by the following factors (in order of importance):

**Determinants of Transfer Prices**

1. Market conditions in the foreign country
2. Competition in the foreign country
3. Reasonable profit for foreign affiliate
4. U.S. federal income taxes
5. Economic conditions in the foreign country
6. Import restrictions
7. Customs duties
8. Price controls
9. Taxation in the foreign country
10. Exchange controls.[43]

Other surveys have come up with different rankings.[44] However, a recurring theme appears to be the importance of market conditions (especially, the competitive situation), taxation regimes, and various market imperfections (e.g., currency control,

---

[42]Saeed Samiee and Patrik Anckar, "Currency Choice in Industrial Pricing: A Cross-National Evaluation," *Journal of Marketing*, 62 (July 1998), pp. 112–27.

[43]Jane Burns, "Transfer Pricing Decisions in U.S. Multinational Corporations," *Journal of International Business Studies*, vol. 11, no. 2, Fall 1980, pp. 23–39.

[44]See, for example, Seung H. Kim and Stephen W. Miller, "Constituents of the International Transfer Pricing Decision," *Columbia Journal of World Business*, Spring 1979, p. 71.

custom duties, price freeze). Generally speaking, MNCs should consider the following criteria when making transfer-pricing decisions:[45]

- **Tax regimes.** Ideally, firms would like to boost their profits in low-tax countries and dampen them in high-tax countries. To shift profits from high-tax to low-tax markets, companies would set transfer prices as high as possible for goods entering high-tax countries and vice-versa for low-tax countries. However, manipulating transfer prices to exploit corporate tax rate differentials will undoubtedly alert the tax authorities in the high-tax rate country and, in the worst case, lead to a tax audit. Most governments impose rules on transfer pricing to ensure a fair division of profits between businesses under common control. We will revisit the taxation issue shortly.

- **Local market conditions.** Another key influence is local market conditions. Examples of market-related factors include the market share of the affiliate, the growth rate of the market, and the nature of local competition (e.g., non-price- versus price-based). To expand market share in a new market, multinationals may initially underprice intra-company shipments to a start-up subsidiary.[46]

- **Market imperfections.** Market imperfections in the host country, such as price freezes and profit repatriation restrictions, hinder the multinational's ability to move earnings out of the country. Under such circumstances, transfer prices can be used as a mechanism to get around these obstacles. Also, high import duties might prompt a firm to lower transfer prices charged to subsidiaries located in that particular country.

- **Joint venture partner.** When the entity concerned is part of a joint venture, parent companies should also factor in the interests of the local joint venture partner. Numerous joint venture partnerships have hit the rocks partly because of disputes over transfer pricing decisions.

- **Morale of local country managers.** Finally, firms should also be concerned about the morale of their local country managers. Especially when performance evaluation is primarily based on local profits, transfer price manipulations might distress country managers whose subsidiaries' profits are artificially deflated.

**Setting Transfer Prices**

There are two broad transfer-pricing strategies: market-based transfer pricing and nonmarket-based pricing. The first perspective uses the market mechanism as a cue for setting transfer prices. Such prices are usually referred to as **arm's length prices**. Basically, the company charges the price that any buyer outside the MNC would pay, as if the transaction had occurred between two unrelated companies (at "arm's length"). Tax authorities typically prefer this method to other transfer pricing approaches. Since an objective yardstick is used—the *market price*—transfer prices based on this approach are easy to justify to third parties (e.g., tax authorities). The major problem with arm's length transfer pricing is that an appropriate benchmark is often lacking, due to the absence of competition. This is especially the case for intangible services. Many services are only available within the multinational. A high-stakes dispute between the U.S. Internal Revenue Service and GlaxoSmithKline PLC, the British pharmaceuticals company, illustrates the issue of valuing intangibles vividly.[47] According to the IRS, Glaxo's U.S. subsidiary overpaid its European parent for the royalties associated with scores of drugs, including its blockbuster Zantac drug. Glaxo allegedly had overvalued the drugs' R&D costs in Britain and undervalued the value of marketing activities in the United States, thereby artificially cutting the U.S. subsidiary's profits and tax liabilities. Glaxo vehemently denied this charge. As you can see, the case centered on the issue of where value is created and where credit is due—on the marketing or on the R&D front?

[45]S. Tamer Cavusgil, "Pricing for Global Markets," *Columbia Journal of World Business*, Winter 1996, pp. 66–78.
[46]Mohammad F. Al-Eryani, Pervaiz Alam, and Syed H. Akhter, "Transfer Pricing Determinants of U.S. Multinationals," *Journal of International Business Studies*, vol. 21, Third Quarter 1990, pp. 409–25.
[47]"Glaxo Faces Allegations of Tax Underpayment in U.S.," *Asian Wall Street Journal* (December 8, 2002), p. A7.

Nonmarket-based pricing covers various policies that deviate from market-based pricing, the most prominent ones being: **cost-based pricing** and **negotiated pricing**. Cost-based pricing simply adds a markup to the cost of the goods. Issues here revolve around getting a consensus on a "fair" profit split and allocation of corporate overhead. Further, tax authorities often do not accept cost-based pricing procedures. Another form of nonmarket based pricing is negotiated transfer prices. Here conflicts between country affiliates are resolved through negotiation of transfer prices. This process may lead to better cooperation among corporate divisions.[48]

One study showed that compliance with financial reporting norms, fiscal and custom rules, anti-dumping regulations prompt companies to use market-based transfer pricing.[49] Government imposed market constraints (e.g., import restrictions, price controls, exchange controls) favor nonmarket-based transfer pricing methods. To the question, which procedure works best, the answer is pretty murky: there is no "universally optimal" system.[50] In fact, most firms use a mixture of market-based and non-market pricing procedures.

Cross-country tax rate differentials encourage many MNCs to set transfer prices that shift profits from high-tax to low-tax countries to minimize their overall tax burden. This practice is sometimes referred to as international tax arbitrage. At the same time, MNCs need to comply with the tax codes of their home country and the host countries involved. Non-compliance may risk accusations of tax evasion and lead to tax audits. In January 2004, GlaxoSmithKline, the pharmaceuticals company, was presented with a $5.2 billion bill for extra taxes and interest by the US government following an investigation of the firm's transfer pricing policies. According to one estimate, the total tax loss in the United States due to "creative" transfer pricing was $53 billion in 2001.[52] Therefore, the issue that MNCs face can be stated as follows: how do we as a company draw the line between setting transfer prices that maximize corporate profits and compliance with tax regulations?

To avoid walking on thin ice, experts suggest to set transfer prices that are as close as possible to the Basic Arm's Length Standard (BALS). This criterion is now accepted by tax authorities worldwide as the international standard for assessing transfer prices. In practice, there are three methods to calculate a BALS price: comparable/uncontrollable price, resale price, and cost-plus. The first rule—comparable/uncontrollable—states that the parent company should compare the transfer price of its "controlled" subsidiary to the selling price charged by an independent seller to an independent buyer of similar goods or services. The problem is that such "comparable products" are often not around. The resale price method determines the BALS by subtracting the gross margin percentage used by comparable independent buyers from the final third-party sales price. Finally, the cost-plus method fixes the BALS by adding the gross profit mark-up percentage earned by comparable companies performing similar functions to the production costs of the controlled manufacturer or seller. Note that this rule is somewhat different from the cost method that we discussed earlier since, strictly speaking, the latter method does not rely on mark-ups set by third parties. The OECD has drawn up guidelines on transfer pricing that cover complex taxation issues. The latest version of these rules is presented in *Transfer Pricing Guidelines for Multinational Enterprises and for Tax Administrations.*[53]

**Minimizing the Risk of Transfer Pricing Tax Audits[51]**

---

[48]R. Ackelsberg and G. Yukl, "Negotiated Transfer Pricing and Conflict Resolution in Organization," *Decision Sciences*, July 1979, pp. 387–398.

[49]M. F. Al-Eryani, et al., "Transfer Pricing Determinants," p. 422.

[50]Jeffrey S. Arpan, "International Intracorporate Pricing: Non-American Systems and Views," *Journal of International Business Studies*, Spring 1972, p. 18.

[51]This section is based on John P. Fraedrich and Connie Rae Bateman, "Transfer Pricing by Multinational Marketers: Risky Business," *Business Horizons*, Jan.–Feb. 1996, pp. 17–22.

[52]"A Big Squeeze for Governments: How Transfer Pricing Threatens Global Tax Revenues," *Financial Times* (July 22, 2004): 11.

[53]A hard copy of this document is available via http://www.oecdbookshop.org/oecd/display.asp?sf1=identifiers&st1=232001041P1. The most recent version came out in early 2006 and also includes an electronic version.

**EXHIBIT 12-7**
DECISION-MAKING MODEL FOR ASSESSING RISK OF TP STRATEGY

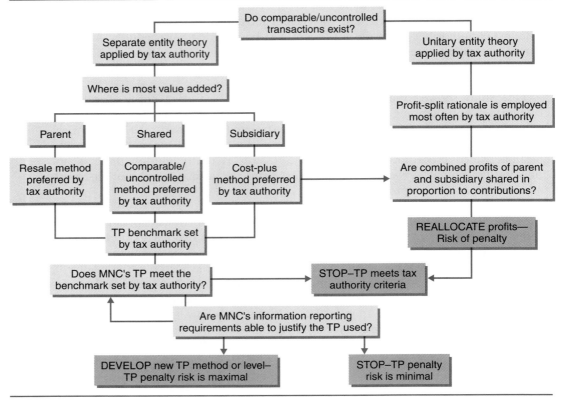

*Source:* John P. Fraedrich and Connie Rae Bateman, "Transfer Pricing by Multinational Marketers: Risky Business." Reprinted from *Business Horizon,* January–February 1996 by the Foundation for the School of Business at Indiana University. Used with permission.

**Exhibit 12-7** gives a flowchart that can be used to devise transfer-pricing strategies that minimize the risk of tax audits. Decisions center around the following five questions:

1. Do comparable/uncontrolled transactions exist?
2. Where is the most value added? Parent? Subsidiary?
3. Are combined profits of parent and subsidiary shared in proportion to contributions?
4. Does the transfer price meet the benchmark set by the tax authorities?
5. Does the MNC have the information to justify the transfer prices used?

◆ ◆ ◆ ◆ ◆ ◆ ◆ ◆ ◆  **GLOBAL PRICING AND ANTI-DUMPING REGULATION**

The anti-dumping laws that most governments use to counter dumping practices present a potential minefield for global pricing policies. **Dumping** occurs when imports are being sold at an unfair price. To protect local producers against the encroachment of low-priced imports, governments may levy countervailing duties or fines. Thus, it is important for exporters to realize that pricing policies, such as penetration pricing, may trigger anti-dumping actions. The number of anti-dumping initiatives has staggered in recent years. Most of the action takes place in the United States and the European Union. However, anti-dumping cases are increasingly initiated in Japan, India and other developing countries. Economists often refer to this trend as a rise in protectionism.[54]

Several possible reasons can explain the growing popularity of anti-dumping litigation. The removal of traditional trade barriers (tariffs, quotas) has encouraged several countries to switch to non-tariff barriers such as anti-dumping to protect their local industries. A World Bank study showed that the impact of dumping duties in the U.S. manufactured goods sector has boosted average tariffs in that sector from a nominal 6 percent rate to 23 percent.[55] There is also a huge imbalance between plaintiffs (local producer[s]) and defendants (importer[s]) in anti-dumping cases. Plaintiffs typically face no penalties for frivolous complaints. Moreover, plaintiffs clearly have a home advantage (local legislation, local judge).[56] Anti-dumping action is often utilized as a tactical tool to foster voluntary export restraints (VER). Foreign competitors, faced with the prospect of anti-dumping action, may decide to fall back on VERs as the lesser of two evils.[57] Finally, the concept of a "fair" price is usually pretty murky. The U.S. trade law defines dumping to occur when imports are sold below the home-country price (price discrimination) or when the import price is less than the "constructed value" or average cost of production ("pricing below cost"). Either concept can be very vague. In some situations, the imported good is not sold in the home country so that no basis of comparison exists (absence of domestic price).

Anti-dumping actions will persist in the future. Multinationals need to take anti-dumping laws into account when determining their global pricing policy. Aggressive pricing may trigger anti-dumping measures and, thus, jeopardize the company's competitive position. Global companies should also monitor changes in anti-dumping legislation and closely track anti-dumping cases in their particular industry.

To minimize risk exposure to anti-dumping actions, exporters might pursue any of the following marketing strategies:[58]

- **Trading-up.** Move away from low-value to high-value products via product differentiation. Most Japanese carmakers have stretched their product line upwards to tap into the upper-tier segments of their export markets.

- **Service enhancement.** Exporters can also differentiate their product by adding support services to the core product. Both moves—trading up and service enhancement—are basically attempts to move away from price competition, thereby making the exporter less vulnerable to dumping accusations.

- **Distribution and communication.** Other initiatives on the distribution and communication front of the marketing mix include: (1) the establishment of communication channels with local competitors, (2) entering into cooperative agreements with them (e.g., strategic alliances), or (3) reallocation of the firm's marketing efforts from vulnerable products (that is, those most likely to be subjected to dumping scrutiny) to less sensitive products.

## PRICE COORDINATION    ◆ ◆ ◆ ◆ ◆ ◆ ◆

When developing a global pricing strategy, one of the thorniest issues is how much coordination should exist between prices charged in different countries. This issue is especially critical for global (or regional) brands that are marketed with no or very few cross-border variations. Economics dictate that firms should price discriminate between markets such that overall profits are maximized. So, if (marginal) costs were

[54]Jagdish Bhagwati, *Protectionism*, Cambridge, MA: The MIT Press, 1988, Chapter 3.

[55]"Negotiators down in the dumps over US draft," *The Financial Times*, November 25, 1993, p. 6.

[56]J. Bhagwati, *Protectionism*, pp. 48–49.

[57]James E. Anderson, "Domino Dumping, I: Competitive Exporters," *American Economic Review*, vol. 82, no. 1, March 1992, pp. 65–83.

[58]Michel M. Kostecki, "Marketing Strategies between Dumping and Anti-dumping Action," *European Journal of Marketing*, vol. 25, no. 12, 1991, pp. 7–19.

roughly equivalent, multinationals would charge relatively low prices in highly price sensitive countries and high prices in insensitive markets. Unfortunately, reality is not that simple. In most cases, markets cannot be perfectly separated. Huge cross-country price differentials will encourage gray markets where goods are shipped from low-price to high-price countries by unauthorized distributors. Thus, some coordination will usually be necessary. In deciding how much coordination, several considerations matter:

1. **Nature of customers.** When information on prices travels fast across borders, it is fairly hard to sustain wide price gaps. Under such conditions, firms will need to make a convincing case to their customers to justify price disparities. With global customers (e.g., multinational clients in business-to-business transactions), price coordination definitely becomes a must. General Motors applies "global enterprise pricing" for many of the components it purchases. Under this system, suppliers are asked to charge the same universal price worldwide.[59] In Europe, Microsoft sets prices that differ by no more than 5 percent between countries due to pressure from bargain-hunting multinational customers.[60]

2. **Amount of product differentiation.** The amount of coordination also depends on how well differentiated the product is across borders. Obviously, the less (cross-border) product differentiation, the larger the need for some level of price coordination and vice versa. Stains in Southern Europe differ from stains in Scandinavia because of different food habits. Also, the spin speed of washing machines varies across Europe. In cold, wet countries (e.g., Great Britain) the average spin speed is 1200 rpm – twice as fast as the 600-rpm speed of washers in Spain.[61] Henkel, the German conglomerate, adjusts the formula for its Persil laundry detergent brand to suit local market conditions. As a result, a detergent sold in one European country may not be suitable for washers elsewhere in Europe. Thus, product differentiation can pose a barrier for cross-border price comparison shopping.

3. **Nature of channels.** In a sense, distribution channels can be viewed as intermediate customers. So, the same logic as for end consumers applies here: price coordination becomes critical when price information is transparent and/or the firm deals with cross-border distribution channels. Pricing discipline becomes mandatory when manufacturers have little control over their distributors.

4. **Nature of competition.** In many industries, firms compete with the same rivals in a given region, if not worldwide. Global competition demands a cohesive strategic approach for the entire marketing mix strategy, including pricing. From that angle, competition pushes companies toward centralized pricing policies. On the other hand, price changes made by competitors in the local market often require a rapid response. Should the subsidiary match a given price cut? If so, to what extent? Local subsidiaries often have much better information about the local market conditions to answer such questions than corporate or regional headquarters. Thus, the need for alertness and speedy response to competitive pricing moves encourages a decentralized approach toward pricing decisions.

5. **Market integration.** When markets integrate, barriers to cross-border movement of goods come down. Given the freedom to move goods from one member state to another, the pan-European market offers little latitude for perfect price discrimination.[62] Many of the transaction costs plaguing parallel imports that once existed, have now disappeared. In fact, the European Commission imposes heavy penalties against companies that try to limit gray market transactions. The Commission fined Volkswagen almost $110 million when it accused VW of competition abuses. VW

[59]"GM Powertrain suppliers will see global pricing," *Purchasing* (February 12, 1998).

[60]"European Software-Pricing Formulas, Long Abstruse, Develop a Rationale," *Wall Street Journal*, June 11, 1993.

[61]"A Shopping Contest for the Euro," *Financial Times* (January 5/6, 2002), p. 7.

[62]Wolfgang Gaul and Ulrich Lutz, "Pricing in International Marketing and Western European Economic Integration," *Management International Review*, vol. 34, no. 2, 1994, pp. 101–24.

had ordered its Italian dealers not to sell cars to citizens from outside Italy. Austrian and German shoppers tried to buy VW cars in Italy where they were 30 percent cheaper.[63]

Several multinationals doing business in the European Union harmonize their prices to narrow down price gaps between different member states. Mars and Levi Strauss reduced their pan-European price gaps to no more than 10 percent.[64]

6. **Internal organization.** The organization setup is another important influence. Highly decentralized companies pose a hurdle to price coordination efforts. In many companies, the pricing decision is left to the local subsidiaries. Moves to take away some of the pricing authority from country affiliates will undoubtedly spark opposition and lead to bruised egos. Just as with other centralization decisions, it is important to fine-tune performance evaluation systems, as necessary.

7. **Government regulation.** Government regulation of prices puts pressure on firms to harmonize their prices. A good example is the pharmaceutical industry. In many countries, multinationals need to negotiate the price for new drugs with the local authorities. Governments in the European Union increasingly use prices set in other EU member states as a cue for their negotiating position. This trend has prompted several pharmaceutical companies, such as Glaxo, to negotiate a common EU-price for new drugs.

Increasingly, purchasers demand **global-pricing contracts** (GPCs) from their suppliers. There are several reasons behind the shift toward GPCs: centralized buying, information technology that provides improved price monitoring, standardization of products or services. GPCs, however, can also benefit suppliers: global customers can become showcase accounts; a GPC can offer the opening toward nurturing a lasting customer relationship; small suppliers can use GPCs as a differentiation tool to get access to new accounts.

**Global-Pricing Contracts (GPCs)[65]**

However, before engaging in a GPC with a purchaser it is important do your homework. To achieve successful GPC implementation, Narayandas and his colleague provide the following guidelines:

1. Select customers who want more than just the lowest price.

2. Align the supplier's organization with the customer's. Ideally, the supplier's account-management organization should mirror the client's procurement setup.

3. Hire global account managers who can handle diversity. Get team members who cannot just handle sales, but also market intelligence gathering, problem spotting, contract compliance monitoring.

4. Reward those global-account managers and local sales representatives who make the relationship work.

5. Allow for some price flexibility.

6. Build information systems to monitor the key variables (e.g., cost variations, competitive situation).

In the late 1990s Procter & Gamble was facing a severe parallel imports situation in Russia for its Always feminine protection brand. The price for Always was much higher than in the other Central European countries, especially Poland from which most parallel imports originated. To resolve the problem, P&G lowered the price for Always in Russia and increased it in Poland so that the cross-border price variation became no more than 10 percent. Given the pressure toward increased globalization, some degree

**Aligning Pan-Regional Prices**

[63]"On the road to price convergence," *Financial Times*, (November 12, 1998), p. 29.

[64]"Counting Costs of Dual Pricing in the Run-Up to 1992," *Financial Times*, July 9, 1990, p. 4.

[65]This section benefited from Das Narayandas, John Quelch, and Gordon Swartz. "Prepare Your Company For Global Pricing," *Sloan Management Review*, (Fall 2000), pp. 61–70.

**EXHIBIT 12-8**
PAN-EUROPEAN PRICE COORDINATION

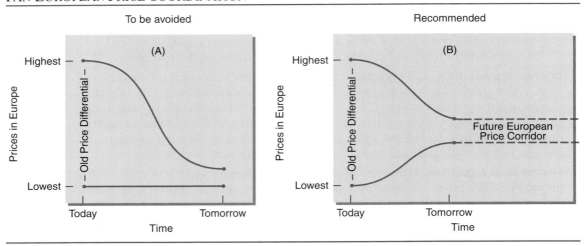

Courtesy Professor Hermann Simon

of price coordination becomes often very necessary. In some cases, firms set a uniform pricing formula that is applied by all affiliates. Elsewhere, coordination is limited to general rules that only indicate the desired pricing positioning (e.g., premium positioning, middle-of-the road positioning).

Simon and Kucher[66] propose a three-step procedure to align prices in regional markets with arbitrage opportunities. Pressure to narrow down price gaps could lead to two scenarios (see **Exhibit 12-8**). The disaster scenario (panel (A) in Exhibit 12-8) is a situation where all prices sink to the lowest price. Calculations by Lehman Brothers, an investment bank, have shown that, if all car prices in the euro area fell to the lowest levels, the revenues of the French carmakers, Peugeot and Renault would drop by 12 percent and 9 percent respectively.[67] At the other extreme, companies may try to sustain cross-border price gaps. The desired scenario (panel (B) in Exhibit 12-8) tries to find the middle ground by upping prices in low-price countries and cutting them in high-price countries. To pursue this scenario, firms should set a **pricing corridor** within the region.

The procedure works as follows:

**Step 1:** *Determine optimal price for each country.* Find out what price schedules will maximize overall profits. Given information on the demand schedule and the costs incurred in each market, managers are able to figure out the desirable prices in the respective markets.

**Step 2:** *Find out whether parallel imports ("gray markets") are likely to occur at these prices.* Parallel imports arise when unauthorized distributors purchase the product (sometimes repackaged) in the low-price market and then ship it to high-price markets. The goal of step 2 is not to pre-empt parallel imports altogether but to boost profits to the best possible degree. Given the "optimal" prices derived in the first step, the manager needs to determine to what extent the proposed price schedule will foster parallel imports. Parallel imports become harmful insofar as they inflict damage on authorized distributors. They could also hurt the morale of the local sales force or country managers. Information is needed on the arbitrage costs of parallel importers. For instance, in the European drug industry, parallel importers target drugs with more than 20 percent price differentials. Conceivably, firms might decide to abandon (or

[66]Hermann Simon and Eckhard Kucher, "The European Pricing Time Bomb—And How to Cope With It," *Marketing and Research Today*, February 1993, pp. 25–36.
[67]"Faster forward," *The Economist* (November 28, 1998), pp. 83–84.

not enter) small, low-price markets thereby avoiding pricing pressure on high-price markets. MNCs should also consider the pros and cons of non-pricing solutions to cope with parallel imports. Possible strategies include: product differentiation, intelligence systems to measure exposure to gray markets, creating negative perceptions in the mind of the end-user about parallel imports.[68] In 1996 P&G changed the name in Northern Europe for one of its cleaner products from *Viakal* to *Antikal* to fight parallel imports sourced from Italy where the product was 30 percent cheaper.

**Step 3:** *Set a pricing corridor.* If the "optimal" prices that were derived in Step 1 are not sustainable, firms need to narrow the gap between prices for high-price and low-price markets. Charging the same price across-the-board is not desirable. Such a solution would sacrifice company profits. Instead, the firm should set a pricing corridor. The corridor is formed by systematically exploring the profit impact from lowering prices in high-price countries and upping prices in low-price countries, as shown in panel (B) of Exhibit 12-8. The narrower the price gap, the more profits the firm has to sacrifice. At some point, there will be a desirable trade-off between the size of the gray market and the amount of profits sacrificed.

Of course, this method is not foolproof. Competitive reactions (e.g., price wars) need to be factored in. Also, government regulations may restrict pricing flexibility. Still, the procedure is a good start when pricing alignment becomes desirable.

Global marketers can choose from four alternatives to promote price coordination within their organization, namely:[69]

**Implementing Price Coordination**

1. **Economic Measures.** Corporate headquarters are able to influence pricing decisions at the local level via the transfer prices that are set for the goods that are sold to or purchased from the local affiliates. Another option is rationing, that is, headquarters sets upper limits on the number of units that can be shipped to each country. To sustain price differences, luxury marketers like Louis Vuitton set purchase limits for customers shopping at their European boutiques. Louis Vuitton products bought in Europe or Hawaii are often resold in Japan by discount stores as "loss leaders."

2. **Centralization.** In the extreme case, pricing decisions are made at corporate or regional headquarters level. Centralized price decision-making is fairly uncommon, given its numerous shortcomings. It sacrifices the flexibility that firms often need to respond rapidly to local competitive conditions.

3. **Formalization.** Far more common than the previous approach is formalization where headquarters spells out a set of pricing rules that the country managers should comply with. Within these norms, country managers have a certain level of flexibility in determining their ultimate prices. One possibility is to set prices within specified boundaries; prices outside these bounds would need the approval from the global or regional headquarters.

4. **Informal Coordination.** Finally, firms can use various forms of informal price coordination. The emphasis here is on informing and persuasion rather than prescription and dictates. Examples of informal price coordination tactics include discussion groups, "best-practice" gatherings.

Which one of these four approaches is most effective is contingent on the complexity of the environment in which the firm is doing business. When the environment is fairly stable and the various markets are highly similar, centralization is usually preferable over the other options. However, highly complex environments require a more decentralized approach.

---

[68]Peggy A. Chaudhry and Michael G. Walsh, "Managing the Gray Market in the European Union: The Case of the Pharmaceutical Industry," *Journal of International Marketing*, vol. 3, no. 3, 1995, pp. 11–33.

[69]Gert Assmus and Carsten Wiese, "How to Address the Gray Market Threat Using Price Coordination," *Sloan Management Review*, Spring 1995, pp. 31–41.

# ◆◆◆◆◆◆◆◆ COUNTERTRADE

**Countertrade** is an umbrella term used to describe unconventional trade-financing transactions that involve some form of non-cash compensation. During the last decade, companies have increasingly been forced to rely on countertrade. Estimates on the overall magnitude of countertrade vary but the consensus estimate is that it covers 10 to 15 percent of world trade.[70] One of the most publicized deals was PepsiCo's $3 billion arrangement with the former Soviet Union to swap Pepsi for profits in Stolichnaya vodka and ocean freighters and tankers.[71] Given the growth of countertrade, global marketers should be aware of its nuts and bolts.

**Forms of Countertrade**

Countertrade comes in six guises: barter, clearing arrangements, switch trading, buyback, counterpurchase, and offset. **Exhibit 12-9** classifies these different forms of countertrade.

**EXHIBIT 12-9**
CLASSIFICATION OF FORMS OF COUNTERTRADE

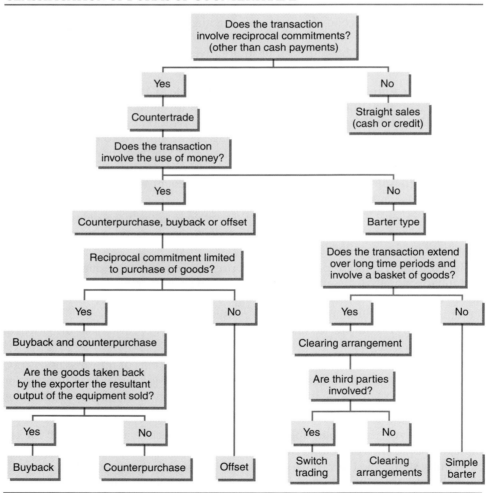

*Source:* Jean-François Hennart, "Some Empirical Dimensions of Countertrade," *Journal of International Business Studies* Second Quarter 1990, p. 245.

---

[70]Jean-François Hennart and Erin Anderson, "Countertrade and The Minimization of Transaction Costs," Working Paper no. 92-012R, The Wharton School, University of Pennsylvania, Philadelphia, PA.
[71]"Worldwide Money Crunch Fuels More International Barter," *Marketing News*, March 2, 1992, p. 5.

The main distinction is whether or not the transaction involves monetary compensation. Let us look at each form in more detail:[72]

- **Simple barter.** Simple barter is a swap of one product for another product without the use of any money. Usually, no third party is involved to carry out the transaction. A single contract covers the entire transaction. Though one of the oldest forms of countertrade, it is very seldom used these days. It is most common in deals that involve subsistence economies. Barter is also sometimes introduced into existing contracts to recover debt through goods when the debtor cannot pay cash.

- **Clearing arrangement.** Under this form, two governments agree to import a set specified value of goods from one another over a given period. Each party sets up an account that is debited whenever goods are traded. Imbalances at the end of the contract period are cleared through payment in hard currency or goods. One clearing agreement between Indonesia and Iran specified that Indonesia would supply paper, rubber, and galvanized sheets in exchange for 30,000 barrels per day of Iranian crude oil.[73]

- **Switch trading.** This is a variant of clearing arrangements where a third party is involved. In such deals, rights to the surplus credits are sold to specialized traders (**switch traders**) at a discount. The third party uses then the credits to buy goods from the deficit country.

    None of these types entail cash payment flows. The remaining forms involve some use of money. They lead to two parallel agreements: the original sales agreement between the foreign customer and supplier, and a second contract where the supplier commits himself to purchase goods in the customer's country.

- **Buyback (compensation).** Buyback arrangements typically occur with the sale of technology, turnkey plants, or machinery equipment. In such transactions, the seller provides the equipment and agrees to be paid (partially or fully) by the products resulting from using the equipment. Such agreements are much more mutually beneficial than the other forms of countertrade. A typical example of a buyback contract is an agreement that was settled between PALMCO Holdings, Malaysia's biggest palm oil refiner, and Japan's Kao Corporation. The contract set up a $70 million joint venture to produce palm oil byproducts in Malaysia. Kao was to be compensated by 60 percent of the output that it could use as inputs for producing detergents, cosmetics, and toiletries.[74]

- **Counterpurchase.** Counterpurchase is the most popular form of countertrade. Similar to buyback arrangements, two parallel contracts are set up. Each party agrees to buy a specified amount of goods from the other for hard currency over a set period. Contrary to buybacks, the products are unrelated. Typically, the importer will provide a shopping list from which the exporter can choose. In October 1992, PepsiCo set up a joint venture in Ukraine with three local partners. Under the agreement, the partnership was to market ships built in Ukraine. Proceeds from the ship sales were to be used to buy soft-drink equipment, to build bottling plants, and to open Pizza Hut restaurants in Ukraine.[75]

- **Offset.** Offset is a variation of counterpurchase: the seller agrees to *offset* the purchase price by sourcing from the importer's country or transferring technology to the other party's country. Offset is very common with defense contracts but is also becoming more common in other sectors. There are two different types: direct and indirect offset. With **direct offset**, the supplier agrees to use materials or components sourced from the importing country. **Indirect offset** refers to a contractual arrangement that involves goods or services unrelated to the core goods to be exported. An offset contract between Indonesia and General Dynamics to buy F-16 aircraft, stipulated that some of the parts would be supplied by PT Nusantara, an Indonesian manufacturer.

[72]Costas G. Alexandrides and Barbara L. Bowers, *Countertrade. Practices, Strategies, and Tactics*, New York: John Wiley & Sons, 1987, Chapter 1.

[73]Aspy P. Palia, "Countertrade Practices in Indonesia," *Industrial Marketing Management*, vol. 21, 1992, pp. 273–79.

[74]Aspy P. Palia, "Countertrade Practices in Japan," *Industrial Marketing Management*, vol. 22, 1993, pp. 125–32.

[75]"PepsiCo to finance Ukraine expansion with ship exports," *Financial Times*, October 23, 1992.

**Motives behind Countertrade**

Companies engage in countertrade for a variety of reasons. The most commonly cited benefits are:

- **Gain access to new or difficult markets.** Countertrade in many ways is a "necessary evil." It can be very costly and risky. Nevertheless, being prepared to accept countertrade deals offers for many companies a competitive edge that allows them to penetrate markets with a lack of hard currency cash. Many exporters accept countertrade arrangements because their rivals offer it. A UK survey found that 80 percent of the exporters' competitors were also involved in countertrade.[76]

- **Overcome exchange rate controls or lack of hard currency.** Shortages of hard currency often lead to exchange controls. To navigate around government imposed currency restrictions, firms use countertrade.

- **Overcome low country creditworthiness.** This benefit applies to trade with parties located in countries with low credit ratings. Under such conditions, the other party faces high interest rates or difficult access to credit financing. Countertrade allows both parties to overcome such hurdles.

- **Increase sales volume.** Firms with a substantial amount of overheads face a lot of pressure to increase sales. Despite the risks and costs of countertrade, such deals provide a viable opportunity to achieve full capacity utilization. Also, companies often engage in countertrade to dispose of surplus or obsolete products.

- **Generate long-term customer goodwill.** A final payoff is that willingness to accept countertrade deals fosters long-term customer goodwill. Once the credit and/or currency situation in the client's country improves, sellers will be able to capitalize on the customer goodwill cemented over the years.

Among these marketing objectives, a survey of industrial firms located in twenty-three countries showed that the most important ones are: (1) sales increase (mean response of 3.91 on a 5-point scale), (2) increased competitiveness (3.90), and (3) entry to new markets (3.54).[77] A study of U.S. companies countertrading with Latin America found that the main reasons included (ranked in order of importance):[78]

1. Customers' inadequate reserves of foreign currency
2. The only way business could be done
3. Demanded by customers
4. To gain a competitive advantage
5. Facilitating transactions with government and expanding business contacts
6. To achieve growth
7. Better capacity utilization
8. Expansion of distribution channels in significant markets
9. To release blocked funds
10. To avoid the impact of protectionist regulations.

Note that several of the motives listed above are long-term oriented (e.g., gaining entry to new markets, generate goodwill), while some of the other motives are short-term oriented (e.g., use excess production capacity). Firms that are driven by long-term benefits tend to be much more proactive in soliciting countertrade business and pursuing countertrade transactions than short-term oriented firms.[79] Whatever the

---

[76]David Shipley and Bill Neale, "Industrial Barter and Countertrade," *Industrial Marketing Management*, vol. 16, 1987, pp. 1–8.

[77]Dorothy A. Paun, "An International Profile of Countertrading Firms," *Industrial Marketing Management*, vol. 26, no. 1, 1997, pp. 41–50.

[78]John P. Angelidis, Faramarz Parsa, and Nabil A. Ibrahim, "Countertrading with Latin America: A Comparative Analysis of Attitudes of United States Firms," *International Journal of Management* 21 (December 2004): 435–44.

[79]Dorothy A. Paun and Aviv Shoham, "Marketing Motives in International Countertrade: An Empirical Examination," *Journal of International Marketing*, vol. 4, no. 3, 1996, pp. 29–47.

motive for entering a countertrade agreement, it is important to realize the drawbacks of such arrangements.

Not every exporter is willing to jump on the countertrade bandwagon. In many cases, the risks and costs of a countertrade deal far outweigh its potential advantages. Some of the shortcomings that have been identified by exporters include:[80]

**Shortcomings of Countertrade**

- **No "in-house" use for goods offered by customers.** Exporters often face the problem of what to do with the goods they are offered. Goods that cannot be used in-house need to be resold. Getting rid of the goods can be a major headache, especially when the quality of the merchandise is poor or when there is an oversupply. Some firms will rely on specialist brokers to sell their goods.

- **Timely and costly negotiations.** Arranging a countertrade deal requires a time-consuming and complex bargaining process. A prospective customer with a long track record usually has a tremendous edge over an exporter with little negotiation skills. Parties will need to haggle over the goods to be traded, their respective valuation, the mixture cash/merchandise, the time horizon, and so on.

- **Uncertainty and lack of information on future prices.** When some of the traded goods involve commodities, firms run the risk that the price sinks before the goods can be sold. Apart from price uncertainty, there is uncertainty about the quality of the goods.

- **Transaction costs.** Costs flowing from countertrade quickly add up: cost of finding buyers for the goods (if there is no in-house use), commissions to middlemen (if any), insurance costs to cover risk of faulty or non-delivery, hedging costs to protect against sinking commodity prices.

The study of countertrading with Latin America cited earlier found that the most serious problems were (ranked in order of importance):[81]

1. Time-consuming negotiations
2. Complicated negotiations
3. Product mismatch
4. Cost increases
5. Inferior quality of goods
6. Difficulty in selling the received products
7. Profitability reduction
8. Price setting problems
9. Involvement of third parties
10. Loss of purchasing flexibility.

Given the potential risks and costs an exporter might run, one of the key questions is whether to handle deals in-house or to use specialist middlemen. This decision will basically be driven by a trade-off of the benefits of using outsiders (reduction of risks and transaction costs) with the costs to be incurred (mainly commission).

Countertrade has probably reached its peak now. In fact, some former East Bloc countries are trying to avoid such trade in order to signal their commitment to free markets.[82] Still, countertrade will survive, as many countries remain strapped for hard-currency cash.[83] Highly useful online resources on countertrade include the following websites:

---

[80]D. Shipley and B. Neale, "Industrial Barter and Countertrade," pp. 5–6.

[81]John P. Angelidis, et al., "Countertrading with Latin America."

[82]"A Necessary Evil," *The Economist*, November 25, 1989, p. 79.

[83]"Worldwide money crunch fuels more international barter," *Marketing News*, March 2, 1992, p. 5.

- www.barternews.com
- www.londoncountertrade.org
- www.apcatrade.org (Asia Pacific Countertrade Association)

Finally, here are a few guidelines:[84]

1. Always evaluate the pros and cons of countertrade against other options.
2. Minimize the ratio of compensation goods to cash.
3. Strive for goods that can be used in-house.
4. Assess the relative merits of relying on middlemen versus an in-house staff.
5. Check whether the goods are subject to any import restrictions.
6. Assess the quality of the goods.

---

[84]Based on D. Shipley and B. Neale, "Industrial Barter and Countertrade," *Industrial Marketing Management*, 16, 1987 and J. R. Carter and J. Gagne, "The Dos and Don'ts of International Countertrade," *Sloan Management Review*, Spring 1988.

## SUMMARY ◆ ◆ ◆ ◆ ◆ ◆ ◆ ◆ ◆ ◆ ◆ ◆ ◆ ◆ ◆ ◆ ◆ ◆ ◆ ◆ ◆ ◆ ◆ ◆

Two types of mistakes can be made when setting the price in foreign markets: pricing the product too high and pricing it too low. When the price is set too high, customers will stay away of the firm's products. As a result, profits will be far less than they might have been. In India, Procter & Gamble's Ariel detergent brand initially created huge losses, partly because P&G charged a retail price far higher than Unilever's Surf Ultra.[85] Setting prices too low might also generate numerous pains. Local governments may cry foul and accuse the firm of dumping. Local customers might view the low price as a signal of low quality and avoid your product. Local competitors may interpret the low price as an aggressive move to grab market share and start a price war. Or, they may see it as an opportunity to launch a knock-off version of your product. And when the price is far lower than in other markets, distributors (local and nonlocal) might spot an arbitrage opportunity, and ship the product from the low-price to your high-price markets,

---

[85]"Ariel share gain puts P&G India through the wringer," *Advertising Age International*, November 8, 1993, pp. I–3, I–22.

thereby creating a gray market situation. Making pricing decisions is one of the most formidable tasks that international marketers face. Many different elements influence global pricing decisions. Aside of the roles played by the 4 Cs (customers, competition, channels and company), marketers also need to factor in the impact (direct or indirect) of local government decisions.

In this chapter, we covered the major global pricing issues that matter to marketers: export price escalation, inflation, currency movements, anti-dumping regulations, and price coordination. Even though pricing is typically a highly decentralized marketing decision, cross-border price coordination becomes increasingly a prime concern. We introduced several approaches through which international marketers can implement price coordination. Especially in industrial markets, firms increasingly become aware of the long-term rewards of countertrade as a way of doing business in the global arena. In many cases, countertrade is the sole means for gaining access to new markets. Companies that decide to engage in countertrade should bear in mind the numerous road bumps that these transactions involve.

## KEY TERMS ◆ ◆ ◆ ◆ ◆ ◆ ◆ ◆ ◆ ◆ ◆ ◆ ◆ ◆ ◆ ◆ ◆ ◆ ◆ ◆ ◆ ◆ ◆ ◆

| | | | |
|---|---|---|---|
| Arm's-length price | Countertrade | Local-currency price stability | Simple barter |
| Buyback | Dumping | Offset (direct, indirect) | Switch trade |
| Clearing arrangement | Dynamic incremental pricing | Price corridor | Transfer price |
| Cost-plus pricing | Exchange rate pass through | Price escalation | |
| Counterpurchase | Global-pricing contract | Pricing-to-market | |

## REVIEW QUESTIONS ◆ ◆ ◆ ◆ ◆ ◆ ◆ ◆ ◆ ◆ ◆ ◆ ◆ ◆ ◆ ◆ ◆ ◆ ◆ ◆ ◆ ◆

1. What mechanisms can exporters use to curtail the risks of price escalation in foreign markets?

2. How does competition in the foreign market affect your global pricing decisions?

**3.** A study quoted in Chapter 13 reports that there was much more pass-through by German carmakers than their Japanese counterparts in the U.S. car market when both currencies depreciated against the U.S. dollar. What might explain these different responses?

**4.** Should MNCs always try to minimize their transfer in high corporate tax countries? Why (or why not)?

**5.** What measures might exporters consider to hedge themselves against anti-dumping accusations?

**6.** Explain why countertrade is often viewed as a necessary evil.

## DISCUSSION QUESTIONS ✦ ✦ ✦ ✦ ✦ ✦ ✦ ✦ ✦ ✦ ✦ ✦ ✦ ✦ ✦ ✦ ✦ ✦ ✦ ✦

**1.** Many multinational companies that consider entering emerging markets face the issue that the regular price they charge for their goods (that is, the retail price in developed markets) is far beyond the buying power of most local consumers. What strategic options do these companies have to penetrate these markets?

**2.** Company XYZ sells a body-weight control drug in countries A and B. The demand schedules in the two countries are:

Country A: Sales in A $= 100 - 10 \times$ Price in A
Country B: Sales in B $= 100 - 6.67 \times$ Price in B

The marginal costs are 4 in both countries. There are no fixed costs.

a. What prices should XYZ set in A and B if it optimizes the price in A and B individually? What would be total profits?

b. Suppose that due to parallel imports, prices in the high-price countries drop to the level of the low-price country? What would be total profits under that scenario?

c. Suppose now that the two countries are treated as one big market? What would be the optimal price then? What would be total profits?

d. Set a pricing corridor between A and B by completing the following table:

**3.** Countertrade accounts for a substantial proportion of international trade. Do you foresee that the share of countertrade will increase or decline? Why?

**4.** How will a weakening of the euro versus the Japanese yen affect German carmakers such as BMW and Volkswagen in Japan? What measures do you suggest German carmakers might consider taking to cope with a weaker euro?

**5.** A major bone of contention in recent years has been the prices charged for AIDS drugs in the developing world by Western pharmaceutical giants such as Merck and Glaxo-SmithKline. Several makers of AIDS drugs, such as Merck, have now agreed to provide AIDS drugs in developing nations such as South Africa at a price that is roughly equivalent to the manufacturing costs. What potential hurdles do you see with this new pricing scheme?

**6.** How can local competitors use anti-dumping procedures as a competitive tool against foreign competitors?

**7.** In Russia, Procter & Gamble markets Tide, its U.S. premium laundry detergent brand, as an economy brand with the slogan "Tide is a guarantee of clean clothes." Except for the brand name and the product category, all aspects of the products (formula, price, positioning) are different between the U.S. and the Russian product. What might be the rationale behind this strategy? Was this strategy a good idea?

| Price Corridor (in %) | Price in A | Price in B | Sales Revenue in A | Sales Revenue in B | Profits in A | Profits in B | Total Profit | Profit Sacrifice (in %) |
|---|---|---|---|---|---|---|---|---|
| 0 | | | | | | | | |
| 5 | | | | | | | | |
| 10 | | | | | | | | |
| 20 | | | | | | | | |
| 25 | | | | | | | | |

# SHORT CASES

## CASE 12-1

### WHISTLE BLOWERS RAISE SOME SERIOUS QUESTIONS ABOUT SWATCH'S TRANSFER PRICING POLICIES

Swatch Group is one of the world's leading watchmakers. The group owns a stable of 17 watch brands, including Breguet and Omega. Just as many other multinational companies do, Swatch devotes considerable energy to devising tax arrangements that minimize its overall tax burden. In general, such practices (sometimes referred to as international tax arbitrage) are perfectly legal. However, in the summer of 2004, two whistleblowers who had left the company were asking U.S. tax authorities to have a closer look at Swatch's tax policies. They had built up their case with a stash of internal e-mails and company documents.

Concern had been raised about the activities of Swatch Group (Asia), a subsidiary based in Hong Kong and registered in the tax haven of the British Virgin Islands. Invoices indicated that goods shipped through this subsidiary received a major markup before being sent to other units of Swatch. For instance, Omega watches were given a 40 percent markup if they went out to Singapore and a 50 percent markup when bound for Japan. One company e-mail stated: "Externally for tax reasons we credit only 60 percent. That means that we have an internal credit note and different external credit note . . . The advantage of this procedure is that we have absolutely no negative impact on the internal [reporting] figures in Japan."

Tax lawyers interviewed about the matter said that to justify the mark-up differences as they pass through the subsidiary,

*Source:* "A Swiss Movement on Tax Bills," *Financial Times* (August 13, 2004): 18 and "Swatch Group Defends its Pricing Policy," *Financial Times* (August 13, 2004): 18.

the intermediary has to be adding value to the product, or incurring some risk by its role in the transaction. If not, the tax rate of the jurisdiction of origin should apply. Also, the values attributed to goods internally should be close to their market prices at the destination.

The e-mails signaled that Swatch staff had concerns about its transfer-pricing practices and how they might appear to tax authorities. One e-mail from a finance department official stated: "We have to be very cautious when the source is Swatch Group internal. I have not the intention to endanger the whole system." Mr. Rentsch, the group's general counsel, denied any wrongdoing. According to him, the two whistleblowers were former disgruntled employees who "were trying to build up something against the company." Still, the company was concerned about the allegations and decided to set up an internal investigation. In comments to the press, Swatch pointed out that transfer pricing is a very complex issue that depends on a large number of variables including: exchange rates, working conditions in different countries, and differing distribution structures. Also, as a matter policy, Swatch tries to avoid major price gaps between markets in order to minimize the risks of gray markets where local traders sidestep authorized distributors.

### DISCUSSION QUESTIONS

**1.** Explain why transfer pricing is so complicated especially for a company like Swatch.

**2.** What measures could Swatch implement to avoid similar predicaments in the future?

## CASE 12-2

### CARLSBERG MALAYSIA—SELLING BEER IN A 60 PERCENT MUSLIM NATION

Malaysia's beer market has been under heavy pressure lately. From 2004 to 2006, the industry saw heavy increases in excise duties. With an excise duty of RM7.40 (US$2) per liter, Malaysia now has the second highest beer tax in the world (Norway ranks first). The price increases have narrowed the price gap between

*Sources:* www.euromonitor.com/Beer_in_Malaysia; "Guinness Confident of Warding Off Newcomer," www.theedgedaily.com, accessed on February 19, 2009; and "Malaysian Beer Brands Facing Pricing Problem," *Media*, November 27, 2008, p. 21.

beer and other alcoholic drinks such as wine. Beer drinkers have balked: consumption dropped from 1.4 million (2004) to 1.2 million hectoliters (2006) as a result of the price increases. Many beer and stout customers have turned to wine and liquor due to the narrowed price gap for these products with beer.

The tax increases have also reshaped the competitive landscape. Carlsberg bore the brunt of the price increases. Until recently, two big brewers carved up Malaysia's beer market: Carlsberg, which has been operating in Malaysia for over 35 years, and Guinness Anchor Berhad (GAB), the maker of Guinness,

Tiger and Anchor beer. In 2000 Carlsberg had a 55 percent market share while GAB had the remaining 45 percent. By mid-2006, GAB's share had risen to 55 percent. In 2007 a new local beer-maker under the name of Napex Corporation joined the two brewers selling a beer named Jaz Beer. Differences between the brand portfolios of GAB and Carlsberg partly explain the market share reversal. GAB sells pricier brands such as Guinness and Heineken while most of Carlsberg's sales came from the lower-priced Carlsberg green label. Buyers of premium brands are wealthier and less price sensitive than cheap beer consumers. Soren Jensen, managing director of Carlsberg Malaysia, explained the situation as follows: "Once you have high duties, you don't have much cheap beer. The premium brands have strengthened because the relative price difference is smaller." (*Media*, Nov. 27, 2008) Charles Ireland, the head of GAB, said: "We sell premium brands, they sell brands which are of lower prices; we have different business models and our consumer markets are different." (www.theedgeasia.com).

To shore up Carlsberg's position, the firm overhauled its brand stable by adding new high-end offerings such as Tuborg, Skol Super, and Carlsberg Gold as well as importing Corona from Mexico. GAB also outspent Carlsberg in advertising during 2007: RM10.4 million ($2.8 million) for GAB versus RM6.8 million ($1.8 million) spent by Carlsberg on its core brand (see Table A). Television, radio, and outdoor are not used. Print accounts for 70 percent of all advertising spending, cinema 19 percent, and point-of-sale 11 percent. Other promotional activities include relationship marketing, trade promotions, and sponsorships. Global brands such as Heineken and Carlsberg also get exposure through global sponsorship activities: Carlsberg with Liverpool, Heineken with the UEFA Champions soccer league.

**Top five brands by adspend (000's)**

| | |
|---|---|
| Carlsberg | RM6,780 (Carlsberg) |
| Heineken | RM5,867 (GAB) |
| Tiger Beer | RM2,967 (GAB) |
| Skol | RM1,884 (Carlsberg) |
| Anchor | RM1,603 (GAB) |

## DISCUSSION QUESTIONS

**1.** What do you see as the main challenges that Carlsberg is facing in Malaysia?

**2.** From 2004 to 2006, the beer and stout market in Malaysia saw heavy increases in duties. Carlsberg bore the brunt of these increases, losing market share to GAB. What strategic initiatives would you recommend to Soren Jensen to meet the challenges Carlsberg is facing?

# FURTHER READING ◆ ◆ ◆ ◆ ◆ ◆ ◆ ◆ ◆ ◆ ◆ ◆ ◆ ◆ ◆ ◆ ◆ ◆ ◆ ◆

Adler, Ralph A., "Transfer Pricing for World-Class Manufacturing," *Long Range Planning*, vol. 29, no. 1, pp. 69–75.

Assmus, Gert and Carsten Wiese, "How to Address the Gray Market Threat Using Price Coordination," *Sloan Management Review*, Spring 1995, pp. 31–41.

Carter, Joseph R. and James Gagne, "The Dos and Don'ts of International Countertrade," *Sloan Management Review*, vol. 29 no. 3, Spring 1988, pp. 31–37.

Cavusgil, S. Tamer, "Unraveling the Mystique of Export Pricing," *Business Horizons*, vol. 31 May–June 1988, pp. 54–63.

Cavusgil, S. Tamer, "Pricing for Global Markets," *The Columbia Journal of World Business, Winter* 1996, pp. 66–78.

Chintagunta, Pradeep K., and Ramarao Desiraju. "Strategic Pricing and Detailing Behavior in International Markets." *Marketing Science* 24 (Winter 2005): 67–80.

Fraedrich, John P. and Connie RaeBateman, "Transfer Pricing by Multinational Marketers: Risky Business," *Business Horizons, Jan.–Feb.* 1996, pp. 17–22.

Kostecki, Michel M., "Marketing Strategies between Dumping and Anti-Dumping Action," *European Journal of Marketing*, vol. 25, no. 12, 1991, pp. 7–19.

Narayandas, Das, John Quelch, and Gordon Swartz. "Prepare Your Company for Global Pricing," *Sloan Management Review* (Fall 2000), pp. 61–70.

Paun, Dorothy, "An International Profile of Countertrading Firms," *Industrial Marketing Management*, vol. 26, 1997, pp. 41–50.

Paun, Dorothy and Aviv Shoham, "Marketing Motives in International Countertrade: An Empirical Examination," *Journal of International Marketing*, vol. 4, no. 3, 1996, pp. 29–47.

Rabino, Samuel and Kirit Shah, "Countertrade and Penetration of LDC's Markets," *The Columbia Journal of World Business, Winter* 1987, pp. 31–38.

Samiee, Saeed, "Pricing in Marketing Strategies of U.S.- and Foreign-Based Companies," *Journal of Business Research*, vol. 15, 1987, pp. 17–30.

Shipley, David and Bill Neale, "Industrial Barter and Countertrade," *Industrial Marketing Management*, vol. 16, 1987, pp. 1–8.

Simon, Hermann and Eckhard Kucher, "The European pricing time bomb—and how to cope with it," *Marketing and Research Today,* February 1993, pp. 25–36.

Sims, Clive, Adam Phillips, and Trevor Richards, "Developing a global pricing strategy," *Marketing and Research Today,* March 1992, pp. 3–14.

*Transfer Pricing Guidelines for Multinational Enterprises and Tax Administrations.* OECD Publishing, 2006.

Weekly, James K., "Pricing in Foreign Markets: Pitfalls and Opportunities," *Industrial Marketing Management*, vol. 21, 1992, pp. 173–79.

# COMMUNICATING WITH THE WORLD CONSUMER

13

## CHAPTER OVERVIEW

1. GLOBAL ADVERTISING AND CULTURE

2. SETTING THE GLOBAL ADVERTISING BUDGET

3. CREATIVE STRATEGY

4. GLOBAL MEDIA DECISIONS

5. ADVERTISING REGULATIONS

6. CHOOSING AN ADVERTISING AGENCY

7. OTHER MEANS OF COMMUNICATION

8. GLOBALLY INTEGRATED MARKETING COMMUNICATIONS (GIMC)

To promote its Temptations range of chocolates in India, Cadbury, the British chocolate maker, put out a print ad that was timed to coincide with India's Independence Day.[1] The ad showed a map of India with the words "Too good to share" printed across the state of Jammu and Kashmir. The reference to Kashmir, which is at the center of a longstanding dispute between India and Pakistan, did not please Hindu nationalists. Cadbury was forced to issue a statement apologizing for the advertisement. One of Procter & Gamble's biggest advertising blunders happened in Japan when the firm introduced its disposable diapers Pampers brand. Around that time, P&G aired a TV commercial in the United States showing an animated stork delivering Pampers diapers at home. P&G's American managers in Japan figured that this could be an excellent piece of advertising they could transplant into the Japanese market to back up the launch of Pampers. The copy was dubbed in Japanese and the Japanese package replaced the American one. Unfortunately, this cute commercial failed to seduce Japanese mothers. After some consumer research, P&G discovered that Japanese consumers were confused about why a bird was delivering disposable diapers. Contrary to Western folklore, storks in Japan are not supposed to deliver babies. Instead, babies allegedly arrive in giant

---

[1]"Anger over Kashmir Chocolate Ad," http://news.bbc.co.uk, August 21, 2002.

peaches that float on the river to deserving parents.[2] After the debacle, P&G used a more relevant advertising model to promote Pampers to Japanese consumers: the testimonial of a nurse who also happens to be a mother—the "expert mom."[3] As both the Cadbury and the P&G cases illustrate, international advertising can prove to be very tricky.

The first part of this chapter will focus on global advertising. We first cover the cultural challenges that advertisers face. We examine the major international advertising planning decisions that marketers need to address. In particular, we cover budgeting and resource allocation issues, message strategy, and media decisions. One hurdle that advertisers face is the maze of advertising regulations across the world. We highlight the different types of regulations and discuss several mechanisms to cope with them. Next we address another important global advertising concern: advertising agency selection for foreign markets. The second part of this chapter explores other forms of communication tools that global marketers have access to.

## GLOBAL ADVERTISING AND CULTURE ◆ ◆ ◆ ◆ ◆ ◆ ◆

Advertising is to a large extent a cultural phenomenon. On the one hand, advertising shapes a country's popular culture. At the same time, the host country's culture may also influence the creation of an ad campaign and its effectiveness. As the P&G example in the introduction demonstrated, when advertising appeals are not in sync with the local culture, the ad campaign will falter. In the worst-case scenario, the ad might even stymie the advertised product's sales or damage the brand image. Effective ad campaigns also do a great job in leveraging local cultural phenomena. A TV ad created for Unilever's Vaseline brand in India is an excellent example.[4] The commercial shows the distress of a local woman buying shoes. As the woman prepares to try out a shoe, the salesman spots cracks in her feet and tells her that the shoe is not within her budget. An onscreen message then asks: "Why should someone peep in your life because of cracks in the skin of your feet?" An image of Vaseline cream follows, with the promise that it will soften hard skin and get rid of cracks. The ad cleverly plays on Indian women's embarrassment of a) having cracked feet and b) not being able to afford servants. **Global Perspective 13-1** gives another nice example. Because most advertising has a major verbal component, we first look at the language barriers.

Language is one of the most daunting barriers that international advertisers need to surmount. Numerous promotional efforts have misfired because of language related mishaps. Apart from translation, another challenge is the proper interpretation of ideas. The IBM global slogan "Solutions for a Small Planet" became "small world" in Argentina as "planet" failed to convey the desired conceptual thrust there.[5] Given the bewildering variety of languages, advertising copy translation mistakes are easily made. One can identify three different types of translation errors: simple carelessness, multiple-meaning words, and idioms.[6] Some typical instances of translation blunders that can be ascribed to pure carelessness are the following examples:

**Language Barriers**

> Original slogan: "It takes a tough man to make a tender chicken."
> Translation: "It takes a sexually excited man to make a chick affectionate."

---

[2]The story goes as follows. A long time ago—in the Japan of the fourteenth century—an old man and his wife had been childless. They were very sad. When the old lady went to a nearby river to do the laundry, she saw a huge "momo" (peach) floating on the river. She brought it back home. And lo and behold, the peach suddenly broke into two halves and a baby came out from inside. They named this baby "Momotaro"—meaning: a boy from a peach.

[3]"Even at P&G, only 3 brands make truly global grade so far," *Advertising Age International* (January 1998), p. 8.

[4]"Vaseline plays on Indian women's embarrassment of not having a servant," http://www.adageglobal.com, accessed on December 24, 2002.

[5]David A. Aaker and Erich Joachimsthaler, "The Lure of Global Branding," *Harvard Business Review* (Nov.-Dec. 1999), p. 144.

[6]David A. Ricks, *Blunders in International Business*, Cambridge, MA: Blackwell Publishers, 1993.

◆ ◆ ◆ ◆ ◆ ◆ ◆ ◆ ◆ ◆ ◆ ◆ ◆ ◆ ◆ ◆ ◆ ◆ ◆ ◆ ◆ ◆ ◆ ◆ ◆ ◆ ◆ ◆ ◆ ◆ ◆ ◆ ◆ ◆

# GLOBAL PERSPECTIVE 13-1

## DUNKIN' DONUTS "LONGEST LOVE MESSAGE TO MOMS" CAMPAIGN IN THAILAND

Dunkin' Donuts entered Thailand in 1981 and now operates almost 130 outlets, serving more than 300,000 customers a week. In fact, Thailand is home to the chain's largest shop in the world, with a seating capacity of 130. Dunkin' Donuts portrays itself as a company that cares for society and honors the family. Contrary to Western countries, a Thai Dunkin' Donuts restaurant tends to be a meeting place where people come with their family and friends to relax and socialize.

In the summer of 1999, Dunkin' Donuts ran a 5-week promotional campaign centered on Thailand's Queen birthday (August 12), which coincides with national mother's day. The goal of the promotion was twofold. One objective was to increase the chain's market share by 2 percent. The second goal was to increase brand loyalty among its target consumers, teenagers and young adults. The cornerstone of the "Longest Love Message to Moms" campaign was an invitation to Thais to come to the stores and pen a love note to their mothers on a

special banner. Customers could also participate in a contest where they could win cash and product prizes. The grand prize was a company-sponsored lunch hosted by the winner and his/her mother for underprivileged children in Bangkok.

The campaign received a lot of publicity. A mile-long banner marked with 50,000-plus love-to-mom messages was carried around by more than 400 Dunkin Donuts store employees in the national parade for the queen's birthday. The promotion did an excellent job in billing Dunkin' Donuts as a company that, though foreign, cares about the local culture, Thai people, and Thailand's royal family. Overall, the company only spent $14,000 on the promotion. Did the chain achieve its objectives? You bet. Sales increased by $373,000 over normal sales volume during the promotion period. Dunkin' Donuts' market share in the doughnut category rose from 67 percent (May 1999) to 71 percent (September 1999)—twice the 2 percent share-increase-target. An ACNielsen survey also found that Dunkin' Donuts was perceived as a "caring corporate citizen, dedicated to the Thailand market and its people."

*Source:* "Thais Sweet on Mom, 'Love' Campaign," *Marketing News* (September 11, 2000), pp.6–7.

---

Original slogan: "Body by Fisher."
Translation: "Corpse by Fisher."

Original slogan: "When I used this shirt, I felt good."
Translation: "Until I used this shirt, I felt good."

The second group of translation mishaps relates to words that have multiple meanings. Consider a campaign ran by the Parker Pen Company in Latin America. When entering Latin America, Parker used a literal translation of a slogan the company was using in the United States: "Avoid embarrassment—use Parker Pens." However, the Spanish word for "embarrassment" has also the meaning of pregnancy. As a result, Parker was unconsciously advertising its products as a contraceptive.[7]

The third class of language-related advertising blunders stems from idioms or local slang. Idioms or expressions that use slang from one country may inadvertently lead to embarrassing meanings in another country. One U.S. advertiser ran a campaign in Britain that used the same slogan as the one that was used back home: "You can use no finer napkin at your dinner table." Unfortunately, in Britain, the word *napkin* is slang for "diapers."[8] **Exhibit 13-1** lists the different words that Goodyear has singled out for saying *tires* in Spanish.

So, what are the solutions for overcoming language barriers? One obvious cure is to involve local advertising agencies or translators in the development of your promotional campaigns. Their feedback and suggestions are often highly useful.

Another tactic is simply not to translate the slogan into the local language. Instead, the English slogan is used worldwide. The Swiss luxury watchmaker TAG Heuer used the tag line "Don't crack under pressure" without translating it in each of its markets,

---

[7]David A. Ricks, *Blunders in International Business.*
[8]ibid.

**EXHIBIT 13-1**
FIVE DIFFERENT WAYS OF SAYING TIRES IN SPANISH

| Spanish Word for Tires | Countries Using Each Word |
|---|---|
| Cauchos | Venezuela |
| Cubiertas | Argentina |
| Gomas | Puerto Rico |
| Llantas | Mexico, Peru, Guatemala, Colombia, and elsewhere in Central America |
| Neumaticos | Chile |

*Source:* D. A. Hanni, J. K. Ryans, Jr. and I. R. Vernon, "Coordinating International Advertising—The Goodyear Case Revisited for Latin America." This article originally appeared in *Journal of International Marketing*, 3(2), 1995, published by Michigan State University Press, p. 84.

even Japan, where over 60 percent of the audience had no clue of the slogan's meaning.[9] Other examples of universally used slogans that were left untranslated are "You and us: UBS," "Coke is it" and "United Colors of Benetton." For TV commercials, one can add subtitles in the local language. This is exactly what the U.S. Meat Export Federation (USMEF) did with the "aisareru" beef or "desire beef" campaign in Japan.[10] The campaign was launched in March 2002 by the USMEF to deliver messages of safety, taste, and nutrition to the Japanese consumers, who had become worried about mad cow disease. The TV commercials featured three U.S. women, working in the U.S. beef industry, who share the concerns of their Japanese counterparts about the safety of the food that they serve to their families.

For radio or TV commercials, voice-overs that use the local slang often become necessary. However, this rule cannot be generalized. For instance, while Egyptian consumers prefer colloquial Egyptian Arabic in their advertising, use of local slang is less advisable for Gulf Arabs.[11] Finally, meticulous copy research and testing should enable advertisers to pick up translation glitches.

Many of the trickiest promotional issues occur in the domain of religion. In Saudi Arabia, for example, only veiled women can be shown in TV commercials, except from the back. As you can imagine, such restrictions lead to horrendous problems for haircare advertisers. Procter & Gamble navigated around that constraint by creating a spot for Pert Plus shampoo that showed the face of a veiled woman and the hair of another woman from the back. Early 2007, the start of the "Year of the Pig," CCTV, China's national broadcaster, banned the use of advertising containing pig images out of respect for the country's Muslim minority (2 percent of the population).[12] The ban meant that advertisers would have to re-shoot their Chinese New Year spots. Coca-Cola had prepared two spots—one featuring a piglet and another with a panda bear. After a great deal of pressure CCTV relaxed the ban and decided to review ads on a case-by-case basis.

As Cadbury's Kashmir gaffe described at the beginning of this chapter shows, political sensitivities are also crucial. Canon came under fire in the Chinese media for a promotional CD-ROM that mistakenly referred to Taiwan and Hong Kong as countries—a major affront to China's one-country policy.[13] For similar reasons, Toyota ran into trouble in China with a print ad campaign for the Land Cruiser. One of the print ads showed stone lions saluting a passing Land Cruiser. Stone lions are a symbol of power and authority in China. The campaign caused outrage among the Chinese media and public as it was seen as a display of Japanese imperialism.[14]

**Other Cultural Barriers**

---

[9]"TAG Heuer: all time greats?" *Director*, April 1994, pp. 45–48.

[10]http://animalrangeextension.montana.edu/Articles/Beef/Q&A2002/Promote.htm

[11]"Peace process forges new Middle East future," *Advertising Age International*, April 1996, p. I13.

[12]"Ban Thwarts 'Year of the Pig' Ads in China, www.npr.org, accessed on February 10, 2009.

[13]"China's Paper Tigers Swift to Bite," *Financial Times* (August 23, 2000), p. 9. Part of the animosity stemmed also from the fact that Canon is a Japanese company. Many Chinese still feel very ambivalent toward Japan.

[14]"Toyota Looks for Road to Recovery in China," *Media* (March 12, 2004): 19.

**Communication and Cultural Values**

The effectiveness of a communication campaign often depends on the extent to which the values evoked by the campaign match the cultural values of the target audience. One framework that helps in understanding the influence of culture on advertising is the Hofstede cultural grid discussed in Chapter 4. As you may recall, the schema classifies cultures based on five dimensions: power distance, uncertainty avoidance, individualism/collectivism, masculinity, and long-termism. The schema has been applied in several cross-cultural studies to assess the effectiveness of different advertising approaches. One study explored the link between the values portrayed in Benetton advertising and consumers' values in Norway, Germany and Italy. The study concludes that when consumers' values match the values expressed by the advertising, the liking for the brand increases.[15] Another study examined the effectiveness of antismoking messages targeted to teenagers in different cultures. According to the study, advertisements that are framed in a negative manner by pointing out the threats of smoking are more effective in high uncertainty-avoidance (UA) countries than ads with positive messages. However, positively framed anti-smoking ads that stress the benefits of cutting smoking may be more effective in low-UA countries such as Denmark, Russia, the United Kingdom, and the United States.[16] The schema can also be used to assess the effectiveness of comparative advertising within a particular cultural environment. Such ads favorably compare the promoted brand against the competing brand(s) (identified or unidentified). While forbidden or heavily restricted in many countries, comparative advertising is legal in major markets such as the United States and Japan. In group-oriented (collectivist) cultures (e.g, Japan, Thailand), comparison with the competition may not be acceptable because the other party risks losing face. In feminine cultures (e.g., Scandinavia, Thailand), comparative advertising could be viewed as too aggressive and bold. In cultures that are a combination of individualistic and feminine values, comparative advertising could work as long as it is done in a subtle, non-aggressive manner. A good example is the well-known tag line used by the Danish beer brand Carlsberg: "Probably the best beer in the world." Cultures where comparative advertising is likely to be most effective are those that embrace masculinity and individualism as values.[17]

◆ ◆ ◆ ◆ ◆ ◆ ◆ ◆ ## SETTING THE GLOBAL ADVERTISING BUDGET

One of the delicate issues that marketers must grapple with when planning their communication strategy centers on the "money" issue. Advertising spending worldwide is considerable. **Exhibit 13-2** ranks the top 15 global advertisers in 2007. Not surprisingly, the biggest spenders are the major multinational consumer goods companies. The largest ad spending categories are: Automotive ($23.7 billion), personal care ($23.4 billion), food ($11.0 billion), entertainment ($9.7 billion), and drugs ($9.4 billion).[18] **Exhibit 13-3** shows that most of the spending occurred in the United States, followed by Europe.

The key spending questions for global marketers are twofold: (1) How much should we spend? and (2) How should we allocate our resources across our different markets? Let us first look at the budgeting amount question. Companies rely on different kinds of advertising budgeting rules, notably percentage of sales, competitive parity, and objective-and-task.[19]

[15]Rosemary Polegato and Rune Bjerke, "The Link between Cross-Cultural Value Associations and Liking: The Case of Benetton and Its Advertising," *Journal of Advertising Research*, September 2006, pp. 263–73.

[16]James Reardon, Chip Miller, Irena Vida, and Liza Rybina, "Antismoking Messages for the International Teenage Segment: The Effectiveness of Message Valence and Intensity Across Different Cultures," *Journal of International Marketing*, 14(3), 2006, pp. 115–38.

[17]Marieke de Mooij, *Global Marketing and Advertising,* Thousand Oaks, CA: SAGE Publications, 1998, pp. 252–54.

[18]*Advertising Age's Global Marketers*, December 8, 2008, p. 6.

[19]See, for instance, Rajeev Batra, John G. Myers and David A. Aaker, *Advertising Management*, Upper Saddle River, NJ: Prentice Hall, 1996 (5th Edition).

**EXHIBIT 13-2**
TOP 15 GLOBAL ADVERTISERS—MEASURED MEDIA ONLY (2007)

| Rank | Company | Home country | Spending amount (billions of $) |
|------|---------|--------------|--------------------------------|
| 1 | Procter & Gamble | USA | $9.36 |
| 2 | Unilever | UK/Netherlands | $5.29 |
| 3 | L'Oréal | France | $3.43 |
| 4 | General Motors | USA | $3.34 |
| 5 | Toyota | Japan | $3.20 |
| 6 | Ford Motor | USA | $2.90 |
| 7 | Johnson & Johnson | USA | $2.36 |
| 8 | Nestlé | Switzerland | $2.18 |
| 9 | Coca-Cola | USA | $2.18 |
| 10 | Honda Motor | Japan | $2.05 |
| 11 | Time Warner | USA | $2.02 |
| 12 | Reckitt Benckiser | UK | $1.98 |
| 13 | Sony Corp. | Japan | $1.89 |
| 14 | Kraft Foods | USA | $1.85 |
| 15 | Nissan Motor | Japan | $1.83 |

*Source:* Compiled from *Advertising Age's Global Marketers* (December 8, 2008)

## Budgeting Rules

***Percentage of Sales.*** The rule based on **percentage of sales** simply sets the overall advertising budget as a percentage of sales revenue. The base is either past or expected sales revenues. The obvious appeal of this decision rule is its simplicity. One nagging question though is what percentage to choose. The biggest downside of this rule is that sales revenue (past or projected) drives advertising spending, whereas the purpose of advertising is to impact sales. The method is clearly not a sound strategy for markets that were recently entered, especially if the percentage base is historical sales revenue.

***Competitive Parity.*** The principle of the **competitive parity** rule is extremely simple: Use your competitors' advertising spending as a benchmark. For instance, a company could simply match its lead competitor's spending amount to get a similar amount of share-of-voice.[20] The rationale for this approach is that the competitors' collective wisdom signals the "optimal" spending amount. It is not surprising that the three biggest global advertising spenders (P&G, Unilever, and L'Oréal) are global rivals. Likewise, four of the largest spenders in the top-10 are car companies: General Motors (4), Toyota (5), Ford (6), and Honda (10) (see Exhibit 13-2). The competitive

**EXHIBIT 13-3**
MEASURED ADVERTISING SPENDING BY REGION (2007)

| Region | Amount (billions of $) | Percentage of worldwide amount |
|--------|------------------------|-------------------------------|
| Africa | $0.74 | 0.7 |
| Asia-Pacific | $16.15 | 15.0 |
| Europe | $37.71 | 35.0 |
| Latin America | $3.63 | 3.4 |
| Middle East | $0.70 | 0.7 |
| Canada | $2.09 | 1.9 |
| USA | $46.61 | 43.3 |
| World | $107.63 | 100.0 |

*Source:* Compiled from *Advertising Age's Global Marketers* (December 8, 2008)

---

[20]Share of voice is a brand's advertising weight as a percentage of the total category advertising.

parity rule also allows the company to sustain a minimum "share of voice"[21] without rocking the boat. Advertising scholars have pointed out several shortcomings of competitive parity as a budgeting norm. The industry's spending habits may well be very questionable: collective wisdom is not always a given. Also, marketers that recently entered a new market probably should spend far more relative to the incumbent brands to break through the clutter.

**Exhibit 13-4** contrasts the spending levels in several countries around the world of two global rivals Procter & Gamble and Unilever, the number one and two top global

**EXHIBIT 13-4**
MEASURED AD SPENDING COMPARISON P&G VERSUS UNILEVER (2007)

| Country | Procter & Gamble | Unilever | Spending Ratio: Column (2): Column (3) |
|---|---|---|---|
| **Asia** | | | |
| China | $1,097.5 | $446.5 | 2.46 |
| India | 80.2 | 254.6 | 0.31 |
| Kazakhstan | 72.9 | 24.7 | 2.95 |
| Malaysia | 38.3 | 36.7 | 1.04 |
| Pakistan | 10.2 | 20.2 | 0.50 |
| Philippines | 38.9 | 55.5 | 0.70 |
| Taiwan | 21.3 | 12.0 | 1.77 |
| Thailand | 53.4 | 164.2 | 0.32 |
| Vietnam | 17.9 | 41.9 | 0.43 |
| | | | |
| **Europe** | | | |
| Belarus | 28.9 | 13.5 | 2.14 |
| Belgium | 114.2 | 56.0 | 2.04 |
| Croatia | 30.7 | 16.5 | 1.86 |
| Czech Republic | 67.2 | 58.6 | 1.15 |
| Finland | 12.1 | 21.2 | 0.57 |
| Germany | 314.1 | 205.1 | 1.53 |
| Greece | 66.8 | 47.2 | 1.41 |
| Hungary | 90.3 | 93.9 | 0.96 |
| Ireland | 25.6 | 31.6 | 0.81 |
| Italy | 147.0 | 129.2 | 1.14 |
| Netherlands | 136.8 | 237.9 | 0.57 |
| Poland | 161.9 | 196.0 | 0.83 |
| Russia | 190.0 | 84.7 | 2.24 |
| Serbia | 75.1 | 24.9 | 3.02 |
| Sweden | 69.7 | 82.6 | 0.84 |
| Switzerland | 52.2 | 35.3 | 1.49 |
| United Kingdom | 462.0 | 285.0 | 1.62 |
| | | | |
| **Americas** | | | |
| Argentina | 26.8 | 77.5 | 0.34 |
| Chile | 8.4 | 15.1 | 0.55 |
| Colombia | 8.9 | 10.1 | 0.88 |
| Mexico | 124.0 | 79.4 | 1.56 |
| United States | 3,700.3 | 910.3 | 4.06 |
| | | | |
| **Africa & Middle East** | | | |
| Kuwait | 15.1 | 9.0 | 1.67 |
| Morocco | 14.0 | 10.0 | 1.40 |
| South Africa | 33.9 | 48.1 | 0.70 (2004) |
| Turkey | 295.0 | 237.3 | 1.24 |

*Note:* Figures are in millions of U.S. dollars; italics are countries were P&G outspends Unilever.

*Source:* Compiled from *Advertising Age's Global Marketers,* December 8, 2008 and *Advertising Age Annual 2009,* December 29, 2008.

[21]Share of voice refers to the amount of ad spending on the brand as a proportion of the total category ad-spending amount.

advertisers, respectively. Glancing at the figures, it seems P&G prevails in China, the NAFTA[22] region, East and Central Europe (except Poland), most of Western Europe (except the Netherlands) and the Middle East. Unilever dominates in Scandinavia, South and Southeast Asia, and South America.

***Objective-and-Task Method.*** The most popular budgeting rule is the so-called **objective-and-task** method. Conceptually, this is also the most appealing budgeting rule: it treats promotional efforts as a means to achieve the advertiser's stated objectives. This method was found to be used by almost two-thirds of the respondents in the one survey mentioned earlier.[23] The concept of this budgeting rule is very straightforward. The first step of the procedure is to spell out the goals of the communication strategy. The next step is to determine the tasks that are needed to achieve the desired objectives. The planned budget is then the overall costs that the completion of these tasks will amount to. The objective-and-task method necessitates a solid understanding of the relationship between advertising spending and the stated objectives (e.g., market share, brand awareness). One way to assess these linkages is to use field experiments. With experimentation, the advertiser systematically manipulates the spending amount in different areas within the country to measure the impact of advertising on the key objectives of the campaign (e.g., brand awareness, sales volume, market share).

The budgeting process also involves the allocation of resources across the different countries in which the firm operates. **Exhibit 13-5** shows the allocation of advertising dollars (percentage-wise) by the world's top three advertisers in 2007: Procter &

**Resource Allocation**

**EXHIBIT 13-5**
2007 AD SPENDING ALLOCATION BY 3 BIGGEST
ADVERTISERS IN KEY MARKETS

| Country | P&G | Unilever | L'Oréal |
|---|---|---|---|
| **Europe** | | | |
| France | 2.4% | NA | 12.7% |
| Germany | 3.3 | 3.9% | 6.7 |
| Italy | 1.6 | 2.4 | 3.3 |
| Russia | 2.0 | 1.6 | 2.7 |
| Spain | 1.8 | NA | 4.1 |
| United Kingdom | 4.9 | 5.4 | 6.9 |
| | | | |
| **Asia** | | | |
| China | 11.7 | 8.4 | 5.7 |
| India | 0.8 | 4.8 | 1.0 |
| Indonesia | NA | 3.8 | NA |
| Thailand | 0.6 | 3.1 | 1.1 |
| | | | |
| **Americas** | | | |
| Brazil | NA | 3.7 | NA |
| Canada | 1.9 | NA | 1.9 |
| Mexico | 1.3 | 1.5 | NA |
| USA | 39.5 | 17.2 | 22.8 |
| **Total Ad Spending Amount** (in million of dollars) | $9,358 | $5,295 | $3,426 |

*Source*: Percentages calculated based on ad spending figures reported in *Advertising Age's Global Marketers*, December 8, 2008, and *Advertising Age Annual 2009*, December 29, 2008.

---

[22]North American Free Trade Agreement countries are the United States, Canada, and Mexico.

[23]N. E. Synodinos, C. F. Keown and L. W. Jacobs, "Transnational advertising practices," *Journal of Advertising Research*, April/May 1989, pp. 43-50.

Gamble, Unilever, and L'Oréal. Not surprisingly, all three of them allocate a large chunk of their advertising dollars to China and the United States.

There are three approaches that companies use to make advertising allocation decisions. At one extreme are companies like Microsoft and FedEx where each country subsidiary independently determines how much should be spent within its market and then requests the desired resources from headquarters. This is known as **bottom-up budgeting. Top-down budgeting** is the opposite approach. Here headquarters sets the overall budget and then splits up the pie among its different affiliates. EDS, a U.S.-based information technology consulting company, allocated advertising budgets proportional to the revenue contribution of the different regions for a major global ad campaign.[24] Motorola also centralizes budget decisions. The company puts its budget together centrally and then allocates it depending on regional and local needs. Other companies that centralize budgeting decisions include Sun Microsystems, Bausch & Lomb, and Delta Airlines.[25] A third approach, which becomes increasingly more common, takes a regional angle. Each region decides the amount of resources that are needed to achieve its planned objectives and then proposes its budget to headquarters. A survey conducted by *Advertising Age International* in 1995 found that the most favored approaches are bottom-up (28 percent of respondents) and region-up budgeting (28 percent). Only 20 percent of the responses indicated that the headquarters office has direct control over funding decisions. The survey also indicated substantial cross-industry differences in resource allocation practices.

---

◆ ◆ ◆ ◆ ◆ ◆ ◆ ◆    ## CREATIVE STRATEGY

**The "Standardization" versus "Adaptation" Debate**

On March 4, 2009, Visa rolled out its first-ever global ad campaign for its debit card.[26] The $140 million campaign, which ran in the United States and 43 countries (e.g., India, Mexico, Japan), was designed to persuade consumers that debit cards are more convenient and safer than cash. The ads promote the use of Visa card for small purchase transactions: "Our prime objective was to create a campaign that would migrate consumer and business spending from cash and cheques to the better form of electronic payment, Visa. We also wanted a campaign that would work on a global scale while also connecting locally, and 'Go' is one of those few universal words that is broadly understood around the world."[27] In Asia the ads show people from different places enjoying what the world has to offer.[28]

One of the thorniest issues that marketers face when developing a communication strategy is the choice of a proper advertising theme. Companies that sell the same product in multiple markets need to establish to what degree their advertising campaign should be standardized. *Standardization* simply means that one or more elements of the communication campaign are kept the same. The major elements of a campaign are the message (strategy, selling proposition, platform) and the execution.

The issue of standardize-versus-adapt has sparked a fierce debate in advertising circles. A truly global campaign is uniform in message and often also in execution (at least, in terms of visuals). When necessary, minor changes must be made in the execution to comply with local regulations or to make the ad more appealing to local audiences (voice-overs, local actors). Typically, global campaigns heavily rely on global or pan-regional media channels. "Truly" global campaigns are still relatively rare.

---

[24]"EDS in global push to boost understanding of who it really is," *Media* (October 1, 1999), p. 30.

[25]"U.S. Multinationals," *Advertising Age International* (June 1999), pp. 39–40.

[26]"Visa is Seeking to Usurp Cash as King," *The Wall Street Asia*, March 4, 2009, p. 16.

[27]"Visa Rolls Out First Global Campaign," www.brandrepublic.asia, accessed on March 4, 2009.

[28]See http://www.brandrepublic.asia/Media/The-Workarticle/2009_03/Visa--Visa-Gofesto--Global/34580 for a clip.

◆ ◆ ◆ ◆ ◆ ◆ ◆ ◆ ◆ ◆ ◆ ◆ ◆ ◆ ◆ ◆ ◆ ◆ ◆ ◆ ◆ ◆ ◆ ◆ ◆ ◆ ◆ ◆ ◆ ◆ ◆ ◆ ◆ ◆ ◆ ◆ ◆

## $\mathcal{G}$LOBAL PERSPECTIVE 13-2

### NISSAN'S GLOBAL "SHIFT" ADVERTISING CAMPAIGN

In the past, Nissan Motor's advertising messages varied enormously across markets. In Europe, it had no tagline. In the U.S. the tag line was "Driven" and in Japan it used the slogan "Bringing more to your life every day." To beef up its global brand image, Nissan kicked off its global "Shift" campaign in 2002. In the United States, where the campaign coincided with the launch of the Nissan 350Z sports car, the tag line varies, including "Shift passion," "Shift joy," and "Shift forward." One TV ad in the United States shows a baby trying to make its first steps with the tag line "Shift achievement." In Europe, the slogan is "Shift expectations." In Japan, the tag line is "Shift the future."

*Source:* "Nissan Shifts Focus to Unified Strategy For Its Global Campaign," *Asian Wall Street Journal* (October 10, 2002), p. A7.

The "Shift" campaign was born from a cooperative process between Nissan managers from advertising and marketing divisions worldwide. Brainstorming over a 10-month period spawned hundreds of candidates for a global tagline. One major obstacle was that many of the most common words (e.g., "power," "exciting") were already pre-empted by copyright somewhere. In the end, "Shift" was the winning idea. The "shift" slogan appeared to best convey the sense of change message that Nissan hoped to get across. Moreover, it could be easily understood in non-English speaking countries. To give local subsidiaries some amount of control, Nissan allowed local variations for the second half of the tag line.

---

Ricoh is one of Xerox's biggest rivals; in the United States, for instance, Ricoh's market share was 14.5 percent in 2001, slightly below Xerox's 14.9 percent.[29] In recent years, the Japanese office-machine company has grown by buying up competing brands such as Lanier and Savin. Still, despite its rise, only 15 percent of the consumers outside Japan recognize its name. As price competition intensifies in Ricoh's core businesses, the company aspires to move into higher-margin products such as networked office equipment systems. To grab the attention of senior executives, Ricoh kicked off a global advertising campaign in 2002. The ads showed communicators in unlikely places. For instance, one ad featured an African chieftain who uses clicks and whistles to communicate with his tribe. The message tried to make people wonder whether their business communications are as effective as they can be (see **Global Perspective 13-2** for another example of a global campaign). What makes the case of standardization so compelling in the eyes of many marketers? A variety of reasons have been offered to defend global, if not pan-regional, advertising campaigns. The major ones are listed here.

**Merits of Standardization**

***Scale Economies.*** Of the factors encouraging companies to standardize their advertising campaigns, the most appealing one is the positive impact on the advertiser's bottom line. The savings coming from the economies of scale of a single campaign (as opposed to multiple country-level ones) can be quite eye-catching. Levi Strauss reportedly saved around $2.2 million by shooting a single TV ad covering six European markets.[30] Several factors lie behind such savings. Producing a single commercial is often far cheaper than making several different ones for each individual market. Savings are also realized because firms can assign fewer executives to develop the campaign at the global or pan-regional level.

***Consistent Image.*** For many companies that sell the same product in multiple markets, having a consistent brand image is extremely important. Consistency was one of the prime motives behind the pan-European campaign that Blistex, a U.S.-based lipcare manufacturer, started to run in 1995. Prior to the campaign, advertising themes varied from country to country, often highlighting only one item of Blistex's product

---

[29]"Ricoh Wants World to Know Its Name," *Asian Wall Street Journal* (November 18, 2002), p. A8.

[30]"A universal message," *The Financial Times*, May 27, 1993.

line. The entire product range consists of three items, each one standing for a different need. In many of its markets, brand awareness was dismally low. The objectives for the pan-European campaign were (1) to increase brand awareness and (2) to have the same positioning theme by communicating the so-called "care-to-cure" concept behind Blistex' product line.[31] Campbell's pan-European advertising strategy for the Delacre cookie brand was also driven by a desire to establish a single brand identity across Europe. The brand's platform is that Delacre is a premium cookie brand with the finest ingredients based on French know-how. The same campaign was aired in English reaching 30 million people in more than 20 countries.[32] Message consistency matters a great deal in markets with extensive media overlap or for goods that are sold to global target customers who travel the globe.

***Globalization of Media.*** Another force that drives global communication campaigns is the rise of global media groups. Global conglomerates dominate almost all media forms: television (e.g., Time Warner, News Corp., Viacom), print (e.g., News Corp., Time Warner, Condé Nast, Pearson), cinema (e.g., AMC Cinemas), and outdoor (Clear Channel, JC Decaux).

***Global Consumer Segments.*** Cross-cultural similarities are a major catalyst behind efforts toward a standardized advertising approach. The "global village" argument often pops up in discussions on the merits of global or pan-regional advertising campaigns. The argument of cultural binding especially has clout with respect to product categories that appeal to the elites or youngsters as observed by David Newkirk, a consultant with Booz Allen & Hamilton: "The young and the rich have very similar tastes the world over, and that's what's driving the convergences in advertising and media."[33] High-tech and business-to-business products and services typically also have global customer needs. When Microsoft launched its new operating system, Vista, the company initiated a $500 million global marketing blitz, which was expected to make 6.6 billion impressions worldwide. According to the software giant, Vista satisfies global needs of its target customers: "They have lots of information on their PCs, they are always on the go, and they need tools which allow them to make decisions quickly."[34]

***Creative Talent.*** Creative talent among ad agencies is a scarce supply. It is not uncommon that the most talented people within the agency are assigned to big accounts, leaving small accounts with junior executives. The talent issue matters especially in countries that are plagued with a shortage of highly skilled advertising staff. By running a global campaign, small markets can benefit of having the same high-quality, creative ads as larger ones have.

***Cross-Fertilization.*** More and more companies try to take advantage of their global scope by fostering cross-fertilization. In the domain of advertising, cross-fertilization means that marketers encourage their affiliates to adopt, or at least consider, advertising ideas that have proven successful in other markets. This process of exploiting "good" ideas does not even need to be restricted to global brands. Nestlé used the idea of a serialized "soap-mercial" that it was running for the Nescafé brand in the United Kingdom for its Tasters Choice coffee brand in the United States. The campaigns, chronicling a relationship between two neighbors that centers on coffee, were phenomenally successful in both markets. Likewise, a recent Johnnie Walker campaign ("Pact") developed in China was adapted for the rest of the Asia-Pacific region. The campaign involved a five-part series of spots, shown on television and a

---

[31]Mark Boersma, Blistex, Personal Communication.
[32]"Rebuilding in a crumbling sector," *Marketing*, February 18, 1993, pp. 28–29.
[33]"A universal message," *The Financial Times*, May 27, 1993.
[34]"Vista Unveils Global Blitz," *Media*, February 9, 2007, p. 5.

designated website, and targeted 25- to 35-year-old males. Its storyline centered on a young architect who pursues his dream to become a film director with the support of his close friends. The use of the "Pact" campaign in other Asian countries was driven by the insight that the themes of personal fulfillment and goal achievement through friendship also resonate in those countries.[35] Coming up with a good idea is typically very time consuming. Once the marketer has hit on a creative idea, it makes common sense to try to leverage it by considering how it can be transplanted to other countries.[36]

In addition to these motivations, there are other considerations that might justify standardized multinational advertising. A survey conducted among ad agency executives found that the single brand image factor was singled out as the most important driver for standardizing multinational advertising. Two other critical factors are time pressure and corporate organizational setup.[37] Obviously, developing a single campaign is less time-consuming than creating several ones. The firm's organizational setup also plays a major role, in particular the locus of control. In general, if the multinational's control is highly centralized, it is extremely likely that theme-development is largely standardized. Advertising is usually very localized in decentralized organizations. Also, for many small companies, local advertising is typically the responsibility of local distributors or franchisees. The shift toward regional organizational structures is definitely one of the major drivers behind the growing popularity of regional campaigns.

Faced with the arguments listed above for standardization, advocates of adaptation can easily bring forward an equally compelling list to build up the case for adaptation. The four major barriers to standardization relate to: (1) cultural differences, (2) advertising regulations, (3) differences in the degree of market development, and (4) the "Not Invented Here" (NIH) syndrome.

## Barriers to Standardization

***Cultural Differences.***   Contrary to the "global village" (or "flat world") cliché, cultural differences still persist for many product categories. Cultural gaps between countries may exist in terms of lifestyles, benefits sought, usage contexts, and so forth. A case in point is the use of references to sex in ad campaigns. While references to sex are not unusual in many Western ads, sex is rarely used in Asia to promote products, due to both regulations and market acceptance. The U.S. version of an ad for personal care brand Herbal Essences, full of sexual innuendo, was also used in Australia. However, the ad was re-shot for Thailand, showing girls having a fun time rather than an erotic experience. Unless it is done in a funny manner, sex is not used in Thai advertising for it runs counter to Buddhist values and Thai culture.[38]

Cultural gaps may even prevail for goods that cater toward global segments. A case in point involves luxury goods that target global elites. The user benefits of cognac are by and large the same worldwide. The usage context, however, varies a lot: in the United States cognac is consumed as a stand-alone drink; in Europe, often as an after-dinner drink; and in China it is consumed with a glass of water during dinner. As a result, Hennessy cognac adapts its appeals according to local customs while promoting the same brand image.[39]

***Advertising Regulations.***   Local advertising regulations pose another barrier for standardization. Regulations usually affect the execution of the commercial. Countries like Malaysia and Indonesia impose restrictions on foreign made ads to protect their local advertising industries. As a result, Ray-Ban had to adapt a pan-Asian campaign in

---

[35]"Whisky Label Makes Pact," *Media*, March 6, 2008, p. 6. See http://www.youtube.com/watch?v=Vd0mCjsbrgM for a sample spot of the series.

[36]T. Duncan and J. Ramaprasad, "Standardizing Multinational Advertising: The Influencing Factors," *Journal of Advertising*, vol. 24, no. 3, Fall 1995, pp. 55–68.

[37]Ibid.

[38]"Pushing the Sex Envelope," *Media* (September 20, 2002), pp. 16–17.

[39]"Cachet and Carry," *Advertising Age International*, February 12, 1996, p. I–18.

Malaysia by re-shooting the commercials with local talent.[40] Later in this chapter, we cover the regulations hurdle in more detail.

***Market Maturity.*** Differences in the degree of market maturity also hamper a standardized strategy. Gaps in cross-market maturity levels mandate different advertising approaches. When Snapple, the U.S.-based "New Age" beverage, first entered the European market, the biggest challenge was to overcome initial skepticism among consumers about the concept of "iced tea." Typically, in markets that were entered very recently, one of the main objectives is to create brand awareness. As brand awareness builds up, other advertising goals gain prominence. Products that are relatively new to the entered market also demand education of the customers on what benefits the product or service can deliver and how to use it.

***"Not-Invented-Here" (NIH) Syndrome.*** Finally, efforts to implement a standardized campaign often also need to cope with the NIH-syndrome. Local subsidiaries and/or local advertising agencies could block attempts at standardization. Local offices generally have a hard time accepting creative materials from other countries. Later on in this chapter we will suggest some guidelines that can be used to overcome NIH attitudes.

## Approaches to Creating Advertising Copy

Marketers adopt several approaches to create multinational ads. At one extreme, the entire process may be left to the local subsidiary or distributor, with only a minimum of guidance from headquarters. At the other extreme, global or regional headquarters makes all the decisions, including all the nitty-gritty surrounding the development of ad campaigns. The direction the MNC takes depends on the locus of control and corporate headquarters' familiarity with the foreign market. MNCs that fail to adopt a learning orientation about their foreign markets risk being challenged by the local subsidiaries when they attempt to impose a standardized campaign.[41] In any event, most MNCs adopt an approach that falls somewhere in between a purely standardized and purely localized campaign. McDonald's China, for instance, ran an ad campaign to promote beef that mimicked a famous U.S. TV commercial that featured basketball legends Michael Jordan and Larry Bird. The Chinese version showed a duo of Chinese basketball stars, Yi Jian and Zhu Fang Yu, engaged in a friendly competition. Although the commercials were very similar, local celebrities were used for the Chinese version. Let us look at the main approaches for developing and executing global concepts.

***"Laissez-Faire."*** With the "laissez-faire" approach, every country subsidiary simply follows its own course developing its own ads based on what the local affiliate thinks works best in its market. There is no centralized decision-making.

***Export Advertising.*** With **export advertising**, the creative strategy is produced in-house or by a centrally located ad agency and then "exported" without inputs from the foreign markets. Usually the ad agency is based in the advertiser's home country. A universal copy is developed for all markets. The same positioning theme is used worldwide. Visuals and most other aspects of the execution are also the same. Minor allowances are made for local sensitivities, but by and large the same copy is used in each of the company's markets. Obviously, export advertising delivers all the benefits of standardized campaigns: (1) the same brand image and identity worldwide, (2) no confusion among customers, (3) substantial savings, and (4) strict control over the planning and execution of the global communication strategy.[42] On the creative front, a centralized message demands a universal positioning theme that travels worldwide. The Visa "More

---

[40]"Ray-Ban ogles 16–25 group in Southeast Asia blitz," *Advertising Age International*. June 1996, p. 1–30.
[41]Michel Laroche, V. H. Kirpalani, Frank Pons, and Lianxi Zhou, "A Model of Advertising Standardization in Multinational Corporations," *Journal of International Business Studies*, 32 (2) (Second Quarter 2001), pp. 249–66.
[42]M. G. Harvey, "Point of view: A model to determine standardization of the advertising process in international markets," *Journal of Advertising Research*, July/August 1993, pp. 57–64.

**EXHIBIT 13-6**
EXAMPLES OF UNIVERSAL APPEALS

- *Superior quality.* Clearly, the promise of superior quality is a theme that makes any customer tick. A classic example here is the "Ultimate Driving Machine" slogan that BMW uses in many of its markets.

- *New product/service.* A global rollout of a new product or service is often coupled with a global campaign announcing the launch. A recent example is the marketing hype surrounding the launch of Windows Vista by Microsoft.

- *Country of origin ("made in").* Brands in a product category with a strong country stereotype often leverage their roots by touting the "Made In" cachet. This positioning strategy is especially popular among fashion and luxury goods marketers.

- *Heroes and celebrities.* Tying the brand with heroes or celebrities is another popular universal theme. A recurring issue on this front is whether advertisers should use "local" or "global" heroes. When sports heroes are used, most advertisers will select local, or at least regional, celebrities. With movie personalities the approach usually differs. The Swiss watchmaker SMH International promoted its Omega brand with a TV commercial featuring the actor Pierce Brosnan after the release of the James Bond movie "GoldenEye."

- *Lifestyle.* The mystique of many global upscale brands is often promoted by lifestyle ads that reflect a lifestyle shared by target customers, regardless of where they live. The execution of the ad may need to be customized for the different markets. A celebrated example is Johnnie Walker's award winning "Keep Walking" campaign that centers on the concept of 'progress.'

- *Global Presence.* Many marketers try to enhance the image of their brands via a "global presence" approach—telling the target audience that their product is sold across the globe. Obviously, such a positioning approach can be adopted anywhere. The "global scope" pitch is often used by companies that sell their products or services to customers for whom this attribute is crucial, though the concept is used by other types of advertisers as well. Warner-Lambert created commercials for its Chiclets chewing gum brand that tried to project the cross-cultural appeal of the brand. One spot showed a young man in a desert shack rattling a Chiclets box. The sound of Chiclets triggers the arrival of a cosmopolitan group of eager customers.

- *Market Leadership.* Regardless of the country, being the leading brand worldwide or within the region is a powerful message to most consumers. For products that possess a strong country image, a brand can send a strong signal by making the claim that it is the most preferred brand in its home country or even around the world.

- *Corporate Image.* Finally, corporate communication ads that aspire to foster a certain corporate image also often lend themselves to a uniform approach.

People Go with Visa" 2009 global ad campaign, for instance, taps in the global need for security and safety. **Exhibit 13-6** offers some other examples of universal appeals. Export advertising is very common for corporate ad campaigns that aim to create awareness, to reposition the company, or reinforce an existing company image. It is also very popular when the country-of-origin is an important part of the brand image.

***Prototype Standardization.***   With **prototype standardization**, advertising instructions are given to the local affiliates concerning the execution of the advertising. These guidelines are conveyed via the company's website, manuals or multimedia materials (e.g., DVD, CD-ROM). Mercedes uses a handbook to communicate its advertising guidelines to the local subsidiaries and sales agents. Instructions are given on the format, visual treatment, print to be employed for headlines, and so on.[43] Likewise, the Swiss watchmaker TAG Heuer has a series of guidebooks covering all the nuts and bolts of their communication approach, including rules on business card design.[44] Wrigley, the Chicago-based candy maker, produced a video for its international advertising program. The video offers guidelines on ad execution, including minutiae such as: how the talent should put the gum in his or her mouth, the background of the closing shot, tips on the handling of the gum before the shooting of the commercial, and so forth. It

---

[43]Rijkens.
[44]"TAG Heuer: all time greats?" pp. 45–48.

shows examples of clips that follow and do not follow the guidelines. The video also tells under what circumstances deviations from the norms are acceptable.

***Regional Approach.*** According to the regional approach, every region produces its own interpretation and execution of the campaign. In that sense, this approach is a compromise between centralized decision-making and "laissez-faire." One company that adopted the regional approach is Nokia.[45] Strategic decision-making for the Nokia brand is done centrally by a "brand forum." Regional affiliates decide on the execution of marketing communications.

***Concept Cooperation.*** With **concept cooperation** headquarters spells out guidelines on the positioning theme (platform) and the brand identity to be used in the ads. Worldwide brand values are mapped out centrally. Responsibility for the execution, however, is left to the local markets. That way, brand consistency is sustained without sacrificing the relevance of the ad campaign to local consumers. Similar to the prototype standardization approach, instructions on proper positioning themes and concepts are shared with the local agencies and affiliates through manuals, videotapes, or other communication tools. Nestlé's classic "Have a break, have a KitKat" campaign is a good illustration of this approach. Originally, the slogan referred to the institutionalized British tea break at 11 a.m. This notion did not apply to consumers in other countries where the "Have a break" concept was extended. Instead, different interpretations of the break concept were developed in the various countries where the campaign was run. One approach that companies and ad agencies increasingly use to strike the balance between thinking global and acting local is the **modular approach**. With this approach, the in-house advertising team or the ad agency develops several variations of the campaign around the same theme. A global Intel campaign that aired in 2005 showed combinations of six celebrities[46] sitting on the laps of ordinary laptop-computer users. Country affiliates could choose which celebrities to use for their campaigns.

---

◆ ◆ ◆ ◆ ◆ ◆ ◆ ◆  **GLOBAL MEDIA DECISIONS**

Another task that international marketers need to confront is the choice of the media in each of the country where the company is doing business. In some countries, media decisions are much more critical than the creative aspects of the communication campaign. In Japan, for instance, media buying is crucial in view of the scarce supply of advertising space. Given the choice between an ad agency that possesses good creative skills and one that has enormous media-buying clout, most advertisers in Japan would pick the latter.[47]

International media planners have to surmount a wide range of issues. The media landscape varies dramatically across countries or even between regions within a country. Differences in the media infrastructure exist in terms of media availability, accessibility, media costs, and media habits.

**Media Infrastructure**    Most developed countries offer an incredible abundance of media choices. New media channels emerge continuously. Given this embarrassment of riches, the marketer's task is to decide how to allocate the company's promotional dollars to get the biggest bang for the buck. In other countries, though, the range of media channels is extremely limited. Many of the media vehicles that exist in the marketer's home country (e.g., broadband, digital TV) are simply not available in the foreign market. Government controls can

---

[45]"Fight to the Finnish," *Ad Age Global* (June 2002): 13–15.

[46]The six celebrities were actors Tony Leung, John Cleese, and Lucy Liu, skateboarder Tony Hawk, soccer star Michael Owen, and singer Seal

[47]"The enigma of Japanese advertising," *The Economist*, August 14, 1993, pp. 59–60.

# $\mathcal{G}$LOBAL PERSPECTIVE 13-3

## SMS ADVERTISING IS HOT

Short messaging service (SMS) lets mobile phone subscribers send text messages quickly and cheaply. According to one survey, SMS ranked as the most highly used mobile phone feature among many Asian consumers. The rise of SMS, especially among tech-savvy youth, has turned it into a communication channel that marketers cannot ignore. The most successful uses of SMS marketing is for digital coupons and event-based messages. The latter often involve other media.

SMS has several appeals for marketers. First, costs can be fairly low. The costs of a campaign range from a few cents to 50 cents per customer, depending on a wide range of factors, such as whether an ad agency was involved, third-party costs (e.g., telecom carriers), the cost of the software being used, the complexity of the campaign. SMS enables personalized, one-on-one marketing. As such, SMS is an excellent vehicle to communicate brand values. Response to SMS campaigns can also be very easily tracked. There are a few obstacles though. One major hurdle is often the telecom carrier. Carriers can be reluctant to give away phone numbers, even though they often stand to benefit from such campaigns with the revenues being generated each time consumers respond. In countries like the Philippines where prepaid phone cards are prominent, mobile phone users are hard to profile, and hence, difficult to target. SMS is often also simply treated as another mass medium,

instead of a personalized one. As a result, SMS promotions often create backlash when the receivers of the messages view them as *spam*. Hence, SMS campaigns should allow the prospect to opt in (or opt out) to be more effective.

Still, in spite of these obstacles, several companies have been very creative and successful in using SMS as an advertising medium. In summer 2007, PepsiCo ran the very creative "1-in-5 Panalo" SMS campaign in the Philippines. During the two-months campaign, participants could win various prizes (e.g., ring tones, handsets) by sending in an SMS code found on the bottom of Pepsi bottle caps. Pepsi received over 15,000 messages per day and sales increased over 58 percent.

Mobile marketing is also on the rise in India. The most common approach is SMS contests in which consumers are invited to participate in contests through traditional media and to respond using SMS. Kellogg's India extended an advertising campaign for Kellogg's Corn Flakes (KCF) with an SMS campaign. The goal of the campaign was to drive home the benefits of "Iron Shakti," the main ingredient of corn flakes. The campaign used a contest that targeted adults 25 and up. Participants had to answer questions based around KCF's product features and send in their answers through SMS.

The next advance will be the jump from SMS to MMS—multimedia messaging services. The advent of MMS adds a whole new layer by allowing advertisers to incorporate audio and video images with traditional text messages. Advertisers in India like Cadbury have been experimenting with so-called *mobisodes*—30-second video clips that can be downloaded on mobile phones.

*Source:* "Text Messaging Ads on Fast Track in Asia," *Advertising Age* (December 2, 2002), p. 12; "U.S. Lags Behind," *Advertising Age* (December 2, 2002), p. 12; "Kellogg's Adopts SMS for Corn Flakes Boost," *Media* (February 13, 2004): 14; "Engaging the Mobile Consumer," *Media*, April 17, p. 28.

---

heavily restrict the access to mass media options such as television in a host of countries. In Germany, for instance, TV advertising is only allowed during limited time frames of the day.

The media infrastructure can differ dramatically from country to country, even within the same region. Whereas TV viewers in the West can surf an abundance of twenty-five TV channels, their Asian counterparts have access, on the average, to a measly choice of two to three channels. The standard media vehicles such as radio, cinema, and TV are well established in most countries. New media, such as cable, the internet, mobile phones, satellite TV, and pay-TV, are steadily growing (see **Global Perspective 13-3** for a discussion of SMS advertising). Given the media diversity, advertisers are forced to adapt their media schedule to the parameters set by the local environment.

One of the major limitations in many markets is media availability. The lack of standard media options challenges marketers to use their imagination by coming up with "creative" options. Intel, the U.S. computer chip maker, built up brand awareness in China by distributing bike reflectors in Shanghai and Beijing with the words "Intel Inside Pentium Processor." Advertisers in Bangkok have taken advantage of the city's

**Media Limitations**

**EXHIBIT 13-7**
AVERAGE COST OF A PRIME-TIME 30 SECOND TV SPOT (2007)

| Country | Cost of a prime-time ad (in U.S. dollars) | Per capita income (2008E)* |
|---|---|---|
| China | $23,233 | $6,100 |
| Hong Kong | 33,555 | 45,300 |
| India | 10,096 | 2,900 |
| Indonesia | 3,226 | 3,900 |
| Japan | 21,693 | 35,300 |
| Malaysia | 2,436 | 15,700 |
| Philippines | 4,548 | 3,400 |
| Singapore | 4,739 | 52,900 |
| Thailand | 5,970 | 8,700 |
| Vietnam | 2,364 | 2,900 |

*Note: Per capita GDP is in purchasing power parity (PPP) terms

Sources: MindShare and https://www.cia.gov/library/publications/the-world-factbook/geos/vm.html, accessed on March 4, 2009.

notorious traffic jams by using media strategies that reach commuters. Some of the selected media vehicles include outdoor advertising, traffic report radio stations, and three-wheeled taxis (*tuk-tuks*).[48]

Marketers must also consider media costs. For all types of reasons, media costs differ enormously between countries. **Exhibit 13-7** shows the costs of a prime-time 30-second TV spot in several Asian countries. In general, high costs-per-thousand (CPMs)[49] are found in areas that have a high per capita GNP. Other factors that influence the local media cost include the amount of media competition (e.g., the number of TV stations) and the quality of the media effectiveness measurement systems in place. Advertising rates for free-to-air satellite TV channels in the Arab world are relatively low due to the rapid proliferation of TV stations and the lack of a good television rating system.[50]

A major obstacle in many emerging markets is the overall quality of the local media. Take China, for instance. For many print media, no reliable statistics are available on circulation figures or readership profiles. Print quality of many newspapers and magazines is appalling. Newspapers may demand full payment in advance when the order is booked and ask for additional money later on. There are no guarantees that newspapers will run your ad or TV broadcasters will show your spot on the agreed date. The rise of new technologies, however, is rapidly improving media monitoring in many countries.

**Recent Trends in the Global Media Landscape**

In the last two decades the global media environment has changed dramatically. Below we pinpoint some of the major trends:

- *Growth of commercialization and deregulation of mass media.* One undeniable change in scores of countries is the growing commercialization of the mass media, especially the broadcast media. In Belgium, for example, commercial TV was basically non-existent. Advertisers who wanted to air a commercial to promote their goods either had to rely on cinema as a substitute for TV or TV channels from neighboring countries (the Netherlands, Germany, France, and Luxembourg). Following the launch of several commercial TV and radio stations, the media environment is entirely different now. Similar trends toward commercialization and deregulation of the media can be observed in many other countries. Note that

---

[48]"Bangkok is bumper to bumper with ads," *Advertising Age International*, February 20, 1996, p. I–4.

[49]CPM is the cost per thousand viewers of a particular ad.

[50]Morris Kalliny, Grace Dagher, Michael S. Minor, and Gilberto De Los Santos, "Television Advertising in the Arab World: A Status Report," *Journal of Advertising Research*, June 2008, pp. 215–23.

this trend is not universal: From January 2009, primetime advertising was banned on all public-broadcasting channels in France.[51]

- *Rise of global and regional media.* One of the most eye-catching developments in the media world has been the proliferation of global and regional media. Several factors explain the appeal of global media to international advertisers. By using such media, advertisers can target customers who would otherwise be hard to reach. International media also facilitate the launch of global or pan-regional ad campaigns. Another major asset is that most international media have well-defined background information on their audience reach and profile. The major barrier to advertising on global media has been the cultural issue. Many satellite TV broadcasters, for instance, initially planned to broadcast the same ads and programs globally. Because of that, viewership for many satellite channels was extremely low. As a result, very few advertisers were interested in airing spots on these channels. Lately, however, more and more satellite networks such as Star TV, ESPN, and MTV have started to customize the content of their programs by adding voice-overs, subtitles or even local content to their offerings. A push toward localization also exists among many publishing houses of international magazine titles. In Japanese kiosks, magazine racks offer Japanese editions of titles such as *GQ*, *National Geographic*, and *Cosmopolitan*.

- *Growth of non-traditional (NT) interactive media.* One remarkable trend is the growing popularity of non-traditional (NT) interactive media among international advertisers. By coming up with innovative approaches, marketers hope to be able to break through the advertising clutter associated with traditional media and grab the target customer's attention. Interactive media also enable the advertiser to customize the message to the target audience. Obviously, the most visible form is the internet (see Chapter 19). Many other forms of NT marketing tools exist, however. To promote the Xbox videogame player in Europe, Microsoft gave away 2 million DVDs with an interactive commercial.[52] At various points, viewers could click on text or icons to get information about the Xbox or upcoming videogame releases. Targeting the 16- to 34-year-old males, the DVDs were distributed by adding them to videogame magazines and holiday catalogs. Global Perspective 13-3 describes how firms leverage text messaging to come up with creative communication campaigns.

- *Improved media monitoring.* To plan a communication campaign, access to high-quality coverage, circulation or viewership data on the media vehicles to be considered is an absolute must. Moreover, companies would also like to be able to track how much, when, and in what media their competitors advertise. In many countries, marketers were plagued with a lack of solid, reliable monitoring systems. Fortunately, the situation is improving rapidly. The advent of new technologies has led to monitoring devices that allow far more precise data collection than in the past, even for very traditional media such as outdoor. To track reach, frequency, and ratings data along with demographics, Nielsen Outdoor launched a new device called Npod (http://www.nielsen.com/solutions/nielsenoutdoor.html).[53] The new monitoring system was first launched in Chicago and then in South Africa and China. Consumers in the sample group are asked to carry the device, the size of a mobile phone, for a set period of time. Through the GPS satellite network, the system allows for time and date stamping of consumers, as well as their direction and speed of travel.[54] Strides have also been made in the area of TV ratings data that measure the viewership for TV programs. TNT and AGB Nielsen Media Research, two of the major players in this area, now run ratings panels in scores of countries, including China and India. Although in some countries like Vietnam data Nielsen relies on panel members filling out diaries about their daily TV viewing behavior, in numerous countries the firm

---

[51]"France Bans Advertising on State TV during Primetime, www.guardian.co.uk, accessed on March 5, 2009.

[52]"Microsoft, Others Target Teenagers Via Interactive DVDs," *Asian Wall Street Journal*, December 30, 2002, p. A5.

[53]Nielsen Personal Outdoor Device.

[54]"China Pilots OOH System," *Media*, October 20, 2006, p. 15.

now collects the data through state-of-the-art peoplemeters that are hooked up to the panel member's television set. India is home now to one of the biggest TV panels in the world with 30,000 panel members.[55]

## ♦ ♦ ♦ ♦ ♦ ♦ ♦ ♦   ADVERTISING REGULATIONS

A Toyota ad that featured Hollywood actor Brad Pitt as celebrity endorser was banned by the Malaysian government. According to Malaysia's then Deputy Information minister: "Western faces in advertisements could create an inferiority complex among Asians . . . [The advertisement] was a humiliation against Asians . . . Why do we need to use [Western] faces in our advertisements? Are our own people not handsome?"[56] **Exhibit 13-8** lists some of the other strict rules and regulations that advertisers should

### EXHIBIT 13-8
MALAYSIA'S ADVERTISING CODE OF ETHICS (*KOD ETHIKA PENGIKLANAN*)—EXTRACTS:

**Rules and regulations**

- Advertisements must not project and promote an excessively aspirational lifestyle.
- Adaptation or projection of foreign culture that is not acceptable to a cross-section of the major communities of the Malaysian society either in the form of words, slogans, clothing, activity, or behavior is not allowed.
- The use of man or woman as principal agent by highlighting characteristics that appeal to the opposite sex as the main ingredient in the selling of products should not be allowed.
- The body of the female model should be covered until the neckline, which should not be too low. The length of a skirt worn should be below the knees. Arms may be exposed up to the edge of the shoulder but armpits cannot be exposed. Costumes, although complying with the above, must not be too revealing or suggestive. Women in swimming costumes or shorts and men in swimming trunks or shorts will only be allowed in scenes involving organized sporting or outdoor activities provided that they are generally decently dressed on groups and only in long shots. A "long shot" is technically described as a shot with full frame.
- Scenes involving models (including silhouettes) undressing or acts that could bring undesirable thoughts will not be allowed.
- Strong emphasis on the specialty of the country of origin of an imported product is not allowed. Any reference should only state the name of the foreign country. Words should not be used to suggest superior quality or promise a greater benefit.
- All scenes of shots must be done in Malaysia. If foreign footage is deemed necessary, only 20 percent of the total commercial footage is allowed and prior approval from this Ministry must be obtained. However, foreign footage for advertisements on tourism to ASEAN* countries can be approved up to 100 percent.
- Musicals and other sounds must be done in Malaysia.
- Promos of foreign programs/events that are not telecast in this country are not allowed.
- All advertisements on food and drinks must show the necessity of a balanced diet.

**Unacceptable products, services, and scenes:**

- Liquor and alcoholic beverages.
- Blue denims—jeans made from other material can be advertised provided the jeans are clean and neat.
- Promotions of any contest, except in sponsored programs.
- Application of a product to certain parts of the body such as armpits.
- Clothes with imprinted words or symbols that could convey undesired messages or impressions.
- Scenes of amorous, intimate or suggestive nature.
- Disco scenes.
- Feminine napkins.
- The use of the word 1 (one) either in numeric or in words.
- Kissing between adults.

*Source:* "The Malaysian Advertising Code of Ethics for TV and Radio," http://www.asianmarketresearch.com, accessed on May 16, 2002.

---

[55]"Millions are Watching, We Think," *Media*, August 10, 2007, p. 11.

[56]"Malaysia Bans Toyota Ad," http://www.asiamarketresearch.com, accessed December 20, 2002.

comply with in Malaysia. While some of the rules make sense given Malaysia's Muslim background, others border on absurdity. No wonder that Malaysian TV commercials have a hard time winning awards in international advertising contests.

A major roadblock that global advertisers face is the bewildering set of advertising regulations advertisers need to cope with in foreign markets. **Advertising regulations** are the rules and laws that limit the way products can be advertised. Regulators are usually government agencies (e.g., the Federal Trade Commission in the United States). In many countries, however, the local advertising industry may also be governed by some form of self-regulation. Self-regulation can take various forms.[57] One possibility is that local advertisers, advertising agencies, and broadcast media jointly agree on a set of rules. Although such bodies typically cannot enforce their rules, they can sanction offenders through soft power tools. For instance, the Advertising Standards Authority (ASA) in Great Britain blacklists each week violating ads on its website (http://www.asa.org.uk/asa/adjudications/public/). Several reasons lie behind self-regulation of the advertising industry, including protection of consumers against misleading or offensive advertising, protection of legitimate advertisers against false claims, or accusations made by competitors. Another forceful reason to set up self-regulatory bodies is to prevent more stringent government-imposed regulation or control of the advertising industry. This section summarizes the major types of advertising regulations.

### *Advertising of "Vice Products" and Pharmaceuticals.*

Tough restrictions, if not outright bans, apply to the advertising of pharmaceuticals and so-called *vice* products in many countries. Japan, for example, prohibits the use of the word "safe" or "safety" or any derivatives when promoting over-the-counter drugs (e.g., pain relievers, cold medicines).[58] Despite opposition of advertising agencies, advertisers and media channels, rules on the advertising of tobacco and liquor products are becoming increasingly more severe. For instance, in 2006 the Thai government banned all alcohol advertising and sales promotions.

### *Comparative Advertising.*

Another area of contention is comparative advertising, where advertisers disparage the competing brand. While such advertising practices are commonplace in the United States, other countries heavily constrain or even prohibit comparative advertising. In China, for instance, advertisers are not allowed to compare their products with their competitors' or to include superlative terms such as "best." Anheuser-Busch, however, was able to air a commercial with Budweiser's slogan that it was "America's favorite beer" after it supported the claim with statistical evidence.[59] In Japan, comparative advertising—though not illegal—is a cultural taboo. It is seen as immodest and underhanded. Often the Japanese side with the competitor![60]

### *Foreign Made Ads.*

Several countries also protect their local advertising production industry and acting talent by clamping down on foreign-made ads. For example, Malaysia requires that 80 percent of an ad's production cost should be spent in that country. There are exceptions though for campaigns that incorporate global icons (e.g., the cowboy used in Marlboro advertising). One problem is that the local talent can be scarce and, as a result, the quality of the locally produced commercials may suffer.[61]

### *Content of Advertising Messages.*

The content of advertising messages could be subject to certain rules or guidelines. In Australia, Toyota was forced to withdraw a series of spots advertising the Celica model because of their content. One of the spots was a "Jaws" spoof in which shark-like Celicas speed down a jetty. The ad violated the

[57]Marieke de Mooij, *Advertising Worldwide,* 2nd Edition, New York: Prentice Hall, 1994.

[58]John Mackay, McCann-Erickson Japan, private communication.

[59]"China's Rules Make a Hard Sell," *International Herald Tribune* (August 18, 2000), p. 13.

[60]John Mackay, McCann Erickson Japan, private communication.

[61]"Anti-foreign Ad Laws Bite," *Media,* May 18, 2007, p. 5.

Advertising Standards Council's guidelines on "dangerous behavior or illegal or unsafe road usage practices."[62] A Volkswagen commercial in Sweden that showed a VW car being driven over lots of food was banned for portraying wasteful behavior.[63]

Ads may also be banned or taken off the air because they are offensive or indecent. A campaign for Unilever's Axe deodorant brand was suspended by the Indian government because of the commercial's steamy nature. The ad showed a man morph into a walking chocolate figure after spraying himself with Axe's Dark Temptation deodorant. Women throw themselves at him, licking and biting parts of his body.[64] Many countries also have regulations against sexist advertising or ads with exaggerated ("puffery") claims.

Ad campaigns in China are also very vulnerable to censorship due to cultural or political insensitivities. A recent example of a banned commercial was an ad for Unilever's skincare brand Pond's. Even though the ad had complied with China's censorship regulations, it was taken off the air because it starred Tang Wei, a leading actress. Tang Wei was blacklisted by Sarft,[65] the agency that supervises China's TV and radio channels, for her role in the controversial movie *Lust, Caution*, in which she displayed full frontal nudity.[66] In general, China forbids ads showing environmental degradation, bad behavior, pornography, violence, gambling, and superstition. Advertising content is not allowed to use national symbols (e.g., flag, national leader's images and voice, national anthem), to disrespect religion and traditional culture, or to denigrate women and disabled people.[67]

***Advertising Targeting Children.*** Another area that tends to be heavily regulated is advertising targeted to children. Korea and Malaysia, for example, bans fast food TV ads targeted toward children, blaming such ads for rising obesity levels among youngsters.[68] In Europe, rules to curb advertising to children are widespread. Greece bans all TV advertising of toys between 7 a.m. and 10 p.m.[69] In Finland, children cannot speak or sing the name of a product in commercials. In Turkey, children are only allowed to watch TV ads with "parental guidance." Italy bans commercials in cartoon programs that target children. China poses a series of rules that advertisers to children need to respect. Contrary to regulations in Western countries, most of the standards center on cultural values: respect for elders and discipline. For instance, one of the rules bans ads that "show acts that children should not be doing alone."[70]

Although many ad regulations often sound annoying or frivolous, having a clear set of advertising rules and restrictions is a boon for consumers and advertisers alike. If no rules govern the advertising environment, the law of the jungle applies. In China, most of the advertising malpractice cases in the past involved ads for drugs, medical services, and food. It was not unusual to have some soaps claim to help people lose weight and some tonics promise to make users smarter.[71]

How should marketers cope with advertising regulations? There are a couple of possible actions:

1. *Keep track of regulations and pending legislation.* Monitoring legislation and gathering intelligence on possible changes in advertising regulations are crucial. Bear in mind that advertising regulations change continuously. In many countries the prevailing mood is in favor of liberalization with the important exception of tobacco and alcohol advertising. European Union member states are also trying to bring their

---

[62]"ASC slams brakes on Australian Toyota ads," *Advertising Age International*, May 16, 1994, p. I–6.

[63]http://www.youtube.com/watch?v=xu0hgrKZ66Q

[64]"As the Ads Heat Up, India Tries to Keep Cool," *The Wall Street Journal Asia*, September 10, 2008, p. 27.

[65]State Administration for Radio, Film, and Television.

[66]"Director Lee Defends Actor Banned from Chinese Media," http://www.guardian.co.uk/film/2008/mar/11/news.

[67]"China's Regulation Minefield," *Media*, February 23, 2007, p. 11.

[68]"Malaysia Bans Fast Food Ads Targeted At Children," *Media*, May 4, 2007, p. 2.

[69]"Kid Gloves," *The Economist* (January 6, 2001), p. 53.

[70]Louisa Ha, "Concerns about advertising practices in a developing country: An examination of China's new advertising regulations," *International Journal of Advertising*, 15, 1996, pp. 91–102.

[71]"China's Rules Make a Hard Sell."

rules in line with EU regulations. Many ad agencies have in-house legal counsels to assist them in handling pending advertising legislation.

2. *Screen the campaign early on.* Given the huge budgets at stake, it is important to get feedback and screen advertisements as early as possible to avoid costly mistakes. In China, TV commercials must be submitted to each regional office of the State Administration for Industry and Commerce prior to airing. To be on the safe side, many companies submit their storyboards and script before producing the commercial. Sometimes, however, CCTV, China's main TV channel, wants to see the finished ad first before granting approval.

3. *Lobbying activities.* A more drastic action is to lobby local governments or international legislative bodies such as the European Parliament. Lobbying activities are usually sponsored jointly by advertisers, advertising agencies, and the media. China's national broadcaster relaxed a ban on advertising containing pig images during the 2009 Chinese New Year after a great deal of pressure from ad agencies and their clients.[72] As usual, too much lobbying carries the risk of generating bad publicity, especially when the issues at hand are highly controversial.

4. *Challenge regulations in court..* Advertisers can consider fighting advertising legislation in court. In Chile, outdoor board companies, advertisers and sign painters filed suit in civil court when the Chilean government issued new regulations that required outdoor boards to be placed several blocks from the road.[73] In European Union member states, advertisers have sometimes been able to overturn local laws by appealing to the European Commission or the European Court of Justice. For instance, a host of retailers (including Amazon.com), ad agencies, and media in France filed a complaint with the European Commission in an attempt to overturn a 40-year old French law that bans TV advertising by retailers. They argued that the law runs counter to EU rules.[74]

5. *Adapt marketing mix strategy.* Tobacco marketers have been extremely creative in handling advertising regulations. A widely popular mechanism is to use the brand extension path to cope with tobacco ad bans. For instance, the Swedish Tobacco Co., whose brands have captured more than 80 percent of the Swedish cigarette market, started promoting sunglasses and cigarette lighters under the Blend name, its best-selling cigarette brand, to cope with a complete tobacco ad ban in Sweden.[75] In the United Kingdom, Hamlet, the leading cigar brand, shifted to other media vehicles following the ban on all TV tobacco advertising in the United Kingdom in October 1992. Hamlet started using outdoor boards for the first time, installing them at 2,250 sites. It ran a sales promotion campaign at a horse race where losing bettors got a free Hamlet cigar. It also developed a video with about twenty of its celebrated commercials. The video was made available for purchase or rent.[76] South Korea is the only country where Virginia Slims is pitched as the successful man's cigarette. Why? Because Korean law forbids advertising cigarettes to women and young adults.[77]

## CHOOSING AN ADVERTISING AGENCY    ◆ ◆ ◆ ◆ ◆ ◆ ◆

Although some companies like Benetton, Diesel, Avon, and Hugo Boss develop their advertising campaigns in-house, most firms heavily rely on the expertise of an advertising agency. Over the years, the advertising agency industry has consolidated through mergers and globalized leading to global mega agencies. **Exhibit 13-9** lists the

---

[72]"China's Regulation Minefield," *Media*, February 23, 2007, p. 11.

[73]"Chilean fight for outdoor ads," *Advertising Age International*, April 27, 1992, p. I-8.

[74]"Retailers Fight French Law That Bans Advertising on TV," *Asian Wall Street Journal* (February 22, 2001), p. N7.

[75]"Swedish marketers skirt tobacco ad ban," *Advertising Age International*, June 20, 1994, p. I-2.

[76]"Hamlet shifts to other media since TV spots are banned," *Advertising Age International*, April 27, 1992, p. I-8.

[77]"Real Men May Not Eat Quiche . . . But in Korea They Puff Virginia Slims," *Asian Wall Street Journal*, December 27/28 1996, pp. 1, 7.

**EXHIBIT 13-9**
WORLD'S TOP 10 AD AGENCIES (2007)

| Rank | Agency | Headquarters | Revenue | % of Revenue Outside the U.S. |
|------|--------|--------------|---------|------------------------------|
| 1 | Omnicom Group | New York | $12,694 | 47.2 |
| 2 | WPP Group | London | 12,383 | 63.3 |
| 3 | Interpublic Group | New York | 6,554 | 44.3 |
| 4 | Publicis | Paris | 6,384 | 58.0 |
| 5 | Dentsu | Tokyo | 2,932 | 97.7 |
| 6 | Aegis Group | London | 2,215 | 76.9 |
| 7 | Havas | Suresnes, France | 2,094 | 67.0 |
| 8 | Hakuhodo | Tokyo | 1,392 | 100.0 |
| 9 | MDC | Toronto/New York | 547 | 19.7 |
| 10 | Alliance Data Systems | Dallas | 469 | 6.2 |

*Note:* Revenue figures are in millions of U.S. dollars.

*Source:* Based on figures reported in "World's Top 50 Agency Companies" www.adage.com/datacenter, accessed on February 22, 2009.

top-10 advertising agencies in the world in order of their worldwide revenue. Note that several of the leading ad agencies are located outside the United States. In selecting an agency, the international marketer has several options:

1. Work with the agency that handles the advertising in the firm's home market.
2. Pick a purely local agency in the foreign market.
3. Choose the local office of a large international agency.
4. Select an international network of ad agencies that spans the globe or the region.

When screening ad agencies, the following set of criteria can be used:

• *Market coverage.* Does the agency cover all relevant markets? What is the geographic scope of the agency?

• *Creative talent.* What are the core skills of the agency? Does the level of these skills meet the standards set by the company? Also, is there a match between the agency's core skills and the market requirements? Good creative talent is in short supply in many countries. In most developing markets, expatriates usually take up senior positions at agencies, while locals provide support.

• *Expertise with developing a central international campaign.* When the intent of the marketer is to develop a global or pan-regional advertising campaign, expertise in handling a central campaign becomes essential. One survey suggests, however, the agency's lack of international expertise and coordination ability is still a sore point for many companies.[78]

• *Creative reputation.* The agency's creative reputation is often the most important criterion for many advertisers when choosing an ad agency.

• *Scope and quality of support services.* Most agencies are not just hired for their creative skills and media buying. They are also expected to deliver a range of support services, like marketing research, developing other forms of communication (e.g., sales promotions, public relations, event-sponsorships).

• *Desirable image ("global" versus "local").* The image—global or local—that the company wants to project with its communication efforts also matters a great deal. Companies that aspire to develop a "local" image often assign their account to local ad agencies. One risk though of relying on local agencies is that their creative spark may lead to off-message, provocative advertising. Coke's senior executives were not too amused with an Italian campaign that featured nude bathers on the beach. A Singapore ad made for McDonald's to promote a new Szechuan burger featured a brothel-like "mama-san," not exactly in tune with McDonald's core family values.[79]

---

[78]"Clients and Agencies Split over Ad Superstars," *Ad Age Global* (May 2001), p. 16.

[79]"A Little Local Difficulty," *Ad Age Global* (February 2002), p. 4.

- *Size of the agency.* Generally speaking, large agencies have more power than small agencies. This is especially critical for media buying where a healthy relationship between the media outlet and the ad agency is very critical. On the other hand, the creative side of advertising does not always benefit from scale. Many award-winning ad campaigns have been designed by smaller boutique-like agencies.

- *Conflicting accounts.* Does the agency already work on an account of one of our competitors? The risk of conflicting accounts is a major concern to many advertisers. There are two kinds of risks here. First of all, there is the confidentiality issue: marketers share a lot of proprietary data with their advertising agency. Second, there is also the fear that the ad agency might assign superior creative talent to the competing brand's account, especially when that account is bigger.

Note that sometimes these criteria may conflict with one another. A characteristic of the Japanese agency industry is that the large agencies service competing brands. Hence, companies that approach a big Japanese ad agency like Dentsu or Hakuhodo may need to accept the fact that the agency also handles the accounts of competing brands.

## OTHER MEANS OF COMMUNICATION

◆ ◆ ◆ ◆ ◆ ◆ ◆

For most companies, media advertising is only one part of the communication package. While advertising is the most visible form, the other communication tools play a vital role in a company's global marketing mix strategy. In this section, we discuss the following alternative promotion tools: sales promotions, direct marketing, sponsorships, mobile marketing, trade shows, product placement, and public relations/publicity. Personal selling and internet marketing, both of which can be regarded to some extent as promotion tools, are discussed in later chapters.

*Sales promotions* refer to a collection of short-term incentive tools that lead to quicker and/or larger sales of a particular product by consumers or the trade. There are basically two kinds of promotions: consumer promotions that target end-users (e.g., coupons, sweepstakes, rebates) and trade promotions that are aimed at distributors (e.g., volume discounts, advertising allowances). For the majority of MNCs, the sales promotion policy is a local affair. Several rationales explain the local character of promotions:[80]

**Sales Promotions**

- *Economic development.* Low incomes and poor literacy in developing countries make some promotional techniques unattractive but, at the same time, render other tools more appealing. One study of promotional practices in developing countries found above-average use of samples and price-off packs.[81]

- *Market maturity variation.* For most product categories, there is a great deal of variation in terms of market maturity. In countries where the product is still in an early stage of the product life cycle, trial-inducing tools such as samples, coupons, and cross-promotions are appropriate. In more established markets, one of the prime goals of promotions will be to encourage repeat purchase. Incentives such as bonus packs, in-pack coupons, and trade promotions that stimulate brand loyalty tend to be favored.

- *Cultural perceptions.* Cultural perceptions of promotions differ widely across countries. Some types of promotions (e.g., sweepstakes) may have a very negative image in certain countries. According to one study, Taiwanese consumers have less-favorable attitudes toward sweepstakes than consumers in Thailand or Malaysia. Nor are Taiwanese concerned about losing face when using coupons. Malaysians, on the other

---

[80]K. Kashani and J.A. Quelch, "Can sales promotions go global?" *Business Horizons*, vol. 33, no. 3, May–June 1990, pp. 37–43.
[81]J. S. Hill and U. O. Boya, "Consumer goods promotions in developing countries," *International Journal of Advertising*, vol. 6, 1987, pp. 249–64.

hand, favor sweepstakes over coupons.[82] Shoppers in Europe redeem far fewer coupons than their counterparts in the United States.[83]

• *Trade structure.* One of the major issues companies face is how to allocate their promotional dollars between consumer promotions—which are directly aimed at the end-user ("pull")—and trade promotions ("push")—which target the middlemen. Because of differences in the local trade structure, the balance of power between manufacturers and trade is tilted in favor of the trade in certain countries. When Procter & Gamble attempted to cut back on trade promotions by introducing every-day-low-pricing in Germany, several major German retailers retaliated by de-listing P&G brands.[84] Differences in distributors' inventory space and/or costs also play a role in determining which types of promotions are effective.

• *Government Regulations.* When C&A, a Brussels-based clothing retailer, offered a 20 percent discount to German customers paying with a credit card instead of cash, it was threatened with huge fines by a German court.[85] C&A's scheme was apparently in violation of a 70-year old German law regulating sales and special offers.[86] By the same token, Lands' End, the U.S. mail order retailer, was forced to withdraw a lifetime guarantee offer in Germany. According to Germany's supreme court, the offer violated the 1932 German Free Gift Act and was anti-competitive.[87] Probably the most critical factor in designing a promotional package is local legislation. Certain practices may be heavily restricted or simply forbidden. In Germany, for instance, coupon values cannot be more than 1 percent of the product's value. Vouchers, stamps, and coupons are banned in Norway.[88] **Exhibit 13-10** shows which promotion

### EXHIBIT 13-10
#### WHICH TECHNIQUES ARE ALLOWED IN EUROPE

*Key: Y = permitted X = not permitted ? = may be permitted*

| Promotion Technique | UK | NL | B | SP | IR | IT | F | G | DK |
|---|---|---|---|---|---|---|---|---|---|
| On-park promotions | Y | Y | ? | Y | Y | Y | ? | Y | Y |
| Banded offers | Y | ? | ? | Y | Y | Y | ? | Y | Y |
| In-pack premiums | Y | ? | ? | Y | Y | Y | ? | Y | ? |
| Multipurchase offers | Y | ? | ? | Y | Y | Y | ? | Y | Y |
| Extra product | Y | Y | Y | Y | Y | Y | ? | ? | Y |
| Free product | Y | ? | Y | Y | Y | Y | Y | X | ? |
| Reusable/other use packs | Y | Y | Y | Y | Y | Y | Y | Y | Y |
| Free mail-ins | Y | Y | ? | Y | Y | Y | ? | Y | Y |
| With purchase premiums | Y | ? | Y | Y | Y | Y | ? | ? | ? |
| Cross-product offers | Y | Y | X | Y | Y | Y | ? | Y | Y |
| Collector devices | Y | Y | Y | Y | Y | Y | Y | Y | Y |
| Competitions | Y | ? | ? | Y | Y | ? | Y | Y | ? |
| Self-liquidating premiums | Y | Y | Y | Y | Y | Y | Y | Y | Y |
| Free draws | Y | X | ? | Y | Y | Y | Y | Y | Y |
| Share outs | Y | Y | ? | Y | Y | ? | ? | Y | ? |
| Sweepstake/lottery | ? | X | ? | Y | X | ? | ? | Y | X |
| Money off vouchers | Y | Y | Y | Y | Y | Y | Y | ? | Y |
| Money off next purchase | Y | Y | Y | Y | Y | Y | Y | ? | Y |
| Cash backs | Y | Y | Y | Y | Y | X | Y | X | Y |
| In-store demos | Y | Y | Y | Y | Y | Y | Y | Y | Y |

*Source:* The Institute of Sales Promotion, www.isp.org.uk 2006.

[82]Lenard C. Huff and Dana L. Alden, "An Investigation of Consumer Response to Sales Promotions in Developing Markets: A Three-Country Analysis," *Journal of Advertising Research,* (May–June 1998), pp. 47–56.

[83]"Coupon FSIs dropped," *Advertising Age International,* October 11,1993, p. I–8.

[84]"Heat's on value pricing," *Advertising Age International,* January 1997, pp. I–21, I–22.

[85]The purpose of this somewhat unusual promotion was to cut cash register lines during the euro introduction period.

[86]"Defiant C&A reignites debate on German shopping laws," *Financial Times* (January 9, 2002), p. 2.

[87]"Lands' End to File Brussels Complaint," *Financial Times* (January 11, 2000), p. 2.

[88]"Coupon FSIs dropped."

techniques are allowed in nine European countries. As you can see, Germany appears to be one of the most restrictive environments for promotion campaigns. The United Kingdom, on the other hand, seems to be very liberal.

Kashani and Quelch suggest that multinational companies appoint an international sales promotion coordinator. The manager's agenda would involve tasks such as these:[89]

- Promote transfer of successful promotional ideas across units.
- Transplant ideas on how to constrain harmful trade promotional practices.
- Gather performance data and develop monitoring systems to evaluate the efficiency and effectiveness of promotions.
- Coordinate relations with the company's sales promotion agencies worldwide.

## Direct Marketing

*Direct marketing* includes various forms of interactive marketing where the company uses media that enable it to get direct access to the end-consumer and establish a one-to-one relationship. The most prominent forms of direct marketing are direct mail, telemarketing, door-to-door selling, internet marketing (see Chapter 18), and catalogue selling. In a sense, direct marketing is a hybrid mix of promotion and distribution. For companies such as Avon, Amazon.com, Dell, Mary Kay, and Amway, direct marketing goes even beyond just being a marketing mix instrument: It is basically a business model for them.

Direct marketing is growing very rapidly internationally. Many of the celebrated firms in the area have been able to successfully transplant their direct marketing model to other markets. About one year after Dell entered China, it managed to become one of the leading PC-brands there, despite skepticism that its practice of selling direct would not work in a country where salesmanship centers on connections.[90]

Though still rare, some firms have been able to successfully implement global direct marketing campaigns. A good illustration was a campaign run by Unisys, a U.S.-based information technology company. Its "Customer Connection" program was a million-dollar-plus, multilingual program that combined direct mail and telemarketing worldwide. Every quarter, Unisys sent out direct mail to key decision-makers in 23 countries. The mailing described product and technology offerings in seven languages and came with a personalized letter signed by a Unisys region or country-manager. Native-speaking tele-marketers would then follow up asking if the client manager recalls the mailing, if they had any queries, and if they would like to remain on the mailing list. Follow-up surveys showed that 70 percent of the contacted executives responded positively to the program.[91]

As with other promotion tools, direct marketing might also encounter hurdles in foreign markets. A notorious case was the complete ban on direct selling that the Chinese government imposed in the spring of 1998 due to a series of sales scams and pyramid schemes. Well-established selling companies such as Avon, Amway, and Mary Kay basically had to shut down their operations. As a result, these companies had to rethink their way of doing business in China and focus on retail outlets and sales representatives. Avon, for example, struck a deal with Watson's, a Hong Kong-based drugstore chain, to set up small counters in its stores.[92] In 2005, the Chinese government relaxed its ban on personal selling and instituted a highly monitored licensing schema in which Avon was given the first permit.[93]

## Global Sponsorships

Sponsorship is one of the fastest growing promotion tools. Global spending on sponsorship is estimated to be around $43.5 billion in 2008.[94] Given the global appeal of sports, big

---

[89]Kashani and Quelch, "Can sales promotions go global?"

[90]"Chasing the China Market," *Asiaweek* (June 11, 1999), p. 46.

[91]"Unisys cuts clear path to int'l recovery," *Marketing News* (September 27, 1999), pp. 4–6.

[92]"Avon scrambles to reinvent itself in China after Beijing's ban on direct selling," *Far Eastern Economic Review* (October 22, 1998), pp. 64–66.

[93]"Avon Given Direct-selling Nod in China," www.chinadaily.com.cn, accessed on February 25, 2009.

[94]www.sponsorship.com, accessed on February 24, 2009.

multinationals increasingly use sports sponsorships as their weapon of choice in their global battle for market share. Adidas, the German sportswear maker, paid a hefty $80 million to $100 million in cash and services for sponsorship of the Beijing 2008 Summer Olympics. As part of the deal, adidas could outfit Chinese athletes at the medal ceremonies even if the athletes competed in garb from other companies. Other multinationals that shelled out huge amounts of sponsorship money for the Beijing Summer Olympics, included Lenovo, Samsung, Volkswagen, and Johnson & Johnson. These companies saw the Olympics as key to shoring up their competitive position in China.[95] Sponsorship also stretches to other types of events, such as concert tours, festivals, charity, and art exhibitions.

Ideally, the sponsored event should reinforce the brand image that the company is trying to promote. Red Bull, one of the dominant energy drink brands, is a case in point. From its very launch onwards, Red Bull has strived to promote a daring macho image by sponsoring *extreme* sports events ranging from wind surfing to hang gliding.[96] In 2004, Red Bull acquired the Jaguar Formula One racing team. With these sponsorships, Red Bull is able to reinforce its image as the brew that gives "Wings to Body and Mind." Formula One can also help the company to get more visibility in the United States, the Middle East, and Central America, where its brand is less established.[97]

Event sponsorship carries four major risks. First, the organizers of the event could sell too many sponsorships, leading toward clutter. Second, the event may be plagued by controversy or scandal. Following the 1998 drug-plagued Tour de France, Coca-Cola drastically scaled down its sponsorship activities for that cycling event.[98] High profile sponsors of the 2008 Beijing Olympics like Coca-Cola also faced a balancing act when their sponsorship of the Games attracted scrutiny from anti-China activists around the world. Third, the payback of the sponsorship can prove elusive. A survey of 1,500 Chinese citizens in 2008 found that only 15 percent could name two of the global sponsors and just 40 percent could name one.[99] The fourth risk is known as *ambush marketing*. With ambush marketing, a company seeks to associate with an event (e.g., the Olympics) without any payments to the event organizer. The culprit hereby steals the limelight from its competitor that officially sponsors the event. By associating with the event, the ambushing company misleads the public by creating the impression that it is a legitimate sponsor. While Coca-Cola was the official sponsor of the 2002 World Cup Soccer, Pepsi managed to sign up some of the biggest soccer celebrities, including England's David Beckham. Likewise, Nike was Brazil's sponsor even though adidas was the official tournament sponsor. In fact, research done after the 1998 World Cup Soccer found that Nike had better recall among TV viewers than adidas, the official sponsor.[100] To stamp out ambush marketing, organizers often place severe restrictions on the marketing activities of non-sponsors. For instance, Heineken handed out green hats to its customers during the Euro 2008 soccer tournament. However, anyone who tried to enter a stadium wearing such a hat was asked to remove it, as Carlsberg was the official sponsor.[101]

Apart from these four pitfalls,[102] there is also the issue of response measurement. In general, measuring the effectiveness of a particular sponsorship activity is extremely

[95] http://www2.chinadaily.com.cn/english/doc/2006-01/28/content_516253.htm

[96] "Extreme Sports and Clubbers Fuel Energetic Rise," *Financial Times* (November 23, 2001), p. 10.

[97] "Red Bull Charges into Ailing Jaguar," *Financial Times* (April 22, 2004): 16.

[98] "Sponsors Rethink the Tour," *Ad Age Global* (March 2001), p. 48.

[99] "Are Olympics Sponsorships Worth It?" http://www.businessweek.com/globalbiz/content/jul2008/gb20080731_125602.htm

[100] "Sponsors' Asian Gamble," *Ad Age Global* (March 2002), pp. 24–25.

[101] "Playing the Game," *The Economist*, July 5, 2008, p. 73.

[102] Note that the sponsored event or sports team also runs certain risks, the main one being that the sponsor can no longer honor the sponsorship commitment due to financial problems or even bankruptcy. Some recent examples include the sponsorship of the Houston Astros Stadium by Enron, AIG's shirt sponsorship of the Manchester United soccer team, and the shirt sponsorship of Anderlecht, a leading Belgian soccer team, by the Belgian bank Fortis. Luckily, new sponsors emerged in all three cases: Coca-Cola for the Houston stadium (renamed the Minute Maid Park), the insurer Aon for Manchester United, and BNP Paribas (a French bank that took over Fortis) for Anderlecht.

hard. Some firms have come up with very creative procedures to do just that. In Asia, Reebok[103] tested out a campaign on Star TV's Channel V music channel in which the vee-jays wear Reebok shoes. To gauge the impact of the campaign, TV viewers were directed to Reebok's website. At the site, the viewer was able download a coupon that could be used for the next Reebok shoe purchase.[104]

Mobile phones are part of everyday life for many people around the planet. Worldwide the number of mobile-phone subscribers was more than 3.3 billion in 2007.[105] In many developed countries 3G-technology is well established and several countries are planning to launch 4G-technology. The combination of the web and advances in portable device technology has spurred a new communication approach: **mobile marketing** or **brand-in-the-hand marketing**. Brand-in-the-hand marketing is a communication strategy that leverages the benefits of mobile devices (at this stage primarily mobile phones) to communicate with the target consumers. One good example is a mobile marketing campaign that BMW ran for its Series 3 car in China during summer 2006. To view the BMW mobile website, customers clicked on BMW banner ads that appeared on the portals of mobile phone carriers such as China Mobile. Within the BMW site, visitors could customize their favorite Series 3 car with preferred colors and features. The site also had a click-to-call feature that enabled visitors to schedule test drive appointments. Tracking results for the 2-month campaign showed more than 500,000 unique visitors and more than 2 million page views.[106]

**Mobile (Brand-in-the-Hand) Marketing**

Mobile marketing differs from traditional communication marketing in two key respects: (1) it can be executed customized to the consumer's location (e.g., shopping location) or consumption context and (2) the marketer is able to interact with the target customer. Sultan and Rohm recognize three important roles for mobile marketing:

1. Foster top-of-mind brand awareness
2. Increase consumer involvement and interaction (e.g., through content downloads, viral marketing)
3. Directly influence consumer actions[107]

Despite the rich potential of mobile marketing, marketers are still reluctant to embrace mobile marketing due to several issues. One hurdle is the wide regional variation in technology. Most European countries and several Asian markets have a much more advanced mobile phone technology infrastructure than the United States and China. One solution is a phased approach: a company could test a mobile marketing campaign in a country with a highly developed infrastructure (e.g., Korea, Singapore) and then fine-tune it before rolling it out at a later stage in a less advanced but more crucial market (e.g., China, India). Another issue that mobile marketers must grapple with relates to privacy concerns and laws, which can also vary greatly across countries. Finally, the implementation of mobile marketing relies on a series of partners (e.g., wireless carriers, distributors) with possibly conflicting interests. Needless to say, setting up such partnerships in different countries can be a daunting task.

*Trade shows* (trade fairs) are a vital part of the communication package for many international business-to-business (B-to-B) marketers. According to one survey, trade shows account for 17 percent of the typical B-to-B marketer's marketing budget.[108]

**Trade Shows**

[103]Reebok was acquired by adidas in 2005.

[104]"Reebok sets strategy to get sales on track in fast-growing Asia," *The Asian Wall Street Journal*, May 31–June 1, 1996, p. 12.

[105]http://www.itu.int/ITU-D/ict/statistics/

[106]"How to Find Focus Online," *Media*, October 20, 2006, p. 26–27.

[107]Fareena Sultan and Andrew Rohm, "The Coming Era of 'Brand in the Hand' Marketing," *MIT Sloan Management Review*, Fall 2005, pp. 83–90.

[108]"Study Finds Online, Trade Shows Dominate B-to-B Spending," www.mediapost.com, accessed on February, 22, 2009.

Trade shows have a direct sales effect—the sales coming from visitors of the trade show booth—and indirect impacts on the exhibitor's sales.[109] Indirect sales effects stem from the fact that visitors become more aware of and interested in the participating company's products. The indirect effects matter especially for new products. Trade fairs are often promoted in trade journals. Government agencies, like the U.S. Department of Commerce, also provide detailed information on international trade fairs.

There are some notable differences between overseas trade shows and North American ones.[110] Overseas fairs are usually much larger than the more regional, niche-oriented shows in the United States. Because of their size, international shows attract a much wider variety of buyers. Hospitality is another notable difference between trade show affairs in the United States and in foreign markets. For instance, even at the smallest booths at German shows, visitors are offered a chair and a glass of orange juice. Larger booths will have kitchens and serve full meals. Empty booths are filled with a coffee table and water cooler. In the United States, trade show events tend to be pure business.

When attending an international trade show, the following guidelines could prove useful:[111]

• Decide on what trade shows to attend at least a year in advance. Prepare translations of product materials, price lists, and selling aids.
• Bring plenty of literature. Bring someone who knows the language or have a translator.
• Send out, ahead of time, direct-mail pieces to potential attendees.
• Find out the best possible space, for instance in terms of traffic.
• Plan the best way to display your products and to tell your story.
• Do your homework on potential buyers from other countries.[112]
• Assess the impact of trade show participation on the company's bottom line.[113] Performance benchmarks may need to be adjusted when evaluating trade show effectiveness in different countries since attendees might behave differently.[114]

One recent phenomenon is the emergence of "virtual trade shows," which allow buyers to walk a "show floor," view products, and request information without physically being there.[115] Unisfair is one example of a company that hosts online expos. Its website (www.unisfair.com) also offers several showcases of such events. An excellent highly informative online resource on international trade shows is the website of Federation of International Trade Associations (FITA): www.fita.org. **Global Perspective 13-4** discusses a non-traditional approach Siemens took to promote its products through a mobile trade show.

## Product Placement

**Product placement** is a form of promotion where the brand is placed in the context of a movie, television show, video games, or other entertainment vehicles. The marketer might pay for the placement or may offer the good free of charge (e.g., cars in action movies). One survey estimated that companies spent $2.9 billion on paid product

---

[109]S. Gopalakrishna, G. L. Lilien, J. D. Williams, and I. K. Sequeira, "Do trade shows pay off?" *Journal of Marketing*, vol. 59, July 1995, pp. 75–83.

[110]"Trading Plätze," *Marketing News* (July 19, 1999), p. 11.

[111]B. O'Hara, F. Palumbo, and P. Herbig, "Industrial trade shows abroad," *Industrial Marketing Management*, vol. 22, 1993, pp. 233–37.

[112]"Trading Plätze."

[113]See S. Gopalakrishna and G. L. Lilien, "A three-stage model of industrial trade show performance," *Marketing Science*, vol. 14, no. 1, Winter 1995, pp. 22–42 for a formal mathematical model to assess trade show effectiveness.

[114]Marnik G. Dekimpe, Pierre Franois, Srinath Gopalakrishna, Gary L. Lilien, and Christophe Van den Bulte, "Generalizing About Trade Show Effectiveness: A Cross-National Comparison," *Journal of Marketing*, 61(October 1997), pp. 55–64.

[115]"All trade shows, all the time," *Marketing News* (July 19, 1999), p. 11.

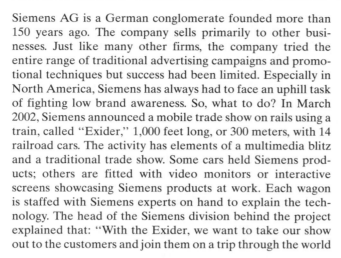

## GLOBAL PERSPECTIVE 13-4

### SIEMENS EXIDER – A TRADE SHOW ON WHEELS: "SIEMENS IS REALLY COOL!"

Siemens AG is a German conglomerate founded more than 150 years ago. The company sells primarily to other businesses. Just like many other firms, the company tried the entire range of traditional advertising campaigns and promotional techniques but success had been limited. Especially in North America, Siemens has always had to face an uphill task of fighting low brand awareness. So, what to do? In March 2002, Siemens announced a mobile trade show on rails using a train, called "Exider," 1,000 feet long, or 300 meters, with 14 railroad cars. The activity has elements of a multimedia blitz and a traditional trade show. Some cars held Siemens products; others are fitted with video monitors or interactive screens showcasing Siemens products at work. Each wagon is staffed with Siemens experts on hand to explain the technology. The head of the Siemens division behind the project explained that: "With the Exider, we want to take our show out to the customers and join them on a trip through the world

*Sources:* "Siemens Makes Tracks Toward Higher Profile," *International Herald Tribune* (March 27–28, 2004): 11; http://www2.automation .siemens.com/mes/simatic_it/html_76/download/adbv200203215e.pdf; and http://www.frost.com/prod/servlet/market-insight-top.pag?docid= 19829104&ctxixpLink=FcmCtx3&ctxixpLabel=FcmCtx4.

of modern industrial automation, drive, switching, and installation technology."

The train journey started in Spain. Siemens' market share rose 3 percentage points after the Exider passed through. Other destinations included Britain, China, Singapore, and ultimately the United States. Invitations to visit the train went out to anyone Siemens deemed to be a potential customer. Siemens hoped that people taking the tour would ask questions, pick up brochure, attend technical seminars, and exchange business cards with a Siemens salesperson. For Siemens, the train is a vehicle to bring its technology close to the customers, even those in remote areas. A vice president of Polo Ralph Lauren visited the train "to see what other things I might buy from them." Customers on the train were overheard saying that they had never realized that Siemens had such a broad portfolio of solutions in so many industry segments. Some customers looking at a display in one of the coaches said: "Oh? This is really cool!" Stephen Greyser, a Harvard Business School professor, said: "Anyone who steps inside that train becomes a willing collaborator in the process of learning more about what Siemens is and does." Likewise, Michael Watras, a brand consultant, noted: "It's out-of-the-box thinking that positions the brand as cutting-edge."

---

placement in 2007.[116] For many marketers product placement can be a very effective tool to target audiences that are less exposed to traditional media advertising. Products that are often featured include cars, luxury goods, consumer electronics, and computers. The none-too-subtle use of product placement in movies such as *Casino Royale* and *I, Robot* has triggered a fair amount of criticism. One British website[117] even has a ranking of the ten worst movies for product placement,[118] with the *Fantastic Four* being singled out for "the most company logos in one shot" award. In terms of product placement as a global marketing tool, one notable example is the 1993 sci-fi movie *Demolition Man*. In the U.S. version of the movie, the hero played by Sylvester Stallone refers to Taco Bell as being the sole survivor of the "franchise wars." In many foreign releases of the movie Taco Bell is replaced with Pizza Hut, which is also owned by Yum! Brands. The reason for the change was that Taco Bell is not present in most of Yum! Brands' non-American markets. **Global Perspective 13-5** discusses how Unilever used product placement in the Chinese *Ugly Betty* series to promote its brands.

## Viral Marketing

**Viral marketing** refers to marketing tools that try to achieve marketing objectives such as increased brand awareness by boosting a self-replicating viral process through a social network, similar to the spread of a real-world virus. The social network can be virtual (e.g., Facebook, email contacts) or offline (or some combination).[119] Other terms that are sometimes used are *buzz marketing* and *word-of-mouse marketing*. The message can be spread through text messages, images, music or video clips, or games.

---

[116] http://www.pqmedia.com/about-press-20080212-bemf.html.

[117] http://www.theshiznit.co.uk/feature/top-10-worst-movies-for-product-placement.php

[118] Number 1 is *I, Robot*, number 2 is *The Island*, and number 3 is *Blade: Trinity*.

[119] http://en.wikipedia.org/wiki/Viral_marketing, accessed on February 21, 2009.

## $\mathcal{G}$LOBAL PERSPECTIVE 13-5

### THE CASTING OF DOVE SOAP IN "UGLY WUDI"

*Ugly Betty*, the American television hit series based on a Colombian telenovela, now has a remake in China called *Ugly Wudi*. Unilever is turning to the Chinese series to pitch three of its famous brands in China: Dove soap, Lipton tea, and Clear anti-dandruff shampoo. Although Dove's global "Real Beauty" campaign has been very successful in most markets elsewhere in the world, it struggled to gain traction in China. The campaign, which showed "real" non-model-like faces, was much admired by feminists and advertising groups in Europe and the United States. A senior Unilever marketing executive explained that Chinese women really feel they can achieve the beauty portrayed in ads, if they have stamina to work at it. Therefore, Unilever decided to axe the "real women" campaign in China and try out something totally new: branded entertainment. Mindshare, Unilever's media buying agency, brokered a deal with the Chinese broadcaster of the Ugly Wudi TV series which offers the multinational the right

to exclusive ads and product placements during the show. The show promotes the three Unilever brands as part of the story-line. Unilever marketing staff worked with the show's writers to integrate 3,300 seconds of the Dove brand into the first show's first season. Dove commercials around the character show Wudi with a perfect skin, but wearing braces and over-sized glasses to match her ugly traits. Unilever sees a strategic fit between the show and the "real beauty" concept of Dove soap.

The show premiered in September 2008. For the Chinese version, the writers dropped the Chinese Betty's siblings to conform to China's one-child policy and had her work at an ad agency instead of a fashion magazine. The Chinese Betty uses Lipton during office tea breaks and her boss, Fernando, washes his hair with Clear shampoo. Unilever hopes that the show will boost sales in China's hinterland. Initial measurement data looked encouraging. A survey conducted at the end of the show's first season found that Dove's unaided awareness rose 44 percent among target consumers generally. Mindshare estimates that the product placement delivered four times the value Unilever would have got with traditional media advertising.

*Sources:* "Unilever Casts Dove Soap in 'Ugly Wudi'," *The Wall Street Journal Asia*, December 30, 2008, p. 20; "Unilever Turns Ugly Betty into Chinese Brand Vehicle, *Media*, May 1, 2008; and "Unilever Sponsors 'Ugly Betty' in China," *Advertising Age*, April 21, 2008, p. 12.

---

The key for the viral campaign to be effective is twofold: (1) identify people with a high networking influence and (2) create a message that is so compelling that it will be passed on through the network.

Scores of major brands have embraced viral marketing as a communication tool. Some recent examples include Unilever's Axe, Volkswagen, and Carlsberg. Yet, to be successful viral marketers must grapple with several challenges. As more and more marketers jump on the bandwagon, the biggest issue is to come up with something that stands out and breaks through the clutter. The creative bar can be much higher than for traditional marketing tools. One consultant points out that a viral marketing campaign has to be "extremely good, absolutely hilarious or shocking. The trouble is that most companies are not willing to take risks or to break taboos."[120] Another concern is to make sure that the campaign does not offend the global online community by being seen as a blatant commercial infringement. Virtual marketers also have little control over how the message is spread and where it ends up. When a viral message is circulated in a geographic area where the brand is not available, the campaign would be wasteful. Netizens could also subvert the campaign. When Carlsberg ran a viral e-mail campaign that spoofed its ad slogan during the Euro 2004 Soccer campaign,[121] netizens came up with an altered negative version which became much more visible than the original.[122]

**Global Public Relations (PR) and Publicity**

For global marketers building up good relationships with various stakeholders (e.g., employees, press, distributors, customers, government authorities) is an important part of their communication strategy. *Public relations (PR)* consists of managing the flow of

---

[120]"Viral Advertisers Play with Fire," *Financial Times*, August 29, 2006, p. 6.

[121]The message was: "Carlsberg don't send e-mails, but if they did they'd probably be the best e-mails in the world."

[122]"Viral Advertisers . . . "

**EXHIBIT 13-11**
EXAMPLES OF INTERNATIONAL PR CAMPAIGNS

**Example 1: adidas Chinese women's volleyball team**

- *Brief.* To strengthen adidas' association with the Chinese women's volleyball team
- *Target audience.* 14- to 24-year-olds in China
- *Challenge.* Although the Chinese women's volleyball players were stars in the 1980s with world championship wins, the team had lost its appeal with youth: it was widely perceived as non-feminine and unfashionable.
- *Campaign.* The goal of the campaign was to make women's volleyball "cool." The PR agency launched a yearlong campaign of viral elements and publicity stunts. To change the drab image, glamour shots of the players were taken and angled for various publications, mostly lifestyle media. Stylish video clips of the team were shot and posted online. Adidas also organized a "chant" competition to boost enthusiasm and pride in the national team. Adidas' PR agency also set up a blog.
- *Results.* The total media value received was worth Rmb 36 million ($4.6 million), worth more than 13 times the original investment. The blog received more than 20,000 page views on the first day of the launch.

**Example 2: Pantene Shine**

- *Brief.* To instill the spirit of Pantene shampoo's new platform.
- *Target audience.* 15- to 35-year-old women in India
- *Challenge.* In autumn 2006, P&G launched a new global positioning for Pantene shampoo with a new logo, packaging, and tagline: "Shine, I believe I can."
- *The campaign.* The cornerstone was India's first Pantene Shine Awards. The inaugural award was a high-profile award attended by celebrities from all over India. Six women in the beauty industry were honored at the award show and designated as brand ambassadors, including Bollywood star Sushmita Sen. Pantene's PR agency also organized India's first branded chat shows, called *Shine. I believe I can—Sush speaks out*. The brand also launched a reality TV show, inviting entries from women aged 18 to 30 across India to compete for the "dream job" of TV news anchor.
- *Results.* The award show got nearly 500 mentions in print and TV, reaching 90 percent of the target audience.

*Source:* "Are Clients Ready for Breakthrough Creative?" *Media*, April 20, 2007, p. 8; and "Pantene Rolls Out Reality TV Show," *Media*, May 4, 2007, p. 2.

information between an organization and its publics.[123] *Publicity* is spreading information about a product or company to gain awareness. Most of that communication is "free" although most companies will often engage a PR agency to manage the information flow. Effective PR management often leads to high publicity. A well-executed PR campaign needs to fulfill two requirements: (1) it should be creative and (2) it should be based on insights about the target audience derived from solid research. **Exhibit 13-11** summarizes two well-executed PR campaigns.

# GLOBALLY INTEGRATED MARKETING COMMUNICATIONS (GIMC)

◆ ◆ ◆ ◆ ◆ ◆ ◆

In a pan-European campaign to promote Sony Ericsson's new T300 mobile phone, hundreds of drooling dogs were walked several times a day during a six-week period in major European cities.[124] The dogs, as well as their walkers, were wearing specially designed branded clothing. The walking activity was part of an integrated campaign centering on the "drooling" theme. Other elements included TV, the internet, posters, viral e-mail, radio, and sponsorships. According to one of Sony Ericsson's European marketing manager: "The drool campaign is about creating lust for THE BAR (the

---

[123]James E. Grunig and Todd Hunt, *Managing Public Relations* (Orlando, FL: Harcourt Brace Jovanovich, 1984).

[124]"Packs of Dogs Provide 'Ad Space' for Euro Launch of Sony T300 Handset," http://www.adageglobal.com, accessed on December 16, 2002.

handset's nickname) . . . The entire drool campaign has a real edge to it—something that the target audience (16- to 24-year-olds) all over Europe will relate to."

For most companies, media advertising is only one element of their global communications efforts. As we saw in the previous section, marketers use many other communication tools. In recent years, advertising agencies and their clients have recognized the value of an **integrated marketing communications (IMC)** program—not just for domestic markets but globally. The "drool" campaign is just one example of the push toward IMC. IMC goes beyond taking a screenshot from a TV ad and plastering it everywhere: the core idea should be integrated, not the execution. By coordinating the different communication vehicles—mass advertising, sponsorships, sales promotions, packaging, point-of-purchase displays, and so forth—an IMC campaign can convey one and the same idea to the prospective customers with a unified voice.[125] Instead of having the different promotional mix elements send out a mish-mash of messages with a variety of visual imagery, each and every one of them centers on that single key idea. By having consistency, integration, and cohesiveness, marketers will be able to maximize the impact of your communication tools.

A five-nation survey of ad agencies found that the use of IMC varies a lot. The percentage of client budgets devoted to IMC activities was low in India (15 percent) and Australia (22 percent). The percentage was far higher in New Zealand (40 percent) and the United Kingdom (42 percent).[126] One study also revealed cross-country differences in the evaluation of the IMC concept: U.S. PR and advertising agencies seem to consider IMC as a way to organize the marketing business of the firm while Korean and U.K. agencies view it as coordination of the various communication disciplines.[127]

A **globally integrated marketing communications (GIMC)** program goes one step further. GIMC is a system of active promotional management that strategically coordinates global communications in all of its component parts, both horizontally (country-level) and vertically (promotion tools).[128]

To run a GIMC program effectively places demands on both the advertiser's organization and the advertising agencies involved. Companies that want to pursue a GIMC for some or all of their brands should have the mechanisms in place to coordinate their promotional activities vertically (across tools) and horizontally (across countries). By the same token, agencies in the various disciplines (e.g., advertising, PR) should be willing to integrate and coordinate the various communication disciplines across countries. GIMC also requires frequent communications both internally and between ad agency branches worldwide.[129] Unfortunately, in many countries it is difficult to find ad agencies that can provide the talent to collaborate on and execute integrated campaigns.

---

[125]"Integrated Marketing Communications: Maybe Definition Is in the Point of View," *Marketing News* (January 18, 1993).

[126]Philip J. Kitchen and Don E. Schultz, "A Multi-Country Comparison of the Drive for IMC," *Journal of Advertising Research*, (Jan.–Feb. 1999), pp. 21–38.

[127]Philip J. Kitchen, Ilchul Kim, and Don E. Schultz, "Integrated Marketing Communications: Practice Leads Theory," *Journal of Advertising Research*, 48 (December 2008), pp. 531–46.

[128]Andreas F. Grein and Stephen J. Gould, "Globally Integrated Marketing Communications," *Journal of Marketing Communications*, 2(3) (1996), pp. 141–58.

[129]Stephen J. Gould, Dawn B. Lerman, and Andreas F. Grein, "Agency Perceptions and Practices on Global IMC," *Journal of Advertising Research*, (Jan.–Feb. 1999), pp. 7–20.

# SUMMARY ◆ ◆ ◆ ◆ ◆ ◆ ◆ ◆ ◆ ◆ ◆ ◆ ◆ ◆ ◆ ◆ ◆ ◆ ◆ ◆ ◆ ◆ ◆

Global communications presents for many marketers some of the most daunting challenges. A multitude of decisions need to be carried out on the front of international advertising. This chapter gave you an overview of the major ones: creating advertising campaigns, setting and allocating the budget, selecting media vehicles to carry the campaign, choosing advertising agencies, and coordinating cross-country advertising programs. The development of a global advertising plan involves many players—headquarters, regional and/or local offices, advertising agencies—typically making the entire process frustrating. However, the potential rewards of a brilliant and well-executed international advertising strategy are alluring.

One of the front-burner issues that scores of international advertisers face is to what degree they should push for pan-regional or even global advertising campaigns. The arguments for standardizing campaigns are pretty compelling: (1) cost savings, (2) a coherent brand image, (3) similarity of target groups, and (4) transplanting of creative ideas. By now, you should also be quite familiar with the counterarguments: (1) cultural barriers, (2) countries being at different stages of market development, (3) role of advertising regulations, and (4) and variations in the media-environment. Most global marketers balance between the two extremes by adopting a compromise solution.[130]

Overall, there seems to be a definite move towards more pan-regional (or even global) campaigns. Numerous explanations have been put forward to explain this shift: the "global" village rationale, the mushrooming of global and pan-regional media vehicles, restructuring of marketing divisions and brand systems along global or pan-regional lines. Another important development is the emergence of new media outlets, including the internet. While it is hard to gaze into a crystal ball and come up with concrete predictions, it is clear that international advertisers will face a drastically different environment ten years from now.

---

[130]Ali Kanso and Richard Alan Nelson, "Advertising Localization Overshadows Standardization," *Journal of Advertising Research*, (Jan.–Feb. 2002), pp. 79–89.

## KEY TERMS

Advertising manual (brand book)
Bottom-up budgeting
Brand-in-the-Hand Marketing
Competitive parity

Concept cooperation
Export advertising
Globally integrated marketing communications (GIMC)

Integrated Marketing Communications (IMC)
Mobile Marketing
Modular approach
Objective-and-task

Product Placement
Prototype standardization
Percentage of sales
Top-down budgeting
Viral Marketing

## REVIEW QUESTIONS

1. Most luxury products appeal to global segments. Does that mean that global advertising campaigns are most appropriate for such kind of products?

2. Discuss the major challenges faced by international advertisers.

3. Spell out the steps that international advertisers should consider in order to cope with advertising regulations in their foreign markets.

4. What factors entice international advertisers to localize their advertising campaigns in foreign markets?

5. What are the major reasons for standardizing an international advertising program?

6. What will be the impact of satellite TV on international advertising?

7. What do you see as the major drawbacks of the internet as a communication tool from the perspective of an international advertiser.

8. What mechanisms should MNCs contemplate to coordinate their advertising efforts across different countries?

## DISCUSSION QUESTIONS

1. Poland recently imposed a ban on alcoholic drinks advertising. How do you think brewers like United Distillers and Seagram should adjust their marketing mix strategy to cope with this ban?

2. One of the hottest topics in advertising is whether it is ethical to advertise to children. On side of the debate are the moralists who claim that children up to the age of ten cannot distinguish advertising from programming. By this logic, the state should intervene and protect children from advertising. Some researchers disagree, however. One British study showed that the idea that children under the age of 12 fail to understand the purpose of advertising is just plain wrong. Lego, the Danish toy group, favors industry self-regulation. The company claims that Lego's toys are designed to educate and entertain. Advertising allows the firm to explain the virtues of its toys. Some people also argue that advertising bans and regulations are often matters of vested interests dressed up as moral causes. Sweden's restrictions on toy advertising may explain why Swedish toys are at least 30 percent more expensive than elsewhere in Europe. Likewise, some claim that the real purpose of Greece's ban on TV toy advertising was to protect the local toy industry from cheap Asian imports that have to advertise their way into the marketplace. What is your viewpoint in this debate? Is self-regulation the ultimate solution here as Lego claims?

3. The allocation of promotional dollars between "pull" (consumer promotions + media advertising) and "push" varies

drastically for many advertisers across countries. What are the factors behind these variations?

4. In emerging markets such as India, consumers shop far more frequently than in most Western countries—often on a daily basis. As a result, consumers there have many more chances to switch brands. What does this buying behavior imply in terms of communication approaches in case a foreign firm such as Unilever or Colgate tries to foster repeat purchase and brand loyalty?

5. Pick a particular global brand. Search for TV commercials of the brand on YouTube.com or the brand's website in different regions—try to find at least three different spots. What do the commercials have in common? How do they differ? Speculate about the reasons behind the commonalities and differences that you found for the ads.

# SHORT CASES

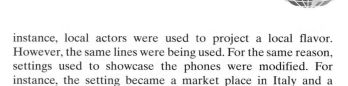

## CASE 13-1

### NOKIA: 1,001 REASONS TO GO GLOBAL?

In the fall of 2004, Nokia, the world's largest mobile phone maker, rolled out its first truly global corporate advertising campaign in TV, print, and online with the slogan "1,001 reasons to have a Nokia imaging phone." The aim of the campaign was to create a stronger, more consistent brand identity. The campaign shed a landmark for Nokia. In the past, Nokia typically created different images and messages for its different markets.

The ad agency Grey Worldwide created the ads for Europe, the Middle East, and Africa. Bates Advertising in Singapore, part of the WPP Group, was responsible for the Asia-Pacific area. The two agencies collaborated to come up with one single campaign.

The ad does not actually spell out 1,001 reasons for having a Nokia imaging phone, it just says that there are 1,001 of them. Some of the ads and commercials use the face of cherubic baby to suggest using a Nokia phone to store favorite pictures. Nokia localized some aspects in the execution of the campaign. For

*Source:* "Advertising: One World, One Message: Nokia Goes Global With Ads," *Asian Wall Street Journal* (September 27, 2004): A6 and http://www.nokia.be/UK/Phones/Imaging/downloads.html.

instance, local actors were used to project a local flavor. However, the same lines were being used. For the same reason, settings used to showcase the phones were modified. For instance, the setting became a market place in Italy and a bazaar in the Middle East.

Nokia argues that the case for a global ad campaign is strong these days. Most countries now use the same mobile phone technology (GSM). As a result, new products can now be rolled out globally simultaneously.

### DISCUSSION QUESTIONS

1. What are the benefits of a global advertising campaign such as the Nokia 1,001 reasons described in the case?

2. What are the risks of such a campaign? Do you think Nokia is on the right track?

3. How do you assess the campaign (message strategy, slogan, visuals)? Overall, do you judge Nokia's approach a success or a failure?

4. Do you believe global advertising campaigns will become more prominent in the future? For which products or services?

## CASE 13-2

### P&G CHINA — A LEGAL CLOUD OVER SK-II

SK-II is an ultra-premium skincare range that originated from Procter & Gamble's Japan division. According to P&G's product literature, the SK-II product combines the magic of nature with the advances of science. A Japanese monk visiting a sake brewery noticed that brewery workers had very soft and youthful hands. Even an elderly wrinkled man had the silky smooth hands of a young boy. A team of skincare scientists discovered the secret: a clear liquid that could be extracted during the yeast fermentation process. The liquid became known as the "Secret Key" to beautiful skin.

De-Wrinkle Active, the latest launch in China from P&G's SK-II skincare line, attracted unwelcome publicity

*Sources:* http://www.sk2.co.uk/our_legend1.htm; "P&G accepts fine for 'bogus' advertising, *China Daily* (April 11, 2005); "Famous brands lose face," www.en.ce.cn (October 7, 2005); "P&G acts fast to calm legal cloud over SK-II," *Media* (April 8, 2005).

in early March 2005 when Lu Ping, a woman from Jiangxi province, filed a lawsuit against P&G, China's biggest advertiser, the company that distributed it, and even Carina Lau, the celebrity who endorsed SK-II in P&G's advertising. The plaintiff said she had spent Rmb. 840 (US$100) on a 25-gram bottle of SKII anti-aging De-Wrinkle Essence in the hope that "the concentrated treatment would work to help iron out 47 percent of deep lines and wrinkles after 28 consecutive days of usage," as the product's promotional materials had promised.

Unfortunately for Mrs. Lu, the "miracle cure" failed to remove her wrinkles. Instead, it triggered an allergic reaction, which left the woman in pain. Lu alleged that she was misled by the brand's advertising. A local industrial watchdog claimed that P&G's statistics for SK-II's claims came from a lab experiment on 300 Japanese women and lacked authoritative

Xinhua/Landov LLC

proof. After a 20-day investigation into SK-II, the Nanchang Commercial and Industrial Bureau fined P&G with a penalty of Rmb. 200,000 (US$24,000) for making false advertising claims.

Initially P&G considered Lu's case as a spiteful act to draw media attention. P&G insisted that all of its cosmetic products had undergone stringent tests and were well received in Japan and the U.S. On March 25, the firm softened its tone and admitted that its advertising had been misleading. In April, P&G paid the fine and made an apology to consumers. Lu, on the other hand, lost her case because of insufficient evidence. She said she would appeal the verdict. Sales of SK-II brand had slipped by nearly 30 percent. P&G planned to launch a new SK-II campaign in September 2005. The SK-II case underlines an emerging trend in China—consumer activism, which has become a major force in Chinese society today.

## DISCUSSION QUESTIONS

**1.** What lessons does P&G's mishap with SK-II in China inspire for advertisers in China?

**2.** Did P&G handle the SK-II case correctly? What would you recommend to P&G China for the marketing of its SK-II product line?

---

## $\mathcal{C}$ASE 13-3

### COCA-COLA'S TORCH RELAY SPONSORSHIP: MARKETING YOUR BRAND WITHOUT ALIENATING THE WORLD

With less than six months to go before the opening of the Beijing Olympics, the TV images being aired worldwide about the clashes in Tibet were worrisome for Coca-Cola. Coca-Cola, whose Olympic involvement dates back to 1928, had also been a sponsor for the 1936 Games in Berlin when the Nazis were in power. Neville Isdell, the company's chairman, said in an interview with the BBC that he would have agreed to that deal also if had he been in charge: "What we support is not actually the individual governments but the whole aura that surrounds the Olympics and the credo of the Olympic movement." (news.bbc.co.uk)

To sponsors of the Games such as Coca-Cola, the Beijing Olympics represents a golden opportunity to tap into China's vast market and to nurture good relationships with the country's decision-makers. Still, there is a growing concern that the widespread protests about the clashes in Tibet and other China-related issues could distract from the commercial success of the Games. Eliot Cutler, a managing partner of a law firm that provides advice on crisis management, said: "They [the sponsors] have an interest in making sure the Games are free of controversy—and in taking themselves out of the middle" (*Wall Street Journal*, 3/17/2008).

*Sources:* "Olympic Sponsors Face a Balancing Act," *The Wall Street Journal Asia*, March 17, 2008, p. 29; "Coca-Cola Defends Olympics Deal," news.bbc.co.uk, accessed on February 22, 2009; and "Corporate Sponsors Nervous as Tibet Protest Groups Shadow Olympic Torch's Run," http://www.nytimes.com/2008/03/29/business/world business/29torch.html?_r=1&ref=us&pagewanted=print.

For Coca-Cola there is a more immediate worry: the company is one of three corporate sponsors of the Olympics torch relay—the other two are Samsung and Lenovo. China had been criticized for its support of the genocidal Sudan regime, its treatment of ethnic minorities (e.g., Tibetans), and its dealing with political and religious dissidents. Western activists have been particularly incensed about the relay's planned route through Tibet. "To a lot of people, Tibet has this mythic power, this Shangri-La image," noted John Ackerly, president of the International Campaign for Tibet (www.nytimes.com). Coca-Cola was estimated to have paid as much as $15 million to sponsor the relay. "These types of protests can cause deep heartache [for sponsors]," said Eric Denzenhall, the president of a crisis PR firm based in Washington. Mr. Isdell declared that Coca-Cola remains committed to the Games. He observed that Coca-Cola's sponsorship strategy was based on moral principles: "The Olympic torch was a symbol of peace. It was developed originally around the Greek Olympics to stop the warring that was going on between different factions in Greece. There are people who want it to communicate something different and are trying to use that symbolism for issues that may have a fair resonance. But I don't believe it is right to use those symbols of peace for another cause. I believe the Olympics are a force for good and if they were not a force for good, we would not sponsor them." On the other hand, one commentator pointed out that sponsors like Coca-Cola have to have "some responsibility to humanity" and should react to current events.

## DISCUSSION QUESTIONS

1. Was Coca-Cola right to continue with the sponsorship in spite of all the protests and controversy surrounding the torch relay? Is Coca-Cola correct in asserting that the Olympics is only about sports?

2. How should Coca-Cola proceed? Should the firm scale back its plans for the torch relay? What do you recommend?

# $\mathcal{C}$ASE 13-4

## KIWI SCHOOLGIRLS FIND ALMOST NO VITAMIN C IN RIBENA DRINK

Ribena is a famous brand of fruit-based health drinks sold by global drugs company GlaxoSmithKline (GSK). In 2004 Ribena hit a major snag due to its advertising campaign in New Zealand. The campaign stated that the black currants in Ribena have four times the vitamin C of oranges.

The controversy surrounding the ad campaign started with a simple school project. That year, two New Zealand high school students conducted a science experiment to determine the vitamin C levels of their favorite fruit drinks. They hypothesized that cheaper brands would be less healthy. The students were surprised to discover that Ribena contained virtually no trace of vitamin C, contrary to the brand's advertising claims. Instead, their lab test found that Ribena contained a tiny amount of vitamin C, while a cheaper rival product "Just Juice" contained almost four times as much. After contacting the company, the students' concerns of "intentionally misleading and quite inappropriate" claims were dismissed. "They didn't even really answer our questions. They just said it's the black currants that have it, and then hung up," one of the students said (www.guardian.co.uk).

Their case was taken up by a television consumer affairs show, Fair Go, which suggested the girls take their findings to the New Zealand Commerce Commission, a government watchdog. The commission's investigation confirmed the girls' findings: Ribena had no detectable level of vitamin C even though black currants have more vitamin C than oranges. The commission brought 15 charges in the Auckland District Court against GSK under the Fair Trading Act. On 27 March 2007 GSK pleaded guilty to all 15 charges and was fined NZ$217,500 (about $156,000) for misleading consumers and ordered to run a one-month corrective advertisement campaign in New Zealand's leading print titles in addition to a message on its website. After the verdict, one of the girls told a local radio

station: "We feel quite proud . . . blown away. If we hadn't done that science test three years ago, Ribena could have been promoted as Vitamin C full forever." (www.iht.com)

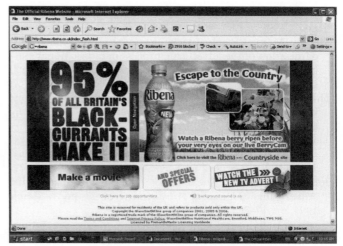

Clearly, GSK had not handled the PR crisis well. New Zealand media reports indicated sales dropped by 10 to 12 percent in 2007 compared to sales a year ago. Questions over Ribena's vitamin C content were raised also in other markets. GSK maintains that the issue only affected Australia and New Zealand and that Ribena drinks sold in other markets contain the levels of vitamin C stated on the product label.

## DISCUSSION QUESTIONS

1. What are the lessons to be drawn from Ribena's crisis in New Zealand?

2. How can GSK salvage the Ribena brand in New Zealand?

*Sources: "Schoolgirls Rumble Ribena Vitamin Claims,"*www.guardian. co.uk, accessed on January 1, 2009; "GlaxoSmithKline Fined for False Ribena Advertisements in New Zealand," www.iht.com, accessed on January 2, 2009; www.ribena.co.uk, and "Are Consumers Ready to Forgive Ribena's Lie?" *Media*, April 20, 2007.

# FURTHER READING ✦ ✦ ✦ ✦ ✦ ✦ ✦ ✦ ✦ ✦ ✦ ✦ ✦ ✦ ✦ ✦ ✦ ✦ ✦

Al-Makaty, Safran S., G. Normanvan Tubergen, S. Scott Whitlow and Douglas A. Boyd, "Attitudes toward Advertising in Islam," *Journal of Advertising Research*, May/June 1996, pp. 16–26.

Davison, Andrew and Erik Grab, "The contributions of advertising testing to the development of effective international advertising: The KitKat case study," *Marketing and Research Today*, February 1993, pp. 15–24.

De Mooij, Marieke, *Advertising Worldwide*, 2nd Edition, Englewood Cliffs, NJ: Prentice Hall, 1994.

Domzal, Teresa J. and Jerome B. Kernan, "Mirror, Mirror: Some Postmodern Reflections on Global Advertising," *Journal of Advertising*, vol. 22, no. 4, December 1993, pp. 1–20.

Duncan, Tom and Jyotika Ramaprasad, "Standardizing Multinational Advertising: The Influencing Factors," *Journal of Advertising*, vol. 24, no. 3, Fall 1995, pp. 55–68.

Hanni, D. A., J. K. Ryans, Jr., and I. R. Vernon, "Coordinating international advertising—The Goodyear case revisited for Latin America," *Journal of International Marketing*, vol. 3, no. 2, 1995, pp. 83–98.

Harvey, M. G., "Point of view: A model to determine standardization of the advertising process in international markets," *Journal of Advertising Research*, July/August 1993, pp. 57–64.

Hill, John S. and Unal O. Boya, "Consumer goods promotions in developing countries," *International Journal of Advertising*, vol. 6, 1987, pp. 249–64.

James, W. L. and J. S. Hill, "International advertising messages: To adapt or not to adapt (That is the question), *Journal of Advertising Research*, June/July 1991, pp. 65–71.

Johansson, Johny K. "The Sense of "Nonsense": Japanese TV Advertising," *Journal of Advertising*, vol. 23, no. 1, March 1994, pp. 17–26.

Kashani, Kamran and John A. Quelch, "Can sales promotions go global?" *Business Horizons*, vol. 33, no. 3, May–June 1990, pp. 37–43.

Kaynak, Erderer, *The Management of International Advertising*, New York, NY: Quorum Books, 1989.

Laroche, Michel, V. H. Kirpalani, Frank Pons, and Lianxi Zhou. "A Model of Advertising Standardization in Multinational Corporations," *Journal of International Business Studies*, 32(2) (Second Quarter 2001): 249–66.

McCullough, Wayne R., "Global Advertising which Acts Locally: The IBM Subtitles Campaign," *Journal of Advertising Research*, May/June 1996, pp. 11–15.

Maynard, Michael L. and Charles R. Taylor, "A Comparative Analysis of Japanese and U.S. Attitudes toward Direct Marketing," *Journal of Direct Marketing*, 10, Winter 1996, pp. 34–44.

Meenaghan, Tony. "Current Developments & Future Directions in Sponsorship." *International Journal of Advertising*, 17(1), pp. 3–28.

Mehta, Raj, Rajdeep Grewal, and Eugene Sivadas, "International Direct Marketing on the Internet: Do Internet Users Form a Global Segment?" *Journal of Direct Marketing*, 10, Winter 1996, pp. 45–58.

Mueller, Barbara, "An Analysis of Information Content in Standardized vs. Specialized Multinational Advertisements," *Journal of International Business Studies*, First Quarter 1991, pp. 23–39.

O'Hara, B., F. Palumbo, and P. Herbig, "Industrial trade shows abroad," *Industrial Marketing Management*, vol. 22, 1993, pp. 233–37.

Plummer, Joseph T., "The Role of Copy Research in Multinational Advertising," *Journal of Advertising Research*, Oct./Nov. 1986, pp. 11–15.

Quelch, John A. and Lisa R. Klein, "The Internet and International Marketing," *Sloan Management Review*, Spring 1996, pp. 60–75.

Rijkens, Rein, *European Advertising Strategies*, London: Cassell, 1992.

# SALES AND CROSS-CULTURAL MANAGEMENT

HAPTER OVERVIEW

1. MARKET ENTRY OPTIONS AND SALESFORCE STRATEGY

2. CULTURAL CONSIDERATIONS

3. IMPACT OF CULTURE ON SALES MANAGEMENT AND PERSONAL SELLING PROCESS

4. CROSS-CULTURAL NEGOTIATIONS

5. EXPATRIATES

Think of two major markets in Asia: Japan and China. Japan is a well-established developed country similar to the United States. One might assume that foreign firms can sell products pretty much the same way as they do in the United States. Such an assumption may prove to be very wrong! For example, U.S. automakers still have great difficulty making inroads into the Japanese market, even though Japan does not impose any tariffs or quotas on foreign products, and even though BMW, Mercedes-Benz, and Volkswagen have become familiar names in Japan. One major, yet little known, reason is in the way cars are sold in Japan. Unlike in the United States where customers visit car dealers, in Japan, door-to-door salespeople sell a majority of cars, much the same way Avon representatives sell personal care and beauty products. However, now the situation is gradually changing, and Japanese dealers are diversifying. They are investing more money in significantly larger American-style dealership operations and less in door-to-door sales and small one-car showrooms. The reason for this shift in sales strategies is that Japanese consumers increasingly dislike at-home sales calls, especially women, who today play a major role in new car purchasing decisions. However, traditional door-to-door sales remain effective in offering a high level of service that continue to determine which cars will eventually be sold, and will not disappear any time soon.[1]

---

[1] Alexandra Harney, "Death of the Salesman Spells Boost For Japan," *Financial Times* (January 5, 1999), p. 6; and Masataka Morita and Kiyohiko G. Nishimura, "Information Technology and Automobile Distribution: A Comparative Study of Japan and the United States," A working paper, University of Tokyo, August 25, 2000.

## ❖ ❖ ❖ ❖ ❖ ❖ ❖ ❖ ❖ ❖ ❖ ❖ ❖ ❖ ❖ ❖ ❖ ❖ ❖ ❖ ❖ ❖ ❖

### 𝒢LOBAL PERSPECTIVE 14-1

### FOREIGN BUSINESS IN CHINA: SALESFORCE IS CRUCIAL

The world's top soy sauce producer, Kikkoman Corp. of Japan, opened a plant in Kunshan, Jiangsu Province, near Shanghai in May 2002 to produce high-end soy sauce. The leader of the company places high hopes on the Chinese operation, since potential consumers of soy sauce in China, albeit a mere 1 percent of the country's population, are as many as 13 million, equal to the population of Tokyo in Japan. But the company, which makes and sells soy sauce in the United States and Europe, does not engage in marketing in China, leaving sales activities to a local joint venture with Ton Yi Industrial Corp., Taiwan's leading food processor, which has significant experience in China and has its own sales network there. "We have realized that bill collection and other sales-related jobs in China are beyond our ability," said the president of Kikkoman.

Many foreign companies are repeating the process of trial and error in their attempts to take control of distribution, a key

to conquering the puzzling Chinese market. Some focus on increasing the local network; some ally with partners with the aim of selling products through partners' sales channels; and some are terminating joint venture contracts with local state-run firms with weak marketing muscle in an attempt to build up sales networks of their own.

Under the circumstances, foreign manufacturers, which fear getting bogged down in the local distribution system, are getting forced to take an approach in which they sell a small amount of expensive products to China's new rich through foreign sales agents, who may be inferior in marketing ability but reliable in regard to paying for the goods they purchase. Currently the company sells its soy sauce at five or six times the price of the Chinese local product. According to its chairman and CEO, it will be another ten years before increased purchasing power allows Chinese consumers to trade up to Kikkoman. To grow businesses in China, only those who have a strong sales network, just like the Kikkoman-Ton Yi joint venture, are more likely to control and market to the mass consumers in China.

*Sources:* "China Market Huge but Hard to Crack," *Nikkei Weekly,* http://www.nni.nikkei.co.jp, July 1, 2002; "Kikkoman to Diversify Ops Abroad," *Nikkei Weekly,* June 20, 2005.

China, on the other hand, is an emerging economic and political giant. Foreign and local companies are fighting an increasingly fierce battle for a slice of the potentially lucrative Chinese market with its 1.3 billion potential consumers. However, it is not easy for foreign enterprises to establish a presence in the unfamiliar, rapidly changing market, where old and modern social systems coexist. The truth is that selling products is far more difficult in China than manufacturing them there. Business morals and practices have yet to develop sufficiently in the distribution sector. It is quite common for sales agents to channel products into the black market or for manufacturers' salespeople to discount prices for agents in exchange for secret rebates. Faced with China's labyrinthine sales channels, which even local manufacturers find difficult to manage, foreign businesses are often at a loss as to how to maneuver in them. In such a market, the local salesforce is crucial in penetrating the market (See **Global Perspective 14-1**). All these examples vividly illustrate the importance of international sales management.

What does the salesperson do in a company? We can think of many different types of salespeople, from entry-level laborers who stand behind the counter at an ice cream store to industrial experts who work entirely within the offices of a corporate client. Some salespeople sell products and others sell services. Some are focused on the immediate sale; some take overall responsibility for all aspects of a global business customer's business literally on a global basis. Salespeople take orders, deliver products, educate buyers, build relationships with clients, and provide technical knowledge.

In all cases the salesperson is the front line for the company. The customer sees only the salesperson and the product. Through the salesperson, the customer develops an opinion of the company. And the success or failure of the company rests largely on the ability of the salesforce. We cannot overstate the importance of making good decisions when those decisions affect the quality and ability of the company's salesforce. This chapter investigates how the processes of sales management and personal selling are changed when taken overseas into another culture.

**EXHIBIT 14-1**
INTERNATIONAL SALES STRATEGY AND INTERCULTURAL
CONSIDERATIONS

| International Sales Strategy Issues | Intercultural Issues within the Foreign Country |
| --- | --- |
| Global/International vs. local account management | Motivation |
| Salesforce skill availability | Cultural sensitivity |
| Country image | Ethical standards |
| Expatriate recruiting | Fairness |
| Centralized training | Relationship building |
| Home to host communications | Selling style differences |

So what is international about sales management and personal selling? First, we can break international sales management issues into two categories that provide a clarification of the use of the term *international* (1) *international strategy considerations*—issues that analyze more than one country's assets, strengths, and situations, or that deal directly with cross-border coordination and (2) *intercultural considerations*—issues that focus on the culture of the foreign country and its impact on operations within that country.

Although these two categories are not mutually exclusive, they help to clarify what makes international sales management considerations different from domestic sales management. A list of examples appears in **Exhibit 14-1**.

In this chapter, we highlight issues related to the choice of market entry method and the sales management step to setting salesforce objectives. In relating foreign entry choices to sales management, we provide a framework for thinking about the effects of various salesforce management issues. Subsequently, we ask the student to carefully consider the cultural generalizations that influence international decisions and interactions. Poor generalizations will produce flawed sales management. Good tools for generalizing about cultures can help the international manager make decisions that accurately take into account cultural differences.

We discuss how cultural differences, in general, affect issues central to sales management. We consider cultural impacts on recruiting, training, supervising, and evaluating salespeople, as well as on the personal sales process. We also examine a special form of cross-cultural interactions: international negotiations.

Finally, we discuss the complex issues involved when a company sends its employees overseas. A company that uses expatriates successfully has significant advantages, but the process requires careful selection, training, supervision, and evaluation of personnel.

## MARKET ENTRY OPTIONS AND SALESFORCE STRATEGY ◆ ◆ ◆ ◆ ◆ ◆ ◆

In the salesforce management "process," we start with setting objectives and strategy. These steps include determining the goals and purposes of the salesforce and the structure that will best meet those goals. To a large extent, these initial steps determine the requirements for the subsequent steps in the process—recruiting, training, supervising, and evaluating.

The question of *how to enter the market* is central to marketing. As a company decides what form its market entry will take, it is making a decision that limits and defines key underlying aspects of its future salesforce management. For example, if a company decides to sell its products in the United States through a large, integrated distributor, it may only need a small, highly mobile salesforce.

In international sales, the form of entry has even greater implications in international sales. The form of entry determines how large the salesforce needs to be, and will influence how much training it will require. It also influences whether the salesforce is predominantly local foreign citizens or whether it is primarily expatriates. This composition then influences the compensation scale required. Clearly, the form of entry directly influences many of the *downstream* salesforce management options. This section reviews various options for entering a foreign market and summarizes the principal implications and questions each option raises.

The entry method we have been referring to is also termed the *level of integration* in the market. Forward integration suggests greater ownership and control of the distribution channel. For example, a company might begin its foreign sales by exporting through a merchant distributor who takes title to the product and performs all necessary foreign sales functions. Later, the company might integrate forward into the distribution channel by hiring its own commissioned sales agents in the foreign country. Still greater forward integration might consist of the company purchasing a sales subsidiary and establishing product warehouses abroad.[2]

Determining the best level of integration is an issue more appropriate for a chapter on international strategy than sales management. However, in determining the entry form, the company must consider the subsequent influences it will have on their sales management options. In general, a greater forward integration is preferred when: (1) the operation is large enough to spread out the overhead costs of owning and maintaining infrastructure and training and supervising employees; (2) an inability to enforce contractual obligations on outside intermediaries or some other need for greater control of the sales process requires a strong presence in the host country; and (3) sales of a service usually require a presence in the country earlier than would otherwise be considered.

A number of typical entry approaches and the sales management concerns each raises are presented in **Exhibit 14-2.**

Selling through an Export Management Company (EMC) or an Export Trading Company (ETC) is considered a low-involvement approach to international sales. **Export management companies (EMCs)** in general, serve the needs of their clients in entering a market or sourcing goods from a market. They are characterized by their "service" nature and efforts to interact with and meet the needs of the exporter client. Many EMCs have specific expertise in selecting markets abroad and finding customers due to their language capabilities, previous business experience in the country, or a network of their business contacts. The EMC works with an exporter in one of two ways. First, the EMC may act as an agent distributor performing marketing services for the exporter client, responsible primarily for developing foreign business and sales strategies and establishing contact abroad. For this prospecting role, the EMC earns its income from a commission on the products it sells on the exporter's behalf. Second, the EMC can act as a merchant distributor, who purchases products from the domestic exporter, takes title, sells the product in its own name, and consequently assumes all trading risks. The domestic exporter selling directly to the merchant EMC receives its money without having to deal with the complexities and trading risks in the international market. On the other hand, the exporter is less likely to build its own international experience. Many inexperienced exporters use EMCs services mainly to test the international arena, with some desire to become direct participants once a foreign customer base has been established. This can cause conflict between the interests of the EMC and those of the client exporter.

Since the late-1990s, the rapid growth of the internet and the recent proliferation of e-business have generated threat to the future of EMCs. The impact of e-business on the survival of EMCs has been a subject of serious debate for some time. However,

---

[2]Saul Kline, Gary L. Frazier, and Victor J. Roth, "A Transaction Cost Analysis Model of Channel Integration in International Markets," *Journal of Marketing Research*, 27 (May 1990), pp. 196–208.

**EXHIBIT 14-2**
DEGREE OF INVOLVEMENT AND SALES MANAGEMENT ISSUES

| Degree of Involvement | Examples | Description | Sales Management Concerns |
|---|---|---|---|
| Limited Foreign Involvement and Visibility | Export Management Companies (EMC), Export Trading Companies (ETC), direct exporting, licensing | • Concerned with contract for sales from the United States<br>• No salesforce or representatives abroad<br>• Little or no control over foreign marketing process | • Goals of the company may not take precedence<br>• Low foreign image and stability<br>• Impossibility of training salesforce |
| Local Management and Salesforce | Piggybacking, selling through chains | • Little attempt to make foreign sales imitate U.S. sales culture<br>• May "borrow" a salesforce or sell via direct contracts from abroad with multidistributor outlets | • Ineffective customs (lack of influence)<br>• Low product knowledge<br>• Control (trust, commitment)<br>• Poor communications |
| Expatriate Management and Local Salesforce (Mixed) | Selling through chains with locals, direct selling with locals | • Expatriates oversee sales regions, lead training | • Perceptions of equality and fairness<br>• Cultural interactions |
| Heavy to Complete Expatriate Salesforce | Traveling global salesforce, high technology experts | • Client-by-client sales by expatriate salesforce | • Lack of local understanding of insiders and market workings<br>• High cost<br>• Difficulty in recruiting expatriates<br>• Country limits on expatriates or rules, such as taxes, which vary depending on foreign presence |

according to a recent research, this might not be the case. Based on the resource-based perspective of the firm, this study suggests that the primary reason underlying the survival of the EMCs in the past has been their market-based resources and capabilities accumulated over time and this would also be the primary reason of their survival and re-intermediation in the future. By appropriately weaving e-business into their market-based resources and capabilities, the well-established EMCs can acquire a superior position of value creation vis-à-vis their suppliers in their value chains. As a result, the EMCs are expected to continue to play an important mediator role for inexperienced exporters.[3]

**Export trading companies (ETCs)** are usually large conglomerates that import, export, countertrade, invest, and manufacture in the global arena. The ETC can purchase products, act as a distributor abroad, or offer services. Mitsubishi, Mitsui, Sumitomo, and Marubeni, among others, are major examples of an ETC, which are known in Japan as **sogoshosha** (general trading companies).[4] ETCs utilize their vast size to benefit from economies of scale in shipping and distribution. In the United States, the Export Trading Company Act of 1982 exempted ETCs from antitrust laws.[5] The intent was to improve the export performance of small and medium-sized companies by allowing them joint participation with banks in an ETC. ETCs offer the exporting

---

[3]Varinder M. Sharma, "Export Management Companies and E-Business: Impact on Export Services, Product Portfolio, and Global Market Coverage," *Journal of Marketing Theory & Practice*, 13 (Fall), 2005, pp. 61–71.

[4]Lyn S. Amine, S. Tamer Cavusgil, Robert I. Weinstein, "Japanese Sogo Shosha and the U.S. Export Trading Companies," *Journal of the Academy of Marketing Science*, 14 (Fall 1986), pp. 21–32.

[5]Daniel C. Bello and Nicholas C. Williamson, "The American Export Trading Company: Designing A New International Marketing Institution," *Journal of Marketing*, 49 (Fall 1985), pp. 60–69.

company a stable, known distributor, but they do not give the exporting company much control over or knowledge about the international sales process.

A recent empirical study, which estimates the determinants of the manufacturing exports demand from 1978 to 2004 to identify the effect of this exemption on the real value of exports, indicates that the program created by the ETC Act to provide limited antitrust immunity for joint export activity appears to have no statistically significant effect on the real value of U.S. exports. However, it also concludes that, although ETC Act has limited impact on the country's economy, it does present anecdotal evidence that shows its facilitation on some business cases to increase industry exports.[6]

Licensing also represents a low-involvement approach to foreign sales. The company licenses its product or technology abroad and allows the contracting foreign company to coordinate the production and foreign distribution of the product.

Limited involvement approaches to international market entry simplify sales management greatly by reducing it to a predominantly domestic activity. There is little need to recruit, train, supervise, or evaluate a foreign or expatriate salesforce. However, companies that follow a limited involvement approach sacrifice the benefits that hiring and training their own salesforce can provide. These benefits include the ability to motivate and monitor the salesforce and to train them to better serve the customer, the customer loyalty that a dedicated salesforce can generate, and the perception of permanence and commitment that a dedicated salesforce conveys. Many foreign companies look for such an indication of stability and commitment when selecting suppliers.

Mid-level involvement approaches to foreign sales are those in which the company controls some portion of the distribution process. Thus, the company must employ some management or salesforce abroad. This work force may be either predominantly host country employees, or it may include a large share of expatriates. In either case, the company deals face to face with the foreign culture, and intercultural communication becomes a significant issue. Training can help reduce misunderstandings and miscommunications, and can provide both sides with tools to understand the perspectives of the others. For example, training helps the local salespeople better understand the company's policies by reviewing its history and goals. Training also helps the expatriates understand the local market by reviewing the norms of business within their industry and country.

The choice of whether to rely on expatriate involvement is not an easy one. Without expatriate involvement, the company could decide that it is difficult to control the sales process, even though it owns part of the process. With expatriate involvement, local nationals could envy the expatriates' higher levels of pay or resent the limitations on their career opportunities with the company.

High involvement approaches are those in which the company substantially controls the foreign distribution channels. The company could own warehouses to store products and outlets where the products are sold, and it could manage a large, dedicated salesforce abroad. Typically, if a domestic company is highly involved in a foreign market, at least some of that presence will be expatriates. For some companies only the top officer abroad is an expatriate. For others, the expatriate presence is much stronger.

The benefits of controlling distribution include the ability to recruit, train, and supervise a foreign salesforce that can best represent the company abroad. However, controlling distribution requires that the sales volume be large enough to justify the costs, and it also requires enough experience to avoid costly errors.

## Role of Foreign Governments

At the time the company is considering its entry strategy, it should consider foreign government rules and practices. Many host country governments design regulations to

---

[6]Margaret C. Levenstein and Valerie Y. Suslow, "The Economic Impact of the U.S. Export Trading Company Act," *Antitrust Law Journal*, 2007, 74 (2), pp. 343–86.

protect local firms from international competition and ensure that local citizens benefit from experience in management positions at international companies. Thus, governments limit the number of international companies they allow to sell in the market, and they require that foreign companies fill a large number of positions with local citizens. Even the United States follows such practices. The U.S. Immigration and Naturalization Service does not let foreign managers enter the United States to work when it believes that there are U.S. citizens capable of performing the same jobs. Foreign countries also often dictate who can enter, for how long, and for what jobs. These requirements can determine which entry strategy makes sense for a company.

A second issue in deciding the entry approach is the role expected of companies as "corporate citizens" in the country. If a company sets up a complete sales and distribution subsidiary, it may be expected to build local infrastructure, support local politicians, or take part in local training initiatives. Such considerations will weigh in on the choice of the sales approach.

## CULTURAL CONSIDERATIONS

◆ ◆ ◆ ◆ ◆ ◆ ◆

**Personal Selling**

At the level of **personal selling** there is little true *international* selling. The sales task tends to take place on a national basis. Generally, salespeople perform the majority of their sales within one country—probably even within one region or area of a country. A salesperson selling big-ticket items, such as airplanes or dam construction, could sell to many countries. But even then, each sale is a sale within one country, and the entire sales process takes place in one country. Furthermore, despite growing "international sales," salespeople typically work in only one region. Even in the European Union (EU), for example, where close borders and similar economies could encourage salespeople to work over larger areas, personal selling activities still remain bound mostly to a country or a region. Thus, an analysis of *international* personal selling is a study of how differences in culture impact the forms, rules, and norms for personal selling within each country.[7]

Personal selling is predominantly a personal activity. It requires that the salesperson understand the customer's needs and wants. The salesperson must understand local customs well enough to be accepted and be able to form relationships with the customers. Do customers require a close, supportive relationship where the salesperson regularly checks up on them and knows the names of relatives? Does the customer expect some favors to "lubricate the process"? Each culture has different norms for the process of selling and buying.[8]

Throughout this chapter, we refer to the need to adapt sales and management techniques to the local culture to be successful.[9] It would be wonderful if a diagram were available that could help managers plot the appropriate solutions for each country. Although such a diagram is too much to hope for, we can look at some common generalizations and categorizations of cultural traits and consider how they could affect our sales approach. We must take care, however, not to imply that any culture can be described accurately in a few words or categories.

---

[7] See, for example, Joel Herche and Michel J. Swenson, "Personal Selling Constructs and Measures: Emic versus Etic Approaches to Cross-National Research," *European Journal of Marketing*, 30 (7) 1996, pp. 83–97; Ravi Sohi, "Global Selling and Sales Management-Cross Cultural Issues-National Character," *Journal of Personal Selling & Sales Management*, 19 (Winter 1999), pp. 80–81; and Nina Reynolds and A. Simintiras, "Toward an Understanding of the Role of Cross-Cultural Equivalence in International Personal Selling," *Journal of Marketing Management*, 16 (November 2000), pp. 829–51.

[8] Bruce Money, Mary C. Gilly, and John L. Graham, "Explorations of National Culture and Word-of-Mouth Referral Behavior in the Purchase of Industrial Services in the United States and Japan," *Journal of Marketing*, 62 (October 1998), pp. 76–87.

[9] Chanthika Pornpitakpan, "The Effects of Cultural Adaptation on Business Relationships: Americans Selling to Japanese and Thais," *Journal of International Business Studies* 30 (Second Quarter 1999), pp. 317–38.

R. Lord/The Image Works

An Avon sales representative selling to customer in a rural area in São Paulo, Brazil. This local sales rep has good personal knowledge of this rural community and customers.

## Cultural Generalization

As an example of a cultural generalization with both helpful insights and misleading oversights, consider the foreign view of Germans. Germans are typically viewed as scientifically exacting and industrious people. We could therefore approach sales in Germany by building a small core of technically trained, independent sales agents. However, if we think Germans look at work the same way Americans do, we will be misguided! The typical German manufacturing workweek is only thirty hours. Also, Germans jealously guard their free time and show little interest in working more to earn more.[10]

We must also be careful not to group people from what may appear to us as very similar cultures, but who consider themselves, and react to situations, in a very distinct manner. Consider, for example, South Korea and Japan. We may think that Koreans would be accustomed to the same bottom-up, consensual decision-making approach for which the Japanese are known. Korean workers, however, tend to work within a top-down, authoritarian leadership structure,[11] and require a higher level of definition in their job structure to avoid suffering from role conflict. A Korean salesperson might accept as normal a short-term position with few prospects for long-term progress, whereas a Japanese salesperson would not dream of it.[12]

Another example is the differences in the orientation of salespeople in Australia and New Zealand. Most of us tend to think that their cultures are very similar. However, salespeople in New Zealand tend to be more committed to, and generally more satisfied with, their work than their Australian counterparts. Additionally, there are differences in preferences toward compensation (Australians preferring greater security in the form of larger salary) and special incentives (New Zealanders having a much higher preference for travel with other winners and supervisory staff).[13] In a way, salespeople in New Zealand share more similarities in their value system with their Japanese counterparts than their Australian neighbors.

These and other observations suggest that cultural generalizations may be risky even among seemingly similar countries, particularly at the operational level. As explained earlier in Chapter 4, one of the most widely used tools for categorizing cultures for managerial purposes is Hofstede's scale of five cultural dimensions (i.e., power/distance; uncertainty/avoidance; individualism/collectivism; masculinity/

---

[10]Daniel Benjamin and Tony Horwitz, "German View: You Americans Work Too Hard—And For What?" *Wall Street Journal* (July 14, 1994), p. B1.

[11]Hak Chong Lee, "Managerial Characteristics of Korean Firms," in K. H. Chung and H. C. Lee, eds. *Korean Managerial Dynamics* (New York: Praeger, 1989), pp. 147–62.

[12]Alan J. Dubinsky, Ronald E. Michaels, Masaaki Kotabe, Chae Un Lim, and Hee-Cheol Moon, "Influence of Role Stress on Industrial Salespeople's Work Outcomes in the United States, Japan, and Korea," *Journal of International Business Studies*, 23 (First Quarter 1992), pp. 77–99.

[13]William H. Murphy, "Hofstede's National Culture as a Guide for Sales Practices across Countries: The Case of a MNC's Sales Practices in Australia and New Zealand," *Australian Journal of Management*, 24 (June 1999), pp. 37–58.

femininity; long-term/short-term orientation). Hofstede's scale uses many questions to determine where countries, not individual people, stand on each dimension.

As also explained in Chapter 4, companies also have their own distinct **corporate (organizational) cultures**. The culture at a company helps determine the norms of behavior and the mood at the workplace. This corporate culture acts in conjunction with national or country culture to set the values and beliefs that employees carry in the workplace.

**Corporate (Organizational) Culture**

The differences between the cultures of any two companies have been found to be determined significantly by the *practices* of those already in the company, especially the founders. By contrast, the differences between the cultures of companies in two countries are based more in the ingrained cultural *values* of the employees.[14] Values are learned earlier in life and are much more difficult to change than practices. Consider an example of the difference in trying to modify each. We might expect to initiate novel work practices without strong negative reactions from the employees. For example, we might ask salespeople to report to a group instead of to a boss in an effort to instill a sense of group responsibility. However, if we attempt to change procedures that are strongly rooted in the values of a country's culture, we may be asking for a negative response. Consider the troubles we might encounter if we attempted to integrate men and women in the salesforce in Saudi Arabia. At the very least we would not bring out the best the salesforce has to offer.

Thus, although corporate cultures determine much about the working environment and even the success of an organization, the practices that characterize them are fairly malleable. Country cultures, and more specifically, the values people build at an early age in life, also greatly influence which management practices will succeed. However, cultural values are fairly fixed—do not underestimate the importance of cultural values and people's unwillingness to change them.[15]

In the last twenty years, influenced by Japan's vertical *keiretsu* (a closely knit group affiliation among the principal company, upstream suppliers of components and other materials, and downstream retailers for its finished products along the value chain), an increasing number of companies, such as Bose, Compaq, and Motorola, have begun to station their engineering personnel in their independent parts suppliers for more effective product development and to station their sales personnel work in the retailer's offices. The principal companies can track demand at store levels directly and place orders on a just-in-time basis. Both up-stream and down-stream involvements by the principal companies along the value chain can manage information flow from the retailers and customers more effectively and step up the pace of new product development.[16]

**Relationship Marketing**

This type of buyer-seller relationship is a win-win situation because both sides gain from the deal (albeit in different ways). Thus, they start out with the intention of producing a mutually beneficial arrangement. An increasing number of organizations have, indeed, come to see the relationship as one of interdependence; the two sides adopt a peer-to-peer relationship.

Indeed, the relationship between a seller and a buyer seldom ends when the sale is made. In an increasing proportion of transactions, the relationship actually intensifies subsequent to the sale. This becomes the critical factor in the buyer's choice of the seller the next time around. How good the seller-buyer relationship is depends on how well the seller manages it.[17] Again, many companies are finding that adoption of the personal computer technology in maintaining product, pricing, and technical data for effective customer relationships is crucial for their success.

---

[14]Geert Hofstede, Bram Neuijen, Denise Daval Ohayv, and Geert Sanders, "Measuring Organizational Cultures: A Qualitative and Quantitative Study Across Twenty Cases," *Administrative Science Quarterly*, 35 (1990), pp. 286–316.
[15]Ibid.
[16]Michiel R. Leenders and David L. Blenkhorn, *Reverse Marketing: The New Buyer-Supplier* Relationship, New York: Free Press, 1988.
[17]Gila E. Fruchter and Simon P. Sigué, "Transactions vs. Relationships: What Should the Company Emphasize?" *Journal of Service Research*, 8 (August 2005), pp. 18–36.

It is almost a decade since management consultancy Bain & Co carried out its groundbreaking research into the key differences between customer acquisition and customer retention.[18] By considering the real costs and long-term returns, the research revealed that most companies often understate acquisition costs, while cross-selling to an existing customer cost one-sixth of the price of making a sale to a prospect. Bain introduced one of the most famous equations in marketing: a 5-percent increase in customer retention would increase the value of each customer by between 25 and 100 percent. The potential implied in that finding led directly to customer relationship marketing.[19]

Good customer relationships are important by any means in any market. However, they tend to be more conspicuous in high-context cultures, such as Asian and Latin American countries. As discussed in Chapter 4, people in high-context culture countries tend to prefer group-oriented decision-making processes, unlike low-context culture countries, such as the United States and Western and Northern European countries, where decision-making processes are individualistic. In many firms, salespeople are also the primary source of information exchange within a customer-seller relationship and thus play a critical role in the formation and sustainability of customer relationships. To the extent customer relationship marketing is important, the personal traits of sales managers need to be carefully examined, particularly when they engage in "selling" to corporate clients in other countries.

## Myers–Briggs Type Indicator

All business is personal. Despite all the time that marketing departments put into persuasive press releases and snazzy computer presentations, in the end, people do business with people. It means that prospective customers have to like and trust salespersons from the get-go.

One popular tool for characterizing people that addresses their cognitive styles is the **Myers–Briggs Type Indicator (MBTI)** (See **Exhibit 14-3**). The MBTI is based on the

**EXHIBIT 14-3**

MYERS–BRIGGS TYPE INDICATOR OF PERSONAL CHARACTERISTICS

| Personal Dimension | Description |
| --- | --- |
| Extrovert vs. Introvert | An extrovert tends to rely on the environment for guidance, be action-oriented, sociable, and communicate with ease and frankness. |
| | An introvert tends to show a greater concern with concepts and ideas than with external events, relative detachment, and enjoyment of solitude and privacy over companionship. |
| Sensing vs. Intuitive | A sensing person tends to focus on immediate experience, become more realistic and practical, and develop skills such as acute powers of observation and memory for details. |
| | An intuitive person tends to value possibility and meaning more than immediate experience, and become more imaginative, theoretical, abstract, and future oriented. |
| Thinking vs. Feeling | A thinking person tends to be concerned with logical and impersonal decision-making and principles of justice and fairness, and is strong in analytical ability and objectivity. |
| | A feeling person tends to make decisions by weighing relative values and merits of issues, be attuned to personal and group values, and be concerned with human, rather than technical, aspects of a problem. |
| Judging vs. Perceiving | A judging person tends to make relatively quick decisions, be well planned and organized, and seek closure. |
| | A perceiving person tends to be open to new information, not move for closure to make quick decisions, and stay adaptable and open to new events or change. |

*Source:* Constructed from Neil R. Abramson, Henry W. Lane, Hirohisa Nagai, and Haruo Takagi, "A Comparison of Canadian and Japanese Cognitive Styles: Implications for Management Interactions," *Journal of International Business Studies*, 24 (Third Quarter 1993), pp. 575–87.

---

[18]Frederick Reichheld, *The Loyalty Effect*, Boston, MA: Harvard Business School Press, 1996.

[19]David Reed, "Great Expectations," *Marketing Week*, April 29, 1999, pp. 57–58.

following four personal dimensions: (1) extrovert versus introvert, (2) intuitive and sensing, (3) thinking versus feeling, and (4) judging versus perceiving.

Using this scale, Abramsom, Lane, Nagai, and Takagi[20] found significant cognitive distinctions between Canadian and Japanese MBA students. The English-speaking Canadian students preferred intuition, judgment, and thinking, whereas the Japanese students preferred sensing, perceiving, and thinking, but were more feeling-oriented than the Canadian students. In summary, the English-speaking Canadians displayed a logical and impersonal, or objective, style that subordinates the human element. The Japanese displayed a more feeling style, which emphasized the human element in problem solving such as being sympathetic and trust building in human relations. English-speaking Canadians have a tendency to seek fast decisions and rush to closure on data collection. The Japanese were found to resist quick decision-making because of their preference for obtaining large amounts of information. A recent study also shows that French-speaking Canadians in Quebec, unlike the English-speaking Canadians, are indeed a bit more similar to Japanese in terms of their emphasis on trust building.[21] Indeed, Japanese salespeople, who emphasize trust building, use more word-of-mouth referrals in consummating sales than American counterparts.[22]

Although the Myers-Briggs Type Indicator categorizes personal style and traits, there is some similarity to the national culture classification schemes such as Hall's high versus low context cultures and Hofstede's five components of culture (explained earlier in Chapter 4). People from low-context (individualistic) culture tend to be extrovert, intuitive, thinking, and judging, while those from high-context (group-oriented) culture tend to be introvert, sensing, feeling, and perceiving in orientation. Of course, the interpretation of cultural characteristics at the personal level may border on stereotyping. Rather, think of cultural traits as a general tendency in evaluating personal style and traits.[23]

Differences in style and traits must be taken into consideration whenever two cultures interact. In international sales, cross-cultural interaction takes place between the home office and the subsidiary, between expatriate managers and the salesforce, or between an expatriate salesperson and the customer. If the cultural norms and cognitive styles of both sides are more clearly understood, it will help reduce misconceptions and miscommunications.

## IMPACT OF CULTURE ON SALES MANAGEMENT AND PERSONAL SELLING PROCESS

♦ ♦ ♦ ♦ ♦ ♦ ♦

In general, the human resource practices of multinational corporations (MNCs) closely follow the local practices of the country in which they operate.[24] These human resource practices include: time off, benefits, gender composition, training, executive bonuses, and participation of employees in management. However, human resource practices

---

[20]Neil R. Abramson, Henry W. Lane, Hirohisa Nagai, and Haruo Takagi, "A Comparison of Canadian and Japanese Cognitive Styles: Implications for Management Interactions," *Journal of International Business Studies*, 24 (Third Quarter 1993), pp. 575–87.

[21]Joseph P. Cannon, Patricia M. Doney, and Michael R. Mullen, "A Cross-Cultural Examination of the Effects of Trust and Supplier Performance on Long-Term Buyer-Supplier Relationships," *Enhancing Knowledge Development in Marketing*, 1999 American Marketing Association Educators' Proceedings, Summer 1999, p. 101.

[22]R. Bruce Money, Mary C. Gilly, and John L. Graham, "Explorations of National Culture and Word-of-Mouth Referral Behavior in the Purchase of Industrial Services [FN] in the United States and Japan," *Journal of Marketing*, 62 (October 1998), pp. 76–87.

[23]See, for example, William J. Bigoness and Gerald L. Blakely, "A Cross-National Study of Managerial Values," *Journal of International Business Studies*, 27 (Fourth Quarter 1996), pp. 739–52; and Kwok Leung; Rabi S. Bhagat, Nancy R. Buchan, Miriam Erez, and Cristina B. Gibson, "Culture and International Business: Recent Advances and their Implications for Future Research," *Journal of International Business Studies*, 36 (July 2005), pp. 357–78.

[24]Philip M. Rosenzweig, and Ritin Nohria. "Influences on Human Resource Management Practices in Multinational Corporations," *Journal of International Business Studies*, 25 (Second Quarter 1994), pp. 229–51.

also depend on the strategy desired, the culture of the company, and even the country from which the company originated.

Thus, although we can say that the sales management process should adapt to the local environment,[25] we acknowledge the difficult give-and-take involved in adapting a company's culture and procedures with the sales and management practices of a foreign country.

> When host-country standards seem substandard from the perspective of the home country (manager), the manager faces a dilemma. Should the MNC implement home country standards and so seem to lack respect for the cultural diversity and national integrity of the host (country)? Or, should the MNC implement seemingly less optimal host country standards?[26]

One recent study suggests that international differences in the effectiveness of different sales management should be incorporated into the design of control systems, should involve local personnel in the decision, and should allow local countries' flexibility in the implementation of control strategy. The transfer of sales management practices across different countries without careful attention to local differences is very risky.[27] One good exemplary hiring policy is presented in **Global Perspective 14-2**.

The process of salesforce management provides a framework for a closer look at the challenges involved in adapting management practices to a new culture. Salesforce management consists of the following six steps:

1. Setting salesforce objectives
2. Designing salesforce strategy
3. Recruiting and selecting salespeople
4. Training salespeople
5. Supervising salespeople
6. Evaluating salespeople

## Salesforce Objectives

Setting salesforce objectives depends on having already determined the larger, strategic objectives of the company. A company can have the strategic objective of adding value by providing the customer more understanding of a product's use. Or the company could want to enter the market as the low-cost provider. Once such strategic objectives are decided upon, the company can evaluate what roles the salesforce will play in reaching these goals. These roles are the salesforce objectives. They explicitly state *what* the salesforce will be asked to do, whether it is solving customer complaints or pushing for publicity of the product.

Salesforce objectives will then influence much of the rest of the sales management process. If a salesforce objective is to expand market share, then the salesforce will be designed, recruited, trained, supervised, and evaluated using that objective as a guideline. Salesforce objectives will guide how much salesforce time and effort will be required for digging up leads versus working with existing customers, or how much effort will be placed on new products versus older products, or how much effort will be spent on customer satisfaction compared to sales volume.

---

[25] A recent study proves that when management practices are adapted to the national culture of a country in which the company operates, its financial performance tends to improve. See Karen L. Newman and Stanley D. Nollen, "Culture and Congruence: The Fit between Management Practices and National Culture," *Journal of International Business Studies*, 27 (Fourth Quarter 1996), pp. 753–79.

[26] Thomas Donaldson, "Multinational Decision-Making: Reconciling International Norms," *Journal of Business Ethics*, 4 (1985), pp. 357–66.

[27] Nigel F. Piercy, George S. Low, and David W. Cravens, "Consequences of Sales Management's Behavior—and Compensation-Based Control Strategies in Developing Countries," *Journal of International Marketing*, 12 (3), 2004, pp. 30–57.

**GLOBAL PERSPECTIVE 14-2**

**TGI FRIDAYS, INC.**

In setting up overseas, the restaurant chain, TGI Fridays, an American bar and diner concept, follows a key series of guidelines:

- Choose a local development partner to guide through government obstacles, local hiring practices, and on-site business hurdles.
- Concentrate on hiring fun employees who "fit" the company's image—"fun" people willing to sing "Happy Birthday" to a customer.
- Entrust the entire operation to the overseas management after business practices and philosophy have been completely transferred.
- In seeking new overseas managers, look for foreign nationals on assignment or pursuing studies in the United States and offer them an opportunity to return home, bringing back with them the knowledge they have acquired about U.S. culture, and business and service standards. But just as important, they are experts in the traditions, ethics, and ways of life of the customers (we) want to serve in foreign markets.

An example of these guidelines put into practice is TGI Fridays' expansion into England. Its success can be attributed

*Sources:* Mark Hamstra, "Operators Bullish about Opportunities in Overseas Markets, Despite Turmoil," *Nation's Restaurant News* (October 5, 1998), p. 86; and Conrad Lashley, "Empowerment through Involvement: A Case Study of TGI Fridays Restaurants," *Personnel Review*, 29 (5/6, 2000), pp. 791–815.

to the chain's strong local partner, Whitbread PLC, successfully operating under license from the parent company in the United States.

The company's own research shows that 25 percent of customers return to the restaurant at least once per month. During weekdays the typical customer is female in her thirties and is in a professional, managerial, or white-collar occupation. However, the typical customer profile changes throughout the day: business lunches, families in the afternoon and early evening, couples and young adults in the later evening. At the weekend customers typically include large numbers of families. There are also some significant differences between customer profiles in London and the provinces.

In these circumstances, employee performance, particularly of front-line staff, has a crucial role to play. The success of the service depends on the worker's ability to construct particular kinds of interactions. "Dub-Dubs," as the waiting staff are called, have to advise customers on the menu and how best to structure their meal. They also have to identify the customer's service requirements and deliver what is needed. In some cases, having a good laugh with the customers is needed. At other times they have to entertain restive children. Employee performance requires more than the traditional acts of greeting, seating and serving customers. Employees have to be able to provide both the behaviors and the emotional displays to match with customer wants and feelings. In other words, the ability to "connect with others" is a crucial ingredient for high employee performance.

Setting salesforce objectives will require a very similar approach internationally as it does domestically. In fact, many "international" salesforce issues are really local issues in a foreign country. However, setting the best international salesforce objectives depends not only on the company goals, but also on an analysis of the culture and values of the country it is entering. The company could use a standardized approach for all countries, or it might customize its salesforce management approach from the ground up for each country. Most companies will probably customize some aspects of each country's salesforce objectives, but will follow previously held beliefs about the purpose of the salesforce to decide most objectives. Once the objectives are known, the company can begin designing the structure of the proposed salesforce.

With the salesforce's objectives set, the company can concentrate on the strategies needed to achieve those objectives. Salesforce strategy addresses the structure, size, and compensation of the salesforce.

**Salesforce Strategy**

The structure determines the physical positioning and responsibilities of each salesperson. A company selling one product to a dispersed client base might consider a *territorial salesforce*, with each salesperson responsible for a particular area and reporting up the line to regional sales managers. Another company, with numerous, unrelated, complex products, could consider a *product salesforce* structure, where each salesperson sells only one product or product line, even when selling to a single customer. A third company, which requires close contact with its customers to keep up with customer needs and build tight relationships, could employ a *customer sales-force* structure, in which account managers are responsible for particular clients. Each of these approaches has advantages and disadvantages. Choosing the most appropriate international salesforce strategy requires analyzing many of the same considerations as it does domestically. However, additional considerations could arise concerning the lack of capable local salespeople, the cultural expectations of clients, and the dramatically increased costs of maintaining expatriate personnel abroad.

The size of the salesforce depends on the sales structure. The company often calculates how many salespeople are needed by determining how many visits or calls each type of customer should receive and how many salespeople will be needed to make the necessary number of visits. In a foreign culture, customers' distinct expectations may modify the calculations. Although a client in the United States could be satisfied with buying large quantities of a product and hearing from the salesperson every six months, the foreign client could expect a salesperson to be in regular contact and could want to buy smaller quantities more regularly. Such considerations impact the salesforce size. For example, Wal-Mart, the world's largest company, has recognized that the key to its growth lies in rapidly growing China. Unlike Western consumers, Chinese customers tend to buy in smaller quantities and are accustomed to going to supermarket every one or two days. Thus, Wal-Mart Supercenters have to devote more floor space and sales associates to food than to other departments. Furthermore, because Chinese customers need to "feel" the merchandise (put their hands on it) before making the purchase, salesforce assignments need to be carefully examined in order to cater to Chinese consumers' characteristics. When Wal-Mart opened its Supercenter in Chongqing, a metropolis of 31 million in southwest China, it had to open 75 checkout lanes and embrace roughly 120,000 visitors in one single day.[28]

Salesforce compensation is the chief form of motivation for salespeople. However, companies do not pay salesforces equally in all countries. The purchasing power of the "same" quantity of money may not be the same. And more important, pay expectations, or the "going rate," varies dramatically from country to country. The company must carefully consider the social perceptions of its compensation scale. A commission-based compensation could not motivate salespeople in some other countries. A salary scale with large rewards for success could be viewed as unfair. The company must evaluate the impact that the compensation system will have on the employees and then consider what impact the system will also have on the final customer. The pay system must motivate salespeople to leave customers with the appropriate, desired perceptions of the company.

## Recruitment and Selection

In order to successfully recruit and select salespeople, the company must understand what it wants in its salespeople and know how to find and attract people with the necessary skills. The first decision is whether the company will recruit from the local, foreign labor force for the jobs it is creating or whether it will fill them by sending domestic employees overseas. The company could find a strong cultural bias against salespeople in the local market and find it difficult to recruit the necessary talent. Even if it can recruit "talented" people, the company could not clearly know what skills and character traits will work the best in the unfamiliar culture. If the company tries to recruit employees at home, it may have a tough time convincing salespeople or managers with the necessary skills to take the time off from the "fast track" at home.

Complicating the search for talent is the fact that the desired skills and characteristics are not as clear as it first appears. Employers could base their expectations for salespeople on their domestic standards. For example, the employer could look for candidates with an outgoing attitude. However, in some cultures a quieter, more patient

---

[28]"The Great Wal-Mart of China," *Fortune*, July 25, 2005, pp. 104–116.

approach will truly maximize sales. The skills required for success as a salesperson depend on the culture in which the sales take place.

Finally, the employer must consider the strong influences of tribal, religious, or other group relations within a country. A Hindu might not want to make purchases from a Muslim. English companies might do better to hire Irish salespeople to make sales in Ireland. History could give one group a distinct advantage, especially where they have become accepted as a strong business force. For example, the Parsees in India manage an unusually large portion of the nation's business, and Chinese salespeople, the descendants of the Chinese merchant clan, are prominent throughout Asia.[29] A wise sales manager will look for and recruit a salesforce that takes advantage of each country's natural distinctions.

One way for the company to accelerate the difficult process of building a salesforce from scratch is to establish a joint venture with or acquire a local company that already has a functional salesforce. For example, when Merck wanted to expand its pharmaceutical business in Japan, it acquired Banyu Pharmaceutical instead of building its subsidiary and distribution channel from scratch. Merck had immediate access to Banyu's field salesforce of more than a thousand. In Japan, where personal relationships probably weigh more in importance than the quality of products per se, personal selling is all the more critical in relationship-building and -maintaining purposes. Similarly, When Wal-Mart wanted to expand into Europe, its first move was to buy out Wertkauf, a German national chain store, in order to have instant distribution channel members working for it and supply channels already established, as well as a beachhead for the rest of Europe.[30]

Most sales training takes place in the country where staff members reside. The company determines how much technical, product knowledge, company history and culture, or other training its local salesforce requires. However, this country-by-country approach usually fails to develop a globally consistent sales and marketing strategy for MNCs. Therefore, an increasing number of globally oriented companies are now developing a globally consistent sales and marketing program to serve customers and foster long-term partnerships that would engage customers and meet their specific local needs and preferences. For example, BSC, a U.S. manufacturer of medical devices, selected AchieveGlobal in Tampa, Florida, to train its international sales and marketing staff. The two companies have developed a comprehensive training program, consisting of a three-day sales program for all employees and a two-day coaching seminar for sales managers. The sales training program incorporates product knowledge orientation with needs-satisfaction selling, extensive role-playing, and case studies. The session for managers shows them effective ways to coach their teams without handholding. Both companies ensure that BSC's entire sales and marketing staff is trained in the language of their specific country and that the program can be adapted to meet each local culture. This means not only translating the program's language into the local vernacular but also making sure the whole approach meets each country's specific needs. As a result, those sales managers are transferred to local markets with more consistent sales and marketing programs internationally.[31]

**Training**

An additional consideration with regard to international sales training is adapting the training to the needs of the local market. For example, Carrefour, the French retail giant, has created the Carrefour China Institute to train its staff in China to engender the "Carrefour Spirit." Before opening stores in China, the company conducted in-depth research for store location, understanding of the local culture and traditions, and local consumer purchasing behaviors. Inevitably, Carrefour's concepts of "localization

[29]See an excellent treatise, Min Chen, *Asian Management Systems: Chinese, Japanese and Korean Styles of Business* (London: Routledge, 1995), pp. 69–83.

[30]John Fernie and Stephen J. Arnold, "Wal-Mart in Europe: Prospects for Germany, the UK and France," *International Journal of Retail & Distribution Management*, 30 (2/3) 2002, pp. 92–102.

[31]Slade Sohmer, "Emerging as a Global Sales Success," *Sales & Marketing Management*, 152 (May 2000), pp. 124–25.

management" and "low price and high quality" have worked in the Chinese world. The company was rewarded with $1.9 billion revenue in 2004.[32] The training that the salesforce receives must reflect cultural differences in purchasing patterns, values, and perspective of the selling process.

Although international companies often benefit in the local market by offering their employees better training than local competitors, they face the problem of protecting their investment in their employees. National companies often "raid" companies with well-trained salesforces for employees. To protect their investments, the MNCs must offer higher compensation and better promotion opportunities than their competitors.

**Supervision** Supervising the salesforce means directing and motivating the salesforce to fulfill the company's objectives and providing the resources that allow them to do so. The company can set norms concerning how often a salesperson should call each category of customer, and how much of his or her time the salesperson should spend with each of various activities. The company can motivate the salesperson by establishing a supportive, opportunity-filled organizational climate, or by establishing sales quotas or positive incentives for sales. The company often provides the salesperson with tools, such as laptop computers or research facilities, to provide better chances to achieve his or her goals. International sales management addresses how each of these supervising approaches will be received by the salesforce, and what the cultural implications are. For example, cultures that value group identity over individuality will probably not respond well to a sales contest as a motivator.

***Motivation and Compensation.*** Financial compensation is one of the key motivators for employees in all cultures. However, successful sales programs use a wide variety of motivators. The sales manager will want to adapt the incentive structure to best meet local desires and regulations. The use of commissions in motivating salespeople is not publicly acceptable in many countries.[33] Commissions reinforce the negative image of the salesperson benefiting from the sale, with no regard for the purchaser's well-being. Salary increases can substitute for commissions to motivate salespeople to consistently perform highly. However, under certain circumstances, large salary discrepancies between employees are also not acceptable. Strong unions can tie a company's hands in setting salaries, the "collectivist" culture of a country such as Japan cannot accept that one person should earn substantially more than another in the same position. Koreans, for example, are used to working under conditions in which compensation is not directly contingent on performance but rather on seniority. When financial rewards are not acceptable, the company must rely more heavily on nonfinancial rewards, such as recognition, titles, and perquisites for motivation.

Foreign travel is another reward employed by international companies. For example, Electrolux rewards winning sales teams in Asia with international trips. When necessary, companies can combine an international trip with training and justify it as an investment in top salespeople.

***Management Style.*** Management style refers to the approach the manager takes in supervising employees. The manager can define the employee's roles explicitly and require a standardized sales pitch or set broad, general goals that allow each salesperson to develop his or her own skills. A number of studies have found that the best management approach varies by culture and country. For example, Dubinsky and colleagues[34] found that role ambiguity, role conflict, job satisfaction, and organizational

---

[32]"Carrefour China: A Local Market," *China Business*, April 28, 2005.

[33]Michael Segalla, Dominique Rouzies, Madeleine Besson, and Barton A. Weitz, "A Cross-National Investigation of Incentive Sales Compensation," *International Journal of Research in Marketing*, 23 (4): 419–33.

[34]Alan J. Dubinsky, Ronald E. Michaels, Masaaki Kotabe, Chae Un Lim, and Hee-Cheol Moon, "Influence of Role Stress on Industrial Salespeople's Work Outcomes in the United States, Japan, and Korea," *Journal of International Business Studies*, 23 (First Quarter 1992), pp. 77–99.

commitment were just as relevant to salespeople in Japan and Korea as in the United States, and that role conflict and ambiguity have deleterious effects on salespersons in any of the countries. However, specific remedies for role ambiguity, such as greater job formalization (or more hierarchical power, defined rules, and supervision), have a distinct effect on the salespeople in different countries.

One fair generalization is that greater formalization invokes negative responses from the salesforce in countries in which the power distance is low and the individualism is high (such as in the United States). Greater formalization also invokes positive responses from the salesforce in countries in which the power distance is high and the individualism is low (such as in India).[35]

***Ethical Perceptions.*** Culture, or nationality, also influences salespeople's beliefs about the ethics of common selling practices and the need for company policies to guide those practices. Why is this important? Salespeople need to stay within the law, of course, but more importantly, in order to maintain the respect of customers, salespeople must know what is ethically acceptable in a culture. For example, in the United States, giving a bribe is tantamount to admitting that your product cannot compete without help. However, in many cultures, receiving a bribe is seen as a privilege of having attained a position of influence. An understanding of the ethical norms in a culture will help the company maintain a clean image and will also help the company create policies that keep salespeople out of the tense and frustrating situations where they feel they are compromising their ethical standards.

As an example of differences in ethical perceptions, consider the results of a study by Dubinsky and colleagues.[36] The study presented salespeople in Korea, Japan, and the United States with written examples of "questionable" sales situations. Examples of the situations used follow:

- Having different prices for buyers for which you are the sole supplier

- Attempting to circumvent the purchasing department and reach other departments directly when it will help sales

- Giving preferential treatment to customers whom management prefers or who are also good suppliers

The salespeople were asked to rate the extent to which it was unethical to take part in the suggested activity. The results indicated that in general, U.S. salespeople felt that the situations posed fewer ethical problems than did salespeople from Japan and Korea. Another interesting finding of the study—the assumption that Japanese "gift-giving" would extend into the sales realm was found to be untrue. In fact, Japanese salespeople felt that giving free gifts to a purchaser was more an ethical problem than did U.S. salespeople. For Koreans, however, gift-giving was less an issue.

Paradoxically, U.S. salespeople indicated that they wanted their companies to have more policies explicitly addressing these ethical questions. Why? Apparently, salespeople in the United States feel more comfortable when the ethical guidelines are explicitly stated, whereas in other countries (Korea and Japan here), the cultural exchange of living in a more community-oriented society provides the necessary guidelines. Similarly, in countries like Mexico, where power relationships are explicit, salespeople may simply accept and follow management's ethical discretions regardless of their personal ethical standards.[37]

---

[35]Sanjeev Agarwal, "Influence of Formalization on Role Stress, Organizational Commitment, and Work Alienation of Salespersons: A Cross-National Comparative Study," *Journal of International Business Studies*, 24 (Fourth Quarter 1993), pp. 715–40.

[36]Alan J. Dubinsky, Marvin A. Jolson, Masaaki Kotabe, and Chae Un Lim, "A Cross-National Investigation of Industrial Salespeople's Ethical Perceptions," *Journal of International Business Studies*, 22 (Fourth Quarter 1991), pp. 651–70.

[37]William A. Weeks, Terry W. Loe, Lawrence B. Chonko, Carlos Ruy Martinez, and Kirk Wakefield, "Cognitive Moral Development and the Impact of Perceived Organizational Ethical Climate on the Search for Sales Force Excellence: A Cross-Cultural Study," *Journal of Personal Selling & Sales Management*, 26, (Spring 2006), pp. 205–17.

**Evaluation**

Evaluating salespeople includes requiring them to justify their efforts and provide the company with information about their successes, failures, expenses, and time. Evaluations are important to motivate the salesforce, to correct problems, and to reward and promote those who best help the company achieve its goals. Two types of evaluations are common: *quantitative* and *qualitative* evaluations. Examples of quantitative evaluations are comparisons of sales, sales percents, or increases in sales. Examples of qualitative evaluations include tests of the knowledge and manner of the salesperson. Because net profit is often the company's primary objective, evaluations should serve to promote long-term net profits. In some foreign cultures, however, evaluations could be seen as an unnecessary waste of time, or they may invade the sense of privacy of salespeople.

Evaluations help management keep up on sales progress and help employees receive feedback and set goals. International salesforce evaluations must consider the culture's built-in ability to provide feedback to employees. For example, in Japan the "collectivist" nature of the culture may provide the salesperson with much more sense of performance feedback than the "individualistic" culture in the United States would. Thus, it makes sense that U.S. sales managers use more regular, short-term performance evaluations than Japanese sales managers in order to provide their salesforce with more feedback.[38]

Evaluations in international sales management can provide useful information for making international comparisons. Such comparisons can help management identify countries where sales are below average and refine the training, compensation, or salesforce strategy as necessary to improve performance.

◆ ◆ ◆ ◆ ◆ ◆ ◆ ◆ ◆ **CROSS-CULTURAL NEGOTIATIONS**

Conducting successful cross-cultural negotiations is a key ingredient for many international business transactions. International bargaining issues range from establishing the nuts and bolts of supplier agreements to setting up strategic alliances. Negotiation periods can run from a few hours to several months, if not years of bargaining. Bargaining taps into many resources, skills, and expertise. Scores of books have been devoted to negotiation "dos and don'ts."[39] Cross-cultural negotiations are further complicated by divergent cultural backgrounds of the participants in the negotiation process.[40] In this section, we discuss the cultural aspects of international negotiations and bargaining.

**Stages of Negotiation Process**

Roughly speaking, four stages are encountered in most negotiation processes:[41] (1) non-task soundings, (2) task-related information exchange, (3) persuasion, and (4) concessions and agreement. Non-task soundings include all activities that are used to establish a rapport among the parties involved. Developing a rapport is a process that depends on subtle cues.[42] The second stage relates to all task-related exchanges of information. Once the information exchange stage has been completed, the negotiation parties typically move to the persuasion phase of the bargaining process. Persuasion is a

---

[38]Susumu, Ueno and Uma Sekaran, "The Influence of Culture on Budget Control Practices in the U.S. and Japan: An Empirical Study," *Journal of International Business Studies*, 23 (Fourth Quarter 1992), pp. 659–74.

[39]See, for example, Mel Berger, *Cross Cultural Team Building: Guidelines for More Effective Communication and Negotiation*, New York: McGraw-Hill, 1996.

[40]For those interested in learning more about the complexities of cross-cultural negotiations, see a recent special issue on this topic, edited by Yahir H. Zoubir and Roger Volkema, in *Thunderbird International Business Review*, 44 (November/December 2002).

[41]John L. Graham and Yoshihiro Sano, "Across the Negotiating Table from the Japanese," *International Marketing Review*, 3 (Autumn 1986), 58–71.

[42]Kathleen K. Reardon and Robert E. Spekman, "Starting Out Right: Negotiation Lessons for Domestic and Cross-Cultural Business Alliances," *Business Horizons*, Jan.–Feb. 1994, 71–79.

give-and-take deal. The final step involves concession making, intended to result in a consensus. Not surprisingly, negotiation practices vary enormously across cultures. Japanese negotiators devote much more time to nurturing rapport than U.S. negotiators. For Americans, the persuasion stage is the most critical part of the negotiation process. Japanese bargainers prefer to spend most of their time on the first two stages so that little effort is needed for the persuasion phase. Japanese and American negotiators also differ in the way they make concessions. Americans tend to make concessions during the course of the negotiation process, whereas Japanese prefer to defer this stage to the end of the bargaining.[43] See **Exhibit 14-4** for negotiation styles in five other countries.

**Exhibit 14-5** represents a framework of culturally responsive negotiation strategies, driven by the level of cultural familiarity that the negotiating parties possess about one another's cultures. Cultural familiarity is a measure of a party's current knowledge of his counterpart's culture and ability to use that knowledge competently. Depending on the particular situation, eight possible negotiation strategies can be selected. Let us briefly consider each one of them:

## Cross-Cultural Negotiation Strategies[44]

***Employ an Agent or Adviser.*** Outside agents, such as technical experts or financial advisors, can be used when cultural familiarity is extremely low. These agents can be used to provide information and to advice on action plans.

***Involve a Mediator.*** Whereas the previous strategy can be used unilaterally, both parties can also jointly decide to engage a mutually acceptable third party as a mediator. Successful mediation depends on maintaining the respect and trust of both parties.

***Induce the Counterpart to Follow One's Own Negotiation Script.*** Effective negotiators proceed along a *negotiation script*—the rules, conduct, ends they target, means toward those ends, and so forth. When the counterpart's familiarity with your culture is high, it could be feasible to induce the other party to follow your negotiation script. This strategy is especially useful when cultural knowledge is asymmetrical: the other party is knowledgeable about your culture, but you are not familiar with his or hers. Inducement could be via verbal persuasion or subtle cues.

***Adapt the Counterpart's Negotiation Script.*** With moderate levels of familiarity about the counterpart's cultural mindset, it becomes possible to adapt to his negotiation script. Adaptation involves a deliberate decision to adjust some common negotiation rules.

***Coordinate Adjustment of Both Parties.*** When the circumstances lend themselves, both parties can jointly decide to arrive to a common negotiation approach that blends both cultures. Occasionally, they might propose to adopt the negotiation script of a third culture.

***Embrace the Counterpart's Script.*** With this strategy, the negotiator volunteers to adopt the counterpart's negotiation approach. This demands a tremendous effort from the negotiator. It can be effective only when the negotiator possesses a great deal of familiarity about the other party's cultural background.

***Improvise an Approach.*** This strategy constricts a negotiation script over the course of negotiating. This approach is advisable when both parties feel very

---

[43]Graham, John L., "Negotiating with the Japanese (Part 1)," *East Asian Executive Reports*, (November 15, 1988), pp. 8, 19–21.
[44]Stephen E. Weiss, "Negotiating with "Romans"—Part 1," *Sloan Management Review* (Winter 1994), pp. 51–61; Stephen E. Weiss, "Negotiating with "Romans"—Part 2," *Sloan Management Review* (Spring 1994), pp. 85–99.

**EXHIBIT 14-4**
NEGOTIATION STYLES AND GUIDELINES IN FIVE COUNTRIES

| | France | Poland | Turkey | Russia | Spain |
|---|---|---|---|---|---|
| Language | – Younger people: English acceptable<br>– Older people: French—if necessary, agree at early stage to use an interpreter | – English or German<br>– Do not overestimate fluency<br>– Be willing to use an interpreter | – Be careful with terminology; allow extra time for language problems<br>– Be clear and succinct<br>– Avoid being negative | – Do not expect partner speaks English (especially outside big cities); find good interpreter | – Do not assume command of English<br>– Consider using interpreter<br>– Documents and business cards should be in Spanish, not just English |
| Sequence | – General principles →rough outline→details | – Goal-directed<br>– Little small talk<br>– Prepare for lengthy delays | – Small talk matters a lot<br>– Wait to talk business until host brings it up | – Negotiations can be protracted<br>– Starting times not always respected<br>– Frequent interruptions | |
| Communication style | – Abstract and elaborate<br>– Relish in logic, battle of wits<br>– Straightness = blunt, rude<br>– Avoid hard sell | – Unemotional<br>– Lack of flexibility of Polish counterparts | – Be flexible to manage delays; factor in unexpected<br>– Avoid bluntness<br>– Stick to main message; avoid weakening arguments with minor points<br>– Listen first, then ask questions; don't put words into counterpart's mouth | – Personal relationships play vital role<br>– Russian partners can be "slow" | – Personal relationships play vital role; regard personal invitations as a partnership investment<br>– Be prepared for delays<br>– Interruptions common<br>– Several people may talk at once<br>– Discussions can be lively<br>– Spanish people rely on quick thinking, spontaneity<br>– Negotiations can be lengthy |
| Contract | – Very formal, flowery<br>– Fairly brief | – Technical<br>– Very detailed | | – Avoid any changes to contracts; if necessary you will need to make a strong case | |
| Context | – Entertaining matters a great deal but usually done at restaurants<br>– Do not raise issues until end of meal | | – Entertaining important, often at host's home | – Usually at restaurants<br>– Toasting important ritual but be careful | – Can invite partner for lunch or dinner<br>– Deals with top executives often agreed during meals, middle managers trash out details later |

*Sources:* Constructed from "Enjoy a Battle of Wits and a Good Lunch," *Financial Times* (September 11, 2000), p. 9; "Crossing Cultural Barriers," *Financial Times* (September 25, 2000), p. 11 (Poland); "Contacts that Make or Break Turkish Ventures," *Financial Times* (November 6, 2000), p. 14 (Turkey); "A Market Emerging from a Country in Turmoil," *Financial Times* (February 19, 2001), p. 7 (Russia); "Formality, Feasting and Patience," *Financial Times* (October 9, 2000), p. 12 (Spain).

**EXHIBIT 14-5**
CULTURALLY RESPONSIVE STRATEGIES AND THEIR
FEASIBILITY

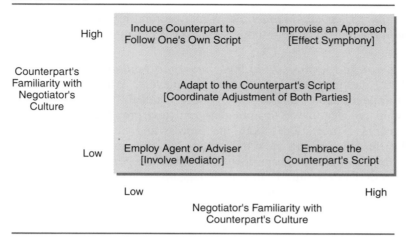

| | | |
|---|---|---|
| High | Induce Counterpart to Follow One's Own Script | Improvise an Approach [Effect Symphony] |
| Counterpart's Familiarity with Negotiator's Culture | Adapt to the Counterpart's Script [Coordinate Adjustment of Both Parties] | |
| Low | Employ Agent or Adviser [Involve Mediator] | Embrace the Counterpart's Script |
| | Low                                          High | |
| | Negotiator's Familiarity with Counterpart's Culture | |

comfortable with their counterpart's culture. It might be effective when bargaining with members from a high-context culture in which mutual bonding and other contextual cues are at least as important (nontask-related aspects) as the immediate negotiation concerns.

*Effect Symphony.* The final strategy capitalizes on both parties' high cultural familiarity by creating an entirely new script or by following some other approach atypical to their respective cultures. For instance, the coordination could select parts from both cultures.

"REMEMBER—WALK IN SIDEWAYS, DON'T LOOK AT THE CEILING, IF YOU AGREE WITH HIM, DON'T SMILE IF YOU DON'T AGREE WITH HIM, SMILE..."

©Sidney Harris

Cultural adaption may be necessary when doing business abroad.

The choice of a particular strategy partly depends on how familiar the negotiators are with the other party's culture. To pick a particular strategy, consider the following steps:

1. *Reflect on your culture's negotiation practices.* What negotiation model do you use? What is the role of the individual negotiator? What is the meaning of a satisfactory agreement?

2. *Learn the negotiation script common in the counterpart's culture.* This involves reflecting on these questions such as: Who are the players? Who decides what? What are the informal influences that can make or break a deal?[45] Answers to these questions will help the negotiator to anticipate and interpret the other party's negotiating behaviors. Expectations about the process and the outcome of the bargaining will differ. People can view the process as win-win or win-lose. The approach to building an agreement can focus first on either general principles or specifics. The level of detail required can vary. Perspectives on the implementation of an agreement can also differ. In some cultures renegotiation is frowned upon. In other cultures, an agreement is seen as a starting point of an evolving relationship.[46]

3. *Consider the relationship and contextual clues.* Different contexts necessitate different negotiating strategies. What circumstances define the interaction between the negotiation parties? Contextual clues include considerations such as the life of the relationship, gender of the parties involved, balance of power.

4. *Predict or influence the counterpart's approach.* Prediction could be based on indicators such as the counterpart's pre-negotiation behavior, track record. In some cases, it is desirable to influence the other party's negotiation strategy via direct means (e.g., explicit request for a negotiation protocol) or through more subtle means (e.g., disclosing one's familiarity with the counterpart's culture).

5. *Choose a strategy.* The chosen strategy should be compatible with the cultures involved, conducive to a coherent pattern of interaction, in line with the relationship and bargaining context, and ideally acceptable to both parties.

◆ ◆ ◆ ◆ ◆ ◆ ◆ ◆ ◆    # EXPATRIATES

Most companies with a salesforce abroad will, at the very least, send a few expatriates abroad as operations begin in a new country. **Expatriates** are home country personnel sent overseas to manage local operations in the foreign market. The general trend among U.S. multinationals since the 1990s has been a decreasing use of expatriate managers overseas and an increasing reliance on local foreign talent.[47] This trend reflects the increasingly international perspective of MNCs, increasing competence of foreign managers, and the relatively increasing competitive disadvantage of the cost of maintaining home country personnel abroad. Despite the relative decline, more employees than ever are involved in international assignments due to the increase in international sales and production. According to a recent study of international assignments, 38 percent of companies surveyed increased the number of international transfers from headquarters in 2004 and 2005. Another 47 percent are still sending the same number abroad. The biggest increases were among companies (both foreign and indigenous) in Asia and Latin America, regions that are home to a new wave of

---

[45] Sebenius, James K. "The Hidden Challenge of Cross-Border Negotiations," *Harvard Business Review* 80 (March 2002), pp. 76–85.

[46] Sebenius, 2002, p. 84.

[47] Gunter K. Stahl, Edwin L. Miller, and Rosalie L. Tung, "Toward the Boundaryless Career: A Closer Look at the Expatriate Career Concept and the Perceived Implications of an International Assignment," *Journal of World Business*, 37 (Autumn 2002), pp. 216–27.

internationally mobile employees. In addition, 44 percent of all firms reported an increase in international transfers between places other than headquarters.[48]

Expatriates have a number of advantages over foreign nationals for companies that sell their products internationally. In general, a successful expatriation starts with a selection of good candidates who are willing to try new things and persist in exhibiting an open-minded and flexible personality to accept the host country's norms. Therefore, firms should select expatriates whose personal values are in line with those of the host countries so that expatriates would have more social interaction with host nationals. For example, when U.S. expatriates possess collective norms that are similar to those of Asian and Latin American cultures, they would have more social interaction with the locals and are more attitudinally attached to the host culture.[49]

Jack Welch, the former CEO of General Electric stated in his speech to GE employees:

**Advantages of Expatriates**

> The Jack Welch of the future cannot be me. I spent my entire career in the United States. The next head of General Electric will be somebody who spent time in Bombay (Mumbai), in Hong Kong, in Buenos Aires. We have to send our best and brightest overseas and make sure they have the training that will allow them to be the global leaders who will make GE flourish in the future.[50]

His statement clearly summarizes the importance of expatriates and their international experiences for improved communications between the company's headquarters and its foreign subsidiaries and affiliates, and development of talent within the company.

*Better Communication.* Expatriates understand the home office, its politics, and its priorities. They are intimately familiar with the products being sold and with previously successful sales techniques. Expatriates can rely on personal relationships with home office management, which increases trust on both sides of the border and can give the expatriate the ability to achieve things that a third-country national or a host country national could not achieve. With an expatriate abroad, communications with the home country will be easier and more precise owing to the groundwork of cultural and corporate understanding. The expatriate will also give the home office the confidence that it has someone in place who understands the company's intent and expectations.

*Development of Talent.* Sending employees abroad provides the company another advantage that hiring foreign locals may not provide: The company develops future managers and executives who can later use their international perspective in management. For example, the leaders of General Motors, Avon, Campbell Soup, Ford, Gillette, Tupperware, Goodyear, General Mills, Case, and Outboard Marine all have significant overseas experience in their careers.[51] According to research by Gregersen, Morrison, and Black, senior executives of multinationals who have had international assignments indicated that those jobs provided their single most influential leadership experience.[52] Thus, by sending their most promising rising stars overseas, companies are sowing the seeds to harvest the next generation of executives.

---

[48]"Traveling More Lightly—Staffing Globalization," *Economist*, June 24, 2006, pp. 77–80.

[49]Sunkyu Jun and James W. Gentry, "An Exploratory Investigation of the Relative Importance of Cultural Similarity and Personal Fit in the Selection and Performance of Expatriates," *Journal of World Business*, 40 (February 2005), pp. 1–8.

[50]Mansour Javidan and Robert J. House, "Leadership and Cultures around the World: Findings from GLOBE," *Journal of World Business*, 37 (Spring 2002), pp. 3–10.

[51]Mason A. Carpenter and Gerard Sanders, "International Assignment Experience at the Top can Make a Bottom-Line Difference," *Human Resource Management*, 39 (Summer/Fall 2000), pp. 277–85.

[52]Hal B. Gregersen, Allen J. Morrison, and J. Stewart Black, "Developing Leaders for the Global Frontier," *Sloan Management Review*, 40 (Fall 1998), pp. 21–32.

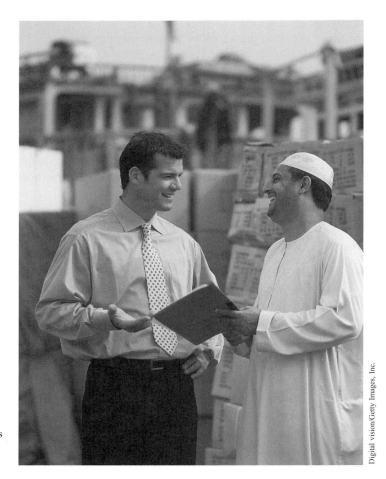

Digital vision/Getty Images, Inc.

Cultural differences do exist. In many cases, your willingness to accept differences is a key to your success in business.

***Difficulties of Sending Expatriates Abroad.***   Although the benefits of sending expatriates abroad are clear, difficulties can also arise for various reasons ranging from organizational to personal ones and even to security risk. Some of the major difficulties are as follows.

***Cross-Cultural Training.***   As with so many other complex situations in life, a little shared understanding goes a long way. In the case of the expatriate, training can significantly help in understanding the cultural differences of the foreign country. U.S. companies used to overlook such "cultural sensitivity training"; expatriates were expected to "pick it up as they go." Cultural misunderstandings can have a large impact, however. About 6 percent of expatriate assignments failed prematurely.[53] As a result, **cross-cultural training** has been on the rise in recent years as more globally oriented companies moving fast-track executives overseas want to curb the cost of failed expatriate stints.

According to GMAC Global Relocation Services' 2008 survey, 67 percent of respondents cited an increase in the expatriate population during 2008. It also reported that 11 percent of all expatriates were new hires and 9 percent of expatriates had previous international experience. Companies are becoming more flexible about the length of international assignments, and are moving away from long-term assignments to a variety of short-term alternatives. The survey found that more companies have embraced a global perception of their entire workforce, therefore utilizing their human resources more effectively and have chosen to outsource their relocation programs to achieve higher levels of financial return, expatriate performance, and satisfaction.

---

[53]*Global Relocation Trends 2008 Survey Report*, GMAC Relocation Services, http://www.gmacglobalrelocation.com/, 2008.

Formal cross-cultural training was mandatory at 23 percent of companies, but 81 percent of them rated it as having great or good value.[54]

Once the expatriate is abroad, it becomes more difficult to provide training, but doing so is even more important. The expatriates are not in constant contact with colleagues, and may not be picking up the newest technology in their company's field. They could be missing out on important policy or procedural changes that the company is undertaking. Ongoing training, whether in a foreign or the home country, can make a huge difference in the success of an overseas assignment.

During the first year of the assignment, having an executive coach with deep country-specific experience can add incalculable benefits to the new expatriate. A competent coach is able to provide feedback to executives on how others perceive them, and to provide a local perspective on problem solving that might otherwise not occur to someone who is new to the region. Such a coach is often able to help the executive in question see potential issues before they arise.[55] Today, host countries are also taking measures to help foreign expatriates get used to their culture. For example in India, there are end-to-end expatriate-services companies offering a range of relocation and cross-cultural services. A company named Global Adjustments even publishes India's only expatriate cultural monthly magazine called *At a Glance— Understanding India*. Headquartered in Chennai, this company has offices in all six major cities in India: Bangalore, Chennai, Kolkata, Mumbai, Pune, and Delhi, helping expatriates from 74 countries ease the passage to and from India.[56]

It is advised that the more different the culture into which people are venturing, the more specific and rigorous the training needs to be, and the more the training needs to incorporate experiential tactics such as simulations and role plays aimed at specific differences.[57]

However, expatriates must recognize that within an average two- to four-year assignment abroad, they will never internalize enough of the local culture to overcome all social and communication concerns. Even with appropriate training, the expatriates are the product of their home culture. They will eat with a fork when a hand is more polite, shake on a deal and thereby show their lack of faith, or require that a contract with all possible legal contingencies spelled out be signed in triplicate when honor and trust dictate that the deal go through on a shared local drink. These could appear to be small social problems, but such social problems can keep the expatriate out of important deals. As Black and Porter[58] noted in their article title, "a successful manager in Los Angeles may not succeed in Hong Kong." The expatriate could find after some time that the best place to make sales is not at the client's offices but at the bar watching soccer with other executives.

***Motivation.*** Motivating expatriates to accept and succeed at positions abroad requires a combination of carefully planned policies and incentives. Appropriate policies help make the prospects of going overseas attractive before, during, and after it takes place. Expatriates often express dissatisfaction that their stints abroad hinder their career progress. Companies should set up and publicize career paths for expatriates that reward and use skills acquired overseas. Additionally, while expatriates are overseas, regular communication with the home office will help allay fears that "out of sight, out of mind" will hinder their career progress.[59] Intranet websites for expatriates will help facilitate such communication.

---

[54]Ibid.

[55]"Preparing Execs for Asia Assignments," *BusinessWeek.com*, April 1, 2008.

[56]"Helping the U.S. and India Work Together," *BusinessWeek.com*, April 29, 2008.

[57]J. Stewart Black, Mark Mendenhall, and Gary Oddou, "Toward a Comprehensive Model of International Adjustment. An Integration of Multiple Theoretical Perspectives," *Academy of Management Review*, 16 (April 1991), pp. 291–317.

[58]J. Stewart Black and Lyman W. Porter, "Managerial Behaviors and Job Performance: A Successful Manager in Los Angeles May Not Succeed in Hong Kong," *Journal of International Business Studies*, 22 (First Quarter 1991), pp. 99–113.

[59]Thomas F. O'Boyle, "Little Benefit to Careers Seen in Foreign Stints," *Wall Street Journal* (December 11, 1989), p. B1, B4.

A recent study also shows that employees who choose an expatriate assignment place a high intrinsic value on the overseas experience *per se*, especially on the opportunities it brings for personality development and enrichment of their personal lives. They also believe that their overseas assignment will help improve their professional and management skills and enhance their careers, although not necessarily within their current company.[60]

***Compensation.*** The average cost of maintaining a home-country executive can cost three to five times what it costs to maintain an employee at home.[61] Compensation packages include various premiums including overseas premiums, housing allowances, cost-of-living allowances, tax equalizations, repatriation allowances, all-expense-paid vacations, and performance-based bonuses. Most compensation premiums are paid as a percentage of base salary. Yet despite this, according to GMAC's Global Relocation Trend 2008 Survey, 32 percent of candidates for expatriate posts rated inadequate compensation packages as the most common reason for turning down their assignments.[62]

When it comes to their wallets, worldly expatriates often moan about Tokyo, London, or New York. This is undoubtedly understandable. However, in many other countries such as those in Africa where the cost of living people think should be low, expatriates find it even more expensive to work and live there. A recent survey by ECA International, which advises multinational companies on how to look after their expatriate staff, rates Harare the most expensive city for such foreigners in the world. Angola's Luanda comes second and Congo's Kinshasa fifth, just behind Oslo and Moscow. Even Gabon's Libreville is deemed more expensive than Tokyo. On the other hand, in cases such as Luanda, where the economy is booming and inflation a mere 12 percent, living costs for foreigners are still incredibly expensive. After decades of war, not much is produced at home, bar oil and diamonds, so most things are imported and command high prices. Foreigners tend to eat at just a handful of restaurants where dinner for two costs more than $150. Actually, expatriates feel ripped off in Angola, Zimbabwe, or Congo. This make it even more difficult to decide satisfactory compensation packages for expatriates.[63] How much should overseas assignments pay?

One approach has been to pay expatriates a premium for their willingness to live in adverse conditions. Such special "hardship packages" can cause problems, however. Overseas employees could notice the discrepancy in remuneration among expatriates, local nationals, and third-country nationals.[64] An expatriate sales manager in Japan could be motivated by an incentive system through which he or she would earn a higher salary for stellar performance. However, such an individual approach would not sit well with Japanese colleagues who subscribe to a collective approach that does not favor standing out from others of similar seniority. Furthermore, expatriates who receive a generous compensation package while abroad may lose motivation on returning home to their previous salary scale.[65] A more recent approach has been to consider the overseas assignment a necessary step for progress within the company. In other words, it is viewed more as a learning experience than as a hardship.

The company must also consider the impact of the family life cycle on compensation. An expatriate with a spouse and children will encounter higher needs abroad due

---

[60]Gunter K. Stahl, Edwin L. Miller, and Rosalie L. Tung, "Toward the Boundaryless Career: A Closer Look at the Expatriate Career Concept and the Perceived Implications of an International Assignment," *Journal of World Business*, 37 (Autumn 2002), pp. 216–27.

[61]Eric Krell, "Evaluating Returns on Expatriates," *HR Magazine*, 50 (March 2005), pp. 60–65.

[62]*Global Relocation Trends 2008 Survey Report*, GMAC Relocation Services, http://www.gmacglobalrelocation.com/, 2008.

[63]"Costly Postings," *Economist*, December 16, 2006, p. 48.

[64]So Min Toh and Angelo S. DeNisi, "A Local Perspective to Expatriate Success," *Academy of Management Executive*, 19 (1), 2005, 132–47.

[65]Michael Harvey, "Empirical Evidence of Recurring International Compensation Problems," *Journal of International Business Studies*, 24 (Fourth Quarter 1993), pp. 785–99.

to the loss of a spouse's income and the cost of enrolling children in private schools. A program must be flexible enough to adjust to the varying needs of different employees.

***Family Discord.*** The typical candidate for an international assignment is married, has school-age children, and is expected to stay overseas for three years. In this age of two-career families, an international assignment means that a spouse could have to suspend a stateside career. Thus, many employees are reluctant to move abroad. Others who accept transfers grow frustrated as they find that their spouses cannot get jobs or even work permits abroad. Schools where the international assignee's home language is spoken must be found, or children must learn the local language. Concerns about the safety and happiness of family members can keep the candidate from accepting an overseas position. A recent study found that concerns about children and spouses' careers were the two main reasons why employees turned down jobs abroad.[66] Given such complexities, it is clear why it could be difficult to motivate typical candidates to accept an overseas stint.

Unsuccessful family adjustment is the single most important reason for expatriate dissatisfaction compelling an early return home. Expatriates as well as their family members are in crisis because of culture shock and stress. As a result, marriages break up and some people become alcoholic.

Thus, international companies try to cut costs by reducing the problems that can hurt expatriates' job satisfaction and performance. Having an experienced and empathetic counselor who can work with all family members in a constructive manner on confusing or negative experiences can greatly improve the chance for success. Many expatriate families in China, for example, isolate themselves from Chinese society because it is intimidating to cope with a steep language barrier as well as unfamiliar cuisine and even unfamiliar transportation or healthcare systems. A guide can give family members the confidence they need to function on their own wherever they are.[67] In addition, firms such as AT&T have begun putting prospective expatriates through management interviews, a written test, and a self-assessment checklist of "cultural adaptability," as well as interviews with a psychologist (see **Global Perspective 14-3**). To

**GLOBAL PERSPECTIVE 14-3**

## SCREENING CANDIDATES FOR EXPATRIATION

An increasing number of companies are screening prospective expatriates and their spouses for cross-cultural adaptability. The following are some of the questions asked at AT&T.

1. Would your spouse's career be put on hold to accompany you on an international assignment? If so, how would this affect your spouse and your relationship with each other?

2. Would you enjoy the challenge of making your own way in new environments?

*Source:* Adapted from Gilbert Fuchsberg, "As Costs of Overseas Assignments Climb, Firms Select Expatriates More Carefully," *Wall Street Journal* (January 9, 1992), p. B1.

3. How would you feel about the need for networking and being your own advocate to secure a job upon return from your foreign assignment?

4. How willing and able are you in initiating and building new social contacts abroad?

5. Could you live without television?

6. How important is it for you to spend a significant amount of time with people of your own ethnic, racial, religious, and national background?

7. Have you ever been genuinely interested in learning about other peoples and cultures?

8. Do you like vacationing in foreign countries?

9. Do you enjoy ethnic and foreign cuisine?

10. How tolerant are you of having to wait for repairs?

---

[66] "Traveling More Lightly—Staffing Globalization," *Economist*, June 24, 2006, pp. 77–80.

[67] "Preparing Execs for Asia Assignments," *BusinessWeek.com*, April 1, 2008.

help spouses find jobs abroad, Philip Morris Company hired an outplacement firm to provide career counseling and job leads.[68]

***Security Risk.*** Since the September 11, 2001 terrorist attacks in the United States, security risk has become a serious issue. Clearly, these terrorist attacks, among others, have had an impact on human resource management. Particularly, expatriate executives from U.S. companies and their families are not as eager to take on international assignments, especially in countries viewed as security risks. Perceived or real security risk concern requires more development, training, and recruiting of local executives, which in the long run should be beneficial to all.

Despite such an anxiety factor causing some dent in the globalization movement, the forces of market and financial globalization are unlikely to be reversed. In fact, more executives have been trained to believe that international experience is critical to their long-term career success. Because of the increased number of international MBA students in many business schools around the world, they are increasingly being placed in countries in which they fit right in culturally, religiously, and racially. These "indigenized" managers increase the frequency of international travel, cross-border migration, and lower communication costs across national boundaries.[69]

## The Return of the Expatriate — Repatriation

Repatriation is the return of the expatriate employee from overseas. Although companies are making efforts to prevent this, many returning expatriates have difficulty finding good job assignments when their foreign positions end. The post-return concern that an overseas assignment can damage a career back home can discourage employees from taking a foreign position. Repatriation is distinct from other forms of relocation. After an average absence of 3.5 years, expatriates themselves have changed, adopting certain values, attitudes, and habits of their host countries. According to GMAC Relocation Services' 2008 survey, 69 percent of respondents held repatriation discussions, and 77 percent of companies identified new jobs within the company for repatriating employees.[70] This is a far cry from its 2001 survey reporting a deplorable picture that 66 percent of companies surveyed indicated that they offered no post-expatriate employment guarantees.[71] In the past decade, U.S. companies have made a measurable improvement in their repatriation policies.

Expatriates face a long list of difficulties upon returning home. Their standard of living often declines. And they often face a lack of appreciation for the knowledge they gained overseas. Without a clear use for their skills, returned expatriates often suffer from a lack of direction and purpose. New stateside assignments often do not give the repatriated employee the same responsibility, freedom, or respect that was enjoyed overseas. It is difficult to adjust to being just another middle manager at home. And poor communications with the home office while abroad leave the returnee cut off from the internal happenings and politics of the company, limiting opportunities for career growth.[72]

GMAC Relocation Services' 2008 survey also reported a number of effective ways to reduce attrition rates. These include providing (1) chances to use international experience, (2) position choices upon return, (3) recognition, (4) repatriation career support, (5) improving performance evaluation, and (6) family repatriation support. Pre-trip training should state the details for the candidate, including future training expected, help the company will provide, and, importantly, the career path that the

[68]Carla Joinson, "Relocation Counseling Meets Employees' Changing Needs," *HRMagazine*, 43 (February 1998), pg. 63–70.

[69]Sevgin Eroglu, "Does Globalization Have Staying Power?" *Marketing Management*, 11 (March/April 2002), pp. 18–23.

[70]*Global Relocation Trends 2008 Survey Report*, 2008.

[71]*Global Relocation Trends 2003/2004 Survey Report*, GMAC Relocation Services, http://www.gmacglobalrelocation.com/, May 2004.

[72]Aaron W. Andreason and Kevin D. Kinneer, "Bringing Them Home Again," *Industrial Management*, 46 (November/December 2004), pp. 13–19.

move will help. The effort and cost of such comprehensive planning sends a strong signal of the importance of foreign assignments to expatriate candidates.

Expatriates are important whenever communication with the home country office is at a premium. Communication is facilitated among managers of the same nationality. Thus, the company is better off with a stronger expatriate base abroad when the overseas situation puts pressure on communications with the home office. Thus, expatriates are especially important in complex operating environments, when elevated political risk requires constant monitoring, or when a high cultural distance separates the home and host countries. On the other hand, in very competitive environments, local nationals could provide important links to the local business community and perhaps play a key strategic role in gaining business.

**Generalizations about When Using Expatriates Is Positive/ Negative**

## SUMMARY ◆ ◆ ◆ ◆ ◆ ◆ ◆ ◆ ◆ ◆ ◆ ◆ ◆ ◆ ◆ ◆ ◆ ◆ ◆ ◆ ◆ ◆ ◆ ◆ ◆

No matter how global a company becomes, its salesforce remains its front line. On the other hand, actual sales activities are truly local activities, far detached from decision making at headquarters. Particularly, in Latin European, Latin American, and Asian countries, salespeople's ability to build trust with prospective customers prior to sales is extremely important. An effective salesforce management is most elusive yet crucial to developing a coherent international marketing and distribution strategy.

Because sales activities are local activities, they tend to be strongly affected by cultural differences (e.g., shopping habit, negotiation style) around the world, making it difficult, if not impossible, for the international marketing manager to integrate overseas sales operations. Many companies rely on merchant distributors at home or sales agents in the foreign market who have more intimate knowledge of the marketplace. As sales increase, these companies begin to increase their commitment to developing their own distribution and salesforce in the foreign market.

The development of an effective sales organization requires salesforce objectives and a salesforce strategy adapted to local differences and calls for careful recruiting, training, supervising, motivating, and compensating local salespeople. We also provided some background on a very complex form of cultural interface: cross-cultural negotiations. Several strategies are introduced to assist you in international bargaining situations.

Furthermore, an increasing number of expatriate managers are sent to overseas posts to directly manage the company's local salesforce. Expatriate managers function as a bridge between headquarters and local operations, and must be culturally adaptive and versatile. Although international assignments have increasingly become a necessary requirement for fast-track managers, cultural adaptability is not always an inborn qualification of many expatriate managers. Cross-cultural training is crucial, because failed expatriate assignments cost the company dearly in terms of lower business performance and dejected employee morale. Use of expatriate managers with personal profiles that fit in well with local cultures is also on the increase for reasons of political correctness. Companies recently have also begun to develop a repatriation program to ease returned expatriates back into their stateside positions. Such a well-organized repatriation program is important to encourage managers to take up expatriate assignments.

## KEY TERMS ◆ ◆ ◆ ◆ ◆ ◆ ◆ ◆ ◆ ◆ ◆ ◆ ◆ ◆ ◆ ◆ ◆ ◆ ◆ ◆ ◆ ◆ ◆ ◆ ◆ ◆

| | | | |
|---|---|---|---|
| Corporate culture | Export management | Myers–Briggs Type Indicator | Sogoshosha (General trading |
| Cross-cultural training | company (EMC) | (MBTI) | company) |
| Expatriate | Export trading company | Personal selling | |
| | (ETC) | Repatriation | |

## REVIEW QUESTIONS ◆ ◆ ◆ ◆ ◆ ◆ ◆ ◆ ◆ ◆ ◆ ◆ ◆ ◆ ◆ ◆ ◆ ◆ ◆ ◆

1. In what ways does international sales management differ from domestic sales management?

2. Discuss why mode of entry and sales management are closely related.

3. For what type of business does a company employ a traveling global salesforce?

4. How could a foreign government affect a company's salesforce management?

5. Why is it generally considered difficult to adopt a U.S.-style commission-based salesforce management in such countries as Japan and Mexico?

6. Discuss why expatriate managers are important to a parent company despite the enormous cost of sending them overseas.

7. Suppose you are developing a cultural training program for employees to be sent to overseas posts. What courses would you include in your two-week program? Why?

## DISCUSSION QUESTIONS ◆ ◆ ◆ ◆ ◆ ◆ ◆ ◆ ◆ ◆ ◆ ◆ ◆ ◆ ◆ ◆ ◆ ◆ ◆ ◆

1. One feature in international selling that is becoming more common is the idea of piggybacking; i.e., tying up with existing sales channels to distribute and sell your products. Examples include Dunkin' Donuts (as the name suggests, the confectionery chain) combining with Baskin-Robbins (the ice-cream chain) units to sell in Canada, Mexico, and Indonesia. According to business proponents of piggybacking, it allows a significant reduction in costs and risks by sharing resources such as dining space, staff, etc., leading to better profitability. However, the concern is that a foreign partner, often chosen as the piggybacking partner (unlike the example just stated) could devote less attention to the foreign product. If the piggybacking is with a unit in the same business, considerable cannibalization can also take place. Discuss the conditions under which a piggyback strategy would be appropriate and under which conditions it would not be appropriate.

2. Many U.S. companies such as Home Depot, Intel, Kodak, Nike, and Whirlpool have set up sales offices in China. One thing sales managers must be aware of is that the differences in sales styles between the United States and China are vast. For example, relationship building is very important in sales and in hiring sales people in China. Further, more companies need to figure out what part of the country and what market segments they are to enter. Generally speaking, Chinese consumers are more price-conscious than Japanese and Korean consumers. However, Chinese youth are less likely to follow the traditional values of collectivism, restraint, and harmony, but exhibit strong tendencies of individualism and self-reliance. They worship more western brands in comparison to domestic brands. If U.S.-based companies were to set up sales office in China, what would be their challenges and opportunities? Given the differences in sales styles between the United States and China, what should the company do to enhance its sales management?

3. Domino's Pizza International, the Ann Arbor, Michigan, based pizza chain, is known worldwide for its delivery service. Its policy of giving away its pizza free if not delivered within half an hour was a legendary service theme, and it earned them a unique position in the consumer's mind. However, the company's foray into Poland in 1994 proved how modifications to positioning strategies might become essential in certain international markets. In 1994, the company wanted to open franchises in Poland. It was keen on opening delivery units as it has in most other countries. However, the lack of reliable and appropriate infrastructure in terms of telephone service in Poland posed a problem. Its delivery concept would not ride very far if potential customers could not phone in their orders. So, in stark contrast to its policy in other countries, Domino opened a sit-in restaurant in Poland in March 1994, followed by another one several months later. Only after some time did it open its standard delivery unit. While this was one way of tiding over the selling constraints peculiar to this market, there was the risk that it was deviating from their most salient positioning theme. Do you think the strategy adopted by Domino's was a wise one? If so, give reasons. If not, provide an alternate strategy, giving your justification for the same.

4. Many firms in the past have followed an incremental approach to the sales channels used in international markets. Typically, these companies started by selling in foreign markets through sales agents or distributors. Following this, they opened liaison offices to assist and monitor the activities of the appointed distributors. With subsequent growth in business, the company would set up its own sales subsidiary to manage sales and customer service. This incremental strategy has worked quite effectively for many companies in the past. In your opinion, would the current emphasis being placed on globalization have any bearing on the effectiveness of this incremental strategy? If so, what would this effect be, and why?

5. Today many companies talk about localization, but find it difficult to do. Sometimes expatriate managers are unable or unwilling to train their successors. This can be a particular problem for Japanese companies. The standard practice in Japanese multinationals has been to rely on people sent from the home office, even for mid-level technical jobs. In part, this stems from a tradition of apprentice-style training, which can mean Japanese firms "struggle to get new people up to speed quickly," says Rochelle Kopp, principal of Japan Intercultural Consulting, a training firm. Language is often an added complication in going abroad. A further difficulty is that many Japanese expatriates and their families prefer to stay in America, say, rather than return home. As a result, Japanese employees abroad tend to hand over little responsibility to their local colleagues. Discuss the advantages and disadvantages of localization of executives. Do you think Japanese situation is applicable to other regions? Why or why not? Discuss strategic solutions regarding difficulties of localization for Japanese companies.

# SHORT CASES

 ASE 14-1

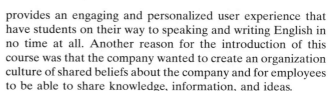

## HILTON UNIVERSITY — FOR EMPLOYEES ONLY!

Products-based multinational firms with worldwide operations— and therefore a diverse workforce—face a major task in the training of employees in different regions in order to maintain a uniform organizational culture throughout the global company. But for multinational service firms, maintaining an educated, well-trained workforce is even more challenging. That is why many service firms have made it a priority to establish training programs. Take the hospitality industry for example. In the pre-World Wide Web era, these training programs used to be face to face and carried out in various foreign locations. The downside of this form of classroom instruction was costs, time and the wide disparity in teaching methods in different places. Today, however more and more global service firms are taking their classrooms online. Not only does this form of training lower overall costs but also attempts to transfer the image of corporate culture.

Premier hotel group Hilton International launched its Hilton University in 2002, solely for training and educating its global employees. Prior to this initiative, employee training was conducted on every Hilton hotel's premises in more than 65 countries. Needless to say, the costs of training, time taken and the training programs differed to a certain extent based on location. Also, not all Hilton hotels are owned by the company. Some hotels are managed by outsiders. The company felt the need to consolidate employee training and introduced online training. Another reason for establishing Hilton University was that corporate headquarters felt the need to monitor and control training programs, mainly the content of the training program and its effect on employee skills.

Hilton University conducts several different online training programs. Its employees worldwide are expected to get training for at least 40 hours in a year. One of the businesses' primary needs is the ability of its hotel staff to effectively communicate with its customers. Given that many of its hotels are located in non-English speaking countries, the English training program has become one of its most important one. Hilton's main clientele is comprised of high-income, educated travelers, who are willing to pay a premium for good service and comfort. A large number of its patrons are also from its home country (U.S.). Hence, a majority of its customers are English speaking and with the establishment of Hilton University, the company announced that English would be its official language for conducting business in all parts of the globe.

Accordingly, Hilton University started an English course. It uses GlobalEnglish, the leading online English learning and service provider for business communication. This course

provides an engaging and personalized user experience that have students on their way to speaking and writing English in no time at all. Another reason for the introduction of this course was that the company wanted to create an organization culture of shared beliefs about the company and for employees to be able to share knowledge, information, and ideas.

The results of the English training program were good. The GlobalEnglish is used by many team members of Hilton to improve their proficiency in English. On average, more than 75 percent of Hilton's foreign employees commended the program and claimed that it had given them the necessary language skills to be able to confidently perform their jobs. Better communication with guests improves their satisfaction, a good way to greet them more often as they come back. As mentioned earlier, Hilton had set a target of 40 hours per employee, but the number of hours actually clocked in by employees exceeded the target by 10 hours on average.

Since 2005, Hilton University has offered more online language learning, including French, Spanish, Italian, German, and Dutch. However, most of the courses other than language provided by Hilton University are still in English. Since less than 10 percent of Hilton's foreign staff is fluent in English, most of these courses are not comprehensible to the majority of its employees. A possible solution to this problem is to introduce courses in different languages. In addition to the complexity of this task, the company was unable to provide similar learning opportunities to its non-English speaking staff.

In spite of the problem of course language, Hilton University still witnesses great success. From 2002 to 2005, nearly 10,000 Hilton people have completed over 100,000 e-Learning programs. 93 percent of these learners said that they would recommend this form of learning to their friends and colleagues. The strongest "likes" were the chance to learn at a time, place, and speed that is suited the learner.

Boosted by the success of its online programs, Hilton University has introduced several others that the company expects will increase employee productivity and improve service at its hotels all over the world. This initiative by the company has also raised its image in the eyes of employees and the company has gotten a whole lot closer to its objective of maintaining a global service-oriented organization culture.

### DISCUSSION QUESTIONS

**1.** Should the salesforce of service multinationals have a global service strategy like Hilton's or should it be more locally oriented to serve the needs of regional customers? Why?

**2.** How is saleforce training in manufacturing firms different from that in service firms?

**3.** What are the pros and cons of online training versus face-to-face classroom based training?

*Source:* John Guthrie, "Hilton International: Creating a Global Service Culture," *Chief Learning Officer*, 4 (January 2005), pp. 54–56; www.hiltonuniversity.com, accessed August 1, 2009.

# $\mathscr{C}$ASE 14-2

## PROGEON CALL CENTER SERVICES

Western firms have been outsourcing manufacturing operations to low-cost countries for more than five decades now. Business Process Outsourcing, or BPO as it is commonly known, is a relatively new practice and highly controversial at best. The volume of this form of outsourcing has grown exponentially in the last few years. BPO has mainly gone to firms in emerging economies that can provide low cost services. This has led to the establishment of call centers in countries such as India, where a significant part of the population is able to communicate in English. A call center is any organization or a part of an organization that handles incoming and outgoing telephonic calls for consumers. Until some years back, Western multinationals operated their own call centers in their home countries. Recently, these operations have shifted to emerging countries.

Indian information systems company Infosys, one of the fastest growing companies in Asia, set up a subsidiary in April 2002 to respond to this growth in demand for services. The unit, known as Progeon, is jointly owned by Infosys, which owns around 80 percent of the company with the rest being owned by one of Citigroup's finance companies. Since its establishment, Progeon has nabbed BPO contracts with Western firms such as Cisco and British Telecom. Today, the company has more than 20 such large contracts. Progeon provides services related to insurance, banking, finance, and telecom to its customers. These services are grouped into voice jobs and data jobs. Voice jobs are housed in a call center. Most of the firm's clients also have information technology related contracts with one of its parent companies, Infosys.

Progeon's call center operations cater to customers of its Western client firms. The way a call center works is that calls to a company such as Cisco from customers in the United States for example, are routed to call centers such as Progeon in Bangalore, India. Progeon's employees address these calls. Sometimes Progeon's staff is also required to make calls to its client's customers overseas. This enables Western firms to provide services round the clock to their customers and also avail them of such services at lower costs. Thus, call center employees indirectly make up a part of the foreign salesforce of Western firms.

*Source:* Charlotte Huff, "Accent on Training," *Workforce Management*, 84 (March 2005), p. 54.

When Western customers dial a phone number to reach a company such as Cisco, oftentimes they are unaware that their call has been routed overseas. A major part of the task for call center employees all over India then is to perfect the American or British accent depending on where their corporate client is based. While most call center employees are hired subject to their ability to speak and write English, very often, their language is heavily accented. This is true in the case of India, which has over 15 different main languages and more than 100 dialects. Therefore, training of call center personnel is important before allowing them to get on the job. Most call centers have rigorous training programs that last around a month for new employees before putting them on the job. These programs include training through singing, skits, conversation simulations, and so on, all with the required accent. Quick learners among new employees are often given awards to motivate them.

Progeon developed its own version of the new salesforce training program, for which it won the Optimas Award given by Workforce Management magazine in the year 2005. Whereas call center employees in other firms are also accent and language trained, Progeon's new recruits, in addition to accent training, are also taught about the industry in which their client firm operates. They are also educated about the firm's history, common usage terms, recent news, and strategies so that they are well versed in the firm's operations. New recruits are made to perfect their accents based on instructions and a thorough analysis of their recorded voices. Recently hired employees are given a course on variation in social behavior in different cultures. As a result, the company has considerably improved the overall quality of their staff. Progeon has significantly reduced employee turnover and enabled the company to gain an upper hand over its rivals. In a country where call centers have sprung up in nearly every corner of major cities, Progeon has managed to differentiate itself.

### DISCUSSION QUESTIONS

1. What are some of the problems that Progeon's well-trained staff could still face, given that their clients are from culturally distant countries?

2. What are the drawbacks for multinational firms of BPO through call centers in far-off locations?

---

# FURTHER READING

Attia, Ashraf M., Earl D. Honeycutt, Jr., and M. Asri Jantan, "Global Sales Training: In Search of Antecedent, Mediating, and Consequence Variables," *Industrial Marketing Management*, 37 (April 2008): 181–90.

Blodgett, Jeffrey G., Long-Chuan Lu, Gregory M. Rose, and Scott J. Vitell, "Ethical Sensitivity to Stakeholder Interests: A Cross-Cultural Comparison," *Academy of Marketing Science*, 29(2), 2001: 190–202.

Brashear-Alejandro, Thomas, "International Salesforce Management," in Masaaki Kotabe and Kristiaan Helsen,ed., *The SAGE Handbook of International Marketing*, London: Sage Publications, 2009: 430–48.

DeCarlo, Thomas E., Raymond C. Rody, and James E. DeCarlo, "A Cross National Example of Supervisory Management Practices in the Sales Force," *Journal of Personal Selling & Sales Management*, 19 (Winter 1999): 1–14.

Elahee, Mohammad N., Susan L. Kirby, and Ercan Nacif, "National Culture, Trust, and Perceptions About Ethical Behavior in Intra-and Cross-Cultural Negotiations: An Analysis of NAFTA Countries," *Thunderbird International Business Review*, 44 (November/December 2002): 799–818.

Engle, Robert L., "Global Marketing Management Scorecard: A Tale of Two Multinational Companies," *Problems & Perspectives in Management*, 2005 Issue 3, pp. 128–36.

Evans, Jody and Felix T. Mavondo. "Psychic Distance and Organizational Performance: An Empirical Examination of International Retailing Operations," *Journal of International Business Studies*, 33(3) (2002) 515–32

Gorchels, Linda, Thani Jambulingam, and Timothy W. Aurand, "International Marketing Managers: A Comparison of Japanese, German, and U.S. Perceptions," *Journal of International Marketing*, 7(1) (1999): 97–105

Kotabe, Masaaki and Crystal Jiang, "Three Dimensional: The Markets of Japan, Korea, and China are Far from Homogeneous," *Marketing Management*, 15(2) (2006) 39–43

Lenartowicz, Tomasz and Kendall Roth, "Does Subculture Within a Country Matter? A Cross-Cultural Study of Motivational Domains and Business Performance in Brazil," *Journal of International Business Studies*, 32(2) (2001) 305–25

Neale, Margaret E. *Business Week's Guide to Cross-Cultural Negotiating. Maximizing Profitability in Intra- and Inter-Cultural Negotiations*, New York: McGraw-Hill, 1995.

Palich, Leslie E., Gary R. Carini, Linda P. Livingstone, "Comparing American and Chinese Negotiating Styles: The Influence of Logic Paradigms," *Thunderbird International Business Review*, 44 (November/December 2002): 777–98.

Piercy, Nigel F., George S. Low, David W. Cravens, "Consequences of Sales Management's Behavior- and Compensation-Based Control Strategies in Developing Countries," *Journal of International Marketing*, 12(3), 2004: 30–57.

Sebenius, James K., "The Hidden Challenge of Cross-Border Negotiations," *Harvard Business Review*, 80 (March 2002): 76–85.

Shankarmahesh, Mahesh N., John B. Ford, and Michael S. la Tour, "Determinants of Satisfaction in Sales Negotiations with Foreign Buyers: Perceptions of US Export Executives," *International Marketing Review*, 21(4/5), 2004: 423–46.

Ulijn, Jan and Dean Tjosvold, "Innovation in International Negotiation: Content and Style," *International Negotiation*, 9(2), 2004: 195–99.

Zoubir, Yahir H. and Roger Volkema, "Special Issue: Cross-Cultural Negotiations," *Thunderbird International Business Review*, 44 (November/December 2002).

# GLOBAL LOGISTICS AND DISTRIBUTION

**15**

Companies have to deliver products to customers both *efficiently* and *effectively*.[1] First of all, global logistics, also referred to as global supply chain management,[2] has played a critical role in the growth and development of world trade, and in the integration of business operations on a worldwide scale. Its primary objective is to develop a cost-efficient delivery mechanism. In fact, the level of world trade in goods and, to some extent, services, depends to a significant degree on the availability of economical and

---

[1] For a philosophy of efficiency- vs. effectiveness-seeking in business orientation, see Masaaki Kotabe, "Efficiency vs. Effectiveness Orientation of Global Sourcing Strategy: A Comparison of U.S. and Japanese Multinational Companies," *Academy of Management Executive*, 12, November 1998, 107–19; and Shelby D. Hunt and Dale F. Duhan, "Competition in the Third Millennium: Efficiency or Effectiveness?" *Journal of Business Research*, 55 (February), 2002, pp. 97–102.

[2] Some authors (including the authors of this book) use logistics and supply chain management interchangeably, while others generally define supply chain management somewhat more broadly than logistics. Although, in this chapter, we try not to engage in this definitional debate over what functions are included in each, the Council of Logistics Management offers the following definitions. **Logistics management** typically includes inbound and outbound transportation management, fleet management, warehousing, materials handling, order fulfillment, logistics network design, and inventory management of third party logistics services providers. To varying degrees, the logistics function also includes sourcing and procurement, production planning and scheduling, packaging and assembly, and customer service. **Supply chain management** is an integrating function with primary responsibility for linking major business functions and business processes within and across companies into a cohesive and high-performing business model. It includes all of the Logistics Management activities noted above, as well as manufacturing operations, and it drives coordination of processes and activities with and across marketing, sales, product design, finance, and information technology.

reliable international transportation services. Decreases in transportation costs and increases in performance reliability expand the scope of business operations and increase the associated level of international trade and competition.[3] Second, the use of appropriate distribution channels in international markets increases the chances of success dramatically. Its primary objective is to develop a task-effective delivery mechanism for customer satisfaction. Coca-Cola's success relies largely on its global distribution arm, Coca-Cola Enterprises, the world's largest bottler group. It helps Coca-Cola market, produce and distribute bottled and canned products all over the world. The group also purchases and distributes certain non-carbonated beverages such as isotonics, teas and juice drinks in finished form from the Coca-Cola Company to satisfy the diverse needs of its consumers.[4]

As far back as 1954, Peter Drucker had said that logistics would remain "the darkest continent of business"[5]—the least well understood area of business—and his prediction proved true until well into the 21st century. It is not too difficult to demonstrate the importance of the physical handling, moving, storing, and retrieving of material. In almost every product, more than 50 percent of product cost is material related, while less than 10 percent is labor. Yet, over the years this fact has not received much attention. In 2006, the total logistics cost represented about 10 percent of the GDP, or $1.3 trillion, in the United States. Among them, transportation costs alone accounted for $635 billion in 2006.[6] As of 2006, Europe's logistics cost represented 11 percent of GDP. It was some 13 percent of GDP for India. For China, the Council of Supply Chain Management Professionals puts the figure at around 21 percent of GDP—a huge improvement since 1991, when it was around 25 percent.[7]

Since the 1990s, a variety of issues have been driving the increased emphasis on logistics and distribution management. It was epitomized in 1998 by General Motors' lawsuit against Volkswagen over the defection of José Ignacio Lopez, the former vice president of purchasing at General Motors and one of the most renowned logistics managers in the automobile industry.[8] His expertise is said to have saved General Motors several billion dollars from its purchasing and logistic operations, which would directly affect the company's bottom line. The importance of distribution channels is further evidenced by the recent mergers in the auto industry, in which giant multinationals are gobbling up smaller manufacturers with strong brand names, but inadequate global distribution, such as Ford's acquisition of Volvo.[9]

As firms start operating on a global basis, logistics managers need to manage the shipping of raw materials, components, and supplies among various manufacturing sites at the most economical and reliable rates. Simultaneously, these firms need to ship finished goods to customers in markets around the world at the desired place and time. The development of intermodal transportation and electronic tracking technology has caused a quantum jump in the efficiency of the logistic methods employed by firms. Intermodal transportation refers to the seamless transfer of goods from one mode of transport (e.g., aircraft or ship) to another (e.g., truck) and vice versa without the hassle of unpacking and repackaging the goods to suit the dimensions of the mode of transport being used. Tracking technology refers to the means for keeping continuous tabs on the exact location of the goods being shipped in the logistic chain—this enables quick

[3] John H. Dunning, "Reappraising the Eclectic Paradigm in an Age of Alliance Capitalism," *Journal of International Business Studies*, 26 (Third Quarter 1995), pp. 461–91.

[4] Coca-Cola Enterprises, http://www.cokecce.com, Accessed on March 11, 2009.

[5] Peter F. Drucker, *The Practice of Management* (New York: Harper & Brothers, 1954).

[6] "Business logistics costs rise to 9.9 percent of GDP in 2006," *Logistics Management*, http://www.logisticsmgmt.com/, June 6, 2007.

[7] "Cargo Cults," *Economist*, June 17, 2006, Special Section, pp. 9–14.

[8] "No Ordinary Car Thief," *U.S. News & World Report*, June 5, 2000, p. 52.

[9] Salama, Alzira, Wayne Holland, and Gerald Vinten, "Challenges and Opportunities in Mergers and Acquisitions: Three International Case Studies—Deutsche Bank-Bankers Trust; British Petroleum-Amoco; Ford-Volvo," *Journal of European Industrial Training*, 27(6), 2003, pp. 313–21.

reaction to any disruption in the shipments because (a) the shipper knows exactly where the goods are in real time and (b) the alternative means can be quickly mobilized.

## ◆◆◆◆◆◆◆◆ DEFINITION OF GLOBAL LOGISTICS

**Global logistics** is defined here as the design and management of a system that directs and controls the flows of materials into, through and out of the firm across national boundaries to achieve its corporate objectives at a minimum total cost. As shown in **Exhibit 15-1**, global logistics encompasses the entire range of operations concerned with products or components movement, including both exports and imports simultaneously. Global logistics, like domestic logistics, encompasses materials management, sourcing, and physical distribution.[10]

**Materials management** refers to the inflow of raw materials, parts, and supplies in and through the firm. **Physical distribution** refers to the movement of the firm's finished products to its customers, consisting of transportation, warehousing, inventory, customer service/order entry, and administration. **Sourcing strategy** refers to an operational link between materials management and physical distribution, and deals with how companies manage R&D (e.g., product development and engineering), operations (e.g., manufacturing), and marketing activities. Although the functions of physical distribution are universal, they are affected differently by the tradition, culture, economic infrastructure, laws, topography, and other conditions in each country and each region. In general, in geographically large countries, such as the United States, where products are transported over a long distance, firms tend to incur relatively more transportation and inventory costs than firms in smaller countries. On the other hand, in geographically concentrated countries, such as Japan and Britain, firms tend to incur relatively more warehousing, customer service/order entry, and general administrative costs than in geographically larger countries. This is so primarily because a wide variety of products with different features have to be stored to meet the varied needs of customers in concentrated areas. The results of a recent survey of physical distribution costs in various European countries relative to the United States are presented in **Global Perspective 15-1**. Although it is possible to attribute all cost differences to topography, customs, laws of the land, and other factors, the cost differences could also reflect how efficiently or inefficiently physical distribution is managed in various countries and regions.

**EXHIBIT 15-1**
GLOBAL LOGISTICS

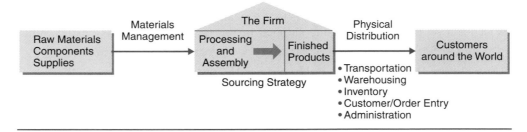

---

[10]Donald J. Bowersox, David J. Closs, and M. Bixby Cooper, *Supply Chain Logistics Management, 3rd ed.* (Boston: McGraw-Hill, 2010).

## $\mathcal{G}$LOBAL PERSPECTIVE 15-1

## REGIONAL VARIATIONS IN PHYSICAL DISTRIBUTION COSTS IN EUROPE AND ROOM FOR IMPROVEMENT

The physical distribution costs consist of transportation, warehousing, inventory, customer service/order entry, and administration. Let us make a comparison in terms of these components of the distribution costs between the two continents across the Atlantic. The following table shows cost comparisons (as a percentage of revenue).

The largest disparity was in warehousing, where European costs measured 3.03 percent, almost a third of total distribution costs, compared to 1.98 percent in the United States. These expenses are the cost of both plant and field warehouses including labor, space, direct materials, etc. Similarly, a large difference was observed in customer service/order entry—the cost of people, space and materials needed to take orders and handle inquiries—with 0.83 percent in Europe, compared to 0.49 percent in the United States.

| | European Union | The United States |
|---|---|---|
| Transportation | 2.79% | 3.23% |
| Warehousing | 3.03% | 1.98% |
| Inventory | 1.73% | 1.93% |
| Customer Service/ Order Entry | 0.83% | 0.49% |
| Administration | 0.79% | 0.44% |
| Total | 9.17% | 8.07% |

European governments have begun to privatize transportation services. Since January 1, 1993, the European Union (EU) movement presents opportunities for reducing logistics costs and boosting efficiency. And it is not just Europeans but also foreign manufacturers, including those in North America, who are finding that political changes in Europe have created opportunities for greater efficiency and lower costs in their logistics.

However, there still are many political, legal, and technical issues to be settled before Europe truly is unified. Across the region, borders have all but disappeared with the advent of high-speed passenger trains, highways without customs posts and now a single currency. Europe's state-owned phone monopolies, electric utilities, airlines and other national franchises have all been pried open to competition. However, rail freight remains a bastion of Europe's old ways, a patchwork of protected, antiquated national

networks. No two European countries use the same signaling systems or electric current for their trains. For example, Trains in Britain and France run on the left side of dual-track lines, while those in the rest of Europe run on the right. Since Britain and France, however, use two different gauges of track, trains crossing their shared border along the Channel Tunnel must stop to let each car be lifted so that its wheels can be changed.

As a result, European industry has taken to the highways for transportation. Railways' share of goods transport with the EU has fallen to about 14 percent now from 32 percent in 1970. In the United States, railways account for 41 percent of freight traffic. The downside to the increase in truck traffic is increased traffic congestion, which hampers efficient transportation despite the unified European economy. The most conservative estimate of the cost of traffic jam is a little over 2 percent of Europe's GDP at minimum. And it could be as high as 6 percent.

Further, with the expansion of the EU in May 2004, traditional distribution hubs in western and central Europe faced tougher competition. In the process of integrating the candidate countries into all the systems and practices of the EU, the EU has to restrict access to road and rail networks in some countries for two to three years. Meanwhile, European government and the EU have developed programs and initiatives to reduce road congestion and encourage companies to move goods transport away from roads to ensure the important infrastructure development.

Thus, logistics managers must plan how to respond to changes as they occur. Here are some of the many changes reshaping European logistics strategies:

*Customs procedures.* For the most part, customs check points as a shipment crosses each nation's border have been eliminated. Duties and trade statistics now are a matter strictly between the originating and destination countries, and intermediate countries no longer are involved. Consequently, transit times and paperwork between EU countries, particularly for truck traffic, are steadily being reduced.

*Harmonized product standards.* Prior to unification, each European country had its own manufacturing, packaging, labeling, and safety standards for almost every item sold within its borders. Under the European Union, pan-European harmonized standards are being developed and replacing most of those country-by-country regulations. As a result, companies can manufacture a single version of a product for sale in all parts of the EU, rather than design and manufacture different versions of the same item for each member country. Product harmonization will allow shippers to redesign not only their distribution patterns and facilities, but also their customer-service strategies.

*Sources:* "Logistics Strategies for a New Europe, *Traffic Management*, 33, (August, 1994), p. 49A; "In the Unified Europe, Shipping Freight by Rail is a Journey into the Past," *Wall Street Journal*, (March 29, 1999), p. A1 and A8; "European Transport Policy," *Logistics & Transport Focus*, 4 (July/August 2002), pp. 40–41; and "Distribution Hubs Face Competition," *Logistics and Transport Focus*, May 2004, p. 6.

(*continued*)

$\mathcal{G}$LOBAL PERSPECTIVE 15-1

(CONTINUED)

*Transportation deregulation.* The European Commission is deregulating transportation in Europe in order to open markets in member states to competition and to eliminate conflicting regulations that impede the flow of traffic between EU countries. The deregulation promises to promote the development of efficient, cost-effective services in all modes.

*Transportation infrastructure.* As in Japan and the United States, growing demand for just-in-time deliveries increases traffic and exacerbates transportation bottlenecks (particularly, inter-regional trucking). The European Commission and individual governments are actively encouraging private development of rail and water alternatives.

## ◆◆◆◆◆◆◆◆ MANAGING PHYSICAL DISTRIBUTION

Physical distribution is inextricably tied with international trade, multinational manufacturing and sourcing of raw materials, components, and supplies. Physical distribution has become considerably more complex, more costly, and as a result, more important for the success of a firm. A variety of factors contribute to the increased complexity and cost of global logistics, as compared to domestic logistics.

- **Distance.** The first fundamental difference is distance. Global logistics frequently require the transportation of parts, supplies, and finished goods over much longer distances than is the norm domestically. A longer distance generally suggests higher direct costs of transportation and insurance for damages, deterioration, and pilferage in transit and higher indirect costs of warehousing and inventory.

- **Exchange Rate Fluctuation.** The second difference pertains to currency variations in international logistics. The corporation must adjust its planning to incorporate the existence of currencies and changes in exchange rates. For example, in the mid-1990s when the Japanese yen appreciated faster than the U.S. dollars against key European currencies, Honda found it much more economical to ship its Accord models to Europe from its U.S. plant in Marysville, Ohio, rather than from its plants in Japan.

- **Foreign Intermediaries.** Additional intermediaries participate in the global logistics process because of the need to negotiate border regulations of countries and deal with local government officials and distributors. Although home country export agents, brokers, and export merchants work as intermediaries providing an exporting service for manufacturing firms, those home-based intermediaries do not necessarily have sufficient knowledge about the foreign countries' market conditions or sufficient connections with local government officials and distributors. In Asian countries such as Japan, Korea, and China, personal "connections" of who knows whom frequently seem to outweigh the Western economic principle of profit maximization or cost minimization in conducting business.[11] Therefore, working with local distributors has proved very important in building initial connections with the local business community as well as local government regulators.

- **Regulation.** A bulk of international trade is handled by ocean shipping. Because the United States is the world's largest single trading country in both exports and imports, and most of its trading partners are located across the Pacific and the Atlantic Oceans, U.S. regulations on ocean transport services directly affect foreign exporters to the

---

[11]See, for example, Jean L. Johnson, Tomoaki Sakano, and Naoto Onzo, "Behavioral Relations in Across-Culture Distribution Systems: Influence, Control, and Conflict in U.S.–Japanese Marketing Channels," *Journal of International Business Studies*, 21 (Fourth Quarter 1990), 639–55; and Chris Rowley, John Benson, and Malcolm Warner, "Towards an Asian Model of Human Resource Management?: A Comparative Analysis of China, Japan and South Korea," *International Journal of Human Resource Management*, 15 (June/August 2004), pp. 917–33.

Courtesy Kristiaan Helsen

United States (as well as U.S. importers of foreign goods) in terms of shipping costs and delivery time. In the United States, the Merchant Marine Act of 1920 (also known as the Jones Act) forbids foreign-owned freighters from transporting passengers and merchandise from one domestic port to another by restricting foreign access to the domestic shipping market. The act requires passengers and merchandise being transported by ship in the United States to travel on U.S.-built, U.S.-owned and U.S.-staffed vessels, while allowing unilateral retaliatory action against restrictions imposed by other countries. In March 2003, more than 50 nations, including Australia, Canada, China, the European Union, and Japan, filed a joint statement with the World Trade Organization calling for the liberalization of international marine transport services during the WTO's new round of multilateral trade negotiations.[12] Until resolved by the WTO, the barriers imposed by this act continue to add to the costs of logistics in and around the United States.

- **Security.** Security was not an acutely serious concern until September 11, 2001, when the blatant terrorist attacks in the United States awakened the world to the importance of domestic and international security measures. Transportation costs for exporters have increased because of the extra security measures that shipping lines and terminal operators face.[13] However, if the government-imposed user fees or carrier surcharges are too high or come without sufficient advance notice, some exporters could even lose their overseas markets due to increased shipping costs and insurance premiums (Refer to **Terrorism and the World Economy** in Chapter 5).

## Modes of Transportation

The global logistics manager must understand the specific properties of the different modes of transport in order to use them optimally. The three most important factors in determining an optimal mode of transportation are the value-to-volume ratio, perishability of the product, and cost of transportation. The **value-to-volume ratio** is determined by how much value is added to the materials used in the product. **Perishability** of the product refers to the quality degradation over time and/or product obsolescence

---

[12]"Japan Joins Call for Opening Marine Services Market In WTO Talks," *NikkeiNet Interactive*, http://www.nni .nikkei.co.jp/, March 4, 2003.

[13]Robert Spich and Robert Grosse, "How Does Homeland Security Affect U.S. Firms' International Competitiveness?" *Journal of International Management*, 11 (December 2005), pp. 457–78.

along the product life cycle. The **cost of transportation** should be considered in light of the value-to-volume and perishability of the product.

*Ocean Shipping.* Ocean shipping offers three options. **Liner service** offers regularly scheduled passage on established routes; **bulk shipping** normally provides contractual service for pre-specified periods of time; and the third category is for *irregular runs*. Container ships carry standardized containers that greatly facilitate the loading and unloading of cargo and intermodal transfer of cargo. Ocean shipping is used extensively for the transport of heavy, bulky, or nonperishable products, including crude oil, steel, and automobiles. Over the years, shipping rates have been falling as a result of a price war among shipping lines. For example, an average rate for shipping a 20-foot container from Asia to the United States fell from $4,000 in 1992 to as low as $1,680 by 2009.[14] Although most manufacturers rely on existing international ocean carriers, some large exporting companies, such as Honda and Hyundai, have their own fleets of cargo ships. For example, Honda, a Japanese automobile manufacturer, owns its own fleet of cargo ships not only to export its Japan-made cars to North America on its eastbound journey but also to ship U.S.-grown soybeans back to Japan on its westbound journey. This strategy is designed to increase the vessels' capacity utilization.[15] Indeed, Honda even owns a number of highly successful specialty tofu restaurants in Tokyo frequented by young trendsetters in Japan.[16]

*Air Freight.* Shipping goods by air has rapidly grown over the last thirty years. Although the total volume of international trade using air shipping remains quite small—it still constitutes less than 2 percent of international trade in goods—it represents more than 20 percent of the value of goods shipped in international commerce. High-value

Hong Kong is the busiest container port in the world and a hub of global distribution.

[14]Drewry Independent Maritime Advisor, http://www.drewry.co.uk/, accessed on September 1, 2009.
[15]"Engineers Rule," *Forbes*, September 4, 2006, pp. 112–16.
[16]The first author's personal knowledge; also visit Honda's Soybean Division, http://www.hondatrading-jp.com/english/business/soybeen.shtml.

goods are more likely to be shipped by air, especially if they have a high value-to-volume ratio. Typical examples are semiconductor chips, LCD screens, and diamonds. Perishable products such as produce and flowers also tend to be air freighted. Changes in aircraft design have now enabled air transshipment of relatively bulky products. Three decades ago, a large propeller aircraft could hold only 10 tons of cargo. Today's jumbo cargo jets carry more than 30 tons, and medium- to long-haul transport planes (e.g., the C-130 and the AN-32) can carry more than 80 tons of cargo. These super-size transport planes have facilitated the growth of global courier services, such as FedEx, UPS, and DHL. Of all world regions, the entire Asia-Pacific is the most popular airfreight market today, with double-digit, year-on-year growth. Asia has become the world's factory floor to outsource the manufacture of goods and services. The top five commodities moving from the Asia Pacific area to the United States include office machines and computers, apparel, telecom equipment, electrical machinery and miscellaneous manufactured products. The westbound (from the United States to Asia/Pacific) commodities mainly include documents and small packages, electrical machinery, and fruits and vegetables. In the next 20 years, westbound and eastbound air cargo traffic will grow at roughly the same pace, an estimated 7 percent.[17]

***Intermodal Transportation.*** More than one mode of transportation is usually employed. Naturally, when shipments travel across the ocean, surface or air shipping is the initial transportation mode crossing national borders. Once on land, they can be further shipped by truck, barge, railroad, or air. Even if countries are contiguous, such as Canada, the United States, and Mexico, for example, various domestic regulations prohibit the unrestricted use of the same trucks between and across the national boundaries. When different modes of transportation are involved, or even when shipments are transferred from one truck to another at the national border, it is important to make sure that cargo space is utilized at full load so that the per-unit transportation cost is minimized.

Managing shipments so that they arrive in time at the desired destination is critical in modern-day logistics management. Due to low transit times, greater ease of unloading and distribution, and higher predictability, many firms use airfreight, either on a regular basis or as a backup to fill in when the regular shipment by an ocean vessel is delayed. For footwear firms Reebok and Nike and fashion firms such as Pierre Cardin, the use of airfreight is becoming almost a required way of doing business, as firms jostle to get their products first into the U.S. market from their production centers in Asia and Europe. The customer in a retail store often buys a product that could have been air freighted in from the opposite end of the world the previous day or even the same day. Thus, the face of retailing is also changing as a result of advances in global logistics.

Distance between the transacting parties increases transportation costs and requires longer-term commitment to forecasts and longer lead times. Differing legal environments, liability regimes, and pricing regulations affect transportation costs and distribution costs in a way not seen in the domestic market. Trade barriers, customs problems, and paperwork tend to slow the cycle times in logistics across national boundaries. Although this is true, the recent formation of regional trading blocs, such as the European Union, the NAFTA (North American Free Trade Agreement), and the MERCOSUR (The Southern Cone Free Trade Area), is also encouraging the integration and consolidation of logistics in the region for improved economic efficiency and competition.

A firm's international strategy for logistics management depends, in part, on the government policy and on the infrastructure and logistic services environment. The traditional logistics strategy involves anticipatory demand management based on forecasting and inventory speculation.[18] With this strategy, a multinational firm

**Warehousing and Inventory Management**

---

[17]Roger Morton, "Something in the Air," *Logistics Today*, 46 (July 2005), pp. 23–26.

[18]Louis P. Bucklin, "Postponement, Speculation, and the Structure of Distribution Channels," *Journal of Marketing Research*, 2 (February 1965), pp. 26–31.

estimates the requirements for supplies as well as the demand from its customers and then attempts to manage the flow of raw materials and components in its worldwide manufacturing system and the flow of finished products to its customers in such a manner as to minimize holding inventory without jeopardizing manufacturing runs and without losing sales due to stockouts.

In the past, the mechanics and reliability of transportation and tracking of the flow of goods was a major problem. With the increasing use of information technology, electronic data interchange and intermodal transportation, the production, scheduling and delivery of goods across national borders is also becoming a matter of just-in-time delivery although some structural problems still remain. For instance, current restrictions on U.S.–Canada air freight services and U.S.–Mexico cross border trucking restrain the speed of goods flow, add to the lead times, and are examples of government restrictions which need to be changed to facilitate faster movement of goods across borders.

Despite those restrictions, forward-looking multinational companies can still employ nearly just-in-time inventory management. For example, Sony's assembly plant in Nuevo Laredo, Mexico, just across the Texas border, imports components from its U.S. sister plants in the United States. While cross-border transportation across the U.S.–Mexico international bridges experiences traffic congestion and occasionally causes delays in shipment, Sony has been able to manage just-in-time inventory management with a minimum of safety stock in its warehouse.

### Hedging against Inflation and Exchange Rate Fluctuations.

Multinational corporations can also use inventory as a strategic tool to deal with currency fluctuations and to hedge against inflation. By increasing inventories before imminent depreciation of a currency instead of holding cash, a firm can reduce its exposure to currency depreciation losses. High inventories also provide a hedge against inflation, because the value of the goods/parts held in inventory remains the same compared to the buying power of a local currency, which falls with devaluation. In such cases the international logistics manager must coordinate operations with that of the rest of the firm so that the cost of maintaining an increased level of inventories is more than offset by the gains from hedging against inflation and currency fluctuations. Many countries, for instance, charge a property tax on stored goods. If the increase in the cost of carrying the increased inventory along with the taxes exceeds the saving from hedging, increased inventory could not be a good idea.

### Benefiting from Tax Differences.

Costs can be written off before taxes in creative ways so that internal transit arrangements can actually make a profit. This implies that what and how much a firm transfers within its global manufacturing system is a function of the tax systems in various countries to and from which the transfers are being made. When the transfer of a component A from country B to country C is tax-deductible in country B (as an export) and gets credit in country C for being part of a locally assembled good D, the transfer makes a profit for the multinational firm. Access to and use of such knowledge is the forte of logistics firms that sell these services to the multinational firm interested in optimizing its global logistics.

### Logistical Integration and Rationalization.

**Logistical integration** refers to coordinating production and distribution across geographic boundaries—a radical departure from the traditional country-by-country based structure consisting of separate sales, production, warehousing, and distribution organizations in each country. **Rationalization**, on the other hand, refers to reducing resources to achieve more efficient and cost-effective operations. Although conceptually separate, most companies' strategies include both aspects of the logistics strategy.

For example, DuPont expects to save millions annually by centralizing logistics management and consolidating its logistics spending to get better pricing and service from its providers. The company currently uses a wide range of freight carriers, logistics providers, and freight forwarders to handle its shipments. By centralizing its logistical activities, DuPont can optimize its shipments and combine small shipments into larger ones (integration). The company has replaced the disconnected legacy mainframe logistics system used by 70 percent of its individual strategic business units, subsidiaries, joint ventures, and affiliates with Global Logistics Technologies Inc.'s G3 Web-based transportation and logistics-management software (rationalization). Since 2001, the company has been able to manage almost all of its operations using the software, including shipments for U.S. domestic, Europe domestic, and some intra-Asia areas. DuPont's logistic management has not only enhanced its product delivery time but also ensured security of shipments, a significant factor because more than 40 percent of what the company ships are classified as hazardous materials. Furthermore, the company has benefited from shortened inventory through improved visibility and standardization of data.[19]

As presented earlier in Global Perspective 15-1, dramatic economic integration is taking place in the enlarged European Union. However, a word of caution is in order. Remember that although the laws of the European Union point toward further economic integration, there still are and will continue to be political, cultural, and legal differences among countries as well. Similarly, as shown in **Global Perspective 15-2**, the North American Free Trade Agreement is not free of arcane regulations, either. Consequently,

## $\mathcal{G}$LOBAL PERSPECTIVE 15-2

### CABOTAGE RULES IN THE NORTH AMERICAN FREE TRADE AGREEMENT

Cabotage refers to the right of a trucker to be able to carry goods in an assigned territory. Traditionally, countries have restricted cabotage rights of foreign truckers. If a U.S. trucking company has a scheduled load to the United States from Toronto, then the truck may carry the load but the driver must be Canadian. Similarly, a U.S. trucker, after delivering goods in Toronto, cannot pick up another load and deliver it in Ottawa—that is a violation of current cabotage rules. Even under the North American Free Trade Agreement (NAFTA), Canada, the United States, and Mexico have varying degrees of—even sometimes confusing—regulations on cabotage rights. In theory, the NAFTA should have worked out truly free mobility of goods by allowing the cabotage rights of truckers from Canada, the United States, and Mexico. But the reality is still far from it, although it is improving.

The U.S. government refused to allow Mexican truckers to have full access to the United States until recently. Safety concerns were cited in keeping Mexican trucks from operating throughout the country, although those fears may not be supported by facts. Similarly, the Mexican trucking association, Camara Nacional del Autotransporte de Carga, continues to oppose opening up cabotage to allow point-to-point coverage in Mexico by U.S. trucking companies.

*Source:* "U.S. Transportation Department Implements NAFTA Provisions for Mexican Trucks, Buses," FDCH Regulatory Intelligence Database, November 27, 2002; "DOT Eyes Truck Inspection Harmony for All of North America," *Occupational Health & Safety*, December 2002, p. 10; and John C. Taylor, Douglas R. Robideaux, George C. Jackson, "U.S.-Canada Transportation and Logistics: Border Impacts and Costs, Causes, and Possible Solutions," *Transportation Journal*, 43 (Fall 2004), pp. 5–21.

In March 2002, President Bush finally modified the moratorium on granting operating authority to Mexican motor carriers. This action means that the United States has fulfilled its obligations under the North American Free Trade Agreement and that Mexican truck and regular-route bus service into the U.S. interior can begin. As a practical matter, this service will begin only after the U.S. Department of Transportation's Federal Motor Carrier Safety Administration (FMCSA) reviews Mexican carrier applications and grants provisional operating authority to qualified Mexican truck and bus companies seeking this authority.

The United States does not have a coherent cabotage regulation with Canada. The U.S. Immigration and Naturalization Service is going after Canadian drivers who have "violated" cabotage rules by moving trailers within the United States even though U.S. Customs permits such movements. A number of Canadian drivers have had their trucks seized, have been fined, and then kicked out of the United States. Under an agreement engineered by the Canadian and U.S. trucking associations, Canadian officials have been allowing U.S. drivers to perform cabotage movements in Canada. Now the Canadian government is thinking about retaliating against the United States by mounting a crackdown on U.S. truck drivers entering Canada to parallel the aggressive treatment Canadian drivers are facing from the U.S. Immigration and Naturalization Service.

Despite these arcane regulations still in place in the NAFTA countries, the U.S. Department of Commerce hopes to establish conformity among Canada, Mexico and the U.S. in cargo securement regulations in compliance with the North American Cargo Securement Standard Model Regulations.

---

[19]"DuPont Streamlines Logistics and IT Costs with Centralized, Web-Based System," *Manufacturing Systems*, April 2004, p. 52.

despite the promised benefit of logistics integration and rationalization, international marketers as well as corporate planners have to have specialized local knowledge to ensure smooth operations. Customer service strategies particularly need to be differentiated, depending on the expectations of local consumers. For example, German buyers of personal computers may be willing to accept Dell Computer's mail-order service or its Web site ordering service, but French and Spanish customers could assume that a delivery person will deliver and install the products for them.

***E-Commerce and Logistics.*** Another profound change in the last decade is the proliferation of the internet and electronic commerce ("e-commerce"). The internet opened the gates for companies to sell easily directly to consumers across national boundaries. We stated in Chapter 1 that manufacturers that traditionally sell through the retail channel *can* benefit the most from e-commerce. Furthermore, customer information no longer is held hostage by the retail channel.

We emphasize "can" because *in reality, logistics cannot go global as easily as e-commerce.* This revolutionary way of marketing products around the world is epitomized by Dell Computer, which put pressure on the industry's traditional players with a simple concept: sell personal computers directly on the internet to customers with no complicated channels. Michael Dell successfully introduced a new way for PC companies to compete—not by technology alone, but by recognizing customers' needs and emphasizing Dell's ability to satisfy and serve them quickly and efficiently, above and beyond the traditional national boundary. Now, major PC companies are compressing the supply chain via such concepts as "build to order" rather than "build to forecast." However, order taking can take place globally, but shipping of PCs needs to be rather local or regional for various reasons.

You may ask why most e-businesses do not ship overseas if the Web makes any company instantly global. Also, why do more companies not make their internet-powered supply chains globally accessible? The answer is that it remains very difficult to manage the complex logistics, financial, linguistic, and regulatory requirements of global trade. E-businesses operating from one central location could not also address logistical problems associated with local competition and exchange rate fluctuations. For example, in Australia, OzBooks.com sells 1.2 million books and Dymocks, Australia's largest bookseller, offers just over 100,000 books online. These Australian companies are no comparison in size to Amazon.com with some 5 million books available online. These smaller Australian online booksellers have a competitive advantage over Amazon.com, however. They have a comprehensive offering of books published in Australia while Amazon.com does not. Furthermore, competing on price for international sales without local distribution is tricky as exchange rates fluctuate. When the Australian dollar depreciated during the Asian financial crisis, buying from Amazon.com and other U.S. Web retailers became more expensive in Australia. Australian consumers log on to local alternatives such as OzBooks.com instead. As a result, leading e-commerce sites now offer regional Web sites to handle sales in various parts of the world. For example, Amazon.com now has eight regional websites around the world to cater to these regional and local differences.

Another example is Compaq Computer in Latin America. The company has been extremely successful in selling computers over the internet throughout Latin America since October 1999. The company guarantees delivery within 72 hours of placing orders online. Latin Americans shopping online can buy the computers in local currency and do not have to bring the computers through customs. This requires local assembly of Compaq computers. Compaq has assembly plants in Mexico, Ecuador, Argentina, Brazil, Venezuela, Chile, Puerto Rico, Colombia, and Peru.[20]

The Web may have dispensed with physical stores, but local adaptation of product offerings and setting-up of local distribution centers remain as crucial as ever. The local

---

[20]"IT Watch," *Business Latin America*, September 13, 1999, p. 7; and "Latin American PC Market Continues to Grow," *World IT Report*, February 19, 2002, p. N.

competition has forced Amazon.com and other American e-commerce companies to reassess what it means to operate globally on the internet.

**Third-Party Logistics (3PL) Management**

Good logistics can make all the difference in a company's ability to serve its customers. The crucial factor is not just what the company makes or how the product is made. It is also how quickly the company can get the parts together or shift finished products from its factories to markets. Despite the immense competitive advantage that logistics can generate for the organization, manufacturers often find that logistics operations are usually faster and less expensive if they are outsourced and organized by specialists and professionals who have competence in integrated logistics management and the ability to service multiple clients and products. According to management consultants at McKinsey, tracking the logistics outsourcing industry, U.S. companies currently spend around $100 billion a year on **third-party logistics (3PL) services**. This 3PL market is growing rapidly in the United States.[21] Although no new data are currently available, the European 3PL market was worth around $147 billion in 2001, and is growing at a similar rate as in the United States.[22] The largest 3PL sector is the value-added warehousing and distribution industry. Survey statistics show two important factors: (1) the 3PL industry has a tremendous untapped opportunity for growth with the Fortune 500 companies, and (2) the mid-sized companies are making the best use of savings and service advantages that outsourcing can offer.[23]

To stay with the trend, Ford established a contract with TPG, a Dutch logistics company, to service its Toronto factory. This plant produces 1,500 Windstar minivans a day. To keep it running virtually round the clock, TPG organizes 800 deliveries a day from 300 different parts manufacturers. Its software must be tied into Ford's computerized production system. Shipments have to arrive at 12 different points along the assembly lines without ever being more than 10 minutes late. Parts must be loaded into trucks in a pre-arranged sequence to speed unloading at the assembly line. This upstream procurement capability is extremely important when it comes to addressing the ever-changing needs of consumers in the downstream marketing activities. Another example is an arrangement between Maxtor, a maker of computer disk drives, and Exel, the world's leading logistics firm. Exel, formed from a merger of a shipping line and a trucking company, now owns no ships or trucks, focusing instead on logistics contracts. The Maxtor deal requires it to shift computer drives from factories in Asia to companies such as Dell, Compaq and HP in Asia and the United States, all within 48 hours.[24]

Multinational companies also benefit from 3PL arrangements particularly in culturally and/or geographically diverse markets, such as India and China. For example, in India, Whirlpool Corporation, a leading U.S. manufacturer of major household appliances, works with Quality Express, whose national delivery network serves over 10,000 retailers and 50,000 construction sites scattered all over India. The result was ERX Logistics, a joint venture that provides Whirlpool with full logistics service for its finished products from warehousing to final delivery. Whirlpool has been able to lower its minimum order quantity form about one-third of a truckload to five or six pieces.[25]

Interestingly, with more companies resorting to 3PL, the range of logistics businesses the express operators are moving into is broadened. In the United States, one service offered by UPS's local branches is a drop-off facility for broken Toshiba laptops. Most laptop owners think that when they have told Toshiba about their problem and put their laptop into a UPS box, it is sent to the Japanese company to be repaired and

[21]"Travel Infrastructure Logistics: Executive Insight," *McKinsey.com*, accessed September 30, 2008.

[22]Bernard L. Bot and Carl-Stefan Neumann, "Growing Pains for Logistics Outsourcers," *McKinsey Quarterly*, no. 2, 2003.

[23]"1999 Annual Report—Third-Party Logistics: No End to the Good News," *Logistics Management and Distribution Report*, 38 (July 1999), pp. 73–74.

[24]"A Moving Story," *Economist*, December 7, 2002, pp. 65–66.

[25]"India: Logistics Gives the Competitive Edge," *Businessline*, November 5, 2001.

then returned by UPS. But what really happens is that when the laptop arrives at UPS's Louisville hub, it is taken to a vast estate of warehouses near the airport and mended in a repair shop owned and run not by Toshiba but by UPS. The UPS technicians are trained by Toshiba and the warehouse holds Toshiba spare parts. Even the people in the Toshiba call center that deals with inquiries work for UPS. The delivery company has been contracted to provide a complete repair and customer-service operation. And having done this for one company, UPS could capitalize on its investment by providing a similar service for others.

## Logistical Revolution with the Internet

The trend toward third-party logistics is a result of the internet and the Intranet (a specialized secure internet channel established between the companies) as well as concentrating on core competencies. The internet and the Intranet facilitate on-time inventory and distribution coordination without constraint of geographical boundaries. Core competencies refer to the mix of skills and resources that a firm possesses that enable it to produce one set of goods and/or services in a much more effective manner than another firm. Also, competent logistics firms can save money for a multinational firm shipping components between its facilities in different countries, because shipping costs paid internally can vary according to the fluctuation of foreign currencies.

We illustrate how some major companies take advantage of the internet and the Intranet for streamlining their logistics. At Dell Computer, the international logistics manager makes certain that the third-party logistics provider has state-of-the-art logistics and keeps it involved in Dell's strategic planning. Dell buys monitors finished and packaged, ready to deliver directly to the customer the world over. It does not add any value to the monitor itself, so Dell tries to avoid handling the monitor, preferring instead to have the logistic provider warehouse it and move it to Dell when the information system link with Dell drops an order into the warehouse computer. This saves Dell inventorying costs and gives it more operational flexibility.[26]

Pharmaceutical giant, Eli Lilly, has gradually outsourced more of its global logistics to Swiss-based Danzas AEI Intercontinental. This e-logistics company's famed "MarketLink" system manages seamless logistics services driven by the real-time flow of data between the company and its customers. Danzas AEI was recently put in charge of handling customs and the delivery of Eli Lilly's airborne and ocean imports. Based in the pharmaceutical hub of Basel, Switzerland, Danzas AEI Intercontinental has increasingly specialized in pharmaceutical products, working also with SmithKline Beecham and Hoffman-La Roche.[27]

As the market for third-party logistics has increased substantially since the 1990s, many traditional shippers, such as UPS, Federal Express, DPWN, and TNT, have developed large business units solely devoted to integrated logistics. Many logistic companies are now moving to provide tailored logistic solutions in international markets for their clients. One major player is UPS Logistics Group, a subsidiary of United Parcel Service, founded in 1995. UPS Logistics offers a full spectrum of supply chain services and logistics expertise throughout the world. Now its operations in North America, Europe, Asia, and Latin America include over 500 distribution facilities and strategic stocking locations. The subsidiary is composed of industrial engineers, software systems integrators and developers, facility designers, operations managers, high-tech repair technicians, logisticians, and transportation, financial, e-commerce, and international trade experts.[28]

Even online companies, such as Amazon.com, rely increasingly on 3PL services in foreign markets. Amazon.com launched its Canadian website (www.amazon.ca) in July 2002, but logistics is handled by Canada Post Corp. In 2001, more than 250 thousand Canadians ordered products from Amazon's U.S. site, and Canada represents Amazon's largest export market. Now Amazon.ca features bilingual Canadian

---

[26]Silvia Ascarelli, "Dell Finds U.S. Strategy Works in Europe," *Wall Street Journal* (February 3, 1997), p. A8.

[27]Robert Koenig, "Danzas Expands Pharmaceutical Logistics Business with Eli Lilly," *Journal of Commerce* (December 7, 1998), p. 14A; and "Danzas AEI Intercontinental," *Journal of Commerce*, November 25, 2002, p. 32.

[28]UPS Logistics Group, http://www.upslogistics.com, accessed January 20, 2006.

content and 1.5 million items, and Canada Post handles domestic deliveries. Canada Post's subsidiary, Assured Logistics, handles supply chain services such as warehousing, inventory management, and online fulfillment. This has proved to be mutually beneficial arrangement. Canada Post is establishing itself as a competent player in the online world, and as a result, its business is picking up with about 300 Canadian companies now using its online logistical services. On the other hand, Amazon spent US$200 million a year on technology to keep its U.S. operation running, but dies not incur that cost in its Canadian operation through Amazon.ca. Furthermore, this arrangement permits Amazon to better cater to the local market needs in Canada.[29]

Some distribution companies even find that the best way to be successful is to create a distribution alliance, and pool their logistics resources together. An example is the global distribution alliance between three international electronics distribution companies: the U.S. company Pioneer-Standard, the British company Eurodis, and Taiwan's World Peace Industrial. The alliance's ability to cover almost the entire globe has enabled it to obtain worldwide exclusive distribution contracts from electronics manufacturers such as Philips Semiconductors.[30] Similarly, six European logistics companies have joined forces to launch Eunique Logistics, a new pan-European alliance that provides customers a single point of contact for a range of distribution and logistics services throughout Europe.[31]

## MANAGING SOURCING STRATEGY

International logistics covers both the movement of raw materials and components into a manufacturing plant and the movement of finished products from the plant to the firm's customers around the world. Of these aspects of global logistics, it has become imperative for many companies to develop an efficient international sourcing strategy as they attempt to exploit their capabilities in R&D, operations, and marketing globally.

The design of international sourcing strategy is based on the interplay between a company's competitive advantages and the comparative advantages of various countries. **Competitive advantage** influences the decision regarding what activities and technologies a company should concentrate its investment and managerial resources in, relative to its competitors in the industry. **Comparative advantage** affects the company's decision on where to source and market, based on the lower cost of labor and other resources in one country relative to another.[32]

Over the last 30 years or so, gradual yet significant changes have taken place in international sourcing strategy. The cost-saving justification for international procurement in the 1970s and 1980s was gradually supplanted by quality and reliability concerns in the 1990s. Most of the changes have been in the way business executives think of the scope of international sourcing for their companies and exploit various resultant opportunities as a source of competitive advantage. Naturally, many companies that have a limited scope of global sourcing are at a disadvantage over those that exploit it to their fullest extent in a globally competitive marketplace. Six reasons are identified as to why companies adopt an international sourcing strategy.[33] These are:

- Intense international competition
- Pressure to reduce costs
- The need for manufacturing flexibility

[29]"Amazon Lands in Canada, Outsources Logistics," *Computing Canada*, (July 5, 2002) p. 6.

[30]"Arrow Hooks US Components Division," *Electronics Weekly*, January 22, 2003, p. 3.

[31]"New European Alliance," *Logistics and Transport Focus*, June 2002, p. 13.

[32]Bruce Kogut, "Designing Global Strategies: Comparative and Competitive Value-Added Chains," *Sloan Management Review*, 26 (Summer 1985), pp. 15–28.

[33]Joseph R. Carter and Ram Narasimhan, "Purchasing in the International Marketplace," *Journal of Purchasing and Materials Management*, 26 (Summer 1990), pp. 2–11.

- Shorter product development cycles
- Stringent quality standards
- Continually changing technology

Toyota's global sourcing operations illustrate one such world-class case. The Japanese carmaker is equipping its operations in the United States, Europe, and Southeast Asia with integrated capabilities for creating and marketing automobiles. The company gives the managers at those operations ample authority to accommodate local circumstances and values without diluting the benefit of integrated global operations. Thus, in the United States, Calty Design Research, a Toyota subsidiary in California, designs the bodies and interiors of new Toyota models, including Lexus and Solara. Toyota has technical centers in the United States and in Brussels to adapt engine and vehicle specifications to local needs.[34] Toyota operations that make automobiles in Southeast Asia supply each other with key components to foster increased economies of scale and standardization in those components—gasoline engines in Indonesia, steering components in Malaysia, transmissions in the Philippines, and diesel engines in Thailand. Toyota has also started developing vehicles in Australia and Thailand since 2003. These new bases develop passenger cars and trucks for production and sale only in the Asia-Pacific region. The Australian base is engaged mainly in designing cars, whereas the Thailand facility is responsible for testing them.[35]

## Procurement: Types of Sourcing Strategy

Sourcing strategy includes a number of basic choices that companies make in deciding how to serve foreign markets. One choice relates to the use of imports, assembly, or production within the country to serve a foreign market. Another decision involves the use of internal or external supplies of components or finished goods.

Sourcing decision-making is multifaceted and entails both contractual and locational implications. From a contractual point of view, the sourcing of major components and products by multinational companies takes place in two ways: (1) from the parents or their foreign subsidiaries on an "intra-firm" basis and (2) from independent suppliers on a "contractual" basis. The first type of sourcing is known as **intra-firm sourcing**. The second type of sourcing is commonly referred to as **outsourcing**. Similarly, from a locational point of view, multinational companies can procure components and products either (1) domestically (i.e., *domestic sourcing*) or (2) from abroad (i.e., *offshore sourcing*). Therefore, as shown in **Exhibit 15-2**, four possible types of sourcing strategy can be identified.

In developing viable sourcing strategies on a global scale, companies must consider not only the costs of manufacturing and various resources as well as exchange rate fluctuations but also the availability of infrastructure (including transportation, communications, and energy), industrial and cultural environments, ease of working with foreign host governments, and so on. Furthermore, the complex nature of sourcing strategy on a global scale spawns many barriers to its successful execution. In particular, logistics, inventory management, distance, nationalism, and lack of working knowledge about foreign business practices, among others, are major operational problems identified by both U.S. and foreign multinational companies engaging in international sourcing.

Many studies have shown, however, that despite, or perhaps as a result of, those operational problems, *where* to source major components seems much less important than *how* to source them. Thus, when examining the relationship between sourcing and competitiveness of multinational companies, it is crucial to distinguish between sourcing on a "contractual" basis and sourcing on an "intra-firm" basis, for these two types of sourcing will have a different impact on the firm's long-run competitiveness.

---

[34]Fumiko Kurosawa and John F. Odgers, "Global Strategy of Design and Development by Japanese Car Makers—From the Perspective of the Resource-Based View," *Association of Japanese Business Studies 1997 Annual Meeting Proceedings*, June 13-15, 1997, pp. 144–46.

[35]"Toyota Design Breaks from Clay and Foam," *Automotive News Europe*, April 4, 2005, p. 38.

**EXHIBIT 15-2**
TYPES OF SOURCING STRATEGY

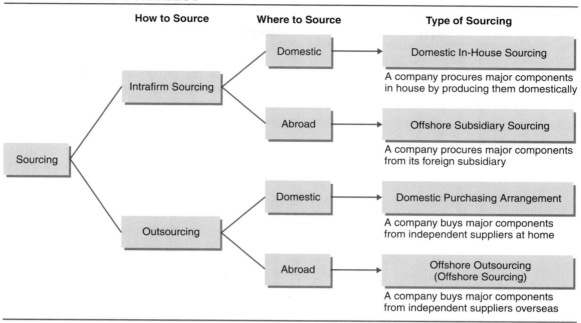

*Intra-Firm Sourcing.* Multinational companies can procure their components in-house within their corporate system around the world. They produce major components at their respective home base and/or at their affiliates overseas to be incorporated in their products marketed in various parts of the world. Thus, trade takes place between a parent company and its subsidiaries abroad, and also between foreign subsidiaries across national boundaries. This is often referred to as **intra-firm sourcing**. If such in-house component procurement takes place at home, it is essentially **domestic in-house sourcing**. If it takes place at a company's foreign subsidiary, it is called **offshore subsidiary sourcing**. Intra-firm sourcing makes trade statistics more complex to interpret, since part of the international flow of products and components is taking place between affiliated companies within the same multinational corporate system, which transcends national boundaries. About 30 percent of U.S. exports is attributed to U.S. parent companies transferring products and components to their affiliates overseas, and about 40 percent of U.S. imports is accounted for by foreign affiliates exporting to their U.S. parent companies. For both Japan and Britain, intra-firm transactions account for approximately 30 percent of their total trade flows (exports and imports combined), respectively.[36] Although statistics on intra-firm trade between foreign affiliates are limited to U.S. firms, the share of exports to other foreign affiliates in intra-firm exports of foreign affiliates rose from 37 percent in 1977 to 60 percent in 1993, and has been stable since then. This also suggests the increased role of foreign affiliates of U.S. multinational firms outside the United States.[37]

*Outsourcing (Contract Manufacturing).* In the 1970s, foreign competitors gradually caught up in a productivity race with U.S. companies, which had once commanded a dominant position in international trade. It coincided with U.S. corporate

---

[36]United Nations Center on Transnational Corporations, *Transnational Corporations in World Development: Trends and Perspectives* (New York: United Nations, 1988).

[37]*World Investment Report 1996*, pp. 13–14; and *World Investment Report 1998* (New York: United Nations, 1996 and 1998, respectively).

strategic emphasis drifting from manufacturing to finance and marketing. As a result, manufacturing management gradually lost its organizational influence. Production managers' decision-making authority was reduced so that R & D personnel prepared specifications with which production complied and then marketing personnel imposed delivery, inventory, and quality conditions. In a sense, production managers gradually took on the role of outside suppliers within their own companies.[38]

Production managers' reduced influence in the organization further led to a belief that manufacturing functions could, and should, be transferred easily to independent contract manufacturers, depending on the cost differential between in-house and contracted-out production. A company's reliance on domestic suppliers for major components and/or products[39] is basically a **domestic purchase arrangement**. Furthermore, in order to lower production costs under competitive pressure, U.S. companies turned increasingly to outsourcing components and finished products from abroad, particularly from newly industrialized countries including Singapore, South Korea, Taiwan, Hong Kong, Brazil, and Mexico. Initially, subsidiaries were set up for production purposes (i.e., offshore subsidiary sourcing), but gradually, independent foreign contract manufacturers took over component production for U.S. companies. This latter phenomenon is known by many terms, usually called **offshore outsourcing** (or more casually, **outsourcing**). For example, Apple, Dell, and Gateway outsource 100 percent of their laptop computers from Quanta Computer Inc., a Taiwanese company and the world's largest maker of laptop computers. Dell Computer alone accounts for half of Quanta's sales.[40]

In recent years, an increasing number of companies have used the internet to develop efficient B2B procurement (outsourcing) systems on a global scale. On February 25, 2000, General Motors, Ford, and DaimlerChrysler made history by jointly forming Covisint (www.covisint.com), which is probably the largest global online B2B procurement system dedicated to the auto industry. The Big Three have been joined by partners Nissan Motor, Renault, Commerce One, Inc., and Oracle Corp. in an effort to provide procurement, supply-chain, and product-development services to the auto industry on a global scale. The auto industry was an early adopter of the B2B procurement business model for a number of marketing-related reasons. First, automakers could develop products with a relatively short life cycle. Second, they would require a fast response time to market. Third, automakers were early adopters of outsourcing, one primary reason for which is the auto industry's drive for change from a push model to a pull model—their desire to achieve customized make-to-order marketing feasible.[41] However, by 2004, it was clear that Covisint had not been able to build a trust relationship between the participating automakers and their suppliers as it had on paper, and was eventually sold to Compuware Corp. as a messaging data service and portal.[42] Covisint's failure illustrates how difficult it is to manage outsourcing relationships.[43] The near-term benefits of outsourcing are clear. Among the most important reasons for outsourcing, according to a recent survey (see **Exhibit 15-3**), are cost reduction, focus on core competencies, access to special expertise, improved financial performance, delivery speed, reduction of resource constrains, and access to new technologies.

---

[38]Stephen S. Cohen and John Zysman, "Why Manufacturing Matters: The Myth of the Post-Industrial Economy," *California Management Review*, 29 (Spring 1987), pp. 9–26.

[39]Rodney Ho, "Small Product-Development Firms Show Solid Growth," *Wall Street Journal* (April 22, 1997), p. 32: This article shows that entrepreneurial companies have begun to fill a void of new product development role as large companies trim their internal R & D staff and expenditures in the United States. Although it makes financial sense, at least in the short term, those outsourcing companies will face the same long-term concern as explained in this chapter.

[40]"Quanta's Quantum Leap," *Business Week*, November 5, 2001, pp. 79–81; and "The Laptop Trail," *Wall Street Journal*, June 9, 2005, p. B1, B8.

[41]Beverly Beckert, "Engines of Auto Innovation," *Computer-Aided Engineering*, 20 (May 2001), pp. S18–S20.

[42]"Rule of the Road Still Apply to Covisint," *InformationWeek*, February 9, 2004. p. 32.

[43]Martina Gerst and Raluca Bunduchi, "Shaping IT Standardization in the Automotive Industry—The Role of Power in Driving Portal Standardization," *Electronic Markets*, 15 (December 2005), pp. 335–43.

**EXHIBIT 15-3**
MAJOR REASONS FOR
OUTSOURCING

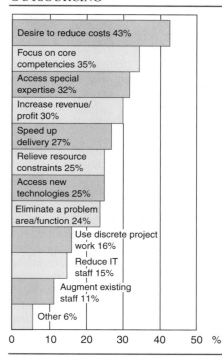

Desire to reduce costs 43%
Focus on core competencies 35%
Access special expertise 32%
Increase revenue/profit 30%
Speed up delivery 27%
Relieve resource constraints 25%
Access new technologies 25%
Eliminate a problem area/function 24%
Use discrete project work 16%
Reduce IT staff 15%
Augment existing staff 11%
Other 6%

0  10  20  30  40  50  %

*Source:* Survey results reported in "Outsourcing: Directions and Decisions for 2003," *2003 Outsourcing Trends*, CIO, http://www.cio.com, accessed February 16, 2006.

However, cultural differences are one of the biggest reasons why offshore outsourcing deals fail or run into problems in the long run.[44]

The short-term benefits of outsourcing are clear. Lower production costs, better strategic focus and flexibility, avoiding bureaucratic costs, and access to world-class capabilities are among the most important reasons for outsourcing. Long-term implications are not so clear, however. In particular, procurement from independent foreign suppliers (i.e., offshore outsourcing) has received quite a bit of attention, for it not only affects domestic employment and economic structure but sometimes also raises ethical issues (See **Global Perspective 15-3**). Companies using such a strategy have been described pejoratively as **hollow corporations**.[45] It is occasionally argued that those companies are increasingly adopting a "designer role" in global competition by offering innovations in product design without investing in manufacturing and process technology. Re-visit some caveats for contract manufacturing discussed in Chapter 9.

Even Covisint, the global B2B procurement business founded by the Big Three automakers discussed earlier, was not able to generate results that the companies had initially expected. Typical B2B procurement systems, including Covisint, have tended to rely on auctions that emphasize the lowest bids on a global basis. This internet-era emphasis on low cost could border on the cost emphasis of the 1960s and 1970s that ignored the importance of quality, technological superiority, delivery, and other non-cost aspects of competitive advantage. In fact, for superior product development when working jointly with external suppliers, automakers need to emphasize the importance

---

[44]"Culture Clashes Harm Offshoring," *BusinessWeek.com*, July 17, 2006.

[45]"Special Report: The Hollow Corporation," *Business Week* (March 3, 1986), pp. 56–59; and Robert Heller, "The Dangers of Deconstruction," *Management Today*, (February 1993), pp. 14, 17.

◆ ◆ ◆ ◆ ◆ ◆ ◆ ◆ ◆ ◆ ◆ ◆ ◆ ◆ ◆ ◆ ◆ ◆ ◆ ◆ ◆ ◆ ◆ ◆ ◆ ◆ ◆ ◆ ◆ ◆ ◆ ◆ ◆ ◆

## 𝒢LOBAL PERSPECTIVE 15-3

### OFFSHORE SOURCING AND SWEATSHOPS OVERSEAS: AN ETHICAL ISSUE

At least 80 people died and another 100 were seriously injured when a garment factory collapsed in Dhaka, Bangladesh in 2004. The factory made sweaters for European retailers Carrefour and Zara. These people were working in unsafe conditions to produce goods for consumers in the West. It is part of what corporate critics invariably call a "race to the bottom." Multinational companies seek places where labor is cheap, and safety, health, and environmental laws are lax.

The rapid globalization linking manufacturing companies, investors, and consumers around the world has touched off some ethical questions in recent years. Offshore sourcing is the practice of companies manufacturing or contracting out all or parts of their products abroad. Outsourcing makes it possible for those companies to procure products and components much more cheaply than manufacturing them in their home country. In many cases, labor cost savings are a strong motive for companies to engage in offshore sourcing. For example, Nike, the leading U.S. footwear company, has subcontractors in Taiwan, South Korea, and Indonesia, which collectively run twelve factories in Indonesia, producing 70 million pairs of Nike sneakers a year. Today, Nike's contractor network involves some 800,000 workers. Like any other footwear factories everywhere in Asia, work conditions are tough, with mandatory overtime work and constant exhaustion. Although these factories may be modern, they are drab and utilitarian, with vast sheds housing row upon row of mostly young women working many hours. The basic daily wage in Indonesia for

these workers is a mere $2–3 a day. There a pair of Pegasus running shoes costs about $18 to put together, and retails for $75 once shipped to the United States. The condition is similar in Vietnam, where 35,000 workers producing Nike shoes at five plants put in 12 hours a day to earn $1.60—less than the $2 or so it costs to buy three meals a day.

Although working conditions at these subcontractors' factories have improved over time at Nike's initiation, the company has a long way to go before it lives up to its stated goal of providing a fair working environment for all its workers. In Indonesia, police and factory managers have a not-so-subtle cozy relationship whereby police help keep workers under control. Despite its strong political clout, Nike has not challenged the Indonesian government's control over labor. Nike's code of conduct seems to remain vague, despite its intentions.

The linking of a firm's private interests with the larger public good has been referred to as corporate citizenship. Multinational companies cannot claim ignorance about the workers who produce the products they buy or the conditions in which they work. Large companies have the resources to investigate those with whom they do business. Ethically speaking, they should set standards that their contractors have to meet to continue their contracts. Indeed, in recent years, socially responsible investing (SRI) has increasingly become the practice of making investment decisions on the basis of both financial and social performance. The SRI movement has grown into a $1.185 trillion business, accounting for about 1 in 10 U.S. invested dollars.

A new, exhaustive academic review of 167 studies over the past 35 years concludes that there is in fact a positive link between companies' social and financial performance—but only a weak one. But this does not mean that it is not worth the effort because companies will benefit a lot in building a better brand reputation, making decisions that are better for business in the long term, being more attractive to potential and existing employees, etc.

*Sources:* R. Bruce Hutton, Louis D'Antonio, and Tommi Johnsen, "Socially Responsible Investing: Growing Issues and New Opportunities," *Business and Society*, 37 (September 1998), pp. 281–305; "Labor Standards Clash with Global Reality," *New York Times*, April 24, 2001; "Cops of the Global Village," *Fortune*, June 27, 2005, pp. 158–66; "The Next Question," *Economist*, January 19, 2008, Special Section, pp. 8–10; and "A Stitch in Time," *Economist*, January 19 2008, Special Section, pp. 12–14.

---

of technical collaborations, such as product design, as well as building trust in supplier-buyer relationships.[46]

This widespread offshore outsourcing practice could have a deleterious impact on companies' ability to maintain their initial competitive advantage based on product innovations.[47] Indeed, keeping abreast of emerging technology through continual improvement in operations and process seems to be essential for the company's

---

[46]Kotabe, Masaaki, Xavier Martin, and Hiroshi Domoto, "Gaining from Vertical Relationships: Knowledge Transfer, Relationship Duration, and Supplier Performance Improvement in the U.S. and Japanese Automobile Industries," *Strategic Management Journal*, 24 (March 2003), pp. 293–316.

[47]Constantinos Markides and Norman Berg, "Manufacturing Offshore is Bad Business," *Harvard Business Review*, 66 (September-October 1988), pp. 113–20; and Masaaki Kotabe, Michael J. Mol, and Janet Y. Murray, "Outsourcing, Performance, and the Role of E-Commerce: A Dynamic Perspective," *Industrial Marketing Management*, 37(1), 2008, pp. 37–45.

continued competitiveness. This may explain why Sharp, one of the world's largest liquid-crystal-display (LCD) panel manufacturers, is building a $9 billion factory to make LCD panels and solar panels in Japan instead of moving factories offshore to places like China, where products could be made more cheaply. Actually, while Apple Inc. is leading a trend in the electronics industry to outsource hardware manufacturing and focus on design and software, Sharp is making a huge bet that keeping manufacturing of LCD and solar panels in-house will give it a big competitive advantage. If Sharp continues to be successful, the focused-manufacturing strategy could be a model for other Japanese electronics makers, which find Apple's outsourcing model a turnoff and are still trying to figure out a way to remain a manufacturer while growing its profit in an industry that is rapidly commoditizing[48] (See **Global Perspective 15-4** for other potential hazards of relying on outsourcing).

## GLOBAL PERSPECTIVE 15-4

### BEING TOO LEAN IS A DANGEROUS THING

There are two types of risk in a supply chain, external and internal. For the external, there is never a scarcity of examples, such as a dock strike in California, a typhoon in Taiwan, a tsunami in Asia, and a hurricane in New Orleans. More recently a huge explosion at the Buncefield oil storage terminal in Britain's Hertfordshire caused widespread problems for businesses not just locally but across a large part of England.

Sometimes even a political wrangle in Brussels will bring a supply chain to a shuddering halt. In the fall of 2005, some 80 million items of clothing were impounded at European ports and borders because they exceeded the annual import limits that the European Union and China had agreed on only months earlier. Retailers had ordered their autumn stock well before that agreement was signed, and many were left scrambling to find alternative suppliers. The negative impact was large although a compromise was reached eventually.

Besides the external ones, most supply-chain disruptions often have internal causes as well. Undoubtedly, it is great when companies run supply chains "lean." However, too much leanness and meanness can severely hurt companies. The cost of such disruptions is huge. Typically a company's share price drops by around 8 percent in the first day or two after companies announce supply-chain problems, according to a research by Vinod Singhal, a professor of operations management at the Georgia Institute of Technology. This is worse than the average stock market reaction to other corporate bad news, such as a delay in the launch of a new product (which triggers an average fall of 5 percent), untoward financial events (an average drop of 3-5 percent) or IT problems

(2 percent). And the effects can be long-lasting: operating income, return on sales and return on assets are all significantly down in the first and second year after a disruption.

If leanness is not controlled appropriately, it can cause a calamity when external risk happens. A striking example involves Philips. It began on a stormy evening in New Mexico in March 2000 when a bolt of lightning hit a power line. The temporary loss of electrical power knocked out the cooling fans in a furnace at a Philips semiconductor plant in Albuquerque. A fire started, but was put out by staff within minutes. By the time the fire brigade arrived, there was nothing for them to do but inspect the building and fill out a report. The damage seemed to be minor: eight trays of wafers containing the miniature circuitry to make several thousand chips for mobile phones had been destroyed. After a good cleanup, the company expected to resume production within a week.

That is what the plant told its two largest customers, Sweden's Ericsson and Finland's Nokia, which were vying for leadership in the booming mobile-handset market. Nokia's supply-chain managers had realized within two days that there was a problem when their computer systems showed some shipments were being held up. Delays of a few days are not uncommon in manufacturing and a limited number of back-up components are usually held to cope with such eventualities. But whereas Ericsson was content to let the delay take its course, Nokia immediately put the Philips plant on a watch list to be closely monitored in case things got worse.

They did. Semiconductor fabrication plants have to be kept spotlessly clean, but on the night of the fire, when staff were rushing around and firemen were tramping in and out, smoke and soot had contaminated a much larger area of the plant than had first been thought. Production could be halted for

*Source:* "When the Chain Breaks," *Economist*, June 17, 2006, Special Section, pp.18–20.

*(continued)*

---

[48]Yukari Iwatani Kane, "Sharp Focuses on Manufacturing; A $9 Billion Plant In Japan Will Make LCD, Solar Panels," *Wall Street Journal*, July 9, 2008. p. B1.

$\mathcal{G}$LOBAL PERSPECTIVE 15-4

(CONTINUED)

months. By the time the full extent of the disruption became clear, Nokia had already started locking up all the alternative sources for the chips.

That left Ericsson with a serious parts shortage. The company, having decided some time earlier to simplify its supply chain by single-sourcing some of its components, including the Philips chips, had no plan B. This severely limited its ability to launch a new generation of handsets, which in turn contributed to huge losses in the Swedish company's mobile-phone division. In 2001 Ericsson decided to quit making handsets on its own. Instead, it put that part of its business into a joint venture with Sony.

This example has become a classic case study for supply-chain experts and risk consultants. Unfortunately, such disruptions in supply chains seem to be happening more often. In order to avoid such disruptions, some people suggest that supply chains should be regulated, a bit like public utilities, because countries have become so highly dependent on private-sector production infrastructure. Barry Lynn, author of a book on this subject, *End of the Line*, thinks that perhaps companies should be required to limit their outsourcing and use more than one supplier of essential items. In his book, he argues that globalization and outsourcing provide only a temporary benefit to consumers because the companies that form part of supply chains will buy each other up in pursuit of ever greater efficiency, and thus lose most of their flexibility.

There are signs that some companies are already alert to these concerns and may be planning to reorganize their supply chains to make them safer. That process could speed up if disruptions become more common. A critical way to achieve a resilient supply chain is to create flexibility--and that flexible companies are best placed to compete in the marketplace. For larger firms, that could mean adopting so-called the "continental strategy": having a spread of suppliers in different continents for added flexibility, as Dell and Cisco do. Smaller firms may not be able to achieve a geographical spread. But in any case, companies do not want to go back to carrying lots of inventory in different locations. They need to do something in-between, carrying a little more cost than an absolutely lean model so as to get protection.

Nowadays, more and more multinationals go to Asia, in particular to China and India, for leanness. However, there are very legitimate, very good business reasons not necessarily to complete and ship from Asia to avoid supply chain disruptions. Companies may consider other options in other parts of the world although these may look more expensive. A higher cost structure can make supply chain more robust and reliable.

All in all, there will always be natural disasters, as well as corporate mistakes. In order to insulate themselves from the consequences, companies will have to spread their risks more widely. That does not necessarily mean fewer aircrafts will be queuing up to land at Louisville and Memphis, or that fewer container ships will set sail from Asia's bustling ports. But it does mean that in the future, companies may spend rather more to maintain a number of different supply chains, and some of those may be closer to home.

**Outsourcing of Service Activities**

In 2007, the United States was ranked the largest exporter and importer of services, providing $454 billion of services to the rest of the world and receiving $440 billion worth of services from abroad. Furthermore, according to a recent government estimate, approximately 16 percent of the total value of U.S. exports and imports of services were conducted across national boundaries on an intra-firm basis (i.e., between parent companies and their subsidiaries). Increasingly, U.S. companies have expanded their service procurement activities on a global basis in the same way they procure components and finished products. Spending on offshore services is three times higher in North America than in Western Europe but the gap is closing, with Indian providers becoming more popular in 2007, growing 40 percent in the United States and 60 percent in Europe annually.[49]

As discussed, firms have the ability and opportunity to procure components/finished goods that have proprietary technology on a global basis. This logic also applies equally to service activities. The technological revolution in data processing and telecommunications (trans-border data flow, telematics, etc.) either makes the global tradability of some services possible or facilitates the transactions economically. Furthermore, because the production and consumption of some services do not

---

[49]"Global Outsourcing to Grow 8% in 2008," *BusinessWeek.com*, January 10, 2008.

need to take place at the same location or at the same time, global sourcing could be a viable strategy.

Thanks to the development of the internet and e-commerce, certain service activities are increasingly outsourced from independent service suppliers. The internet will also accelerate growth in the number of e-workers. This net-savvy and highly flexible corps will be able to perform much or all of their work at home, or in small groups close to home, regardless of their locations. International e-workers can also operate in locations far from corporate headquarters. They will be part of the growth in *intellectual outsourcing*. Already such e-workers can write software in India for a phone company in Finland, provide architectural services in Ireland for a building in Spain, and do accounting work in Hong Kong for an insurance company in Vancouver. Globalization of services through the internet is likely to expand considerably in the future.[50]

Bangalore, India should particularly be noted. The region is described as the Silicon Valley of that country. Bangalore has rapidly evolved to become the center of offshore programming activities. Many U.S. companies have started outsourcing an increasing portion of software development to companies in Bangalore. Established software vendors, including IBM, Microsoft, Oracle, and SAP, already employ Indian talent no longer just to write software code but also to help design and develop commercial offerings that are higher up in the software design food chain. Increasingly, Indian software entrepreneurs want to put their own companies' brand names on products, at home and abroad, by capitalizing on their country's highly educated and low-cost workforce to build and sell software for everything from back-office programs to customer-facing applications.[51] According to Indian tech industry body, National Association of Software and Services Companies (NASSCOM), services and software exports contributed around $41 billion in 2008. The Indian tech industry is aiming to hit total revenues for software and services of US$75 billion by 2010.[52] NASSCOM is recognized to represent an alternative to the government in shaping the industry landscape in India.[53] Similarly, China is catching up in this role. Microsoft has four research laboratories located around the globe: Redmond, Washington; Cambridge, UK; Beijing, China and San Francisco, California, with the goal to invent Microsoft's future, by focusing on technologies and technology trends in the next 5–10-year time frame. For example, Microsoft Research (MSR) Asia, founded in 1998 in Beijing, has already produced many research results that have been transferred to Microsoft products, including Office XP, Office System 2003, Windows XP, and Longhorn — the next major release of Windows.[54]

Outsourcing of service activities has been widely quoted in the popular press as a means to reduce costs and improve the corporate focus; that is concentrating on the core activities of the firm. However, outsourcing may also serve (a) as a means of reducing time to implement internal processes, (b) as a means of sharing risk in an increasingly uncertain business environment, (c) to improve customer service, (d) to get access to better expertise not available in-house, (e) for headcount reduction, and (f) as a means of instilling a sense of competition, especially when departments within firms develop a perceptible level of inertia.[55]

In the case of service companies, the distinction between core and supplementary services is necessary in strategy development. **Core services** are the necessary outputs of an organization that consumers are looking for, while **supplementary services** are

---

[50]Robert D Hormats, "High Velocity," *Harvard International Review*, 21 (Summer 1999), pp. 36–41.

[51]"India's Next Step," *InformationWeek*, August 8, 2005, pp. 34–39.

[52]"Indian Tech Industry Looking at 33% Growth," *BusinessWeek.com*, February 14, 2008.

[53]Nir Kshetri and Nikhilesh Dholakia, "Professional and Trade Associations in a Nascent and Formative Sector of a Developing Economy: A Case Study of the NASSCOM Effect on the Indian Offshoring Industry," *Journal of International Management*, 15(2), 2009.

[54]"Labs: Asia," Microsoft Research, http://research.microsoft.com/aboutmsr/labs/asia/, accessed February 20, 2006.

[55]Maneesh Chandra, "Global Sourcing of Services: A Theory Development and Empirical Investigation," a Ph.D. dissertation, The University of Texas at Austin, 1999.

either indispensable for the execution of the core service or are available only to improve the overall quality of the core service bundle. Using an example of the healthcare industry, the core service is providing patients with good-quality medical care. The supplementary services may include filing insurance claims, arranging accommodation for family members (especially for overseas patients), handling off-hour emergency calls, and so on. The same phenomenon arises in the computer software industry. When the industry giant, Microsoft, needed help in supporting new users of Windows operating software, it utilized outsourcing with Boston-based Keane, Inc. to set up a help desk with 350 support personnel.

Core services may gradually partake of a "commodity" and lose their differential advantage vis-à-vis competitors as competition intensifies over time. Subsequently, a service provider may increase its reliance on supplementary services to maintain and/or enhance competitive advantage. "After all, if a firm cannot do a decent job on the core elements, it is eventually going to go out of business."[56] In other words, a service firm exists in order to provide good-quality core services to its customers; however, in some instances, it simply cannot rely solely on core services to stay competitive. We can expect that core services are usually performed by the service firm itself, regardless of the characteristics of the core service. On the other hand, although supplementary services are provided to augment the core service for competitive advantage, the unique characteristics of supplementary services may influence "how" and "where" they are sourced.[57]

The bottom line is that the quality of the service package that customers experience helps service companies differentiate themselves from the competition. One important category of quality is the variability of the product or service's attributes—its reliability. As in manufacturing, service companies that choose to differentiate themselves based on reliability must consistently maintain it, or else they will undermine their strategic position by damaging the reputation of their brand name. There is empirical evidence that outsourcing of some service activities for the sake of economic efficiency tends to result in less reliable service offerings.[58] The same concern about the advantages and disadvantages of outsourcing in the manufacturing industry appears to apply in the services industry.

## ◆ ◆ ◆ ◆ ◆ ◆ ◆ ◆ ◆   FREE TRADE ZONES

A **free trade zone** (FTZ) is an area located within a nation (say, the United States) but is considered outside of the customs territory of the nation. The use of FTZs has become an integral part of global sourcing strategy as they offer various tax benefits and marketing flexibility on a global basis.

Many countries have similar programs. In the United States, a free trade zone is officially called a Foreign Trade Zone. FTZs are licensed by the Foreign Trade Zone Board and operated under the supervision of the Customs Service. The level of demand for FTZ procedures has followed the overall growth trend in global trade and investment. Presently, some 700 FTZs are in operation and, as part of their activity, about 540 manufacturing plants are operating with subzone status. Subzones are adjuncts to the main zones when the main site cannot serve the needed purpose and are usually found at manufacturing plants. Across the United States, about 335,000 jobs are directly related to activity in FTZs, Companies operating in FTZs are saving

[56]C. H. Lovelock, "Adding Value to Core Products with Supplementary Services," in C. H. Lovelock, ed., *Services Marketing*, 3rd ed., Englewood Cliffs, NJ: Prentice Hall, 1996.

[57]Terry Clark, Daniel Rajaratnam, and Timothy Smith, "Toward a theory of international services: Marketing intangibles in a world of nations," *Journal of International Marketing*, 4(2), 1996, pp. 9–28; and Janet Y. Murray and Masaaki Kotabe, "Sourcing Strategies of U.S. Service Companies: A Modified Transaction-Cost Analysis," *Strategic Management Journal*, 20 (September 1999), pp. 791–809.

[58]C. M. Hsieh, Sergio G. Lazzarini, Jack A. Nickerson, "Outsourcing and the Variability of Product Performance: Data from International Courier Services," *Academy of Management Proceedings*, 2002, pp. G1–G6.

**EXHIBIT 15-4**

BENEFITS OF USING A FOREIGN TRADE ZONE (FTZ) IN THE UNITED STATES

1. *Duty deferral and elimination.* Duty will be deferred until products are sold in the United States. If products are exported elsewhere, no import tariff will be imposed.
2. *Lower tariff rates.* Tariff rates are almost always lower for materials and components than for finished products. If materials and components are shipped to an FTZ for further processing and finished products are sold in the United States, a U.S. import tariff will be assessed on the value of the materials and components, rather than on the value of the finished products.
3. *Lower tariff incidence.* Imported materials and components that through storage or processing undergo a loss or shrinkage may benefit from FTZ status as tariff is assessed only on the value of materials and components that actually found their way into the product.
4. *Exchange rate hedging.* Currency fluctuations can be hedged against by requesting customs assessment at any time.
5. *Import quota not applicable.* Import quotas are not generally applicable to goods stored in an FTZ.
6. *"Made in U.S.A." designation.* If foreign components are substantially transformed within an FTZ located in the United States, the finished product may be designated as "Made in U.S.A."

money, improving cash flow, and increasing logistical efficiency.[59] Legally, goods in the zone remain in international commerce as long as they are held within the zone or are exported. In other words, those goods (including materials, components, and finished products) shipped into an FTZ in the United States from abroad are legally considered not having landed in the customs territory of the United States and thus are not subject to U.S. import tariffs, as long as they are not sold outside the FTZ in the United States (See **Exhibit 15-4**).

An FTZ provides many cash flow and operating advantages as well as marketing advantages to zone users. Even when these goods enter the United States, customs duties can be levied on the lesser of the value of the finished product or its imported components.

Operationally, an FTZ provides an opportunity for every business engaged in international commerce to take advantage of a variety of efficiencies and economies in the manufacture and marketing of their products. Merchandise within the zone can be unpacked and repacked; sorted and relabeled; inspected and tested; repaired or discarded; reprocessed, fabricated, assembled, or otherwise manipulated. It can be combined with other imported or domestic materials; stored or exhibited; transported in bond to another FTZ; sold or exported. Foreign goods can be modified within the zone to meet U.S. import standards and processed using U.S. labor.

Aging imported wine is an interesting way to take advantage of an FTZ. A U.S. wine importer purchases what is essentially newly fermented grape juice from French vineyards and ships it to an FTZ in the United States for aging. After several years, the now-aged French wine can be shipped throughout the United States when an appropriate U.S. import tariff will be assessed on the original value of the grape juice instead of on the market value of the aged wine. If tariff rates are sufficiently high, the cost savings from using an FTZ can be enormous.

Another effective use of an FTZ is illustrated by companies such as Ford and Dell Computer. These companies rely heavily on imported components such as auto parts and computer chips, respectively. In such a case, the companies can have part of their manufacturing facilities designated as subzones of an FTZ. This way, they can use their facilities as they ordinarily do, yet enjoy all of the benefits accruing from an FTZ. Furthermore, if foreign components are substantially transformed within an FTZ located in the United States, the finished product may be designated as "Made in

---

[59]"US Foreign-Trade Zones Boost Employment, Exports," *Journal of Commerce*, September 5, 2005, p. 24.

the U.S.A." To the extent customers have a favorable attitude toward the "Made in the U.S.A." country-of-origin, such labeling has additional marketing advantage.

At the macro-level, all parties to the arrangement benefit from the operation of trade zones. The government maintaining the trade zone achieves increased investment and employment. The firm using the trade zone obtains a beachhead in the foreign market without incurring all costs normally associated with such an activity. As a result, goods can be reassembled, and large shipments can be broken down into smaller units. Duties could be due only on the imported materials and the component parts rather than on the labor that is used to finish the product.

In addition to free trade zones, various governments have also established export processing zones and special economic areas. Japan, which has had a large trade surplus over the years, has developed a unique trade zone program specifically designed to increase imports rather than exports (see **Global Perspective 15-5**). The common dimensions of all of these zones are that special rules apply to them, when compared with other regions of the country, and that the purpose of these rules is the desire of governments to stimulate the economy—especially the export side of international trade. Export processing zones usually provide tax- and duty-free treatment of production facilities whose output is destined for foreign markets. The *maquiladoras* of Mexico is one example. (For those interested in Mexico's maquiladoras, see Appendix to this chapter.)

For the logistician, the decision of whether to use such zones is framed by the overall benefit for the logistics system. Clearly, transport and re-transport are often

## $\mathcal{G}$LOBAL PERSPECTIVE 15-5

### JAPAN'S FOREIGN ACCESS ZONE TO INCREASE IMPORTS AND INWARD DIRECT INVESTMENT RATHER THAN EXPORTS

Japan has made some of its major trading partner countries turn protectionist because it has run a huge trade surplus over the years. To increase imports into Japan rather than to encourage exports from Japan, the Japanese government announced a basic plan for the expansion of imports in 1993. It is a $20 billion program that created a national network of 31 import promotion areas scattered across the country, or as the Japanese call them "foreign access zones," where importers and foreign investors get special tax breaks and other advantages. The foreign access zones provide a major opportunity for U.S. and other foreign businesses setting up beachhead in Japan.

Operations based in the access zones also get around most, if not all, of the existing impediments to foreign investment in Japan. The zones provide inexpensive warehousing and storage, free or low-cost translation and marketing assistance, access to less expensive regional labor, and most important of all, local marketing opportunities that bypass the large

*Source:* Ronald A. Morse, Alan Kitchin, "Japan: A Place in the Sun," *Director*, 51 (September 1997), pp. 77–80; "Kitakyushu: Transportation and Distribution," http://www.city.kitakyushu.jp//page/english/02transport/index.html, accessed August 3, 2006; and "Measures to Promote Imports," the Ministry of Economic, Trade, and Industry's website, http://www.meti.go.jp/english/report/data/cFDI071e.html, accessed September 1, 2009.

trading companies and their traditional keiretsu distribution channels.

Kyushu, Japan's southernmost island, has been one such testing ground for this open approach. It is being promoted as the "crossroads of Asia" (it is closer to Shanghai and Seoul than it is to Tokyo). Also known as "Silicon Island," Kyushu hosts a clutch of US high-tech manufacturers (including Texas Instruments which employs 1,000 people at its Hiji plant). The island's two main cities, Fukuoka and Kitakyushu have fully espoused the Japanese government's foreign access zone concept. Across Kyushu, cities and prefectures are competing with one another to offer the best incentives to incoming business.

In late 1990s, Kitakyushu raised its cash incentives for building new factories and software houses from $1.8 million to $4.5 million. Other incentives include discounted office space in a newly-constructed Asian trade center, a land leasing program at 8 percent of evaluated cost, and joint venture opportunities with local companies boasting private electricity supplies.

Kitakyushu's port, Hibikinada, is being deepened and a new $1.5 billion international airport is being constructed on reclaimed land nearby. Kyushu is committed to a future role as an Asian production base —but for the moment it is more likely to be used as an entry point for the Japanese market.

required, warehousing facilities need to be constructed, and material handling frequency increases. However, the costs could well be balanced by the preferential government treatment or by lower labor costs.

## INTERNATIONAL DISTRIBUTION CHANNEL

◆ ◆ ◆ ◆ ◆ ◆ ◆

Both consumer and industrial products go though some form of distribution process in all countries and markets. International distribution channels are the link between a firm and its customers in markets around the world. For a firm to realize its marketing objectives, it must be able to make its product accessible to its target market at an affordable price. A firm cannot do this if its distribution structures are inflexible, inefficient, and burdensome. Creating a reliable and efficient international distribution channel can be one of the most critical and challenging tasks that an international marketing manager can face.

In essence, companies have two options when it comes to configuring their international distribution systems:

**Channel Configurations**

1. A firm may decide to sell direct to its customers in a foreign market by using its own local salesforce or through the internet.

2. A firm may decide to use the resources of independent intermediaries, most often at the local level.

An Australian company, ResMed, a manufacturer of medical respiratory devices, is an example of a firm that uses the first option. Most of ResMed's foreign sales are generated by its own sales staff operation from its own sales offices in the United States, the United Kingdom, and throughout Europe and South-East Asia. Although this direct distribution channel may appear to be the most effective, it is only successful if customers are geographically homogeneous, have similar consumption patterns and are relatively few.[60] Dell and Hewlett-Packard are two examples of multinational companies in the same personal computer industry with different distribution systems. Dell distributes its PCs directly from its assembly factories to end-users anywhere in the world, while Hewlett-Packard users international agents and retailers. Dell customers may have to wait several days or weeks to get a PC, whereas Hewlett-Packard customers can walk away from a retailer with a PC immediately. In deciding which distribution channels to adopt, a firm needs to consider the cost of meeting customer needs. Therefore, a firm needs to evaluate the impact on customer service and cost as it compares different international distribution options.

**EXHIBIT 15-5**
INTERNATIONAL DISTRIBUTION CHANNEL ALTERNATIVES

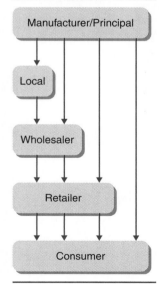

Distribution channels that use intermediaries, agents, or merchants positioned between the manufacturer and customers in a distribution channel, can often have several levels and employ several intermediaries, each with its own specific purpose within the distribution channel. The use of intermediaries can be a relatively easy, quick and low-cost entry strategy into a new foreign market, therefore their frequent use by many companies, particularly small-to-medium companies that do not have the resources to operate their own marketing and distribution system in a foreign market. **Exhibit 15-5** shows some of the distribution channel configurations.

Within a distribution channel, a firm can elect to go through one or more agent or merchant intermediaries. The basic difference between agent and merchant intermediaries is the legal ownership of goods. An *agent intermediary* does not take title (ownership) to the goods. Rather, it distributes them on behalf of the principal company in exchange for a percentage of the sale price. *Merchant intermediaries* hold title to the goods they exchange and operate in their own right as independent

---

[60]Bruce Seifert and John Ford, "Export Distribution Channels," *Columbia Journal of World Business*, 24(2), 1989, pp. 15–22.

businesses. The names given to intermediaries can vary from country to country and from industry to industry in the same country.

Apart from meeting customer needs and costs, several other factors influence the choice of distribution channel configuration used by a firm to gain access to its international markets, including the characteristics of the company's customers; the range and choice of intermediaries; competitors; marketing environment; and the strengths and weaknesses of the company itself.[61] However, these factors stand out as being particularly important in selecting a proper distribution channel in terms of market coverage, control and cost.

Coverage refers to the market segments or geographic area a firm's products are represented in. Although full market coverage may be the company's objective, it is not always possible in a foreign market; nor may it be desirable. In some countries, such as China and Brazil, three or four major cities contain the country's most affluent and viable market segments for foreign products. If a firm wishes to attempt full market coverage, it may have to use several intermediaries.

The more intermediaries in the distribution channel, the more likely the firm loses control over all aspects the marketing of its products. If a firm wishes to have complete control over such aspects of its marketing as establishing prices, the types of outlets its products should be available in, inventory levels and promotion, it has little choice but to develop its own company-controlled distribution system.

Although direct distribution by a firm may allow it to have complete control over all aspects of the marketing of its products, it brings significant cost issues. This is particularly true if the sale base is relatively small. Channel costs include the margins, markups or commissions payable to the various intermediaries. Although these costs may inflate a product's price in a foreign market, companies may be disappointed in believing that they can reduce channel costs by using a direct distribution strategy. Local costs associated with maintaining a salesforce, inventory, providing credit and advertising may offset any cost savings.

In reality, most often, no one factor is more important than another in configuring an international distribution channel. A channel with optimum coverage and control at a minimum cost is the preferred choice but, in practice, a balance has to be struck.

## Channel Management

Use of an indirect distribution channel always results in loss of some control over a company's marketing operations. This loss of control can be greater in international distribution channels than in domestic ones because the company has no permanent presence in the foreign market and must rely heavily on the actions of its foreign intermediaries. Differences in expectations and goals between the company and its foreign intermediaries can lead to channel conflict. To deal with this, companies must actively manage the relationship between themselves and their intermediaries, and often among intermediaries themselves, in an effort to create a harmonious relationship characterized by loyalty, trust, cooperation, and open communication.[62]

The selection of intermediaries becomes crucial to the process of maintaining harmonious channel relationships for a company that wishes to achieve its foreign sales and other marketing objectives. Some guidelines for selecting and dealing with foreign intermediaries include:[63]

• Search for intermediaries capable of developing markets, not just those with good contacts.

• Regard intermediaries as long-term partners, not as a temporary means of market entry.

---

[61]Bert Rosenbloom and Trina L. Larsen, "International Channesls of Distribution and the Role of Comparative Marketing Analysis," *Journal of Global Marketing*, 4(4), 1991, pp. 39–54.

[62]Leonidas C. Leonidou, Constantine S. Katsikeas, and John Hadjimarcou, "Building Successful Export Business Relationships: A Behavioral Perspective," *Journal of International Marketing*, 10(3), 2002, pp. 96–115.

[63]David Arnold, "Seven Rules of International Distribution," *Harvard Business Review*, 78 (November/December), 2000, pp. 131–37.

- Actively search for and select intermediaries; do not let them select you.
- Support your intermediaries by committing resources such as marketing ideas, funds and know-how.
- Ensure intermediaries provide the information you need, including up-to-date market information and detailed sales performance data.
- Attempt to maintain as much control as possible over the marketing strategy.
- Try to make links with national intermediaries as soon as possible after entering a foreign market.

In addition, the company should always maintain a genuine interest in both the intermediary and the foreign market, be prepared to adapt to the local competitive conditions, and attempt to minimize disagreements with an intermediary as quickly as possible.

# INTERNATIONAL RETAILING

◆ ◆ ◆ ◆ ◆ ◆ ◆

The face of distribution that consumers interact with is the retail store at which they shop. In developed parts of the world, retailing employs between 7 percent and 12 percent of the workforce and wields enormous power over manufacturers and consumers. **International retailing** is any retailing activity that transcends national borders. Over the last two decades, retailers have grown into some of the world's largest companies, rivaling or exceeding manufacturers in terms of global reach. They have been growing much faster abroad than in their domestic markets. The world's top 10 retailers' international operations are summarized in **Exhibit 15-6**.

In search of new opportunities, retailers have not only diversified across geographical market boundaries but also across product boundaries. First, most leading retailers have developed their own private-label product lines as well as sell the products of leading national- and international-brand manufacturers. Second, retailers have increasingly adopted the discount format. As a result, more consumers are getting used to their streamlined, no-frills retail format. Third, retailers have also increasingly embraced the virtual store (e-commerce) format.[64]

Take a look at the world's largest discount store chain, Wal-Mart of the United States. Wal-Mart has become the largest company in the United States and the world's

**EXHIBIT 15-6**
INTERNATIONAL OPERATIONS OF THE WORLD'S TOP 10 RETAILERS

| Rank | Retail Company | Country of Origin | Total Sales (in $ billion) | Foreign Sales (%) | Number of Foreign Markets |
|------|----------------|-------------------|----------------------------|-------------------|---------------------------|
| 1 | Wal-Mart | United States | 376.4 | 22 | 14 |
| 2 | Carrefour | France | 122.2 | 53 | 37 |
| 3 | Metro Group | Germany | 87.4 | 55 | 32 |
| 4 | Tesco | Britain | 86.8 | 25 | 13 |
| 5 | Seven & I | Japan | 79.1 | 34 | 8 |
| 6 | Ahold | Netherlands | 77.5 | 82 | 8 |
| 7 | Kroger | United States | 69.5 | 0 | 0 |
| 8 | Sears | United States | 64.8 | 12 | 2 |
| 9 | Costco | United States | 64.7 | 20 | 8 |
| 10 | Target | United States | 62.6 | 0 | 0 |

*Source:* Global Retail Intelligence, www.planetretail.net, and *Fortune*, 2006.

[64]Katrijn Gielens and Marnik G. Dekimpe, "Global Trends in Grocery Retailing," in Masaaki Kotabe and Kristiaan Helsen, ed., The SAGE Handbook of International Marketing, London: SAGE Publications, 2009, pp. 413–28.

largest retailer with annual revenues of about $376.4 billion in 2006. As of September 2008, the company had 914 Wal-Mart stores, 2,576 Supercenters, 594 SAM'S Clubs, and 143 Neighborhood Markets in the United States. Internationally, the Company operated units in Argentina (24), Brazil (315), Canada (305), Central America (461), China (206), Japan (392), Mexico (1,045), Puerto Rico (54), and the United Kingdom (344). Despite its aggressive foreign expansion, however, Wal-Mart experienced continued difficulties in such markets as Argentina and Puerto Rico, pulling out of Germany and South Korea, as well as declining sales in Japan.

Wal-Mart is Procter & Gamble's single largest customer, buying as much as the household product giant sells to Japan. Wal-Mart is extremely successful in the NAFTA region, but not necessarily the most global retailer. Actually only 10 percent of its sales are generated outside its core NAFTA market, compared to Carrefour, which generates more than 20 percent of sales outside Europe. Wal-Mart's success lies in low tariffs in the NAFTA zone, cheap labor and low-cost logistics, with savings passed on to consumers.[65] In other foreign markets, however, Wal-Mart's performance has been lackluster, primarily due to its unwillingness to adapt to local market conditions (See, for example, the case study on Wal-Mart operations in Brazil, included in the textbook).

Retailing involves very locally entrenched activities, including stocking of an assortment of products that local consumers prefer, catering to local shopping pattern (e.g., shopping frequency, time of shopping, and traffic jam), and seasonal promotion as well as meeting local competition on a daily basis. International retailers that are willing to adapt their strategy to local ways of doing things while taking advantage of their managerial and information technology capabilities seem to be more successful than those that try to extend their ways of doing things abroad. In general, European retailers tend to be more willing to customize their marketing and procurement strategies to various local market peculiarities than are U.S. or Japanese retailers.[66] Wal-Mart, which tended to extend its U.S.-based procurement and product assortment strategies in its earlier foreign expansion, resulting in a huge market adjustment problem, is now moving slowly to convert the stores it has acquired in Europe into retailers unlike anything Americans would recognize as Wal-Marts.[67]

Wal-Mart also began its entry into the difficult Japanese retail market in mid-2002. It increased its equity stake in Seiyu, Japan's fourth-largest supermarket group, paving the way for a low-cost strategy in Japan. However, Wal-Mart is expected to have an upward battle in Japan as quality-conscious Japanese consumers associate its emphasis on "Everyday Low Price" with poor quality, or "yasu-karou, waru-karou," which is a Japanese phrase used to express the feeling that "you get what you pay for" or conversely, the more you pay, the better quality you must be getting. Take organic food as one example. Japanese consumers tend to be less tolerant of skin blemishes and lack of size and shape uniformity in organic produce.[68] Consequently, Wal-Mart in Japan suffered continued declining sales and increasing losses in 2007.[69]

On the other hand, Carrefour, as a typical European retailer willing to be more accommodating to local needs and culture, approaches foreign markets differently. With some 10 years of experience in the Chinese market and a good understanding of the Chinese consumer, the French retailer understands that Chinese consumers are eager to learn about Western products and has incorporated numerous signs providing detailed product information in its supermarkets in China. For example, in the bakery department, Carrefour provides detailed explanation regarding the different flours used and their associated benefits. To promote French wine to consumers, Carrefour

[65]"How NAFTA Helped Wal-Mart Reshape the Mexican Market," *Wall Street Journal*, August 31, 2001, p. A1.

[66]Brenda Sternquist, *International Retailing, 2nd ed.*, New York: Fairchild Publications, 2007.

[67]Earnest Beck and Emily Nelson, "As Wal-Mart Invades Europe, Rivals Rush to Match Its Formula," *Wall Street Journal Interactive Edition*, http://interactive.wsj.com/, October 6, 1999.

[68]Hatakeyama Noboru, "Highly Demanding Japanese Consumers," *Japan Spotlight Bimonthly*, 23 (September/October 2004), pp. 2–5; and "Wal-Mart to Make Seiyu A Group Company," *NikkeiNet Interactive*, http://www.nni.nikkei.co.jp/, November 2, 2005.

[69]"Wal-Mart Expects Bigger 2007 Loss in Japan," *Wall Street Journal*, February 13, 2008, p. B14.

**EXHIBIT 15-7**

SWOT ANALYSIS OF CARREFOUR'S OPERATIONS IN CHINA AND WORLDWIDE

**Strengths (in the Chinese market)**

- 10 years of experience in China
- Good understanding of the Chinese consumer
- Clear leader in the Shanghai market
- First mover advantage in many of the primary and secondary cities
- Chinese managers have been trained in its own in-house training center
- Corner on the expatriate and high-end market in primary cities
- Good competition on price, putting pressure on both international and domestic retailers
- Dia format expansion plans to enable Carrefour to compete in growing convenience market

**Weakness (in the Chinese market)**

- Tailored hypermarkets to the upper end of the market, which could be a problem when penetrating less affluent cities
- Received negative media coverage regarding its relationship with the government, local supplier management, and store opening strategy impact on local retailers

**Opportunities (in the global market)**

- Dominant "enlarged home market" position
- Unrivalled international presence and experience of emerging markets
- Multi-format strategy
- Global vision and organization
- World-class merchandising
- Customer knowledge

**Threats (in the global market)**

- Key gaps in international presence (i.e. United States, United Kingdom, and Germany)
- Relatively small turnover in comparison with Wal-Mart
- Slow pace of expansion in some emerging markets
- Lack of scale in Central European markets

*Source:* "Carrefour 2005," Retail Analysis, iReport series, http://www.igd.com/analysis/, accessed February 20, 2006.

had a French wine specialist provide advice and offer wine tasting to passing shoppers. The company was a clear market leader in Shanghai and other primary and secondary cities (See **Exhibit 15-7** for Carrefour's SWOT analysis of its China and global operations). After all, it is crucial for retailers to understand that there is no such a thing as a homogenous consumer market. For example, each Asia Pacific market is different and presents a different level of opportunity. Because each consumer has his or her own purchasing habits, there is no one winning Asian retail formula for both retailers and suppliers.[70]

**Private-Label Branding (Store Brands)**

Retailers increasingly rely on **private-label brands (store brands)** to appeal to price-conscious customers as well as to broaden their product offerings. Worldwide, the share of private labels as a percentage of all consumer packaged goods has grown from 14 to 18 percent.[71] For example, European retail chains such as Tesco sell goods under their own name made by a manufacturer called McBride, based near Manchester, England. McBride is not a household name although European consumers nearly spend $1 billion on household cleaners and personal care goods made by the company.[72] Private labels come under various guises. At one extreme are the generic products that are packaged very simply and sold at bottom prices. At the other extreme are premium store brands that deliver quality sometimes superior to national brands. Private labels

---

[70]"Carrefour 2005," Retail Analysis, iReport series, http://www.igd.com/analysis/, accessed February 20, 2006.

[71]Nirmalya Kumar and Jan-Benedict Steenkamp, *Private Label Revolution* (Cambridge, MA: Harvard Business School Press, 2006).

[72]"The Big Brands Go Begging," *Business Week* (March 21, 2005): 24–25.

have made big inroads in several European countries. In Japan and most other Asian countries, on the other hand, store brands are still marginal players. Consumers in this region tend to be extremely brand loyal.[73]

As a branding strategy, private labeling is especially attractive to MNCs that face well-entrenched incumbent brands in the markets they plan to enter. Under such circumstances, launching the product as a store brand enables the firm to get the shelf space access that it would otherwise be denied. In Japan, manufacturers that do not have the resources to set up a distribution channel network have tied up with local retailers to penetrate the market. Agfa-Gevaert, the German/Belgian photographic filmmaker agreed to supply a store brand film to Daiei, a major Japanese supermarket chain.[74] Eastman Kodak also decided to offer private-label film in Japan. Most of the distribution system is locked up by the local competitors, Fuji and Konica. Kodak hoped to grab a larger share of the Japanese film market by making a private-label film for the Japanese Cooperative Union, a group of 2,500 retail stores.[75]

## "Push" versus "Pull"

At the heart of this retailing revolution is the fundamental change in the way goods and services reach the consumer. Previously, the manufacturer or the wholesaler controlled the distribution chain across the world. The retailer's main competitive advantage lay in the merchandising skills of choosing the assortment of goods to sell in the store. The retailer's second advantage—closeness to the customer—was used to beat the rival retailer across the street. The manufacturer decided what goods were available and, in most countries, at what price they could be sold to the public.

That distribution system of earlier times has been turned upside down. The traditional supply chain powered by the manufacturing *push* is becoming a demand chain driven by consumer *pull*—especially in the developed countries where the supply and variety of goods is far above base-level requirements of goods and services. In most industrialized countries, resale price maintenance—which allows the supplier to fix the price at which goods can be sold to the final customer—has either been abolished or bypassed. The shift in power in the distribution channel is fundamentally a product of the application of information technology to store management.

Many multinational companies from industrialized countries are now entering markets and developing their distribution channels in developing countries. A study by New York University's Tish Robinson showed that companies from Western countries seem to have difficulty competing with Japanese companies in fast-growing Southeast Asian markets and attributed this to different styles in managing distribution channels. In just three decades, for example, the consumer electronics distribution systems in Malaysia and Thailand have come to be characterized by a striking presence of exclusive dealerships with Japanese multinational manufacturers such as Panasonic, Sanyo, and Hitachi.

For example, Panasonic practices a push strategy with 220 exclusive dealerships in Malaysia and 120 in Thailand. In Malaysia, these exclusive dealerships represent 65 percent of total Panasonic sales, although these numbers represent only 30 percent of the retailers selling Panasonic products. On the other hand, General Electric and Philips use a pull strategy, relying on the multivendor distribution system without firm control of the distribution channel as practiced in Western countries. Competitors from the United States and Europe are feeling locked out of Japanese companies' tightly controlled distribution channels in Southeast Asia.[76] This information suggests that a push strategy is more effective than a pull strategy in emerging markets.

---

[73]"No global private label quake—yet," *Advertising Age International*, January 16, 1995, p. I–26.

[74]"Japan's brands feel the pinch, too," *Financial Times*, April 28, 1994, p. 9.

[75]"Kodak pursues a greater market share in Japan with new private-label film," *Wall Street Journal*, March 7, 1995, p. B-4.

[76]Patricia Robinson, "The Role of Historical and Institutional Context in Transferring Distribution Practices Abroad: Matsushita's Monopolization of Market Share in Malaysia," *The American Marketing Association and the Japan Marketing Association Conference on the Japanese Distribution Strategy*, November 22–24, 1998.

Cutting down on stocks in inventory is a tempting thing to do to achieve cost savings. The chief reason for holding stocks is to smooth out bumps in the supply chain. However one of the biggest sources of inefficiency in logistics occurs exactly because distribution channel members just do so independently of each other. It is known as the "**bullwhip effect**"—after the way the amplitude of a whiplash increases down the length of the whip when it is cracked. Procter & Gamble discovered this effect more than a decade ago. The company noticed an odd thing about the shipment of Pampers, its well-known brand of disposable diapers. Although the number of babies and the demand for diapers remained relatively stable, orders for Pampers fluctuated dramatically. This was because information about consumer demand can become increasingly distorted as it moves along the supply chain. For instance, when a retailer sees a slight increase in demand for diapers, it orders more from a wholesaler. The wholesaler then boosts its own sales forecast, causing the manufacturer to scale up production. But when the increase in demand turns out to be short-lived, the distribution channel is left with too much stock and orders are cut back.[77]

**On-Time Retail Information Management**

Computer systems can now tell a retailer instantly what it is selling in hundreds of stores across the world, how much money it is making on each sale, and increasingly, who its customers are. This information technology has had two consequences.

*Reduced Inventory.* First, a well-managed retailer no longer has to keep large amounts of inventory—the stock burden has been passed upstream to the manufacturer. In addition, the retailer has a lower chance of running out of items. For a company such as Wal-Mart, with more than 60,000 suppliers in the United States alone, keeping everyone informed is critical. The company does this through its Retail Link system, which suppliers can tap into over a secure internet connection. They can check stock levels and sales down to the level of individual stores. Wal-Mart may have a brutal reputation for driving down costs, but its investment in information systems has played a large part in building one of the world's most efficient supply chains, capable of handling more than $300 billion of annual sales.[78] Another good examples involves 7-Eleven stores in Japan. The moment a 7-Eleven store customer in Japan buys a soft drink or a can of beer, the information goes directly to the bottler or the brewery and immediately goes into the production schedule and the delivery schedule, actually specifying the hour at which the new supply must be delivered and to which of the 4,300 stores. In effect, therefore, 7-Eleven controls the product mix, the manufacturing schedule and the delivery schedule of major suppliers such as Coca-Cola or Kirin Breweries. The British retailer Sainsbury's supply chain is geared to provide inputs on demand from the stores with a scheduled truck service to its 350 stores. The stores' ordering cycle is also set to match the loading and arrival of the trucks, which run almost according to a bus schedule.

Further attempts to reduce inventory can also be made jointly by retail chains for their mutual benefit. For example, in February 2000, Sears, Roebuck & Co., and Carrefour, joining the rush to the business-to-business electronic-commerce arena, announced a joint venture to form an online purchasing site where the retailers will buy about $80 billion in combined purchases. The venture, called GlobalNetXchange (GNX), creates the industry's largest supply exchange on the internet. GNX is an e-business solution and service provider for the global retail industry. Now suppliers can monitor retailers' sales, reduce inventory levels to a minimum, and better plan manufacturing of products on a hosted platform. It makes money by charging fees to suppliers or retailers using the exchange and is set up as a separate entity with its own management, employees and financing.[79]

*Market Information at the Retail Level.* Second, the retailer is the one that has real-time knowledge of what items are selling and how fast. This knowledge is used to

---

[77] "Shining examples," *Economist*, June 17, 2006, Special Section, pp. 4–6.

[78] Ibid.

[79] "Leading Trading Exchanges Link Together," *Food Logistics*, June 2005, p. 8.

extract better terms from the manufacturers. This trend in the transfer of power to the retailer in the developed countries has coincided with the lowering of trade barriers around the world and the spread of free-market economies in Asia and Latin America. As a result, retailers such as the United States' Toys 'R' Us, Tower Records, and Wal-Mart; Britain's Marks & Spencer and J. Sainsbury; Holland's Mark; Sweden's IKEA; France's Carrefour; and Japan's 7-Eleven Stores are being transformed into global businesses.

A firm can use strong logistics capabilities an offensive weapon to help gain competitive advantage in the marketplace by improving customer service and consumer choice, and by lowering the cost of global sourcing and finished goods distribution.[80] These capabilities become increasingly important as the level of global integration increases, and as competitors move to supplement low-cost manufacturing strategies in distant markets with effective logistic management strategies. This point is well illustrated by Ito-Yokado's takeover in 1991 of the Southland Corporation, which had introduced 7-Eleven's convenience store concept in the United States and subsequently around the world. Seven & I (formerly, Ito-Yokado) of Japan licensed the 7-Eleven store concept from Southland in the 1970s and invented just-in-time inventory management and revolutionized its physical distribution system in Japan. The key to Ito-Yokado's success with 7-Eleven Japan has been the use of its inventory and physical distribution management systems to accomplish lower on-hand inventory, faster inventory turnover, and most importantly, accurate information on customer buying habits. 7-Eleven Japan now implements its just-in-time physical distribution system in 7-Eleven stores in the United States.[81]

Thus, distribution is increasingly becoming concentrated; manufacturing, by contrast, is splintering. Thirty-five years ago, the Big Three automakers shared the U.S. auto market. Today the market is split among 10—Detroit's Big Three, five Japanese carmakers, and two German carmakers. Thirty-five years ago, 85 percent of all retail car sales occurred in single-site dealerships; even three dealership chains were uncommon. Today, a fairly small number of large-chain dealers account for 40 percent of the retail sales of cars.

Given the increased bargaining power of distributors, monitoring their performance has become an important management issue for many multinational companies. Although information technology has improved immensely, monitoring channel members' performance still remains humanistic. In general, if companies are less experienced in international operations, they tend to invest more resources in monitoring their channel members' activities.[82] As they gain in experience, they may increasingly build trust relationships with their channel members and depend more on formal performance-based control.[83]

**Retailing Differences across the World**

The density of retail and wholesale establishments in different countries varies greatly. As a general rule, industrialized countries tend to have a lower distribution outlet density than the emerging markets. Part of the reason for this difference stems from the need in emerging markets to purchase in very small lots and more frequently because of low income and the lack of facilities in homes to keep and preserve purchased items. At the same time, the advanced facilities available in the developed world allow a much higher square footage of retail space per resident, due to the large size of the retail outlets.

[80]Roy D. Shapiro, "Get Leverage from Logistics," *Harvard Business Review*, 62 (May–June 1984), pp. 119–26.

[81]Masaaki Kotabe, "The Return of 7-Eleven . . . from Japan: The Vanguard Program," *Columbia Journal of World Business*, 30 (Winter 1995), pp. 70–81.

[82]Esra F. Gencturk and Preet S. Aulakh, "The Use of Process and Output Controls in Foreign Markets," *Journal of International Business Studies*, 26 (Fourth Quarter, 1995), pp. 755–86.

[83]Preet S. Aulakh, Masaaki Kotabe, and Arvind Sahay, "Trust and Performance in Cross Border Marketing Partnerships: A Behavioral Approach," *Journal of International Business Studies*, 27 (Special Issue 1996), pp. 1005–1032.

Japan's retail industry has a number of features that distinguish it from retailing in western countries. The major ones are a history of tight regulation—albeit being increasingly deregulated—less use of cars for shopping, and the importance of department stores in the lives of most people. For more than forty years until recently, the Large-Scale Retail Store Law[84] in Japan helped to protect and maintain small retail stores (12 retail stores per 1,000 residents in Japan vs. 6 retail stores per 1,000 residents in the United States in 1994) and, partly in consequence, a multilayered distribution system. Consequently, Japan has experienced relatively poor proliferation of mega-stores and large-scale shopping centers. Since Japan's urban areas are crowded, roads are congested and parking is expensive or non-existent, many people use public transport to shop. Consequently, shopping is usually within a rather small radius of the home or workplace and products, especially food, generally are bought in small quantities. Shopping, therefore, is more frequent. This situation is further encouraged by Japanese cooking's requirement for fresh ingredients. Retail stores that not only stay open 24 hours a day throughout the week but also practice just-in-time delivery of fresh perishable foods, such as 7-Eleven and Lawson, are extremely popular in Japan. Discount stores have also gained in popularity among recession-weary, now price-conscious Japanese consumers. Similarly, department stores are crucial in everyday Japanese life. The variety of goods and services offered by the average department store ranges well beyond that in most retail outlets abroad. Large department stores stock everything from fresh food and prepared dishes, to discount and boutique clothing, and household and garden goods. Many have children's playgrounds and pet centers—some with displays resembling a miniature zoo. Museum-level art and craft exhibitions often are housed on upper floors, and both family and exquisite restaurants usually on the top floor. It is a very different--and often difficult--market for foreign retailers to enter. See **Global Perspective 15-6** for information on international retailers entering the Japanese market.

In Germany, store hours are limited. Stores may not open on Sundays and generally close on weekdays by 6 p.m. They can be open one Saturday in a month until 2:30 p.m. The IFO Economic Research Institute in a German government-commissioned report has recommended that stores be allowed to remain open from 6 a.m. to 10 p.m. on weekdays and until 6 p.m. on Saturdays; however, stores are still expected to be closed on Sundays.[85] Hence, although these laws are now being reviewed, the proposed changes contrast with the situation in the United States, where retail stores may remain open seven days a week, 24 hours a day. Keeping stores open in this manner requires very strong logistics management on the part of retailers and the manufacturing firms supplying the retailers. The sending organization, the receiving organization, and the logistics provider (if applicable) have to work very closely together.

In China, basket shopping is still considered the norm for most consumers, and they spend on average $5 per visit. Retailers adjust their store layouts to cope with a large number of basket shoppers. Wal-Mart, for instance, has set up basket-only checkouts in its Supercenters to enable faster checkout. Because low price is the most competitive advantage, retailers spread a strong price message throughout most of the stores, in both Chinese and English that promote both everyday low prices and promotional items throughout food and non-food departments. As a result, high volumes of goods are heavily merchandised by large promotions in bins and in bulk floor stacks. In general, a store flyer is a major marketing tool and is designed to drive foot traffic by presenting discounts for household commodities. Recent research analysts summarized the following key differences between hypermarkets in China and those in the West. In China:

---

[84]Jack G. Kaikati, "The Large-Scale Retail Store Law: One of the Thorny Issues in the Kodak-Fuji Case," *The American Marketing Association and the Japan Marketing Association Conference on the Japanese Distribution Strategy*, November 22–24, 1998.

[85]Marco Grühnhagen, Robert A. Mittelstaedt, and Ronald D. Hampton, "The Effect of the Relaxation of 'Blue Laws' on the Structure of the Retailing Industry in the Federal Republic of Germany," presented at 1997 AMA Summer Educators' Conference, August 2–5, 1997.

## GLOBAL PERSPECTIVE 15-6

### FOREIGN RETAILERS AND DIRECT MARKETERS ENTERING INTO JAPAN EN MASSE

In Japan, until early 1990s, the Large-Scale Retail Store Law gave small retailers and wholesalers disproportionate influence over the Japanese market by requiring firms planning to open a large store to submit their business plan to the local business regulation council, the local chamber of commerce (made up of those small retailers and wholesalers to be affected), and the Ministry of Economy, Trade and Industry (METI). As a result of this "Catch-22" requirement, the process would take between 12 and 18 months, and was seen by foreign retailers as an almost insurmountable entry barrier.

Under U.S. government pressure, the Large-Scale Retail Store Law was relaxed in 1992 and in 1994. Under the amendments, the task of examining applications for new stores was transferred from the local business regulation council to the Large-Scale Retail Store Council, a government advisory board under the METI. Consequently, the maximum time required for various applications and approvals is now set at 12 months. These two revisions of the Large-Scale Retail Store Law have contributed to the increase in the number of applications requesting approval to establish a large retail store. According to the Japan Council of Shopping Centers estimate, shopping centers have opened at the rate of more than 100 per year since 1992.

Toys 'R' Us exploited this opportunity and was ultimately successful in cracking the Japanese market. It boasted a total of 37 stores in 1996, and planned to open an average of 10 more per year across the country. Following the success of Toys 'R' Us, other foreign-based retailers have begun to crack the Japanese market. Nearly a dozen other such foreign retailers have opened their stores in Japan in the last decade. Foreign firms face more difficulties when opening a general merchandise store than one for a niche product because the large Japanese general merchandise stores, such as Daiei and Ito-Yokado are well entrenched and dominate the market. Despite such difficulties, Wal-Mart (U.S.) with a partial acquisition of Japan's struggling Seiyu, Carrefour (France), and Metro (Germany) entered the Japanese market. As attested by Carrefour's early departure, whether they can take root there is too early to tell, however.

On the other hand, foreign niche retailers, including Toys 'R' Us, which face few competitors, have been fairly successful. For example, U.S.-based Tower Records, U.K.-based HMV, and Virgin Megastores have opened comparably large stores,

selling both imported and domestic music tapes and CDs at competitive prices. Specialty retailers of outdoor goods and clothes are other retailers to pour into the Japanese market in the last ten years. Among them, U.S.-based L.L. Bean and Eddie Bauer are the market leaders.

While Toys 'R' Us and Tower Records have a wholly owned subsidiary in Japan, L.L. Bean and Eddie Bauer teamed up with a well-known Japanese company. L.L. Bean Japan is a Japanese franchise 70 percent owned by Japan's largest retailing group, Seibu, and 30 percent by Panasonic. Eddie Bauer Japan is a joint venture of Otto-Sumitomo, a Sumitomo Group mail-order retailer, and Eddie Bauer USA. In general, forming a joint venture or a franchise allows new entrants to start faster, although they could lose control of the company's operation in Japan. Future would-be entrants should bear in mind that Japan is not an easy place to do business because, in addition to regulations, land and labor costs are extremely high.

On the other hand, direct marketing—another form of retailing—has blossomed into a $20-billion industry despite Japan's continued recession. Ten percent of this market belongs to foreign companies including Lands' End, an outdoor clothing maker, and Intimate Brands, which distributes Victoria's Secret catalogs. "For those companies and individuals who say that Japan is a closed market, I really can't think of an example of an easier market entry than catalog sales," says Cynthia Miyashita, president of mail-order consultant Hemisphere Marketing Inc. in Japan. In high-context cultures like Japan, however, less direct, low-key approaches in which a mood or image is built in an attempt to build a relationship with the audience is considered more appropriate in approaching prospect customers than in low-context cultures such as the United States.

Foreign mail-order companies sidestep Japan's notoriously complex regulations, multilevel distribution networks and even import duties. Here are a few cases in point:

- Japan's post offices are unequipped to impose taxes on the hundreds of thousands of mail-order goods that flood the postal system, making direct marketing products virtually duty-free. Local competitors who import products in bulk have to pay duties, forcing up their prices.
- Many products, such as vitamins and cosmetics, are subject to strict testing regulations in Japan, but those rules do not apply if the products are sold through mail order for personal consumption. That gives direct-mail customers in Japan access to a wide array of otherwise unavailable products.
- Mail costs in the United States are so low that it is more economical to send a package from New York to Tokyo than from Tokyo to Osaka, which reduces overhead costs for direct-mail products.
- Although Japanese companies are not allowed to mail goods from foreign post offices for sale at home, foreign companies face no such restrictions.

*Sources:* Joji Sakurai, "Firms Challenge Image of Japan's Closed Markets," *Marketing News*, (July 20, 1998), p. 2; Jack G. Kaikati, "The Large-Scale Retail Store Law: One of the Thorny Issues in the Kodak-Fuji Case," in Michael R. Czinkota and Masaaki Kotabe, *Japanese Distribution Strategy* (London: Business Press, 2000), pp. 154–63; and "Attitudes toward Direct Marketing and Its Regulation: A Comparison of the United States and Japan," *Journal of Public Policy & Marketing*, 19 (Fall2000), pp. 228–37; and "Wal-Mart to Make Seiyu A Group Company," *NikkeiNet Interactive*, http://www. nni.nikkei.co.jp/, November 2, 2005.

- The majority of hypermarkets are located on two floors, normally with non-food items located on the upper floor and food on the lower.
- Many hypermarkets are located inside shopping centers in the heart of the city.
- They have high staffing levels due to the presence of suppliers' staff working as in-store "merchandisers."
- Retailers provide courtesy buses to bring customers from residential areas into the center city because China has a low car ownership.[86]

***E-Commerce and Retailing.***    Despite those cultural differences and regulations in retailing still in place, countries such as Japan and Germany have warmed up to the same electronic commerce revolution as the United States has already experienced. In Japan, for example, Rakuten Ichiba Internet Mall (http://www.rakuten.co.jp) has achieved stellar growth since its launch with a mere $500,000 in capital and just 13 stores in May 1997. The mall had increased to over 22,400 stores by the end of 2007, and generated total sales revenue of $1.77 billion with net profits of $304 million in 2007.[87] In Germany, SAP already dominates the market for so-called enterprise software (i.e., enterprise resource planning and customer relationship software). Some 82,000 of the world's largest organizations in more than 120 countries now automate everything from accounting and manufacturing to customer and supplier relations using SAP software, making it by far the leading source of large corporate programs with a record revenue of $11.3 billion and operating profits of more than $3.4 billion in 2007.[88]

E-commerce is not limited to developed countries. China is already the fastest growing internet market in Asia. The internet community in China increased by more than 260 times within the ten years from 1997 to 2007, soaring from just 620,000 users in 1997 to 253 million by the second quarter of 2008, far beyond the United States' 215 million as of the same period.[89] As a result of the unfortunate outbreak of the severe acute respiratory syndrome (SARS) in China in 2003, the Chinese government began to take advantage of the internet to encourage business transactions without unnecessary human contacts, This government effort further helped build the internet market in China.[90] In Brazil, the number of people using the internet grew rapidly from 14 million in 2002 to 42.6 million by December 2007, making it South America's most wired nation, and accounting for 46.3 percent of the region's internet users.[91] A similar growth in entrepreneurial e-commerce operators is expected with the growing internet access.

As explained earlier in this chapter, despite the rapid increase in internet users and e-commerce participants around the world, the need for the local or regional distribution of products remains as important as it was before the internet revolution.

---

[86]"Retailing in China," Retail Analysis, iReports, www.igd.com/analysis, accessed January 10, 2006.

[87]Rakuten Ichiba, http://www.rakuten.co.jp/, 2007 Annual Report.

[88]SAP, http://www.sap.com/about/investor/inbrief/index.epx, accessed March 20, 2009.

[89]Internet Word Stats, http://www.internetworldstats.com/, accessed September 30, 2008.

[90]"China has World's 2nd Largest Number of Netizens," *XINHUA*, January 16, 2003; and "China takes Steps to Ensure SARS Does Not Hinder Construction Plans," *XINHUA*, May 23, 2003.

[91]Internet Word Stats.

---

# SUMMARY ✦ ✦ ✦ ✦ ✦ ✦ ✦ ✦ ✦ ✦ ✦ ✦ ✦ ✦ ✦ ✦ ✦ ✦ ✦ ✦ ✦ ✦ ✦ ✦ ✦ ✦ ✦ ✦ ✦ ✦ ✦ ✦ ✦

Logistics, or supply chain management, has traditionally been local issues and related to getting goods to the final customer in a local market. However, while the intent of serving the customer remains, retailers have been transformed into global organizations that buy and sell products from and to many parts of the world. At the same time, with the increase in the globalization of manufacturing, many firms are optimizing their worldwide production by sourcing components and raw materials from around the world. Both of these trends have increased the importance of global logistic management for firms.

The relevance of global logistics is likely to increase in the coming years because international distribution often accounts for between 10 percent and 25 percent of the total landed cost to obtain an international order. The international logistics manager has to deal with multiple issues, including transport, warehousing, inventorying, and the connection of these activities to the firm's corporate strategy. Inflation, currency exchange, and tax rates that differ across national boundaries complicate these logistics issues, but international logistics managers can exploit those differences to their advantage, which are not available to domestic firms.

Logistics management is closely linked to manufacturing activities, even though logistics management is increasingly being outsourced to third-party logistics specialists. Many companies, particularly those in the European Union, are trying to develop a consolidated production location so that they can reduce the number of distribution centers and market their products from one or a few locations throughout Europe. Firms such as Federal Express, Airborne Express, and TNT have evolved from document shippers to providers of complete logistics functions; indeed, all of these firms now have a business logistics division whose function is to handle the outsourced logistics functions of corporate clients.

Various governments, including the United States, have developed free trade zones, export processing zones, and other special economic zones designed chiefly to increase domestic employment and exports from the zone. Various tax and other cost benefits available in the zones attract both domestic and foreign firms to set up warehousing and manufacturing operations.

In the area of international distribution, marketing managers need to make careful decisions on the configuration of their distribution channel. Issues such as cost, coverage, and control determine how many intermediaries there should be and where. The ongoing management of the distribution channel can be a challenge, with channel conflict being an ever-present issue for many international marketing managers.

Retailing has long been considered a fairly localized activity subject to different customer needs and different national laws regulating domestic commerce. Nevertheless, some significant change is taking place in the retail sector. Information technology makes it increasingly possible for large retailers to know what they are selling in hundreds of stores around the world. Given this intimate knowledge of customers around the world, those retailers have begun to overtake the channel leadership role from manufacturers. The United States' Wal-Mart and Toys 'R' Us, Japan's 7-Eleven, and Britain's Tesco are some of the major global retailers changing the logistics of inventory and retail management on a global basis.

Finally, e-commerce is increasingly dispensing with physical stores. However, local adaptation of product offerings and setting-up of local distribution centers remain as important as it was before the internet revolution. Furthermore, complex international shipping requirements and exchange rate fluctuations hamper smooth distribution of products around the world.

## KEY TERMS ◆ ◆ ◆ ◆ ◆ ◆ ◆ ◆ ◆ ◆ ◆ ◆ ◆ ◆ ◆ ◆ ◆ ◆ ◆ ◆ ◆ ◆ ◆

| | | | |
|---|---|---|---|
| Agent intermediary | Global logistics | Materials management | Rationalization |
| Air freight (Airfreight) | Intermodal transportation | Merchant intermediary | Third-party logistics (3PL) services |
| Bulk shipping | Liner service | Ocean shipping | Value-to-volume ratio |
| Bullwhip effect | Logistic integration | Perishability | |
| Free trade zone (FTZ) | Maquiladora operation | Physical distribution | |

## REVIEW QUESTIONS ◆ ◆ ◆ ◆ ◆ ◆ ◆ ◆ ◆ ◆ ◆ ◆ ◆ ◆ ◆ ◆ ◆ ◆ ◆

**1.** Define the term global logistics. Enumerate and describe the various operations encompassed by it.

**2.** What factors contribute to the increased complexity and cost of global logistics as compared to domestic logistics?

**3.** What role do third-party logistics companies play in international trade? What are the advantages of using these companies over internalizing the logistics activities?

**4.** Describe the role of free trade zones (FTZs) in global logistics.

**5.** What are the reasons for the dramatic increase in cross-border trade between the United States and Mexico?

**6.** How is information technology affecting global retailing?

**7.** The United States and Japan have similar income and purchasing-power levels, yet, the retail structures between the two countries have significant differences. Describe some reasons for these differences.

## DISCUSSION QUESTIONS ◆ ◆ ◆ ◆ ◆ ◆ ◆ ◆ ◆ ◆ ◆ ◆ ◆ ◆ ◆ ◆

**1.** Some economists have brought attention to the importance of the role of geography in international trade. One example of this is the dramatic rise in trade between the United States and Mexico. This increase is attributed primarily to wage differences between the two countries and the proximity, with both countries sharing a joint border over 2,000 miles in length. Geographic proximity allows for the relative cheap movement of goods by train from the heart of Mexico to any corner of the United States within three to four days. On the other hand, advocates of globalization claim that the role of geography in international trade is limited and is reducing constantly. They contend that direct transportation costs as a percentage of the total value of the goods for most goods is low and is declining. Furthermore, it is not actual transportation costs, but the coordination of managerial resources and information that is the key to savings through global logistics. This reduces the role of geography in international trade to a minimal level. Comment on the two views.

2. Beginning in 2000 with the announcement by the Big Three automakers of plans for a single online supplier exchange Newco, major manufacturers in at least a half-dozen industries have followed suit. In the wake of the Big Three's announcement, other corporations have come together—on customer-facing and supplier-facing initiatives—to create online joint ventures. Among the most prominent are liaisons between: DuPont, Cargill and Cenex Harvest States Cooperative; Sears and Carrefour, and Kraft, H. J. Heinz Co., and Grocery Manufacturers of America with other major food companies. This represents an enormous shift in online business strategy, and raises major challenges for marketers and market makers. The question is, will these e-marketplaces be the kind founded by consortia of manufacturers, by independent, third-party companies, or by a combination of both? At least in the auto industry, there is no question that both material management (supply chains) and distributions (dealerships) are more concentrated, while manufacturing is splintering. What does this implicate for other manufacturing industries and what does this mean in terms of international marketing strategies?

3. The world is moving closer to an era of free trade and global economic interdependence. The worldwide reduction in tariff and non-tariff barriers and the increasing levels of world trade are testimony to this fact. These reductions in trade barriers will in the very near future make free trade zones an anachronistic concept. Hence, if you were making an investment decision, on behalf of your company, to establish a manufacturing facility in a developing country, placing too much emphasis on investing in free trade zones may be a short-term workable proposition, but a long-term mistake. Do you agree or disagree with this statement? Give reasons for your answer.

4. We learned from the text that with the expansion of the European Union in May 2004, traditional distribution hubs in western and central Europe faced tougher competition. For instance, despite integration of all the candidate countries into the systems and practices of the EU, it would take two to three years for those countries to open their road and rail networks under the transition arrangements. Even though governments and EU have developed programs and initiatives to reduce road congestion and advised the use of other transport networks as alternatives to roads, companies that operate in Bulgaria, Czech Republic, Estonia, Hungary, Latvia, Poland, and Slovakia, are still concerned about the costs and benefits of transporting goods from roads and the viability of alternative modes of transport. What opportunities and threats does the new EU body offer to transporters, freight-forwarders, and exporters?

5. Reduced trade barriers and saturation of domestic markets are two market forces that are encouraging large retail chains to move overseas. Large retail chains in the United States, Japan, and Europe are aggressively making forays into international markets, although there is a significant regional bias in these efforts. U.S. retail chains such as Wal-Mart have primarily focused on Canada and have now turned their focus to Mexico. Japanese retail chains such as JUSCO and Daimaru have made significant inroads into Southeast Asia, while Western European chains such as Julius Meinl (Austria), Promodes (France), Ahold (The Netherlands), and TESCO (U.K) are diversifying into Eastern Europe and other countries within Europe. Industry analysts point out that this internationalization of retail business will significantly alter the nature of competition. Significant rationalization through acquisitions of retail businesses is bound to take place. The verdict on the expected effects of this rationalization and increased competition on specialty chains is still unclear. What would you predict the retail business to look like ten years from now? What would be the role of specialty stores and specialty chains?

6. The concept of "one-stop-shopping" for global logistics is fast catching on. There are now more than thirty large logistic companies, called "mega-carriers," who can provide truly global and integrated logistic services. What are the opportunities and threats that these trends offer to small and large transporters, freight-forwarders, and shippers (exporters)?

7. As presented in Global Perspective 15-4, in order to avoid supply chain disruptions, some people suggest that supply chains should be regulated, a bit like public utilities, because countries have become so highly dependent on private-sector production infrastructure. Do you agree with it? Why or why not? Also, it states that there are very legitimate, very good business reasons not necessarily to complete and ship from Asia to avoid supply chain disruptions. Companies may consider other options in other parts of the world even though these may look more expensive. A higher cost structure can make supply chain more robust and reliable. Besides the reason provided there, are there any other possible reasons? What are they? Please discuss and give some examples.

# SHORT CASES

## 𝒞ASE 15-1

### DELL: SURVIVING A LOGISTICAL NIGHTMARE

Well-known U.S.-based computer maker Dell seems to have perfected the art of making just-in-time computers and supplying them to its consumers. The company is known to keep costs under control by directly reaching the consumer without the additional expense on intermediaries. Dell owns no warehouses but manages to assemble over 75,000 computers a day and its build-to-order business model is a case study in itself. Add to that an effective after sales service and Dell has itself a competitive advantage that has been almost unbeatable. But maintaining this position takes work, especially when you have a company that sources its computer parts from numerous suppliers all over the world.

Companies such as Dell usually ship computer parts to various U.S. and international ports from their suppliers. So, what happens when dockworker unions on the west coast of the United States go on strike for days at a stretch? Well, most companies lose millions due to this kind of unexpected disruption in the supply chain. But, not Dell! Dell faced this situation in the recent past. While many U.S. firms faced adversity, Dell managed to get by with the fewest scratches. This is how.

When the strike prevented parts sourced internationally from reaching Dell's plants in the United States, the company was faced with the probability that as the strike continued, its U.S. factories would run out of parts. Dell would soon be unable to put together its computers without the necessary parts and the company would then be left idling like so many others.

However, unlike a hurricane or a tsunami that is hard to predict, most U.S. firms were aware of the impending dockworkers strike a few months in advance. So, Dell started getting itself ready by having a plan in place in case its supply chain did get disrupted. One important move was up-to-the-hour communication with the concerned parties, such as its international suppliers, most of them from Asia, the port authorities and the sea transport companies that it relied on to ship the products.

At the time, the dockworkers formally announced the strike Dell was able to put its plan into action. The measures Dell took were no different from those taken by other firms. Obviously, most firms use sea transport for shipping their parts and products from overseas because it is the cheapest form of transport. However, when that route got eliminated temporarily due to a dock strike,

*Source:* Bill Breen, and Michael Aneiro, "Living in Dell Time," *Fast Company Magazine,* November 2004, pp. 86–96.

most firms sought the expensive but fastest air transport. Thus, most U.S. firms started booking airlines to transport their much-needed parts from abroad. Consequently, there were high costs of flying in parts with several firms vying for flights from logistics firms such as UPS and FedEx and other major airlines as well. Dell had already accounted for the use of air travel well in advance and as a result it was able to charter planes to ship its foreign parts to the United States at almost half the cost of other companies. Furthermore, up to minute communication with its suppliers ensured that parts were always ready and waiting to be shipped to the United States so the aircraft that shipped those parts did not have to wait in the hangars until the parts were there.

Next came the part when the strike was over and the tens of ships arrived with Dell-destined parts. The company had planned for this as well. It calculated the unloading cycle so that company associates could collect the company's containers as they arrived rather than waiting to sort through the backup and waste time later on. During the week and a half that the dock closings lasted, Dell was on time to deliver every single computer. Consumers thus had no reason to even doubt that the company was right in the middle of a logistical crisis.

Global firms with their global operations are able to reap the benefits of low cost sourcing, etc. but what comes with the territory is a constant threat to operations and having contingency plans in place plays an important role in successfully combating such hard times. The dockworkers' strike and the terrorist attacks on the United States in 2001 brought home to some global firms the need to either maintain warehouses and spare inventory, or keep their suppliers close by or then be prepared to face these situations the way Dell did.

### DISCUSSION QUESTIONS

**1.** Would it be a good strategy for Dell to own some warehouses in case of unforeseen events? How would that affect their business model?

**2.** What were the important elements of their contingency plan that made it successful?

**3.** Dell spent a considerable amount of time and money planning in advance in case of a disruption in its supply chain. What should the company do to avoid the additional expenditure in case of future disruptions?

## 𝒞ASE 15-2

### FRENCH RETAILER CARREFOUR: LOSES IN JAPAN BUT WINS IN CHINA?

For Western firms in general and more recently, global retailers in particular, succeeding in the Japanese market has always

been challenging and international business history abounds with stories of their struggles. Noted examples of global retailers that have faced difficulties in Japan include Wal-Mart affiliate, Seiyu and Germany's Metro Group whereas U.K.'s Boots and France's Sephora exited Japan just two years after entering it, which made the retailing industry, sit up and take notice. The latest casualty of the hard to please Japanese market is France's Carrefour, the largest retailer in Europe and the second largest in the world (after U.S.-based giant Wal-mart) with worldwide sales of over 82.1 billion euros (2007). Carrefour operates around 11,000 stores in 30 different countries. As of 2007, 45.8 percent of its sales come form its home country France, 37.5 percent from operations in other European countries, 10 percent from Latin America, and 6.7 percent in Asian economies.

To start at the very beginning, Western retailers started eyeing the Japanese market in the 1990s when the Japanese government finally revoked its Large-Scale Stores Law that prevented foreign entry by retailers and when real estate prices in Japan started falling. At the dawn of the 21st century, several global retailers set up shop in Japan. These firms include Boots, Sephora, Wal-Mart, and finally U.K.'s Tesco in 2003. Carrefour made its entry into Japan in the year 2000 and initially opened four stores in cities such as Tokyo, Osaka, Saitama and Hyogo, followed by four more in Kansai. At the time of its entry, it planned to have a total of around 15 stores by the end of the year 2003. But not only was it unable to reach that number, by the beginning of 2005, the company had started denying rumors that it was going to quit Japan only to exit the Japanese market a few months later. Industry experts claim that the low price focus of firms like Carrefour and Wal-Mart do not meet the expectations of discerning Japanese consumers who prefer better quality over lower price. Also, the establishment of specialized retailers and changes in the consumption patterns has exacerbated the situation for foreign retailers.

Carrefour, which engages in all types of retailing with a focus on food retailing at competitive, low prices, runs stores in three main formats in foreign markets, namely "hypermarkets," "supermarkets," and "hard discounters" with hypermarkets being the largest in terms of floor area and stock and hard discounters being the smallest of the three formats. When Carrefour's first few stores opened up in Japan, there were large spaces filled with piles of products that did not allow consumers to easily find an item they needed. Furthermore, according to some, Japanese consumers saw Carrefour as a French retailer and expected to see more French-style clothing and products. Tapping into this perception of their stores, Carrefour revamped its stores in Japan and brought in more French-made products but even then, it failed to carve a niche for itself in the mature Japanese market. On the supply side,

Carrefour originally planned to source its products directly from manufacturers but with inadequate purchase orders, it was unable to secure purchase contracts directly from producers. Thus, it was forced to approach wholesalers for products. However, it was unable to break through the tight-knit network between local suppliers and the homegrown Japanese supermarkets and therefore could not offer a wide range of products to its Japanese clients. Finally, motivated by a drop in worldwide revenues and unprofitable stores in Japan and four years after its entry into the market, Carrefour made the decision to sell off all its stores in Japan. Contenders for the acquisition included many but ultimately Carrefour sold its stores to Japan's largest retailer Aeon Co. Ltd. Now Carrefour Japan is run by **Aeon Marché Co.**

On the other hand, Carrefour's experience in Mainland China has been very different and it is now one of the top five retailers in the country. Carrefour entered China in 1995 with a store in Beijing and by the year 2000, it had over 25 stores in 15 major cities in Mainland China. Since then, Carrefour has developed rapidly in this country. By August 2008, Carrefour has opened 116 stores on the mainland with a total floor area of nearly 1 million square meters and is employing almost 50,000 people. The company's sales in China amounted to 30 billion yuan in 2007, accounting for about 5 percent of total group revenue. In China, Carrefour's formula of low prices, huge stores and a high degree of localization seemed to have worked out so much so that it has now gone down in global management books as Carrefour's Chinese success story. Moreover, Carrefour has decentralized store operation in China and also established the Carrefour China Institute for employee training.

The company's success in China in spite of periodical run-ins with protective Chinese regulatory authorities has come as both a surprise and an important lesson to global firms. China, like Japan, has not been an easy market for foreign firms to conduct business in, given its varying cultures within the same country, the stark differences between lifestyles in urban cities as compared to that in provinces and its political set up. With China's entry into the World Trade Organization (WTO) and spurred by Carrefour's accomplishments in China, the company's ambitious plans for the market include opening a store a month and investing more than $750 million in its stores in China. So, the company still has something to smile about!

*Sources:* Carrefour.com home page; "Carrefour at the Crossroads," *Economist*, October 22, 2005, p. 71; "Carrefour's Expansion in China," *China Daily*, August 12, 2008, and various other sources.

## DISCUSSION QUESTIONS

**1.** Do you think it was the right decision for Carrefour to leave Japan? Could it instead have adopted other strategies that perhaps would have led to a different outcome?

**2.** Carrefour, being the second largest retailer in the world, what are implications of its pull-out from Japan for other global retailers such as Wal-Mart which is struggling to survive?

**3.** Why did Carrefour exit Japan but succeed in China?

# CASE 15-3

## WHICH DISTRIBUTOR TO CHOOSE IN COSTA RICA?

Not long ago, TransMotors (a disguised name), an American export management company that had a joint venture in China manufacturing motorcycles began to search for new distributors in Central America. During previous years, TransMotors had been highly successful in South America and Africa locating distributors for its line of basic transportation motorcycles. Using Honda technology, the Chinese motorcycles were proven to be of high quality and reliability. Most important, they sold for less than a third of the cost of the competing Japanese models.

The first stop in Central America was Costa Rica, the most prosperous country in the region. A growing economy and political stability provided the kind of market conditions that were optimal for successful sales: a rising lower middle class that could now afford a dependable motorcycle for its transportation needs. Such a formula had worked very well in Colombia, Ethiopia, Venezuela, Burkina Faso, Argentina, South Africa, Brazil, Nigeria, Peru, and Cameroon. For TransMotors, like most others seeking to gain entry into high-growth, emerging markets, the key to success was selecting and recruiting the right kind of distributors for its products.

Robert Grosse, the executive in charge of developing entry strategy for TransMotors, was able to locate two possible distributors in Costa Rica. Full of pride because of success in the above-mentioned markets and others, Grosse believed himself invincible when it came to identifying who would be the best representative for his company's products.

Harvey Arbelaez, the first candidate for the Costa Rican distributor, was a young, upstart entrepreneur who had cut his teeth in the agriculture business—importing farm implements and fertilizers. Arbelaez had built a nice network that covered the entire market in Costa Rica and was interested in the Chinese motorcycles because he felt they would complement his existing product lines.

Jaime Alonso Gomez, the other candidate appeared to be the better fit. Gomez was one of the richest individuals in the country and had made his fortune as the exclusive distributor of Honda cars, Scania trucks, and Komatsu heavy equipment. He had sold some Honda motorcycles in the past and was interested in getting back into the low-end transportation business. To the U.S. executive, this appeared to be the logical choice.

When it came time to travel to San Jose to interview the two prospects, Grosse had as his goal the sale of 250 motorcycles a year for each of the first three years. According to his research, the annual sale of motorcycles for the entire country was approximately 2,700 units and growing nicely at a rate of 10 percent per year. The sale of 250 units annually would establish a foundation that could be leveraged down the road to build market share to ultimately 20-25 percent.

*Source:* This case was provided by Professor Timothy J. Wilkinson of Montana State University based on Andrew R. Thomas and Timothy J. Wilkinson, "It's the Distribution, Stupid!" *Business Horizons,* 48 (2005), 125–34.

The first stop on the trip was at Arbelaez's office. On a personal level, the two did not hit it off; although, it was clear to Grosse that Arbelaez was wildly enthusiastic about the opportunity to offer the Chinese motorcycles throughout his network. Any positive feelings on the American executive's part soon evaporated, however, when the young man showed projections that the annual sale would be no more than 100 units for the first couple of years. Arbelaez said it would take a long while for the marketplace to adjust to a Chinese-branded product, but once it did, the potential would be tremendous. At this point, Grosse ended the conversation and told his counterpart, "I will take your plan under advisement." Twenty minutes later, the American executive was dropped off by a taxi in front of the sparkling offices of the Honda/Scania/Komatsu distributor, Jaime Alonso Gomez.

Within an hour of their meeting, Grosse and Gomez agreed that the dealer would become the exclusive distributor for the Chinese motorcycles. It was clear that there existed the sales staff, service capability, financial resources, and knowledge of distribution to handle the motorcycles. And, if that wasn't enough, the first order was to be 1,000 units—four times what the American executive thought it would be! Dinner that night was a celebration of the new relationship at San Jose's most prestigious private club. All that was needed was an exclusive distribution agreement giving the Costa Rican sole rights for the Chinese motorcycles for five years. Then, once the agreement was in place, a revolving Letter of Credit would be opened to begin shipping the motorcycles in 125 unit increments over the first year.

After the exclusive agreement was consularized and notarized, the first 125 units were shipped from China to Costa Rica without incident. The Letter of Credit went smoothly and communication between the two firms was regular and efficient. However, everything changed when it came time to ship the next 125 units. To re-initiate the revolving Letter of Credit a document was required from the distributor to the confirming bank. For more than a month the U.S. firm called, e-mailed, and faxed its exclusive distributor. The only individuals the Americans could get in touch with were administrative assistants, who generated the same, pat answers. "He's away on a trip . . . in a meeting . . . away from his desk." With the second lot of motorcycles languishing at the dock in Shanghai and the other 700 units ready for production, pressure was building.

Unannounced, Grosse grabbed a plane and flew to San Jose to see what was going on. He took a taxi at the airport and went right to his new distributor's office. Not surprising, his new distributor was "in meetings all day and unavailable." Nor were any of the motorcycles or promotional material anywhere to be found on the showroom floor.

Distraught, the American executive took a cab to his hotel. During the 30-minute trip, he was startled to see so many small motorcycles on the streets of San Jose—something that was not the case during his last visit a few months earlier. Many of them were the models of one of his leading competitors from Taiwan.

After a couple of stiff drinks at the hotel bar, Grosse swallowed his pride and called Harvey Arbalaez, the young entrepreneur whom he had rejected earlier as the exclusive distributor. Half-expecting to be hung up on, the American executive was shocked when the young man agreed to join him for dinner to discuss what was happening with the motorcycles. Not gloating too much, the young Costa Rican showed pictures of TransMotors' motorcycles still sitting in a bonded warehouse at the port. He further showed photos of a brand new motorcycle distribution company located in the heart of San Jose that was importing small motorcycles from Taiwan. Because of no competition, newspaper articles stated that sales of the Taiwanese products might exceed 500 units that year. In scanning the articles, Grosse recognized the last name of the distributor. The name was Gomez—turns out, he was the brother of the Honda guy.

## DISCUSSION QUESTIONS

**1.** What mistakes did Robert Grosse make in selecting a distributor?

**2.** What steps should Robert Grosse have taken that could have helped in doing a better job in distributor selection?

# FURTHER READING • • • • • • • • • • • • • • • • • • • • • •

Barnes, Paul and Richard Oloruntoba, "Assurance of Security in Maritime Supply Chains: Conceptual Issues of Vulnerability and Crisis Management," *Journal of International Management*, 11 (December), 2005: 519–40.

Bowersox, Donald J., David J. Closs, and M. Bixby Cooper, *Supply Chain Logistics Management*, New York: McGraw-Hill, 2002.

Colla, Enrico and Marc Dupuis, "Research and Managerial Issues on Global Retail Competition: Carrefour/Wal-Mart," *International Journal of Retail & Distribution Management*, 30(2/3), 2002: 103–11.

Dawson, John and Jung-Hee Lee. "International Retailing in Asia," *Journal of Global Marketing*, 18(1/2), 2004, Special Issue.

McGurr, Paul T., "The Largest Retail Firms: A Comparison of Asia-, Europe- and U.S.-based Retailers," *International Journal of Retail & Distribution Management*, 30(2/3), 2002: 145–47.

"Global Department Stores," DATAMONITOR, www.datamonitor.com, Reference Code: 0199-2037, May 2005.

Grieger, Martin, "Electronic Marketplaces: A Literature Review and A Call for Supply Chain Management Research," *European Journal of Operational Research*, 144 (January), 2003: 280–94.

Hanks, George F. and LucindaVan Alst, "Foreign Trade Zones," *Management Accounting;* 80 (January), 1999: 20–23.

Harryman, Roy, "Foreign Trade Zones Give Companies A Competitive Edge," *Expansion Management*, 20 (June), 2005: 25–28.

Haytko, Diana L., John L. Kent, and Angela Hausman, "Mexican Maquiladoras: Helping or Hurting the US/Mexico Cross-Border Supply Chain?," *International Journal of Logistics Management*, 18(3), 2007: 347–63.

Hult, G. Tomas M., David J. Ketchen, Jr., and Ernest L. Nichols, Jr., "An Examination of Cultural Competitiveness and Order Fulfillment Cycle Time within Supply Chains," *Academy of Management Journal*, 45 (June), 2002: 577–86.

Lieb, Robert and Brooks A. Bentz, "The Use of Third-Party Logistics Services by Large American Manufacturers: The 2004 Survey," *Transportation Journal*, 44 (Spring), 2005: 5–15.

Mathur, Lynette Knowles and Ike Mathur, "The Effectiveness of the Foreign-Trade Zone as an Export Promotion Program: Policy Issues and Alternatives," *Journal of Macromarketing* 17 (Fall), 1997: 20–31.

Samiee, Saeed and Peter G.P. Walters, "Supplier and Customer Exchange in International Industrial Markets: An Integrative Perspective," *Industrial Marketing Management*, 35 (July), 2006: 589–99.

# APPENDIX: MAQUILADORA OPERATION • • • • • • • • • • • • • • •

The maquiladora industry, also known as the in-bond or twin-plant program, is essentially a special Mexican version of a free trade zone. Mexico allows duty-free imports of machinery and equipment for manufacturing as well as components for further processing and assembly, as long as at least 80 percent of the plant's output is exported. Mexico permits 100 percent foreign ownership of the maquiladora plants in designated maquiladora zones.

Mexico's Border Industrialization Program developed in 1965 set the basis for maquiladora operations in Mexico. It was originally intended to attract foreign manufacturing investment and increase job opportunities in areas of Mexico suffering from chronic high unemployment. Most of them are located along the U.S.–Mexico border, such as Tijuana across from San Diego, Ciudad Juarez across from El Paso, and Nuevo Laredo across from Laredo. Over the years, however, Mexico has expanded the maquiladora programs to industrialized major cities such as Monterrey, Mexico City, and Guadalajara, where more skilled workers can be found. This duty-free export assembly program has helped transform Mexico, once a closed economy, into the world's 9th largest exporter.[92] Automobile and electronics product assembly makes up the bulk of maquiladora industries.

The competitive pressures of the world economy forced many large manufacturing companies to abandon their assembly plants in the United States and move to Mexican maquiladoras. Furthermore, to meet local content requirements imposed by NAFTA, foreign firms, too, expanded manufacturing operations in maquiladoras. Particularly, Asian companies, such as Panasonic, Sanyo, Sony, Samsung, and Daewoo, have invited some of their traditional components suppliers to join them in maquiladoras to increase local procurement.

Mexico had long been an attractive location for labor-intensive assembly because its hourly labor cost declined in dollar terms from $2.96 in 1980 to $1.20 in 1990 and to about $0.50 in 1999. This decline resulted from a series of peso depreciations beginning in 1976, including the devastating depreciation that shook the Mexican economy in late 1994 and 1995. However, since 1999, the Mexican economy has grown rapidly and the Mexican peso has started appreciating against the U.S. dollar, driving up the costs of maquiladora operations over time. In addition, rising wages are also making maquiladora operations less attractive. Furthermore, as part of the NAFTA agreement, which took effect in 1994, maquiladoras have also been stripped of many of the tax and tariff exemptions.[93] By 2002, the average labor cost in Mexico had

risen to $2.45 per hour, losing cost competitiveness to China, where the average labor cost was 68 cents in the interior region and 88 cents in the eastern coastal region. As recently as 2000, 90 percent of all maquiladora inputs in Mexico came from the United States, 9 percent came from Asia, and China contributed only 1 percent of the total. By 2003, however, the U.S. share of maquiladora inputs had declined to 69 percent, while Asia's share had increased to 28 percent, including 8 percent from China. In other words, instead of manufacturing materials in Mexico's maquiladoras, U.S.-based suppliers (both domestic and foreign companies operating in the United States) are increasingly having their materials partially or completely manufactured in Asia to take advantage of cheaper labor and then sending them to Mexican maquiladoras for final assembly for eventual export to the United States.[94] Although maquiladora exports had continued to grow from $14 billion in 1990 to nearly $105 in 2005, the role of the maquiladora as a cheap manufacturing location is ending. As a result, the only companies that are still operating successfully on the U.S.-Mexican border are high-tech plants. Mexico should become more capital-intensive with efforts toward more value-added production by attracting and retaining high-tech plants tailored to high-end customers, and offering just-in-time delivery.[95]

[92]*World Trade Report 2005: Exploring the Link between Trade, Standards, and the WTO,* Geneva, World Trade Organization, 2005.

[93]The dramatic growth of maquiladoras in Mexico is not entirely attributed to Mexico's Border Industrialization Program and inexpensive labor cost. Special U.S. tariff provisions have also encouraged U.S.-based companies to export U.S.-made components and other in-process materials to foreign countries for further processing and/or assembly and subsequently to re-import finished products back into the United States. U.S. imports under these tariff provisions are officially called **U.S. imports under Items 9802.00.60 and 9802.00.80 of the U.S. Harmonized Tariff Schedule** (the 9802 tariff provisions for short).

The 9802 tariff provisions permit the duty-free importation by U.S.-based companies of their materials previously sent abroad for further processing or assembly (i.e., tariffs are assessed only on the foreign value-added portion of the imported products). More specifically, item 9802.00.60 applies to re-importation for further processing in the United States of any metal initially processed or manufactured in the United States that was shipped abroad for processing. Item 9802.00.80 permits re-importation for sale in the United States of finished products assembled abroad in whole or in part made up of U.S.-made components. Therefore,

the higher the U.S. import tariff rates, the more beneficial it is for U.S.-based companies to be able to declare U.S. imports under the 9802 tariff provisions. Consequently, many U.S.-based companies have taken full advantage of both the 9802 tariff provisions of the United States and the maquiladora laws of Mexico in pursuit of cost competitiveness.

Under the provisions of NAFTA, however, U.S. import tariffs on products originating from Canada and Mexico continue to be reduced over the next decade or so. As a result, the tariff advantage for products re-imported from Mexico into the United States under the 9802 tariff provisions will eventually diminish over time. However, as many items still have five-, ten-, and some fifteen-year phase-in periods before elimination of tariffs, the 9802 tariff provisions will remain useful even within the NAFTA for the foreseeable future. Keep in mind that these tariff provisions still benefit U.S.-based companies manufacturing *outside of the NAFTA region* as long as U.S.-made materials and components are used in production.

[94]"No Rest for the Weary," *Journal of Commerce*, February 21, 2005, pp. 20–22.

[95]"NAFTA Helps Mexico Compete Globally," *Expansion Management*, October 2005, p. 20.

# EXPORT AND IMPORT MANAGEMENT

## CHAPTER OVERVIEW

1. ORGANIZING FOR EXPORTS

2. INDIRECT EXPORTING

3. DIRECT EXPORTING

4. MECHANICS OF EXPORTING

5. ROLE OF THE GOVERNMENT IN PROMOTING EXPORTS

6. MANAGING IMPORTS—THE OTHER SIDE OF THE COIN

7. MECHANICS OF IMPORTING

8. GRAY MARKETS

Exporting is the most popular way for many companies to become international. The main reasons for this are: (1) exporting requires minimum resources while allowing high flexibility and (2) it offers substantial financial, marketing, technological, and other benefits to the firm. Because exporting is usually the first mode of foreign entry used by many companies, exporting early tends to give them first-mover advantage.[1] However, exporting requires experiential knowledge. Exporters must acquire foreign market knowledge (i.e., clients, market needs, and competitors) and institutional knowledge (i.e., government, institutional framework, rules, norms, and values) as well as develop operational knowledge (i.e., capabilities and resources to engage in international operations).[2] Selling to a foreign market involves numerous high risks arising from the lack of knowledge of and unfamiliarity with foreign environments, which can be heterogeneous, sophisticated and turbulent. Furthermore, conducting market research across national boundaries is more difficult, complex, and subjective than for its domestic counterpart.

---

[1]Yigang Pan, Shaomin Li, and David K. Tse, "The Impact of Order and Mode of Market Entry on Profitability and Market Share," *Journal of International Business Studies*, 30 (First Quarter 1999), pp. 81–104.

[2]Kent Eriksson, Jan Johanson, Anders Majkgård, D. Deo Sharma, "Effect of Variation on Knowledge Accumulation in the Internationalization Process," *International Studies of Management and Organization*, 30, 2000, pp. 26–44.

For successful development of export activities, systematic collection of information is critical. Market information can be well-documented and come from public and private data sources, but it can also be so tacit that only seasoned marketing managers with international vision and experience could have a "gut-feel" in understanding it.[3] Market information helps managers to assess the attractiveness of foreign markets and decide whether to engage in exporting. After a firm has decided to start exporting, it requires information on how to handle the mechanics of it, including how to enter overseas markets and what adaptations to make to the marketing mix elements.[4] A recent study, which compared export leaders—defined as companies that distribute products or services to six or more countries—to export laggards, also shows that the more companies export, the more they spend in information technology. According to the same study, much of the investment the leading export companies make in IT is for e-business, from Web-based commerce and supply-chain networks to electronic marketplaces. This focus seems to be paying off.[5]

As presented in Chapter 2, the nature of international exports and imports has also improved since the beginning of this new century. From 1997 to 2007, global GDP grew more than 30 percent, while total global merchandise exports increased by more than 60 percent.[6] However, growth in world output and trade has decelerated since 2007. In 2007, weaker demand in the developed economies reduced global economic growth to 3.4 per cent from 3.7 per cent, roughly the average rate recorded over the last decade. Lower imports than in the preceding years were observed in North America, Europe, Japan, and the net oil importing developing countries in Asia. This downward trend outweighed the rapid import growth momentum observed in Central and South America, the Commonwealth of Independent States (CIS or former Soviet Republics), Africa, and the Middle East. The developing countries as a group accounted for more than one half of the increase in world merchandise imports in 2007. The excess of regional export growth over import growth can be attributed largely to the United States, where import volumes increased only marginally (1 percent), while exports expanded by 7 percent in 2007. Europe's real merchandise export and import growth of 3.5 percent in 2007 continued to lag behind the global rate of trade expansion, as has been the case since 2002.[7] Then since late 2008, U.S. financial turmoil has spread throughout the world, resulting in an unprecedented global recession with plummeting international trade.[8] Weaker demand in the developed countries now provides a less favorable framework for the expansion of international trade than in preceding years.[9]

Although the United States is still relatively more insulated from the global economy than other nations (See Chapter 2), exports of goods and services combined represented 8.3 percent of the U.S. GDP as of 2007, yet account for more than 25 percent of U.S. economic growth in the past decade.[10] Roughly 10 percent of all U.S. jobs (approximately 12 million) rely on exports. In general, one factory job in five depends on international trade in the United States. Between 1990 and 2000, export-related jobs grew by 56 percent, an increase that is three times faster than the rate of job growth in the rest of the economy. These facts demonstrate that export is an important source of U.S. economic growth and job creation. Furthermore, jobs that depend on

---

[3]Gary A. Knight and Peter W. Liesch, "Information Internalization in Internationalizing the Firm," *Journal of Business Research*, 55 (December 2002), pp. 981–95.

[4]Leonidas C. Leonidou and Athena S. Adams-Florou, "Types and Sources of Export Information: Insights from Small Business," *International Small Business Journal*, 17 (April–June 1999), pp. 30–48.

[5]Mary E. Thyfault, "Heavy Exporters Spend Big on Leading-Edge IT," *InformationWeek*, Apr 23, 2001, p. 54.

[6]*World Trade Report 2007*, http://www.wto.org/, Geneva, World Trade Organization, 2007.

[7]*World Trade Report 2007* and *World Trade Report 2008*, http://www.wto.org/, accessed October 10, 2008.

[8]"World Trade to Shrink in 2009: World Bank," newsroomamerica.com, December 9, 2008.

[9]"A Turn for the Worse," *Economist*, September 13, 2008, pp. 71–72.

[10]Computed from statistics in Central Intelligence Agency, *World Factbook 2008*, https://www.cia.gov/library/publications/.

trade pay between 13 to 18 percent more than the average wage, indicating that these employees generally earn more than the others.[11]

This chapter primarily considers the export function; it attempts to explain the import function as the counterpart of the export function, because for every export transaction there is, by definition, an import transaction as well. Aside from some differences between the procedure and rationale for exports and imports, both are largely the same the world over.

## ORGANIZING FOR EXPORTS ◆ ◆ ◆ ◆ ◆ ◆ ◆

For a firm exporting for the first time, the first step would be to research potential markets using available secondary data. Increasingly international marketing information is available in the form of electronic databases ranging from the latest news on product developments to new material in the academic and trade press. Well over 6,000 databases are available worldwide, with almost 5,000 available online. The United States is the largest participant in this database growth, producing and consuming more than 50 percent of these database services. When entering a culturally and linguistically different part of the world, managers need to understand a completely new way of commercial thinking that is based on a different culture and works on a different set of premises. Often seasoned managers' flexibility and adaptability acquired through experience and learning, prove to be important in building export contracts.[12] It is also to be noted that export research for markets such as China and the CIS must still be done largely in the field because very little prior data exist for them and when they are available, they are often not reliable.[13] See **Global Perspective 16-1** for how complex the task of exporting is relative to domestic sales.

**Research for Exports**

The identification of an appropriate overseas market and an appropriate segment involves grouping by the following criteria:

1. Socioeconomic characteristics (e.g., demographic, economic, geographic, and climatic characteristics)
2. Political and legal characteristics
3. Consumer variables (e.g., lifestyle, preferences, culture, taste, purchase behavior, and purchase frequency)
4. Financial conditions

On the basis of these criteria, an exporter can form an idea of the market segments in a foreign market.[14] First, regions within countries across the world are grouped by macroeconomic variables indicating the levels of industrial development, availability of skilled labor, and purchasing power. For example, from an exporter's point of view the Mumbai–Thane–Pune area in Western India has more in common with the Monterrey area and the Mexico City area in Mexico and the Shanghai–Wuxi area in China than with other areas in India. All three areas already have a well-developed industrial base and purchasing power that is equal to that of the middle class in developed nations. Such economically homogeneous groups across the world are a result of the globalization of markets. These apparently similar markets can, however, differ along political and legal

---

[11]National Council on Economic Education http://www.econedlink.org/lessons/index.cfm?lesson=EM208; Trade Resource Center http://trade.businessroundtable.org/trade_2005/wto/us_economy.html; and Trade Resource Center http://trade.businessroundtable.org/trade_basics/trade_jobs.html, accessed January 15, 2006.

[12]Amal R. Karunaratna, Lester W. Johnson, and C. P. Rao, "The Exporter-Import Agent Contract and the Influence of Cultural Dimensions," *Journal of Marketing Management*, 17 (February), 2001, pp. 137–58.

[13]Peter G. P. Walters and Saeed Samiee, "Marketing Strategy in Emerging Markets: The Case of China," *Journal of International Marketing*, 11(1), 2003, pp. 97–106.

[14]For a comprehensive review of the export development process, see Leonidas C. Leonidou and Constantine S. Katsikeas, "The Export Development Process: An Integrative Review of Empirical Models," *Journal of International Business Studies*, 27 (Third Quarter 1996), pp. 517–51.

◆ ◆ ◆ ◆ ◆ ◆ ◆ ◆ ◆ ◆ ◆ ◆ ◆ ◆ ◆ ◆ ◆ ◆ ◆ ◆ ◆ ◆ ◆ ◆ ◆ ◆ ◆ ◆ ◆ ◆ ◆

## $\mathcal{G}$LOBAL PERSPECTIVE 16-1

### THE COMPLEXITIES OF EXPORTING VS. DOMESTIC SALES

Major differences exist in processing domestic and export sales but the two most important may be the complexity and the number of people involved in exporting products. These differences are also major contributors to new and better paying jobs for the domestic labor market.

*The Process for Domestic Sales*: The order is entered or given to a salesperson via e-mail, fax, internet, or phone. If the product is in stock, the salesperson sends the request to the shipping department where the order is filled and then boxed, crated, or skidded. The box is marked, labeled, and put on a truck for delivery the next day or as soon as possible.

*The Process for Export Sales*: An order entry person (usually bilingual) enters the order that is received via e-mail, fax, internet, or phone. An export compliance officer reviews all foreign inquiries, requests, and purchase orders. The officer also monitors Export Administration Regulations (EAR), tariffs, harmonized codes, export licenses, boycott, language, checklists for denied parties, and Shipper's Security Endorsement, etc. Engineering department reviews for compliance and product certifications. These tasks are usually outsourced to labs. Companies can use separate production lines designated specifically for export because of major differences in technical specifications, certifications, and designs. Different sources of outside suppliers may also be needed for exported goods. Drawings, designs, and instructions need to be translated and printed in several foreign languages. The Export Shipping Department is experienced in export packing, containerizing, and creating detailed packing lists. The department also references metric weights and measurements

*Source:* Richard Gref, "Are Export Sales Really Good for the U.S. Economy?" *Business Credit*, September 2000, p. 52.

while providing export labeling and routing that identifies the terms of shipment.

A freight forwarder is an export documentation specialist who handles Export Declarations, Certificates of Compliance, Consular, Origin, Chambers of Commerce signatures, export insurance, and airway and ocean bills of lading. In terms of transportation, trucks and railroad cars are used to deliver export containers to domestic ports in order to meet shipping schedules. The banking sector handles foreign open account payments, wire transfers, letters of credit, drafts and financing (short, medium and long term). Factoring houses, forfeiting agencies and insurance agencies (public and private) augment this process as well. U.S. government employees including U.S. Customs officers, Export Administration personnel (at the Bureau of Industry and Security), and Ex-Im Bank, Small Business Administration, World Bank, and USAID representatives, also may contribute to the export sales process. Other government agencies represented in this process include the Department of Commerce, Department of Treasury and Export Assistance. The monitoring of export sales (analysis and statistics) is completed by the Departments of State and Defense as well as the Nuclear Energy Commission and the Central Intelligence Agency. Other service providers include international telecommunications and foreign travel service agents as well as international newspapers, magazines and publications, and international credit reporting agencies such as FCIB. Finally, attorneys, accounting firms, tax experts, and consultants specializing in international markets provide their services.

So, the next time someone asks you the question whether export sales really are easy to handle, you may want to share a copy of this article.

---

dimensions. An exporter or importer that violates terms has legal recourse in India, and the court of adjudication is in India. Legal recourse is still largely wishful thinking in China. By addressing consumer and macroeconomic variables, the exporter can successfully segment the international market into homogenous segments where similar elements of the marketing mix can be applied.

Data for grouping along macroeconomic criteria are available from international agencies such as the World Bank, which publishes the *World Development Report*. In addition, the United Nations produces a series of statistical abstracts on a yearly basis covering economic, demographic, political, and social characteristics that are very useful for grouping analysis. The International Monetary Fund publishes data on international trade and finance quarterly and annually. Both the Organization for Economic Cooperation and Development (OECD—a group of advanced nations) and the European Union (EU) publish a variety of statistical reports and studies on their member countries.

**Export Market Segments**

As discussed in Chapter 7, the grouping of countries and regions among countries enables a firm to link various geographical areas into one homogeneous market segment that the firm can cater to in meeting its export objectives. The next task is to develop a product strategy for the selected export markets. The export market clusters obtained by clustering regions within different nations would fall into various levels: at the country level would be countries with the same characteristics as the U.S. market; at the regional level within nations, there would be geographical and psychographic segments in many different countries to which the firm can export the same core product it sells in domestic markets without any significant changes. It is a form of market diversification in which the firm is selling a standardized, uniform product across countries and regions.[15] Mercedes-Benz automobiles and Rolex watches sell to the same consumer segment worldwide. Another standardized product that sells worldwide is the soft drink. The Coca-Cola Company markets essentially one Coke worldwide.

Products that can be standardized could satisfy basic needs that do not vary with climate, economic conditions, or culture. A standardized product is the easiest to sell abroad logistically because the firm incurs no additional manufacturing costs and is able to use the same promotional messages across different regions in different countries across the world. If those different regions have comparable logistics and infrastructural facilities, the distribution requirements and expenses would also be similar.

Where it is not possible to sell standardized products, the firm could need to adapt its products for the overseas marketplace. In such instances, either the firm's product does not meet customer requirements or it does not satisfy the administrative requirements of foreign countries. Such markets can require modification of the product if it is to succeed in the foreign market.[16] Brand names, for example, need to be changed before a product can be sold, because the brand name could mean something detrimental to the product's prospect. Ford recently released its new European Ka model in Japan. Ka means "mosquito" in Japanese, a less than popular disease-carrying pest. Analysts called the Ka dead on arrival.[17] Beauty-products giant Estée Lauder found out that its perfume Country Mist would not sell in Germany because mist means manure in German slang. Sometimes, a new product has to be developed from a manufacturing viewpoint because the product is not salable as it is in the export market. For example, room air conditioner units being exported to Egypt must have special filters and coolers and have to be sturdy enough to handle the dust and heat of Egyptian summer.

# INDIRECT EXPORTING

◆ ◆ ◆ ◆ ◆ ◆ ◆

**Indirect exporting** involves the use of independent intermediaries or agents to market the firm's products overseas. These agents, known as export representatives, assume responsibility for marketing the firm's products through their network of foreign distributors and their own salesforce. It is not uncommon for a U.S. producer who is new to exporting to begin export operation by selling through an export representative. Many Japanese firms have also relied on the giant general trading companies known as sogoshosha. Use of agents is not uncommon when it is not cost effective for an exporter to set up its own export department. Such firms can initiate export operations through export representatives who know the market and have experience in selling to them. There are several types of export representatives in the United States. The most common are the combination export manager (CEM), export merchant, export broker, export commission house, trading company, and piggyback exporter.

The **combination export manager** (CEM) acts as the export department to a small exporter or a large producer with small overseas sales. CEMs often use the letterhead of

[15]Lloyd C. Russow, "Market Diversification: "Going International," *Review of Business*, 17 (Spring 1996), pp. 32–34.

[16]Roger J. Calantone, S. Tamer Cavusgil, Jeffrey B. Schmidt, and Geon-Cheol Shin, "Internationalization and the Dynamics of Product Adaptation—An Empirical Investigation," *Journal of Product Innovation Management*, 21 (May 2004), pp. 185–98.

[17]Keith Naughton, "Tora, Tora, Taurus," *Business Week* (April 12, 1999), p. 6.

the company they represent and have extensive experience in selling abroad and in the mechanics of export shipments. CEMs operate on a commission basis and are usually most effective when they deal with clients who have businesses in related lines. Because credit plays an increasingly important role in export sales, CEMs have found it increasingly difficult to consummate export sales on behalf of clients without their credit support. As more and more firms begin exporting on a regular basis, CEMs are becoming a vanishing breed. A list of CEMs can be found in the *American Register of Exporters and Importers* and in the telephone yellow pages.

**Export merchants**, in contrast to the CEM, buy and sell on their own accounts and assume all responsibilities of exporting a product. In this situation, the manufacturers do not control the sales activities of their products in export markets and depend entirely on the export merchant for all export activities. This loss of control over the export marketing effort is a major drawback to using export merchants. The **export broker**, as the name implies, is someone who brings together an overseas buyer and a domestic manufacturer for the purpose of an export sale and earns a commission for establishing a contact that results in a sale.

Foreign buyers of U.S. goods sometimes contract for the services of a U.S. representative to act on their behalf. This resident representative is usually an **export commission house** that places orders only on behalf of its foreign client with U.S. manufacturers and acts as a finder for its client to get the best buy. A **trading company** is a large, organization engaged in exporting and importing. It buys on its own account in one country and exports the goods to another country. Most of the well-known trading companies are Japanese or Western European in origin. Japanese trading companies, known as sogoshosha, such as Mitsui, Mitsubishi, Sumitomo, and Marubeni operate worldwide and handle a significant proportion of Japanese foreign trade. United Africa Company, a subsidiary of Unilever, operates extensively in Africa. Another European trading company is Jardine Matheson in Hong Kong, a major trading force in Southeast Asia. See **Exhibit 16-1** for the major types of trading companies.

**Piggyback exporting** refers to the practice by which carrier firms that have established export departments assume, under a cooperative agreement, the responsibility of exporting the products of other companies. The carrier buys the rider's products and

**EXHIBIT 16-1**
MAJOR TYPES OF TRADING COMPANIES AND THEIR COUNTRIES OF ORIGIN

| Type | Rationale for Grouping | Some Examples by Country of Origin |
|---|---|---|
| General Trading Company | Historical Involvement in generalized imports/exports | C. Itoh (Japan), East Asiatic (Denmark), SCOA (France), Jardine Matheson (Hong Kong) |
| Export Trading Company | Specific mission to promote growth of exporters | Hyundai (Korea), Interbras (Brazil), Sears World Trade (US) |
| Federated Export Marketing Group | Loose collaboration among exporting companies supervised by a third party and usually market specific | Fedec (UK), SBI Group (Norway), IEB Project Group (Morocco) |
| Trading arm of MNCs | Specific international trading operations in parent company operations | General Motors (US), IBM (US) |
| Bank-based or affiliated trading group | A bank at the center of a group extends commercial activities | Mitsubishi (Japan), Cobec (Brazil) |
| Commodity trading company | Long standing export trading in a specific market | Metallgesellschaft (Germany), Louis Dreyfus (France) |

*Source:* Adapted from Lyn Amine, "Toward a Conceptualization of Export Trading Companies in World Markets," in S. Tamer Cavusgil, ed., *Advances in International Marketing*, vol. 2 (Greenwich, CT: JAI Press, 1987), pp. 199–208.

markets them independently. The rider plays a peripheral role in the export marketing overseas. Piggybacking can be an option to enter an export market, but is normally avoided by firms who wish to be in exports over the long haul because of the loss of control over the foreign marketing operations.

# DIRECT EXPORTING

**Direct exporting** occurs when a manufacturer or exporter sells directly to an importer or buyer located in a foreign market. It requires export managers' full commitment both in their attitudes and in their behavior for export success.[18] Direct exporting can manifest in various organizational forms, depending on the scale of operations and the number of years that a firm has been engaged in exporting. In its most simple form, a firm has an export sales manager with some clerical help responsible for the actual selling and directing of activities associated with the export sales. Most of the other export-marketing activities (advertising, logistics, and credit, for example) are performed by a regular department of the firm that also handles international trade transactions.

As export activities grow in scale and complexity, most firms create a separate **export department** that is largely self-contained and operates independently of domestic operations. An export department can be structured internally on the basis of function, geography, product, customer, or some other combination. Some firms prefer to have an **export sales subsidiary** instead of an export department in order to keep export operations separate from the rest of the firm. In terms of internal operations and specific operations performed, an export sales subsidiary differs very little from an export department. The major difference is that the subsidiary, being a separate legal entity, must purchase the products it sells in the overseas markets from its parent manufacturer. This means that the parent has to develop and administer a system of transfer pricing. A subsidiary has the advantage of being an independent profit center and is therefore easier to evaluate; it can also offer tax advantages, ease of financing, and increased proximity to the customer.

Instead of a foreign sales subsidiary, a firm also has the option of establishing a **foreign sales branch**. Unlike a subsidiary, a branch is not a separate legal entity. A foreign sales branch handles all of sales, distribution, and promotional work throughout a designated market area and sells primarily to wholesalers and dealers. Where it is used, a sales branch is the initial link in the marketing channel in the foreign market. Often the branch has a storage and warehousing facility available so it can maintain an inventory of products, replacement parts, and maintenance supplies.

Indirect exporting and direct exporting are compared in **Exhibit 16-2**. Both have advantages and disadvantages, although over the long-term, that is, for a firm

**EXHIBIT 16-2**
COMPARISON OF DIRECT AND INDIRECT EXPORTING

| *Indirect Exporting* | *Direct Exporting* |
| --- | --- |
| • Low set up costs | • High set up costs |
| • Exporter tend not to gain good knowledge of export markets | • Leads to better knowledge of export markets and international expertise due to direct contact |
| • Credit risk lies mostly with the middlemen | |
| • Since it is not in the interest of the middlemen doing the exporting, customer loyally rarely develops | • Credit risks are higher especially in the early years |
| | • Customer loyalty can be developed for the exporter's brands more easily |

[18]Rodney L. Stump, Gerard A. Athaide, and Catherine N. Axinn, "The Contingent Effect of the Dimensions of Export Commitment on Exporting Financial Performance: An Empirical Examination," *Journal of Global Marketing*, 12(1) (1998), pp. 7–25; and David L. Dean and Bulent Menguc, "Revisiting Firm Characteristics, Strategy, and Export Performance Relationship," Industrial Marketing Management, 29 (September 2000), pp. 461–77.

desiring a permanent presence in international markets, direct exports tend to be more useful.

<hr>

♦ ♦ ♦ ♦ ♦ ♦ ♦ ♦   ## MECHANICS OF EXPORTING

The paperwork involved in export declaration forms can be time-consuming, no matter how useful information provided on the forms may be. In the United States, to expedite the exporting process, the U.S. Commerce Department's Census Bureau launched a new system, the **Automated Export System (AES)**, on October 1, 1999. AES is a computer system that collects Electronic Export Information (EEI), which is the electronic equivalent of the export data formerly collected as Shipper's Export Declaration (SED) information. AES enables exporters to file export information at no cost over the internet; it is part of an effort to make government more efficient and boost U.S. exports.[19]

AES is a joint venture between the U.S. Customs Service, the Foreign Trade Division of the Bureau of the Census (Commerce), the Bureau of Industry and Security (Commerce), the Office of Defense Trade Controls (State), other federal agencies, and the export trade community. It was designed to improve trade statistics, reduce duplicate reporting to multiple agencies, improve customer service, and to ensure compliance with and enforcement of laws relating to exporting. It is the central point through which export shipment data required by multiple agencies is filed electronically on the internet to Customs, using the electronic data interchange (EDI). AES is a completely voluntary system that provides an alternative to filing the paper Shipper's Export Declarations. AES export information is collected electronically and edited immediately, and errors are detected and corrected at the time of filing. AES is a nationwide system operational at all ports and for all methods of transportation.

This internet-based system allows exporters, freight forwarders, and consolidators to file shippers' export declaration information in an automated, cost-free way. AES has the goal of paperless reporting of export information.[20] The new system reduces the paperwork burden on the trade community, make document storage and handling less costly, improve the quality of export statistics, and facilitate exporting in general. Before AES, the export system was paper bound, expensive, labor intensive, and error prone.

However, a large number of firms still did not want to switch to AES until it was mandatory. Following a three-year standoff, Customs & Border Protection (CBP) and the Census Bureau have resolved their turf war over mandatory filing of export data through the AES. The newly published Foreign Trade Regulations that require electronic filing of export declarations, which took effect on July 1, 2008, brings an end to paper shippers export declaration, and make the AES the only legal means for filing export data. While the formal effective date of the final rule is July 2, 2008, Census did not commence implementation until September 30, 2008—in effect providing a three-month "grace period" of "informed compliance" to learn the new rules. "Enforced compliance" then began on September 30. With regard to penalties, fines for noncompliance with the new AES rule have increased tenfold, to a maximum of $10,000 per incident for criminal violations. Criminal penalties under AES are currently $1,000. Fines can be levied on the exporter or its forwarder, carrier, or other agent authorized to file on its behalf. In addition, civil penalties of up to $1,000 per day up to a total of $10,000 may be imposed. Described in Subpart H, criminal and civil penalties can be levied for submission of false or misleading information or furtherance of illegal activities and forfeiture penalties. Civil penalties can be levied for failure to file or delayed filing.[21]

<hr>

[19]"Two Major Export Compliance Changes Coming in Early 2006," *Managing Exports & Imports*, October 2005, pp. 1–13.

[20]David Biederman, "AES A Must for Dual-Use Goods," *Traffic World*, January 3, 2000, p. 30.

[21]R. G. Edmonson, "Here Comes Mandatory AES," *Journal of Commerce*, June 9, 2008, p. 21; and "Filing of Export Data via AES Made Mandatory," *Managing Imports & Exports*, August 2008, p. 1, 10–12.

Exporting starts with the search for a buyer abroad. It includes the research to locate a potential market, a buyer, and information concerning the process of closing a sale. We covered the process of getting an order earlier in this chapter. Once an export contract has been signed, the wheels are set in motion for the process that results in the export contract. The *first* stage has to do with the legality of the transaction. The exporter must determine whether the goods can actually be imported by the importing party — importing country licensing law can halt a transaction unless it is studied in advance.

**Legality of Exports**

Standard specifications for products and services are especially important in Europe and Japan as far as U.S. exporters are concerned. As far as export transactions to third-world countries are concerned, the convertibility of the importing country's currency must be determined even in this day of liberalization. If the country's currency is not convertible, the importing party must have permission to remit hard currency. Finally, the exporter must ensure that there are no export restrictions on the goods it proposes to export from the United States. Security concerns on encryption technology, for example, permit the exports of encryption technology that incorporates no more than 40 bits. All exports from the United States (except those to Canada and U.S. territories) require an **export license**, which can be a general export license or a validated export license. A **general license** permits exportation within certain limits without requiring that an application be filed or that a license document be issued. A **validated license** permits exportation within specific limitations; it is issued only on formal application. Most goods can move from the United States to the free world countries under a general license. A validated license is required to export certain strategic goods regardless of their destination. For most goods, the license is granted by the U.S. Department of Commerce's Bureau of Industry and Security. For certain specific products, however, the license is granted by other U.S. government agencies (See **Exhibit 16-3**).

As onerous as export validation procedure appears, large companies are proactively dealing with it. For example, Philips, with $4 billion in annual exports to over 150 countries from some 260 U.S. locations, has automated its export process to a significant degree by implementing its PROTECT system, which is a database that permits export

## EXHIBIT 16-3
### U.S. GOVERNMENT DEPARTMENTS AND AGENCIES WITH EXPORT CONTROL RESPONSIBILITIES

| *Licensing Authority* | *Responsibility* |
|---|---|
| Department of State, Office of Defense Trade Controls (DTC) | Licenses defense services and defense (munitions) articles. |
| Department of the Treasury, Office of Foreign Assets Control (OFAC) | Administers and enforces economic and trade sanctions against targeted foreign countries, terrorism sponsoring organizations, and international narcotics traffickers. |
| Nuclear Regulatory Commission, Office of International Programs | Licenses nuclear material and equipment. |
| Department of Energy, Office of Arms Controls and Nonproliferation, Export Control Division | Licenses nuclear technology and technical data for nuclear power and special nuclear materials. |
| Department of Energy, Office of Fuels Programs | Licenses natural gas and electric power. |
| Defense Threat Reduction Agency — Technology Security | Responsible for the development and implementation of policies on international transfers of defense-related technology, and reviews certain dual-use export license applications. |
| Department of the Interior, Division of Management Authority | Controls the export of endangered fish and wildlife species. |
| Drug Enforcement Administration, International Drug Unit | Controls the import and export of listed chemicals used in the production of control substances under the Controlled Substances Act. |
| Food and Drug Administration, Office of Compliance | Licenses medical devices. |
| Food and Drug Administration, Import/Export | Licenses drugs. |
| Patent and Trademark Office, Licensing and Review | Oversees patent filing data sent abroad. |
| Environmental Protection Agency, Office of Solid Waste, International and Special Projects Branch | Controls toxic waste exports. |

*Source:* Bureau of Industry and Security, U.S. Department of Commerce, http://www.bis.doc.gov/reslinks.htm, accessed August 5, 2009.

managers to simulate their export transaction before it is approved. The PROTECT database includes: 1) all Philips products that fall under any type of export control; 2) a full listing of proscribed or sensitive countries and customers; 3) all export control laws and regulations; and 4) concrete instruction on how to act in specific export control matters. In general, the Philips export management system clearly identifies who are its customers, how it takes orders, and who is responsible for exports to ensure that export activities follow the company's export compliance guidelines and procedures.[22]

Similarly, exporters from other countries also need to get export license in their countries in order to sell their products in foreign markets. For example, although many Chinese automobile companies planned to increase the number of vehicles they export, their efforts were not taken into realty because the Chinese government announced that it would limit the number of export licenses available to domestic automotive companies by 2008.[23] Triggered by the safety issues of Mattel toy made in China, the toy industry and government in China paid a lot of attention to efforts to correct problems that led to widespread recalls in 2007. One of the Chinese government's efforts was to revoke export licenses for hundreds of its estimated 3,500 export-oriented toy factories.[24]

## Export Transactions

The second pillar of an export transaction involves the logistics of the export transaction, which includes (1) the terms of the sale, including payment mode and schedule, dispute settlement mechanism, and service requirements (if applicable); (2) monitoring the transportation and delivery of the goods to the assigned party—the assignee in the bill of lading and obtaining proof of delivery—the **customs receipt**; and (3) shipping and obtaining the bill of lading.

When a company has a firm order for exports, it must execute the order by delivering the product or service promised to the overseas customer. A **bill of lading** is a contract between the exporter and the shipping company indicating that the shipping company has accepted responsibility for the goods and will provide transportation in return for payment. The bill of ownership can also be used as a receipt and to prove ownership of the merchandise, depending on the type of the bill of lading. A **straight bill of lading** is non-negotiable and is usually used in prepaid transactions. The goods are delivered to a specific individual or company. A **shipper's order bill of lading** is negotiable; it can be bought, sold, or traded while the goods are still in transit, (i.e., title of the goods can change hands). The customer usually needs the original or a copy of the bill of lading to take possession of the goods (depending on the terms of the export contract).

A **commercial invoice** is a bill for the goods stating basic information about the transaction, including a description of the merchandise, total cost of the goods sold, addresses of the buyer and the seller, and delivery and payment terms. The buyer needs the invoice to prove ownership and to arrange payment terms. Some governments also use commercial invoices to assess customs duties. Other export documentation that may be required includes export licenses, certificates of origin, inspection certification, dock and/or warehouse receipts, destination control certificates (to inform shippers and other foreign parties that the goods can be shipped only to a particular country), shippers' export declaration, and export packaging lists. To ensure that all required documentation is accurately completed and to minimize potential problems, firms entering the international market for the first time with an export order should consider using **freight forwarders** who are shipping agents and specialists in handling export documentation.

## Terms of Shipment and Sale

The responsibilities of the exporter, the importer, and the logistic provider should be spelled out in the export contract in terms of what is and what is not included in the price quotation and who owns title to the goods while in transit. **INCOTERMS 2000**,

---

[22]"AAEI Conference Highlights: How Microsoft, Philips Meet New Post-9/11 Compliance Requirements," *Managing Exports*, August 2004, pp. 1–4.

[23]Christie Schweinsberg and Sol Biderman, "China Aims to Rein in Auto Exports," *Ward's Auto World*, November 2006, pp. 34–34.

[24]Steve Toloken, "Toy Makers Reaping What They Have Sown," *Plastics News*, February 4, 2008, p. 6.

**EXHIBIT 16-4**

TERMS OF SHIPMENT

| | |
|---|---|
| **Ex-works** (EXW) at the point of origin | The exporter agrees to deliver the goods at the disposal of the buyer to the specified place on the specified date or within a fixed period. All other charges are borne by the buyer. |
| **Free Alongside Ship** (FAS) at a named port of export | Title and risk pass to buyer including payment of all transportation and insurance cost once delivered alongside ship by the seller. Used for sea or inland waterway transportation. The export clearance obligation rests with the seller. |
| **Free on Board** (FOB) at a named port of export | The exporter undertakes to load the goods on the vessel to be used for ocean transportation and the price quoted by the exporter reflects this cost. |
| **Free Carrier** (FCA) at a named place | It is mainly quoted for air transport and multimodal transport; the pricing conditions are very similar to those of FOB. |
| **Cost and Freight** (CFR) to a named overseas port of disembarkation | The exporter quotes a price for the goods including the cost of transportation to a named overseas port of disembarkation. The cost of insurance and the choice of the insurer are left to the importer. |
| **Carriage Paid To** (CPT) at named place of destination | It is mainly quoted for air transport and multimodal transport; the pricing conditions are very similar to those of CFR. |
| **Cost, Insurance and Freight** (CIF) to a named overseas port of disembarkation | The exporter quotes a price including insurance and all transportation and miscellaneous charges to the port of disembarkation from the ship. CIF costs are influenced by port charges (unloading, wharfage, storage, heavy lift, demurrage), documentation charges (certification of invoice, certification of origin, weight certificate) and other miscellaneous charges (fees of freight forwarder, insurance premiums) |
| **Carriage and Insurance Paid To** (CIP) at named place of destination | It is mainly quoted for air transport and multimodal transport; the pricing conditions are very similar to those of CIF. |
| **Delivery Duty Paid** (DDP) to an overseas buyer's premises | The exporter delivers the goods with import duties paid including inland transportation from the docks to the importer's premises |

which went into effect on January 1, 2000 and is an acronym for International Commercial Terms, are the internationally accepted standard definitions for the terms of sale by the International Chamber of Commerce.[25] The commonly used terms of shipment are summarized in **Exhibit 16-4**.

The terms of shipment used in the export transaction and their acceptance by the parties involved are important to prevent subsequent disputes. These terms of shipment also have significant implications on costing and pricing. The exporter should therefore learn what terms of shipment importers prefer in a particular market and what the specific transaction requires. A CIF quote by an exporter clearly shows the importer the cost to get the product to a port in a desired country. An inexperienced importer may be discouraged by an EXW quote because the importer may not know how much the EXW quote translates in terms of landed cost at home.

**Payment Terms**

The financing and payments of an export transaction constitute the third set of things to do with regard to an export transaction. For example, is export credit available from an Export-Import Bank (discussed later in the chapter) or a local agency supporting exports? What payment terms have been agreed on? Customary payment terms for noncapital goods transactions include advance payment, confirmed irrevocable letter of credit, unconfirmed irrevocable letter of credit, documents against payment (D/P), documents against acceptance (D/A), open account, and consignment basis payments. These terms are explained in **Exhibit 16-5**. The terms of payment between the exporter and the importer are a matter of negotiation and depend on a variety of factors including the buyer's credit standing, the amount of the sale transaction, the availability of foreign exchange in the buyer's country, the exchange control laws in the buyer's

---

[25]http://www.iccwbo.org/incoterms, accessed August 10, 2009.

**EXHIBIT 16-5**
TERMS OF PAYMENT IN AN EXPORT TRANSACTION

| | |
|---|---|
| **Advance Payment** | An importer pays exporter first; an exporter sends goods afterwards. |
| **Confirmed irrevocable letter of credit** | A letter of credit issued by the importer's bank and confirmed by a bank usually in the exporter's country. The obligation of the second bank is added to the obligation of the issuing bank to honor drafts presented in accordance with the terms of credit. |
| **Unconfirmed irrevocable letter of credit** | A letter of credit issued by the importer's bank. The issuing bank still has an obligation to pay. |
| **Documents against payment (D/P)** | An importer pays bills and obtains documents and then goods. Therefore, the exporter retains control of the goods until payment. |
| **Documents against acceptance (D/A)** | An importer accepts bills to be paid on due date and obtains documents and then goods. Therefore, the exporter gains a potentially negotiable financial instrument in the form of a document pledging payment within a certain time period. |
| **Open account** | No draft drawn. Transaction payable when specified on invoice |
| **Consignment** | A shipment that is held by the importer until the merchandise has been sold, at which time payment is made to the exporter. |

*Sources:* Lakshman Y. Wickremeratne, *ICC Guide to Collection Operations: For the ICC Uniform Rules for Collections,* (URC 522) (Paris, International Chamber of Commerce, 1996), pp. 22–26; and "Documentary Collections DC Payment Terms Offer Intermediate Level of Risk for International Collections," *Managing Exports*, December 2002, pp. 4–5.

country, the risks associated with the type of merchandise to be shipped, the usual practice in the trade, and market conditions (i.e., a buyer's market or a seller's market and payment terms offered by competitors).

When negotiating payment terms with an importer, an exporter must consider the risks associated with the importer and the importer's country, including credit risks, foreign exchange risks, transfer risks, and the political risks of the importer's country. **Credit risk** is the risk that the importer will not pay or will fail to pay on the agreed terms. The exporter must consider this risk. **Foreign exchange risk** exists when the sale is in the importer's currency and that currency can depreciate in terms of the home currency, leaving the exporter with less in the home currency.[26] **Transfer risk** refers to the chances that payment will not be made due to the importer's inability to obtain foreign currency (usually, U.S. dollars) and transfer it to the exporter. **Political risk** refers to the risks associated with war, confiscation of the importer's business, and other unexpected political events.

If an exporter sells for cash, there is virtually no risk. The possible nominal risk is associated with the timing of the order, as compared to the receipt of payment. A sale on a **confirmed irrevocable letter of credit** has slightly more risk. The confirmation places a home bank or other known bank acceptable to the seller; the payment risk assumed by the exporter devolves almost completely to this bank. If the sale is in a foreign currency, the exporter is still exposed to the risk of depreciation of the foreign currency relative to the dollar. An **unconfirmed irrevocable letter of credit** exposes the exporter to the creditworthiness of the buyer's bank in the foreign country because the exporter's home bank is no longer guaranteeing payment. The exporter thus faces the additional risk of a change in the value of the foreign currency (if the sale is not in the exporter's home currency), the risk that the payment cannot be transferred to the exporter's

---

[26]A recent study shows that exporters who accept foreign currency as a medium of payment tend to sell a higher volume and have more satisfied customers (i.e., importers) but tend to have lower profit margins than those exporters who accept domestic currency. This is due probably to foreign exchange rate risk. For detail, see Saeed Samiee and Patrik Anckar, "Currency Choice in Industrial Pricing: A Cross-National Evaluation," *Journal of Marketing*, 62 (July 1998), pp. 112–27.

home bank, and the risk that the political conditions in the buyer's country will change to the exporter's detriment.

**Documents against payment** (D/P) and **documents against acceptance** (D/A) are an importer's IOUs, or promises to pay. These payment terms (D/P and D/A) are much less expensive and easier for both exporters and importers to use than securing letters of credit. D/P and D/A are employed widely around the world but are historically underutilized by U.S. exporters.[27] Exports on a D/P are paid for by an importer at the time it accepts the exporter's export documents. Exports on a D/A are paid for by an importer on the due date of bill. Relative to a sale on a letter of credit, D/P basis increases the payment risk in an export transaction because no financial institution such as a bank has assumed the risk of payment. A D/A further escalates the risk because the buyer, by "accepting the bill," will receive the title documents and can pick up the goods without payment. Finally, an **open account** sale has no evidence of debt (promissory note, draft, etc.) and the payment may be unenforceable. Usually, conducted only on the basis of an invoice, an open account transaction is recommended only after the exporter and the importer have established trust in their relationship.

**Currency Hedging**

The fourth task of an exporter is to arrange a foreign exchange cover transaction with the banker or through the firm's treasury in case there is a foreign exchange risk in the export transaction. Such arrangements include reversing the forward currency transaction if required and hedging the foreign exchange risk using derivative instruments in the foreign exchange markets, for example, currency options and futures. In general, customer-oriented exporters tend to use invoicing in foreign currency. Thus, currency hedging becomes all the more important to customer-oriented exporters.[28] When the exporter is receiving some currency other than its domestic currency, covering a trade transaction through forward sales, currency options, and currency futures enables the exporter to lock in the domestic currency value of the export transaction up to a year in the future, thus ensuring more certain cash flows and forecasting. Due care needs to be exercised in the use of currency hedging, because an unwary or uninformed firm can lose large amounts of money. (See Chapter 3 for detail.)

# ROLE OF THE GOVERNMENT IN PROMOTING EXPORTS[29]  ◆ ◆ ◆ ◆ ◆ ◆ ◆

Government export promotion activities generally comprise (1) export service programs (e.g., seminars for potential exporters, export counseling, how-to-export handbooks, and export financing) and (2) market development programs (e.g., dissemination of sales leads to local firms, participation in foreign trade shows, preparation of market analysis, and export news letters).[30] In addition, program efforts can be differentiated as to whether the intent is to provide informational or experiential knowledge. Informational knowledge typically is provided through "how-to" export assistance, workshops, and seminars, while experiential knowledge is imparted through the arrangement of foreign buyers' or trade missions, trade and catalog shows, or participation in international market research.

---

[27]"Documentary Collections DC Payment Terms Offer Intermediate Level of Risk for International Collections," *Managing Exports*, December 2002, pp. 4–5.

[28]Patrik Anckar and Saeed Samiee, "Customer-Oriented Invoicing in Exporting," *Industrial Marketing Management*, 29 (November 2000), pp. 507–20.

[29]This section draws from Esra F. Gencturk and Masaaki Kotabe, "The Effect of Export Assistance Program Usage on Export Performance: A Contingency Explanation," *Journal of International Marketing*, 9(2), 2001, 51–72.

[30]William C. Lesch, Abdolreza Eshghi, and Golpira S. Eshghi, "A Review of Export Promotion Programs in the Ten Largest Industrial States," in S. Tamer Cavusgil and Michael R. Czinkota, eds. *International Perspectives on Trade Promotion and Assistance* (New York: Quorum Books, 1990), pp. 25–37.

U.S. government-sponsored trade-show exhibits. The government is actively involved in export promotion.

As stated at the beginning of this chapter, export is an important source of economic growth and job creation. Furthermore, jobs that depend on trade pay between 13 to 18 percent more than the average wage. Therefore, government efforts to promote exports seem to make sense. Although exports may be considered a major engine of economic growth in the U.S. economy, many U.S. firms do not export. Many firms, particularly small- to medium-size ones, appear to have developed a fear of international market activities. Their management tends to see only the risks—informational gaps, unfamiliar conditions in markets, complicated domestic and foreign trade regulations, absence of trained middle managers for exporting, and lack of financial resources—rather than the opportunities that the international market can present. These very same firms, however, may well have unique competitive advantages to offer that may be highly useful in performing successfully in the international market.

For example, small- and medium-size firms can offer their customers short response times. If some special situation should arise, there is no need to wait for the "home office" to respond. Responses can be immediate, direct, and predictable to the customer, therefore providing precisely those competitive ingredients that increase stability in a business relationship and reduce risk and costs. These firms also can often customize their operations more easily. Procedures can be adapted more easily to the special needs of the customer or to local requirements. One could argue that in a world turning away from mass marketing and toward niche marketing, these capabilities may well make smaller-size firms the export champions of the future.

Through the **Export Enhancement Act** of 1992, the U.S. government announced the National Export Strategy, a strategic, coordinated effort to stimulate exports.[31] In pursuit of this objective, the International Trade Administration of the U.S. Department of Commerce has devoted a substantial amount of the tax dollars allocated to it to help U.S. firms export their goods and services. For instance, the Japan Export Information Center (JEIC), established in April 1991, is the primary contact point within the Department of Commerce for U.S. exporters seeking business counseling and commercial information necessary to succeed in the Japanese market. The JEIC's principal function is to provide guidance on doing business in Japan and information on market entry alternatives,

---

[31]Richard T. Hise, "Globe Trotting," *Marketing Management*, 6 (Fall 1997), pp. 50–58.

market data and research, product standards and testing requirements, intellectual property protection, tariffs, and non-tariff barriers. The Japanese External Trade Organization (JETRO), affiliated with Japan's Ministry of Economy, Trade and Industry has also in recent years switched from promoting Japanese exports to helping U.S. and other foreign companies export and invest in Japan. The new emphasis on import promotion is part of the Japanese government's broader strategy to pull more foreign business into Japan, particularly from small to mid-size companies. These efforts are also an attempt to chip away at Japan's trade surplus with the United States and hopefully encourage a greater balance of trade for the future.[32]

In the United States, the Department of Commerce (DOC) also has industry specialists and country specialists in Washington, D.C. The industry specialists are available to give exporters information on the current state of the exporter's products overseas; comment on marketing and sales strategies; inform on trade missions, trade shows, and other events; and give other counsel. The country specialists are available to give information on the target country, any current trade issues with the United States, customs and tariff information, insight on the business climate and culture, and any other information on a country required by the exporter. For example, Purafil, a company based in Doraville, Georgia, that produces a dry chemical filtration system, benefited handsomely by participating in a DOC-sponsored trade mission to the Middle East for the first time. As part of the trade mission, the DOC provided a venue for Purafil and other companies to network and establish business relationships with prospective clients. One area in which the DOC is particularly helpful is in establishing credibility for the company marketing overseas. As a result, Purafil has been able to increase exports to 60 percent of all its revenues.[33]

Similarly, the DOC's Commercial Service has developed *BuyUSA.com*, an e-marketplace with a worldwide network of offices and expertise. The service offers online access to U.S. trade specialists who can assist buyers and sellers with exporting issues. For example, J. D. Streett & Company, a small auto lubricant and antifreeze manufacturer based in Maryland Heights, Missouri, spent some $400 to list its products on BuyUSA.com, resulting in major sales to Vietnam in 60 days.[34] Clearly, the government helps exporters find business leads in foreign markets.

Other countries also develop governmental programs to promote exports. For example, China recently raised tax rebates for certain textile and garment exports to help producers cope with the paper-thin profit margins squeezed by the yuan's appreciation and higher costs. Export tax rebates for some textile and garment items, are increased by two percentage points to 13 percent from August 1, 2008. The country's textile and clothing exports rose 11.1 percent to US$81.7 billion in the first half of 2008 from a year earlier. The tax rebate aims to increase would ease pressure and help boost exports.[35] Some governments even proactively engage in attracting inward foreign direct investment in the hope that their countries could increase exports. For example, Argentina, home to one of Latin America's most educated workforces and modern telecommunications, has the potential to become one of the region's leading software exporters. Hoping to lure software makers, the Argentine government enacted a law in 2005, offering technology companies tax benefits. The law has helped draw commitments of new investments of $60 million over the next three years from Intel and Microsoft to develop software in Argentina. Software company executives have lauded Argentina as a potential software-producing leader.[36]

---

[32]Rosalind McLymont, "In an About Face, Japanese Group Provides Help to Foreign Exporters," *Journal of Commerce*, (April 19, 1999), p. 5A.

[33]"Clearing the Air," *Export America*, 3, September 2002, pp. 6–7.

[34]"Speeding to New Global Markets," *Export America*, 3, March 2002, p. 9.

[35]"China Increases Export Tax Rebates for Textile, Garment Product," *ChinaView*, July 31, 2008.

[36]"Argentina Has Potential to be Software Leader," *Reuters*, November 25, 2005.

**Export–Import Bank**

The **Export-Import Bank (Ex-Im Bank)** is an independent U.S. government agency that plays a crucial role in promoting exports helping finance the sale of U.S. exports primarily to emerging markets throughout the world by providing loans, guarantees and insurance. In fiscal year 2007, Ex-Im Bank of the United States authorized $12.6 billion in financing to support an estimated $16 billion of U.S. exports worldwide.[37] Ex-Im Bank is not an aid or development agency, but a government held corporation, managed by a board of directors consisting of a chairman, vice chairman and three additional board members. Members serve for staggered terms and are chosen and serve at the discretion of the president of the United States.

Ex-Im Bank is designed to supplement, but not compete with private capital. Ex-Im Bank has historically filled gaps created when the private sector is reluctant to engage in export financing. Ex-Im Bank 1) provides guarantees of *working capital loans* for U.S. exporters, 2) guarantees the *repayment of loans* or makes loans to foreign purchasers of U.S. goods and services, and 3) provides *credit insurance* against non-payment by foreign buyers for political or commercial risk. To carry out the U.S. government's strategy for continuing export growth, the Ex-Im Bank is focusing on critical areas such as emphasizing exports to developing countries, aggressively countering the trade subsidies of other governments, stimulating small business transactions, promoting the export of environmentally beneficial goods and services, and expanding project finance capabilities.

The Ex-Im Bank also helps large U.S. companies to win contracts for major infrastructure projects, especially in the emerging markets. For example, it approved two long-term loan guarantees totaling $57 million in 2002 to support the export by Siemens Transportation Systems Inc., Sacramento, CA, of $62 million of equipment for light rail mass transportation systems in two Venezuelan cities.[38]

The Ex-Im Bank is also combating the "trade distorting" loans of foreign governments through the aggressive use of its Tied Aid Capital Projects Fund. The idea is that the Ex-Im Bank is willing on a case-by-case basis to match foreign tied-aid offers that are commercially viable and pending to be able to preemptively counter a foreign tied-aid offer. For instance, if a highway project in China gets a bid from a European or Japanese consortium of firms that offer to give concessional aid for the project but stipulate that in return for the aid the Chinese should buy machinery and materials from suppliers to be specified by the Europeans (or the Japanese), a U.S. firm bidding for the same project can depend on being able to provide concessional financing through the resources of the Ex-Im Bank. In addition, the U.S. government is no longer shy about openly representing U.S. firms and about being powerful advocates on behalf of U.S. businesses. Cabinet secretaries in the U.S. government have led groups of top business executives to many emerging markets. Accompanying administration officials on foreign missions give business executives a chance to get acquainted with decision makers in foreign governments, which awarded many infrastructure projects. The U.S. government lobbied hard to obtain airplane orders for Boeing from Singapore Airlines, Cathay Pacific, and Saudia, all of which were being lobbied hard by the French government to buy from the Airbus–European consortium.

Critics may cavil at this active role of the U.S. government in promoting exports; however, if U.S. firms are to retain their position in existing markets and if they are to gain access to new markets, they must have the same facilities that are available to firms from other nations. The Export-Import Bank of China, the third largest official credit institution in the world, following Japan Bank for International Cooperation (JBIC) and Export-Import Bank of the United States, inaugurated its Paris office in 2005 which would serve all the French-speaking countries in Western Europe, Northern Europe, and Africa. The Paris office plays a key role in promoting the bank's official loan business on behalf of the Chinese government to French-speaking countries, those in

---

[37]The Annual Report of the Export Import Bank of USA, http://www.exim.gov, accessed September 21, 2008.

[38]Press Releases from Export-Import Bank's web site, www.exim.gov, accessed February 20, 2002.

Africa in particular, under favorable terms.[39] For this reason, the policy of advocacy on behalf of U.S. firms fighting to enter new markets or to retain existing markets is a cornerstone of the national export policy.

Other areas in which the government plays a role in promoting exports include the establishment and maintenance of foreign trade zones (FTZs) and the Export Trading Company Act of 1982.

***Foreign Trade Zone.*** As discussed in detail in Chapter 15, foreign trade zones (free trade zones) enable businesses to store, process, assemble, and display goods from abroad without paying a tariff. Once these goods leave the zone and enter the United States, they are charged a tariff, but not on the cost of assembly or profits. If the product is re-exported, no duties or tariffs apply. Thus, a U.S. firm can assemble foreign parts for a camera in a Florida FTZ and ship the finished cameras to Latin America without paying duty.

**Tariff Concessions**

***American Export Trading Company.*** The Export Trading Company Act of 1982 encourages businesses to join together and form export-trading companies. The act provides antitrust protection for joint exporting and permits banking institutions to own interests in these exporting ventures. This act makes it practical for small- and medium-size exporting firms to pool resources without the fear of antitrust persecution and inadequate capitalization. A bank may hold up to 100 percent stock in an export trading company and is exempted from the collateral requirements contained in the Federal Reserve Act for loans to its export trading company.[40]

Although the U.S. government has become earnest in promoting exports, it also takes a hand in regulating exports. The Foreign Corrupt Practices Act of 1977 (as amended in 1986) imposes jail terms and fines for overseas payoffs that seek to influence overseas government decisions, although payments to expedite events that are supposed to take place under local laws are no longer illegal. Many U.S. exporters, especially exporters of big-ticket items, believe that the Foreign Corrupt Practices Act provides an unfair advantage to exporters from Europe and Japan that have been able to make such payments and get tax write-offs for the payments under export expenses. In 1996, under newly agreed provisions of WTO, firms from other countries were no longer allowed to make such payments without incurring penalties, thus leveling the playing field somewhat for U.S. exporters. Under the Wassenaar Arrangement of 1995 (see Chapter 5), domestic laws also exist that restrict exports of security-sensitive technology such as sophisticated machine tools and encryption technology for computer software and hardware (see **Global Perspective 16-2**).

**Export Regulations**

Antitrust laws prevent U.S. firms from bidding jointly on major foreign projects. Human rights legislation and nuclear nonproliferation policies require that every year the federal government recertify the Normal Trade Relations (NTR)[41] status of major foreign trade partners (e.g., China). These are examples of the U.S. exporting its own rules to other nations under the aegis of WTO. To the extent that such actions result in the same rules for all nations engaging in international trade, such behavior benefits trade; however, such behavior can also be perceived as an infringement of national sovereignty by many nations.

Sometimes the actions of a foreign government can affect exports. These actions relate to tariffs and local laws relating to product standards and classification. For example, computer-networking equipment exported from the United States to the European Union is charged a 3.9 percent tariff. A recent EU ruling decided that computer

---

[39]"Export-Import Bank of China Opens Paris Office," *Peoples' Daily Online*, June 20, 2005.

[40]William W. Nye, "An Economic Profile of Export Trading Companies," Antitrust Bulletin, 38 (Summer 1993), pp. 309–25.

[41]See Chapter 2 for details.

## GLOBAL PERSPECTIVE 16-2

### EXPORT CONTROL IN THE UNITED STATES: THE BALANCING ACT BETWEEN FREE TRADE AND TIGHT SECURITY

Control of high-tech exports has been regulated under a continuing executive order since 1994 when the Export Administration Act (EAA) of 1979 expired. In the past several years, the technology industry has argued that the current export control regime is outmoded. Current export control rules use a performance rating called "millions of theoretical operations per second" (MTOPS) to determine which microprocessors and computers must apply for export licenses to certain countries. Computing power has become so prolific, however, that it is nearly impossible to regulate by using performance-based controls such as MTOPS.

Indeed, the federal government has had to race with the market over the past several years to keep export control regulations from barring the export of readily available, mass-market computers. For example, as recently as 1999, microprocessors with an MTOPS rating of 1,200 and computers with a rating of 2,000 were subject to controls. Those limits have been raised repeatedly over the past few years. The limits on chips apply to export to certain countries such as China and the former Soviet countries. The limits on computers apply to so-called Tier III countries, which include China, Russia, Israel, Pakistan, and India.

In 2001, key senators introduced the Export Administration Act of 2001, aimed at balancing competing priorities: free trade and tight security. The bill attempted a narrower, more surgical application of controls on dual-use items—commercial exports

in aerospace, computers, encryption and machine tools that could be diverted to military use by overseas companies or countries. The bill would stiffen fines and prison terms for violators, both individual and corporate, in an attempt to bolster control of advanced technologies that are less widely dispersed. The bill also contained a provision that would eliminate the requirement that computer export controls be based on MTOPS levels. The House of Representatives was unable, however, to pass a similar bill.

The failure of Congress to enact a new EAA requires the president to continue to use his authority under the International Economic Emergency Powers Act (IEEPA) to regulate export controls. The Department of Commerce is currently working to establish a new metric to replace the MTOPS standard for high-performance computers. Meanwhile, the Bush Administration raised the MTOPS limit on computers from 85,000 to 190,000 MTOPS in March 2002. This rating would allow for the export of multi-processor servers with up to 32 Intel Itanium CPUs.

Since the September 11 terrorist attacks, U.S. companies have had to adjust to new export control challenges because license applications take longer, are rejected more often, and require more backup information. Microsoft, for instance, has outsourced certain export functions through partnering to achieve export efficiency in all processes. Furthermore, the company has implemented the SAP GTS system to conduct a country-screening process. Currently, Microsoft is proactively partnering with the U.S. government to secure global supply chains by participating in the C-TPAT (customers-Trade partnership Against Terrorism) program. Evidently, Microsoft is not the only company that has to adjust to the post 9/11 export paradigm shift.

*Sources:* Tam Harbert, "One Step Forward on Export Control," *Electronic Business*, March 2002, p. 36; "AAEI Conference Highlights: How Microsoft, Philips Meet New Post–9/11 Compliance Requirements," *Managing Exports & Imports*, August 2004, pp. 1–4; and "OEE 2005 Enforcement Actions and Fines Expected to Easily Surpass 2005," *Managing Exports & Imports*, May 2005, p. 8.

---

networking equipment (e.g., adapters, routers, and switches) do not crunch data but transport them and so should be classified as telecommunication equipment. Telecommunication equipment, however, carries a higher tariff rate of 7.5 percent, increasing the landed price of these products in Europe.[42] Such actions by foreign governments are usually attempts to provide protection to local industry.

Finally, a government could tax exports with the purpose of satisfying domestic demand first or of taking advantage of higher world prices. For example, in 1998, two typhoons damaged trees in the northern Philippines, stripping away mature coconuts. Coconut oil shipments during the fourth quarter of 1998 were 60 percent below their normal level. The coconut oil market continued to face production declines and the threat of higher prices and Indonesia, the second largest producer, continued to impose

---

[42] "Europe's Computer Networking Tariffs May Lead to U.S. Complaint to WTO," *Wall Street Journal* (May 1, 1996), p. B7.

high export duties on coconut oil.[43] The goal of such measures was to curb exports and try to keep a lid on internal food industry costs as coconut oil prices soared. Similarly, a government could devise a mechanism by which to enforce collection of sales and/or value added tax owed by customers abroad. For instance, Australian exporters like Seawind International are influenced by the export regulations in Australia. One example is that Australian Tax Office will not allow buyers located in foreign countries to take delivery of their boat and cruise for months before shipping the boat home unless they pay value-added tax.[44]

## MANAGING IMPORTS—THE OTHER SIDE OF THE COIN ◆ ◆ ◆ ◆ ◆ ◆ ◆

So far the chapter has been devoted exclusively to exports, and we now turn to imports. For organizations in the United States importing is considerably easier than for most firms in the rest of the world. One of the primary reasons for this is the fact that unlike importers in most of the rest of the world, U.S. importers can pay the seller abroad in their own currency—the U.S. dollar—because the U.S. dollar is an internationally accepted denomination of exchange. Thus, unlike importers in Brazil or Indonesia who must find U.S. dollars (or other hard currencies) to pay for imports, an importer in the United States can manage by shelling out U.S. dollars. About 60 percent of the world's trade is still denominated in U.S. dollars; exporters want dollars in return for the goods or services sold.

However, denomination of trade in dollars is changing, especially in Europe, where the euro has emerged as the currency in which trade is denominated. Most of the time, therefore, a U.S. importer does not have to bother to hedge foreign exchange transactions or try to accumulate foreign currency to pay for imports. On occasion, a U.S. importer does not even need a letter of credit. This same advantage has become available to the European Union (EU) member countries. EU member countries are now able to pay in euro for their imports from other member countries. Similarly, in Asia the Japanese yen is emerging as the currency in which trade is denominated. Japan benefits from this on a more limited geographical basis. Japan is now able to pay in Japanese yen for much of its imports from Southeast Asia.

This is not to suggest that a firm can import anything for sale in the United States. There are restrictions on trade with countries such as Iran, Libya, Iraq, and Cuba. Iran and Libya are thought to be supporters of state-sponsored terrorism. The United States has been at war with Iraq (at the time of this writing), and Cuba has been a pariah for the United States since 1959. The same restrictions exist with respect to North Korea since the Korean War that ended in 1953. Production and marketing considerations also limit what can be imported and sold profitably in the United States. For soaps and cosmetics, for example, the demand for imports is minimal. However, the United States is a surplus producer of many categories of goods including aircraft, defense equipment, medical electronics, computer software, and agricultural goods.

Importing any good is thus predicated upon the existence of a situation in which the domestic production of the good in question is not sufficient to satisfy demand. For example, annual sales of cut flowers in the U.S. is nearly $10 billion, but domestic production meets only about 30 percent of the demand, with Americans purchasing flowers not just for special occasions but also for sending messages, as a token of friendship, as a get-well wish, or just to convey "have a nice day" to someone. Imports of cut flowers are primarily from Colombia, Mexico, Costa Rica, Ecuador, Peru, and Kenya.[45] The

---

[43]Jim Papanikolaw, "Coconut Oil Market Tightens because of Bad Weather in 1998," *Chemical Market Reporter*, (January 25, 1999), p. 8.
[44]" . . . But GST Puts a Damper on Exports," *Manufacturers' Monthly*, December 2007, p. 18.
[45]"Say it with Flowers," *New Statesman*, February 16, 2004, pp. 22–23.

**EXHIBIT 16-6**
MODEL OF IMPORTER BUYER BEHAVIOR

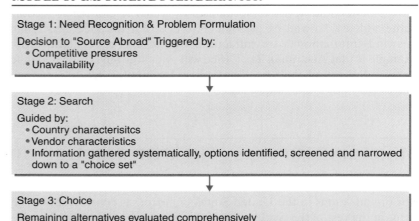

Stage 1: Need Recognition & Problem Formulation

Decision to "Source Abroad" Triggered by:
• Competitive pressures
• Unavailability

Stage 2: Search

Guided by:
• Country characterisitcs
• Vendor characteristics
• Information gathered systematically, options identified, screened and narrowed down to a "choice set"

Stage 3: Choice

Remaining alternatives evaluated comprehensively
• Compensatory process used to evaluate remaining vendors
• Highest ranked overseas vendor(s) selected

*Source:* Neng Liang and Rodney L. Stump, "Judgmental Heuristics in Overseas Vendor Search and Evaluation: A Proposed Model of Importer Buyer Behavior," *International Executive*, Copyright (November, 1996), pp. 779–806. Reprinted by permission of John Wiley & Sons, Inc.

imported flowers must satisfy the selective U.S. consumer and must comply with the U.S. Plant Protection Quarantine Inspection Program and antidumping regulations. Because the product is highly perishable, air transportation and rapid transit through customs must be ensured. Thus, the importer of flowers has to go through many hoops to locate a reliable seller and arrange the logistics. Importer behavior will, of course, depend on the category of goods being purchased abroad.

However, importer buyer behavior is a relatively under-researched area in the field of international trade partly because most nations are more interested in maximizing exports rather than imports, and restricting imports is relatively simple as compared to being a successful exporter. The most important of the organizational buying models is the BuyGrid model.[46] Besides elaborating on how the purchasing process evolves and highlighting the role of buyers' search in choice decisions, this framework was the first to categorize buy decisions as (1) straight buys, (2) modified rebuy, and (3) new tasks.

Although this framework was developed primarily for domestic purchases, it is applicable to import decisions as well. Applying the framework for an import decision and taking into account the increased uncertainty in international markets would translate into a procedure presented in **Exhibit 16-6**. This sequence of actions in an import situation appears logical, as it does for exports, but many international supplier relationships start with an "unsolicited export order" in which importers place an order with a selected foreign vendor without any systematic vendor search and evaluation. The lack of a systematic approach to vendor identification and evaluation can stem from a difficulty in accessing all relevant information and from the idea of bounded rationality—the notion that, due to limited cognitive abilities, humans tend to satisfy, not optimize. Thus, given the information available, which cannot be complete, managers will not be able to make the best decision.[47]

---

[46]Patrick J. Robinson, Charles W. Faris, and Yoram Wind, *Industrial Buying and Creative Marketing*, (Boston: Allyn and Bacon, 1967).

[47]Neng Liang and Rodney L. Stump, "Judgmental Heuristics in Overseas Vendor Search and Evaluation: A Proposed Model of Importer Buyer Behavior," *International Executive*, 38 (November/December 1996), pp. 779–806.

# MECHANICS OF IMPORTING

An import transaction is like looking at an export transaction from the other end of the transaction. Instead of an exporter looking for a prospective buyer, an importer looks for an overseas firm that can supply it the raw materials, components, or finished products that it needs for its business. Once an importer locates a suitable overseas exporter, it negotiates with the exporter the terms of the sale including, but not restricted to the following:

- Finding a bank that either has branches in the exporter's country or has correspondent bank located in the exporter's country and establishing a line of credit with the bank if this has not already been done.
- Establishing a letter of credit with a bank stating the terms of payment and how payment is to be made. This includes terms of clearing the goods from the docks/customs warehouse (sometimes with title for goods going temporarily to the bank), insurance coverage, terms of transfer of title, and so on.
- Deciding on the mode of transfer of goods from exporter to importer and transfer of funds from importer to exporter. Transportation partly provides proof of delivery to the exporter's bank or the exporter. The exporter (or its bank) presents the proof of delivery to the importer's bank (branch in importer's own country/correspondent bank). The importer's bank transfers funds to the exporter's bank and simultaneously debits the importer's account or presents a demand draft to the importer.
- Checking compliance with national laws of the importing country and the exporting country. Import restrictions into the U.S. include quotas on automobiles, textiles and steel and quarantine checks on food products as well as a ban on imports from Cuba, North Korea, and Iran.
- Making allowances for foreign exchange fluctuations by making covering transactions through the bank so that the dollar liability for the importer either remains fixed or decreases.
- Fixing liability for payment of import duties and demurrage and warehousing in case the goods are delayed due to congestion at ports. These payments are normally the responsibility of the importer.

An examination of these mechanics of an import transaction reveals that the transaction is materially the same as an export transaction. The differences that are of interest to managers involved in the import of goods into the United States include these:

- A difference in risk profile, meaning that an exporter faces the risk of receiving no payment due to a variety of factors, whereas nonpayment is not an issue in imports. However, the quality of goods and services imported can be an issue for imports, but this is not usually an issue in exports.
- The facility of being able to pay in its own currency (most of the time), which is not available to importers in almost any other country.
- Everything else being equal, the ease for a U.S. firm to import rather than to export because of the primacy of the U.S. dollar despite the gradual depreciation of the U.S. dollar over time.

**Import Documents and Delivery**

When a shipment reaches the United States, the consignee (normally the importer) files entry documents with the port director at the port of entry. The bill of lading properly endorsed by the consignor in favor of the consignee serves as the evidence of the right to make entry. The entry documents also include an entry manifest, Customs Form 7533, Customs Form 3461, packing lists if appropriate, and the commercial invoice. The entry should be accompanied by evidence that a bond is posted with customs to cover any potential duties, taxes, and penalties that may accrue. A **bond** is a guarantee by someone that the duties and any potential penalties will be paid to the customs of the importing country. In the event that a custom broker is employed for the purpose of making entry, the broker can permit the use of the bond to provide the required coverage.

Entry can be for immediate delivery, for ordinary delivery, or for a warehouse, or it can be not entered for a period of time. Merchandise arriving from Canada and Mexico, trade fair goods, perishable goods and shipments assigned to the U.S. government almost always utilize the **Special Permit for Immediate Delivery** on Customs Form 3461 prior to the arrival of the goods to enable fast release after arrival. An entry summary must be filed within 10 days of the release of the goods. Imported goods coming in under ordinary delivery use normal channels including Form 7533. Under warehousing, goods are placed in a custom-bonded warehouse if it is desired that the entry of the imported goods be delayed. The goods can remain in a bonded warehouse for a period of five years. At any time during the period warehoused goods may be re-exported without payment of duty or may be withdrawn for consumption upon the payment of duty. If the importer fails to enter the goods at the port of entry or the port of destination within five working days after arrival, they may be placed in the general warehouse at the risk and expense of the importer.

**Import Duties**

Import duties that have to be paid are ad valorem, specific, or compound. An **ad valorem duty**, which is applied most frequently, is a percentage of the value of the merchandise, such as 5 percent ad valorem. Thus, an auto shipment worth $100 million that has an ad valorem rate of 3.9 percent will pay $3.9 million as customs duty. A **specific duty** rate is a specified amount per unit of weight or other quantity, such as 5.1 cents per dozen, 20 cents per barrel or 90 cents per ton. A **compound duty** rate is a combination of an ad valorem rate and a specific rate, such as 0.7 cents per kilogram plus 10 percent as valorem. Average import duty rates in Japan (3.4%), the United States (5.2%), and the European Union (7.7%) are relatively low compared to those in many other countries (e.g., Mexico with 18.0%),[48] but used to be much higher. After the Uruguay Round, the major global trade negotiations from 1986 to 1994, developed countries—the most important buyers of developing countries' exports—were opening their markets further. Their import duties for industrial products fell from 6.3 percent on average before the Uruguay Round to 3.8 percent afterward. Also due to the Uruguay Round, significantly more products exported to developed countries will enjoy zero import duties. The entry of imported merchandise into a foreign country is complete after customs clears the goods from the port of entry or the port of destination.

**Antidumping import duties** are assessed on imported merchandise sold to importers in a foreign country at a price that is less than the fair market value. The fair market value of merchandise is defined under articles of the World Trade Organization as the price at which the good is normally sold in the manufacturer's home market. In the United States, countervailing duties are assessed for some imported goods to counter the effects of subsidies provided by foreign governments, because without the **countervailing duty** the price of these imported goods in the U.S. market would be artificially low, causing economic injury to U.S. manufacturers.

The U.S. importer could even avoid payment of import duties by applying for a **duty-drawback** refund under Temporary Importation under Bond (TIB) in the United States. A duty drawback is a refund of up to 99 percent of all ordinary customs duties. It can be a direct identification drawback or a substitution drawback. *Direct identification drawback* provides a refund of duties paid on imported merchandise that is partially or totally used within five years of the date of import in the manufacture of an article that is exported. *Substitution drawback* provides a refund of duties paid on designated imported merchandise upon exportation of articles manufactured or produced with the use of substituted domestic or imported merchandise that is of the same quality as the

---

[48]"Trends in Market Openness," *OECD Economic Outlook*, 65 (June 1999), pp. 207–21.

designated import merchandise.[49] All countries have procedures allowing for the temporary importation of goods for across their borders.[50]

As explained in Chapter 15, importing firms can also utilize foreign trade zones profitably. They can set up facilities in an FTZ to import finished goods, component parts, or raw materials for the eventual domestic consumption or import of merchandise that is frequently delayed by customs quota delays or import merchandise that must be processed, generating significant amounts of scrap. An important feature of foreign trade zones for foreign merchants entering the U.S. market is that the goods may be brought to the threshold of the market, making immediate delivery certain and avoiding the possible cancellation of orders due to shipping delays.

## GRAY MARKETS

◆ ◆ ◆ ◆ ◆ ◆ ◆

**Gray market** channels refer to the legal export/import transaction involving genuine products into a country by intermediaries other than the authorized distributors. From the importer's side, it is also known as a **parallel import**. Distributors, wholesalers, and retailers in a foreign market obtain the exporter's product from some other business entity. Thus, the exporter's legitimate distributor(s) and dealers face competition from others who sell the exporter's products at reduced prices in that foreign market. High-priced branded consumer goods (cameras, jewelry, perfumes, watches, and so on) whose production lies principally in one country are particularly prone to gray market imports. Brand reputation is a critical element in gray market goods exports, and the distribution is typically through exclusive wholesalers and distributors.[51]

In the information technology (IT) sector alone, gray market sales accounted for between 5 percent and 30 percent of total IT sales in 2007, with a value of about $58 billion, according to a new report by audit firm KPMG LLP and The Alliance for Gray Market and Counterfeit Abatement.[52] A study of manufacturers of health and beauty aids determined that gray market sales amounted to 20 percent of authorized sales in some markets and as much as 50 percent of authorized sales in others. The gray market problem is so serious that multinational companies such as Motorola, HP, DuPont and 3M devote full-time managers and staff to dealing with gray market issues.[53] Gray market is pervasive across all industries. For example, if purchased on the gray market, a $92,000 brand-new Mercedes-Benz SL55 AMG Convertible, which meets all U.S. safety and pollution control requirements, can be purchased for 20 percent less than the price ($114,580) charged by the local authorized dealer. Similarly, in the luxury boat market, many foreign dealers of U.S. manufacturers are seriously affected by gray market activity. To avoid higher prices abroad, foreign retailers too often come to the United States and purchase their boat from a U.S. dealer, and then arrange their own transportation, circumventing the licensed dealer in their own home country.[54]

---

[49]Michael V. Cerny, "More Firms Establish Drawback Programs as $1.5B Goes Unclaimed." *Managing Exports*, (October 2002): pp. 1–6.

[50]Lara L. Sowinski, "Going Global in a Flash," *World Trade*, 18 (August 2005), pp. 28–32.

[51]This section draws from Dale F. Duhan and Mary Jane Sheffet, "Gray Markets and the Legal Status of Parallel Importation," *Journal of Marketing*, 52 (July 1988), pp. 75–83; Tunga Kiyak, "International Gray Markets: A Systematic Analysis and Research Propositions," A paper presented at 1997 AMA Summer Educators' Conference, August 2–5, 1997; and Michael R. Mullen, C. M. Sashi and Patricia M. Doney, "Gray Markets: Threats or Opportunity? The Case of Herman Miler vs. Asal GMBH," in Tiger Li & Tamer S. Cavusgil, ed., *Reviving Traditions in Research on International Market*, Greenwich, CT: JAI Press, 2003.

[52]Scott Campbell, "Gray Matter," *VARbusiness*, July 28, 2008, p. 11.

[53]Kersi D. Antia, Mark Bergen, and Shantanu Dutta, "Competing with Gray Markets," *Sloan Management Review*, 46 (Fall 2004), pp. 63–69.

[54]Frank Reynolds, "Senior Management Apathy Could Sink U.S. Pleasure Boat Exports," *Journal of Commerce*, (March 24, 1999), p. 9A.

Although gray market products look similar to their domestic counterparts, they could not be identical and not carry full warranties. Nevertheless, the volume of gray market activities is significant. Three conditions are necessary for gray markets to develop. *First*, the products must be available in other markets. In today's global markets, this condition is readily met. *Second*, trade barriers such as tariffs, transportation costs, and legal restrictions must be low enough for parallel importers to move the products from one market to another. Again, under the WTO principles, the trade barriers have been reduced so low that parallel importation has become feasible. *Third*, price differentials among various markets must be great enough to provide the basic motivation for gray marketers. Such price differences arise for various reasons, including currency exchange rate fluctuations, differences in demand, legal differences, opportunistic behavior, segmentation strategies employed by international marketing managers, and more recently, the World Wide Web's information transparency.

- **Currency fluctuations.** The fluctuating currency exchange rates among countries often produce large differences in prices for products across national boundaries. Gray marketers can take advantage of changes in exchange rates by purchasing products in markets with weak currencies and selling them in markets with strong currencies.

- **Differences in market demand.** Similarly, price differences can be caused by differences in market demand for a product in various markets. If the authorized channels of distribution cannot adjust the market supply to meet the market demand, a large enough price difference could develop for unauthorized dealers to engage in arbitrage process, that is, buying the product inexpensively in countries with weak demand and selling it profitably in countries with strong demand. For example, Apple Corp.'s international marketing strategy of 3G iPhone attempts to extract different prices from different countries—the situation is more attractive as iPhones become a better value to Asian gray-market entrepreneurs[55] (see **Global Perspective 16-3**).

- **Legal differences.** Different prices across different markets due to different legal systems similarly motivate gray marketing activities. For example, as explained in Chapter 5, copyright protection lasts only 50 years in the European Union and Japan compared with 95 years in the United States. In other words, even if the music recordings were originally made and released in the United States, the recordings made in the early- to mid-1950s by such figures as Elvis Presley and Ella Fitzgerald are entering the public domain in Europe, opening the way for any European recording company to release albums that had been owned exclusively by particular labels. Although the distribution of such albums would be usually limited to Europe, CD-store chains and specialty outlets in the United States routinely stock cheaper foreign imports via gray markets.[56]

- **Opportunistic behavior.** Opportunistic behavior by distributors tends to occur when the distributor's gross margin is disproportionately large relative to the marketing task performed and is particularly attractive if the transaction occurs outside the distributor's assigned territory. For example, if the sale takes place in a neighboring foreign country (i.e., outside the territory), the opportunistic distributor could lower the selling price in that market because the sale is not made at the expense of the distributor's own full markup sales in its domestic market. In other words, this opportunistic behavior typifies the attitude, "somebody else's problem is not my problem."

- **Segmentation strategy.** Although currency exchange rates and differences in market demand could be beyond the control of international marketing managers, segmentation strategy can result in 1) planned price discrimination and 2) planned product differentiation among various markets. Even for an identical product, different

---

[55]Mark Ritson, "iPhone Strategy: No Longer a Grey Area," *Marketing*, June 11, 2008, p. 21.

[56]"Companies in U.S. Sing Blues As Europe Reprises 50's Hits," *New York Times*, January 3, 2003, Late Edition, p. A1.

## GLOBAL PERSPECTIVE 16-3

### ACCOUNTING FOR iPHONE GRAY MARKETS

Apple created a fad for iPhone from the very beginning. However, unfortunately, a large part of the handsets sales come from gray markets. Why?

When it was launched in the United States in 2007, the iPhone was locked into the AT&T network. The only way to own one was by signing a contract with the carrier. The deal gave AT&T exclusive rights to the handset, and ensured that Apple could maintain premium prices and receive an unprecedented 15 percent of the operator's revenues from each user. Apple repeated the arrangement with O2 in the UK and Orange in France. But this groundbreaking strategy also created the perfect conditions for a gray market. This middle ground, between a brand's official "white" sales channels and the clearly illegal black market in counterfeit or stolen goods, offers genuine products through non-official channels.

Within hours of launch, the internet was awash with offers of unlocked iPhones that would work with any SIM. Apple had a goal of selling 10 million iPhones by the end of 2008. While gray-market sales count in the tally, the loss of subsequent share of sales from network usage on the approved mobile network could cost Apple up to $500 million in lost revenues. If only taking sales into consideration, it is estimated that a quarter of the 5 million iPhones sold to date have been through the gray market—more than four times the number officially sold in Europe. But it is not surprising when you review the factors that turned the iPhone into the perfect gray-market product.

First, there was Apple's attempt to maintain exclusivity. Using a single operator in each market ensured maximum

control of the offer to the consumer, but it also increased the potential for gray-market activity. The more control a company tries to exert over the way its brand is retailed, the more likely gray markets are to emerge.

Second, the product's international rollout was also a factor. The company wanted to stagger the launch, partly because of the limited number of handsets that were initially made available to consumers and partly to maximize the impact in each country. With today's global markets, however, it is almost impossible to prevent consumers in one market from accessing a product in another.

Third, Apple's international marketing strategy also attempted to extract different prices from different countries. Again, this makes sense in theory, but gray markets flourish in the spaces between different prices. The currency fluctuations of the past 12 months made this situation even more attractive as iPhones became a better value to Asian gray-market entrepreneurs, who were buying them in U.S. dollars but selling them on in Chinese Yuan.

Fourth, Apple also encouraged the gray market by using multiple retail channels. If it had allowed consumers to buy the phone only through operator channels, where a fixed 18-month contract would have been a stipulation for purchase, the gray market would have been restricted.

So why did Apple insist that its stores would also sell the iPhone, thus enabling consumers to get the handset without an operator contract? The straightforward answer is that Apple wanted to showcase the sexy new phone in its own stores to drive sales and ensure brand consistency. The more suspicious marketer might also suggest that it wanted a bit of gray-market action to boost sales and spread its super-cool, premium status around the world.

*Source:* Mark Ritson, "iPhone Strategy: No Longer A Grey Area," *Marketing*, June 11, 2008, p. 21.

---

pricing strategy can be adopted for various reasons, including differences in product life cycle stage, customer purchase behavior, and price elasticity across different markets. Different prices across different markets motivate gray marketers to exploit the price differences among the markets.

• **The World Wide Web.** As an information medium, the World Wide Web raises a customer's awareness of special offers that were initially designed to be limited to specific regions, countries, or classes of customers. Gray-market sales are growing with the popularity of the internet. Web-based gray marketers can also advertise merely by using the product's brand name or model number on their web sites and waiting for search engines to direct consumers there. The internet greatly stimulates gray market activity by presenting different price quotations from multiple merchants. Gray marketers can pay for presence on shopping bots, such as mysimon.com, cnet.com, shopping.yahoo.com, or bottomdollar.com, as well as amazon.com and eBay.com. If you look closely at Amazon's website, you will see that the site sells Seiko (not authorized Seiko retailers) at or below dealer cost. If you click the SAS (Southern Audio Services) name on eBay (not authorized SAS retailers), it will come up thousands of times and sell SAS at 30 percent discounts or more. The explosion of unauthorized e-commerce has hit many sectors, including pharmaceuticals, electronics, and software.[57]

Alternatively, the product can be modified to address the specific needs of different markets. Contradictory to common sense, adaptation of individual products for a specific market also leads to substantially more gray marketing. This occurs for two reasons. First, when, for example, a stripped version of the product is marketed in Europe and an enhanced version is marketed in the United States, some U.S. consumers, who may not be willing to pay for the enhanced model with too many refinements, import the simpler, less expensive version from an unauthorized distributor through a gray marketing channel. Second, some consumers simply want to purchase the product models that are not available in their domestic markets to differentiate themselves from the rest of the consumers. This is increasingly likely as markets around the world become more homogeneous.[58]

Gray marketing activity can also bring about some beneficial effect to manufacturers. Parallel channels foster intrabrand competition that can force authorized channels to do a better job serving their local customers and lead to improved customer satisfaction. It is conceivable that manufacturers can add gray marketers to the authorized channel or even acquire them, provided that such actions do not lead to increased conflict with existing authorized distributors. In industries with high fixed costs where capacity utilization and economies of scale are important, manufacturers may require the incremental sales generated by parallel channels to sustain high production volumes.[59]

A key question for the manufacturer of branded products is whether a gray market will cause a global strategy to become less desirable. Closer control and monitoring of international marketing efforts can certainly reduce the threat of gray market goods to negligible levels. As rule of thumb, firms using independent distributors (e.g., commission agents and merchant distributors) tend to suffer most from gray-market activity while firms with ownership-based control over distribution channels (e.g., joint venture partners, wholly owned subsidiaries, and direct sale of exports to end users) offer more control over the final sale of the product.[60] As presented in **Exhibit 16-7**, international marketers not only try to confront existing gray markets reactively but also are increasingly developing more proactive approaches to gray market problems before they arise.

Cisco decided to offer discounts to combat gray market providers, in an effort to win back sales from small and medium-sized businesses. Although gray market products have been on sale for some time, the networking company's popularity among smaller businesses was starting to affect its revenues. To appeal to smaller businesses, Cisco launched products targeted at companies with fewer than 100 users, and it would be working with its official Select resellers to offer discounts. The company also plans to push its Cisco Certified Refurbished Equipment mark to help differentiate products.[61] In a similar vein, Hyundai dealers in Germany created a trading company. The company would help Hyundai's German dealers buy the brand's cars in low-cost European Union (EU) countries for resale in Germany. The move aims to beat reimporters, who exploit price differences within the EU by purchasing vehicles in low-price countries and reselling them in high-price countries.[62]

---

[57]Steven Sagri, "Don't Give Press Play to Amazon's 'Gray Market' Watch Sales," *National Jeweler*, June 2007, p. 18; and Mina Kimes, "How Middlemen Can Discredit Your Goods," *FSB: Fortune Small Business*, May 2008, pp. 75–78.

[58]Matthew B. Myers, "Incidents of Gray Market Activity among U.S. Exporters: Occurrences, Characteristics, and Consequences," *Journal of International Business Studies*, 30 (First Quarter 1999), pp. 10–126.

[59]Michael R. Mullen, C. M. Sashi, and Patricia M. Doney, "Gray Markets: Threats or Opportunity? The Case of Herman Miller vs. Asal GMBH," in Tiger Li & Tamer S. Cavusgil, ed., *Advances in International Marketing*, Greenwich, CT: JAI Press, 2003, pp. 77–105.

[60]Ibid.

[61]John-Paul Kamath, "Cisco Plans Discounts to Win Back SME Users," *Computer Weekly*, April 17, 2007, p. 40.

[62]Bettina John, "Hyundai's German Dealers Aim to Stop Gray-Market Sales," *Automotive News Europe*, April 16, 2007, p. 8.

# EXHIBIT 16-7

## HOW TO COMBAT GRAY MARKET ACTIVITY

*A. Reactive Strategies to Combat Gray Market Activity*

| Type of Strategy | Implemented by | Cost of Implementation | Difficulty of Implementation | Does It Curtail Gray Market Activity at Source? | What Relief Does It Provide Authorized Dealers? | Long-Term Effectiveness | Legal Risks to Manufacturers or Dealers | Company Examples |
|---|---|---|---|---|---|---|---|---|
| Strategic confrontation | Dealer with manufacturer support | Moderate | Requires planning | No | Relief in the medium term | Effective | Low | Creative merchandising by Caterpillar and auto dealers |
| Participation | Dealer | Low | Not difficult | No | Immediate relief | Potentially damaging reputation of manufacturer | Low | Dealers wishing to remain anonymous |
| Price cutting | Manufacturer and dealer jointly | Costly | Not difficult | No, if price cutting is temporary | Immediate relief | Effective | Moderate to high | Dealers and manufacturers remain anonymous |
| Supply interference | Either party | Moderate at the wholesale level; high at the retail level | Moderately difficult | No | Immediate relief or slightly delayed | Somewhat effective if at wholesale level; not effective at retail level | Moderate at wholesale level; low at retail | IBM; Hewlett-Packard; Lotus Corp.; Swatch Watch USA; Charles of the Ritz Group, Ltd.; Leitz, Inc; NEC Electronics |
| Promotion of gray market product limitations | Jointly, with manufacturer leadership | Moderate | Not difficult | No | Slightly delayed | Somewhat effective | Low | Komatsu, Seiko, Rolex, Mercedes-Benz IBM |
| Collaboration | Dealer | Low | Requires careful negotiations | No | Immediate relief | Somewhat effective | Very high | Dealers wishing to remain anonymous |
| Acquisition | Dealer | Very costly | Difficult | No | Immediate relief | Effective if other gray market brokers don't creep in | Moderate to high | No publicized cases |

*(continued)*

**EXHIBIT 16-7** (CONTINUED)

*B. Proactive Strategies to Combat Gray Market Activity*

| Type of Strategy | Implemented by | Cost of Implementation | Difficulty of Implementation | Does It Curtail Gray Market Activity at Source? | What Relief Does It Provide Authorized Dealers? | Long-Term Effectiveness | Legal Risks to Manufacturers or Dealers | Company Examples |
|---|---|---|---|---|---|---|---|---|
| Product/service differentiation and availability | Jointly with manufacturer leadership | Moderate to high | Not difficult | Yes | Medium to long term | Very effective | Very low | General Motors, Ford, Porsche, Kodak |
| Strategic pricing | Manufacturer | Moderate to high | Complex; impact on overall profitability needs monitoring | Yes | Slightly delayed | Very effective | Low | Porsche |
| Dealer development | Jointly, with manufacturer leadership | Moderate to high | Not difficult; requires close dealer participation | No | Long term | Very effective | None | Caterpillar, Canon |
| Marketing information systems | Jointly, with manufacturer leadership | Moderate to high | Not difficult; requires dealer participation | No | After implementation | Effective | None | IBM, Caterpillar, Yamaha, Hitachi, Komatsu, Lotus Development, Insurance companies |
| Long-term image reinforcement | Jointly | Moderate | Not difficult | No | Long term | Effective | None | Most manufacturers with strong dealer networks |
| Establishing legal precedence | Manufacturer | High | Difficult | Yes, if fruitful | No | Uncertain | Low | COPIAT, Coleco, Charles of the Ritz Group, Ltd. |
| Lobbying | Jointly | Moderate | Difficult | Yes, if fruitful | No | Uncertain | Low | COPIAT, Duracell, Porsche |

*Note:* Company strategies include, but are not limited to, those mentioned here.
*Source:* S. Tamer Cavusgil and Ed Sikora, "How Multinationals Can Counter Gray Market Imports," *Columbia Journal of World Business*, 23 (Winter 1988), pp. 75–85.

## GLOBAL PERSPECTIVE 16-4

### SMUGGLING AND BLACK MARKETS: AN ETHICAL DILEMMA FOR MULTINATIONAL COMPANIES SELLING LAWFUL PRODUCTS

Conventional wisdom has it that trade liberalization (i.e., adopting free*r* trade policy) in many emerging markets would reduce smuggling and black market phenomena because it reduces unnecessary and artificial price differences across countries. Economists call this tendency the "Law of One Price." However, in a seminal work on smuggling in 1996, Kate Gillespie and Brad McBride found quite the opposite: These countries are likely to see the resurgence of organized smuggling and black-market distribution as a result of trade liberalization. A number of reasons may be considered. First, liberalization is rarely complete, and smugglers could still take advantage of evading income, sales, and other taxes as well as tariffs. Second, as the reduced price differences (thanks indeed to trade liberalization) make it difficult for casual smugglers to make enough money, smugglers need to be larger and better organized in pursuit of "economies of scale" in their operations. As a result, smuggling shifted to organized crime and takes on a more sinister aspect. Third, evidence indicates that both the evolution of smuggling into organized crime and the use of smuggling as a way to launder money for international drug cartels and possibly terrorist organizations are increasing.

Smuggling is an illegal importation of either legal products (e.g., TVs, computers, music CDs) or illegal products (e.g., narcotics and child pornographic material). We focus only on smuggling of legal products here. What does smuggling have to do with multinational companies that engage in the business of selling legal products internationally? Nothing directly.

In June 2000, U.S. Customs estimated the global volume of money laundering, much of which is related to the illicit trade in narcotics, to total more than $600 billion a year or between 2 and 5 percent of the world's GDP. The problem is that money is *fungible* (simply stated, money is money wherever it comes from). U.S. exports are often purchased with narcotics dollars. Those exports include otherwise lawful goods, including household appliances, consumer electronics, liquor, cigarettes,

used auto parts, and footwear. The connection between money laundering and smuggled consumer products has been a major concern of U.S. Customs for several years particularly after the government cracked down on money laundering through U.S. banks.

This is how the system works. A drug cartel in a Latin American country exports narcotics to the United States where they are sold for U.S. dollars. The cartel in this Latin American country contacts a third party—a peso broker—who agrees to exchange pesos in the country for the U.S. dollars that the cartel controls in the United States. The peso broker uses contacts in the United States to place the drug dollars purchased from the cartel into the U.S. banking system. Latin American importers then place orders for items and make payments through the peso broker who uses contacts in the U.S. to purchase the requested items from U.S. manufacturers and distributors. The peso broker pays for these goods with cash or drafts drawn on U.S. bank accounts. The purchased goods are shipped to some Caribbean or South American destinations, sometimes via Europe or Asia, and are then smuggled into this Latin American country. The Latin American importer avoids paying high tariffs, and the peso broker profits by charging both the cartel and the importers for services rendered.

The U.S. multinational companies that sell these products have routinely denied having any idea that they were involved in money laundering. Beginning in June 2000, however, a group of corporate executives began a series of meetings at the Justice Department. The companies included Hewlett-Packard, Ford Motor, Whirlpool, General Motors, Sony, Westinghouse, and General Electric (GE). With the exception of GE, the companies called to participate had products appearing in the black market in a Latin American country. GE was invited as the example of a good corporate citizen that was successfully cleaning up the smuggling of its goods into South America. However, GE's shutting down smuggling came at a fairly steep price to the company and to the benefit of those competitors that kept their eyes closed on the fact. Between 1995 and 2000, General Electric estimated that its good corporate citizenship policy cost the company about 20 percent of its sales to South America.

*Sources:* Kate Gillespie and J. Brad McBride, "Smuggling in Emerging Markets: Global Implications," *Columbia Journal of World Business*, 31 (Winter 1996), pp. 40–54; and Kate Gillespie, "Smuggling and the Global Firm," *Journal of International Management*, 9 (3) (2003), pp. 317–33.

---

Gray marketing is a legal trading transaction. On the other hand, smuggling and black market refer to the illegal importation and sales of either otherwise legal goods or illegal products. Although such illegal transactions are outside the scope of this book, we address these issues in **Global Perspective 16-4** to introduce you to some ethical dilemma that multinational companies can face concerning the smuggling and black market activities by independent distributors of what would otherwise be legal products.

# SUMMARY

The national government has a variety of programs to support exports, although many government policies—which are sometimes dictated by political compulsions—also hinder exports. Export markets provide a unique opportunity for growth, but competition in these markets is usually fierce. With the rise of the big emerging markets (Brazil, China, and India), competition is likely to intensify even more.

Procedurally, exporting requires locating customers, obtaining an export license from the federal government (a general or validated license); collecting export documents (such as the bill of lading, commercial invoice, export packing list, insurance certificate); packing and marketing; shipping abroad; and receiving payment—most of the time through a bank. Conversely, importing requires locating a seller, obtaining an import license, usually establishing a letter of credit, turning over import documents (the bill of lading, etc.) to indicate receipt of goods, and making payment through the banking system. Methods of payment include advance payment, open account, consignment sale, documents against payment (D/P), documents against acceptance (D/A), and letter of credit. Of these, the last two are the most popular. Depending on the nature of the payment terms and the currency of payment, the exporter could need to make foreign exchange hedging transactions. The U.S. government is now taking a more active role in promoting the exports of U.S. firms as they bid for big-ticket items in the emerging markets.

Imports are the obverse of exports. A U.S. importer can make payments in U.S. dollars unlike an importer in many other countries. Any good coming in through a U.S. port must pass through customs and pay the appropriate duty and be authorized by customs at the port of entry or the port of destination for entry. Unlike an exporter who faces a payment risk, the importer's risks are associated with delivery schedules and product quality. Foreign exchange risk is common to both imports and exports. Entry of some goods into a country is restricted by bilateral and multilateral quotas as well as by political considerations.

Finally, globalization of markets has spawned gray marketing activities by unauthorized distributors taking advantage of price differences that exist among various countries due to currency exchange rate fluctuations, different market demand conditions, and price discrimination, among other factors. For companies marketing well-known branded products, gray markets have become a serious issue to be confronted proactively as well as reactively.

# KEY TERMS

Ad valorem duty
American Export Trading Company of 1982
Automated Export System
Bill of lading
Bond
Combination export manager (CEM)
Commercial invoice
Compound duty
Credit risk

Customs receipt
Direct exporting
Documents against acceptance (D/A)
Documents against payment (D/P)
Ex-Im Bank (Export-Import Bank)
Export broker
Export commission house
Export department

Export Enhancement Act of 1992
Export license
Export merchant
Export sales subsidiary
Foreign exchange risk
Foreign sales branch
Foreign Trade Zone
Freight forwarder
Gray market (Parallel imports)

Import duty
Indirect exporting
Letter of credit
Open account
Piggyback exporting
Political risk
Specific duty
Trading company
Transfer risk

# REVIEW QUESTIONS

1. How does a prospective exporter choose an export market?

2. What are the factors that influence the decision of the exporter to use a standardized product strategy across countries and regions?

3. What are the direct and indirect channels of distribution available to exporters? Under what conditions would the use of each be the most appropriate?

4. Terms of payment represent an extremely important facet of export transactions. Describe the various terms of payments in increasing order of risk.

5. Describe the various terms of shipment and sale.

6. What is the role of government (home country) in export activities? Explain in the context of U.S. exporters.

7. Managing imports in the United States is by and large easier and less risky than managing export? Give reasons why this is true.

8. What are gray markets? What factors led to the development of gray markets?

# DISCUSSION QUESTIONS ✦ ✦ ✦ ✦ ✦ ✦ ✦ ✦ ✦ ✦ ✦ ✦ ✦ ✦ ✦ ✦ ✦ ✦ ✦ ✦ ✦

1. A friend of yours who owns a small firm manufacturing and selling CD-ROM–based computer games would like to market the company's products abroad. Your friend seeks information from you on the following:

    a. Which markets should the firm target (what sources of information to tap)?

    b. How should it tap these markets (what are the steps you would advise)?

    c. What are the direct and indirect costs involved in exporting?

    d. What kind of assistance can your friend get from governmental and nongovernmental agencies at any of the stages involved? What would your advice be?

2. General trading companies have played and continue to play a leading role in the exports and imports of products from and to Japan. The effectiveness of these companies is evident from the fact that in the recent Fortune 500 list of the world's largest corporations, 5 of the top 10 corporations (including the top three) are Japanese trading firms. Although there is little question about the effectiveness of these firms, various business executives, especially outside Japan, interpret the directing of exports and imports through such firms as adding to significant inefficiencies in terms of higher costs and lost opportunities. Do you agree with this contention? Why or why not? The top three trading houses, Mitsubishi, Mitsui, and Itochu, had profitability ratios (profits after taxes/total revenues) of 0.18 percent, 0.17 percent, and 0.07 percent, respectively. Would this information have any bearing on your answer?

3. You are the manager for international operations of a manufacturer of steel in the United States. You have received an offer to purchase at a very attractive price 5,000 metric tons of wire rods (used to draw wires for the manufacture of nails) from a large nail manufacturer located in a developing country X. What would you deem to be the most appropriate choice of export terms of payment and terms of shipment, given the following information? (Include any precautions that you would take to ensure the successful execution of the order):

    a. The prospective importer has its account at a local bank. Local government rules stipulate making payments only through this bank.

    b. The local bank does not have any international operations/branches.

    c. The currency of country X has been extremely unstable, with its value having depreciated by more than 20 percent recently.

    d. The interest rates are extremely high in this country.

    e. The legal system in this country is weak, but the firm that is willing to place the order has a good reputation

based on past experience with other international manufacturers.

    f. Rain and summer heat can cause the product to deteriorate if kept unused for a time longer than necessary.

    g. This country exports a larger amount by the sea route than it imports. Hence, many ships have to go empty to get cargo from this country to the United States.

4. Non-tariff barriers to international trade have significant implications, for both exporters and importers. One of the most prevalent non-tariff barriers used is antidumping duties or the threat of initiating antidumping investigations. The use of antidumping duties has recently received some criticisms as affecting certain high-growth industries adversely while protecting some smaller inefficient (as claimed) industries. One typical example quoted is the manufacture of laptop computers. Antidumping duties were levied against Japanese manufacturers of flat-panel screens (used in the manufacture of laptop computers) at the behest of would-be flat-panel manufacturers in the United States. It was the contention of these U.S. producers that if the flat panels were not dumped by Japanese manufacturers, the U.S. producers would be able to raise capital to initiate production of this product. As a result of the duties levied, which would have added significant costs to the computers manufactured in the United States, most U.S. manufacturers (many of whom had plans to manufacture laptop computers within the United States) shifted to sites abroad. According to the computer manufacturers, the antidumping decision sacrificed the fastest-growing segment of the computer industry to a nonexistent domestic flat-panel industry. The proponents of antidumping legislation, however, contend that the threat of predatory practices is real and antidumping procedures take care of this threat. Whom would you side with, the proponents or the critics of antidumping actions?

5. The internet has become a powerful place for products, information, and everything you can think of today, and internet retailing has become increasingly accepted by most consumers. While consumers are surfing for the best prices, it is difficult for them to tell a legitimate, authorized dealer from a gray marketer. Assuming that you are a consultant of a famous computer company, what are your recommendations for the firm to be able to combat gray market activities? Could the company continuously attract bargain-seeking consumers by informing consumers of the dark side of gray market retailing?

6. As presented in Global Perspective 16-3, the rampant gray market of iPhone largely resulted from Apple's international strategy. In order to reduce and control gray market, what strategies should Apple use?

# SHORT CASES

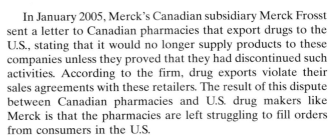

## CASE 16-1

### AN UPSET MERCK

Purchasing medicines through internet pharmacies is the latest trend to hit the drug industry. This channel of distribution has existed for years now but it drew attention to itself when Pfizer's popular drug for erectile dysfunction was released and consumers who were too embarrassed to buy this drug offline, resorted to buying it online. At the time, drug companies were not too distressed at this trend, given that it added one more channel of distribution of their products and drug companies willingly supplied pharmacies with drugs for sale over the internet.

However, the past couple of years have seen major U.S. pharmaceutical companies cutting off drug supplies to some Canadian pharmacies and now second largest U.S. drug company Merck, with sales of over $20 billion worldwide, is the most recent one to join the bandwagon. The reason for this move: Canadian pharmacies that operate through the mail order or online channel, provide drugs not only to Canadian consumers but also indulge in cross-border exports to patients in the United States who demand drugs at lower prices than those offered in the U.S. The Canadian government controls prices of pharmaceuticals in Canada unlike the U.S. government and therefore prices of drugs tend to be cheaper in Canada than the same drugs that are available in the U.S.

According to U.S. pharmaceuticals companies, this export-import practice affects Canadian consumers on one hand because drug exports to the U.S. results in a shortage of medicines for Canadian patients. On the other hand, firms such as Merck argue that such drug exports to patients are essentially risky due to the lack of stringent controls. Furthermore, the emergence of internet pharmacies that sell counterfeit medicines has increased the possibility of health hazards to patients who expect to get genuine products but do not. Also, Merck argued that some of its drugs provided under the U.S.'s Medicaid program are affordably priced and should preclude drug exports by Canadian pharmacies.

*Source:* "Pain of the Pill Market," *Maclean's*, February 21, 2005, pp. 28–29.

In January 2005, Merck's Canadian subsidiary Merck Frosst sent a letter to Canadian pharmacies that export drugs to the U.S., stating that it would no longer supply products to these companies unless they proved that they had discontinued such activities. According to the firm, drug exports violate their sales agreements with these retailers. The result of this dispute between Canadian pharmacies and U.S. drug makers like Merck is that the pharmacies are left struggling to fill orders from consumers in the U.S.

But, this business has proved to be extremely attractive for the pharmacies. Sale of prescription and other drugs over the internet started off on a small scale but over the years, due to the high demand for this method of sale, these firms have grown so much that drug companies are becoming more vigilant and defensive against such activities. Nevertheless such moves by Merck and others have managed to curb drug exports to a certain extent. Since Merck's decision to boycott these pharmacies, internet pharmacies have reduced their workforce. There are some, however, that are still going strong by obtaining drugs from wholesalers and retailers behind closed doors. Still others are now looking toward other foreign countries, mainly in Europe, to supply drugs.

It is interesting to see whether or not drug exports will cease in the future but that might need some strict regulation and governmental interference. Amidst complaints by pharmaceuticals giants, the Canadian government has considered passing a law to shut down internet pharmacies. But, the talks are still on.

### DISCUSSION QUESTIONS

**1.** What else can Merck do to reduce the exports of drugs back into the U.S. by Canadian pharmacies?

**2.** Should the U.S. and Canadian governments step in to solve this problem? If so, what can the governments do in this matter?

**3.** Will Merck's recent move prevent further exports by Canadian pharmacies?

**4.** What does the future likely hold for this retail method for drugs in particular?

## CASE 16-2

### SONY—COMBATING GRAY MARKETS FOR PSPs

Sony Corporation, the famous Japanese consumer electronics company, recently launched its (PlayStation Portable) PSP product, a handheld media system, amidst much hype and publicity. The product is the latest addition to its popular PS (PlayStation) line of products. The company has plans to introduce the product in major markets in the world. However, even before its launch everywhere, the much awaited PSP gadgets are already available in some target markets via the gray market channel and Sony, along with its subsidiary Sony Computer Entertainment Europe is fighting tooth and nail to prevent retailers worldwide from biting into its revenues when the product is officially released for sale.

In the recent past, multinational firms have introduced their innovations in the Triad markets almost simultaneously. But, the PSP system was launched in Japan late 2004 and in the United States in March 2005. Sony planned to launch PSP in the UK market and the rest of Europe months later in September 2005. The reasons for this delay were multifold but it was partly due to the multicultural requirements for software for European consumers and also Europe's stringent safety and standard compliances. Another reason for the deferred European launch was that Sony wanted to ensure that there was sufficient supply to meet demand in the U.S. The company, however, did not offer any apologies for the late launch, stating that Europeans would eventually benefit from a better version of the product, having corrected the bugs well in advance.

However, even before the launch, retailers in the UK were importing PSPs from Japan and the United States and selling them in Europe. In order to keep retailers from selling PSPs, Sony finally brought legal action against these parties in the UK in June 2005. Sony wrote over 500 letters to importers who were selling gray market PSPs in Europe, including some who sold their products on popular online auctioneer eBay. Sony claimed that it wanted confiscation of PSPs and also sought compensation for damages. Pushed to the edge by these sales, Sony also demanded that it be given the identities of retailers and consumers who had indulged in these transactions.

One of the main adversaries in this legal battle in the UK was online retail firm ElectricBirdLand or EBL, which decided to stand up against Sony and fight the charges. Moreover, EBL argued that Sony did not have appropriate trademarks for its PSP product and related technologies in Europe. EBL also claimed that Sony was pursuing action against smaller firms while ignoring larger firms such as music company HMV, which sold PSP add-ons to parties who were importing Sony PSPs. However, HMV was only advertising the products pre-sales but was to make them available to consumers only after the formal launch in September. This controversy surrounding the PSP's launch gave rise to doubts as to whether Sony would in fact be able to stick to its schedule to present the PSP to Europeans on time. End June 2005, Sony won the case against EBL but there were other similar ongoing cases against retailers such as Nuplayer. Nevertheless, some retailers have responded by pulling the products off their real and virtual shelves. There are still others who are pushing Sony's buttons by continuing to sell PSPs because the lucrative margins of over 60 percent make it worthwhile. Sony's headaches were not restricted to the UK only. Gray markets for PSPs exist all over Europe.

Even before the unveiling of the PSP in Europe, it has created a buzz but it is not just Sony that is benefiting from its popularity. In fact, it is gray market sellers who are bringing in the dough right now. Meanwhile, hackers all over the world have busied themselves trying to run unauthorized games and other software on Sony's PSPs. Sony meanwhile is working hard to continuously develop new versions of the PSP to keep hackers at bay. And as Sony awaits the UK High Court's decision, gray marketers are continuing to sell PSPs through their websites.

Technology geeks are the happiest as end consumers. Even though they pay a higher price for the gray market product that comes with no warranties, they get to keep abreast of the latest advances in electronics. There are some who believe there is a difference in the PSPs sold in Japan and the rest of the world because the products sold in Japan are superior in terms of their hardware and software.

## DISCUSSION QUESTIONS

1. What can firms like Sony do to prevent sale of new products in gray markets?

2. Do you think Sony launched the PSP too early and should instead have waited to launch it in the Triad simultaneously? Why did the company then rush to introduce its product?

3. How was the sale of PSPs in Europe through gray markets a threat to Sony?

4. How does the sale of PSPs in Europe through gray markets affect the future of the product itself?

## FURTHER READING ◆ ◆ ◆ ◆ ◆ ◆ ◆ ◆ ◆ ◆ ◆ ◆ ◆ ◆ ◆ ◆ ◆ ◆ ◆ ◆ ◆

Anckar, Patrik and Saeed Samiee, "Customer-Oriented Invoicing in Exporting," *Industrial Marketing Management*, 29 (November 2000): 507–20.

Antia, Kersi D., Mark E. Bergen, Shantanu Dutta, and Robert J. Fisher, "How Does Enforcement Deter Gray Market Incidence?" *Journal of Marketing*, 70 (January 2006): 92–106.

Bello, Daniel C. and Ritu Lohtia. "Export Channel Design: The Use of Foreign Distributors and Agents." *Journal of Academy of Marketing Science*, 23(2) (1995): 83–93

Diana, Tom, "How to Hedge Foreign Exchange Risk," *Business Credit*, 109 (April 2007): 60–62.

Diamantopoulos, Adamantios and Nikolaos Kakkos, "Managerial Assessments of Export Performance: Conceptual Framework and Empirical Illustration," *Journal of International Marketing*, 15(3) (2007) 1–31

Katsikea, Evangelia S., Marios Theodosiou, Robert E. Morgan, and Nikolaos Papavassiliou, "Export Market Expansion Strategies of Direct-Selling Small and Medium-Sized Firms: Implications for Export Sales Management Activities," *Journal of International Marketing*, 13(2), 2005: 57–92.

Katsikeas, Constantine S., Leonidas C. Leonidou, and Saeed Samiee, "Research into Exporting: Theoretical, Methodological, and Empirical Insights," in Masaaki Kotabe and Kristiaan Helsen, ed., *The SAGE Handbook of International Marketing*, London: Sage Publications, 2009, pp. 165–82.

Lages, Luis Filipe, Carmen Lages, and Cristiana Raquel Larges, "Bringing Export Performance Metrics into

Annual Reports: The APEV Scale and the PERFEX Scorecard," *Journal of International Marketing*, 13(3) 2005: 79–104.

Leonidou, Leonidas C., Constantine S. Katsikeas, and John Hadjimarcou, "Building Successful Export Business Relationships: A Behavioral Perspective." *Journal of International Marketing*, 10(3) (2002) 96–115

Moen, Oystein and Per Servais, "Born Global or Gradual Global? Examining the Export Behavior of Small and Medium-Sized Enterprises," *Journal of International Marketing*, 10(3) (2002) 49–72

Moini, A. H., "Small Firms Exporting: How Effective Are Government Export Assistance Programs?" *Journal of Small Business Management*, 36(January 1998): 1–15.

Mullen, Michael R., C. M. Sashi, and Patricia M. Doney, "Gray Markets: Threats or Opportunity? The Case of Herman Miler vs. Asal GMBH," in Tiger Li & Tamer S. Cavusgil, ed., *Advances in International Marketing* Greenwich, CT: JAI Press, 2003.

Myers, Matthew B. and David A. Griffith, "Strategies for Combating Gray Market Activity," *Business Horizons*, 42 (November-December 1999): 2–8.

Seyoum, Belay, *Export-Import Theory, Practices, and Procedures*, London: Taylor & Francis, 2008.

Sharma, Varinder M., "Export Management Companies and E-Business: Impact on Export Services, Product Portfolio, and Global Market Coverage," *Journal of Marketing Theory & Practice*, 13(Fall 2005): 61–71.

# PLANNING, ORGANIZATION, AND CONTROL OF GLOBAL MARKETING OPERATIONS

**17**

## HAPTER OVERVIEW

1. GLOBAL STRATEGIC MARKETING PLANNING
2. KEY CRITERIA IN GLOBAL ORGANIZATIONAL DESIGN
3. ORGANIZATIONAL DESIGN OPTIONS
4. ORGANIZING FOR GLOBAL BRAND MANAGEMENT
5. LIFE CYCLE OF ORGANIZATIONAL STRUCTURES
6. CONTROL OF GLOBAL MARKETING EFFORTS

The capstone of a company's global marketing activities will be its strategic marketing plan. To implement its global plans effectively, a company needs to reflect on the best organizational setup that enables it to successfully meet the threats and opportunities posed by the global marketing arena. Organizational issues that the global marketer must confront cover questions like: What is the proper communication and reporting structure? Who within our organization should bear responsibility for each of the functions that need to be carried out? How can we as an organization leverage the competencies and skills of our individual subsidiaries? Where should the decision-making authority belong for the various areas?

We consider the major factors that will influence the design of a global organizational structure. Multinational companies (MNCs) can choose from a wide variety of organizational structures. In this chapter, we discuss the major alternative configurations. We also highlight the central role played by country managers within the firm's organization. More and more companies try to build up and nurture global brands. We look at several organizational mechanisms that firms can adopt to facilitate such efforts. Because change requires flexibility, this chapter explores different ways that MNCs can handle environmental changes. MNCs must also decide where the decision-making locus belongs. The challenge is to come up with a structure that bridges the gap between two forces: being responsive to local conditions and integrating global marketing efforts. The final section focuses on control mechanisms companies can utilize to achieve their strategic goals.

◆ ◆ ◆ ◆ ◆ ◆ ◆ ◆   ## GLOBAL STRATEGIC MARKETING PLANNING

The vast majority of multinational companies prepare a **global strategic marketing plan** to guide and implement their strategic and tactical marketing decisions. Such plans are usually developed on an annual basis and look at policies over multiple years. The content of a global strategic marketing plan can be very broad in scope but usually covers four areas:[1]

1. **Market situation analysis.** A situation analysis on a global basis of the company's customers (market segments, demand trends, etc.), the competition (SWOT[2] analysis), the company itself, and the collaborators (e.g., suppliers, distribution channels, alliance partners).

2. **Objectives.** For each country, management states goals that are achievable and challenging at the same time.

3. **Strategies.** Once the objectives have been determined, management needs to formulate marketing strategies for each country to achieve the set goals, including resource allocation.

4. **Action plans.** Strategies need to be translated into concrete actions that will implement those strategies. Specific actions are to be spelled out for each marketing mix element.

Although these are the core areas of a global strategic marketing plan, such a plan will also discuss anticipated results and include contingency plans.

**Bottom-Up versus Top-Down Strategic Planning**

International planning can be top-down (centralized) or bottom-up (decentralized). Obviously, hybrid forms that combine both options are also possible. With **top-down planning**, corporate headquarters guides the planning process. **Bottom-up planning** is the opposite. Here, the planning process starts with the local subsidiaries and is then consolidated at headquarters level. The bottom-up approach has the advantage of embracing local responsiveness. Top-down planning, on the other hand, facilitates performance monitoring. A centralized approach also makes it easier to market products with a global perspective. One survey of large multinational corporations found that pure bottom-up planning was most popular (used by 66 percent of the companies surveyed). Only 10 percent of the interviewed companies, on the other hand, relied on a pure top-down planning process. The balance used a hybrid format (11 percent) or no planning at all (12 percent).[3]

**Pitfalls**

Marketing plans can go awry. One survey identified the following obstacles as the main problems in preparing strategic plans for global markets:

1. Lack of information of the right kind (39 percent of the respondents).
2. Too few courses of action; too little discussion of alternatives (27 percent).
3. Unrealistic objectives (22 percent).
4. Failure to separate short/long-term plans (20 percent).
5. Lack of framework to identify strengths/weaknesses (19 percent).
6. Too many numbers (17 percent).
7. Lack of framework to define marketplace threats and opportunities (15 percent).

---

[1]See, for instance, Douglas J. Dalrymple and Leonard J. Parsons, *Marketing Management* (New York: John Wiley & Sons, 2000), Chapter 17.

[2]SWOT analysis is the method used to evaluate the strengths, weaknesses, opportunities, and threats that the company is facing.

[3]Myung-Su Chae and John S. Hill, "The Hazards of Strategic Planning for Global Markets," *Long Range Planning*, 29(6) (1996), pp. 880–91.

8. Senior management de-emphasizing or forgetful about strategic/long-range plans (15 percent).
9. Too little cooperation between headquarters/subsidiaries or among subsidiaries (10 percent).
10. Too much information of the "wrong kind" (4 percent).
11. Too much planning jargon (1 percent).[4]

Obviously, external factors can also interfere with the strategic planning process. Changes in the political and the economic environment can upset the finest strategic plans. China's sudden clampdown on direct selling created upheaval for Avon, Amway, and Mary Kay, among other companies. The 2008-2009 global economic downturn wreaked havoc on the strategic plans of multinationals around the globe. McDonald's, for example, had finalized a three-year strategic plan by October 2008. However, as the global economy worsened, the company revisited its plan in December. McDonald's pressed its managers around the world to closely monitor cost items and data on customer traffic, buying patterns, and the general economic situation (e.g., unemployment rate).[5] As a result, McDonald's U.K. began running more ads for its value-priced Little Tasters menu and McDonald's China slashed prices by up to 33 percent. Other external factors that can hamper strategic marketing planning include changes in the competitive climate (e.g., deregulation), technological developments (e.g., 3G wireless technology), and consumer-related factors.

## KEY CRITERIA IN GLOBAL ORGANIZATIONAL DESIGN ◆ ◆ ◆ ◆ ◆ ◆ ◆

As is true of most other global managerial issues, there is no magic formula that offers the "ideal" organizational setup under a given set of circumstances. Yet there are some factors that companies should consider when engineering their global organizational structure. In the following discussion, we make a distinction between environmental and firm-specific factors. We start with a look at the major environmental factors.

**Competitive Environment.** Global competitive pressures force MNCs to implement structures that facilitate quick decision-making and alertness. In industries where competition is highly localized, a decentralized structure where most of the decision-making is made at the country-level is often appropriate. Nevertheless, even in such situations, MNCs can often benefit substantially from mechanisms that allow the company to leverage its global knowledge base.

**Environmental Factors**

**Rate of Environmental Change.** Drastic environmental change is a way of life in scores of industries. New competitors or substitutes for a product emerge. Existing competitors form or disband strategic alliances. Consumer needs worldwide constantly change. Businesses that are subject to rapid change require an organizational design that facilitates continuous scanning of the firm's global environment and swift alertness to opportunities or threats posed by that environment.

**Regional Trading Blocs.** Companies that operate within a regional trading bloc (e.g., the European Union, NAFTA, MERCOSUR) usually integrate their marketing efforts to some extent across the affiliates within the block area. A case in point is the European Union. In light of the European integration, numerous MNCs decided to streamline their organizational structure. Many of these companies still maintain their local subsidiaries, but the locus of most decision-making now lies with the pan-European headquarters. As other trading blocs such as Asia's APEC and South America's

---

[4]Ibid.
[5]"McDonald's seeks way to keep sizzling," *The Wall Street Journal Asia*, March 11, 2009, pp. 14–15.

MERCOSUR evolve toward the European model, one can expect similar makeovers in other regions.

***Nature of Customers.*** The company's customer base also has a great impact on the MNC's desired organizational setup. Companies such as DHL, IBM, and Citigroup, which have a "global" clientele, need to develop structures that permit a global reach and at the same time allow the company to stay "close" to their customers.

These are the major external drivers. We now turn to the prime firm-specific determinants.

**Firm-Specific Factors**

***Strategic Importance of International Business.*** Typically, when overseas sales account for a very small fraction of the company's overall sales revenues, simple organizational structures (e.g., an export department) can easily handle the firm's global activities. As international sales grow, the organizational structure will evolve to mirror the growing importance of the firm's global activities. For instance, companies may start with an international division when they test the international waters. Once their overseas activities expand, they are likely to adopt an area-type (country- and/or region-based) structure.

***Product Diversity.*** The diversity of the company's foreign product line is another key factor in shaping the company's organization. Companies with substantial product diversity tend to go for a global product division configuration.

***Company Heritage.*** Differences in organizational structures within the same industry can also be explained via corporate culture. Nestlé and Unilever, for example, have always been highly decentralized MNCs. A lot of the decision-making authority has always been made at the local level. When Unilever realized that its marketing efforts required a more pan-European approach to compete with the likes of Procter & Gamble, the company transformed its organization and revised its performance measures to provide incentives for a European focus. One of Unilever's senior executives, however, noted that the changeover "comes hard to people who for years have been in an environment where total business power was delegated to them."[6] As long as a given formula works, there is little incentive for companies to tinker with it. Revamping an organization to make the structure more responsive to new environmental realities can be a daunting challenge.

***Quality of Local Managerial Skills.*** Decentralization could become a problem when local managerial talents are missing. Granted, companies can bring in expatriates, but this is typically an extremely expensive remedy that does not always work out. For instance, expatriate managers may find it hard to adjust to the local environment.

## ◆ ◆ ◆ ◆ ◆ ◆ ◆ ◆ ◆ ORGANIZATIONAL DESIGN OPTIONS

The principal designs that firms can adopt to organize their global activities are:

- **International division.** Under this design, the company basically has two entities: the domestic division, which is responsible for the firm's domestic activities, and the international division, which is in charge of the company's international operations.
- **Product based structure.** With a product structure, the company's global activities are organized along its various product divisions.
- **Geographic structure.** This is a setup where the company configures its organization along geographic areas: countries, regions, or some combination of these two levels.

---

[6]"Unilever adopts clean sheet approach," *Financial Times,* October 21, 1991.

- **Matrix organization.** This is an option where the company integrates two approaches—for instance, the product and geographic dimensions—with a dual chain of command.

We will now consider each of these options in greater detail. At the end of this section, we will also discuss the so-called **networked** organization model.

## International Division Structure

Most companies that engage in global marketing initially start by establishing an export department. Once international sales reach a threshold, the company might set up a full-blown international division. The charter of the international division is to develop and coordinate the firm's global operations. The unit also scans market opportunities in the global marketplace. In most cases, the division has equal standing with the other divisions within the company.

This option is most suitable for companies that have a product line that is not too diverse and does not require a large amount of adaptation to local country needs. It is also a viable alternative for companies whose business is still primarily focused on the domestic market. Over time, as international marketing efforts become more important to the firm, most companies tend to switch to a more globally oriented organizational structure.

## Global Product Division Structure

The second option centers around the company's different product lines or strategic business units (SBUs). Each product division, being a separate profit center, is responsible for managing worldwide the activities for its product line. This alternative is especially popular among high-tech companies with highly complex products or MNCs with a very diversified product portfolio. Ericsson, John Deere, and Sun Microsystems are some of the companies that have adopted this structure. **Exhibit 17-1** shows how John Deere organizes its company.

Several benefits are associated with a global product structure. The product focus offers the company a large degree of flexibility in terms of cross-country resource allocation and strategic planning. For instance, market penetration efforts in recently entered markets can be cross subsidized by profits generated in developed markets. In many companies, a global product structure goes in tandem with consolidated manufacturing and distribution operations. This approach is exemplified by Honeywell, the U.S. maker of control tools, which has set up centers of excellence that span the globe.[7] That way, an MNC can achieve substantial scale economies in the area of production and logistics, thereby improving the firm's competitive cost position. Another appeal is

**EXHIBIT 17-1**
ORGANIZATIONAL STRUCTURE OF JOHN DEERE OF A GLOBAL
PRODUCT STRUCTURE

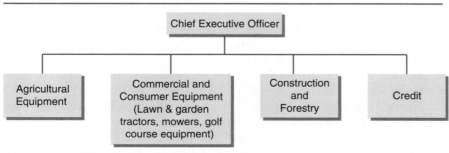

*Source*: www.deere.com

---

[7]Honeywell, *1995 Annual Report.*

**EXHIBIT 17-2**
THE COCA-COLA COMPANY: EXAMPLE OF A GEOGRAPHIC
STRUCTURE

| *Operations* | |
|---|---|
| *Africa* | *Latin America* |
| President | President |
| East and Central Africa | Brazil |
| Nigeria and Equatorial Africa | Latin Center Division |
| North and West Africa | Mexico |
| South Africa | South Latin Division |
| *East, South Asia and Pacific Rim* | *North Asia, Eurasia and Middle East* |
| President | President |
| India | China |
| Philippines | Eurasia and Middle East |
| South Pacific and Korea | Russia/Ukraine/Belarus |
| Southeast Asia and West Asia | Japan |
| *European Union* | *North America* |
| President | President |
| Central Europe | Canada |
| Germany and Nordic Division | Foodservice and Hospitality Division |
| Iberian Division | |
| Mediterranean Division | |
| Northwest Europe | |

*Source*: The Coca-Cola Company, 2005
Annual Report

that global product structures facilitate the development of a global strategic focus to cope with challenges posed by global players.[8]

The shortcomings of a product division are not insignificant. Lack of communication and coordination among the various product divisions could lead to needless duplication of tasks. A relentless product-driven orientation can distract the company from local market needs. The global product division system has also been criticized for scattering the global resources of the company.[9] Instead of sharing resources and creating a global know-how pool, international resources and expertise get fragmented. A too narrow focus on the product area will lead to a climate where companies fail to grasp the synergies that might exist between global product divisions.

**Geographic Structure**    The third option is the geographic structure, where the MNC is organized along geographic units. The units might be individual countries or regions. In many cases, MNCs use a combination of country-based subsidiaries and regional headquarters. There are other variants. Coca-Cola, for instance, has five different regions, each one of them being further divided into subregions, as is shown in **Exhibit 17-2**. Area structures are especially appealing to companies that market closely related product lines with very similar end-users and applications around the world.

***Country-Based Subsidiaries.***    Scores of MNCs set up subsidiaries on a country-by-country basis. To some degree, such an organization reflects the marketing concept. By setting up country affiliates, the MNC can stay in close touch with the local market conditions. The firm can thereby easily spot new trends and swiftly respond to local market developments.

Country-focused organizations have several serious handicaps, however. They tend to be costly. Coordination with corporate headquarters and among subsidiaries can easily become extremely cumbersome. A country-focus often leads to a "not-invented-here" mentality that hinders cross-border collaboration and support. Some critics of

[8]W. H. Davidson and P. Haspeslagh, "Shaping a global product organization," *Harvard Business Review*, July–August 1982, pp. 125–32.
[9]W. H. Davidson and P. Haspeslagh, "Shaping a global product organization," p. 129.

the country-model derisively refer to the country-model as a mini-United Nations with a multitude of local fiefs run by scores of country managers.[10]

### New Role of Country Managers.
Corporate strategy gurus such as Ohmae foresee the demise of the country manager. Major companies have already cut down the role of their country managers within the organization, with power being transferred to a new breed, the "product champion." Often these days, country managers fulfill administrative duties and are described as "hotel managers." Companies such as P&G and Dow Chemical created global business divisions to handle investment strategic decisions. Oracle cut down its country managers to size when the company realized that its country-based organization had become a patchwork of local fiefs that did not communicate with each other: Oracle's logo in France differed from the one in the UK, global accounts like Michelin were treated as different customers, and so forth.[11] Several forces are held responsible for this shift away from strong country managers:[12]

- The threats posed by global competitors who turn the global marketplace into a global chess game.
- The growing prominence of global customers who often develop their sourcing strategies and make their purchase decisions on a global (or pan-regional) basis.
- The rise of regional trading blocs that facilitate the integration of manufacturing and logistics facilities but also open up arbitrage opportunities for gray marketers.
- Knowledge transparency. The internet and other information technologies allow customers and suppliers to become better knowledgeable about products and prices across the globe.

At the same time, several developments create a need for strong country managers.[13] Nurturing good links with local governments and other entities (e.g., the European Union) becomes increasingly crucial. Local customers still represent the lion's share of most companies' clientele. Local competitors sometimes pose a far bigger threat than global rivals. In many emerging markets, strong local brands (e.g., the Baidu search engine in China; the fast food restaurant Jollibee in the Philippines) often have a much more loyal following than regional or global brands. Many winning new-product or communication ideas come from local markets rather than regional or corporate headquarters. Also, if the role of local management is reduced to pen pushing and paperwork, it becomes harder to hire talented people. For these reasons, several firms have increased the clout of their country managers. A good example is 3M. In 1991, 3M set up 30 product-based units. To cut costs, 3M centralized procurement, production, distribution, and service centers (e.g., human resources). However, a decade later, 3M decided to hand power back to its country managers as they can provide a local perspective on group policies. The country managers also play a valuable role in establishing contacts with local customers and spotting opportunities for new businesses.[14]

To strike the balance between these countervailing forces, country managers of the twenty-first century should fit any of the following five profiles depending on the nature of the local market:[15]

- The *trader* who establishes a beachhead in a new market or heads a recently acquired local distributor. Traders should have an entrepreneurial spirit. Their roles include

---

[10]Though some of the major MNCs operate in more countries than the number of UN member states.

[11]"From Baron to Hotelier," *The Economist* (May 11, 2002), pp. 57–58.

[12]John A. Quelch, "The new country managers," *McKinsey Quarterly*, 1992, No. 4, pp. 155–65.

[13]John A. Quelch and Helen Bloom, "The return of the country manager," *McKinsey Quarterly*, 1996, No. 2, pp. 30–43.

[14]"Country Managers Come Back in from the Cold," *Financial Times* (September 24, 2002).

[15]J. A. Quelch and H. Bloom, "The return of the country manager," pp. 38–39 in Michael Goold and Andrew Campbell, *Designing Effective Organizations* (San Francisco, CA: Jossey-Bass, 2002).

sales and marketing, scanning the environment for new ideas, gathering intelligence on the competition.

- The *builder* who develops local markets. Builders are entrepreneurs who are willing to be part of regional or global strategy teams.

- The *cabinet member* who is a team player with profit and loss responsibility for a small- to medium-sized country. Teamwork is key here, since marketing efforts may require a great deal of cross-border coordination, especially for global and pan-regional brands. Major strategic decisions are often made at the regional level rather than by the country subsidiary.

- The *ambassador* who is in charge of large and/or strategic markets. His responsibilities include handling government relations, integrating acquisitions and strategic alliances, coordinating activities across SBUs. In this role, the country manager can provide hands-on parenting for local markets that need more attention than they can get from the global product division. Ideally a seasoned manager, the ambassador should be somebody who is able to manage a large staff. For instance, Asea Brown Boveri, a Swiss/Swedish consortium, views the tasks of its Asia-based country managers as "to exploit fully the synergies between our businesses in the countries, to develop customer based strategies, to build and strengthen relationships with local customers, governments, and communities."[16]

- The *representative* in large, mature markets whose tasks include handling government relations and legal compliance and maintaining good relations with large, local customers. Dow Chemical, for example, realized that it needed to have strong local management in Germany who can talk shop with the German government authorities.

Whatever role is decided upon for the country manager, the main requirement is to clearly define the scope of the job. Some companies are now combining the two jobs of country manager and product champion.[17] This new breed of hybrid manager, referred to by some as a *country prince*, is based in a country that is seen as strategically important for the product category. Paris-based Nexans, the world's biggest maker of electric cables, adopted this approach. Nexans has three country princes. For instance, one heads the global product division for ship cables and is country manager for South Korea. **Exhibit 17-3** shows the job description for the Japan country manager at Twitter, the San Francisco-based social networking service.

## EXHIBIT 17-3
### JOB DESCRIPTION OF JAPAN COUNTRY MANAGER AT TWITTER

*Responsibilities*

- Lead all Twitter business operations in Japan.
- Identify, partner and collaborate with local strategic partner(s) in Japan to drive higher and sustained adoption for Twitter.
- Work closely with Japanese strategic partner to localize/internationalize the Twitter service.
- Construct a working road map for localization, define hiring plan and create a dashboard for Twitter usage and trends in Japan.
- Become the go-to person for all matters concerning Japan Twitter strategy, localization road map and execution.
- Budgetary responsibility and profit/loss leadership over Twitter investments in Japan.
- Liaison between Product and the Japanese Twitter Product, modeling changes and strategies based on analytical reasoning.
- Become a leading and vocal evangelist for the Japanese user base.
- Support the Business Development team in Twitter by identifying, evaluating, and testing revenue-generating strategies for the Japanese Twitter Product.
- Support the internationalization initiatives for Twitter in other regions.

*Source*: Adapted from twitter.jobscore.com, accessed on March 11, 2009.

---

[16]Gordon Redding, "ABB—The battle for the Pacific," *Long Range Planning*, 1995, vol. 28, no. 1, pp. 92–94.

[17]"The Country Prince Comes of Age," *Financial Times* (August 9, 2005): 7.

*Regional Structures.* Many MNCs that do not feel entirely comfortable with a pure country-based organization opt for a region-based structure with regional headquarters. A typical structure has divisions for North America, Latin America, the Asia-Pacific, and EMEA.[18] To some extent, a regional structure offers a compromise between a completely centralized organization and the country-focused organization. The intent behind most region-based structures is to address two concerns: lack of responsiveness of headquarters to local market conditions and parochialism among local country managers. In more and more industries, markets tend to cluster around regions rather than national boundaries. In some cases, the regions are formal trading blocs like the European Union or NAFTA that allow almost complete free movement of goods across borders. In other cases, the clusters tend to be more culture-driven.

A survey done in the Asia-Pacific region singles out five distinct roles for regional headquarters (RHQs):[19]

- **Scouting.** The RHQ serves as a listening post to scan new opportunities and initiate new ventures.
- **Strategic stimulation.** The RHQ functions as a "switchboard" between the product divisions and the country managers. It helps the SBUs in understanding the regional environment.
- **Signaling commitment.** By establishing an RHQ, the MNC signals a commitment to the region that the company is serious about doing business in that region.
- **Coordination.** Often the most important role of the RHQ is to coordinate strategic and tactical decisions across the region. Areas of cohesion include developing pan-regional campaigns in regions with a lot of media overlap; price coordination, especially in markets where parallel imports pose a threat; consolidation of manufacturing; and logistics operations.
- **Pooling resources.** Certain support and administrative tasks are often done more efficiently at the regional level instead of locally. RQH might fulfill support functions like after-sales services, product development, and market research.

## Matrix Structure

Imposing a single-dimensional (product, country, or function-based) management structure on complex global issues is often a recipe for disaster. In the wake of the serious shortcomings of the geographic or product based structures, several MNCs have opted for a matrix organization. The matrix structure explicitly recognizes the multi-dimensional nature of global strategic decision-making. With a matrix organization, two dimensions are integrated in the organization. For instance, the matrix might consist of geographic areas and business divisions. The geographic units are in charge for all product lines within their area. The product divisions have worldwide responsibility for their product line. As a result, the chain of command is often dual with managers reporting to two superiors. **Exhibit 17-4** shows an example of a matrix-like organization. Sometimes, the MNC might even set up a three-dimensional structure (geography, function, and business area). The various dimensions do not always carry equal weight. For instance, at Siemens the locus of control is shifting more and more toward the business areas, away from the geographic areas.

The matrix structure has two major advantages.[20] First, matrices reflect the growing complexities of the global market arena. In most industries MNCs face global *and* local competitors; global *and* local customers; global *and* local distributors. In that sense, the matrix structure facilitates the MNC's need to "think globally and act locally"—to be *glocal*—or, in Unilever's terminology, to be a *multi-local multinational*. The other

---

[18]Europe, the Middle East, and Africa.

[19]Philippe Lasserre, "Regional headquarters: the spearhead for Asia Pacific markets," *Long Range Planning*, vol. 29, February 1996, pp. 30–37.

[20]Thomas H. Naylor, "The international strategy matrix," *Columbia Journal of World Business*, Summer 1985, pp. 11–19.

**EXHIBIT 17-4**
NESTLE'S ORGANIZATIONAL SETUP

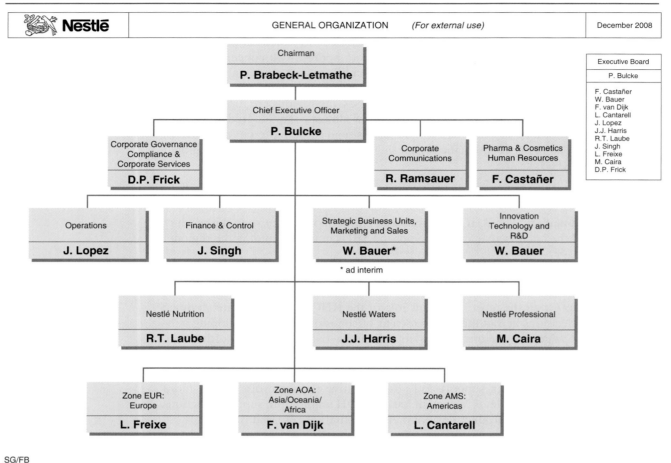

| Nestlé | GENERAL ORGANIZATION | (For external use) | December 2008 |

Chairman
**P. Brabeck-Letmathe**

Chief Executive Officer
**P. Bulcke**

Executive Board

P. Bulcke

F. Castañer
W. Bauer
F. van Dijk
L. Cantarell
J. Lopez
J.J. Harris
R.T. Laube
J. Singh
L. Freixe
M. Caira
D.P. Frick

Corporate Governance
Compliance &
Corporate Services
**D.P. Frick**

Corporate
Communications
**R. Ramsauer**

Pharma & Cosmetics
Human Resources
**F. Castañer**

Operations
**J. Lopez**

Finance & Control
**J. Singh**

Strategic Business Units,
Marketing and Sales
**W. Bauer***

Innovation
Technology and
R&D
**W. Bauer**

* ad interim

Nestlé Nutrition
**R.T. Laube**

Nestlé Waters
**J.J. Harris**

Nestlé Professional
**M. Caira**

Zone EUR:
Europe
**L. Freixe**

Zone AOA:
Asia/Oceania/
Africa
**F. van Dijk**

Zone AMS:
Americas
**L. Cantarell**

SG/FB

*Source*: www.nestle.com

appeal of the matrix organization is that, in principle at least, it fosters a team spirit and cooperation among business area managers, country managers and/or functional managers on a global basis.

In spite of these benefits, companies, such as BP and Philips (see **Global Perspective 17-1**), have disbanded their matrix structure. Others, such as IBM and Dow Chemical, have streamlined their matrix setup.[21] Matrix structures have lost their appeal among many MNCs for several reasons. Dual (or triple) reporting and profit responsibilities frequently lead to conflicts or confusion. For instance, a product division might concentrate its resources and attention on a few major markets, thereby upsetting the country managers of the MNC's smaller markets. Another shortcoming of the matrix is bureaucratic bloat. Very often, the decision-making process gets bogged down, thereby discouraging swift responsiveness toward competitive attacks in the local markets. Overlap among divisions often triggers tension, power clashes, and turf battles.[22]

The four organizational structures that we covered so far are the standard structures adopted by most MNCs. The simplicity of the one-dimensional structures and the

---

[21]"End of a corporate era," *Financial Times* March 30, 1995, p. 15.

[22]Christopher A. Bartlett and Sumantra Ghoshal, "Matrix management, not a structure, a frame of mind," *Harvard Business Review*, July–August 1990, pp.138–45.

## GLOBAL PERSPECTIVE 17-1

### PHILIPS'S QUEST FOR THE RIGHT ORGANIZATION

The Dutch company Philips is one of the world's biggest electronics companies, with 159,000 employees in 60 countries. The firm was one of the earliest adopters of the matrix structure. After World War II, it set up both national units and product divisions. The head of, say, the lighting division in France would report to two superiors: the French country manager and the global head of the lighting unit. Conflicts between the two lines of command were resolved via committees.

The matrix was plagued by numerous problems. One major issue was accountability: Who was to be held responsible for

*Source:* "The New Organization: A Survey of the Company—'The Matrix Master'," *The Economist* (January 21, 2006): 4.

the profit-and-loss account? Should it be the country boss or the product boss? In the early 1990s, Philips started to rethink its organization and created a number of units with worldwide responsibility. These new business units were built around products and based in the company's headquarters. Local country offices became subservient to the new units.

More recently, Philips tinkered further with its organization. To become more customer driven, Philips appointed a chief marketing officer. Under the motto "One Philips," it has launched several low-key changes. Employees are encouraged to work across different business units. They are also expected to rotate in their careers across geographical boundaries and product divisions.

---

shortcomings of the matrix model have led several companies to look for better solutions. Below, we discuss one of the more popular forms: the *networked organization*.

**The Global Network Solution**

Global networking is one solution that has been suggested to cope with the shortcomings associated with the classical hierarchical organization structures. The network model is an attempt to reconcile the tension between two opposing forces: the need for local responsiveness and the wish to be an integrated whole.[23] Strictly speaking, the network approach is not a formal structure but a mindset. That is, a company might still formally adopt, say, a *matrix* structure, but at the same time develop a global network. The networked global organization is sometimes also referred to as a **transnational**.[24] Several features characterize network structures:

- There is much less power at the center of the network than at the top of a hierarchical structure. Ideally, decisions are made through collaboration instead of being imposed from the top.

- Units relate as equals in status and power even though they fulfill different roles.

- The units that form the network relate to any other unit as necessary, they have multiple relationships.

- Within a network, units of similar size or function can perform very different tasks. They may change the role they play within the organization in response to local market needs and opportunities.[25]

According to advocates of the network model, MNCs should develop processes and linkages that allow each unit to tap into a global knowledge pool. A good metaphor for the global network is the atom. At the center is a common knowledge base. Each national unit can be viewed as a source of ideas, skills, capabilities, and knowledge that can be harnessed for the benefit of the total organization.[26] Asea Brown Boveri (ABB),

---

[23]Christopher A. Bartlett and Sumantra Ghoshal, "Organizing for Worldwide Effectiveness: The Transnational Solution," *California Management Review*, Fall 1988, pp. 54–74.

[24]Christopher A. Bartlett and Sumantra Ghoshal, "Organizing for Worldwide Effectiveness: The Transnational Solution."

[25]David Arnold, *The Mirage of Global Markets. How Globalizing Companies Can Succeed as Markets Localize* (Upper Saddle River, NJ: Pearson Education, 2004), pp. 200–201.

[26]Christopher A. Bartlett, "Building and Managing the Transnational: The New Organizational Challenge," in *Competition in Global Industries*, Michael E. Porter, Ed., Boston, 1986, MA: Harvard Business School Press, pp. 367–401.

the Swiss-Swedish engineering consortium, is often touted as a prime example of a global networking.[27] Percy Barnevik, former CEO and one of the major forces behind ABB's transformation, describes ABB's vision as follows:

> Our vision was to create a truly global company that knows no borders, has many home countries and offers opportunities for all nationalities. While we strived for size to benefit from economies of scale and scope, our vision was also to avoid the stigma of the big company with a large headquarters and stifling bureaucracy, countless volumes of instructions, turf defenders and people working far from their customers. With our thousands of profit centers close to customers we wanted to create a small company culture with its huge advantages of flexibility, speed and the power to free up the creative potential of each employee.[28]

Some sample mechanisms to foster cross-border organizational integration without full centralization include the following:

- Best-practice sharing via formal or informal networks.
- Rotating key people within functions from one country to another.
- Training managers who can hold responsibilities over and above those of their main job.
- Developing common work patterns and ethic that facilitate cross-border cooperation. ABB, for instance, uses a company "bible" to tie together the different units within its organization. Its bible describes the firm's mission and values, long-term objectives, and guidelines on how to behave internally.[29] Another well-known example is "The Toyota Way."
- Creating a corporate academy. McDonald's "Hamburger University,"[30] which was founded in 1961, is a celebrated example.[31]

Technological advances have also spurred the creation of so-called "virtual teams" within more and more companies. Spread around the globe, these teams communicate through e-mail, Skype, or videoconferences rather than on a face-to-face basis. **Exhibit 17-5** lists guidelines for global virtual teams to be effective.

**EXHIBIT 17-5**
GUIDELINES ON GLOBAL VIRTUAL TEAMWORK
TIPS FOR TOP PERFORMANCE

---

- Start with face-to-face meeting to kick off trust building.
- Keep the team as small as practical.
- Have a code of practice on how to communicate and behave (e.g., how to respond to e-mails).
- Communicate regularly, but don't overdo it.
- Ensure everyone understands each other's role.
- Have a supportive sponsor who represents their interests at a senior level within the organization.
- Keep strong links with the parent organization.
- Reward results, not how people work.

---

*Source:* "'Virtual Teams' Endeavor to Build Trust," *Financial Times*, September 9, 2004, p. 8.

---

[27]William Taylor, "The Logic of Global Business: An Interview with ABB's Percy Barnevik," *Harvard Business Review*, March–April 1991, pp. 91–105.

[28]Asea Brown Boveri, *1995 Annual Report*, p. 5.

[29]Manfred F.R. Kets de Vries," Making a Giant Dance," *Across the Board*, October 1994, pp. 27–32.

[30]See http://www.mcdonalds.com/corp/career/hamburger_university.html.

[31]Giancarlo Ghislanzoni, Risto Penttinen, and David Turnbull, "The Multilocal Challenge: Managing Cross-border Functions," *The McKinsey Quarterly*, 2008 (2), pp. 70–81.

## ORGANIZING FOR GLOBAL BRAND MANAGEMENT

◆ ◆ ◆ ◆ ◆ ◆ ◆

Global branding is the rage for more and more companies. However, to foster and nurture global brands, companies often find it useful to put organizational mechanisms in place. This is especially so for decentralized companies where local decisions involve global branding strategies. Several options exist: (1) a global branding committee, (2) a brand champion, (3) global brand manager, and (4) informal, ad hoc brand meetings. Let us look at each one of these in detail.

**Global branding committees** are usually made up of top-line executives from corporate (or regional) headquarters and local subsidiaries. Their charter is to integrate and steer global and local branding strategies. Visa International's "Global Branding Marketing Group" exemplifies this approach.[32] The group's goal is to establish better communications among regions and to leverage global media buying power. It is made up of the heads of marketing from each region. HP created a "Global Brand Steering Committee" in 1998. Its primary tasks include brand positioning and vision.[33]

**Global Branding Committee**

The **brand champion** is a top-line executive (sometimes a CEO) who serves as the brand's advocate.[34] The approach works well for companies whose senior executives have a passion and expertise for branding. One practitioner of brand championship is Nestlé. The company has a brand champion for each of its twelve corporate strategic brands. The brand champion approves all brand and line extension decisions,[35] monitors the presentation of the brand worldwide, and spreads insights on best practices within the organization.[36]

**Brand Champion**

The **global brand manager** is a steward of the brand whose main responsibility is to integrate branding efforts across countries and combat local biases. In the corporate hierarchy, the position is usually just below top-line executives. The position is most suitable for organizations where top management lacks marketing expertise, as is often the case with high-tech firms. For the global brand manager to be effective, the following conditions should hold:[37]

**Global Brand Manager**

• Commitment to branding at the top of the organization. Top-line executives—though most likely lacking a marketing background—should share the vision and a belief in strong branding.

• Need to create and manage a solid strategic planning process. Country managers should adopt the same format, vocabulary, and planning cycle.

• Need to travel to learn about local management and best practices and to meet local customers and/or distributors.

• Need for a system to identify, mentor, and train prospects that can fill the role.

Even if for some reason a company decides against a formal structure, it could still find it worthwhile to have informal mechanisms to guide global branding decisions. This usually takes the form of ad-hoc branding meetings. A good example is Abbott International, a U.S.-based pharmaceutical company. Whenever a new product is

**Informal, Ad Hoc Branding Meetings**

---

[32] "U.S. Multinationals," *Advertising Age International* (June 1999), p. 44.

[33] Ibid.

[34] "David A. Aaker and Erich Joachimsthaler, "The Lure of Global Branding," *Harvard Business Review*, (Nov.–Dec. 1999), p. 142.

[35] A brand extension is using the same brand for a new product in another product category; a line extension is launching new varieties (e.g., a new flavor, a new package format) of the brand within the same product category.

[36] Aaker and Joachimsthaler, p. 142.

[37] Aaker and Joachimsthaler, p. 142.

planned, international executives meet with local staff to discuss the global brand. The ad-hoc committee reviews patents and trademarks for each country to decide whether or not to use the U.S. name in the other countries.[38]

---

♦ ♦ ♦ ♦ ♦ ♦ ♦ ♦   ## LIFE CYCLE OF ORGANIZATIONAL STRUCTURES

In December 2008 Dell announced plans to reorganize the company around three major customer segments, namely (1) large enterprise, (2) public (government, education, health care, and the environment), and (3) small and medium businesses. According to Michael Dell, the changeover resulted from listening to customers and responding to their desire for faster innovation and globally standardized products and services: "Customer requirements are increasingly being defined by how they use technology rather than where they use it. That's why we won't let ourselves be limited by geographic boundaries in solving their needs."[39] Organization structures are not set in stone. Change occurs and is not always welcomed by the local staff. Companies need to adapt their organization for several reasons.[40] First, existing structures may have become too rigid or complex with too many divisions and layers of management. A second reason is that the environment changes. To cope with these dynamics, the organization may need an overhaul. Third, managers learn new skills or new senior management is brought in from outside the firm. Fad prone managers are often attracted to new theories or paradigms, regardless of whether they actually serve the organization's purpose. Fourth, a key event such as a merger or major acquisition could force a company to rethink its organizational structure. A good example is Lenovo's takeover of IBM's PC division. The acquisition meant a higher emphasis for Lenovo on international markets and the corporate segment, and led to an overhaul of its organization. Finally, the pursuit of new strategic opportunities or directions often demands also a change in the organization.

Regardless of the reasons, successful restructuring takes time, planning, and resources. Change may imply new relationships, new responsibilities, or even downsizing. Not surprisingly, restructuring is often met with resistance by employees who think they "know better." Hence, apart from the "physical" changes, restructuring often requires a fundamental cultural change.[41]

In some cases companies have moved from one extreme to another before finding a suitable configuration. A case in point is Kraft General Foods Europe (KGFE).[42] In the early 1980s, KGFE tried to impose uniform marketing strategies across Europe. This attempt led to so much ill will among KGFE's local units that Kraft soon abandoned its centralized system. It was replaced by a loose system where country managers developed their own marketing strategies for all Kraft brands, including the regional (e.g., Miracoli pasta) and global brands (e.g., Philadelphia cream cheese). Not surprisingly, this system created a great deal of inconsistency in the marketing strategies used. In the 1990s Kraft was split into a North American and an international division with two chief executives, though the biggest product categories had "global councils" to cover best practices. Still, Kraft was struggling. In 2004, the dual structure was swept away in order to make Kraft truly global, cut costs, and ramp up innovation. The overhaul led to the creation of five global product units (beverages, snacks, cheese and dairy, convenient meals, and grocery) backed by two regional commercial units (one for North America, one for the rest of the world). Kraft also set up global units handling support functions such as supply chain and product development.[43]

---

[38]"U.S. Multinationals," p. 44.

[39]http://www.dell.com/content/topics/global.aspx/corp/pressoffice/en/2008/2008_12_31_rr_000?c=us&l=en&s=corp.

[40]Michael Goold and Andrew Campbell, *Designing Effective Organizations* (San Francisco: Jossey-Bass, 2002), pp. 88–89.

[41]"Be Principled for a Change," *Financial Times* (August 23, 2004): 9.

[42]"Cross-border Kraftsmen," *Financial Times* (June 17, 1993).

[43]"Search for the Right Ingredients," *Financial Times* (October 7, 2004): 8.

**EXHIBIT 17-6**
STOPFORD-WELLS INTERNATIONAL STRUCTURAL STAGES MODEL

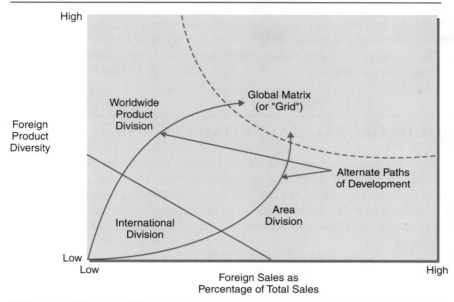

*Source*: Reprinted by permission of Harvard Business School Press. From Christopher A. Barlett, "Building and Managning the Transnational: The New Organizational Challenge," in *Competition in Global Industries*, ed. M.E. Porter (Boston, MA: Harvard University Presss, 1987), p. 368. Copyright (c) 1986 by the President and Fellows of Harvard College.

Several management theorists have made an attempt to come up with the "right" fit between the MNC's environment (internal and external) and the organizational setup. One of the more popular schemas is the stages model shown in **Exhibit 17-6**, which was developed by Stopford and Wells.[44] The schema shows the relationship between the organizational structure, foreign product diversity, and the importance of foreign sales to the company (as a share of total sales). According to their model, when companies first explore the global marketplace they start off with an international division. As foreign sales expand without an increase in the firm's foreign product assortment diversity, the company will most likely switch to a geographic area structure. If instead the diversity of the firm's foreign product line substantially increases, it might organize itself along global product lines. Finally, when both product diversity and international sales grow significantly, MNCs tend to adopt a two-dimensional matrix structure.

The Stopford-Wells staged model has been criticized for several reasons. First, the model is a purely descriptive representation of how MNCs develop over time based on an analysis of U.S.-based MNCs. So, it would be misleading to apply the framework in a prescriptive manner, as several people have done.[45] Second, the structure of the organization is only one aspect of a global organization. Other, equally important, elements are the mindsets of the managers and managerial processes. The MNC's environment is dynamic; it changes all the time. Thus, a fit between the environment and the MNC's organizational structure is not enough. Global organizations also need flexibility.[46]

An in-depth study of a sample of ten successful U.S.-based MNCs showed that the key challenge for MNCs is building and sustaining the right management process instead of looking for the proper organizational structure.[47] According to the study, the installation of such a process moves through three stages. The first step is to recognize the complexity

---

[44]John M. Stopford and Louis T. Wells, Jr., *Managing the Multinational Enterprise: Organization of the Firm and Ownership of the Subsidiary*. New York: Basic Books, 1972.

[45]Christopher A. Bartlett, "Building and Managing the Transnational: The New Organizational Challenge," in *Competition in Global Industries*, M.E. Porter, Ed., 1986, Boston, MA: Harvard Business School Press, pp. 367–401.

[46]Sumantra Ghoshal and Nitin Nohria, "Horses for courses: Organizational Forms for Multinational Corporations," *Sloan Management Review*, Winter 1993, pp. 23–35.

[47]Christopher A. Bartlett, "MNCs: get off the reorganization merry-go-round," *Harvard Business Review*, March–April 1983, pp. 138–46.

of the MNC's environment. Country and regional managers must look at strategic issues from multiple perspectives—a **glocal mindset,** so to speak. During the second stage, the company introduces communication channels and decision-making platforms to facilitate more flexibility. In the final stage, the MNC develops a corporate culture that fosters collaborative thinking and decision-making. Such an agenda could include activities such as formulating common goals and values, developing reward systems and evaluation criteria that encourage a cooperative spirit, and providing role models.

◆ ◆ ◆ ◆ ◆ ◆ ◆ ◆ ◆    **CONTROL OF GLOBAL MARKETING EFFORTS**

To make global marketing strategies work, companies need to establish a control system. The main purpose of controls is to ensure that the behaviors of the various parties within the organization are in line with the company's strategic goals. We will first concentrate on formal control methods. We will then also turn to less formal means to implement control: establishing a corporate culture and management development.

**Formal ("Bureaucratic") Control Systems**

Any formal control system consists of basically three building blocks: (1) the establishment of performance standards, (2) the measurement and evaluation of performance against standards, and (3) the analysis and correction of deviations from standards.

***Establishing Standards (Metrics).*** The first step of the control process is to set standards (metrics). These standards should be driven by the company's corporate goals. There are essentially two types of standards: behavior- and outcome-based. Behavior-based control involves specifying the actions that are necessary to achieve good performance. Managers are told through manuals/policies how to respond to various scenarios. Rewards are based on whether the observed behavior matches the prescribed behavior. Examples of behavior-based standards include distribution coverage, branding policies, pricing rules, and R&D spending. Output-based control depends on specific standards that are objective, reliable, and easy to measure. Outcome standards focus on very specific outcome-oriented measures such as profit-loss statements, return on investment (ROI), market share, sales, and customer satisfaction.

When applied too rigorously, behavior-based standards restrain local management's ability to respond effectively to local market conditions. An example is Johnson & Johnson's experience in the Philippines.[48] In the early 1990s, J&J's managers found out that young Philippine women used J&J's baby talcum to freshen their makeup. To cater toward their needs, local management developed a compact holder for the talcum powder. However, a few days before the planned launch of the new product, corporate headquarters asked the local managers to drop the product, claiming that the cosmetics business is not a core business for J&J. Only after the local marketing head made a personal plea for the product at J&J's headquarters was the subsidiary given the green light. The product became a big hit, though it was never launched in other markets since J&J did not want to run the risk of being perceived as a cosmetics maker.

Output-based standards such as profits can also create problems. For instance, a change in the company's transfer pricing rules[49] could distort profits of the local subsidiary even though its performance does not change.[50] Likewise, a high sales volume target could encourage a country subsidiary to get involved with the gray market in order to boost its numbers.

---

[48]Niraj Dawar and Tony Frost, "Competing with Giants. Survival Strategies for Local Companies in Emerging Markets," *Harvard Business Review,* (March–April 1999), pp. 119–29.

[49]The transfer price is the price charged by one country subsidiary to another country affiliate for delivered goods or services to that affiliate (see also Chapter 12).

[50]Robert D. Hamilton III, Virginia A. Taylor, and Roger J. Kashlak, "Designing a Control System for a Multinational Subsidiary," *Long Range Planning,* 29(6), pp. 857–68.

For most companies, the two types of standards matter. Let us show you why with a simple illustration. Imagine that headquarters wants country A to increase its market share by 3 percentage points over a one-year period. Country A could take different approaches to achieve this target. One path is to do a lot of promotional activities—couponing, price promotions, trade deals, and so on. Another route is to spend more on advertising. Both paths could achieve the desired outcome. However, with the first option—heavy dealing—the company risks tarnishing its brand image. With the second option, the subsidiary would invest in brand equity. Thus, the same outcome can be realized through two totally different behaviors, one of which can ruin the long-term viability of the company's brand assets.

Ideally, standards are developed via a bottom-up and top-down planning process of listening, reflecting, dialoguing, and debating between headquarters and the local units. Standards should also strike a delicate balance between long- and short-term priorities.[51]

***Measuring and Evaluating Performance.*** Formal control systems also need mechanisms to monitor and evaluate performance. The actual performance is compared against the established standards. In many instances, it is fairly straightforward to measure performance, especially when the standards are based on within-country results. To make global or pan-regional strategies work, MNCs also need to assess and reward individual managers' contributions to the "common good." For example, two-thirds of the bonuses payable to Unilever's senior executives in Europe are driven by Unilever's performance in that region.[52] In practice, however, it is tremendously hard to gauge managers' contributions to the regional or global well-being of the firm.

***Analyzing and Correcting Deviations.*** The third element is to analyze deviations from the standards and, if necessary, make the necessary corrections. If actual performance does not meet the set standard, the company needs to analyze the cause behind the divergence. If necessary, corrective measures will be taken. This part of the control system also involves devising the right incentive mechanisms—checks and balances—that make subsidiary managers "tick." While proper reward systems are crucial to motivate subsidiary managers, one study has shown the key role played by the presence of *due process.*[53] Due process encompasses five features: (1) the head office should be familiar with the subsidiaries' local situation; (2) global strategy development should involve a two-way communication; (3) head office is relatively consistent in making decisions across local units; (4) local units can legitimately challenge head-quarters' strategic views and decisions; and (5) subsidiary units receive explanations for final strategic decisions.

Apart from formal control mechanisms, most MNCs also establish informal control methods. Below we cover the two most common informal control tools, namely, corporate culture and human resource development.

## Informal Control Methods

***Corporate Culture.*** For many MNCs with operations scattered all over the globe, shared cultural values are often a far more effective "glue" to bond subsidiaries than formal bureaucratic control tools. Corporate cultures can be *clan-based* or *market-based*.[54] Clan cultures have the following distinguishing features: they embody a long socialization process; strong, powerful norms; and a well-defined set of internalized controls. Market cultures are the opposite: norms are loose or absent; socialization

[51]Guy R. Jillings, "Think Globally, Act Locally," *Executive Excellence*, October 1993, p. 15.

[52]"Unilever adopts clean sheet approach," *The Financial Times*, October 21, 1991.

[53]W. Chan Kim and Renée A. Mauborgne, "Making Global Strategies Work," *Sloan Management Review*, Spring 1993, pp. 11–24.

[54]David Lei, John W. Slocum, Jr., and Robert W. Slater, "Global Strategy and Reward Systems: The Key Roles of Management Development and Corporate Culture," *Organizational Dynamics*, Winter 1989, pp. 27–41.

processes are limited; and control systems are purely based on performance measures. For most global organizations where integration is an overriding concern, a clan-like culture is instrumental in creating a shared vision.

Corporate values are more than slogans that embellish the company's annual report. To shape a shared vision, cultural values should have three properties:[55]

1. **Clarity.** The stated values should be simple, relevant, and concrete.

2. **Continuity.** Values should be stable over time, long-term oriented, not flavor-of-the-month type values.

3. **Consistency.** To avoid confusion, everyone within the organization should share the same vision. Everybody should speak the same language. Everyone should pursue the same agenda.

***Human Resource Development.*** Another major informal control tool is a company's program for management development. These programs have three critical roles.[56] First and foremost, training programs can help managers worldwide in understanding the MNC's mission and vision and their part in pursuing them. Second, such programs can speed up the transfer of new values when changes in the company's environment dictate a "new" corporate mentality. Finally, they can also prove fruitful in allowing managers from all over the world to share their best practices and success stories.

**"Soft" versus "Hard" Levers**

A joint research project conducted by the Stanford Business School and McKinsey aimed to uncover what sort of tools multinationals rely on to resolve the global vs. local tensions.[57] The project, dubbed the "Globe Project," studied 16 multinational companies through in-depth interviews, questionnaires, and network analysis. Based on company interviews, the researchers identified seven management tools or "levers" that companies use to resolve the global/local trade-offs:

- *Organizational structure.* Creating formal positions and lines of authority.
- *Process.* Defining workflows and procedures.
- *Incentives.* Reward systems that encourage outcomes in line with the desired balance between global and local priorities.
- *Metrics.* Measurement systems that focus on desired outcomes.
- *Strategy.* The extent to which the central strategy guides local decisions.
- *Networks.* Building personal relationships that help resolve disputes and encourage sharing of knowledge and resources.
- *Culture.* Shared values that encourage a common approach among all members of the organization.

As you can see, there is some overlap between these levers and the control methods we discussed earlier. Three of the tools—process, incentives, and metrics—are *hard levers*; three other tools—strategy, networks, and culture—are *soft lever* (formal versus informal methods). Structure is a hybrid. The study scored each company that participated in the project on each of these levers. Depending on the score, a company could be classified as a "hard" or "soft" firm. 3M, the conglomerate with its unique innovation culture leans very heavily toward soft levers. Toyota, on the other hand, with its heavy focus on quality control is a prototypical "hard" company.

---

[55]Christopher A. Bartlett and Sumantra Ghoshal, "Matrix Management: Not a Structure, a Frame of Mind," *Harvard Business Review*, July–August 1990, pp. 138–45.

[56]David Lei and colleagues, "Global Strategy and Reward Systems: The Key Roles of Management Development and Corporate Culture," *Organizational Dynamics*, Winter 1989, p. 39.

[57]"Corporations with Hard and Soft Centres," *The Financial Times* (February 20, 2002), p. 11.

# SUMMARY ◆ ◆ ◆ ◆ ◆ ◆ ◆ ◆ ◆ ◆ ◆ ◆ ◆ ◆ ◆ ◆ ◆ ◆ ◆ ◆ ◆ ◆ ◆ ◆ ◆ ◆ ◆

Running a multinational organization is a tremendous challenge. Local managers need empowerment so that the local unit is able to respond rapidly and effectively to local market threats, grab opportunities, and stay in tune with local market developments. Yet, a "laissez-faire" situation will easily evolve into a patchwork of local barons who will inevitably jeopardize the interests of the group as a whole. Too much centralization, however, will straitjacket the country manager, create resentment, and stifle local creativity and responsiveness. This tension global (integration, scale) versus local (market responsiveness) tension needs to be addressed. In this chapter we discussed the structures and control mechanisms that MNCs can use to shape a global organization. Companies can pick from a variety of structures, ranging from a single international division to a global network operation. Formal and informal (culture, management development) control mechanisms are available to run global operations. However, the dynamics of the global marketing arena means that building a global organization is much more than just choosing the "right" organizational configuration and control systems. Global players constantly need to reflect on how to strike the balance between centralization *and* decentralization, local responsiveness *and* global integration, center *and* periphery. As with many other challenges in global marketing, there are no one-size-fits-all solutions. In their search for the proper structure and strategic coherence, countless MNCs have come up with schemes that led to confusion, frustration, and ill will among subsidiary managers. We can, however, offer some pieces of advice though:

- **Recognize the need for business asymmetry.** Due to relentless environmental changes, power sharing between the centre and the periphery will vary over time, over business units and even across activities (product development, advertising, pricing) within business units. Different business units within the organization have different needs for responsiveness and global coordination.[58] Especially widely diversified companies should recognize that each business unit needs a different format, depending on its particular circumstances and needs. For instance, Asea Brown Boveri has businesses that are *superlocal* (e.g., electrical installation) and *superglobal* (e.g., power plant projects). P&G's model treats countries differently based on their income. In high-income countries, the business unit is in charge of resource allocation; in low-income countries (e.g., China, Eastern Europe) the region is responsible. The reason is that low-income countries are more challenging and less familiar business environments. However, the global product unit makes production and marketing decisions for products such

as Pantene shampoo, which are global in nature—in terms of consumer buying habits and usage.[59]

- **Adopt a bottom-up approach.** Getting the balance right also requires democracy. When building up a global organization, make sure that every country subsidiary has a "voice." Subsidiaries of small countries should not be concerned about getting pushed over by their bigger counterparts.

- **Importance of a shared vision.** Getting the organizational structure right—the "arrows" and "boxes" so to speak—is important. Far more critical though is the organizational "psychology."[60] People are key in building an organization. Having a clear and consistent corporate vision is a major ingredient in getting people excited about the organization. To instill and communicate corporate values, companies should also have human resource development mechanisms in place that will facilitate the learning process.

- **Invest heavily in horizontal communication channels and information flows.** Very often multinational corporations focus primarily on vertical communication channels going from the country unit to corporate (or regional) headquarters but neglect horizontal information flows among the different country affiliates. As a result, country units become isolated and try to achieve their own profit goals instead of the overall company profit.[61]

- **Ensure that somebody has a global overview of each product line or brand.** Global oversight of a product line or brand is needed to facilitate transfer of learning and knowledge among markets and to leverage new product and marketing mix programs. The central hub could be corporate or regional headquarters or the lead market with the category's most sophisticated customers and/or distributors and in which most product innovations debut.[62] Lenovo's global marketing hub is located in Bangalore: Lenovo's India team develops global marketing campaigns targeted for dozens of countries, including the United States, France, and Brazil.

- **Need for a good mix of specialists of three types— country, functional, business.** There is no such a thing

---

[58]"Fashionable federalism," *The Financial Times*, December 18, 1992.

[59]"From Baron to Hotelier," *The Economist* (May 11, 2002), pp. 57–58.

[60]Christopher A. Bartlett and Sumantra Ghoshal, "Matrix Management: Not a Structure, a Frame of Mind," *Harvard Business Review*, July-August 1990, pp. 138–45.

[61]David Arnold, *The Mirage of Global Markets. How Globalizing Companies Can Succeed as Markets Localize* (Upper Saddle River, NJ: Pearson, 2004), pp. 205–206.

[62]Ibid.

as a *transnational manager*. Companies should breed specialists of three different kinds: country, functional and global business (SBU). Country managers in particular—once feared to become part of the endangered species list—play a key role. As we discussed earlier in this chapter, the country manager's skills and role will differ from country to country. Some subsidiaries need a "trader"; others need an "ambassador."

- **Moving unit headquarters abroad seldom solves the organization's problems.** In recent years, several companies (e.g., IBM, HP, and Siemens) have moved business unit headquarters abroad. Several of these moves were done for very sensible reasons: getting closer to the customer or supplier, being in the big guys' backyard, cutting costs. For instance, the Japanese company Hoya,

one of the world's largest makers of spectacle lenses, moved the headquarters of its vision care business to the Netherlands. The move was prompted by Europe's technological prowess in this sector.[63] Unfortunately, in many cases the relocation typically turns out to be mere window-dressing in a drive to become more global-oriented. Sometimes transfers can even be counterproductive, weakening the corporate identity or the "authenticity" of the brand when it is strongly linked to the firm's home country.[64]

---

[63] "A European Move with Global Vision," *Financial Times* (January 12, 2006): 10.
[64] "Home Is Not Always Where the Heart Is," *Financial Times* (January 10, 2005): 6.

---

# KEY TERMS ◆ ◆ ◆ ◆ ◆ ◆ ◆ ◆ ◆ ◆ ◆ ◆ ◆ ◆ ◆ ◆ ◆ ◆ ◆ ◆ ◆ ◆ ◆

Bottom-up (top-down) planning
Brand champion
Clan culture
Geographic structure

Global brand manager
Global networking
Global strategic marketing plan
International division

Market culture
Matrix structure
Networked organization
Product-based structure

Transnational

---

# REVIEW QUESTIONS ◆ ◆ ◆ ◆ ◆ ◆ ◆ ◆ ◆ ◆ ◆ ◆ ◆ ◆ ◆ ◆ ◆ ◆ ◆ ◆ ◆

**1.** How does a global networked organization differ from the matrix structure?

**2.** Describe how external environmental drivers influence the organizational design decision.

**3.** What are the pros and cons of a regional organization structure?

**4.** What mechanisms can companies use to foster a global corporate culture?

**5.** What does it take for an MNC to be a "multi-local multinational"?

---

# DISCUSSION QUESTIONS ◆ ◆ ◆ ◆ ◆ ◆ ◆ ◆ ◆ ◆ ◆ ◆ ◆ ◆ ◆ ◆ ◆ ◆ ◆

**1.** Do an online search for country manager jobs on the web (see Exhibit 17-3 for an example). Discuss the profile in the job description (e.g., responsibilities, qualifications).

**2.** In his book, *The End of the Nation State* (New York: The Free Press, 1995), Kenichi Ohmae makes the following observations about country-based organization structures:

*One of the prime difficulties of organizing a company for global operations is the psychology of managers who are used to thinking by country-based line of authority rather than by line of opportunity. Lots of creative ideas for generating value are overlooked because such managers are captive to nation state-conditioned habits of mind. Once that constraint is relaxed . . . a nearly infinite range of new opportunities comes into focus: building cross-border alliances, establishing virtual companies, arbitraging differential costs of labor or even services. . . . I strongly believe that, as head-to-head battles within established geographies yield less and less incremental value, changing the battleground from nation to cross-border region will be at the core of 21st-century corporate strategy.*

Do you agree or disagree with these comments? Why?

## SHORT CASES

### CASE 17-1

#### REVAMPING PROCTER & GAMBLE: "ORGANIZATION 2005"

Until the late 1990s, Procter & Gamble was split into four regional divisions: North America; Europe, Middle East, and Africa; Asia; and Latin America. Each division was responsible for its profits and losses. Despite heavy R&D spending, P&G failed through the 1990s to develop and successfully launch innovative products. After a lackluster sales performance during the mid-1990s, P&G decided to embark on a self-improvement plan. Top executives of the firm traveled around the country, visiting the CEOs of a dozen major companies such as Kellogg, Hewlett-Packard, and 3M in search for advice. The result of the whole exercise was "Organization 2005" a new bold plan to revamp the P&G organization. The goal of the restructuring exercise was to boost sales and profits by launching an array of new products, closing plants, and cutting jobs. The plan was spearheaded by then CEO Durk Jager. According to Jager, P&G's management had become too conservative: "Speed builds sales. But, speed has been an issue for us."

Under Organization 2005, P&G was to be remolded from a geographically based organization to one based on global product lines. The key elements of the program were:

- **Global Business Units (GBUs).** P&G moved from four geographic units to seven so-called GBUs based on product lines. Each GBU would have all the resources it needs to understand consumer needs in its product area and to do product innovation. By shifting the focus to products, P&G hoped to boost innovation and speed. The GBUs were to develop and sell products on a worldwide basis. They would replace a system where country managers ruled their local fiefs, setting prices and devising product policies as they saw fit. By 2000, P&G had consolidated into five GBUs: paper ($12 billion in net sales in FY 2001), fabric and home care ($11.7 billion), beauty care ($7.3 billion), health care ($4.4 billion), and food and beverage ($4.1 billion), such

as baby care, laundry detergents, shampoos, and beauty care.
- **Global Business Services (GBSs).** This new unit would bring support services such as accounting, information technology, and data management under one roof.
- **Market Development Organizations (MDOs).** The MDOs were created to tailor global marketing programs to local markets.
- **Corporate functions.** Corporate functions were streamlined Most of the corporate staff was transferred to one of the new business units.
- **Overhaul of reward systems and training programs.**

P&G saw the revamped organization as a continuation of the strategy it started in the 1980s when it moved from brand management to category management. With the new setup, category management would be run on a global basis. Durk Jager, P&G's CEO, made the case for Organization 2005 as follows: "Organization 2005 is focused on one thing: leveraging P&G's innovative capability. Because the single best way our growth . . . is to innovate bigger and move faster consistently and across the entire company. The cultural changes we are making will also create an environment that produces bolder, more stretching goals and plans, bigger innovations, and greater speed."

However, in FY 2000, P&G was struggling. Results were below plan. Core earnings (earnings excluding restructuring charges) grew a modest 2.0 percent. Durk Jager commented: "I am proud of our vision of Organization 2005, and we've made important progress. It's unfortunate our progress in stepping up top-line sales growth resulted in earnings disappointments." Jager resigned in June 2000, after less than two years on the job. A. G. Laffey, the new CEO, said: "In hindsight, it is clear that we have changed too much too fast, all with the right intent of accelerating growth—but still, too much change too fast."

#### DISCUSSION QUESTIONS

1. What went wrong with Organization 2005? Do you agree with Laffey's comments of "too much too fast"?

2. Is Organization 2005 fundamentally right for P&G? Or, should P&G nip Organization 2005 in the bud and if so, why?

*Sources:* "P&G's Hottest New Product: P&G," *Business Week* (October 5, 1998), pp. 58–59; "The what, not the where, to drive P&G," *Financial Times* (September 3, 1998), p. 18; www.pg.com/investor/news/recentnews_newsrel.html; http://www.indiainfoline.com/fmcg/feat/pgga.html.

## FURTHER READING

Arnold, David. *The Mirage of Global Markets. How Globalizing Companies Can Succeed as Markets Localize.* Upper Saddle River, NJ: Pearson, 2004.

Bartlett, Christopher A., "Building and Managing the Transnational: The New Organizational Challenge," in

*Competition in Global Industries*, M. E. Porter, Ed., Boston, MA: Harvard University Press, 1986, pp. 367–401.

Bartlett, Christopher A. and Sumantra Ghoshal, "Organizing for Worldwide Effectiveness: The Transnational Solution," *California Management Review*, Fall 1988, pp. 54–74.

Corstjens, Marcel, and Jeffrey Merrihue. "Optimal Marketing." *Harvard Business Review* 81 (October 2003): 114–21.

Davidson, W. H. and P. Haspeslagh, "Shaping a Global Product Organization," *Harvard Business Review*, July–August 1982, pp. 125–32.

Ghislanzoni, Giancarlo, Risto Penttinen, and David Turnbull, "The Multilocal Challenge: Managing Cross-border Functions," *McKinsey Quarterly*, 2(2008), pp. 70–81.

Goold, Michael and Andrew Campbell. *Designing Effective Organizations*. San Francisco: Jossey-Bass, 2002.

Hamilton, Robert D., III, Virginia A. Taylor, and Roger J. Kashlak. "Designing a Control System for a Multinational Subsidiary." *Long Range Planning*, 29(6): 857–68.

Lasserre, Philippe, "Regional Headquarters: The Spearhead for Asia Pacific Markets," *Long Range Planning*, 29, February 1996, pp. 30–37.

Naylor, Thomas H., "The International Strategy Matrix," *Columbia Journal of World Business*, Summer 1985, pp. 11–19.

Quelch, John A., "The New Country Managers," *The McKinsey Quarterly*, no. 4, 1992, pp. 155–65.

Quelch, John A. and Helen Bloom, "The Return of the Country Manager," *The McKinsey Quarterly*, no. 2, 1996, pp. 30–43.

Roberts, John. *The Modern Firm*. Oxford: Oxford University Press, 2004.

Snow, Charles C., Sue C. Davison, Scott A. Snell, and Donald C. Hambrick, "Use Transnational Teams to Globalize Your Company," *Organizational Dynamics*, Spring 1996, pp. 50–67.

Solberg, Carl Arthur. "Standardization or Adaptation of the International Marketing Mix: The Role of the Local Subsidiary/Representative," *Journal of International Marketing*, 8(1) (2000): 78–98.

"The New Organization. A. Survey of the Company," *The Economist* (January 21, 2006).

Tennant, Nancy, and Deborah L. Duarte. *Strategic Innovation*. San Francisco: Jossey-Bass, 2003.

Theuerkauf, Ingo, David Ernst, and Amir Mahini. "Think local, organize . . . ?" *International Marketing Review*, 13(3) (1996): 7–12.

# MARKETING STRATEGIES FOR EMERGING MARKETS

**18**

HAPTER OVERVIEW

1. EMERGING MARKETS

2. COMPETING WITH THE NEW CHAMPIONS

3. TARGETING/POSITIONING STRATEGIES IN EMERGING
   MARKETS—BOP OR NO BOP?

4. ENTRY STRATEGIES FOR EMERGING MARKETS

5. PRODUCT POLICY

6. PRICING STRATEGY

7. THE DISTRIBUTION CHALLENGE

8. COMMUNICATION STRATEGIES FOR EMERGING MARKETS

As developed countries are getting saturated, multinationals have increasingly set their sights on the fast-growing emerging markets (EMs) in Asia, Latin America, the former East Bloc countries, and Africa. McDonald's restaurant in central Moscow's Pushkin Square is the chain's busiest one in the world.[1] Mars sells more cat food in Russia than anywhere else in the world.[2] Inditex of Spain, one of Europe's leading clothes retailers, owns the fashionable Zara brand. In March 2009, the retailer announced that half of the 125 to 135 new Zara stores that it planned to open would be in Asia, with a heavy emphasis on China. In 2010, the company would also start rolling out Zara stores in India under a joint venture with the Tata Group.[3] Around the same time, Lenovo, the personal computer maker, revealed a new organizational structure with the creation of two new business units, with one unit focusing on customers in emerging markets and the other centered around consumers in mature markets.[4]

---

[1] "Russia's Consumers Come of Age," www.ft.com, accessed on April 2, 2009.

[2] "Brands Make a Dash into Russia," www.ft.com, accessed on April 2, 2009.

[3] "Inditex Chief Tailors Its Strategy," *Financial Times*, March 26, 2009, p. 19.

[4] "Lenovo Restructures Into Two Units," www.scmp.com, accessed on March 27, 2009.

Given their growing middle classes and rising incomes, the siren call of emerging markets is hard to resist. Several large Western multinationals now derive the bulk part of their revenues from such markets. The global economic downturn has spurred companies even more to explore prospects in that part of the globe. Still, MNCs face daunting obstacles when doing business in these countries. At the same time, a more recent phenomenon has been the steady but undeniable emergence of strong local companies. Several of these firms have been able to prove their mettle in competing with the big multinationals in their home country. In this chapter we focus on emerging markets. We first highlight the key characteristics of emerging markets. We then turn to the competitive landscape: we look at how companies from these countries have been able to compete successfully against the big multinationals in their home-markets and also in the global market place. Next we explore targeting and positioning strategies for emerging markets. In particular, we discuss strategies to reach the so-called bottom-of-the-pyramid segments. The remainder of the chapter examines how the characteristics of emerging markets can influence marketing strategies.

## ◆◆◆◆◆◆◆◆ EMERGING MARKETS

**Definition**    **Emerging markets (EMs)** refer to economies that are in the process of rapid growth and industrialization.[5] The "emerging markets" moniker was first introduced in 1981 by Antoine van Agtmael at an investor conference in Thailand. Van Agtmael, who at that time was a deputy director at the World Bank's IFC, thought that the term would resonate more with prospective investors in Thailand than the "Third World" label. Today it is not entirely clear which countries qualify as emerging markets. Loosely speaking, the countries that fall under the rubric are those that can be neither classified as developing, nor as developed. Morgan Stanley's Emerging Market Index currently consists of 25 countries.[6] The list includes the usual suspects such as Brazil, China, Indonesia, and India but also a few countries that could be easily classified as developed economies (e.g., Taiwan, Israel, Korea) given that their per-capita income is at least $20,000.[7] The London-based FTSE Group distinguishes between four types of countries, namely: (1) Developed (e.g., most Western countries, South Korea), (2) Advanced Emerging (e.g., Brazil, Hungary, Mexico, South Africa), (3) Secondary Emerging, which largely overlaps with the MSCI group, and (4) Frontier countries (e.g., Bahrain, Kenya, Serbia, Vietnam). Another term that is gaining some traction is **transition economies**: countries that are changing from a centrally planned economy to a free market economy.[8] The International Monetary Fund classified 25 countries as transition economies. Most of these are countries that belonged to the former East Bloc but the list also includes four Asian countries, namely Cambodia, China, Laos, and Vietnam.[9] However, for the purpose of this chapter we stick with the emerging market label. Among the emerging markets, for many global marketers the most promising and exciting ones are the four that constitute the **BRIC**, namely: Brazil, Russia, India, and China.[10] By 2007, the BRIC nations already accounted for 15 percent of global GDP.[11] Jim O'Neill, a Goldman Sachs economist who coined the BRIC acronym, predicts that the BRIC economies combined will be larger than the G7, the Group of Seven (G7)

---

[5]http://en.wikipedia.org/wiki/Emerging_markets#cite_note-1, accessed on March 22, 2009.

[6]http://www.mscibarra.com/products/indices/licd/em.html#EM, accessed on March 22, 2009.

[7]The complete list consists of the following countries: Argentina, Brazil, Chile, China, Colombia, Czech Republic, Egypt, Hungary, India, Indonesia, Israel, Jordan, Korea, Malaysia, Mexico, Morocco, Pakistan, Peru, Philippines, Poland, Russia, South Africa, Taiwan, Thailand, and Turkey.

[8]http://en.wikipedia.org/wiki/Transition_economy, accessed on March 19, 2009.

[9]http://www.imf.org/external/np/exr/ib/2000/110300.htm, accessed on March 19, 2009.

[10]The BRIC is a term coined in 2001 by Jim O'Neill, the chief economist at investment bank Goldman Sachs.

[11]"When Are Emerging Markets No Longer 'Emerging'," knowledge.wharton.upenn.edu, accessed on March 19, 2009.

industrialized nations,[12] by 2027.[13] In 2005, Goldman Sachs introduced the concept of the **Next Eleven** (N-11). These are 11 countries that, as the acronym suggests, will follow in the footsteps of the BRIC in rivaling the G7. The eleven countries is a very diverse mix that includes: Bangladesh, Egypt, Indonesia, Iran, Korea, Mexico, Nigeria, Pakistan, Philippines, Turkey, and Vietnam.[14]

As we hinted above, the term "emerging markets" has lost some of its meaning given the wide mix of countries that are often classified as such. As a result, it is hard to find common ground among emerging markets. Even classifying them as high-growth countries has become questionable in recent years. During the Asian financial crisis in 1997/98, many of the so-called Asian Tigers stopped roaring. The economies of some of them rebounded a bit after the crisis but most of them never fully recovered. More recently, the global economic downturn did not spare the emerging markets: except for China and maybe a few other emerging markets. Most EM economies became very weak and started submerging with negative growth rates. Still emerging markets share certain characteristics. In particular, they seem to have the following properties:

**Characteristics of Emerging Markets**

1. *Low per capita incomes but rapid pace of economic development.* Per capita incomes are still much lower in most EMs than in developed nations (see column 3 of Exhibit 18-1). Obviously, low incomes pose an upper limit on purchases. Still, the incomes in most of these countries are surging rapidly, as shown in **Exhibit 18-1** (column 4), leading to a strong and growing middle-class population. Goldman Sachs estimates that the global middle class, defined as people with annual incomes ranging from $6,000 to $30,000, is growing by 70 million per year. The bank foresees that another 2 billion people will join the group by 2030.[15]

2. *High income inequalities.* The last column of Exhibit 18-1 shows the Gini index, a statistic often used to measure the degree of income inequality in a country. The higher the value of the Gini coefficient, the more income inequality.[16] As you can see, most EM countries register much higher values for the Gini index than developed nations.

3. *High rates of emigration to the developed world.* Many low per-capita income EMs also export their people. Mexico and other Latin American countries export agriculture workers to the United States; the Philippines exports nurses and teachers to North America and Western Europe; South Asian countries export construction workers to the Middle East. Money sent home by these migrants ("remittances") is an important part of their home countries' economies. For instance, remittances accounted for 13 percent of the Philippines' GDP in 2007.[17] Globally, the World Bank estimated that money sent home by these immigrants was $305 billion in 2008.[18] Apart from their financial impact, these immigrants also form global diasporas, which companies can leverage.

4. *Populations are youthful and growing.* Populations in most emerging markets are younger and growing much more rapidly than in the Triad region.[19] This is illustrated in Exhibit 18-1, which shows the population growth rate (column 2) and median age (column 3) for several emerging markets. Most of these countries have population growth rates of 1 percent or more, with a median population age between 20 and 30 years. The exceptions are the former Communist East Bloc countries.

5. *Weak and highly variable infrastructure.* The infrastructure in many of the countries is underdeveloped. Transportation networks such as roads, airports, and railroads

---

[12]The G7 consists of Canada, France, Germany, Italy, Japan, the United Kingdom, and the United States.

[13]Jim O'Neill, "The New Shopping Superpower," *Newsweek*, March 30, 2009, p. 17.

[14]http://www2.goldmansachs.com/ideas/brics/BRICs-and-Beyond.html

[15]"The Expanding Middle: The Exploding World Middle Class and Falling Global Inequality," Goldman Sachs, Global Economics Paper No: 170, July 7, 2008.

[16]http://en.wikipedia.org/wiki/Gini_coefficient.

[17]http://siteresources.worldbank.org/INTPROSPECTS/Resources/334934-1199807908806/Top10.pdf

[18]http://peoplemove.worldbank.org/en/content/remittances-expected-to-fall-by-5-to-8-percent-in-2009

[19]The United States, Japan, and Western Europe.

**EXHIBIT 18-1**
ECONOMIC AND DEMOGRAPHIC COMPARISON EMERGING MARKETS
VERSUS G7 COUNTRIES

| Countries | Population Growth (09 est.) (%) | Median Age (09 est.) | Per Capita GDP (PPP) (08 est.) (US$) | GDP—Real Growth Rate (08 est.) (%) | Gini Index |
|---|---|---|---|---|---|
| Emerging Market Countries | | | | | |
| Argentina | 1.05 | 30 | 14,500 | 6.6 | 49 |
| Brazil | 1.20 | 28.6 | 10,300 | 5.2 | 56.7 |
| Chile | 0.90 | 31.4 | 15,400 | 4.0 | 54.9 |
| China | 0.66 | 34.1 | 6,100 | 9.8 | 47 |
| Colombia | 1.38 | 27.1 | 9,000 | 3.5 | 53.8 |
| Czech Republic | −0.09 | 40.1 | 26,800 | 3.9 | 26 |
| Egypt | 1.64 | 24.8 | 5,500 | 7.0 | 34.4 |
| Hungary | −0.26 | 39.4 | 20,500 | −1.5 | 28 |
| India | 1.55 | 25.3 | 2,900 | 7.3 | 36.8 |
| Indonesia | 1.14 | 27.6 | 3,900 | 5.9 | 39.4 |
| Malaysia | 1.72 | 24.9 | 15,700 | 5.5 | 46.1 |
| Mexico | 1.13 | 26.3 | 14,400 | 2.0 | 47.9 |
| Morocco | 1.48 | 25 | 4,000 | 5.3 | 40 |
| Pakistan | 1.95 | 20.8 | 2,600 | 4.7 | 30.6 |
| Philippines | 1.96 | 22.5 | 3,400 | 4.6 | 45.8 |
| Poland | −0.05 | 37.9 | 17,800 | 5.3 | 34.9 |
| Russia | −0.47 | 38.4 | 15,800 | 6.0 | 41.5 |
| South Africa | 0.28 | 24.4 | 10,400 | 3.7 | 65 |
| Thailand | 0.61 | 33.3 | 8,700 | 3.6 | 42 |
| Turkey | 1.31 | 27.7 | 12,900 | 4.5 | 43.7 |
| G7 countries | | | | | |
| Canada | 0.82 | 38.1 | 40,200 | 0.7 | 32.1 |
| France | 0.55 | 39.4 | 32,700 | 0.7 | 32.7 |
| Germany | −0.05 | 43.8 | 34,800 | 1.7 | 27 |
| Italy | −0.05 | 43.3 | 31,000 | 0.0 | 32 |
| Japan | −0.19 | 44.2 | 35,300 | 0.7 | 38.1 |
| United Kingdom | 0.28 | 40.2 | 37,400 | 1.1 | 34 |
| USA | 0.97 | 36.7 | 48,000 | 1.4 | 45 |

*Source:* Based on figures reported on https://www.cia.gov/library/publications/the-world-factbook/, accessed on March 26, 2009.

are low in coverage and fragile. Likewise, basic utilities such as water supply and electricity are in short supply. Telecommunications networks and internet access often lag far behind the grids of mature markets in terms of coverage and technology. This is indicated in **Exhibit 18-2**, which contrasts mobile phone and internet penetration between ten emerging markets and the G7 countries. Multinationals doing business in these areas need to come up with creative solutions to cope with these kinds of infrastructure weaknesses.

6. *Technology is underdeveloped.* Most of the countries also lag behind mature markets in the area of technology. This is the case both on the supply side (infrastructure, innovation) and the demand side (adoption of new technologies). On the supply side, most R&D spending and innovation are still centered in developed countries. This is especially true in high-tech industries such as information technology, biotech, and telecommunications. However, without the legacy of old technologies, companies doing business in the countries often can leapfrog old technologies. Indeed, a recent study that analyzed the mobile technology in various countries found that the BRIC countries appear to lead in mobile technology service breadth through innovation and the introduction of a wider variety of services than developed nations.[20] Research

---

[20]Alina Chircu and Vijay Mahajan, "Revisiting Digital Divide: An Analysis of Mobile Technology Depth and Service Breadth in the BRIC Countries," University of Texas Austin, working paper, 2007.

**EXHIBIT 18-2**
MOBILE PHONE, INTERNET & BROADBAND PENETRATION IN TEN
EMERGING MARKET COUNTRIES VERSUS THE G7 COUNTRIES (2007)

| Country | Mobile Phone Subscribers Per 100 Inhabitants | Internet Subscribers per 100 Inhabitants | Broadband Subscribers per 100 Inhabitants |
|---|---|---|---|
| *Emerging Market Countries* | | | |
| Brazil | 63.1 | 35.2 | 3.5 |
| China | 41.2 | 16.0 | 5.0 |
| Egypt | 39.8 | 13.9 | 0.6 |
| India | 20.0 | 6.9 | 0.3 |
| Indonesia | 35.3 | 5.6 | 0.1 |
| Mexico | 62.5 | 20.7 | 4.2 |
| Nigeria | 91.5 | 6.7 | – |
| Russia | 114.6 | 21.0 | 2.8 |
| South Africa | 87.1 | 8.1 | 0.8 |
| Turkey | 82.8 | 16.2 | 6.1 |
| *G7 Countries* | | | |
| Canada | 61.7 | 73.0 | 27.6 |
| France | 89.8 | 51.2 | 25.2 |
| Germany | 117.6 | 72.0 | 23.7 |
| Italy | 153.1 | 54.3 | 18.4 |
| Japan | 83.9 | 68.8 | 22.1 |
| United Kingdom | 118.5 | 72.0 | 25.7 |
| USA | 83.5 | 72.5 | 23.9 |
| Worldwide | 50.1 | 20.9 | 5.4 |

*Source*: www.itu.int

studies done by Tellis and his colleagues also shows that consumers in emerging markets tend to be less eager to adopt new products than their counterparts in developed countries. One measure his team developed is the mean time-to-takeoff for new products, meaning the number of years for sales of the new product to start taking off (see also Chapter 10). Developed countries have relatively low time-to-takeoff: 5.4 years for Japan, 5.7 years for Norway, and 6.1 years for the Netherlands, Denmark, and the United States. Countries with fairly long time-to-takeoffs are all EMs: 12.4 years for India, 12.6 years for the Philippines, 13.6 years for Indonesia, and 13.9 years for Vietnam and China.[21]

7. *Weak distribution channels and media infrastructure.* Compared to developed countries, distribution and media infrastructures in EM countries are largely under-developed. Especially in rural areas, distribution is often very inefficient. Lack of adequate distribution channels means that companies often have to set up their own distribution. However, the distribution environment is changing dramatically, even in the poorer emerging markets. For instance, the shopping mall phenomenon that originated in the United States is, for better or worse, spreading to dozens of emerging markets. Nine out of the ten largest shopping malls in the world are located in emerging markets: four in China, one in Malaysia, one in Turkey (the biggest mall in Europe), and three in the Philippines (see **Exhibit 18-3**).[22]

Most of these characteristics are numbers-based (income, population, and so forth). However, we would like to add one final element that relates to a country's

---

[21]Deepa Chandrasekaran and Gerard J. Tellis, "Global Takeoff of New Products: Culture, Wealth, or Vanishing Differences?" *Marketing Science*, 27 (Sept.-Oct. 2008), pp. 844–60.
[22]"The World's Largest Malls," www.forbes.com, accessed on March 26, 2009.

**EXHIBIT 18-3**
THE WORLD'S LARGEST SHOPPING MALLS

| Ranking | Name | Location | Gross Leaseable Area (in million sq. feet) | Year Opened |
|---|---|---|---|---|
| 1 | South China Mall | Dongguan, China | 7.1 | 2005 |
| 2 | Golden Resources Shopping Mall | Beijing, China | 6.6 | 2004 |
| 3 | SM Mall of Asia | Pasay City, Philippines | 4.2 | 2006 |
| 4 | Cevahir Istanbul | Istanbul, Turkey | 3.8 | 2005 |
| 5 | West Edmonton Mall | Edmonton, Canada | 3.8 | 1981 |
| 6 | SM Megamall | Mandaluyong City, Philippines | 3.6 | 1991 |
| 7 | Berjaya Times Square | Kuala Lumpur, Malaysia | 3.4 | 2005 |
| 8 | Beijing Mall | Beijing, China | 3.4 | 2005 |
| 9 | Zhengjia Plaza | Guangzhou, China | 3 | 2005 |
| 10 | SM City North Edsa | Quezon City, Philippines | 3 | 1985 |

*Source*: Compiled from "World's 10 Largest Shopping Malls," www.forbes.com

Courtesy: Mr. Romualdo Leones

SM Mall of Asia in Pasay City, Philippines

institutional framework: EMs are economies that are coming of age as they evolve from a system based on informal relationships to a more formal system with rules that are transparent and apply equally to all market players.[23] This involves strong economic, political, and legal institutions with rigorous regulatory controls (e.g., anti-trust, intellectual property rights), rule of law, corporate governance, and contracts that are binding and enforced.

[23]"When Are Emerging Markets No Longer 'Emerging'?" knowledge.wharton.upenn.edu, accessed on March 27, 2009.

## COMPETING WITH THE NEW CHAMPIONS

◆ ◆ ◆ ◆ ◆ ◆ ◆

Conventional wisdom tells us that as trade barriers crumble and emerging economies take off, multinationals can grab opportunities in these countries and prosper. The boons of these markets include cheap labor, rising incomes, and weak local competitors. These days, however, in many rapidly developing countries the competitive environment does not always live up to this premise. Local players have been able to keep multinationals at bay. One sign is the growing number of companies that are rooted in that part of the world showing up in the *Fortune Global 500* ranking. In the 2008 ranking, 29 companies hailed from China, 7 from India, 5 from Brazil, 5 from Mexico, and 5 from Russia.[24] Another telling sign is the global banking sector. In 1999, 11 of the 20 largest (in terms of market capitalization) banks in the world were U.S. based with Citigroup being the largest bank and Bank of America coming second. In 2009, barely one decade later, 5 of the largest banks hailed from China and only 3 from the United States. The top spot now belongs to ICBC, China's biggest bank; Citigroup meanwhile languishes at the bottom of the list.[25] Obviously, the global economic downturn played a big role here, but still.

A more recent development is that several of the so-called new champions are also wielding their clout outside their home market. In this section we first look at strategies used by local companies in emerging markets. We then examine how multinationals can bolster their competitive position against the onslaught of the new champions.

In the Philippines, many lunch crowd people longing for a burger do not head to a McDonald's or a Burger King restaurant. Instead, they buy their fast food at Jollibee's, a local chain with a cute-looking bee as a mascot (see **Exhibit 18-4**). The company,

**The New Champions**

**EXHIBIT 18-4**
JOLLIBEE—THE LEADING FAST FOOD CHAIN IN THE PHILIPPINES

Courtesy: Mr. Romualdo Leones

[24]http://money.cnn.com/magazines/fortune/global500/2008/.
[25]"The Fearsome Become the Fallen," www.ft.com, accessed on March 26, 2009.

which started as an ice cream parlor in 1975, now dominates the fast food scene in the Philippines. It has become popular by creating the image of a warm, friendly, family-bonding place. In 1986, it opened its first store overseas, in Taiwan. Today, Jollibee outlets can be found across Asia (e.g., Brunei, Hong Kong, Indonesia, Vietnam) as well as in the United States.[26] Jollibee is just one example of a so-called **new champion**, a company created in an emerging market that has been able to humble multinationals. Looking at China, the fastest growing EM, local champions throw their weight in dozens of industries. In the IT industry alone, some of the highfliers that are leaders in their respective fields include Baidu for online search, Taobao (owned by Alibaba) for online auctions, youku.com for online video-sharing, Shanda for online gaming, and QQzone (owned by Tencent) for social networking.

Dozens of the new champions have also become credible challengers outside their home market. Taiwan-based HTC is now one of the leading smart-phone brands. The company is also the manufacturer of the first smart phone that uses Google's Android software. Acer, another Taiwanese high-tech company, is the leading brand in Europe's personal computing market. Some of these challengers have made forays overseas by buying up global brands. Recent high-profile examples include the purchase of the Miller beer brand by South African brewer SAB and the Budweiser brand by Brazil's InBev,[27] the acquisition of IBM's PC division by Chinese computer maker Lenovo, and the purchase of the Jaguar and Land Rover luxury car brands by India's Tata Group. Some also have made strides in the global arena through global ad campaigns or multimillion dollar sponsorship deals: in 2004 Emirates Air, the Dubai-based airline, signed a £100 million ($165 million) deal to name the new stadium of English soccer team Arsenal;[28] India's Tata Consultancy Services became a sponsor of the Formula One Ferrari team for the 2009 season.[29]

What makes emerging-markets firms so successful? Bhattacharya and Michael identify six strategies that the new champions employ to stave off multinational companies:[30]

1. *Create customized offerings.* Savvy local companies often have built up an intimate knowledge of their customers. By leveraging their customer information, these firms have been able to develop customized products or services that appeal to their clients. A case in point is Shenzhen-based Tencent and its QQ online messaging service. With a registered user base of 150 million, Tencent dominates China's messaging and social networking site (SNS) market. Foreign internet brands, such as MSN, Yahoo!, and MySpace, lag far behind. Apart from investing very heavily in building up the QQ-brand name, another reason for QQ's dominance is features such as digital avatars that can be personalized. These avatars allow users to personalize their online messaging presence, thereby tapping into Chinese people's desire for freedom of expression. By the same token, Jollibee localized its burgers to taste like stronger-flavored meatballs instead of pure beef patties, which Filipinos find too bland. The chain's menu also includes favorite Filipino items such as sweet spaghetti, palabok (vermicelli noodles), and arroz caldo (a chicken rice dish).[31]

2. *Develop business models to overcome obstacles.* Local champions are adept in identifying key challenges and then developing business models to surmount them. Multinational firms can always copycat them but savvy local players always sustain their edge by honing their first-mover advantage. A good example is the computer gaming industry in China. For companies such as Sony and Microsoft, product piracy is a key challenge in China. Shanda and other Chinese players have developed a

---

[26]"A Filipino Sting for McDonald's," *International Herald Tribune*, May 31, 2005, p. 10.

[27]Strictly speaking, InBev is a Belgium/Brazil company but the CEO and key managers are Brazilian. After the Anheuser-Busch acquisition, InBev changed its name to Anheuser-Busch InBev.

[28]http://news.bbc.co.uk/sport2/hi/football/teams/a/arsenal/3715678.stm

[29]http://news.bbc.co.uk/sport2/hi/motorsport/formula_one/7788830.stm

[30]Arindam K. Bhattacharya and David C. Michael, "How Local Companies Keep Multinationals at Bay," *Harvard Business Review*, 86 (March 2008), pp. 84–95.

[31]"A Filipino Sting for McDonald's."

**EXHIBIT 18-5**

Tata Group chairman Ratan Tata poses with a Nano car.

thriving business by developing multiplayer online role-playing games where the issue of piracy is moot. Another important obstacle is the lack of a credit card culture. Shanda overcame that stumbling block by introducing off-line payment mechanisms such as pre-paid cards.

3. *Deploy latest technologies.* Given that local players are typically still very young companies, they are not hampered by the legacy of old technologies and can leapfrog to the latest technologies instead. This enables them to keep their operating costs low and to provide good-quality products or services. Some of these companies have also become very innovative. Safaricom is Kenya's leading mobile phone service provider. The company developed a mobile banking service called M-PESA that allows clients to transfer money via SMS and handle their mobile phone as an electronic wallet. The product became so successful that Vodafone, a British mobile carrier that holds a stake in Safaricom, rolled it out to other developing countries (see **Exhibit 18-5**).

4. *Take advantage of cheap labor and train staff in-house.* Labor costs in most emerging markets are still much lower than in developed countries. Rather than relying on capital-intensive modes of business, many of the new champions have developed business models that leverage the cheap labor cost advantage in their home country. Huawei and ZTE, two leading Chinese telecom infrastructure firms, have been able to undercut the likes of Cisco and Alcatel/Lucent in international markets because of their access to a massive pool of Chinese engineers who are willing to accept salaries far lower than their Western counterparts. By the same token, BYD, the biggest Chinese manufacturer of rechargeable batteries, claims that its "human resource advantage" is the key element of its strategy.[32] The company's business model relies on a huge army of migrant workers to assemble its products instead of the robotic arms used on Japanese assembly lines. BYD employs about 10,000 engineers

[32]"Buffett Takes Charge," *Fortune Asia Edition* (April 27, 2009), pp. 36–42.

who come from China's best schools. The firm can afford to recruit so many of them because salaries are only $600 to $700 a month. Companies from emerging markets are also often much more capable in dealing with the bare minimum of resources than their rivals from the developed world, a skill that Carlos Ghosn, the head of Renault-Nissan, describes as "frugal engineering."

5. *Scale up rapidly.* Many homegrown champions distinguish themselves by building up scale very quickly. Typically, this happens through a combination of organic growth and absorbing smaller rivals. Several new champions go a step further and take their innovative business models to other emerging markets or sometimes even the Western world. A case in point is Pearl River Piano, China's leading piano manufacturer. The company grew over the last 30 years by out-investing local rivals. Currently, the company has the world's largest piano factory with a capacity of 100,000 pianos per year. In 2000, the firm bought up Rittmuller, a German piano maker, to boost its reputation and to broaden its price points.[33] The firm is now the leader at the low end of the U.S. upright piano market.

6. *Invest in talent to sustain growth.* The new challengers also grow by their willingness to invest in managerial talent. Several of their top executives left senior positions with multinationals to join them. Even though the salaries may not always match those paid by multinationals, there are other ways to attract talent: the prospect of rapid career advancement, the joy of being part of an entrepreneurial culture, shares in the company.

One challenge that the emerging-market champions face is whether they should focus on their home market or expand into the global marketplace. Li Ning, for example, is a Chinese athletic wear company named for its founder, who won three gold medals in gymnastics during the 1984 Los Angeles Olympics. The sneaker company has been very successful in China. It intends to export its shoes to Europe and the United States and compete head-on with the likes of Nike and adidas.[34] Deciding which strategy to pursue hinges on two parameters: the strength of globalization pressures and the degree to which a company's assets can be transferred internationally.[35] Combining these two parameters generates a set of four strategic options, as is illustrated in **Exhibit 18-6**. If globalization pressures are high in the industry but the company's assets are only valuable in its home market, then the best course of action is to enter into a joint venture or sell out to a multinational. This option is the *dodging* strategy. In 2008, Huiyuan Juice, China's leading pure juice brand, agreed to allow Coca-Cola to acquire it., However, the Chinese government ultimately rejected the proposed buy-out deal due to anti-trust concerns. If a company's assets are transferable, it can use its success at home as a platform for expansion in foreign markets. Under this scenario, the company can compete head-on with the large multinationals and become a *contender*. To overcome the first-mover status of established multinationals, the contender should start by benchmarking the global players to search for ways to innovate. The insights derived from the benchmarking exercise can then be used to navigate around the leading global players. This could be done by tapping into niches that have been neglected by the existing multinationals so far.[36] The switch to greener technologies in the car industry gives newcomers from emerging markets an opening to compete with incumbent carmakers. In particular, BYD, a Chinese battery maker, can leverage its expertise in battery design to compete in the electric car niche. By the same token, India's Tata Group aspires to launch its super-cheap fuel-efficient Tata Nano car in Europe and the United States. In Tata's case, a key transferable asset is the company's expertise in developing ultra-cheap cars. When there is little pressure to globalize and the company's assets are not transferable, the firm should focus on defending its home turf advantage. Companies finding themselves in

---

[33] www.pearlriverusa.com

[34] "China Tries to Solve its Brand X Blues," www.nytimes.com, accessed on March 28, 2009.

[35] Niraj Dawar and Tony Frost, "Competing with Giants. Survival Strategies for Local Companies in Emerging Markets," *Harvard Business Review*, March–April 1999, pp. 119–29.

[36] Christopher A. Bartlett and Sumantra Ghoshal, "Going Global. Lessons from Late Movers," *Harvard Business Review*," March–April 2000, pp. 133–42.

**EXHIBIT 18-6**
STRATEGIC OPTIONS FOR EMERGING-MARKET COMPANIES

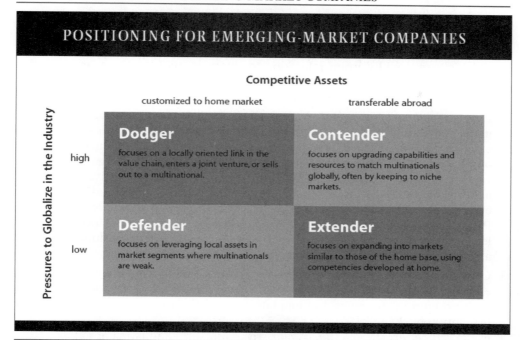

such a situation are *defenders*. Li Ning, the Chinese athletic wear company that we mentioned earlier, could be an example of such a company. One of the firm's assets is Mr. Li Ning, the founder and former gymnast, who personifies the brand. While Li Ning is well recognized in China,[37] the brand personality does not resonate with sports fans outside China. Furthermore, given the size of China's athletic apparel market, there is very little pressure for Li Ning to globalize. The fourth scenario arises when globalization pressures are weak but the company's assets are transferable. Under such circumstances, the company can generate extra revenues and scale economies by leveraging its asset in markets similar to its home market. A case in point is Lenovo, the Chinese personal computing firm. With its dominance of the PC market in China, Lenovo has learned how to effectively compete in emerging markets. Lenovo's strategy is to expand aggressively in emerging markets, including the other three BRIC countries, by transferring its China business model.[38]

Multinationals from the developed world can fight off the challenge posed by emerging-market newcomers but it may take some innovative thinking. Usually, multinationals from developed countries defend themselves against emerging giants by focusing on the high-end segments of the market. Such a move may allow them to sustain margins but at the expense of lower volumes. Another option is to take a leaf out of the new champions' book and try to beat them at their own game by pursuing value-for-market strategies. The competitive response that IBM delivered to the onslaught on its service business provides a good illustration of this approach. A threesome of Indian outsourcing upstarts, Tata Consulting Services, Infosys, and Wipro, posed a serious threat to IBM's service business. To fight off the assault, IBM bought Daksh, a smaller rival of the trio, and built it into a large business to compete on cost and quality with its Indian rivals.[39] In general,

**Competing Against the Newcomers**

[37] Li Ning lit the Olympic flame during the opening ceremony of the 2008 Beijing Summer Olympics.
[38] "Lenovo Ousts CEO, Returns to Roots," www.wsj.com, accessed on March 28, 2009.
[39] "A Special Report on Globalization," *The Economist*, September 20, 2008.

multinationals can choose from five value-for-money strategies to fend off threats from the emerging giants in their industry:[40]

1. *Go beyond low-cost sourcing in emerging markets.* Western multinationals should view developing countries as more than cheap manufacturing bases. They should examine the entire value chain from R&D to customer service support and see which stages would warrant relocation to emerging markets. For example, Nokia Siemens Network, a joint venture between Nokia and Siemens, set up an innovation center in China to develop software technologies for the telecom industry.

2. *Develop products in emerging markets and bring them home.* Companies could launch in their developed markets new products that were developed by their subsidiaries in emerging markets. The reason is that these affiliates often have an intimate knowledge of value-oriented consumers and, thereby, honed their skills for this segment. Unilever views its Indian subsidiary Hindustan Lever as a major font for innovative ideas. Pureit, a cheap home water purification system that Hindustan Lever introduced in 2008, is one example of a brilliant innovation that Unilever plans to transplant to other markets.[41] M-PESA is an innovative mobile payment solution developed by Safaricom, Kenya's leading mobile phone carrier. Vodafone, the British mobile communications group and a partner of Safaricom, is now taking the breakthrough service to other countries.

3. *Copy branding tactics used in emerging markets.* Emerging giants often use cost-effective tactics to build up their brand image. Western companies could learn from such promotion strategies and emulate such tactics to get more bang for their promotion buck.

4. *Team up with the new emerging giants.* Traditionally, multinationals would form a joint venture with a local firm to penetrate the host market. The local partner would help the multinational through its distribution knowledge or knowledge of local consumers. A more radical approach is to tie up with a new emerging giant and harness its capabilities in delivering value-for-money (cost innovation). This would allow the multinational to share the risks with the local partner and to grow in tandem with the partner. One example is IBM's partnership with AirTel in the Indian mobile-phone market. IBM manages much of AirTel's back-office operations and shares the financial risk with the firm. Such partnerships would not just focus on the emerging-market firm's home market but also include other emerging markets or even developed countries.

5. *Invest in growing mass markets in developing countries.* Most Western multinationals focus on the high-end segments of the market when competing in developing countries and leave the mass markets to their local competitors. However, such strategy enables local players to build up scale and experience. To pre-empt them, multinationals must broaden their scope and also go for the mass markets.

◆ ◆ ◆ ◆ ◆ ◆ ◆ ◆   ## TARGETING/POSITIONING STRATEGIES IN EMERGING MARKETS—BOP OR NO BOP?

Just as with developed markets, choosing the right target markets is one of the key strategic issues multinationals grapple with in emerging markets. As income levels in most of these countries tend to be low, MNCs doing business in this part of the world have typically focused on the wealthy consumers and businesses while ignoring the rest of the population. These days, however, several MNCs realize that there could also be huge market opportunities at the so-called "bottom of the pyramid." The **bottom of the pyramid (BOP)** is defined as the 4 billion people living on less than $2 per day. C. K.

---

[40]Peter J. Williamson and Ming Zeng, "Value-for-Money Strategies for Recessionary Times," *Harvard Business Review*, 87 (March 2009), pp. 66–75.
[41]"Unilever CEO Looking at India for Growth Tips," www.business-standard.com, accessed on March 29, 2009.

Prahalad, a management guru and professor at the University of Michigan, popularized the concept in his 2004 book, *Fortune at the Bottom of the Pyramid*. The BOP paradigm can be summarized as follows:[42]

- First, there is a lot of untapped money at the BOP. The poor represent a substantial reservoir of pent-up demand.
- Second, the BOP offers a new growth opportunity for value creation and a forum for innovation.
- Third, BOP markets must become an integral part of the firms' core businesses. They will be critical for the long-term growth and vitality of MNCs.

Catering to the BOP in EMs can be very rewarding for MNCs. Some of the benefits include the following:[43]

1. Some BOP markets are large and attractive as stand-alone entities.
2. Many local innovations can be leveraged across other BOP markets, thereby creating a global opportunity for such innovations.
3. Some innovations that originate in BOP markets can also be launched in the MNC's developed markets.
4. The learning experience from the BOP markets can also benefit the MNC. Pursuing the BOP forces an MNC to deliver value for money, which requires relentless cost discipline. Cost discipline goes beyond cost cutting techniques. To succeed in a BOP market, the MNC should pursue **cost innovation**, meaning, innovation efforts that focus on re-engineering cost structures (instead of new functions or features) so that the firm can offer the same or even much more value at a lower cost for consumers.[44]

Nokia's experience in China illustrates how an MNC can thrive in a BOP market environment. Nokia views China's less-developed regions as a major driving force behind its future growth: while mobile phone subscription growth in China's big cities is slowing, the country's smaller cities and rural area still offer tremendous market opportunities. Most new users from these regions buy handsets for the first time. To tap into China's BOP, Nokia has developed a wide variety of ultra-cheap handsets that can be sold for as little as $30. As a result, Nokia was able to outmaneuver domestic handset manufacturers and prevail in the low-end segment, while still maintaining dominance in the upper-end of China's mobile phone market.[45]

One fallacy marketers often make is that value for the BOP consumers means low price. Low-income consumers have similar perceptions and needs as their richer neighbors. They are often attracted to international brands due to their perceived quality image. One market researcher in the region notes: "A low-income mother sending her child to school may see the fact that he or she has a very clean white shirt as the only way she can express love. So she will choose her soap powder brand in a much more considered way than a middle-income mother who can afford to express her love in other ways."[46]

Although the case for marketing to the BOP sounds compelling, some scholars find the BOP proposition to be too good to be true. In particular, professor Karnani, incidentally a colleague of C. K. Prahalad, argues that the whole concept of marketing to the BOP is a mirage. Karnani claims that the BOP market (1) is very small and (2) is unlikely to be profitable for most MNCs as they overestimate the buying power of poor

---

[42]C. K. Prahalad, *The Fortune at the Bottom of the Pyramid* Upper Saddle River, NJ: Wharton School Publishing, 2004, pp. 4–6.
[43]Ibid., Chapter 3.
[44]"Value-for-Money Strategies," pp. 68–70.
[45]"Nokia Sees Chance in Underdeveloped Areas," www.chinadaily.com.cn, accessed on March 30, 2009.
[46]"A Fresh Look at the Low Earner," *Media*, March 9, 2007, p. 8.

## $\mathcal{G}$LOBAL PERSPECTIVE 18-1

### HINDUSTAN LEVER — STRADDLING THE PYRAMID

In 2008, Hindustan Unilever Ltd (HUL), Unilever's subsidiary in India, celebrated its 75th anniversary. The company is the largest soap and detergent manufacturer in India. India's current socioeconomic structure looks like a pyramid: a narrow top of high-income households — the "affluent," a broader middle layer of middle-income people — the "aspirers," and huge bottom layer of low-income households, the "strivers." However, HUL foresees that the shape of India's society will evolve from a pyramid to a diamond by 2013 (see Table A). Furthermore, India has a very young population.

Instead of simply selling premium brands to the top-end of the pyramid, HUL grows its business by "straddling the pyramid." This vision involves offering premium brands to the affluent, value-for-money brands to middle-income consumers, and affordable pricing to low-income consumers. HUL recognizes that India's BOP consumers do not simply look for cheap products but quality products that are affordable.

### India's Changing Income Pattern — From a Pyramid to a Diamond

| Socioeconomic class | Number of households in 2003 (in millions) | Number of households projected by 2013 (in millions) |
| --- | --- | --- |
| Rich Classes | 3 | 11 |
| Aspiring Classes | 46 | 124 |
| Strivers (BOP) | 131 | 96 |
| Total | 181 | 231 |

*Source:* National Council of Agriculture & Economic Research

To straddle the pyramid, HUL's marketing strategy rests on six pillars:

*Sources:* Harish Manwani, "Winning in Developing & Emerging Markets," http://www.hul.co.in/mediacentre/speeches/Hll_Agm_Speech_Booklet_2006.pdf, "Hindustan Unilever Limited," Merrill Lynch India Conference Investor Presentation, 2nd February 2009.

1. An unmatched brand portfolio to serve the many Indias
2. Innovation and R&D capabilities
3. A track record of building large and profitable mass markets
4. A versatile distribution network that is capable of handling both traditional and modern trade
5. A good record of devising strategies that aid rural development in India
6. A strong local talent base.

For each core category, HUL has a brand portfolio that covers all three income groups. A case in point is the soap category in which the firm sells three major brands: at the bottom, Lifebuoy for the strivers; in the middle, Lux for the aspirers; and at the top, Dove for the affluent. HUL's 2008 (value) market share of the soap category was 51.6 percent, compared to 9.4 percent for the nearest competitor.

Innovation at HUL is not only new product development but also stretches to business processes, packaging, distribution channels, and delivery mechanisms. To develop the BOP market, HUL introduced the single-use, one Rupee sachet of shampoo. The firm extended this so-called low unit price concept to other categories (e.g., detergents, tea, toothpaste). To cope with India's lack of water supply, HUL scientists developed a detergent powder (Surf Excel Quick Wash) that requires much less water than regular powders. Unilever plans to launch the brand in other markets where water scarcity is a major issue.

Diarrhea is a major disease among India's poor. Almost twenty percent of India's children suffer from diarrhea. In 2002, HUL initiated a campaign to combat this disease, which illustrates how the firm combines its business strategy with economic development. Studies had shown that washing hands with soap lowers the risk of the disease by almost half. Unfortunately, there is little awareness among India's poor of basic hygiene habits such as washing hands. To spread the message of health and hygiene to India's countryside, HUL launched the Lifebuoy Swasthya Chetana initiative in 2002.

people. Instead of viewing the poor as consumers, the best antidote to poverty according to the critics of the BOP premise is to focus on them as producers. Private firms can help here by upgrading the skills and productivity of the poor and creating more job opportunities for them.[47]

One fundamental difference between developed countries and the EMs is that segments are usually much coarser in the latter markets. Most categories in developed countries are highly segmented catering to a wide variety of preferences or tastes. Such

---

[47]Aneel Karnani, "The Mirage of Marketing to the Bottom of the Pyramid: How the Private Sector Can Help Alleviate Poverty," *California Management Review*, 49(4), Summer 2007, pp. 90–112.

high level of product differentiation tends to be very costly for most product categories. Given the low incomes in most EMs, such finely refined level of segmentation is not effective. Also, the targeted media (e.g., niche cable channels) that enable highly refined segmentation simply do not exist in many EMs. **Global Perspective 18-1** discusses some of the strategies being used by Hindustan Lever to conquer India's BOP market.

## ENTRY STRATEGIES FOR EMERGING MARKETS

◆ ◆ ◆ ◆ ◆ ◆ ◆

Given their volatile market environment, choosing the proper entry strategy becomes a crucial task for a successful performance in EMs. As we saw in Chapter 9, setting up an entry strategy involves many different aspects. In this section we focus on two key decisions: the timing and the mode of entry.

Despite the appeal of EMs, especially the huge BRIC countries, early entry can hurt performance even for mighty brands. When the cereal industry of Western countries matured in the 1990s, it did not take long for Kellogg's to decide to enter India. A country with one billion people presents an alluring prospect for many consumer goods companies. Further, the company would have very few direct competitors. In 1994, Kellogg's ventured into India with a $65 million investment. Unfortunately, Indian consumers found the whole concept of eating breakfast cereal odd. Although initial sales were encouraging, sales never really took off. Apparently, many people bought Corn Flakes for its novelty value but then went back to more familiar breakfast entrees. Even if they liked the taste, the product was too expensive for most households.[48] Most likely, India was not yet ready for Western-style cereals and Kellogg's entry may have been too hasty and aggressive.

**Timing of Entry**

There are several reasons why first movers in emerging markets can fail.[49] As the Kellogg's example shows, early entrants may not be aware of the pitfalls of newly opened emerging markets. Second, returns on investment can be low when the infrastructure is not yet fully developed. For instance, when distribution channels are dysfunctional or missing, the MNC typically needs to build up its own distribution network. Such an endeavor demands heavy investments that may be hard to recover in the short or medium term. Third, later entrants have a flatter learning curve as they can learn from the mistakes made by earlier entrants.

On the other hand, powerful arguments can also be made for early entry.[50] First, government relations are usually far more influential in EMs than in developed countries. Nurturing of these relationships could lead to favorable treatment and tangible benefits (e.g., tax holidays, licenses) that buffer the early entrant against incursions of later entrants. Second, the huge pent-up demand for previously unavailable Western brands can lead to very high initial sales. Third, early entrants can lock up access to key resources such as media access, brand endorsers, distributors or suppliers. Such resources are often much scarcer in EMs than in developed countries. Fourth, early entrants can enjoy higher productivity of their marketing dollars. In early stages of economic development, advertising rates and competitive marketing spending are relatively low. Therefore, marketing dollars can deliver much more bang-for-the-buck in the form of high awareness, share-of-mind, or brand preference compared to later stages. A final aspect is the potential for smaller players to outmaneuver their larger slower-moving rivals. EMs have less well-established brand preferences and higher growth rates than their developed counterparts. As a result, gaining a foothold in these markets can be much less difficult for the challengers than in more mature developed countries.

---

[48] http://brand-failures.kuntau.net/culture-failures/kelloggs-in-india.html

[49] Joseph Johnson and Gerard J. Tellis, "Drivers of Success for Market Entry into China and India," *Journal of Marketing*, 72 (May 2008), pp. 1–13.

[50] David J. Arnold and John A. Quelch, "New Strategies for Emerging Markets," *Sloan Management Review*, 40 (Fall 1998), pp. 7–20.

**Entry Mode**  An MNC that plans to enter a new EM can choose from several modes of entry (discussed in Chapter 9): exporting, licensing/franchise, joint venture, wholly-owned subsidiary. As you may remember, the key tradeoff among these choices is that between risk and control over marketing resources. Risk has both a financial (e.g., currency volatility, getting paid) and marketing (e.g., sales volume) component. In general, risk levels tend to be much higher in EMs than in developed countries. However, control can also be very critical for an MNC entering an EM. First, control protects resources from leakage, such as patent theft. Second, success in the EM often rests on strict control over scarce resources such as distribution or supply. One very important factor for the mode choice is the institutional framework in the EM. These institutions include items such as the legal framework and its enforcement, property rights protection, regulatory regimes (e.g., anti-trust). A recent study compared the entry choices of MNCs in four emerging economies: Vietnam, Egypt, South Africa, and India. The authors found that the stronger the institutional framework, the more likely the MNC would prefer an acquisition or greenfield entry mode over joint ventures.[51]

Given the large risks and the firm's lack of knowledge, MNCs usually first enter with a low-risk entry mode (e.g., licensing, minority JV) to minimize risks. The focus is on sales rather than marketing. There is little adaptation, as the small volumes cannot support potential adaptation costs. Over time, as sales take off, the MNC increases its commitment and shifts toward a higher-control entry mode. In case the MNC entered the market via a joint venture, it might raise its stake or even buy out the partner if the country's legal framework allows that.[52]

When developing an entry strategy, the ultimate yardstick is the firm's performance in the host country. Clearly many factors play a role in driving the entry's success or failure. A recent study examined the drivers of success for market entry into China and India, the two biggest emerging markets. Its main conclusions were the following:[53]

- Success is greater for entry into China than for entry into India.
- Success is greater for smaller firms than for bigger ones.
- Success is greater for entry into emerging markets with less openness and less risk and those that are economically similar to the multinational's home market.
- The greater the control of the entry mode, the larger the success.

Once the MNC has decided on an entry strategy, the firm has to develop a marketing strategy to penetrate the EM. Simply replicating strategies that served the company well in developed countries could be a recipe for disaster. In the remainder of this chapter, we discuss the different elements of the marketing mix in an EM environment.

◆ ◆ ◆ ◆ ◆ ◆ ◆ ◆  **PRODUCT POLICY**

Offering the right product mix is a major requirement to thrive in the EM. Scores of MNCs failed in this regard. In what follows, we highlight three facets of the product policy: product design, branding, and packaging.

**Product Design**  Often, when first entering an EM, the multinational is reluctant to adapt its product offerings to the host market. Adaptation costs money and is time consuming. Given the high market risks, adaptation could be a gamble that the firm is not willing to make.[54]

---

[51]Klaus Meyer, Saul Estrin, Sumon Bhaumik, and Mike W. Peng, "Institutions, Resources, and Entry Strategies in Emerging Economies," *Strategic Management Journal*, 30(1), 2009, pp. 61–80.

[52]*The Mirage of Global Markets*, pp. 85–90.

[53]Joseph Johnson and Gerard J. Tellis, "Drivers of Success for Market Entry into China and India," *Journal of Marketing*, 72 (May 2008), pp. 1–13.

[54]David J. Arnold and John A. Quelch, "New Strategies in Emerging Markets," *MIT Sloan Management Review*, 40 (1), Fall 1998, pp. 7–20.

Instead, the MNC might sell a narrow range of existing products and position them as premium products targeted at the affluent EM customers. Another option MNCs often pursue is **backward innovation**: offer a stripped-down version of the product that is sold in developed markets. Such a basic product could then be sold at a much lower price than the original product being sold in developed markets. Panasonic's so-called "Emerging Markets Win" (EM-WIN) products exemplify this approach. These products are mostly appliances and electronics designed in Japan, but with fewer features (e.g., fewer refrigerator doors) and modified slightly for local customers. The line targeted upper-middle income consumers (the "next rich") in fast-growing developing countries.[55]

Companies following such product policies believe that products that are at or near maturity in the developed markets, could act as anchors for the product policy in EMs. The underlying premise is that the market conditions that prevailed in the developed countries when these products were first introduced are similar to the ones that exist now in the EMs. A further payoff is that the product or its stripped-down version gets an extra lease to life by selling them in the EM. While this policy may have been effective in the twentieth century, it could go badly wrong in today's information age. Consumers in EM often want the latest products now instead of products that have become mature or obsolete in developed countries.[56] Rapid information flows via the internet and other channels imply that EM customers are often very familiar with the latest trends in EM markets.

Products designed for the mass market in EMs need to surmount two barriers, namely (1) low incomes and (2) poor infrastructure (e.g., unreliable power supply, poor roads).[57] Low incomes imply that products should be affordable, functional and built to last. Quality consistency is also crucial. Following China's melamine milk scandal, many Chinese mothers switched to foreign milk powder brands because of their safety image and consistent quality.[58] To cope with infrastructure shortcomings, the product must be sturdy and long lasting. Products may also need to be designed to handle a dysfunctional infrastructure. Whirlpool redesigned its washers for India so that they could restart from the point in the washing cycle where they had left off when the power or water supply was interrupted.[59] Surf Excel is a HUL[60] laundry detergent that is mostly used for washing clothes by hand. Water is scarce resource in India, especially in the dry southern states. HUL improved the detergent formulation so that the water used for washing could be reduced.[61] Also in India, HUL developed Pureit, an in-home water purifier that removes harmful germs from water. At Rps. 2000 (approx. $45), Pureit costs much less than most other water purifiers in India. The water purifier does neither require continuous electricity supply (it uses a battery instead), nor pressurized tap water.[62] **Global Perspective 18-2** discusses Nokia's product strategy for EMs.

**Branding**

Local brands have often humbled global brands in EMs. Assuming that consumers in EMs, even the affluent ones, will pay a premium for global brands can be a fatal mistake. One McKinsey study prescribes a two-pronged branding strategy for MNCs doing business in EMs. For the wealthy segment, the MNC can pursue sophisticated, brand-building strategies. Especially among youth segments, the global brand can offer a passport to global citizenship and thereby foster a global identity.[63] However, to capture the BOP market, MNCs should try to emulate their local competitors. This may

[55]"Panasonic Eyes Emerging Market," *The Wall Street Journal Asia*, July 10-12, 2009, p. 4.

[56]"New Strategies in Emerging Markets," p. 16.

[57]Niraj Dawar and Amitava Chattopadhyay, "Rethinking Marketing Programs for Emerging Markets," *Long Range Planning*, 35 (2002), pp. 457–74.

[58]http://news.bbc.co.uk/2/hi/asia-pacific/7620812.stm.

[59]Ibid.

[60]HUL (Hindustan Unilever Limited) is Unilever's India subsidiary.

[61]http://www.unilever.com/innovation/productinnovations/indiasavingwaterwithsurfexcel.aspx

[62]http://www.pureitwater.com/about/affordable_price.asp

[63]Yuliya Strizhakova, Robin A. Coulter, and Linda L. Price, "Branded Products as a Passport to Global Citizenship: Perspectives from Developed and Developing Countries," *Journal of International Marketing*, 16 (4), 2008, pp. 57–85.

◆ ◆ ◆ ◆ ◆ ◆ ◆ ◆ ◆ ◆ ◆ ◆ ◆ ◆ ◆ ◆ ◆ ◆ ◆ ◆ ◆ ◆ ◆ ◆ ◆ ◆ ◆ ◆ ◆ ◆ ◆ ◆ ◆ ◆ ◆

# $\mathcal{G}$LOBAL PERSPECTIVE 18-2

## NOKIA'S PRODUCT LINEUP FOR EMERGING MARKETS

With penetration rates in most developed regions close to 90 percent or even higher, handset makers increasingly focus on emerging markets. Nokia, the world's leading mobile phone company, has long recognized the potential of this part of the world. The firm is already the market leader in China and India, the two biggest prizes.

To make handsets practical for people living in EMs, Nokia traveled to the far corners of the globe. The company designed rugged, low-cost handsets with features such as dustproof cases (crucial in dry areas) and flashlights (useful in places with power outages). Through conversations with slum dweller in places such as Nairobi, Nokia learnt that many people often share handsets. It designed phones that allow owners to set limits on how much time users can talk or how much money they can spend. The phones also permit multiple contact lists.

*Sources:* "First Mover in Mobile," www.businessweek.com, accessed on March 30, 2009; "Nokia Brings the Web to Emerging Markets," www.businessweek.com, accessed on April 1, 2009; "Nokia Unveils 4 New Phones for Emerging Markets," www.reuters.com, accessed on April 1, 2009; and http://www.nokia.com/NOKIA_COM_1/Microsites/Entry_Event/phones/Nokia_Life_Tools_datasheet.pdf.

In Spring 2008, Nokia unveiled a whole range of new phone models for EM consumers. One new phone is the Nokia 5000, a low-end entry-level multimedia phone which sells for around 90 euros (around $120). Another new model is the Nokia 1680 Classic camera phone which retails for 50 euros (around $65). On November 4, 2008, Nokia announced a series of new devices and services that would facilitate web access in EMs. The new devices allow users to set up an e-mail account on Nokia's Ovi web portal without ever going near a PC. The new phone models are a boon for the numerous mobile-phone users who live in areas without reliable electricity or internet connections. Nokia also aspires to improve the lives of rural mobile phone users through a new information service, Nokia Life Tools. This service would offer information on a range of topics such as market prices, weather, prices of pesticides and fertilizers, tips on new agricultural techniques. It would also provide educational services (e.g., learning English, exam results) and entertainment (e.g., cricket scores, astrology, music). A basic subscription costs about $1.20 a month. Nokia planned to roll out this new service first in India and then elsewhere in Asia and Africa.

---

involve acquiring a local brand. Focus should be on keeping the best local managers, cost reduction, operational efficiencies, and simplicity rather than product reformulations.[64] One recent study that compared the performance of foreign and local brands in China found that the most critical element were the brands' local advantages such as access to local resources and government support.[65]

Unilever's branding strategy in India is a good illustration of some of the tactics discussed above. The company dominates India's shampoo market with a 46.3 percent market share in 2008. HUL sells global brands (e.g., Dove, SunSilk) in the category. Indian women often oil their hair before washing it, so Western shampoos that do not remove oil have not done well in India. Unilever reformulated its shampoos for India and dropped the conditioner.[66] Unilever also dominates the laundry detergent category with a 38.1 percent market share. The company's global Surf brand targets the upper crust of India's society. In response to a low-cost competitor, it launched an inexpensive brand called Wheel. The product is less refined than the premium brands but it costs much less. Wheel rapidly gained market share, matching the key competitor's share.[67]

**Packaging**    MNCs operating in EMs should pay close attention to packaging. The presence of cash-strapped consumers means that global players often must offer smaller package sizes in order to make their products affordable for the mass-market. For example, Colgate MaxFresh toothpaste is typically sold in 40-gram, 80-gram, and 150-gram tubes in India

---

[64]Gilberto Duarte de Abreu Filho, Nicola Calicchio, and Fernando Lunardini, "Brand Building in Emerging Markets," www.mckinseyquarterly.com, accessed on March 29, 2009.

[65]Gerald Yong Gao, Yigan Pan, David K. Tse, and Chi Kin Yim, "Market Share Performance of Foreign and Domestic Brands in China," *Journal of International Marketing*, 14 (2), 2006, pp. 32–51.

[66]"The Legacy that Got Left on the Shelf," *The Economist*, February 2, 2008, pp. 66–68.

[67]"Brand Building in Emerging Markets."

while it is sold in 6-oz. (170 gram) and 8-oz. (227 gram) tubes in the United States.[68] To address the needs of different segments, MNCs typically offer a variety of pack sizes at different price points. The smaller unit sizes cater toward the single-purchase buyers. The larger sizes target the bulk purchasers. Often though, local merchants buy the family-pack size and resell it in loose form (e.g., single cigarettes from open boxes).

Because of their freshness and safety (e.g., sealed packaging), brands sold by MNCs are often favored by local consumers. The pharmaceutical company Pfizer, for instance, benefits from the belief in much of the developing world that branded medicines are worth paying a premium for because they are safer and more effective than generics. Pfizer's prices in Venezuela, though far below U.S. prices, are still 40% to 50% more than generics.[69] Poor local infrastructure forces firms to re-engineer the packaging to ensure the safety and freshness of their products. The packaging must be sturdy enough to allow shipping in sub-optimal conditions to areas that are not always accessible via motorized transport. Storage facilities that are standard in developed countries such as refrigeration do not always exist.

Finally, MNCs should strive for sustainability regarding packaging. In many EMs, packaging materials are scarce and costly. Furthermore, waste treatment facilities are often inadequate. Therefore, packaging should ideally rely on local materials and be recyclable or biodegradable.[70]

## PRICING STRATEGY ◆ ◆ ◆ ◆ ◆ ◆ ◆

Not surprisingly, given the low per-capita income levels in most EMs, setting the right price is an important element of the marketing strategy. In general, strategies that rely on thin margins and big volumes tend to succeed. Large volumes can make even small-ticket items that retail at one cent (e.g., gum) hugely profitable.[71] To capture sustainable sales volume, an MNC should try to saturate all price points instead of simply focusing on the upper-end of the market. If it fails to do so, local competitors who cater to the mass market could achieve economies of scale and use their favorable cost position to attack the MNC in the higher-priced segment at some point in the future. In India, Unilever dominates most of the product categories in which it competes. In all of these categories, Unilever markets at least one brand in each price tier (see **Exhibit 18-7**). Likewise, Nokia rolls out handsets at different price points in EMs: ranging from cheap entry-level phones for low-income, first-time buyers to premium priced full-feature sets for well-heeled replacement buyers. It makes profits at all ends of the market.[72]

To sustain profit margins, MNCs should focus on cost innovation ("frugal engineering") to improve the product's cost structure instead of continuous product innovation. By lowering fixed and variable costs, the firm can make its products affordable while still enjoying a healthy profit margin. At the same time, marketers should keep in mind that EM consumers are not always obsessed with price. Unilever's experience with Omo in Vietnam is a telling example.[73] In 1995, Unilever launched the laundry detergent brand Omo in Vietnam. During its first 8 years, Omo was preoccupied with a bitter price war against P&G's Tide. When its market share started to slip in 2002, Unilever decided to shift its strategy for Omo from price-led to brand-led. The firm tried to create an emotional bond by weaving heritage, family, and compassion into the core of Omo's brand proposition. For instance, during the 2004 Tet New Year, it ran a commercial around the local superstition that touching the clothes of loved ones would

---

[68]Sameer Mathur, "Package Sizing and Pricing in an Emerging Market," Carnegie Mellon University working paper, 2008.

[69]"Drug Firms See Poorer Nations as Cure for Sales Problems," *The Wall Street Journal Asia*, July 8, 2009, pp. 14–15.

[70]Kelly L. Weidner, Jose Antonio Rosa, and Madhubalan Viswanathan, "Marketing to Subsistence Consumers: Contemporary Methodologies and Initiatives," University of Illinois at Chicago working paper, 2008.

[71]"Rethinking Marketing Programs for Emerging Markets," p. 465.

[72]"Nokia's Big Plans for India," www.businessweek.com, accessed on March 29, 2009.

[73]"Brands at the Starting Gate," *Media*, February 23, 2007, pp. 20–21.

**EXHIBIT 18-7**
HINDUSTAN UNILEVER'S BRAND PORTFOLIO

### Portfolio straddling the pyramid

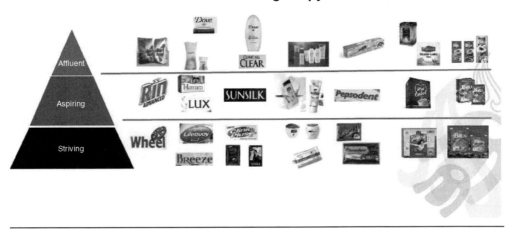

*Source:* Hindustan Unilever Limited

send a message to call them back home. By 2005, Omo had become the number one recalled brand and seized category leadership in Vietnam.

In rural areas, people often practice **demand pooling**: they join their resources together to buy a particular product or service. For instance, Nokia learned that Nairobi slum dwellers organize buying clubs where the members pool their money to buy handsets one at a time until every member has one.[74] Demand pooling can also occur among groups of small businesses or entrepreneurs.

## THE DISTRIBUTION CHALLENGE

Distribution is typically one of the biggest challenges for MNCs doing business in EMs. The lack of a suitable distribution infrastructure coupled with the sheer land size of many EMs has deterred several MNCs from early entry. Distribution in many EMs also varies enormously between urban and rural areas. In urban areas, even the small retailers carry a wide assortment of brands in spite of limited shelf space. At the same time, modern distribution formats (e.g., shopping malls, hyper/supermarkets, discount stores) are on the rise. The needs of the modern trade differ greatly from those of the traditional trade. MNCs need to develop skills in supply chain management, in-store merchandising, and key account management to cater to the needs of the modern trade. Doing this without rupturing the ties with the traditional retailers poses a big challenge.[75] Rural retailers often carry only a single brand for each category. Therefore, being first on the shelf and building a close relationship with these retailers can create a competitive edge.[76]

Compared to developed countries, distribution also tends to be much more labor intensive in EMs, especially in rural areas. In most cases, local regulations or lack of local market knowledge force the MNC to partner with a local distributor. Middlemen in EMs often fulfill roles which elsewhere are fulfilled by the country subsidiary such as choosing target segments, setting the pricing policy, or promoting the brand.[77]

---

[74]"First Mover in Mobile," www.businessweek.com, accessed on March 30, 2009.

[75]Harish Manwani, "Winning in Developing and Emerging Markets," Speech at Hindustan Unilever Limited Annual General Meeting, May 29, 2006.

[76]"Rethinking Marketing Programs for Emerging Markets," p. 469.

[77]"New Strategies in Emerging Markets," pp. 17–18.

**EXHIBIT 18-8**
PROJECT SHAKTI

*Source:* www.hllshakti.com

If a suitable distribution infrastructure is lacking, one solution is to establish a distribution system from scratch. In many of the former communist East Bloc countries, government-controlled distribution collapsed after the fall of the Berlin Wall. In Russia and Poland, P&G decided to build its own distribution operations, known within the company as the *McVan model*. In both countries, the company identified a number of promising distributors and provided them with vans, working capital, and extensive training. Each distributor was granted territorial exclusivity. In exchange, the distributors made a commitment to distribute only P&G products. In Russia, this distribution system gave P&G coverage of some 80 percent of the population at a time when most MNCs were still restricted to the two main cities of Moscow and St. Petersburg. As a result, P&G gained leadership in many categories.[78] Unilever's approach to distributing its products in rural India is another good example. The company's challenge was how to reach 500,000 villages in the remote areas of India. Unilever's solution, called *Project Shakti*,[79] was to tap into the growing number of women's self-help groups, of which about one million now exist across India (see **Exhibit 18-8**). Unilever rolled out the project in 2001. Company representatives give presentations at self-help group meetings and invite their members to become direct-to-consumer sales distributors selling Unilever products. Unilever provides participants support with training in selling, commercial knowledge, and bookkeeping. Those who complete the training program can then choose to become *Project Shakti* entrepreneurs. Each distributor invests 10,000 to 15,000 rupees ($220–330) in stock at the outset—usually borrowed from the self-help group or micro-finance banks—and aims to get around 500 customers. Most of them generate 10,000 to 12,000 rupees sales revenues a month, which translates into a monthly profit of 700 to 1,000

**Creating Distribution Systems**

---

[78]David Arnold, "Procter & Gamble: Always Russia," Harvard Business School Case Study, No. 9-599-050, 1998.
[79]Shakti means strength in Sanskrit.

rupees (\$15–22).[80] As of early 2009, the project had over 45,000 distributors covering over 135,000 villages across 15 states. Unilever plans to expand the Shakti distribution model to other EM countries, including Sri Lanka, Vietnam, and Bangladesh.[81] Establishing an innovative distribution system such as P&G's *McVan model* or Unilever's *Project Shakti* in EM countries can generate an unassailable competitive advantage.

**Managing Distributor Relationships**

Even when the MNC can locate distribution partners, managing the relationship is a critical task. A breakdown of the MNC/distributor partnership can often turn disastrous. Professors Arnold and Quelch identified four areas of distribution policy in which MNCs should adapt the approaches used in developed markets:[82]

1. *Distributor partner selection criteria.* In developed markets, product-market knowledge is often one of the main criteria for choosing a distributor. However, for EMs, competence in working with MNCs tends to be more promising as a selection criterion. The industry experience criterion may exclude more entrepreneurial candidates.

2. *Direct selling.* Faced with the absence of a suitable distribution infrastructure, scores of MNCs have adopted a direct selling business model in EMs. The relative low-cost of labor makes such a format viable. For business-to-business (B2B) selling, EMs can also rely on the internet as a channel. Indeed, China-based Alibaba is now the world's largest online global trading platform with 38.1 million registered users (see **Exhibit 18-9**). The bulk of the site's customers are Chinese companies seeking buyers

**EXHIBIT 18-9**
ALIBABA–THE WORLD'S LARGEST ONLINE GLOBAL TRADING PLATFORM

*Source:* www.alibaba.com

---

[80]http://www.hllshakti.com, accessed on April 2, 2009.

[81]"Rustic Wisdom: Unilever to Take Project Shakti Global," economictimes.indiatimes.com, accessed on April 6, 2009.

[82]"New Strategies in Emerging Markets," pp. 18–19.

overseas. Still, the internet firm plans to become the online trading house of choice for small and medium sized enterprises around the world.[83]

3. *Local autonomy.* MNCs are usually very unfamiliar with the EM's local market environment. As a result, they delegate control over many marketing tasks (e.g., pricing, promotion) to their local distributor. However, the local distributor typically focuses on short-term sales revenues instead of long-term objectives such as building up the business. To safeguard the firm's interest in the development of the business, it is better off to retain some control over some of the most critical marketing decisions.

4. *Exclusivity.* Local distributors often insist on territorial exclusivity. However, for rapid market development, having multiple distributors is often much more preferable.

## COMMUNICATION STRATEGIES FOR EMERGING MARKETS

Communication strategies are an important driver behind the performance of a brand in EMs. For categories that are novel to the local consumers, marketing activities must accomplish several tasks: educating the consumers about the product use and benefits, raising brand awareness, and creating a brand image. A challenge for MNCs in EMs is to prioritize these tasks. Another communication-related issue for EMs is who to target—current existing users of the product or non-users. Most MNCs concentrate on increasing demand from current users, as this is much easier to do. Still, the payoffs from converting non-users into users can be huge.[84]

**Push versus Pull Activities**

A recurring resource allocation dilemma that marketers face in EMs is the pull-versus-push issue: should the company focus on consumer-oriented promotions (e.g., media advertising) or trade-directed promotions instead? Getting this balance right can be a make-or-break decision for the product's success. In most EMs, the emphasis must often be on trade-directed push-type promotions. There are several reasons. First, in many of these countries, the trade has immense power, especially in rural areas. Consumers interface directly with the retailers and often rely on their brand recommendations. Second, people shop much more frequently than in the West, often on a daily basis. As a result, the opportunities to switch brands arise much more often. Therefore, in-store promotions (e.g., point-of-purchase displays, video-demonstrations) have a heavy influence on their buying decisions.

For consumer-oriented pull promotion activities, mass media like TV and radio are often ineffective, especially in a country like India with its very diverse consumer groups. Instead, targeted media are much more useful. Billboards can be used to straddle India's pyramid: they can reach the poor who do not have TVs and do not read newspapers as well as the rich who are bored being stuck in city traffic.[85] Consumers in EM countries can also process advertisements very differently from those in the West. In China, for instance, ads tend to be read literally; people want credible evidence before they believe claims made in the ads.[86] **Exhibit 18-10** provides some insights on how to communicate with consumers in rural India.

**Mass Media versus Non-Traditional Marketing Approaches**

In general, mass media in EMs have much less clout than in the developed world. One hurdle for mass media promotions is that the local infrastructure is often a shambles. Basic data on matters such as magazine circulation or TV viewership is often missing or highly inaccurate. Also, in rural areas, coverage by the mass media is often very poor. For instance,

[83]"Alibaba Prepares for Global Expansion," www.ft.com, accessed on April 6, 2009.

[84]"Rethinking Marketing Programs for Emerging Markets," p. 466.

[85]"In India, Billboard Ads Scale New Heights," *The Wall Street Journal Asia,* April 26, 2007, p. 30.

[86]"One Country, Different Systems," *Media,* March 9, 2007, p. 5.

**EXHIBIT 18-10**
GUIDELINES ON REACHING RURAL INDIA

1. Rural India is not a consolidated entity. It is impossible to reach everybody. Due to vast cultural and language differences, common programs, even within the same state, are often not doable.

2. Mass media (e.g., TV, press, radio) are not effective as rural communities are mostly oral societies with low literacy rates. Stalls or vans parked in rural areas are much more valuable tools. They provide both brand building and sampling opportunities.

3. Opinion leaders (e.g., retailers, school teachers, *panchayats*—village heads) represent an important rural marketing channel. Such channels can be powerful brand ambassadors; consumers often trust their recommendations.

4. A key step is to identify prominent social occasions and use them to build brands. Examples include market days (*haats*), festivals. Setting up a stall costs very little; the average turnout for a *haat* could be 5,000 people.

5. Some successful rural programs rely on local youths who sell brands in 10 to 15 villages on bicycles. Examples of brands that deployed such programs include Colgate, Heinz, and Eveready. The seller gets a small monthly stipend of around $35.

6. Product trial at a minimal charge can be very effective.

*Sources*: "Reaching Rural India," *Media*, May 4, 2007, p. 13; and "Countryside Competition," *Media*, June 29, 2007, p. 25.

500 million Indians lack TV and radio.[87] Other factors that hamper the effectiveness of mass media in countries such as India are illiteracy and language diversity. In the urban areas, on the other hand, consumers are bombarded with TV ads for many competing brands. Given that the tastes of EM consumers tend to be very fickle, attracting and keeping them through mass media advertising tools like TV or radio often turns out to be very difficult.

Given these limitations, non-traditional communication approaches can be much more rewarding. Also, with labor being relatively cheap, people-intensive communication modes can deliver more bang-for-the-buck. They also enable the marketer to spend more time on educating the customer and to customize the message. Just as with distribution, savvy marketers such as Nokia, P&G, and Unilever have set up their own non-traditional communication systems. Nokia, for example, deploys a fleet of vans painted in the brand's signature blue across rural India as advertisements on wheels. Nokia staff park the vans in villages and then explain the basics of how mobile phones work and how to buy them.[88] **Global Perspective 18-3** discusses some of the aspects of the marketing strategy that made Nigeria the second-largest market for Guinness beer.

## *G*LOBAL PERSPECTIVE 18-3

### NIGERIA OVERTAKES IRELAND TO BECOME THE SECOND-LARGEST MARKET FOR GUINNESS BEER

In 2007, Nigeria had the distinction of overtaking Ireland as the second-largest market for Guinness, the Irish beer brand owned by Diageo (Britain is the stout's biggest market).

*Sources:* "My Goodness: Nigeria Overtakes Ireland in Guinness Sales," www.guardian.co.uk, accessed on April 4, 2009; http://en.wikipedia.org/wiki/Michael_Power_(Guinness_character); and "The Power of a Campaign with a Local Flavour," *Financial Times*, February 12, 2004, p. 9.

Guinness Nigeria's success stems from several factors: development of products customized to the local market, aggressive marketing, brand heritage, and lack of strong competition. The brand thrives in Nigeria despite numerous challenges such as the logistical problems of operating in Africa, political instability, the rise of born-again Christianity, and strict enforcement of Islamic laws in Nigeria's Muslim regions.

(*continued*)

---

[87]Hindustan Unilever Limited, Merrill Lynch India Conference Investor Presentation, February 2, 2009.

[88]"First Mover in Mobile," www.businessweek.com, accessed on April 6, 2009.

European colonizers introduced the brand more than 200 years ago in west and central Africa. While Guinness Nigeria uses the brand's familiar harp logo, the product formulation is customized to local tastes. The main ingredient for the Nigerian brew is sorghum, a common African cereal. As a result, the Nigerian stout has a sweeter flavor. In fact, a significant share of sales comes from exports to the Nigerian diaspora in Britain. The brewer also launched Malta Guinness, a non-alcoholic beer that targets the light-beer drinking segment of the population.

Guinness Nigeria owes part of its success to the brilliant "Michael Power" campaign. The campaign centered on a fictional James Bond-like action figure. Guinness ran the campaign in Africa from 1999 to 2006. Instead of having Michael Power make a standard sales pitch, the ad agency created a series of Michael Power short films used as vehicles for Guinness product placement. As the films were free, they were very popular with many African TV stations. In 2003, Guinness took the Power campaign to a higher level with the action movie *Critical Assignment* in which the hero fights a corrupt African politician. However, given the lack of cinemas in Nigeria, the company had to spend heavily on its own screenings. It dropped the campaign in 2006 to comply with the parent company's worldwide code on marketing. The code involves cutting back on words with a potential sexual connotation, including "power." Instead, Guinness ran a new TV ad campaign that promotes the brand as "the home of greatness."

## SUMMARY ✦ ✦ ✦ ✦ ✦ ✦ ✦ ✦ ✦ ✦ ✦ ✦ ✦ ✦ ✦ ✦ ✦ ✦ ✦ ✦ ✦ ✦ ✦ ✦ ✦

Scores of MNCs are salivating over the prospect of selling their goods to the billion-plus consumers located in emerging markets. Yet, emerging markets are very distinctive from developed countries. Business models that were honed in industrialized countries can fail miserably in this part of the world. The challenges faced in EMs are manifold: low incomes, lack of adequate distribution and media systems, cultural diversity, to mention just a few. The market opportunities clearly do exist but assailing these markets is not for the faint-hearted. In this chapter we covered the key characteristics of such markets. We then discussed a recent phenomenon—the rise of the so-called new champions—companies rooted in EMs that have outperformed large MNCs in their home turf. Increasingly, several of these challengers pose a threat to incumbent MNCs in the global arena.

To thrive in EMs, MNCs need to rethink their basic business models. Just focusing on the upper crust of the market while leaving the mass market to local firms can prove a fatal blunder. Instead, successful companies have been able to tap into the so-called bottom-of-the-pyramid market. Finally, we examined how the distinctive characteristics of the EM's market environment force MNCs to create new strategic marketing approaches.

## KEY TERMS ✦ ✦ ✦ ✦ ✦ ✦ ✦ ✦ ✦ ✦ ✦ ✦ ✦ ✦ ✦ ✦ ✦ ✦ ✦ ✦ ✦ ✦ ✦

| | | | |
|---|---|---|---|
| Backward innovation | Cost innovation | Emerging market | Next Eleven (N-11) |
| BRICs | Demand pooling | New champions | Transition Economies |

## REVIEW QUESTIONS ✦ ✦ ✦ ✦ ✦ ✦ ✦ ✦ ✦ ✦ ✦ ✦ ✦ ✦ ✦ ✦ ✦ ✦ ✦ ✦

**1.** What are the characteristics of emerging markets? What is the meaning of BRIC and N-11? What is so special about the groups of countries falling under these two rubrics? How do the BRIC countries differ from the N-11 ones?

**2.** What are the key characteristics of emerging markets?

**3.** Explain what is meant by "backward innovation." What are its pluses and minuses?

**4.** How do you explain the rise of the new champions? How can MNCs compete against them?

**5.** Explain the bottom-of-the-pyramid paradigm. From the multinational's perspective, the BOP a golden opportunity or is it simply a mirage?

**6.** What are the challenges posed by EMs in the area of distribution/communications? What are some of the solutions?

## DISCUSSION QUESTIONS ✦ ✦ ✦ ✦ ✦ ✦ ✦ ✦ ✦ ✦ ✦ ✦ ✦ ✦ ✦ ✦ ✦ ✦

**1.** What do you think will be the impact of the global economic downturn on the developing world's emerging champions? Will it strengthen or weaken them? Explain.

**2.** The chapter discussed the rise of the so-called emerging giants. Several Chinese companies are trying to expand overseas by acquiring foreign brands. The most visible example of this phenomenon was Lenovo's purchase of IBM's PC division. Geely, a leading Chinese carmaker, is reportedly interested in buying the Volvo brand from Ford. Not all of these acquisitions have been successful. One analyst made the following comment on this trend: "Acquisitions are no substitute for great marketing, and they actually demand more branding effort." (*Media*, March 26, 2009). Do you agree with his assessment? What are the drivers behind the acquisition spree? What are some of the possible risks?

3. Tata recently launched the Nano in India, the company's home market. The Nano is the world's cheapest cars. Tata has ambitious plans, including introducing the car in Europe and the United States. Is Tata daydreaming or do you feel there is a viable market opportunity for the Nano in Western countries. If they go ahead, how should they position the Nano? What target markets? What marketing mix strategy (to address this question, do some online research about the Nano).

4. Many companies assume that emerging markets are technology backwaters. Do you agree or this just a myth? Explain.

# SHORT CASES

### *C*ASE 18-1

## BARBIE GOES TO CHINA

In March 2009, Barbie celebrated its 50th birthday. In spite of her youthful appearance, sales of the iconic doll were down 21 percent. However, Mattel hopes that Barbie will make a splash in China. The company recently opened its first-ever Barbie 40,000 square-feet flagship store in Shanghai. The store opening was a gala event starring movie actors Jet Li and Christy Chung. The store includes a Design Center where children can create their own dolls, a spa, a fashion runway, a café, and, of course, many dolls.

Mattel is betting big on China: most families have just one child. Mattel's target is the so-called "little Emperor (Empress?)" generation. There are some competitors (e.g., Hello Kitty, Snoopy) but no big brands. Also, the focus in China is not just children but also includes young adults and adult women. Mattel sells Barbie-branded apparel and accessories

*Sources:* "Barbie's off to China amid falling sales," http://marketplace.publicradio.org/display/web/2009/03/06/pm_barbie_china/#; and "Barbie Seeks Local Appeal Through Shanghai Makeover," *Media*, March 26, 2009, p. 18.

for women. Cute is big in China: many young people have a whole range of cartoon characters and stuffed animals in their office or car.

Laura Lai, general manager at Barbie (Shanghai) Commercial, explains the strategy as follows: "Barbie is a relatively new brand to the market so we needed a way to condense almost five decades of brand history into a single experience. As China as a whole isn't a television advertising-reliant market for children's brands, we needed an innovative approach to reaching girls and their parents that could create an almost immediate relationship for the brand with consumers." (*Media*, March 26, 2009).

### DISCUSSION QUESTIONS

**1.** Mattel is expanding the Barbie brand beyond young girls to parents and young adults in China, a tactic it has never used in other markets. What is its motivation? Is it a smart move in your judgment? What are some possible risks?

**2.** Could the approach Mattel is taking for Barbie work for other brands in China as well? If so, what kind of brands?

Courtesy Kristiaan Helsen

### CASE 18-2

## TATA NANO—THE MODEL T FOR THE TWENTY-FIRST CENTURY?

In March 2009, six years after the concept was hatched, India's much-hyped super-cheap Tata Nano went on sale. With 7 million motorbikes sold in 2008 in India, Tata has big hopes for the Nano. Initially, the launch date would have been in the fourth quarter of 2008 but violent protests from farmer groups over land compensation for the factory site in West Bengal derailed Tata's plans. In the end, Tata decided to relocate the production to a plant in Pantnagar and build a dedicated plant in the western state of Gujarat. The Gujarat factory will have an annual capacity of 250,000 cars, but its opening is slated for 2010. In the mean time, Tata can only build 50,000 Nanos a year. The revised schedule meant that the car was to be shipped from July 2009 in phases to 100,000 customers chosen via a lottery.

The mission to develop the world's cheapest car began back in 2003. At the time, Ratan Tata, the chairman of India's Tata Group, gave his engineering team three requirements: (1) the car should be low-cost, (2) adhere to regulatory requirements, and (3) achieve performance targets such as fuel efficiency and acceleration capacity. Five years later, on January 10, 2008 Mr. Tata unveiled the Tata Nano at the 2008 Auto Expo in New Delhi. The Tata Nano has been nicknamed the Model T for the 21st century. During the ceremony, Mr. Tata commented: "I observed families riding on two-wheelers—the father driving the scooter, his young kid standing in front of him, his wife seated behind him holding a little baby. It led me to wonder whether one could conceive of a safe, affordable, all-weather form of transportation for such a family. Tata Motors' engineers and designers gave their all for about four years to realise this goal. Today, we indeed have a People's Car, which is affordable and yet built to meet safety requirements and emission norms . . . . We are happy to present the People's Car to India and we hope it brings the joy, pride and utility of owning a car to many families who need personal mobility." (www.tatamotors.com). Tata expects that the Nano will improve Indians' life: "People want to change their quality of life, and through the roads, will go from one place to another. It will be explosive growth, and Nano will be an answer. Nano is not an urban product, it is a product for the country." (USA Today)

The four-seater Nano is 3 meters (a little over 10 feet) long and 1.5 meters wide (about 5 feet). It can reach a speed of 65 miles per

**WHAT MAKES THE TATA NANO SO CHEAP?**

No air conditioning on standard model — Windows wind down by hand — Height 1.6m (5ft) — Manual steering, no air bag — 624cc two-cylinder engine in boot giving max speed of 105km (65mph) — Plastic and adhesive replaces welding — Bodywork made of sheet-metal and plastic — Length 3.1m (10ft) — Width 1.5m (5ft)

INDRANIL MUKHERJEE/AFP/Getty Image, Inc.

*Source*: news.bbc.co.uk

hour and has a fuel efficiency of 5 liters per 100 kilometers 9 (or 47 miles per gallon). The base model is priced at 100,000 rupees (around $2,500), the same price as a DVD player in a Lexus. The basic model has no airbags, air conditioning, radio, or power steering. However, more luxurious versions are available.

Not everyone is pleased with the Nano. Green campaigners in India point to India's poor road infrastructure and rising pollution levels. One local pollution specialist pointed out that: "Even if they claim it will be fuel efficient, the sheer numbers will undermine this. India's infrastructure doesn't have the capacity." (www.timesonline.co.uk) India's capital Delhi already registers 1,000 new vehicles per day. The average speed at peak times has dropped to 7 miles per hour. Mr. Tata, however, dismissed environmentalists' concerns: "We need to think of our masses. Should they be denied the right to an individual form of transport?" (www.timesonline.co.uk).

Despite its limitations, the Nano's fans outweigh its critics so far. It already has a dedicated Facebook group. Mr. Goyal, a 35-year old accountant, had been planning to buy the Nano since it debuted at the Delhi car show. By paying 50,000 rupees more, he can switch from a motorbike to a four-wheeler. The Nano will allow him to take along his wife and two children and would be more comfortable and safer than a motorbike. Hormazd Sorajbee, the editor of Autocar India, predicts, "The success of [the Nano] will change the rules of carmaking in the world." (*New York Times*, March 23, 2009). Because of the economic downturn, some expect that the Nano will appeal beyond the first-time market as consumers may trade down.

Tata Motors plans to introduce the car in other emerging markets in Latin America, Southeast Asia, and Africa. The company also plans to launch a plusher, more expensive Nano in Europe in 2011. The Nano Europe will meet stricter European safety and emission standards. The carmaker even ponders to

*Sources:* http://www.tatamotors.com/our_world/press_releases.php? ID=340&action=Pull; "Inside the Tata Nano Factory," www.business-week.com, accessed on February 19, 2009; "Tata Nano—World's Cheapest New Car Is Unveiled In India," www.timesonline.co.uk, accessed on February 19, 2009; "Maybe Tata, Jaguar/Land Rover is not such an odd couple," www.usatoday.com, accessed on February, 19, 2009; "2,000 Dollar Question: Can the Nano Deliver?" www.nytimes.com, accessed on April 27, 2009; "The New People's Car," The Economist, March 28, 2009, pp. 59–60; "World's Cheapest Car is Launched," news.bbc.co.uk, accessed on April 27, 2009; and "Tata Nano Goes on Sale," www.wsj.com, accessed on April 27, 2009.

roll out the car in the United States a few years after the European introduction.

Other carmakers are joining the fray. Renault-Nissan is teaming up with Indian motorcycle maker Bajaj to launch an ultra-cheap model by the end of 2012. A Nissan top-executive said: "We're working with Bajaj to make use of their frugal engineering skills and technology, while we're supplying some financial backing, a strong distribution system and potential expansion to other markets." (*Media*) Hyundai and several Chinese manufacturers are also looking into the segment.

**DISCUSSION QUESTIONS**

**1.** Does the so-called *one lakh* (100,000 rupees) car really have potential beyond India? What criteria should Tata Motors use for deciding which countries to enter? Should Tata also launch the Nano in developed countries? Why or why not?

**2.** What challenges do you envision in launching the Nano?

**3.** How should the Nano be positioned? Would you apply the same positioning strategy in, say, India and Germany or would you adjust it? If so, why and how?

# FURTHER READING ✦ ✦ ✦ ✦ ✦ ✦ ✦ ✦ ✦ ✦ ✦ ✦ ✦ ✦ ✦ ✦ ✦ ✦ ✦ ✦ ✦ ✦ ✦ ✦ ✦

Arnold, David J. and John A. Quelch, "New Strategies for Emerging Markets," *Sloan Management Review*, 40 (Fall 1998): 7–20.

Dawar, Niraj and Tony Frost, "Competing with Giants. Survival Strategies for Local Companies in Emerging Markets," *Harvard Business Review*, March-April 1999: 119–29.

Dawar, Niraj and Amitava Chattopadhyay, "Rethinking Marketing Programs for Emerging Markets," *Long Range Planning*, 35 (2002): 457–74.

Johnson, Joseph and Gerard J. Tellis, "Drivers of Success for Market Entry into China and India," *Journal of Marketing*, 72 (May 2008): 1–13.

Mahajah, Vijay. *Africa Rising. How 900 Million African Consumers Offer More Than You Think*. Upper Saddle River, NJ: Wharton School Publishing, 2009.

Mahajan, Vijay and Kamini Banga. *The 86% Solution. How To Succeed In the Biggest Market Opportunity of the 21st Century*. Upper Saddle River, NJ: Wharton School Publishing, 2006.

Prahalad, C. K. *The Fortune at the Bottom of the Pyramid. Eradicating Poverty Through Profits*. Upper Saddle River, NJ: Wharton School Publishing, 2005.

Williamson, Peter J. and Ming Zeng, "Value-for-Money Strategies for Recessionary Times," *Harvard Business Review*, 87 (March 2009): 66–75.

# GLOBAL MARKETING AND THE INTERNET

**19**

$\mathcal{C}$HAPTER OVERVIEW

1. BARRIERS TO GLOBAL INTERNET MARKETING

2. COMPETITIVE ADVANTAGE AND CYBERSPACE

3. GLOBAL INTERNET CONSUMERS

4. GLOBALLY INTEGRATED VERSUS LOCALLY RESPONSIVE INTERNET MARKETING STRATEGIES

5. THE INTERNET AND GLOBAL PRODUCT POLICY

6. GLOBAL PRICING AND THE WEB

7. GLOBAL DISTRIBUTION STRATEGIES AND THE INTERNET

8. THE ROLE OF THE INTERNET FOR GLOBAL COMMUNICATION STRATEGIES

Although the obituaries of numerous dot-com companies were written during the 2001 tech-bust, the internet remains a technological marvel for global marketers. The internet has reshaped the global marketplace for international marketers both on the demand- and the supply-side. The web clearly provides a unique distribution and communication channel to marketers across the globe. It is the ultimate marketplace to buy and to sell goods and services. The challenge for many global multinationals is to wring out the benefits that the web offers. For scores of internet startups that initially focused on their home market, going global can provide an avenue for further growth. Amazon foresees that Europe could ultimately prove to be a better place for doing e-commerce than the United States for two reasons: with Europe's high population density (1) delivery is faster and (2) real estate prices are high in high traffic city areas, leading to a cost advantage to virtual retailers over their brick-and-mortar competitors.[1] EBay has already planted its foot in thirty countries across the globe. Other web firms are following suit. Small and medium sized enterprises (SMEs) also participate in

---

[1] "Jeff Bezos' Amazon Adventure," *Ad Age Global* (February 2002), pp. 16–17.

**EXHIBIT 19-1**
TOP 15 COUNTRIES IN INTERNET USAGE

| Country | Internet Users (in millions) | % of World Users | Penetration (as % of country's population) | User Growth (2000-2008) |
|---|---|---|---|---|
| 1. China | 253.0 | 17.3 | 19.0 | 1,024.4 |
| 2. United States | 220.1 | 15.0 | 72.5 | 130.9 |
| 3. Japan | 94.0 | 6.4 | 73.8 | 99.7 |
| 4. India | 60.0 | 4.1 | 5.2 | 1,100.0 |
| 5. Germany | 52.5 | 3.6 | 63.8 | 118.9 |
| 6. Brazil | 50.0 | 3.4 | 26.1 | 900.0 |
| 7. United Kingdom | 41.8 | 2.9 | 68.6 | 171.5 |
| 8. France | 36.1 | 2.5 | 58.1 | 325.3 |
| 9. South Korea | 34.8 | 2.4 | 70.7 | 82.9 |
| 10. Italy | 34.7 | 2.4 | 59.7 | 162.9 |
| 11. Russia | 32.7 | 2.2 | 23.2 | 954.8 |
| 12. Canada | 28.0 | 1.9 | 84.3 | 120.5 |
| 13. Turkey | 26.5 | 1.8 | 36.9 | 1,225.0 |
| 14. Spain | 25.6 | 1.8 | 63.3 | 375.6 |
| 15. Indonesia | 25.0 | 1.7 | 10.5 | 1,150.0 |
| Worldwide Total | 1,463.6 | 100.0 | 21.9 | 305.5 |

*Source:* http:www.internetworldstats.com/top20.htm, accessed on March 9, 2009.

the flurry. In fact, for many SMEs, the internet has proven to be a welcome opportunity for overseas expansion.

Although the internet originated in the United States, it has rapidly morphed into a global phenomenon. The worldwide internet population surpassed the 1 billion milestone in 2005 — up from only 45 million users 10 years earlier and 420 million in 2000. The total number of users was nearly 1.5 billion in mid-2008. Exhibit 19-1 presents a geographic breakdown of internet usage worldwide. As you can see, the internet population in China is larger now than the number of U.S. internet users. Another notable fact is the rapid increase of the internet population, with growth rates of around 1,000 percent for each of the four BRIC countries (see last column of **Exhibit 19-1**).[2]

Until the early 1990s, the internet was primarily the preserve of the military and academic researchers. However, the development of new software (e.g., Java, Netscape) during the early 1990s has turned the internet into a commercial medium that has transformed businesses worldwide. In the advent of the forces unleashed by this new technology, this final chapter focuses on the role of the internet in global marketing. We first highlight the main challenges that international marketing managers face with the internet. The remainder of the chapter explores the impact of the web on global marketing strategies.

# BARRIERS TO GLOBAL INTERNET MARKETING          ◆ ◆ ◆ ◆ ◆ ◆ ◆

Although most forecasts about the future of global e-commerce are rosy, there are several structural barriers that might slow down its expansion. In particular, the following hurdles might interfere: (1) language barriers, (2) cultural barriers, (3) infrastructure (e.g., penetration of personal computers, broadband, or 3G), (4) knowledge barriers, (5) access charges, and (6) government regulations. Let us look at each one of these in turn.

When Avis Europe PLC set up its global car-rental website in 1997, clients could rent a car almost anywhere in the world, as long as they spoke English. Avis soon found out

**Language Barriers**

---

[2]Brazil, Russia, India, and China.

that its English-only website was not enticing to non-English speakers. To win customers, it rolled out localized sites in the client's language.[3] The multilingual sites were also customized in other ways. For instance, the German site targets the business segment whereas the Spanish site focuses on leisure bookings. Given the internet's origins in the United States, it is not surprising that much of the content is U.S.-focused and that the English language has dominated the web so far. According to the latest data, English still prevails as the leading language on the internet (450 million users), followed by Chinese (321.3 million) and Spanish (122 million).[4]

One survey of 186 U.S. online merchants found that 74 percent use only English on their sites and 79 percent present prices in U.S. dollars only.[5] However, more than 70 percent of the world's internet population now lives outside English-speaking countries.[6] A study by Forrester research found that business users on the web are three times more likely to purchase when the website "speaks" their native language.[7] Hence, a company that plans to become a global e-business player may need to localize its websites in order to communicate with target customers in their native tongue. In some cases, companies can stick to English, especially if they operate in an industry that is primarily Anglo-Saxon (e.g., aerospace). However, in most cases translation becomes necessary if the firm wants to sell to non-English speakers. As Willy Brandt, a former German Chancellor, once put it: "If I'm selling to you, I speak your language. If I'm buying, *dann müssen Sie Deutsch sprechen*"—then you must speak German.

Companies that want to localize their websites by translating the content into other languages have several options. One approach is to hire a third party to do the translation job. One example is Translation Services USA (http://www.translation-services-usa.com/), which is a company that specializes in website translation. The company, whose clients range from small businesses to Fortune 500 companies, translates websites into 150 languages including dialects such as Creole, Corsican, Basque, and Greenlandic. A second option is to use an online translation tool such as Yahoo! Babel Fish (http://babelfish.yahoo.com/), which can translate blocks of text and also an entire webpage. These tools are usually free but their results can be very inaccurate. Their range of languages is also very limited. Another alternative is to use specialized software to do the translation. A market leader in this area is SYSTRAN, a company head-quartered in Paris. SYSTRAN develops software products that enable instantaneous translation of web pages, internet portals into and from 52 language pairs. Several major internet portals such as Yahoo!, Google, and AltaVista also use SYSTRAN's translation technology.[8]

## Cultural Barriers

Cultural norms and traditions can also hinder the spread of the internet. In Confucian-based cultures (most East Asian nations), business is routinely conducted on a personal basis. Networking and personal relationships play a major role in business transactions. Nonetheless, Dell was able to gain a foothold in markets like China and Hong Kong with its Dell Online business concept. One major impediment in numerous markets is the lack of a credit card culture and security concerns. In many countries outside North America, credit card penetration is still very low. In countries like Egypt, only the upper-class people use a credit card to buy goods.[9] Companies that use the internet as a distribution channel in such countries are usually forced to offer a range of payment options such as cash on delivery, wire transfers, and e-money. China has about 50 online payment systems now. The leader is AliPay, a service developed by China's top auction site, Taobao. With the AliPay system, the seller gets the money only after the buyer

[3] "Learning Local Languages Pays Off for Online Sellers," *Asian Wall Street Journal* (November 24–6, 2000), p. 12.

[4] http://www.internetworldstats.com/stats7.htm, accessed on March 15, 2009.

[5] www.imediaconnection.com/global/5728.asp?ref=http://www.imediaconnection.com/content/6090.asp.

[6] http://www.internetworldstats.com/stats7.htm, accessed on March 15, 2009.

[7] www.internetindicators.com/global.html

[8] www.systransoft.com, accessed on March 15, 2009.

[9] Ibrahim Elbeltagi, "E-commerce and Globalization: An Exploratory Study of Egypt," *Cross Cultural Management: An International Journal*, 14(3, 2007), pp. 196–201.

obtains the goods.[10] Even where credit card penetration is high, online shoppers who are worried about credit card fraud are reluctant to release their credit card number and other personal data online. Instead, internet users end up giving the information through fax or over the phone to the online merchant. Advances in encryption- and smart card-technology should provide a solution on this front. However, even with all the enhanced security features, many internet users still prefer to pay for their transactions offline.

Culture sensitivity also matters in website design.[11] Websites must include content and have a structure that conforms to the cultural values, symbols, and heroes of the site's visitors.[12] On the U.S. site of Amazon.com, book delivery is promised with "Usually ships within 24 hours." On the British site the wording is "Usually dispatched within 24 hours." Books chosen go into a "shopping cart" on Amazon.com's U.S. site and into a "shopping basket" on the British site. These are subtle distinctions but they can be very important if a global web marketer wants to lure foreign customers. By failing to respect the local cultural norms, companies run the risk of antagonizing the customers they are trying to attract. For instance, in the male-dominated Arab world, websites should avoid portraying women in roles of authority. In countries with strong individualism (e.g., the United States), the website should show how the product can improve the individual's life; in countries with a strong group-sense (e.g., many East Asian countries), a sales pitch may need to reveal how the product can benefit the group as a whole. Attitudes toward privacy vary widely, with Americans far less concerned than most Europeans and the Japanese.

Patriotism is another important consideration. In China, several websites have triggered public fury by, for instance, listing Taiwan and Hong Kong/Macao as "countries" instead of as a province or territories, respectively. Being sensitive to national identity could imply having a country-specific website for each country instead of bundling smaller countries with larger ones (e.g., New Zealand with Australia, Ireland with the United Kingdom). IBM, for instance, has a huge menu of country sites including for tiny countries such as Montserrat and Bermuda. These are essentially the same but they show that IBM is being sensitive to smaller markets.[13]

Symbols very familiar in the home market do not necessarily have a universal meaning or may even offend foreign customers. A thumbs-up icon would indicate something good to U.S. consumers but would be insulting in Italy. Website colors also convey different meanings. In Japan, soft pastels are effective, whereas in the United States bold and sharp tones work better in connecting with consumers.

One concern is that managers may overlook the need for cultural alertness when setting up a global online business operation. Traditionally, managers would scout local markets and communicate with local partners to become familiar with the local culture. With a virtual business, face-to-face contacts are minimal, especially for small and medium-sized enterprises (SMEs). One suggestion here is for managers to join internet discussion groups and bulletin boards to gain knowledge about cultural norms and values in the foreign market.[14] **Global Perspective 19-1** discusses how Dell surmounted cultural sensitivity issues for its websites.

**Infrastructure**

In many countries, the local information technology (IT) infrastructure imposes constraints on e-commerce market opportunities. One measure of interest here is the Economist Intelligence Unit's annual ranking of e-readiness.[15] A country's e-readiness measures the extent of internet connectivity and technology (ICT) infrastructure in the

---

[10]"China's E-tail Awakening," *Business Week International*, November 19, 2007, p. 44.

[11]"Global website Design: It's All in the Translation," *International Herald Tribune* (March 22, 2001), p. 17.

[12]David Luna, Laura A. Peracchio, and Maria D. de Juan, "Cross-Cultural and Cognitive Aspects of Web Site Navigation," *Journal of the Academy of Marketing Science*, 30(4), pp. 397–410.

[13]"Looking Local Can Make a Big Difference on the Web," *Financial Times*, February 11, 2008, p. 2.

[14]John Q. Quelch and Lisa R. Klein, "The internet and International Marketing," *Sloan Management Review* (Spring 1996), pp. 60–75.

[15]http://graphics.eiu.com/files/ad_pdfs/2005Ereadiness_Ranking_WP.pdf

## $\mathcal{G}$LOBAL PERSPECTIVE 19-1

### LESSONS FROM DELL'S WEB GLOBALIZATION PROJECT

In October 2003, Dell Inc (www.dell.com) launched an enhanced global e-commerce site, followed by an upgraded service and support site in July 2004. The project had taken 3 years to complete and involved the joint efforts of 30 business teams. A key challenge of the web globalization project was the creation of a global online brand communication. To implement this task, Dell formed a core team, Global Brand Management (GBM), in spring 2002 with participants from the Americas, Asia, and Europe/Middle East. The main goal of their assignment was to develop a coherent visual interface design (VID) standard for Dell's websites balanced with local adaptations if necessary. The key issues in this endeavor centered around five VID components: corporate logotype and brand tagline; country names; national flags and country selection menu; language selection.

#### CORPORATE LOGOTYPE AND TAGLINE

The first VID issue dealt with the degree of localization of Dell's corporate icon. For regions not using Latin alphabets, westernized corporate names are typically phonetically transcribed for legal registration and to ease customer pronunciation. For some languages, choosing a proper phonetic equivalent is rarely easy. For instance, picking Chinese characters purely based on phonetics might lead to meaningless or even bizarre combinations. For the Dell brand name, the following character groupings all have a similar *dai er* sound: 怠饵 (*idle pastry*), 歹儿 (*evil child*), and 呆二 (*imbecile two*). In the case of Dell China, the corporate name in local script was rendered by 戴尔 *dai er* (*honor thus*), which projects a positive corporate image.

Although localizing the corporate icon could have benefits, it violates the spirit of a coherent imagery in terms of geometric dimensions, color schema, and typeface. A well-recognized and valued logotype can communicate a range of positive marketing messages (e.g., trust, product quality, prestige). For that reason, local Dell websites incorporate the blue corporate logotype with an angled E character even in regions not using Latin alphabets.

Another important brand element is the brand tagline. In October 2001, Dell had introduced the *Easy as Dell* slogan. For the homepages of many countries, Dell simply settled on the

English tagline. However, for some countries, Dell opted to create an equivalent localized tagline. This was not always an easy task. For example, for the Japanese tagline, Dell's team came up with a pool of 60 candidates. In the end, the localized tagline became シンプルをあなたにデル *Sinpuru Anata ni Deru (Simple for you, Dell)*.

#### COUNTRY NAMES

Choosing the right country name for Dell's websites was far less trivial than it sounds. Part of the discussion centered on using a country's official name or its short-form equivalent. The short form was chosen as the standard (e.g., *México* instead of *Estados Unidos Méxicanos*). For some regions, Dell also needed to navigate around delicate political issues. For instance, to avoid controversy with Mainland China, Dell chose for Taiwan the provincial name 台灣 *tai wan* was written in traditional Chinese characters, not the simplified script used in Mainland China.

#### FLAG IDENTIFIERS AND COUNTRY SELECTOR MENU

Another delicate issue is the usage of flag identifiers. Flags carry many meanings. While for most countries flag identifiers are not controversial, Greater China poses obstacles. Focus group research showed that Mainland Chinese might lodge objections over the display of the Taiwanese flag. As a result, no flag identifier is used for the Taiwan website. Likewise, the Korean website does not display any flag. A similar issue arose with the design of the country selector menu. For markets like Taiwan or Canada, the team inserted the phrase "Choose a country/region" to take a neutral stance. For other regions, it kept the original "Choose a country" phrase.

#### LANGUAGE SELECTION

Countries with multiple languages also needed a language toggle. Toggle options were decided for the respective regions based on socioeconomic factors. For instance, the Dell-Canada website displays the "English/Français" toggle, the Dell-Belgium website contains a "Nederlands/Français" toggle. Given the significance of English as a language of commerce, websites for markets such as Hong Kong, Taiwan, and Switzerland also include "English" as an option for the language toggle.

*Sources:* Leon Z. Lee, "Creating Worldwide Brand Recognition," *Multilingual Computing & Technology* 16 (1): 41–46; and Leon Z. Lee, "Virtual Teams: Formation, Flexibility, and Foresight in the Global Realm," *The Globalization Insider*, www.localization.org, accessed on April 16, 2005.

country. Obviously, a key component of the measure relates to the hardware infrastructure: number of Wi-Fi hotspots, broadband penetration, security of internet connections, and mobile phones in the country. The index also captures other elements such as citizens' ability to utilize technology skillfully, the transparency of the country's business and legal environment, the extent to which the government encourages the

**EXHIBIT 19-2**

EIU E-READINESS RANKINGS BY COUNTRY, 2008

| Country | 2008 e-readiness rank | 2005 e-readiness rank | 2008 e-readiness score (max. = 10) |
|---------|-----------------------|-----------------------|------------------------------------|
| USA | 1 | 2 | 8.95 |
| Hong Kong | 2 | 6 | 8.91 |
| Sweden | 3 | 3 | 8.85 |
| Australia | 4 | 10 | 8.83 |
| Denmark | 4 (tie) | 1 | 8.83 |
| Singapore | 6 | 11 | 8.74 |
| Netherlands | 6 (tie) | 8 | 8.74 |
| United Kingdom | 8 | 5 | 8.68 |
| Switzerland | 9 | 4 | 8.67 |
| Austria | 10 | 14 | 8.63 |
| Norway | 11 | 9 | 8.60 |
| Canada | 12 | 12 | 8.49 |
| Finland | 13 | 6 | 8.42 |
| Germany | 14 | 12 | 8.39 |
| South Korea | 15 | 18 | 8.34 |
| New Zealand | 16 | 16 | 8.28 |
| Bermuda | 17 | NA | 8.22 |
| Japan | 18 | 21 | 8.08 |
| Taiwan | 19 | 22 | 8.05 |
| Belgium | 20 | 17 | 8.04 |

*Source:* Economist Intelligence Unit, 2008.

use of digital technologies.[16] **Exhibit 19-2** shows the e-readiness rankings and scores for 2008.

Not surprisingly, the leading countries in this ranking have high per capita incomes. Most emerging markets rank very low in terms of e-readiness. For instance, all four BRIC countries' e-readiness rank very lowly: Brazil comes 42nd, Russia 57th, India 54th, and China 56th. The bottom spots in the ranking are taken by Algeria, Indonesia, Azerbaijan, and Iran. This split between rich and poor countries is often referred to as the **digital divide** between rich and poor nations.[17]

A critical component for international internet marketing is the digital literacy level of the host country. Digital literacy is defined as the ability to locate, understand and create information using digital information.[18] Digital literacy matters both on the demand and supply side. On the demand side, low computer literacy could limit consumers' willingness to engage in e-commerce transactions. On the supply side, setting up an e-business often requires recruiting people with high computer literacy skills that in many countries are often in short supply. Especially in emerging markets, scarcity of proper talent and skills can restrain the development of a digital economy.

Governments around the world do recognize the crucial importance of having digitally savvy human resources to compete in the global marketplace. Several governments have launched initiatives to improve digital literacy within their society. The Philippine government, for instance, launched an ambitious project in 2008 to improve the digital literacy skills of more than 100,000 teachers. The project is carried out with the assistance of Intel, Microsoft, and the USAID, the U.S. government's foreign aid organization.[19] Several non-profit organizations also help out in bridging the digital divide between developed and developing countries. One example is Silicon

**Knowledge Barrier**

---

[16]The scoring criteria and weights are: connectivity and technology infrastructure (20%), business environment (15%), cultural environment (15%), legal environment (10%), government policy (15%), and consumer/business adoption (25%).

[17]http://news.bbc.co.uk/2/hi/technology/4296919.stm

[18]http://en.wikipedia.org/wiki/Digital_literacy, accessed on March 16, 2009.

[19]www.pia.gov.ph, accessed on March 16, 2009.

Valley-based Inveneo, a non-profit social enterprise that helps to provide access to information communications technology (ICT) to underprivileged communities, primarily in sub-Saharan Africa.[20]

**Access Charges**

Early in 1999, the Campaign for Unmetered Telecommunications (CUT) organized a web boycott in several European countries. Internet users in Belgium, France, Italy, Poland, Portugal, Spain, and Switzerland were asked to go offline for 24 hours in protest of high access charges. In October 1998, Italian internet users repeatedly downloaded information from the website of Telecom Italia, thereby blocking access to the site for other users. The move was organized to protest an increase in local telephone rates. Similar campaigns have occurred in other countries as a means to protest against high telecommunication charges.

In numerous countries, high internet access charges are a sore point. Until March 1999, the cost to Chinese internet users was 30 times higher than in the United States. The cost of surfing the web typically consists of two parts: internet subscription rates and telephone charges. While internet subscription fees are often low or free of charge, telephone charges can be prohibitive. In markets with excessive access charges, comparison-shopping becomes very costly. For instance, while eBay's U.S. customers may spend hours browsing the auction site, this is less likely in Europe where most people pay per-minute phone charges for internet access.[21] Furthermore, shoppers are less likely to complete a purchase transaction.

Government deregulation, increased competition, and new access alternatives (e.g., through cable TV) should put downward pressure on the cost of going online. Internet users in Germany used to pay between $6 and $28 per month to their local Internet Service Providers (ISPs), and then pay Deutsche Telekom 4 cents for each minute on the phone to their ISP. Even for moderate users, these charges easily led to bills of over $50 per month. New competitors now offer internet access at much lower rates. Access to the web in Japan used to be dominated by NTT, which charged sky-high fees. However, as new rivals entered the web access market in Japan, access rates have been falling rapidly.[22]

**Legal Environment and Government Regulations**

The host country's legal environment is another critical factor that affects international internet marketing. Most governments are very enthusiastic about the internet and the opportunities that the digital industry offers. Yet, red tape and government regulations typically stifle the industry in dozens of countries. Regulations differ on issues such as data protection, customs, acceptance of the use of digital signatures and e-mailed contracts as legally binding.

E-commerce is global; the law, on the other hand, is mostly local. Hence, one of the fundamental issues is the question of jurisdiction: Whose contract and consumer laws apply? These issues remain largely unsolved. Problems related to national laws are compounded by a shortage of legal precedents and experts who can interpret existing legislation. In general, companies have two alternatives to handle legal concerns. They can either set up separate websites that comply with local laws or one mega-site that copes with every conceivable local legal requirement.[23]

To see how fragmented government regulations and laws affect e-commerce, consider the experience in Europe of Gateway, the U.S.-based PC maker.[24] When Gateway wanted to sell computers in Europe online, it initially planned to set up a single electronic storefront with different views for each separate market listing a different price. However, differences in value added tax rates, currencies, and culture in

---

[20]http://www.inveneo.org/

[21]"EBay Steams Into Europe," *Business Week (Asian Edition)* (October 16, 2000), p. 32.

[22]"Finally, Japan's Netizens May Be Able to Afford the Net," *Business Week* (November 22, 1999).

[23]"Global E-commerce Law Comes Under the Spotlight," *Financial Times* (December 23, 1999), p. 4. Gateway pulled out of Europe in the late 1990s.

[24]Gateway was acquired in October 2007 by Acer, the Taiwanese computer company.

the end forced Gateway to create separate websites for each individual European market.[25]

Several governments have been trying to come to terms with global e-commerce issues by enacting legislation that covers the various areas of concern. Legal conflicts also arise about domain names. AOL, for example, was engaged in a lengthy legal battle over the use of the "aol.com.br" domain name in Brazil with Curitiba America, a small local internet concern.[26] One attempt to resolve such domain disputes was the establishment of ICANN.[27] This non-governmental body handles such disputes through a process of mandatory arbitration.[28]

Although government over-regulation can discourage the digital industry, some amount of regulation is clearly necessary, especially to defend intellectual property rights (IPR) and to stamp out cybercrime. Some countries have gone the extra mile to defend IPR: Denmark, for instance, made history when a court ruled that local ISPs must block access to The Pirate Bay website, a Sweden-based website that facilitates illegal downloading.[29]

Apart from the barriers we discussed above, there are others. Geographical distances can be a major constraint when goods need to be stocked and shipped. Shipping costs easily become a major hurdle for many e-shoppers, especially for bulky items. Delivery delays also increase with distance. Getting paid is another complicating factor. Credit card fraud and lack of trust in general is another challenge. Several e-tailers have a blacklist of countries to which they refuse to ship because of past fraud problems.

---

# COMPETITIVE ADVANTAGE AND CYBERSPACE

◆ ◆ ◆ ◆ ◆ ◆ ◆

The internet offers two major benefits to companies that use the tool as a gateway to global marketing: cost/efficiency savings and accessibility ("connectivity"). Compared to traditional communication tools (e.g., media advertising, catalogs) and distribution channels, the costs of the internet as a delivery channel are far lower. The internet also offers access to customers around the world. As a result, the value of some of the pre-internet sources of competitive advantage has been deflated. One of these potential sources is scale. Some observers have argued that one of the major consequences of the internet is that small and large firms are on an equal footing now as far as global competition is concerned. Barriers to entry due to size have been dismantled. The advantages of size will disappear.[30] Barriers due to geographical space and time zones are no longer relevant.[31]

Although size-related advantages will probably lessen, claims that the internet provides a level playing field to small and large global players alike are somewhat overblown. Large multinationals will still maintain an edge in most industries over their smaller competitors, especially in the global arena. Large firms still enjoy a substantial competitive advantage because of larger resources and more visibility among prospective customers worldwide. Deep pockets allow them to hire the best talent and buy the latest technologies in the area. Large multinationals can also tap into their global expertise to cope with the countless challenges that going international poses: the logistics of getting tangible goods to the customers, differing payment methods and currencies, a maze of rules and regulations, coping with customs, and so forth. It is also

---

[25] "Net Marketers Face Hurdles Abroad," *Advertising Age International* (June 1999), p. 42.

[26] "AOL Waltzes Into Brazil, Unprepared for the Samba," *The New York Times* (December 11, 1999), p. B2.

[27] Internet Corporation for Assigned Names and Numbers (www.icann.org).

[28] "Global E-commerce," p. 4.

[29] "Pirate Bay to Remain Blocked in Denmark," http://www.macworld.co.uk/digitallifestyle/news/index.cfm? RSS&NewsID=23799.

[30] "The internet and International Marketing," p. 71.

[31] "The Integration of internet Marketing," p. 13–14.

more likely that target customers will find the website of a well-known large multi-national rather than of a small upstart.[32]

Instead of size, technology is now being touted as a key source for competitive advantage. Although technology matters, marketing skills will still play a major role in global marketing: "A site with the latest technologies but one that doesn't meet customer expectations will not make the cut."[33]

◆ ◆ ◆ ◆ ◆ ◆ ◆ ◆ ◆     # GLOBAL INTERNET CONSUMERS

One of the tasks facing global marketers who plan e-commerce endeavors is to gain a solid understanding of their prospective customers. One question that arises is to what extent online customers differ from offline ones. A second issue is to what degree internet users differ across cultures or countries: Do global internet users prefer to browse and buy from standardized global web sites or do they prefer websites adapted to their local cultures? Do their preferences and buying motivations overlap or do they differ and, if so, how? If they are indeed similar, companies can standardize their e-commerce strategies on a global or pan-regional basis, except for a few minor changes, such as language or shipping policies. If, on the other hand, there are significant differences, then a standardized internet strategy might be a recipe for disaster.

Internet usage patterns clearly differ across countries. A survey conducted by the Pew Research Center finds that internet use is on the rise in both industrialized and developing countries. According to the study, most people in the United States, Canada, and Western Europe are internet savvy. However, fewer than 10 percent went online in Pakistan and Indonesia. Internet use was also relatively low in India, Russia, and Turkey.[34] Not surprisingly, in all the countries surveyed, internet use rises with higher education and incomes.

Internet users also differ in terms of their online buying behavior. One study sponsored by Accenture, an international management consulting firm, looked into cross-country internet shopping patterns.[35] The study sampled 515 individuals from 20 countries. The key finding of the study was that there are enormous regional differences. However, differences between countries *within* the same region were minimal. North Americans have a greater affinity for the web, more trust, less anxiety, enjoy shopping more, and look for branded products more than internet users from most other regions. They also showed the highest commitment to return to websites for purchases. Asians had the least favorable attitude toward the web and the greatest fear about internet shopping. Their intent to purchase through the web and to return to websites was fairly low, despite their affinity for technology.

Consumers can also vary in the "perceived value" that they derive from visiting a brand's website. One large-scale study that involved 8,500 website visitors and 30 websites found that:

1. The most important driver of perceived value is the utilitarian experience associated with the website. Companies can increase that experience by offering useful, truthful, and new information about their products or brands. The second most critical factor is the amount of pleasure provided by the site, with visual material being a major component. Customization ranks third. Examples of the latter include the ability for the visitor to personalize the content or look/feel of the site, online

---

[32]Saeed Samiee, "The internet and International Marketing: Is There a Fit?" *Journal of Interactive Marketing*, 12 (Autumn 1998), pp. 5–21.

[33]"The Integration of internet Marketing," p. 15.

[34]www.pewglobal.org, accessed on March 16, 2009.

[35]Patrick D. Lynch and John C. Beck, "Profiles of internet Buyers in 20 Countries: Evidence for Region-Specific Strategies," *Journal of International Business Studies*, 32 (4) (Fourth Quarter 2001), pp. 725–48.

consultation, or personally addressing the visitor. Especially website visitors living in more individualistic countries put high weight on customization.

2. The effect of privacy/security protection on perceived value is strongest for people living countries high on individualism and where the rule of law is weak.

3. Not surprisingly, websites should be adapted to the local context for countries where consumers take pride in their country's symbols, culture, and language.[36]

## $\mathcal{G}$LOBAL PERSPECTIVE 19-2

### EBAY — A GLOBAL FLEA MARKET

A *New Yorker* cartoon shows a woman driving a huge tractor into her living room to show it to friends. Its caption: "I got it from eBay." An *eBay* search on the magazine's cartoon-bank produces five other cartoons. Clearly, eBay has become part of the cultural landscape. EBay, the online auction group, was founded in the mid-1990s by Pierre Omidyar, a young French computer programmer. To most venture capitalists, the idea of an online flea market was not exactly captivating. And yet, eBay managed to do something that very few other dot-coms were able to: it has always made a profit. Its business model is basically very simple: match individual buyers and sellers online and take a cut of the transaction. What is behind eBay's profit potential? A mixture of no cost of goods, no inventories, low marketing costs, and no huge capital investments. EBay has turned into one of the world's most successful internet enterprises with 84 million active users. Meg Whitman, eBay's former CEO, managed to turn the firm from a purely domestic company with auctions in 300 categories into a global empire spanning 21 countries and 16,000 categories. Categories now include computers, used cars, time-share holidays. EBay has truly become a global trading platform.

EBay's biggest strength has been its willingness to its customers incessantly. Early on, it introduced buyer and seller feedback ratings and showed pictures of the goods being sold. When the firm launched Billpoint, many customers resented the new payment service. EBay quickly redesigned the site and explained that Billpoint was optional. EBay also constantly scans the site to see whether any new opportunities arise in the

*miscellaneous* category. EBay users also have an emotional attachment to the site; a community sense which translates into strong site loyalty. As one eBay customer explained: "There a lot of people who are afraid to take the chance of leaving eBay because they have built up thousands of positive recommendations from buyers which they cannot transfer to a competitor." The company bills itself as "a community by nature, not by design." It imposes very few restrictions on the merchandise being traded. For instance, it stopped the auction of a human kidney and has banned the sales of guns, alcohol, and tobacco.

EBay has patched together a global empire via a string of acquisitions (e.g., Alando in Germany, France) and start-ups from scratch (e.g., Japan, the U.K.). It dominates most of its markets. Not all overseas forays have been successful. In Japan Yahoo! has pre-empted eBay and now claims leadership. EBay made two mistakes in Japan: it came in late (5 months after Yahoo! Japan launched its auction site) and it charged a commission for every transaction (Yahoo! Japan didn't). The company claims that as a whole its international business is profitable. In France eBay was ordered by a court to pay a $61 million fine for selling fake luxury goods from Louis Vuitton and Dior on its site.

China is the auction house's big ambition. In March 2002, the firm took a cautious first step by investing $30 million for a one-third stake in EachNet, a Shanghai-based online auction company. EBay acquired the company fully in June 2003. Unfortunately, eBay failed to gain traction in China, particularly against local incumbent Taobao, which is part of the Alibaba group. In December 2006, eBay folded EachNet into a new joint venture it set up with China-based Tom Online. The move gave eBay access to Tom Online's user base of 75 million along with its local market expertise. EBay hoped that the new partnership would enable it to crack the Chinese market. The firm imposed strict restrictions on sellers to stamp out sales of counterfeit goods. It also launched creative campaigns to build up its image in China. One campaign, Jigsaw Puzzle, consisted of a virtual puzzle where users were invited to upload puzzle pieces to eBay's local website. For each piece submitted, eBay donated Rmb 1 (about 15 cents) to a local charity that builds libraries.

*Sources:* "EBay, the flea market that spanned the globe," *Financial Times* (January 11, 2002), p. 18; "The community that listens to customers," *Financial Times* (January 11, 2002), p. 18; "Success depends on rapid growth abroad," *Financial Times* (January 11, 2002), p. 18; "EBay Bids for a Piece of China," *Asian Wall Street Journal* (March 18, 2002), p. A12; "Auction Brawl," *Business Week (Asian edition)* (June 4, 2001), pp. 18-19; http://www.ecommerce-guide.com/essentials/ebay/article.php/3578921; "How to Find Focus Online," *Media*, October 20, 2006, p. 27; "EBay Shifts China Strategy," http://www.washingtonpost.com/wp-dyn/content/article/2006/12/20/AR2006122000234_pf.html; and "EBay Returning to China," http://www.iht.com/articles/2007/06/21/technology/ebay.php.

---

[36]Jan-Benedict E. M. Steenkamp and Inge Geyskens, "How Country Characteristics Affect the Perceived Value of Web Sites," *Journal of Marketing*, 70 (July 2006), pp. 136–50.

# GLOBAL PERSPECTIVE 19-3

## PLANET GOOGLE?

Google, the Silicon Valley-based internet juggernaut, dominates the search engine market in most Western countries. However, there are still several major markets where Google has made little headway against well-entrenched local search companies. In China, which comprises the world's largest internet population, Baidu, a NASDAQ-listed Chinese internet firm, handles more than 60 percent of all internet searches compared to only 11 percent for Google China. Other countries where Google lags behind include the Czech Republic, Russia, Japan, and South Korea (see Table A). In these markets, Google has been kept at bay by local firms who have capitalized their first-mover advantage. These local players have been able to consolidate their lead by building up a strong brand reputation and combining search with a range of other portal-like services. In Russia and the Czech Republic, Google did not initially match the locals in the quality of local language search results. Also, initially with few local language web documents available, Google's computer algorithm technology proved to be less of a competitive advantage in those markets.

Source: "The Plucky Local Groups Who Dare to Defy Planet Google," *Financial Times*, September 17, 2008, p. 18.

### TABLE A
### Google's Share in the Non-Google World

| Country | Number 1 | Number 2 | Number 3 |
|---|---|---|---|
| Czech Republic | Seznam: 62.5% | Google: 24.8% | Centrum: 4.8% |
| China | Baidu: 66.5% | Google: 11.3% | Alibaba: 7.4% |
| Russia | Yandex: 45.9% | Google: 33% | Rambler Media: 8.8% |
| South Korea | Naver: 57.7% | Lycos: 18.4% | Google: 8.5% |
| Japan | Yahoo! Japan: 51.0% | Google: 39.5% | Rakuten: 2.0% |

*Sources*: ComScore; e-3internet

Google counts on its ability to invest more in technology to get an edge over the competition. The firm expects that as the number of web documents in local languages explodes, its local rivals will find it harder to keep up. Google is also willing to change its game plan to reflect local preferences. Several local firms such as Naver in South Korea and Seznam in the Czech Republic have created a very successful service where users answer questions posed by others, similar to the service offered by Yahoo! Answers. Google has copycatted this service in several of its emerging markets, including Thailand and China. Google also launched an Arabic version (and the first non-English version) of Knol, a site that posts user-written articles on a range of topics.

# GLOBALLY INTEGRATED VERSUS LOCALLY RESPONSIVE INTERNET MARKETING STRATEGIES

◆ ◆ ◆ ◆ ◆ ◆ ◆

At the core of any global web marketing strategy is the conflict between local responsiveness and global integration. By being in tune with the local market's demands, the multinational can do a better job in satisfying its overseas customers. Research shows that consumers have a higher purchase intention and better attitude toward highly adapted websites compared to sites that are medium or low on cultural adaptation.[37] **Global Perspective 19-3** discusses some of the initiatives that Google took to make its service more locally responsive. However, localization comes at a price. By global or regional integration, the global web marketer can achieve operational efficiencies—in terms of setup, learning, and maintenance costs. Multinationals can leverage these efficiencies to gain a competitive edge over local players or global rivals that use a different business model. These cost savings can be passed on to the distributors and end-customers in the form of lower prices. Just as with global ad campaigns, an integrated web marketing strategy can also ensure cross-country consistency in building up a global brand image.

**Exhibit 19-3** provides a useful framework for deciding on the most suitable global internet marketing strategy. The schema is based on two dimensions: global integration and local responsiveness. By combining these two dimensions, four possible types of internet marketing strategies become possible: (1) a nationally differentiated strategies, (2) pure local adaptation, (3) global cost leadership, and (4) transnational cost adaptation strategies. Which of these four strategies is most suitable depends on the nature of the product or service. The first class of goods covers "look and feel" products. These are products where no gains can be made from global integration (e.g., because the local markets are large enough to get economies of scale). Multinationals pursue a strategy of national differentiation for this class of products (Cell 1). Adapting to unique characteristics of each individual country can help develop a competitive edge. Adaptations may be in terms of website design, language, shipping policies, assortment, and so forth. Given that such strategy can easily become expensive, MNCs should carefully deliberate whether market presence is really justified. The second class covers goods where neither local sensitivity nor global integration offers a competitive edge. A typical example is commodity-like products that are very local in nature because of perishability or bulkiness. Cell 3 involves goods where there is no need for localization but there are

## EXHIBIT 19-3
GLOBAL INTERNET STRATEGIES ACCORDING TO NATURE OF GOOD OR SERVICE BEING SOLD

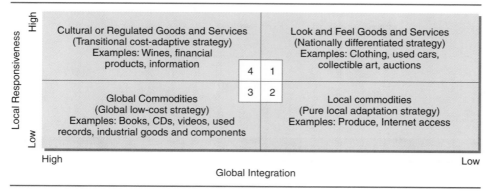

*Source:* Reprinted with permission from *Business Horizons,* May–June 2002. Copyright (2002) by the Trustees at Indiana University, Kelley School of Business.

---

[37]Nitish Singh, Olivier Furrer, and Massimiliano Ostinelli, "To Localize or to Standardize on the Web: Empirical Evidence from Italy, India, Netherlands, Spain, and Switzerland," *The Multinational Business Review*, 12 (Spring 2004), pp. 69–87.

opportunities for global integration. As with the previous case, these are mostly commodity-like products. However, here a competitive advantage is achievable via global scale efficiencies. The last category involves products or services that require both global integration and local sensitivity. A global web marketing strategy for these goods demands a balancing act that allows the company to achieve scale economies while coping with local peculiarities. On the product side, a transnational strategy could be accomplished via mass-customization.[38]

What do companies do in practice? One study looked at 206 websites to explore how American brands standardize their websites in four European countries (the UK, France, Germany, and Spain).[39] Most U.S. MNCs tailored the specific content of their country websites, especially textual information and visual images. However, a minimum level of standardization was found for logos, colors, and layouts. Further, the amount of web standardization was larger for durable goods than for non-durables. As with global new product development, firms can strike a balance between globalization and localization of their website using a core-product like strategy: create a global portal for the brand's (or company's) website that channels website visitors to nationally tailored sites.[40] The BMW website is a good illustration of this approach: the BMW portal—www.bmw.com—offers two broad choices: an "international website" available in English and German with various topics covering the different BMW models and other information, and highly customized country sites (see **Exhibit 19-4**). Another good example is the website for Nivea, the German skincare brand (see **Exhibit 19-5**). The Nivea portal gives visitors access to around 60 country, territory, and

**EXHIBIT 19-4**
INTERNATIONAL WEBSITE OF THE BMW BRAND

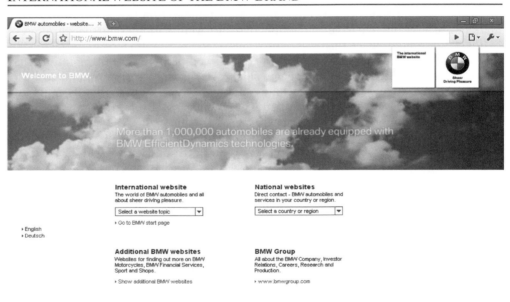

*Source:* www.bmw.com

---

[38]Mauro F. Guillèn, "What is the Best Global Strategy for the Internet?" *Business Horizons*, 45(3), pp. 39–46.

[39]Shintaro Okazaki, "Searching the Web for Global Brands: How American Brands Standardise Their Web Sites in Europe," *European Journal of Marketing* 39, 1/2(2005): 87–109.

[40]"How Country Characteristics Affect the Perceived Value of Web Sites," pp. 146–47.

## EXHIBIT 19-5
### WEBSITES OF THE NIVEA BRAND

*Source:* www.nivea.com (Nivea international portal)

*Source:* www.nivea.ie (Nivea Ireland website)

(*Continued*)

*Source:* www.nivea.co.th (Nivea Thailand website)

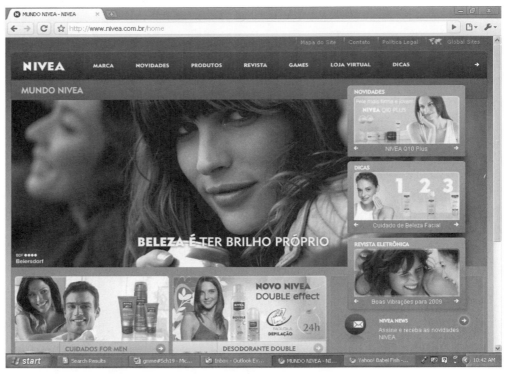

*Source:* www.nivea.com.br (Nivea Brasil website)

*(Continued)*

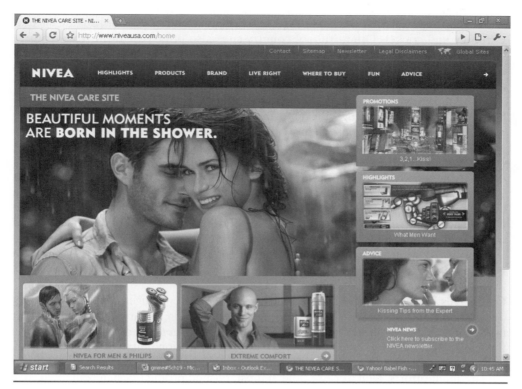

*Source:* www.niveausa.com (Nivea U.S.A. website)

regional sites. Each country site has Nivea's signature blue with the same visuals and imagery and similar features (e.g., Highlights, Brand, Advice). The sites are localized in several respects: the models used in the images, language (several country sites have multiple language choices), the products displayed. Some features are also unique to or relabeled on a particular country site (e.g., the "Games" feature on European sites is called "Fun" on Nivea's U.S. site).

## THE INTERNET AND GLOBAL PRODUCT POLICY ◆ ◆ ◆ ◆ ◆ ◆ ◆

From a product policy perspective, the internet offers tremendous opportunities. Given the intrinsic nature of the internet, the medium can be used to foster global brand building. The internet can also be leveraged as a platform for global new product development. Furthermore, the internet can also be a major driver in the diffusion of new products or services. Below we elaborate more the role of the internet in global product policy.

Management of global brands on the web is one of the challenges that global internet marketers face.[41] Many MNCs allow their local subsidiaries to set up their own websites. Cultural fragmentation is often the main driver behind customization. Yahoo! deliberately puts its country managers in charge of the local website's content.[42] Yahoo! portals around the world carry the Yahoo! logo on top and offer standard services (e.g., Answers, Movies, Finance, Maps), but differences do exist. In India, online auctions and online shopping are not offered as few people have credit cards. On the other hand, the

**Global Branding and the Internet**

[41]"The internet and International Marketing," p. 70.
[42]"Yahoo Uses Local Road In Drive to Expand Its Brand Across Asia," *Asian Wall Street Journal* (March 1, 2001), p. N1.

India Yahoo! portal includes topics that most other countries do not provide such as astrology and cricket. Other Yahoo! country sites also offer very distinctive features such as online courses in Australia and topics on gourmet, clothing/beauty, and real estate in Japan. By granting autonomy to its country managers, Yahoo! hopes to capitalize on its technology and global brand while catering to local customers.

Often, however, websites lack coordination and oversight. As a result, they can become a collage projecting different images, visuals, content, and messages for the brand and/or company. Consequently, consumers who visit sites associated with the brand or the company may get confused. With global cult brands (e.g., Land Rover, Harley Davidson), the issue of multiple sites becomes further compounded as individual distributors and brand enthusiasts set up their own websites featuring the brand. This problem becomes especially thorny when the company tries to broadcast a single brand or corporate image. Therefore, just as with more traditional communication media such as advertising, some amount of coordination of the content and tone of websites under the MNC's control is a must when a consistent brand or company image is desirable. Unfortunately, consumer-generated websites related to the brand are beyond the firm's control.

## Web-based Global New Product Development

Companies increasingly use the web to support the different stages of the new product development (NPD) process.[43] The internet plays a role in the area of global product innovation on at least three fronts: global product design, generating new product ideas through consumer *co-creation*, and new product diffusion. First of all, companies increasingly rely on geographically distributed innovation centers for their new product development efforts. Dell, for example, has established product design centers in four locations around the world: Austin, Singapore, Bangalore, and Shanghai. By using the web as a platform, multinationals like Dell and Lenovo can streamline their product development management, lower overall global development costs, and shorten the time to market. Advances in computer-aided design (CAD) software have turned web-based global NPD more efficient. One example is the PTC Windchill® suite[44] of web-based software products that has been used by firms like Dell to facilitate NPD in a global environment. This software uses a single repository for all product-data and enables engineers and managers alike to access product data from anywhere in the world through a simple web-based interface.[45]

The internet is also a driving force behind the rise of **consumer co-creation** which refers to innovation processes where consumers co-create value with the company. Instead of the consumers simply being passive and only giving feedback on new product concepts (e.g., via focus groups), they actively become involved in the NPD process. The internet makes this process more powerful by offering a massive, worldwide pool of people to tap into and by providing information access to those people. Co-creation has been applied by numerous companies including Dell ("IdeaStorm"—see **Exhibit 19-6**), Nike, Diageo, and Starbucks. P&G, for instance, aims to have one-third of its innovations being spurred through co-creation with customers or former employees. Jacques Bughin, a McKinsey partner, provides the following five tips to make co-creation effective:

1. *Signal credibility to potential contributors.* This can be done by signaling the reputation of the brand or the presence of third-party funding.

2. *Create incentives to participate.* Such incentives could be monetary (cash, revenue sharing) but also non-monetary (e.g., public acknowledgements). Dell's IdeaStorm website includes a listing of the top-20 idea contributors.

---

[43]Muammer Ozer, "Using the Internet in New Product Development," *Research Technology Management* 46, 1 (Jan/Feb 2003): 10–16.

[44]http://www.ptc.com/products/windchill/

[45]"How Dell Accelerates Product Development Worldwide," www.dell.com/powersolutions, accessed on March 18, 2009.

**EXHIBIT 19-6**
EXAMPLE OF CONSUMER CO-CREATION—DELL'S IDEASTORM

*Source:* www.ideastorm.com

3. *Establish a clear model of leadership in co-creation networks.* Decide who is in charge of the co-creation network and how to manage it.

4. *Get the brand right before engaging in co-creation.* People need to trust the brand before they are willing to engage in consumer co-creation.[46]

Finally, the internet can also play a critical role in the diffusion of new products within and across countries.[47] Companies can use the web to inform potential adopters of new products or planned launches around the world. Online hype or buzz can also stoke interest about the innovation, even long before the product is released in a particular market, as demonstrated by recent high-profile new product launches such as Apple's iPhone, Amazon's Kindle e-book reader, and Sony's PSP. On the other hand, negative online chatter from consumers where the new product has already been introduced can hamper the adoption of the innovation in later markets.

The internet heralds changes in the marketing of international services. Services differ from goods in four respects: (1) intangibility, (2) simultaneity, (3) heterogeneity, and (4) perishability. *Intangibility* means that services cannot be stored, protected through patents or displayed. *Simultaneity* refers to the fact that services are typically produced and consumed at the same time. Service delivery is also *heterogeneous*, meaning that it depends on many uncontrollable factors. There is no guarantee that the service delivered will match the service that was promised. The final characteristic, *perishability*, refers to the fact that services usually cannot be saved, stored, resold, or returned. In

**Web-based Marketing of Services**

---

[46]"Innovation and Co-Creation," *MSI Conference Summary*, June 16–18, 2008.

[47]Venkatesh Shankar and Jeffrey Meyer, "The Internet and International Marketing," in *The Sage Handbook of International Marketing*, Masaaki Kotabe and Kristiaan Helsen (eds.), London: Sage, 2009.

the global marketplace, these issues become even more taxing because of environmental differences between the foreign markets and the company's home market.

The internet allows global service marketers to break the logjam posed by these challenges.[48] Consider the tangibility issue first. International service providers can use the web to substantiate the service promises they make. For instance, international travelers who rent a car or book a hotel online can print out the confirmation note. Thereby, they can get instant tangible evidence of the transaction. Another way to manage intangibility is by offering samples of the service online. Visitors of Amazon's website can sample music or read book extracts before placing their order.

The web also offers solutions to overcome the simultaneity issue. The fact that services in general need to be "manufactured" at the point of sale makes mass production difficult. However, simultaneity becomes less of an issue with the internet. Indeed, mass customization is one of the major pluses of the web based on information technology, data storage, and data processing capabilities. Services can very easily be tailor-made via the internet to the individual needs of the customer.

The web also makes it easier for international service marketers to deal with the heterogeneity issue. The medium offers opportunities to standardize many aspects of the service provision, thereby making service transactions less unpredictable and more consistent. Elements such as greetings, reminders, and thank-you expressions can easily be standardized. Obviously, one risk here is that in some cultures customers might resent having the human element removed from service encounters. Therefore, one of the dilemmas that international service firms face is what elements of the service provision could be standardized. Because of cultural differences, these choices may differ across countries.

Finally, the web also enables companies to manage perishability. Marketers can use their website to balance demand and supply.[49] A website gives service marketers the ability to offer 24-hour/7 day service to customers around the world. Geographic boundaries and time zones no longer matter. Marketers can also use their site to manage demand. Airlines occasionally use their website to sell seats via online auctions.

---

## ◆ ◆ ◆ ◆ ◆ ◆ ◆ ◆ GLOBAL PRICING AND THE WEB

Many MNCs that have set up a web presence find that a downside of the internet is that it makes global pricing decisions less flexible. The internet creates **price transparency** for customers and distributors alike by opening a window on a company's prices for a particular item around the world. It now takes only a few mouse clicks to gather and compare price and product attribute information for a given product from the different markets where the product is sold. Various websites like Germany's DealPilot.com or Britain's shopguide.co.uk offer price comparisons of different shopping sites, thereby lowering the search effort for e-shoppers. Customers can also sample the "price floor" through various auction sites hosted by firms such as eBay in Western countries or Taobao in China. The information advantage that sellers traditionally enjoyed over buyers has dissipated due to the very nature of the internet technology.

For global marketers, price transparency creates several issues.[50] First and foremost, it severely impairs the firm's ability to price discriminate between countries. Transparency may also transform differentiated products into commodity-like goods, where the only point of difference is price. A third consequence, coupled to the previous one, is that price transparency might undermine consumers' brand loyalties and make them more price conscious. The number-one purchase criterion becomes price. Rather than being

---

[48]Pierre Berthon, Leyland Pitt, Constantine S. Katsikeas, and Jean Paul Berthon, "Virtual Services Go International: International Services in the Marketspace," *Journal of International Marketing* 7(3) (1999), pp. 84–105.

[49]Leyland Pitt, Pierre Berthon, and Richard T. Watson, "Cyberservice: Taming Service Marketing Problems with the World Wide "web," *Business Horizons*, (Jan.-Feb. 1999), pp. 11–18.

[50]Indrajit Sinha, "Cost Transparency: The Net's Real Threat to Prices & Brands," *Harvard Business Review*, 78 (March/April 2000), pp. 43–50.

loyal to a particular brand, consumers become more and more deal-prone, buying the cheapest brand available within their consideration set of acceptable brands. Finally, price transparency may also raise questions among consumers about price unfairness. Because of various restrictions, customers in one country may not be able to order via the internet the same product at a lower price from another country. However, when they realize that the product is much cheaper outside their country, consumers in high-price markets may feel that they are being taken for a ride, unless the price gaps can be fully justified. Some of these issues are illustrated by Apple's experience with the pricing of iTunes downloads in Europe. Until early 2008, Apple charged much more for iTunes downloads in the United Kingdom than in euro-zone countries: whereas iTunes customers in Britain had to pay 79p to download a song, those in Germany and France had to fork out 68p (€0.99). In early 2008, following public outcry in the United Kingdom, Apple decided to lower its U.K. prices by almost 10 percent to bring them in line with the rest of Europe.[51]

To cope with price transparency due to the internet, companies can pursue various routes. First, as we discussed in Chapter 12, firms can align their prices by, for instance, cutting prices in high-price countries and/or raising them in low-price markets. This was the route taken by Apple for iTunes downloads in the United Kingdom: the company narrowed the price gap between the U.K. and the euro-zone. Second, companies can also "localize" their products so that they differ across countries and comparison-shopping becomes less feasible. In some industries (e.g., pharmaceuticals, consumer electronics), manufacturers can also alert buyers about the adverse consequences of buying from low-price overseas suppliers. Risks that consumers might run into include limited or no warranty coverage, lack of service support, buying products that are not suitable (e.g., wrong technology standard) or that turn out to be counterfeit. Finally, outright refusal to handle orders from overseas buyers is another tactic. For instance, some country websites (e.g., iTunes) only allow payment for shipping orders through credit cards registered in that particular country.

---

## GLOBAL DISTRIBUTION STRATEGIES AND THE INTERNET ◆ ◆ ◆ ◆ ◆ ◆ ◆

The internet has also brought momentous changes for international distribution strategies. Firms that plan to make the internet an integral part of their international distribution channel, need to reflect on questions such as these: Should internet distribution complement or replace our existing channels? Will the role of our current distributors change as a result of having the internet as an additional channel medium? Should we allow our distributors to set up their own internet channels? Global retailers, facing the onslaught of online sellers, need to decide whether they should remain a brick-and-mortar business or transform themselves into a click-and-mortar business by setting up a web presence.

**Role of Existing Channels**

Connectivity means that in many industries buyers can now hook up directly through the internet with manufacturers, thereby bypassing existing channels. Some observers have gone so far as to claim that the internet heralds the end of the middleman. Especially in Japan, where there are sometimes up to seven layers of distribution between the manufacturer and the end user, the internet has the potential to cut out scores of middlemen.

Although the internet could diminish the role of intermediaries in certain businesses, in most industries distributors can still play a vital role. Manufacturers that plan to add the internet to their existing international channels need to ponder the effects of this new medium on the incumbent channels. In general, there are two possibilities: a **replacement effect** or a **complementary effect**. With the former, the internet primarily cannibalizes existing distribution channels. With the latter, on the other hand, the internet expands the overall business by offering a more attractive value proposition to

---

[51]"Apple to Cut UK Prices for iTunes Tracks," www.guardian.co.uk, accessed on March 6, 2009.

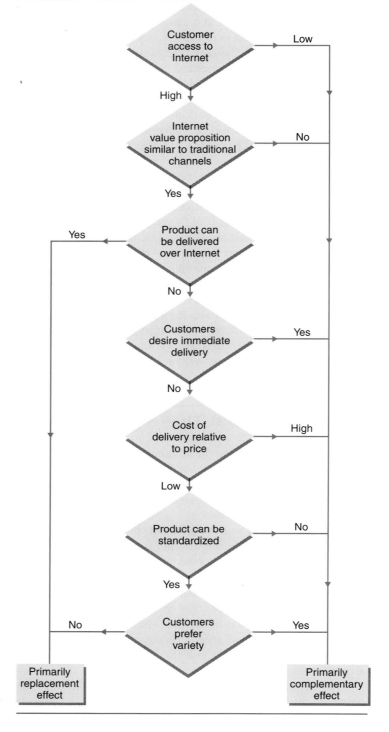

**EXHIBIT 19-7**
COMPLEMENTARY VERSUS REPLACEMENT EFFECT OF
THE INTERNET

*Source:* Courtesy of
Professor Nirmayal Kumar,
London Business School.

prospective buyers. The extent to which the internet has mostly a replacement or complementary impact will depend on the nature of the industry (see **Exhibit 19-7**).[52]

---

[52]"Internet Distribution Strategies: Dilemmas for the Incumbent," *Mastering Information Management. Part Seven–Electronic Commerce.* Supplement to the *Financial Times* (March 15, 1999), pp. 6–7.

Most likely, the effects will also depend on the country. Manufacturers may have different distribution channels in place in the various countries where they operate. Also, when the product life cycle stage varies across markets, the effect of the internet on incumbent channels will probably differ.

The most successful distributors will be those that are able to build up new competences that leverage the internet. The reason for having a distribution channel in the first place is the value-added that the middleman offers. Traditionally, sources of value-added might have been scale, inventory, assortment, and so forth. With the rise of the internet, distributors will need to look into novel ways to build competences. For instance, one potential downside of the internet is "information overload." Intermediaries can add value for their customers by collecting, interpreting, and disseminating information.[53]

Manufacturers who decide to incorporate the web in their international distribution strategy also need to ponder what approach to adopt.[54] One choice is not to use the internet for purchase transactions and also forbid distributors from using the internet as a sales medium. In that case, websites accessible to outsiders would merely function as a product information and/or communication tool. A second approach consists of allowing middlemen to sell goods over the internet. However, the manufacturer itself would not sell directly via the internet. One downside with this strategy is that sales from middlemen via the internet may impinge on existing pricing policies and territorial restrictions. In the worst-case scenario, internet sales might spur gray market activity. The third strategy is the complete opposite of the previous one. Here, internet sales are restricted to the manufacturer. A major risk here is that sales thus generated simply cannibalize incumbent resellers, thereby leading to channel conflicts. One way to counter such a risk is by selling different product lines through the various channels. However, resellers may dislike such differentiation strategy if it turns out that the product lines sold directly over the internet are more popular than the ones allocated to them. Finally, companies can also pursue a free-for-all strategy where goods are sold direct through the internet and manufacturers allow their resellers to sell online. It is then up to the market to settle on the ultimate winning combination.

Some people see the battle between conventional bricks-and-mortar retailers and internet retailers as a beauty contest with the cards stacked in favor of the latter. Consumers enjoy the convenience, the broad product assortment, and the product information provided by shopping websites. There are three e-tailing business models. First, there is the manufacturer's direct website where the manufacturer sells directly to the end-customer. Second, there are the pure web-only retailers. Pure web retailers often have a price advantage over traditional retailers because they have lower property and warehousing costs. The third possibility is the hybrid **click-and-mortar retailing model** in which the online presence becomes an extension of the traditional channel. Dozens of large retail chains have been trying to meet the challenge posed by pure web retailers by setting up a website presence. By going online, these chains are able to combine the advantages of having a website presence with those of a physical presence.[55] Click-and-mortar retailers can cross-market between their website and their store outlets, thereby adding value for their clients. Customers have the advantage of being able to touch the goods or even try them out before buying them online. They can pick up the goods ordered online at the local retail outlet to save shipping costs. Click-and-mortar retailers also often enjoy substantial brand equity whereas most pure web retailers still need to invest a lot to build up a brand. As a result, their customer acquisition costs are generally much higher than for their click-and-mortar competitors. Most hybrid retailers also have a financial advantage. Whereas retailers such as Wal-Mart, FNAC or Bertelsmann have plenty of cash available, many pure cyber-retailers often have had huge losses or minuscule profits so far. One final benefit is that local chains

**E-Tailing Landscape**

---

[53]"The internet and International Marketing," p. 66.

[54]"Internet Distribution Strategies: Dilemmas for the Incumbent," p. 7.

[55]"The Real internet Revolution," *The Economist* (August 21, 1999), pp. 53–54.

often have a better feel of the local culture. Most of the well-known brands in pure web retailing (e.g., E-trade, Amazon.com) still have rather limited international expertise.

A good example of the clash between click-and-mortar and pure internet retailers was the rivalry in France between FNAC, a leading French music and bookstore chain, and CDNOW, a U.S.-based online music vendor.[56] When CDNOW entered France and Germany it added local language "gateways" to its U.S. website. For instance, French shoppers could place orders in French and pay in their local currency. FNAC launched a pre-emptive strike by setting up a music website to compete with CDNOW. CDNOW enjoyed several competitive advantages. Sony and AOL Time Warner, two leading music content companies, had a major stake in CDNOW (37 percent each). This enabled CDNOW to offer international internet shoppers the latest releases at bargain prices. As one of the pioneers in online retailing, CDNOW also enjoyed a technology advantage over FNAC. FNAC, on the other hand, also had several competitive advantages. It was able to use its website as an extension of its store network and vice versa. Furthermore, in France and other European countries, the FNAC brand name is a trusted brand with much more familiarity among consumers than the CDNOW brand name.[57]

Whether the e-tailing business model will succeed in a particular country, depends on a wide range of factors:[58]

- *Consumer behavior.* Will consumers value a website component? Does it add value (e.g., customization, information, bigger selection, price)? Are there any valuable benefits of being part of an online community (e.g., eBay)? Are there concerns about releasing personal data or paying via a credit card online?

- *Cost structure.* Are the costs of distribution (shipping, logistics) and marketing acceptable?

- *Government policies.* What are the tax rules for buying online? Are they likely to change? Are there (or will there be) any restrictive privacy legislation or customs policies?

---

♦ ♦ ♦ ♦ ♦ ♦ ♦ ♦     ## THE ROLE OF THE INTERNET FOR GLOBAL COMMUNICATION STRATEGIES

From a communication perspective, global marketers can leverage the internet in two ways. The first role is as a pure advertising medium. This can be done via banner ads, search engine advertising, or more sophisticated forms of online advertising. The second—and probably far more crucial—role is as a communication medium that enables the company to build customer ties. **Global Perspective 19-4** discusses a recent digital pan-Asian marketing campaign launched by Unilever for its Yellow Label Lipton tea brand.

**Online Advertising**     One use of the web is as an advertising tool. In that function, internet advertising would complement other forms of promotion such as TV, radio, outdoor. Online advertising spending, although still marginal, is growing rapidly. By 2009, JupiterResearch forecasts that advertising spending will grow to about $16.1 billion in the US and $3.9 billion in Europe.[59] Overall, in almost all countries internet advertising still is a very tiny slice of the global advertising pie, even in the developed world.

As a global, interactive broadcast medium, the internet offers several advantages to international advertisers. One potent quality is the internet's global reach. Online

---

[56]"Storming a CD Bastille," *Business Week* (November 15, 1999), pp. 46–47.

[57]CDNOW was ultimately absorbed by Amazon.

[58]Diane D. Wilson, "The Future of internet Retailing: Bigger than Catalogs? Bigger than Bricks and Mortar?" in *The World According to E: E-Commerce and E-Customers*, MSI Report No. 00-102, pp. 5–8.

[59]http://news.bbc.co.uk/2/hi/business/4203805.stm

## GLOBAL PERSPECTIVE 19-4

### LIPTON HIRAMEKI—MAKING TEA TRENDY AMONG YOUNG OFFICE WORKERS IN ASIA

In early 2007, Unilever launched a major regional digital campaign dubbed "Hirameki Park" in Asia with the aim to persuade young office workers to switch their drink of choice from coffee to Unilever's Yellow Label Lipton tea brand. The initial campaign was developed in Japan. The campaign's concept refers to the Japanese word *hirameki,* which roughly translates to "I've got an idea" in English. More specifically, the *hirameki* campaign tries to make tea trendy among young office workers: "The strategy was about inspiring a new generation of tea drinkers, so it doesn't seem old-fashioned, but rather a healthy alternative to energy drinks like Red Bull or coffee" (adage.com). To woo the target consumers, the campaign touts the benefits of tea. One of ad agency executives behind the campaign explained its basis as follows:

*Sources:* "Lipton Ads to Go Regional," *Media,* March 23, 2007, p. 5 and "Lipton Hirameki Launch Hits China," adage.com, accessed on March 23, 2009.

"Asians know there is goodness in tea. What is not commonly known is tea contains theanine, and this has been found to create a relaxed but alert mental state . . . .The idea is that Hirameki brightens my day with new perspectives and inspirational moments." (*Media*, March 23, 2007).

The campaign included TV commercials but also had a major digital element. Unilever's ad agency created a regional website—hiramekipark.com—as well as customized country sites for 11 countries. The sites have a range of activities that encourage consumer interaction around an inspiration theme, including blogs, downloads, quizzes, and videos. For instance, one application would ask the consumer every day at a designated time what type of break they would like to have among three categories: inspiration, flash of mind, or new perspective. After the consumer picks a choice, the site would then stream content from the internet based on the chosen selection. Unilever also ran online banner ads on MSN Messenger as part of the campaign.

advertising is not restricted by geographic boundaries or time zones. In principle, customers anywhere around the world can be targeted via web advertisements. Online advertising is also far less expensive than more traditional forms of advertising, even though its rates are rising rapidly. The internet also allows precision as online marketers can get very precise information about website visitors based on visitor feedback, browsing behavior, and historical buying patterns. Advertising messages can be customized to individual prospects. Advertisers can save money by sending the right message to the right people.[60] As a result, the relevance of an online ad can be much higher than for ads using traditional media tools. One more useful characteristic that sets the internet apart from conventional advertising media is the fact that advertisers can instantly assess whether or not a particular advertisement is working. Online advertisers can experiment with different creative messages. Based on the experimental findings, they can replace overnight one message with another one.

Internet advertising uses a wide spectrum of techniques. One form that is still very popular is banner advertising. By clicking on the **banner ad**, users are taken to the advertiser's website where they can obtain more product information. Unfortunately, banner advertising is one of the least effective online advertising techniques. One form of online advertising which is gaining increasing popularity is **search engine advertising**— either based on keyword search or website context. Keyword search advertising allows the company to have a link to its website when people are looking for product-related information. Advertisers only pay a fee to the search engine provider when users click on the link or place an order. Website publishers can also earn advertising money by allowing the search engine company to display targeted advertising on their website related to the content of the website. Other internet advertising forms include e-mail ads, video ads that precede a video clip being downloaded, wallpaper ads, and Google map ads.

A very effective form of online campaigns is the microsite that marketers often create to promote a particular brand. Such campaigns are often integrated with other communication tools. Dockers India created a new microsite (www.dockersindia.com)

---

[60]"Advertising that Clicks," *The Economist* (October 9, 1999), pp. 75–81.

to promote a new line of Never-Iron 100-percent cotton pants in India. The site targeted 25 to 35-year-old urban males. To drive visitors to the site, Dockers did online advertising on websites such as Yahoo! India, Rediff.com, and tech-oriented Zdnetindia.com. The campaign also had a viral marketing element by encouraging visitors via a lucky drawing to spread word-of-mouth about the site to their friends.[61]

Despite the appeal of internet advertising as a medium, many advertisers are still quite wary about its potential as a global promotion tool. For one thing, there is the annoyance factor: Most people find online ads pretty irritating. Audience measurement is still a major issue. To monitor the effectiveness of an online campaign, what should be the right metric? Should it be the number of views of the page that contains the ad or should it be the *click-through rate*, that is, the number of times that surfers click on the ad?[62] Too often, advertisers simply look at the click through rate to determine whether an online ad campaign is working. What metric to use, will depend on the purpose of the campaign.[63] If the goal is to sell or to gather a database, then click-through rates, cost per acquisition, or cost per sale could be possible metrics. However, if the campaign's purpose is to build the brand, then gross impressions will be more appropriate.

Several forms of online advertising take a long time to download. This can be irritating to users in countries where access and/or phone charges are high, especially in places where internet access is slow. In many countries, access to the internet and especially broadband is still quite limited. Therefore, the scope of internet advertising may be restricted to a very narrow segment of the target population. Also, the agency talent to create attractive internet advertisements is lacking in many countries. Finally, international marketers that plan to use the web as an advertising tool should familiarize themselves with advertising regulations and restrictions that apply in the foreign markets.[64] The ultimate success of an online campaign hinges on three factors:

- **The nature of the product.** For some product, online advertising is much more suitable than for other categories. For example, online campaigns would work for high involvement goods where buyers engage in product research and price comparisons (e.g., mortgages, travel).

- **The targeting.** Whether or not a campaign will work also depends on how well the target markets have been chosen. For mass-market campaigns, the web is usually not the right medium.

- **Choice of site.** Picking the right sites is also vital. Ads on low-traffic niche sites are often more effective than ads on high-traffic general portals (e.g., Yahoo!).

- **Execution of the ad.** The quality of the production is also an important variable. No matter how many sites the banner ads appears on, if the banner is boring, it will fail to grab viewers' attention or build strong brand impressions.[65]

**Non-Traditional (NT) Web-based Communication**

Apart from online advertising, global online marketers can also use the web for non-traditional communication campaigns to build up their brand image. A good example is an internet contest that Coca-Cola organized for its Coke Zero line in China in November 2008. In the campaign, called "Be Bond for a Day" visitors of Xiaonei. com, a local social networking site, were asked why they deserved to be the next James Bond. Winners received a "Day of James Bond," including a ride in a helicopter and in Bond's signature Aston Martin car.[66] Several marketers have created web-based global NT marketing campaigns. An excellent example is the Olympic-themed "The Lost Ring" campaign (www.thelostring.com) that McDonald's released in March 2008. The

---

[61]"Dockers Goes Online to Hit Target," *Media* (August 12, 2005): 16.

[62]"Caught in a tangled "web of confusion," *Financial Times* (January 21, 2000).

[63]"Clients Must Look at Available Tools for Better Online Results," *Media* (August 9, 2002), p. 9.

[64]Richard C. Balough, "Websites Shouldn't Advertise Trouble," *Marketing News* (August 16, 1999), p. 15.

[65]"Netting Gains As Hype Dies Down," *Media* (August 23, 2002), pp. 16–17.

[66]"Slump May Help China's Online-Ad Market," *The Wall Street Journal Asia*, December 11, 2008, p. 18.

campaign centered on an Olympic-themed online game. Players searched for clues to uncover a secret tied to the Games. Ten characters provided clues via channels such as YouTube, blogs, and Twitter updates. Gradually the puzzle revealed that McDonald's was behind the game. The game, which was available in seven languages, attracted more than 150,000 players, with 70 percent of the traffic coming from outside the United States.[67] **Global Perspective 19-5** discusses how Hewlett-Packard leverages the web in China to build up HP's brand image.

# *G*LOBAL PERSPECTIVE 19-5

## "MY COMPUTER. MY STAGE" — HEWLETT-PACKARD TRIES TO CEMENT ITSELF AS THE COMPUTER BRAND OF CHOICE IN CHINA

In 2008, Hewlett-Packard (HP) ran a major digital campaign in China in its drive to become the computer brand of choice among Chinese youth. HP had become China's second most popular computer brand, behind Lenovo. The first phase of the campaign, called "My computer. My stage" involved an art competition that attracted 36,000 entries. HP relied on partners such as Mingshen Bank, which offered customers the option to create their personalized credit card using a design submitted for the competition.

*Source:* "HP Seeks Online Rappers in User-generated Drive," *Media,* July 10, 2008, p. 8

For the second phase, which ran until the end of 2008, HP launched a user-generated campaign around hip-hop music. HP's ad agency in China created a website, called hpmystage.com, to invite aspiring Chinese rappers to create their own hip-hop tracks using an online studio and design avatars to perform them. Somewhat surprisingly maybe, hip-hop culture is big among Chinese youngsters. The campaign was inspired by a Chinese movie titled *Kungfu Hip-Hop*, which prominently featured a strategic HP laptop product placement. HP's target audience was the 18- to 25-year-old Chinese. Other elements of the campaign included dance competitions at universities and malls.

*Source:* www.hpmystage.com

---

[67]"An Online Game So Mysterious Its Famous Sponsor Is Hidden," www.nytimes.com, accessed on March 19, 2009.

Besides company-generated content, the internet also enables user-generated communication. Several cult brands have spawned global or local online brand communities of loyal customers. Through these forums, customers can discuss the various aspects of the brand or the company. A recent example of branded social networks is the launch by BMW of the MyBMWClub.cn site in China in April 2009. The goal of the site is to foster brand loyalty among China's BMW drivers. Users of the site create profiles, share tips and owner-experiences, and upload videos.[68] The rise of YouTube has created a forum for user-generated ads. Several companies have used YouTube as a platform for ad-creation contests. Unfortunately, the downside of user-generated content is lack of control. Netizens can denigrate the brand or spread false rumors. Several people have also used their creative juices to develop online ads that spoof or mock the brand. A case in point is the "funny terrorist" Volkswagen hoax spot[69] that spread like wildfire on the internet. The spoof ad opens with a suicide bomber jumping into his VW Polo and then parking in front of a busy London restaurant to detonate his bomb. The bomb goes off but the blast is contained within the car. The ad ends with the punch line: "Polo. Small but tough."[70]

**Online Monitoring**     International marketers who rely on the internet need have access to high-quality data to make informed decisions for their web-based communication strategies. Data is needed on areas such as website visitor traffic, visitor demographics, competitor's online ad spending. Two companies currently dominate the internet audience tracking industry: Nielsen Online and comScore. Although both firms are U.S.-based, they are rapidly expanding overseas. In October 2008 Nielsen formed a joint venture, called CR-Nielsen, with a local company to track internet use in China. One issue with online measurement is that standard yardsticks are in short supply. The most popular measure still is the page view metric, which counts the number of times an entire page is loaded. However, this metric has limited use for media-rich portals such as YouTube. Reliable online portal auditing is also missing for many developing countries. For these markets, online advertisers need to trust claims made by the portal on metrics such as visitor traffic.[71]

While numbers are useful, the real challenge is to measure sentiment ("buzz"), including items such as what was said, the authority of the contributor, where the website links to, and the number of links. Several tools exist such as Nielsen Buzzmetrics and CRMMetrix. One difficulty is that the relevant types of sites depend on the market. For instance, in the Asia-Pacific region Chinese consumers love bulletin boards, Koreans embrace social networks, Singaporeans crave blogs, Thais build online communities, Japanese social media are built around the mobile phone.[72]

---

[68]"BMW China Launches Social Network," www.brandrepublic.asia, accessed on April 20, 2009.

[69]See http://www.youtube.com/watch?v=u1irD0c9K34&feature=related.

[70]"Spoof Suicide Bomber Ad Sparks Global Row," guardian.co.uk, accessed on March 19, 2009.

[71]"Online Measurement," Media, August 10, 2007, p. 13.

[72]"Tools that Track Buzz," Media, April 20, 2007, p. 6.

# SUMMARY ◆ ◆ ◆ ◆ ◆ ◆ ◆ ◆ ◆ ◆ ◆ ◆ ◆ ◆ ◆ ◆ ◆ ◆ ◆ ◆ ◆ ◆ ◆

The internet offers international marketers a platter full of promises. It can be leveraged to save costs and time and to generate revenues. Customers previously outside the marketer's reach now become easily accessible. The medium can be used to build up brand equity or to showcase new products or services. For scores of business around the world, it has proven to be a cost-efficient distribution channel. The internet also

offers great potential as a global interactive advertising channel. One-to-one marketing to customers anywhere in the world is no longer a pipe dream.

In spite of all these goodies, marketers should not overlook the challenges that international internet marketing poses. Some of those barriers are structural and may be difficult to overcome: government regulations, cultural barriers, lack of internet/broadband access, the knowledge barrier, and so forth. Other challenges are strategic. Companies who want to embrace the internet have to think about the implications of this medium for their global marketing strategy. Building a website does not automatically mean that consumers worldwide will beat a path to your door. Customers need to be lured to the site. Also, the site should be continuously updated and refreshed to entice first-time visitors to come back. Global marketers also need to balance off the advantages of customized content versus the rewards of having a consistent worldwide image.

The internet has brought profound changes for businesses around the world. It has created a new business paradigm: e-commerce. In a cover article in *The Atlantic* magazine, the late Peter Drucker wrote: "In the mental geography of e-commerce, distance has been eliminated. There is only one economy and only one market . . . every business must be globally competitive . . . the competition is not local anymore—in fact, it knows no boundaries."[73] For marketers, probably the biggest consequence of the web is indeed that competition is no longer local. Any firm can set up a global business on the internet from day one. Having an internet presence has become for scores of companies a matter of survival. Suppliers who are reluctant to go online risk losing out to those who are not. Companies that do not develop a website presence soon risk having their customers browsing their competitors' sites for information.

---

[73]Peter Drucker, "Beyond the Information Revolution," *The Atlantic* (October 1999), pp. 47–57.

## KEY TERMS ◆ ◆ ◆ ◆ ◆ ◆ ◆ ◆ ◆ ◆ ◆ ◆ ◆ ◆ ◆ ◆ ◆ ◆ ◆

| | | | |
|---|---|---|---|
| Banner ad | Cost transparency | Knowledge barrier | Search engine advertising |
| Click-and-Mortar retailer | Digital divide | Online survey | |
| Complementary effect | E-commerce | Replacement effect | |

## REVIEW QUESTIONS ◆ ◆ ◆ ◆ ◆ ◆ ◆ ◆ ◆ ◆ ◆ ◆ ◆ ◆ ◆ ◆ ◆ ◆ ◆ ◆ ◆

**1.** What structural barriers impact the use of the internet as an international marketing medium?

**2.** What advantages do click-and-mortar retailers have over pure web retailers? What are the disadvantages?

**3.** Explain the notion of price transparency in the context of the internet. What are the possible solutions that marketers can have to cope with the problem?

**4.** In many countries, the internet infrastructure is far less sophisticated than in the United States. Phone lines are of poor quality. Transmission rates are slow. What does poor infrastructure imply for "internationalizing" e-commerce?

**5.** For international web marketers, one major dilemma is to what degree they should localize their websites. What forces favor centralization? Which factors might tilt the balance toward localization?

## DISCUSSION QUESTIONS ◆ ◆ ◆ ◆ ◆ ◆ ◆ ◆ ◆ ◆ ◆ ◆ ◆ ◆ ◆ ◆ ◆

**1.** Some observers claim that the internet revolutionizes the way small and medium-sized companies (SMEs) can compete in the global market place. In essence, the internet has created a level playing field for SMEs. Where before SMEs had a hard time to internationalize, now any mom-and-pop outfit can open an electronic storefront with a global reach. Do you agree? What downsides do small e-businesses face vis-à-vis large companies

**2.** Dozens of internet research firms such as Forrester Research and International Data Corp. issue projections and studies about the future of e-commerce and the internet market in general. The figures usually vary wildly. For instance, when forecasts were made for the number of internet users worldwide during 2000, predictions ranged from a low of 157 million (Morgan Stanley) to a high of 327 million users (internet Industry Almanac). What explains this huge data disparity?

**3.** While numerous brands have created pages on existing social networking sites such as Facebook and MySpace, a handful of brands (e.g., BMW, Mercedes-Benz, MTV) have taken the idea a step further and created their own networking domains from scratch. One example is the MyClubBMW.cn site that BMW launched in April 2009 in China. The goal of such sites is to strengthen brand loyalty among brand users. Is setting up a branded social site instead of using an existing mainstream networking site something other brands should consider? What are the key advantages? What are possible downsides? For what kind of brands and in what type of countries would branded social networks be a worthwhile strategy?

**4.** Select a global brand (e.g., Ray-Ban, SK-II, Lenovo). Visit the brand's international portal and then visit 4 to 5 country sites, preferably from distinct continents. If necessary, you can

654 • Chapter 19 • Global Marketing and the Internet

translate the site into English using babelfish.yahoo.com. How is the global portal organized? What are the differences and similarities among the individual country sites? Do they tend to be very localized or globalized? What could be the reasons for either outcome?

5. Web companies that rely on advertising are booming in developing countries. YouTube's audience nearly doubled in India and Brazil. This sounds like good news. Unfortunately, many of these big web players with huge global audiences and renowned brands are struggling to make even tiny profits in that part of the world. Operating costs to deliver images and videos to users are high in countries where bandwidth is limited, especially for sites that have a lot of user-generated content. At the same time, advertising rates are low. One extreme approach would be to "shut off" all those countries. Few internet companies have taken that option. What other ways would you suggest to raise revenue and/or lower costs for internet companies in developing countries?

# SHORT CASES

## CASE 19-1

### YAHOO! AND ALIBABA: SEEKING DOMINANCE IN CHINESE CYBERSPACE

People who thought that the internet craze had died during the dot-com bust of the late 1990s may have had groundhog-day feelings in the summer of 2005. Early August 2005, shares of Baidu, a search engine company heralded as China's answer to Google, went up some 350 percent on the day of its US$4bn IPO. Then, on August 11, 2005, Yahoo!, the U.S. portal, announced it would pay $1bn for a 40 percent stake in Alibaba, a Chinese B2B portal, owned by Jack Ma. With 15 million registered users, Alibaba clearly offers great reach. Its two B2B websites generated around $5bn worth of transactions in 2005. However, the portal had revenues of only $46m in 2004. Taobao, its online auction website, rapidly became China's number 2 consumer auction website, behind EachNet, the auction site owned by eBay. The quick market share increase, though, was partly due to Taobao's free services.

Jack Ma once compared local e-commerce companies such as Alibaba to crocodiles in the Yangtze River. He claimed that foreign "sharks" who swim up from the sea would have a hard time fighting the local crocodiles lurking in the river as "the smell of the water is different." Such logic must have resonated with Yahoo!. So far, foreign internet players have had little success with their standalone operations. Most of the top players in China's internet market are homegrown: Sina is the top portal; Baidu dominates the search engine market; Shanda Interactive is the largest gaming company.

Jerry Yang, Yahoo!'s co-founder, said: "We are playing for the long term. We believe the prize is huge." No doubt, the Chinese internet sector offers great promise. The value of all e-commerce transactions is expected to rise to around $217.5bn by 2007. Online advertising is predicted to go up from $208m in 2004 to $1bn by 2009. And China's online auction market could rise from $425m in 2004 to $2.7bn in 2007. However, riches are not guaranteed. Credit card usage, though on the rise, is still very limited. Foreign companies also need to cope with the challenges of cultural and linguistic differences. Also, the Beijing government exercises

strict control over the internet. Policy or regulatory changes are a constant hazard for China's internet companies. For instance, Communist party officials recently expressed unease over the spread of multiplayer role-playing games.

The Alibaba/Yahoo! deal closely resembles the cooperation model that Yahoo! used in Japan and which worked out very well in that market. According to the deal, Alibaba would take control of Yahoo's assets in China. The diversity of Alibaba's business might prove a clear strength. The company commands a strong position in B2B e-commerce. Other assets include Alipay, an online payment facility similar to eBay's Paypal, and Taobao, an eBay-like auction site. The assets thrown in by Yahoo! included its internet portal, its email service, a search engine (3721), and an online auction site (1Pai). The new operation covers almost all major internet areas, except for online gaming.

Skeptics view the diversity as a lack of focus. Some analysts also suggested that Yahoo! overpaid for its 40 percent share of Alibaba. Rival eBay's aspirations for China most likely triggered the deal. Meg Whitman, eBay's CEO, declared that China is a "must win" for the company. Rumor had it that eBay was courting Jack Ma.

There are immediate branding considerations on the horizon for the newly formed entity. The combination owns a mishmash of brands. Whether the Sino-U.S. marriage will be a success remains to be seen. Yahoo! offered a huge pile of cash and its Chinese brand portfolio. Alibaba already has a critical mass of 15 million registered users. The task for Jack Ma is to turn those eyeballs into profits.

### DISCUSSION QUESTIONS

1. Was Yahoo! right to outsource its future in China to Alibaba.

2. The case points out that the Alibaba/Yahoo! combination led to a mishmash of internet brands. How should Alibaba manage this mix of brands?

3. What other marketing actions would you prescribe for the Alibaba/Yahoo! combination to succeed?

4. Do you agree with some of the critics that the new entity lacks focus? What might be some of the advantages that diversity offers to internet players in China?

*Sources:* "Yahoo Search Is Complete: Alibaba Finds a Way to Reap the Riches of Online China," *Financial Times* (August 12, 2005): 9; "Crocodile Amid the Pebbles," *Financial Times* (August 12, 2005): 9; *China Hand*, Chapter 12 (December 1, 2005); "Seeking to Dominate Chinese Cyberspace," *Media* (December 2, 2005): 20.

## CASE 19-2

### VW POLO – HOAX AD SPREADS LIKE A WILDFIRE

In January 2005, Volkswagen was at the center of a big controversy after a spoof advert featuring a suicide bomber spread across the world on the internet. The spoof ad opens

with the suicide bomber leaving his home and hopping into his VW Polo. The driver wears the signature scarf made famous by the late Palestinian leader Yasser Arafat. He parks his car in front of a busy London restaurant and then detonates his bomb. The blast is contained within the car, saving the diners. The ad ends with the slogan: "Polo. Small but tough." The clip became the most watched viral ad of 2005, with over 2.3 million downloads.[74]

The hoax created quite a stir as the ad flashed around the world on the internet. Many people were confused and thought the ad was for real given its high production values showing the VW logo. An investigation by the British newspaper *The Guardian* revealed that the hoax was created by a duo of maverick advertisers, Lee and Dan (leeanddan.com). The ad was shot on 35mm film and a shoestring budget of £40,000 (around $65,000). In an interview with *The Guardian*, a British newspaper, Lee said that "We made the advert for Volkswagen. We never really intended it for public consumption. It was principally something we made to show people in the industry but it got out somehow . . . .The ad's a comment on what's

*Sources:* "Suicide Bomber Sells VW Polo—Hoax Ad Takes Internet by Storm," guardian.co.uk; "Spoof Suicide Bomber Ad Sparks Global Row," guardian.co.uk, and "Infectious Humor," guardian.co.uk, all accessed on March 15, 2009.

---

[74]See http://www.youtube.com/watch?v=HnL-7x4n4d8 for a clip.

happening at the moment. People see this on the news every day . . . the car comes out as a hero" as it stops the blast. Viral ads are often produced by creative talent looking for work. Apparently the duo had sent the spoof to DDB, Volkswagen's ad agency.

Volkswagen was not amused. A company spokesperson said that "We were horrified. This is not something we would consider using: it is incredibly bad taste to depict suicide bombers." He added that VW was considering legal action and blamed the advert on "two young creatives who are trying to make a name for themselves."

This was not the first time that a spoof ad wreaked havoc for a famous car brand. A year earlier, Ford had to distance itself from a viral e-mail showing a cat's head being cut off by a Ford car's sunroof.

### DISCUSSION QUESTIONS

1. What could be the impact of the viral "suicide bomber" ad for Volkswagen? Is the company right to be concerned about the hoax?

2. What should VW do? Should they indeed take legal action and sue the makers of the ad? Or is there a better course of action?

---

## CASE 19-3

### MYSPACE IN CHINA

When News Corporation brought MySpace to China in April 2007, the launch seemed to make perfect sense: the world's leading social networking site (SNS) in the world's fastest growing internet market. Although MySpace was a relative latecomer, News Corp. was betting that it could overcome that handicap through heavy investment and by competing unconventionally as a start-up in China. News Corp. entered China's SNS scene by setting up a joint venture with a venture capital firm and a local Chinese investment firm. News Corp. was aware that China had been a hard nut to crack for international internet brands. Examples of famous foreign web brands that failed miserably in China include Amazon, Yahoo!, and eBay.

Upfront, News Corp. decided to set up the Chinese MySpace venture as a wholly localized entity. Luo Chan, a former Microsoft executive who used to run the MSN portal, was hired to become the CEO. He and his local team would have total control of the site's operations, and, being native Chinese, would understand how to build up the site in the local environment. William Bao, a partner at Softbank China & India, explained: "By putting a local manager in, they give the company a fighting chance. This is a very crowded area, with at least 100 companies competing in the same space that MySpace entered."

*Sources*: "MySpace China Struggles for a Niche," Media, October 2, 2008; "Murdoch Is Taking MySpace to China," www.nytimes.com, accessed on March 6, 2009; and "MySpace China Looks for Answers after Setback," www.businessweek.com, accessed on March 6, 2009.

MySpace's competition is indeed very diverse. One competitor, Xiaonei, started out as a campus-based site. It is often referred to as the 'Chinese Facebook' given the very similar interface. Xiaonei's owner received $430 million funding in May 2008. Another SNS operator with campus roots is 51.com. Kaixin001 is popular among white-collar workers in China because of its microblogging platform, its gigabyte storage space, and popular applications such as Friends for Sale and Parking Wars. Probably MySpace's most formidable competitor is Qzone, an instant messaging service ("QQ") developed by Shenzhen-based Tencent. Although not a Western-style social network site, Qzone shares many features and is highly popular among adolescents and online gamers.

About a year after its entry, MySpace.cn had not much to show for its effort and heavy investments. By 2008, the site claimed around 5 million members. Also, less than 18 months after entering the market, its CEO left. Chinese reports speculated that Luo Chan left because News Corp. had not given him the autonomy he had hoped for. Rumor has it that News Corp. targeted 50 million users by 2010. If this were indeed the case, MySpace could face an uphill struggle. Market leader Qzone already has 105 million registered users and 51.com has 95 million.

The Western-style social networking format was slow to take off in China partly because of the need to use one's real name. Bulletin boards, which allow anonymity, are much more popular among Chinese netizens. These typically focus on specific topics of interest.

*Source:* www.MySpace.cn

Some observers doubt whether MySpace's business model will ever succeed in China. Brad Greenspan, chairman of BroadWebAsia, said: "Everybody knows it's a U.S. brand. If you want to spend time on a site that's about you, it's harder to pull that off with a U.S. brand. It just doesn't feel authentic." (www.businessweek.com) Others concur and argue that SNS is an entirely local game in China. Furthermore, Chinese users may be reluctant to switch to a newcomer. Many young Chinese students may also have trouble simply spelling the name MySpace.

One observer of the industry commented that: "Given the brand name, amount of money behind it, and team it has put together, MySpace China has no choice but to go after the massive mainstream social networking market to reach critical volume. However, in the long run, I don't think that Chinese online habits or preferences will support general social networking sites." (Media, October 2, 2008) Others suggest that MySpace China needs to differentiate itself from its wide range of competitors and come up with a niche and unique services. Another challenge, which MySpace also faces in other countries, is how to monetize the site.

### DISCUSSION QUESTIONS

**1.** Is there a market opportunity for MySpace in China? Why or why not?

**2.** Why is MySpace.cn struggling? Is News Corp. overambitious with its 50 million users goal?

**3.** What should by the business model for MySpace China? Should the site indeed go for a niche? If so which one? How to "monetize" (generate revenue) the site?

**4.** Why do you think well-known global website brands find it hard to crack China's internet market?

## FURTHER READINGS ✦ ✦ ✦ ✦ ✦ ✦ ✦ ✦ ✦ ✦ ✦ ✦ ✦ ✦ ✦ ✦ ✦ ✦ ✦ ✦

Berthon, Pierre, Leyland Pitt, Constantine S. Katsikeas, and Jean Paul Berthon. "Virtual Services Go International: International Services in the Marketspace." *Journal of International Marketing*, 7(3) (1999): 84–105.

Cronin, Mary J. *Global Advantage on the Internet. From Corporate Connectivity to International Competitiveness.* New York: Van Nostrand Reinhold, 1996.

Dodd, Jonathan. "Market Research on the Internet—Threat or Opportunity?" *Marketing and Research Today*, (February 1998): 60–67.

Okazaki, Shintaro. "Searching the Web for Global Brands: How American Brands Standardise Their Web Sites in Europe." *European Journal of Marketing* 39 1/2 (2005): 87–109.

Pitt, Leyland, Pierre Berthon, and Richard T. Watson. "Cyberservice: Taming Service Marketing Problems with the World Wide Web." *Business Horizons*, (January/February 1999): 11–18.

Quelch, John A. and Lisa R. Klein. "The Internet and International Marketing." *Sloan Management Review*, (Spring 1996): 60–75.

Samiee, Saeed. "The Internet and International Marketing: Is There a Fit?" *Journal of Interactive Marketing*, 12(4) (Autumn 1998): 5–21.

Shankar, Venkatesh and Jeffrey Meyer. "The Internet and International Marketing," in *The SAGE Handbook of International Marketing*, Masaaki Kotabe and Kristiaan Helsen (eds.). London: SAGE, 2009.

Steenkamp, Jan-Benedict E. M. and Inge Geyskens. "How Country Characteristics Affect the Perceived Value of Web Sites". *Journal of Marketing*, 70 (July 2006), pp. 136–150.

# CASES

ASES OUTLINE

# $\mathscr{C}$ASE 1

## CARREFOUR: ENTRY INTO INDIA*

Carrefour is a French international hypermarket chain that has grown to become one of the world's leading retail groups over the past 40 years. It is the world's second-largest retailer in terms of revenue after Wal-Mart and the largest in Europe. The reasons for its phenomenal success throughout the world include the facilities it offers at its hypermarkets, such as one-stop shopping, low prices, self-service, and free parking. After mixed success in Asia, the company is now on the brink of expanding into India and its Managing Director, Herve Clech, is worried about the best way to make this move.

### WHY INDIA?

The company's marketing research team has underscored the huge potential in conducting retail business in India. Retail is India's largest industry, accounting for over 10 percent of the country's GDP and around 8 percent of employment. This industry is expected to grow at an annual rate 25 percent driven by strong income growth, changing lifestyles, and favorable demographic patterns. About 50 percent of population in India is under 25 and is more welcoming of large and modern shopping malls than the country's traditional small stores.

Traditionally, India has had a very unorganized retail sector consisting of small shops housing a store in the front and the owner's house at the back. More than 99 percent of retailers function in less than 500 ft² (46.5 m²) of shopping space. The Indian retail sector is estimated at around Rs 900,000 crore[1] (US $174 billion) of which the organized sector accounts for a mere 2 percent, indicating a huge potential market opportunity for the consumer-savvy organized retailer. With this, India's retail sector is witnessing rejuvenation as traditional markets make way for new formats such as department stores, hypermarkets, supermarkets and specialty stores and local retailers as well as global competitors have already reorganized themselves to take advantage of this. However, due to the policies of only 51 percent foreign direct investment (FDI) allowance for one-brand stores but 0 percent FDI for multi-brand retail stores, global giant retailers are either waiting to determine the best time to enter or searching for potential reliable business partners. The country's huge market potential as well as stiff competition has forced Clech to ponder the best strategic plans for Carrefour's entry in India. The company's marketing research team has underscored the importance of evaluating Carrefour's performance in the existing Asian market. Specifically, the lessons Carrefour should have learned from its two major markets in Asia: China and Japan.

### CARREFOUR'S HISTORY

Carrefour was founded by the Fournier and Defforey families, opening its first supermarket in 1959 in Annecy, Haute-Savoie, France. The group initiated the new store concept of "hypermarket," stressing the need for mass-sales, low delivery costs and everyday discounts to achieve high sales turnover. The first hypermarket was opened in 1963 in Sainte-Geneviève-des-Bois, offering food and nonfood items with a floor area of 2,500 m². Well-established in France, Carrefour started its expansion in 1969, setting up the first hypermarket in Belgium. Then in 1970 Carrefour became a publicly traded company listed on the Paris Stock Exchange. In the following decades, Carrefour entered South America and Asia with its first stores in Brazil and Taiwan.

### CARREFOUR TODAY

The Carrefour group currently operates four main grocery store formats: hypermarkets, supermarkets, hard discount, and convenience stores (see **Case Exhibit 1-1**). It currently has over 15,000 company-operated or franchise stores. Examples of slogans for store formats are: Hypermarkets: *The appeal of the new*; Supermarkets: *Making life easier*; Hard Discount Stores: *Grocery products at low, low prices*. Besides these traditional modes, e-commerce in the form of Ooshop and CarrefourOnline.com (*Everything you need in non-food, online*) was created in 1999 and 2005, benefiting from Carrefour's hypermarket expertise and offering the broadest selection available in the marketplace with over one million listings.

**CASE EXHIBIT 1-1**
SALES BY FORMAT (DECEMBER 31, 2007)

|  | Hypermarkets | Supermarkets | Hard Discount | Others |
|---|---|---|---|---|
| Number of stores | 1,163 | 2,708 | 6,166 | 4,954 |
| Sales (in millions of euros) | 60,573 | 24,071 | 9,948 | 7,850 |
| % of group sales | 59.1% | 23.5% | 9.7% | 7.7% |

*Source:* Carrefour Group/2007 Financial Report.

A pioneer in countries such as Brazil (1975) and China (1995), Carrefour currently operates in three major markets: Europe, Latin America, and Asia (see **Case Exhibit 1-2**) and with a presence in 30 countries, over 54 percent of group turnover is derived from outside of France. The group sees strong potential for further international growth in the future, particularly in such large national markets as India, China, Brazil, Indonesia, Poland, and Turkey.

---

*This case was prepared by Clare Downer, Masahiro Shono, Yi "Helen" Ye and Xuan Zhang of the Fox School of Business and Management at Temple University under the supervision of Professor Masaaki Kotabe for class discussion rather than to illustrate either effective or ineffective management of a situation described (2009).

[1] A **crore** is a unit in the numbering system used in India and other countries. An Indian crore is equal to 10 million.

## CASE EXHIBIT 1-2
### BREAKDOWN BY GEOGRAPHIC REGION
### (DECEMBER 31, 2007)

| (In %) | 2007 | Number of Stores (All Formats) |
|---|---|---|
| France | 45.8% | 5,515 |
| Europe (excluding France) | 37.5% | 7,860 |
| Latin America | 10.0% | 1,096 |
| Asia | 6.7% | 520 |
| Total | 100.0% | 14,991 |

Source: Carrefour Group/2007 Financial Report

During the late 1980s, the economies of several Asian countries such as Taiwan, Singapore, and South Korea were rapidly growing and Carrefour decided to expand its presence in the Asia Pacific Region to compete head-on with Wal-Mart and other Western and Asian mass retailers. Although sales in the Asian market account for only 6.7 percent of Carrefour's global sales, this market shows great potential, accounting for 17.3 percent of growth in sales in 2007 (see **Case Exhibit 1-3**).

## CASE EXHIBIT 1-3
### GROWTH RATE IN NET SALES BY GEOGRAPHIC REGION

| (in millions of euros) | 2007 | 2006 | 2007/2006 Rate | 2007/2006 at Constant % Var. exchange |
|---|---|---|---|---|
| France | 37,621 | 37,212 | 1.1% | 1.1% |
| Europe (excluding France) | 30,837 | 28,835 | 6.9% | 6.6% |
| Latin America | 8,211 | 5,928 | 38.5% | 38.0% |
| Asia | 5,480 | 4,911 | 11.6% | 17.3% |
| Total | 82,148 | 76,887 | 6.8% | 7.0% |

Source: Carrefour Group/2007 Financial Report

### CARREFOUR'S SUCCESS IN CHINA

Carrefour entered the Chinese market in 1995 when the Government had partially opened up the retail sector. By the end of 2007, the company had grown from less than 5 retail stores in 1995 to 109 stores across 39 cities (mainly hypermarkets with some supermarkets and convenience stores). Carrefour has been the largest foreign retailer in China since 2003 and its success has been attributed to its localization policy and government marketing.

The Chinese version of "Carrefour" is "家乐福" (Jia Le Fu), which was derived from the translation of its English pronunciation and three commonly used Chinese characters, which show the company's respect for local culture. "Jia" is "Family," "Le" is "Happiness," and "Fu" is "Good fortune." The combination implies that this supermarket can provide happiness and pleasure, which is Carrefour's mission. In contrast, the translation of "Wal-Mart"—"沃尔玛" (Wo Er Ma), following the pronunciation principle, has no substantial meaning in Chinese. Carrefour knows that in this region, what people want most are familiarity, friendliness, and satisfaction of local tastes.

Carrefour has always been committed to localization wherever it exists. To this end it entered China as a large supermarket with its low-cost discounts being the most important offering to the price conscious consumers. Also, the company offers its merchandise in a traditional Chinese fashion. For example, customers can pull their own seafood from tanks or select fresh produce from bins. Carrefour has employed a large number of locals, and has created greater local career-development opportunities. Furthermore, the stores rely on locally purchased goods in order to ensure product freshness.

Carrefour's strong bargaining power with suppliers helps guarantee its price advantage. Besides strict price control, a supplier-to-be is required to pay a number of fees, including shop entry fee, bar code fee, on-shelves fee, promotion fee, festival fee, and information systems use fee. However, those suppliers are still willing to cooperate with the company, because Carrefour holds a significant position in the retail market. In brief, the price advantage ensures rapid turnover in goods, reducing the cost of capital.

Carrefour's success in China, especially its amazing new store-opening rate, to a great extent is due to "government marketing." Since reforms and the opening-up of China in the late 1970s, the Chinese government has offered preferential tax rates to attract overseas investment. The idea of Super National Treatment of the foreign investment has been prevalent in Chinese top down society. Thus, once Carrefour expressed interest in a particular area, the local government and the media would generate publicity. Besides, the local government would provide protection for the enterprise especially aimed at adverse regulation. Carrefour for its part, would try to establish good relationships with the governments by leading economic development and increasing employment.

However, behind Carrefour's glorious story in China, potential problems exist. For example, Carrefour has recently been involved in some issues, such as its violation of current commercial rules in opening new stores, unjustifiable charges forced on suppliers, as well as trademark issues. To some extent, government's overprotection may have negative consequences in the long term for a short-term gain. Also, due to over-valuing market penetration, Carrefour has yet to establish a distribution system in China, and its computer system development has also fallen behind its rivals for several years.

Despite its successes, Carrefour is currently facing stiff competition in the Chinese retail market. Global giant, Wal-Mart, is expanding in provincial capitals and small cities delivering local favorites alongside foreign brands. Britain's largest retailer, Tesco, is undergoing a period of aggressive growth after purchasing a 50 percent stake in the local hypermarket giant, Ting Hsin. Smaller local retailers are now realizing that changes need to be made in the way they do business in order to remain relevant to their customers and retailers such as Lianhua and Jiayou have recently merged to try to stave off the threat of companies such as Carrefour.

### FAILURE IN JAPAN

Despite the successes, high on the mind of Clech is the company's dismal entry into Japan a few years earlier. Despite being among the giants of global retailers, it is estimated that total sales for its 8 Japanese stores for the fiscal year ending March 2004 had resulted in a loss of 32.3 billion yen (235.9 million euros). The three main reasons for Carrefour's failure to conquer the Japanese market are its ignorance of Japanese retail culture, its inability to expand its business, and the lack of consumer trust.

First, Carrefour failed to meet the needs of Japanese consumers with its existing competencies. In Western business practices, (e.g. Wal-Mart), growth is accelerated mainly by mass marketing the products across all stores and using high volume purchasing savings to create "Every Day Low Prices." In contrast, Japanese consumers are very "trend sensitive," and due to lack of storage space prefer to purchase smaller amounts more frequently. Aside from the fact that sales trends typically do not last long, Carrefour also had to deal with the regional differences in Japan and their effects on local culture.

Second, Carrefour failed to expand its business in Japan because it did not choose a local partner. Other competitors, such as Wal-Mart and Tesco, are competing in Japan through joint ventures with local players, receiving assistance in launching operations at existing stores, as well as in purchasing store properties. However, since Carrefour decided to invest without a partner, it faced several problems including finding real estate with enough space to build its huge stores.

Third, trust became an issue in 2004, when the company got caught mislabeling substandard Japanese pork as higher-quality American produce. Several months later, to make the situation worse, Carrefour was again charged with selling ham products with expired dates. After this incident, it was discovered that check sheets, used to confirm labeling information, had not been filled out properly—a shortcoming that was supposed to have been addressed after the earlier deceptive labeling incident. The result was a drop in consumers' trust of the Carrefour store brand.

Added to these factors was the drop in popularity in Japan of the General Merchandise Store (GMS) format. **Case Exhibit 1-4** shows that GMS sales have been declining, and specialty supermarkets and e-commerce retailing are growing rapidly in Japan. Carrefour's major competitors have also been feeling the pinch in Japan's changing retail landscape. Dwindling revenues indicate that Wal-Mart's "Everyday Low Prices" slogan does not have the same appeal in Japan as it does in the US and its local unit Seiyu, Ltd will be closing at least 20 unprofitable stores and re-organizing its workforce in order to stay in business.

## CARREFOUR'S FORMULA FOR VICTORY

By comparing Carrefour's performances in both China and Japan, Clech has come to understand his company's own pattern of success. Countries in which Carrefour has been successful include Taiwan, China, Brazil, Argentina, Italy, and Belgium, where Carrefour became a top retailer by displacing local retailers. Although these countries had many local department stores and small-scale supermarkets, there were no large-scale chain stores or large-scale discount shops selling electrical household appliances or clothing. Therefore, the common attributes of these countries were (1) the fact that small-scale retail has not progressed and the absence of large scale retail, (2) the absence of potential competitors that carry specialty items, (3) inexpensive retail space, and (4) "developer-friendly" government laws and regulations. Japan does not fall into any of the above criteria and based on the changing trends in consumer needs (e.g., the decline in popularity of GMS) Carrefour had to admit defeat after just a few years of operation.

So, what makes India the next step in the region? Clech's strategic marketing team has been keeping an eye on India's economy and social trends for the past several years and feels that now is the time to make a move. India's market size and current growth trends make it one of the best retail opportunities in the world. Nevertheless, gaining entry to India's retail industry will not be easy and Clech needs to consider its many cultural, political, economic, and financial characteristics in order to find out whether it fits into Carrefour's success pattern.

## INDIA'S CULTURAL ENVIRONMENT— CUSTOMER BEHAVIOR

Recent research from the McKinsey Global Institute indicates that India will be a nation of upwardly mobile middle class households within the next generation and will eventually pass Germany as the world's fifth largest consumer market. According to NCAER (National Council for Applied Economic Research), the term "middle class" applies to those earning between US$4,000 and 21,000 (US$20,000–120,000 at PPP). However, this definition suits only about 60 million of India's population. In considering simple consumer-based criterion for ownership of a telephone, a vehicle, or a color TV, the middle class makes up nearly 200 million persons—the size of a country. Middle class upward movement has forced brands like Mercedes Benz and Louis Vuitton to stake their claim early in the country anticipating a boom in the consumption of high value products and brands.

According to Nielsen's Retail Track, the Consumer Packaged Goods market (branded, packaged groceries, food and toiletries market) in India stood at US$21.25 billion for the year 2007 with a growth of 16 percent over the previous year (see **Case Exhibit 1-5**). The increase in disposable income as well as the country's booming economy has caused Indian households to gradually increase consumption of durable goods, and the growth in ownership of mobile phones is remarkable compared to any other product category.

## CASE EXHIBIT 1-4
### 5–YEAR GROWTH BY RETAIL SEGMENT IN JAPAN
1997–2003

| Retail Segment | 2002 sales (Yen 100K) | Growth Rate (5 years to 2002) |
|---|---|---|
| CVS | 67,137 | 20 |
| Specialty Supermarkets | 261,254 | 17 |
| Mid-level retailers | 261,920 | Δ8 |
| GMS | 85,151 | Δ15 |
| Dept. Stores | 84,269 | Δ22 |
| Specialty Shops | 524,147 | Δ24 |

| (Yen 100K) | 1998 | 1999 | 2000 | 2001 | 2002 | 2003 | Y/Y |
|---|---|---|---|---|---|---|---|
| B2C/Electronic Commerce | 645 | 3,360 | 8,240 | 14,840 | 26,850 | 44,240 | 164.8% |

*Source:* METI, research on Electronic Commerce Transactions

## CASE EXHIBIT 1-5
### INCREASE IN DURABLE GOODS PENETRATION ACROSS THE COUNTRY

| Product | 2005 (%) | 2006 (%) |
|---|---|---|
| Color TV | 27.3 | 29.5 |
| Black & White TV | 24.1 | 21.9 |
| Two Wheelers | 17.4 | 16.2 |
| Four Wheelers | 2.4 | 3.6 |
| Refrigerator | 13.9 | 14.4 |
| Washing Machine | 4.2 | 4.7 |
| Air Cooler/Conditioner | 7.8 | 7.3 |
| Telephone | 12.3 | 15.0 |
| Mobile Phone | 3.1 | 12.5 |

*Source:* Spring 2006 India Retail Digest

The Nielsen's Annual Shopper Trends Study in 2006 indicates several interesting points. First, traditional stores continue to account for a dominant share (nearly 75%) of all food and grocery purchases; however, they are in decline. Second, recent usage of hypermarkets/supermarkets has increased and consumers tend to welcome these kinds of modern shopping stores. Third, Indian shoppers value large formats, a wide selection, efficient loyalty programs, pricing and visual merchandising, store accessibility, and quality products. Fourth, awareness of private labels increased from 63 percent in 2005 to 75 percent in 2006. Also, women dominate as main shoppers and influencers in household purchases and primarily belong to the age range of 25 to 40 years. The favorable consumer buying patterns are positive for Carrefour's entry into Indian market.

### INDIA'S POLITICAL ENVIRONMENT

Carrefour needs to consider several issues related to India's political system when considering investing there, including government structure, political activism, and security issues. Weighing these issues will help the company determine whether or not India's political system is stable enough to risk heavy investment as decades of political uncertainty have earned the country an unfavorable reputation.

India, with a population of 1 billion, is the second most populous country in the world and has the distinction of being the world's largest democracy. However, its varied ethnic groups, languages, and religions have created a somewhat unstable political system with ramifications for potential foreign investors. Aside from the 28 states and 7 union territories, the government currently recognizes 18 languages, although the official language is Hindi (English is also widely spoken). One result of its diverse cultures is a political system made up of the majority India National Congress as well as four other parties called the United Progressive Alliance. Also included in the mix are several communist parties known as the "Left Bloc"; and with such a mix of political ideologies and a heavily bureaucratic government, the country continues to suffer from corruption and stalled political initiatives. This has in the past been a stumbling block to major foreign companies but the current government has been trying to encourage foreign direct investment (FDI) projects by initiating political and social reforms.

Terrorist attacks in India have traditionally been blamed on the country's long-standing dispute with Pakistan but recent events have shown that some attacks have also been fueled by poverty. The U.S. Department of State has called India one of the "world's most terror afflicted countries" with over 2,000 persons being killed in the first quarter of 2008 alone. This is an issue that companies like Carrefour need to take into account when deciding whether to invest.

### THE INDIA'S ECONOMIC ENVIRONMENT

According to the Global Insight Country Risk Summary, by the end of 2007 India's economy had grown to about US$ 1.1 trillion and was the third largest in Asia after Japan and China. Overall, India is the world's twelfth largest economy. The country's nominal GDP per capita is steadily growing and is currently at US $1,096 and this is projected to keep growing through 2012. In the past, India suffered from high inflation but this has been brought somewhat under control during the recent years by tight monetary measures. However, confronted with the huge recession this year, a surge in inflation of 11.03 percent hit the 13-year high above 11 percent, with Reliance Industries, telecoms and banks bearing the brunt of investor despair.

Although the country's average per capita income is low, India's middle and upper classes have been steadily growing. Private consumption grew 8.3 percent in the fourth quarter of fiscal year 2007 and it is projected to grow over the next few years due mainly to income growth. Although Indians have been benefiting from this rise in prosperity, wealth distribution is very uneven and 25 percent of the population still lives below the poverty line with the country's unemployment rate currently at 9.8 percent. With this in mind, the majority of the population still mostly patronizes the 15 million small "mom-and-pop" stores but this custom is expected to change eventually as the country sees an increase in larger big box stores and foreign investment.

According to statistical data released by the World Bank, India has had a high constant fiscal deficit for the past four decades and there is no sign that the gulf between imports and exports is narrowing. The cash deficit has also remained for the past 20 years, ranging mainly from 2 percent to 4 percent of its GPD. Among most Asian countries, India has a low ratio of exports to GDP, which implies that it may have a lower interdependent ratio. However, due to insufficient confidence and increased anxiety from investors, the short-term vibration on economic environment is still inevitable. After hitting a record high rate of 39.285 against the US dollar in January 2008, the rupee has depreciated by 27.3 percent in less than one year accompanied by the global financial crunch.

### THE INDIAN FINANCIAL MARKET

The Indian financial market is more complete and mature than those of many other developing countries. Its stock market is over 100 years old and there are currently 27 stock markets regulated by the Securities and Exchange Board of India. The stock market has shown considerable vitality and its growth performance has ranked in the top 5 worldwide during the past years. India's financial services sector plays a major role in the country's economic and social development. Between 1969 and 1976, almost all the Indian commercial banks were nationalized, which greatly facilitated central control and effective management. Meanwhile, the nationalized banks also have a high level of marketization. Over the past 10 years, India has continued to reduce the state's intervention in interest-rate structure, and now the interest rate is mainly determined by the market.

Since the beginning of the 1990s, the Indian financial market has carried out a series of reform measures in order to encourage investors. In 1992, the Indian Government instituted the FII (Foreign Institutional Investors) system, which allowed Indian companies to issue equity securities to foreign investors through convertible bonds so that they could invest directly in India's corporate securities.

Nowadays, the relationship between India and the global financial liquidity is pretty closed. This is mainly because on one hand, India's rapid economic development requires private and public financing, but India's domestic capital supply falls far short of its urgent needs, making it highly dependent on the global financial liquidity. On the other hand, as India's financial market has a high level of liberalization, marketization and openness, global capital is willing to invest in India's market financially when the economic situation allows. One consideration Carrefour should take into account is the welcoming and openness of Indian market recently.

## INDIA — RETAIL INDUSTRY OVERVIEW

Retail has become one of the most dynamic and fast-paced industries with several players entering the market. But all of them have not yet tasted success because of the heavy initial investing that is required in order to compete with existing companies. However, the market is growing, government policies are becoming more favorable and emerging technologies are facilitating operations.

The retailing configuration in India is developing quickly, as shopping malls are increasingly becoming familiar in large cities. When it comes to development of retail space such as malls, the country's Tier II cities are growing in importance. Furthermore, the governments of several states are encouraging the use of land for commercial development (see **Case Exhibit 1-6**).

## CASE EXHIBIT 1-6
### PREDICTED MALL DISTRIBUTION SPACE IN INDIA

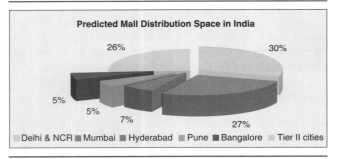

*Source:* M. Dhanabhakyam and A. Shanthi, "Indian Retail Industry—Its Growth, Challenges and Opportunities," www.fibre2fashion.com, accessed December 20, 2008.

## ORGANIZED RETAIL SECTOR IN INDIA

Retailing in India is currently (2008) estimated to be a US$ 312 billion industry, of which organized retailing makes up only 3 percent, or US$ 9.4 billion, though it is expected to reach US$

23 billion by 2010. It is expected that by 2016 modern retail industry in India will be worth US$ 175–200 billion. Most of the organized retailing is recent and concentrated in metropolitan cities such as Mumbai, Delhi, Bangaluru, and Kolkata.

Factors driving the growth of India's organized retail sector include the booming economy, the rise in the relatively young working population, growing salaries, more nuclear families in urban areas, the rising number of working women, Western influences, and growth in expenditure on luxury items. In addition, the Indian government in 2005 allowed foreign direct investment (FDI) in single brand retail to 51 percent, which has opened up many opportunities for foreign investors.

Food is the most dominant sector in the Indian retail industry, growing at a rate of 9 percent annually and since 60 percent of the Indian grocery shopping consists of non-branded items, the branded food industry is trying to convert Indian consumers to branded products. The Food Retail Industry in India is dominant and food and beverage sales account for the largest percentage increase in retail sales every year (see **Case Exhibit 1-7**).

## CASE EXHIBIT 1-7
### RETAIL SALES IN INDIA

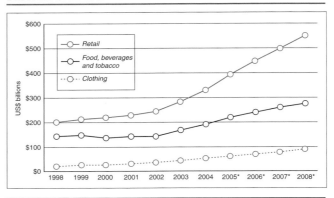

*Source:* Economist Intelligence Unit and A. T. Kearney analysis
*Data for 2005–2008 is based on estimates

## CHALLENGES FACING AN INDIAN ORGANIZED RETAIL SECTOR

The biggest challenges facing the Indian organized retail sector include the lack of retail space and rising real estate prices due to increased demand. Trained manpower shortage is also a challenge as it is still difficult and expensive to find and retain well-educated persons. The allowance of only one-brand stores does not allow FDI in multi-brand retail and this has made the entry of global retail giants into the Indian organized retail sector challenging. The country, however, allows multi-brand retailers to enter the market through franchise agreements and so 51 percent FDI in single-brand retail, 100 percent in cash and carry, and 0 percent in multi-brand retail is currently allowed.

Due to the potential lucrative benefits for players in the Indian Retail Market, Carrefour will face several competitors. Local Indian competitors include Reliance Industries Ltd., which plans to invest US$6 billion in opening 1,000 hypermarkets and 1,500 supermarkets, Pantaloons, which plans to increase its retail space to 30 million ft² with a US$1 billion investment and Bharti Telecoms, which is in talks with British global giant Tesco for a $750 million joint venture. Also, other international competitors such as Wal-Mart and Metro AG are also undergoing discussions to set up shop in India and since the allowance of only one-brand stores has made the entry of global retail giants difficult, Wal-Mart and Metro AG are trying to enter this sector indirectly through franchise agreements and cash-and-carry wholesale trading.

The growth of the retail sector is heavily dependent on the role of supply chain and as such, the Indian Supply Chain Council has been formed to explore the challenges faced by retailers and to find possible solutions. The role of the supply chain in the organized retail sector should be a shelf-centric partnership between the retailer and the manufacturer, as this will create operations that are loss free. The infrastructure in India in terms of road, rail, and air transportation is presently in bad shape and so warehousing will play a major role in supply chain operations. To overcome these problems, the Indian retailer is trying to reduce transportation costs and is investing in logistics directly or through partnerships. Overall, as the Indian organized retail sector grows the role of supply chain is becoming all the more important.

## CARREFOUR'S DECISION TO DATE

Carrefour is still struggling to finalize an Indian partner after six years of persistent search. After two years of market

evaluation, Carrefour decided to postpone its plans due to the country's lack of clarity and direction on foreign direct investment. However, in 2007, the company rekindled its Indian retail plans and resumed looking for a local partner. Carrefour now plans to enter the Indian retail market through the franchise route by 2009, and three potential local partners are being considered. The company has now formed Carrefour WC&C India and Carrefour India Master Franchise Company to begin both Cash-and-Carry and front-end retailing in India, and up until now, talks are still ongoing with Bharti Enterprises, the Wadia Group, and Delhi-based realty companies such as Parsvnath and DLF to finalize plans.

## DISCUSSION QUESTIONS

**1.** What lessons should Carrefour India learn from the Japanese and Chinese markets?

**2.** Is it the right time to enter the Indian retail market? If so, what is the best entry mode?

**3.** Due to the cultural diversity in India, how should Carrefour segment the market and cater to customer needs?

**4.** How can Crrefour improve and make use of the current infrastructure in India?

---

# CASE 2

## WAL-MART'S RISING SUN? A CASE ON WAL-MART'S ENTRY INTO JAPAN*

Ed Kolodzeiski stares across Tokyo's northern suburb of Akabane from his office at the Seiyu headquarters wondering what to do with Seiyu, the struggling, wholly-owned Japanese subsidiary of Wal-Mart. Mounting pressures of competition, supply chain inefficiencies, and the inability to offer Wal-Mart's trademark everyday low prices have resulted in perennial losses for the retailer in the world's second largest economy—and the outlook is not improving.

Following in the footsteps of retail giants including Carrefour, Costco, and Metro, Wal-Mart, the world's largest retailer, entered Japan in 2002. Wal-Mart replicated its usual foreign entry strategy and purchased a 6.1 percent stake in the floundering Japanese retailer Seiyu. Seiyu is now the fifth largest retail store by revenue in Japan. Wal-Mart gradually took control of the Japanese giant away from its previous owner, Saison Group—one of Japan's most successful conglomerates—and purchased all remaining Seiyu shares in 2008.

Kolodzeiski knows he has made a few mistakes, he knows the retailing market is stagnating and that Japanese consumers are not and never were who he thought they were. With rampant criticism and scalding inquiry on both sides of the Pacific,

Kolodzieski must deliver a change. Yet Wal-Mart's time-honored success has usually stemmed from a focus on core competencies and a precise business model. For Kolodzieski, the question is what to change and how?

## WAL-MART AS AN ORGANIZATION

In 1962, Sam Walton founded Wal-Mart on the premise of getting deals from suppliers, passing the savings to his customers, and earning profits through volume. If there was one competitive element that differentiated Wal-Mart from its competitors it was EDLP, or *everyday low pricing*. To successfully execute EDLP, Wal-Mart ran a "best price, no deal" business: no markdowns, no allowances, and no promotional money. This meant no promotion-driven inventory holding and no need to change store layout. The company spent under one percent of sales on advertising—dramatically less than its main competitors who spent up to six or seven percent. It is savings like these that Wal-Mart was able to pass on to its customers through low prices.

Although Wal-Mart bargained hard with its suppliers, it also built partnerships. One key initiative was the sharing of electronic information. Wal-Mart has used electronic data interchange since the 1980s to communicate with suppliers. At roughly the same time, Wal-Mart developed Retail Link, a state-of-the-art retail and supply chain distribution system. Retail Link reportedly cost Wal-Mart $4 billion to develop and perfect; suppliers had to make substantial investments to

*This case was prepared by Colin England, Mitika Khera, Benjamin Presseisen, and Bhuvan Wadhwa of the Fox School of Business and Management at Temple University under the supervision of Professor Masaaki Kotabe for class discussion, rather than to illustrate either effective or ineffective management of a situation described (2009).

implement the new system as well. Wal-Mart's technology-driven transformation of retailing shrank inventory lags from months in the 1950s to weeks in the 1970s and close to real time by the 1990s. By 2002, it took less than 10 minutes for information captured by point-of-sale scanners in the stores to move into the data warehouses. By reducing theS of goods sold, Retail Link allowed Wal-Mart to raise margins and still under-price the competition.

Wal-Mart also innovated in their use of retail formats. Wal-Mart started out with a traditional 60,000–80,000 square foot discount department store format—a model that was nearing maturity in the 1980s. Then in the early 1990s, Wal-Mart rolled out the supercenter format, combining groceries with other departments and as a result, became the largest grocery retailer in the world. Wal-Mart's store managers, charged with monitoring local competitors, had the authority to roll back prices if another retailer was selling at a discount.

All of these factors—Retail Link, the pricing policies, the supplier relationships, and the inventory management systems—provided Wal-Mart with extremely high productivity rates. The company was not only growing the number of stores, it was also growing its sales per store.

## WAL-MART'S INTERNATIONAL EXPANSION

Wal-Mart's global expansion activity began in the early 1990s, and has been met with enthusiasm, protest, and outright rejection across foreign markets (see **Case Exhibit 2-1** for a timeline of Wal-Mart's international expansion). Below, the selected foreign market reports provide a framework for a better understanding of its Japanese retailing efforts. These countries were chosen to give an unbiased view of the company's international operations by exploring two markets in which it is successful (Mexico and Canada), two markets in which it failed (Indonesia and Germany), and a market where it is similarly struggling (the UK). In addition to these, Wal-Mart had operations in China, Nicaragua, El Salvador, Guatemala, Honduras, Brazil, Argentina, and India, and had exited South Korea by the time of the case. Further data showed Wal-Mart examining a potential move into Russia.

## Successful Expansions: Mexico and Canada

*Mexico.* Wal-Mart's international expansion efforts began in Mexico in November of 1991 when it opened Club Aurrera (like a scaled-down Sam's Club) in a joint venture with Mexico's biggest retailer, Cifra, in the suburbs of Mexico City. The company first attempted its now-trademark international strategy—partnering with, and ultimately taking control of, local retailers to assimilate them to the Wal-Mart model.

In 2000, Wal-Mart purchased the controlling interest in Cifra, resulting in a new conglomerate, Wal-Mart de Mexico, or Walmex. This tactic was successful. In fact, Walmex was hailed as the company's biggest international victory by growing organically and placing more and more Mexicans into gainful employment. Most recently, Walmex's first quarter 2008 earnings posted an 11 percent increase from that of 2007 and the company operated 1,033 locations across the country. Walmex, however, was sharply criticized for undermining local economies, especially agriculture. The retailer sold 50 percent of the country's produce, and imposed quality standards that farmers often found impossible to meet. Other issues Walmex faced included unreliable supplier relationships, legislative and political issues, and accusations of unfair wages. Despite the criticism, Walmex continued to collect record annual revenues and touted plans for 30 new locations in 2009.

*Canada.* Wal-Mart entered Canada in 1994 through acquisition of Woolco, the Canadian remainder of the Ohio-based F.W. Woolworth Company's discount retail chain. The resulting company, Wal-Mart Canada, was consistently successful in this market, having operated a growing network of 310 retail outlets in multiple formats. Wal-Mart Canada, which employed 77,500 by 2008, also encountered its share of challenges in this market – primarily relating to unions. In April 2005, the company closed one of its locations and terminated 200 jobs when union contract arbitration began. Wal-Mart also closed a Quebec Tire and Lube Express in October 2008, citing that the union contract "did not fit with the company's business model." Wal-Mart Canada, though condemned for its behavior towards unionization, remained one of the top two retailers in this market.

## CASE EXHIBIT 2-1
### WAL-MART'S INTERNATIONAL EXPANSION TIMELINE

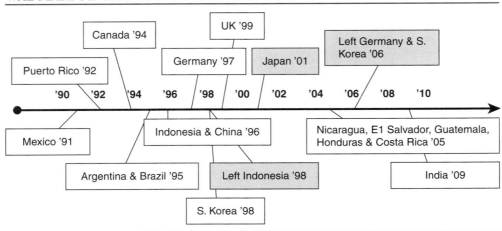

## Failed Markets: Indonesia and Germany

*Indonesia.* Wal-Mart entered Indonesia in August 1996 through a partnership with Multipolar, a subsidiary of Lippo, a powerful Indonesian conglomerate. Wal-Mart's licensing deal resulted in two new Jakarta Supercenter franchises by January of 1997. The entry was met with some indifference, but gave Wal-Mart its first experience with dense and complicated Asian supply chains. In 1998, however, Wal-Mart left Indonesia following the Asian financial crisis and a vicious legal dispute with Lippo. This was the first instance of a Wal-Mart departure from an overseas market.

*Germany.* Wal-Mart entered Germany in December of 1997 through an acquisition of the 21-store Wertkauf hypermarket chain. The following year, Wal-Mart increased its German footprint to 95 units through acquisition of the 74-store Interspar hypermarket chain. Wal-Mart's aggressive price-cutting efforts in this market resulted in $200M in losses for the company in 1999. Subsequent struggles in this highly regulated and unionized country included strikes, fines, and consequent PR challenges. With a poor reputation and embarrassing 2 percent market share in Germany, Wal-Mart was downtrodden. Further, it devastated employee morale when it issued a staff handbook that banned workplace romance, required workers to smile in a non-smiling culture, and instituted the "Wal-Mart chant" every morning before store openings. Critics assert that Wal-Mart never understood German culture, neither from a consumer nor human resources perspective. Wal-Mart sold off all of its 85 German units in 2006 to competitor Metro at a steep discount and exited the market at an estimated cost of $1 billion.

## Continued Market Struggle: Great Britain.
In 1999 Wal-Mart acquired the 300-unit British supermarket chain Asda, the second largest retailer in this market next to Tesco. As Wal-Mart's largest non-U.S. subsidiary, revenues from Asda made up nearly half of the company's international sales. Asda accomplished a 16 percent market share in grocery spending but had still not been able to overtake Tesco. Industry specialists pointed to Tesco's variety of store formats compared to Asda's rather monotonous hypermarket chain. The primary inhibitor that prevented Wal-Mart's trademark growth strategy from taking root in British soil, however, was one particularly inconvenient piece of legislation called Planning Policy Statement 6 (PPS6), which limited retail development to town centers rather than outskirts. Wal-Mart's continued lobbying to amend this law invariably failed. Asda also saw two lawsuits in the mid-2000s, millions in related fines, and strikes at its distribution centers by workers citing poor working conditions. At the time of the case, Asda operated 356 stores across the UK and employed 160,000.

### WAL-MART IN JAPAN

In May 2002, Wal-Mart purchased a 6.1 percent stake in Japanese retailer Seiyu, which operated more than 400 retail units across Japan, the world's second-largest economy. Seiyu, which focused on the apparel and grocery verticals, became a wholly owned subsidiary of Wal-Mart in 2008 after a six-year gradual stock acquisition process. Wal-Mart continued to operate in Japan under the Seiyu brand name. By the time of the case, Wal-Mart had invested over $3 billion in Seiyu's chain stores. Below is a chronology of Wal-Mart's involvement with Seiyu in Japan from 2003 to 2008. **Case Exhibit 2.2** shows the financial struggles of Seiyu in this same time period.

In early 2003, Seiyu began reorganizing its structure and implemented point-of-sale and SMART inventory tracking systems across 53 stores in Japan. These platforms increased store efficiencies by capturing consumer trends. In the same year, Wal-Mart acquired a 34 percent stake and became Seiyu's biggest shareholder. By the end of 2003, its net income fell to its lowest level in the 2002–2007 timeframe, a loss of ¥91B ($772M), even though 9 new stores opened that year.

### CASE EXHIBIT 2-2
SEIYU'S NET INCOME 2002–2007

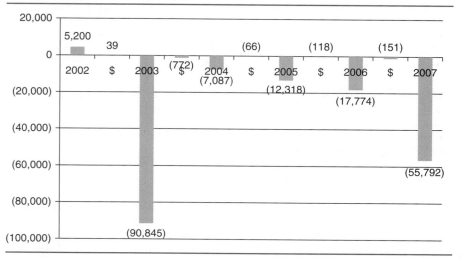

Euromonitor International

In April 2004, Seiyu opened its first pilot superstore in Japan. During the course of the year, Seiyu installed Wal-Mart's computer systems (Retail Link) in more than half of its 400 stores to enhance their inventory management and distribution. In this year, Seiyu managed to cut costs 6.1 percent by trimming payrolls, distribution expenses and advertising. Wal-Mart simultaneously saw the need to reduce headcounts in its Japanese operations, and persuaded Seiyu management to lay off 25 percent of headquarters staff, including 1,500 employees and managers. This resulted in negative publicity for the company. In spite of these efforts to cut costs and improve efficiency, Seiyu reported an annual loss of ¥7B ($66M), more than triple its projections for that year. Seiyu's management blamed unseasonable weather, stiff competition from rivals, and difficulties with Retail Link for lack of sales. By the end of 2004, Wal-Mart owned a 38 percent controlling stake in the company.

In 2005, Seiyu announced a loss of over ¥12B ($118M) even though it expected to break even by year-end. Masao Kiuchi, Seiyu's CEO, resigned after taking responsibility for the company's poor performance and Wal-Mart increased its ownership to 42 percent this year.

In August 2006, Wal-Mart built and opened a U.S.-style distribution center in Misato to improve its distribution. This year was the first time in 15 years that individual store sales of Seiyu turned positive. In spite of this, by the end of the year 2006, Seiyu reported a ¥18B loss ($151M) in net income as Wal-Mart boosted its share again to 54 percent of Seiyu.

By 2007, Wal-Mart had implemented the SMART system in more than three quarters of its 392 stores in Japan to capture consumer demands and better meet consumer needs. This helped Seiyu enhance its product assortments to increase sales. But by year-end, Seiyu announced a loss of ¥56B ($469M).

The relationship between Seiyu and Wal-Mart grew rapidly between 2002 and 2007, as Wal-Mart integrated more of its policies and systems into the subsidiary, took more and more control of the company, but was still unable to turn a profit from its operations. This begs a deeper question: What were the underlying causes for Wal-Mart's perennial failures in Japan? The following sections explore pre-existing attributes that had a direct effect on Wal-Mart's performance in Japan, including Seiyu before Wal-Mart's acquisition, the competitive environment of Japanese retailing, and the unique consumer culture in this market. This investigation will provide a deeper understanding of what Wal-Mart was up against in this market, as well as how it should proceed if it seeks to become profitable in Japan.

### Seiyu Before Wal-Mart.

Seiyu was founded in 1956 as the supermarket arm of the privately owned Seibu Distribution Companies, later renamed the Saison Group. As Tokyo and its suburbs grew swiftly throughout the 1960s, so did Seiyu. The company became a chainstore business, developed the retail strategy of self-service department stores, and offered household and food items at a discount. Store sizes ranged between 900 and 3,000 square meters depending on the site.

Seiyu, with more than 80 units in greater Tokyo, diversified its operations and went public with a listing on the Tokyo Stock Exchange in the 1970s. By 1978, Seiyu had established the highly successful Family Mart Company that became the third largest convenience store chain in Japan.

By the 1980s, the Japanese economy was booming and consumer tastes ascended to higher quality goods and services. Seiyu's low-price, low-quality store brands were no longer acceptable. To respond to this shift in consumer preference, Seiyu improved the quality of its supermarket brands and private label foodstuffs. During this same period, Seiyu pursued overseas expansion and investments in non-retailing ventures.

The 1990s were a decade marked by sustained economic sluggishness after Japan's economic bubble burst in 1991. Seiyu felt the effects of these difficulties and closed 13 stores in 1997 and another six the following year. Seiyu remained a troubled firm at the dawn of the millennium, burdened by a debt in excess of ¥911.5 billion ($7.46 billion), a figure equivalent to 52 times the total shareholders' equity of ¥17.28 billion ($144 million). The company also could not expect any assistance from the Saison Group, as Saison was facing its own financial crisis. This forced Seiyu to look for outside financing, and in April 2000 the company raised ¥15.62 billion through the sale of additional shares. Sumitomo purchased about half of this offering, giving the trading company a 12 percent stake in Seiyu. Still a struggling operation, Seiyu was well poised and enthusiastic for rescue by the world's largest retailer when talks with Wal-Mart began in 1999.

### Competition in Japan.

The competitive landscape of retailers in Japan was characterized by several international and domestic players with multiple outlets spanning the country. Among the domestic contenders in the market, 7-Eleven Japan Co. Ltd., Aeon Co. Ltd., and Ito-Yokado Co. Ltd. were the top challengers to Seiyu. **Case Exhibit 2-3** provides the market shares of the retailers in Japan from 2004 to 2007 (% retail value).

### CASE EXHIBIT 2-3
#### RETAIL MARKET SHARES BY STORE, 2004–207

| Company | 2004 | 2005 | 2006 | 2007 |
|---|---|---|---|---|
| 7-Eleven Japan Co Ltd | 2.1 | 2.2 | 2.2 | 2.2 |
| Edion Corp | 1.6 | 1.8 | 1.8 | 2 |
| AEON Co Ltd | 1.5 | 1.6 | 1.6 | 1.6 |
| Ito-Yokado Co Ltd | 1.2 | 1.3 | 1.3 | 1.3 |
| Yamada. Denki Co Ltd | 0.9 | 1 | 1.2 | 1.3 |
| Lawson Inc | 1.2 | 1.2 | 1.2 | 1.2 |
| Family Mart Co Ltd | 0.9 | 0.9 | 0.9 | 0.9 |
| Mitsukoshi Ltd | 0.8 | 0.8 | 0.7 | 0.9 |
| Daiei Inc. The | 1.3 | 1.1 | 0.9 | 0.8 |
| Circle K Sunkus Co Ltd | 0.8 | 0.8 | 0.8 | 0.8 |
| Takashimaya Co Ltd | 0.8 | 0.7 | 0.8 | 0.8 |
| Yodobashi Camera. Co Ltd | 0.5 | 0.6 | 0.6 | 0.6 |
| Uny Co Ltd | 0.6 | 0.6 | 0.6 | 0.6 |
| Seiyu. Ltd. The | 0.6 | 0.6 | 0.6 | 0.6 |
| Others | 85.2 | 84.8 | 84.2 | 84.2 |
| **Total** | **100** | **100** | **100** | **100** |

*Source:* Euromonitor International estimates

### Seven-Eleven Japan Co. Ltd. (7-Eleven).

7-Eleven Japan Co. Ltd. became a subsidiary of Seven & I Holdings Co. Ltd. In September 2005. By the time of this case, it operated over 11,500 stores in Japan and accounted for 21.7 percent of all convenience store sales. Its convenience-based product offerings consisted mainly of grocery items, which included packaged food, fast food, beverages, and daily necessities. In addition to regular convenience store services, the company also offered value-added services including door-to-door delivery requests and photocopiers in its stores.

7-Eleven's philosophy was to integrate its convenience stores and differentiated products into consumers' daily lives. 7-Eleven targeted the mass segment, and aimed at serving certain sub-targets such as health-conscious consumers and working professionals. 7-Eleven sought to generate a consumer pull-factor toward its stores, competing on price with national brands. **Case Exhibit 2-4** provides a summary of 7-Eleven performance from 2006 to 2007.

## CASE EXHIBIT 2-4
2006–2007 PERFORMANCE SUMMARY: 7-ELEVEN JAPAN

|  | 2006 | 2007 |
|---|---|---|
| **Year end February** | | |
| Net sales (¥ billion) | 2,533.5 | 2,574.3 |
| Operating profit (¥ billion) | 172.7 | 168.2 |
| Outlets | 11,735 | 12,034 |
| Selling area ('000 sq m) | 1,364.0 | 1,383.3 |
| Number of employees | n/a | 5,294 |
| Sales of grocery (%) | 80.2 | 79.9 |

*Source:* Euromonitor estimates

*AEON Co. Ltd. (AEON).* AEON operated in a vast number of retail channels: mass merchandisers, hypermarkets, supermarkets, convenience stores, and clothing and footwear stores. Almost 90 percent of AEON's revenue was generated in Japan, the remainder from operations in China, Hong Kong, Malaysia, Taiwan, Thailand, and the United States.

The company was the third largest retailer in Japan in 2007. Its ability to adapt to changing market conditions was enhanced by a strong presence across a wide range of retailing categories. Over the years, AEON has made significant efforts to improve the efficiency of its operations, including acquiring stakes in other Japanese retailers in order to develop synergies and economies of scale. AEON is quickly adapting to changes in Japan's market dynamics of low birth rate, aging population and deflation through its organic and acquisition-based growth strategies. As a result of its scale of operations, AEON leveraged significant purchasing power in negotiations with suppliers. **Case Exhibit 2-5** presents its performance from 2006 to 2007.

## CASE EXHIBIT 2-5
2006–2007 PERFORMANCE SUMMARY: AEON CO. LTD.

|  | 2006 | 2007 |
|---|---|---|
| **Year end February** | | |
| Net sales (¥ billion) | 4,430 | 4,824 |
| Operating profit (¥ billion) | 166 | 189 |
| Outlets | 4,407 | 4,212 |
| Selling area('000 sq m) | 3,100.0 | 3,110.4 |
| Number of employees | 71,171 | 76,318 |
| Sales of grocery (%) | 82.2 | 79.5 |

*Source:* Euromonitor International estimates

*Ito-Yokado Co. Ltd. (Ito-Yokado).* Ito-Yokado, established in 1920, focused on mass merchandising outlets, convenience stores, restaurants, and financial services until Seven & I Holdings Co. Ltd. acquired it in September 2005 through stock transfers. It sold apparel, grocery, and household items. Ito-Yokado was major player in mass merchandising with the fourth largest market value share of 19 percent in 2007 behind AEON Co. Ltd. (23%). Ito-Yokado focused on a regional store management strategy rather than a national method in order to meet the diverse customer needs from region to region. Each store also actively collaborated with local farmers to provide the freshest produce and express its product value to customers. **Case Exhibit 2-6** summarizes Ito-Yokado's 2006–2007 performance.

## CASE EXHIBIT 2-6
PERFORMANCE SUMMARY: ITO-YOKADO CO. LTD.

|  | 2006 | 2007 |
|---|---|---|
| **Year end February** | | |
| Net sales (¥ billion) | 1,487.5 | 1,464.1 |
| Operating profit (¥ billion) | 18.3 | 17.1 |
| Outlets | 174 | 176 |
| Selling area ('000 sq m) | 1,733.41 | 1,751.61 |
| Number of employees | 44,299 | 43,137 |
| Sales of grocery (%) | 45.2 | 45.8 |

*Source:* Euromonitor International estimates

Beyond the domestic companies, Wal-Mart's primary competitors in Japan were international entrants, including Carrefour from France and Tesco from the United Kingdom.

*Carrefour.* Carrefour, the world's second-largest retailer, entered Japan in 2000 without a partner, unlike Wal-Mart and Tesco who entered joint ventures to begin business in this market. The French company opened its first hypermarket in Tokyo and its footprint grew sluggishly to seven stores across the country by 2003. It had expected nearly twice that number of locations by the three-year mark, and cited difficulties in securing suitable real estate as the cause of expansion impediments.

The retailer also struggled to effectively market to Japanese consumers. Industry critics claim the retailer's poor returns in Japan were due to cultural misunderstanding and the inability to provide the variety of new, novel, and high-quality products Japanese consumers demanded. To further complicate efforts for success, in 2004 the Ministry of Agriculture charged Carrefour with mislabeling meat products and selling expired ham. These events devastated Carrefour's brand equity among Japanese shoppers. The company was simultaneously struck with an increasing decline in its European sales; it decided to trim its unprofitable and unnecessary operations in Japan and Mexico to free up capital for investment in its domestic market and its successful Chinese operations. Carrefour sold all eight of its stores to AEON and departed the Japanese market indefinitely with losses of $264 million.

*Tesco.* Tesco entered Japan through a strategic $340 million acquisition of C Two-Network in 2003, which operated 78 discount supermarkets in greater Tokyo. Tesco has been able to sustain its success in Japan, and many attribute this success to the company's thorough understanding of Japanese consumer culture. Tesco continued to grow in the years following market entry, acquiring 25 Fre'c stores in August of 2004 and 8 Tanekin stores in 2005. Tesco has banked on small-format stores, stocking the freshest of produce and prepared foods, as well as a sufficient selection of consumers' daily needs, in a space small enough for the ultra-urban environs of congested Tokyo, Osaka, Kyoto, and other cities. The British retailer spent millions in market research and is proceeding cautiously but optimistically in the famously complicated Japanese retail market. Tesco has 109 stores and employs 3,300 in Japan.

## *The Retail and Consumer Environment in Japan.*

Japan is the world's second-largest economy, with a population of 127 million and has one of the highest per-capita incomes in the world, making it a highly attractive market for retailers. However, Japanese retail culture is very different from that of other developed nations. Japan is a country with strong and close-knit supplier webs that are extremely difficult for foreign companies to penetrate. As a result of this, it was difficult for retailers like Wal-Mart to cut costs enough to pass on discounts to customers. One major roadblock to cutting costs was the fact that Japanese consumers buy more fresh produce than shoppers elsewhere. That made lowering costs difficult since most farms and fisheries in Japan are small, family-run operations that frequently offer better deals on smaller orders rather than on larger ones. This increased the number of small suppliers that a company needed to deal with frequently, making it difficult for large companies to cut costs and increase efficiencies.

Another aspect of the Japanese market was the need for local customization since what sells well in Hokkaido is often eschewed in Kyushu, creating logistical headaches for large retailers that cut into profits. In order to successfully customize merchandise offerings to suit the varying needs of Japanese customers in different regions, companies needed to establish relationships with several small local suppliers in each region, making the distribution network complex for international companies with limited experience in this area of operation.

Some of the popular types of retail stores in Japan include department stores, general supermarkets, specialty supermarkets, convenience stores, drug stores, and other specialty stores. The highest sales growth among these had been in the specialty stores category. Supermarkets as well as specialty supermarkets are very popular shopping destinations for day-to-day products among the Japanese consumers. There has been a rising trend towards consolidation in this segment. AEON Co. Ltd. and 7-Eleven Japan Co. Ltd. have been among the most popular supermarkets in Japan. These supermarkets are typically approximately 108 square meters in size, located in every neighborhood across cities and towns in Japan. The concept of larger retail stores located in the suburbs was new to the Japanese population and had been introduced in recent years by international retail chains such as IKEA, Wal-Mart, Carrefour, and Toys 'R'Us.

Japanese consumers are very different in their tastes and preferences for retail products as compared with consumers in other parts of Asia, as well as other developed countries. They have an affinity for luxury products as they consider a high price to be synonymous with high quality products. Japanese consumers are willing to pay premium prices for quality products. They are also known to be the most stringent in terms of quality standards. Japanese supermarkets imposed strict quality checks on all incoming grocery products since consumers would not buy food products that had marks or stains on them. Japanese food products are individually packed, as appearance plays an important role in the purchasing decision of the consumers.

Similarly, Japanese consumers are willing to pay huge sums of money to purchase brands such as Louis Vuitton, Gucci, Fendi, and the like. Japanese consumers purchased 40 percent of the world's luxury goods annually. They consider high-end branded products to be status symbols and refrain from purchasing unbranded or private label products. As a result of this, when Japanese consumers read "Everyday Low Prices," they refrain from buying those products since they consider them to be of poor quality.

Another aspect of Japanese consumers that differentiated them from those of the rest of the world is the fact that Japanese consumers tend to buy small quantities of products. This is due to the limited space in many Japanese homes. Additionally, Japanese consumers prefer purchasing fresh groceries and small quantities of household products at regular intervals rather than purchasing large quantities and stocking up for long periods of time.

This exploration of Seiyu's history, the competitive landscape and the consumer culture in Japan shows the dynamics of the Japanese retailing sector, and should provide a better familiarity of Wal-Mart's challenges in this market. Explained below are the current states and future plans for Wal-Mart and Seiyu's Japanese operations.

### *Wal-Mart Takes Over.*

On April 25, 2008, Wal-Mart raised its stake in Seiyu to 100 percent despite the fact that the company had yet to turn an annual profit. Wal-Mart acquired the remaining stake in Seiyu Ltd. for approximately $875 million and made the company a full-fledged subsidiary. In turn, Wal-Mart operated Seiyu with greater flexibility in a range of activities, including merchandising, distribution and logistics. Many analysts believed that AEON's purchase of eight Japanese stores from Carrefour, which prevented Wal-Mart from taking control of Daiei, another struggling supermarket chain, was the reason behind Wal-Mart's further investment in Seiyu. So far, Wal-Mart has invested over $3 billion in the Seiyu venture.

Because of the continuous losses it has realized since its initial investment in the company, Wal-Mart decided to close almost 20 outlets and cut 6 percent of its workforce to trim its losses in 2008. Seiyu is now the fifth largest retail store in Japan in terms of revenue. The company currently operates out of Kita-Ku, Tokyo, and has approximately 393 stores under its flagship. Wal-Mart enjoyed a dominant market position and strong financial results in the United States and other countries between 2002 and 2007, but its investment in Japan proved that the company's formula for success was ill equipped for survival in this market.

### FINAL THOUGHTS WITH THE CEO

Ed Kolodzeiski considers the future of Seiyu. He wonders if Japan will be another Germany for the world's number-one retailer, or if he can revitalize the venture and make it something like Canada for Wal-Mart. Regardless of his decision, and the path of Seiyu going forward, the last seven years have been an utter disappointment, and big decisions are still on the table for the struggling Japanese subsidiary.

## DISCUSSION QUESTIONS

1. Was Seiyu the best partner for Wal-Mart?
2. What were Wal-Mart's cultural oversights and how could they more effectively adapt to meet the needs of Japanese consumers?

3. Given the competitive landscape in the Japanese Market, do you think Wal-Mart should consider converting to/adopting the convenience store format?

4. Should Wal-Mart leave Japan? If so, what would be the implications on Wal-Mart as a corporation and a brand? If not, how can Wal-Mart remain competitive and become profitable?

# CASE 3

## ARLA FOODS AND THE MOHAMMED CARTOON CONTROVERSY*

### COMPANY BACKGROUND

Founded in 1881, Arla Foods is one of the world's largest Dairy producers based in Århus, Denmark. The company is a cooperative that is owned by approximately 10,600 dairy farmers in Denmark and Sweden. In 2007, Arla had approximately US $8.4 billion in revenues, turned a profit of US$164 million and had a workforce of 16,559 employees.

Arla Foods has achieved its immense size through a series of mergers and acquisitions. In 2000, the Danish dairy company MD Foods and the Swedish dairy company Arla merged and formed the company Arla Foods. The fusion of two dairy giants allowed the resulting company to view the Nordic countries as a single large market as opposed to four distinctly separate entities. In 2003, Arla Foods again decided to join forces with another dairy producing juggernaut, the British owned Express Dairies. Arla Foods was now the leading supplier of dairy products in the United Kingdom.

Today, Arla Foods is the largest dairy company in Europe and considers Denmark, Sweden, Finland, and the UK its home markets. The corporation exports to more than 100 countries throughout Europe, the United States, Canada, and the Middle East and aims "to provide modern consumers with milk-based products that create inspiration, confidence and well-being."

Arla Foods has a robust portfolio of brands that touches most parts of the dairy market (**Case Exhibit 3-1**). Some of its more well-known brands include Anchor Dairy Cream, Denmark's Finest Cheese, Cravendale Milk, and Lurpak Butter. Lurpak butter has twice won the award for "Best tasting butter in the world" at the world championships for dairy products. For many products, such as cheese, Arla has multiple brands to address different segments of the market. In addition to its consumer-targeted brands, Arla also manufactures milk-based ingredients for businesses in the food industry. These products include whey protein and cheese powder. Arla is also known to be on the cutting edge of new dairy technology development, as well as leading the push towards organic products.

### CASE EXHIBIT 3-1
### ARLA'S BRANDS

Nulman Group/ARLA FOODS

For years, Arla had branded itself as a grass-roots Danish company. Correspondingly, the advertising strategy the company employed highlighted its Danish cooperative origins (**Case Exhibit 3-2**). Arla so vehemently believed in creating a strong Danish association with its brands that it sponsored the Danish National Football team.

Arla's organizational structure is split into four main businesses: Consumer Nordic, Consumer International, Consumer UK, and Global Ingredients. In addition, there is a Corporate Center whose main goal is to integrate the four businesses effectively. Each division is responsible for virtually all the

---

*This case was prepared by Stine Ludvig Bech, Bartosz Fratczak, Jonathan Lane, and Nadine Oei at the Hong Kong University of Science and Technology under the supervision of Professor Kristiaan Helsen for class discussion, rather than to illustrate either effective or ineffective management of a situation described (2009).

## CASE EXHIBIT 3-2
### ARLA'S PRINT ADVERTISEMENTS

**(A)**

**(B)**

Consumer Nordic/ARLA FOODS

day-to-day activities in its region. By supervising all activities from production, to marketing, to sales, Arla hopes to deliver a consistent product to the end consumer.

### ARLA IN THE MIDDLE EAST

In Arla's mind, Middle Eastern markets represented an area of particular interest. The high per-capita dairy consumption and large population of the region made it a prime suitor for Arla's diverse mix of dairy products. For over 40 years Arla had been targeting this area, and by 2004 the Middle East had evolved

into a US$480 million market, accounting for 6–8 percent of the company's gross profits. The company viewed the Middle East as "one market with similar customs regulations, language and cultural background." Finn Hansen, Executive Director of Arla Foods' Overseas Division, stated, "for many years, Arla has traded, and enjoyed good relations with consumers in the Middle East. In fact, we have more Muslim than Danish consumers." Arla had established itself as the sixth largest dairy firm in the region.

Arla's expansion strategy in the Middle East involved forming various joint ventures with local partners. According to Mr. Hansen, a "joint venture provides us with full control of the distribution of our own products which means that we'll be able to take charge of the company's future development in the Middle East." In the early stages of 2005, the company decided to make a direct investment of approximately US$64 million into the region. The plan was to double the size of the local workforce from 1,000 to 2,000, and to increase production at its state-of-the-art cheese spread plant in Saudi Arabia.

***The Mohammed Cartoons.*** Up until the end of 2005 Arla's prospects in the region looked bright. Sales were strong and the company was perceived as a high-quality dairy producer. On September 30, 2005, however, Arla's Middle Eastern fortunes would take a turn for the worse for reasons out of the company's control. On that day, the Danish newspaper Jyllands-Posten published a series of 12 editorial cartoons depicting the Islamic prophet Mohammed. Each caricature was meant to be an artist's representation of what Mohammed meant to them. Many of the depictions were viewed as controversial, but in one of the more inflammatory drawings, Mohammed was shown hiding a bomb underneath his turban.

The resulting maelstrom was well beyond anything that Jyllands-Posten could have possibly anticipated. Many Muslims called for the Danish government to apologize to the Islamic community over the cartoons, but high-ranking Danish officials refused, claiming that an apology would tarnish their citizens' right to freedom of expression (**Case Exhibit 3-3**).

Incensed by the cartoons, the Muslim world responded with great conviction. Some more moderate Muslim leaders, like the Afghan President Hamid Karzai, simply denounced the cartoons. He stated that "any insult to the Holy Prophet is an insult to more than 1 billion Muslims and an act like this must never be allowed to be repeated." Some reactions, however, were far more extreme. In Pakistan, a protest of 70,000 irate Muslims resulted in serious violence. The mêlée lead to cars, shops, and offices being burned. Globally, approximately 20 people were killed during protests. The situation became so dire that Danish Prime Minister Anders Fogh Rasmussen described the controversy as "Denmark's worst international crisis since World War II."

***Danish Industry Crippled.*** In addition to the protests, many throughout the Muslim world decided to boycott all Danish goods. Although Danish exporters had nothing to do with the publishing of the inflammatory cartoons, many Muslims viewed the rejection of Danish products to be the best way to express their disapproval. According to Data from the Danish National Statistical Office, between February and June of 2006, exports to Saudi Arabia and Iran fell by 40 percent and 47 percent respectively. On an online blog, a

**CASE EXHIBIT 3-3**
DANISH GOVERNMENT'S RESPONSE TO THE CONTROVERSY

Royal Danish Embassy
Riyadh

# THE DANISH GOVERNMENT RESPECTS ISLAM

Ambassador Hans Klingenberg, Ambassador of Denmark to the Kingdom of Saudi Arabia, announces that the Danish Prime Minister. Mr. Anders Fogh Rasmussen, in a televised speech on the occasion of the New Year condemned any expression, action or indication that attempts to demonise groups of people on basis of their religion or ethnic background.

These comments were a reaction to a heated debate about freedom of expression and limits to freedom of expression following the publication of 12 caricature drawings of The Prophet Mohammed in one Danish newspaper, Jyllands Posten. This paper is a private and independent newspaper that is neither owned by, nor affiliated to, the Government or any political party in Denmark.

In some contexts the issue has unfortunately been portrayed as if the drawings were part and parcel of a smearing campaign against Muslims in Denmark. This is certainly not the case. The Danish Government respects Islam as one of the world's major religions.

In letters of January 6th 2006 addressed to the Secretary General of the Arab League, H.E. Amr Moussa, and to the Secretary General of the Organisation of The Islamic Conference, H.E. Professor Ekmeleddin Ihsanoglu, the Danish Minister for Foreign Affairs, H.E Per Stig Moller, expressed that the Danish Government understood that Muslim circles had felt hurt and offended by the Danish Newspapeis' drawings. The Danish Minister for Foreign Affairs has personally in an Op Ed on January 4th in a Danish national newspaper warned against disrespect among religions. It was, however, also underlined that freedom of expression is a vital and indispensable element of Danish society and that the Danish Government cannot influence what an independent newspaper chooses to bring.

The Prime Minister's speech has been transmitted to all concerned authorities namely the Ministry of Foreign Affairs of the Kingdom of Saudi Arabia, the Organisation of Islamic Conference and to the Arab League.

The speech as well as the Foreign Minister's letters of January 6, 2006 is available on the Embassy website www.ambriyadh.um.dk

Embassy of Denmark; Riyadh, January 28, 2006

Muslim woman from Kabul stated, "If one wants to show outrage, boycotting seems to be the most logical way to go rather than issuing fatwas and burning down buildings." Dr. Ahmad Abdul Aziz al Haddad, Department of Islamic Affairs and Charitable Works, stated, "this is the power of the Islamic people, the power to boycott." The boycott manifested itself differently throughout the Middle East. Some retailers placed yellow tape that read "Danish Products" around all Danish goods that they offered to consumers. Other stores removed Danish goods altogether and posted signs saying, "Danish products were here." To make matters worse, the boycotts were not limited to individuals. Some governments, like that of Qatar, suspended their country's trade missions to Denmark.

As one may expect, the boycott of Danish goods had a much more lasting and meaningful effect on Danish companies than did the protests and violence. The scope of the sanctions became so large that even *non-Danish* multinational corporations were forced to respond. For example, the French retailing giant Carrefour proactively removed all Danish products from the shelves of its Middle Eastern stores. Similarly, the Swiss multinational Nestlé was forced to respond to a rumor that two of its products were of Danish origin. To combat the false claim, Nestlé printed an advertisement in a Saudi Arabian newspaper reassuring consumers that their products are not Danish-made. According to a Nestlé spokesperson, "we noticed that after a day or so the situation normalized." The effectiveness of this "non-Danish" clarification is a testament to the staunch anti-Danish sentiments that were pervasive throughout Saudi Arabia and the rest of the Middle East.

### The Effect on Arla Foods.

Predictably, Arla was not immune to the backlash against all things Danish. According to data from the Danish National Statistical Office, the country's dairy exports fell by 85 percent in February 2006, and top Arla executives estimated that the company would lose about US$75 million due to the boycotts. Finn Hansen, a divisional director at Arla, summarized the situation when he said, "this has been a tough time for everyone at Arla Foods involved in our Middle East business." According to a press release issued by Arla Foods, "All Arla's customers in the region have cancelled their orders and sales have come to a standstill in almost all markets. Arla's warehouses are full." The company later conceded that the approximately US$2 million per day loss would force them to re-consider its previously announced investment into the region.

The situation became so serious that it even forced Arla to scale back its operations outside of the Middle East. According to Jacob Mikkelsen, an Arla manager, the situation "not only affects us in the market here—it affects our employees, it affects our partners." He went on to say, "we've had to lay off employees in the production sites in Denmark right now because, obviously, we cannot send any products [to the Middle East]—as we don't have any sales."

The anti-Arla sentiment reached such a fevered pitch that the company even decided to suspend its sponsorship agreement with the Danish National Football Team. Arla spokeswoman Astrid Gade-Nielsen said: "We would like to maintain the focus on football, so we will hold off with putting on the Arla logo."

Clearly, Arla was in an unenviable predicament. Entirely due to external factors, one of the company's main businesses had shut down. Despite the fact that Arla had nothing to do with creating the situation, the company had no choice but to try and fix it. Arla had sunk far too much company time, money, and employee time into establishing itself as a premier dairy company in the Middle Eastern market to allow this controversy to ruin one of its prized businesses. At this point, Arla's directors were faced with some tough decisions. They could attempt to completely disassociate the company from its Danish roots and project Arla Foods as a global corporation, or they could staunchly support the right of the Danish citizens to express themselves freely. No matter what course of action they take, however, Arla's future in the Middle East was about to dramatically change course.

## DISCUSSION QUESTIONS

**1.** How do you anticipate the incident will affect Arla's brand image? Specifically, in Islamic countries versus the Western world?

**2.** Should Arla Foods restructure the existing promotional strategy globally? Only in Muslim countries?

**3.** What are the advantages and disadvantages of being a multinational company in such a situation?

**4.** How should Arla respond to the boycott in the Middle East?

**5.** What lesson can be learned from these events?

# CASE 4

## CLUB MED: GOING UPSCALE*

Club Méditerranée (Club Med), a corporation in the all-inclusive resort market, manages over 100 resort villages in Mediterranean, snow, inland, and tropical locales in over 40 countries. Its resorts do business under the Club Med, Valtur,

*This case was prepared by Karen Bartoletti, Alexandra Doiranlis, Steven Kustin, and Sharon Salamon of New York University's Stern School of Business and further updated by Dan Zhang of Temple University under the supervision of Professor Masaaki Kotabe for class discussion, rather than to illustrate either effective or ineffective management of a situation described (2008).

Club Med Affaires (for business travelers), and Club Aquarius brand names. Club Med also operates tours and 2 cruise liners: Club Med 1 cruises the Caribbean and the Mediterranean and Club Med 2 sails the Pacific. The company also arranges specialized sports facilities. Club Mediterranee's clientele is about one-third French, with the rest being mainly from North America and Japan.

Club Med found that its all-inclusive price is not as widely accepted as it has been in the past. The firm has found that consumers' preferences have changed. Vacationers are not willing to spend large amounts of money for vacations that include many activities the vacationers are not using as much as they had in the past. This change in preference poses a problem for the company because Club Med's competition has been able to customize travel packages for each consumer at prices that vacationers feel more comfortable with.

Though it appears easy for Club Med to also customize travel packages, the company is at a disadvantage compared to its competition. Most of the competitors are found in a small number of locations, while Club Med has resorts scattered all over the world. Currency devaluation and political boycotts are some of the situations that Club Med faces worldwide on an ongoing basis. These external factors are reducing the company's ability to increase sales and gain new customers.

## BACKGROUND AND HISTORY

Club Mediterranée, otherwise known as "Club Med," was originally founded by a group of travelers, headed by Gerald Blitz, in 1950. However, through the years, as this group was increasing in size, it became increasingly more difficult to manage. Therefore, in 1954 Blitz took the opportunity to turn this "association" into a business, with the aid of Gilbert Trigano. Trigano sought to establish this organization and by 1985 Club Mediterranée S.A. was transformed into a publicly traded company on the Paris Stock Exchange. Club Med Inc. became the U.S.-based subsidiary of Club Mediterranée, headed by Trigano's son Serge. Today, Club Med encompasses over 80 villages, on five continents, with its GOs (Club Med staff are called "GOs," or Gentils Organisateurs, i.e., Guest Officers) representing around a hundred nationalities speaking over 30 languages (see **Case Exhibit 4-1**). In addition, Club Med has two cruise ships.

The Club Med style can be best described by the sense of closeness found among the managers. All managers are former village chiefs and are therefore knowledgeable of the company's everyday operations. This immediately reflects on the "friendly" relationships that the GO's (Club Med speak for assistants or gracious organizers) and GM's (Club Med speak for guests or gracious members) have with each other making every vacationer's experience a memorable one. A distinguishing feature of a Club Med resort is the living area, which is much simpler than that of a typical hotel chain. Rooms are sparsely decorated (i.e., no phones, televisions, etc.). Unlike typical hotel chains, Club Med measures its capacity in each resort by the number of beds, not the number of rooms, since singles have roommates. This simpler approach has made Club Med very successful. Another key to success was Club Med's image as a place to go when you want to escape. However, in the year 2004, after years of trying to make higher profits, the company altered

## CASE EXHIBIT 4-1
### THE CLUB MEDITERRANÉE GROUP VILLAGES WORLDWIDE

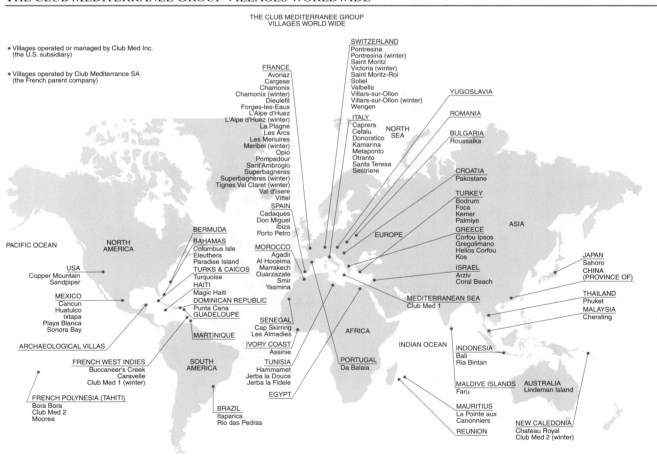

its strategy hoping to make a comeback. The new strategy aimed at giving consumers a differentiated product that was more upscale and luxurious, especially in the Americas.

## INDUSTRY STRUCTURE

Until 1986, Club Med had a very strong position in the all-inclusive resort market. The corporation's level of bargaining power with buyers, suppliers, and labor was high (see **Case Exhibit 4-2**). During that time period a client interested in duplicating "the Club Med experience" would have had to pay an additional 50 to 100 percent to have an identical experience at other resorts (see **Case Exhibit 4-3**). With regard to suppliers, companies that provided vacation-related services, such as airlines, were willing to give Club Med significant discounts in exchange for mass bookings. In keeping with the advance in information technology and the value of the web, Club Med launched a website www.clubmed.com at the end of 2003. The internet now accounts for around 20 percent of its sales. This proved to be a huge boon to travel agents who could check availability, prices, airfares, and even make bookings online. The website also allows travel agents to block reservations rather than book and confirm them for up to 48 hours. In 2004, Club Med developed a specialist program for travel agents.

## CASE EXHIBIT 4-3
### COST COMPARISON

| Average Costing of a 7-day holiday in Don Miguel | Normal Marbella Prices | Typical Club Med Holiday |
|---|---|---|
| Return airfare London/Málaga | ₤199 | Included |
| Coach transfer to resort | ₤20 | Included |
| U.K. government departure taxes | ₤5 | Included |
| Hotel (3-star equivalent) & breakfast | ₤300 | Included |
| Seven three-course lunches (@ ₤15) | ₤105 | Included |
| Wine with lunch and dinner (7 bottles @ ₤5) | ₤35 | Included |
| Seven three-course dinners (@ ₤17) | ₤119 | Included |
| Cycling (6 days @ ₤5/hr) | ₤30 | Included |
| Tennis lessons (6 days @ ₤8/hr) | ₤48 | Included |
| Night club entrance (6 × ₤5) | ₤30 | Included |
| Tips to staff (7 × ₤2) | ₤14 | Included |
| Child care facilities (6 × 4hrs @₤5/hr) | ₤120 | Included |
| Total | ₤1,025 | From ₤569 |

## CASE EXHIBIT 4-2
### USE FORCES DRIVING INDUSTRY COMPETITION

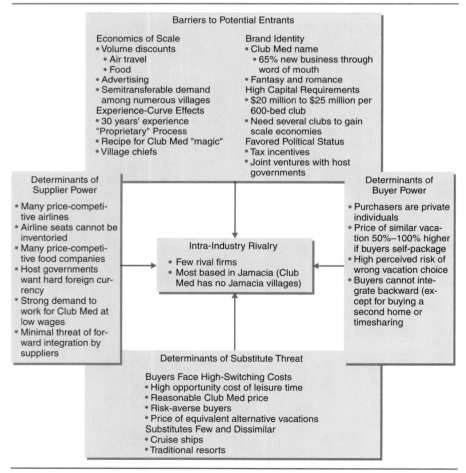

Under the program, the company certified 12,000 travel agents and apparently the certification has enabled travel agents to increase bookings significantly. Finding labor was not a problem for this resort chain because thousands of people were interested in working at such a pleasurable location.

## COMPETITION

As of 1986, Club Med began facing competition. This company was no longer the only all-inclusive resort. Many of the firm's competitors were realizing similar success. In 1986, most of the all-inclusive competitors had adopted Club Med's style of recreational activities with staff members acting as directors of these organized games. By then, the only major difference that Club Med maintained was the fact that their price did not include drinks. At the start of the year 2004, after several years of listening to agents complain that vacationers were skeptical about booking Club Med resorts due to its exclusive prices, Club Med reverted to an all inclusive deal and launched its "Total" All-Inclusive package in most of its villages. In the first part of the 2005, the company declared the Alps area, in which it operates 22 villages, a "cash-free zone," meaning that it was an all-inclusive package with snacks and drinks available round the clock. That area of the world being a major ski locale, it attracts thousands of people every year. Therefore, Club Med has also launched ski programs for its members at its resorts around the Alps.

One competitor, Jack Tar Village, the Jamaica-based company, operates resorts located mostly in the Caribbean. Jack Tar positions the resorts as more glamorous and modern than those of Club Med. This can be seen in advertisements where the company implicitly criticizes the spartan rooms and methods of Club Med. Jack Tar's claim to fame in relation to Club Med is its open bar policy.

Another competitor that the firm must consider is the Super-Clubs Organization, which operates four resorts in Jamaica. These resorts have reputations for being the most uninhibited and sexually oriented resorts. SuperClubs also follow a system of having drinks included in their price, but the other distinction from Club Med is the vacation's packaging and distribution. Club Med bundles the ground transportation with the rest of their packages while air transportation was to be distributed directly to consumers or travel agencies. SuperClubs, on the other hand, bundled ground transportation packages to be sold through large tour wholesalers, who in turn grouped these packages to be sold to the travel agencies.

Activities that Club Med and their competition offer are similar, but the way they are offered is somewhat different. Club med's competitors offer the same activities but do not include them in the initial price of the vacation. A few of the included SuperClubs activities were tennis, basketball, exercise rooms, and the like, but jet skiing and parasailing were available for an additional fee. This allowed Club Med's competitors to offer lower prices and take away potential clients from Club Med. This concept has worked for the competition because consumers find that they are not using all the activities offered. Therefore, there is no reason to pay an all-inclusive price. Club Med, on the other hand, suffers from ecological, economic, and political constraints that prevent the firm from using this individual pricing method, which could lead to customized packages for vacationers.

## THE SERVICE CONCEPT

Club Med has a worldwide presence in the resort vacation business that has allowed the firm to grow and dominate this industry. The original mission statement includes the idea that the company's goal is to take a group of strangers away from their everyday lives and bring them together in a relaxing and fun atmosphere in different parts of the world. This feeling can be expected in any of the more than 100 resorts. This mission is the key to Club Med's competitive advantage. Consumers anywhere in the world know they will get the same preferential treatment while they are in the Club Med villages.

The company's strategy for assuring that guests come back is carried out by having their guests join a club as members by paying an initiation fee as well as annual dues. With the membership, they receive newsletters, catalogs featuring their resorts, and discounts on future Club Med vacations. This makes people feel more like a part of Club Med and creates strong brand loyalty. In fact, an average Club Med vacationer revisits four times after their initial stay at one of its resorts.

All Club Med villages are similar in their setup regardless of what part of the world they are in. The resort sites are carefully chosen by taking into consideration the natural beauty (i.e., scenic views, beachfront, woodland, no swampland, etc.), good weather, and recreational potential. Each resort has approximately 40 acres to accommodate all the planned activities: windsurfing, sailing, basketball, volleyball, tennis, and so on. The resorts' secluded atmosphere is further exemplified by the lack of daily "conveniences" such as TV, clocks, radios, even writing paper. This is done to separate individuals from civilization so they can relax as much as possible. However, under the new luxury experience model, Club Med is in fact adding room facilities in some of its resorts.

Club Med organizes everything in a manner that encourages social interaction between guests. The rooms are built around core facilities such as the pool. Meals are done buffet style and the tables seat six to eight people so guests can sit and meet with many different people at every meal.

All activities and meals are included in the fee paid before the vacation begins. The only exceptions are bar drinks and items purchased in the small shops; those items are put on a tab and paid for at the end of the vacation as guests check out. The goal behind this all-inclusive price is to limit the amount of financial decisions made by the guests so, once again, they do not have to think of the pressures of the "real world."

Each day the guests have a choice of participating in a variety of activities. As evening sets in there are choices for after dinner activities like dancing and shows. All activities are designed to encourage guests to join in. Even the shows allow for audience participation.

## PROBLEMS

Until 1996, Club Méditerranée was predicted to have strong sales growth due to successful market penetration in other countries. However, the same expansion that helped the firm become famous may be the cause of the firm's disadvantage in relation to its competitors. Club Med did not have as great of an increase in sales as it had anticipated. This is due to economic and ecological disasters in countries where Club Med resorts are located. This makes it difficult for Club Med to maintain its beautiful resorts in countries that suffer from such disasters.

With this knowledge taken into consideration, contracts are drawn up between Club Med and the government of the corresponding country. The key clause in these contracts states that if Club Med is allowed to enter the country, the firm will increase tourism in the area. In turn, the government will provide financial aid to help pay for the costs of maintaining the new resort facilities.

Joint ventures with host governments have proven to be not as profitable as expected. An example of such a disappointment is when the Mexican government agreed to maintain Club Med's facilities if the corporation would increase Mexico's tourism level. However, unexpected occurrences, such as depreciation in the country's currency, limited the amount of capital the Mexican government could allocate to maintain the resort's facilities. This put Club Med in a difficult situation, as the firm had to suddenly maintain its facilities with less government funding than expected. Though Club Med's resorts are very profitable in Mexico, the devaluation of the peso has caused Club Med's maintenance costs to rise dramatically. This in turn prevents Club Med from reducing its prices and offering customized packages to its vacationers.

A second example of how international resorts reduce the firm's ability to compete effectively is Club Med's penetration into France. The resorts in the area had been doing well until March 1996. At that time, it became known that France had been conducting nuclear tests in the South Pacific. This caused Club Méditerranée to receive fewer bookings than expected in its Tahiti-based resorts. These resorts were avoided by tourists because of riots among residents who were concerned about the testing; this resulted in negative publicity in this part of the world. The riots, which occurred often in airports, deterred potential tourists from flying into this region.

Another significant event in the history of Club Med was the September 11 attacks in the United States that caused a considerable reduction in travel the world over. For Club Med, however, it was followed by the closure of 15 of its villages. Since then, it has reopened 6 and opened 4 new villages.

The hurricanes in the Caribbean in 2004 also caused some serious damage to Club Med's resorts in those regions. The company had to rebuild its Punta Cana village and at the time, it gave out Hurricane Protection Certificates that allowed guests who had lost out on vacation days due to a category 1 hurricane. Guests can exchange those certificates for travel to that destination sometime in the future.

Worse still, the terrible tsunami disaster in Southeast Asia devoured most of its coastline and Club Med's properties in Malaysia, Phuket, and the Maldives. Furthermore, the region has experienced a huge reduction in tourism.

The effects in one area where Club Med is based, often indirectly affects other Club Med resorts as well. With a lower clientele in its Tahiti-based resorts and surrounding territories, Club Med experiences lower revenue and therefore acquires less money to maintain these resorts. As a result, the firm compensates for such losses by using the profits from other resorts that have not suffered from similar disasters. Problems such as these prevent Club Med from reducing prices by implementing a customized travel package, which would enable the firm to compete more effectively in the vacation resort market.

## WHAT LIES AHEAD?

Club Med fell on hard financial times through much of the 1990s, a result of rundown properties, a reputation for mediocre food and amenities, the aging of the baby boomers, a backlash against the sexual revolution and an inconsistent message that was filtered through eight advertising agencies in different countries.

In 1998, Philippe Bourguignon, who is credited with turning around Euro Disney, was brought in as new chairman to stem the decline. He immediately instigated a $500-million, three-year rescue program. Unprofitable villages and some sales offices were closed, and older resorts are being refurbished. Thanks to the new chairman's leadership, Club Med is making a comeback. Attendance is rising, the company turned a modest profit last year and 74 of its villages have undergone a $350 million restructuring. In April 1999, after the growth strategy was put into action, the stock bounced back from a 12-month low of $63.67 to close at $84.17. Occupancy rose to 72.3 percent last year, up from 69.1 percent in the 1997 fiscal year and 66.9 percent in the 1996 fiscal year to 73.7 percent in 2000. In fiscal 1998, attendance at Club Med rose 5 percent, to almost 1.6 million, although it is still well below the record 1.8 million set in 1989. Equally important, after huge losses in both 1997 ($215 million) and 1996 ($130 million), the company earned $30 million in revenue of $1.5 billion in sales. In 2001, revenues were up 5.1 percent, to 1.985 billion euros. While there are still many problems confronting the resort club, such as a 10 percent loss of room space due to renovations, Club Med appeared to be back on track to success. The company finally reported a net profit of 3 million euros for the six months ended April 2005 compared with a loss of 4 million euros the previous year, its first time in four years, in spite of calamities such as the devastating tsunami in the Indian Ocean and the continuous storms in the Caribbean, which caused a drop of 4.3 percent in sales. The company also attributed this positive profitability to a slight change in its strategy away from "two-trident" properties to a more upscale position. Boosted by these results, the company aimed at an operating profit of 100 million in the year 2006. However, unfortunately, Club Med posted a net loss of 8 million euros for 2006-07, compared with a 5 million euro profit in the previous year.

After serious losses and cash problems in 2002, former chairman Bourguignon resigned and Henri Giscard d'Estaing was appointed as the new chairman. With this new appointment, the company started looking toward a change in strategy and a brighter future. Current management is well aware of the strong brand recognition that Club Med holds. It is synonymous with the pursuit of pleasure. However, management would like to alter this perception. It would like to eliminate the perception of Club Med as a "swingers" paradise. Even if Club Med wanted it to be such a resort, it would be virtually impossible to compete with resorts that have sprung up in Europe, Asia, and the Caribbean in recent years catering exclusively to hedonistic life styles. But Club Med has not just been renovating properties. A big change is the decision to concentrate its sales and marketing efforts on France, the United States, Canada, Belgium, Japan, Italy, Germany and Switzerland. These countries account for 74 percent of visitors. Club Med also plans to enter the Chinese market once again. It tried to enter China a few times before but the effort was largely unsuccessful. Therefore, this time it will not open a resort until it has developed brand familiarity in China by opening a sales office first. The company intends to follow this similar strategy it adopted while entering the South Korean market, which has been growing every year. In January 2005, the company announced that it was opening its first report in Albania. The company's next step is opening villages in Italy and Brazil.

The United States is Club Med's No. 1 target. To increase U.S. visitors, Club Med is considering opening three new resorts around the United States, one of them being a resort for couples in the Dominican Republic, another being a family report in the Yucatan Peninsula near Mexico, and the third being a family resort in Brazil. It has invested over $350 million from 1998 to 2004 in advertising to rejuvenate their strong brand name in the United States, which has been misunderstood because of poor advertising campaigns. Each village is now ranked with two, three or four tridents, based on amenities and comfort level, with the result that the 13 budget Club Aquarius villages are being folded into the two-trident category. A major expansion is under way around the Pacific Rim, including new resorts in Indonesia, China, the Philippines, and Vietnam. As part of its agenda to promote itself and leverage occupancy, Club Med has started entering strategic alliances with firms all over the world. In November 2002, it signed a deal with match.com, an online dating company and a part of USA Interactive, to offer vacation packages for singles to "casually" meet people in a different setting. This was part of its focus on the American customer.

In the year 2004, Club Med executed its new upmarket strategy, rebranding itself as upscale and family-oriented. Prior to that, French hospitality group Accor had acquired a 28.9 percent stake in Club Med, becoming the largest shareholder. Although it sold most of its stake in 2006, announcing that it wished to refocus on its core businesses, Accor's affiliation once provided Club Med with the much needed financial assistance and association with a powerful ally. To start with, it changed its brand identity and logo with a makeover expenditure of more than 500 million euros. The company believed that with consumers' changing preferences, there were looking for a different vacation experience and it launched its "New Luxury" product. This included major renovations at its U.S. locations, namely Club Med Columbus Isle, Club Med Buccaneer's Creek, and Club Med Turkoise. Club Med Columbus Isle went through a $5 million upgrade to include more luxury features including king-sized beds, flat screen TVs, and well-stocked mini fridges, among many other such facilities. Add to that three new dining options and a poolside with eclectic music, daybeds, and lounges and it hopes to offer an experience like none other. The company also spent $50 million on refurbishing its resorts at Buccaneer's Creek and $6 million on the one at Turkoise.

Among the new experiences that Club Med is trying to bring to its members are the unique gym facilities in some of its resorts and the "Seven Senses of Summer Program" offering a different activity every day of the week (including art classes, movie nights, dancing, and meditation). In early 2005, the company launched its first flagship store in London, UK, known as the "The Travel Boutique."

With its sights set on providing guests with nothing less than the best, Club Med continues to move its resorts further upscale. Renovations and remodeling efforts across our properties have added a new level of luxury, while innovative programs have made each location even more enjoyable than before. In 2006 and 2007, Club Med and its partners dedicated a total of $530 million to renovate and revamp the group's portfolio of offerings. 2006 saw Club Med close five of its more rudimentary resorts and upgrade seven others (Club Med Cancun Yucatan, Mexico; Club Med Caravelle, Guadeloupe; Club Med La Plagne, French Alps; Club Med Opio in Provence, France; and soon Club Med Albion, Mauritius; Club Med Ixtapa Pacific, Mexico; and Club Med Buzios, Brazil). For the future, Club Med is scanning for new properties in the Americas that it can convert into boutique style luxury properties like the one on Columbus Isle.

## DISCUSSION QUESTIONS

1. Given Club Med's current problems, do you feel the company could have avoided its pricing scheme problems through different expansion plans?

2. Why is Club Med unable to offer competitive prices?

3. Given Club Med's current problems, do you think that "the Club" will be able to survive by keeping its current pricing strategy or do you think a new strategy should be implemented?

4. How can Club Med continue to differentiate itself in order to sustain its competitive advantage against its competitors who seem to be imitating its service concepts?

5. Club Med has changed its strategy recently to a more luxury driven one. By the end of 2008, the company hopes to have most of its villas operating as luxurious boutiques. Spending $50 million a villa to refurbish it, how does that affect costs and eventually profits? In other words, what is the justification for these high expenditures?

# CASE 5

## HONDA IN EUROPE*

### INTRODUCTION

The Honda Motor Company first entered the European market in the early 1960s through the sale of its motorcycles. The

*This case was prepared by Jong Won Ko, Peter Wirtz, Mike Rhee, and Vincent Chan of the University of Hawaii at Manoa and further updated by Dan Zhang of Temple University under the supervision of Professor Masaaki Kotabe for class discussion, rather than to illustrate either effective or ineffective management of a situation described (2008).

company's motor vehicles were introduced into Europe at a much later date. Honda's motor vehicle sales in Europe have been relatively poor, especially in the previous five years. Despite its huge success in the North American market, Honda is struggling to gain a significant foothold in the European market. Honda executives wonder why their global strategy is sputtering. Is global strategy just a pipe-dream, or is something wrong with Honda's European strategy?

## HISTORY OF HONDA

In 1946 Souichiro Honda founded the Honda Technology Institute. The company started as a motorcycle producer and by the 1950s had become extremely successful in Japan. In 1956, Honda entered the U.S. market and was able to position itself effectively, selling small sized motorcycles. In the early 1960s, the company commenced automobile manufacturing and participated in Formula-1 racing (F-1) to assist its technology development. Thanks mainly to its F-1 efforts, Honda became recognized as a technologically savvy company, not only in Japan but in the rest of the world as well.

Until the early 1990s the company experienced serious organizational mismanagement resulting from tension between the technology side and the marketing-sales side. The situation became so dire that the technology biased president and founder, Souichiro Honda, was forced out, as a result of his neglect in important marketing decisions. After Souichiro Honda's departure, the company became more marketing-technology balanced, and by 1999 it was second in sales only to Toyota in the Japanese market. The company's underlying success is best summarized in its mission statement, "pleasure in buying, selling and producing," and "Beat GM, not Toyota." Honda currently has 25 separate factories in the world, and its operations cover automobiles, motorcycles, financial services, power products, and power tools. In fiscal 2008, 83 percent of Honda's revenues came from its automobile sector, as outlined in **Case Exhibit 5-1**.

### CASE EXHIBIT 5-1
HONDA'S BUSINESS PORTFOLIO
(IN MILLION YEN)

| | |
|---|---|
| Motor Cycle | 1,558,696 |
| **Automobile** | **9,489,391** |
| Others | 421,194 |
| **TOTAL** | **11,469,281** |

## AUTOMOBILE INDUSTRY

The automobile industry worldwide is in the mature stage of its life cycle. By the 1990s, an oversupply of motor vehicles became such a problem to the industry that a number of mergers and acquisitions (M&A) and alliances took place. In the late 1990s, industry experts stated that only six or seven companies would remain global players, while other companies would be forced to sell in niche markets. In the last decade, DaimlerChrysler acquired a major share of Mitsubishi, GM became the controlling shareholder of Fiat and Saab, Ford acquired Volvo, Jaguar, and a major share of Mazda, and Renault became the controlling shareholder of Nissan. Global scale production and sales became important as a way to cut cost through developing a common platform or engines as well as global procurement. Unlike their European and American counterparts, Japanese automobile companies, including Honda, did not adopt the M&A strategy for expansion. To remain a global competitor, Honda instead expanded its operations by setting up plants in regional markets. **Case Exhibit 5-2** shows that Honda is currently ranked sixth in the world.

### CASE EXHIBIT 5-2
THE WORLD'S TOP 10 AUTOMOBILE MAKERS IN SALES IN THE FIRST HALF OF 2008

| Ranking | Name | Sales (in million units) |
|---|---|---|
| 1 | Toyota | 4.818 |
| 2 | General Motors | 4.540 |
| 3 | Volkswagen | 3.266 |
| 4 | Ford | 3.217 |
| 5 | Hyundai | 2.187 |
| **6** | **Honda** | **2.022** |
| 7 | Nissan | 2.014 |
| 8 | PSA Peugeot Citroen | 1.697 |
| 9 | Renault | 1.326 |
| 10 | Suzuki | 1.283 |

***Honda in Europe.*** Currently, Honda has five regional operations: North America, South America, Japan, Asia-Oceania, and Europe. The European operation covers Europe, the Middle East, and Africa. Honda entered the European market in 1961 as a motorcycle manufacturer, with its automobile operations following several years later. In 1986, Honda started engine production in the UK, and six years later it launched its European production at Swindon in Somerset, UK. Honda opened production facilities in Turkey in 1999 to target the Middle East and Eastern European markets. The European operation accounts for a small portion of Honda's global operation, as shown in **Case Exhibit 5-3**.

### CASE EXHIBIT 5-3
HONDA'S GLOBAL SALES BY REGION

| Net Sales (in billion yen) | Year 2007 | Year 2008 | Unit Sales (in thousands) | Year 2007 | Year 2008 |
|---|---|---|---|---|---|
| North America | 5,179 | 5,209 | North America | 1,788 | 1,850 |
| Japan | 1,413 | 1,321 | Japan | 672 | 615 |
| **Europe** | **917** | **1,183** | **Europe** | **324** | **391** |
| Asia (excl. Japan) | 862 | 1,048 | Asia (excl. Japan) | 620 | 755 |
| Other | 518 | 728 | Other | 248 | 314 |

There are a number of reasons for the low sales in Europe. Honda entered the European market rather late, and its first production facility in the region was built in 1992, at a time when Honda was still only a minor player in the Japanese market. Prior to 1992, Honda Europe was forced to import its vehicles from the United States, making it impossible for the company to aggressively attack the European market. One of the most important reasons for the lack of success was that the European market was highly saturated with locally owned car manufacturers. Companies such as Saab, Volvo, BMW, Audi, Volkswagen, DM, Opel, Renault, Peugeot, and Fiat have been dominating the European market for a considerable number of years. In addition, other foreign companies, such as Toyota, Nissan, Ford, and Hyundai make the European market extremely competitive.

In 2001, Volkswagen was ranked number one in Europe with 17.6 percent of the market and Peugeot number 2 with

15.8 percent. Renault, Ford, Fiat, and GM had approximately 10 percent of the market each, and Toyota, BMW, and Audi had a market share in the region of 5 percent. Honda captured only 2.4 percent of the European market. The competitive industry map (**Case Exhibit 5-4**) shows Honda's current position in the European automobile market.

## CASE EXHIBIT 5-4
### BRAND IMAGE IN EUROPE

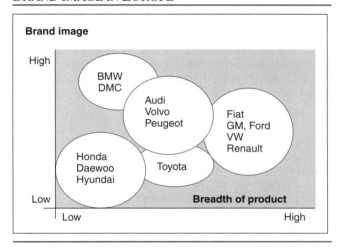

The Honda brand image in Europe is relatively weak and the product line is narrow compared to the other major players in the market. The company needs to expand its sales and production in order to survive in global scale competition.

### *Honda's European Marketing.*
The four largest markets within the European market are those of Germany, the UK, Italy, and France.

*Product.* Honda's European manufacturing plant is located in the UK and as a result the country has more Honda models than any other country in Europe, with a total of 20. Germany, the country with the highest number of vehicle registrations, has the next largest number of models, 16. Italy and France, both similar in size to the UK, have 11 and 9 models, respectively. The products found in Italy and France are also found in Germany and the UK. The UK has a number of automobiles that cannot be found in the other three countries, including diesel-powered cars.

*Price.* The prices of Honda's vehicles in Europe are comparable to those of similar cars produced by local manufacturers. **Case Exhibit 5-5** compares the price in euros of Honda's new 1.4-liter Jazz, with similar cars offered in the European market.

## CASE EXHIBIT 5-5
### AUTOMOBILE PRICES

| Vehicle | Honda Jazz | Peugeot 307 | VW Polo | Renault Clio | Opel Astra | Fiat Stilo |
|---|---|---|---|---|---|---|
| **Price (euro)** | 13,800 | 13,250 | 13,930 | 13,650 | 13,400 | 13,500 |

The exhibit clearly implies that Honda is attempting to price its product at a similar level to that of the competition.

*Distribution.* The image of Honda's vehicles and motorcycles in Europe is aligned together. Consequently, Honda vehicles throughout Europe are distributed at the same locations that their motorcycles are. Vehicles produced in the UK and Turkey are distributed throughout Europe, the Middle East, and Africa. Recently, because of the depreciating euro vis-à-vis the U.S. dollar, cars manufactured in the UK have also been exported to the United States.

*Promotion.* The promotion of Honda's motor vehicles is essentially the same throughout Europe, whether in France, Germany, Italy, or the UK. The company spends very little time and money in promotion, however. It believes that its success in Formula-1 racing, together with its ability to produce high-mileage, fuel-efficient products that exhibit great engineering, is enough to make it a popular in the European market. It relies on word of mouth by its customers to potential customers and, to a lesser extent, on the internet and the company's various websites.

In the recent 2002 launch of the Jazz (known as the Fit in Japan), the company relied heavily on word of mouth and on a website created especially for the occasion. The website, using the same design for all European countries, promoted the car as suitable for young working women. The website attempted to give the car a cool, young image by associating it with Feng Shui, Yoga, and other relatively hip activities. A sense of fun was also attached to the website in an attempt to draw in young women. Once inside the Jazz website, the user could easily find the nearest dealership to purchase the vehicle.

### *European Sales.*
**Case Exhibit 5-6** shows the sales figures for Honda's eight most popular motor vehicles from 1996 to

## CASE EXHIBIT 5-6
### HONDA'S UNIT SALES IN EUROPE: 1996–2002

| Year | Civic | Accord | Shuttle | CR-V | HR-V | Logo | S2000 | Stream | Total |
|---|---|---|---|---|---|---|---|---|---|
| **1996** | 150,783 | 44,248 | 3,255 | 11 | | | | | 203,276 |
| **1997** | 160,530 | 39,410 | 3,278 | 16,502 | | | | | 232,242 |
| **1998** | 151,270 | 31,536 | 4,670 | 41,886 | 88 | | | | 240,489 |
| **1999** | 99,156 | 48,835 | 4,261 | 35,923 | 26,257 | 12,856 | 1,179 | | 234,942 |
| **2000** | 74,653 | 46,579 | 2,956 | 29,751 | 28,537 | 10,593 | 3,948 | | 201,284 |
| **2001** | 83,024 | 28,822 | 320 | 24,381 | 17,726 | 4,145 | 2,195 | 7,283 | 169,922 |

2001 (detailed sales by automobile model are not available thereafter). During this period, Honda's most successful year was in 1998; since then, however, sales had declined dramatically for a number of years. However, despite the stagnant markets in Western Europe, the growth of the markets in Central and Eastern European countries as well as Russia, since around 2005, has helped Honda increase its total sales to 391 thousand units by 2008. Factors accounting for this performance were: the expansion in sales of diesel-powered cars; favorable sales for the new model *CR-V*, which was introduced in January 2007; the three-door Type S as well as Type R models in the *Civic* series; and strong sales of the sedan-type models, such as the *Accord* and *Civic* four-door sedans, especially in Russia.

Honda's motor vehicles have been relatively unpopular in the majority of Western Europe, in particular Italy and France. The company's best sales have occurred in the UK and Germany as shown in **Case Exhibit 5-7** (no sales information by country is available after 2003).

and Italy are all European, cultural differences abound among them. One theory that explains the differences between the four nations is that of high-context versus low-context cultures. In a high-context culture, the interpretation of messages depends on contextual cues like gender, age, and balance of power, and not on physical written text. In a high context culture, things may be understood, rather than said. Countries considered to be high-context cultures include those of China, Japan, Italy, France, Spain, and Latin America.

Conversely, a low-context culture emphasizes a distinctive written text or spoken words, where ideas are communicated explicitly. Low-context cultures expect others to say what they mean and do what they say. There is far less emphasis on contextual cues, such as ranking and balance of power. Examples of countries that fall within this category are the United States, the Scandinavian nations, and Germany. A graphical

**CASE EXHIBIT 5-7**
HONDA'S UNIT SALES IN EUROPE BY COUNTRY: 1994–2003

| Country | 1994 | 1995 | 1996 | 1997 | 1998 | 1999 | 2000 | 2001 | 2002 | 2003 |
|---|---|---|---|---|---|---|---|---|---|---|
| U.K. | 38,187 | 45,772 | 50,075 | 55,611 | 61,044 | 65,290 | 68,736 | 63,459 | 77,942 | 81,858 |
| Germany | 53,687 | 52,614 | 54,550 | 55,918 | 48,247 | 43,610 | 33,536 | 31,868 | 32,590 | 34,251 |
| France | 14,411 | 11,848 | 13,260 | 12,585 | 14,095 | 15,270 | 8,717 | 6,495 | 6,392 | 5,547 |
| Italy | 12,063 | 14,101 | 15,014 | 25,406 | 24,532 | 22,031 | 18,570 | 13,732 | 15,509 | 18,887 |

***European Culture.*** Honda's relatively poor showing in Europe may be explained by a number of reasons. The main problem was that the company failed to truly understand the culture of Europe, and more importantly, it treated Europe as one giant single market. Although France, Germany, the UK,

view of high-context and low-context countries is presented in **Case Exhibit 5-8**.

Successful advertising in low-context cultures differs from that in high-context cultures. An advertisement for a high-context culture is based on an implicit style where the emphasis is on the

**CASE EXHIBIT 5-8**
CULTURAL CONTEXT

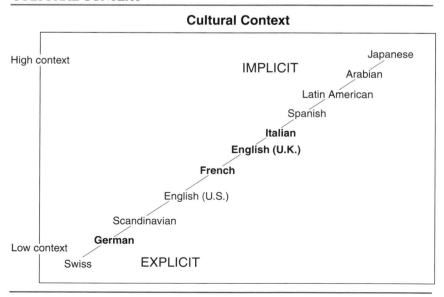

overall feel and outlook rather than on the feeding of pure information. In this type of advertisement, the actual product may not even be shown. The audience may only be given implied images and sublime messages. Honda's Jazz website contained a large amount of information that would have been too much for high-context cultures such as the French and the Italians. In addition, high-context cultures have been much slower than their low context counterparts in adopting the internet.

On the other hand, the advertisement for a low-context culture includes the actual product, together with a large amount of information. Low-context nations such as Germany would have most likely been able to appreciate Honda's Jazz website. It is therefore unlikely that an advertisement/promotion campaign created for a high-context culture will be effective in a low-context culture country and vice versa. Since Europe consists of both high-context and low-context culture countries, companies such as Honda, intending to expand its business, should take into consideration two separate market segments when planning its marketing strategy. Honda's situation in France, Italy, Germany, and the UK in regard to their culture are outlined in the following sections.

**France.** France is a high-context culture where style and image is of the utmost importance. The perceived quality of a product means that the French have a bias toward the style and image of a product. The image of Japanese cars in France is relatively poor, dating back to the 1930s when Japanese manufacturers entered the European market with low quality products. Since that time, Japanese carmakers, in particular Honda, have not understood the concept of style and image in marketing. They appear to show a car only in a factual way, which is extremely low-context. Japanese carmakers in France have recently tried to alter their image, though with limited success.

Today France's image of Japanese cars, and in particular of Honda, is that of a small, low-quality car, suitable only for a second car. Most buyers of Japanese cars are young career women who have just entered the workforce and housewives with limited cash. The main family car is likely to be a Renault or Peugeot and is driven by the man in the family. In addition, the French are risk-averse people, who dislike trying new things. They are also highly patriotic, supporting and purchasing their national products, such as Renault and Peugeot cars.

The patriotism and risk averseness of the French, together with their low image of Japanese cars and the large number of other European automobiles available in the market, makes it extremely difficult for Honda to be successful in this market.

**Italy.** Italy, like France, is a high-context culture where a great deal of emphasis is placed on feeling and style. The Italian culture is reflected in their daily lifestyle, which gives a sense of romance to the people living there. As in France, the Italians view Japanese cars as small, low-quality vehicles, suitable only as a second family car. The most popular automobile in Italy, especially for families, is the Fiat. The Fiat is dominant because the Italians, like their high-context cousins the French, being very patriotic.

Italians are also risk-averse and are not adventurous in sampling products outside of Europe. Italians, like the majority of Europeans, love to drive diesel automobiles. Only the French

enjoy driving diesel cars more than the Italians. However, Honda still lags behind in the production of diesel cars relative to competition in Europe. As shown in **Case Exhibit 5-9**, the trend in the popularity of diesel cars relative to gasoline-powered cars is clear in Europe. Diesel cars are hugely popular because of the high gasoline prices in those countries. Diesel engine cars are cheaper to maintain in the long run, compared to gasoline engine cars.

**CASE EXHIBIT 5-9**
MARKET SHARE OF DIESEL CARS IN WESTERN EUROPE

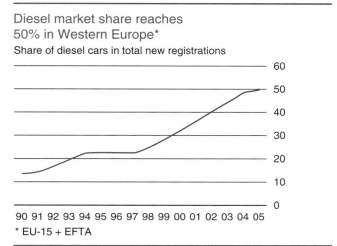

Diesel market share reaches 50% in Western Europe*
Share of diesel cars in total new registrations

90 91 92 93 94 95 96 97 98 99 00 01 02 03 04 05
* EU-15 + EFTA

*Source:* ACEA

A large number of European cars compete in Europe, particularly at the luxury end. BMW, Mercedes, and Audi are very popular for the very rich, as are Ferrari, Lamborghini, and Porsche. It is difficult for Japanese cars to enter the European market, especially at the higher end. The only Japanese cars that are selling reasonably well are Toyota's Yaris, Nissan's Micra, and Jazz from Honda. All three models compete in the 1.4 liter and under segment.

**Germany.** Of the four main European countries in which Honda is sold, Germany has had the second highest sales volume. Germany is a low-context culture where practicality and durability is one of the main concerns of a product. Consumers are concerned with every detail regarding a product and wish to know all relevant information before making a purchase. The promotion style used by Honda on the internet, bursting with information on their automobiles, seems to be an appropriate form of promotion for the low-context nature of the Germans.

Another factor that should place Honda's products in a better position in Germany is the Germans' greater willingness to take risks and to purchase new products. As a result, Honda would not have to spend additional resources to change the image of their vehicles in Germany, as it should probably do in France and Italy. If Honda's promotion is in line with the German's low context nature, why could Honda not improve its sales position further? There must be another reason for its lackluster sales increase. One of the most logical reasons is the perceived nature of Honda's quality. The company needs to use its marketing to promote quality because competitors such as Mercedes (under DaimlerChrysler), Audi, Volvo, Jaguar (under Ford), and Volkswagen, to name a few, are seen as high-quality carmakers.

### The United Kingdom.

English culture is moderately high, focusing on tradition and class. Accordingly, the type of advertising and marketing promotion that will appeal to the English is similar to that popular in France and Italy but is more conservative in nature. On the other hand, the English are more individualistic and less risk averse than the French and Italians. Hence, it should be easier for Honda to introduce its range of cars in the UK and to improve sales. The fact that the manufacturing plant is located in the UK helps in the promotion of the cars. The construction of a second assembly plant should also help Honda's position in the UK.

The existence of the assembly plant, together with the risk taking nature of the English, has increased the number of Hondas sold in the UK to such a level that it is easily Honda's best market. The number sold in the UK as of 2001 was twice that of Germany, which only five years before recorded more sales than the UK. However, no Honda vehicle has entered the list of the top ten cars sold in the UK or throughout Europe, as shown in **Case Exhibit 5-10**.

### CASE EXHIBIT 5-10
TOP 10 CARS SOLD IN EUROPE IN 2007

| Rank | Make & Model | No. of Cars Sold |
| --- | --- | --- |
| 1 | Peugeot 207 | 437,505 |
| 2 | VW Golf | 435,055 |
| 3 | Ford Focus | 406,557 |
| 4 | Opel/Vauxhall Corsa | 402,044 |
| 5 | Opel/Vauxhall Astra | 402,173 |
| 6 | Renault Clio | 382,041 |
| 7 | Fiat Punto | 377,989 |
| 8 | Ford Fiesta | 355,933 |
| 9 | VW Passat | 300,566 |
| 10 | BMW 3 Series | 295,312 |

### Possible Entry Wedge.

A possible entry wedge exists in Europe that could help Honda recover some of its lost ground. The European automotive industry is committed to a voluntary agreement to reduce $CO_2$ emissions by 25 percent from the 1995 levels by 2008 for all new cars. As an incentive for individuals to drive low-emission cars, special tax brackets will be given to drivers of low emission cars.

In 2001, Honda's Insight produced the lowest levels of $CO_2$ emission of any car in Europe. **Case Exhibit 5-11** shows the five cars with the lowest $CO_2$ emission.

### CASE EXHIBIT 5-11
TOP 5 CARS WITH THE LOWEST $CO_2$ EMISSION

| Rank | Car | Engine | Gas Type | $CO_2$ g/km |
| --- | --- | --- | --- | --- |
| 1 | Honda Insight | 1 liter | Gasoline | 80 |
| 2 | Peugeot 206 | 1.4 liter | Diesel | 113 |
| 3 | Toyota Prius | 1.5 liter | Gasoline | 114 |
| 4 | Renault Clio | 1.5 liter | Diesel | 115 |
| 5 | Audi A2 | 1.4 liter | Diesel | 116 |

The ranking is an excellent opportunity for Honda to promote its cars in Europe, where people (especially in Germany) are obsessed with the environment and are burdened with high taxes. In addition, Honda introduced the Civic Hybrid in 2003. It is a gasoline-electric power train, fuel-efficient car with a low $CO_2$ emission level. Although the car has an electric engine, it does not need to be plugged in and recharged. The battery pack recharges itself automatically as the car is running.

Aiming at further business expansion in Europe, Honda is promoting product development that meets regional needs by establishing a broad-based local network of company facilities and R&D offices. In 2004, Honda released a diesel version of the Accord, the first car to be fitted with Honda's own diesel engine and designed to meet EU environmental performance standards for emission control (Euro 4). The diesel lineup expanded rapidly thereafter with the addition of diesel CR-V, FR-V, and Civic models. Targeting local customer needs, Honda subsequently launched a European version of the Civic in 2006, which has been well received by a wide range of customers. Further, in July 2008 at the British Motor Show, Honda unveiled its low-emission roadster concept, the OSM, the design of which was out of the company's R&D facility in Offenbach, Germany.

### The Issue.

Honda is currently at the crossroads of its European expansion in the automobile market. It has been successful in managing to market essentially the same cars in many parts of the world, particularly in the North American and Japanese markets. Honda executives are wondering whether or not they should adopt more localized product development in Europe.

### DISCUSSION QUESTIONS

**1.** Does adapting the promotion of its motor vehicles to suit each country's culture make sense for Honda?

**2.** Is it wise for Honda to market its products the same way in every country?

**3.** Is pricing its vehicles similar to the competition a good strategy for Honda?

**4.** Should Honda change its product mix from country to country?

**5.** Is distributing its motor vehicles together with its motorcycles a good strategy for Honda?

**6.** Is the European market too competitive for Honda?

# CASE 6

## ANHEUSER-BUSCH INTERNATIONAL, INC.: MAKING INROADS INTO BRAZIL AND MEXICO*

### HISTORY

In 1852 George Schneider started a small brewery in St. Louis. Five years later the brewery faced insolvency. Several St. Louis businessmen purchased the brewery, launching an expansion financed largely by a loan from Eberhard Anheuser. By 1860 the enterprise had run into trouble again. Anheuser, with money already earned from a successful soap-manufacturing business, bought up the interest of minority creditors and became a brewery owner. In 1864 he joined forces with his new son-in-law, Adolphus Busch, a brewery supplier, and eventually Busch became president of the company. Busch is credited with transforming it into an industry giant and is therefore considered the founder of the company.

Busch wanted to break the barriers of all local beers and breweries, so he created a network of railside icehouses to cool cars of beer being shipped long distances. This moved the company that much closer to becoming one of the first national beers. In the late 1870s, Busch launched the industry's first fleet of refrigerated cars, but needed more to ensure the beer's freshness over long distances. In response, Busch pioneered the use of a new pasteurization process.

In 1876 Busch created Budweiser and today the company brews Bud the same way it did in 1876. In 1896 the company introduced Michelob as its first premium beer. By 1879 annual sales rose to more than 105,000 barrels, and in 1901 the company reached the one million barrel mark.

In 1913, after his father's death, August A. Busch, Sr. took charge of the company, and with the new leadership came new problems: World War I, Prohibition, and the Great Depression. To keep the company running, Anheuser-Busch switched its emphasis to the production of corn products, baker's yeast, ice cream, soft drinks, commercial refrigeration units, and truck bodies. They stopped most of these activities when Prohibition ended. However, the yeast production was kept and even expanded to the point that Anheuser-Busch became the nation's leading producer of compressed baker's yeast through the encouragement of the company's new president in 1934, Adolphus Busch III.

August A. Busch, Jr. succeeded his brother as president in 1946 and served as the company's CEO until 1975. During this time eight branch breweries were constructed, and annual sales increased from 3 million barrels in 1946 to more than 34 million in 1974. The company was extended to include family entertainment, real estate, can manufacturing, transportation, and major league baseball.

August A. Busch III became president in 1974 and was named CEO in 1975. From that time to the present, the company opened three new breweries and acquired one. Other acquisitions included the nation's second-largest baking company and Sea

World. The company also increased vertical integration capabilities with the addition of new can manufacturing and malt production facilities, container recovery, metalized label printing, snack foods, and international marketing and creative services.

***Corporate Mission Statement.*** Anheuser-Busch's corporate mission statement provides the foundation for strategic planning for the company's businesses:

> The fundamental premise of the mission statement is that beer is and always will be Anheuser-Busch's core business. In the brewing industry, Anheuser-Busch's goals are to extend its position as the world's leading brewer of quality products; increase its share of the domestic beer market 50 percent by the late 1990s; and extend its presence in the international beer market. In non-beer areas, Anheuser-Busch's existing food products, packaging, and entertainment will continue to be developed.

The mission statement also sets forth Anheuser-Busch's belief that the cornerstones of its success are a commitment to quality and adherence to the highest standards of honesty and integrity in its dealings with all stakeholders.

### BEER AND BEER-RELATED OPERATIONS

Anheuser-Busch, which began operations in 1852 as the Bavarian Brewery, ranks as the world's largest brewer and has held the position of industry leader in the United States since 1957. Currently, more than four out of every ten beers sold in the United States are Anheuser-Busch products.

Anheuser-Busch's principal product is beer, produced and distributed by its subsidiary, Anheuser-Busch, Inc. (ABI), in a variety of containers primarily under the brand names Budweiser, Bud Light, Bud Dry Draft, Michelob, Michelob Light, Michelob Dry, Michelob Golden Draft, Michelob Gold, Draft Light, Busch Light, Natural Light, and King Cobra, to name just a few. In 1993 Anheuser-Busch introduced a new brand, Ice Draft from Budweiser, which is marketed in the United States and abroad as the preferred beer because it is lighter and less bitter than beer produced in foreign countries. Bud Draft from Budweiser was first introduced in the United States in late 1993 in 14 states, with a full national rollout in 1994 in the United States and abroad.

***Sales.*** Anheuser-Busch's sales grew slowly after a sales decline in 1994. Net sales increased consistently from 1993 to almost $13.3 billion in 1998 but fell again to $11.8 billion in 1999. Net sales were up again in the next five years to $14.9 billion in 2004. Thanks to a portfolio of products that expanded in 2007, Anheuser-Busch reported U.S. shipments of 104.4 million barrels in 2007, up 2.1 million barrels over 2006. The net sales in 2007 increased 6.2 percent, reaching $16.7 billion.

---

*This case was prepared and updated by Masaaki Kotabe with the assistance of Dan Zhang of Temple University for class discussion, rather than to illustrate either effective or ineffective management of a situation described (2008).

## ANHEUSER-BUSCH INTERNATIONAL, INC.

Anheuser-Busch International, Inc. (A-BII) was formed in 1981 to explore and develop the international beer market. A-BII is responsible for handling the company foreign beer operations and for exploring and developing beer markets outside the United States. Its activities include contract and license brewing, export sales, marketing and distribution of the company's beer in foreign markets, and equity partnerships with foreign brewers.

A-BII has a two-pronged strategy: (1) build Budweiser into an international brand and (2) build an international business through equity investments and creating partnerships with leading foreign brewers (see **Case Exhibit 6-1**). In seeking growth, Anheuser-Busch International emphasizes part-ownership in foreign brewers, joint ventures, and contract-brewing arrangements. These elements give the company opportunities to use its marketing expertise and management practices in foreign markets. The success of these growth opportunities depends largely on finding the right partnerships that create a net gain for all parties involved. Other options for international expansion include license-brewing arrangements and exporting. In addition to its domestic breweries in the United States, the company operates two international breweries in China and the United Kingdom, respectively. Budweiser beer is locally brewed through partnerships in seven other countries, Argentina, Canada, Italy, Ireland, Spain, Japan, and South Korea.

A-BII is currently pursuing the dual objectives of building Budweiser's worldwide presence and establishing a significant international business operation through joint ventures and equity investments in foreign brewers. Anheuser-Busch's beer products are sold in more than 80 countries and U.S. territories. A-BII now sells about 35 percent of its total beer volume outside the United States. Anheuser-Busch's total beer volume was 157 million barrels in 2006, up 5.6 percent from 2005. Domestic beer volume rose a meager 1.2 percent. International volume from Anheuser-Busch brands produced overseas and exports from the company's U.S. breweries rose 9.3 percent to 23 million barrels for 2006. International volume via partnerships with foreign brewers grew near 20 percent to 32 million barrels, principally due to sales of Tsingtao brand in China and Modelo beer in Mexico.

***Market Share.*** The top 20 beer brands in worldwide market share for 2007 are shown in **Case Exhibit 6-2**. Most recently, Anheuser-Busch has announced several agreements with other leading brewers around the world, including Modelo in Mexico, Antarctica in Brazil, and Tsingtao Brewery in China. These agreements are part of A-BII's two-pronged strategy of investing internationally through both brand and partnership development. Through partnerships A-BII will continue to identify, execute, and manage significant brewing acquisitions and joint ventures, partnering with the number-one or number-two brewers in growing markets. This strategy will allow A-BII to participate in beer industries around the world by investing in leading foreign brands, such as Corona in Mexico through Modelo. A-BII's goal is to share the best practices with its partners, allowing an open interchange of ideas that will benefit both partners.

## CASE EXHIBIT 6-1
### ANHEUSER-BUSCH INTERNATIONAL PARTNERSHIPS

| Country | Partner | Investment | Date |
|---|---|---|---|
| Argentina | Compañía cervecerías Unidas S.A.-Argentina (CCU - Argentina) | Equity investment (of which 28.6% Is direct and indirect); licensed brewing and joint marketing | 1995 |
| Canada | Labatt | Licensed brewing, distribution, and marketing agreement | 1980 |
| Central America (Costa Rica El Salvador Guatemala Honduras Nicaragua Panama) | (Cervecería Costa Rica –La Constancia –Cervecería Centroamericana –Cervecería Hondureña –Compañía de Nicaragua –Cervecería Nacional) | Import, distribution | 1994 |
| Chile | Compañía Cervecerías Unidas (CCU) | 20% Equity investment | 2001 |
| China | –Tsingtao | –27% equity investment | 1993 |
| | –Budweiser Wuhan International Brewing Co. | –98% A-B Owned brewery | 1995 |
| | –Harbin Brewery | A-B Sales, marketing, distribution –100% ownership | 2005 |
| Denmark | Carlsberg Breweries A/S | Import, distribution | 1998 |
| France | Brasseries Kronenbourg | Import, distribution, packaging | 1996 |
| India | Crown International | Joint venture | 2007 |
| Ireland | Diageo (Guinness Ireland Ltd.) | Licensed brewing; joint marketing | 1986 |
| Italy | Heineken Italia | Licensed brewing; joint marketing | 2003 |
| Japan | Kirin Brewery Co. Ltd. | Licensed brewing; joint marketing Kirin sales, distribution | 2000 |
| Mexico | Grupo Modelo | Import, distribution | 1989 |
| | | Equity investment (of which 50% is direct and indirect) | 1993 |
| Russia | Heineken Russia | Licensed brewing; joint marketing | 2006 |
| South Korea | Oriental Brewery Co. Ltd. | Licensed brewing; joint marketing | 1986 |

**CASE EXHIBIT 6-2**
TOP 20 BEER BRANDS WORLDWIDE, 2007

| Rank | Brand | Company/Brewer | Shipments (Barrels) |
|------|-------|----------------|---------------------|
| 1 | **Bud Light** | **Anheuser-Busch** | **40.9** |
| 2 | **Budweiser** | **Anheuser-Busch** | **33.7** |
| 3 | Skol | InBev | 28.5 |
| 4 | Snow | China Resources Snow Breweries | 25.9 |
| 5 | Corona | Grupo Modelo | 25.8 |
| 6 | Brahma | InBev | 21.6 |
| 7 | Heineken | Heineken | 21.4 |
| 8 | Miller Lite | SABMiller | 18.2 |
| 9 | Coors Light | Molson Coors Brewing Co. | 16.8 |
| 10 | Asahi Super Dry | Asahi Breweries | 14.8 |
| 11 | Yanjing | Beijing Yanjing Beer Group Corp. | 12.8 |
| 12 | Tsingtao | Qingdao Brewery (Holdings) Corp. | 12.6 |
| 13 | Polar | Cerveceria Polar | 11.2 |
| 14 | Antarctica Pilsen | InBev | 10.4 |
| 15 | Amstel | Heineken | 10.4 |
| 16 | Carlsberg | Carlsberg Breweries | 10.4 |
| 17 | Baltika | Baltic Beverages Holding | 10.0 |
| 18 | Guinness | Guinness Brewing Worldwide (Diageo) | 9.2 |
| 19 | **Natural Light** | **Anheuser-Busch** | **9.0** |
| 20 | Sedrin | Fujian Sedrin Brewery Co./InBev | 8.6 |
| | Total Top 20 | | 352.2 |

***Latin America.*** The development of Budweiser in Latin America is one of the keys to long-term growth in the international beer business, for it is one of the world's fastest growing beer markets and is a region with a growing consumer demand for beer. Anheuser-Busch products are sold in 11 Latin American countries—Argentina, Belize, Brazil, Chile, Ecuador, Mexico, Nicaragua, Panama, Paraguay, Uruguay, and Venezuela—with a total population of over 380 million consumers. Particularly, the three countries showing the fastest growth in total beer consumption in the period between 1990 and 2000 are Brazil (+200%), Colombia (+130%), and Mexico (+100%). In Brazil and Mexico–the two largest beer markets in Latin America, Anheuser-Busch International acquired an equity position in their major local breweries.

***Brazil.*** In 1995, Anheuser-Busch International made an initial investment of 10 percent in a new Antarctica subsidiary in Brazil that would consolidate all of Antarctica's holdings in affiliated companies and control 75 percent of Antarctica's operations. Anheuser-Busch had an option to increase its investment to approximately 30 percent in the new company in the future. The amount of the initial investment was approximately $105 million. The investment has established a partnership that gave Antarctica a seat on the board of Anheuser-Busch, Inc. and gave Anheuser-Busch International proportionate representation on the board of the new Antarctica subsidiary. The two brewers also explored joint distribution opportunities in the fast-growing South American beer market. A-BII desired to sign a deal that calls for establishing an Anheuser-Busch-controlled marketing and distribution agreement between the two brewers to support sales of Budweiser in Brazil.

The second component of the partnership was a licensing agreement in which Antarctica would brew Budweiser in Brazil. The joint venture would be 51 percent owned and controlled by Anheuser-Busch, 49 percent by Antarctica. Antarctica's production plants would produce Budweiser according to the brand's quality requirements. Local sourcing of Budweiser would allow more competitive pricing and increased sales of the brand in Brazil.

Antarctica, based in São Paulo, controlled 35 percent of the Brazilian beer market. Its annual production in 1998 was about 20 million barrels of beer. Antarctica had a network of nearly 1,000 Brazilian wholesalers. Prior to its investment in Antarctica, Budweiser had achieved a distribution foothold in the Brazilian beer market in cooperation with its distributor, Arisco. Brazil has a population of 180 million people, with per capita beer consumption in Brazil estimated to be 40 liters per year. With Brazil's population growing by 1.7 percent a year, reduced import duties, and free market reforms, Anheuser-Busch was expected to do well in the Brazilian market over the next decade.

However, the Antarctica–Anheuser-Busch partnership stayed rocky at best, and ended up breaking apart in 1999, putting an end to the contract which permitted the U.S. company to acquire up to 29.7 percent of the partnership. And in the same year, Antarctica merged with another Brazilian brewery, Brahma, creating Brazil's largest and the world's third largest brewery, Companhia de Bebidas das Américas (AmBev), effectively forcing out Anheuser-Busch out of the Brazilian market at that point. And, in 2004, when AmBev joined hands with Belgium's Interbrew, the combined firm InterbrewAmBev (InBev) became the world's largest brewer with a global market share of 14 percent and revenues of over $12 billion. And further in 2008 (at the time of this writing), InBev announced an agreement to acquire Anheuser-Busch. The combination of Anheuser-Busch and InBev will create the global leader in the beer industry and one of the world's top five consumer products companies. On a pro-forma basis for 2007, the combined company would have generated global volumes of 460 million hectoliters, revenues of $36.4 billion (€26.6 billion) and earnings before interests, taxes, depreciation and amortization (EBITDA) of $10.7 billion (€7.8 billion). Anheuser-Busch and InBev together believe that this transaction is in the best interests of both companies' shareholders, consumers, employees, wholesalers, business partners and the communities they serve.

***Mexico.*** In a further move to strengthen its international capabilities, Anheuser-Busch companies purchased a 37 percent direct and indirect equity interest for $980 million in Grupo Modelo (located in Mexico City) and its subsidiaries, which thus far are privately held. Modelo is Mexico's largest brewer and the producer of Corona, that country's best-selling beer. The brewer has a 51 percent market share and exports to 56 countries. In connection with the purchase, three Anheuser-Busch representatives have been elected to the Modelo board, and a Modelo representative has been elected to serve on the Anheuser-Busch board. As of 2002, Anheuser Busch owned approximately 50 percent of Grupo Modelo (directly and indirectly). Its brands Budweiser and Bud Light sales volume grew 25 percent in Mexico in 2003. Mexico is now the company's largest export market as well. In 2003, Anheuser-Busch's sales volume in Mexico saw double-digit growth for the fifth consecutive year.

In addition, the agreement includes the planned implementation of a program for the exchange of executives and management personnel between Modelo and Anheuser-Busch in key areas, including accounting/auditing, marketing, operations, planning, and finance. Modelo will remain Mexico's exclusive importer and distributor of Budweiser and other Anheuser-Busch brands, which have achieved a leading position in imported beers sold in Mexico. These brands will continue to be brewed exclusively by Anheuser-Busch breweries in the United States. Currently, Anheuser-Busch brews beer for Mexico at its Houston and Los Angeles breweries, which are not very far away from Mexico and add to the markup of ABI brands.

All of Modelo's brands will continue to be brewed exclusively in its seven existing Mexican breweries and a new brewery in North Central Mexico. U.S. distribution rights for the Modelo products are not involved in the arrangement. Corona and other Modelo brands will continue to be imported into the United States by Barton Beers and Gambrinus Company and distributed by those importers to beer wholesalers.

Modelo is the world's tenth-largest brewer and, through sales of Corona Modelo Especial, Pacifico, Negra Modelo and other regional brands, holds more than 51 percent of the Mexican beer market. Its beer exports to 56 countries in North and South America, Asia, Australia, Europe, and Africa account for more than 69 percent of Mexico's total beer exports.

Modelo is one of several companies that distribute Budweiser besides Antarctica in Brazil and other local import-export companies in other Latin American countries. Modelo is the exclusive importer and distributor of Anheuser-Busch beers in Mexico. The newest brand, Ice Draft, will be the fourth ABI brand distributed in Mexico by Modelo, joining Budweiser, Bud Light, and O'Douls.

The Modelo agreement is significant because beer consumption has grown 6.5 percent annually in Mexico in the past few years. Mexico's beer consumption is the eighth largest in the world but still only half of U.S. consumption. The per capita beer consumption rate in Mexico is estimated at 44 liters, compared to 87 liters per person in the United States, which is high given that Mexico's per-capita income is one-tenth that of the United States. The Mexican market is expected to grow at a rapid rate.

Anheuser-Busch does not have control over pricing. The local wholesalers and retailers set prices for Budweiser. A-BII also does not have plans to set up a full-scale production facility in Mexico at this time.

At present Budweiser is imported, which makes it two to three times higher in price than local beers. So it is largely an upscale, niche market brand at this time. An equity arrangement in another brewery or an agreement with Modelo could lead to local production and make ABI brands more competitive with the local beer brands. In 2002, Budweiser brands made up 34 percent of the beer imports in Mexico. In 2002, net income for the company's international beer operations rose 6.3 percent in the third quarter, which the company claimed was due to the performance of Grupo Modelo.

Besides the 11 Latin American countries mentioned, Anheuser-Busch has signed agreements with the largest brewers in Costa Rica, El Salvador, Guatemala, and Honduras to distribute and market Budweiser in their respective countries. Local breweries (Cerveceria Costa Rica in Costa Rica, La Constancia in El Salvador, Cerveceria Centroamericana in Guatemala, and Cerveceria Hondurena in Honduras) distribute Budweiser in the 12-ounce bottles and 12-ounce aluminum cans.

These distribution agreements will allow Budweiser to expand its distribution throughout the rest of Central America. These countries have an extensive national distribution network and, more important, have local market expertise to develop Budweiser throughout the region. Under the agreements, the Central American brewers will import Budweiser from Anheuser-Busch plants in Houston, Texas, and Williamsburg, Virginia. Anheuser-Busch will share responsibility for Budweiser's marketing with each of its Central American partners, supported by nationwide advertising and promotional campaigns.

### Advertising.
Event Sponsorship. Given Budweiser's advertising approach, which is traditionally built around sports, the decision to hold the 1994 World Cup soccer tournament in the United States gave A-BII a perfect venue to pitch Budweiser to Latin Americans. The company signed a multimillion-dollar sponsorship deal with the World Cup Organizing Committee, making Budweiser the only brand of beer authorized to use the World Cup logo. "The World Cup has become a vehicle for us to reach Latin America," said Charlie Acevedo, director of Latin American marketing for Anheuser-Busch International.

For ten months, soccer fans in South America saw the Bud logo on everything from soccer balls to beer glasses. Soccer fans collected a World Cup bumper sticker when they purchased a 12-pack of Bud. When they watched the game on television, they saw Budweiser signs decorating the stadiums and a glimpse of the Bud blimp hovering overhead. According to Charlie Acevedo, the goal is to make Budweiser a global icon, like McDonald's or Coca-Cola.

Anheuser-Busch just signed its second two-year agreement with ESPNLatin America. "Being able to buy on a regional basis gives a consistent message that is very reasonable in terms of cost," said Steve Burrows, A-BII's executive vice president of marketing.

Latin America offers promise with its youthful population and rising personal income. Half of Mexico's population is under 21, and other Latin American countries have similar profiles, offering opportunities for advertisers to reach the region's 450 million population.

The biggest new advertising opportunities in the Latin American market are Fox Latin America, MTV Latino, Cinemax Ole (a premium channel venture with Caracas cable operator Omnivision Latin American Entertainment), USANetwork, and Telemundo (a 24-hour Spanish-language news channel). Marketers will have yet another pan-regional advertising option. Hughes (the U.S. aerospace company) and three Latin American partners—Multivision in Mexico, Televisao Abril in Brazil, and the Cisneros Group in Venezuela—launched a $700 million satellite that will beam programs in Spanish and Portuguese into homes across the continent. The service is called DirectTV. Because of this satellite, Central and South America have added 24 new channels; with digital compression technology, its capability could reach 144 cable channels.

In the past Anheuser-Busch used CNN international as its only ad vehicle, but with all the new opportunities, "the company will begin adding a local media presence throughout Latin America," said Robert Gunthner, A-BII's vice president of the Americas region (see **Case Exhibit 6-3**).

### CASE EXHIBIT 6-3
PENETRATION OF PAID CABLE TV CHANNELS

| TV Location | Households (in millions) | Paid subscribers | Penetration rate |
| --- | --- | --- | --- |
| Brazil | 30.0 | 3,300,000 | 15% |
| Mexico | 14.0 | 1,700,000 | 12 |
| Argentina | 9.0 | 4,300,000 | 47 |
| Chile | 3.4 | 200,000 | 6 |
| Venezuela | 3.3 | 90,000 | 3 |
| Uruguay | 0.7 | 35,000 | 5 |
| Ecuador | 0.5 | 25,000 | 5 |
| Paraguay | 0.5 | 45,000 | 9 |

Anheuser-Busch will be using ads originally aimed at U.S. Hispanics, most of which were created by Carter Advertising of New York. A-BII will let the local agencies pick its messages, customize advertising, and do local media planning. In the past, there has been much criticism of ABI's ethnocentric approach to marketing Budweiser; however, because of the world obsession with American pop culture, A-BI executives feel they do not need to tone down the company's American image. In Costa Rica, A-BII will use JBQ, San Jose; in El Salvador, Apex/BBDO, San Salvador; in Guatemala, Cerveceria's in-house media department; and in Honduras, McCann-Erickson Centroamericana, San Pedro.

Imported beers cost two or three times as much as locally brewed beers in South America, but thanks to cable television and product positioning in U.S. movies, Budweiser was already a well-known brand in South America when the company began exporting to the continent.

***Strategy.*** Anheuser-Busch has seen double-digit increases in Latin American sales in the past five years. The gains came from both an increase in disposable income and increasingly favorable attitudes toward U.S. products, especially in Argentina, Brazil, Chile, and Venezuela. Because Latin America has a very young population, Anheuser-Busch expects this market to grow at 4 percent annually. Furthermore, with NAFTA and a free-trade zone, the company expects to see a significant rise in personal income in Latin American countries, which translates to great growth potential for Anheuser-Busch brands. The GDP (gross domestic product) per capita in 2007 is presented in **Case Exhibit 6-4**.

North American products and lifestyles are very much accepted in South America, but beer consumption still lags far behind U.S. levels. Argentines consume about 30 liters annually per capita. Brazilians 40 liters, Chileans 50 liters, and Venezuelans 65 liters, compared to 87 liters per person annually in the United States.

"The international focus will be almost completely on Budweiser because there is a worldwide trend toward less-heavy,

### CASE EXHIBIT 6-4
GDP PER CAPITA IN SELECTED LATIN AMERICAN COUNTRIES (2007)

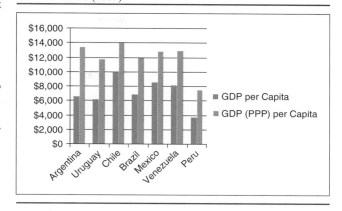

less-bitter beers," and Jack Purnell, chair and chief executive officer of Anheuser-Busch International. The company is counting on the American image to carry its beer, therefore opting for a universal campaign with American themes as opposed to tailoring Budweiser's image for local markets.

In the past, ABII has tinkered with its formula and marketed Budweiser under different names to give a local flavor to their beer but had absolutely no success. Purnell said: "What the market does not need is an American brewery trying to make up from scratch, new European-style beers. Bud should be Bud wherever you get it."

***Opportunities.*** Mexico offers the U.S. exporter a variety of opportunities encompassing most product categories. Mexico is continuing to open its borders to imported products. Mexico's population of approximately 109 million is the eleventh largest in the world and the second largest in Latin America (after Brazil and Argentina). Mexico is a young country, with 69 percent of its population under 30 years of age. In addition the Mexican government has adopted new privatization policies decreasing its involvement in the country's economy. As a result, private resources, both local and foreign, are playing a greater role in all areas of the Mexican economy.

NAFTA, which aims to eliminate all tariffs on goods originating from Canada and the United States, is expected to create a massive market, with more than 360 million people and $16 trillion in annual output.

***Demographics.*** Mexico's overall population in 2007 was estimated at 109 million people. The age breakdown is as follows: under 15, 38 percent; 15–29, 29 percent; 30–44, 17 percent; 45–59, 9 percent; 60–74, 5 percent; 75 and over, 2 percent. The average age of the Mexican population was 23.3 years.

Between 1970 and 1990 the ratio of the population living in localities with between 100,000 and 500,000 inhabitants grew from 12 to 22 percent. This was largely due to rural-urban migration. More than 71 percent of the population lives in urban areas of Mexico. In 1990, 22 percent of the national population lived in Mexico City and the State of Mexico. The Mexican population is expected to rise to 112 million in the year 2010.

# SUBJECT INDEX

## A

A-B-C-D paradigm of buying behavior, 105e
Absolute advantage, 25–26
Acquisitions, 59, 312, 313–15
ACTA. *See* Anti-Counterfeiting Trade Agreement
Adaptation
  cultural, in China, 125
  dual, 333
  product, 333
  in product policy decisions, new products, 333
  standardization *vs.*, 268
Adhocracy cultures, 131
Ad valorem duty, 562
Advertising, 265, 332. *See also* Budgets, advertising; Communication; Marketing
  agency selection, 447–49, 448e
  ASA, 445–46
  banner ad, 649
  blunders, 426–27
  in China, 362, 429, 446, 456gp
  communication/cultural barriers and, 430
  creative strategy, 434–40
  culture and, 427–30
  export, 438–39
  increasing regional, 92
  in India, 426–29
  in Japan, 426–27
  language barriers, 427–28
  manual, 439–40
  media decisions, 440–44
  online, 648–50
  search engine advertising, 649
  standardization, 434–38, 459
  targeting children, 446–47
*Advertising Age International*, 434
Advertising copy creation, 435–37
  concept cooperation, 440
  export advertising, 438–39
  laissez-faire, 438
  by MNCs, 438
  modular approach, 440

prototype standardization, 439–40
  regional approach, 440
  universal appeals, 439e
Advertising regulations, 437–38
  for ads targeting children, 446–47
  comparative advertising, 445
  defined, 445
  EU, 446–47
  foreign made ads, 445
  Malaysia, 444–45, 444e
  message content, 445–46
  for puffery claims, 446
  for vice products/ pharmaceuticals, 445
Advertising Standards Authority (ASA), 445–46
AES. *See* Automated Export System
Aesthetics
  in Asia, 112
  color, 112, 113e, 114
  as culture element, 112–14
  food preferences and, 114
Africa, 142, 178
African Regional Industrial Property Organization (ARIPO), 178
Agent intermediary, 523
Aggregate segmentation, 225
Air freight, 504–5
Alliance for Gray Market and Counterfeit Abatement, 563
American Export Trading Company of 1982, 557
Analogy method, 207–10
Andean Group, 54–55
Anti-Counterfeiting Trade Agreement (ACTA), 180
Antidumping regulation
  compliance, 560
  import duties, 562
  pricing and, 412–13, 422
Antiglobalization, 33, 50gp, 228
*Antitrust Guidelines for International Operations*, 181
Apartheid, 142

APEC. *See* Asia Pacific Economic Cooperation
Appropriability regime, 30
Arbitration, 167, 171
Argentina, 193
  Brazil and, 87
  debt, 87
  financial crisis, 33, 70, 86
  inflation in, 89gp
  price index, 199
ARIPO. *See* African Regional Industrial Property Organization
Arm's length prices, 410–11
ASA. *See* Advertising Standards Authority
ASEAN. *See* Association of Southeast Asian Nations
Asia, 136, 290, 291, 294e. *See also* Association of Southeast Asian Nations
  aesthetics in, 112
  APEC, 47gp
  Asian Tigers, 599
  case study, 139
  donuts in, 127
  e-commerce in, 251
  EMs, 597
  financial crisis, 33, 67, 70, 72, 85–86, 85e, 91, 98
  FTAs, 57gp
  GDP, 86
  marketing surveys in, 203
  NTBs in, 152gp
  SAARC, 54–55
  skin color in, 128
  value systems, 117–18
  yen in, 74
Asian Tigers, 599
Asia Pacific Economic Cooperation (APEC), 47gp, 183, 577
Assertiveness, 123
Association of Southeast Asian Nations (ASEAN), 42–43, 54, 56–57
  exports/imports, 152gp

# AUTHOR INDEX

# COMPANY INDEX